3

Robert Ph. Dollfus

THE ZOOLOGY OF TAPEWORMS

by

Robert A. Wardle

and

James Archie McLeod

UNIVERSITY OF MANITOBA, WINNIPEG, CANADA

"Such as for their belly's sake
Creep and intrude and climb into the fold."
JOHN MILTON

Published for the University of Manitoba by
THE UNIVERSITY OF MINNESOTA PRESS, Minneapolis

PRINTED AT THE NORTH CENTRAL PUBLISHING COMPANY, ST. PAUL

London • Geoffrey Cumberlege • Oxford University Press

Library of Congress Catalog Card Number: 52-5324

DEDICATED *as a tribute of admiration to Robert Ph. Dollfus who, with indomitable energy, amidst the discomforts and dangers and difficulties of an enemy-held city, crystallized for posterity the knowledge of a lifetime devoted to pure science*

Preface

This book describes the tapeworms of the world. It attempts to summarize what is known about their classification, structure, life histories, and ways of life. It discusses the probable origin of tapeworms from free-living worms and the lines along which they may have diverged from one another. It provides descriptions of and identification keys for all the known families and genera of tapeworms and the majority of the known species.

The names of the men and women whose labors indirectly made this summary possible are listed at the end of the book. Among the many who have helped directly by sending copies of published articles, unpublished manuscripts, original drawings, photographs, tapeworm specimens, and advice on doubtful points, our particular thanks are due to the late Theodor Pintner in Vienna; J. D. Smyth, Thomas Southwell, and W. N. F. Woodland in Britain; T. W. M. Cameron, W. A. Clemens, R. E. Foerster, A. G. Huntsman, R. B. Miller, and D. S. Rawson in Canada; Robert Ph. Dollfus, J. Guilhon, Jules Guiart, and M. G. Lemaire in France; Hans Vogel in Germany; Satyu Yamaguti in Japan; L. W. Wisniewski in pre-1939 Poland; G. K. Petruschevsky and Viktor Tarassow in Russia; Jean G. Baer and Hans A. Kreis in Switzerland; Ralph V. Bangham, Asa C. Chandler, W. N. Cort, Hiram E. Essex, Ernest Carroll Faust, the late John E. Guberlet, R. Chester Hughes, George William Hunter III, George La Rue, Thomas Magath, Harold W. Manter, Justus F. Mueller, William A. Riley, Robert Rausch, Victor B. Scheffer, Horace W. Stunkard, H. V. Van Cleave, Carl E. Venard, Teunis Vergeer, and the late Henry Baldwin Ward in the United States of America.

We acknowledge with gratitude those university library staffs, notably those of McGill, Michigan, Minnesota, Toronto, and Yale, who so readily lent volumes not otherwise accessible, or provided microfilms. For abstracts of articles which due to war conditions could not be consulted in the original journals, *Biological Abstracts* and *Helminthological Abstracts* were indispensable.

The generous financial help of the National Research Council of Canada, the University of Manitoba, and the University of Minnesota alone made publication possible.

Last, but by no means least, must be mentioned the editorial staff of the University of Minnesota Press whose patience and skill produced order out of the chaos of a crude manuscript.

Robert Arnold Wardle
James Archie McLeod

Winnipeg, 1951

Contents

PART I

Chapter I. GENERAL FEATURES 3
Chapter II. LIFE CYCLE 45
Chapter III. BIOLOGY 92
Chapter IV. ORIGIN AND EVOLUTION 142
Chapter V. HISTORY AND CLASSIFICATION 155

PART II

Tapeworm Classification Used in This Book 173
Order PROTEOCEPHALA 175
Family Proteocephalidae 187
Order TETRAPHYLLIDEA 227
Family Phyllobothriidae 232
Family Onchobothriidae 254
Order DISCULICEPITIDEA 270
Family Disculicepitidae 272
Order LECANICEPHALA 273
Family Lecanicephalidae 275
Family Cephalobothriidae 276
Order TRYPANORHYNCHA 286
Family Tentaculariidae 299

Family Hepatoxylidae 301

Family Sphyriocephalidae 303

Family Dasyrhynchidae 305

Family Lacistorhynchidae 308

Family Gymnorhynchidae 311

Family Pterobothriidae 312

Family Eutetrarhynchidae 315

Family Gilquiniidae 316

Family Otobothriidae 317

Order CYCLOPHYLLIDEA 321

Family Mesocestoididae 325

Family Tetrabothriidae 333

Family Nematotaeniidae 343

Family Anoplocephalidae 347

Family Catenotaeniidae 381

Family Taeniidae 388

Family Davaineidae 428

Family Biuterinidae 446

Family Hymenolepididae 449

Family Dilepididae 475

Family Acoleidae 521

Family Amabiliidae 523

Family Dioicocestidae 526

Family Diploposthidae 528

Order APORIDEA 534

Family Nematoparataeniidae 534

Order NIPPOTAENIIDEA 538

Family Nippotaeniidae 538

Order CARYOPHYLLIDEA 540

Family Wenyonidae 541

Family Caryophyllaeidae 541

Family Lytocestidae 548

Family Capingentidae 550

Order SPATHEBOTHRIDEA 552

Family Spathebothriidae 552

Family Cyathocephalidae 554

Family Diplocotylidae 555

Order PSEUDOPHYLLIDEA 559

Family Haplobothriidae 567

Family Dibothriocephalidae 572

Family Ptychobothriidae 618

Family Bothriocephalidae 623

Family Echinophallidae 634

Family Triaenophoridae 636

Family Amphicotylidae 641

Orders AMPHILINIDEA, GYROCOTYLIDEA, BIPOROPHYLLIDEA 653

Order Amphilinidea 653

Family Amphilinidae 656

Order Gyrocotylidea 658

Family Gyrocotylidae 658

Order Biporophyllidea 664

Family Biporophyllaeidae 664

References 669

Index 775

ILLUSTRATIONS

1. Holdfast of *Cysticercus fasciolaris* 5
2. Sucker of *Choanotaenia iola* 7
3. Skin of *Ligula* 14
4. Skin of *Archigetes* 18
5. Holdfast of *Ophiotaenia filaroides* 21
6. Expanded holdfast of *Anthobothrium auriculatum* 21
7. Longitudinal muscle fibers of *Avitellina centripunctata* 21
8. Holdfast of *Grillotia erinaceus* 21
9. Cross section of *Grillotia erinaceus* through neck 21
10. Skin and underlying tissues of *Grillotia erinaceus* 21
11. Expanded holdfast of *Anthobothrium auriculatum* 25
12. Holdfast of *Proteocephalus torulosus* 25
13. Flame cell of *Avitellina centripunctata* 25
14. Holdfast of *Avitellina centripunctata* left half of osmoregulatory system 25
15. Lateral osmoregulatory canals in plerocercoid of *Proteocephalus torulosus* 27
16. Osmoregulatory canals in holdfast of *Calliobothrium coronatum* 27
17. Holdfast of *Grillotia erinaceus* showing nervous system 29
18. Neurochords from *Pterobothrium microcephala* 30
19. *Triaenophorus*, sectional views of proglottis 33
20. *Ophiotaenia filaroides*, male genitalia 34

21. Genital atrium of *Anthocephalus elongatus* 34
22. Cirrus apparatus of *Dibothriocephalus latus* 34
23. Cirrus pouch and vaginal end section of *Raillietina echinobothrida* 34
24. Cirrus apparatus of *Caryophyllaeus laticeps* 35
25. Female reproductive ducts of *Proteocephalus parallacticus* 37
26. Genitalia of *Triaenophorus stizostedionis* 37
27. Female genital ducts of *Dibothriocephalus latus* 37
28. Female genital ducts of *Dibothriocephalus latus* 37
29. Stages in development of uterus of *Dibothriocephalus latus* ... 41
30. Development of egg of *Hydatigera taeniaeformis* 49
31. Embryo of *Hydatigera taeniaeformis* 50
32. Early development of *Dibothriocephalus latus* 52
33. Embryonated egg and coracidium of *Spirometra erinacei* 53
34. Oncosphere of *Dibothriocephalus latus* 55
35. Procercoid of *Dibothriocephalus latus* 60
36. Early development of *Ophiotaenia perspicus* 62
37. Plerocercoid larval forms 67
38. Plerocercoids of *Nybelinia sp.* 69
39. *Sparganum proliferum* 71
40. *Urocystidium gemmiparum* 71
41. *Ilisha parthenogenetica* 71
42. Tetraphyllidean plerocercoids 72
43. Early developmental stages of anoplocephaline tapeworms 74
44. Life cycle of *Dipylidium caninum* 76
45. Cysticercoids of *Choanotaenia infundibulum* 80
46. *Catenotaenia pusilla*, egg development 81
47. *Catenotaenia pusilla*, larval stages in *Glyciphagus* 82
48. *Catenotaenia pusilla*, young worms 83
49. Types of bladder worms 84
50. Development of a cysticercus 86
51. Apparatus for viewing tapeworms in vitro 95
52. Tissues of a ligulid plercercoid before and after cultivation in Locke's solution 97

53. Appearance of *Nybelinia* plerocercoids in different media 112
54. Rate of movement of larval *Nybelinia* in favorable media 113
55. Respiratory responses of *Moniezia expansa* to pH values of medium 116
56. Rate of growth of *Dibothriocephalus latus* 120
57. Ascites in fingerling Salmonoid infested with intrahepatic dibothriocephalid larvae 128
58. Phylogeny of tapeworms 148
59. *Ophiotaenia filaroides* 181
60. *Proteocephalus torulosus* 181
61. Types of genitalium arrangement among Proteocephala 183
62. Arrangement of genitalia among subfamilies of Proteocephalidae 185
63. *Marsypocephalus*, pattern of genitalia 190
64. *Marsypocephalus tanganyikae*, holdfast 190
65. *Peltidocotyle rugosa*, holdfast and genitalia 190
66. *Peltidocotyle rugosa*, holdfast 190
67. *Rudolphiella*, genitalia 190
68. *Amphilaphorchis*, holdfast and mature proglottis 190
69. *Ephedrocephalus* 190
70. Species of *Monticellia* 191
71. *Endorchis* 194
72. *Zygobothrium*, genitalia 194
73. *Amphoteromorphus* 194
74. *Amphoteromorphus* 194
75. *Nomimoscolex* 195
76. *Corallobothrium* larva 196
77. *Corallobothrium fimbriatum* and *C. giganteum* 197
78. *Lintoniella adhaerens* 197
79. Holdfast differences within *Proteocephalus* 199
80. Internal diagnostic differences within *Proteocephalus* 199
81. *Proteocephalus pearsei* 199
82. *Proteocephalus parallacticus* 200
83. *Proteocephalus arcticus* 200

84. *Proteocephalus ptychocheilus* 200
85. *Proteocephalus laruei* 200
86. *Proteocephalus stizostethi* 201
87. *Proteocephalus wickliffi* 201
88. *Proteocephalus osculatus* 204
89. *Megathylacus jandia* 209
90. *Gangesia parasiluri* 209
91. *Acanthotaenia sandgroundi* 209
92. *Acanthotaenia shipleyi* 209
93. *Silurotaenia siluri* 211
94. *Electrotaenia malopteruri* 211
95. *Ophiotaenia alternans* 214
96. *Ophiotaenia saphena* 214
97. *Ophiotaenia olor* 220
98. *Ophiotaenia magna* 220
99. Comparison of normal proteocephalid and solenotaeniid gravid uteri 222
100. *Crepidobothrium gerrardii minus* 225
101. *Sciadocephalus megalodiscus* 225
102. *Manaosia bracodemoca* 225
103. *Phyllobothrium marginatum* 230
104. Distinctions between Trypanorhyncha, Tetraphyllidea, and Proteocephala tapeworms 230
105. *Scolex pleuronectis* 230
106. *Scyphophyllidium giganteum* 235
107. *Pithophorus tetraglobus* 235
108. *Myzophyllobothrium rubrum* 235
109. *Pelichnibothrium speciosum* 237
110. *Echeneibothrium myzorhynchum* 239
111. *Echeneibothrium tobijei* 239
112. *Carpobothrium chiloscyllium* 239
113. *Anthobothrium cornucopia* 239
114. *Dinobothrium planum* 245
115. *Dinobothrium septaria* 245

116. *Phyllobothrium lactuca*, holdfast 247
117. *Phyllobothrium magnum* 250
118. *Phyllobothrium radioductum* 250
119. *Phyllobothrium* plerocercoid (*P. tumidulum*?) 250
120. *Orygmatobothrium plicatum* 254
121. *Pedibothrium brevispine* 256
122. *Uncibilocularis trygonis* 256
123. *Uncibilocularis mandleyi* 256
124. *Thysanocephalum thysanocephalum* 256
125. *Spiniloculus mavensis* 256
126. *Yorkeria parva* 259
127. *Calliobothrium verticillatum* 259
128. *Onchobothrium* 259
129. *Acanthobothrium coronatum* 259
130. *Platybothrium hypoprioni* 265
131. *Balanobothrium* 266
132. *Cylindrophorus lasium* 266
133. *Tetracampos ciliotheca* 266
134. *Ceratobothrium xanthocephalum* 266
135. *Disculiceps* 271
136. *Lecanicephalum peltatum* 271
137. *Tetragonocephalum* 271
138. *Parataenia medusiae* 276
139. *Cephalobothrium aetiobatidis* 277
140. *Hexacanalis abruptus* 278
141. *Tylocephalum dierama* 279
142. *Tylocephalum dierama* 280
143. *Polypocephalus radiatus* 280
144. *Adelobothrium aetiobatidis* 281
145. *Anthemobothrium pulchrum* 281
146. *Staurobothrium aetiobatidis* 281
147. *Diplobothrium simile* 283
148. Diplobothriid plerocercoids 283

149. *Eniochobothrium gracile* 283
150. *Phanobothrium monticellii* 283
151. *Discobothrium japonicum* 283
152. *Prosobothrium armigerum* 285
153. *Prosobothrium japonicum* 285
154. *Echinobothrium typus* 285
155. *Pillersium owenium* 285
156. *Diagonobothrium asymmetrum* 285
157. "*Anthocephalus elongatus*" 287
158. Internal features of trypanorhynchan and tetraphyllidean tapeworms 294
159. Tetraphyllidean and trypanorhynchan larval forms 296
160. Trypanorhynchan larval types 297
161. *Tentacularia coryphaenae* 300
162. *Nybelinia lingualis*, hooks 300
163. *Nybelinia pintneri*, holdfast 300
164. *Hepatoxylon trichiuri*, postlarva 300
165. *Sphyriocephalus tergestinus* 304
166. *Dasyrhynchus talismani* 304
167. *Floriceps saccatus* 304
168. *Callitetrarhynchus gracilis* 307
169. *Lacistorhynchus tenuis* 307
170. *Grillotia erinaceus* 307
171. *Grillotia* species 307
172. *Gymnorhynchus gigas* 313
173. *Pterobothrium* plerocercus 313
174. *Eutetrarhynchus lineatus*, holdfast 313
175. *Eutetrarhynchus ruficollis*, armature 313
176. *Gilquinia squali* 313
177. *Otobothrium*, holdfasts 319
178. *Diplootobothrium springeri* 319
179. *Poecilancistrium caryophyllum*, holdfast and retractile organ . . 319
180. *Mesocestoides lineatus f. lineata* 326

181. Tetrabothriid genera, holdfasts 336
182. *Baerietta baeri* 345
183. *Nematotaenia dispar* 345
184. *Cylindrotaenia americana* 345
185. *Distoichometra bufonis* 345
186. *Cylindrotaenia quadrijugosa* 345
187. *Aporina delafondi* 349
188. *Stilesia hepatica* 349
189. *Andrya primordialis* 356
190. *Monoecocestus americanus* 356
191. *Diandrya composita* 356
192. *Moniezia expansa* 356
193. *Anoplocephala perfoliata* 356
194. *Moniezia monardi* 356
195. *Anoplocephala spatula* 356
196. *Paranoplocephala mamillana* 356
197. *Bertiella studeri* 363
198. *Bertiella fallax* 363
199. *Paronia pycnonoti* 363
200. *Cittotaenia pectinata americana* 363
201. *Oochoristica osheroffi* 370
202. *Oochoristica taborensis* 370
203. *Oochoristica bivitellolobata* 370
204. *Oochoristica gracewileyae* 370
205. *Oochoristica parvovaria* 371
206. *Oochoristica whitentoni* 371
207. *Oochoristica oklahomensis* 373
208. *Oochoristica procyonis* 373
209. *Catenotaenia pusilla* 385
210. *Catenotaenia linsdalei* 387
211. *Echinococcus oligarthrus* 392
212. Echinococcid hooks 392
213. *Echinococcus granulosus* 393

214. *Echinococcus lycaontis* 393
215. *Echinococcus granulosus* 394
216. Hydatid cyst 394
217. *Fossor angertrudae* 400
218. *Paracladotaenia acciptris* 402
219. *Taeniarhynchus saginatus* 404
220. *Taeniarhynchus saginatus* 404
221. *Dasyurotaenia robusta* 405
222. *Cladotaenia foxi* 407
223. *Hydatigera taeniaeformis* 409
224. *Hydatigera taeniaeformis*, hooks 409
225. *Hydatigera balaniceps* 409
226. *Hydatigera lyncis* 409
227. *Hydatigera laticollis* 409
228. *Multiceps packi* 415
229. *Multiceps twitchelli* 415
230. Hooks of *Multiceps macracantha* 415
231. Hooks of *Multiceps otomys* 415
232. Hooks of *Multiceps glomeratus* 415
233. Typical taeniid hooks 417
234. Typical taeniid gravid segments 418
235. *Taenia pisiformis* 420
236. *Taenia hydatigena*, gravid segment 420
237. *Taenia hydatigena*, mature segment 420
238. *Taenia solium*, gravid segment 420
239. *Taenia rileyi*, gravid and mature segments 420
240. *Raillietina echinobothrida* 429
241. *Raillietina cesticillus*, oncosphere 432
242. *Raillietina cesticillus*, cysticercoids 432
243. *Ophryocotyle proteus* 434
244. *Cotugnia polytelidis* 434
245. *Cotugnia taiwanensis* 434
246. *Davainea proglottina*, mature segment 434

247. *Davainea proglottina*, entire worm 434
248. *Raillietina* (*Paroniella*) *centuri* 438
249. *Raillietina* (*Raillietina*) *bakeri* 438
250. *Raillietina* (*Skrjabinia*) *cesticillus* 440
251. *Raillietina* (*Fuhrmannetta*) *leoni*, mature segments 440
252. *Raillietina equatoriensis*, mature segments 440
253. *Houttuynia torquata* 443
254. *Houttuynia struthionis* 443
255. *Idiogenes buteonis* 445
256. *Chapmania tapika* 445
257. *Schistometra conoideis* 445
258. *Sphyronchotaenia uncinata* 445
259. *Neyraia intricata* 447
260. *Deltokeras multilobatus* 447
261. *Cyclorchida omalancristrota* 447
262. Phylogenetic relationships between *Wardium*, *Hymenolepis*, and *Weinlandia* 451
263. Arrangement of testes in various hymenolepidids 452
264. Typical hymenolepidid hook 453
265. *Hymenolepis filumferens* 459
266. *Hymenolepis nana*, eggs 462
267. *Hymenolepis nana* var. *fraterna*, cysticercoid-host relationships 462
268. *Hymenolepis nana* var. *fraterna*, holdfasts of young individuals . 462
269. *Oligorchis longivaginosis* 464
270. *Hymenolepis mastigopraedita* 464
271. *Hymenolepis stolli* 464
272. *Hymenolepis dafilae* 464
273. *Diorchis nyrocae* 464
274. *Hymenolepis citelli* 464
275. Life cycle of *Hymenolepis cantaniana* 468
276. *Diorchis spp.*, hooks 470
277. *Fimbriaria fasciolaris*, holdfast and pseudo-holdfast 473
278. *Fimbriaroides intermedia* 473
279. *Fimbriariella falciformes* 473
280. *Fimbriaroides* species 473

281. *Cotylorhipis furnarii* ... 480
282. *Echinorhynchotaenia tritesticulata* ... 480
283. *Pentorchis arkteios* ... 480
284. *Angularella beema* ... 480
285. *Unciunia trichocirrosa* ... 480
286. *Amoebotaenia setosa* ... 480
287. *Amoebotaenia sphenoides* ... 480
288. *Valipora mutabilis* ... 483
289. *Valipora parvispine* ... 483
290. *Trichocephaloidis megalocephala* ... 483
291. *Lateriporus biuterinus* ... 483
292. *Laterorchites bilateralis* ... 483
293. *Paricterotaenia cirrospinosa* ... 483
294. *Liga brasiliensis* ... 486
295. *Dilepis undula* ... 486
296. *Paradilepis brevis* ... 486
297. *Dendrouterina nycticoracis* ... 490
298. *Gryporhynchus tetrorchis* ... 490
299. *Anomotaenia nycticoracis* ... 493
300. *Similuncinus totani-ochropodos* ... 493
301. *Choanotaenia iolae* ... 493
302. *Dipylidium caninum* ... 506
303. *Diplopylidium nolleri* ... 506
304. *Joyeuxiella pasqualei* ... 512
305. *Joyeuxiella echinorhynchoides* ... 512
306. *Joyeuxiella sp.* of Kofend ... 512
307. *Southwellia ransomi* ... 513
308. *Malika pittae* ... 513
309. *Anonchotaenia globata* ... 515
310. *Anonchotaenia globata*, nematodiform embryos ... 515
311. *Metroliasthes lucida* ... 515
312. *Metroliasthes lucida*, life cycle stages ... 518
313. *Octopetalum longicirrosum* ... 519
314. *Rhabdometra similis* ... 519
315. *Paruterina angustata* ... 519

316. *Sphaeruterina punctata* 519
317. *Acoleus vaginatus* 523
318. *Amabilia lamelligera* 523
319. *Tatria duodecacantha* 523
320. *Dioicocestus spp.* 527
321. *Shipleya inermis* 527
322. *Gyrocoelia perversa* 527
323. *Diploposthe laevis* 529
324. *Diplophallus polymorphus* 529
325. *Jardugia paradoxa* 529
326. *Diplogynia americana* 529
327. *Progynotaenia evaginata* 531
328. *Proterogynotaenia rouxi* 531
329. *Protogynella blarinae* 531
330. *Leptotaenia ischnorhyncha* 531
331. *Nematoparataenia southwelli* 535
332. *Gastrotaenia cygni* 536
333. *Nippotaenia chaenogobii* 536
334. *Wenyonia virilis* 542
335. *Archigetes cryptobothrius* 542
336. *Biacetabulum infrequens* 542
337. *Biacetabulum meridianum* 542
338. *Caryophyllaeides fennica* 542
339. *Hypocaryophyllaeus paratarius* 545
340. *Monobothrium wageneri* 545
341. *Caryophyllaeus laticeps* 546
342. *Caryophyllaeus laticeps* 546
343. *Glaridacris spp.* 547
344. *Lytocestus indicus* 547
345. *Balanotaenia bancrofti* 547
346. *Capingens singularis* 550
347. *Spartoides wardi* 550
348. *Pseudolytocestus differtus* 550
349. *Spathebothrium simplex* 553
350. *Cyathocephalus truncatus* 555

351. *Diplocotyle olrikii* 556
352. *Bothrimonus fallax* 557
353. *Haplobothrium globuliforme* 577
354. *Pyramicocephalus anthocephalus* 577
355. *Digramma alternans* 577
356. Plerocercoids of *Ligula intestinalis* 578
357. *Ligula intestinalis* 580
358. *Bothridium pithonis* 580
359. *Duthiersia fimbriata* 580
360. *Duthiersia expansa* 580
361. *Adenocephalus pacificus* 582
362. *Glandicephalus antarcticus* 584
363. *Diphyllobothrium stemmacephalum* 586
364. Yamaguti's "*Diphyllobothrium stemmacephalum*" 586
365. *Diphyllobothrium fuhrmanni* 586
366. *Diplogonoporus balaenopterae* 587
367. *Cordicephalus phocarus* 589
368. *Cordicephalus arctocephalinus* 589
369. "*Diphyllobothrium arctocephalinus*" 590
370. "*Diphyllobothrium arctocephali*" 590
371. *Spirometra* species 594
372. *Spirometra gracile* 596
373. *Spirometra bresslauei* 596
374. *Spirometra mansonoides* 601
375. *Dibothriocephalus latus* 606
376. *Dibothriocephalus laruei* 610
377. *Dibothriocephalus oblongatus* 610
378. *Schistocephalus solidus* 616
379. *Cephalochlamys namaquensis* 618
380. *Senga besnardi* 621
381. *Clestobothrium crassiceps* 621
382. *Polyonchobothrium gordoni* 621
383. *Ptychobothrium belones* 622
384. *Polyonchobothrium cylindraceum* 622
385. *Polyonchobothrium polypteri* 622

386. *Bothriocephalus scorpii* 626
387. *Bothriocephalus claviceps* 626
388. *Bothriocephalus cuspidatus* 626
389. *Bothriocephalus cuspidatus*, life cycle 627
390. *Bothriocephalus cuspidatus*, subspecies 628
391. *Bothriocephalus manubriformis* 630
392. *Bothriocephalus occidentalis* 630
393. *Bothriocephalus rarus* 631
394. Japanese bothriocephalid holdfasts 633
395. *Onchodiscus sauridae* 633
396. *Taprobothrium japonensis* 633
397. *Parabothriocephalus gracilis* 633
398. *Parabothriocephaloides segmentatus* 633
399. *Echinophallus japonicus* 635
400. *Triaenophorus* species 637
401. Triaenophorid larvae *in situ* 639
402. Attachment of adult triaenophorids to host gut lining 639
403. *Fistulicola plicatus* 640
404. *Anchistrocephalus microcephalus* 640
405. *Anonchocephalus chilensis* 640
406. *Eubothrium rugosum* 644
407. *Eubothrium crassum* 646
408. *Eubothrium salvelini* 646
409. *Eubothrium oncorhynchi* 646
410. *Abothrium gadi* 651
411. *Bathybothrium rectangulum* 651
412. *Parabothrium bulbiferum* 651
413. *Marsipometra* species 652
414. *Amphilina foliacea* 657
415. *Gephyrolina paragonopora* 657
416. *Gigantolina magna* 657
417. *Gyrocotyle urna*, expanded and contracted 660
418. *Gyrocotyle urna* 660
419. *Biporophyllaeus madrassensis* 664

PART I

· CHAPTER I ·

General Features

The word "tapeworm" is used by naturalists, farmers, physicians, and veterinarians for certain worms which infest the alimentary tracts of farm livestock, game animals, birds, fishes, and even at times of human beings. The word seems to have come into popular use about 1824 and is probably a direct translation of the German word "Bandwurm" (ribbon worm), which was being commonly used around the beginning of the nineteenth century by early German and Dutch parasitologists in their writings. Zoologically speaking, such worms are Platyelminthes (flatworms) of the classes Cestoda and Cestodaria.

The various hypotheses as to the origin and evolution of tapeworms are purely conjectural. Their anatomy, gross or microscopic, their physiology, their life cycles, their habits – all are far from being fully understood. The keys to an understanding of many obscure biological phenomena may lie within these animals, but the investigator is baffled by the fragility of his material, by its brief existence when removed from its normal habitat, and by the complexity of its environmental requirements. Yet a vast literature has accumulated around them – a literature polylingual, scattered, and fragmentary. It is our aim in the following pages to present from this literature and from our own observations a coherent story of this group of animals and to make clear the gaps and imperfections in our knowledge of them.

The body of the tapeworm is as a rule a long, flattened cylinder, often so much so as to make clear the origin of the vernacular terms tapeworm, Bandwurm, and cestode (from the Greek word for ribbon), and such zoological terms as Cestoda and Cestodaria. The two flat body surfaces will be termed in these pages the surficial surfaces and will be regarded as dorsal and ventral in orientation, although it is not always possible to say which is dorsal and which is ventral. The edges will be termed the marginal surfaces.

The tapeworm is thus a "depressed" animal; that is to say, it is an animal which is flattened from above downward, flattened in a dorsoventral plane. In surficial view, the tapeworm body is a long and very narrow triangle. The apex of the triangle may be regarded for convenience of description as being anterior, since if the worm is able to travel at all it does so with this end foremost. However, as will be seen later, there are grounds for believing that this foremost end is homologous with the posterior end of other animals.

A tapeworm is usually white, but occasionally is gray, yellow, or cream in color as a result of absorption of substances in its environment. The surface of its body is rarely perfectly smooth but is commonly cross-wrinkled or grooved longitudinally. Frequently it shows a succession of transverse, parallel grooves which divide it into somewhat squarish segments. The intersegmental grooves provide anterior and posterior borders to each such segment. Should the posterior border of a segment overlap the anterior border of the segment following, the first segment is said to be "craspedote"; if such overlapping does not occur, the segment is "acraspedote."

Like any other animal, a tapeworm shows a mixture of features shared in common with the other members of the zoological group to which it belongs – in this case Platyelminthes, or flatworms – and of adaptive features which are peculiar to tapeworms and which result from a long adaptation to a parasitic method of life. Thus, like other flatworms, a tapeworm is depressed, headless, and limbless. In place of a body cavity there is a spongelike tissue, the parenchyma. Although readily permeable to water, and containing in fact about 90 per cent water, a system of water-expulsion organs – the osmoregulatory system – prevents it from becoming utterly waterlogged. There is neither a distinct circulatory system nor a distinct excretory system. Its nervous system is well developed, surprisingly so for such a sluggish animal; but specialized sense organs are lacking. Its reproductive system is complex and hermaphroditic.

Only with other tapeworms, however, does the individual tapeworm share its peculiarities of body elongation and serial segmentation, its absence of an alimentary system, its deep-seated system of muscle fibers, its peculiar and characteristic embryonic stage, and some other features which will be brought out in the following pages. With one exception – the genus *Archigetes* – a tapeworm can come to maturity and continue to exist only in the alimentary tract of a vertebrate animal which may be termed the primary or definitive host. Usually the worm is specific; that is to say, it will live only within this one species of host or within a group of closely related species. Its immature or larval stages, however, are less specific and may occur within a wide range of both vertebrate and invertebrate hosts, the so-called secondary or intermediate hosts. Rarely do the larval stage and the adult stage coexist within the same host individual.

Holdfast

What appears to be the anterior end of a tapeworm is a small, spherical or egg-shaped "holdfast organ" by which the worm is anchored to the lining of the host intestine in which it lives. The nature of this holdfast organ was not clearly understood by the early students of tapeworm structure, and for a long time it was regarded as a head.

The earliest suggestion that a tapeworm has a head seems to have been made by a London physician, Edward T. Tyson (1650–1708), in 1683, possibly in reference to *Taenia pisiformis*, a common tapeworm of dogs. The holdfast organ was described again by Nicholas Andry (1658–1742) in 1700 for the common beef tapeworm of man *(Taeniarhynchus saginatus)* and by Charles Bonnet (1720–93), a Swiss naturalist, in 1762 for the common broad tapeworm of man *(Dibothriocephalus latus)*. The holdfast organs of proteocephalan and trypanorhynchan tapeworms were also familiar to eighteenth-century observers. Francesco Redi (1626–98) remarked on the presence of four cuplike structures on the proteocephalan holdfast, and Karl Asmund Rudolphi (1771–1832), regarding such cups as mouths, applied to them the term "suckers" and thus originated a common and long-persistent but erroneous belief that through them the animal took in food.

Since, however, the "head" of an animal is an aggregation of food-perceiving and food-catching organs, the holdfast end of a tapeworm is not a head; for there are upon it neither organs for perceiving nor for handling food, although admittedly there is within it a concentration of the nervous system. It is rather a modification of the originally posterior end, modified to anchor the worm either permanently or, it may be, only temporarily to the wall of the cavity within which it lives. Following the suggestion made by P. J. van Beneden in the middle of the last century, this holdfast end is commonly called by zoologists a "scolex," the rest of the worm being referred to as the "strobila." We prefer here to use the terms "holdfast" and "body."

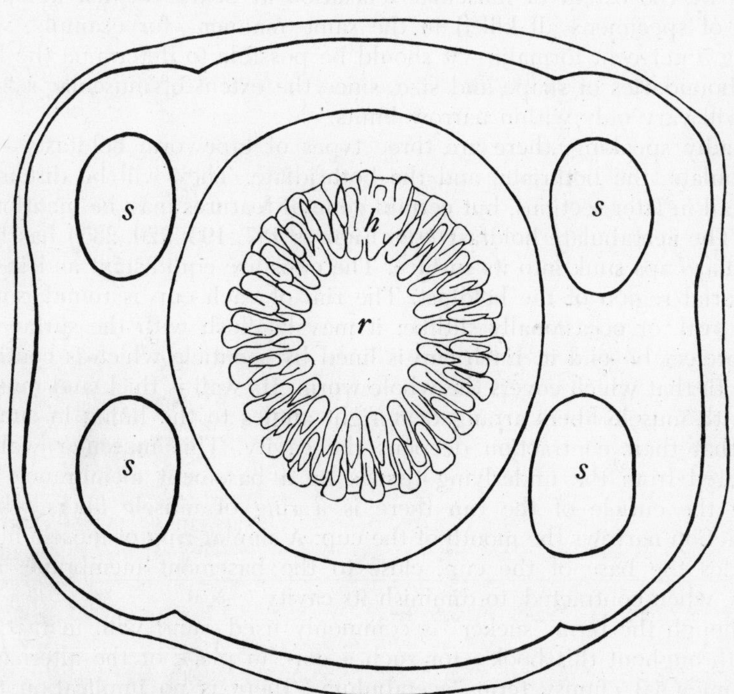

FIG. 1. Holdfast of *Cysticercus fasciolaris*. After Dollfus, 1938. *h*, hooks; *r*, rostellum; *s*, suckers.

Among tapeworms in general there is a wide variety of holdfast shapes and holdfast sizes. In some forms it can scarcely be distinguished from the body; in others, it is represented by a persistent larval structure; in still other forms, it is lost early in the life cycle and replaced by a modification of the first segment, for which the term "pseudo-holdfast" will be used. The holdfast may be spherical, ovoid, cubical, rhomboidal, pyramidal – always, of course, with the edges and corners rounded. In size it varies from one to two millimeters in length and breadth. Compared with the body, it is minute. It reaches full size toward the end of larval life. Apparent increase after that is due rather to degeneration and consequent relaxation of the muscle fibers within it.

The shape and size of the holdfast, in a living tapeworm newly removed from the host and observed in an artificial medium, change continually since there is no internal skeleton. The extent of the change varies with the chemical nature, the hydrogen-ion concentration, and the temperature of the medium; with the length of time that the worm has been divorced from its normal habitat; and, to some extent, with the species of worm to which it belongs. In dead, preserved specimens no two individuals are identical in shape and size, even when they were approximately so when alive. Meticulous descriptions of the dimensions and shape of any particular holdfast are therefore of little value. On the other hand, the post-mortem shape and size of the holdfast are determined by the extent of muscular relaxation at death, so that among a range of specimens all killed in the same manner – for example, with boiling 5 per cent formalin – it should be possible to determine the limiting boundaries of shape and size, since the extent of muscular relaxation will vary only within narrow limits.

Broadly speaking, there are three types of tapeworm holdfasts – the acetabulate, the bothriate, and the bothridiate. They will be discussed in detail in later sections, but certain general features may be mentioned here. The acetabulate holdfast (see Figures 187, 193, 220, 235) has four muscular cups sunk into its surface. The cups are equidistant and in the equatorial region of the holdfast. The rim of each cup is round, sometimes oval, or occasionally slitlike; it may lie flush with the surface or may project beyond it. Each cup is lined by a cuticle which is continuous with that which covers the whole worm. Its wall is thick and muscular, with muscle fibers arranged at right angles to the lining in such a way that their contraction deepens the cavity. This muscular wall is separated from the underlying tissues by a basement membrane. Just below the cuticle of the rim there is a ring of muscle fibers whose contraction narrows the mouth of the cup. A similar ring of muscle fibers encircles the base of the cup, close to the basement membrane, and serves, when contracted, to diminish its cavity.

Although the term "sucker" is commonly used – and will, in fact, be used throughout this book – for such a cup, in place of the alternative but somewhat clumsy term "acetabulum," there is no implication that it serves for the intake of food. It is quite definitely a holdfast structure. It works by gripping the plug of gut lining that fills the cavity when the cup is pressed to the lining of the host gut. No doubt if it were applied to a firm, unyielding surface it would stick to it as a conical rubber cup sticks to a smooth surface by reason of the lower air pressure within it; but the gut lining of a vertebrate is not firm and smooth, and it is doubtful whether normally the sucker adheres to the gut lining in the fashion of a vacuum cup.

The suckers are as much organs of locomotion as of fixation. The continuous expansion, contraction, and torsion of the holdfast end bring the suckers in contact with the gut lining and so provide fulcra toward which the tapeworm body can be pulled forward by muscular action. When the holdfast is relatively immobile, as may be the case in cyclophyllidean tapeworms, the suckers are small and may be assisted by accessory holdfast structures. Commonly the apical end of the holdfast

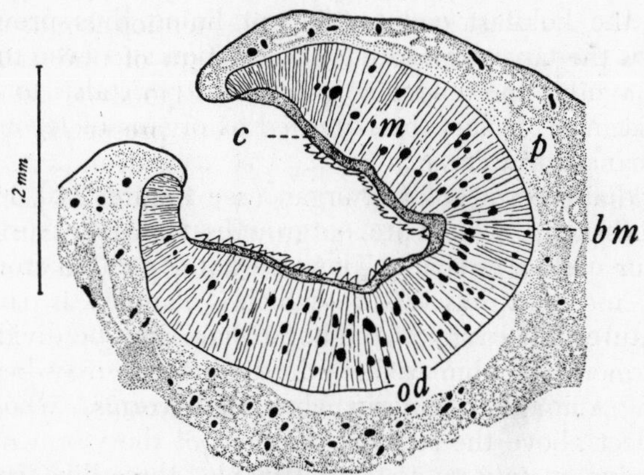

FIG. 2. Sucker of *Choanotaenia iola* in cross section. After Lincicome, 1939. *bm*, basement membrane; *c*, cuticle; *m*, radial muscles; *od*, an osmoregulatory duct; *p*, parenchyma.

region projects like a dome or a finger, as a so-called "rostellum." The rostellum may be a permanent projection, or it may be withdrawable into the holdfast end. If it is withdrawable, it may be either solid or hollow, its withdrawability in the latter case being effected much in the way a hollow glove finger can be withdrawn within the palmar part of the glove. Upon the rostellum there is commonly a continuous covering of thornlike hooks or of spines, or there may be one or more circles of such hooks or spines. Rarely, the sucker rims are spinose also.

The bothriate type of holdfast end has two surface depressions which are referred to as "bothria." In shape, each bothrium may be a shallow saucer, a groove, or a slit, or, by fusion of the margins of the slit, the bothrium may be a tube open at one or both ends. Only two such bothria are present, but among caryophyllaeids three or more pseudobothria may occur (see Figures 343 A, 362, 375). Each bothrium is surficial in orientation, and since it is not separated from the underlying tissues by any basement membrane but is merely a surface depression, it probably represents the widening or deepening of a mid-dorsal or mid-ventral groove, still evident in some forms, that in the proto-tapeworm ran along the middle of each flat surface. In some forms, *Pyramicocephalus* for example, the bothria seem rather to be continuations of former marginal grooves.

The gripping power of a bothrium is weak. Where the two bothria are wide and shallow, the fixation of the worm to the host gut wall is accomplished mainly through hooks or spines on the tip of the holdfast end (as in *Triaenophorus, Anchistrocephalus, Polyonchobothrium*; see Figures 401, 403), or by means of a four-lobed or two-lobed platelike structure, the apical disk or Scheitelplatte, which occurs on the tip of the holdfast region, although just how such an apical disk fixes itself is not clear. When the bothrium is groovelike, the mobility of its margins allows it to grip a fold of gut lining. However, even the slight, temporary adhesion of the holdfast end to the gut lining thus provided by the bothria allows the tapeworm to hold its position and even to make headway slightly against the tendency of host gut peristalsis to force it rearward. Bothria must, in fact, be regarded as organs of locomotion rather than of permanent fixation.

The bothridial type of holdfast organ (see Figures 110, 119, 124, 135) has four "bothridia," which are outgrowths from the surface and are trumpetlike or earlike in shape. They are not separated from the underlying tissues, and their musculature, which is complex, is part of the general musculature. The cavity of the bothridium may be divided by ridges into compartments. Within each bothridium there may be a small but true sucker. Among trypanorhynchan tapeworms, whose bothridia scarcely project above the surface, the hold of the worm upon the host gut wall is due mainly to four protrusible, threadlike structures, the "tentacles," which are armed with spiral rows of thornlike hooks and which can be withdrawn into tubular sheaths.

The chief problem which confronts a living tapeworm, of course, is that of holding its position in the host gut against the tendency for gut peristalsis to expel it. This is particularly a problem when the worm is young and its length a matter of millimeters. The large tapeworm, several meters long, can keep its station merely by the muscular pressure of its flat surfaces against the gut lining, but a small worm must either burrow into the mucosa or possess efficient holdfast structures. Many caryophyllaeid tapeworms, with smooth, weak bodies, burrow almost completely into the host gut mucosa. *Eubothrium rugosum*, one of the smaller species of Amphicotylidae, embeds its apical disk within the host gut lining and develops a *scolex deformatus*, a distorted holdfast end, the apical disk becoming like an inverted pyramid and locking the body of the worm firmly to the gut wall (Figure 409).

The power of such structures as suckers, bothria, and bothridia to hold the worm to the gut lining depends mainly upon the gripping power of their margins, and to a much less extent upon the zone of low pressure set up within them when they press against the mucosal surface. That such anchorage cannot be the primary function of these organs is suggested by the elaborate provision of accessory fixation structures such as armed rostella and tentacles. The original function of suckers, bothria, and bothridia must have been to provide sufficient traction for the small proto-tapeworm to travel over the yielding walls of its habitat in order to reach a favorable position. The rapidity and purposeful activity with which a trypanorhynchan larva can travel over the smooth surface of a glass dish merely by stretching, shortening, and twisting its body and bringing first one bothridium and then another in contact with the glass surface do not suggest that the function of such bothridia is merely that of passively anchoring the worm to its habitat.

Body

The term "strobila" (from the Greek word for chain) was suggested by van Beneden for the region following the holdfast organ, the region that we shall call here the body. The holdfast is separated from the body only by an imaginary line tangential to the posterior borders of the bothria or suckers. The most characteristic feature of a tapeworm body is the linear series of sets of reproductive organs. To such metameric repetition of the reproductive organs, the term "proglottisation" is commonly given. Each set of reproductive organs is called a "genitalium," and the area that immediately surrounds it is called a "proglottis." Such proglottisation is absent from those orders grouped as Cestodaria, but characterizes tapeworms of the class Cestoda except for the order Caryophyllidea and the family Nematotaeniidae.

If for the moment we exclude the order Pseudophyllidea, it can be said that in the great majority of cestodan tapeworms each proglottis is separated from its neighbors fore and aft by membranous partitions, or, in the few cases where such membranes are absent, by zones from which longitudinal muscle fibers are lacking. Further, corresponding with such internal interproglottidal zones, transverse grooves mark off the outer surfaces of the worm into "segments." In such cases segmentation corresponds with proglottisation, a segment being identical with a proglottis. It must be emphasized, however, that such is not always the case, and that the terms "segment" and "proglottis" are not synonymous.

The proglottides are budded off *apparently* in orderly succession from a region of unsegmented body which immediately follows the holdfast. To this region such terms as "neck," "growth-zone," and "Keimzone" are given. The oldest proglottis is thus the one farthest from the neck. Similarly, sexual development progresses in extent as the proglottides shift from the neck, so that the last proglottis of the body is gravid, being mainly an egg-filled sac, before the rest. Quite commonly the shape of the proglottis may change as it is pushed farther from the neck region. The early proglottis may be rectangular, with a length greater than its width; a medianly placed proglottis may be square; while a proglottis in the posterior third of the body may be linear, its width greatly exceeding its length.

Usually when the terminal proglottis becomes gravid it drops from the body. This phenomenon has been termed by Pintner (1913) "apolysis."

After such apolysis, the proglottis degenerates and liberates its eggs; even its ragged anterior and posterior borders do not heal. In some forms, however, the gravid proglottis leaves the body and keeps on growing; its torn borders heal; it may show mobility; it may even develop a pseudo-holdfast and may alter in shape. For this type of apolysis Pintner reserved the term "euapolysis." In other forms, again, the end proglottis leaves the body before it is completely gravid and completes its development while free. Pintner suggested for such cases the term "hyperapolysis."

When we consider the body of a pseudophyllidean tapeworm, the picture is less clear. Segmentation may be completely lacking, and even when segments are present, they may not correspond with the proglottides. There is no evidence of orderly budding of proglottides from a post-holdfast zone. The final larval stage, the plerocercoid larva, is unsegmented and unproglottised. After it reaches the gut of its definitive host, proglottisation may occur quickly but segmentation may never occur. Such is the case, for example, in the family Cyathocephalidae (see Order Spathebothridea). On the other hand, in many forms segmentation may appear before proglottisation, and a series of transverse grooves appearing apparently simultaneously may mark off a "primary body." Proglottisation then takes place, but one, two, or even three proglottides may correspond with a single segment. Secondary transverse grooves now appear and bring about a coincidence between proglottides and segments.

In the majority of pseudophyllidean tapeworms, the proglottides are not separated by membranous partitions or by areas of weakened or absent longitudinal musculature. Correlated with this fact, perhaps, is the absence of apolysis. All the segments in the posterior half of the strobila may become egg-producing simultaneously and discharge their eggs through permanent uterine pores. However, the egg-producing powers of such proglottides are not unlimited, and eventually the proglottides become exhausted. Strips of such exhausted proglottides may break away from the strobila in what may be termed "pseudapolysis." Even pseudapolysis seems to be limited to unusually long-bodied pseudophyllideans such as Dibothriocephalidae and Amphicotylidae. Short-bodied forms apparently leave the host in an intact condition when sexually exhausted, sometimes only a few days after becoming gravid.

The physiological reasons for proglottisation and segmentation are far from clear. The American zoologist C. M. Child and his pupils have shown (1926) that for several free-living flatworms a *series* of axial gradients of metabolic activity may follow one another along the flatworm body, and that among such flatworms there is a tendency toward asexual reproduction by transverse divisions which coincide with the boundaries between the metabolic zones. Commonly the products of such divisions break free and develop into complete individuals, but a temporary union of such individuals in chain fashion has been recorded in some forms. If we assume, as seems justifiable from other evidence, that the holdfast is embryologically the posterior end of a tapeworm, the chain of proglottides must be regarded as a chain of individuals formed by transverse budding.

On this view, the maximum value of metabolic activity should be found at the pole of the larval tapeworm farthest from the holdfast, and the minimal value at the holdfast end. Such differences in axial gradient should also be demonstrable in individual proglottides. On this view, too, we cannot regard new proglottides as being cut off from a growth-zone but must regard each new proglottis as cut off from the first formed proglottis. With regard to this point, it may be noted that no histological evidence of active nuclear metabolism can be seen in the growth-zone. Segmentation should follow proglottisation as a response to the strains placed upon an elongated structure, fixed at one end and free at the other, by the peristaltic movements of the host gut. Such strains would be opposed by the contraction of the longitudinal musculature in each proglottis; the nonmuscular areas between successive proglottides would in that event appear as depressed transverse grooves.

The irregularity of proglottisation and segmentation among pseudophyllidean tapeworms is explicable only on the view, to be elaborated later, that certain families – notably Cyathocephalidae, Triaenophoridae, and Amphicotylidae – are neotenic larvae of segmented ancestral forms. Dibothriocephalidae show an internal separation of the proglottides and marked external segmentation; Bothriocephalidae show an internal separation only here and there, and the primary segmental grooves correspond with the internal interproglottidal zones. On the other hand, among Cyathocephalidae – which will be regarded here as neotenic larvae of proto-Dibothriocephalidae – proglottisation appears early, even in the procercoid larval stage, but both internal demarcation and external segmentation are absent. In Amphicotylidae – to be regarded as neotenic larvae of proto-tetraphyllidean forms – proglottisation is delayed, appearing only after the worm is fully grown; and internal demarcation is absent, though external segmentation may not only be well marked but may appear even before proglottisation.

Such irregularities are to be explained only by regarding them as irregular types of embryonic recapitulation, possibly as examples of "heterochronism" – that is to say, time-displacement in development which leads to organs appearing earlier or later in individual development than is the case in ancestral phylogeny – or of "abbreviation," in which the end stages of ancestral phylogeny are omitted from the ontogeny so that the definitive adult stage of the descendent resembles an adult stage of a remote rather than of a recent ancestor. Cases of neoteny fall under the latter heading.

Teratological distortions of the holdfast and the segments are not infrequent among tapeworms. Excessive numbers of suckers on the holdfast of cyclophyllidean worms are common, as well as additional margins or ridges on the body such that in cross section it appears Y-shaped (triradiate), H-shaped (tetraradiate), or star-shaped (pentaradiate). Many such cases have been described by Vigener (1903), Foster (1916), Faust (1925), Dobrovolny and Dobrovolny (1935), and Clapham

(1939b), who summarized the whole subject to that date. Apparently, according to Barker (1916), such deformities are not inherited but arise from partial separation of the early blastomeres of the developing egg.

Also common is a doubling of genitalia in each segment, suggesting the possibility that genera which normally show such diplogonadism have arisen as mutations from monogonadic forms (cf. *Cordicephalus*). Vergeer (1935) has reported such doubling in *Dibothriocephalus* producing an appearance strongly recalling the allied and diplogonadic *Diplogonoporus*. Williams (1939) described multiplication of genitalia in *Moniezia expansa* with incomplete delimitation of segments such that in what appeared to be two consecutive segments, there were two complexes of genitalia on the left side, representing three complete sets, and on the right side one normal set and a complex representing two sets of genitalia. Roudabush (1941) described multigenitalial and agenitalial segments of *Taenia pisiformis*. Honigberg (1944) described a segment of *Dipylidium caninum* with double genitalia on the left side only and reviewed other cases of teratology in this form.

Until the discovery and application of methods of staining and preparing animal tissues for microscopical study, relatively little was known about the nature of the skin and the internal organs of tapeworms. The 1870's, however, saw the pioneer observations of Schiefferdecker (1874) and Leuckart. In the 1880's and 1890's came those of Pintner (1880), Zschokke (1888c), Rindfleisch (1885), Linstow (1891, 1893a), Kraemer (1892), Blochmann (1896, 1897), and Zernecke (1895) on tapeworm anatomy and histology. To this period belong also the classic studies of Fraipont (1880, 1881) on the flatworm osmoregulatory system; of Lang (1881), Niemec (1885, 1888), and Ludwig Cohn (1898a) on the nervous system; of Lühe (1893, 1895a, 1897b) on the muscles; of Moniez (1880b) and F. Schmidt (1888) on the reproductive system.

The early years of this century saw the contributions of Bugge (1902) on the osmoregulatory system; Minckert (1905) on tapeworm histology generally; Maclaren (1903), Ziegler (1905), and Pratt (1909) on the skin; Young (1908) and Gough (1911) on the muscles; Ziluff (1912) on scolex muscles; Balss (1908) and Johnstone (1912) on genital ducts; Wagner (1917), Nybelin (1922), and Prenant (1922) on the parenchyma. Noteworthy in recent years have been the contributions of the Illinois school under H. Baldwin Ward; the Polish schools of Janicki and Wisniewski; the Swiss school of Fuhrmann, Joyeux, and Baer; and in Britain, the studies of Beddard, Meggitt, Southwell, and Woodland.

However, as Young (1935) has stressed, there is still a vast uncertainty about many details of tapeworm structure and development. Tapeworms are unfavorable objects for histological study since the groundwork of their bodies is a loose syncytium in which "the true relations of various cellular elements (i.e., muscle and connective tissue fibrils, nerves, and excretory tubes) are difficult to distinguish, and which is easily distorted by fixatives, producing puzzling artifacts."

Young has suggested ten main problems of tapeworm structure and development:

1. What is the cestode individual – the proglottis or the chain of proglottides?

2. Are germ layers present, and if so, what is their origin?

3. What is the status of the subcuticular layer? Is it an epithelium, or merely a specialized part of the general parenchyma?

4. What is the origin of the sex cells? Is there anything comparable to a "germ-track" in cestodes, or are their germ cells, like other tissues, merely specialized parts of a primarily undifferentiated tissue? And can germ cells, once they have been differentiated, become de-differentiated and secondarily give rise to somatic tissues?

5. What is the origin of the problematical cell, associated with the fertilized egg in some cestodes, which has been variously interpreted as a yolk cell, polar body, or cleavage cell?

6. What is the method of cell division – mitotic, amitotic, or both?

7. Is there any evidence of chromosome continuity in these worms?

8. In oogenesis and spermatogenesis, is there reduction of chromosomes, and in the former process, is there formation of polar bodies?

9. What is the structure of the cestode sperm? Can anything comparable to head, middle piece, or tail be differentiated in it? Can its origin be traced back to a definite spermatid?

10. In those rare cases in which there is sexual differentiation in cestodes, what are the possible determining factors?

In the following pages, some attempt will be made to provide answers to the questions listed above.

Skin

The descriptions of tapeworm skin structure by various students of the question are in many respects confusing and contradictory. There is, however, a general agreement that this skin comprises, from the outer surface inward, the following layers: (*a*) cuticle, (*b*) basement membrane, (*c*) subcuticular muscles, (*d*) neuromuscular cells, and (*e*) subcuticle. The cuticle is delicate, transparent, and readily shed. According to Wisniewski (1930) it consists, in *Archigetes sieboldii*, a caryophyllaeid tapeworm, of two layers, possibly of several. These layers are very thin and transparent. In material fixed in Fleming's solution and doubly stained with safranin and Lichtgrün, the cuticle stains green. If stained with Mallory's stain and fuchsin, the cuticle stains light blue. It is without pore canals, and the passage of water, glucose, etc., through it can only be by osmosis. Presumably its laminated nature favors such osmosis.

The basement membrane, according to Wisniewski (1930), also consists of two layers. They stain respectively red and dark green with the safranin-Lichtgrün combination; yellowish gray and dark blue with the Mallory-fuchsin combination; and brilliant red and bright blue with the usual eosin-haematoxylin combination. The outermost layer appears in many places to contain granules and refractive, nonstainable vacuoles. Granules appear also in the innermost layer but are scarcer. Below the basement membrane lies a fairly thick protoplasmic layer in which cell

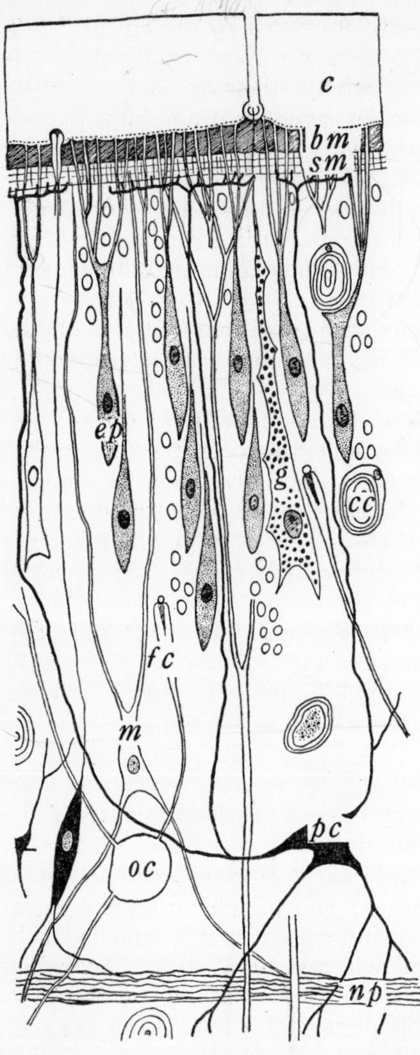

FIG. 3. Skin and underlying tissues of *Ligula* as interpreted by Blochmann, 1897. *c*, cuticle; *bm*, basement membrane; *sm*, subcuticular muscles; *ep*, epidermal cells; *g*, gland cells; *cc*, calcareous corpuscle; *fc*, flame cell; *m*, myoblast; *pc*, parenchyma; *np*, nerve plexus.

outlines cannot be distinguished; within it may occur disintegrating nuclei.

The subcuticular muscles, according to Gough (1911), comprise two layers of muscle cells (myoblasts), each cell having lateral, fiberlike outgrowths (fibrillae). The two layers are so arranged that the fibrillae of the outermost layer run approximately transversely to the long axis of the worm, thus forming "circular" or "transverse" muscle fibers, while the fibrillae of the innermost layer run longitudinally so as to form "longitudinal" muscle fibers.

The neuromuscular cells appear as a layer of flattened, multipolar cells lying just below the subcuticular muscle fibrillae and in the same plane as the basement membrane. Some authors refer to them as Sommer-Landois cells. Each cell sends out several processes which seem to join the tips of the subcuticular muscle fibrillae. Others appear to join the tips of processes from adjacent neuromuscular cells. Still others seem to join the tips of neurofibrillae from the nerve network.

The subcuticle consists of a layer of elongated cells, each roughly at right angles to the plane of the cuticle. The individual cells may be widely spaced or densely packed, according to the state of contraction of the worm. The cells taper at each end and fray out into branches. The branches from the uppermost poles of the cells penetrate the cuticle and may even appear on the body surface as "pseudo-cilia" or even as spines; by early observers these processes were termed "pore canals." The processes from the lowermost poles converge, according to Gough (1911), to form bundles of dorso-ventral muscle fibers, or along the margins of the worm to form bundles of transverse muscle fibers; according to this observer, the subcuticular cells are bipolar muscle cells.

One of the most controversial questions of comparative histology concerns the relation of the flatworm skin to that of other animals and the relation of its various layers to one another. Certain postulates may be laid down:

1. Turbellaria – from which both Trematoda and Cestoda have undoubtedly originated, though possibly along independent lines – have a true epithelial skin, derived from the ectoderm layer of the embryo, using the term "epithelial skin" in the sense laid down by Blochmann (1896): "Ich verstehe also unter äusserem Epithel eine Zellenschicht, die entweder selbst die äussere Oberfläche des Thierkörpers begrenzt, oder auf ihrer Oberfläche eine vom Zellplasma chemisch mehr oder weniger differentierte Membran erzeugt, die dann ihrerseits den aüsseren Überzug des Körpers bildet. Wie diese Membran gebildet wird, durch eine Art von Sekretion, oder durch chemische Umwandlung der peripheren Plasmapartien ist für unsere Frage einerlei; ebenso ob diese Membran besondere Strukturverhältnisse hat oder nicht."

2. This turbellarian ectoderm is represented by the coverings of the developing embryo of Trematoda and Cestoda, and by the coverings of the earliest postembryonic stage of Trematoda and Cestoda – namely, the trematode *miracidium* and the cestode *coracidium*.

3. These coverings are definitely cast off, or they degenerate, when these early postembryonic forms pass into the next postembryonic stage. This observation, made originally by Schauinsland (1886), has been confirmed by almost every student of the question.

"In all forms in which the development has been adequately studied, two layers of cells are formed during cleavage, which are subsequently cast off, releasing the embryo, which consists of an undifferentiated mass, out of which the tissues of the larva are formed by a process of differentiation in situ without the formation of any subsequent layers. Some writers (Leuckart, 1881, and Schauinsland, 1886) regard these two layers as ectoderm only, or as ectoderm and mesoderm; while others (Beneden, 1881; Zograf, 1890), admitting that these layers are ectodermal in origin, believe that some ectoderm remains and takes part in development.

"Monticelli (1892c) and Bresslau (1904) consider the desquamated membranes as structures formed by the embryo (Monticelli) or the yolk cells (Bresslau), but not forming any part of the germ layers of the former, which latter develop subsequent to membrane formation out of the embryonic mass (Monticelli); and yet others (St. Remy, 1901b; Young, 1908) believe that any comparison between the 'germ layers' of cestodes and other Metazoa is futile in view of the degeneracy of the former." Young (1935).

4. The cuticle of the adult trematode or cestode cannot, therefore, be homologous with the ciliated epithelium that covers the turbellarian

body. It must be considered either (*a*) as a secretion of the subcuticle, or (*b*) as a secretion of the parenchyma, the spongelike mesh that fills up the interior of the flatworm body, apart from the subcuticular cells which, as already stated, are considered by Young (1908) and by Gough (1911) as muscle cells.

The view that the cuticle is formed from the subcuticle was put forward originally by Blochmann (1896) and has received support from many later observers, notably from Fuhrmann (1931). Some divergence of opinion, however, is found among these observers as to whether the subcuticular cells are really ectoderm cells that have sunk in from the surface – the view of Blochmann – or whether they are cells of the parenchyma, which itself, according to one group of students represented by Ziegler (1905), is of ectodermic origin, or, according to another group of students represented by Balss (1908), is of mesodermic origin. The latter view thus regards cuticle formation in flatworms as of mesodermic origin and so providing an exception to the germ layer hypothesis. A reconciliation between the several views is possible if, as Young (1908) concluded from a study of cuticle formation in the larval *Taenia pisiformis*, the cuticle is formed by a deposition of cement substance, derived presumably from the subcuticle, among a groundwork of simple parenchyma fibrillae. According to this observer, the cuticle is formed before the differentiation of subcuticular cells.

The view that the tapeworm cuticle is a purely parenchymal secretion was put forward originally by Pratt (1909) and is sometimes called "Pratt's theory." In recent years it has been supported by Wisniewski (1930), by Vogel (1930), and by Venard (1938). Wisniewski believed that during the development of *Archigetes* neither epithelium nor subcuticle is present in the early procercoid larval stage. Where such an epithelium occurs, as in the genital ducts, no sinking inward of surface epithelium can be observed. He believed the cuticle of the adult worm to be a "pseudodermis" – as Poche (1924) termed it – that is, a skin formed from the mesoderm, in this case represented by the parenchyma.

Vogel (1930), likewise, studying cuticle formation in the procercoid larva of *Dibothriocephalus latus*, found no subcuticle below the delicate larval cuticle. He believed this cuticle to be a secretion of the parenchymal surface and to be homologous with the basement membrane of the turbellarian skin. Later, however, this early cuticle becomes underlaid by a new cuticle formed by the condensation of a layer of cells which have an affinity for the dyestuff pyronin, and can thus be seen to invade the future subcuticular zone from the nucleated internal tissue that underlies the procercoid cuticle. These cells become the subcuticle, and the early cuticle is shed when the procercoid loses its cercomer and undergoes metamorphosis. That is to say, the tapeworm during its life has three successive cuticles. First, it has an embryonic covering homologous with the cuticle of Turbellaria and derived from the embryonic ectoderm; second, a larval cuticle, homologous with the basement membrane of Turbellaria and derived from the parenchyma; and third, an adult cuticle derived from the subcuticular cells.

The absence of subcuticular cells from the suckers of cyclophyllidean tapeworms, as asserted by Young (1908) and Gough (1911), and the presumption therefrom that the cuticle of the cyclophyllidean holdfast is an early larval one that has persisted, support the view—arguable on other grounds—that the cyclophyllidean tapeworms are more primitive than the pseudophyllidean ones, and that the holdfast of the latter is a new structure, a pseudo-holdfast derived from the body of the ancestral pseudophyllidean.

The possibility that the subcuticular cells represent *embryonic ectoderm* rather than ectoderm that has sunk inward from the surface, as Blochmann thought, that they represent in fact ectoderm that never reached the embryonic surface, is suggested by the observations of many students that a nucleated epithelium appears early as a lining for the genital ducts but degenerates later and is replaced by a cuticle similar to that of the body surface. Such a view would harmonize skin formation in tapeworms with that in other animals and with the germ layer hypothesis.

"On the one hand the cuticle is considered as a much modified epithelium, and certain bodies found therein have been interpreted as nuclei or the remains thereof (Salensky, 1874). On the other hand, the subcuticular cells are regarded as an epithelium which secretes the cuticle (Blochmann, 1896, *et al.*), while yet another interpretation regards the cestodes and trematodes as entirely lacking an epithelium, the subcuticula representing parenchymal cells specialized as absorptive, sensory, and neuro-muscular elements (Pratt, 1909; Young, 1908, *et al.*).

"In support of the first of these hypotheses, besides the observations above cited on the presence of nuclear remnants in the cuticula of *Amphilina*, may be mentioned my own work (1912) on the epithelium of certain turbellarians, in which I found evidence of a progressing degeneration, from that of forms like *Planocera* to that of *Bdelloura* in which nuclei are apparently entirely absent. These observations suggest rather strongly that the cuticle of trematodes and cestodes has developed from the epithelium of the turbellaria by condensation and loss of cellular structure, with resultant absence of a true epithelium in the former worms.

"If this interpretation be correct the embryonic membranes of cestodes and trematodes would appear to be either ectodermal derivatives or layers specialized in these groups, and without homologs in other forms; while the embryonic mass itself is composed of a greatly modified ectoderm remnant (cuticle), and an undifferentiated tissue (parenchyma), representing the mesoderm and entoderm of other worms, from which all the tissues of the adult are developed, including the nervous system, which is ordinarily of ectodermal origin." Young (1935).

Parenchyma

The skin of the tapeworm encloses a loose, spongelike mass of tissue, usually termed "parenchyma," within which are embedded the muscles, nerves, osmoregulatory organs, and reproductive organs. The histology of this parenchyma is obscure. All observers are agreed that it is a faintly stainable network enclosing polyhedral spaces. One group of observers (Looss, Stieda, Linstow, Sommer, Landois, *et al.*) has regarded these spaces as being *intracellular* and formed by the coherence of bladderlike cells. Another group (Pintner, Prenant, Schmidt, Zernecke, *et al.*) has regarded the parenchymal spaces as *intercellular*, formed by the meeting and coalescence of branching processes of embryonic cells.

Actually, as one might expect, the parenchyma is formed in both ways, so that the spaces are both intracellular and intercellular. Wisniewski, who has studied the development of parenchyma in the larval development of *Archigetes*, describes the following steps in the process (Figure 4):

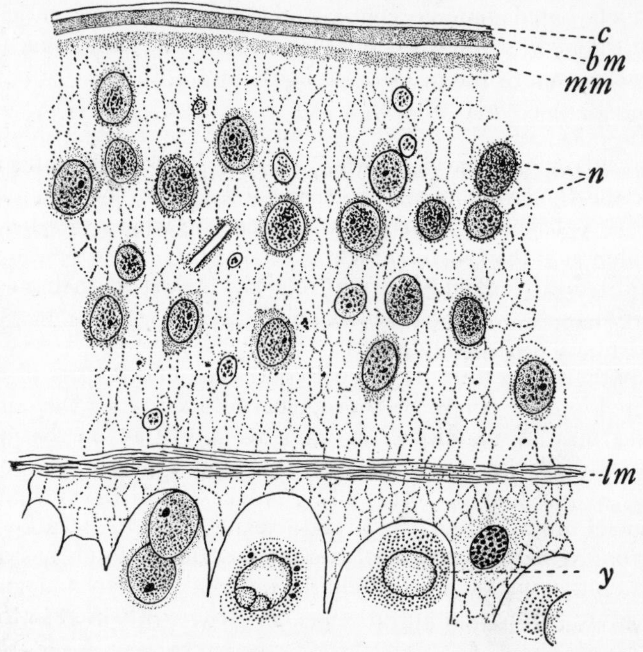

FIG. 4. Skin and underlying tissues of *Archigetes* as interpreted by Wisniewski, 1930. *c*, cuticle; *bm*, basement membrane; *mm*, matrix sheath of circular muscles; *n*, nuclei of degenerating somatic cells; *lm*, longitudinal parenchymal muscles; *y*, yolk glands.

1. In the youngest stages the surface cuticle encloses about 120 cells, which are of two types. One type, distinguished on the grounds of their career as "germinative cells," have large, weakly staining nuclei surrounded by scanty cytoplasm; they give rise to the testes, ovaries, and yolk glands. The other type, distinguished as "somatic cells," have smaller, intensively staining nuclei, divide rapidly, and come to outnumber greatly the germinative cells.

2. As the larva grows, the rate of division of the somatic cells declines

and they become larger, more cytoplasmic, and basophilic in staining reaction. Another type of cell appears, distinguished as "somatic-germinative cells" and originating apparently from the germinative cells. They resemble somatic cells but have large, weakly staining nuclei, in contrast with the compact, intensively staining nuclei of the true somatic cells.

3. The somatic and the somatic-germinative cells begin to swell; their cytoplasm becomes fibrous; vacuoles appear inside them; they tend to unite with one another by cytoplasmic bridges or by fusion of their walls, thus forming an intracellular network in which intercellular lacunae are present.

In the central region of the tapeworm, the somatic cells lose their nuclei and form a purely cytoplasmic network within which the reproductive organs begin to appear. The development of these organs exerts pressure upon the network and brings about its partial degeneration; much of it goes to form membranes around the reproductive organs. In the cortical region of the tapeworm, on the other hand, nuclei are plentiful in the parenchyma, although not every nucleus corresponds with a cell.

Scattered through the parenchymal network of most tapeworms are relatively large, round or oval cells, each with a large nucleus. These presumably are cells of the subcuticle that have sunk into the parenchyma. Among them are so-called "calcareous corpuscles," composed of concentric layers of a mixture of the phosphates and carbonates of calcium and magnesium cemented together by an organic cement and enclosed within a cell membrane.

Musculature

Two zones of muscle fibers may be seen in the majority of tapeworms – a subcuticular zone and a parenchymal zone. The subcuticular zone of muscle fibers lies between the basement membrane of the skin and the layer of flattened neuromuscular cells. There is some uncertainty as to whether or not these subcuticular muscles represent true myoblasts, distinct from the neuromuscular cells of Young (1908), or whether they represent processes from those neuromuscular cells. They comprise an outer layer of fibers, fine and closely parallel to one another, arranged approximately transversely to the long axis of the worm; and an inner layer of fibers arranged in loosely parallel bundles in the antero-posterior axis of the worm. These layers are usually referred to as the circular and the longitudinal subcuticular muscles respectively.

Among Turbellaria and Trematoda such subcuticular muscles are the only muscles of the animal, and the circular and longitudinal fibers are supplemented by diagonally running fibers between the two layers and by dorso-ventral fibers. It is probable, therefore, that the complicated arrangement of muscle fibers found within the tapeworm holdfast is derived from the subcuticular system.

La Rue (1909), describing the holdfast musculature of *Ophiotaenia filaroides*, a primitive suckered type, analyzed the arrangement as follows:

1. In the holdfast, in front of the suckers, there is a series of diagonal fibers running from the right and left sides of the holdfast to the dorsal and ventral sides (Figure 5). In cross sections through the holdfast tip, these fibers appear as a faintly staining rhomboid figure.

2. Posterior to this rhomboid and extending to the posterior level of the suckers, there is a cross-shaped series of dorso-ventral and ventral fibers producing in cross sections the so-called "muscle cross."

3. At the level of the suckers, a diagonal muscle cross is produced in transverse sections by fibers which run from the anterior sucker of each side to the posterior sucker of the opposite side. The juxtaposition of this cross upon the muscle cross mentioned above produces the effect of an eight-pointed star, the "Muskelstern" of Riggenbach (1896a).

4. Within the wall of each sucker just below the cuticle, there is a band of fibers running around the sucker margin. Essex (1927a), discussing the sucker musculature of the proteocephalan genus *Corallobothrium*, described this layer as being peculiarly thick around the inner half of the sucker rim, and as acting to some extent as a sphincter muscle. At right angles to this band of circular fibers, a zone of radial fibers runs to the internal limiting membrane of the sucker; just within this latter membrane, around the base of the sucker, another zone of circular fibers is found.

Gough (1911), discussing the sucker muscles of the anoplocephalid tapeworm *Avitellina centripunctata*, described similar muscle patterns as seen in cross sections through the holdfast; but owing to the suckers occupying the anterior face of the holdfast, these patterns are produced somewhat differently from those described by La Rue. The rhomboid figure in *Avitellina* is produced by the juxtaposition of (*a*) a diagonal cross, *anterior* to the terminal loops of the osmoregulatory canals and produced by fibers running from the front face of the left ventral sucker to the front face of the right dorsal sucker, crossing fibers from the front face of the right ventral sucker to the front face of the left dorsal sucker; and (*b*) a rhomboid system of fibers situated *posteriorly* to the terminal osmoregulatory loops and connecting the lateral face and the median face of each ventral sucker with the median and lateral faces of each dorsal sucker.

Posterior to the rhomboid is a tetragon of fibers which connect the median faces of the left suckers, median faces of the right suckers, median faces of the dorsal suckers, and median faces of the ventral suckers. A second tetragon of fibers occurs near the bases of the suckers and comprises fibers arranged as in the first tetragon. The juxtaposition of rhomboid and tetragon will give in certain planes of cross sectioning the "Muskelstern." Near their bases the suckers are also connected by muscle fibers which connect the two dorsal suckers with each other and the two ventrals with each other, but do not seem to connect the dorsals with the ventrals.

Gough describes each sucker as separated from the holdfast parenchyma by a delimiting membrane. Directly within this membrane are two sets of fibers running parallel with it – the first set forms concentric

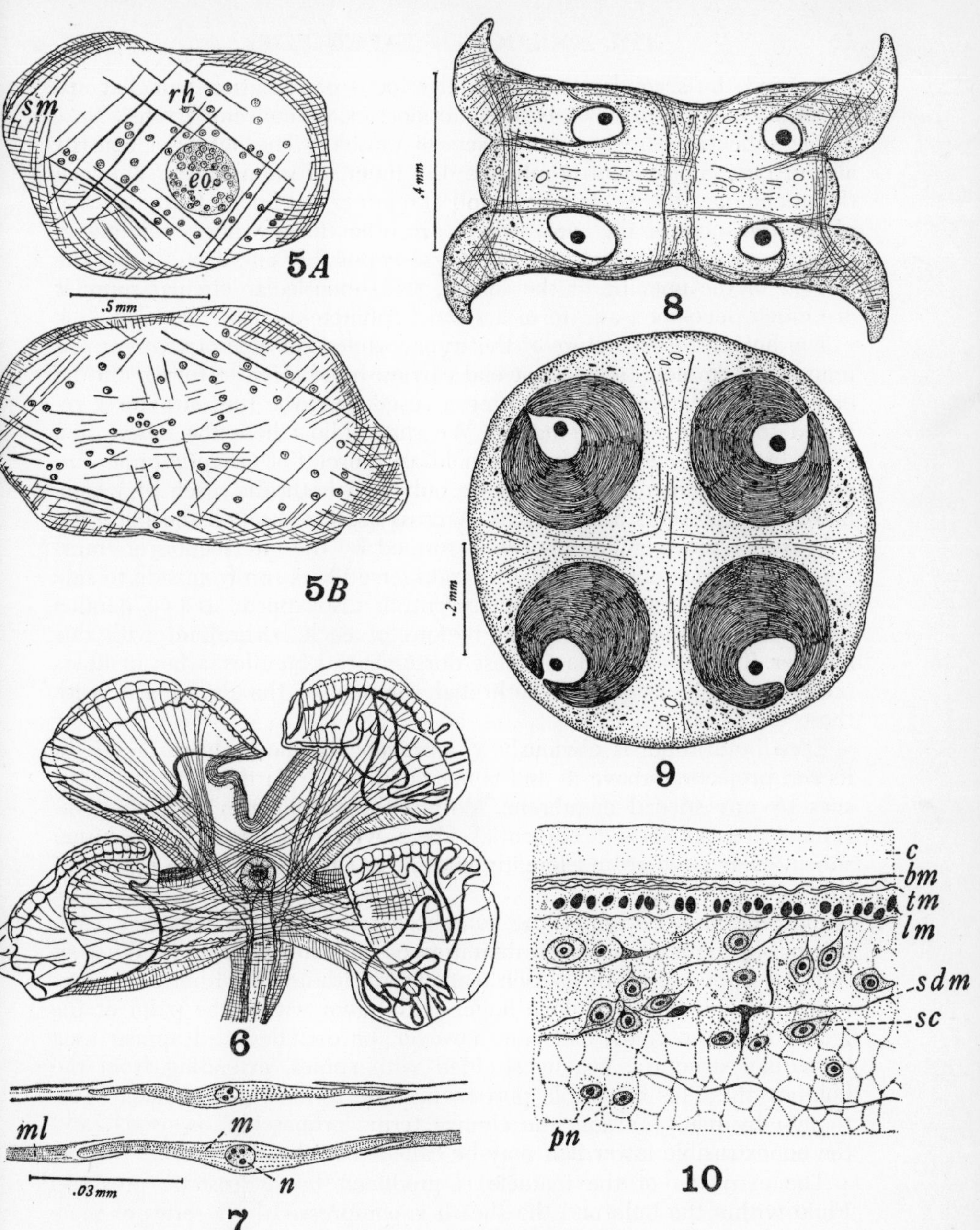

FIG. 5. *Ophiotaenia filaroides*, cross sections of holdfast. After La Rue, 1909. *sm*, subcuticular muscles; *rh*, muscle rhomboid; *eo*, end organ. FIG. 6. *Anthobothrium auriculatum*, expanded holdfast to show muscle fibers. After Rees, 1943. FIG. 7. *Avitellina centripunctata*, longitudinal muscle fibers. After Gough, 1911. *m*, myoblast; *n*, nucleus; *ml*, muscle. FIGS. 8 and 9. *Grillotia erinaceus*, cross sections through holdfast at level of bothridia (8) and at the level of tentacle bulbs (9). After Johnstone, 1912. FIG. 10. *Grillotia erinaceus*, skin and underlying tissues. After Johnstone, 1912. *c*, cuticle; *bm*, basement membrane; *tm*, transverse subcuticular muscles; *sc*, subcuticular cell; *lm*, longitudinal subcuticular muscles; *sdm*, subdermal muscles; *pn*, parenchymal nuclei.

rings, and the second set radiates, the focus of radiation being at approximately the same spot as the innermost of the concentric rings. Next to the subcuticle are found two sets of muscles. The outer set consists also of circular, concentric muscles; the inner, of radial fibers. Between the cuticle and the delimiting membrane are radial fibers. In the middle of the thickness of the sucker there are other muscle fibers running at right angles to the radials, whose course is possibly circular. Around the margin of the opening of the sucker, the subcuticular circular muscles are much developed and form a sort of sphincter.

The holdfast musculature of the trypanorhynchan type of tapeworm is unusually complex. Its holdfast end carries, in addition to four bothridia or two bothridia each representing a fused pair, the four structures referred to previously as tentacles. We shall follow here the description given by Johnstone (1912) of the holdfast muscles of *Grillotia erinaceus*, a trypanorhynchan with apparently only two bothridia, each of which, however, represents a fused pair. A cross section through the bothridia (Figure 8) shows a "muscle cross" formed by the intersection of transverse and dorso-ventral fibers. The transverse fibers run from side to side in two parallel bundles; the dorso-ventrals also appear as two parallel bundles connecting the median regions of each bothridium with one another. To the outer side of these dorso-ventral bundles, a fan of fibers on each side links up the bothridial surfaces of the dorsal side with those of the ventral.

Each bothridium is obviously a depression of the body surface with its rim projecting above it, and is not delimited from the underlying tissues by any special membrane. Within the mobile rim of each bothridium are radial and tangential fibers which supplement the usual subcuticular circular and longitudinal fibers that underlie the cuticle of the bothridia.

In addition to bothridia, the holdfast has four tubular tentacles, each originating from a cylindrical dilatation or bulb deep within it. When at rest, the uppermost half of each tentacle is withdrawn within the lowermost half, much like a glove finger withdrawn within the palm of the glove. This uppermost half can, however, be extruded and appear as a threadlike structure, heavily studded with spines, extending from the holdfast tip. This extrusible portion may be termed the "tentacle" (although by many authors the clumsy term "proboscide" is used), and the nonextrusible lower half may be called the "sheath."

The extrusion of the tentacle is produced by hydrostatic pressure. Fluid within the bulb and the sheath is compressed by a series of muscular sheaths or laminae that surround the bulb. Four such muscle sheaths may be recognized: (1) Extrinsic tangential fibers which run from the floors of the bothridia to the sheath. (2) Extrinsic longitudinal muscle fibers which are inserted in the outer wall of each bulb and are continuous with the longitudinal fibers of the parenchymal muscles. (3) Intrinsic tentacular fibers within the bulb wall. This wall consists of an outer cuticle, a thick layer of such muscle fibers, and an inner wall continuous with the sheath. The muscle fibers are in two series, each running obliquely around the bulb but crossing each other at angles of 45°. Their contraction reduces the cavity of the bulb so that by hydrostatic pressure the tentacle is extruded from the sheath. (4) Retractor muscles of the tentacles, comprising a bundle of fibers from the posterior wall of each bulb to the internal wall of its tentacle, near the tip. They run axially through bulb and sheath.

Enough evidence has been given to indicate that the holdfast musculature of a tapeworm is a greatly modified part of the subcuticular musculature of the rest of the body. Some further idea of its complexity may be gained from Figure 6, based upon Gwendolen Ree's figure of the holdfast muscles of the tetraphyllidean, *Anthobothrium.* A review of holdfast musculature, based upon modern microtechnical methods and covering a wide range of tapeworm types, is urgently needed.

Peculiar among flatworms is the so-called "parenchymal musculature" of tapeworms. It may be described as a band or zone of muscle fibers which encircles the worm about midway between its outer surface and its central axis, and which divides the parenchyma into cortical and medullary regions. This zone consists of a band of bipolar, spindle-shaped myoblasts of relatively enormous lengths which lie within longitudinally running bundles of fibers, produced by the myoblasts themselves. According to the studies of Gough (1911) on *Avitellina*, the muscle fibers on the margin of the zone are tubular, and the ends of the myoblasts are inserted into the tubular fiber ends (Figure 7). The contractile fibers have presumably been deposited upon the outer surface of the myoblasts. The tubular cavity of the muscle fiber gradually fills with muscle substance, and the myoblast disappears from the axial region of the fiber and comes to lie lateral to it. Those fibers which lie within the muscle zone, internal to the marginal tubular fibers, are solid.

On the inner side of the band of longitudinal muscle fibers are two parallel bands of transverse fibers which have been secreted by myoblasts with lateral fibrillaę. The two bands lie dorsally and ventrally, respectively, and enclose between them the medullary parenchyma. Their ends fray out, and the divergent fiber ends of each band cross those of the other band before proceeding to be inserted in the cuticle.

The extent to which the zone of longitudinal muscle fibers is developed varies greatly among tapeworms, even within the limits of a single genus. In some forms, the muscle fibers form stout bundles which encircle the segment and fill up almost all the cortical region. In other forms, the fibers occur singly and scattered through the cortex, being barely visible as minute granules in a stained transverse section of a segment.

It is possible that the parenchymal musculature is a reminiscence of a former alimentary canal musculature in the ancestral stock from which tapeworms have evolved. But until evidence is available from a detailed comparison of tapeworm and turbellarian histology such speculation is profitless. The uniform pattern of this parenchymal musculature among tapeworms and the predominance of longitudinal fibers over transverse ones are explicable when the function of the parenchymal musculature is considered. That function, located especially in the longitudinal fibers of the zone, is the very important one of holding the worm in its condition of tonus, or partial muscular contraction, which is its main protection against the tendency of the peristaltic movements of the host intestine to expel it. However, the differences in the thickness of the parenchymal muscle zone shown by closely allied species are difficult to account for in terms of variations in strength of gut peristalsis among the respective hosts. It is difficult, too, to understand such phenomena as the double parenchymal muscle zone of the dibothriocephalid tapeworm *Schistocephalus,* which lives under almost the same host conditions, both as larva and as adult, as the closely allied genus *Ligula,* whose parenchymal muscle zone is single.

The zone of parenchymal muscles, forming as it does a sheath which surrounds the reproductive organs and which takes up biological stains with great avidity, impedes considerably the morphological study of tapeworms, since it is rarely possible to prepare for microscopical study such beautifully clear preparations of tapeworm segments as are possible with trematodes.

Osmoregulatory System

The term "osmoregulatory" will be used throughout this book in preference to the usual term "excretory" for the system of organs described below. There is no experimental evidence that these organs are exclusively excretory in function, or even that they are excretory at all. On the other hand, there is strong presumptive evidence that they serve to maintain within the worm a degree of hydrostatic pressure that helps the tapeworm in extensory movements of the body and holdfast, and that they serve to regulate the water balance of the animal.

The osmoregulatory system was one of the earliest anatomical systems of the tapeworm body to be described. Reference may be made to the studies of Fraipont (1880, 1881), Pintner (1880, 1896b, 1906, 1933), Köhler (1894), Bugge (1902), Wagner (1917), Gough (1911), Essex (1927a), Wisniewski (1930), Vogel (1930), and Rees (1943). This system of organs comprises two types of structures – (1) "collecting canals," and (2) the "flame cell."

1. The collecting canals, typically four in number, run the full length of the worm and lie just inside the margin of the medullary parenchyma. On each side, a vessel lying somewhat ventrally in the parenchyma and usually of wide lumen carries a fluid – presumably water – in a direction *away from* the holdfast. This is commonly termed the ventral vessel or ventral canal. Dorsal to it, or lying lateral to it, between it and the lateral nerve cord, there may be a dorsal vessel, narrower in lumen and carrying fluid *toward* the holdfast. Within the holdfast end itself, the four vessels may be connected by a network of vessels each at least as wide in diameter as the longitudinal canals (Figures 11, 12, 14, 16).

This would seem to be the primitive arrangement. The network within the holdfast may, however, be represented by a single ring vessel – the condition in taeniid tapeworms – by a transverse vessel, or, as in anoplo-

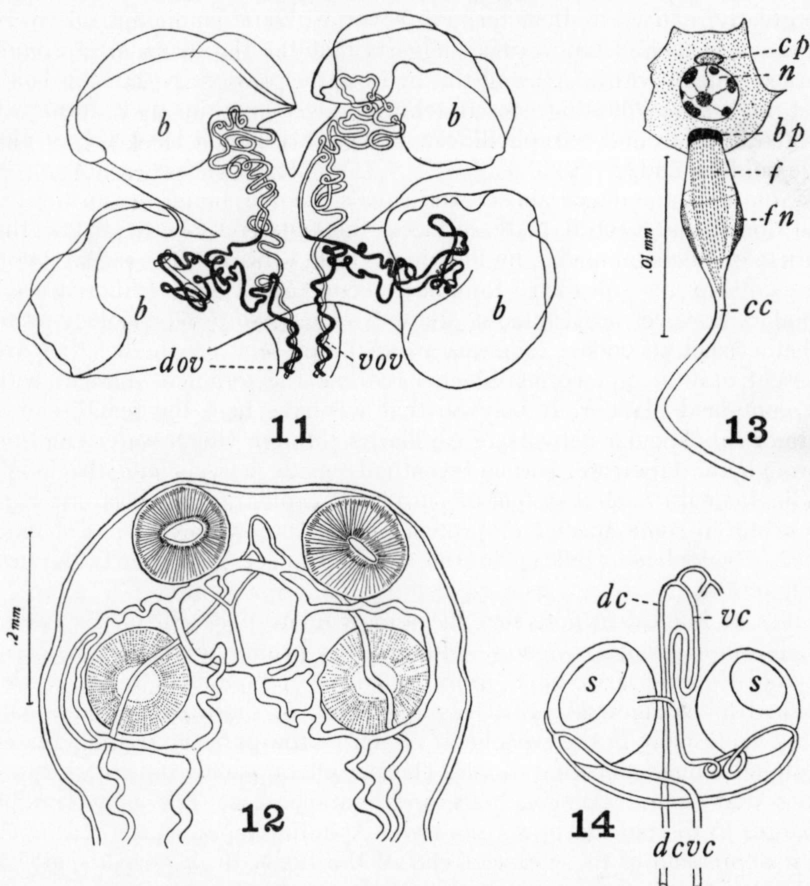

FIG. 11. *Anthobothrium auriculatum*, holdfast expanded to show osmoregulatory canals. After Rees, 1943. *b*, bothridia; *dov*, dorsal osmoregulatory canal; *vov*, ventral osmoregulatory canal. FIG. 12. *Proteocephalus torulosus*, holdfast showing osmoregulatory canals. After Wagner, 1917. FIG. 13. *Avitellina centripunctata*, a flame cell. After Gough, 1911. *cp*, corpuscle; *n*, nucleus; *bp*, basal plate; *f*, flame cell; *fn*, funnel; *cc*, capillary canal. FIG. 14. *Avitellina centripunctata*, holdfast with left half of osmoregulatory system, viewed laterally. After Gough, 1911. *dc*, dorsal canal; *vc*, ventral canal; *s*, suckers.

cephalid tapeworms, the dorsal and ventral vessels of one side may be connected by a loop, but no cross connection between right and left longitudinal canals is ever found.

There appears to be no connection between the dorsal and ventral vessels of any one side during their course through the body. Between the pair of ventral vessels, however, and occasionally between the pair of dorsal canals, there may be in each segment, just in front of the posterior border, a transverse connecting vessel that may be actually wider than the longitudinal canals it connects. In the last segment, this transverse vessel is represented by a bladderlike structure which opens to the outside by a short duct. The tendency for dorsal canals to be absent or to be greatly reduced in diameter in tapeworms whose holdfast is relatively rigid, as in taeniid tapeworms, suggests that the dorsal canals are concerned chiefly with increasing the hydrostatic pressure within the holdfast and so facilitating its stretching movements in such forms as proteocephalan and tetraphyllidean tapeworms, which have a very mobile holdfast end.

From both the dorsal and ventral canals twiglike branches run toward the dorsal and ventral body surfaces, there to end blindly below the cuticle or to communicate by fine ducts, from a bladderlike ending, with the outside by so-called "foramina secundaria." Some difference of opinion, however, exists among students of tapeworm morphology as to whether such secondary foramina are really present, or whether they are present only in tapeworms which have lost the terminal segment with its contained bladder. It may be that we have here the remains of a former subcuticular network of capillaries through which water entering through the tapeworm surface eventually made its way into the longitudinal canals. Such a system of peripheral capillaries has been asserted to occur in some species of proteocephalan tapeworms (see Kraemer, 1892; Riggenbach, 1896a) in the holdfast, neck, and newly formed proglottides.

It is of interest to note that the osmoregulatory system of the caryophyllid tapeworm, *Archigetes* – either a very primitive type of tapeworm or the neotenic larva of a primitive ancestral tapeworm form – is described by Wisniewski (1930) as a network of short, connected canals lying exclusively in the peripheral region of the parenchyma. There are no longitudinal collecting canals. The peripheral canals run in all directions and bound polygonal areas of parenchyma. The network discharges to the outside by six somewhat spindle-shaped canals that open in a depression of the posterior end of the body. In the trunk region a second network lies somewhat irregularly deeper than the first network. Characteristic of the network is its clarity in some regions at one moment and its near invisibility at other moments. Possibly the phenomenon is associated with the expansion and contraction of the worm, the canals of the network tending to fill when the worm expands and to empty when it contracts. The movements of the worm thus tend to fill and empty, alternately, any particular area of the net.

However, Wagner (1917) described the osmoregulatory system of the plerocercoid larva of *Proteocephalus torulosus*, again to be regarded as a relatively primitive type of tapeworm, as having the four characteristic longitudinal collecting canals. From them, straight, unbranching vessels come off to the body surface, there to end blindly or to open by secondary foramina (Figures 12, 15). Pintner (1933), describing trypanorhynchan forms, believed that there were no dendritic, blindly ending branches of the longitudinal canals, but that through fusion of the outer walls of the canals here and there with the parenchyma, tiplike portions of the canals are pulled outward. The part of the vessel wall *opposite* the outgrowth then grows into it, and eventually the outgrowth widens out as a bend or a curve in the course of the canal (Figure 16).

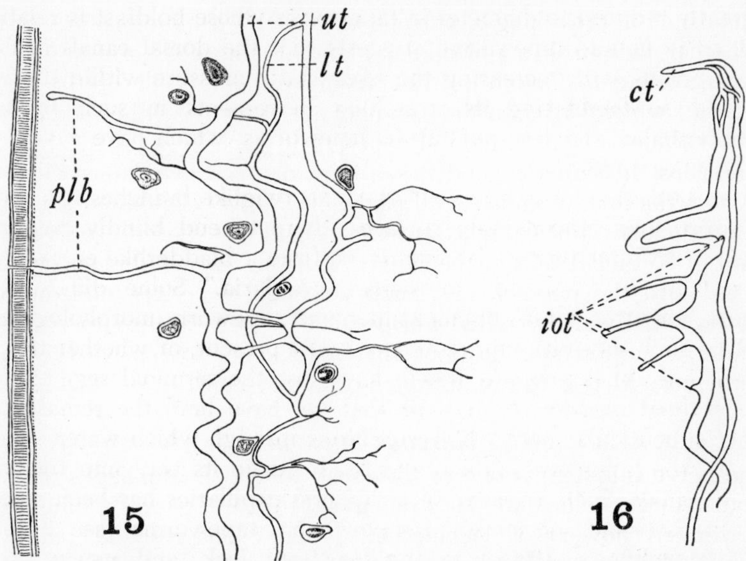

FIG. 15. Lateral osmoregulatory canals in plerocercoid of *Proteocephalus torulosus.* After Wagner, 1917. *ut,* upper trunk; *lt,* lower trunk; *plb,* peripheral lateral branches. FIG. 16. Osmoregulatory canals in holdfast of *Calliobothrium coronatum.* After Pintner, 1933. *ct,* common anterior termination; *iot,* irregular outgrowing tubules.

Rees (1943), in the tetraphyllidean form, *Anthobothrium auriculatum* (L.), found the usual four longitudinal canals with the dorsal ones narrower in diameter than the ventrals. The arrangement in the holdfast is simple. Each vessel passes into the stalk of the nearest bothridium, then loops back upon itself, and at the base of the stalk joins the other vessel of its side, each dorsal thus joining each ventral. There is no ring vessel (Figure 11).

2. The second component of the osmoregulatory system is the flame cell. Studies by later observers have added little to the descriptions of tapeworm flame cells given by Bugge (1902). They are irregularly star-shaped cells, each provided with a granular cytoplasm and with a nucleus that stains conspicuously. Each nucleus has a nucleolus and several chromatin bodies. The "flame" is a bundle of long cilia which comes off from the cell fairly near to the nucleus, but is sometimes separated from the cell proper by a "neck" of protoplasm. The cilia arise from a basal plate, a lens-shaped body whose concave side is turned toward the flame. The flame is enclosed in a funnel-like widening of the end of a capillary vessel which comes off from a ventral canal (Figure 13). The flame cells occur in groups of four. According to some authors (Schiefferdecker, 1874; Haman, 1885; Gough, 1911; Wagner, 1917), they lie in the medullary parenchyma, in the vicinity of the ventral vessel. Other authors (Pintner, 1880; Zschokke, 1888c; Zernecke, 1895) believed them to be most numerous in the cortical parenchyma.

There is still some doubt as to whether the flame cell is merely a mechanism for provoking a current within the osmoregulatory system, or whether it is itself a unicellular gland. Flame cells appear to originate, according to Gough (1911), from epithelial cells of the ventral canal wall which sink into the parenchyma away from the membranous lining of the canal but remain attached to it, each by a radial fibril. The cell nucleus then divides, and three, four, or even five flame cells originate from the first, modified epithelial cell. Flame cells do not arise from the dorsal canals, but Gough has described in the ventral canals a withdrawal of epithelial cells of the canal wall from the membrane they have secreted into the parenchyma. Such cells, however, remain connected with the canal wall by radial fibrillae. These cells appear to swell and to undergo certain modifications that led Gough to believe they were nephrocytes – that is to say, nitrogen-excretory cells.

Nervous System

The nervous system is one of the most difficult anatomical systems of the tapeworm to elucidate. It is remarkably complex for an animal with such limited powers of locomotion. It does not respond readily to methods of differential staining. Considerable discrepancies, therefore, are found between the accounts of different authors. There is, however, general agreement that the nervous system comprises: (1) two longitudinal nerve cords running the full length of the body, each lying lateral to the osmoregulatory collecting canals of its side; (2) a thick transverse bundle of fibers, called the "posterior" or "cerebral commissure," connecting the two longitudinal cords in the holdfast; and (3) in front of this commissure, a rectangle or circle of nervous tissue – the "anterior commissure" – on which are four structures that recall in appearance the nerve ganglia of other animals. From these four structures, nerves run forward and backward to supply the holdfast.

One of the clearest descriptions of a tapeworm nervous system was that given by Johnstone (1912) in his description of the trypanorhynchan tapeworm *Grillotia erinaceus*. In this form, the four ganglionoid structures lie in pairs, one pair on the right side and one on the left, lying as it were at the corners of a rectangle whose long sides represent the anterior commissure. Behind the origins of this commissure, the ganglia of each pair fuse, and the right and left points of fusion are connected by a thick posterior commissure (Figure 17).

Each of the four ganglia gives off a stout "anterior bothridial nerve" to the antero-lateral region of the nearest bothridium. Each ganglion is continued backward as a very short longitudinal connective which soon enlarges to form a "posterior ganglion"; from each of these comes off a "posterior bothridial nerve" to the postero-lateral region of the nearest bothridium. Beyond the ganglia thus formed, the connectives continue backward and on each side are joined by another connective from the posterior commissure. Still within the holdfast, the three connectives on each side now fuse to form the beginning of a lateral nerve cord.

Just opposite the posterior margins of the bothridia, but still of course within the axial region of the holdfast, each lateral nerve cord swells

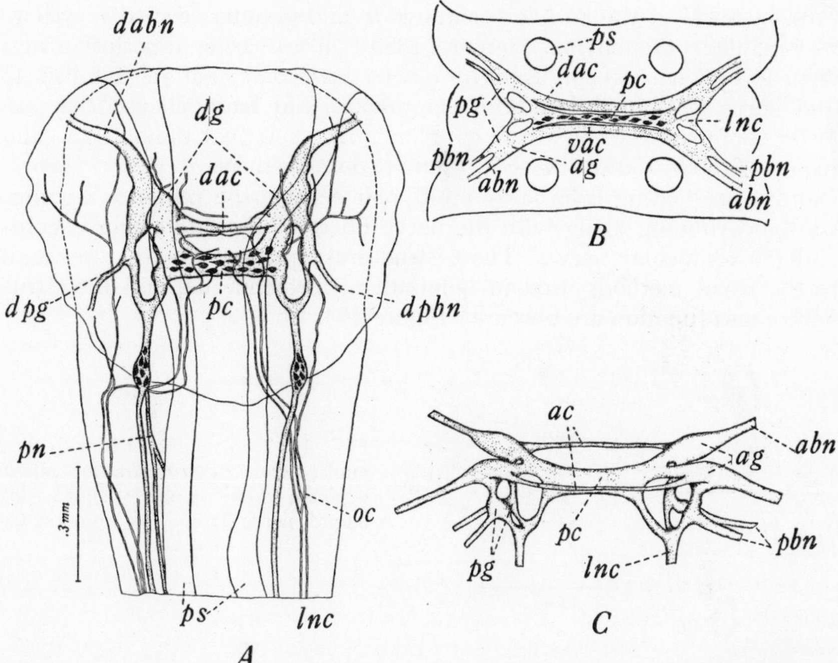

FIG. 17. Arrangement of ganglia, commissures, and nerves within the holdfast of *Grillotia erinaceus*. After Johnstone, 1912. *abn*, anterior bothridial nerve; *ac*, anterior commissure; *ag*, anterior ganglion; *dabn*, dorsal anterior bothridial nerve; *dac*, dorsal anterior commissure; *dg*, dorsal ganglia; *dpbn*, dorsal posterior bothridial nerve; *dpg*, dorsal posterior ganglion; *lnc*, lateral nerve cord; *oc*, osmoregulatory canal; *pbn*, posterior bothridial nerve; *pc*, posterior commissure; *pg*, posterior ganglion; *pn*, proboscidial nerve; *ps*, proboscidial sheath; *vac*, ventral anterior commissure.

again to form what appears to be a short, columnar ganglion, from which comes off a stout nerve. The two nerves thus formed – the "tentacular nerve trunks" (Johnstone calls them the "proboscidial" nerve trunks) – run backward and inward toward the central axis of the holdfast and soon fork. The two branches of each fork run backward between the tentacle sheaths, still enclosed in the same sheath of parenchyma, and supply a strip of tissue of an obscure nature which lies close to the outer wall of each bulb. Presumably the nerve fibers penetrate the walls of the bulbs and end in the muscle fibers of the bulbs. For a more detailed summary of the trypanorhynchan nervous system, reference should be made to Dollfus (1942).

Although the terms "ganglion" and "commissure" are used freely in descriptions of tapeworm nervous systems, it is far from certain that any homologies can be drawn between these structures and the similarly named structures in chordate animals. Johnstone (1912) asserted that he found no nerve cells in the ganglia of *Grillotia* nor any trace of nerve fibers in the commissures and connectives. Only in the unpaired posterior commissure and in the short columnar ganglion at the beginning of each lateral nerve cord were any nerve cells to be found. The structural material of the anterior commissure and ganglia seemed in fact to be modified parenchyma. Pintner (1880), in an earlier description of a trypanorhynchan worm, *Eutetrarhynchus ruficollis*, had also failed to find nerve cells in the anterior commissure but had believed the posterior commissure to be a true ganglionic mass. At that time and in later papers (1893, 1925a, 1934b), Pintner described giant fibers (neurochords) originating from large multipolar cells in the posterior commissure and running along with the nerve fibers of the lateral nerve cords and the tentacular nerves. These structures appear somewhat resistant to the usual methods used in helminth microtechnique, and their true nature and function are obscure (Figure 18).

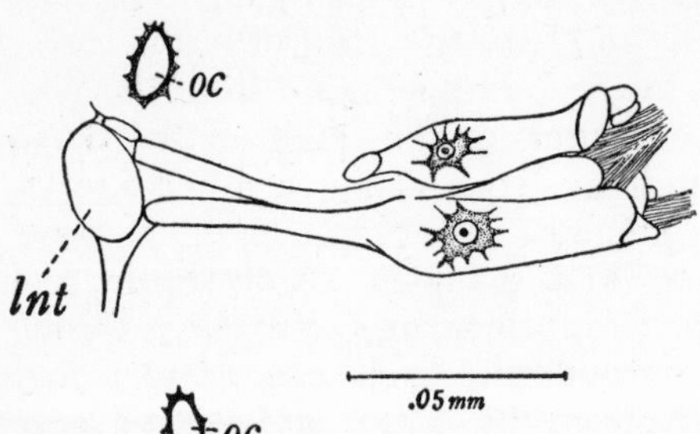

FIG. 18. Two neurochords with their nuclei from *Pterobothrium microcephala*. After Pintner, 1934a. *lnt*, lateral nerve trunk; *oc*, osmoregulatory canal.

Gough (1911) described the arrangement of the nervous system in the holdfast of the anoplocephalid worm *Avitellina*. At the level of the bases of the four suckers, there are four anterior ganglia. If the suckers are regarded as dorso-lateral and ventro-lateral in position, these ganglia may be oriented as dorso-median, ventro-median, and lateral in position. They are connected by transverse commissures which form, as it were, a rhomboid figure. The dorso-median and ventro-median ganglia are connected similarly by a dorso-ventral commissure, and the lateral ganglia by a transverse commissure, so that a cross of fibers occupies the central area of the rhomboid. The center of this cross is swollen as a central ganglion, which corresponds, perhaps, with the posterior commissure of Johnstone's description. Each of the peripheral ganglia gives off two nerves. These at first run forward, then bend and unite with the nerves from the neighboring ganglion, so that the eight nerves form four loops which connect neighboring ganglia.

Gough described the ganglia as containing large and prominent bipolar and multipolar nerve cells, and the nerves as made up of parallel bundles of neurofibrillae – in the case of the trunk nerve cords – and of large bipolar nerve cells and neurofibrillae in the case of the holdfast nerves. Gough also described large multipolar cells within the sucker walls, similar perhaps to those described by Spätlich (1909) in the bothridia of the tapeworm genus *Tetrabothrium*.

Reference to Niemec's (1885) description of the nervous system of *Taenia* shows that here, again, there is a basic arrangement similar in principle to that in trypanorhynchan and anoplocephalid worms. A rhomboid anterior commissure connecting two dorsal and two ventral ganglia is crossed transversely by a thick posterior commissure that connects the swollen ends of the lateral nerve cords. These swollen ends (possibly analogous to columnar ganglia) each give off an "accessory nerve" that runs parallel with the lateral nerve cords and would seem to correspond with the tentacular nerve of Johnstone's description, although of course no tentacles or bulbs occur in *Taenia.* In front of the commissure and situated in the base of the rostellum, there is a nerve ring from which small nerves run forward into the rostellar tissue.

Rees (1943) found in *Anthobothrium auriculatum* a very simple arrangement. The brain is represented by a dorso-ventrally flattened mass. The broad dorsal and ventral commissures lie close together and at each end enlarge to form a ganglion. The dorsal and ventral ganglia of each side fuse with one another posteriorly, and from the point of fusion comes the lateral nerve cord. The nerves to the bothridia arise from the posterior region of each ganglion, just in front of the origin of the nerve cords, and run forward into the bothridial stalks where each nerve forks. From the anterior region of each ganglion emerges an anterior nerve which runs forward and divides into three branches. Of these, the two inner branches supply the rostellum (myzorhynchus); the outer branch extends over the anterior face of the bothridial stalk nearest to it and runs just below the surface of it. Noteworthy is the presence of large nerve cells in each of the ganglia and commissures.

It may be added in conclusion that of all the anatomical systems of the tapeworm, the nervous system is the one most deserving of a comprehensive and detailed study with modern methods of microtechnique.

Male Reproductive System

Protandrous hermaphroditism is almost universal among tapeworms. The mature proglottis contains both male and female organs, and the male organs ripen before those of the female system. Separate sexes are known to occur only in the genus *Dioicocestus*, a parasite of grebes and ibises. In this genus, in addition to well-developed males and females, it is of interest to note that many individuals are asexual or imperfectly sexed. Clerc (1930) has compared such individuals with the "intersexes" described by Baltzer (1926) in the gephyrean worm *Bonellia.*

"The 'intersexual females' are apparently only immature females, which later may become sexually mature. In the case of the intersexual males, however, the presence of female organs in all, but of varying degrees of development, would seem to support Clerc's contention. How this condition has arisen, the sex determining factors therein, and what are the differentiating factors of male and female organs in the hermaphroditic forms, are questions for the future to decide. But so long as the whole subject of hermaphroditism and of sex in general remains in the present state of confusion, speculation regarding sex determination in the tapeworms is unprofitable." Young (1935).

Another point concerning which investigations are urgently desirable is the origin of the germinal tissue itself. Young (1935) believes that such evidence as is available indicates a common origin of soma plasm and germ plasm in tapeworms. All of the organs, he thinks, including the sexual ones, arise from a common embryonic parenchyma. From the earliest cleavage to the time when the sex organs become distinct, he finds no indication whatever of a difference between soma and germ plasm. He quotes further, in support of this view, the observations of Child (1907) on the development of testes from neuromuscular cells in *Moniezia* and similar findings by himself (1919b) on several other tapeworm species, notably *Dipylidium caninum* and *Rhyncobothrium bulbifer*. In one tapeworm species, Young found differentiated flame cells enclosed in developing testes, an observation certainly suggestive of a common origin for both somatic and germinal cells.

However, Vogel (1930), in the embryo of *Dibothriocephalus latus*, was able to distinguish by special staining techniques cells which he regarded as definitely somatic, and other cells which he believed to be of the nature of germ cells; and Wisniewski (1933) described protogenitalial tissue in procercoid larvae of *Cyathocephalus* as small as four millimeters.

So varied and so complex are the patterns of the reproductive system among tapeworms that it is difficult to present a picture whose details will apply to all. There is, however, ample material for the construction of such a picture. The observations and descriptions of such early workers as Sommer (1874), Leuckart (1879), Meyner (1895), Jacobi (1896a), Mrazek (1897), and Wolffhügel (1900a), though of great value, were limited by the imperfections of their microtechnique; but the later contributions of Balss (1908), Gough (1911), Johnstone (1912), Wagner (1917), Nybelin (1922), Pintner (1880–1935), Wisniewski (1933), and the Illinois school of workers, using particularly methods of serial sectioning, buffered staining, and reconstruction, have done much to fill the gaps in the earlier narratives. It is unfortunate, perhaps, that so much of our information is based upon the study of pseudophyllidean forms; for it would seem preferable to base a general picture upon the arrangements of the reproductive system found in such admittedly primitive tapeworm groups as the orders Proteocephala and Tetraphyllidea and the cyclophyllidean family Anoplocephalidae. However, some reference to pseudophyllidean arrangements is unavoidable in any discussion of the tapeworm reproductive system.

The male system in a mature tapeworm proglottis consists of testes, vasa efferentia, and sperm duct. These organs may be referred to collectively as the male genitalia. These structures appear to originate from strands and clusters of epithelioid cells that appear at points where later the genital components will appear. There is some difference of opinion as to whether sperm duct and vagina have a common origin or whether they are separate from the beginning; some difference of opinion also exists as to whether the gonad ducts are continuous with the gonads right from the beginning or whether their union is secondary.

The testes vary in number among different tapeworm genera from one to several hundreds. The approximate number of testes per segment is commonly used as a character for differentiating genera and species. It

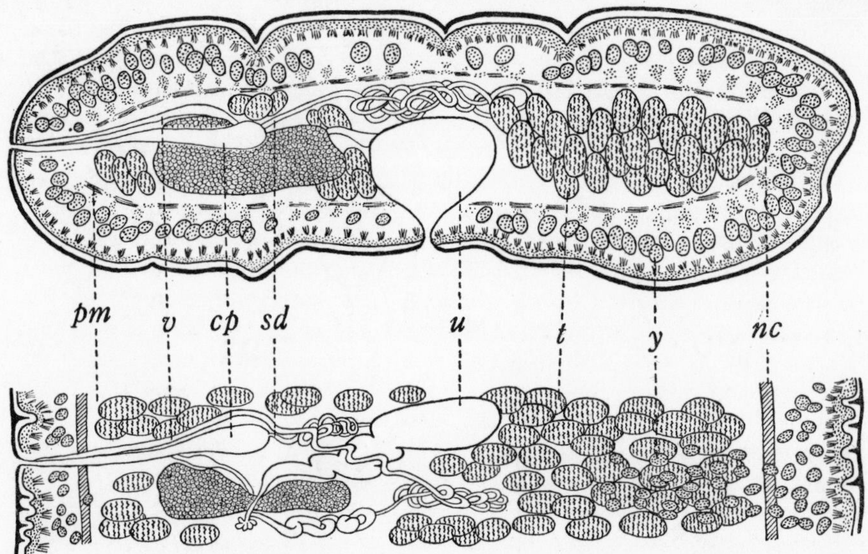

FIG. 19. *Triaenophorus,* sectional views of a proglottis to show the arrangement of the genitalia. After Newton, 1932. *cp,* cirrus pouch; *nc,* nerve cord; *pm,* parenchymal muscle sheath; *sd,* sperm duct; *t,* testes; *u,* uterus; *v,* vagina; *y,* yolk glands.

can be computed approximately by counting the cross sections of testes seen in a successive series of serial cross sections through a proglottis, and dividing the figure thus obtained by the actual number of proglottis sections required to show the whole of an individual testis. Another method is to arrive at the average number of testes per cross section of proglottis – as counted in a series of such sections – and multiply the figure by the average number of testes seen in a sagittal section, similarly estimated.

In the majority of tapeworms the testes lie in one or two horizontal rows within the parenchymal muscle sheath. That is to say, they are medullary in position. However, in the proteocephalan subfamilies Marsypocephalinae, Ephedrocephalinae, Othioscolecinae, and Monticellinae, which on other grounds may be regarded as very primitive tapeworms, the testes form a continuous layer between the parenchymal muscle sheath and the subcuticular muscle layer of one of the flat surfaces. The testes in such a case are cortical in position, and the flat surface to which they approximate is conventionally regarded as dorsal.

Each testis, in the immature proglottis, is a spherical or ovoid mass of undifferentiated cells which, as development proceeds, become enclosed within a delicate limiting membrane of pavement epithelium, the "tunica propria." The tunica propria of each testis is continued as a minute, delicately walled duct – the vas efferens. These vasa efferentia usually lie in one horizontal plane dorsal to the testes and run into one another to form a network (Figure 20). From this network the sperm duct emerges and runs in sinuous fashion from about the center of the proglottis toward the genital pore.

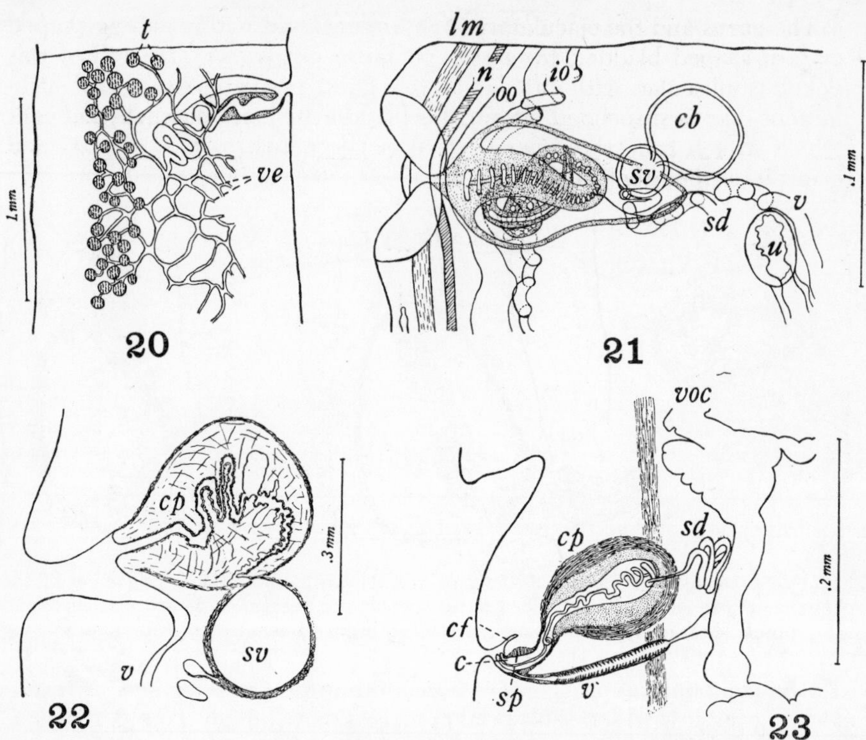

FIG. 20. *Ophiotaenia filaroides*, male genitalia. After La Rue, 1909. FIG. 21. *Anthocephalus elongatus*, genital atrium. After Pintner, 1913. FIG. 22. *Dibothriocephalus latus*, cirrus apparatus. After Nybelin, 1922. FIG. 23. *Raillietina echinobothrida*, cirrus pouch and vaginal end section. After Lang, 1929. *c*, cirrus; *cb*, cirrus bladder; *cf*, cloacal fold; *cp*, cirrus pouch; *io*, inner osmoregulatory canal; *lm*, longitudinal parenchymal muscles; *n*, lateral nerve cord; *oo*, outer osmoregulatory canal; *sd*, sperm duct; *sp*, sphincter muscle of cirrus pouch; *sv*, seminal vesicle; *t*, testes; *u*, uterus; *v*, vagina; *ve*, vasa efferentia; *voc*, ventral osmoregulatory canal.

The genital pore may be marginal in position, or, less commonly, superficial. It is the mouth of a basin-shaped depression of the proglottis surface. Such terms as genital atrium, genital sinus, genital cloaca, and cirro-vaginal atrium are applied to it. Its margin commonly is thickened and projects somewhat above the proglottis surface. The sperm duct and the vagina open side by side on the bottom of the basin.

The sperm duct originates as a solid cord of epithelioid cells surrounded by a basement membrane. This cord later becomes tubular and, as in other flatworms, may be regarded as consisting of a long, thin-walled, ciliated vas deferens and a short, muscular vas intromittens, whose lining appears to be a continuation of the surface cuticle. The vas intromittens can be partly protruded through the genital pore in such a fashion that it becomes everted, turned inside out. This protrusible portion is referred to as the "cirrus." The nonprotrusible portion of the intromittent duct, whose lumen becomes the lumen of the everted cirrus, is better termed the "ejaculatory duct."

The cirrus and the ejaculatory duct are enclosed within an egg-shaped or pear-shaped bladder, the cirrus pouch or cirrus sac. The wall of this pouch is muscular, with circular muscle fibers predominating. The intromittent duct is suspended within this bladder by loose parenchymal cells which stretch from the inner surface of the pouch to pass around and grip the intromittent duct (Figures 19–24, 26).

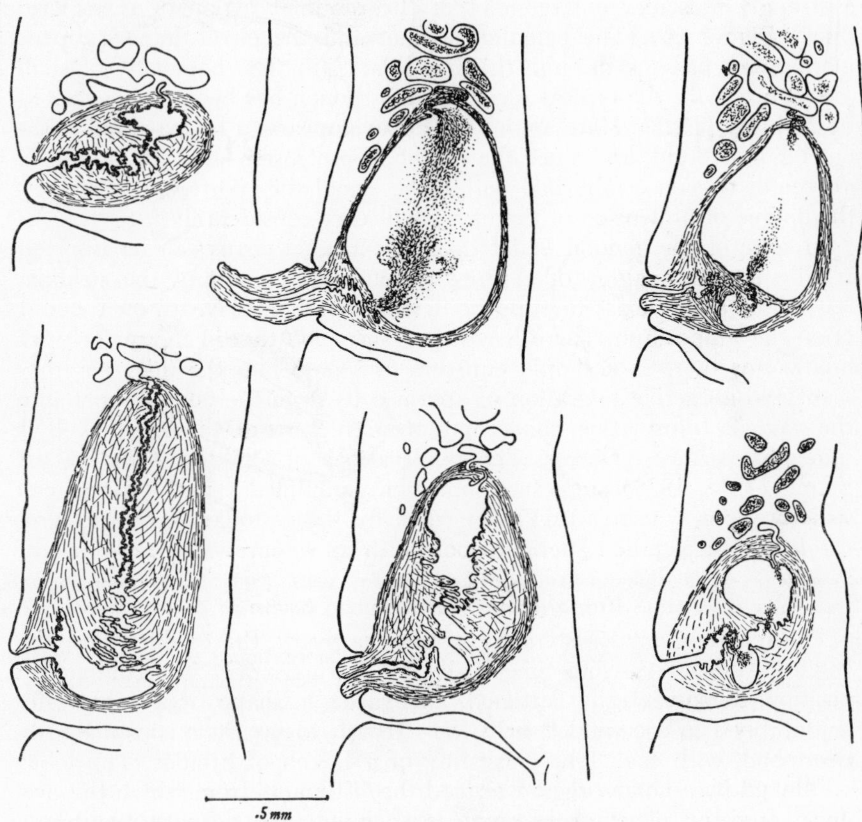

FIG. 24. Cirrus apparatus of *Caryophyllaeus laticeps* in various states of contraction. After Nybelin, 1922.

The mature sperm duct may show two dilatations. One of these, on the vas deferens just before it enters the cirrus pouch, is called the "external seminal vesicle"; the other, on the ejaculatory duct and so within the cirrus pouch, is called the "internal seminal vesicle" (Figures 22, 26). Pintner (1913) described in several trypanorhynchan worms a condition in which the internal seminal vesicle is so large that its wall is in contact with the wall of the cirrus pouch, the intervening parenchyma becoming obliterated. The cirrus pouch then appears as if it were a bladderlike dilatation of the terminal region of the sperm duct, receiving at its inner end the vas deferens and giving off at its outer end the cirrus. A pouchlike outgrowth from this bladder pierces the cirrus pouch wall and comes to lie close to the external seminal vesicle. To the contraction of this "Cirrusmotionsblase" Pintner ascribed the extrusion of the cirrus. Presumably in such a case the cirrus is extruded without being everted (Figure 21).

In some caryophyllaeid tapeworms, the parenchyma within the cirrus pouch is replaced by muscular tissue, so that the cirrus pouch appears as a strongly muscular enlargement of the terminal region of the sperm duct (Figure 24). The ejaculatory duct and the cirrus lumen appear merely as a passage through this muscular bulb. The homology of such a structure with the typical form of cirrus pouch has been demonstrated by Nybelin (1922). Here again, the cirrus appears to be extruded without being everted, and since the extent of protrusion depends upon the degree of tension established within the ejaculatory portion of the duct, the degree of protrusion of the cirrus will vary considerably.

In spite of the general belief that an extruded cirrus can be inserted readily into the vagina of a proglottis in another part of the strobila, few observations exist to support it. Some authors have thrown doubt upon the supposition. There is a strong suspicion that in the majority of tapeworms there is a simple emission of semen into the fluid environment and an active migration of sperm cells from the environment into the vagina. Information concerning the structure of the sperm cell is somewhat scanty however. The observations of Child (1907) and of Young (1913, 1923) suggest a somewhat simplified type of sperm cell structure, but Watson (1911) described for the cestodarian genus *Gyrocotyle* a typical tailed spermatozoon with an intensely staining "head."

Female Reproductive System

The female genital system comprises the ovary, the oviduct, and the vagina. The ovary – sometimes called a "germarium" – is medullary in position, dorso-ventrally flattened, and varies in shape from a butterfly or dumbbell to a capital H or a fan – that is to say, it is conspicuously two-lobed, with each lobe consisting of a bunch of tubules. The lobes are linked by a hollow region termed the "isthmus," from which the oviduct comes off. The whole ovary is enclosed in a delicate membrane which, according to Johnstone (1912), describing *Grillotia erinaceus*, is without nuclei, but which, according to La Rue (1911), describing *Ophiotaenia filaroides*, is nucleated.

The term "oviduct" will be used here in a broad sense to mean the egg-conducting tube, from ovary to ultimate birth pore, or to ultimate blind termination. It begins at the isthmus, being apparently continuous with the ovarian membrane. It then runs backward in the ventral plane almost to the posterior border of the proglottis, then loops toward the dorsal surface. Before reaching the dorsal cortical parenchyma it turns forward to run in the dorsal plane of the medulla nearly to the anterior border of the proglottis (Figures 25–28).

Several regions of the oviduct may be recognized. The beginning of the duct may be enlarged and muscular, constituting the so-called "oocapt" (egg swallower) – or "Schluckapparat" (Pintner, 1889) or the

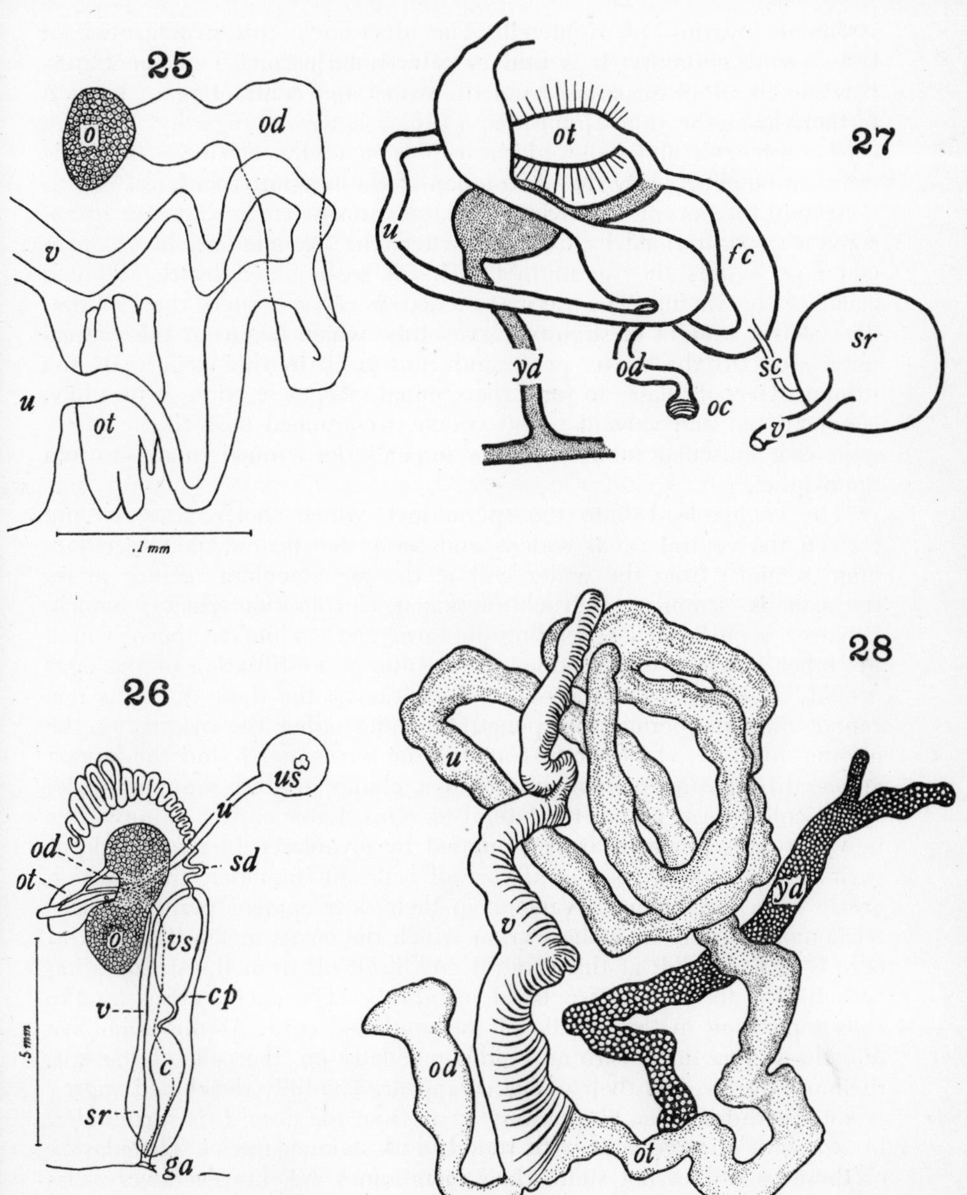

FIG. 25. Female reproductive ducts of *Proteochephalus parallacticus*. After MacLulich, 1943. FIG. 26. Genitalia of *Triaenophorus stizostedionis*, exclusive of yolk glands and testes. After Miller, 1945. *c*, cirrus; *cp*, cirrus pouch; *ga*, genital aperture; *o*, ovary; *od*, oviduct; *ot*, ootype; *sd*, sperm duct; *sr*, seminal receptacle; *u*, uterus; *us*, uterine sac; *v*, vagina; *vs*, vesicula seminalis. FIG. 27. *Dibothriocephalus latus*, female genital ducts (diagrammatic). After Nybelin, 1922. FIG. 28. Same (reconstruction). After Magath, 1929a. *fc*, fertilization canal; *oc*, oocapt; *od*, oviduct; *ot*, ootype; *sc*, seminal canal; *sr*, seminal receptacle; *u*, uterus; *v*, vagina; *yd*, common yolk duct.

"sphincter ovarius" of Monticelli. The function of this structure is not known with certainty. It is said to carry out rhythmic movements, expanding to admit an ovum from the ovary and contracting to force it farther down the tube. Johnstone (1912), however, regarded it as an elastic sphincter and believed the expulsion of the egg cells from the ovary to be effected by the contraction of the proglottis muscles.

Beyond the oocapt, the oviduct enlarges somewhat in diameter to become a region termed by German writers the "Keimleiter," by English-language writers the "germiduct." This is soon joined by the seminal canal of the vagina. The vagina — called by some writers the "spermiduct" — is a straight or slightly curved tube which begins at the vaginal pore, close to the cirrus pore, and runs back to the vicinity of the isthmus. Here it dilates to form the seminal receptacle, the exit of which is constricted and valvelike, and which is continued as a thick-walled, somewhat muscular tube of narrow lumen — the seminal canal — to join the oviduct.

"The vagina leads into the spermiduct, which shortly after having crossed the ventral canal widens and forms the pear-shaped receptaculum seminis; from the wider end of the receptaculum seminis arises the canalis seminis (Befruchtungskanal — fertilisation duct), which, however, soon branches, sending one arm, the oviduct, to the ovarium, the other arm, the uterine duct, to the uterus. Fertilisation of the eggs probably takes place at the point of junction of the three ducts, as one cannot observe spermatozoa penetrating into either the oviduct or the uterine duct. . . . In their first anlage the cirrus-pouch and the vagina appear to have a common origin in a clump of dark-staining nuclei which collect near one of the lateral margins. Later on this clump splits into two masses, which are surrounded by myoblasts. In the middle of each of these masses a central core of cells differentiates, those which are to form the vagina advancing in their development perhaps somewhat more rapidly than those from which the cirrus arises. The central core is at first solid; at this stage it cuts itself off from the surrounding cells by the formation of a basal membrane. The cavity arises by the cells separating in the middle of the epithelial cord. At this stage we find the vagina lined with an epithelium; later on, the cells of the epithelium atrophy, and their nuclei disappear. The fully developed vagina is lined with fine cilia, all pointing away from the pore; it is surrounded by a sheath of large cells with round, dark-staining nuclei. The plasma of these cells does not stain; their membranes are, however, very distinct. In shape, the cells are prismatic, with all the sides delimited by planes, the ends of the cells bordering on the parenchyma generally forming pyramids. These cells surround the vagina in a single layer; their function may be glandular (?), and they certainly help to give greater rigidity to the vagina.

"The female sexual canals, spermiduct, oviduct, uterine duct, canalis seminalis and the receptaculum seminis all arise as solid cords of epithelial cells, which, after having produced a basal membrane, become hollow. As is the case with the vagina, the epithelium atrophies, and finally disappears. Oviduct, canalis seminalis and uterine duct are, when completely developed, lined with cilia. The receptaculum seminis is not a simple dilation of the spermiduct due to the action of the contents, but arises out of a clump of cells which already show the final shape of the organ." Gough (1911).

"The vagina is a fairly wide and thin walled tube running back from the genital aperture. It is thickest nearest to the genital opening and consists of a structureless membrane bearing nuclei on its outer surface with some muscle fibers running mostly in a longitudinal direction, though some of them are also transverse and oblique. The vagina runs back nearly in the middle line of the proglottis towards the space between the anterior lobes of the ovary, but it is not nearly so much convoluted as the uterine canal. Near the ovary and approximately in the middle line of the segment, it enlarges considerably to form the receptaculum seminis. In the immature proglottis this dilated part of the vagina may be empty, but in segments approaching sexual maturity (in the female organs) all the canal and particularly the dilated receptaculum contain spermatozoa received from the same proglottis by self-fertilisation or from another by copulation. The wall of the receptaculum is much thinner than that of the rest of the vaginal tract, being of course only a dilated part of the latter. Near the median part of the ovary, and beyond the receptaculum, the vagina decreases considerably in diameter and its wall becomes much thicker. There is now a thick basement membrane with close, but rather irregular layers of nuclei on the inner and outer surfaces. The duct passes either over or under the median ovarian bridge and, just posterior to the latter, its calibre diminishes very suddenly and from its extreme posterior boundary a small tube takes its origin. This is the canalis seminalis. It has a thick wall consisting of very dense fibers running circularly or obliquely. It runs very nearly at right angles to the former direction of the vagina and joins the oviduct very close to the junction of the latter with the vitelline duct." Johnstone (1912).

The function of the cilia that line the vaginal lumen would seem, according to Pintner (1934b), to be that of a nonreturn valve mechanism, since they are not motile. The region of the oviduct which immediately follows the junction of the seminal canal is usually referred to by such terms as "fertilization canal" or "Befruchtungskanal." It may be regarded as extending from the entrance of the seminal canal to the entrance of the common yolk duct.

The term "yolk glands" or "vitellaria" is given to a number of scattered bodies which form a layer in the cortical parenchyma parallel to the body surface, or form a longitudinal band on each side. They are grouped around a pair of ducts which combine eventually as the common yolk duct. They communicate with these ducts by minute canals, each running from an individual yolk gland. Comparison with the reproductive system of rhabdocoel Turbellaria suggests that such yolk glands are in reality detached portions of the ancestral ovaries. That is to say, the yolk glands represent modified ovarian tissue, and the yolk cells represent modified oocytes.

Among many cyclophyllidean forms, the yolk glands are represented by a compact mass of tissue situated in the medulla between the ovary and the posterior border of the proglottis. In the cyclophyllidean subfamily Avitellinae (Anoplocephalidae), such a compact yolk gland is not present, but it is represented by scattered cells within the ovary itself, termed by Gough (1911) "ovarial nutritive cells" and regarded by him as modified oocytes. They lie among the oocytes proper and send out plasmatic processes along and over the surface of the oocytes, thus presumably supplying them with nutriment. The connection between the yolk cells and the oocytes in this case is therefore temporary, since the yolk cells apparently do not leave the ovary; whereas in other tapeworms where a separate yolk-producing mass occurs, the yolk cells attach themselves to an oocyte and remain so attached to it within the egg shell.

The course of the oviduct, following the entrance of the common yolk duct, may be compared to the upper limb of a letter U standing on its side in a dorso-ventral plane. The oviduct, that is to say, now turns toward the dorsal surface and then runs forward in the mid-dorsal region of the medullary parenchyma. This U-shaped region, where the oviduct bends upward and forward, is termed the "ootype," or primary uterus. It is surrounded by numerous elongated, club-shaped cells, the so-called "shell glands" or Mehlis' glands of early descriptions. Johnstone (1912) described each cell as having a distal bulbous region, in which lies the nucleus, and a proximal stalklike region from which filamentous processes penetrate the cells of the ootype wall.

It seems well established that these cells are unicellular glands, and that they discharge into the cavity of the ootype a watery, eosinophilic fluid; but the extent to which this fluid forms the future egg shell is uncertain. The consensus of opinion among such observers as Hofsten (1912), Todtmann (1913, 1914), and Burr (1912) on Turbellaria; Henneguy (1902) and Goldschmidt (1909) on Trematoda; and Nybelin (1922) on pseudophyllidean tapeworms suggests that the shell of the flatworm egg is formed by the coalescence of shell granules, seen as yellow, refractive droplets within the yolk cells of the forming egg. The function of the shell glands would seem rather that of secreting a cementing fluid to hold together the fertilized egg cell and its yolk cells until such coalescence has formed the shell.

From the ootype, the oviduct runs forward in the mid-dorsal line of the medullary parenchyma. It now contains fully formed eggs – that is to say, matured ova which have been fertilized and supplied with yolk cells and shells. This final region of the oviduct may be termed the "uterine tract," or secondary uterus. The eggs escape to the outside either through permanent birth pores (uterine pores, tocostomes), or through temporary openings in the ventral surface of the proglottides – possibly preformed – or by the disintegration of the whole proglottis.

It is in the pattern of the uterine tract that tapeworms differ so greatly from one another in the arrangement of the reproductive organs. Shelled eggs accumulating within the uterine tract tend to deform it in directions established by evolution and so preformed in the immature proglottis, and the pattern of deformity appears to vary only within narrow limits for each particular tapeworm species.

If we assume that the original type of uterine tract was a simple tube — a part of the oviduct that ran from the ootype forward to end at the uterine pore — we may classify the main patterns of gravid uterine tract as follows:

1. The uterine tract remains a tube throughout, but, growing rapidly while fixed at each end, it is forced into a spiral course (Figure 29). Owing to the depressed nature of the proglottis — its dorso-ventral flattening — the whorls of the spiral become "loops" to the right and left of the middle line. The loops may lie roughly parallel to one another, but

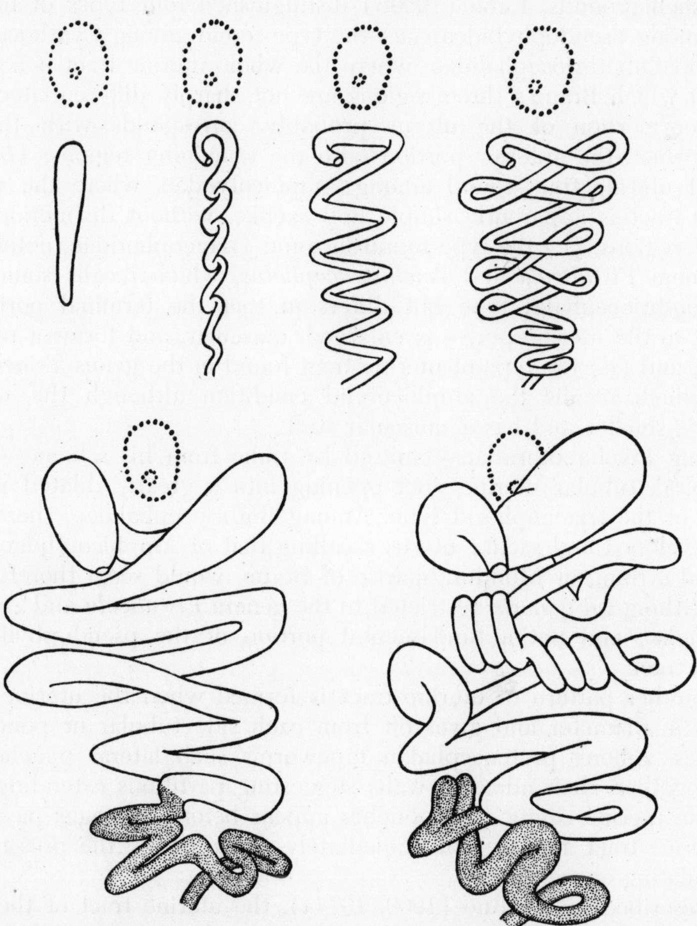

FIG. 29. Stages in the development of the uterine tube of *Dibothriocephalus latus.* After Wardle and McColl, 1937.

if the proglottis becomes foreshortened, they will group themselves much like the loops of a rosette of ribbon around the area where the uterus opens to the outside. Such a spiral-loop-rosette arrangement, for example, is very characteristic of the pseudophyllidean tapeworms of the families Cyathocephalidae and Dibothriocephalidae (see Orders Spathebothridea and Pseudophyllidea).

2. A second pattern of uterine distortion is produced by the gravid uterus becoming a wide, shallow bag. The gravid tract of the tapeworms of the pseudophyllidean family Amphicotylidae, for example, is such a wide, shallow bag – "saclike" is the term – funneling on its ventral surface toward a uterine pore situated on the ventral surface of the proglottis. Braun (in Bronn's "Thierreich," 1896–1900) regarded the uterine tract of pseudophyllidean tapeworms in general as showing typically three regions: (*a*) the uterine duct (Uteringang); (*b*) the uterus proper (Uterushöhle); and (*c*) the uterine atrium (Mündungspartie).

On such grounds, Lühe (1900b) distinguished four types of uterine tract among Pseudophyllidea: (*a*) the type found among Cyathocephalidae and Dibothriocephalidae, where the whole uterine tract is a spiral tube in which Braun's three regions are not sharply differentiated; the posterior portion of the uterus probably corresponds with Braun's uterine duct, the anterior portion with the remaining regions; (*b*) the type of uterine tract found among Amphicotylidae, where the whole uterine tract is apparently simple and saclike, without distinction into Braun's regions; (*c*) the type found in some Triaenophoridae, notably in the genera *Fistulicola* and *Anchistrocephalus*, which recalls somewhat the dibothriocephalid type but differs in that the terminal portion – nearest to the uterine pore – is enlarged, muscular, and forms a uterine atrium; and (*d*) the type of uterine tract found in the genus *Triaenophorus,* which recalls the amphicotylid condition although the saclike uterus is smaller and has a muscular wall.

Among Ptychobothriidae – omitted by Lühe from his scheme – there is a spiral, tubular uterine duct opening into a greatly dilated uterus proper of the triaenophorid type. Among Bothriocephalidae, there is a well-developed and saclike uterus recalling that of Amphicotylidae. The terminal atrium, or Mündungspartie of Braun, would seem therefore to be something *sui generis*, restricted to the genera *Fistulicola* and *Anchistrocephalus,* and not a fundamental portion of the pseudophyllidean uterine tract.

3. Another pattern of uterine tract is formed when the uterine tube widens in diameter and gives off from each side tubular or pouchlike branches. Among proteocephalan tapeworms such lateral pouches lie close together, their adjacent walls suggesting partitions extending into a saclike uterine cavity. The pouches appear before any eggs pass into the uterine tract and are not immediately produced by the pressure of accumulating eggs.

As described by La Rue (1909, 1914a), the uterine tract of the proteocephalan arises from a median rod of deeply staining cells which originate from the parenchyma of the young proglottis. The rod becomes a tube but gives off solid branches to right and left. Later these also become hollow. A few of the pockets are directed ventrally, eventually to pierce the body wall and act as temporary uterine pores. Connecting the ootype to the base of the uterine stem there is a spiral tube with weakly muscular wall, which La Rue terms the "uterine passage"; it would seem to be analogous, if not homologous, with the "uterine duct" of the pseudophyllidean pattern.

Among Trypanorhyncha, similar side branching from a central stem is to be seen. There is again a spiral uterine duct to carry the shelled eggs from the ootype to the uterine stem. Johnstone (1912) described the uterine stem of *Grillotia* as a cylindrical tube which grows in diameter as it becomes filled with eggs until it occupies by far the greater part of the proglottis in front of the genital pore. Its wall consists at first of a thin, structureless membrane lined internally by a single-layered syncytium and covered externally by several layers of cells. In the fully expanded uterus, however, the wall consists merely of the basement membrane. Expansion of the uterus is produced by the formation of lateral pockets which tend to fuse with one another.

Among Tetraphyllidea, the uterine tract of mature segments is a sinuous, thick-walled tube running from the ootype forward almost to the anterior border of the proglottis. In the gravid proglottis, it is a wide sac with lobulated walls but never with side branches. Side branching from a median uterine stem is seen again, however, in the uterine pattern of Taeniidae. Here the median stem is relatively undilated and the branching is commonly complex, due to the formation of secondary and tertiary sub-branches. The simplest condition is seen in the genus *Echinococcus* (Figures 211–15), where the lateral branches appear as blunt, short outpocketings. The extreme condition is seen in the genus *Taenia* (Figure 234), where the medullary parenchyma of the gravid proglottis appears to be almost filled with a ramifying mass of uterine branches.

4. A final type of uterine distortion occurs when the proglottides, approaching the gravid condition, become shorter, changing from quadrangular to linear in shape. Among a number of cyclophyllidean families, notably the "davaineid group" (Davaineidae, Hymenolepididae, Dilepididae, etc.), such foreshortening of the gravid proglottis is common. We find, possibly as a result of this, an extraordinary variety of patterns. The uterus may appear as a transverse tube or as a sac with irregular side branches; or it may appear as a network of tubes or even as a tubular ring with short outpocketings. It may, again, discharge its eggs into a pouchlike structure derived presumably from the parenchyma and lying close beside the uterus; such a "paruterine organ" is found in a range of forms, where quite possibly it has evolved independently and so may provide an example of evolutionary convergence. Again, the uterus may degenerate and never function, the eggs in such cases being held within pouchlike cavities of the parenchyma, the so-called "egg capsules."

Among cyclophyllidean tapeworms it is well established that the uterine tract does not open to the outside either permanently or temporarily. The eggs escape only when the proglottis disintegrates or tears. However, among tetraphyllidean tapeworms – in the old sense of the term, comprising Proteocephala, Lecanicephala, Tetraphyllidea, and Trypanorhyncha – Pintner (1913) distinguished three types of communication between the uterine tract and the outside.

First, there is the true uterine pore or tocostome, which is formed by an invagination of the outer surface fusing with an evagination of the uterine wall. Second, there is the involutive pseudo-uterine pore, which Pintner described as a funnel-like depression of the proglottis wall at a point where the gravid uterus presses against it. Through the tip of the funnel the uterus eventually establishes communication with the outside. Pintner (1913) says: "Under the pressure of the uterus, the body wall tissues form a funnel-like depression from inside outwards which, under continual pressure, finally breaks through to appear externally as a papilliform swelling. The cuticle however shows no kind of extension into the aperture. The whole process has the appearance of what was formerly referred to as 'dehiscence' of the tissues, the uterine pore being formed, not by active cell growth, but by involution, by a kind of resorption process correlated with mechanical factors such as the pressure from inside outwards." Third, there may be a splitting of the proglottis wall, without any appearance of a uterine pore.

Nybelin (1922), surveying the question among pseudophyllidean worms, regarded the uterine pore of Cyathocephalidae, Dibothriocephalidae, and Bothriocephalidae as a true uterine pore. Among Amphicotylidae and most other pseudophyllidean tapeworms, the apparent uterine pore corresponds with Pintner's involutive pseudo-uterine pore.

· CHAPTER II ·

Life Cycle

Our knowledge concerning the development and the life cycle of tapeworms has accumulated more slowly than that relating to their general anatomy, and few tapeworm life cycles are known completely. This phase of tapeworm study began in earnest with the publication by Siebold (1850) of his hypothesis that certain parasites of hog muscles, called at that time Blasenwürmer (bladder worms), are produced from eggs, and are not provoked *in situ* by tissue inflammation. On Siebold's view, they were tapeworms that had got into the wrong definitive host.

A further landmark in the progress of investigations into tapeworm life histories was the published description, by the gynecologist G. Friedrich Küchenmeister (1852), of the results of a series of experiments that established conclusively the true relationship between bladder worms and taeniid tapeworms. The belief, still current among many parasitologists, that Küchenmeister heroically demonstrated, by experiments upon himself, the true nature of *Cysticercus cellulosae*, the bladder worm of hog muscles, is not correct. His first successful experiments appear to have concerned the rearing in dogs of the tapeworm *Taenia pisiformis* from bladder worms taken from the body cavities of rabbits. His experiments with *Cysticercus cellulosae* were carried out upon a condemned murderer.

"Lastly, the direct proof of these assertions has been furnished by myself in making the following experiments upon a murderer condemned to death. Seventy-two, sixty, thirty-six, twenty-four and twelve hours before execution, 12, 18, 15 and 18 specimens of *Cysticercus cellulosae* were administered to the criminal, partly in rice or vermicelli soup cooled to blood heat, partly in blood puddings from which the fat was removed and replaced by cysticerci. The cysticerci had already lain seventy-two hours in a cellar before I discovered them by chance; the last ones administered had consequently lain about 130 hours out of the living organism. I hardly believed that those which had lain more than 80 hours were still capable of development . . . on dissection, 48 hours after execution, I found ten young taeniae." Küchenmeister (1852).

Küchenmeister's experiments and the pioneer studies of G. R. Wagener (*Die Entwicklung der Cestoden*, 1854) bore fruit in R. Leuckart's *Die Blasenwürmer und Ihre Entwicklung* (1856); Willemoes-Suhm's study of the life cycle of *Schistocephalus* (1869); Donnedieu's classic study of the life cycle of *Ligula* (1877a, 1877b); Villot's descriptions of the bladder worm larvae of taeniid tapeworms (1883a, 1883b); Max Braun's *Zur Entwicklungsgeschichte des breiten Bandwurms, Bothriocephalus latus* (1883b); Schauinsland's description of the embryonic development of *Dibothriocephalus latus* (1885); the studies of Grassi (1887) on the life cycle of *Hymenolepis nana*; of Grassi and Rovelli (1892) and of Schmidt (1894) on the life cycles of various cyclophyllidean tapeworms.

The early years of the present century saw the studies of St. Remy on *Anoplocephala* (1900) and *Hydatigera taeniaeformis* (1901a); of Bartels on *Cysticercus fasciolaris* (1902); Wolf on *Cyathocephalus* (1906); Child on *Moniezia expansa* (1904–11); Janicki on *Hydatigera taeniaeformis* (1906c, 1907); Young on *Cysticercus pisiformis* (1908); La Rue on *Ophiotaenia filaroides* (1909); Cooper on *Proteocephalus ambloplites* (1915); Meggitt on *Proteocephalus filicollis* (1914a); Wagner on *Proteocephalus torulosus* (1917); Janicki and Rosen on *Dibothriocephalus latus* (1917); Rosen on various pseudophyllidean forms (1919, 1920); Joyeux's *Cycle évolutif de quelques cestodes* (1920); Goette's *Die Entwicklungsgeschichte der Cestoden* (1921); and Woodland's study of *Hymenolepis fraterna* (1924a).

Among noteworthy contributions to the subject of tapeworm embryology in recent years have been those of Gauthier (1923) on *Cyathocephalus*; Ruszkowski (1925) on *Drepanidotaenia*; Ruszkowski (1932a, 1934) on *Echinobothrium, Grillotia*, and *Gyrocotyle*; Essex (1927a, 1927b, 1928a) on *Dibothriocephalus, Bothriocephalus*, and *Corallobothrium*; Vogel (1929c, 1930) on *Dibothriocephalus*; Wisniewski (1930, 1932) on *Archigetes* and *Cyathocephalus*; Jones and Alicata (1935) on *Hymenolepis cantaniana*; Hunninen (1935c) on *Hymenolepis fraterna*; Vergeer (1936) on *Dibothriocephalus*; Reid and Ackert (1937) on *Choanotaenia*; Reid, Ackert, and Case (1938) on *Raillietina*; Stunkard (1934–41) on various Anoplocephalidae; Mueller (1935–41) on *Spirometra*; Michajlow (1932a–33b) on *Triaenophorus*; Miller (1943–46) on *Triaenophorus*; and so on. The list is not intended to be complete and many other contributions of note will be mentioned in the pages that follow.

Egg

Within the tapeworm ovary, the egg cell is in that phase of oogenesis termed the "primary oocyte." Its transformation to a "secondary oocyte" and thence to a ripe egg may take place before it leaves the ovary (*Avitellina centripunctata*) or within the fertilization canal (*Hydatigera taeniaeformis*). In the latter event the egg cell may be fertilized before it has completed oogenesis.

The evidence concerning tapeworm oogenesis is conflicting. The developing oogonia can readily be followed in the ovaries of various cestodes through the prophase and in some cases the metaphase stages, after which mitosis apparently stops and the nuclei go back to the resting condition, or break up into chromidia from which cleavage cells arise.

Young (1935) comments with regard to this remarkable phenomenon:

"Chromidial cell formation has been described by many workers on Protozoa and while denied by some (Kofoid, 1921) its probability is maintained by Calkins (1933) who says '. . . the gamete nuclei which arise from the chromidial net represent chromatin which is manufactured by a cytoplasmic substance of the same nature as the karyolymph and a substance which, possibly, may be derived from the nucleus'; and Wilson (1925) who says '. . . [it] seems to be established decisively in some species . . . that at certain stages of the life-history true individualized nuclei may be formed by aggregation or growth of the chromidial granules and may later in their turn give off such granules or break down into them.' A similar method of nuclear development has been described by Griggs (1909) in *Synchitrium decipiens*, a parasite of the peanut, and by Baird (1924) in the moulds, *Phycomyces nitens* and *Rhizopus nigricans*. It is, I believe, significant that these accounts are given either of unicellular or parasitic forms.

"Now if cell multiplication by chromidia may occur in protozoa and fungi, it is not unlikely that it may occur also in tapeworms; and that many of the mitoses which have been described here, especially in gametogenesis, where they occur most frequently, are in reality abortive ones to be followed later by chromidial development. If my observations be correct they 'support the view that polar bodies are not formed and that maturation of both sperm and egg are degenerating in cestodes' (Young, 1913). In any case it seems to me that the whole subject of cell division, gametogenesis and the role of chromosomes in these worms is badly in need of an exhaustive and thorough examination." Young (1935).

In the majority of tapeworms, segmentation, gastrulation, and embryogeny of the egg take place while the egg is within the uterine tract, but in many pseudophyllidean forms the egg does not begin to segment until it has left the uterus.

The fertilized egg cell is spherical, transparent, and yolkless. In addition to the periplasm, the modified surface layer of protoplasm, the egg is covered by a membrane. Whether this is a true vitelline membrane, a nonliving product of the cell, whether it is a true fertilization membrane – split off from the vitelline membrane after the entrance of the sperm cell – or whether it is a combination of both, is not clear. The egg cell lies amidst a group of yolk cells, relatively large in size and few in number. The egg is thus extralecithal, its deutoplasm (yolk) lying outside its cytoplasm (egg protoplasm). These yolk cells may break down into a darkly granular mass shortly before segmentation begins.

Surrounding the egg cell and its satellite yolk cells is the "shell." Whether this is produced by the shell glands or whether it is produced from yolk cells – opinions differ – it is a secondary membrane and, zoologically speaking, is therefore a chorion and not a shell. It is comparable in fact to the outer covering of the arthropod egg.

The embryonic development of the tapeworm egg has attracted few investigators, and little has been added in recent years to the descriptions given by Schauinsland (1885) of the developing *Dibothriocephalus* egg and by Janicki (1907) of the developing *Taenia* egg. If the details of egg development in these forms are typical of tapeworms in general, the course of development appears similar to that described in other flatworms. The segmentation is complete but unequal, a few macromeres and a relatively large number of micromeres being produced. The macromeres give rise to a cellular membrane which encloses the segmenting egg cell and the surrounding yolk mass. This membrane is thus a blastoderm – an extraembryonic blastoderm certainly, but a cellular layer surrounding the yolk. Presumably when first formed, this blastoderm lies close to the inner surface of the chorion and is thus analogous, though not of course homologous, with a true vitelline membrane; but as the yolk is slowly consumed by the developing embryo, the blastoderm shrinks away from the chorion.

The micromeres form a loose, spherical mass, which is described as giving rise by epibole to a gastrula. During gastrulation another, and apparently double, cellular layer is formed, surrounding this time the forming gastrula. This double membrane may be referred to as the embryonic envelope (Figure 30). The gastrula undergoes embryogenic transformation into a type of embryo termed an "oncosphere." Thus at the end of embryonic development the tapeworm egg may be said to comprise, from the outside inward: (*a*) the chorion, (*b*) the extraembryonic blastoderm, (*c*) the embryonic envelope, and (*d*) the oncosphere.

The chorion – called by some authors the egg shell or Eihülle – is seen in its highest development among pseudophyllidean and tetraphyllidean tapeworm eggs, where it is a relatively stout, ovoid, yellow-brown structure. Among these forms, the chorion is commonly operculate – that is to say, it has at one pole a circular lid which, when opened, allows the oncosphere to swim out or to creep out. In other tapeworms, however, the chorion is delicate and transparent and has no such lid. The space between chorion and blastoderm may be filled with a clear gelatinous substance or with a mucoid fluid (see Essex, 1927a; Magath, 1929b). Only rarely does the chorion show ridges or outgrowths. Exceptional is the cyclophyllidean form *Liga*, in which the chorion has a tubular outgrowth from each pole ending in a globular expansion. Among taeniid tapeworms, the chorion and probably the blastoderm are shed while the egg is within the uterine tract, and the apparent "shell" of the egg, as seen in host feces, represents the embryonic envelope.

The extraembryonic blastoderm – variously termed the yolk envelope, vitelline membrane, Hüllmembran – is probably present in all tapeworm eggs, although, according to the amount of yolk enclosed, it may lie in close proximity to the chorion or closely applied to the embryonic envelope, producing the effect in either case of apparently only two egg membranes instead of the usual three.

The cellular nature of the blastoderm is less apparent as development of the egg proceeds. Wagner (1917) described the membrane in *Proteocephalus torulosus* as being double contoured, with elongated nuclei along its inner margin. This observer took the view that the membrane

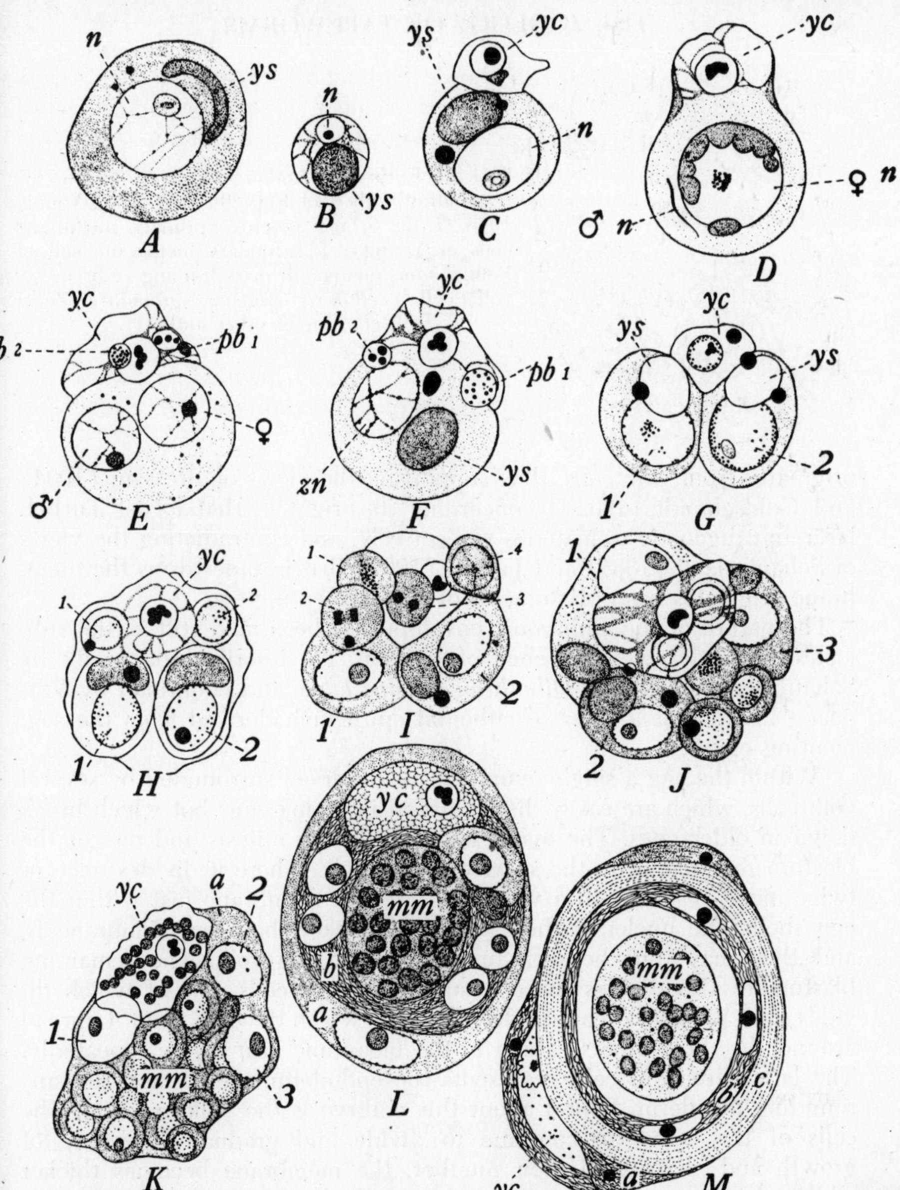

FIG. 30. Embryonal development of *Hydatigera taeniaeformis*. After Janicki, 1906c, 1907. A. Ripe oocyte in ovary. B. Ripe yolk cell in yolk gland. C. Egg cell in oviduct. D. Intrauterine egg just after entrance of sperm cell. E. Later intrauterine egg showing polar body formation. F. Later intrauterine egg with zygote nucleus. G. 2-cell stage. H. 4-cell stage, 2 macromeres, 2 micromeres. I. 6-cell stage, 2 macromeres, 4 micromeres. J. Formation of third macromere (3). K. Beginning of formation of outer membrane (*a*) and multiplication and massing of micromeres (*mm*). L. Embryo with outer (*a*) and inner (*b*) membranes. M. Completion of chitinous shell (*c*) formation. *a*, outer membranes; *b*, inner membrane; *c*, chitinous shell; *mm*, massed micromeres; *n*, egg cell nucleus; ♂ *n*, sperm cell nucleus; ♀ *n*, female nucleus; *pb*, polar body; *yc*, yolk cell; *ys*, yolk substance; *1*, *2*, *3*, *4* (small), micromeres; *1*, *2*, *3* (large), macromeres; *zn*, zygote nucleus.

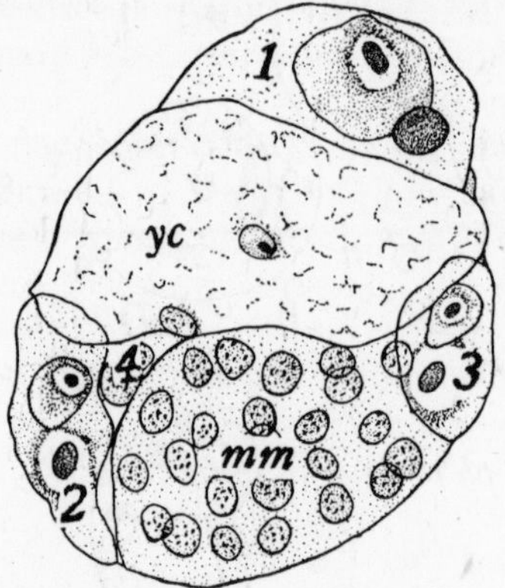

FIG. 31. Embryo of *Hydatigera taeniaeformis*, corresponding with K of Fig. 30. After R. T. Young, 1935. *1, 2, 3,* macromeres (primary membrane cells of Young); *4,* secondary membrane cell of Young; *mm,* micromere mass forming embryo; *yc,* yolk cell (*cellule granuleuse, granulirte Zelle, Vitellogène* of other authors).

originates from yolk cells, thus supporting the views of Bresslau (1904) and Goldschmidt (1902b) concerning its origin in rhabdocoel Turbellaria and digenetic trematodes respectively, and contradicting the views of Schauinsland (1885) and Janicki (1907) that in tapeworms the membrane originates from blastomeres of the segmenting egg.

The nature of the embryonic envelope has been, and still is, the subject of considerable difference of opinion. As described originally by Schauinsland (1885) in *Dibothriocephalus latus*, and confirmed by Vergeer (1936), it is a layer of cuboidal epithelium derived from the segmenting egg.

"Within the egg a single ovum can be observed surrounded by several yolk cells, which are easily distinguished in young eggs but which break down in older eggs. The ovum soon divides by mitosis and one of the blastomeres escapes to the surface of the yolk, where it divides once or twice more, resulting in a very thin vitelline membrane just within the egg shell. The nuclei of these cells are thicker than the membrane is, and they may thus be seen projecting into the yolk. The remaining blastomere also divides twice, resulting in four cells, one of which divides later in such a manner that the cells which develop from it spread around the three others, which in the meantime also divide repeatedly. The latter group of cells represents the endoderm, the former, the surrounding ectoderm. Round about this embryo is the yolk material. The cells of the ectoderm continue to divide and gradually, because of growth and increase in their number, the membrane becomes thicker while on its outer surface cilia develop, which at first are short but become longer. This, then, is the ciliated outer membrane or embryophore. The inner mass becomes the onchosphere. As the embryo grows the yolk decreases but not all of it is ever used up. When the egg hatches, a few of the yolk cells are sometimes still intact, although the nuclei have generally broken down. Occasionally one can see also part of the vitelline membrane remaining within the empty shell. If we accept Schauinsland's interpretation then, the onchosphere and the forms which develop from it, consist of endoderm and mesoderm only; the outside of the onchosphere and consequently of the adult worm, is endoderm and through it food from the contents of the intestine of the host is absorbed. The reproductive organs and other inner tissues must be mesodermal derivatives." Vergeer (1936) (Figure 32).

A re-examination of this embryonic structure in *Dibothriocephalus latus* by Vogel (1929c, 1930) suggested that while originally it appears to be a true cuboidal epithelium, its cellular nature is eventually lost. In the "coracidium" – the term given to the oncosphere when surrounded by its embryonic envelopes, after emergence from the egg shell – the so-called embryophore appears to be limited externally and internally by a delicate membrane. Observed microscopically, by dark ground illumination, the space between the two membranes is seen to be divided by protoplasmic partitions in which refractive droplets can be seen. These droplets are used up during the short life of the coracidium and may serve as sources of energy for the cilia that cover the coracidial envelope. They appear to be of a fatty nature and resemble the droplets within yolk cells. Within the compartments thus formed are fluid-filled vacuoles. The cilia on the anterior half of the coracidium – the half that moves foremost during the progress of the coracidium – are longer than those on the posterior half. Each consists of a basal portion, thick and very active, and a delicate continuation which is not motile but remains stiff during the movement of the cilium. Presumably the continuation represents the axial fiber of the cilium, and the basal portion may have a contractile sheath. It is interesting thus to note a condition that is to be seen also in the cilia of many infusorian Protozoa and in the tail of spermatozoa.

Wisniewski (1930), describing the developing egg of *Cyathocephalus truncatus*, found the embryo to be enclosed by a nonciliated membrane which fits so closely to the embryo that it can be distinguished only with difficulty. It consists at first of stratified epithelium, but in the fully grown embryo the cellular appearance is lost and the membrane appears as a strongly refractive, homogeneous structure which differs from the embryophore of *Dibothriocephalus* not only in lacking cilia, but in having two layers, external and internal.

Both Essex (1927a) and Magath (1929b), in the primitive proteocephalan forms *Corallobothrium fimbriatum* and *Crepidobothrium testudo,* described the embryonic membrane as being a *single* membrane, with a granular layer between it and the surface of the oncosphere. However, it is very definitely figured by many authors as a double membrane (see Wagner, 1917: *Proteocephalus torulosus*; Ransom, 1909: *Hymenolepis cantaniana*; Stiles, 1906: *Hymenolepis fraterna*; Reid *et al.*, 1938: *Raillietina cesticillus*); and the probability that the double-contoured effect is not an optical illusion is suggested by Reid's findings that the two membranes can be separated by dialyzing the developing egg in distilled water.

A more comprehensive examination of the embryonic envelopes of a range of tapeworms might be directed toward the possibility that there exists here something similar to the double cellular envelope which covers the developing insect embryo, where the outer serosa is derived from

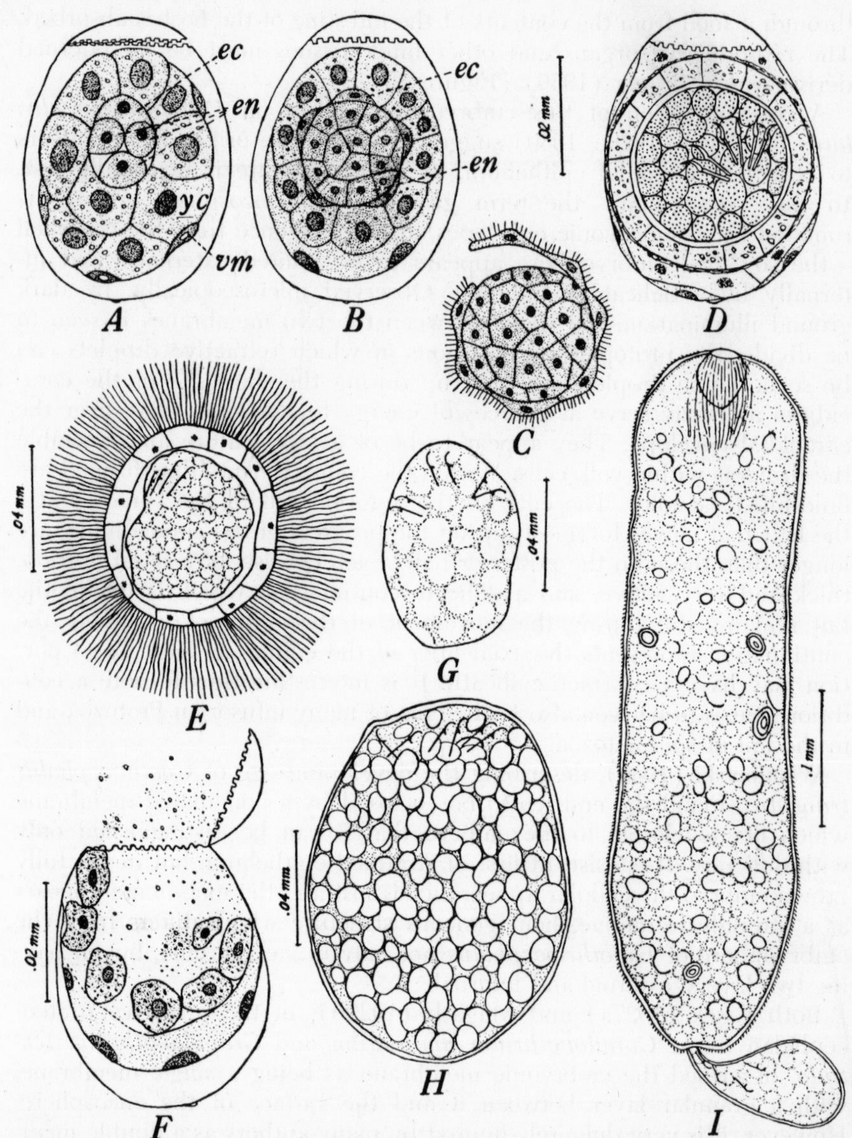

FIG. 32. Early development of *Dibothriocephalus latus*. A and B. Segmented eggs. After Vergeer, 1936. *ec*, ectodermal cell; *en*, endodermal cell; *yc*, yolk cell; *vm*, vitelline membrane. C. Immature embryo with cilia developing. After Schauinsland, 1886a. D. Egg shortly before hatching. After Vergeer, 1936. E. Liberated coracidium. After Essex, 1927b. F. Egg after escape of coracidium. After Vergeer, 1936. G. Procercoid from body cavity of *Diaptomus* 5 hours after ingestion of coracidium. H. Procercoid at 7 days. I. Procercoid at 14 days. All after Essex, 1927b.

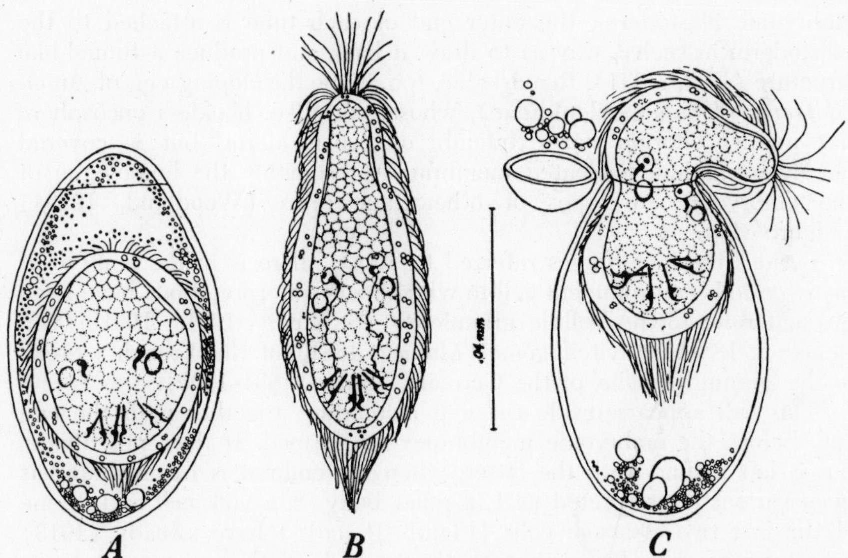

FIG. 33. *Spirometra erinacei.* After Neveu Lemaire, 1936. A. Embryonated egg. B. Coracidium. C. Escape of coracidium.

yolk cells and the inner amnion from extraembryonic ectoderm. Such a finding would reconcile, to some extent, the divergent views that have been expressed on the question, and, by bringing the organogeny of tapeworms into harmony with that of other animals, would reconcile it with the germ layer hypothesis.

The ciliated type of outer embryonic membrane, so far as present knowledge goes, characterizes only certain pseudophyllidean families (Dibothriocephalidae, Bothriocephalidae, Triaenophoridae) and possibly some, or all, families of Trypanorhyncha. Ruszkowski (1934) has described this type of ciliated embryophore in the developing egg of *Grillotia erinaceus.*

Among taeniid tapeworms, the two embryonic membranes are connected by radially directed fiberlike structures, possibly corresponding with the protoplasmic strands of the dibothriocephalid embryophore. This striated structure forms the outer "shell" of the taeniid egg after it leaves the uterus. Skvortsov (1942) has claimed, however, that the egg of *Taeniarhynchus saginatus* has four membranes. The first is mucoid and colorless; the second is made up of proteins of large molecular weight and is soluble in both pepsin and trypsin; the third is like the second in chemical composition, but is much thinner; and the fourth is transparent, semipermeable, and lipoid in nature.

Among anoplocephalid tapeworms, the outermost embryonic envelope may be prolonged as a pair of spines or even as tip-crossing pincers—the so-called "pyriform apparatus" (Figure 43). In the davaineid form *Raillietina cesticillus,* the innermost embryonic membrane is prolonged as two, or even three or five, tubular structures which reach to the extraembryonic blastoderm; the outer end of each tube is attached to the blastoderm in such a way as to draw it back and produce a funnel-like structure (Figure 241). Remarkable, too, is the developing egg of *Anonchotaenia globata* (Dilepididae), whose wormlike, hookless oncosphere has neither chorion nor extraembryonic blastoderm, but is covered closely by a thin, nucleated membrane, presumably the homologue of the embryonic envelopes of other tapeworms (Woodland, 1929a) (Figure 310).

"Besides the membranes referred to above, there is in the embryo of many cestodes a prominent cell to which many interpretations have been given. I refer to the 'cellule granuleuse' (St. Remy, 1901a, 1901b; Van Beneden, 1881) or 'vitellogène' (Moniez, 1881) of the French writers, or the 'granulirte Zelle' of the Germans (Braun, 1894–1900).

"This cell appears inside the egg membrane, together with the egg cell, before the embryonic membranes are formed. It does not divide, but is left behind with the latter, when the embryo is hatched. It has been variously interpreted as 1, a polar body; 2, a yolk cell and 3, one of the first two cleavage cells [Figure 31, *yc*]. I have already (1913) given my reasons for accepting the second of these interpretations, which is that of Leuckart (1856) and will only briefly recapitulate them here.

"First, the occurrence of compound eggs, i.e., an egg cell surrounded by a mass of yolk cells, is of frequent occurrence in flatworms, which type occurs in the cestode, *Bothriocephalus latus*; while in other forms (i.e., *B. rugosus*) these cells are replaced by a mass of non-cellular yolk.

"Second, in some cases in *Taenia pisiformis* (Young, 1913) the cell in question is double and is attached to 'oocytes in the uterus resembling in every way ovarian oocytes, and which therefore probably had not yet undergone maturation or fertilization.' (l.c.p.395).

"Third, it occasionally contains a darkly staining mass, similar to the yolk masses in the cells of yolk glands.

"Fourth, it appears shortly after, but not before the egg cell has passed the yolk ducts on its way to the uterus.

"Fifth, in those cestodes which lack a yolk gland (i.e., *Thysanosoma*, Young, 1919a) this cell is also lacking." Young (1935).

Oncosphere

The tapeworm oncosphere appears when alive as a grayish mass of granular protoplasm, ovoid or irregularly spherical in shape, recalling somewhat an amoeba, and contracting and expanding in a fashion reminiscent of that animal. It is enveloped by a delicate protoplasmic membrane. The term is derived from the Greek "onkos," a tumor or swelling, and "sphaira," a sphere, and is sometimes, though erroneously, spelled "onchosphere."

Characteristic of the oncosphere are three pairs of hooklike structures in the posterior half of the creature, the tips of the hooks projecting through the protoplasmic membrane during oncospheric expansion. The term "hexacanth embryo," sometimes given to the oncosphere, refers to these hooks. Two pairs of the hooks are lateral in position, the third pair lying between them. The shape of each hook is very similar in all oncospheres observed and consists of a straight, rodlike structure and a shorter, curved, bladelike portion. At the junction of rod and blade there may be a slight enlargement.

Hookless oncospheres have been described. Wisniewski (1930) was unable to see hooks in the oncospheres of *Cyathocephalus truncatus*, although such hooks were definitely figured by Gauthier (1923). The peculiar, elongated, wormlike oncospheres of certain species of *Anonchotaenia* lack such hooks.

Very little differentiation of the internal structures of the oncosphere, beyond the presence of large cells and small cells, can be demonstrated by the usual methods of microtechnique. Vogel (1929c, 1930), however, making use of the methyl green–pyronin technique of Pappenheim, was able to show in the oncosphere of *Dibothriocephalus latus* a complexity of internal structure which had not been suspected by earlier observers (Figure 34). He found the oncosphere to consist in this case mainly of

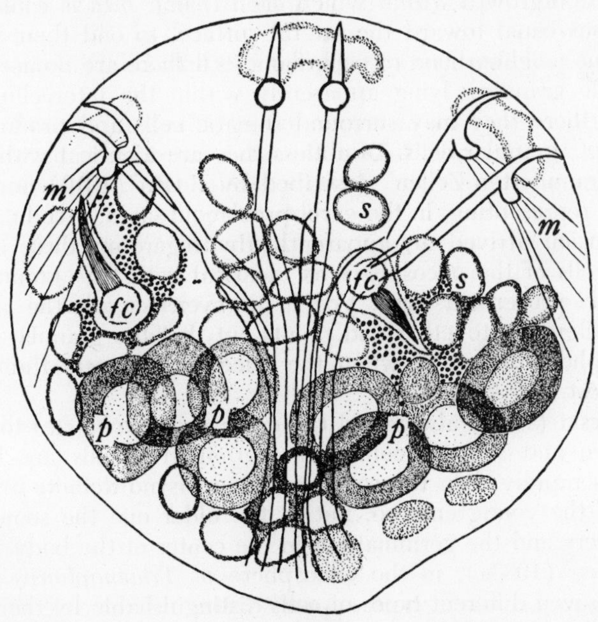

FIG. 34. Oncosphere of *Dibothriocephalus latus*. After Vogel, 1929c, 1930. *fc*, flame cell; *m*, muscle fibers of hooks; *p*, plastin cells; *s*, somatic cells.

a loose mass of small *somatic* cells, each with an elongated, chromatin-rich nucleus that stains intensively bluish-green, and a cytoplasm that remains colorless after staining. In addition, in the anterior half of the oncosphere are from four to twelve relatively larger cells which Vogel terms "plastin" cells, as they stain intensively with the pyronin constituent of the double stain, a constituent which is believed to have an affinity with a hypothetical substance "plastin" in cell cytoplasm. The large, round nucleus of each plastin cell stains only faintly green and is presumably chromatin-poor. The resemblance in staining properties of such plastin cells to the so-called "germinal cells" of the trematode miracidium suggests that they may be in the nature of germ cells.

From the bases of the six hooks, bundles of contractile fibers converge toward the anterior pole of the oncosphere. From the base of the blade-like portion of each hook, similar fibers converge toward the lateral surfaces of the oncosphere. It may be noted that when the oncosphere contracts, the two lateral pairs of hooks appear horizontal and in one straight line, while the central pair remains at right angles to the laterals. When the oncosphere expands, the three pairs of hooks lie almost parallel with one another (see Magath, 1929b: *Crepidobothrium testudo*).

When the oncosphere of *Dibothriocephalus latus* is compressed beneath a cover glass and examined with an oil immersion lens under strong illumination, a pair of flame cells can be seen lying right and left within it, close to the bases of the outer hooks of the lateral pairs. The funnel-like outgrowth within which each "flame" lies is continued as a fine, sinuous canal toward the lateral surface, to end there as a small pore. In the neighborhood of each flame cell there are numerous refractive, motile granules, lying apparently within the intercellular spaces. Here and there they may surround somatic cells and produce the appearance of granular cells. Doubtless they are identical with the "zwei bis drei granulierten Zellen" described by Rosen (1919) and regarded by him as representing, in the early procercoid larva, a rudimentary gut —a conclusion arrived at, apparently, by regarding these supposedly granular cells of the oncosphere as identical with true granulated cells in the early procercoid larva. Vogel, however, regards the latter structures as different altogether and points out that the granular clusters of the oncosphere disappear when the oncosphere enters the first intermediate host.

Wisniewski (1930) also found the embryo of *Archigetes* to consist of germinative and somatic cells. The germinative cells are larger and divide less rapidly than the somatics. There is no definite arrangement of cells in the young embryo, but in the older one the somatics lie at the periphery and the germinatives in the center of the body.

Michajlow (1933a), in the oncosphere of *Triaenophorus nodulosus*, described seven different types of cells distinguishable by their reactions to Mallory's stain, methyl green–pyronin, and iron haematoxylin. The majority are somatic cells, with nuclei staining green and cytoplasm colorless with methyl green–pyronin. Less numerous, and situated among the somatic cells, were what Michajlow called "lambda cells," closely resembling somatics but distinguishable by their reaction to Mallory's stain. Their nuclei stained blue in contrast to the red-to-yellow staining of somatic cell nuclei; their cytoplasm stained red with iron haematoxylin staining, while that of the somatics remained colorless. Scattered through the oncosphere, according to this observer, there are also 9–23 cells whose nuclei stain bright reddish-brown, with nucleoli red and cytoplasm red, with methyl green–pyronin. These were regarded as identical with Vogel's plastin cells and Wisniewski's germinative cells. Near these cells, in a subcuticular position, Michajlow recognized what he called, in imitation of Wisniewski, "germinative-somatic cells," which had several nucleoli in each nucleus and whose cytoplasm was unstainable by either methyl green–pyronin or iron haematoxylin. Granular cells of two different sizes were located in the posterior half of the oncosphere, and flame cells and muscle cells attached to the hooks were also described.

In the oncospheres of *Cittotaenia*, which are only about half the size of those of *Dibothriocephalus, Archigetes*, and *Triaenophorus*, Stunkard (1934) was able, by the methyl green–pyronin technique, to distinguish two types of cells – numerous small somatic cells and 10–20 larger plastin cells. The refractive granules described by Vogel in *Dibothriocephalus* were also seen, but no flame cells could be found.

Venard (1938), in the oncospheres of *Dipylidium caninum*, also found two types of cells distinguishable by morphology and staining properties. Of the 75–100 cells that make up the average oncosphere, about 40 corresponded with the somatic cells of other observers. They were 3–5 μ in diameter, had spherical or elliptical nuclei that stained deeply with Heidenhain's iron haematoxylin, green with methyl green–pyronin, and red with Mallory's stain. An equal number of larger cells, up to 10 μ in diameter, had nuclei each with one large nucleolus and several smaller nucleoli, all staining deep red with pyronin. Two types of such cells were distinguishable: (*a*) about 30 cells distributed uniformly through the oncosphere, but with 4 or 5 occupying a central position; they have spherical or ovoid nuclei, each with a very conspicuous nucleolus; these Venard identifies with Vogel's plastin cells and Wisniewski's germinatives; and (*b*) 10–15 cells with cytoplasm colorless, except with pyronin, whose nuclei have two or more nucleoli. Venard identifies these with Wisniewski's germinative-somatics.

Reid (1948) has described, in oncospheres of *Raillietina cesticillus, Choanotaenia infundibulum, Moniezia expansa*, and *Hymenolepis sp.*, a pair of unicellular glands, each extending the full length of the oncosphere from its posterior end to pores in its anterior tip, from which the movements of the oncosphere produce an exudation of fluid. From comparison with similar structures in trematodan cercariae and miracidia, Reid believes these to be "penetration glands" whose secretion erodes host cells in the neighborhood of the invasion. Alternatively, the secretion may be adhesive, anchoring the oncosphere to the host tissue and so permitting the hooks to secure a better purchase.

Metacestode

The term "metacestode" is a convenient one to indicate the stage, or the succession of stages, of the tapeworm life cycle that is passed within an intermediate host – that is to say, within a host in which the worm does not come to sexual maturity. There are, of course, no abrupt transitions between oncosphere, metacestode, and adult; there is rather a very gradual transition from one to the other. Where a succession of metacestode stages occurs, the stages may be referred to as larval phases of the metacestode stage.

Four types of metacestode may be recognized – the acystic or solid procercoid and plerocercoid types, and the cystic or bladderlike cysticercoid and cysticercus types. However, by a process of external budding of the solid types, and of external or internal budding of the bladderlike types, a number of variations of the four basic types may be produced, so that the variety of larval forms among tapeworms is considerable.

PROCERCOID

The procercoid may be described as a solid-bodied larva in which the oncospheric hooks are retained and in which the future holdfast has not yet differentiated. It characterizes the pseudophyllidean and proteocephalan life cycles. The procercoid larval stage was described for the first time by Janicki and Rosen (1917) in the life cycle of *Dibothriocephalus latus*; their description has been amplified by Essex (1927b) and Vogel (1930). Okumura (1919) and Kobayashi (1931) have described the procercoid stage of *Spirometra mansoni*; Mueller (1938a) of *Spirometra mansonioides*; Essex (1928a) of *Bothriocephalus cuspidatus*; Michajlow (1933a) of *Triaenophorus nodulosus*; Wisniewski (1930, 1933) of *Archigetes* and *Cyathocephalus*. Descriptions of proteocephalan procercoids are less available but have been published by Essex (1927a) for *Corallobothrium*; Magath (1929b) for *Crepidobothrium*; Wagner (1917) for *Proteocephalus torulosus*; Cooper (1915) for *Proteocephalus ambloplitis*; and Kuczkowski (1925) for *Proteocephalus percae*. The list is not complete, of course, and will be supplemented by further references in the sections that deal with the classification of the various families.

In few tapeworms does the procercoid appear to be as differentiated as in *Dibothriocephalus*. Baer (1940b) would apply the term broadly to that part of the tapeworm life cycle that comes between the entrance of the oncosphere into the first intermediate host and its transition to plerocercoid, plerocercus, cysticercoid, or cysticercus larva. The procercoid stage begins, in *Dibothriocephalus latus*, soon after the oncosphere – still enclosed by the ciliated embryophore – is ingested by a species of *Diaptomus* or *Cyclops* (Copepoda, Crustacea). From the ingestion of the ciliated larva by *Diaptomus vulgaris* to the end of procercoid development there is, according to Vogel (1930), an interval of 16–18 days. Essex (1927b), however, obtained fully formed procercoids in *Diaptomus oregonensis* after 14 days.

After entering the gut of the *Diaptomus*, the oncosphere sheds the ciliated envelope and forces its way through the gut wall of the crustacean host to arrive in the hemocoel. The speed with which this is carried out saves the parasite from destruction by the digestive enzymes of the host, but, according to Vogel, such destruction often occurs. Particularly is this so in species of *Cyclops* rather than of *Diaptomus*. Vogel, in Germany, found that the procercoids of *Dibothriocephalus latus* developed readily in *Cyclops strenuus*, *Diaptomus gracilis*, and *Diaptomus vulgaris*, but not in *Cyclops viridis, C. albidus, C. bicuspidatus*, or *C. serratulus.* Although *Cyclops strenuus* was regarded by Rosen and Janicki as the most important intermediate host of *D. latus* in Switzerland, Vogel found this copepod to be only occasionally infected, and diaptomid species to be the chief German hosts. Essex, in northern Minnesota (U.S.A.), found *Cyclops brevispinosus* and *C. prasinus* to be infectible only with difficulty, but *Diaptomus oregonensis* to be readily infectible.

Reaching the hemocoel within a few hours of being swallowed, the oncosphere – or procercoid as it now is – takes up a position parallel with and close beside the crustacean gut, in the cephalothoracic region. Internally, the clusters of granules that surrounded the flame cells now disappear, and the plastin cells begin to multiply so fast that the larva rapidly increases in size. These cells begin to form a dense, parenchyma-like mass, from which will develop later the cuticle, subcuticle, muscle fibers, and osmoregulatory system.

At the end of 16–18 days the procercoid is full grown. It is 500–600 μ long, a rapid increase indeed over the average 30 μ diameter of the oncosphere. In shape it is like an elongated pear. At its narrow end, and partly attached to the body by a narrow stalk that emerges from a funnel-like invagination, there is an oval or club-shaped structure on which are the three pairs of oncospheric hooks. This is the cercomer. At first it is solid, or at any rate filled with parenchymal tissue; but later it becomes bladderlike. At the opposite or broad end of the pear there is another funnel-like structure, deep or shallow according to the degree of muscular contraction of the larva.

At the beginning of its career, the procercoid is covered by a delicate cuticle beneath which lie, without any special arrangement, the nuclei of body cells whose outlines are indistinct. No typical subcuticle can be recognized. In later development, plastin cells wander into the marginal region of the larva, come to lie parallel to one another beneath the cuticle, and become flattened, spindle-shaped, or polygonal. This cellular layer is not separated from the underlying plastin cells by any visible boundary. When the larva is 8–10 days old, these cells become arranged in palisade fashion and form a typicle subcuticle from which protoplasmic outgrowths extend to the cuticle. Beneath the old cuticle a new one forms which, in contrast to the existing one, is minutely spinose. After 12 days the spinose nature of the new cuticle is clearly to be seen. This spiny cuticle covers the body surface except for the cercomer and the cavities of the anterior and posterior funnels. Over the cercomer a new cuticle also forms, but it is thinner than that over the body and without spines. The old cuticle comes away from the body and is eventually lost when the cercomer is discarded. A similar molting of the larval cuticle has also been described by Li (1929) in the procercoids of *Spirometra decipiens* and *S. erinacea.*

As mentioned earlier, there are two prevalent opinions concerning the flatworm ectoderm. According to one view, flatworms are animals without an ectoderm, the ectoderm being cast off during larval development as the embryophore. From another viewpoint, the adult subcuticle is seen as a true ectoderm. Fuhrmann (1931), for example, pointed out that the shedding of embryonic ectoderm is no evidence that the adult flatworm lacks ectoderm, for undifferentiated ectoderm cells may lie beneath the embryonic ectoderm and later differentiate and develop. Vogel, also, demonstrating that the procercoid subcuticle is formed from a group of undifferentiated cells, does not accept the shedding of the ciliated embryonic envelope of the oncosphere as proof that the adult worm lacks a true ectoderm.

In the oncosphere, muscle fibers are visible. They move the hooks and probably, according to Vogel, bring about the stretching and contract-

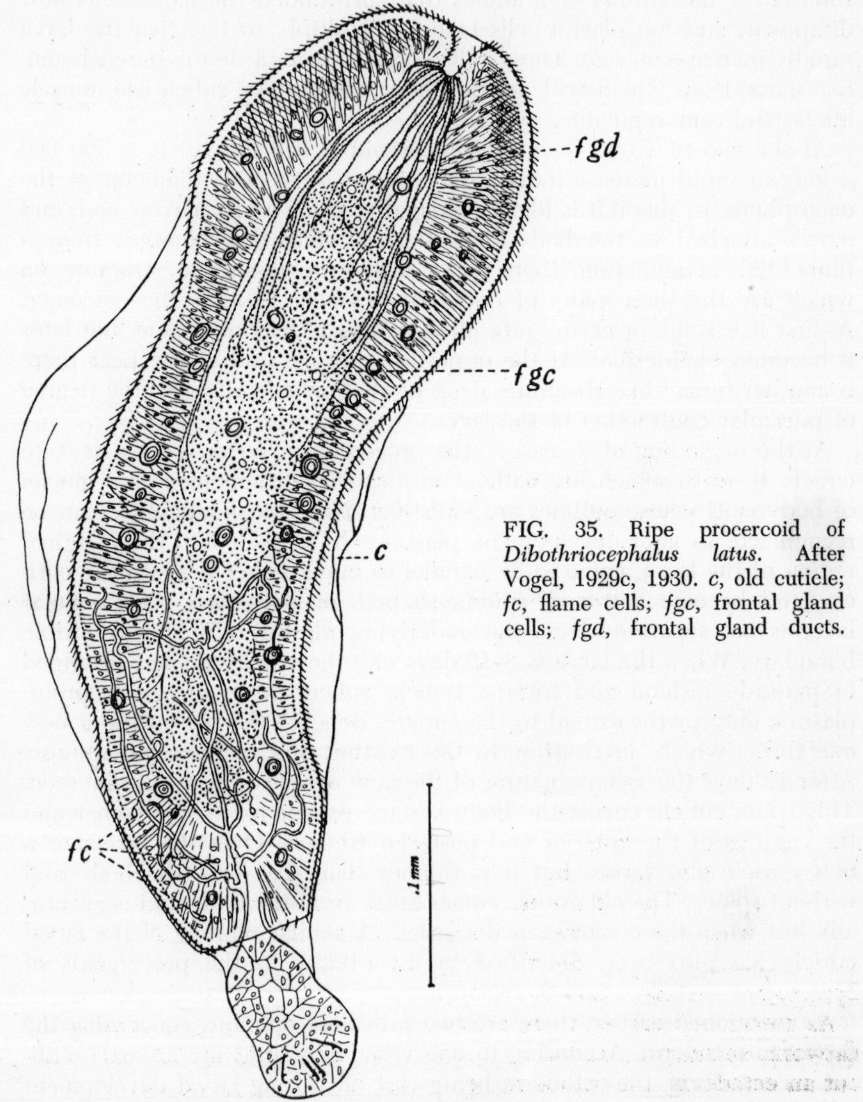

FIG. 35. Ripe procercoid of *Dibothriocephalus latus*. After Vogel, 1929c, 1930. *c*, old cuticle; *fc*, flame cells; *fgc*, frontal gland cells; *fgd*, frontal gland ducts.

ing movements of the oncosphere. In the early procercoid they disappear; but in the ten-day procercoid circular muscle fibers appear below the cuticle, and the procercoid, up to now motionless, begins to show active expansion and contraction. Calcareous structures appear at the end of one week and increase considerably in number during later development.

Of considerable interest among the internal structures of the procercoid are the "frontal glands." Eleven days after development begins, a number of fine lines may be seen radiating from a circular area of the anterior end – where later the anterior funnel will appear – and running somewhat parallel to one another into the interior of the procercoid. Later they can be seen to be in reality fine canals filled with minute drops. Each canal appears to be the outlet for a pear-shaped gland cell which is filled with minute granules. The canals discharge into the anterior funnel. These frontal glands form a thick mass that takes up a great deal of the internal body space, almost to the hinder end (Figure 35).

Similar structures were described by Janicki and Rosen (1917) in the procercoids of *Dibothriocephalus* and of *Triaenophorus*, and by Essex (1928a) in the procercoid of *Bothriocephalus cuspidatus*. None of these observers seems to have noticed that the glands communicate with the outside, but Rosen described a rosettelike mass of cells which opened into the base of the anterior funnel and were presumably the terminal sections of the canals described later by Vogel. Rosen's view that this central cellular mass in the procercoid represents a vestige of a former alimentary tract was not supported either by Essex or Vogel. Fuhrmann (1931) was inclined to homologize the frontal glands of pseudophyllidean procercoids with those of adult Trypanorhyncha, and to homologize both with the head glands of Turbellaria.

Up to the tenth day, the osmoregulatory system of the procercoid shows the same primitive arrangement as in the oncosphere, consisting as it does of a pair of flame cells, each continued as a capillary, sinuous duct to the external surface. After the tenth day, however, a considerable increase takes place in the number of flame cells, as many as 10–12 appearing by the twelfth day and 30–50 by the end of procercoid development. Three or four wide, main canals open to the exterior at the bottom of the posterior funnel, and between them and the flame cells there is a complex network of vessels of small to medium caliber. A number of fine osmoregulatory capillaries open in numerous places on the upper body surface by secondary foramina. There is no noticeable symmetry, however, in the arrangement of either the flame cells or the conducting canals.

Surveying the course of development described above, it is evident that during procercoid development there is both progression and regression. The very considerable difference in size between the initial and the end phases somewhat disguises the regressive changes that take place. The increase in size is due entirely to multiplication of the plastin cells. From them come the subcuticle, the new cuticle, the parenchymal muscles, and the osmoregulatory and glandular cells. The smaller body cells of the oncosphere seem to play no part in the construction of the procercoid. The primitive osmoregulatory system is taken over from the oncosphere and later on is built up considerably. The regressive changes, on the other hand, are the loss of the ciliated embryophore, the shedding of the oncosphere cuticle, the disappearance of the hooklet muscles, and the later degeneration of the cercomer.

The transition of the oncosphere into the procercoid consists, if we ignore the osmoregulatory system, not in a gradual unfolding of organs already present but in a comprehensive new construction from the ground up. It is a true metamorphosis. While the internal tissues of the maturing procercoid are differentiating, it goes through a kind of rest-

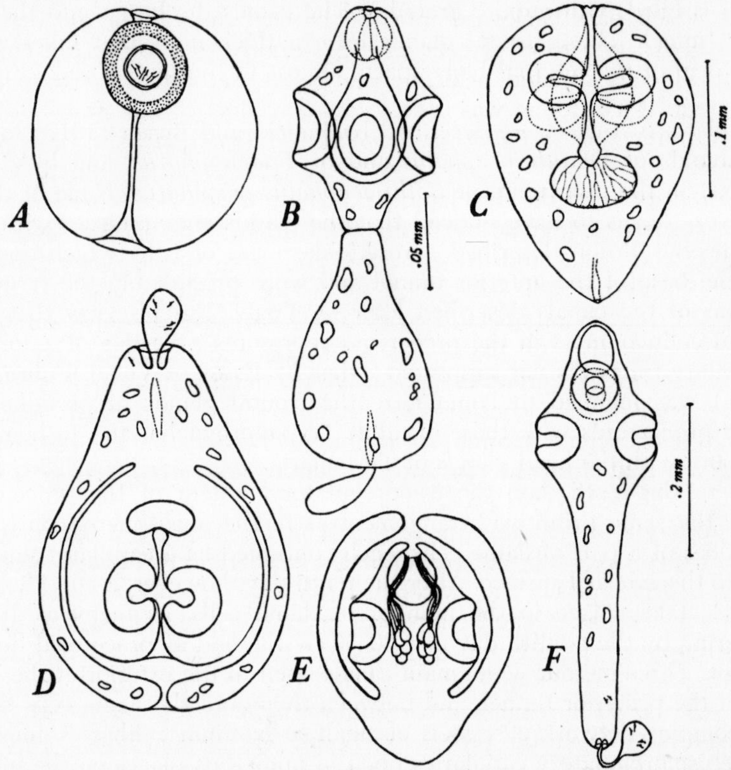

FIG. 36. Early development of *Ophiotaenia perspicus*. After Herde, 1938. A. Oncosphere within embryophore. B. 8-day procercoid showing multicellular end organ with vestibule, calcareous corpuscles, urinary bladder, and cercomer. C. 10-day procercoid with "inverted" holdfast and longitudinal flattened end organ. D. Mature procercoid with "doubly invaginated" holdfast and finely hooked and partially retracted cercomer. E. Much shortened procercoid showing "retracted" holdfast and unicellular glands associated with the end organ. F. Mature procercoid with holdfast freshly everted, suggesting alternate manner in which the couplets of opposed suckers are used, and showing the 4-hooked cercomer nearly ready to detach and the acetabulum larger than the end organ.

ing period that recalls the pupal stage of insects. Thus we might with correctness refer to the metamorphosis of *Dibothriocephalus latus* as "holometabolous" (see Vogel, 1930, p. 642).

The description given by Essex (1928a) of the development of the procercoid of *Bothriocephalus cuspidatus* recalls, although with less detail, Vogel's account of the dibothriocephalid procercoid. Here also there is a striking increase in larval growth, from the 30-micron diameter of the oncosphere to the 450-micron length of the full-grown procercoid. The bladderlike cercomer begins to differentiate from the larval body at the seventh day of development. Anterior and posterior funnels, so marked in *Dibothriocephalus*, are not described for *Bothriocephalus cuspidatus*. In the region where the anterior funnel appears in *Dibothriocephalus* there are in *B. cuspidatus* a number of fine, fiberlike structures which pass backward into the parenchyma. From the region of these fibers, two rows of cells pass posteriorly to a brownish, compact group of cells situated near the middle of the body. No trace of an osmoregulatory system was observed at any time in this procercoid, nor did the cuticle, as in *Dibothriocephalus* and *Triaenophorus*, bear bristles or spines.

A description of the development of the procercoid of *Cyathocephalus truncatus* has been given by Wisniewski (1933). The earliest procercoids are 0.18 mm. long and are spherical and transparent. They have two types of internal cells — smaller ones in the majority, and larger ones relatively few in numbers. The cells are arranged loosely and not in masses suggestive of tissue formation. At the 0.15–0.20 mm. stage, strongly refractive granules appear in the intercellular spaces and increase gradually to considerable numbers. The procercoid begins to darken and become opaque. According to Wisniewski, the granules are formed within the cells, are fatty in nature, and disappear almost entirely as the procercoid grows.

At a length of 0.20 mm. the larva begins to elongate; at 0.50 mm. it is pear-shaped; at 1 mm. it is cylindrical. As in the oncosphere, there are no embryonic hooks. The cercomer begins to appear when the larva is 0.20 mm. long as a small outgrowth from the posterior end, appearing and disappearing with the body movements. Gradually it increases in length, and on reaching a length of 0.15 mm. it begins to be constricted from the body. It reaches a maximum length of 0.55 mm. and degenerates rapidly when the procercoid passes into its final host.

Cyathocephalus is peculiar in being in the adult stage a neotenic procercoid larva — that is to say, in being precociously sexual. The rudiments of the reproductive system appear early in procercoid life. When the larva is only 4 mm. long, a strip of tissue appears in the posterior region of the body, extends as far as the middle region, and proceeds to divide into as many segments as later there will be genitalia. Thus the number of genitalia is predetermined from the beginning. About this time, too, there appears at the anterior end of the larva a funnel-like invagination, clearly visible when the larva is contracted but less so when it is expanded. Finally, the osmoregulatory canals appear in the body and the cercomer simultaneously. With the appearance of the osmoregulatory system there appear also calcareous corpuscles, at first in the anterior region but later throughout the whole body.

This phase of procercoid development – characterized by granular opacity, cercomer formation, the beginnings of genitalia, and the appearance of the anterior funnel and the osmoregulatory system – is termed by Wisniewski the first phase of the middle procercoid stage. A second phase follows when the body becomes clearer and the anterior funnel, osmoregulatory system, and genital ducts are completely formed.

The mature procercoid is characterized not only by its greater length (14 mm.) and perfection of body structure, but also by the appearance of horizontal wrinkles when the body is contracted. At first sight they suggest segmentation, but in reality they are only superficial folds that do not demarcate the areas of the genitalia. *Cyathocephalus* has, in fact, neither external nor internal segmentation. In the mature procercoid there appear genital pores, opening alternately, without any regularity, first on one flat surface, then on another. There are 18–34 genital pores in all when the genitalia are fully developed. The ability of the mature procercoid to produce eggs is lacking, however, until it arrives within the gut of the fish host. Gammarid crustacea serve as intermediate hosts, and it may be that the fish is the second host of three and that the original final host was some Mesozoan reptile that has become extinct.

The term "plerocercoid" is often used for the cyathocephalid stage in the fish host, but this is erroneous. The only differences between the final, mature procercoid in the gammarid crustacean and the stage in the fish are the absence of the cercomer and the presence of fertilized eggs in the uteri. Intensity of egg production is apparently not correlated with the age of the proglottis. One might expect that in *Cyathocephalus* – whose genitalia, if not completely developed, do at any rate take form simultaneously in the procercoid – egg production would occur simultaneously in all the proglottides. Actually, however, eggs may be produced first in the anterior proglottides, the middle proglottides, or in the posterior proglottides. The number of eggs produced is relatively small for a tapeworm. They pass out from the worm very early after its entrance into the fish.

The internal features of the body are scarcely visible in the gravid, egg-producing procercoid. Only the genital pores and the egg-filled uteri are clearly discernible. Calcareous bodies, present in such great numbers in the earlier stages, are now only sparsely represented. In length, the sexual procercoid ranges from 4–8 mm. up to 25 mm., the majority being between 9 and 15 mm. long and 1.1 to 2.2 mm. broad.

The tendency toward a telescoping of procercoid development, seen in *Cyathocephalus*, is carried still further in the life cycles of proteocephalan tapeworms, although in this group developmental abbreviation does not proceed as far as neoteny. Thus Essex (1927a), describing the procercoid development of the presumably primitive proteocephalan *Corallobothrium fimbriatum*, states: "Four days after feeding [i.e., after feeding *Cyclops* with tapeworm eggs], 12 oncospheres were removed from the body cavity of one *Cyclops*. . . . [The] saclike body [of the most highly developed individual] showed considerable differentiation. A cuticular membrane surrounded the body and beneath it the tissue had a striated appearance, due to the development of the subcuticular musculature. Large cells surrounded by more or less heavy granules were evident."

Six-day procercoids had the hooks located at one pole, which was narrower than the rest of the body, partly constricted from it, and extremely transparent. On the eighth and ninth days, the procercoid showed three distinct regions, marked off from one another by constrictions. One constriction delimited the transparent region; the other occurred about one-third of the body length from the pole opposite that which bore the hooks. By the tenth day, outlines of the developing suckers could be seen in this portion of the body, which was therefore a potential holdfast. Larvae studied on the eleventh day after the *Cyclops* was fed showed the four suckers well developed and, at the anterior end, a distinct end organ. The large globular cells of the holdfast region had disappeared. In their place a network of minute, rounded cells with an occasional muscle fiber had appeared. The calcareous corpuscles, five or six in number, were restricted with a few exceptions to the middle region of the larva. The transparent region, more differentiated from the middle region, formed a bladderlike cercomer.

Development on the twelfth and thirteenth days differed from that of the eleventh day in the following respects: the holdfast, which had differentiated by the eleventh day, was invaginated; the number of calcareous corpuscles was greater; and the larval length, by reason of the invagination of the holdfast, was less. Development in *Cyclops* is complete by the fourteenth or fifteenth day after ingestion of the eggs. The best indication of this is the invagination of the holdfast and the loss of the cercomer.

Magath (1929b), discussing the life cycle of another proteocephalan, *Crepidobothrium testudo*, also described a procercoid in which the holdfast of the future adult coexisted with a cercomer. The procercoid elongates and the hooks move to the posterior end when the larva is between four and five days old. Between the fifth and sixth days, a cuplike invagination, an "urnlike structure," appears at the pole opposite to that which bears the hooks. This urnlike structure can be protruded or withdrawn. At this time the cercomer forms. Between the eighth and ninth days, four suckers make their appearance. At twelve or thirteen days, the holdfast invaginates within the body of the pear-shaped larva. At fourteen days the cercomer is lost.

A similar coexistence of holdfast with cercomer, or, at any rate, with embryonic hooks, was described in *Proteocephalus torulosus* by Wagner (1917) and in *P. percae* by Kuczkowski (1925). The phenomenon may be general among Proteocephala. In such species of *Proteocephalus* as have been studied, however, the cercomer is absent or rudimentary — in the latter case, not carrying the hooks, which are found on the posterior region of the body — and the holdfast is never completely invaginated.

In *Corallobothrium* and *Crepidobothrium* there is a distinct cercomer, to which the hooks are restricted, and the holdfast is completely invaginated.

PLEROCERCOID

Strictly speaking, a plerocercoid is a *solid* larval tapeworm in which the future holdfast is present as an invaginated structure, but from which the embryonic hooks have disappeared. The stage begins with the shedding of the cercomer – or loss of the hooks – and it ends with the beginning of proglottisation. Anatomically it is identical with the adult in all respects except for the absence of segmentation, of proglottisation, and of genitalia. It is, in fact, an immature tapeworm, analogous with the nymphal stage of an ametabolous insect rather than with the larval stage of a metabolous insect. Such a plerocercoid stage is found in the life cycles of all pseudophyllidean, proteocephalan, tetraphyllidean, and trypanorhynchan tapeworms whose life cycles are known, either wholly or partially, except the members of the family Cyathocephalidae and, possibly, of the family Caryophyllaeidae. Among cyclophyllidean tapeworms, a plerocercoid larva occurs in the families Mesocestoididae and Nematotaeniidae.

In the case of *Dibothriocephalus latus*, whose life cycle is better known than that of any other pseudophyllidean, the transition from procercoid to plerocercoid takes place when the crustacean containing the former is eaten by an appropriate intermediate host – in this case, some species of fresh-water fish. In Europe, it might be the pike (*Esox lucius*), perch (*Perca fluviatilis*), burbot (*Lota vulgaris*), salmon (*Salmo umbla*), trout (*Trutta vulgaris*), lake trout (*Trutta lacustris*), or grayling (*Thymallus vulgaris*); in Japan, the trout (*Oncorhynchus perryi*); in Madagascar, the barbel (*Barbus vulgaris*); in North America, the jackfish (*Esox lucius*), wall-eyed pike (*Stizostedion vitreum*), sauger (*Stizostedion canadense*), yellow perch (*Perca flavescens*).

When an infected crustacean is swallowed by such a fish, the contained procercoid is not digested but loses its cercomer and migrates from the fish stomach directly to the muscles; or possibly it is carried by the blood stream, although its relatively wide diameter would seem to oppose this method. At any rate, it appears within a few hours attached to the membranous covering of the viscera and from there eventually reaches the body wall muscles.

The histological and anatomical changes that occur during this transition have not to our knowledge been studied with the care and detail that mark the descriptions of the oncosphere-procercoid transition. The completely formed plerocercoid is cylindrical or club-shaped in outline, a glistening, opaque white in color, slightly wrinkled but not segmented – except in occasional specimens – and has each end tucked within the body, the future holdfast being indicated by a short groove at one end. Unlike the plerocercoids of other species of the genus, it is not enclosed by a membranous bag formed by the host tissues, but lies free, slowly expanding and contracting, between the muscle fibers, its future holdfast lying cephalad in the fish. In size it ranges from 1.0 to 17.5 mm., the average length (measured on 56 specimens by Wardle and Green, 1941b) being 3.7 mm.

The distance between myocommata – the membranous partitions which separate the muscle fibers into short blocks – measured in an adult jackfish is about 5–8 mm. Plerocercoids less than 8 mm. long lie parallel with the muscle fibers and are straight; those which exceed this length usually have the anterior third of the body turned back upon the rest of the body in hooklike fashion. The longest plerocercoids may be considerably twisted (Figure 37).

Now if such plerocercoids are fed to kittens and recovered after an

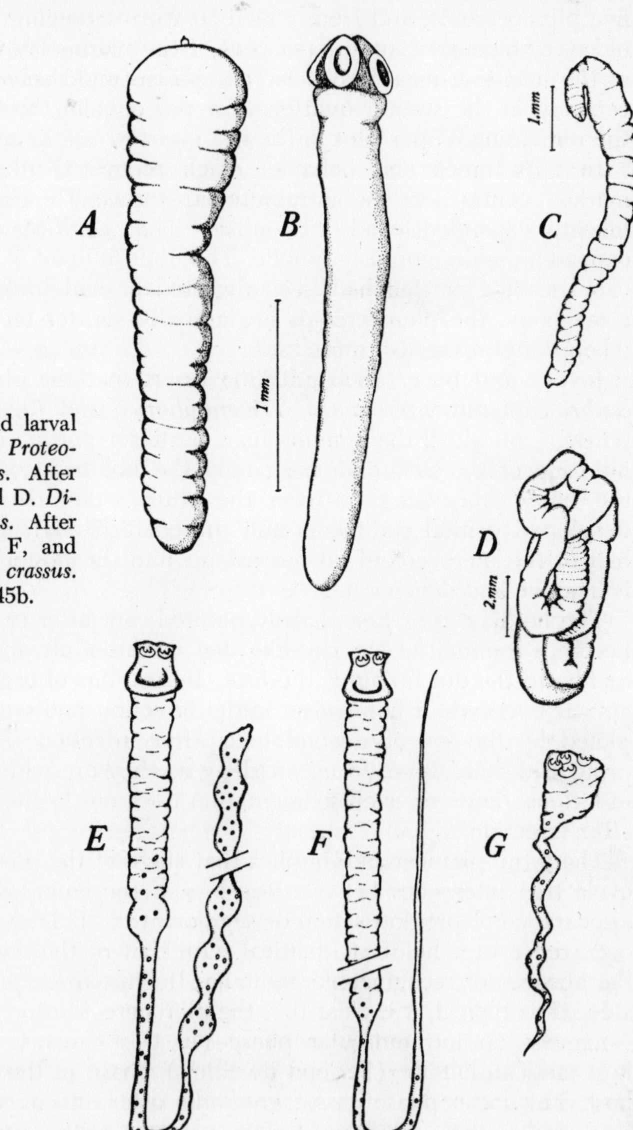

FIG. 37. Plerocercoid larval forms. A and B. *Proteocephalus ambloplitis.* After Cooper, 1915. C and D. *Dibothriocephalus latus.* After Vergeer, 1929a. E, F, and G. *Triaenophorus crassus.* After Miller, 1945b.

interval by post-mortem examination of the hosts, they are found to be in the small intestine. In observations by one of the present authors, 13 hours after initial infection the worms lay at distances of 7, 11, 12, 13, and 16 inches from the pylorus, in a gut measuring 33 inches from pylorus to ileocolic valve. After 25 hours the worms lay at distances of 7.5 to 36 inches from the pylorus in a gut measuring 56 inches from pylorus to ileocolic valve. These observations suggest that scattering of individuals of an age group along the gut is as characteristic of the first few hours of an infection as of later days of infection. In a series of observations on dogs that had all been infected simultaneously, each with five plerocercoids, and from which 80 worms ranging from 3 to 98 days old were recovered, only 5 per cent of the worms lay in the first quarter of the host gut, measured between pylorus and ileocolic valve; 37.5 per cent lay in the second quarter, 22.5 per cent in the third quarter, and the remaining 35 per cent in the last quarter.

In appearance and behavior, such recovered plerocercoids are in marked contrast to the intramuscular forms. They are smooth, translucent, expanded, and ribbonlike. The holdfast is fully everted, expanded, and vigorously mobile. The opposite end of the worm is truncated as if a portion had been digested or had broken away, and for some hours the plerocercoids are actually shorter on the average than when lying in the fish muscles.

Joyeux and Baer (1938a, 1938b) assert that the plerocercoids of *Dibothriocephalus, Spirometra, Triaenophorus*, and *Ligula* consist of two portions, of which the nonmuscular, posterior portion degenerates in the intestine of the definitive host, only the holdfast and anterior part of the body proceeding to form the adult worm. In *Ligula* the well-developed genital rudiments and muscular bands seen in the anterior half of the plerocercoid do not extend into the posterior portion, which is inactive and degenerate.

The holdfast is at first sharply pointed, but after twenty-four hours it becomes rounded at the tip, like that of the adult; it adheres, although feebly, to the gut lining of the host. Indications of segmentation usually appear twenty-four hours after initial infection, and segmentation is completed by the seventy-second hour after infection. The newly formed proglottides are 1.5–2.0 times as long as they are wide. In plerocercoids in kittens, however, such segmentation does not begin until the fifth day after infection.

The term "plerocercoid" implies that stage of the pseudophyllidean life cycle that intervenes between the loss of the embryonic hooks and the appearance of proglottisation or segmentation. It is characterized by the occurrence of a holdfast identical with that of the adult worm, and by the absence of recognizable genitalia. If *Dibothriocephalus latus* is considered as typical, it is clear that the plerocercoid can exist in two phases – namely, an intramuscular phase (in this case) in the intermediate host, and an enteric (i.e., gut-dwelling) phase in the final or definitive host. This latter phase passes *gradually* after an interval of hours, or it

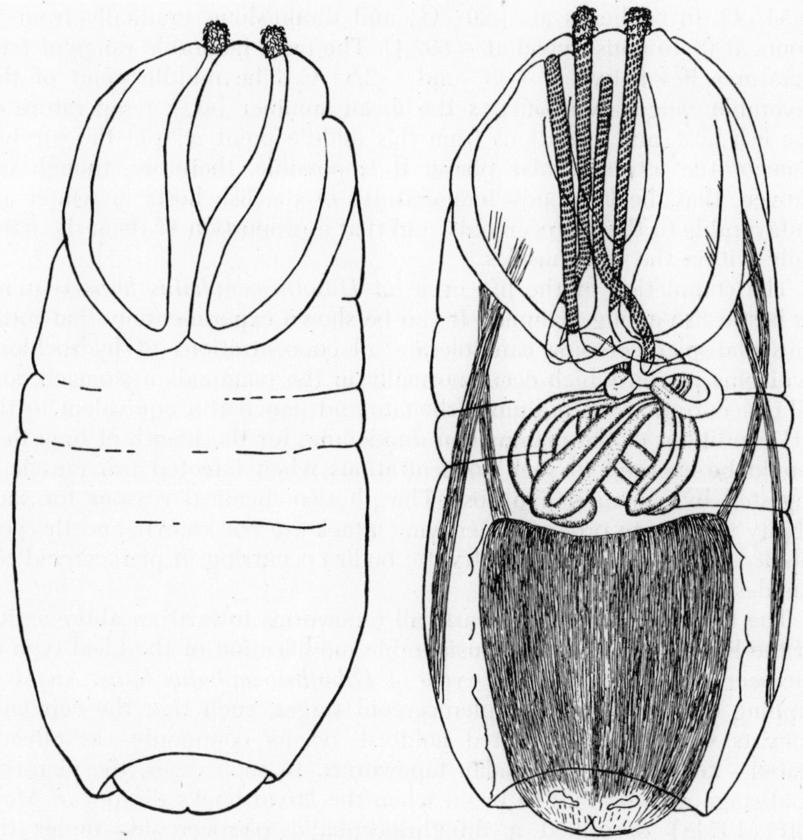

FIG. 38. Plerocercoids of *Nybelinia sp.* After Dollfus, 1929a.

may be days, into the condition of proglottisation that characterizes the adult tapeworm.

The transition from one phase to the other is a transition from one set of physico-chemical values, favorable to the intramuscular phase, to another set of such values favorable to the enteric phase; a transition in this case from the wide range of temperature values of the fish's body to the narrower range of higher temperatures of the mammal's body; from the low electrolytic concentration of fish-muscle juice to the relatively high electrolytic concentration of mammalian intestinal contents. During such transition, the plerocercoid is exposed to the varying values of hydrogen-ion concentration, osmotic pressure, and gastric and duodenal enzyme action.

When intramuscular plerocercoids of *Dibothriocephalus latus* are removed from a fish and placed in physiological saline (0.2 molar sodium chloride), they assume in appearance and behavior the characteristics of the enteric phase. They are found to tolerate temperatures between —8° C. and +55° C., the survival time varying from 15 minutes at

+54° C. to 60 hours at +20° C., and diminishing gradually from 24 hours at 0° to nonsurvival at —89° C. The most favorable range of temperatures lies between +38° and —2.8° C. The middle point of this favorable range approximates the mean summer body temperature of the fish host, and variations from this middle point restrict the survival time of the intramuscular phase. It is possible, therefore, though unproven, that the low body temperatures of the fish hosts in winter are unfavorable to the plerocercoids, and that a proportion of them die naturally within the fish muscles.

The completion of the life cycle of *Dibothriocephalus latus* requires as host a fish-eating mammal. It can be shown experimentally that intramuscular plerocercoids can tolerate all concentrations of hydrochloric acid plus pepsin which occur normally in the mammalian stomach, and all concentrations of sodium carbonate and pancreatin equivalent to the pH conditions of the mammalian duodenum, for the length of time they would be exposed to such concentrations when infected fish muscle is ingested by a mammalian host. The physico-chemical reasons for such ability to tolerate proteolytic enzyme attack are not known, and the possibility of antipeptic and antitryptic bodies occurring in plerocercoid tissue deserves investigation.

The tendency shown by nearly all tapeworms toward an abbreviation of the life cycle has led to considerable modification of the ideal type of plerocercoid seen in the life cycle of *Dibothriocephalus latus.* An overlapping of procercoid and plerocercoid stages, such that the cercomer coexists with the invaginated holdfast, occurs commonly—as already stated—among proteocephalan tapeworms. In such cases, the plerocercoid stage may be said to begin when the larval hooks disappear. Meggitt (1924e) described a dibothriocephalid plerocercoid—under the name of *Sparganum reptans*—in which neither cercomer nor holdfast was present, the latter being represented functionally by the extremely mobile anterior end.

One of the most striking modifications of the plerocercoid stage is brought about by a phenomenon termed "exogenous budding." Ijima (1905) reported the occurrence, in a Japanese woman resident of Tokyo, of what was apparently a subcutaneous dibothriocephalid plerocercoid which had an irregularly branching shape and was able to throw off numerous buds. These buds separated from the parent plerocercoid, migrated to other locations, and in their turn proliferated and branched. Ijima suggested for it the term *Sparganum proliferum.* A similar case was reported by Stiles (1908) in the United States, and other cases have been observed, particularly in Japan (Figure 39).

The morphology of this peculiar plerocercoid has been fully studied (see Ijima, 1905; Stiles, 1908; Yoshida, 1914; Iwata, 1934; Mueller, 1938b). This form differs from other subcutaneous dibothriocephalid larvae—usually given the collective term *Sparganum*—(1) in having no holdfast but only a slender, pointed extremity capable of slight retraction and expansion; (2) in being cylindrical and not flat in shape, a consequence, according to Mueller (1938b), of the transverse and dorso-

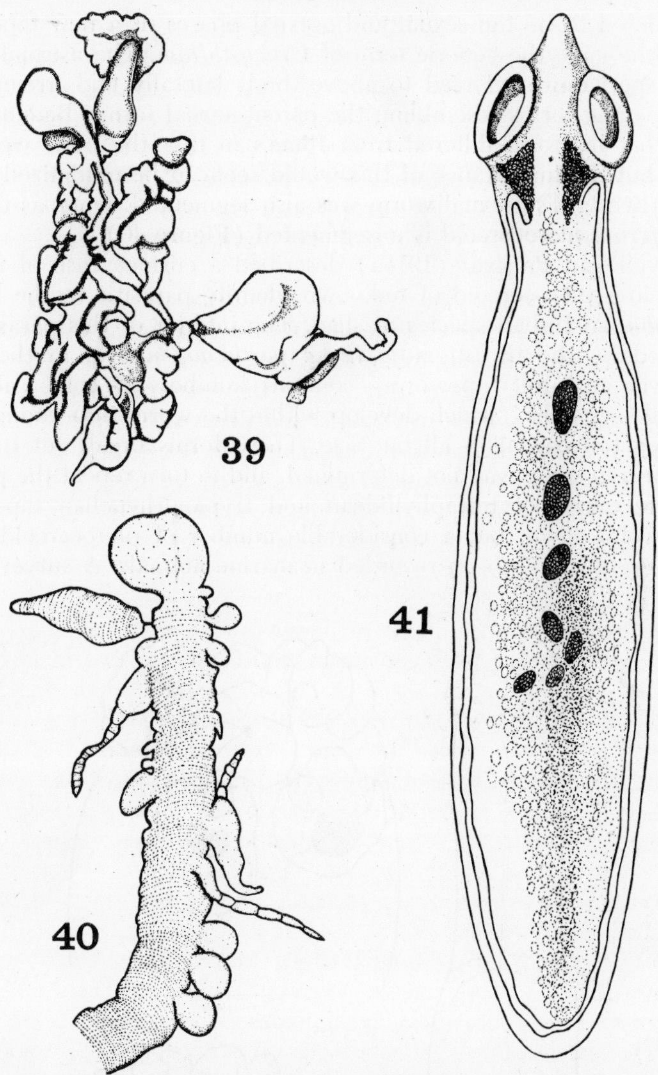

FIG. 39. *Sparganum proliferum.* After Stiles, 1908. FIG. 40. *Urocystidium gemmiparum.* After Beddard, 1912d. FIG. 41. *Ilisha parthenogenetica.* After Southwell, 1929a.

ventral muscles not being differentiated from each other as in other spargana; and (3) in not developing in later sparganid life the two lateral nerve cords and the two longitudinal osmoregulatory canals that characterize other spargana. The former view that *proliferum* represents a distinct dibothriocephalid species is not now held, and the general belief is that it is an aberrant plerocercoid of some species of the *Spirometra mansoni* group.

External budding of a plerocercoid was also found by Beddard (1912d) in two tapeworms from a muskrat (*Ondatra zibethica*). These he considered to be the sexual and asexual phases of a new tapeworm, to which he gave the generic term of *Urocystidium*. The asexual phase, like the sparganum referred to above, buds laterally and irregularly a series of young forms resembling the parent sexual forms. Beddard considered that his form differed from Ijima's in that the buds were segmented; but the importance of this would seem to be minimized by the fact that Beddard's asexual worm was also segmented, whereas the parent *proliferum* plerocercoid is unsegmented (Figure 40).

Southwell and Prashad (1918a) described a curious case of internal budding in a plerocercoid of unknown identity parasitic in the liver of *Hilsa ilisha*, an Indian species of shad. The interior of this parasite – at first called by the investigators *Ilisha parthenogenetica*, in the belief that it was an adult tapeworm – contains numbers of cells, called by Southwell "egg-cells," which develop within the worm into young forms resembling the parent in all but size. These forms break out from the parent form in some way not determined, and in turn repeat the process.

The life cycles of tetraphyllidean and trypanorhynchan tapeworms are not well known, but a considerable number of plerocercoid larvae of these groups have been recorded in marine animals. A survey of the

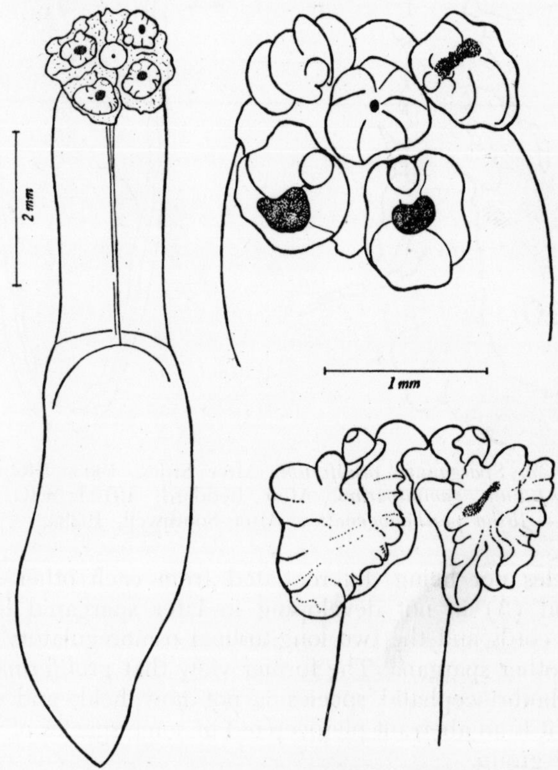

FIG. 42. Tetraphyllidean plerocercoids.
After Dollfus, 1931.

extensive literature on the question has been published by Dollfus (1923b, 1929a, 1931). However, reference to the scanty information available concerning tetraphyllidean and trypanorhynchan life cycles may be postponed to the sections dealing with those groups.

The preferred position of the majority of plerocercoid larvae within the host is in the musculature. Quite a number of plerocercoids, however, habitually embed themselves in the wall of the stomach or intestine or within the liver. Others may be found enclosed within a bladder-like cyst attached to the mesenteries that suspend such organs as the liver and gut to the wall of the body cavity. The method by which such a soft-bodied organism, lacking anything in the nature of a penetrant mechanism and relying mainly upon its own turgidity, can travel from the alimentary canal of its host to an intermuscular position, or to a position within the layers of the gut wall, is far from clearly understood. Mueller (1938b) fed plerocercoid larvae of *Spirometra mansoni* to mice and found that two hours after feeding, the larvae had already penetrated to the host's body cavity.

"Penetration is made mainly in the region of the duodenum and evidently begins shortly after the sparganum leaves the stomach and is completed within a period of 20–30 minutes. After penetrating the mucosa the sparganum does not pass immediately into the body cavity but migrates tangentially beneath the serosa for a distance and finally escapes, usually in the region where the mesentery joins the gut. But in some cases it travels upward between the two coats of the mesentery and may reach the muscles via that route. Thus no direct communication is formed between the cavity of the intestine and the outside and hence the infective contents of the gut do not escape into the coelom. Once out of the intestine, spargana migrate rapidly, often reaching the neck region in mice less than 24 hours after being fed. Only the head of the sparganum escapes from the intestine. The posterior part fragments and passes out with the faeces." Mueller (1938b, pp. 306–8).

CYSTICERCOID

The word "Cysticercoidei," as a group term for certain types of tapeworm larvae, is usually attributed to Leuckart. The term "cysticercoides," similarly as a larval group term, is attributed to R. Blanchard. As understood today, the term refers to a type of tapeworm larva which consists typically of a double-walled bladder enclosing an invaginated holdfast and having a bladderlike "tail" upon which are the three pairs of embryonic hooks.

The general way in which the cysticercoid is formed is as follows. Within the oncosphere, a cavity – the primitive lacuna – arises through the degeneration of the internal cells. The oncosphere elongates and becomes pear-shaped, with the embryonic hooks located at the narrow end. Rudiments of the four future suckers and of the future rostellum now appear at the opposite end. The narrow posterior portion of the larva now elongates further and is invaded by the primitive lacuna so that it becomes a bladder, joined to the rest of the body only by a nar-

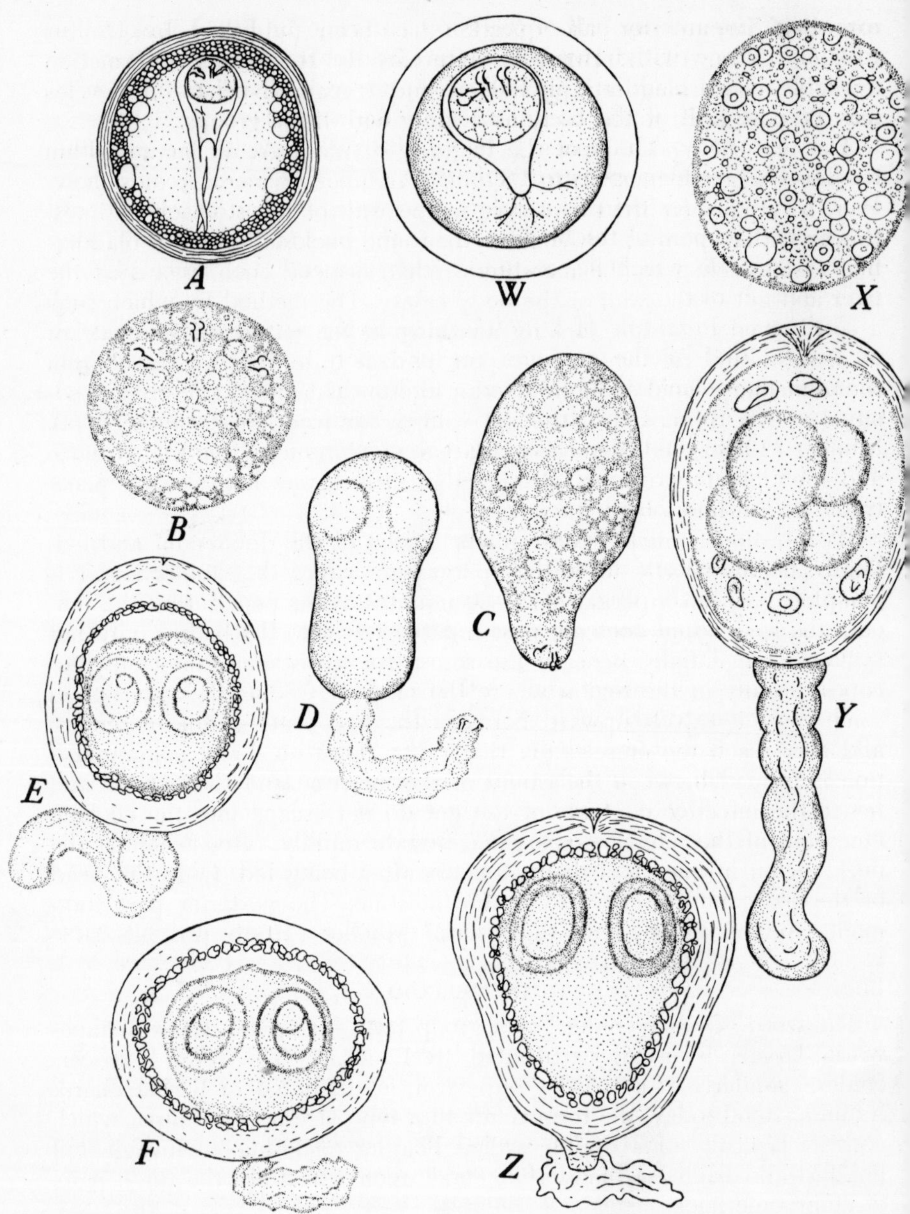

FIG. 43. Early developmental stages of anoplocephaline tapeworms. A to F. *Cittotae ctenoides*. After Stunkard, 1939d. W to Z. *Bertiella studeri*. After Stunkard, 1940a, 19

row stalk. The anterior half of the body, carrying the future suckers and rostellum, is now withdrawn within the bladderlike posterior half so that a double-walled bladder is formed, the outer wall of which is the original posterior half of the body and the inner wall the original anterior half of the body. The space between the two walls is the primitive lacuna. This bladder opens to the outside at its anterior pole by a pore. Within the bladder there is a holdfast, so oriented that its anterior end is opposite the pore of the bladder. From the bladder comes off the long hollow "tail" on which lie, scattered and separated, the three pairs of embryonic hooks.

The classical example of a life cycle involving a cysticercoid stage is, of course, that of the common cat and dog tapeworm, *Dipylidium caninum*, first elucidated by Grassi and Rovelli (1889a). The embryology and life cycle of this form have been restudied by Venard (1938) from whose account the following abbreviation is presented (Figure 44). The cucumber-shaped proglottides do not disintegrate in the gut of the mammalian host but emerge intact. The first evidence of an intermediate host was discovered by Melnikow (1869). While working in Leuckart's laboratory, he found in the body cavity of the biting louse, *Trichodectes*, of the dog, a cysticercoid whose holdfast resembled that of the adult *Dipylidium caninum*. After feeding *Dipylidium* eggs to specimens of *Trichodectes*, Melnikow recovered, a week later, four oncospheres from one insect and "flask-shaped individuals" from another.

The restricted distribution of *Trichodectes* opposed the view that it might be the true intermediate host of this tapeworm. The dog flea appeared to fulfill the distributional requirements better. After a long search, Grassi (1888a) found cysticercoids in the hemocoel of this flea, and later (Grassi and Rovelli, 1892; Sonsino, 1889a) the ability of the dog flea and the human flea to act as hosts of *Dipylidium caninum* was fully confirmed. The method by which the flea ingested the tapeworm eggs remained to be solved. The mouth-parts are obviously too narrow to admit them. Sonsino suggested that either the flea is penetrated by a liberated oncosphere, or that the flea larva becomes infected by ingesting eggs and passes the infection on through its metamorphosis to the adult flea. It remained for Joyeux (1916) to confirm this second hypothesis for *Ctenocephalides canis* and *Pulex irritans*. Chen later added *Ctenocephalides felis* as another intermediate host.

According to Venard's observations, the *Dipylidium* eggs in the gravid proglottis are spherical, 35–60 microns in diameter, and occur in bundles of 2–63, with the majority containing 15–25 eggs. These bundles are termed "egg capsules." Each egg contains an infective oncosphere, 25–30 microns in diameter. The oncosphere shows two distinct membranes—an inner one, closely applied to it, which is the embryonic envelope, and an outer one, which is the extraembryonic blastoderm. The origin of these membranes is as follows. After fertilization, the egg cell receives *one* yolk cell from the yolk glands. The egg cell, plus this yolk cell, passes into the ootype and there develops a chorion. This chorion is deciduous and is absent from the mature egg. Egg cell and yolk cell,

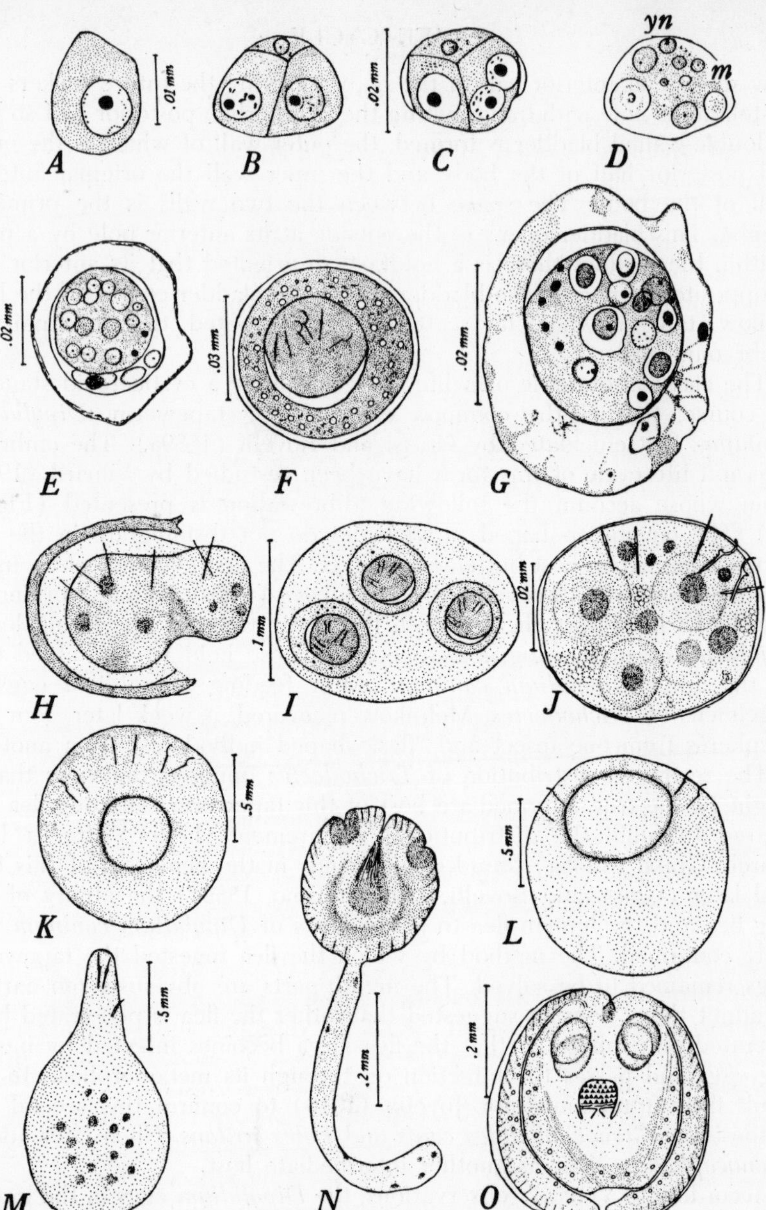

FIG. 44. Life cycle of *Dipylidium caninum*. After Venard, 1938. A. Mature egg. B. 2-cell stage. C. 3-cell stage. D. Further stage in segmentation; the 4 macromeres and yolk cell nucleus (*yn*) will form the yolk shell, the micromeres (*m*) will form the embryo and embryophore. E. Formation of the embryophore. F. Egg from gravid proglottis. G. Section through mature oncosphere showing cells, cuticle of embryo, embryophore, albuminous layer, and yolk shell. H. Hatching of embryo. I. Egg capsule with 3 eggs. J. Oncosphere, 7 days after flea infection. K and L. Oncospheres from flea pupae showing primitive lacuna. M. Oncosphere with forming cercomer. N. Young cysticercoid with rostellum and sucker primordia. O. Fully developed cysticercoid.

within this chorion, now pass into the uterus. Segmentation begins there, the first cleavage producing two approximately equal blastomeres around which the chorion enlarges to form a loose covering. The nucleus of the yolk cell now becomes visible, and in its vicinity there appear small bodies, resembling yolk particles, varying in shape, size, and number. Moniez (1881) interpreted the apparent yolk cell nucleus as a blastomere resulting from abnormal segmentation, and at least two of the smaller bodies he believed to be polar bodies.

Of the two blastomeres, one – containing a nucleus 8.5–9.6 microns in diameter – does not divide, although its nucleus increases in size and becomes vesicular in appearance, and its cytoplasm contains many yolk granules. The entire cell disintegrates and contributes to the formation of the blastoderm. The other blastomere, with a nucleus slightly smaller (7.5–8.5 microns), divides to form three macromeres and a number of micromeres. The former contribute to the formation of the blastoderm; the latter go to form the embryo and embryonic membrane, or embryonic envelope. The blastoderm is thus formed from four macromeres, plus the yolk cell nucleus, plus portions of yolk. In mature eggs it is 2.5–3.2 microns thick, forms the outer covering of the egg, and in the literature is commonly called the "shell." After this "shell" has begun to form, five peripheral micromeres separate from the rest, become flattened, and unite to form an envelope around the remaining micromeres. This envelope is the embryonic envelope.

The oncosphere escapes when the egg – not the proglottis – is eaten by a flea larva. It emerges from the egg membranes in the fore-gut or the mid-gut of the insect and actively penetrates the gut wall to wander in all directions among the host's internal organs. The mature oncosphere at first contains 75–100 cells. Of these, 40 are 3–5 microns in diameter and have spherical or elliptical nuclei staining deeply with iron haematoxylin, green with methyl green–pyronin, and red with Mallory's stain; these, therefore, are somatic cells. The remaining cells are larger, up to 10 microns in diameter, and the cytoplasm and certain granules in the nucleus stain deeply red with pyronin. Venard identified among them two types: 4 or 5 of the cells apparently correspond with the plastin cells of Vogel (germinative cells of Wisniewski) already mentioned; 10–15 others correspond with Wisniewski's germinative-somatic cells.

Within the intermediate host, the somatic cells of the oncosphere gradually disappear and the germinative cells multiply rapidly, producing a marked growth of the organism. At 10 days it has a diameter of approximately 65 microns. In the pupal stage of the flea, the oncosphere is 40–80 microns in diameter and is growing rapidly. Within a day or two after pupation of the insect host, a cavity or "lacuna primitiva," as Grassi and Rovelli termed it, appears in the oncosphere, brought about by a migration of cells from the center to the periphery. As this cavity enlarges it progressively approaches the anterior end of the oncosphere – where the hooks are – and becomes located close to the hooks. The oncosphere becomes ovoid, slightly wider at the hook-bearing end, and its body consists almost entirely of germinative cells with a few scattered germinative-somatics. Almost the entire body of the cysticercoid larva will be formed from these germinative cells, which divide rapidly. The germinative-somatic cells do not contribute appreciably to the larval body. The somatic cells, as Vogel found in *Dibothriocephalus*, degenerate and disappear, in contrast with *Triaenophorus*, where Michajlow found them to divide rapidly and to fill much of the oncosphere body.

When the infected flea emerges from its pupal cocoon, the ovoid oncospheres are in the hemocoel of the abdominal region as white, opaque, granular bodies, 50 by 85 microns in dimension, showing no movement. From now onward the hook-bearing region becomes delimited from the rest of the body as a tail-like appendage, the cercomer. Approximately 10 days are required for this cercomer to reach full development, whereupon it is shed. There is now a reversal of polarity, the end opposite the cercomer becoming the foremost end during locomotion. As the cercomer develops, an invagination appears at this pseudo-anterior end, and the cells below it divide rapidly to form a dense cluster of cells which give rise to the future rostellum. Four ingrowths of the cuticle, symmetrically arranged around this invagination, mark the site of the future suckers. The invagination deepens until the primordia of the rostellum and the suckers are within the larval body.

The rostellum develops first, as a dense, cylindrical bundle of cells covered with a cuticle armed with hooks. It is not in an inverted position, but has the same relationship to the cysticercoid body that it will have in the adult tapeworm. Suckers develop from dense masses of germinative cells. Their concave surfaces face the center of the cysticercoid and are covered, or lined, with cuticle continuous with that which covers the rest of the body. On all other surfaces, the sucker is delimited from the underlying cells, in which it is supported, by a thin layer of cuticle. Rostellum and suckers take 18 days to develop in the adult flea.

The first suggestion of the future osmoregulatory system is a small cavity within a mass of germinative cells dorsal to the attachment of the cercomer. This cavity elongates, makes contact with the cuticle at the posterior end, and develops an outlet. Anteriorly, the cavity is divided into one dorsal and two ventral portions which extend forward by intracellular extension to form the osmoregulatory canals. The whole system is lined by a cuticle. Flame cells are not visible until the bladder and canals have formed. Each flame cell develops from a germinative cell.

After the cysticercoid is eaten by the definitive host, the cystoid body containing the holdfast becomes the first segment. This segment, which contains the osmoregulatory bladder, does not grow as rapidly as the following one and usually drops from the body before a length of three centimeters is reached.

One of the most recent descriptions of cysticercoid development has been given by Wisseman (1945) for the fowl tapeworm *Raillietina cesticillus*. The intermediate host of this tapeworm was shown by Cram (1928a) to be a common ground beetle, *Anisotarsus agilis*. The structure of the cysticercoid was described by Wetzel (1933, 1934), Ackert and Reid (1936), and Joyeux and Baer (1937a, 1938c). Further observations were contributed by Reid, Ackert, and Case (1938). With the account given by Wisseman, we now have a fairly complete story of the development of this form.

Active oncospheres may be obtained from beetles after twelve hours from the time of egg ingestion. Some of these have already increased in size by multiplication of the germinative cells. As the oncosphere grows, a primitive lacuna develops and cellular proliferation begins at the pole opposite to the embryonic hooks. Progressive growth at this pole is accompanied by the formation of a small projection at the hook-bearing pole which develops into a weakly attached, spherical mass of cellular tissue containing a cavity and the hooks. This incipient cercomer is soon lost.

By the growth of the hook-free pole the cysticercoid lengthens. Two bands of nuclear condensation at this pole indicate the future rostellar hooks. A marked constriction just behind them establishes the future rostellum, and another constriction indicates the boundary between holdfast and body. A condensation of nuclei between these two constrictions forecasts the suckers. The primitive lacuna soon fills with parenchymatous tissue formed by the proliferation of the cells that compose its wall. Further development is like that described for *Dipylidium* and need not be reiterated.

Among cysticercoid larvae the primitive lacuna is commonly small and may be restricted to the tail region, the bladder wall appearing solid. Again, the space that surrounds the holdfast – that is to say, the actual bladder cavity – may be the merest chink. The tail region may be long – even excessively so, as in *Drepanidotaenia lanceolata* – or it may be short and stumpy as in *Hymenolepis nana*, or it may be absent altogether. If it is present during early development but absent from later development, the larva is sometimes called a "Cryptocystis." If no trace of tail region is present at any time during development, the larva is a "Cercocystis." Two abnormal species are *Aploparaksidis crassicollis*, whose whole body is invaginated within the base of the tail so that the latter appears to surround the body, and *Anomotaenia pyriformis*, a tailless form, in which the invaginated holdfast floats freely within the enclosing bladder. Rarely, the whole cysticercoid is enclosed within a thin bladder formed as a host reaction product. Such is the case, for example, in *Choanotaenia infundibulum* (Figure 45), whose larva occurs in houseflies (see Guberlet, 1916a; Reid and Ackert, 1937).

"The living cysticercoid is subspherical or ovoid in shape and milky white. Examination with the low power compound microscope shows the walls of the cyst proper and at one side an elongate scolex with the four suckers and a rostellum armed with hooks similar to those of the adult *C. infundibulum*. In one case the scolex was retracted within the cyst walls and did not evaginate until pressure had been applied. Very prominent are the numerous calcareous granules scattered through the cyst and frequent in the larval neck which is attached to one end of the cyst. The whole cysticercoid is encapsulated by a thin, nearly transparent membrane, which ruptures readily and frees the larval scolex,

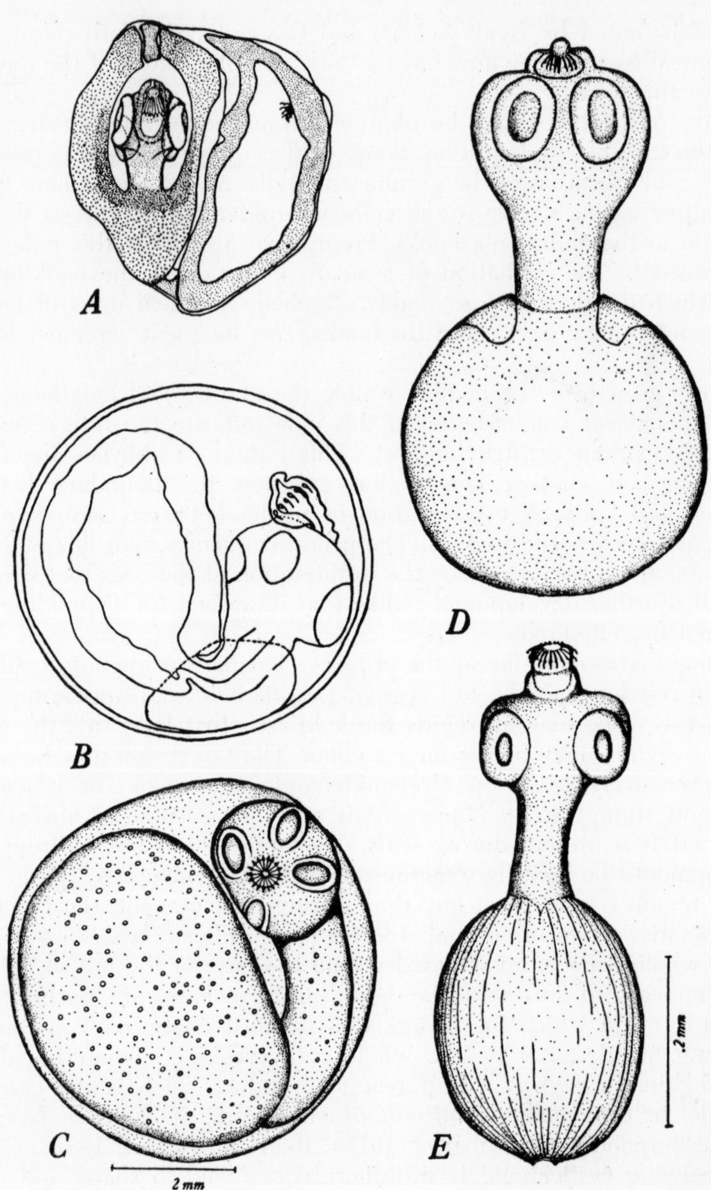

FIG. 45. Cysticercoid of *Choanotaenia infundibulum*. A. After Guberlet, 1916a. B. After Woodger, 1921. C. After Reid and Ackert, 1937. D. After Grassi and Rovelli, 1892. E. Freed cysticercoid. After Reid and Ackert, 1937.

neck, and cyst proper. Upon the rupture of this membrane, the scolex and cyst walls swing apart and tend to straighten out in the position shown in the figure. Prominent also are the numerous converging striations in the cyst walls." Reid and Ackert (1937) (see Figure 45).

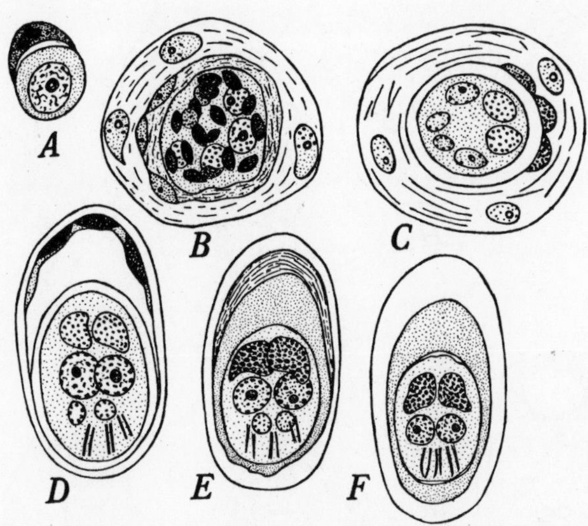

FIG. 46. *Catenotaenia pusilla,* egg development. After Joyeux and Baer, 1945. A. Zygote with yolk cells. B. Beginning of envelope formation. C. Embryonic mass of 6 cells. D. 3 cells of inner envelope still visible. E and F. Ripe embryonated eggs.

Occasionally, as in plerocercoids, a process of budding from the original larva may produce a multiple type of cysticercoid. External budding (exogenous budding) was described by Haswell and Hill (1893) in a cysticercoid — whose adult form is unknown — occurring in an earthworm, *Didymogaster sylvatica.* To this cysticercoid the observers gave the name *Polycercus sp.*

"The hooked embryo in *Polycercus* develops into a rounded, cellular body which becomes enclosed in a cyst, probably entirely of an adventitious character. Buds are given off from the periphery of the mass and develop into cysticercoids, which soon become free in the interior of the cyst. The head, with its hooks and suckers, is developed from the central portion of the solid body, the middle layers form the 'body' and the outermost, the 'caudal vesicle'." Haswell and Hill (1893).

In a cysticercoid — again unknown as to the adult form — which was described by Villot (1883a) as *Staphylocystis glomeridis,* successive branching and external proliferation of secondary cysticercoids produce a grape-bunch mass of cysticercoids. No external surrounding membrane is present (Figure 49).

The best authenticated and best described case of cysticercoid budding is that of *Hymenolepis cantaniana,* a common fowl tapeworm

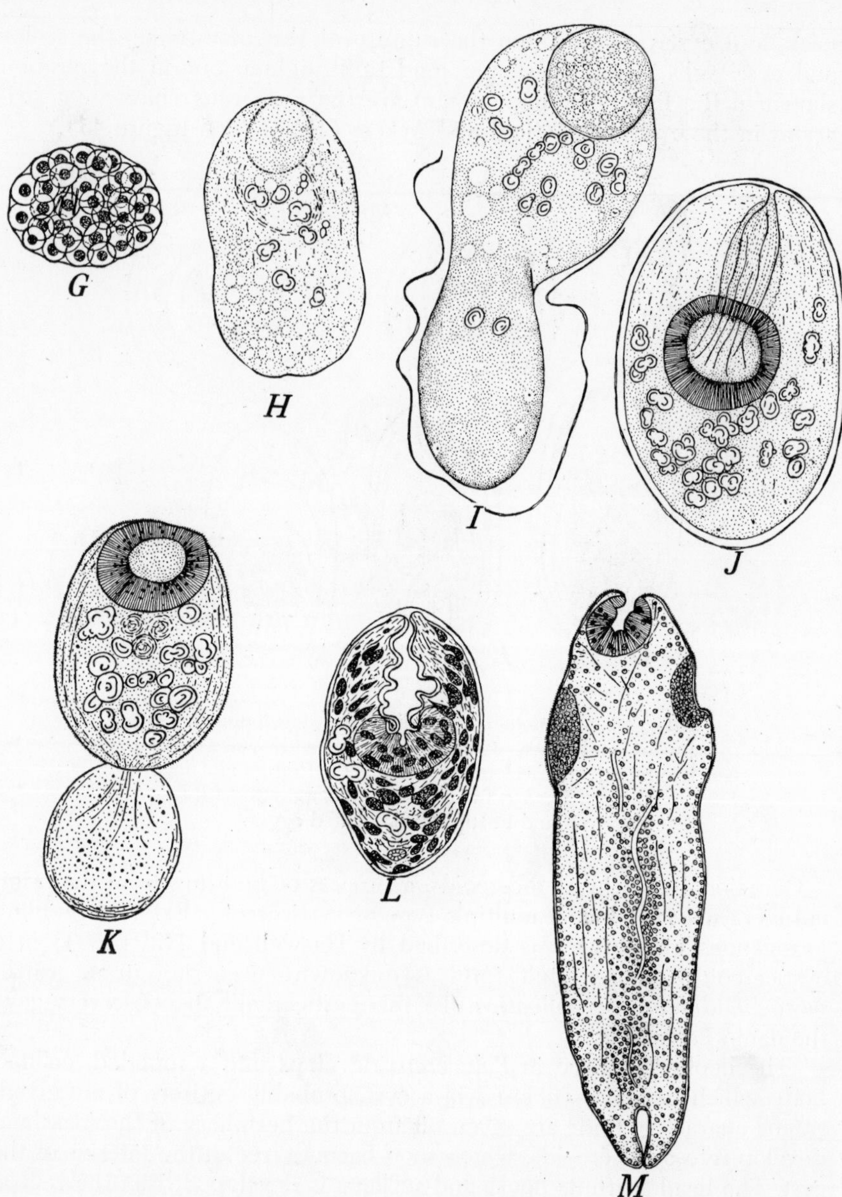

FIG. 47. *Catenotaenia pusilla*, larval stages in *Glyciphagus domesticus* and in mouse. After Joyeux and Baer, 1945. G. 8-day larva. H. Older larva from a spontaneous infestation. I. Larva partly extracted from its cyst, with apical sucker well delimited. J. Ripe larva within cyst, showing invaginated apical sucker. K. Larva escaped from cyst under influence of succus entericus of mouse, with calcareous corpuscles massed in anterior half. L. Longitudinal section through ripe larva within intermediate host. M. Longitudinal section of young larva fixed in gut of mouse.

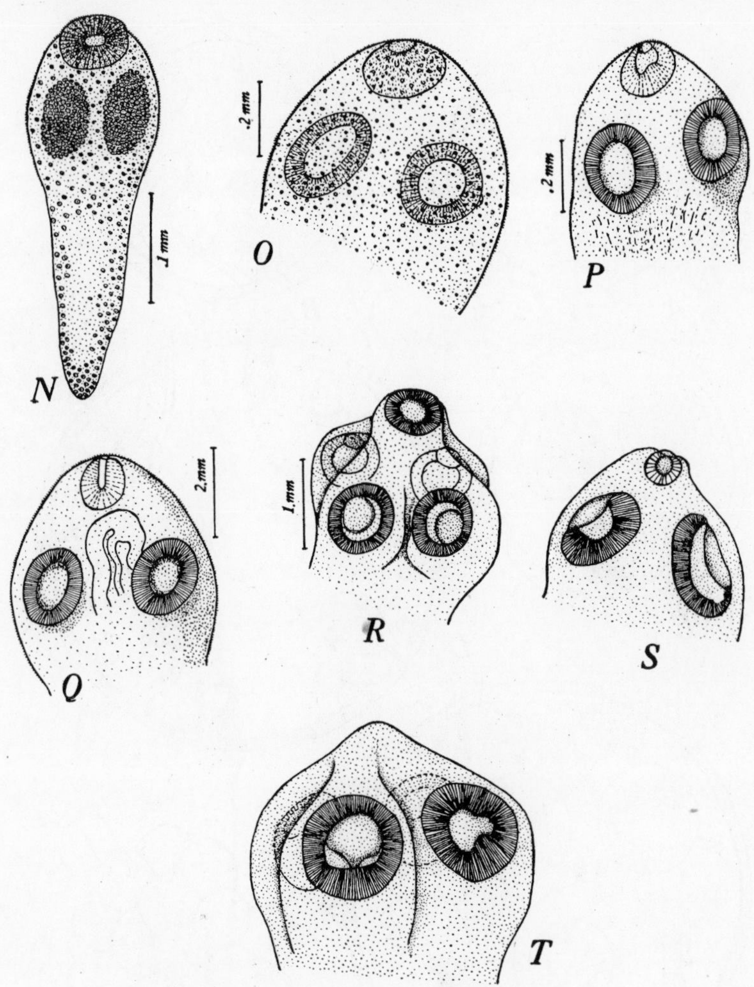

FIG. 48. *Catenotaenia pusilla,* holdfasts of young worms to show the gradual appearance of suckers and the gradual regression of the apical sucker. After Joyeux and Baer, 1945. N to R. Immature worms, from 35μ to 2.5 mm. in length. S. A subadult. T. An adult.

whose larva occurs in dung beetles (*Ataenius cognatus*). The phenomenon has been described in detail by Jones and Alicata (1935). The oncosphere develops into a larva with several lobes, which lengthen to form a branched mycelium. Buds arise from the branches of the mycelium and develop into new branches, or into cysticercoids each containing the unarmed holdfast characteristic of the species. The process of cysticercoid formation is like that described in other hymenolepidid larvae. There is the usual lengthening of the bud, the appearance of a small primitive lacuna, the differentiation of the anterior half of the larva as a holdfast, and the invagination of this holdfast within the posterior half of the larva to produce a rounded, tailless cysticercoid (Figure 275).

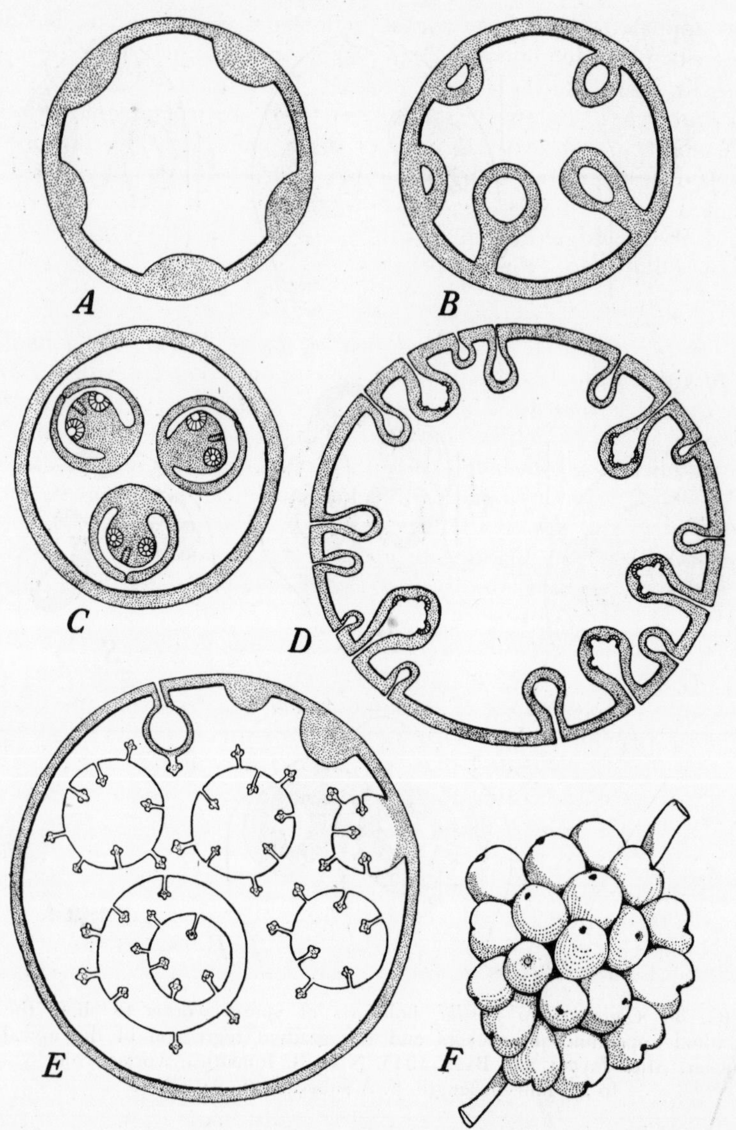

FIG. 49. Types of bladder worms. After Benham, 1901. A, B, and C. *Polycercus* from the coelom of the earthworm, larva of "*Taenia nilotica.*" D. *Coenurus* from the brain of a sheep. E. *Echinococcus* with secondary bladders. F. *Staphylocystis,* an example of external budding.

What appears to have been a case of internal (endogenous) budding was described by Metchnikow (1869) in a form that may have been the larva of Krabbe's (1869) *Taenia nilotica.* Unfortunately, Krabbe's species is *inquirenda,* unless it is identified with *Paricterotaenia nilotica,* and Metchnikow's observation has not been confirmed. He described a thin-walled bladder containing a number of freely floating cysticercoids of a tailed type. These he believed to have begun as buds from the lining of the bladder. For this form Villot (1883a) proposed the general term *Polycercus* (Figure 49).

CYSTICERCUS

The term "cysticercus" was used first by Zeder (1800) for a bladder worm that was probably the larva of the common dog tapeworm *Taenia hydatigena.* It is now used as a general term for a type of tapeworm larva (Figure 50) which is restricted to the family Taeniidae and has the appearance of a translucent bladder from the size of a pea to that of a small cherry. Into this bladder a small pocket projects from the outer surface. Within this pocket the future holdfast develops in such a fashion that pressure upon the bladder, or change in the osmotic pressure of the fluid within it, causes the formed holdfast to be everted through the mouth of the pocket.

Although in many features a cysticercus recalls a tailless cysticercoid, it is fundamentally different. No tail ever appears during cysticercus development. The presence of osmoregulatory canals within the bladder wall shows it to correspond with the posterior region of the cysticercoid body, enormously distended with fluid. The invagination within which the holdfast develops corresponds with the anterior region of the cysticercoid body. The cavity of the cysticercus is therefore a hypertrophied primitive lacuna and does not correspond with that of the cysticercoid, which is the cavity of the anterior body region.

Taeniid tapeworms, to which cysticercus larvae are restricted, have been the most studied of all tapeworms, and there is available a wealth of published information concerning their life cycles. We may note in passing the classical contributions to the question by Küchenmeister (1852), Siebold (1853), Leuckart (1855, 1856), Beneden (1870a, 1881), Linstow (1872a), Moniez (1880a), Raum (1883), Vincentiis (1887), Braun (1897), Goldschmidt (1900), Hofmann (1901), Bartels (1902), St. Remy (1901a), Janicki (1906c, 1907), Young (1908), Mrazek (1916), Dew (1925a), Coutelen (1927a, 1927b, 1931), Dévé (1927, 1933a), Mlodzianowska (1931), Yoshino (1933), and Waele (1934, 1936).

Most modern textbooks of helminthology exemplify the general features of the tapeworm life cycle by reference to that of a taeniid, but it is rare to find any description of the embryogeny of the taeniid egg. Some notes on the subject may appropriately be inserted here.

The egg cells in the mature ovary are, of course, primary oocytes, formed from the oogonia of the immature organ. In a series of papers on the development of the reproductive organs and reproductive cells

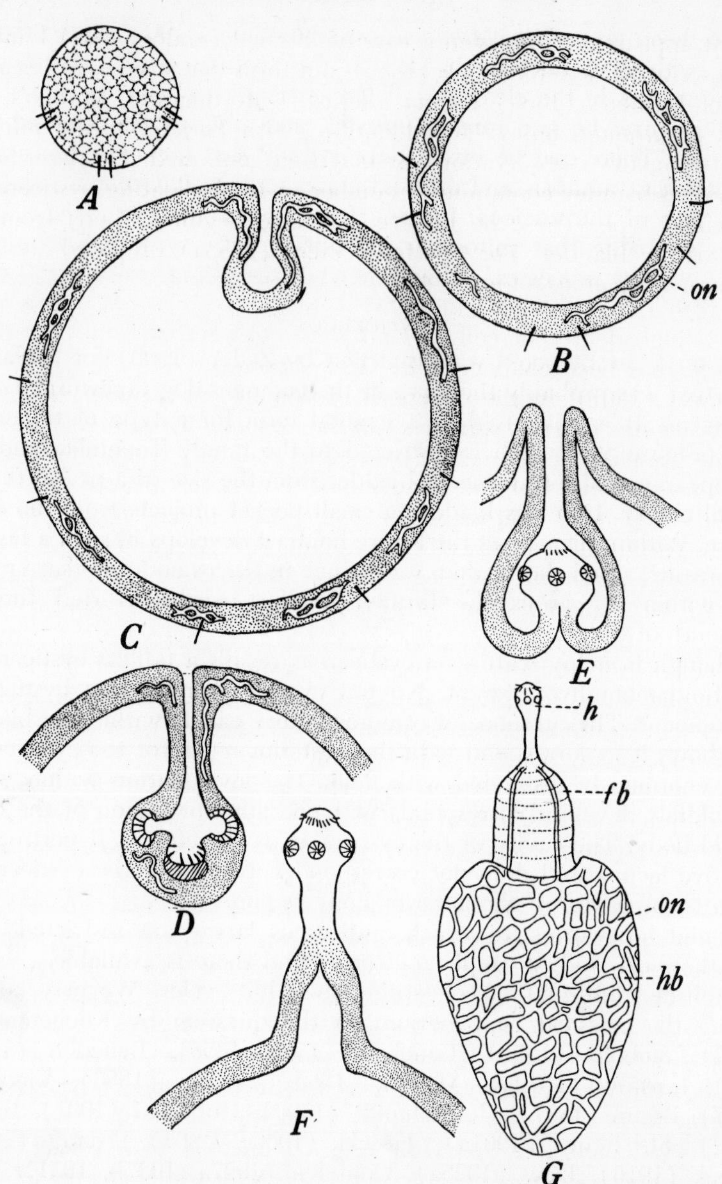

FIG. 50. Development of a cysticercus. After Benham, 1901. A. Solid oncosphere. B. Oncosphere after primitive lacuna has appeared (*on*, osmoregulatory network). C. Further hydrotropic distension and invagination of bladder wall at one point to form a "fore-body." D. Invagination proceeding, suckers and rostellum arising by evagination at the bottom of the tubular fore-body. E. Holdfast beginning to evaginate. F. Evagination of holdfast completed. G. Entire cysticercus (*C. pisiformis*) with holdfast everted. *fb*, fore-body; *h*, holdfast; *on*, osmoregulatory network; *hb*, hind-body.

of the sheep tapeworm, *Moniezia expansa,* Child (1907) stated that the chief method of nuclear division in the spermatogonial and oogonial divisions, and in the cleavages of the fertilized egg, was amitosis. True mitotic figures he had rarely observed, and amitosis he believed to be the rule. "There can be little doubt I think that the two forms of cell division [i.e., amitosis and mitosis] correspond to different physiological conditions of the nucleus. Judging from the visible phenomena, it also seems probable that mitosis is associated with cyclical, and amitosis with acyclical processes." This somewhat surprising conclusion – out of line with the prevalent belief that amitosis is abnormal, is connected with a high degree of cell specialization, and accompanies cell degeneration – has been challenged by later observers.

Janicki (1907), in the oogenesis of *Hydatigera taeniaeformis*, found mitotic figures (skeins, spiremes) in the oogonia of the immature ovary, and occasionally in the mature ovary, but could see no mitotic figures in the formed oocytes of the mature ovary. Richards (1909) was unable to find evidence of amitosis in the oogenesis of taeniid forms. He states: "In the early stages of sex cell development mitosis unquestionably occurs (probably periodically) while amitosis is not evident in my preparations [of *Moniezia*]; and finally there cannot be the slightest doubt that the cleavage of the ovum takes place by mitosis." Harman (1913) could find no evidence of amitosis in *Hydatigera taeniaeformis* and *Moniezia expansa,* and found no condition that could not be explained as the result of mitosis. In the oogonial divisions mitotic figures were frequent. The maturation of the oocytes was definitely mitotic.

The primary oocyte is described by Janicki (1907), for *Hydatigera taeniaeformis,* as a spherical cell of 160 microns diameter, with a large blisterlike nucleus sharply demarcated from the cytoplasm. The nucleus has a clear appearance, its stroma is sparse, and its chromatin is concentrated mainly in a deeply staining nucleolus; the homogeneous cytoplasm contains a crescentic mass, or two spherical masses, of something which seems identical with the yolk material of yolk cells (see Figure 30 A). This primary oocyte leaves the ovary via the oocapt and enters the germiduct. From there it passes into the fertilization canal where it is entered by a sperm cell; thence it passes into the ootype and attracts a yolk cell, one of those brought there by the common vitelline duct (Figure 30 B).

This yolk cell is a spherical cell, 70 microns in diameter, with a rounded nucleus placed eccentrically. Characteristic of the nucleus is the central concentration of the chromatin, giving the appearance of a chromatin nucleolus. The chief constituent in the yolk cell cytoplasm is a large spherical mass of yolk material.

A single yolk cell attaches itself to each oocyte and gives up to it its yolk mass (Figure 30 C). This yolk mass fuses with the yolk structure already present in the oocyte. The yolk-emptied yolk cell remains adhering to the surface of the oocyte, and around the two cells there appears a thin, transparent, structureless membrane, apparently a secretion from the glands of the ootype. The sperm cell, though undoubtedly within the oocyte, remains invisible.

For a detailed description of the changes which now take place in the oocyte and bring about the expulsion of first and second polar bodies and the fusion of male and female pronuclei into a zygote nucleus, reference may be made to Janicki. Suffice it to say that at the end of these changes, the egg is ready to segment and is a spherical cell, with a spherical mass of yolk material and a spherical zygote nucleus. Still adherent to its outer surface are the remains of the yolk cell and the polar bodies (Figure 30 F).

The first cleavage is in line with the adherent yolk cell and divides the egg cell into two equal blastomeres, each with an ovoid yolk mass and a large spherical nucleus. In each blastomere, in the cytoplasm, are one or sometimes two chromatin masses. During the cleavage the yolk disappears, to reform again as an ovoid mass in each blastomere (Figure 30 H). During the second cleavage, the yolk again disappears temporarily. This cleavage is horizontal and cuts off two small micromeres from two larger macromeres. By further divisions of each macromere, two further micromeres are formed (Figure 30 I). The division of one of the micromeres and the longitudinal division of one of the macromeres bring about a condition where a cap of five micromeres lies on top of three macromeres (Figure 30 J). The three macromeres are dissimilar, one being larger than the other two. The appearance of the macromere nuclei is characteristic, each having a well-stained central nucleolus and only sparse chromatin granules.

The three macromeres run together so that their outlines are lost in a sort of syncytium. This syncytium flattens out and surrounds the mass of micromeres as the extraembryonic blastoderm. The yolk content of these macromeres goes to nourish the embryonic mass of micromeres. Among the eighteen or so micromeres, three stand out from the rest in being a little larger and having chromatin-poor nuclei and large nucleoli. These three now proceed to form the embryonic envelope (Figure 30 L). Meanwhile, the cells of the blastoderm lose their contours and form a homogeneous membrane whose original cellular nature is evident only from the three original nuclei still present as bulges from the outer surface of the membrane. The central mass of micromeres groups together to form the oncosphere.

As previously stated, the apparent "shell" of a tapeworm egg, when found in host fecal material, is in reality the double embryonic envelope, with its two membranes connected by radially running, fiberlike structures. Yoshino (1933), discussing the escape of eggs from *Taenia solium*, described the gravid proglottides as actually wriggling or creeping after emergence from the host. Their movements cause slits to form at the anterior end of each proglottis, and through such slits the majority of the uterine eggs emerge. When evacuated into water, what Yoshino calls the thin, colorless mother embryonic membrane – presumably the chorion – was usually intact, but in feces this membrane is usually lost. Occasionally this membrane has one or two delicate polar filaments. Between it and the shell proper, Yoshino speaks of a colloidal albuminoid layer—presumably the blastoderm. The egg proper measures 32–36 microns in diamater (larger) and 28.8–30.4 microns in diameter (lesser). The "shell" is thick, pale yellow in color, and radially striated.

The egg must be swallowed by the secondary host, usually a mammal but in some taeniid species a bird. Apparently the "shell" is not attacked by the digestive juices of the host, or at any rate not by the gastric juice. Waele (1933) believed the stimulus to egg hatching to be the action of the pancreatic juice of the particular intermediate host or range of intermediate hosts in which the cysticercus is usually found, and that the true intermediate host of any taeniid might be ascertainable by comparison of the times of egg hatching in pancreatic juice from a range of potential mammalian or avian hosts. Penfold *et al.* (1937a), in the case of *Taeniarhynchus saginatus*, liberated oncospheres from their embryonic envelopes by exposing the eggs alternately to artificial gastric and pancreatic juices (presumably simulating those of cattle) or by exposing them to sodium hypochlorite. The latter solution (0.05 per cent available chlorine) induced hatching within four minutes but killed the emerging oncospheres. Waele and Dedeken (1936), for *Cysticercus bovis*, found the germ bud with the holdfast and its immediate protecting membrane to be expelled from the cyst in either physiological saline or in gastric juice. The holdfast would evaginate only in neutral or alkaline fluids, however, and was stimulated to do so by bile salts. If the holdfast is exposed directly to gastric juice through injury of its protecting membranes, it is subsequently digested in the duodenum or the jejunum.

It is probable that in the true intermediate hosts the eggs hatch within the duodenum, and the oncospheres force their way through the mucosa into the submucosal blood vessels and eventually arrive in the liver. The occurrence, in the case of *Taenia pisiformis*, of early cysticerci in the mesenteric ganglia of the intermediate host—in this case the rabbit—suggests that some larvae may travel via the lymphatic vessels.

The final lodging of the oncosphere varies with different taeniid species. With *pisiformis* it is most commonly in the liver; with *solium*, whose preferred intermediate host is the pig, the cysticerci are found most commonly in the tongue, neck muscles, and shoulder muscles. In the case of *solium* cysticerci in man, the preferred sites, according to Vosgien (1911) (see Brumpt, 1936), are as follows: eyeball (46 per cent), nervous system (40.9 per cent), skin and cellular tissue (6.32 per cent), muscles (3.47 per cent), and other organs (3.22 per cent). Among ocular cysticerci, the order of location preference is: retina, lens, vitreous humor, anterior chamber, and orbit; occasionally they occur in the pupil, cornea, and iris. Among nervous system cysticerci, the order of location preference is: brain and meninges (90 per cent), and brain ventricles (1.5 per cent).

The cysticerci of *Taeniarhynchus saginatus* in the ox occur mainly in the adipose connective tissue that surrounds the voluntary muscles and the cardiac muscles. It is possible that some mathematical relationship between the diameter of the cysticercus and the diameter of the vascular and lymphatic capillaries determines such apparent preferences, but Brumpt (1936) suspected a definite tropic response on the part of the larva to particular locations of the intermediate host.

Taking as an example the oncosphere of *Taenia pisiformis*, the majority of the larvae appear to end their preliminary migration within the liver. There they grow rapidly and by the sixth day appear as small, transparent, pearly bodies, without hooks and surrounded by a mass of host leucocytes. At this stage the larva is not bladderlike but is a parenchymatous mass, surrounded by a thin cuticle. Toward the 22nd day, according to Moniez (1880a), when the larval mass is about 1 cm. long by 1 mm. wide, a constriction appears at about half its length. One portion of the larva then atrophies and disappears, the remainder developing at one pole an invagination, at the base of which a holdfast begins to differentiate. Toward the 30th day, the larva actively leaves the liver and falls into the body cavity of the host where it remains free and unattached for several days. Meanwhile, degeneration of the central cells of the larva makes it bladderlike. At this stage it becomes fixed to the peritoneal surface of coelom and mesenteries through inflammatory adhesion. At the end of several weeks it is fully formed and capable of infecting a primary host.

The fully formed cysticercus is enclosed by a membrane formed as an inflammatory reaction product by the tissues of the host. It may be termed an "adventitious membrane." Between this membrane and the true wall of the larva there is a film of thick, viscous, somewhat reddish fluid. The body wall proper consists of a *cuticle,* laminated and without cellular structure, internal to which is a granulated, nucleated *germinative layer.* Within the larval body there is a limpid fluid of somewhat complex chemical composition (see Chapter III). The shape of the cysticercus varies according to its location, being spherical when attached to the coelomic lining, elongated when lying between muscle fibers, and lens-shaped when in subcutaneous tissue. The death of the larva is followed by a clouding of the internal fluid and by a gradual calcification of the bladder wall. It is difficult to say whether calcification precedes or follows larval death, but the probabilities suggest the latter phenomenon.

The term "cysticercus" usually implies a bladder of small size containing only one developing holdfast. The term "coenurus" is used for a larger type of bladder worm in which a number of invaginated and developing holdfasts are present. The term "hydatid" is used to indicate a bladderlike larva varying in size from a hazelnut to a child's head, in which daughter cysts are budded off from the germinative membrane, each being coenurus-like in having a number of invaginated and developing holdfasts.

What appears to be a case of external budding on the part of a bladder worm was described by Hölldobler (1937) under the term *Cysticercus multiformis.* The parasite occurred in the subcutaneous connective tissue of a fox in Germany. There was an interconnected mass of bladders of various sizes, showing varying degrees of budding – usually from the pole opposite the holdfast. The latter was always invaginated, had the usual four taeniid suckers, and had a crown of hooks, possibly single.

In three important articles, published since the foregoing account was written, Crusz (1948a and 1948b) has added considerably to our knowledge of cysticercus development. He describes in detail a process of annular constriction of *Cysticercus pisiformis* whereby two or even three separate individuals are produced, the posterior individuals being without a holdfast, however. By using differential staining, polarized light, and histochemistry, Crusz has been able to demonstrate chemical differences between cuticle and hooks, and between base and blade of hooks, in *C. pisiformis* and *C. fasciolaris.* A specimen of *tenuicollis* is described which contained many daughter cysts in various stages of development, one being fully developed. They would seem to be formed by invagination of the parent cyst wall and consequent pinching off from the inner surface of the parent bladder. They are thus homologous with brood capsules of *Echinococcus.*

In recent years, medical and physiological interest in the nature of hydatid cysts has greatly broadened our knowledge of taeniid larvae. We shall postpone to later sections an account of the advances thus made. A similar postponement of discussion will also be made regarding tapeworm life cycle stages that do not appear to correspond closely with the four main tapeworm larval types we have discussed—procercoid, plerocercoid, cysticercoid, and cysticercus.

· CHAPTER III ·

Biology

The study of tapeworm biology concerns two sorts of problems: (1) those that concern the tapeworm as an *individual* – its growth, activities, alimentation, respiration, and so forth; problems, that is to say, of *autecology*; and (2) those that concern the tapeworm as a member of a partnership – its relationships with other parasites and with its host, the effects it may have upon its host, and the effects the host may have upon it; problems, that is to say, of *synecology*.

Problems of Tapeworm Autecology

The precision with which experimental investigations concerning growth, nutrition, respiration, and so on can be conducted with free-living animals is not possible with tapeworms. Such animals cannot be observed continuously within their hosts. They cannot be kept alive outside them for more than a few hours, and even in the most favorable artificial media their life is, as a rule, brief and abnormal, particularly so because they are extremely susceptible to the attack of bacteria and fungi. Relatively little attention has been directed to overcoming these experimental difficulties, and in consequence the biology of these parasites is very inadequately understood and published information on the subject is scanty.

The foremost technical problem confronting the student of tapeworm biology is to maintain a larval or an adult tapeworm outside its host for a period of time approximating the average time that the tapeworm would live were it in its host, and in a condition such that the creature remains, in shape and movements, in growth and development, unchanged from what it would be were it living *in situ*.

The problem demands (1) the establishment and maintenance of a sterile or nearly sterile artificial medium – whether it be a molar electrolytic solution, a colloidal gel, or a colloidal sol – which can serve as a carrier for the food requirements of the animal; (2) the elimination of microorganisms from the tapeworm surface during its passage from host to medium; and (3) the provision of the appropriate food requirements. The criteria of favorability of various artificial media for tapeworms have been stated as *longevity, normality of movement, growth*, and *rate of development* of the tapeworm under experiment (Wardle, 1937b). The various attempts that have been made to cultivate tapeworms, or to keep them alive, outside their hosts are briefly summarized below.

Frisch (1734b): plerocercoids of *Schistocephalus solidus* live more than 2 days in river water. Fabricius (1780): *Proteocephalus percae* can live several days in sea water. Abildgaard (1793): plerocercoids of *Schistocephalus solidus* live 8 days in fresh water. Dujardin (1837): isolated proglottides of *Dipylidium caninum, Taenia pisiformis, Proteocephalus percae,* and *Hymenolepis fringillarum* live several days in a saturated atmosphere. Knoch (1862): holdfasts of bothriocephalid tapeworms from fishes live 8 days in aqueous solutions of egg albumin. Pintner (1880): many tapeworms from marine fishes live 5 to 6 days in sea water plus a trace of egg white. Zschokke (1888c): tapeworms from selachian fishes live 24 hours in sea water plus host gut mucus.

Loennberg (1892b): *Triaenophorus* lives 3–4 weeks in a slightly acid pepsin-peptone solution of sodium chloride at 10° C. in total darkness, 14 days when glucose is added, 4 days in peptone alone. Tower (1900): *Moniezia expansa* lives 5 days in 10 per cent albumin, plus 5 per cent beef extract, plus 2 per cent glucose in tap water. Le Bas (1924): plerocercoids of *Dibothriocephalus latus* live 7 days in Ringer-Locke solution. Dévé (1926): bladder worms of *Echinococcus granulosus* live at least 12 days at 37° C. in aseptic hydatid fluid plus fresh unheated horse serum and increase in volume. Coutelen (1926, 1927a, 1927b): holdfasts from bladder worms of *Echinococcus granulosus* live for 31 days in hydatid fluid plus ascitic serum and reach a volume of 24–35 times that of the original. Coutelen (1929): individual coenurids of *Multiceps serialis* remain alive for 20 days and double their volume when kept aseptically in sodium chloride solution plus fresh horse serum renewed daily, at 37° C.

Cook and Sharman (1930): *Moniezia expansa,* at 37° C., in carbonate-free Ringer's solution lives 200 hours; in the same medium plus M/10,000 NaOH, it lives 286 hours; plus M/10,000 HCl it lives 175 hours; plus M/1,000 HCl it lives 90 hours; plus M/100 NaOH it lives 44 hours; plus M/100 HCl it lives 36 hours; plus M/10 NaOH it dies immediately; in distilled water it dies immediately. Clarenburg (1932) tested the viability of *Cysticercus bovis* in meat obtained from a calf 9 months after experimental feeding with ripe proglottides. Active evagination of the holdfast was obtained with bile, pancreatic extract, trypsinogen, pancreatin, sodium taurocholate, or sodium glycocholate solutions at 40° C.; this occurred feebly even after the meat had been kept 41 days at just below freezing point, and vigorously (movements of suckers and neck) after 28 days. The cysticerci were very resistant to pancreatic extract. In 2½-inch slices of meat they were killed after freezing for 65 hours at —8° to —10° C., after salting for 5 days in 20 per cent and 25 per cent brine, and after immersion for 15 minutes in boiling water. X rays were without lethal effect.

Wardle (1932e): plerocercoids of *Dibothriocephalus* and *Triaenophorus* and adults of *Bothriocephalus scorpii* tolerate balanced salines better than low molecular concentrations of the component salts. Wardle (1934): in a range of saline and nutrient media, maximum longevity values for plerocercoids of *Nybelinia* were given by sterilized double

Locke's solution (456 hours); the longevity in serum-saline gel was 192 hours; in sterilized Locke-bouillon, 200 hours; in Locke-glucose solution, 408 hours. Lemaire and Ribère (1935a) described a technique for cultivating hydatid holdfasts in vitro aseptically. The holdfasts were withdrawn from the cyst with a veterinary syringe and placed in a glass tube, 9 cm. by 12 mm., the bottom of which was closed by a film of collodion. This tube was placed in a wider (21 mm.) round-bottomed tube having a constriction near the bottom, as used by bacteriologists for cultures on potato. The smaller tube rested on the constriction; the serum or other culture medium was placed in the wide tube to a level above the constriction and thus diffused up through the collodion film, which acted as an ultra-filter. The outer tube was closed by a plug of cotton wool.

Mendelsohn (1935) kept larvae of *Hydatigera taeniaeformis*, removed from rats' livers when 15 days old, alive for 35 days in a sterile nutrient fluid of 7 drops of balanced saline, 2 drops of chicken embryo extract, and 3 drops of filtered horse serum at 35° C. Wardle (1937a): *Moniezia expansa*, in a wide range of saline media, glucose-free and glucose-containing, at pH values of 6.0–9.0 and at 36–38° C., cannot be relied upon to show activity longer than 12 hours, although occasional specimens are active up to 3 days. Markov (1938): plerocercoids of *Dibothriocephalus latus* live longest in fish broth (63 days) and in glucose with vitamins (56 days). In glucose without vitamins they live only 30 days; this solution was the most unfavorable of those tried. Young plerocercoids (1–2 mm.) live only half as long as the more advanced ones; the normal longevity is 46 days, which is sufficient to allow experiments in artificial media. Muñoz Fernández and Saucedo Aranda (1945) maintained *Moniezia expansa* alive in Tyrode's solution at 37–38° C. for 6–24 hours. Wilmoth (1945) recorded the survival of larval *Hydatigera taeniaeformis* under various conditions of in vitro culture. Survival time, longest in simple media (576 hours), was shortened by anaerobiosis, which led to small decreases in the pH of the medium. The effects of pH and temperature changes were noted.

In the experiments noted above, the longevity of the worms in the media was a mere fraction of their longevity when in the host, and in no case do normal growth and activity seem to have been present. Stunkard (1932b), however, obtained some evidence of growth with specimens of *Crepidobothrium loennbergi* removed from the gut of the amphibian *Necturus*, washed in sterile Ringer's solution, and transferred to a sterile, isotonic, salt-glucose solution, the salt content of which had been adapted from Craig's medium for gut protozoa cultivation. The medium was modified by the addition of Hottinger broth (prepared by the digestion of veal), and a series of cultures of pH values varying from 6.5 to 7.8 was used. The culture which varied around pH 7.3 was the most favorable. The worms were kept in Petri dishes at room temperature and transferred to fresh media every 12 hours.

In one experiment, young specimens lived more than 32 days and increased 3 to 4 times in length. The terminal portion of the body became segmented, but the proglottides were abnormal and sterile. Addition to the media of salt extracts of intestinal mucosa, pancreas, and liver of *Necturus*, sterilized by filtration, did not appreciably alter the rate of growth or the time of survival. Exclusion of free oxygen by anaerobic methods did not affect the results. Fresh serum from *Necturus* was definitely toxic to the worms.

Green and Wardle (1941) were able to keep *Hymenolepis fraterna* from rats alive and active for 20 days, thus considerably exceeding the normal longevity (11 days) of the mature worms when in the rats. The medium was a dilution of Baker's tissue culture medium (10 drops to 5 cc. of Tyrode's solution), after the worms had been sterilized by being allowed to fall 10 times in succession through 4-inch columns of sterile Tyrode's solution.

The most promising tapeworm cultivation experiments to come to the notice of the present writers are those of Smyth (1946–50). This worker has elaborated a technique that permits the removal of plerocercoid larvae of *Schistocephalus solidus* from the body cavity of *Gasterosteus aculeatus* without bacterial contamination. The larvae are then cultured in plugged test tubes under completely aseptic conditions in a variety of balanced salines, glucose salines, and in nutrient peptone broth (Figure 51).

The most successful results were obtained with peptone broth at room temperatures (16°–19° C.), in which plerocercoids remained active and showed normal behavior for periods up to 300 days. In ¾-strength

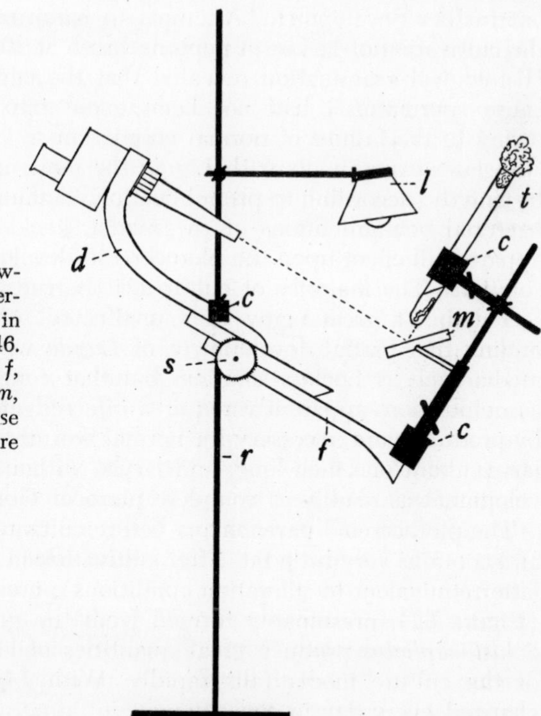

FIG. 51. Arrangement for viewing *Schistocephalus* plerocercoids during cultivation in vitro. After Smyth, 1946. *c*, clamp; *d*, fixed column; *f*, sliding column; *l*, lamp; *m*, mirror; *r*, retort stand; *s*, coarse adjustment wheel; *t*, culture tube containing larvae.

Locke's solution, which was found by experiment to be approximately isotonic with *Schistocephalus* ($\triangle = 0.44° \pm 0.02°$ C.), the mean period of normal behavior was 114 days. In the remaining saline and saline-glucose media, the mean viability and period of normal behavior were considerably less. In the plerocercoid, histological examination revealed that the genitalia were in an immature condition. During cultivation at room temperatures, the genitalia remained in this undifferentiated condition and showed no signs of undergoing spermatogenesis, oogenesis, or vitellogenesis.

Plerocercoids were, however, induced to develop into sexually mature adults by raising the temperature of cultivation in peptone broth to 40° C. (i.e., the body temperature of the final host in the natural life cycle). Oviposition took place after 48–60 hours at this temperature, and histological examination revealed that spermatogenesis, oogenesis, vitellogenesis, and shell formation had taken place in a normal manner. The viability of artificially matured *Schistocephalus* was 4–6 days in vitro – a period equivalent to the viability of the adult in vivo.

The eversion of the cirrus was observed in each proglottis after 40 hours of cultivation at 40° C. During the sexual process, the cirrus everted and invaginated at the rate of about once per second. Cross-fertilization between segments of the same worm or with segments of another worm was not observed. Except for one specimen in ¾-strength Locke's solution which underwent spermatogenesis and partial vitellogenesis, larvae cultured in salines or glucose salines at 40° C. died within 1–3 days without further development. Attempts to hatch out the eggs produced by the cultivation of larvae in peptone broth at 40° C. proved unsuccessful. Histological examination revealed that the eggs were not fertilized because spermatozoa had not been taken into the vagina, presumably owing to the failure of normal copulation.

In later experiments with *Ligula* the most unexpected result obtained by Smyth (according to prepublication communication) was that certain bacterial contaminations of the media, accidentally produced, had no apparent ill effect upon the plerocercoid development in vitro in nutrient solutions. The majority of cultures, it is true, died rapidly when so infected, but a great many were unaffected. Also remarkable is Smyth's finding that partial development of *Ligula* will proceed in *non-nutrient* media such as Locke's solution, but that complete development, as far as oviposition, apparently requires *infected* media, as if some bacterial by-product were necessary for normal worm development. Fragments of larva, about one inch long, and larvae without holdfasts underwent development as readily as complete plerocercoids.

The plerocercoid parenchyma before cultivation is filled with glycogen and contains very little fat. After cultivation in broth or pure salines (the latter equivalent to starvation conditions), great quantities of fat appear (Figure 52), presumably formed from the glycogen. Both *Ligula* and *Schistocephalus* produce great quantities of acids in vitro, and the pH of the culture media falls rapidly. With *Ligula*, the media must be changed every day in consequence.

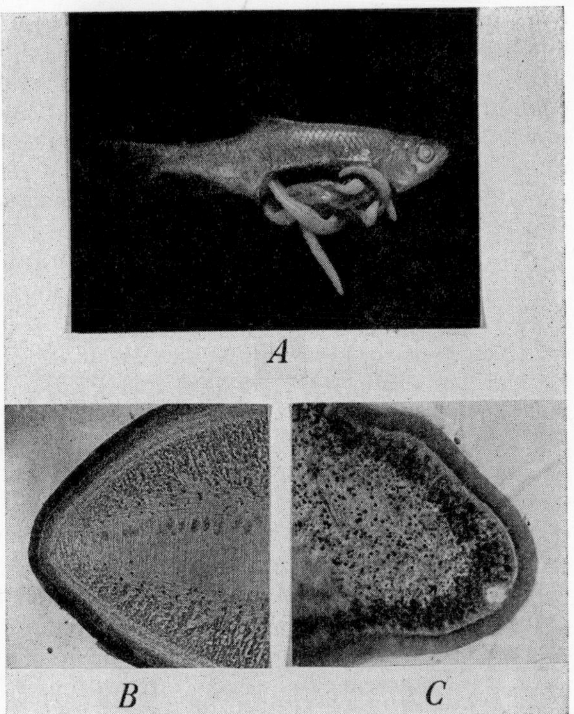

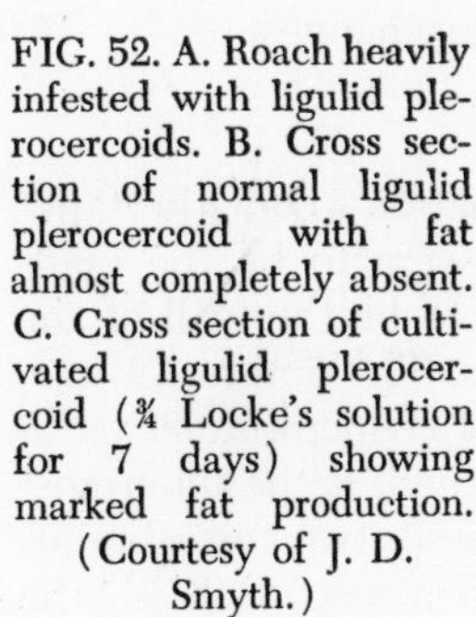
FIG. 52. A. Roach heavily infested with ligulid plerocercoids. B. Cross section of normal ligulid plerocercoid with fat almost completely absent. C. Cross section of cultivated ligulid plerocercoid (¾ Locke's solution for 7 days) showing marked fat production. (Courtesy of J. D. Smyth.)

Using one ligulid larva per tube of 50 cc. of horse serum, renewed every 24 hours, Smyth (1948) succeeded in rearing the larvae to adult stage, with a production of fertile eggs of 6 per cent. These eggs hatched normal coracidia, thus proving the ligulid to be self-fertilizing. Fragments of larva, which were similarly cultivated, developed and produced eggs as efficiently as complete larvae, but there was no regeneration of tissue.

Surveying as a whole the picture of our knowledge of tapeworm cultivation, it is still true to say:

"The inescapable conclusion from the data presented is that the saline media usually employed in physiological studies are useless for the study of tapeworm physiology, and conclusions based upon experiments carried out in such media cannot be accepted as giving an accurate picture of the physiological processes taking place in the worm that is living in the animal gut. That is to say, the bulk of the information already accumulated upon tapeworm physiology, scanty as it is, is practically worthless, and workers in the field of physiology will have to adopt a technique more akin to that of the bacteriologist than that of the physiologist. Successful tapeworm cultivation *in vitro* may require that the animal be embedded in a semi-fluid gel after preliminary aseptic treatment. The technique of such asepsis has yet to be established. On the other hand, the nutritional requirements of such a tapeworm when *in vitro* may prove to be less exacting than has been supposed, and it may not be necessary to duplicate the nutrient complex that surrounds the tapeworm *in situ*." Wardle (1937b).

Tapeworm cultivation is thus essentially a problem of establishing an equilibrium between the tapeworm's internal environment and a laboratory imitation of its external environment. Relatively little information is available, however, about the chemical and physical conditions of the two environments or about the interenvironmental exchanges.

TAPEWORM SURFACE

The most favorable subjects for obtaining information about the tapeworm's internal and external environments would seem to be the bladder worm types of tapeworm larvae. What appears to be the wall of the bladder worm is in reality two separate membranes. The outermost one, the so-called adventitious membrane or pericystic membrane, is a product of host tissue inflammation. The true wall, then, is the innermost membrane, the vesicular membrane. Between these two membranes there is a small quantity – a few drops usually – of a viscous fluid, the external fluid. This represents the external environment – the *milieu extérieur* of French observers.

Within the vesicular membrane there is a relatively larger quantity of a clear, limpid fluid, the internal fluid, representing the internal environment or *milieu intérieur*. The vesicular membrane is thus the skin of the larva, if such a term can be applied to a structure which is not of proved ectodermal origin. Microscopical examination shows the vesicular membrane to be in reality double, with an outer, amorphous, refringent cuticle or laminated membrane, and an inner, syncytial, glycogen-rich, germinal or proligerous membrane. An analysis of the hydatid cuticle by Graña and Oehninger (1944), using the method described by Campbell (1942), showed it to contain an insoluble protein, giving both protein and carbohydrate reactions, which is not dissolved by either pepsin or trypsin but is stained by Best's carmine. It is probably related to hyaloidin. When injected into rabbits it provokes an intense eosinophilia.

When the bladder worm is placed in water at 36–38° C. it can be seen to pulsate rhythmically, the pulsations increasing to a maximum at 40–42° C. and decreasing to a minimum at 32–34° C. Such pulsations also take place when the bladder worm is in its host.

In the case of the plerocercoid type of tapeworm larva, the adventitious membrane may not be present. If present, it is usually well separated from the larva proper as the so-called "cyst," and in such cases the external fluid is relatively voluminous, thick, and almost puslike (cf. *Triaenophorus*). The fluid within the bladder of an encysted plerocercoid such as that of *Triaenophorus* or of some species of *Dibothriocephalus* is therefore not homologous with the fluid within the bladder of the cysticercus or coenurus.

In the adult or strobilar phase of the tapeworm, no such adventitious membrane can be demonstrated. The "skin" of the plerocercoid or the strobilar phase, corresponding with the vesicular membrane, is also essentially double and comprises an outer, noncellular, laminated cuticle and an inner, thin, homogeneous basement membrane. The cuticle is an exudate from a layer of spindle-shaped cells, the subcuticle, that lies below the basement membrane. The homologies of the basement membrane and cuticle with the elements of the vesicular membrane are uncertain. In both the plerocercoid and the strobilar phases, the internal liquid or *milieu intérieur* is represented by the "parenchymal sap," a fluid which fills the interstices of a scleroprotein network termed the parenchyma, in which the remaining organs are embedded.

TAPEWORM CHEMISTRY

Chemico-physical studies of a vesicular tapeworm larva have been made, particularly by the Swiss physiologist, W. G. Schöpfer (1932), using the cherry-sized bladder worm (*Cysticercus tenuicollis*) of a common dog tapeworm, *Taenia hydatigena.* This bladder worm is fairly common in some areas within the abdominal cavity of sheep. There is also available a number of other observations, to be referred to later, on the internal fluid of "hydatids" – that is to say, of larvae of the dog tapeworm *Echinococcus granulosus* – made chiefly by medical workers. Reference should be made to the discussion by Schopfer of previous work in this field.

The external fluid of the bladder worm is essentially an exudate from the host's blood, and differs only in detail from blood serum. In *Cysticercus tenuicollis* it is a viscous, reddish fluid with a density of 1.023, a refractive index of 1.342, and an internal osmotic pressure equivalent to that of blood serum, namely, 7.6 atmospheres. It contains approximately 4 per cent nitrogenous matter, with a trace of cholesterol and somewhat less than 1 per cent inorganic matter. The nitrogen content is thus about half that of sheep blood serum.

The internal fluid of the bladder worm is a transudate from the blood plasma and is comparable in composition to cerebrospinal fluid. It is a clear, limpid fluid with a density of 0.0097, a refractive index of 1.335805, and an osmotic pressure of 8 atmospheres, thus only slightly above that of sheep serum. On evaporation it yields 1.557 per cent solid matter, of which 0.3–0.5 per cent is nitrogenous – chiefly proteins, uric acid, urea, and creatinine, with traces of glucose and cholesterol. The inorganic content consists chiefly of chlorides (0.7 per cent), sulfates and phosphates of sodium, potassium, calcium, magnesium, and iron. The absence from both fluids of fats, fatty acids, and glycogen is noteworthy.

Lemaire and Ribère (1935b), studying the internal fluid of hydatids, were unable in a number of cases to detect any trace of cholesterol or inositol, whereas creatinine, ammonium salts, and lecithin were always present. They further demonstrated proteolytic and glycolytic enzymes, the presence of which supplies an explanation of the results obtained for albumin and glucose. Lemaire (1926) further found that hydatid fluid contains albuminous and peptonic fractions that can be separated by ultrafiltration. When injected intravenously into a dog, the albuminous fraction produced a shock that lasted 8 minutes; the peptonic fraction gave no reaction.

The adventitious membrane would therefore appear to be almost completely permeable to the constituents of the host's serum, and the vesicular membrane to be only selectively permeable, especially toward serum proteins. The evidence for protein degradation shown by the presence of urea, uric acid, and creatinine suggests a metabolism dependent upon oxygen. If a respiratory exchange of oxygen and carbon dioxide takes place through the vesicular membrane, the importance of the characteristic turgescence of the bladder worm is evident, and the attainment of such turgescence by a difference in the electrolyte content between the external and the internal fluids would account for the differences in saline content.

The internal chemistry of the plerocercoid type of larva has not been the subject of any systematic study, but that of the strobilar phase has been investigated, particularly by Brand (1929, 1933) and, to a lesser extent, by Ortner-Schönbach (1913), Vialli (1935), Friedheim and Baer (1933), Smorodinzev and Bebeschin (1935a, 1935b, 1936a, 1936b, 1936c, 1936e, 1939a, 1939b), Smorodinzev, Bebeschin, and Pavlova (1933), Smorodinzev and Pavlova (1936a), and Wardle (1937a). Of considerable interest, also, are the analyses by Salisbury and Anderson (1939) and Lesuk and Anderson (1941) of the larva of *Hydatigera taeniaeformis*, which is not a cystic type, as in other taeniids, but resembles in shape and solidity the adult worm, though of course lacking sexual differentiation.

In the strobilar phase, the holdfast contains approximately 50–75 per cent water, 18–20 per cent organic matter, and 7–20 per cent mineral matter; the remainder of the strobila contains approximately 80–90 per cent water, and the organic matter is distributed equably between nitrogenous, fatty, and carbohydrate matter, with 1–2 per cent mineral salts. Thus, in a series of analyses of *Moniezia expansa* by Wardle (1937a), the mean water content was 86.6 per cent, nitrogenous matter 4.86 per cent, carbohydrate 3.14 per cent, ether-soluble matter 3.8 per cent, and ash 1.4 per cent. Smorodinzev, Bebeschin, and Pavlova (1933), for *Taeniarhynchus saginatus*, found 4 per cent protein (dry weight), 1.36 per cent fat, and 6.19 per cent carbohydrate, assumed to be mainly glycogen. The fats varied considerably (0.29–3.17 per cent) between one specimen and another.

The proportions of protein, fats, and carbohydrate not only vary among individuals of the same species, but considerably so among different species. Reference should be made to the analyses by Brand (1933) of *Taenia hydatigena, Taeniarhynchus saginatus, Moniezia expansa*, and *Anoplocephala magna*, and to the analyses by Smorodinzev *et al.* (1933–39) of *Taeniarhynchus saginatus, Taenia solium*, and *Dibothriocephalus latus*. All strobilar tapeworms agree in having a high carbohydrate content and a high ether-soluble content.

The strobilar ash content is not satisfactorily known. Brand (1933) found the "calcareous bodies" of *Moniezia* to comprise carbonates and phosphates of calcium and magnesium, his figures being CaO 36.13 per cent, MgO 17.07 per cent, P_2O_5 14.09 per cent, and CO_2 33.09 per cent.

Salisbury and Anderson (1939) found the larval content of *Hydatigera taeniaeformis* to be unusually high in percentage of ash (over 16 per cent of dessicated material) and to consist mainly of magnesium and calcium phosphates, although sodium and potassium were present in such large amounts as to make the ash strongly alkaline. Only traces of iron and chlorine were present.

Calcium appears to be taken readily by tapeworms from their environment, but there is no evidence that the internal concentration rises much above the external concentration, that calcium plays any part in tapeworm metabolism, or that the amount taken from the host is pathogenetically significant. Wardle, Gottschall, and Horder (1937) failed to obtain any change in the blood calcium and phosphorus content of dogs infested with *Dibothriocephalus latus* up to periods of three months, although such changes have been demonstrated in rabbits infected with the trematode *Clonorchis sinensis* (Hudimi and Nishizaki, 1934; Shigenobu, 1932). Wardle (1934) commented upon the susceptibility of some tapeworms when in vitro to the lethality of calcium salts, and upon the apparent nonsusceptibility of others, notably the plerocercoid larvae of *Dibothriocephalus* and *Triaenophorus* which, incidentally, do not become calcified when *in situ.* An investigation of the responses of tapeworms, whether strobilar or larval, to environmental calcium might throw some light upon the susceptibility of some larvae to calcification within the host's tissues.

The nitrogenous content of the strobilar phase has not been studied in detail. There is reason to believe that it consists chiefly of scleroproteins that make up the parenchymal network. To what extent albumins, globulins, and specific proteins – serving as antigens to provoke antibody formation – occur in the parenchymal sap cannot be stated. Smorodinzev and Pavlova (1936a) fractionated the proteins of three cestodes, *Taeniarhynchus saginatus, Taenia solium*, and *Dibothriocephalus latus*, and found albumin, globulin, nuclein, keratin, elastin, collagen, and reticulin in amounts they definitely stated. The percentages of phosphorus in the nuclein fraction and of sulfur in the keratin fraction were different for each species.

It is of some significance, possibly, that the products of protein degradation – urea, creatinine, etc. – are absent or undetectable in saline media in which living tapeworms have been immersed. Salisbury and Anderson (1939), in the larval *Hydatigera taeniaeformis*, found 20 per cent of the total nitrogen to be present in aqueous extracts of the defatted, dessicated, powdered material. The amount of protein thus represented was very small, not amounting to more than 7 per cent of the water-soluble nitrogen. Amino nitrogen amounted to 24 per cent, amino acid nitrogen to 9.8 per cent, ammonia to 0.03 per cent, urea to 0.08 per cent, and uric acid to 0.02 per cent of the water-soluble nitrogen. By hydrolysis of the aqueous extract with hydrochloric acid, the amino acid nitrogen rose to 51 per cent, indicating the presence of a large proportion of peptide nitrogen. In the defatted larval powder, 0.04 per cent creatinine, 0.07 per cent creatine, and 0.20 per cent cystine-cysteine were demonstrable. Hexosamine in the aqueous extract amounted to 2.5 per cent of the dried larva.

Kent (1947a) extracted, with doubly distilled water and with saline solutions of different strengths, the proteins from defatted *Moniezia* and found them to be almost entirely associated with relatively large amounts of other organic constituents. He isolated by fractionation a protein-bile acid aggregate which, apparently, is abundantly present, and a protein-glycogen aggregate which he named "baerine" and which contained 60 per cent glycogen. By electrophoresis, baerine and another protein-glycogen aggregate, "moniezine," with 11 per cent glycogen, were obtained. The proteins appear to be quite typical and yield many of the common amino acids. Such an association of proteins with glycogen and bile acids may confer on them their special biochemical and physiochemical properties.

The carbohydrate content of the strobilar phase has been better studied, contributions to the subject having been made by Ortner-Schönbach (1913), Brand (1933), Wardle (1937a), and—for the larval *Hydatigera taeniaeformis*—by Salisbury and Anderson (1939). This phase is entirely polysaccharide in nature, no free sugars having been demonstrated in adult strobilar tissue, although Salisbury and Anderson found 1 per cent reducing sugar in fresh, aqueous extracts of dessicated larval *taeniaeformis*. This polysaccharide content may run as high as 30–40 per cent of the dry weight. There is little doubt that it is identical with mammalian glycogen. Microscopical examination of sectioned strobilar material of *Moniezia*, stained with glycogenophilic stains, shows the glycogen to be uniformly distributed through the parenchyma but to be absent from the cuticle, subcuticle, uterine network, and eggs. There seems to be some correlation between the glycogen content and the degree of muscular tension in the strobila.

The fat content of strobilar material has been studied in detail by several investigators. The earliest study of tapeworm lipids was that made by Faust and Tallqvist (1907) on *Dibothriocephalus latus*. According to these authors, this worm when dried contains 11.5 per cent ether-soluble material comprising lecithin, cholesterol, and palmitic, stearic, and oleic acids. Glycerol was not found, and the fatty acids were believed to occur mainly as cholesterol esters and to a lesser extent as phospholipids.

An analysis of fresh *Dibothriocephalus latus* material by Tötterman and Kirk (1939) reported considerable amounts of phospholipids. The average lipid content of fresh, undried worm was 1.6 per cent, and the phospholipid content was 0.57 per cent. The cephalin fraction made up the major part of the phospholipid content (0.36 per cent), but appreciable amounts of ether-insoluble phospholipids (0.08 per cent) and of lecithin (0.13 per cent) were demonstrated.

The analytical values given by Brand (1933), and Oesterlin and Brand (1933), for *Moniezia expansa* are instructive. The average lipid content was 2.35 per cent of the fresh weight. This percentage was made up, in round figures, of 15 per cent phospholipids; 7 per cent sterols; 8 per cent saturated fatty acids, mainly stearic; 51 per cent unsaturated fatty acids, mainly oleic; and 14 per cent unsaturated hydroxy fatty acids. The hydroxy acids were not identified but had a molecular weight around 250 and yielded, on catalytic reduction, fatty acids with a molecular weight around 270, presumably a mixture of stearic and palmitic acids. The glycerol content of the worm was 4 per cent of the lipid content.

Smorodinzev and Bebeschin (1939b), in *Taeniarhynchus saginatus*, found the proportions of the total lipids to be as follows: cholesterol, 12.39 per cent; neutral fats, 75.42 per cent (with a mean iodine index of 151.31); lecithin, 5.41 per cent; cephalin, 3.78 per cent; and cuorin, 3.13 per cent. The cholesterol–fatty acid ratio was low, indicating a small affinity for water.

Of considerable interest also are the analyses by Salisbury and Anderson (1939) and Lesuk and Anderson (1941) of larval *Hydatigera taeniaeformis*. The lipid content of the dried material was 5.5 per cent, which is extremely low for a tapeworm. This comprised phospholipids, mainly lecithin and cephalin, 30 per cent; free cholesterol, 27 per cent; ester cholesterol, 3 per cent; glycerides, 13 per cent; and cerebrosides, mainly dihydrophrenosin, 20 per cent. The fatty acids occurred mainly as phospholipids. Hydrolysis of the phospholipids yielded about equal amounts of saturated and unsaturated fatty acids. The saturated acids comprised palmitic, 20 per cent; stearic, 52 per cent; arachidic, 23 per cent; and a small amount, 5 per cent, of an unidentified acid. The unsaturated acids, after catalytic reduction, gave mainly stearic acid, but small amounts of palmitic acid and of some acid higher than stearic were present. Lesuk and Anderson (1941) found the ether-insoluble lipids to consist of a mixture of a saturated cerebroside and a hydrolecithin. The cerebroside fraction was made up largely of dihydrophrenosin, which, on hydrolysis, gave galactose, phrenosinic acid, some lower fatty acids, and an unusual cerebroside component which agreed in composition with dihydrosphingosine. The hydrolecithin was essentially dipalmitolecithin, and the products of its hydrolysis were palmitic acid, glycerophosphoric acid, choline, and a substance corresponding in composition with tetracosanoic acid.

Kent and Macheboeuf (1948) extracted dessicated, defatted *Moniezia expansa* with distilled water and obtained, by dialyzing the solution against water at 0° C., a peculiar protein fraction which was insoluble in water. It contained proteins (8.6 per cent nitrogen only), glycogen, cerebrosides, and bile acids. After hydrolysis the amino acids were microchromatographically identified, the glycogen was identified, and the amount of sugar and glucosazone was estimated. The substance associated with the protein is undoubtedly a cerebroside.

According to the analyses given above, tapeworm fatty acids would seem to occur mainly as phospholipids, to a lesser extent as cholesterol esters, and only to a slight extent as glycerides. Deuel and collaborators (1936) demonstrated that triglycerides of fatty acids that have an even number of carbon atoms – such as triacetin, tributyrin, tricaproin, and tricaprylin – and triglycerides with odd-chain fatty acids – such as triproprionin, trivalerin, and triheptylin—are converted readily in the animal organism to glycogen. In view of this fact, the possibility of a correlation between the tapeworm's high glycogen and low glycerol content cannot altogether be ignored, particularly since the habitat of the majority of adult tapeworms is the lower region of the vertebrate ileum, which has been shown by Sperry and collaborators (see Bull. 1937) to be the site of considerable endogenous excretion of fats.

The key to the understanding of many obscure features of tapeworm biology probably lies in a further study of the functions of the phospholipid content. Vaguely as these functions are known, there would seem to be three advantages conferred upon the living tapeworm by their presence: (1) They will enable it to absorb unsaturated fatty acids from the environment with great avidity. (2) They will enable it to make use of an extremely low environmental oxygen content. (3) Its water balance will be controlled by the phospholipid-cholesterol ratio. A low P/C ratio, such as seems indicated by the analyses quoted above, should favor a water-in-oil emulsion within the tapeworm tissues that should greatly increase the possibility of water intake by the worm.

In view of the findings by Bloor (1936) that in smooth muscle the value of the P/C ratio is low, ranging in vertebrate smooth muscle from 3 to 5 as contrasted with values of 10–20 for cardiac and skeletal muscle, it is possible that the extremely low P/C ratio of *Moniezia* and larval *Hydatigera* is a characteristic of any invertebrate animal which lacks skeletal muscle tissue and whose smooth muscle content is considerable. A similarly low P/C ratio has been demonstrated by Lovern (1940) for the annelid worm *Lumbricus*.

INTERENVIRONMENTAL EXCHANGES

A tapeworm, whatever its phase, has no apertures for the intake of food nor for the elimination of waste matter, if we except the external apertures of the main osmoregulatory canals. The substances it utilizes for energy production must pass, probably with the main by-products of such energy production, through the body surface. The tapeworm should therefore be "poikilo-osmotic"—should have, that is to say, an internal osmotic pressure that fluctuates with the fluctuations of the osmotic pressure of the outer environment.

However, such evidence as is available regarding the ratio of external osmotic pressure to internal osmotic pressure is conflicting. Vialli (1925), using thermoelectric methods, determined the internal osmotic pressures of *Taenia pisiformis* and *Taenia hydatigena*, both from the dog, as approximately 13 and 10.6 atmospheres respectively, as compared with 7.5 for the dog gut contents. Schopfer (1932), using cryoscopic methods, found an internal osmotic pressure in *Moniezia expansa* of approximately 8 atmospheres, the mean of 10 determinations, and for the sheep gut contents, an osmotic pressure of nearly 10 atmospheres. For *Eubothrium crassum* of the trout the osmotic pressure was approximately 12 atmospheres, nearly twice that of the host gut contents. In the case of the plerocercoid larva of *Dibothriocephalus latus*, Wardle (1932e), from observation of larval behavior in solutions of known osmotic pressure, suggested an internal osmotic pressure of 3–4 atmospheres, lower than that of the surrounding muscle juice of the pike (approximately 6 atmospheres). Schopfer (1932) suggested an internal osmotic pressure of approximately 8 atmospheres for *Cysticercus tenuicollis*, only slightly above that of sheep serum.

Admittedly, tapeworms readily lose or gain water when the saline content of the surrounding medium is varied. They tend to expand and become turgid in hypotonic saline solutions, and to become increasingly foreshortened and contracted in media whose electrolyte content is increased gradually from isotonicity (Schopfer, 1932; Wardle, 1937a). But the behavior of a tapeworm in an artificial medium cannot be explained altogether on grounds of differences in osmotic gradient between the *milieu intérieur* and the *milieu extérieur*. It is mainly due to a specific effect of the ions in the medium upon muscular irritability, notably the ions K′, Mg″, and Na′, in the order named. The order may not necessarily be one of relative lethality, but one of relative penetrability. Such ions inhibit the region of maximum metabolic activity – H′, K′, Mg″, and Na′ inducing muscular contraction, OH′ and Ca″ inducing muscular relaxation. Penetration of these ions may therefore bring about contraction of the region of maximum activity in salines containing sodium, potassium, or magnesium; or it may bring about relaxation or paralysis in salines containing calcium. Such a hypothesis explains all types of tapeworm behavior (Wardle, 1934) and is in agreement with the findings of Child (1924, 1926) and his co-workers in the case of free-living flatworms.

ALIMENTATION

Very little information is available concerning the food requirements of tapeworms or the methods by which they satisfy such requirements. The assumption is usually made that their food consists of such cell-permeable products of host digestion as amino acids, glucose, and glycerol, diffusing through the strobilar body surface into the parenchyma – or through the vesicular membrane into the internal liquid; and that cell-impermeable substances such as proteins, peptones, disaccharides, polysaccharides, and fats are not utilizable. In the absence of experimental verification of these assumptions, however, any attempts to feed tapeworms in vitro cannot be otherwise than empirical.

Some support for these assumptions, however, has been provided by the accumulation of evidence concerning the physico-chemical nature of the *milieu intérieur* of larval taeniids (*Echinococcus granulosus, Taenia hydatigena, Multiceps serialis*) brought forward by Flössner (1923–25), Hoeden (1925), Mazzocco (1923), Schilling (1904), Wernicke and Savino (1923), and Schopfer (1932). There is general agreement among these investigators that, as already stated, the fluid within the inner membrane of the cysticercus or coenurus type of larval tapeworm is a transudate from the blood plasma of the host, and that it is poorer in proteins and richer in chlorides than is the host plasma. This poverty in proteins is regarded by some observers as evidence that the tapeworm assimilates proteins; but the observations of Schopfer suggest, on the contrary, that the metabolism of the bladder worm is not sufficiently intense to use up proteins so rapidly, and that the protein poverty of the internal milieu is due to low permeability of the inner membrane to proteins of the host plasma. The fundamental nutritive substance appeared to Schopfer to be glucose.

The possibility, however, that the proteins of the internal environment are hydrolyzed as fast as they enter, and may in fact form an important food constituent, is suggested by the demonstration by Smorodinzev and Bebeschin (1936a) of pepsin, cathepsin, and trypsin in the internal milieu of *Taeniarhynchus saginatus* and *Taenia solium.*

The extent to which tapeworms can absorb substances which are in colloidal dispersion, such as fats, is uncertain. That adult tapeworms have a high fatty acid content is well known, and early observers such as Schiefferdecker (1874) postulated the direct passage of fat globules through cuticular pores in the tapeworm surface. It is a striking fact that adult tapeworms have a glycogen-fat content in excess of their protein content — a unique feature among animals. Brand (1933) was inclined to regard the fat content as being of the nature of an accumulated excretory product, a by-product of glycogen degradation. Under anaerobic conditions at 39° C., *Moniezia* in Ringer's solution loses 0.25 per cent of its glycogen in six hours, but loses none of its fat content. The amounts of carbon dioxide (0.11 per cent), succinic acid (0.101 per cent), lactic acid (0.05 per cent), and higher fatty acids (0.05 per cent) excreted into the medium nearly balance the glycogen loss and so support the view that the fatty acid excretion is the result of glycogen degradation. Brand claimed also that sugar-fed tapeworms show an increase in internal fat content.

An interesting approach to the question of tapeworm alimentation has been suggested by Chandler (1943). This observer stresses the possibility that part of the tapeworm's food requirements may be satisfied by absorption of substances from the living mucus membrane of the host gut with which the worms are in contact. In support of this view, Chandler stresses (1) the ability of tapeworm larval phases to absorb nutriment from host tissues, for as a rule they are not bathed in either blood or body-cavity fluid but are embedded in such tissues as the liver, muscles, brain, or under serous membranes, and are sometimes invested by an adventitious connective-tissue capsule long before reaching maturity, through which they are able to absorb nutriment; (2) the location of some adult tapeworms in positions other than the lumen of the vertebrate small intestine, such as the biliary passages of the liver, the pancreatic duct, and the body cavity; and (3) the marked host specificity of some tapeworms.

Experiments carried out by Chandler with *Hymenolepis diminuta* in rats demonstrated (1) that this tapeworm is totally independent of proteins in the host diet but is very sensitive to any restriction of carbohydrate in the host diet; (2) that it is independent of vitamins A, B_1, D, and E in the host diet but affected by any lack of G complex in female though not in male hosts; and (3) that the effects of vitamin G lack are less in hosts deprived of proteins as well as vitamins than in hosts fed a normal amount of proteins. Chandler suggests that the toxic effect of tapeworm infestation may be due in part to absorption of protein and vitamins from the host.

In further investigations, Addis and Chandler (1944, 1946) found that development of the cysticercoids of *Hymenolepis diminuta* in rats is dependent in part on the vitamin G complex of the host. In the absence of this complex, establishment of the larvae becomes difficult, and there is considerable dwarfing of the larvae which do develop. The absence of vitamins A, D, E, and B_1 from the diet of the host apparently has no inhibitory effect upon larval establishment, and the parasites actually grow more rapidly than they do in fully fed control hosts. The suggestion was made that the parasites can synthesize most vitamins but are dependent upon the host for G complex.

It is possible, therefore, that the observed effects of host starvation upon some tapeworms may be due in reality to deprivation of G complex. Thus Levine (1938) showed that the rate of development of *Davainea proglottina* in the fowl is not uniform but is dependent upon the nutritive value of the diet fed to the host. Hager (1941) showed that the egg output of *Hymenolepis diminuta* in rats could be influenced by changes of diet. Partial starvation did not lower the rate, but an absence of vitamin G complex did. Raw milk, wheat middlings, and, to some extent, soybean oil meal supply this factor. Reid's observations (1940, 1942a, 1942b) that starvation of fowls following the intake of mature cysticercoids of *Raillietina cesticillus* does not prevent the establishment of an infection but inhibits their further growth is suggestive of a dependence upon the vitamin content of the host diet. His observation that starvation of the fowl hosts causes passage of the strobilae of this tapeworm but not of the holdfasts – at any rate, in up to 20 days' starvation – supports Chandler's suggestion of direct passage of nourishment from the gut mucosa to the region of the tapeworm in contact with it.

Addis and Chandler (1946) found that a lack of vitamin B_1 had no effect upon the establishment or the development of *Hymenolepis diminuta* in rats, but that fat-soluble vitamins A, D, and E are necessary for establishment though not for normal growth. Some factor in brewer's yeast seems necessary for normal growth. Addis (1946), however, found *Hymenolepis diminuta* to grow normally in male rats fed a vitamin-deficient diet, but in female rats it was stunted. Administration of testosterone to female rats and to castrated male rats permitted normal growth of the worm.

Chance and Dirnhuber (1949) found tissues of *Moniezia benedeni* to contain aneurin (8.6 μg./g. dry weight of worm), nicotinic acid (190 μg.), and pantothenic acid (10.0 μg.) and suggested that the low content of pyridoxine (7.1 μg.) in the anterior proglottides may mean that the tapeworm does not store pyridoxine because the developing proglottides can obtain their vitamin requirements, along with other nutritional compounds, from the intestinal lumen of the host.

RESPIRATION

The phenomenon of tapeworm respiration is comparable to tapeworm alimentation in the indefiniteness of our information. Several investigators, notably Cook and Sharman (1930), Alt and Tischer (1931), Harnisch (1932–37), Friedheim and Baer (1933), and Friedheim, Susz, and Baer (1933), have shown that certain tapeworms in media containing oxygen will absorb such oxygen readily below a temperature limit of 38° C., and that the amount absorbed is proportional to the oxygen tension of the medium. There is no evidence, however, that any more carbon dioxide is produced than under anaerobic conditions, though Cook and Sharman showed the carbon dioxide output to vary with changes in the hydrogen-ion content of the medium.

In the external environment of an adult tapeworm, the oxygen tension is low. The early observation of Fries (1906) of only 0.7 to 1.3 per cent oxygen in the rectal gases of man was opposed by Long and Fenger (1917), who found amounts of oxygen ranging up to 14 per cent in the guts of recently slaughtered hogs, but was confirmed by Brand and Weise (1932). The latter investigators, in a series of Van Slyke measurements of the oxygen content of the bile and gut contents of hogs, sheep, cattle, and dogs, found the maximum oxygen content of bile to be only 0.084 per cent by volume – the amount occurring in water in equilibrium with an atmosphere containing 3.5 per cent – and found the gut contents to be absolutely oxygen-free or to have only a minute oxygen content, except in a few hogs which had swallowed air during slaughter.

It may be stressed, too, that the by-products of tapeworm metabolism – in an artificial medium, at any rate – are carbon dioxide, higher fatty acids, lactic acid, and succinic acid, such as would be produced by glycogen degradation in the absence of oxygen. The proportion of fatty acid produced is practically the same whether the medium is oxygen-free or oxygen-rich (95 per cent). The conclusion may be drawn that energy production in a strobilar tapeworm is independent of oxygen and depends upon the breakdown of glycogen. The strobilar tapeworm is anoxybiotic.

The ready absorption of oxygen from a medium rich in oxygen, by an immersed tapeworm, is explained by Harnisch (1932–37) as the fulfillment of an oxygen debt arising from the accumulation of oxidizable substances produced during anoxybiosis and not completely removed from the body. In the presence of oxygen, such substances will be oxidized at a rate correlated with the oxygen tension of the medium up to a point where an equilibrium is reached between production and oxidation of metabolic products. That the minute oxygen content of the gut lumen may be utilized by the tapeworm is suggested by the demonstration of the oxygen-absorbing pigment, cytochrome, in the tissues of *Dibothriocephalus* and *Triaenophorus* by Friedheim and Baer (1933).

Grembergen (1945) found the tissues of *Moniezia benedeni* to absorb a large amount of oxygen in a manner strictly comparable to that of higher vertebrates.

The fact that anoxybiosis is the normal mode of life among intestinal worms is further suggested by the findings of Flury (1912). He found that the excreted by-products of the metabolism of ascarid roundworms, living under conditions similar to those of tapeworms, consist not of urea, uric acid, creatinine, and purine bases, but of ammonium salts, caproic acid, butyric acid, and especially valeric acid, as much as 0.4 to 0.85 grams of fatty acids per 100 grams of worm being thus excreted. Slater (1925), however, questioned whether the fatty acids are true by-products of ascarid metabolism and suggested that they are formed by contaminative bacteria; but as Brand (1933) has emphasized, in that case the fatty acids produced by unrelated intestinal worms should agree in chemical nature, whereas the contrary is found. Ascarid worms produce chiefly valeric acid; the sheep liver fluke *Fasciola* produces in addition higher, nonvolatile fatty acids; the tapeworm *Moniezia* excretes higher fatty acids, lactic and succinic acids. Succinic acid can also be demonstrated in the bacteriologically sterile fluid of bladder worms (Flössner, 1925).

In one of the most recent contributions to the question, Laser (1944) found the oxygen uptake of whole specimens of *Ascaris suis* to be 80 μl. per gram wet weight per hour, increasing with rising oxygen tension or after periods of anaerobiosis. Though succinic dehydrogenase was present, the accumulation of oxalacetic acid reduced its activity, and this, together with the low concentration of cytochrome, led to the low rate of oxidation. The R.Q. (respiratory quotient) was 1.1 to 1.2 in air and 0.5 to 0.6 in oxygen. The Q_{O_2} of the muscle pulp, 1.3, was not affected by cyanide or azide. The amount of catalase in the worms was low, and the accumulation of hydrogen peroxide, which killed the worms at high oxygen tensions, was demonstrated. Laser concluded that *Ascaris suis* shows a perfect adaptation to the low oxygen tension of its normal environment.

The high glycogen content of tapeworms now becomes explicable, and its origin is a matter of considerable interest. Presumably it is synthesized from glucose, or from glycoproteins or triglycerides withdrawn from the host's body fluids or from the host's gut contents, since the low oxygen tension of the gut lumen or gut contents – if paralleled by a similarly low oxygen content or an actual oxygen lack in the tapeworm tissues – precludes an origin of glycogen from proteins. The source material for the glycogen must enter the worm through the cuticle and be synthesized into glycogen in the parenchymal cells. Ortner-Schönbach (1913) suggested that the glycogen-gorged parenchyma acts as a reservoir of glycogen for the muscles and the gonad ducts, where it is degraded, and as a source of glucose for the ovaries, yolk glands, and germ cells, where it is resynthesized to glycogen.

The admission must be made, however, that the hypothesis of glycogenesis from environmental glucose has received little support from experimental investigations. Ortner-Schönbach could detect no histological evidence of difference in glycogen content between control specimens of the horse tapeworm *Anoplocephala* and specimens that had been kept for seven days in saline solutions and in saline-glucose solutions. Even apart from the possibility that the experimental worms may not have been alive during the whole of the seven days in saline solutions, present histochemical methods of demonstrating glycogen in tissues are far from being sufficiently precise to indicate differences in glycogen content.

Brand (1933) obtained inconclusive results from the immersion of *Moniezia expansa* specimens, under anaerobic conditions, in Ringer-glucose solutions. In four experiments, one worm showed a glycogen gain of 0.13 per cent after six hours' immersion at 37.5° C., but three showed glycogen losses of 0.02, 0.03, and 0.18 per cent. Since the experimental error in experiments of this nature may be as high as 1 per cent – that is to say, two halves of the same worm may differ in glycogen content to that extent – Brand's results suggest merely that *no* glycogen change occurs when *Moniezia expansa* is immersed for six hours in saline-glucose at 37.5° C.

Wardle (1937a), on the other hand, obtained a positive glycogen gain when *Moniezia expansa* was immersed in saline media containing glucose up to 1 per cent in content, but found no gain when other sugars were used or when glycoproteins or amino acids were used. The glycogen was found to become depleted rapidly in media which induced muscular contractions, but to be depleted only slowly in media which induced muscular relaxation or undulant activity. Such changes do not altogether support the view of Ortner-Schönbach that the primary function of tapeworm glycogen is the nourishment of the developing genitalia. Rather, they suggest that glycogen is primarily a source of energy for the longitudinal musculature when the latter is maintaining the condition of muscular tonus which characterizes living tapeworms, and that it is depleted in any artificial medium in which this tonus is maintained, or in which tonus is exaggerated into tetanic contraction; but glycogen is depleted only slowly or scarcely at all when the musculature relaxes completely or undergoes periodically repeated phases of relaxation and contraction, as during undulant activity.

The effects of starvation upon glycogen content are significant. Reid (1942b) found the glycogen content of *Raillietina cesticillus* in chickens to be reduced by 92 per cent after only 20 hours of host starvation. Brand (1933) found that 8 specimens of *Taenia hydatigena* taken from a dog on high carbohydrate diet had a glycogen content of 8.53 per cent, while specimens from a dog on low carbohydrate diet had 4.99 per cent.

MOVEMENT

Because of the arrangement of the parenchymal musculature into longitudinally directed and transversely directed fibers, the movements of a strobilar tapeworm or a plerocercoid larva consist of alternating waves of contraction and expansion. These contractions and expansions are not, however, of uniform intensity throughout the body, but are greatest in that region of the animal where growth is most active—that is to say, the region of maximum metabolic activity. This is the Keimzone, or neck, in worms in which new segments appear to originate in the neck region; but in pseudophyllidean worms, where new segments arise by transverse divisions of the segments of the posterior half of the primary body—using the term "posterior" as a convenient but probably inaccurate term for that half of the body farthest from the holdfast—the region of maximum metabolic activity is approximately at the junction of the first and second thirds of the body length.

The body of a tapeworm is thus alternately shortening and lengthening toward or away from this region of maximum metabolic intensity, and since the region lies nearer to the holdfast than to the other end of the worm, each expansion gives the animal an impetus in the direction toward which the holdfast points.

Rietschel (1935) studied successive, coordinated contraction waves in the body of *Catenotaenia pusilla* by experimental methods. Cutting the nerve cords and osmoregulatory canals did not inhibit the backward progression of the wave of contraction, and any nervous or hydrostatic transmission was thus ruled out. When a segment was compressed, the contraction waves were interrupted at that place and new waves arose behind the compressed segment. On releasing the pressure, contraction waves passed over the segment that had been compressed. Rietschel concluded that the stimulus that produces contractions is not dependent upon the holdfast but may arise in any segment. It is conducted mechanically through the tension of contracting muscle fibers on those situated posteriorly. The physiological significance of the wave of contraction that passes backward over the body is presumably associated with the forward movement of the worm against the flow of material in the gut and the resulting reduction of tension on the holdfast. Perhaps also if the movement of the intestinal contents over the worm is weak, the contraction waves facilitate the passage of material over the segments and aid in the nourishment of the tapeworm (Rietschel, 1935).

The contractions and expansions of the body are particularly vigorous in a short-bodied, muscular form such as a plerocercoid larva when it is placed in a nonlethal medium of low viscosity. The plerocercoid larva of *Nybelinia*, a trypanorhynchan tapeworm in sharks when adult, is particularly common within the stomach wall of hexagrammid fishes in British Columbian waters (Canada). If removed from this habitat and placed in double Locke's solution in a Petri dish, the waves of movement can be seen to begin in a region midway between the posterior borders of the bothridia and the edge of the caudal invagination (Figures 53 and 54). The movements are particularly vigorous. At each expansion the animal doubles its *in situ* length. Friction between the substratum and the worm is necessary for forward progression and is provided by the temporary adherence of one or more bothridia to the bottom of the dish, and by the push of the abothridial end of the worm against the bottom of the dish. Thus the animal actually crawls with fair

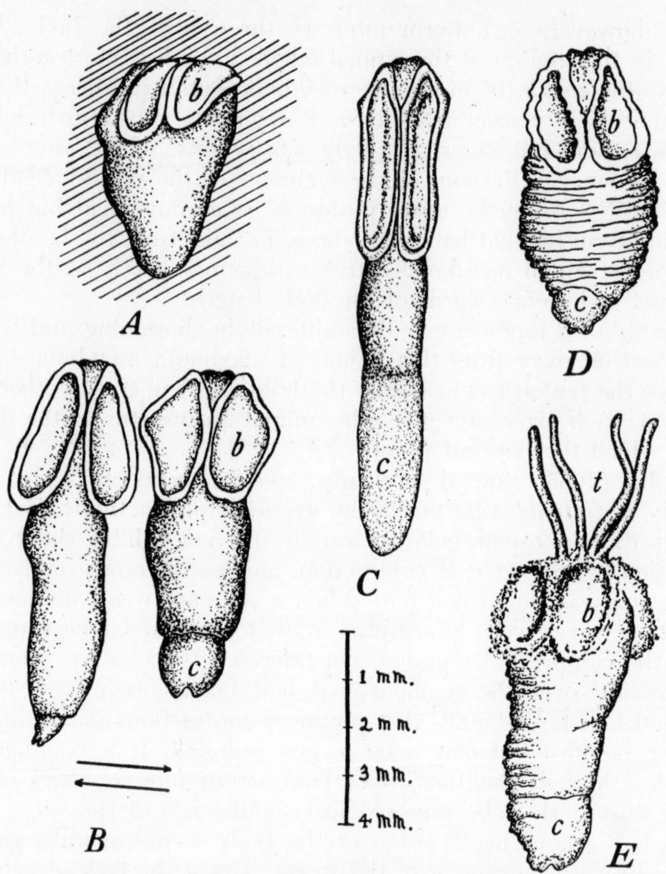

FIG. 53. Appearance of *Nybelinia* plerocercoids in different media. After Wardle, 1934. A. Plerocercoid appearance *in situ*. B. In favorable salines. C. Extreme expansion in resorcinol. D. Tetanic contraction. E. Endosmosis and disintegration. *b*, bothridia; *c*, caudal appendage; *t*, tentacles.

rapidity, moving forward with a slight rotating movement (Wardle, 1934).

Such forward progression is not possible for a long-bodied worm because of the relative inertia of its posterior half. However, in muscular tapeworms such as the pseudophyllidean forms *Bothriocephalus* and *Eubothrium*, the expansions and contractions of the holdfast and anterior segments are most pronounced, and the former may elongate to twice or three times its *in situ* length. In other pseudophyllidean forms, such as *Triaenophorus* and *Dibothriocephalus*, the movements are comparatively sluggish.

When the tapeworm is *in situ* in the host gut, movement is curtailed by the viscosity of the gut contents, by the pressure of the holdfast against the mucosa, by the peristalsis of the gut wall, and, in a long worm, by the inertia of the posterior half of the body. The tapeworm is therefore in a state of partial contraction, of natural tonus, and the rhythm of movement is slow and irregular. The larval *Nybelinia* when *in situ* expands at a mean rate of 4 expansions per minute, as compared with a rate of 24–30 expansions per minute in double Locke's solution. This natural tonus serves to maintain the pressure between holdfast and mucosa, and, in a segmented worm, to maintain the integrity of the interproglottid junctions against the backward drag and disruptive tendency of gut peristalsis.

If, through starvation, through the pressure of maturing genitalia upon the musculature, through toxic elements in the host gut, or through other causes, the tonicity cannot be maintained, the tapeworm may be expelled *in toto*, as weakened fragments of body, or even as isolated segments from its habitat. Such an expulsion of immature individuals of *Eubothrium, Bothriocephalus,* and *Dibothriocephalus* from the host is not uncommon. The expulsion of aged, sexually exhausted tapeworms from the host habitat is probably the normal termination of the tapeworm life cycle. The phenomenon of pseudapolysis – the expulsion of exhausted strips of body – is a common occurrence in infestations of *Dibothriocephalus latus* in human or canine hosts.

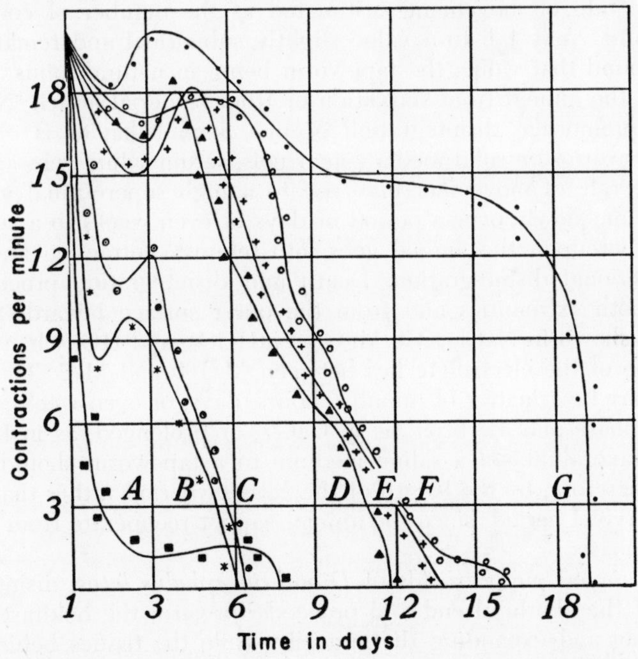

FIG. 54. Curves illustrating rates of movement of larval *Nybelinia* in favorable media and showing first a fall in the initial rate, followed by a recovery, followed by a gradual decline to zero. After Wardle, 1934. A. Serum saline gel. B. Sea water. C. M/10 NaCl. D. Locke's solution × 2, unsterilized. E. Locke's solution × 1, unsterilized. F. Locke's solution × 2 plus glucose, unsterilized. G. Locke's solution × 2, sterilized.

The passage of immature segments from the host is a normal phenomenon of the cyclophyllidean and tetraphyllidean life cycles. The larvae of *Phyllobothrium salmonis*, common as accidental parasites of the gut of Pacific salmon (*Oncorhynchus*), are apparently unable to counteract the peristalsis of their habit and so pass down to the host's rectum. There they accumulate, and when the fish is artificially stripped of its ova in the hatcheries, the larvae may be expelled from the salmon in such numbers as to clog the sieves. On the other hand, if the opposition of the host to tapeworm movement is weak, as in a diseased, moribund, or otherwise abnormal host, the impetus of the worm may throw it into coils – a condition familiar to the collector of tapeworm material – or may move it cephalad along the host gut, probably an uncommon occurrence. In other cases, as in some trypanorhynchan larvae occurring as accidental parasites in the stomachs of teleostean fishes, the worm's movements may help to drive it through the mucosa into the underlying tissues.

When a tapeworm is removed from its natural habitat and placed in an artificial medium, its behavior in terms of movement and distortion may be one of four types. The term "normal," as used below, refers to the rate of movement of the tapeworm when *in situ*.

1. The rate of movement – estimated as the number of contractions per minute – may fall to a value slightly subnormal and remain fluctuating around that value, the tapeworm being in natural tonus, until the death of the animal from starvation or from bacterial attack. No distortion or premortem disintegration occurs. Such behavior is observable with tapeworms on solid media – agar gels, serum saline gels, and so on.

2. The rate of movement may rise to a high supernormal value and then decline slowly over a period of days or even weeks to a subnormal value, whereupon the animal goes into tetanic contraction and undergoes fractional disintegration. Death and disintegration proceed from one or both extremities and from the outer surface inward. Such behavior is shown in NaCl, KCl, $MgCl_2$, $NaHCO_3$, and HCl when the concentration of the electrolyte lies between M/100 and M/2. The activity period may be a matter of minutes, hours, days, or even weeks; the contraction phase may be brief, as in $CaCl_2$, or prolonged, as in HCl. The relative favorability of a saline medium to a tapeworm should be estimated, therefore, by the length of the activity period rather than by the whole survival period, since the animal cannot recuperate from the contraction phase.

In contracted plerocercoids of *Dibothriocephalus latus*, disintegration begins at the abothrial end and proceeds forward; the holdfast may be contracting and expanding rhythmically while the tissues behind it are in a state of disintegration. In the plerocercoid of *Nybelinia*, on the contrary, disintegration begins at the bothridial end and proceeds backward. Thus the caudal invagination may be undergoing rhythmic inversion and eversion when the holdfast is a swollen, disintegrating mass (Figure 53). In adult *Bothriocephalus scorpii* individuals, disintegration proceeds rapidly from the abothrial end forward and less rapidly from the bothrial end backward. The movements of the anterior region of the body in opposition to the relative inertia of the posterior region may throw the body into a tight spiral; and the slower movements of the body margins, as compared with those of the mid-dorsal and mid-ventral regions, may produce "frilling," the margins being partially expanded and pleated while the middle regions are contracted.

3. The animal may pass quickly into a state of tetanic contraction (Figure 53 D). Such is the case in NaCl, KCl, $MgCl_2$, and HCl in molar and supermolar concentrations, and in bactericidal concentrations of most antiseptic compounds. Death in this phase is followed by endosmotic bloating (Figure 53 E), but further dissolution may be inhibited in a bactericidal medium.

4. The animal passes quickly into a condition of extreme relaxation and then proceeds to disintegrate with great rapidity. Such rapid relaxation is induced by water, by NaCl, KCl, and $MgCl_2$ in concentrations below M/100, by calcium compounds, by sodium and potassium hydroxides, and by resorcinol.

It would seem, then, as if the tapeworm surface is permeable to, and susceptible to, the ions OH′, H′, Ca″, K′, Mg″, and Na′ in the order named. As these ions penetrate, there occurs a tonic contraction of the region of maximum activity in worms in salines containing sodium, potassium, and magnesium; and a paralysis or relaxation of this region in worms in pure water, in low concentrations of salines, or in calcium salines. The ends of the worm farthest away from the inhibited region will continue to show rhythmic activity, but eventually death and disintegration will begin, starting in the tissues farthest away from the inhibited region and proceeding gradually toward it.

Such a hypothesis explains all types of tapeworm behavior in aqueous media and is in accordance with the findings of Child (1924, 1926) and his collaborators in free-living flatworms. There the effect of sublethal media is first to inhibit the regions of greatest metabolic activity, and then gradually to inhibit the regions of minimum metabolic activity. The regions of maximum metabolism recuperate somewhat, but the regions of minimum metabolism do not. Thus death and disintegration begin in the tissues farthest from the zone of maximum metabolism and proceed toward it.

The question arises as to whether the order of apparent lethality of ions toward tapeworms is an order of real relative toxicity or merely of relative penetrability. Is the calcium ion really more toxic to tapeworms than the sodium or potassium ion, or does it appear so because it penetrates into the *milieu intérieur* more rapidly? No satisfactory answer can as yet be given to such a question. There is general agreement among workers in this field that the first effects upon an organism of electrolytes in a medium are to alter the normal permeability of the body surface membrane and, in a poikilo-osmotic organism, to induce rapid endosmotic or exosmotic distortion, according to the relative concentrations of the electrolytes on either side of the membrane. Secondly, electrolytes in the medium penetrate into the protoplasm and change it from sol to

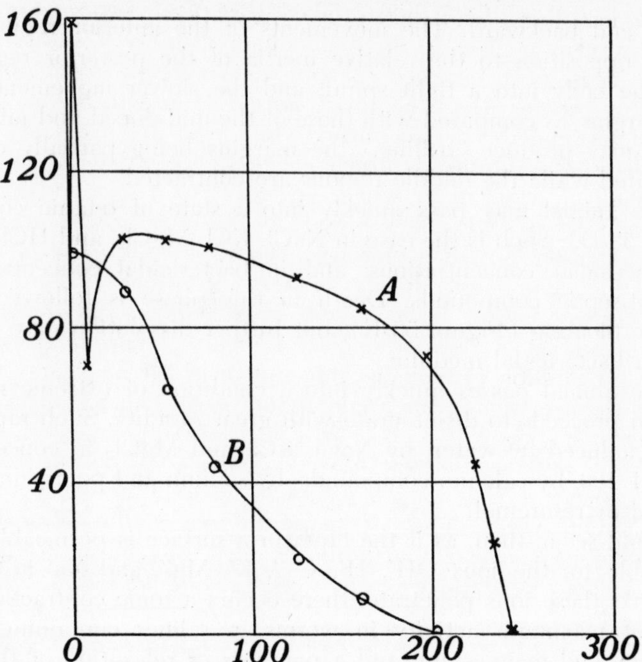

FIG. 55. Respiratory responses of *Moniezia expansa* after the addition to the medium of an acid or a base. After Cook and Sharman, 1930. The points represent the level of respiration determined at the times indicated on the abscissas. Curve A shows worms in M/10,000 NaOH; Curve B shows worms in Ringer's solution. The ordinates represent the percentage of normal respiration in Ringer's solution; the abscissas, the time in hours.

gel. The evidence on the subject is wide and confusing and need not be gone into here. In homoio-osmotic organisms, the distortion is less rapid, an osmotic balance being maintained for a time by energy induced by an increased oxygen intake.

Since free-living flatworms seem quite tolerant of calcium, the apparent susceptibility of tapeworms to calcium salts is worthy of further investigation. Such study may throw light upon the function of the calcareous bodies in tapeworm tissues, and upon the extreme susceptibility of some tapeworm larvae to calcification *in situ*. It may be noted that with plerocercoids of *Dibothriocephalus latus* and *Triaenophorus spp.*, which are intramuscular parasites, no undue susceptibility to calcium salts seems to be present, nor has even partial calcification of such larvae in the host tissues been recorded.

LONGEVITY

Very little accurate information is available concerning the length of life of tapeworms when in their natural habitat. No correlation between size and longevity has been established, and most observations concerning the length of life of the strobilar phase of tapeworms are vitiated by the observer's neglect to eliminate the possibility of host reinfestation and to distinguish between the prepatent and the patent phases – that is to say, between the preliminary period of growth before egg production begins and the period during which eggs are produced.

Perhaps the shortest strobilar longevity recorded is that of *Ligula intestinalis* in water birds, which, according to Joyeux and Baer (1936a), lives only a few days. This brevity of strobilar existence explains why the adult tapeworm is so rarely collected although the plerocercoid is one of the commonest parasites of fresh-water fishes in northern Eurasia and North America. The longest strobilar longevity recorded would seem to be that of *Taeniarhynchus saginatus*, reported by Penfold, Penfold, and Phillips (1937a) as infecting man for 35 years or more. Between these extremes, an accumulation of conflicting longevity data is available.

Broadly speaking, longevity is correlated with apolysis – the shedding of segments – in that annual forms are anapolytic and perennial forms are apolytic. But among anapolytic forms, *Dibothriocephalus latus*, prepatent in man and dog for 18–19 days, may be patent in man for 5 years, and the related species *Spirometra mansoni* may be patent in dogs for 8 years (Leiper, 1936b). *Eubothrium*, in the species of Pacific salmon *Oncorhynchus*, undoubtedly lives up to 5 years in its host, but for the greater part of this time it is probably prepatent, producing eggs perhaps only during the fresh-water migration phase of the salmon life cycle. *Moniezia expansa* of the sheep is prepatent for 37 days and patent for 65–70 days (Seddon, 1931), for 350 days (Gordon, 1932), or for 54 days (Stoll, 1936). *Hymenolepis fraterna* of rats is prepatent for 11–16 days in the rat (15 or more days in the mouse) and patent for 11 days; then it leaves the host (Shorb, 1933). *Raillietina cesticillus* of fowls is patent for 16–20 days according to Wetzel (1934); but Harwood (1938) believed its average life span to be 5 to 6 months in the fowl, with periods of high egg production alternating with periods of no egg production.

The chief difficulty in estimating the survival time of tapeworms in a culture medium is that of deciding the time of death. Absolute figures on tapeworm longevity in vitro are of little value as physiological data, since for part of the time the animal may have been moribund or disintegrating. Nor can it be assumed, as Cook and Sharman (1930) did, that carbon dioxide production is indicative of tapeworm vitality. The experiments of Brand and Weise (1932) suggest that carbon dioxide production by tapeworms is a by-product of glycogenolysis and not of aerobic respiration, and it is possible that such glycogenolysis is as much a post-mortem as a premortem phenomenon. In the light of Brand's findings, the belief of Cook and Sharman that *Moniezia expansa* will live for 200 hours in their saline solutions plus M/10,000 sodium hydroxide must be accepted with caution.

It has already been mentioned that tapeworms when in vitro may pass through a period of undulant activity, sometimes brief, sometimes prolonged, before passing eventually into either a condition of flaccidity or a condition of tetanic contraction, both irreversible. It may be argued, therefore, that the end of the survival time of a tapeworm in an artificial medium could be taken arbitrarily as the moment when undulant activity ceases.

GROWTH

Information concerning the rate of growth of tapeworms is scanty. They cannot of course be continuously observed and measured while within their hosts, and they cannot be kept alive with certainty for more than a few days outside their hosts. The rate of growth, therefore, can only be inferred by measuring groups of individuals of known ages, and the study of tapeworm growth is thus limited to such species as can be reared in laboratory animals or in humans. The only published observations on the subject appear to be those of Petruschewsky and Tarassow (1933b) on *Dibothriocephalus latus*; of Penfold, Penfold, and Phillips (1937) on *Taeniarhynchus saginatus*; of Chandler (1939) on *Hymenolepis diminuta*; and of Wardle and Green (1941b) on *Dibothriocephalus latus*.

The choice of a criterion of growth changes in tapeworms is restricted by the absence from these animals of exoskeleton, endoskeleton, and osmotic rigidity. The living worm rhythmically contracts and expands; it is freely permeable to water, so that its weight and length are affected by the nature of the medium in which it is examined or preserved; and frequently only a fragment of worm may be available for examination.

Linear length, commonly used as a criterion of growth, while applicable to small tapeworms such as hymenolepidid forms and plerocercoid larvae, is less applicable to large tapeworms and not at all to fragments. A similar objection may be raised against the value of *total weight*. The value of *average cross-sectional area*, calculable from average length, average weight, and average specific gravity, offers the advantage of applicability to fragments. Usually, too, in the case of tapeworms preserved in 5 per cent formalin, the value of the specific gravity fluctuates narrowly on either side of unity, so that the average cross-sectional area may be regarded with little loss of accuracy as equivalent to the weight/length ratio.

Using this criterion of growth change, Wardle and Green (1941b) studied the growth changes of *Dibothriocephalus latus* reared in dogs from 5-plerocercoid infections during the first 30 days of life. The data obtained for weight, length, and weight/length ratio of entire worms in successive age groups are given in the accompanying table.

Between the maximum and the minimum values of weight and length there is in each age group a relatively wide spread, and it does not seem possible to determine the probable age of a fragment of *Dibothriocephalus latus* by inspection of the weight/length ratio. Such variations in weight and length within each group arise in part from corresponding variations among the plerocercoids used for initial infection.

The lengths of 56 plerocercoids, killed, preserved, and measured in 5 per cent formalin, ranged from 1.0 to 17.5 mm.; 41 of these had lengths between 1.5 and 6.5 mm., the average length being 3.7 mm. Fifty plerocercoids ranged in weight between 0.1 and 7.16 mg. Thirty-six of them had weights between 0.3 and 2.0 mg., the average weight being 1.4 mg. The W/L ratio of 0.4 is thus much higher than for the worms between 1 and 6 days old. However, if the relatively higher specific gravity of 1.38 of the plerocercoids is taken into consideration, W/L becomes

AVERAGE WEIGHT, LENGTH, AND WEIGHT/LENGTH VALUES FOR *Dibothriocephalus latus* REARED IN DOGS AND KILLED AND PRESERVED IN 5 PER CENT FORMALIN

AGE IN DAYS	NUMBER OF WORMS	AVERAGE WEIGHT IN MILLIGRAMS	AVERAGE LENGTH IN MILLIMETERS	WEIGHT/LENGTH RATIO
3	7	1.44	7.09	0.203
6	5	5.30	20.20	0.262
9	5	43.20	81.20	0.532
12	3	276.30	250.25	1.103
15	4	2350.00	659.00	3.57
18	3	3890.00	698.00	5.57
21	4	2660.00	664.00	4.01
24	3	1676.00	266.20	6.30
27	2	2215.00	660.00	3.36
30	3	9215.00	1436.00	6.42

0.274, which compares closely with that of the 1-day to 6-day worms. It is possible, therefore, that no true growth, in the sense of new tissue formation, occurs in the young worm within the first six days, but that the apparent increase in weight and length is due to water absorption. It may be noted that Chandler (1939) found very slow linear growth in *Hymenolepis diminuta* during the 5-day to 7-day period in the host, as compared with the rapid growth during the 7-day to 18-day period. The average length (20 mm.) given in the table for the 6-day-old worms may be contrasted with the value of 27.0 mm. found by Petruschewsky and Tarassow (1933) for *Dibothriocephalus latus* of the same age in a dog.

Without further knowledge of the food requirements of *Dibothriocephalus latus*, conclusions cannot be drawn as to the influence of its position in the host gut upon available food supply and upon its consequent weight and length. Among 80 worms, ranging from 3 to 98 days old, only 5 per cent lay in the first quarter of the host gut, as measured between pylorus and ileocolic valve; 37.5 per cent lay in the second quarter; 22.5 per cent lay in the third quarter; and the remaining 35 per cent lay in the fourth quarter. In the case of *Hymenolepis diminuta*, Chandler found that the worms take up their initial positions far back in the gut and subsequently move forward. The observations of Wardle and Green upon the positions of young specimens of *Dibothriocephalus latus* in kittens showed that 13 hours after initial infection, the worms lay at distances of 7, 11, 12, 13, and 16 inches from the pylorus in a gut measuring 33 inches between pylorus and ileocolic valve. After 25 hours,

17 worms lay at distances between 7.5 and 36 inches from the pylorus in a gut measuring 56 inches between pylorus and ileocolic valve. These observations suggest that a scattering of the individuals of an age group along the gut is as characteristic of the first few hours of infection as of the later days of infection.

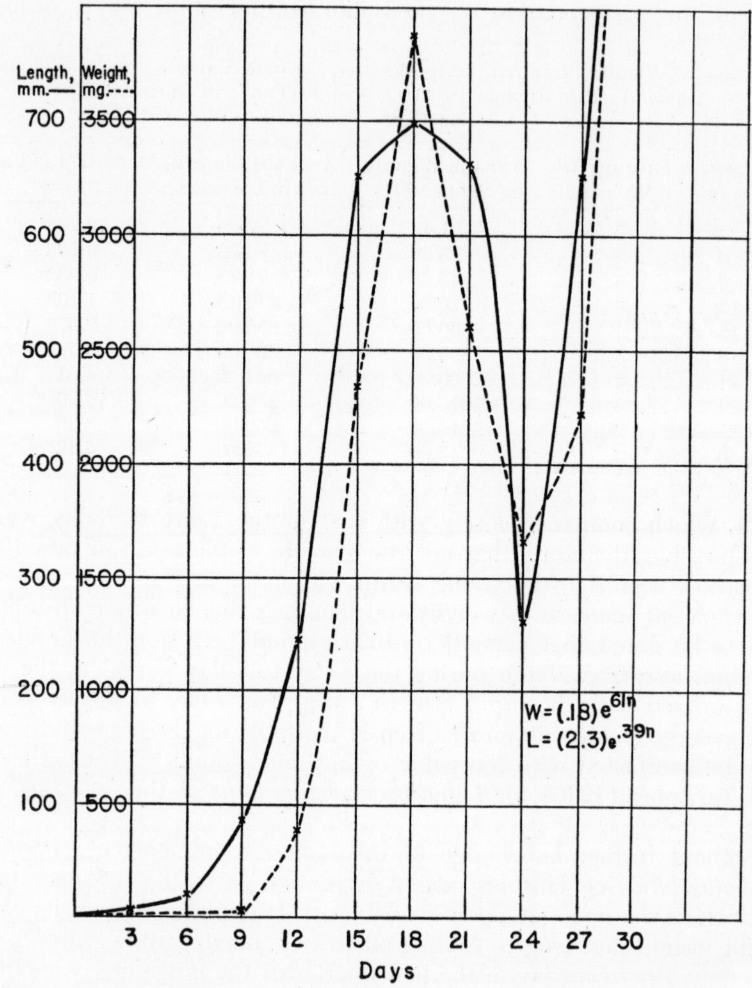

FIG. 56. Increases in length and weight of specimens of *Dibothriocephalus* in dogs. After Wardle and Green, 1941b.

Graphic presentation (Figure 56) of the data tabulated above suggests that the growth of *Dibothriocephalus latus* in dogs during the period 6–15 days after initial infection is rapid and progresses logarithmically according to the formula

$$G = Ae^{kn}$$

where G is the growth value (in millimeters or milligrams), A and k are constants, e is the natural logarithm base (2.71828), and n is the age in days. The actual values of weight (W), length (L), and weight/length ratio (W/L) recorded fit the formulas

$$W = (0.18)e^{0.16n},\ L = (2.3)e^{0.39n},\ W/L = (0.08)e^{0.22n}.$$

During this 6th-to-15th-day period, the average daily increment of length was 48 mm. During the 15th-to-30th-day period, it was 61.5 mm. Petruschewsky and Tarassow found the average daily increment for the 6th-to-36th-day period to be 47 mm. for *Dibothriocephalus latus* in a dog, and 150 mm. for a specimen in man.

Broadly speaking, the worm doubles its weight every 1.13 days and doubles its length every 1.77 days. The logarithmic nature of the growth suggests that most of it is due to cell multiplication. A tapeworm seems to grow more like a population of separate cells than like other multicellular animals.

As Figure 56 indicates, the value of W/L reaches a peak on the 18th day after initial infection. This peak coincides with the appearance in the posterior proglottides of the first batch of eggs. In *Dibothriocephalus latus*, whether in man or dog, the first discharge of eggs occurs between the 18th and the 20th days after initial infection. The exhausted proglottides shrink to one-half or one-third of their former weight, eventually disintegrate, and break free from the strobila. In the table of data, this first egg discharge is clearly indicated by the fall in W/L value in the 21-day specimens. The first apolysis, or shedding of exhausted proglottides, is indicated by the rise in W/L value in the 24-day specimens. Subsequent egg discharges are indicated by lower W/L values; subsequent apolyses are indicated by heightened W/L values.

The conclusion may be drawn that egg discharge and tissue apolysis are not continuous processes but occur spasmodically, as it were, at intervals which, up to 30 days after initial infection, appear to be of three days' duration. The W/L values thus rise and fall between certain limits. An examination of a large number of fragments of *Dibothriocephalus latus* from humans and dogs from various localities suggests that these limits for W/L values are approximately 3 and 5. Exceptions occur however. Clearly, any metabolic features of the host that stimulate egg production will produce an unusually high W/L value. Those that suppress egg production will stimulate linear growth but will lead to an unusually low W/L value. However, the nature of such metabolic factors is at present unknown.

A hint concerning the nature of such factors is given, perhaps, by the findings of Becker (1933) and of Hager (1941) that in rats fed on a milk diet fortified with iron and copper, the egg production of *Hymenolepis fraterna* fell off markedly or even stopped altogether. It will be recalled that Ortner-Schönbach (1913) put forward the suggestion that the primary function of tapeworm glycogen is the nourishment of the developing genitalia. The reduced egg production in the case quoted above may not be due to glycogen starvation, however, since Hager found a similar cessation of egg production when the host was fed a diet free from the vitamin B complex. Elimination of the vitamin G complex alone had a similar effect, but no falling off in egg production resulted when only vitamin B_1 was eliminated.

Wardle and Green's experiments were carried on for too short a time (30 days) to indicate whether new growth exceeds or merely keeps pace with apolytic loss. Penfold, Penfold, and Phillips (1937a), studying *Taeniarhynchus saginatus,* found an increase of 9–12 proglottides per day and a loss of 8–9 proglottides during the same period. Growth thus exceeded apolysis slightly. In an apolytic tapeworm, growth during early life may be expected to exceed apolytic loss, whereas in later life it should merely keep pace with it, and later still should lag behind.

Problems of Tapeworm Synecology

HOST-ONCOSPHERE RELATIONSHIPS

After a tapeworm leaves the egg membranes, it passes during its life cycle through three stages – oncosphere, metacestode, and strobila. The oncosphere – or as some writers call it, the hexacanth embryo – has three pairs of peculiar hooks and no defined internal structures, except perhaps a pair of flame cells. It is present, with scarcely any structural variation, in the life cycle of all tapeworms that have been fully studied, and it provides the strongest argument for an evolutionary origin of the very diverse modern types of tapeworms from a common ancestral stock. However, since it is unknown outside tapeworms, it provides no clue as to what the ancestral stock may have been.

The escape of the oncosphere from its enclosing membranes takes place only in the gut of the appropriate intermediate host under the influence of enzymic digestive juices. There may be some degree of correlation between "shell" thickness and the host digestive powers such that in the wrong type of host the oncosphere is not liberated or is digested entirely.

Within the intermediate host, the oncosphere migrates from the gut lumen through the gut wall to the nearest lymphatic or serous space, or into the blood vascular system. In an insect or crustacean this migration brings it into the hemocoel, where development into the next stage proceeds uneventfully. In a vertebrate host, however, the migration brings the oncosphere into a capillary blood vessel or a capillary lymphatic vessel. In this case it may be carried passively by portal circulation to the liver and impacted there, or it may be carried by the lymphatic system to the general venous circulation. It is then carried by embolism to the lungs, brain, or muscles and impacted there.

The great number of cases in which the late oncosphere or the early metacestode environment is an insect or crustacean hemocoel; the deliberate migration made by many oncospheres, after impaction in the liver, to reach the peritoneal cavity of the host; and the phenomenon of impacted oncospheres which cannot migrate creating their own serous environment within a reaction membrane formed by the host's tissues –

all these circumstances go to suggest that tapeworms were originally parasites in serous or lymph spaces, and that their adaptation to a life in the alimentary tract of vertebrate animals came much later in their evolutionary history.

A high rate of mortality among oncospheres may occur before they leave the egg membranes. According to Essex and Magath (1931), less than 75 per cent of the eggs of *Dibothriocephalus latus* from human hosts, and less than 1 per cent of the eggs from this same species from canine hosts, liberate oncospheres. Wardle and Green (1941b) were unable to confirm this statement, however. The viability of eggs of *Hymenolepis fraterna* produced in the rat declines from a maximum at the time of passage from the rat until it is completely lost by the 11th day after leaving the rat (Shorb, 1933). A high rate of oncosphere mortality may also occur after they reach the intermediate host. Bullock and Curtis (1924), studying the development of oncospheres of the cat tapeworm *Hydatigera taeniaeformis* in the livers of rats, found that a large proportion of the impacted oncospheres died early and were replaced by scar tissue.

That these oncospheres are killed by a host reaction is suggested by the investigations of Miller (1930–34), who has shown that rats can be immunized against infestation by such oncospheres by inoculation with material from adult tapeworms, or with serum from a rat already infested. Such immunization, however, does not prevent oncospheres already firmly established in the liver from developing further. The immunity of the rat to reinfestation will last 167 days, and the offspring of an immunized or a naturally infested female rat will show an immunity for a few weeks after birth. Similar immunization can be provoked by inoculation with material from *Taenia pisiformis*, a dog tapeworm, indicating that the antigen-antibody mechanism is probably a group reaction, called forth against any species of *Taenia* or closely related genera but not against other tapeworm genera.

Campbell (1936) confirmed Miller's findings that intraperitoneal injections of the whole worm (either larval or adult), or of chemical fractions of the whole worm, are able to stimulate resistance of a rat to infestation with larvae of *Hydatigera taeniaeformis*. He found that although extracts of whole worm – or of such chemical fractions of whole worm as the globulins and nucleoproteins, either dilute saline-soluble or saline-insoluble, and the albumins – from fresh material provoked a high degree of resistance, the albumins of dried worm material and the metaproteins provided little if any protection. Total immunity was found to have two parts, as it were – an early immunity and a late immunity – which seemed to vary independently. The latter was also present as a natural reaction in the controls. Thus albumins from fresh material and nucleoproteins of neutral extracts produced a relatively high degree of early immunity but a late reaction less than that of the controls; whereas albumins from dried material and a dilute saline extract produced practically no early immunity but a late immunity which was much greater than that of the controls. It may be noted that reactions which prevent larvae from appearing in the liver of immunized animals constitute what Campbell called "early immunity"; reactions which caused the destruction of larvae already in the liver he called "late immunity."

All the rats in a single experiment, controls and treated, received the same number of oncospheres – the dosages varying between 200 and 700 per rat – passed into the animal's stomach by means of a glass syringe and a rubber catheter. Immunization of the experimental animals was made 8–10 days before the oncosphere-feeding by 6 intraperitoneal injections, on alterate days, of 1 cc. of a 1 per cent suspension of the respective antigen in 0.9 per cent sodium chloride solution. The animals were autopsied 6 to 7 weeks after infection. Living cysts were 3 to 7 mm. in diameter; dead cysts were of pinhead size and hard. Campbell's procedure for estimating quantitatively the degree of immunity is of considerable interest:

"If we assume that the total number of larvae (dead and alive) found in the controls represents the total number of available infective larvae, we can reduce results from the various experiments to a common comparable basis, namely, the ratio (or percentage) of larvae found in treated animals to those found in the controls. The early immunity can then be expressed as the ratio of the number of larvae failing to appear in the liver (total number in controls — total number in immunized) to the number of available larvae (total number of larvae in controls). The late immunity will then be the ratio of the number of dead larvae to the number which could have encysted and been destroyed (total number of larvae in controls). The total immunity (early plus late) therefore becomes the ratio of the difference between total number of cysts in controls and number of living larvae in immunized rats to the total number of cysts in controls.

"These ratios have been given . . . in the following manner:

$$\text{Early immunity} = 1 - \frac{T^i}{T^c} \text{ or } \frac{T^c - T^i}{T^c}$$

$$\text{Late immunity} = \frac{D^i}{T^c} \text{ for immunized animals and}$$

$$\frac{D^c}{T^c} \text{ for controls (natural immunity)}$$

$$\text{Total immunity} = 1 - \frac{A^i}{T^c} \text{ or } \frac{T^c - A^i}{T^c}$$

in which T^i and T^c represent the total number of cysts in the immunized and control animals, respectively, D^i and D^c the number of dead cysts in the immunized and control animals and A^i the number of living larvae in the immunized animals." Campbell (1936).

Thus, for example, a group consisting of eight animals (immunized) showed an average of 29.5 cysts per rat, all of which were dead, while the accompanying controls contained a total of 111 cysts per rat, of which 17.6 were dead. The early immunity of the immunized animals was therefore 111 — 29.5/111, or 0.74. The late immunity was 29.5/111 or 0.26, and the total immunity was 111 — 0/111 or 1.0. The natural immunity of the accompanying controls was 17/111 or 0.15. It may be noted that early immunity for the experiments as a whole varied from 0 to 1.00 (complete), but the late immunity varied only from approximately zero to less than half the possible value. The cause of the differences was not ascertained.

With regard to the occurrence of natural immunity, it is interesting to note that Fortuyn and Feng (1940), using mice for similar experiments, found that not all strains of mice are equally susceptible to infection with *Hydatigera taeniaeformis,* and in one particular strain the female of the species was less resistant than the male. Crossing of the two strains led to offspring which tended to be resistant, but the lower resistance of the female was apparent in the hybrid. Development of the worm in the hybrid mice was often incomplete, producing abortive cysts appearing as spots in the liver. There were often no real cysts. In the parent strains, however, infected livers often showed real and abortive cysts together. It was uncommon to find only aborted cysts (*Helminthological Abstracts*, 1942, of Fortuyn and Feng, 1940).

Larsh (1943–46) was able to produce a similar immunity in mice to infection with *Hymenolepis nana* var. *fraterna* by injecting intraperitoneally suspensions of fresh adult worm tissues. As the result of such treatment, Larsh found that only a quarter of the cysticercoids in the experimental mice were able to develop, as compared with control animals to which an equal number of eggs had been fed. Some degree of protection can be transferred in this way from mother to offspring—transferred both *in utero* and in the milk—but the extent of resistance thus induced in young mice was much less than when the mother was infected naturally with the tapeworm.

It is unfortunate, on the whole, that the physiology of the oncosphere stage has been studied so slightly, as contrasted with that of the metacestode and strobilar stages. It is probable than an investigation of oncosphere physiology would be the most fruitful line of attack upon two important problems of tapeworm biology—the evolutionary origin of tapeworms and the nature of host specificity.

HOST-METACESTODE RELATIONSHIPS

The larval stage begins with the loss of the oncospheric hooks and ends with the appearance of serially arranged genitalia. Since it is derived directly from the oncosphere by tissue differentiation, the solid type of metacestode—whether plerocercoid or plerocercus (a spherical type of solid larva)—should be more primitive than the vesicular or bladder worm type of larva, whether cysticercus, coenurus, or echinococcus. This assumption is supported to some extent by the almost universal occurrence of the solid type – free or encysted – among tetraphyllidean tapeworms, which seem undoubtedly primitive. It may be that the bladder worm types have evolved from solid types which, habitually marooned in nonserous host locations by the narrowing caliber of blood vessels, provided their developing holdfasts with a serous environment by replacing the internal tissue with a transudate from the host blood.

An apparent choice of position within the host is shown by some metacestodes. According to Newton (1932), the intramuscular plerocercoids of *Triaenophorus spp.*, common in western Canada in the fish genus *Leucichthys*, are distributed mainly (80 per cent) in the anterior epiaxonic muscles, only 10 per cent occurring in the posterior epiaxonics and 10 per cent in the hypoaxonics. In the burbot (*Lota*) in the same area, Miller (1944) found such plerocercoids almost exclusively in the liver. Plerocercoids of *Dibothriocephalus latus* in western Canada are found, by some observers, mainly (80–90 per cent) on the peritoneal surface and to a much lesser extent in the musculature, though such is not the experience of the present writers.

In the case of *Cysticercus bovis*, the metacestode of the taeniid form *Taeniarhynchus saginatus* and a common cosmopolitan parasite of cattle, Cousi (1933) found among 621 animals 84.37 per cent with heart muscle infestations, 51 per cent with masseter muscle infestation, and only 42.19 per cent with tongue muscle infestation. Bullock and Curtis (1924), among several thousand metacestodes of *Hydatigera taeniaeformis* occurring in rats, found only one that was not located in the liver. It may be presumed that with this metacestode species, the liver acts merely as a sort of filter for oncospheres traveling in the portal circulation, since they will develop equally well in the subcutaneous tissue when transplanted there.

A similar mechanical explanation may account for the predominance of metacestodes of the dog tapeworm *Echinococcus granulosus* in the liver of humans but in the lungs of sheep and moose, and for the predominance of the metacestodes of the human-frequenting tapeworm *Taenia solium* in the tongue of hogs but in the eye and nervous system of man. Brumpt (1936), discussing the order of preferred locations of this metacestode when using man as a host – the eye (46 per cent), nervous system (40 per cent), skin (6.32 per cent), muscles (3.47 per cent), and other organs (3.22 per cent), as determined by Vosgien (1911) – suggests that such apparent choice of location is due not to the accident of narrowing blood vessels, but to a definite tropic response on the part of the oncosphere. Solomon (1934) has described definite migrations of the metacestode of the dog tapeworm *Taenia pisiformis* from the liver of rabbits to the peritoneal cavity. Bacigalupo (1933) observed similar wanderings by the metacestode of *Echinococcus granulosus* even after the holdfast had formed, although Coutelen (1936) was unable to confirm this.

In the case of the metacestode of *Taenia solium* it seems difficult, if a mechanical explanation is excluded, to account for the definite range of preferred locations within the human eye — they are, in order of occurrence, the retina, lens, conjunctiva, anterior chamber, orbit, and only occasionally the pupil and iris — and to explain why the infested human brain should show seven times as many metacestodes in the brain tissue and meninges as in the brain ventricles.

Metacestode migration is eventually checked by the deposition around the parasite of a zone of fibrosis, the adventitious membrane, left as an inflammatory residue exuded by the irritated host tissue. The formation of this exudate has been described by Bullock and Curtis (1924) for the metacestode of *Hydatigera taeniaeformis*; by Antonow (1932) for the metacestode of *Taenia solium* in the human brain; and by Solomon (1934) for the metacestode of *Taenia pisiformis*.

The inflammation is commonly preceded by a mobilization of eosinophils, and after the inflammation subsides an area of infiltrated "small, rounded" cells is left between the zone of fibrosis and the healthy cells of the surrounding host tissue. The gradual thickening and contraction of the fibrosed layer deprives the parasite of nutriment, and it dies. Permeated by a fluid exudate from the blood, it swells to several times its original volume, becomes gelatinized, and is then destroyed by phagocytosis or replaced by calcium carbonate and calcium phosphate. There is thus the common pathological picture of an inflammatory reaction accompanied by cell proliferation and followed by fibrosis.

Antonow, discussing in detail the formation of the adventitious membrane in the case of cerebral cysticercosis in man, found young cysticerci, which were alive at the time of host death, to be enclosed in a thin membrane composed of an outer layer of granulation tissue containing giant cells. Around older cysticerci, which had died, the membrane was thick and had in addition an inner connective-tissue layer, giant cells appearing in this layer but not in the granulation layer. As a final stage, there was a single layer of hyaline connective tissue. Antonow rejected the hypothesis of membrane formation from nervous tissue or from the walls of the blood vessels, except occasionally, and suggested the possible elaboration of the membrane from plasma cells transformed into fibroblasts.

The absence of such fibrosis around the metacestodes of some tapeworms, notably of *Dibothriocephalus latus*, is worthy of investigation, as is the apparent nonsusceptibility of such metacestodes to calcification. A possible explanation of the difference in degree of inflammatory reaction provoked by different metacestode species may lie in the nature of the internal proteins of the tapeworm. That such proteins can be intensely irritant to the host has been shown in several cases, notably in the case of the hydatid cyst of man — the metacestode of the dog tapeworm *Echinococcus granulosus* — whose rupture commonly provokes anaphylactic shock in the host. In at least 70 per cent of human cases of hydatidosis, an intradermal inoculation of hydatid fluid will provoke a violent dermal reaction, the basis of the Casoni test for hydatidosis (see Kellaway and Fairley, 1932). That the host becomes immunized to the irritant action of hydatid proteins is suggested by the failure of such tests in cases of long-standing infestation, or in cases where previous surgical operation has permitted slight leakage of hydatid fluid into the host tissues, or in the case of ruminant hosts, which presumably are hosts of longer evolutionary standing than humans. The existence of an antigen-antibody mechanism in such cases is demonstrated by the occurrence of precipitins in the blood sera of animals harboring vesicular metacestodes (see Trawinski, 1936), and by the response of 90 per cent of human cases of recurrent or residual hydatidosis to a complement-fixation test similar in principle to the Wassermann test for syphilis.

Due to the early fibrotic isolation of a metacestode, any injury it causes the host is usually functional rather than pathological, and arises chiefly from the mechanical pressure of the growing metacestode – as in the case of hydatid injury – or of the degenerating metacestode – as in the case of human epilepsy induced by cysticercosis – upon the surrounding tissues. The possibility of metacestode irritation being sufficiently intense, in spite of fibrotic isolation, to induce malignancy is illustrated by the common occurrence of cancer of the liver in rats infested by the larvae of *Hydatigera taeniaeformis*, a phenomenon first pointed out by the French observer Borrel (1906) and in recent years studied in some detail by Curtis, Bullock, and Dunning (1920–34) and by Mendelsohn (1934).

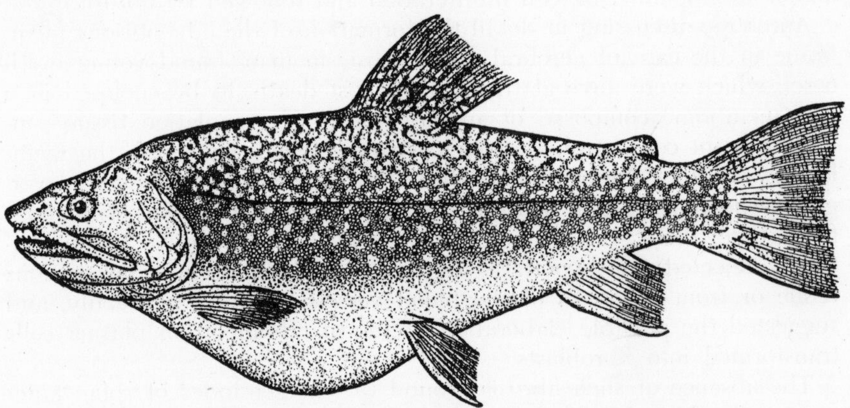

FIG. 57. Ascites in fingerling salmonoid infested with intrahepatic dibothriocephalid plerocercoids.

Following ingestion of the eggs of the taeniid by the rat, such eggs lose their outer membrane through the action of the rat's digestive juices, and the liberated oncospheres attach themselves to the mucosa of the intestine and work their way into blood vessels in the gut wall. Carried to the liver by the portal circulation, each oncosphere becomes lodged within a capillary vessel somewhere between the periphery and the center of a liver lobule. At this stage the oncosphere is very small and solid and is a multicellular, spherical body. The smallest observed by Curtis *et al.* was 15 μ and was found 21 hours after infection.

During the early days of infestation, larval growth and development are very rapid. During the first week there is an exudative inflammation from the host tissues, associated with a degeneration or necrosis of the liver tissues bordering the organism. About the 6th day after infection, the larvae are visible to the naked eye as clear, translucent dots or vesicles on the surface of the liver, sometimes surrounded by a whitish or yellowish opaque ring. Typical host cell proliferation begins from the 8th to the 10th day and reaches maximum activity after the 15th to 20th day, after which the active processes gradually subside. The cells participating in this proliferation are probably both endothelial and connective tissue cells, and the proliferation is accompanied by the formation of a vascular fibrillar matrix.

Larvae which fail to develop do not call forth such cell proliferation, but die early and are replaced by scar tissue. The dead larva is surrounded and penetrated by polymorphs which soon disintegrate. The necrotic zone around the dead larva is replaced by mesothelial cells which grow into and gradually obliterate the space which the larva occupied. Where the larva is alive, cell proliferation subsides after the 16th day, leaving the larva surrounded by the fibrous adventitious layer thus produced. The cyst continues to grow and projects like a blister from the surface of the liver.

According to Bullock and Curtis (1924), among 26,172 experimentally infected albino rats, of which 13,120 had survived the eight-months minimum period before malignancy is evident, 3,285 developed hepatic cancer. Usually only one cyst in the liver became malignant, the rest remaining benign. Cysts from hosts with a single cyst showed a higher percentage of malignancy than cysts from hosts with five or more cysts. The tumors arise in the adventitious layer, nearest the liver, and are mostly spindle-celled or polymorphous-celled sarcomata. According to Mendelsohn (1934) they originate from normal cells resident in the adventitious layer that differ from normal fibroblasts. The stimulus to malignancy does not come from a dying or dead parasite, since nearly all malignant cysts contain a healthy metacestode 12–24 mm. in length. It may be noted, too, that tumors arise only after an infestation of relatively long standing, usually between 248 and 676 days after initial infection. Nearly 80 per cent occur between the 11th and the 17th month after initial infection. Seventy-eight per cent of the cancerous rats are 13–19 months old. Between the earliest appearance of the tumor and the death of the rat a period of 24 days elapses.

HOST-STROBILAR RELATIONSHIPS

The term "strobilar stage" is applied to the wormlike, sexual phase of the tapeworm life cycle, characterized by an everted holdfast and by multiplied reproductive organs arranged in metameric succession. External segmentation may or may not be present – it is not an invariable characteristic of tapeworms – and even when present does not necessarily correspond with the sets of reproductive organs.

With a few exceptions, notably the genera *Stilesia* and *Thysanosoma* in the bile ducts of sheep, the environment of the strobilar stage is the small intestine of a vertebrate animal, usually the middle third of the small intestine, its exact position being determined, possibly, by the degree of saline and glucose concentration optimum to it. That it is influenced by enzyme concentration seems doubtful. Enzyme concentration in the lower small intestine is low, and the strobila is adequately protected by the layer of excreted fatty acids on the body surface and by its chitinoid cuticle. Even during the transition of the metacestode from the intermediate to the definitive host, when it runs the gauntlet of gastric and duodenal enzyme attack, the holdfast and growth zone are adequately protected by their invagination within the metacestode body; and when the holdfast and growth zone evert, under the influence of bile salts in the duodenum, protection from tryptic digestion is ensured by the cuticle (Waele, 1933, 1934). A slight antipeptic, but no antitryptic, activity is shown by aqueous, saline, and alcoholic extracts of fresh tapeworm tissue, and by fractional alcoholic precipitates of saline extracts of fresh and dried strobilar material; but the influence of fatty acids in such extracts cannot altogether be discounted.

The number of strobilae that can live together in a single host individual varies with strobilar size. Small tapeworms such as *Echinococcus* and *Dipylidium* in a dog may number several thousands. The maximum number of individuals of *Dibothriocephalus latus* that one of the present writers (Wardle, Gotschall, and Horder, 1937) could rear in an individual dog was 27, with a total strobilar length of 14 meters. Petruschewsky and Tarassow (1933a, 1933b), investigating the numbers of this tapeworm in human hosts in the Karelia-Murmansk-Leningrad districts of Russia, found among 307 cases that 42 per cent had only a single worm, 22 per cent had two, 13 per cent had three, and the rest had more than three and less than fourteen. The maximum strobilar length in any one case was 90 meters. Tarassow (1934b), however, recorded a unique case of a 23-year-old male with 143 examples of this worm, measuring *in toto* 117 meters. In western Canada, the usual number in any human case is one or two.

The occurrence of premunition — that is to say, the prevention of infestation by an immunity established through an earlier infestation — has been suggested by several observers. On the whole, the results of experimental work have been somewhat conflicting, and the ability of a tapeworm, whether larval or adult, to produce a humoral antibody response has not been demonstrated sufficiently in many cases to permit generalization either for or against the premunition hypothesis. Reference may be made to the summaries of evidence concerning immunity provoked by parasitic helminths published by Taliaferro (1929), Sandground (1929), Clapham (1933), Peters (1936), Cameron (1937), Culbertson (1938), Ackert (1942), and Larsh (1945a).

So far as tapeworms are concerned, it may be said that there is some evidence that tissue-frequenting metacestode stages can provoke some degree of host resistance to further infection. The observations of H. M. Miller (1930–34) on rats infected with larval stages of the cat tapeworm *Hydatigera taeniaeformis* suggest: (1) that rats which harbor one or more larvae can resist completely any tendency toward superinfection when fed a large number of oncospheres; (2) that such resistance persists for more than two months after the larvae have been removed by surgical means; (3) that serum from such immunized rats, when introduced into uninfected rats, will confer protection from infection for a period of 26 to 36 days; (4) that the offspring of such immunized rats are protected from infection for six weeks after birth; and (5) that successful immunization of rats is also obtained by introducing into the body cavity any of a number of other substances. These other substances are: (*a*) fresh *Hydatigera taeniaeformis* material (adult) which has been frozen for three months; (*b*) powdered adult worm from which the lipids have been extracted; and (*c*) fresh material of *Taenia pisiformis, Taeniarhynchus saginatus*, and *Hymenolepis sp.*, but not powdered, dried material of these forms, nor fresh or powdered material of *Dibothriocephalus latus* or *Dipylidium spp.*

Campbell (1936), as stated earlier in this chapter, found that intraperitoneal injections of *Hydatigera taeniaeformis* tissue (adult or larval), or chemical fractions of the whole worm, were capable of provoking in rats varying degrees of resistance to infection with larvae of this worm. Whole worms, or such chemical fractions as globulins and nucleoproteins, either dilute saline-soluble or saline-insoluble, and albumins from fresh worm material, provoked a high degree of resistance. Albuminoid and polysaccharide fractions provoked a significant degree of resistance, but albumins from dried material and metaproteins produced little if any protection.

A similar protection has also been shown by Miller to be induced in rabbits by previous infection with oncospheres of *Taenia pisiformis*, and Kerr (1935) was successful in transferring such immunity to uninfected rabbits by injecting serum from the infected animals.

"Miller's work seems to show quite plainly that we have to do with an antigen-antibody mechanism closely similar to those studied by the bacteriologist. The mechanism is revealed in the form of active immunity, whether naturally or artificially induced, and in the form of a passive immunity, both congenital and artificial. It is not altogether surprising that it shows itself in the case of the larval somatic infection and not in the case of the adult intestinal infection. One point of interest is the successful active immunization with non-specific antigens. This recalls the group reactions so often found in helminthic immunological tests, of which a typical example is the complement-fixation reaction in the genus *Schistosoma* where Fairley, briefly summarised in 1933, has shown that seven species of *Schistosoma* provoke in their respective hosts the formation of antibodies, all of which will react to one antigen, prepared by extracting with alcohol the livers of snails infected with the cercarial stage of *S. spindale*." Peters (1936).

On the other hand, the evidence is conflicting whether or not definitive hosts are protected from further infection by a previous infestation with the strobilar stage. Grassi (1887), and again Joyeux (1920), believed that an infection of rats or of mice with *Hymenolepis fraterna* protected against reinfection. Hunninen (1935c) failed to find any cysticercoids in 38 mice given secondary infections, except in three which were reinfected only three days after the primary infection, and in which he thought the cysticercoids remained from the primary infection as hang-overs resulting from delayed development. Palais (1934) failed to produce superinfection in three rats with *Hymenolepis diminuta.*

Hearin (1941) obtained a high degree of acquired resistance against a second infection in mice as early as 12 hours after an initial infection with *Hymenolepis fraterna.* The immunity thus provoked was absolute for at least 102 days after the initial infection and for at least 141 days after removal of the initial parasite burden by repeated doses of tetrachlorethylene. No demonstrable immunity was obtained by introducing experimentally, by operation, the adult stage of this parasite in mice, which harbored as many as 12 tapeworms for a period of 9 days before the second infection was administered; and no active immunity was obtained by the intraperitoneal injection of as much as 32 cm. of viable adult tapeworm as long as 14 days before infection. An almost complete immunity, however, was produced in previously uninfected mice by repeated intraperitoneal injections of serum from immune animals.

Larsh (1945c) believed the resistance of mice to infestation with *Hymenolepis fraterna* may be due in part to the rapid rate at which the intestine empties itself. Normally, carbon ink will appear in the lower colon within 15 to 20 minutes after entering the mouth; but if opium is administered parenterally the rate of peristalsis is markedly slowed, and in such opiated animals there is an increased percentage development of cysticercoids, due presumably to the delayed passage of eggs.

Brumpt (1936) claimed that human hosts of *Taenia solium* are not subject to reinfection, multiple infections being due to several worms simultaneously acquired. The difficulty in superinfesting dogs with *Dibothriocephalus latus* (Wardle, Gotschall, and Horder, 1937) has been mentioned earlier, and the frequency of human infections with single individuals of *Taenia solium* or *Dibothriocephalus latus* is a matter of common observation. Penfold, Penfold, and Phillips (1936a) have noted the occurrence of only two cases of multiple infestation with *Taeniarhynchus saginatus* in 48 patients who acquired the infection in Victoria (Australia). Seddon (1931) failed to get reinfections in four sheep which had had a *Moniezia* infection and lost it, although these sheep were re-exposed to infection under conditions which resulted in the infection of three control animals. Boughton (1932) found evidence that young rabbits in Manitoba (Canada) were parasitized with *Cittotaenia* to the extent of 100 per cent between May and November, but older rabbits showed no infection.

In regard to artificial immunization, Seddon failed to reinfect sheep which had been fed a suspension of 15 grams of ground, ripe *Moniezia* segments. Turner, Berberian, and Dennis (1933, 1935) claimed to have provoked marked resistance by dogs to infection with *Echinococcus granulosus* by intramuscular injections of dried, powdered hydatid holdfasts. Ohira (1935) partly immunized kittens against *Hydatigera taeniaeformis* and puppies against *Dibothriocephalus latus* by subcutaneous injection or by feeding of an emulsion of the metacestode phases of these worms.

On the other hand, Shorb (1933) believed that breaks in the egg-production rate of naturally acquired *Hymenolepis fraterna* infections of mice merely indicated the loss of old infections and the development of new ones, which in some cases must have been overlapping. He believed he had found evidence of superinfestation when small worms which had shed no proglottides were found in company with larger ones which had lost proglottides in doubly infected mice but not in singly infected mice. Luttermoser (1940) found that chickens acquired little or no resistance against reinfection with *Raillietina cesticillus*, even when the primary infection was light.

Chandler (1939, 1940), from a series of carefully devised experiments, believed that the premunition effect of an existing *Hymenolepis diminuta* infestation in rats is proportional to the bulk of the worms in the intestine and is not influenced by the length of time that the primary infestation has been in existence. When the primary worms were removed by an anthelmintic, or by mechanically washing them out from the intestine after a laparotomy, the protective effect was entirely lost. Further, when some of the worms were removed by an anthelmintic, the worms left behind – freed from competition with their fellows – grew to a size characteristic of an infestation with the number of worms not eliminated. Oral feeding of mashed worms, either in one large dose or in repeated small ones, failed to influence the establishment or the growth of *Hymenolepis diminuta* in rats; and parenteral artificial immunization, either by the implantation of washed, living worms into the body cavity, where they became encapsulated and absorbed, or by a series of subcutaneous injections with saline suspensions of dried, powdered, whole worms, likewise failed to show any influence upon the intestinal worms.

According to Deschiens (1948), pathogenic substances of verminous origin are of two types: (1) toxic polypeptides, not identical with histamine, but including at any rate amine bases, related amino acids, or substances capable of liberating or forming histamine in the host body; and (2) allergenic and anaphylactogenic proteins, glycolipids, and polysaccharides. Such allergenic substances are responsible for the eosinophilia that commonly accompanies helminth infestation.

The influence of the strobilar stage of a tapeworm upon its host is usually benign, although medical and veterinary opinion is prone, on insufficient grounds, to ascribe to tapeworm infestation such host phenomena as gastrointestinal or neuromuscular disturbances, emaciation, and loss of body weight. There seems little evidence to support such assumptions, except where gross superinfestation occurs (Stafseth and Thompson, 1932; Sholl, 1934; Wetzel, 1934), and even then no noticeable metabolic disturbance or pathological change may occur. The presence of 3,000 to 4,000 individuals of *Davainea proglottina* in the intestine of a 12-day-old chick, for example, was reported by Taylor (1933) as causing no evident disturbance.

In the case of *Thysanosoma actinioides*, which lives in the hepatic, bile, and pancreatic ducts of sheep, Curtice (1890) reported that infected lambs were large-headed, with undersized bodies and hidebound skins, that their gait was stiff, and that they had difficulty in cropping the shorter grass. Some did not see well and apprehended danger poorly. The liver was smaller, the kidneys flabbier and paler, the lymphatics somewhat darker, and the muscles thinner and weaker than in normal animals. In all cases he found leanness of muscle and a diminution of fat. The symptoms and pathogenic lesions were in fact those of malnutrition. Hall (1929a) reported that the obstruction of the bile ducts caused inflammation of these ducts, and that the parasites caused alteration of secretion, with digestive disorders resulting. On the other hand, a careful investigation by Christenson (1931), accompanied by over 1,200 post-mortem examinations of infested and uninfested sheep, indicated no grounds for the statements of Curtice and of Hall. In well-organized feed lots no great damage is done to the sheep except where excessively heavy infestations occur, under which conditions the symptoms simulate those of malnutrition.

Penfold (1937a) rejected the popular medical view that the main symptoms of *Taeniarhynchus saginatus* infestation of humans are large appetite, loss of weight, nervous irritability, and pruritis *ani et nasi.* He affirmed that the symptomatology resembled that of duodenal or gastric ulcer, cholelithiasis, and, very occasionally, appendicitis. The most frequent symptoms were digestive disturbances and giddiness. A definite eosinophilia (13 per cent) occurred only once, while there was a relative lymphocytosis in 16 out of 20 patients examined.

Luttermoser and Allen (1942) found that a high protein diet counteracted the assumed ill effects of *Raillietina cesticillus* infestation of chickens, when increase in weight was the criterion. Infected birds fed 26 per cent protein gained weight at the same rate as uninfected controls. However, when the protein intake was limited to 13 per cent, the uninfected birds gained weight over six weeks faster than the infected ones. On the other hand, R. B. Miller (1945d) found whitefish in Alberta (Canada) that were parasitized by plerocercoids of *Triaenophorus spp.* were slightly shorter and lighter than nonparasitized fishes.

Essex, Markowitz, and Mann (1931) found that a marked fall in blood pressure occurred in uninfested dogs that were injected intravenously with dried and powdered *Taenia pisiformis* material, but did not occur in dogs which had previously been infested with this tapeworm. Koropov (1935) obtained similar results by injecting disintegrating strobilar material of the dog tapeworms *Taenia hydatigena* and *Multiceps multiceps.* He ascribed the effects produced to a stimulation of the vagus nerve by a toxin liberated by the tapeworm material and under ordinary conditions of infestation neutralized by the liver.

Tomita (1937), observing human cases of infestation with *Hymeno-*

lepis nana in Formosa, found a varying degree of anemia in all the 50 cases examined. This was due apparently to a diminution of the hemoglobin content of the individual cells. In 18 of the cases there was a leucocytosis. In 38 of the cases there was an eosinophilia, with an associated leucopenia in 35 instances. Lymphocytosis occurred in 23 cases. Where the blood changes were marked, there were symptoms of diarrhea, constipation, hunger pains, fatigue, slight pyrexia, facial pallor, anorexia, headache, melancholia, palpitations, vertigo, insomnia, convulsions, and nocturnal enuresis.

The literature concerning the symptomatology of tapeworm infestation, referring mainly to the infestation of humans with *Dibothriocephalus latus*, suggests that in such infestations, after periods of weeks or months, the host may show mild gastrointestinal or neural disturbances, such as voracious appetite, "creeping feelings," abdominal cramps, alternating diarrhea and constipation, nervousness, insomnia, and so on; and that there may be a fall in the red cell count to a value (in humans) between three and four million cells per cubic millimeter. There may even be a picture of mild hypochromic anemia. Leucopenia and eosinophilia are slight. In the bone marrow picture, erythropoiesis is slightly retarded. The polynuclear count shifts slightly to the left.

In a number of cases of *Dibothriocephalus latus* infestation of humans, ranging from 0.1 to 0.2 per cent according to locality – Finland being the area where the majority of such cases have been recorded – after years of chronic infestation, there appears a fairly rapid progress toward a picture of severe anemia. Glossitis and sclerosis have been observed only rarely, but there is marked gastrointestinal disturbance, achlorhydria, marked deficiency in the secretion of gastric juice, paresthesia of the hands and feet, and jaundice. There is diminished activity of the bone marrow, and leucopenia and thrombopenia may occur. There is a rapid fall in the red cell count to values as low as three million cells per cubic millimeter, and a more gradual fall to values below that, with occasional remissions during which the red cell count may rise again to values above three million. The color index is invariably above unity. The mean cell hemoglobin value is normal (32 micromilligrams or more), the mean cell volume abnormally high (110–160 cubic microns), and the mean cell diameter high (7.5–9.6 microns). Megaloblasts appear in the peripheral blood. Anisocytosis and poikilocytosis are much in evidence.

The resemblance between this extreme picture of tapeworm anemia and the Addison-Biermer type of pernicious anemia was indicated originally by Schapiro (1887) and definitely established by the detailed clinical studies of Schauman (1894). It has been confirmed by the observations of many later students of the question. In fact, the literature on the subject of this so-called "Bothriocephalus anemia" is enormous and cannot be fully analyzed here. Reference may be made to the discussions of the question published by Birkeland (1932), Castle and Minot (1936), and Wardle, Gotschall, and Horder (1937).

Observations upon the symptomatology of animals *experimentally* infected with tapeworm material, dead or alive, are unfortunately few and concern *Dibothriocephalus latus* almost exclusively. Schauman and Tallqvist (1907) fed dogs and rabbits with minced *Dibothriocephalus latus* and injected subcutaneously the products of tryptic digestion of fresh tapeworm material. They observed in some of their dogs, but never in rabbits, a fatally progressive anemia marked by a fall in the red cell count to less than half the normal value. Shikhobalova and Popova (1937) found that the injection of the albuminous and fatty substances of *Dibothriocephalus latus* into cats produced only weak reactions. One cat, after a course of 50 cc. injections of macerated worm for 20 days, developed a marked hypochromic anemia lacking the characteristics of pernicious anemia.

Wardle, Gotschall, and Horder (1937) infected a series of immature dogs with 20–40 plerocercoids of *Dibothriocephalus latus* each and observed over a period of 12 weeks a gradual fall in the red cell count, unaccompanied however by any significant changes in the leucocyte count, color index, serum calcium, or plasma phosphorus. The degree of anemia was never severe, nor were gastrointestinal or neural symptoms noticed. There was a lymphocytosis, attributed by these workers to the use of morphine sulphate, but apparently significantly greater than the control values. There was a slight fall in the polynuclear count and a shift to the left (see Cooke and Ponder, 1927) among the classes of polynuclears that indicated a graded physiological activity of the bone marrow. There was no evidence of eosinophilia or basophilia until the sixth week of infestation.

In a repetition of the experiments, using only 5 plerocercoids per dog for the initial infection, however, there was observed a slight tendency toward a fall in the red cell count, in hemoglobin values, in mature polynuclear count, and in leucocyte count; slight increases occurred in the lymphocyte and eosinophile counts. The changes were so gradual, however, and so subject to remissions, that the average values through 11 weeks of infestation agreed closely with the averages of the control animals. Presumably superinfestation is necessary to provoke changes in the blood picture of dogs within a period of 12 weeks.

Observations upon experimental infections of humans with living or dead *Dibothriocephalus latus* have been made by Le Bas (1924), Tötterman (1937, 1938), Tarassow (1937), and Wardle and Green (1941a). Le Bas infected two persons with two plerocercoids each and one person with one, and made clinical observations during periods of 107, 98, and 270 days, respectively. Diarrhea and constipation occurred during the 15th to the 21st days of infestation, coinciding with the first discharge of eggs. After the 21st day only subjective symptoms were observed, chiefly epigastric and caecal discomfort. General health was only slightly affected. There was no appreciable fall in the red cell count or hemoglobin content. There was a slight leucocytosis but no lymphocytosis. The eosinophile count took weeks to rise, reaching a maximum of 16.6 but soon returning to normal. There was no evidence in the sera of antibodies capable of fixing complement or of giving precipitin reactions with extracts of *Dibothriocephalus*. No undue skin reactions were produced by the intradermal injection of tapeworm material into infected persons.

Tötterman (1937) gave 0.3 g. of powdered tapeworm (*Dibothriocephalus latus*) or its equivalent in alcohol extract – which he believed to contain all of the anemogenic principle – daily during 2 to 4 weeks to 8 patients with *Dibothriocephalus* anemia. Five reacted with a reduction of up to one million in the red cell count, with little or no decrease in the hemoglobin value. Three cases of typical pernicious anemia gave no sign of this reaction, which Tötterman regarded as an allergic one – a hypersensitivity to the tapeworm toxin. Sievers (1938) was able to demonstrate complement fixation, using the sera of *Dibothriocephalus* carriers against alcoholic extract of the tapeworm, in only 10 out of 65 cases, and in 3 of these the reaction was only slight. Forty-four normal sera gave 2 slight positives. *Dibothriocephalus* antibody could be demonstrated only in 2 sera.

Tarassow (1937), after self-infection with 7 plerocercoids, experienced during a period of 36 days nausea, severe abdominal pain, and loss of weight (8 kg.) but no blood changes. In a later experiment with 6 plerocercoids, the red cell count dropped from a pre-experimental value of 4,760,000 to 4,270,000 at the end of two months, and there was a loss of 3 kg. in weight. After expulsion of the worms, the red cell count rose again to 4,750,000. Tarassow regarded this relatively slight fall in the red cell count as of great significance, which "m'a fait hâter l'expulsion des vers."

Wardle and Green (1941a) made 31 consecutive weekly observations upon a male, mature human initially infected with 5 plerocercoids of *Dibothriocephalus latus*. The blood picture on the whole was one of mild hemolytic anemia. The decline in the red cell count was very gradual and subject to remissions. The mean cell volume was higher than normal throughout. Mean cell hemoglobin and mean cell hemoglobin concentration values remained relatively stable. There was a relative lymphocytosis. The gradual increase in the percentage of young polynuclears, unaccompanied by a decrease in the percentage of mature polynuclears, together with the leftward position of the weighted mean throughout, suggested the graded physiological response of the bone marrow that characterizes anemias due to blood destruction. The eosinophile count, as in Le Bas's observations, rose to a maximum fairly early and then declined.

The Scandinavian observer Tötterman (1944a) has brought forward evidence to show that the distribution curves in tapeworm anemia and cryptogenic pernicious anemia are similar. There is no correlation between the size of the mean diameter with either the size of the standard deviation or of the red cell count. There is, however, an agreement between the red cell count and the size of the standard deviation. The distribution curve in severe tapeworm anemia shows tendencies which are characteristic of cryptogenic pernicious anemia. The opinion of Tötterman seems to be that patients carrying *Dibothriocephalus* may become hypersensitive to the cestode protein and develop anemia. Parenteral administration of alcoholic extracts of whole worm to two patients who had suffered from tapeworm anemia brought about a decline in the red cell count, which disappeared, however, when the injections were discontinued. Of the controls, some showed a temporary decline but recovered even though the injections continued.

In seeking an explanation for the blood-destroying influence of *Dibothriocephalus latus*, any direct blood theft or blood loss from mucosal erosion can be ruled out. Any anemogenic agent present must be some substance liberated by the tapeworm during the normal procedure of excretion, or liberated when the tissues of the worm disintegrate and undergo autolysis. The excretory products of *Moniezia expansa*, the only tapeworm whose excretory output has been studied, according to Brand (1929, 1933) consist mainly of carbon dioxide, succinic acid, lactic acid, and certain unidentified higher fatty acids. No myelotoxin has been demonstrated in tapeworm tissues although Essex, Markowitz, and Mann (1931), as stated earlier, demonstrated in *Taenia pisiformis* the presence of a thermolabile toxin that rapidly lowers the blood pressure of dogs when saline extracts of the dessicated worm are injected intravenously.

Seyderhelm (see Kingisepp, 1933), however, some years ago claimed to have isolated from *Dibothriocephalus* material three anemogenic substances which he termed "Bothriocephalin," "Bothriotoxin I," and "Bothriotoxin II." Nyfeldt (*ibid.*) failed to produce anemias in rabbits with Bothriocephalin but obtained anemias of a pernicious type (hyperchromic and megalocytic) with Bothriotoxin I – the fraction precipitated by 50 per cent alcohol from a saline extract of the worm – and with Bothriotoxin II – the fraction soluble in 50 per cent alcohol. Kingisepp (1933) tested the prophylactic effect of liver extract upon anemias produced in rabbits with Bothriotoxin I. Repeated, increasing injections provoked an anemia which was neither hyperchromic nor megalocytic and which was unaffected by liver extract. There was neither eosinophilia nor lymphocytosis. A similar anemia was provoked by a similarly prepared extract of fresh calf's liver and with an aqueous extract of *Gastrophilus* larvae (Insecta). Kingisepp was therefore inclined to attribute anemias of this kind to bacteria, which always contaminate the extracts. Phenolized extracts largely failed to produce any effect, although an effect was produced if injections of normal extracts were preceded by injections of suitably diluted phenol. Thus these experimental anemias are not specific and have no relation to the pernicious anemias of *Dibothriocephalus* carriers.

There is no evidence that a tapeworm interferes with known hemopoietic factors in the host. Bonsdorff (1939) described the results of a series of tests made with autolysates, boiled extracts, and alcohol extracts of *Dibothriocephalus latus* and autolysates of *Taenia* and *Ascaris* to determine the effects, if any, upon the anti-anemic factor of liver extracts. In most cases, the injection of treated liver extract into pernicious anemia patients was followed in a few days by injections of untreated liver extract. The effects produced were measured by reticulocyte and red cell counts and hemoglobin determinations. There was no conclusive evidence that the worm extracts exerted any inhibiting effect upon the efficacy of the liver extracts, a result which Bonsdorff regarded as opposing the allergic hypothesis of "Bothriocephalus anemia."

In a further series of experiments, Bonsdorff endeavored to find out whether the tapeworm interferes in some way with the activity of Castle's "intrinsic factor," which is probably a proteolytic enzyme. The mixing of various tapeworm extracts with gastric juice, trypsin, pepsin, and papain in no way decreased the digestive activity of these enzymes as measured by estimating the nonprotein in nitrogen after incubation, taking into consideration of course the worms own proteolytic activity. Moreover, there was no evidence that anti-enzymes occurred in the worm extracts, and worm protein was readily digested. However, all the extracts inhibited the proteolytic activity of gastric juice at neutral reaction; if the gastric enzyme is identified with Castle's "intrinsic factor," a connection between tapeworm infection and pernicious anemia may possibly occur. The proteolytic activity of the worms themselves—greater in *Dibothriocephalus* than in *Taenia* or *Ascaris*—is believed by Bonsdorff to be maximal at pH 4.0 and to be due to cathepsin.

In later experiments (1940) this same investigator found that fresh or dried *Dibothriocephalus latus* inhibited the digestion of casein by depepsinized gastric juice (human). The antiprotease effect was strongest between pH values of 6 and 9. It was destroyed by heat (80° C. for 20 minutes). The inhibitory substance was insoluble in ether or 96 per cent alcohol (ethyl). It was not dialyzable or precipitated by 50 per cent alcohol, but it was quantitatively precipitated by 90 per cent alcohol. The activity of aqueous extracts was independent of the pH values (between pH 1.7 and pH 9.0) at which they were prepared.

Bonsdorff examined blood and gastric secretions (Ewald-Boa's test meal) from carriers of *Dibothriocephalus latus* who had pernicious anemia. In 9 cases, the removal of the tapeworms caused a definite reticulocyte response and a blood regeneration. No anti-anemic treatment was necessary. The typical pernicious anemia marrow obtained by sternal puncture showed marked macroblastic and normoblastic regeneration 48 hours after the parasites were removed. In these cases, Bonsdorff considered the tapeworms to have been the cause of the anemia. In 5 other cases, however, liver extract was necessary to bring about a complete remission, and in these cases the observer believed the worm infestation to be merely incidental to the anemia. Bonsdorff found further that a proteolytic enzyme, active at pH 7.4 (probably Castle's intrinsic factor), was present in the gastric juice of 7 pernicious anemia patients whose blood picture was attributable to tapeworm infestation, and also in 6 cases of uncomplicated cryptogenic pernicious anemia.

Castle's theory of course postulates the interaction of an endogenous intrinsic factor (possibly a proteolytic enzyme) with an extrinsic factor in the animal's diet for the successful accomplishment of hemopoiesis. It is interesting to note, therefore, that in later work (1943) Bonsdorff found that after expulsion of *Dibothriocephalus latus* from pernicious anemia patients, blood remission failed to appear when substances rich in protein – meat, milk, Hammarsten's casein, yeast, commercial peptone – were omitted from the patients' diet.

A summary of Bonsdorff's views was recently published by him in English (*Journal of Hematology*). He has found only 96 instances of tapeworms associated with anemia among 11,000 medical cases. Cryptogenic pernicious anemia and worm infestation are not uncommon, however, but in the former condition there is no remission after anthelmintic treatment. His observations indicate that where tapeworm and pernicious anemia occur together the gastric juice contains the intrinsic factor, and that lack of the extrinsic factor is not an essential cause. However, there may be a decreased secretion of the intrinsic factor and a relative deficiency of the extrinsic factor. He suggests that the worm interferes with the interaction between the two factors. In manifest pernicious anemia, the worm occurs higher in the intestine than usual – that is to say, in the duodenum or jejunum rather than the ileum; and Bonsdorff believes the interference with the factor interaction to take place only when the worm is thus out of its normal position.

The view that blood destruction may be provoked by the liberation into the blood stream of fatty acids by a disintegrating tapeworm was put forward many years ago by the Scandinavian workers Faust and Tallqvist (1907). Tallqvist demonstrated the presence of hemolytic lipids in the tissues of *Dibothriocephalus latus*, and later, in collaboration with Faust, he identified the hemolytic substance as cholesterol oleate. Hydrolysis of the cholesterid and the absorption of the oleic fraction into the blood stream of the host were therefore assumed to be responsible for "Bothriocephalus anemia." In support of this hypothesis were the experimental findings that a strongly hemolytic chyle, rich in sodium oleate, appeared in dogs fed with oleic acid; and that such feeding with oleic acid over a period of eight months produced in dogs and rabbits an extensive red cell destruction.

The suggestion thus made was that under certain conditions, toxic quantities of unsaturated fatty acids may reach the blood stream by way of the lymphatic system. The conditions under which this might occur are, according to Bloor and Macpherson (1917): (1) an abnormality of the absorptive mechanism that allows excessive amounts of the hemolytic lipids to reach the blood stream; (2) a failure of the assimilative mechanism in the blood or tissues, resulting in an abnormal accumulation of these substances, either free or in the form of toxic derivatives; and (3) a decrease in the antihemolytic substances of the blood – that is to say, in the light of present knowledge, of the cholesterol content.

The percentage lipid content of a tapeworm is not high. In *Dibothriocephalus latus* it averages 12 to 15 per cent of the dessicated tissue. *Dibothriocephalus latus*, however, is an unusually large tapeworm ranging from 1 to 17 meters in length and commonly averaging in humans from 5 to 7 meters. It is characterized by a rapid and continuous disintegration and autolysis of sexually exhausted proglottides. Further, it remains within the host over a period of years. There is thus a steady and constant passage of oleic acid from the disintegrating worm to the blood stream of the host.

It must be admitted that a repetition of the Tallqvist-Faust feeding experiments by Beumer (1919) did not confirm the findings of those workers. Some support to their hypothesis, however, has been given by the findings of Wardle and Green (1941a), who have made the following assertions:

1. The blood picture of dogs and humans infected experimentally with *Dibothriocephalus latus* is one of *increased blood destruction* rather than of macrocytic anemia. The decline in red cell count is very gradual and subject to remissions; mean cell volumes are above normal; and mean cell hemoglobin and mean cell hemoglobin concentration values remain relatively stable. There is a decline in red cell diameter. Some degree of leucocytosis may arise from an increase in the lymphocyte count, and there is some suggestion of a graded physiological response of the bone marrow. Eosinophilia reaches a peak early in the infestation and then declines.

2. A somewhat similar picture is found to occur in rabbits which were fed with fatty acids isolated from the tapeworm *Moniezia expansa* and administered in quantities equivalent to the amounts liberated by the disintegration of 100 grams of tapeworm per week. There were similar marked declines in the red cell counts and white cell counts, high values of mean cell volumes, and declines in average cell diameter values. Mean cell hemoglobin and mean cell hemoglobin concentration values remained relatively stable, however, and no abnormal bone marrow activity was observed.

3. In contrast to acids of tapeworm origin, the administration of stearic, ricinoleic, and oleic acids provoked no changes beyond a decline in red cell diameter values and, in the case of oleic acid only, a decline in red cell counts. No changes were provoked by feeding tapeworm fats.

· CHAPTER IV ·

Origin and Evolution

Common zoological opinion concerning the origin of tapeworms looks upon them as having evolved by way of Cestodaria from some early, primitive stock of digenetic Trematoda. The prevalent hypothesis, formulated originally by Claus (1889) and elaborated by Odhner (1912) and Nybelin (1922), postulates a common ancestral origin of Cestodaria, Cestoda, and digenetic Trematoda from a proto-trematode stock. It is based upon presumed resemblances between (1) the miracidial, cercarial, and adolescarial stages of the trematode life cycle and the coracidial, procercoid, and plerocercoid stages in the life cycle of the caryophyllid, spathebothrid, and pseudophyllid types of tapeworm; (2) the genitalia of digenetic Trematoda and those of the above-mentioned tapeworm groups; and (3) the osmoregulatory systems of digenetic Trematoda and the three tapeworm groups.

Speaking of the genitalial resemblances, Odhner (1912) stated: "It is inconceivable that such a complicated system of ducts could arise a second time independently through mere convergence, and I am forced to see in this a decisive proof, hitherto insufficiently recognized, of the common origin of Cestoda and digenetic Trematoda." In regard to the osmoregulatory systems, Nybelin (1922) wrote: "A fundamental correspondence between the digenetic Trematoda and Cestoda is found in the single, terminal duct of the excretory system which runs to the posterior end of the body and has usually a terminal bladder, whereas the paired dorsal excretory canals of the monogenetic trematode, opening anteriorly, represent a totally different type."

Spengel (1905), on the other hand, argued for a common origin of Cestoda and *monogenetic* Trematoda on the grounds of: (1) the morphological similarities between the cestodarian genus *Amphilina* and the monogenetic types of Trematoda, if the boring apparatus of the amphilinid is assumed to be posterior in position and to be homologous with the posterior holdfast mechanism of the monogenetic trematode; (2) an acceptance of caryophyllid worms as Cestodaria with features in common with spathebothrid and pseudophyllid tapeworms; and (3) a presumed homology between the hook-bearing cercomer of the procercoid larva of certain spathebothrid-pseudophyllid forms and the posterior holdfast mechanism of the monogenetic trematode.

Both hypotheses assume the spathebothrid, caryophyllid, and pseudophyllid tapeworms to be more primitive than the tetrafossate types—

those tapeworms with four suckers or four bothridia. In evidence of this, Spengel stressed the occurrence of permanent uterine apertures in these three tapeworm types, while Nybelin stressed the occurrence among them of thick-shelled and operculated eggs and of ciliated postembryonic stages. Further, since according to both hypotheses the ancestral tapeworms must have been unsegmented, the caryophyllid forms are regarded as the most primitive of present-day tapeworms by those who consider them true tapeworms; but to those who regard Caryophyllidea as Cestodaria, the spathebothrids are the most primitive, since they lack segmentation, have well-developed uterine glands like those of digenetic trematodes, have structures similar to the so-called prostate glands of digenetic trematodes, and have separate male, female, and uterine apertures.

Both hypotheses demand acceptance of the view that proglottisation, segmentation, and apolysis – the shedding of sexually gravid segments from the body – are secondary phenomena, and at least one of the hypotheses demands acceptance of the view that the holdfast of the tapeworm is at its posterior end.

Plausible as the Claus and Spengel hypotheses appear, certain weighty objections can be raised against them. In the first place, the evidence that Cestodaria and Cestoda are closely related is weak, resting as it does chiefly upon the assumption that Caryophyllidea are cestodarian, and that they are intermediate in structure between Cestodaria and the spathebothrid-pseudophyllid tapeworms. This supposition ignores or minimizes the undoubted tapeworm features of Caryophyllidea – for example, the possession of a six-hooked embryo. Even Nybelin (1922) could not ignore such tapeworm features, and he accepted Caryophyllaeidae as a subgrouping of Cyathocephalidae. Hunter (1927b) regarded them as a true family of Pseudophyllidea.

In the second place, the alleged resemblances between the postembryonic stages of digenetic trematodes and those of spathebothrid-pseudophyllid tapeworms do not stand up to close examination. Admittedly both the miracidial and the coracidial types of embryo are ciliated; but whereas the former type has a mouth, gut, eyespots, flame cells, and somatic musculature, the coracidial type is essentially a ciliated, solid blastula with few or no traces of alimentary, sensory, and muscular structures. Furthermore, with the possible exception of *Cyathocephalus*, the coracidial embryo has three pairs of hooks of a type unknown among other flatworm groups. It might be supposed, too, that if the coracidium is an ancestral phase it would occur in the majority of tapeworm life cycles, but actually it is known mainly from four pseudophyllidean families – Bothriocephalidae, Haplobothriidae, Triaenophoridae, and Dibothriocephalidae. It is significantly absent from the life cycles of Caryophyllidea, Spathebothridea, and the pseudophyllidean families Amphicotylidae and Ptychobothriidae. Ruszkowski (1932c), it is true, demonstrated a coracidial embryo in the life cycle of the trypanorhynchan tapeworm *Grillotia erinaceus*, and it may well be that the coracidial phase is more prevalent among tapeworms than seems at present to be the case; but it certainly cannot be widespread.

In the third place, the holdfast organs of Trematoda and Cestoda are fundamentally dissimilar. Among digenetic Trematoda such organs are muscular, cuplike ingrowths of the body surface *(suckers)*, lacking a subcuticle and separated from the underlying parenchyma by a basement membrane. Among Cestoda they may also be cuplike suckers, similar histologically to those of Trematoda; but among the caryophyllid-spathebothrid-pseudophyllid tapeworms the holdfast organs are either lacking completely, are weakly represented, or are in the form of two *bothria* which are merely saucerlike or slitlike depressions of the holdfast surface, histologically similar to the mid-ventral and mid-dorsal grooves of the surficial body surfaces.

Among digenetic trematodes, the holdfast organs typically comprise one terminal sucker, perforated by the mouth – the so-called "oral sucker" – and one nonperforated, ventrally situated sucker – the so-called "ventral acetabulum." Thus the animal clings to its substratum and shifts its position when necessary mainly by movements of the whole body. The holdfast organs of Cestoda, on the other hand, are never confined to one surface but are situated on opposing surfaces around one pole of the body, so that the animal is attached *apically* to its substratum. It seems difficult to derive this arrangement from that prevailing among Trematoda, or to derive the tapeworm bothrium from any known trematode structure.

Finally, the most fundamental characteristic of the tapeworm, the complete absence of an alimentary system, is nowhere foreshadowed among Trematoda, whose evolutionary trend is rather toward an increasing complexity of gut structure.

If we accept the removal by Nybelin and by Hunter of the caryophyllid worms from their former position among Cestodaria and relegate them to a position among tapeworms somewhere near *Spathebothrium* and *Cyathocephalus*, there would seem to be little more in common between Cestodaria and Cestoda, apart from the lack of an alimentary system, than between Trematoda and Cestoda. The view expressed by many authors (cf. Bychowsky, 1937) that the two groups are closely linked – as subclasses Cestodaria and Cestoda of a class Cestoidea – is difficult to justify, although in these pages we have regarded Cestodaria as worthy of inclusion in the general term "tapeworm." The argument of Spengel that tapeworms originated directly from a proto-monogenetic trematode stock, resting as it did upon an assumed relationship between the latter and the caryophyllid worms – which he assumed to be Cestodaria – and the pseudophyllid worms, falls to the ground.

On the other hand, the Claus-Odhner-Nybelin hypothesis that postulates the common origin of present-day digenetic trematodes and present-day tapeworms from a proto-digenetic trematode stock is harder to answer, even if, in the light of present knowledge, we discount the alleged resemblances between the miracidial, cercarial, and adolescarial stages of the trematode and the coracidial, procercoid, and plerocercoid stages of the pseudophyllidean tapeworm as being superficial and adaptative. The gist of this hypothesis is, briefly, that: (1) the two-bothriate tapeworms are the most primitive of present-day tapeworms; (2) they are fundamentally similar to digenetic trematodes in many features, notably the osmoregulatory and reproductive systems; and (3) they have given rise by divergent evolution to the four-suckered and four-bothridiate tapeworms.

Baer (1950b), in an article published since this book was written, has also argued for consideration of a two-bothriate type as the ancestral tapeworm. For this author, Cestoda and Cestodaria represent divergent branches from a common ancestral stock. Just what this stock was – whether trematode or turbellarian – is not stated. From the proto-cestode branch of this stock there emerged what may be termed "proto-haplobothriids" (our term), forms with two bothria and four tentacles, parasitic in those primitive fresh-water fishes, Amioidea, and represented today only by that unique creature, *Haplobothrium globuliforme*. From the proto-haplobothriids there came three lines of evolutionary divergence to produce the present-day tapeworm types. Along one line came the "Diphyllidea" (Baer's term) of selachians, presumably those Tetraphyllidea whose four bothridia fuse in pairs, and the "Tetrarhynchidea" of selachians, presumably Trypanorhyncha. Another line produced disculicepitid forms and went on to terminate as Cyclophyllidea, giving off on the way lines of evolutionary divergence that produced the present-day Tetraphyllidea and Proteocephala. Yet a third line of evolution from the proto-haplobothriid stock gave off successively in time the "Ptychobothriidae," "Caryophyllaeidae," and "Diphyllobothriidae."

It seems clear that any hypothesis which derives tapeworms from a proto-trematode stock must stand or fall on the question of the primitiveness of the two-bothriate types. Unfortunately, in this matter no assistance can be expected from paleontology and very little from embryology. The host distribution and comparative morphology of tapeworms in general are, however, fairly well known, and there is a wealth of pertinent information available.

If the difossate types of tapeworm (Caryophyllidea, Spathebothridea, Pseudophyllidea) are more primitive than the tetrafossate types of tapeworm (Proteocephala, Lecanicephala, Tetraphyllidea, Trypanorhyncha, Cyclophyllidea), they should predominate in the tapeworm fauna of primitive host types – that is to say, in host types which have persisted with relatively slight morphological and presumably slight physiological changes over long periods of time. Further, the majority of the features of difossate tapeworms should show a closer resemblance to those of free-living Platyelminthes than should the features of the tetrafossates, and should foreshadow the latter. Finally, there should be some difossate forms which are aberrant in the direction of Trematoda, and others which are aberrant in the direction of tetrafossates.

Among animal groups which, in the concensus of zoological opinion, are old and persistent, mention may be made of the lampreys, chimaeroid fishes, notidanid and odontaspid sharks, sturgeons, spoonbills, polypterines, lungfishes, bowfins, gar pikes, clupeoids, salmonoids, cyprinoids, siluroids, anguilloids, esocoids, caudate amphibians, chelonians, boid snakes, varanid lizards, iguanid lizards, ratite birds, penguins, divers, petrels, herons, plovers, game birds, monotreme mammals, carnivorous marsupials, edentates, insectivores, bats, toothed whales, and lemurs. The homogeneity of some of these groups is open to question, but whether such groups as the ratite birds and the edentate mammals are regarded as taxonomic units or as groups of such units, their primitiveness must still be accepted.

The tapeworm fauna of many of these groups is incompletely known, but a considerable number of tapeworms have been recorded from some of them. From lampreys and chimaeroid fishes, no tapeworms are known. Those in present-day sharks and rays are mainly tetraphyllidean and trypanorhynchan types; no typical difossates have been recorded from sharks and rays. The tapeworms of the primitive notidanid sharks are unfortunately scarcely known, but *Grillotia erinaceus* has been recorded from *Hexanchus*.

Among primitive fishes, *Polypterus* is host to the aberrant armed difossates *Anchistrocephalus* and *Polyonchobothrium* and to the proteocephalan species *Proteocephalus sulcatus*. *Polyodon* harbors *Marsipometra*, an aberrant difossate. *Amia* has the aberrant difossate *Haplobothrium* as well as the tetrafossate *Proteocephalus ambloplitis*. *Acipenser* has the difossates *Eubothrium crassoides* and the dubious *Bothrimonus*, as well as the tetrafossate form *Proteocephalus singularis*. No tapeworms are known from the herring group with the exception of *Eubothrium fragilis*, nor from lungfishes; but salmonoid fishes harbor the only known species of *Cyathocephalus* and most of the Amphicotylidae except Abothriinae, which are found in the codfishes.

Woodland, in a series of studies, provided a very complete picture of the tapeworm fauna of tropical siluroid fishes. Of 42 tapeworm species found in fishes of the Amazon region, mainly siluroids, 34 were proteocephalan and 8 were tetraphyllidean, the latter belonging to the genera *Anthobothrium* and *Myzophorus*, genera peculiar in showing a tetraphyllidean type of holdfast and a proteocephalan arrangement of the internal musculature.

Among caudate amphibians, the characteristic tapeworm genus is the proteocephalan *Ophiotaenia*, which is also found, however, in colubrine and viperine snakes. In boid snakes the proteocephalan genus *Crepidobothrium* occurs. In varanid lizards – and also in proteroglyphid snakes – is the proteocephalan genus *Acanthotaenia*; the aberrant difossate form *Duthiersia* is restricted to varanid lizards, however.

The ostriches serve as hosts for genera of Davaineidae and Anoplocephalidae; the cassowaries have the dilepidid genera *Anomotaenia* and *Choanotaenia*. Davaineid forms also characterize the tinamous and the galliform birds. The divers and grebes harbor hymenolepidid and tetrabothriid species. Tetrabothriids occur also among the gulls, petrels, penguins, steganopodes, herons, and pigeons. The Charadriiformes (plovers) are rich in cyclophyllidean forms, especially Dilepididae. The difossate forms occurring in birds are members of the family Dibothriocephalidae, notably the genera *Ligula*, *Schistocephalus*, and *Dibothriocephalus*.

Linstowiinae (Anoplocephalidae) characterize monotreme mammals, marsupials, edentates, insectivores, lemurs and even primates. Toothed whales have species of tetrabothriids and also, of course, Cobbold's *Diphyllobothrium.* The difossates of mammals are again species of Dibothriocephalidae.

The above survey is not intended to be exhaustive. Without laboring the argument, further support for which may be found in the lists of hosts given by Meggitt, La Rue, Fuhrmann, Sprehn, and others, the following assertions may be made: (1) Difossate tapeworms occur relatively rarely in primitive host forms, such difossates as are found being in the main forms aberrant in the direction of tetrafossates. The relative absence from primitive hosts of Bothriocephalidae, Triaenophoridae, and Dibothriocephalidae – the families with typical ciliated postembryonic larval stages – is notable. (2) Proteocephalan genera, notably *Proteocephalus, Ophiotaenia, Crepidobothrium, Corallobothrium, Gangesia,* and *Acanthotaenia* are predominant in primitive host types. Common, too, are tetrabothriid forms, davaineid forms, and linstowiine Anoplocephalidae.

The view that Proteocephala are, on the whole, primitive tapeworms is generally accepted, and their close affinities with Tetraphyllidea have been stressed by authoritative students of the group such as La Rue and Woodland. The "collared" Proteocephala seem to be closer in this respect than the noncollared forms. The primitive features of the family Tetrabothriidae, their relative isolation among Cyclophyllidea, and their undoubted points of resemblance to abothriine Pseudophyllidea have been stressed by Nybelin (1922), who regarded them as specialized Pseudophyllidea.

Davaineidae were regarded by Fuhrmann as the most primitive of all the armed, rostellate tapeworms. Linstowiinae were placed by Baer at the foot of the anoplocephalid stem; he derived them directly via ophiotaeniid and oochoristicid forms from Proteocephala. Davaineidae he derived from Anoplocephalidae. Douthitt, on the other hand, placed *Andrya* at the foot of the anoplocephalid stem and derived Linstowiinae from the higher anoplocephalids.

On the basis of host distribution, the conclusion seems inescapable that tetrafossate tapeworms are more primitive than difossate forms, and that the most primitive of present-day tapeworms are the tetraphyllidean forms and the collared proteocephalans, which appear to be the results of divergent evolution from a common ancestral tetraphyllidean-proteocephalan stock. Common to these forms are suckers, proglottisation, segmentation, autotomy of gravid or near-gravid segments, localization of genitalia within the parenchymal muscle ring – although in this respect there is considerable variation of arrangement among Proteocephala – and between the marginal nerve trunks, a follicular condition of the yolk glands and testes, the possession of an apical organ on the holdfast, whether functional or vestigial, a nutritive area of parenchyma (medulla), a saclike uterus with a temporary egg-liberation opening, and a bilobed and compact ovary lying behind the yolk glands.

We must look, therefore, for an ancestral proto-cestode that had an apical organ, follicular testes and yolk glands, interneural genitalia, a compact and posteriorly situated ovary, and a tendency toward gut replacement by digestive parenchyma. Such features characterize to a large extent the present-day alloiocoelous Turbellaria, rather than any type of trematode. Alloiocoela are peculiar among Turbellaria in showing gut degeneration, evolution of follicular testes from compact testes, protrusible proboscis, chain zooid formation, and endoparasitism.

As early as 1897, Loennberg suggested a direct origin of tapeworms from rhabdocoel Turbellaria independent of, and probably earlier in time than, the origin of trematodes from a triclad turbellarian stock. Basing his arguments upon a detailed comparison between the genitalia of tapeworms in general and those of rhabdocoel Turbellaria, Loennberg put forward a phylogenetic scheme – too involved to be adequately discussed here but pictured graphically in Figure 58 – that later knowledge of tapeworm morphology has done much to strengthen. Obsessed, however, with the view that since the sharks are an ancient group, the present-day sharks and their parasites must also be ancient – a view not necessarily correct – he visualized the ancestral proto-cestode as akin to

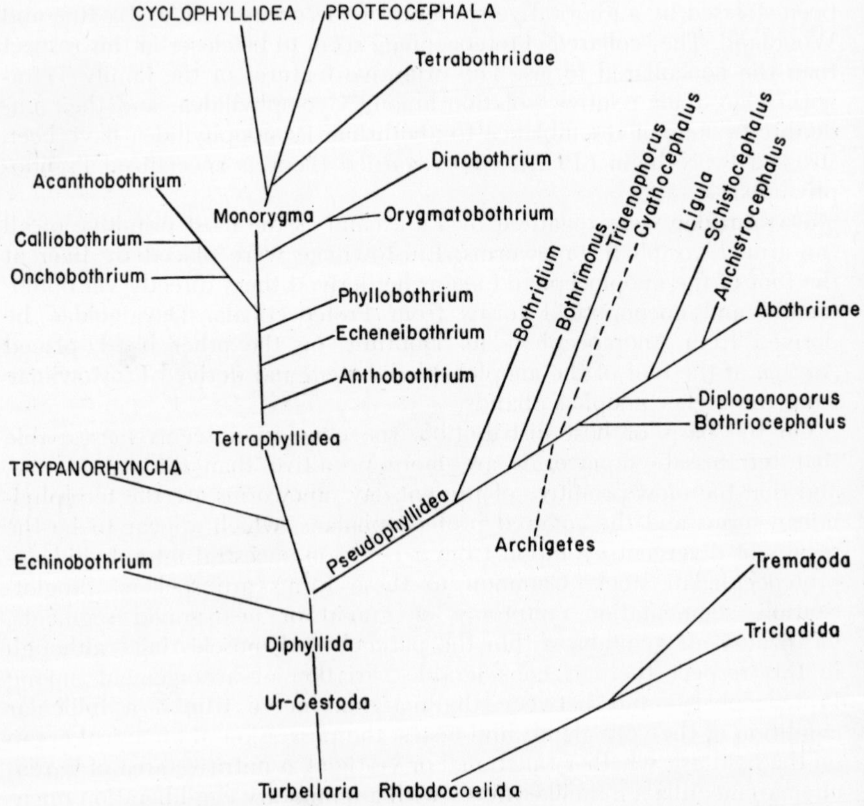

FIG. 58. Phylogeny of tapeworms. After Loennberg, 1897.

present-day Tetraphyllidea in structure, but having only two bothridia, projecting earlike from the dorsal and ventral surfaces of the holdfast end, and used as organs of locomotion rather than of fixation. From such "Ur-Cestoden," according to Loennberg's suggested phylogenetic tree (see Figure 58), the truly difossate types came off early, the trypanorhynchans somewhat later. The main stem continued through Tetraphyllidea to culminate in the taeniids, proteocephalans, and tetrabothriids.

In the light of present knowledge, particularly of Proteocephala, Loennberg's speculations as to the general lines of tapeworm phylogeny are no longer tenable; but his arguments for a turbellarian origin of tapeworms are still in accordance with present-day knowledge of tapeworm morphology.

The main difficulties in the way of any hypothesis of tapeworm origins are posed by (1) the six-hooked embryo; (2) the holdfast; (3) the tetraradiate symmetry; (4) the lack of alimentary organs; (5) the phenomena of proglottisation, segmentation, and apolysis; and (6) the relationship of the difossate and tetrafossate types of tapeworm to one another.

The phylogenetic significance of the six-hooked embryo or oncosphere cannot even be guessed. The views put forward by Stunkard (1937b) as to the origin of flatworms from a hypothetical planulalike ancestor are plausible, but no close comparison can be made between the oncosphere and any known type of planula larva. It can only be said that the situation within the tapeworm egg – with germ cells surrounded by yolk cells, the separation of the daughter cells derived from the first two blastomeres into an epiblast surrounding the yolk cells, on the one hand, and, on the other hand, a hypoblast which differentiates into macromeres and micromeres, and the epibole of the macromeres by the products of micromere division – is in keeping with what little we know of turbellarian embryology.

The holdfast of the typical tapeworm, again, cannot be closely homologized with any corresponding structure among Turbellaria or among Trematoda. Its identification with cestodarian structures has raised much controversy, the details of which will be found in the summaries of the question presented by the authorities quoted in the section dealing with Cestodaria. The orthodox view is that the holdfast represents a true, morphological, anterior end. Supporting this view are the facts that (1) it contains the main nervous mass; (2) it is the only permanent region of the tapeworm; (3) it is foremost during any locomotor movements that the worm is capable of making; (4) it is the most active region of the worm; and (5) gravid detached segments move with that border foremost which was on the holdfast side of the attached segment.

Whether there is any physiological gradient from the holdfast to the opposite end of the tapeworm has not been determined with certainty, but many observations upon tapeworm behavior support such a view. Fuhrmann (1931), a strong proponent of the holdfast as representing the anterior end, homologized it with the rosette organ of gyrocotylid

Cestodaria and believed both to be anterior in position. Ruszkowski (1932b), however, found the rosette organ to originate from the hook-bearing pole of the lycophorid larva of *Gyrocotyle* and so could not homologize it with the tapeworm holdfast, which is generally agreed to originate from that pole of the oncosphere *opposite* to that which bears the hooks.

On the other hand, there is much evidence to indicate that the holdfast is only a *physiological* or functional anterior end, and that morphologically it is posterior. The larval hooks of the oncosphere are always foremost during oncospheric movement. They originate from the opposite pole to that bearing the holdfast or giving rise to the holdfast. A shift of polarity has been shown to take place in many forms when the oncosphere changes to the first larval stage (cf. Essex, 1928a; Stunkard, 1934; Vogel, 1929b; Venard, 1938).

A fundamental bilateral symmetry is shown among tapeworms by the lateral position of the nerve trunks and the main longitudinal osmoregulatory canals, by the tendency for testes and yolk glands to be distributed as lateral bands, by the tendency for the genital apertures to be regularly alternating when marginal, and perhaps by the tendency toward diplogonadism shown by certain genera. Such bilateral symmetry is presumably an inheritance from a crawling ancestral phase. Upon this fundamental bilateral symmetry, however, there is superimposed a secondary tetraradiate symmetry. It is shown by the holdfast musculature, by the location of accessory nerve trunks, by the arrangement of suckers and bothridia, by the body musculature, by the surficial location of the genital apertures in some forms, and by the X-like ovary (in cross section) of some forms. The greater tendency of the muscles to show such tetraradiate symmetry suggests that it is a secondary adaptation to a mode of life not known to the ancestral proto-cestode; a mode of life neither crawling nor swimming, a mode of life that may paradoxically be termed "dynamically static," where a stationary position has to be maintained against a backward thrusting force (in this case gut peristalsis of the host) by continuous muscular tension and by continuous pressure of the apical region of the holdfast against the substratum (see Chapter III).

The absence of an alimentary tract, though paralleled among Cestodaria and Acanthocephala, is one of the most characteristic features of tapeworm anatomy. There is no evidence either from embryology or from morphology of such a structure among tapeworms, but there is some indication of a former digestive tissue such as is found today among certain rhabdocoel Turbellaria. One may cite the loose nature of the central parenchyma in most tapeworms, the wide separation of the lateral nerve trunks and osmoregulatory canals of the medullary region, the occurrence of a ringlike zone of parenchymal muscles (possibly former gut muscles), the ringlike osmoregulatory commissures, and the cortical or partly cortical position of testes, yolk glands and ovary in primitive, collared Proteocephala. There is also the occurrence of two parallel rows of cells starting near the holdfast end of certain larvae and ending at the opposite end in compact groups of brownish cells (see Rosen for *Dibothriocephalus latus, Triaenophorus crassus, Ligula intestinalis*; Essex for *Bothriocephalus cuspidatus*). Rosen regarded these cells as representing a vestigial gut, but Essex objected to this explanation on the grounds that such a large portion of the larva would be involved. If, however, they are regarded as representing not a former gut but a digestive tissue comparable to that of present-day rhabdocoel Turbellaria, Essex's objection is weakened.

The suggestion that the uterus represents a former gut cannot be altogether ruled out. It appears early in the development of a ripe segment, sometimes preceding the genitalia. When a permanent or temporary uterine aperture occurs, it is invariably surficial and median, as is the mouth of many present-day Turbellaria. Meixner (1926), from a close comparison of rhabdocoel morphology with trematode-cestode morphology, argued that the cestode uterus is homologous with the common duct or atrium of Turbellaria, which has become, in adaptation to increased egg production, a long, coiled uterus. This argument may hold good for the uterus of caryophyllid-spathebothrid-pseudophyllid types of tapeworm whose uterine tract would seem, on other grounds, analogous to, rather than homologous with, that of tetrafossate tapeworms; but among the latter forms, the commonest type of uterus is either a sac or a wide, median tube.

If the old mouth is not represented by the uterine aperture or by the line of dehiscence of the ripe tetraphyllidean and proteocephalan segment, it surely cannot be represented, as some authors have suggested, by the so-called "apical organ." This term has of course been used somewhat loosely for any structure in a wormlike animal that is apical or prestomodaeal in position. It has been used for such heterologous structures as the proboscides of Turbellaria, Nemertea, and Acanthocephala, and for the prostomia of annelid worms. Among tapeworms we find a great variety of such structures, not necessarily homologous – apical disks, end organs, apical suckers, retractile or nonretractile rostella, etc., especially among those groups that we regard here as primitive, such as Proteocephala, Tetraphyllidea, Lecanicephala, and Trypanorhyncha. The primary function of such structures is fact-finding – gaining information as to the nature of the environment in front of the animal. Only secondarily do they become a means of anchorage of the animal to its substratum, and only rarely do they become concerned in food-finding.

The commonest type of apical organ among tapeworms is a funnel-like depression of the holdfast end whose lining can be everted as a fingerlike proboscis. Not beyond credibility is the possibility that in a greatly variable, plastic, rapidly evolving proto-cestode stock, true suckers may have begun, as organs of fixation, at the points where such a terminal funnel was invaded by mid-surficial and mid-marginal grooves formed as the worm became secondarily tetraradiate. Bothria and bothridia, however, are organs of locomotion. An active, crawling tapeworm larva holds its holdfast end away from the substratum and maintains contact with the latter by the postholdfast region. Since the worm tends to rotate upon its longitudinal axis, the differential pressure exerted upon those regions that come most heavily and frequently in contact with the substratum may have stimulated the evolution of depressed areas (bothria) and raised areas (bothridia). However, such speculations are profitless since they lack experimental verification. Still, it may be doubted that the cuplike terminal invagination of the procercoid types of larva and of the cyathocephalid adult represent, as some authors have suggested, a former mouth.

The phenomena of proglottisation – repetition of genitalia; of segmentation – the partial division of the body into similar areas by deep grooves; and of apolysis – the tendency for the gravid or near-gravid segments to leave the parent body one by one – seem to the present writers the most cogent arguments in favor of a direct origin of tapeworms from a proto-turbellarian stock. Nybelin, obsessed with his hypothesis of the direct origin of tapeworms from a proto-trematode stock, argued for a primitive, unsegmented proto-cestode which became segmented secondarily as an adaptation to the strains imposed upon a ribbonlike body by host gut peristalsis, the anapolytic condition preceding the apolytic. His arguments ignored the lack of such segmentation among trematodes, its absence from long-bodied roundworms and acanthocephalans similarly exposed to host gut peristalsis, and its absence from many tapeworms, such as *Triaenophorus*. He also ignored the occurrence of a similar phenomenon called "delayed autotomy" among many Turbellaria.

According to Nybelin's view, therefore, a tapeworm is monozootic. It is an individual, originally unsegmented, which by reason of environmental strains becomes segmented secondarily. It thus contravenes Williston's Law of Evolution that there is a general evolutionary tendency from polyisomerism of the parts of a physiological system – the presence of approximately equal units – toward anisomerism – the occurrence of a few unequally developed units. In the present writers' view, the tapeworm is polyzootic. It is a linear colony of highly specialized zooids, originating from proto-cestodes in which new individuals were formed by simple autotomy from the parent body, but in which there appeared a growing tendency toward delayed autotomy, the new individuals tending to remain attached to each other and to the parent body.

The echoes of the mid-nineteenth century controversy as to whether tapeworms are monozootic or polyzootic have died away. Dollfus (1923) summarized the arguments for and against and gave judgment in favor of the monozootic view. Both viewpoints had had brilliant advocates. The monozootic conception of tapeworm individuality had been argued by Claus, Grobben, Hatschek, Hertwig, Haller, Goette, Benham, Ariola, Spengel, Nybelin, and Dollfus. The polyzootic conception had been argued by Beneden, Leuckart, Gegenbaur, Perrier, Boas, Kennel, Kükenthal, and Lang. The arguments of both sides were based upon the conviction that the homologies between difossate and tetrafossate tapeworms are very close, which may not necessarily be the case. We believe that a reconciliation between the two viewpoints is possible.

If a tetrafossate condition of the holdfast and a tendency toward the occurrence of segmentation and apolysis are accepted as primitive proto-cestode characteristics, the difossate forms cannot be more primitive than tetrafossate forms. Judged by host distribution, the most primitive of difossates would seem to be, on the one hand, Abothriinae, and on the other hand, Caryophyllidea. The abothriine forms have been regarded by most students of them as the most aberrant of difossate forms, in the direction of tetrafossates, by reason of their weakly developed, almost nonexistent holdfasts, craspedote and apolytic bodies, medullary testes, and cortical yolk glands. Caryophyllid forms are almost as aberrant in the other direction, showing neither proglottisation, segmentation, nor true, defined holdfast structures. Most typical and most advanced of difossates, so far as proglottisation, segmentation, and holdfast differentiation are concerned, are precisely those families – Bothriocephalidae and Dibothriocephalidae – which are least represented among primitive host forms.

Difossate forms appear to be essentially neotenic forms – persistent, sexually functional larval forms that may have originated independently, not once but many times, from proto-cestode types in which holdfast organs and delayed autotomy had not yet evolved. Such neotenic forms thus never inherited a true holdfast, but evolved what might be better termed a "pseudo-holdfast" of bothria formed by elaboration of mid-surficial grooves. They never possessed a primary segmentation produced by delayed autotomy, but evolved a secondary segmentation in response to strains thrown upon them by host gut movements. The difossate forms may well be regarded, therefore, as monozootic. The tetrafossate forms can only be regarded as polyzootic.

As a basis for further phylogenetic inquiry into the origin and evolution of tapeworms, the following tentative postulates may be suggested:

1. The proto-cestode was a parasitic member of an ancestral stock that gave rise also to the acoelous-alloiocoelous Rhabdocoelida (Turbellaria). It was small, slender, spinose, with neither suckers, bothridia, nor bothria but with a sensory apical organ that had an eversible and spinose lining. The alimentary tract had become replaced by a loose digestive parenchyma into which the eggs were discharged and which opened to the exterior under egg pressure by the dehiscence of a weak, linear area of the body wall, marking the former mouth. Traces of the former alimentary tract and mouth persisted in the larval stage. Premature autotomy led to genital repetition. Delay in the shedding of the ripe zooids produced a chain zooid effect in which the individual zooids became prematurely sexually mature. The ovaries were solid, paired, posteriorly situated, and medullary in position. The yolk glands were marginal and follicular. The testes were medullary, follicular, in two lateral bands. The embryo was hexacanth.

2. The present tetrafossate forms originated from proto-cestodes in which delayed autotomy had become established and in which a secondary tetraradial symmetry had developed. Invasion of the apical organ by mid-surficial and mid-marginal grooves gave rise to the four-suckered

condition. In response to holdfast pressure against the host gut mucosa, many forms evolved a postacetabular fold or collar, such as occurs today in many proteocephalan and lecanicephalan forms. From such collared forms there evolved the bothridiate forms – Trypanorhyncha and Tetraphyllidea. Through anthobothriid forms, there came from the collared proto-cestodes by another evolutionary line the linstowiine Anoplocephalidae, ancestral to present-day Anoplocephalidae. From them the davaineids, hymenolepidids, and dilepidids arose. By another line of evolution came the tetrabothriids, and from them the taeniids.

3. The difossate tapeworms are neotenic, persistent larval forms of the proto-cestode stock. Several lines of evolutionary divergence are represented. Caryophyllidea and Spathebothridea came off before suckers or bothridia or even bothria had evolved. Haplobothriidae may represent neotenic larvae of the proto-Trypanorhyncha. Amphicotylidae, Bothriocephalidae, and Dibothriocephalidae may be descendants of proto-tetraphyllidean forms, the four-lobed apical disk of the former two families being a reminiscence of the proto-bothridia. Segmentation among difossate forms represents not a true delayed autotomy but a response to the strains produced by host gut peristalsis, increasing with body size and with the increased nutritional demand for absorptive surface. The former apical organ is represented by the cuplike invagination of the procercoid stage and the adult cyathocephalid. The pseudoholdfast and its bothria have evolved from the exaggeration of midsurficial grooves.

4. Tetrafossate forms are polyzootic; difossate forms are monozootic. The occurrence of segmentation in both groups is an example of convergent evolution.

5. To the two rules that express the correlation between phylogeny of the host and phylogeny of the parasite – stated by Eichler (1940) as (*a*) Fahrenholz' Rule: the relationships of host animals can usually be determined directly from the systematics of their permanent parasites; and (*b*) Szidat's Rule: the relative phylogenetic age of the host animals can usually be determined directly from the degree of organization of their permanent parasites – we would add a third rule: (*c*) the phylogenetic age of parasites can be determined from the phylogenetic age of their hosts.

6. On these postulates, the most primitive of present-day tapeworms would appear to be Proteocephala. Next in phylogenetic significance are Lecanicephala, Disculicepitidea, Tetraphyllidea, and Trypanorhyncha. Present Cyclophyllidea represent an unwieldy and somewhat polyphyletic assemblage, among which Anoplocephalidae deserve separate ordinal rank. Davaineidae, Hymenolepididae, and Dilepididae also deserve separation as an order. Tetrabothriidae and Taeniidae should constitute a third order.

· CHAPTER V ·

History and Classification

Credit for founding the present zoological classification of tapeworms is usually given to Karl Asmund Rudolphi (1771–1832), author of the term "Entozoa," but actually Rudolphi was anteceded by J. G. H. Zeder, who in 1800 published *Erster Nachtrag zur Naturgeschichte der Eingeweidewürmer, mit Zufassen und Anmerkungen herausgegeben*, a Leipzig publication of 320 pages and 6 plates in which the parasitic worms then known were distributed among five classes. In a further publication, *Anleitung zur Naturgeschichte der Eingeweidewürmer* (1803), of 448 pages and 4 plates, Zeder distributed the adult tapeworms known to him among four families, and the bladder worms among five other families.

Human acquaintance with parasitic worms did not, of course, begin with Rudolphi and Zeder. A brief survey of early references to parasitic worms, compiled by Kreis (1937), points out that a probable though vague reference to the Guinea worm (*Dracunculus medinensis*) occurs in a 1500 B.C. papyrus discovered by George Ebers at Luxor (Egypt) in 1872; that the sheep liver fluke (*Fasciola hepatica*), the Guinea worm, and the Egyptian form of human schistosomiasis may have been known to the compilers of the Mosaic Code; and that from Egypt such early crumbs of helminthological knowledge may have been obtained by the Greeks.

Whether or not the symbol of Aesculapius, the snake coiling around the rod, well known as the cap badge of the British Army Medical Corps, is derived from the ancient practice of extracting the Guinea worm from human flesh by winding it gradually around a cleft twig, there can be little doubt that this worm, as well as the pinworm (*Enterobius vermicularis*), the beef tapeworm (*Taeniarhynchus saginatus*), and some bladderlike types of tapeworm larvae were well known to Hippocrates (460–377 B.C.), "Father of Medicine," and to Aristotle (384–322 B.C.), "Father of Zoology." Plutarch, taking his information from the geographer Agatharchides (*circa* 150 B.C.), described the Guinea worm as emerging from the limbs of inhabitants of the Red Sea regions.

References to parasitic worms in Latin literature are scanty, but Pliny (A.D. 25–79) used the term "Taenia," and Aetius (*circa* A.D. 200) described a method of extracting the Guinea worm without breaking it. Among the early Arabian physicians, inheritors of much of the ancient Greek science, Avicenna (980–1037) in his work "El Kanum" divided the parasitic worms into long worms (e.g., *Ascaris lumbricoides*), tapeworms (*Taeniarhynchus saginatus*), small worms (*Oxyuris*), and roundworms of the small intestine (*Ankylostoma*), and appeared to suspect the filariid origin of the disease elephantiasis. The differences between the tapeworm genera of humans, *Taenia* and *Dibothriocephalus*, seem to have been well known to medieval physicians, and Plater (1656) referred to the latter genus as *Lumbricus latus.*

The first printed work on helminthology was the *Exercitatio de vena Medinensis* of George Hieronymus Welsch (1624–77), published in 1674 at Augsburg. Welsch discussed therein the prevalent view that parasites originate as reaction products of tissue inflammation – the so-called "abiogenesis theory" – and discussed whether or not the Guinea worm was animal in nature. The abiogenesis theory, absurd as it seems to us in the light of present-day knowledge, did much to stimulate interest in the nature and origin of parasitic worms, and from 1683 to the end of the eighteenth century there appeared many works on natural history with descriptions of such worms and observations upon their habits and pathogenicity.

In 1683 Edward T. Tyson (1650–1708) published the first anatomical description of *Ascaris lumbricoides* and established that such roundworms are not insects and do not come from insect eggs. In 1684 Francisco Redi (1626–98) published *Osservazioni intorno agli animali viventi, che si trovano negli animali viventi*, the classic work in which the abiogenesis theory was attacked and overthrown. The Florentine naturalist described the bladder worm type of tapeworm and expressed the view that, like maggots in putrefying meat, such bladder worms originate from eggs. Certain larval tapeworms from fishes were described and systematically arranged. In 1685 the term "taeniae hydatigenae" appeared, coined by the Königsberg physician, Philipp Jacob Hartmann (1640–1707) for the bladder worm now known as *Cysticercus tenuicollis*, whose movements he observed in water. The term survives as *Taenia hydatigena*, whose larva may have been the form Hartmann observed.

Nicolas Andry (1658–1742) published (1700) a *Traité de la generation des vers dans le corps de l'homme* in which *Taeniarhynchus saginatus* is readily recognizable both from text and figure. Erroneously regarding the serially repeated uteri of *Dibothriocephalus latus* as a sort of backbone, Andry referred to this worm as a "Taenia à l'épine," i.e., a spined taenia, or "*Taenia vertebrata*," in contrast with "Taenia sans épine," or backboneless taenia, which was presumably *Taeniarhynchus.* Andry believed the tapeworm to be an individual and not a colony of individuals, and so precipitated an acrimonious controversy that was to confuse the views of students of tapeworm structure through two centuries to come.

In 1753 the theologian and naturalist, Jacob Christian Schäffer (1718–90), established the close zoological relationships between Trematoda and Cestoda. The second half of the eighteenth century saw the publication of many descriptions of tapeworms other than those known to physicians, and a growing accumulation of known plant and animal forms that stimulated the publication of schemes of taxonomic arrangement.

In 1758 the Tenth Edition of Carl von Linné's *Systema Naturae* crystallized, as it were, prevalent views upon the subject of animal and plant classification. The general practice of other writers, and in fact of Linnaeus (as he began to be called) himself in earlier editions of his scheme, was to designate an animal or plant type by an unwieldy Latin phrase. Thus Linnaeus in his Sixth Edition referred to the golden pheasant as *Phasinus crista flava pectore coccineo,* and to the nine-banded armadillo as *Dasypus cingulis novem.* In this Tenth Edition, however, he adopted and consistently followed the practice of allotting to the animal or plant type a *generic* name, which was a Latin noun, and of qualifying the generic name by a *specific* name, which was a Latin adjective. Thus the armadillo became *Dasypus novemcinctus.* The idea was not new. Such a binominal system had been used spasmodically by earlier writers. Plater, as we have seen, used the term *Lumbricus latus* for the broad tapeworm of man. Le Clerc (1715) referred to a common dog tapeworm as *Taenia canina.*

Van Cleave (1935) wrote, in a discussion of pre-Linnaean nomenclature: "One does not have to go far in the study of the history of nomenclature to find that this reputed child of Linnaeus' brain did not spring forth as a fully formed concept, perfect in its earliest inception. The mere fact that the Systema Naturae underwent ten editions over a period of twenty-three years before a 'consistent general application of the binary nomenclature' was attained, gives ample evidence of a development from rather imperfect beginnings. With Linnaeus the system was at first a concept, imperfectly applied, which took years for a genius to perfect. Many would say that even the concept was not original with the great Swedish naturalist." It is possible that even the generic concept – that is to say, the grouping of similar species into genera – originated with Tournefort and other predecessors of Linnaeus.

Even if Linnaeus did not invent the binominal system of animal and plant nomenclature he certainly popularized it, and his influence in this respect is apparent in the natural history writings of the late eighteenth century. The international committee that first laid down the modern rules of animal and plant naming was justified in choosing 1758, the date of the Tenth Edition of *Systema Naturae,* as the starting point, the earliest date for which any specific name could be accepted. Probably the Twelfth Edition of 1766–68, the last edition to receive the author's corrections, would have been a better starting point however.

We may note that Linnaeus included all tapeworms within the one genus *Taenia,* and for a time other naturalists followed this practice. However, Otto Friedrich Mueller, the Danish zoologist (1730–84), erected in 1787 the genus *Caryophyllaeus* for Pallas' *Taenia laticeps.* Among late eighteenth-century contributions of note to the growing accumulation of information about tapeworm types were those of M. E.

Bloch (1779, 1782) on the tapeworms of fishes and birds; of Otto Fabricius (1780) on the tapeworms of Greenland fishes; and of Abildgaard (1790), also on the tapeworms of fishes and birds.

In 1782 another monument in the history of helminthology was erected when J. A. E. Goeze published a 470-page natural history of parasitic worms, the *Versuch einer Naturgeschichte der Eingeweidewürmer thierischer Körper.* This book was remarkable in being the first work on helminthology published in German and for the remarkable accuracy and beauty of its forty-four engraved plates. Tapeworms were described and figured from a great variety of hosts and, following the Linnaean practice, were all placed within the genus *Taenia.* However, Goeze recognized two divisions of this genus, "Taenia visceralis" (cystic forms) and "Taenia intestinalis" (wormlike forms). Goeze described the holdfast of *Echinococcus* and the embryonated egg of *Dipylidium caninum,* and made observations on the development of *Cysticercus fasciolaris.* He pointed out correctly that a tapeworm "grows at one end and dies at the other," possibly the first suggestion of that biological phenomenon, the physiological or axial gradient. One serious flaw in Goeze's views, however, was his belief that tapeworms could be inherited.

In 1790 Gmelin prepared an authoritive Thirteenth Edition of *Systema Naturae* from materials left at Linnaeus' death. In this ten-volume work Gmelin brought within the orbit of the Linnaean scheme the descriptions of animal genera and species made by early but post-Linnaean observers. Gmelin's work was essentially a compendium of known facts rather than a scheme of classification, but there can be little doubt that Rudolphi, when writing his famous *Entozoorum sive vermium intestinalium historia naturalis* (1808, 1809, 1810, 1819), was influenced greatly by Gmelin and Zeder. Rudolphi, however, was ruthless in rejecting the genera and species established by earlier workers in favor of names invented by himself. He introduced the somewhat questionable practice of giving generic rank to life cycle stages. Though such larval genera, so to speak, are now legitimized by the International Rules and are allowed priority over later "adult genera," the question has produced considerable heartburning among zoologists when names made venerable by years of usage must be discarded in favor of some earlier generic name established for an immature form of the animal in question.

The chief merit of Rudolphi's scheme was that it surveyed the whole field of parasitic worms and distributed such worms among the four large groups recognized today—roundworms, thornheads, flukes, and tapeworms. In the final scheme of 1819, five orders were proposed—Nematoidea (roundworms), Acanthocephala (thornheads), Trematoda (flukes), Cestoidea (tapeworms), and Cystica (bladder worms). Rudolphi followed the Linnaean practice of placing all adult tapeworms in the genus Taenia, which in Rudolphi's scheme comprised 116 species. He devoted 172 pages to a valuable bibliography and included extensive chapters on the physiology and pathogenicity of parasites.

Another great impulse was given to the study of helminthology by the publication (1819) by Johann Gottfried Bremser (1767–1827) of *Lebende Würmer im lebenden Menschen*, in which, it is of interest to note, the broad tapeworm was separated from the genus *Taenia* as *Bothriocephalus latus*.

One flaw in Rudolphi's scheme was his failure to realize that the bladder worms are in reality larval tapeworms. Their recognition as tapeworms of a sort was made in the classification schemes proposed by Blainville (1848) and Dujardin (1845), where the bladder worms appeared within the order devoted to tapeworms. However, apart from incorporating a number of new genera and species, these authors contributed little of note toward the unraveling of the problems of tapeworm taxonomy. A closer approach to a scientific arrangement of the tapeworms was made by Beneden (1849b) when, correctly assessing the bladder worms as life cycle stages of tapeworms, he removed them from a scheme in which the tapeworms, mainly on features of the holdfast, were distributed among four orders – Tetraphylles, Diphylles, Pseudophylles, and Aphylles.

A somewhat retrograde step was taken by Diesing in his two-volume *Systema Helminthum* (1850–51) in which the bladder worms were again restored to the rank of a separate order, and in which such a multiplicity of new genera were proposed on grounds so taxonomically worthless that Siebold (1850) was emboldened to protest against "improper genera" and to advocate the deletion of no fewer than ten of Diesing's thirty-two genera. Diesing's later scheme (1863a, 1863b), though abolishing the separate rank of the bladder worms, was far from satisfactory to those zoologists who felt that a rational scheme of animal classification should be formulated on the basis of work in the field and the laboratory rather than work in the library.

However, Diesing's volumes have been called the Bible of parasitologists of the middle nineteenth century, and this period abounded in names of helminthologists of note. It was the period of Leuckart (1822–98), Leidy (1823–91), Carl Theodor von Siebold (1808–85), Theodor Maximilian Bilharz (1825–62), Georg Friedrich H. Küchenmeister (1821–90), T. Spencer Cobbold (1828–86), and Casimir Joseph Davaine (1812–82).

In 1863 the foundations of a scheme of tapeworm classification which has survived with little change to the present day were laid down by Carus. Adopting the term "Platyelminthes" in place of Burmeister's "Platodes" (1856) and Küchenmeister's "Platyelmia" (1855) for the flatworm orders, and recognizing the group as comprising Turbellaria, Trematoda, and Cestoda, Carus divided the known tapeworm genera and species among five families. To designate them he used, with some modifications, Beneden's ordinal terms in Latinized form. The tapeworm families of Carus were named Caryophyllidea, Tetraphyllidea, Diphyllidea, Pseudophyllidea, and Taeniadea. This scheme persisted with little change for thirty years, the principal modification being the subtraction by Monticelli (1892b) from the tapeworms of those forms with a single set of genitalia, formerly termed monozootic tapeworms, and their relegation to a separate class, Cestodaria.

In 1894 there was launched that most ambitious and comprehensive series of zoological monographs, "Bronn's Klassen und Ordnungen des Thierreichs." As is generally the case when authoritative and exhaustive monographs upon animal groups are published, the schemes of classification adopted in "Bronn's Thierreich," as it is commonly called, crystallized zoological opinions and became the accepted taxonomic framework of all later zoological textbooks.

In his treatment of the tapeworms in "Bronn's Thierreich," Braun (1894–1900) adopted the scheme proposed by Carus. By this time Platyelminthes were accepted by zoological opinion as a separate phylum, and the families of Carus were therefore raised by Braun to the rank of orders. Five such orders were recognized – Pseudophyllidea, Tetraphyllidea, Cyclophyllidea, Diphyllidea, and Trypanorhyncha. Caryophyllidea of Carus were submerged within Pseudophyllidea, his Taeniadea became Cyclophyllidea, and Diesing's term Trypanorhyncha was revived for an order containing those tapeworms with four protrusible, hook-covered "proboscides."

In another series of German zoological monographs, "Die Süsswasserfauna Deutschlands," published in the early years of this century, the scheme of Carus again received the accolade of adoption. Lühe (1910a), in the volume dealing with tapeworms, recognized Pseudophyllidea Carus, 1863; Trypanorhyncha Diesing, 1863; Tetraphyllidea Carus, 1863; and Cyclophyllidea Braun, 1900. The order Diphyllidea was not recognized however.

The Braun-Lühe scheme of tapeworm classification has become so entrenched in zoological favor that several attacks upon its blatant defects have failed to find acceptance. Other orders have been added, notably Nippotaeniidea Yamaguti, 1939 and Aporidea Fuhrmann, 1934. In this book we have used what is substantially the Braun-Lühe scheme, mainly for convenience of reference to the literature rather than because of any deep-seated convictions that it is the best scheme devisable. We have preferred to break down to some extent the orders Pseudophyllidea and Tetraphyllidea.

Nevertheless the Braun-Lühe scheme has not been without critics. Most ambitious of the schemes offered in its place have been those of Poche, Pintner, Southwell, and Mola. It is difficult to understand upon just what basis Poche (1926a) founded his scheme of tapeworm classification. The whole of the tapeworms (Cestoidea) were to be distributed between two "sub-sub-classes" (*sic*) – Amphilinoinei (cestodarian forms) and Taenioinei (cestode forms). Taenioinei were divided into four orders – Bothriocephalidea, equivalent to Caryophyllidea and Pseudophyllidea of Carus and Braun; Echinobothriidea, apparently equivalent to that much-criticized "lumber room," Heterophyllidea, proposed by Southwell (1925b); Tetrarhynchidea, equivalent to Trypanorhyncha of Braun; and Taeniidea, within which the proteocephalans, lecanicephalans, tetraphyllideans, and cyclophyllideans found themselves strange bedfellows.

Poche qualified the accepted units of zoological classification – phylum, class, order, family, genus, and species – by such terms as "super-super," "super-sub," "sub-super," "sub-sub," and so forth. His practice appeared to be that of replacing existing names by names of his own invention, not always with happy results. Thus in his scheme Turbellaria became "Turbellares," Nemertea became "Nematarii," Tetrabothriidae became "Tetrabothriodes," and Trypanorhyncha became "Tetrarhynchinae."

Pintner (1928b) recognized in his scheme two orders of a class Cestoidea, namely, Amphilinidea (cestodarian forms) and Cestoda (true tapeworms). The four orders of Lühe – Pseudophyllidea, Cyclophyllidea, Trypanorhyncha, and Tetraphyllidea – were reduced to the rank of families – Bothriocephalidae, Taeniidae, Tetrarhynchidae, and Tetraphyllidae – and some other families were added.

The scheme suggested by Mola (1929b) was as radical and as incomprehensible as that of Poche, and was marked by a confusing and drastic tampering with long-accepted family and subfamily names, and by an obsession with Latin as a medium of explanation. The tapeworms and cestodaria became *Platoda sine extis*, with two classes – Cestodaria Monticelli, 1892 and Cestoda Monticelli, 1892.

Cestodaria were to comprise three orders:

1. Amphilinidea Poche, 1922, with one family, Amphilinidae Claus, 1879
2. Gyrocotylidea Poche, 1925, with one family, Gyrocotylidae Benham, 1901
3. Caryophyllidea Mola, 1929, with one family, Caryophyllaeidae Claus, 1879

Cestoda were to comprise five orders:

1. Pseudophyllidea Mola, 1925, with two families:
   Ligulidae Claus, 1861
   Bothriocephalidae E. Blanchard, 1849
2. Monophyllidea Mola, 1921, with two families:
   Cyathocephalidae Nybelin, 1922
   Discocephalidae Mola, 1929
3. Diphyllidea Mola, 1921, with two families:
   Dibothriophyllidae Mola, 1921
   Dibothriocanthidae Mola, 1921
4. Tetraphyllidea Carus, 1863, with three families:
   Tetraphyllacanthidae Mola, 1921
   Tetraphyllabothridae Mola, 1921
   Ichthyotaeniidae Ariola, 1899
5. Cyclophyllidea Beneden, 1850, with 23 families:
   Tetrabothriidae Fuhrmann, 1929
   Mesocestoididae Fuhrmann, 1907
   Anoplocephalidae Mola, 1929
   Linstowidae Mola, 1929

Thysanosomidae Mola, 1929
Nematotaeniidae Lühe, 1910
Viscoidae Mola, 1923
Davaineidae Mola, 1929
Ophriocotylidae Mola, 1929
Idiogenidae Mola, 1929
Dilepinidae Mola, 1929
Diphyllidiidae Mola, 1929
Paruteriidae Mola, 1929
Phanobothridae Poche, 1925
Taeniidae Perrier, 1897
Hymenolepididae Fuhrmann, 1907
Diploposthidae Poche, 1925
Acoleinidae Fuhrmann, 1907
Amabilinidae Fuhrmann, 1907
Fimbriariidae Wolffhügel, 1900
Echinorhynchotiidae Mola, 1929
Dibothriorhynchidae Mola, 1921
Tetrabothriorhynchidae Mola, 1921

Southwell (1930) recognized two orders, Cestodaria and Eucestoda. The true tapeworms were distributed among six superfamilies—Dibothriocephaloidea Stiles, 1900; Tetrarhynchoidea *nov.*; Phyllobothrioidea *nov.*; Lecanicephaloidea *nov.*; Proteocephaloidea *nov.*; and Taenioidea Zwicke, 1841. A seventh superfamily, Spathebothrioidea, was added by Hart and Guberlet, 1936a.

There are few taxonomic groups of animals in which the validity of established species is more frequently disputed than in Cestoda. To some extent it is to be expected that specific descriptions, established possibly a century ago upon exteromorphic features and upon an exaggerated emphasis on host specificity, should fail to stand the tests imposed by improved methods of microtechnique. Nevertheless, the ephemeral existence of comparatively recently established species raises a suspicion that due attention is not always paid by the creators of these specific descriptions to the extent of variation that occurs among the characters they select as a basis for specific discrimination.

Now the validity of a character as a basis for specific differentiation among Cestoda depends upon the extent and frequency with which (1) a departure from the type description occurs normally among living individuals; (2) a departure from the type description is induced by the technical methods necessary to prepare the character for microscopic observation; and (3) an approach to the type description is induced in forms otherwise dissimilar by common environmental stress. That is to say, the value of the character from the taxonomic standpoint depends upon the extent to which it is an *adaptive* character, functioning merely to keep the organism in tune with its external environment, and thus likely to alter if the environment alters; upon the extent to which it is a *nonadaptive* character, a deep-seated ancestral character, not readily influenced by environmental change; and upon the extent to which the character, whether adaptive or nonadaptive, is susceptible to distortion when exposed to microtechnical agents.

The limitations of a character, therefore, in regard to its value for specific discrimination, can only be determined by the examination of a wide range of specifically uniform material exposed to various methods of microtechnique, and by the examination of a wide range of material that is specifically varied but living under similar conditions of environment. It is significant that the majority of species which fail to stand further inquiry have been established originally upon very limited material, from a very limited host range, in a limited geographical area.

While disclaiming any competency to criticize the specific characters used in the differentiation of cyclophyllidean, tetraphyllidean, or trypanorhynchan material, the writers can claim to have examined critically, and with a wide variety of methods of technique, a range of pseudophyllidean and proteocephalan material – belonging in particular to the genera *Bothriocephalus, Eubothrium, Triaenophorus, Cordicephalus, Dibothriocephalus, Diplocotyle,* and *Proteocephalus* – sufficiently comprehensive to justify the presentation of the following conclusions as to the limitations of the characters commonly used in distinguishing species of these genera.

The first point which merits attention concerns the value that can be assigned to external metromorphic characters – that is to say, to the dimensions and shapes of the various features of the external surface. There is a tendency on the part of some authorities to dismiss the external features of tapeworms as being so uniform in nature among closely related forms as to be of only minor value in the separation of species. Such a view is not wholly justifiable. Many species established over a century ago chiefly upon external characters are still accepted as valid, and such characters are still commonly used as major taxonomic characters by many modern workers in this field. Southwell (1929a) in particular argued strongly in favor of the major value of such characters in opposition to the view, of which Woodland (1925d, 1927b) was a strong protagonist, that the external features of holdfast and body are of minor value and that taxonomic differentiation should rest upon the metromorphic character of some more deeply seated and presumably less variable system of organs, such as genitalia or muscles.

It must be emphasized in the first place that the shape and dimensions of the holdfast, body, and individual segments in an active tapeworm, freshly removed from its host and observed in an artificial medium, are continually altering, due to the absence from cestodes of any system of skeletal tissues. The extent of the alteration is determined by the chemical nature, hydrogen-ion concentration, and temperature of the medium used, and by the length of time that the worm has been divorced from its host habitat. Meggitt (1927b) noted that the body of *Proteocephalus filicollis* increases in length by 30 to 50 per cent if it is kept in water for a few hours before fixation, and that in the same circumstances the body of *Schistocephalus solidus* increases four times in length. The influence of artificial media upon the activity and morphic change of cestodes has already been discussed (Chapter III) and need not be elaborated here.

Even if the fixative employed were to kill the cestode immediately – and probably no fixative can act instantaneously, since its action is impeded by the cuticular thickness and the muscular irritability of the worm – no two specimens when fixed will be identical in shape and size of holdfast and body even if they were approximately so when alive. A great many of the type descriptions of cestode species seem to us, after examining a range of specimens of such species, to have been founded upon distorted material and, so far as external characters are concerned, to be inapplicable to living or undistorted specimens. It must be admitted, however, that many tapeworms vary so slightly in shape and size that the specific descriptions, even if founded upon distorted material, are applicable to living forms.

In the second place, the external metromorphic characters may vary with age. In the case of *Eubothrium oncorhynchi* of the Pacific salmon, for example, there are two types of individual (Figure 409). One type has a holdfast with a conspicuous bilobed terminal disk, rounded bothrial surfaces, deep bothria, and broad anterior segments. The other type has a holdfast with an inconspicuous disk, oval bothrial surfaces, shallow lanceolate bothria, and slender anterior segments. This second type is older and is usually gravid. A similar dimorphism has been noted by the writers in the case of *Eubothrium crassum* in *Myoxocephalus quadricornis*, perhaps an abnormal host, from Hudson Bay. There seems no reason to regard the two types of individual as other than representing two stages of development (Wardle, 1932a, 1932d).

In the case of *Eubothrium rugosum*, common in western Canadian specimens of *Lota lota maculosa*, the young tapeworm has a typical eubothriid holdfast, quadrate to rectangular in outline, with moderately deep bothria and a bilobed terminal disk. Some individuals retain this type of holdfast throughout life, a period of less than one year, but others burrow into the mucosa of the host's pyloric caeca and develop a *scolex deformatus*, the terminal disk becoming relatively enormous and similar in shape to an inverted pyramid (Figure 406). The mucosa forms a cystlike enclosure around the hypertrophied holdfast, the enclosure having a small aperture which surrounds the anterior segments. The body eventually breaks away from the holdfast and passes from the host, whereupon the isolated holdfast becomes completely enclosed and is gradually absorbed by the mucosal cyst. Both types of individual may be found in the same host, and if merely the external metromorphic characters were considered the two types would certainly be regarded as distinct species. Possibly only the absence of the deformed type from European *Lota lota* has prevented the establishment of two such species by early parasitologists. There seems no reason to regard the two forms as other than *morphae* of the species *rugosum.*

The writers were formerly of the opinion that the types of *Triaenophorus* found in western American fishes are examples of morphae of one species *tricuspidatus* (Wardle, 1932d), but the observations of Miller (1943a, 1945, 1946) suggest that three distinct species are present.

In the third place, the external metromorphic characters may vary according to the host distribution of the tapeworm. The genus *Bothriocephalus*, for example, seems particularly susceptible to morphic variation induced presumably by differences in host environment. The long list of species attributed to this genus reflects this susceptibility. In the case of *Bothriocephalus scorpii* (Mueller), widely distributed over the northern hemisphere, there appear to be no structural differences between eastern Atlantic, western Atlantic, and eastern Pacific material sufficiently fundamental to dispute the view that only one species is concerned, but marked differences occur between specimens from different host fishes and from different geographical areas. European authorities recognize a number of forms, notably the *forma bubalidis* and *forma motellae* of Loennberg (1889a, 1893), and the forms described by Schneider (1902b) from *Rhombus maximus* and *Myoxocephalus quadricornis.* In western Atlantic waters a number of types of this same species have been described by Leidy (1855), Linton (1890), Sumner, Osburn, and Cole (1913), and Cooper (1918). In Canadian Pacific waters, Wardle described forms from *Leptocottus armatus* and *Enophrys bison* (Wardle, 1932a). All these forms must be regarded as forms of *Bothriocephalus scorpii* despite the existence of slight but constant differences.

There occurs, also, in hosts as far separated taxonomically and geographically as *Tetrapterus albidus, Histiophorus gladius*, and *Tarpon atlanticus* of the northern Atlantic, *Histophorus sp.* of the Indian and Pacific oceans, and *Leptocottus armatus* and *Sebastodes sp.* of the northern Pacific Ocean, a bothriocephalid cestode characterized by a club-shaped holdfast, a broad, frilled body, and a gravid uterus at least one-third of the segment width. At present, this form is separated according to host distribution and certain alleged differences into a number of species – *plicatus* Rudolphi, *manubriformis* Linton, *occidentalis* Linton, *laciniatus* Linton, *histiophorus* Shipley, and so forth; but it is not improbable that these, again, are merely forms of the originally described species *plicatus.*

In central Canadian waters there occur in species of *Stizostedion* and *Amphiodon* bothriocephalids which, although differing markedly in external characters, agree so closely in their internal features as to suggest that they are merely forms of *Bothriocephalus cuspidatus* Cooper (Figure 390). It may be argued also that there is probably no justification for separating *Cyathocephalus americanus* Cooper from *Cyathocephalus truncatus*, for separating *Diplocotyle nylandica* (Schneider) from *Diplocotyle olrikii* Krabbe, or *Proteocephalus pinguis* La Rue from *Proteocephalus pusillus* Ward. It may be argued, too, that there is no justification for regarding the forms of *Cordicephalus* in northern Atlantic seals as separate species.

The difficulties in the host specificity theory put forward by Fuhrmann (1932) – postulating the natural limitation of any species of cestode to a single host group — are many, and Fuhrmann himself was not always able to regard as distinct species forms which, while anatomically similar, occurred in different host groups. There is the difficulty offered by the ability of some forms to develop in "accidental hosts," a phenomenon that Meggitt (1934a) has termed "pseudoparasitism." It is possible that in some cases species have been established on the characters of such pseudoparasites. There is also the difficulty that the apparent gulf between orders, families, and genera of hosts is of less significance in some host groups than in others. The differences, for example, between *orders* of birds are often less than between *families* of other chordate classes.

Meggitt (1934a), discussing and criticizing the host specificity theory, believed that its adoption would bring about a multiplication of species and even of genera that were anatomically indistinguishable from one another. As he stated, "It appears to the writer that the only safe procedure is to determine the identification solely on the basis of the anatomy of the specimens, and, lacking any grounds of differentiation, to include them in an already existing species, irrespective of the systematic position of the host."

In the fourth place, similarities in external metromorphic characters may be assumed by forms with deep-seated internal differences. The stress laid upon external characters by the early parasitologists has tended to obscure to some extent the existence of convergent adaptations among Cestoda, but some examples are well known. The proteocephalan genera *Corallobothrium* and *Rudolphiella* and the species-groups represented by the old genera *Goezeella* and *Choanoscolex* have holdfasts obscured by folds of skin; but Fuhrmann (1916) showed the existence of fundamental internal differences between the genitalia of these forms. Woodland (1925d) further suggested that this coralla character, one of the most conspicuous holdfast characters found among Proteocephala, had originated independently in these groups.

A belief in the stability of holdfast armature as a taxonomic character has become almost axiomatic among students of tapeworms. In cyclophyllidean forms in particular, the number, shapes, and dimensions of the rostellar hooks or spines, and, among trypanorhynchans, the number, size, and arrangement of the tentacular hooks, are accepted as primary characters for the separation of species. It seems to the writers, however, that considerable caution should be exercised in distinguishing, chiefly on differences of holdfast armature, forms which have a common host distribution, which may coexist in the same host individual, and which show only minor differences in their internal morphology. Nevertheless, as already stated, the separation of the three forms of *Triaenophorus* as distinct species seems thoroughly justified.

Admittedly, many external metromorphic characters are reasonably constant. Although little value can be placed upon precise measurements of the holdfast and holdfast organs, even when the holdfast boundaries are universally agreed upon, which is not always the case, considerable diagnostic value can be ascribed to *relative* measurements — comparing, for example, holdfast dimensions with some given standard such as one millimeter, or expressing dimensions as multiples of holdfast dimensions. Precise measurements of the body are useless for a form which has a wide host distribution; but for a form with restricted host distribution such measurements, or the limiting value of such measurements, may be significant. Such terms as "large," "medium-sized," "fleshy," or "slender," applied to the body, or "cuneiform," "quadrangular," "rectangular," "linear," or "cucurbitiform," applied tc segment shape, although unscientific, may convey to another observer a certain characteristic associated with the species under discussion, and, when regarded purely as supplementary information about commonly variable characters, may be of value. One the whole, however, the majority of external metromorphic characters must be regarded as *adaptive characters*, shaped and colored by the environment; and although undoubtedly valuable in specific differentiation, they can be considered only as supplementing other characters of more stable type.

The second point that merits discussion is the value that can be assigned to metromorphic characters of the internal morphology. It has become the fashion in recent years for students of tapeworm taxonomy to launch into meticulous micrometric descriptions of such internal structures as the cirrus pouch, testes, ovary, yolk glands, and genital ducts, and to provide exhaustively detailed accounts of the cuticle, musculature, nervous system, and so forth. Important as such ponderous and scholarly descriptions must be to the student of comparative histology, it may be doubted whether they are of like value to the systematist, except when they are correlated with peculiarities in the habits and host distribution of the tapeworm under discussion, which is rarely the case.

Just as the validity of external metromorphic characters is weakened by the absence from cestodes of any skeletal support, which would tend to maintain the dimensions of such characters between defined limits, so the validity of internal metromorphic characters is vitiated by the contractibility of such structures as the cirrus pouch, uterine wall, and genital ducts, which makes them susceptible to the distorting effects of chemical and physical stimuli or of technical reagents. Although internal characters are probably less directly adaptive to the external environment and so afford a more stable basis for specific differentiation, they are possibly more susceptible than are external characters to the influence of the internal environment and to the changes induced by the gradual onset of maturity.

On the whole, however, internal metromorphic characters must be regarded as chiefly nonadaptive in character, and so more likely to provide a stable basis for specific differentiation than is the case with the external characters. Nevertheless, internal characters which are subject to muscular contraction and expansion, or to variations with age, are of little more value in this respect than are the dimensional and morphic characters of the holdfast and body. According to Woodland (1925d): "It is evident that for a single character to be regarded as valid for the founding of a genus this character should, as far as possible, be of a deep-seated nature affecting the internal organization. The alternative to deep-seated characters is a constant combination of characters of less importance which are easily recognizable."

Of the characters suggested by Woodland as deep seated, the uterus is notoriously subject to alteration induced by age or by microtechnique. The situation of the yolk glands may also be affected by age, although the writers are inclined to agree with Nybelin (1922) as to the stability of this character. The *relative* dimensions and locations of internal organs are probably fairly stable. It is likely that the characters of the nervous and osmoregulatory systems are more stable than any other characters, but they are impracticable for diagnostic purposes. The dimensional and morphic characters of such structures as the cirrus pouch, ovary, uterus, yolk glands, and testes are probably sufficiently stable to serve as specific characters if the material under comparison is of approximately the same age, has been subjected to identical prefixation and postfixation handling, has been taken from the same host species, and if the measurements are relative to some standard of comparison such as segment width or medullary or cortical depth.

Metromorphic characters break down utterly as a basis for the specific differentiation of tapeworm larval forms. Whatever the type of larva, there are usually only three characteristics available for the systematist – host distribution, shape, and host habitat. Holdfast shape may afford a valuable indication of specific affinity when there is a characteristic armature, as in cyclophyllidean and trypanorhynchan forms or in *Triaenophorus*, or when the holdfast is peculiar to a genus restricted in number of species, as is the case with *Pyramicocephalus*; but otherwise the holdfast is of little value due to its extreme mobility in most cases. Host habitat is also a characteristic of little value to the systematist, as the host range of most tapeworm larvae is wide, and few such larvae are restricted to particular host organs. Similarly, host distribution means little in the identification of tapeworm larvae, since they are notoriously less specific in host distribution than the adult cestodes.

The only method by which larval cestodes can be identified with approximate certainty with adult forms is that of rearing them in sterilized hosts of the suspected adult stage; but such a method, although routine in the investigation of helminths of domesticated animals, is usually impracticable with the cestode fauna of a wide range of wild animals. It may be suggested, therefore, that the description of a larval cestode should emphasize the external metromorphic characters of the organism while *in situ* and the extent of variation from the *in situ* appearance assumed when the larva is transferred to some standard medium such as decimolar NaCl.

If the holdfast characters agree with those of some adult genus or species occurring *in the same area*, it should be reasonable to describe the larval form under the specific or generic name of that adult form, the term *larva inquirenda* being appended to the name to indicate that the crucial test of rearing to maturity in a host animal has not yet been applied. The erection of special generic names for larval cestodes is unnecessary and objectionable. Taxonomic clarity among cestodes has long been obscured by the chaos of synonyms resulting from such procedure, and even such terms as "dibothrium," "cysticercus," "coenurus," and "sparganum" – sanctified though they may be by long usage, and useful in designating morphological types – should be abolished as generic names for well-established cestode larvae.

The question arises, finally, as to the taxonomic position that should be given to cestodes which show a combination of metromorphic similarities and dissimilarities, but in which the similarities are fundamental and the dissimilarities are nonfundamental. Are such forms to be regarded as departures from the type species and distinct species themselves, or are they to be regarded as subspecies of the type species, or merely as morphic variations?

The trinomial system of nomenclature has not as yet become generally adopted for Cestoda, and the system used by students of free-living groups of animals – that of restricting the term "subspecies" to geographical variations, the term "natio" to topographical variations, and the term "morpha" to morphological variations – is not satisfactory for application to internal parasites since the geographical distribution of such forms is of minor importance to the taxonomist. The contention may be made on strong grounds that the host distribution of an internal parasite is equivalent taxonomically to the geographical distribution of a free-living organism. The geographical location of a tapeworm is of very little importance, but the host location is of great significance.

On this contention we would base the following conclusions:

1. The separation of tapeworm species should be based primarily upon nonadaptive characters, such as the correlative positions of the reproductive organs, or such characters of the nervous and the osmoregulatory systems as can readily be observed; and secondarily upon adaptive characters, such as the shape and relative dimensions of the holdfast, body, and individual segments, and upon morphogenetic characters – that is to say, those which change with age, such as the shapes and dimensions of the various reproductive organs. When these characters are used, consideration must be given to the state of development of the specimens, the medium in which they are examined, and the microtechnical treatment they have received. Absolute dimensional values are of little use; relative values, or limiting values, are of great use, especially when associated with given conditions of development, microtechnical treatment, and host distribution.

2. Tapeworms which differ in host distribution, and which agree in nonadaptive characters but disagree in adaptive or morphogenetic characters, should be regarded as subspecies, whether or not the hosts coincide in geographical distribution. As examples may be given: *Bothriocephalus scorpii bubalidis*; *B. s. hemitripteri*; *B. s. leptocotti*; *Bothriocephalus cuspidatus cuspidatus*; *B. c. hiodontos*; and *B. c. stizostedionis.*

PART II

Tapeworm Classification Used in This Book

CLASS CESTODA

1. ORDER PROTEOCEPHALA new order, with one family: PROTEOCEPHALIDAE La Rue, 1914, emended Woodland, 1933, with eight subfamilies: PROTEOCEPHALINAE Mola, 1929; ZYGOBOTHRIINAE Woodland, 1933; MARSYPOCEPHALINAE Woodland, 1933; EPHEDROCEPHALINAE Mola, 1929; PELTIDOCOTYLINAE Woodland, 1934; RUDOLPHIELLINAE Woodland, 1935; ENDORCHIDINAE Woodland, 1934; MONTICELLIINAE Mola, 1929.

2. ORDER TETRAPHYLLIDEA Braun, 1900, with two families: PHYLLOBOTHRIIDAE Braun, 1900; ONCHOBOTHRIIDAE Braun, 1900.

3. ORDER DISCULICEPITIDEA new order, with one family: DISCULICEPITIDAE new family.

4. ORDER LECANICEPHALA new order, with two families: LECANICEPHALIDAE Braun, 1900, emended Pintner, 1928; and CEPHALOBOTHRIIDAE Pintner, 1928.

5. ORDER TRYPANORHYNCHA Diesing, 1863, with two suborders:
   I. SUBORDER ATHECA Diesing, 1854, with seven families: TENTACULARIIDAE Poche, 1926, emended Dollfus, 1930; HEPATOXYLIDAE Dollfus, 1940; SPHYRIOCEPHALIDAE Pintner, 1913; DASYRHYNCHIDAE Dollfus, 1935, with two subfamilies: DASYRHYNCHINAE Dollfus, 1940, and CALLITETRARHYNCHINAE Dollfus, 1940; LACISTORHYNCHIDAE Guiart, 1927, with two subfamilies: LACISTORHYNCHINAE Joyeux and Baer, 1934, emended Dollfus, 1942, and GRILLOTIINAE Dollfus, 1942; GYMNORHYNCHIDAE Dollfus, 1935; PTEROBOTHRIIDAE Pintner, 1931.
   II. SUBORDER THECOPHORA Diesing, 1854, with three families: EUTETRARHYNCHIDAE Guiart, 1927; GILQUINIIDAE Dollfus, 1942, with two subfamilies: GILQUINIINAE Dollfus, 1942, and APORHYNCHINAE Dollfus, 1942; OTOBOTHRIIDAE Dollfus, 1942.

6. ORDER CYCLOPHYLLIDEA Braun, 1900, with fourteen families: MESOCESTOIDIDAE Perrier, 1897; TETRABOTHRIIDAE Linton, 1891, emended Fuhrmann, 1907; NEMATOTAENIIDAE Lühe, 1910; ANOPLOCEPHALIDAE Cholodkovsky, 1902, emended Fuhrmann, 1907, with three subfamilies: ANOPLOCEPHALINAE R. Blanchard, 1891, emended Fuhrmann, 1932, LINSTOWINAE Fuhrmann, 1907, and THYSANOSOMINAE Fuhrmann, 1907; CATENOTAENIIDAE new family; TAENIIDAE Ludwig, 1886; DAVAINEIDAE Fuhrmann, 1907, with three subfamilies: OPHRYOCOTYLINAE Fuhrmann, 1907, DAVAINEINAE Braun, 1900, and IDIOGENINAE Fuhrmann, 1932; BIUTERINIDAE Meggitt, 1927; HYMENO-

LEPIDIDAE Railliet and Henry, 1909, with three subfamilies: HYMENOLEPIDINAE Perrier, 1897, FIMBRIARIINAE Wolffhügel, 1899, emended Webster, 1943, and PSEUDHYMENOLEPINAE Joyeux and Baer, 1935; DILEPIDIDAE Railliet and Henry, 1909, emended Lincicome, 1939, with three subfamilies: DILEPIDINAE Fuhrmann, 1907, DIPYLIDIINAE Stiles, 1896, and PARUTERININAE Fuhrmann, 1907; ACOLEIDAE Ransom, 1909; AMABILIIDAE Ransom, 1909; DIOICOCESTIDAE Southwell, 1930, emended Burt, 1939; DIPLOPOSTHIDAE Poche, 1926, emended Southwell, 1929.

7. ORDER APORIDEA Fuhrmann, 1933, with one family: NEMATOPARATAENIIDAE Poche, 1926.

8. ORDER NIPPOTAENIIDEA Yamaguti, 1939, with one family: NIPPOTAENIIDAE Yamaguti, 1939.

9. ORDER CARYOPHYLLIDEA new order, with four families: WENYONIDAE new family; CARYOPHYLLAEIDAE Leuckart, 1878; LYTOCESTIDAE new family; CAPINGENTIDAE new family.

10. ORDER SPATHEBOTHRIDEA new order, with three families: SPATHEBOTHRIIDAE new family; CYATHOCEPHALIDAE Nybelin, 1922; DIPLOCOTYLIDAE new family.

11. ORDER PSEUDOPHYLLIDEA Carus, 1863, with seven families: HAPLOBOTHRIIDAE Meggitt, 1924; DIBOTHRIOCEPHALIDAE Lühe, 1902; PTYCHOBOTHRIIDAE Lühe, 1902, emended; BOTHRIOCEPHALIDAE E. Blanchard, 1849, emended; ECHINOPHALLIDAE Schumacher, 1914; TRIAENOPHORIDAE Loennberg, 1889, emended; AMPHICOTYLIDAE Nybelin, 1922, with three subfamilies: AMPHICOTYLINAE Lühe, 1900, emended Nybelin, 1922, ABOTHRIINAE Nybelin, 1922, and MARSIPOMETRINAE Cooper, 1917, emended Beaver and Simer, 1940.

CLASS CESTODARIA

12. ORDER AMPHILINIDEA Poche, 1922, with one family: AMPHILINIDAE Poche, 1922, with three subfamilies: AMPHILININAE Poche, 1922, GIGANTOLININAE Poche, 1926, and AUSTRAMPHILININAE Johnston, 1934.

13. ORDER GYROCOTYLIDEA new order, with one family: GYROCOTYLIDAE Benham, 1901.

14. ORDER BIPOROPHYLLIDEA Subramanian, 1939, with one family: BIPOROPHYLLAEIDAE Subramanian, 1939.

Order PROTEOCEPHALA

DESCRIPTION

Of the class Cestoda. Small tapeworms with an extremely mobile holdfast provided with four simple cup-shaped suckers set flush with its surface. A fifth or apical sucker sometimes present. Segmentation usually well marked. Cirro-vaginal atrium opening marginally. Parenchymal muscle zone forming a boundary between cortical and medullary regions of the parenchyma. Yolk glands, ovary, uterus, and testes usually medullary but occasionally cortical. Yolk glands follicular, in lateral bands. Ovary bilobed and posterior in position. Uterus with numerous lateral outgrowths and one or more median ventral apertures. Adults parasitic in fresh-water fishes, in amphibians, and in reptiles.

HISTORY

The first recognition of proteocephalan tapeworms as a major zoological unit was made by Ariola (1899b) when he established the family Ichthyotaeniidae for a genus, *Ichthyotaenia*, founded by Loennberg in 1894 and described in detail by Riggenbach in 1896. To some extent, however, attempts to differentiate such worms generically had been made before these dates. Rudolphi (1808–10), in his comprehensive survey of pre-Rudolphian helminthology, had placed what would today be recognized as proteocephalan forms within that taxonomic lumber room, the genus *Taenia* of Linnaeus (1758). The tendency of students of tapeworms during the first half of the nineteenth century, and even of such later observers as Diesing, Dujardin, Linstow, and Monticelli, was to follow the same practice.

The various phases in the later history of these forms may be listed briefly under outstanding dates.

1858. The first attack upon that quarry of specific material, the genus *Taenia*, was made by D. F. Weinland (1858), curator of the zoological gardens of Frankfurt am Main, Germany. From it he carved the genus *Proteocephalus*, founding it upon the characteristics of the species *ambigua* of Dujardin and placing within it, as additional members, the species *filicollis* of Rudolphi and *dispar* of Goeze.

1891. Linstow pointed out that the species of "Taenia" in fresh-water fishes could be separated from other taeniids by certain constantly occurring characters. In the same year, Monticelli also pointed out that within these fish "Taenias," as then known, some twenty showed such deep-seated differences from the rest – notably in the cortical position of the testes – as to justify their separation as the genus *Tetracotylus*.

1892–1912. In the group of "Taenias" of fishes, amphibians, and reptiles—which we may anticipate by calling Proteocephala, and which now comprised the genera *Proteocephalus* and *Tetracotylus*—other forms were placed, despite certain differences in holdfast characters from the genera of Weinland and Monticelli. Thus Monticelli (1899) added *Crepidobothrium* for Baird's (1860) "Taenia gerrardii" of boid snakes. Riggenbach (1896a) added *Corallobothrium*, a genus established by Fritsch (1886) to accommodate a tapeworm from the Nile catfish. Linstow (1903c) added *Acanthotaenia*, a spiny form from the lizard *Varanus salvator* in Ceylon. La Rue (1911) added *Ophiotaenia* for a worm from the aquatic snake, *Natrix rhombifer*, and *Choanoscolex* for a worm from a South American catfish.

Presumably Weinland was unaware in 1858 that the term "Proteocephala" had been used previously by Blainville (1828a) for a family of tapeworms that included the one genus *Caryophyllaeus*; or possibly he *was* aware of the fact, but believed that the grammatical difference between the terms "Proteocephala" and "Proteocephalus" sufficiently guarded the use of these terms from confusion. Dollfus (1932b), however, pointed out that the term "Proteocephalus" is really an orthographical error or *lapsus* for "Proteocephala," and that since Article 19 of the International Code of Zoological Nomenclature specifically states that an orthographical error shall not be perpetuated, the correct term should be "Proteocephala." There would seem justification, therefore, for Loennberg's abolition of Weinland's term on the grounds of homonymity and its replacement by the term "*Ichthyotaenia*" for a generic group comprising—in 1894—the species *filicollis* Rudolphi, *ocellata* Rudolphi, *torulosa* Batsch, *longicollis* Rudolphi, and *coryphicephala* Monticelli, this latter species being the species of *Tetracotylus* that Monticelli described most completely. If we are to invoke the International Code, however, it may be pointed out that according to Article 8 the generic name may be a Greek substantive *for which the rules of Latin transcription should be followed.* A generic name derivable from the Greek *cephalo* would therefore be "Proteocephalus." Further, as Dollfus admitted, Blainville's term was used not for a genus but for a family. Here we shall use his term to cover the whole order.

1913. Beddard, surveying the forms then comprised within the so-called Ichthyotaeniidae, suggested that the generic term *Acanthotaenia* be restricted to those species found in varanid lizards, and that the generic term *Crepidobothrium* be restricted to those species which have horseshoe-shaped suckers and are found in snakes. To the family he added the genus *Ophidiotaenia*, founded upon a worm from Russell's viper (*Vipera russelli*) which had independent uterine apertures and certain peculiarities of uterine structure, and *Solenotaenia*, founded upon a form from the crossed viper (*Lachesis alternans*) which had a ventral uterine aperture in the form of a permanent slit running almost the full length of the proglottis surface (Figure 99).

1914. The confusion that existed by this time with regard to the classification of this group of tapeworms was clarified considerably by the publication (1914a) of La Rue's *Revision of the Cestode Family*

Proteocephalidae. This writer proposed the retention of Weinland's *Proteocephalus* – with the consequent abolition of Loennberg's *Ichthyotaenia* – on the grounds that Loennberg's type species, which La Rue assumed to be *filicollis* Rudolphi, was synonymous with Weinland's type species *ambigua* Rudolphi. If this assumption be conceded – and most present-day students of the group appear to accept it – then, on grounds of priority of nomenclature, Loennberg's *Ichthyotaenia* and Ariola's Ichthyotaeniidae are no longer acceptable. La Rue suggested for the family the name "Proteocephalidae," a term now used by almost all American and British helminthologists. The possible homonymity of Weinland's term was ignored, but the homonymity of Monticelli's *Tetracotylus* was stressed and the name abolished on the grounds that it had previously been used by Filippi (1854) for a group of larval trematodes. In its place La Rue suggested *Monticellia.*

Two families of proteocephalan tapeworms were recognized, therefore: (1) Proteocephalidae, with the genera *Proteocephalus* Weinland, 1858; *Corallobothrium* Fritsch, 1886; *Acanthotaenia* von Linstow, 1903; *Crepidobothrium* Monticelli, 1899; *Choanoscolex* La Rue, 1911; and *Ophiotaenia* La Rue, 1911; and (2) Monticelliidae, with the one genus *Monticellia* La Rue, 1911.

1915–24. The scheme thus suggested by La Rue persisted with relatively minor changes until 1927 when Woodland suggested the scheme discussed below. Fuhrmann (1916) added to Monticelliidae the genera *Rudolphiella,* founded for Riggenbach's *Corallobothrium lobosum,* and *Goezeella.* Rudin (1917) surveyed the proteocephalan forms from reptiles and added the genus *Batrachotaenia* to Proteocephalidae. Nybelin (1917), describing the tapeworms collected by Mjöberg's Swedish Scientific Expedition to Australia, suggested that the genera *Ophiotaenia, Ophidiotaenia,* and *Solenotaenia* were synonymous with *Crepidobothrium.* It may be noted that this opinion has been supported by Meggitt (1927b) and by Magath (1929b). On the other hand, Fuhrmann (1931), after specially studying *Crepidobothrium gerrardii* (Baird), the type species of Monticelli's genus, was of opinion that *Crepidobothrium* was sufficiently distinguished from *Ophiotaenia* by (*a*) the structure and shape of the heart-shaped suckers; (*b*) the arrangement of the testes as a single field, the lateral fields joining one another in front of the level of the cirrus pouch; and (*c*) the size of the cirrus pouch, greater than in the majority of *Ophiotaenia spp.*

Dollfus (1932b), accepting Fuhrmann's view, pointed out that in any case *Ophiotaenia, Crepidobothrium,* and several other genera of Proteocephalidae are separated from the type genus by very slight and arbitrarily chosen characters which would seem better regarded as merely subgeneric in value, thus justifying to some extent Woodland's classification (discussed below); but that as a matter of practical convenience, Fuhrmann's treatment is preferable.

Woodland (1924) added the genus *Gangesia,* found only in freshwater fishes in India and peculiar in having an armed rostellum. Southwell (1925a) added the genus *Tetracampos* Wedl, 1861, founded by its author on material from the Nilotic siluroid fish *Clarias lazera* and regarded by Southwell as synonymous with his own previously described form *Ophriocotyle bengalensis,* and synonymous also with Woodland's *Gangesia.* It may be noted, however, that the generic distinction of *Gangesia* has been affirmed by later writers such as Verma (1928) and Yamaguti (1934); the latter author asserts, in fact, that *Gangesia* cannot be identified with *Tetracampos* Wedl and that the latter genus should be regarded as doubtful until Wedl's material has been re-examined.

1925–37. Southwell (1925b) in his monograph on Tetraphyllidea placed Proteocephalidae with the family Lecanicephalidae in a suborder, Multivitellata, of an order Cyclophyllidea Braun, emended. To Proteocephalidae he added *Marsypocephalus rectangulus* Wedl, 1861. Fuhrmann and Baer (1925a), describing the tapeworms collected by the Third Cunnington Tanganyika Expedition, redefined the family Monticelliidae and added to it the genera *Loennbergia* Fuhrmann and Baer, *Ephedrocephalus* Diesing, and *Goezeella* Fuhrmann. The genus *Rudolphiella* Fuhrmann, however, was abolished on the grounds of synonymity with *Ephedrocephalus.* According to Woodland (1925d), *Loennbergia* also should be discarded as synonymous with *Marsypocephalus.*

Woodland (1925d) restudied the genus *Solenotaenia* of Beddard (1913) and found that: (*a*) the stunted uterine side branches of this form are seen also in other proteocephalan tapeworms from snakes, for example, in *Proteocephalus marenzelleri, P. calmetti,* and *Crepidobothrium gerrardii;* (*b*) there appears to be every transition between these stunted side branches and fully developed ones; and (*c*) the uterine groove, regarded by Beddard as so characteristic of the genus, represents after all, physiologically if not morphologically, merely a fusion of uterine pores and is therefore only an individual, i.e., a specific, peculiarity of an external character. Therefore he merged the genus *Solenotaenia* within *Proteocephalus.*

Meggitt (1927b) surveyed the families of La Rue's scheme, retained the family Monticelliidae, but revived the term "Ichthyotaeniidae" and the generic term *Ichthyotaenia* in place of La Rue's terms. The family Monticelliidae he regarded as comprising the genera *Ephedrocephalus, Goezeella, Loennbergia, Marsypocephalus,* and *Monticellia.* The family Ichthyotaeniidae he regarded as comprising the four genera *Corallobothrium, Crepidobothrium, Gangesia,* and *Ichthyotaenia.* The unwieldiness of the genera *Crepidobothrium* (58 species) and *Ichthyotaenia* (58 species) he recognized by dividing them into species-groups distinguishable by the nature of the apical organ, the number of testes, width of cirrus pouch, and number of uterine side branches; but no suggestion was made that such groups be given the rank of subgenera. Within each species-group, again, the component species were distinguished by the number of testes, width of cirrus pouch, and number of uterine branches. However, a relatively large number of ichthyotaeniid species that had in the past been established upon dimensional differences of highly contractile structures could not be fitted into any of the species-groups. Despite the occurrence of some errors (see Magath, 1929b) Meggitt's scheme had the advantage of providing a workable if somewhat artificial method of separating the species of Proteocephala.

The most radical departure from La Rue's scheme was put forward by Woodland in a series of articles (1925–37). With the advantage of having before him a mass of material from African and South American siluroid fishes, he surveyed the known proteocephalan tapeworms and suggested their inclusion within one family, Proteocephalidae, which he subdivided into eight subfamilies. Criticizing strongly the use of peculiarities of the holdfast as a basis for differentiating genera, he very materially reduced the list of genera previously recognized. The great majority of proteocephalan forms he placed within a subfamily Proteocephalinae, whose type genus, *Proteocephalus*, he regarded as comprising the former genera *Ophiotaenia, Ophidiotaenia, Acanthotaenia, Solenotaenia, Gangesia, Corallobothrium, Batrachotaenia*, and *Choanotaenia*; and he suggested that these generic terms be discarded.

Acceptance of Woodland's scheme depends upon the view taken as to the value of holdfast characters, a view that is by no means unanimous among students of tapeworms. The genus *Palaia* Shipley, 1900 is *possibly*, according to Woodland, synonymous also with *Proteocephalus*, although its attachment to the host gut wall by the intramucosal enclosure of its holdfast makes such a view doubtful. *Panceria* Sonsino, 1895 is too imperfectly known to be placed with certainty in any scheme of classification, but apparently its double genitalia exclude it from *Proteocephalus*. Fuhrmann (1899c) placed it, as *Pancerina nomen novum*, among linstowine Anoplocephalidae (*q.v.*). Two other genera, however, besides *Proteocephalus*, are admitted by Woodland to Proteocephalinae – namely, *Sciadocephalus* Diesing, 1850 and *Megathylacus* Woodland, 1934.

Since nearly 99 per cent of all proteocephalans are to be placed within the one genus *Proteocephalus*, Woodland's scheme aggravates the difficulty of subdividing this unwieldy assemblage of species; and, since Woodland refused to attach generic or subgeneric values to external characters, he was obliged to confess his inability to substantiate distinct subgenera within the genus *Proteocephalus*. However, he pointed out that the proteocephalan species from fresh-water fishes seem to form a homogeneous group for which the subgeneric term *Teleostotaenia* might be used, a group whose members have an unusually small holdfast (maximum breadth rarely exceeding half a millimeter), a complete lack of spines and hooks, have the testes distributed in one continuous field (except possibly in *Proteocephalus longicollis*), and have the vagina opening always in front of the cirrus pore. This subgroup contains all the proteocephalans from fishes listed by La Rue (1914a) except some from ganoids and siluroids.

A second large group, Woodland admitted, might be labeled *Crepidobothrium*, for forms having a large or a small holdfast, with a small rostellum or without a rostellum, with or without an apical organ, usually devoid of spinelets (except Johnston's *Proteocephalus gallardi*), but having the testes usually to some extent or entirely separated as two lateral fields, and having the vaginal and cirrus pores irregularly alternating as to which is anterior. This group occurs typically in snakes, but may well include many forms from amphibians, chelonians, and siluroid fishes. Nevertheless, Woodland concluded that it is almost impossible to establish subgenera within the genus *Proteocephalus.*

Fuhrmann (1931) followed Woodland's scheme but placed in the subfamily Proteocephalinae the genera *Proteocephalus* Weinland, 1858 (= *Ichthyotaenia* Loennberg, 1894 = *Teleostotaenia* Woodland, 1925 = *Choanoscolex* La Rue, 1909); *Ophiotaenia* La Rue, 1911 (= *Ophidiotaenia* Beddard, 1913 = *Solenotaenia* Beddard, 1913 = *Batrachotaenia* Rudin, 1917); *Acanthotaenia* von Linstow, 1903; *Crepidobothrium* Monticelli, 1899; *Corallobothrium* Fritsch, 1886; *Gangesia* Woodland, 1923; and *Lintoniella* Woodland, 1927. Harwood (1933) also, in accepting Woodland's scheme, placed in Proteocephalinae the genera *Proteocephalus, Ophiotaenia, Acanthotaenia, Crepidobothrium, Corallobothrium, Gangesia,* and *Lintoniella.*

RECOGNITION FEATURES

Probably no tapeworms are better known morphologically and biologically than Proteocephala, due to their common occurrence in European and North American hosts. Although it cannot be said that any exhaustive account of the group as a whole is yet available, there are perhaps more studies available of particular proteocephalan forms than is the case with other groups of tapeworms. The literature on the group is in fact extensive. Contributions to the morphology of Proteocephala in general have been made by: Loennberg (1889a, 1894), Kraemer (1892), Braun (1894–1900), Linstow (1891), Monticelli (1899), Riggenbach (1896a), Benedict (1900), Schneider (1905), Schwarz (1908), La Rue (1911, 1914), Nybelin (1917), Rudin (1917), Southwell (1925a, 1925d, 1930), Kusckowski (1925), Meggitt (1927b), and Woodland (1925–37).

Studies of particular species, varying somewhat in quality of detail, have been published by Fuhrmann (1895b), Linstow (1891, 1903c), Benedict (1900), Barbieri (1909), Zschokke (1884, 1896a), La Rue (1909), Beddard (1913a, 1913b, 1913c), Meggitt (1914a), Cooper (1915), Wagner (1917), Mrazek (1916), Faust (1920), Magath (1924, 1929b), Hannum (1925), Sandground (1928), Verma (1926, 1928), Essex (1927a, 1929a), Hunter (1928, 1929c), Hoff and Hoff (1929), Thomas (1931, 1934a, 1941), Osler (1931), Zeliff (1932), Bangham (1925–42), Larsh (1941), Nybelin (1942), and MacLulich (1943). Present discussion may be limited, therefore, to a survey of such features of proteocephalan morphology as can serve for distinguishing genera and species.

On the whole, these worms are short, slender forms, a few inches in length, and distinctly segmented. The mature and gravid segments are longer than they are broad. The holdfast end is small, ranging in length from 0.1 to 1.0 mm. in material from fishes, and from 0.2 to 1.75 mm. in

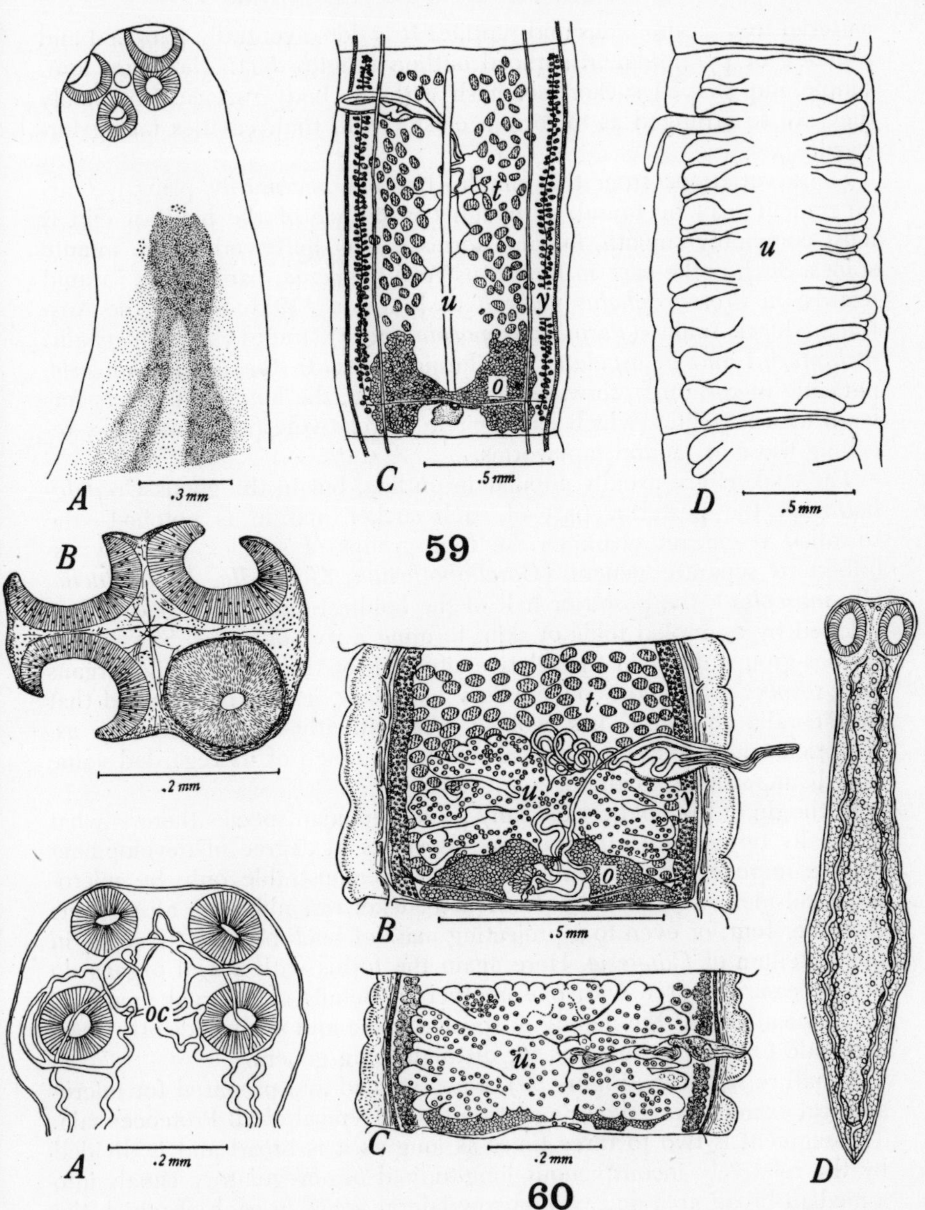

FIG. 59. *Ophiotaenia filaroides*. After La Rue, 1909. A. Holdfast showing suckers and end organ. B. Cross section through the suckers. C. Mature proglottis. D. Gravid proglottis. FIG. 60. *Proteocephalus torulosus*. After Wagner, 1917. A. Holdfast. B. Mature proglottis. C. Gravid proglottis. D. Plerocercoid larva. *o*, ovary; *oc*, osmoregulatory canal; *t*, testes; *u*, uterus; *v*, vagina; *y*, yolk glands.

material from amphibians and reptiles. It is dorso-ventrally flattened and rounded or pyramidal in surficial outline (Figure 59). There are four, simple, cup-shaped suckers set flush with the body surface. Commonly they are so arranged as to form a cluster with their cavities facing forward.

Some variations from this simple, but not necessarily primitive, arrangement may be found. Although the surface of the holdfast end is most commonly smooth, in some forms it may be covered with minute spines. Such is the case in the genus *Acanthotaenia*, parasitic in varanid lizards; in *Proteocephalus gallardi* of Johnston (1911c) from the Australian black snake (*Pseudechis porphyriacus*); and in *Proteocephalus malopteruri* and *P. osculatus* of siluroid fishes. In the genus *Gangesia*, parasitic in certain fresh-water fishes of India, the holdfast projects forward as a rostellum which has a circle of relatively powerful hooks recalling those of taeniid tapeworms.

The suckers are usually circular in outline, but in the genus *Crepidobothrium* the posterior part of each sucker margin is notched—the so-called re-entrant character. In four groups of species, formerly ascribed to separate genera (*Corallobothrium, Goezeella, Rudolphiella, Choanoscolex*), the posterior half of the holdfast end of the body is enveloped by crumpled folds of skin, forming a sort of collar. Since these species-groups differ in the relative situation of the reproductive organs with respect to the cortico-medullary boundary, it may be assumed that this "coralla character" has evolved independently among them, an assumption which detracts from this character much of its regarded value as a distinguishing attribute.

At the tip of the holdfast of many proteocephalan species there is what is usually termed an "apical organ." It varies in degree of development from a mere cluster of embedded cells, demonstrable only by microtechnical methods, to a fully developed sucker resembling in all respects the other four, or even to a projecting mass of hook-bearing tissue, as in the rostellum of *Gangesia.* Here again the forms with apical organs do not necessarily agree with one another in details of internal anatomy. Such apical organs are merely of specific value and not sufficiently characteristic to serve as features for distinguishing genera.

A mature segment (Figure 59), when stained and prepared for microscopical examination, shows a picture that is typical of all Proteocephala. The segment is two to three times as long as it is broad and is divided by the relatively inconspicuous longitudinal osmoregulatory canals into a median broad area and two narrow lateral areas, in each of which the longitudinal nerve cord of its side can be seen. Between the nerve cord and the osmoregulatory canals on each side there is a band of small, intensely staining yolk glands.

The median area shows a central longitudinal tube, the uterus, to each side of which, between it and the osmoregulatory canal, there is an area filled with loosely scattered, rounded testes. The number of testes, between limits, is characteristic of the species and may be used as a specific character. Each testis is enclosed in a delicate sheath, the tunica

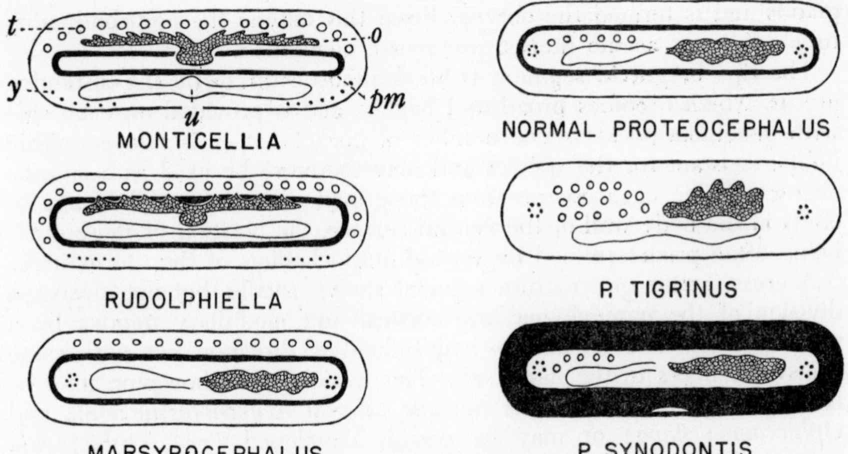

FIG. 61. Types of genitalium arrangement among Proteocephala. After Woodland, 1925d. *o*, ovary; *t*, testes; *pm*, parenchymal musculature; *u*, uterus; *y*, yolk glands.

propria, which is continuous with the walls of a minute efferent duct. The many efferent ducts converge into wider ducts which themselves converge to form a conspicuous vas deferens, or sperm duct, which runs in curved fashion toward one margin. Its terminal portion is thick and muscular and forms a cirrus or copulatory structure whose cavity is the ejaculatory duct. The cirrus is enclosed within a large, oval cirrus pouch which opens into the genital atrium – or cirro-vaginal atrium, or genital sinus – which itself opens to the exterior by the genital pore. When the cirrus pouch contracts, the cirrus is forced into the genital atrium and may project slightly through the genital pore.

Lying within the last fourth of the median area is a conspicuous, darkly stained, butterfly-shaped ovary, comprising two winglike lobes connected by a narrow bridge or isthmus. From the posterior border of this bridge there runs backward a tube which eventually curves on itself to run forward in the middle line as the uterus. The basal portion of this tube is dilated, muscular, and separated from the ovarian bridge by a sphincter muscle; it is usually referred to as the oocapt. The tube now narrows and runs posteriorly as an oviduct until it is joined by the vagina, a tube which runs from the cirro-vaginal atrium in a backward curve, crossing the uterus dorsally, then running directly back to the interovarial space before looping forward again to join the oviduct. Usually on reaching the interovarial space, the vagina dilates somewhat to form a seminal receptacle whose posterior end is apparently valvelike.

The common duct, formed by the junction of vagina and oviduct, is now called the fertilization canal. It continues posteriad, then loops forward as a U-shaped tube and is joined by the common yolk duct, itself formed by the union of a pair of yolk ducts that drain the yolk glands of each side. The junction, as well as the portion of the tube immediately following, is surrounded by numerous finger-shaped Mehlis' glands and is termed the ootype. From this ootype the egg-conducting tube continues as the uterus, previously mentioned.

The ripe or gravid segment is filled almost entirely by the distended uterus, which becomes broad and baglike and is provided on each side with pouchlike pockets. The number of pockets on each side is, within limits, constant for the species and may therefore be used as a specific character. The eggs escape from the gravid uterus through breaks or clefts in the body wall of the ventral surface, the position of these clefts being often predetermined by ventral outpocketings of the uterus itself.

A cross section of a mature segment shows usually, but not always, a division of the parenchyma into cortical and medullary regions by a zone of muscle fibers, mainly longitudinal in direction but with some transverse fibers to the inner side. This muscle zone, however, may be lacking (e.g., *Proteocephalus tigrinus*, several *Acanthotaenia spp.*, and *Ophiotaenia flava*) or may be weakly developed (e.g., *Ophiotaenia marenzelleri*). The position of the reproductive organs with regard to this muscle zone is commonly used as a basis for subdividing the family into subfamilies (Figure 62). The commonest condition is to find all the reproductive organs within this muscle zone, but in *Monticellia* the reproductive organs are mainly outside the zone. In *Endorchis* only the testes lie within it. In quite a number of forms the yolk glands lie outside it.

The life cycle has been studied fairly thoroughly for several species. The observations of Meggitt (1914) on *Proteocephalus filicollis*, Wagner (1917) on *Proteocephalus torulosus*, Kusckowski (1925) on *Proteocephalus percae* and *P. longicollis*, Cooper (1915) and Hunter (1928, 1929) on *Proteocephalus ambloplitis*, Hunter (1929c) on *Proteocephalus pinguis*, Essex (1927a) on *Corallobothrium fimbriatum*, Magath (1929b) on *Crepidobothrium testudo*, Joyeux and Baer (1933a) on *Ophiotaenia racemosa*, Thomas (1931, 1934a) on *Ophiotaenia saphena*, and Herde (1938) and Thomas (1934b, 1941) on *Ophiotaenia perspicua* – all suggest that the proteocephalan egg has to be eaten by a copepod crustacean, in which the oncosphere invades the hemocoel and develops rapidly into a procercoid larva. However, the tail-like cercomer, so characteristic of the typical procercoid, may be lacking, or if it is present it may lack the hooks. A second intermediate host is apparently not needed. The final vertebrate host is infected by swallowing infected Crustacea, and the procercoids invade such organs as the liver, gut, muscles, etc., developing there into typical plerocercoids with invaginated holdfasts (Chapter II). It may be that there is a further wandering of these into the host's alimentary tract, for otherwise – failing habitual cannibalism by the host species – a great many of the plerocercoids would fail to reach the gut and so fail to become adult.

The life cycle may be illustrated in somewhat more detail by reference to the observations of Herde (1938) on *Ophiotaenia perspicua*, parasitic in *Natrix rhombifer* in North America. In this form, the oncosphere is surrounded by three "jackets" – Herde calls them "embryophores." Of these the outermost is a spherical, thin, transparent

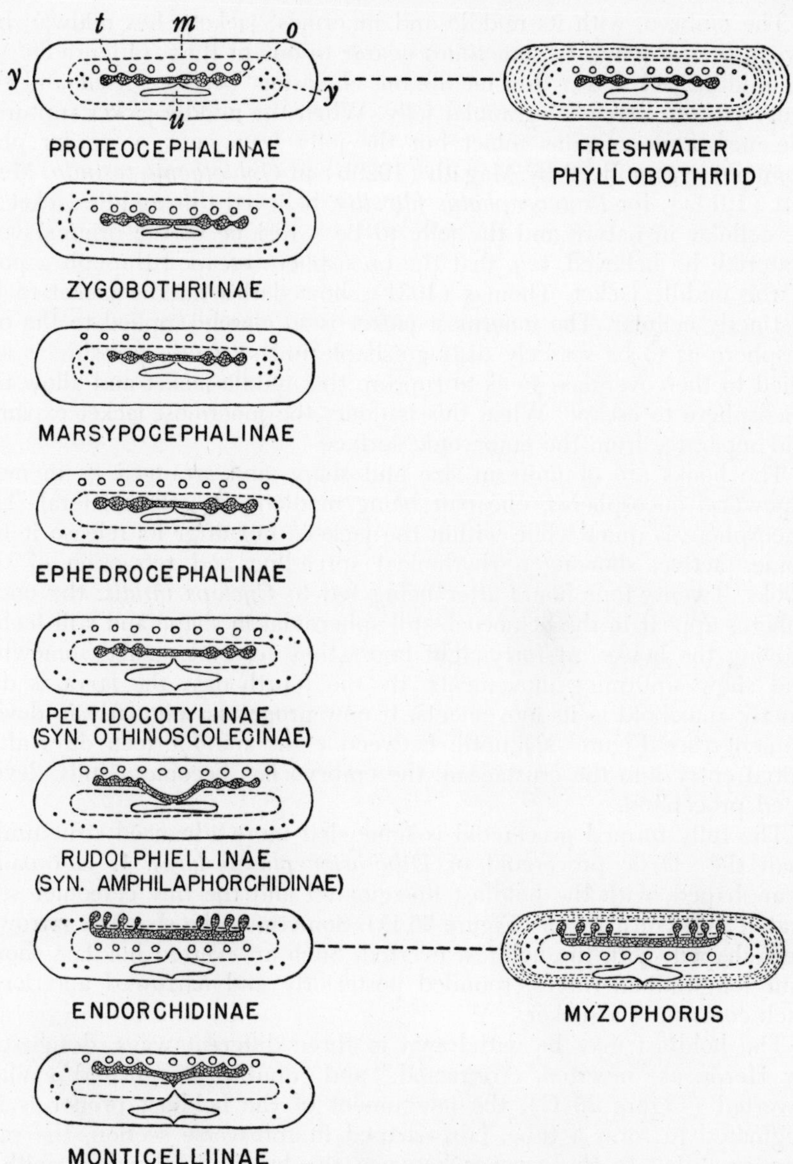

FIG. 62. Arrangement of the genitalia among the subfamilies of Proteocephalidae. After Woodland, 1934a. *m*, parenchymal muscles; *o*, ovary; *t*, testes; *u*, uterus; *y*, yolk glands.

membrane whose surface is pocketed by two "funnels" placed at opposite poles. These funnels reach as far as the middle jacket, but whether they end blindly or meet as a sheath around the middle jacket Herde could not determine. Similar funnels were described by Essex (1927a) in the embryo of *Corallobothrium*.

The embryo, with its middle and innermost jackets, lies midway between these funnels or sometimes nearer to one of them (Figure 36 A). Its middle jacket is a thin membrane enclosing, between itself and the inner jacket, a layer of granular jelly. When the middle jacket ruptures, the membrane remains intact but the jelly fragments. A similar phenomenon was noticed by Magath (1929b) in *Ophiotaenia testudo.* Meggitt (1914a), for *Proteocephalus filicollis,* believed this middle jacket to be cellular in nature and the jelly to be a residue of the original yolk material; he believed, too, that the oncosphere escaped through a pore in the middle jacket. Thomas (1931) showed this middle jacket to be distinctly cellular. The innermost jacket is so closely applied to the oncosphere as to be scarcely distinguishable unless gentle pressure is applied to the coverglass so as to rupture the middle jacket and allow the oncosphere to escape. When this is done, the innermost jacket expands and separates from the embryonic surface.

The hooks are of uniform size and shape and arranged as in most tapeworm oncospheres, one pair being median, the others lateral. The oncosphere is quiet while within the jackets, but after its release it becomes active, showing a rhythmical spreading and retraction of the hooks. Twenty-four hours after being fed to *Cyclops viridis,* the oncospheres appear in the hemocoel, still spheroidal in shape and still feebly moving the hooks. At forty-eight hours they have elongated somewhat and show squirming movements. By the fourth day, the larva is distinctly amoeboid in its movements. It now progresses regularly in development (see Figure 36) until, between eight and fourteen days after initial entry into the crustacean, the embryo has become a fully developed procercoid.

The fully formed procercoid is somewhat more advanced structurally than the classic procercoid of *Dibothriocephalus latus.* It is broadly pear-shaped, with the holdfast invaginated and the tiny cercomer separated by a constriction (Figure 36 D). Sometimes the shape is narrowly pear-shaped, with the holdfast everted. Such an everted holdfast shows four longitudinal ridges, rounded posteriorly and narrowed anteriorly, each containing a sucker.

The holdfast may be withdrawn in three different ways, designated by Herde as "inverted," "retracted," and "doubly invaginated." When inverted (Figure 36 C), the integument of the holdfast proper is invaginated to form a tube, cross-shaped in transverse section, the rays corresponding to the grooves between the longitudinal ridges, with a small, external, mouthlike pore often guarded by four liplike folds, with the end organ at the bottom of the tube, posterior to the suckers, and with the concavities of the suckers directed inward. When retracted, the integument of the neck region is invaginated to form a bladder in which the holdfast proper is withdrawn (Figure 36 E) without change in shape. In double invagination (Figure 36 D), a combination of the two other states occurs. In everted and retracted holdfasts, a little of the apical integument is generally retracted to form a shallow vestibule to the end organ. In extreme extension, the vestibule disappears and the end organ forms a slight apical protrusion. The holdfast changes readily from one invaginated state to another, either without or with intervening eversion.

The end organ is ovoid and longitudinally elongate in the everted holdfast, longitudinally flattened in the inverted holdfast. It is distinctly multicellular with longitudinally elongate, apparently glandular cells. Associated with it are some twenty to thirty unicellular glands arranged in four groups at the level of, and adjacent to, the suckers.

With the doubtful exception of *Lintoniella*, no proteocephalan tapeworm has been recorded from a marine fish, a selachian, a bird, or a mammal. The study of host distribution of tapeworms in general shows a remarkable preponderance of proteocephalan genera – especially of "collared" forms such as *Ophiotaenia, Crepidobothrium, Corallobothrium, Gangesia, Acanthotaenia* – in host groups which zoological opinion regards as primitive and as having persisted with relatively slight morphological changes over long periods of time. Species of Proteocephala occur, for example, in such persistent faunal forms as *Polypterus, Amia, Acipenser,* in siluroid fishes, caudate amphibians, boid snakes, and varanid lizards. It may be accepted that they are on the whole very primitive tapeworms. The tetraphyllidean and trypanorhynchan tapeworms of selachians would seem to be primitive, too, and the deep-seated resemblances between these forms and Proteocephala may therefore be of deep significance.

CLASSIFICATION

We shall adopt here the scheme put forward by Woodland (1925–37) and recognize one family only of Proteocephala, with eight subfamilies. However, since his views concerning the validity of holdfast characters are not everywhere accepted by students of the group, we shall follow, as regards the subfamily Proteocephalinae, the list of genera recognized by Fuhrmann (1931). Within the large genera *Proteocephalus* and *Ophiotaenia* we shall use the concept of species-groups which Meggitt has established.

Family Proteocephalidae La Rue, amended Woodland, 1933

DESCRIPTION

Of the order Proteocephala. With the characters of the order. Holdfast end with true suckers but never with bothridia. Parenchyma usually divided into cortical and medullary regions by distinct layer of longitudinal muscles or by layer of circular muscle fibers, or by a difference in parenchymal texture. Ovaries, testes, yolk glands, and uterus usually in the medulla but in certain genera cortical. Ovary always unilaminate. Vagina dorsal to cirrus pouch. Gravid proglottides not separating from body. Definitive hosts usually fresh-water fishes, amphibians, and reptiles (Figures 12, 15, 20, 25, 36, 59–102).

Woodland's subfamilies may be defined as follows (see Figure 62):

1. Proteocephalinae Mola, 1929. With ovary, testes, yolk glands, and uterus in the medulla. Yolk glands compactly arranged in two lat-

eral bands. Type genus, *Proteocephalus* Weinland. Other genera, *Acanthotaenia* Linstow, *Corallobothrium* Fritsch, *Crepidobothrium* Monticelli, *Gangesia* Woodland, and *Ophiotaenia* La Rue.

2. ZYGOBOTHRIINAE Woodland, 1933. With yolk glands cortical, dispersed, dorsal, lateral, sometimes ventral. Type genus, *Zygobothrium* Diesing. Other genera, *Amphoteromorphus* Diesing, *Nomimoscolex* Woodland.

3. MARSYPOCEPHALINAE Woodland, 1933. With testes cortical. Yolk glands medullary, compactly arranged in two lateral bands. Type and only genus, *Marsypocephalus* Wedl.

4. EPHEDROCEPHALINAE Mola, 1929. With testes and yolk glands cortical. Yolk glands dispersed and ventral. Type and only genus, *Ephedrocephalus* Diesing.

5. PELTIDOCOTYLINAE Woodland, 1934 (=Othinoscolecinae Woodland, 1933). With testes, yolk glands, and uterus cortical, only ovary being medullary. Yolk glands dispersed, arranged as in Zygobothriinae. Type and only genus, *Peltidocotyle* Diesing.

6. RUDOLPHIELLINAE Woodland, 1935. With testes and yolk glands cortical and ovary entirely or partly cortical, only uterus being entirely medullary. Type and only genus, *Rudolphiella* Fuhrmann.

7. ENDORCHIDINAE Woodland, 1934. With only the testes medullary, ovary in large part and uterus (probably) being cortical. Type and only genus, *Endorchis* Woodland.

8. MONTICELLIINAE Mola, 1929. With testes, yolk glands, uterus, and whole or greater part of ovary cortical. Type and only genus, *Monticellia* La Rue.

INCERTAE SEDIS. *Megathylacus, Lintoniella.*

KEY TO GENERA

1.	Testes cortical	2
	Testes medullary	6
2.	Yolk glands cortical	3
	Yolk glands medullary	*Marsypocephalus*
3.	Uterus cortical	4
	Uterus medullary	5
4.	Ovary cortical	*Monticellia*
	Ovary medullary	*Peltidocotyle*
5.	Ovary cortical	*Rudolphiella*
	Ovary medullary	*Ephedrocephalus*
6.	Yolk glands cortical	7
	Yolk glands medullary	10
7.	Uterus cortical	*Endorchis*
	Uterus medullary	8
8.	Each sucker with only one aperture	9
	Each sucker with two apertures	*Zygobothrium*
9.	Each sucker with two compartments	*Nomimoscolex*
	Each sucker normally proteocephalan	*Amphoteromorphus*
10.	Holdfast basally hidden by skin folds	*Corallobothrium*
	Holdfast without skin folds	11

11. Testes in single continuous field 12
Testes in separated lateral bands 13
12. Yolk glands as continuous sheet around other genitalia; forms parasitic in selachians . . . . *Lintoniella*
Yolk glands in separated lateral bands . . . . *Proteocephalus*
13. Holdfast enormous, 2–3 mm. in diameter, with four enormous sacs each opening into an apical depression . . . . *Megathylacus*
Holdfast normal in size and appearance 14
14. Holdfast with spines or hooks 15
Holdfast without spines or hooks 16
15. Holdfast with rostellum armed with hooks . . . . *Gangesia*
Holdfast without rostellum but with small spines . . . . *Acanthotaenia*
16. Suckers oval or circular . . . . *Ophiotaenia*
Suckers with notched posterior margins . . . . *Crepidobothrium*

Incertae sedis: Batrachotaenia, Electrotaenia, Manaosia, Palaia, Sciadocephalus, Silurotaenia, Solenotaenia, Vermaia.

NOTES ON GENERA

Marsypocephalus Wedl, 1861

With four spherical or ovoid suckers. No end organ. Genital apertures irregularly alternating. Testes cortical. Other genitalia medullary. Yolk glands in lateral bands. Genotype, *rectangulus* Wedl, 1861 (Figure 63).

The genotype was recorded from a Nilotic siluroid fish, *Heterobranchus anguillatis*, and was only briefly described. A fuller account was given by Woodland (1925a). Three other species are known: *heterobranchus* Woodland, 1925a from the Nilotic fish *Heterobranchus bidorsalis*; *tanganyikae* Fuhrmann and Baer, 1925a (as *Loennbergia tanganyikae*) from *Clarias lazera* in Lake Tanganyika; and *daveyi* Woodland, 1937 from *Heterobranchus bidorsalis*, Sierra Leone.

Monticellia La Rue, 1911

With four, simple, typical suckers. No end organ. Genital apertures irregularly alternating. Testes, yolk glands, uterus, and greater part of the ovary cortical. Yolk glands ventro-lateral. Genotype, *coryphicephala* Monticelli 1892 (Figure 70).

The host and location of the genotype are unknown. The date 1891 given by Stiles and Hassall (1912) as that of the article by Monticelli establishing this species is incorrect, the article of that date being one on the anatomy of monogenetic trematodes. The correct date should be 1892 (given in our bibliography as 1892a). Eight other species were recognized by Woodland (1935a). The full species list is as follows: *coryphicephala* Monticelli, 1892a (= *Tetracotylus coryphicephala* Monticelli, 1892a = *Ichthyotaenia coryphicephala* Loennberg, 1894; Riggenbach, 1896; Braun, 1894–1900); *siluri* Fuhrmann, 1916 (= *Goezeella siluri* Fuhrmann, 1916); *surubim* Woodland, 1934b (= *Spatulifer surubim* Woodland, 1934a); *piramutab* Woodland, 1933b (= *Goezeella piramutab* Woodland, 1933b); *lenha* Woodland, 1933c; *megacephala* Woodland, 1934b; *rugosa* Woodland, 1935a; *piracatinga* Woodland, 1935a; *spinulifera* Woodland, 1935b. All, with the exception of *coryphi-*

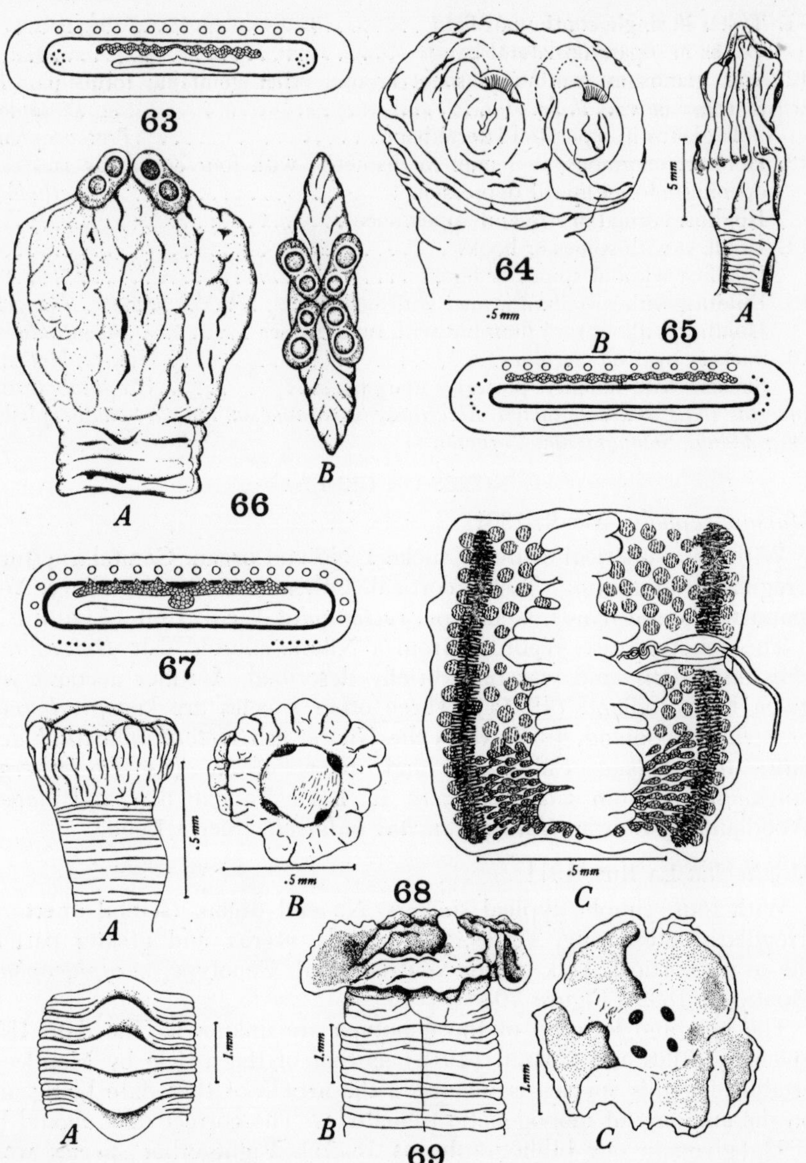

FIG. 63. *Marsypocephalus,* pattern of genitalia. After Woodland, 1933a. FIG. 64. *Marsypocephalus* (= *Loennbergia*) *tanganyikae,* holdfast. After Fuhrmann, 1925a. FIG. 65. *Peltidocotyle rugosa.* After Woodland, 1933a. A. Holdfast. B. Arrangement of genitalia. FIG. 66. *Peltidocotyle rugosa.* After Southwell, 1925b. A. Holdfast, lateral view. B. Holdfast, apical view. FIG. 67. *Rudolphiella,* arrangement of genitalia. After Woodland, 1925d. FIG. 68. *Amphilaphorchis.* After Woodland, 1934a. A. Holdfast, lateral view. B. Holdfast, apical view. C. Mature proglottis. FIG. 69. *Ephedrocephalus.* After Woodland, 1933a. A. Successive segments. B. Holdfast, lateral view. C. Holdfast, apical view.

cephala whose origin is unknown, were recorded from siluroid fishes of the Amazon drainage system of Brazil. The species may be distinguished, according to Woodland, by the features of the holdfast, the distribution of the yolk glands, and the extent of development of the parenchymal muscles (Figure 70).

Peltidocotyle Diesing, 1850

With four suckers and a surface irregularly folded, wrinkled, or

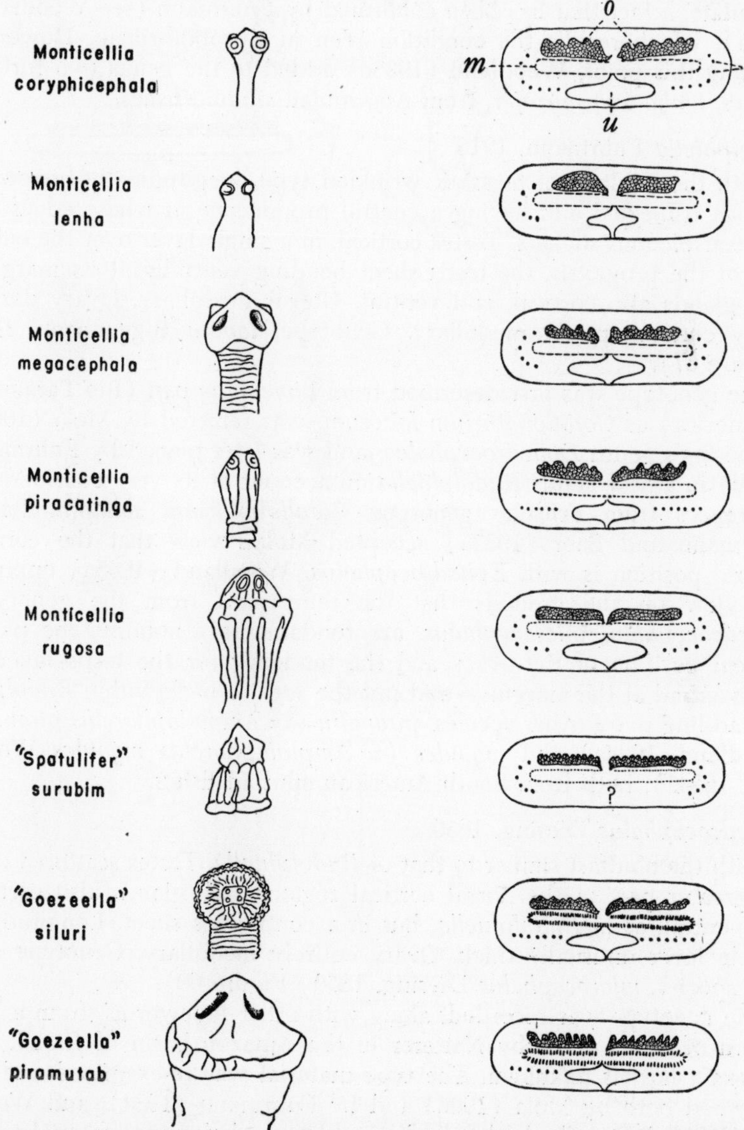

FIG. 70. Distinguishing features of the species of *Monticellia*. After Woodland, 1935a. *m*, parenchymal muscles; *o*, ovary; *u*, uterus; *y*, yolk glands.

grooved. No end organ. Testes, uterus, and yolk glands cortical, only the ovary being medullary. Genotype, *rugosa* Diesing, 1850 (Figures 65, 66).

The genotype was poorly described, and beyond the fact that it was found in *Silurus pintado* (= *Platystoma tigrinum*) in the Amazon region of Brazil, we know little of its origin. Woodland (1933c) identified with it a form he obtained from this host, but decided later that his specimen was a new species of *Monticellia.* Diesing described the suckers as being biloculate, a fact that has been confirmed by Fuhrmann (see Woodland, 1934a), which recalls the condition seen in Zygobothriinae. However, ignoring this point, Woodland (1933c) added to the genus two further species, *lenha* and *myzofer*, from Amazonian siluroid fishes.

Rudolphiella Fuhrmann, 1916

With the holdfast of massive, wrinkled type, longitudinally furrowed, its apex truncated and having a central prominence at whose edges are four conspicuous suckers. Testes cortical, in a single layer over the entire area of the proglottis, the testis sheet bending ventrally at its margins. Yolk glands also cortical, and ventral. Uterus medullary. Ovary dorsal, partly cortical, partly medullary. Genotype, *lobosa* Riggenbach, 1896 (Figure 67).

The genotype was first described from *Pimelodus pati* (Rio Paraguay, S. America) as *Corallobothrium lobosum*; was referred by Mola (1906) to Diesing's genus *Ephedrocephalus*; and was later placed by Fuhrmann (1916) in a new genus *Rudolphiella* on account of its very considerable differences from Fritsch's genotype *Corallobothrium solidum.* Later, Fuhrmann and Baer (1925a) accepted Mola's view that the correct generic position is with *Ephedrocephalus.* Woodland (1935a) opposed this view on the grounds that the differences from the genotype, *Ephedrocephalus microcephalus*, are fundamental – notably, the partly cortical position of the ovary and the tendency for the testis layer to turn ventrad at the margins – and put the species back within *Rudolphiella*, adding two further species, *piranabu* (= *Amphilaphorchis piranabu* Woodland, 1934a) and *myoides* (= *Amphilaphorchis myoides* Woodland, 1934a), both from South American siluroid fishes.

Ephedrocephalus Diesing, 1850

With the holdfast similar to that of *Rudolphiella.* Testes scattered over the greater part of the dorsal cortical region. Yolk glands also cortical and ventral, as in *Rudolphiella*, but in a continuous sheet. Longitudinal muscle layer unusually thick. Ovary entirely medullary. Genotype and only species, *microcephalus* Diesing, 1850 (Figure 69).

The genotype was recorded, along with other tapeworms, from a collection of fishes made by Natterer in the Amazon basin of Brazil, but the exact host is unknown. The type material was re-examined and redescribed both by Mola (1906) and by Fuhrmann (1934); and Woodland (1935c) described what he believed to be holotypic material taken from the fish *Phractocephalus hemiliopterus* of the Amazon region.

Endorchis Woodland, 1934

With the holdfast relatively small, only slightly broader than the body. Holdfast more or less globular with a minute aperture at the apex, the exit of a fine canal leading from a distinct globular end organ. Suckers with mouths somewhat triangular and margins minutely spiny. Genital apertures irregularly alternating. Vagina opening anterior to the cirrus. Yolk glands cortical, in short rows, one dorsal and one ventral on each side. Testes medullary, in a single field, one testis deep, between the yolk glands and the anterior border of the ovary, the field being divided by the narrow vagina. Ovary with its isthmus and large portion of the lateral lobes medullary, but with dorsal projections from the latter penetrating the muscle zone to enter the cortex. Uterus in the ventral cortex (probably). Genotype, *piraeeba* Woodland, 1934c. Additional species, *mandubé* Woodland, 1935a. Both from Amazonian siluroid fishes (Figure 71).

Woodland stressed the close resemblance in the arrangement of the genitalia between *Endorchis* and *Myzophorus,* a tetraphyllidean form from a fresh-water fish in the same area, if we assume that the innermost layer of specially large muscle bundles is homologous with the muscle layer of the proteocephalan (Figure 62).

Zygobothrium Diesing, 1850

With the holdfast large, having "four, hollow, globular parts united centrally to a central column and fused to each other laterally." Each "hollow part" is actually a large sucker the mouth of which is subdivided by a "relatively narrow but conspicuous bridge of tissue disposed tangentially to the scolex circumference" (Woodland 1933a). No end organ present. Genital apertures unilateral, on the right side of the body. Yolk glands cortical, in two lateral semicircles running dorso-ventrally, with a few follicles in the mid-dorsal line. Testes numerous, scattered uniformly through the medullary parenchyma over the dorsal region of the proglottis, between the lateral groups of yolk glands. Ovary and uterus entirely medullary. Genotype, *megacephalum* Diesing, 1850 (Figure 72).

The genotype was recorded by Diesing from material collected, as mentioned earlier, by Natterer in Brazilian siluroid fishes, and the exact host is uncertain. Fuhrmann (1934) redescribed the type material, and Woodland (1933a) claimed to have rediscovered and redescribed the genus from material in *Pirarara bicolor* and *Phractocephalus hemilioptcrus* in the Amazon area.

Nomimoscolex Woodland, 1934

With the holdfast small, with suckers of normal type, and with an end organ. Genital apertures irregularly alternating. Yolk glands marginal, in two rows insufficiently curved to form crescents (in cross sections). In all other respects similar to *Zygobothrium.* Genotype, *piraeeba* Woodland, 1934c in the Amazonian siluroid, *Brachyplatystoma filamentosum.* Other species added by Woodland from the same host type and locality are *piracatinga* Woodland, 1935a; *kaparari* Woodland,

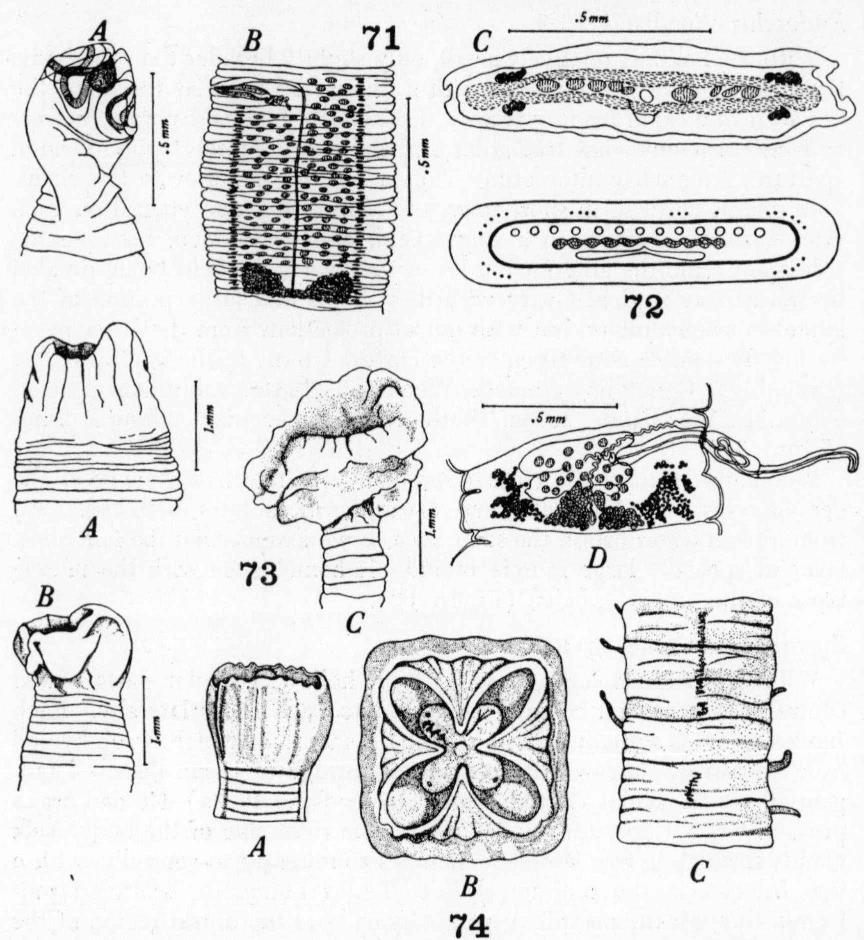

FIG. 71. *Endorchis piraeeba*. After Woodland, 1934c. A. Holdfast in side view (neck twisted). B. Mature proglottis. C. Cross section of mature proglottis. FIG. 72. *Zygobothrium*, arrangement of genitalia. After Woodland, 1933a. FIG. 73. *Amphoteromorphus peniculus*. After Woodland, 1933a. A and B. Contracted holdfasts, unattached. C. Holdfast when attached. D. Mature proglottis with partly developed uterus, dorsal view. FIG. 74. *Amphoteromorphus peniculus*. After Southwell, 1925b. A. Holdfast in profile. B. Holdfast, apical view. C. Successive proglottides.

1935a; *sudobim* Woodland, 1935b; and *lenha* Woodland, 1935 (Figure 75).

Amphoteromorphus Diesing, 1850

With a holdfast having a circular, longitudinally wrinkled surface or wall enclosing a cavity on whose floor are four suckers radially arranged. Or the holdfast may be expanded as an inverted, conical structure with a terminal disk (formed from the lining of the cavity) covered with numerous, delicate, adhesive processes developed from the subcuticle and tending to obscure the suckers. Genital apertures unilateral, on the

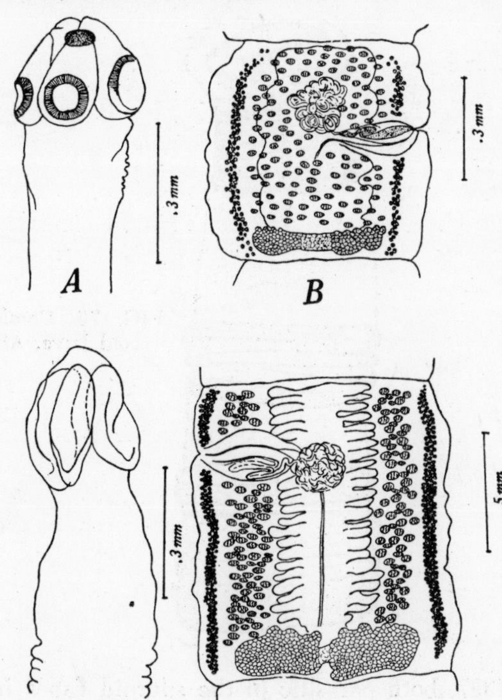

FIG. 75. *Nomimoscolex.* After Woodland, 1934a, 1935b. A. *piraeeba,* holdfast side view. B. *piraeeba,* gravid proglottis (eggs in uterus omitted). C. *sudobim,* holdfast. D. *sudobim,* gravid proglottis.

right side of the body. Cirro-vaginal atria apparently absent. Yolk glands cortical, in two groups on each side, dorsal and ventral. Testes, ovary, and uterus situated as in *Zygobothrium,* with which genus Woodland suggested subfamily relationships. Genotype, *peniculus* Diesing, 1850 (Figures 73, 74).

Diesing's material was obtained from *Brachyplatystoma rousseauxii,* a common large fish of the Amazon river system. Fuhrmann (1934) redescribed the type material, and Woodland (1935c) described material from the same host species, in which the worm is common. Additional species added by Woodland are *piraeeba,* 1934c and *parkarmoo,* 1935a from similar hosts and localities.

Corallobothrium Fritsch, 1886

With the holdfast flattened apically and having its four suckers facing forward. Posterior half of holdfast enveloped by folds of skin, the so-called lappets. No rostellum, hooks, or spines. Genitalia proteocephaline in arrangement, entirely medullary. Testes in one field. Yolk glands in marginal bands, lateral or only slightly dorsal. Adults parasitic in siluroid fishes. Genotype, *solidum* Fritsch, 1886 (Figures 76, 77).

The genotype was recorded from *Malopterurus electricus,* the electric catfish of the Nile. The generic name refers to the resemblance of the holdfast, in Fritsch's opinion, to an oculinid coral. The genus has been monographed by Essex (1927a) on material from North American hosts comprising the species *giganteum* Essex, 1927, and *fimbriatum* Essex,

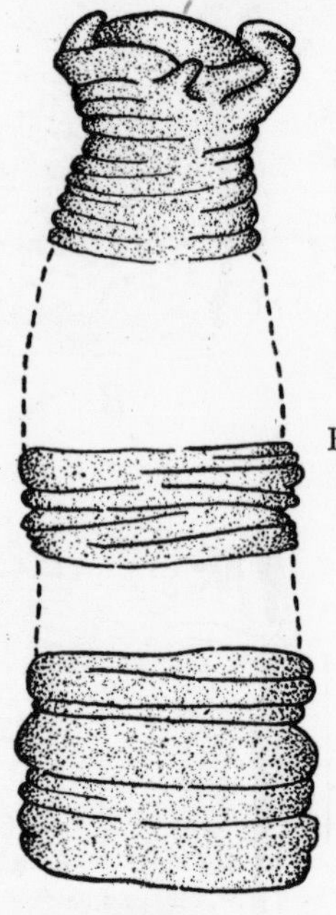

FIG. 76. *Corallobothrium*, plerocercoid larva. After Wardle, 1932a.

1927, both parasitic in the siluroid fishes *Ictaluris punctatus*, *Ameiurus melas*, and *Leptops olivaris* in the Mississippi drainage system. Larsh (1941) added a fourth species, *parvum*, from *Ameiurus nebulosus*, Douglas Lake, Michigan.

The four species are distinguishable as indicated in the accompanying table.

	Maximum Length	Sucker Sphincter	Testes	Second Egg Membrane	Oncosphere
solidum	4 cm.	Absent	140–180	20–24 μ	13–16 μ
giganteum	44 cm.	Present	80–100	14–19 μ	8–13 μ
fimbriatum	8 cm.	Absent	100–125	28–36 μ	16–24 μ
parvum	0.42 cm.	?	18–25	Not stated	Not stated

Lintoniella Woodland, 1927

Holdfast with four normal suckers. No hooks, spines, rostellum, or lappets. Genitalia proteocephaline in arrangement, the chief difference being that the yolk glands form a continuous concentric band around the other genitalia. Genotype, *adhaerens* Linton, 1925 (Figure 78).

The genotype was recorded (as *Ichthyotaenia adhaerens*) by Linton (1925) from *Cestracion zygaenae*, the hammerhead shark, an unusual location for a proteocephalan. The generic name was given by Woodland (1927b).

Proteocephalus Weinland, 1858

With the characters of the subfamily Proteocephalinae. Holdfast with four suckers of normal type. A fifth or apical sucker, functional or ves-

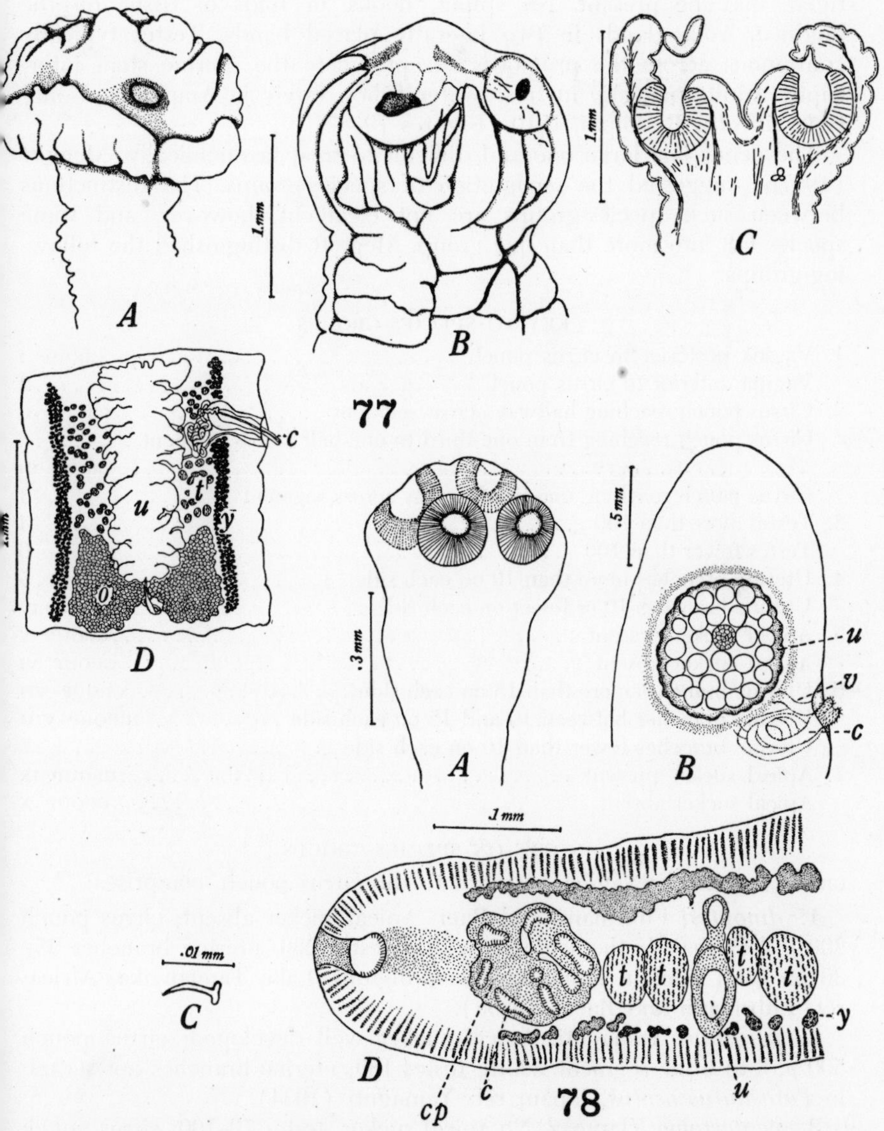

FIG. 77. *Corallobothrium*. After Essex, 1927a. A. *fimbriatum*, expanded holdfast. B. *giganteum*, holdfast showing apical prominence. C. *fimbriatum*, sagittal section of much contracted holdfast. D. *giganteum*, mature proglottis. FIG. 78. *Lintoniella adhaerens*. After Linton, 1924a. A. Holdfast. B. Anterior end of ripe proglottis, ruptured, exposing uterus filled with large segmenting eggs. C. Spine from cirrus. D. Part of transverse section of immature proglottis near genital aperture. *c*, cirrus; *cp*, cirrus pouch; *o*, ovary; *t*, testes; *u*, uterus; *v*, vagina; *y*, yolk glands.

tigial, may be present. No spines, hooks, or folds of tissue on the holdfast. Yolk glands in two laterally placed bands. Testes typically continuous across the proglottis except where the uterine stem interrupts. Adults parasitic in fresh-water fishes, rarely in Amphibia. Genotype, *filicollis* Rudolphi, 1810 (Figures 79–87).

The genus is a large one and difficult to treat taxonomically. Meggitt (1927b) suggested the recognition of species-groups. The distinctions between such species-groups are not clean-cut, however, and some species fall into more than one group. Meggitt distinguished the following groups.

KEY TO SPECIES-GROUPS

1. Vagina posterior to cirrus pouch .... GROUP I
   Vagina anterior to cirrus pouch 2
2. Cirrus pouch reaching halfway across segment .... GROUP II
   Cirrus pouch reaching from one-third to one-half across segment .... GROUP III
   Cirrus pouch reaching one-third or less across segment 3
3. Testes more than 100 4
   Testes fewer than 100 6
4. Uterine branches more than 10 on each side 5
   Uterine branches 10 or fewer on each side .... GROUP IV
5. Apical sucker present .... GROUP V
   Apical sucker absent .... GROUP VI
6. Uterine branches more than 15 on each side .... GROUP VII
   Uterine branches between 10 and 15 on each side .... GROUP VIII
   Uterine branches fewer than 10 on each side 7
7. Apical sucker present .... GROUP IX
   Apical sucker absent .... GROUP X

NOTES ON SPECIES-GROUPS

GROUP I, with the vagina posterior to the cirrus pouch, comprises:

1. *dinopteri* Fuhrmann and Baer. Apical sucker absent; cirrus pouch 290 μ, less than ⅕ the segment width; testes 240; uterine branches 25–30 on each side; in *Dinopterus cunningtoni*, Lake Tanganyika, Africa; ref. Fuhrmann and Baer (1925a).

2. *parasiluri* Yamaguti. Apical sucker well developed; cirrus pouch 500 μ, ¼ to ⅓ the segment width; testes 180; uterine branches not stated; in *Parasilurus asotus*, Japan; ref. Yamaguti (1934).

3. *pentastoma* Klaptocz. No apical sucker; testes 70–100; cirrus pouch not described; uterine branches not described; in *Polypterus bichir*, Sudan; refs. Klaptocz (1906a), La Rue (1914a).

4. *sulcatus* Klaptocz. No apical sucker; testes about 200; cirrus pouch 200–250 μ, extending about ¼ across segment; uterine branches 10–12 on each side; in *Polypterus endlichi, Clarotes laticeps*, Sudan; refs. Klaptocz (1906a), La Rue (1914a).

GROUP II, with the vagina anterior to the cirrus pouch and the latter extending halfway across the segment, comprises:

1. *agonis* Barbieri. No apical sucker; testes 100; cirrus pouch ?;

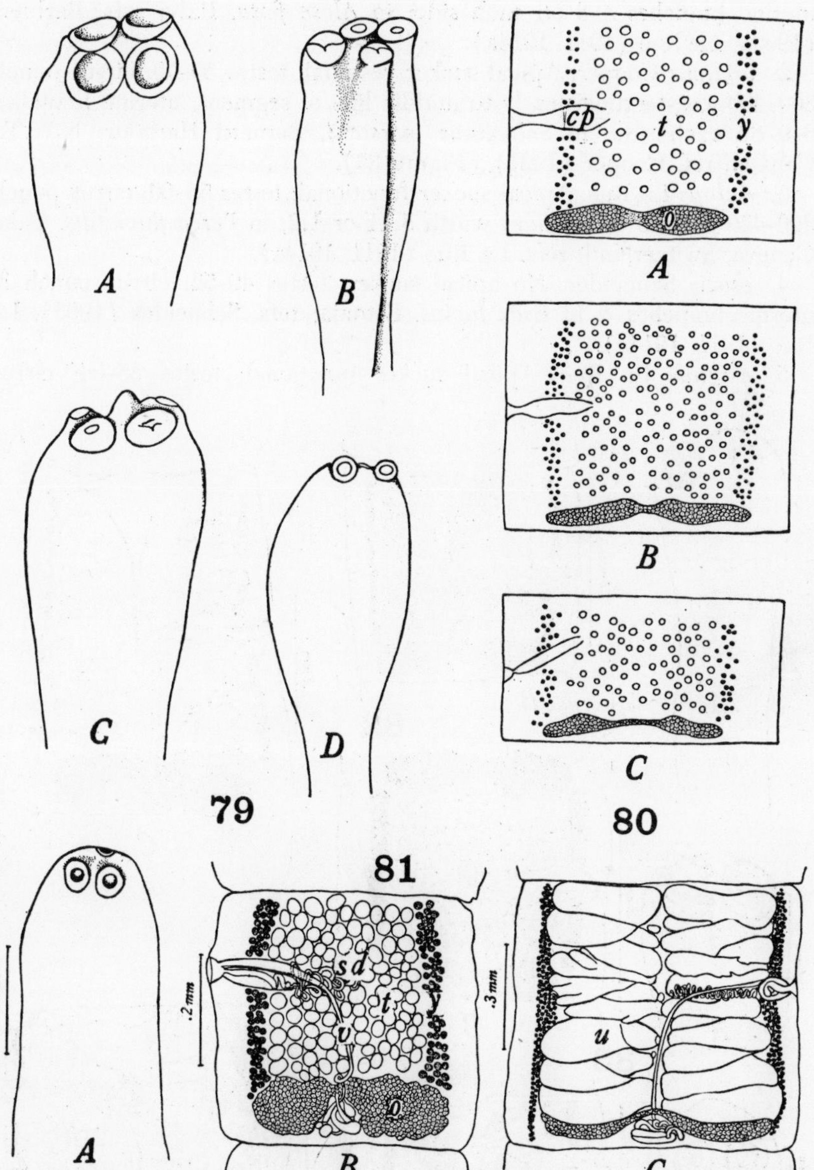

FIG. 79. Holdfast differences within *Proteocephalus*. After Wardle, 1932b. A. *coregoni*. B. *laruei*. C. *luciopercae*. D. *pinguis*. FIG. 80. Internal diagnostic differences within *Proteocephalus*. After Wardle, 1932b. A. *laruei*. B. *coregoni*. C. *luciopercae*. FIG. 81. *Proteocephalus pearsei*. After La Rue, 1919. A. Holdfast. B. Mature proglottis. C. Gravid proglottis. *cp*, cirrus pouch; *o*, ovary; *sd*, sperm duct; *t*, testes; *u*, uterus; *v*, vagina; *y*, yolk glands.

uterine branches 4–8 on each side; in *Alosa finta*, Italy; refs. Barbieri (1909), La Rue (1911, 1914a).

2. *arcticus* Cooper. Apical sucker vestigial; testes 50–70; cirrus pouch 360–400 μ, extending nearly to middle line of segment; uterine branches 6–9 on each side; in *Salvelinus marstoni*, Bernard Harbour, N.W.T., Canada; ref. Cooper (1921) (Figure 83).

3. *dubius* La Rue. Apical sucker functional; testes 55–60; cirrus pouch 260–420 μ, ratio to segment width 5:11 or 1:2; in *Perca fluviatilis*, Lake Geneva, Switzerland; refs. La Rue (1911, 1914a).

4. *esocis* Schneider. No apical sucker; testes 40–52; cirrus pouch ?; uterine branches ?; in *Esox lucius*, Estonia; refs. Schneider (1905), La Rue (1911, 1914a).

5. *exiguus* La Rue. Apical sucker functional; testes 35–54; cirrus

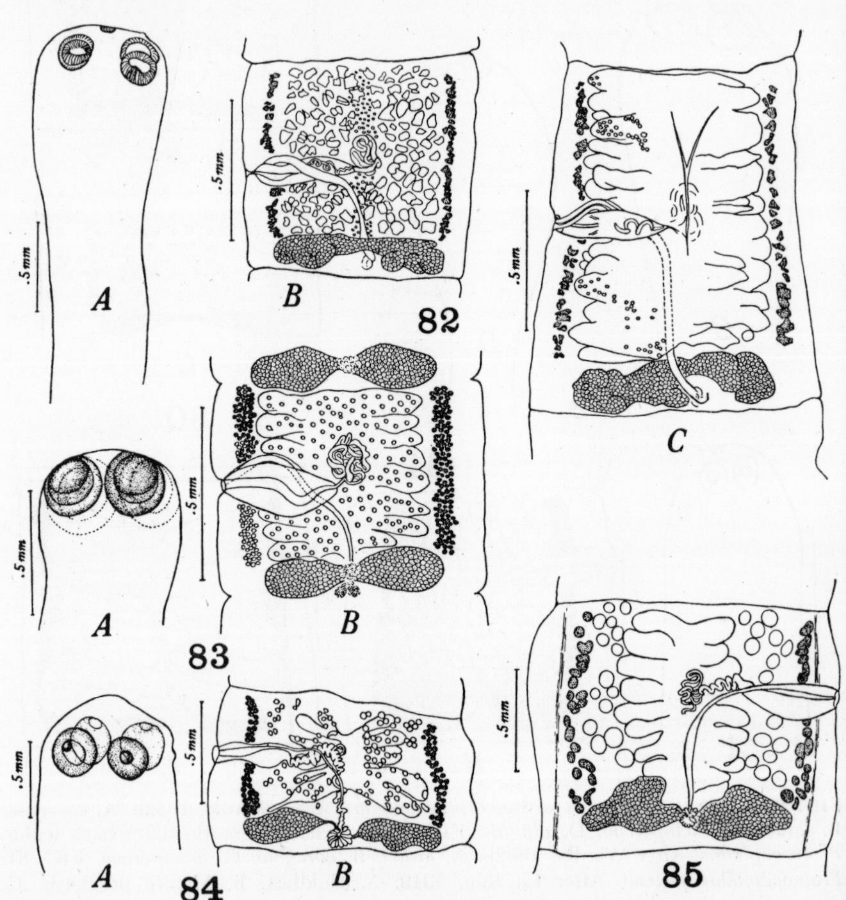

FIG. 82. *Proteocephalus parallacticus*. After MacLulich, 1943. A. Holdfast. B. Mature proglottis. C. Gravid proglottis. FIG. 83. *Proteocephalus arcticus*. After Cooper, 1921. A. Holdfast. B. Gravid proglottis (testes not shown). FIG. 84. *Proteocephalus ptychocheilus*. After Faust, 1920. A. Holdfast. B. Mature proglottis. Fig. 85. *Proteocephalus laruei*, mature proglottis. After Faust, 1920.

pouch 280–340 μ, reaching to middle of segment; uterine branches 9–14 on each side; in *Coregonus spp.*, Michigan, North America; refs. La Rue (1911, 1914a).

6. *fallax* La Rue. Apical sucker functional; testes 30–35; cirrus pouch 370–420 μ, ratio to segment width 1:3 or 1:2; uterine branches 6–8 on each side; in *Coregonus fera*, Lake Lucerne, Switzerland; refs. La Rue (1911, 1914a).

7. *jandia* Woodland. No apical sucker; testes fewer than 100; cirrus pouch 200 μ, about ½ or ⅜ the segment width; uterine branches "numerous" on each side; in *Rhamdia sp.*, Brazil; ref. Woodland (1934b).

8. *salmonis-umblae* Monticelli. Apical sucker functional; testes ?; cirrus pouch ?; uterine branches 6 on each side; in *Salmo umbla*, Lake Geneva, Switzerland; refs. Monticelli (1892a), Riggenbach (1896a), Zschokke (1884, 1896a), Lühe (1910a), La Rue (1911, 1914a).

9. *wickliffi* Hunter and Bangham. No apical sucker; testes 31–51; cirrus pouch 270–350 μ; uterine branches 6–12 on each side; in *Leucichthys artedi*, Lake Erie, North America; ref. Hunter and Bangham (1933) (Figure 87).

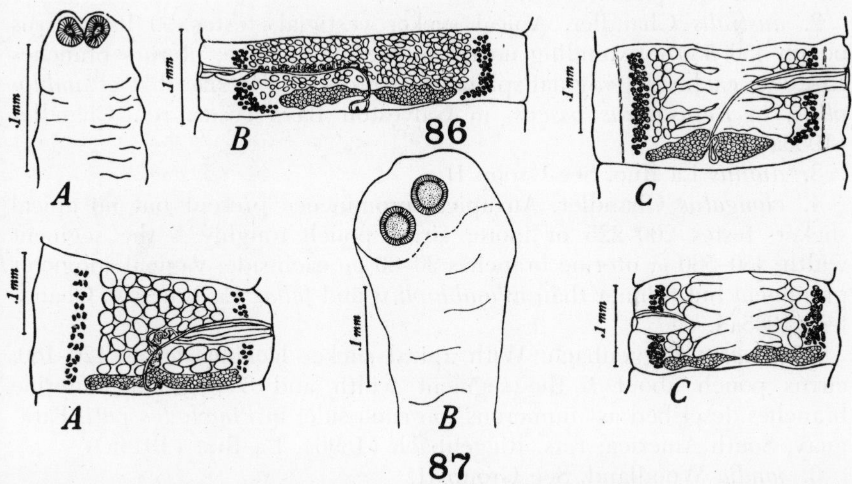

FIG. 86. *Proteocephalus stizostethi.* After Hunter and Bangham, 1933. A. Holdfast. B. Mature proglottis. C. Gravid proglottis. FIG. 87. *Proteocephalus wickliffi.* After Hunter and Bangham, 1933. A. Mature proglottis. B. Holdfast. C. Gravid proglottis.

GROUP III, with the vagina anterior to the cirrus pouch and the latter extending from one-third to one-half across the segment, comprises:

1. *amblopltis* Leidy. Apical sucker vestigial; testes 75–100; cirrus pouch 400–650 μ reaching ²⁄₇ to ⅖ across the segment width; uterine branches 15–20 on each side; in *Amia calva* and bass (*Ambloplites rupestris, Micropterus salmoides, Micropterus dolomieu*), eastern North America; refs. Leidy (1887a), Riggenbach (1896a), Linton (1897b), Benedict (1900), Marshall and Gilbert (1905), La Rue (1911, 1914a).

This form has received much attention from American parasitologists because of its effects upon its hosts (see Cooper, 1915; Bangham, 1927; Hunter, 1928; Venard, 1940). It seems to be essentially a parasite of bowfins in the Red River and St. Lawrence drainage systems, but is reported most commonly from bass. The eggs can readily be distinguished from those of other proteocephalans by their dumbbell shape. The plerocercoids cannot be distinguished from other proteocephalan larvae until the suckers are developed. The vestigial fifth sucker is characteristic. The larvae occur free in the gut of the host fish and encysted in the walls of the gut, mesenteries, spleen, liver, kidneys, and gonads in numbers per fish ranging from a few to as many as 400. The eggs are readily devoured by copepod Crustacea. The second intermediate hosts are young bass fry. The procercoid larvae migrate to the liver, mesenteries, and gonads of the host and become plerocercoids. If infecting the gonads, they may cause parasitic castration of the host. Bass are cannibalistic, and large bass readily devour bass fry. The plerocercoids thus swallowed remain in the upper intestine and develop there to maturity. The adult may be known from other species of *Proteocephalus* by its extremely large vaginal sphincter muscle and by the large number of coils in the ejaculatory duct.

2. *australis* Chandler. Apical sucker vestigial; testes 90–100; cirrus pouch 450–530 μ extending nearly to the middle line; uterine branches 15–20 on each side; vaginal sphincter approaching in size that of *ambloplitis*; in *Lepisosteus osseus*, in Galveston Bay, Texas; ref. Chandler (1935a).

3. *dubius* La Rue. See Group II.

4. *elongatus* Chandler. An apical prominence present but no apical sucker; testes 200–225 or more; cirrus pouch roughly ⅜ the segment width, 480–580 μ; uterine branches 20–30 on each side; vaginal sphincter prominent but thinner than in *ambloplitis* and *fallax* La Rue; ref. Chandler (1935a).

5. *fossatus* Riggenbach. With apical sucker lacking; testes 120–150; cirrus pouch about ⅓ the segment width and 300 μ long; uterine branches described as "numerous" on each side; in *Pimelodes pati*, Paraguay, South America; refs. Riggenbach (1896), La Rue (1914a).

6. *jandia* Woodland. See Group II.

7. *microscopicus* Woodland. With apical sucker lacking; testes about 20; cirrus pouch about ⅖ the segment width and 102–108 μ long; uterine branch number not stated; in *Cichla ocellaris*, Brazil; ref. Woodland (1935c).

8. *parallacticus* MacLulich. With apical sucker small and not functioning; testes 45–92; cirrus pouch more than ⅓ the segment width, reaching nearly to the middle line; uterine branches 7–15 on each side; in *Cristivomer namaycush, Salvelinus fontinalis, Salmo fario*, Ontario, Canada; ref. MacLulich (1943). The specific name refers to the vagina crossing around and under the cirrus pouch (Figure 82).

9. *singularis* La Rue. With apical sucker lacking; testes 75–90; cirrus pouch ⅓ to ⅖ the segment width, 90–100 μ long; uterine branches 20–25 on each side; in *Lepisosteus platystomus*, Illinois, North America; refs.

La Rue (1911, 1914a). The specific name *singularis* refers to the peculiar shape of the holdfast and the suckers. The apex of the holdfast is prolonged as a slender protuberance which is not, however, a true rostellum. Between the suckers are deep grooves which cause the holdfast to appear almost lobate. Each sucker has a pointed apex.

10. *wickliffi* Hunter and Bangham. See Group II.

GROUP IV, with vagina anterior to cirrus pouch, the latter less than one-third the segment width, testes more than 100, and uterine branches fewer than 10 on each side, comprises:

1. *coregoni* Wardle. No apical sucker; testes more than 100; cirrus not exceeding ⅙ of the segment width; uterine branches fewer than 10 on each side; in *Coregonus atikameg*, Hudson Bay; ref. Wardle (1932b) (Figure 80). Of the five species of *Proteocephalus* which have been reported previously from coregonid fishes, the European forms *longicollis, fallax*, and *percae* each possess an apical sucker; so does the American species *exiguus*. The holdfast of *laruei* is unknown. The species *coregoni* clearly differs from *laruei*, however, in the greater number of testes, narrower cirrus pouch, narrower ovarian lobes, and crowded yolk glands. Its closest resemblance is to the European *torulosus*.

2. *macrocephalus* Creplin. Apical sucker vestigial; testes 100–200; cirrus pouch short, about 160 μ; uterine branches 7–11, 12–14 on each side; in *Anguilla vulgaris, A. chrysopa*, Europe and eastern North America; refs. Creplin (1825), Lühe (1910a), La Rue (1914a).

3. *ritae* Verma. Apical sucker represented by a plug; testes 150–200; uterine branches 8–10 on each side; in *Rita rita*, rivers of northern India; refs. Verma (1926), Southwell (1930).

4. *stizostethi* Hunter and Bangham. No apical sucker; testes 90–125; cirrus pouch ⅙ to ¼ of the segment width, 290–470 μ; uterine branches 5–9 on each side; in *Stizostedion glaucum, S. canadense griseum, Micropterus dolomieu*, Lake Erie and St. Lawrence River, North America; ref. Hunter and Bangham (1933) (Figure 86). This species seems closely similar to *perplexus*, differing mainly in size of holdfast, wider proglottides, smaller suckers, lack of division of holdfast into quadrants by grooves, shorter ovarian lobes, location of vagina, smaller number of testes, and fewer uterine branches. *perplexus* and *stizostethi*, however, are the only species of the genus which have L-shaped bands of yolk glands.

5. *torulosus* Batsch. Apical sucker absent; testes 80–150; cirrus pouch extending ⅓ across segment; uterine branches 3–6 on each side; in a range of European cyprinid fishes, in *Lota lota* and *Coregonus fera*; refs. Batsch (1786), Lühe (1910), La Rue (1914), Wagner (1917) (Figure 60).

6. *vitellaris* Verma. Apical sucker absent but represented by an inverted, cuplike or caplike organ, very conspicuous and apparently both glandular and muscular; testes 250–275; cirrus pouch ⅕ to ¼ the segment width; uterine branches 5 on each side; in *Bagarius yarrellii*, Allahabad, India; ref. Verma (1928).

7. *osculatus* Goeze. Apical sucker present; testes 276–291; cirrus pouch ⅙ to ⅕ the segment width; uterine branches 8–14 on each side; in *Siluris glanis*, Europe; ref. Goeze (1782), Nybelin (1942) (Figure 88).

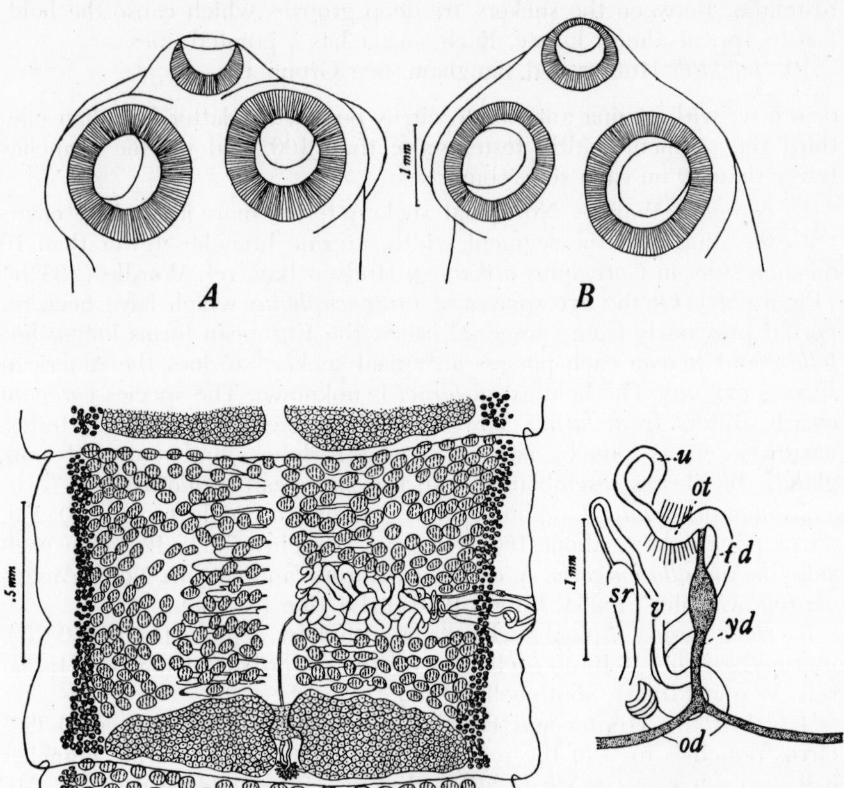

FIG. 88. *Proteocephalus osculatus*. After Nybelin, 1942. A. Holdfast of specimen from *Siluris glanis*, from the Hjalmarsee, Sweden. B. Holdfast of specimen from the Volga, Russia. C. Mature proglottis, ventral view. D. Inner female genital canal. *fd*, fertilization duct; *od*, oviduct; *ot*, ootype; *u*, uterus; *sr*, seminal receptacle; *v*, vagina; *yd*, common yolk duct.

GROUP V, with the vagina anterior to the cirrus pouch, the testes more than 100, the cirrus pouch less than one-third of the segment width, the uterine branches more than 10 on each side, and an apical sucker present, comprises:

1. *osculatus* Goeze. See Group IV.

GROUP VI, with the vagina anterior to the cirrus pouch, the testes more than 100, the cirrus pouch less than one-third of the segment width, the uterine branches more than 10 on each side, and an apical sucker lacking, comprises:

1. *cunningtoni* Fuhrmann and Baer. Testes 200; cirrus pouch 340–380

μ; uterine branches 12–15 on each side; in *Dinopterus cunningtoni*, Lake Tanganyika, Africa; ref. Fuhrmann and Baer (1925a).

2. *dinopteri* Fuhrmann and Baer. The vagina may be either anterior or posterior to the cirrus pouch. See Group I.

3. *perplexus* La Rue. Testes 135–155; cirrus pouch ⅓, ¼, or ⅕ of the segment width; uterine branches 20–25 on each side; in *Amia calva*, Illinois, North America; refs. La Rue (1911, 1914a). This form shows a general resemblance to *ambloplitis* but differs in size, in lack of apical sucker, in size and position of the vaginal sphincter, in the posterior prolongation of the yolk glands, the smaller cirrus pouch, the fewer coils of ejaculatory duct, the greater number of testes, and the size and shape of the eggs.

GROUP VII, with the vagina anterior to the cirrus pouch, the latter extending one-third or less of the segment width, the testes fewer than 100, and the uterine branches more than 15 on each side, comprises:

1. *ambloplitis* Leidy. See Group III.

2. *pusillus* Ward. Apical sucker present; testes 44–70; cirrus pouch ⅓ to ¼ of the segment width, 95–106 μ long; uterine branches 10–16 on each side; in *Salmo sebago*, Maine, and in *Cristivomer namaycush*, Lake Ontario, North America; refs. Ward (1910), La Rue (1911, 1914a). This species somewhat resembles *exiguus* (Group II) but has a larger holdfast and larger sucker mouths. The testes lie in two layers. The cirrus pouch is shorter. Its apical sucker would seem to oppose identification with Linton's insufficiently described species *salvelini*.

3. *singularis* La Rue. See Group III.

GROUP VIII, with the vagina anterior to the cirrus pouch, the cirrus pouch less than ⅓ the segment width, testes fewer than 100, uterine branches 10–15 on each side, comprises:

1. *cernuae* Gmelin. Apical sucker present; testes about 70; cirrus pouch with a ratio to segment width of 2:9 in mature proglottides, 1:5, 1:6, or 1:7 in gravid proglottides; uterine branches 6–8, 9–12 on each side; in *Acerina cernua*, Europe; refs. Gmelin (1790), La Rue (1911, 1914a).

2. *osburni* Bangham. Apical sucker present; testes 50–60; cirrus pouch with ratio to segment width of 0.3:1.0; uterine branches 5–11 on each side; in *Micropterus dolomieu*, Ohio, North America; ref. Bangham (1925).

3. *pearsei* La Rue. Apical sucker present; testes 60–90; cirrus pouch reaching little beyond the yolk glands, 90–113 μ long; uterine branches 7–15, 9–16 on each side; in *Perca flavescens*, Wisconsin, North America; ref. La Rue (1914) (Figure 81).

4. *pinguis* La Rue. Apical sucker present; testes 54–70; cirrus pouch ⅓ or ¼ the segment width, 130–140 μ long; uterine branches 10–14 on each side; in *Esox lucius*, North America; refs. La Rue (1911, 1914a), Wardle (1932b), Hunter (1929c).

5. *pusillus* Ward. See Group VII.

GROUP IX, with the vagina anterior to the cirrus pouch, testes fewer than 100, cirrus pouch less than one-third of the segment width, uterine branches fewer than 10 on each side, and an apical sucker present, comprises:

1. *cernuae* Gmelin. See Group VIII.

2. *fluviatilis* Bangham. Apical sucker muscular and functional; testes 73–98, average 84; cirrus pouch 2/7 to 2/9 the segment width; uterine branches 3, 5, or 7 on each side; in *Micropterus dolomieu*, Ohio, North America; ref. Bangham (1925).

3. *pearsei* La Rue. See Group VIII.

4. *percae* Mueller. Testes 50–60; cirrus pouch 1/3 or 2/5 of the segment width, 340–470 μ long; uterine branches 4, 5, or 9 on each side; in *Perca fluviatilis*, Europe; refs. Mueller (1780), La Rue (1911, 1914a), Lühe (1910a).

5. *pugetensis* Hoff and Hoff. Apical sucker vestigial; testes 30–40; cirrus pouch a little more than 1/4 the segment width, 156–239 μ long; uterine branches 6–7 on each side; in *Gasterosteus cataphractus*, Pacific North America; ref. Hoff and Hoff (1929).

6. *skorikowi* Linstow. Apical sucker present; testes 70–100; cirrus pouch 1/5 to 1/6 the segment width; uterine branches 6–8 on each side; in *Acipenser stellatus*, Caspian Sea; refs. Linstow (1904a), La Rue (1911, 1914).

7. *longicollis* Zeder. Apical sucker present but small; testes 25; cirrus pouch 1/5 the segment width; uterine branches 3 on each side; in *Coregonus spp.*, *Osmerus eperlanus*, *Trutta trutta*, *Salmo spp.*, Europe; refs. Zeder (1800), Rudolphi (1810), Dujardin (1845), Diesing (1850), Linstow (1891), Monticelli (1891), Loennberg (1894), Lühe (1910a), La Rue (1911, 1914a).

GROUP X, with the vagina anterior to the cirrus pouch, the latter less than one-third of the segment width, the testes fewer than 100, the uterine branches fewer than 10 on each side, and the apical sucker lacking, comprises:

1. *beauchampi* Fuhrmann and Baer. Suckers with the outer corners prolonged; testes 80; cirrus pouch 1/9 of the segment width; uterine branches 7–8 on each side; in *Dinopterus cunningtoni*, Sudan; ref. Fuhrmann and Baer (1925a).

2. *filicollis* Rudolphi. Testes 75–90; cirrus pouch 1/4 to 1/3 of the segment width and 130 μ long; uterine branches 5–8 on each side; in *Gasterosteus aculeatus*, *G. pungitius*, Europe; refs. Rudolphi (1802), La Rue (1911, 1914a).

3. *laruei* Faust. Holdfast not observed; testes 40–50; cirrus pouch 1/3 of the segment width; uterine branches 9 on each side; in *Coregonus williamsoni*, Montana, North America; ref. Faust (1920) (Figures 80, 85).

4. *luciopercae* Wardle. Apex of holdfast prolonged as a conical pseudo-rostellum; testes 80–100; cirrus pouch with ratio to segment

width of 1:3; uterine branches 4 on each side; in *Stizostedion vitreum* and *S. canadense*, western Canada; ref. Wardle (1932b) (Figure 80).

5. *neglectus* La Rue. Holdfast unknown; testes 75; cirrus pouch with ratio to segment width of 1:3 to 1:4, 180–340 μ long; uterine branches 7–9 on each side; in *Trutta fario*, Switzerland, *Plecogloccus altiveltis*, Japan; refs. La Rue (1911, 1914a), Kataoka and Momma (1933, 1934).

6. *ptychocheilus* Faust. Testes 60; cirrus pouch with ratio to segment width of 1:3, 420 μ long; uterine branches 6 on each side; in *Ptychocheilus oregonensis*, Montana, North America; ref. Faust (1920) (Figure 84).

7. *stizostethi* Hunter and Bangham. See Group IV.

8. *torulosus* Batsch. See Group IV.

INCERTAE SEDIS. Because of insufficient description, a number of species of *Proteocephalus* cannot be fitted within the above species-groups. They are:

1. *kuyukuyu* Woodland. Only immature specimens observed; body nematodelike in appearance; holdfast pointed terminally, with 4 suckers only; "save at the posterior end the segments are not demarcated by lateral notches, the outline of the body being continuous, but at the posterior end the segments become narrow and distinguishable by intersegmental notches and by secondary transverse creases"; in *Pseudodoras niger* (siluroid), Brazil; ref. Woodland (1935c).

2. *macrophallus* Diesing. Apical sucker lacking; testes 30–40; cirrus pouch 146 μ long; number of uterine branches not stated; in *Cichla monoculus*, Brazil; refs. Diesing (1850), Woodland (1933a).

3. *nematosoma* Leidy. Apical sucker lacking; similar in all respects but diameter of suckers to *ambloplitis*; in *Esox lucius*, North America; ref. Leidy (1888).

4. *plecoglossi* Yamaguti. Apical sucker feebly developed; testes 80–100; cirrus pouch ⅓ or less of the segment width; number of uterine branches not stated; in *Plecoglossus altivelis*, Lake Biwa, Japan; ref. Yamaguti (1934).

5. *salvelini* Linton. Apical sucker lacking; in *Cristivomer namaycush*, Lake Superior, North America; refs. Linton (1897b), La Rue (1911, 1914a).

Other species which must at present be regarded as *species inquirenda* are: *adhaerens* Linton, 1924 (see *Lintoniella*); *cyclops* Linstow, 1877; *eperlani* Rudolphi, 1810; *glandularia* Janicki, 1928; *hemisphaerica* Molin, 1859; *pollachii* Rathke, 1799; *sagitta* Grimm, 1872; *salmonis-omul* Pallas, 1811–12; *simplicissima* Leidy, 1887; and *trionychium* Loennberg, 1894.

Megathylacus Woodland, 1934

With the holdfast large, 2.53 mm. in diameter, quadrilobate, of four enormous sacs whose terminal apertures have each a sphincterlike muscle, differing from true suckers in the feeble development of the radial muscle fibers, whose place is taken by the powerful sphincters. Internal structure typically proteocephaline. Yolk glands in two lateral bands.

Testes in two columns between the yolk gland bands and the median uterine space. Vagina anterior to the cirrus pouch, the latter less than one-third of the segment width. Gravid uterus massive, with numerous lateral branches. Genotype and only known species, *jandia* Woodland, 1934b in the siluroid fish *Rhamdia sp.*, Brazil (Figure 89).

Gangesia Woodland, 1924

With the holdfast conical, its apex rostellumlike and having a circle of 32–37 curved hooks with rounded bases. Internal structure proteocephaline in type (Figure 90). Parasitic in Indian and Japanese fishes. Genotype, *bengalensis* Southwell, 1913.

The genotype was established, as *Ophriocotyle bengalensis*, for material from siluroid fishes, *Ophiocephalus striatus* and *Labeo rohita*, in Bengal, India. *Ophriocotyle*, of course, is an anoplocephalid genus peculiar to birds, and Southwell's identification seems to have been based purely upon the rough similarities between the holdfasts of the two forms. Actually, there is no close resemblance between this form and anoplocephalid tapeworms. In 1925a Southwell referred his species to the genus *Tetracampos* that had been erected by Wedl (1861) for material from *Heterobranchus anguillaris* (Nile catfish) and which also had a holdfast crowned with hooks. To this same genus Southwell referred also two forms described previously by Woodland (1924d) as *Gangesia wallago* and *Gangesia macrones* and believed by him to be Proteocephala with armed, rostellate holdfasts, from Indian siluroid fishes. Woodland (1925d) argued forcibly, upon the basis of Wedl's description and figures, that *Tetracampos ciliotheca* was a bothriocephalid. Unfortunately, Wedl's type material is not available.

The identity of Southwell's material with *Gangesia* was asserted by Verma (1928) and accepted by Southwell (1930). In his review of the genus, Verma recognized six species: (1) *osculata* Goeze, 1782 from *Siluris glanis*, Europe, with rostellar hooks indefinite in number, each less than 10 μ long, and uterine branches 6–8 on each side; (2) *malopteruri* Fritsch, 1886 from the Nile catfish, with rostellar hooks indefinite in number, less than 10 μ long, and uterine branches about 24 on each side; (3) *pseudotropii* Verma, 1928 (according to Southwell, the correct term is *pseudeutropii*) from the siluroid fish *Pseudotropius garua*, Ganges and Jumna rivers of India, with rostellar hooks less than 60 but more than 10 μ long, testes in two lateral fields, yolk glands short, between ovary and genital aperture; (4) *macrones* Woodland, 1924 from *Macrones seengha*, United Provinces of India, with rostellar hooks less than 60 but more than 10 μ long, of two sizes both less than 18 μ long, and testes in two lateral fields; (5) *agraensis* Verma, 1928 from *Wallago attu*, United Provinces of India, with rostellar hooks about 30 to about 22 μ long, testes nearly 100 or more and in one field; and (6) *bengalensis* Southwell (= *wallago* Woodland), with rostellar hooks each about 40 μ long, in two rows, about 50 in number, testes nearly 200 or more in one field.

To the above must be added the species *parasiluri* Yamaguti, 1934

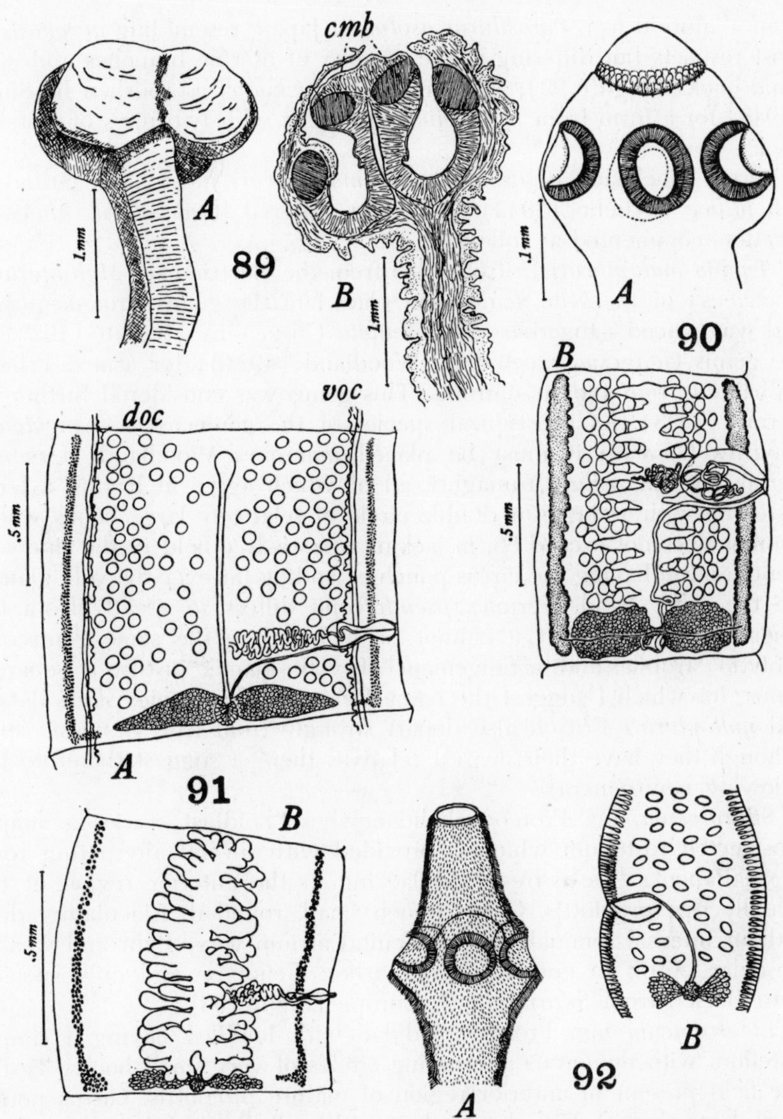

FIG. 89. *Megathylacus jandia*. After Woodland, 1934b. A. Holdfast, lateral view. B. Holdfast, sagittal section to show large size of suckers and circular muscle bands (*cmb*) surrounding their apertures. FIG. 90. *Gangesia parasiluri*. After Yamaguti, 1934. A. Holdfast. B. Mature proglottis, ventral view. FIG. 91. *Acanthotaenia sandgroundi*. After Carter, 1943. A. Mature proglottis, dorsal view. B. Fully gravid proglottis. *doc*, dorsal osmoregulatory canal; *voc*, ventral osmoregulatory canal. FIG. 92. *Acanthotaenia shipleyi*. After Southwell, 1930. A. Holdfast. B. Mature proglottis.

from a siluroid fish, *Parasilurus asotus* in Japan, resembling *agraensis* in most respects but differing in the number of uterine branches and marginal hooks (Figure 90); and the species *lucknowi* established by Singh (1948) for a form from *Eutropiichthys vacha* with two rows of rostellar hooks.

Verma's inclusion of *osculata* and *malopteruri* must be regarded as *sub judice*. Nybelin (1942), reviewing material from *Silurus glanis* in Sweden, commented as follows:

"*Taenia malopteruri* Fritsch, 1886 from the electric eel (*Malopterurus electricus*) of the Nile, cannot be placed in the genus *Proteocephalus* and was placed – together with *osculata* Goeze – by Meggitt (1927) in the genus *Gangesia*, erected by Woodland (1924d) for armed Proteocephalidae from Indian siluroids. This genus was considered further by Verma (1928). As the typical species of the genus is *G. bengalensis* (Southwell) with it must be placed *macrones* Woodland, *agraensis* Verma, and *parasiluri* Yamaguti, all of which agree in having a large rostellum with a single or double circle of relatively large hooks whose number does not exceed 50, in lacking a testis-free field in the ripe segments, and in having the cirrus pouch extending far over the yolk glands. On the other hand, Verma's *pseudotropii* differs so greatly from the other four species that it cannot be included in the same genus. Its apolytic strobila and arrangement of yolk glands justify a separate genus, for which I suggest the name *Vermaia*. The species *siluri* Batsch and *malopteruri* Fritsch also depart strongly from true *Gangesia* spp., although they have their nearest relatives there. I suggest therefore the following new genera:

"*Silurotaenia n.g.* Proteocephalidae whose holdfast carries a simply constructed rostellum which is provided with several alternating rows of small hooks. Testis-free field lacking in the anterior region of the sexually ripe proglottis. Cirrus pouch small, rounded. Ejaculatory duct without internal seminal vesicle. Genital atrium very slight and weakly muscular. Adult in gut of siluroid fishes. Genotype and only species, *siluri* Batsch from *Siluris glanis*, Europe [Figure 93].

"*Electrotaenia n.g.* Proteocephalidae with holdfast having a simple rostellum with numerous alternating circles of very small hooks. Testis-free field present in anterior region of mature proglottis. Cirrus pouch small, bean-shaped. Ejaculatory duct with well developed internal seminal vesicle. Genital atrium muscular, reaching far inwards. Adult in gut of siluroid fishes. Genotype and only species, *electricus* from *Malopterurus electricus*, Africa [Figure 94]."

There is some difference of opinion as to whether one should say *Malapterurus* and *malapteruri* or *Malopterurus* and *malopteruri*. Monticelli (1891) in fact corrected Fritsch's term *malopteruri* to *malapteruri*. We follow here the spelling used by Stiles and Hassall (1912). It may be noted that Nybelin reserved the specific term *osculatus* for *Proteocephalus osculatus*, as he believed that under that term Goeze confused two tapeworms – namely, *P. osculatus* and *Silurotaenia siluri*.

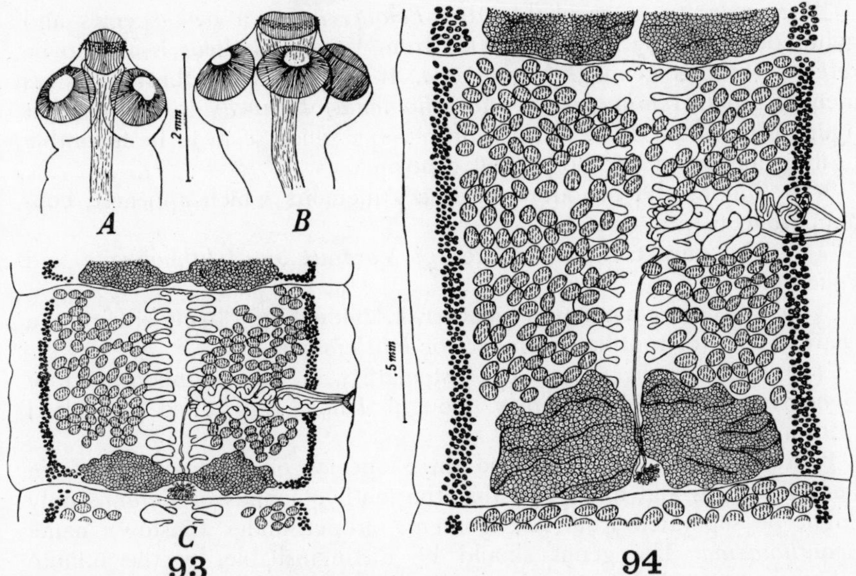

FIG. 93. *Silurotaenia siluri.* After Nybelin, 1942. A. Holdfast with rostellum extended. B. Holdfast with rostellum retracted. C. Mature proglottis, dorsal view. FIG. 94. *Electrotaenia malopteruri,* mature proglottis. After Nybelin, 1942.

Acanthotaenia Linstow, 1903

With holdfast and sometimes rest of body covered with fine spinelets or bristles. Holdfast with four typical suckers and a conical apex. Testes in two fields. Otherwise typically proteocephaline. Genotype, *shipleyi* from *Varanus* (? *salvator*) (Figures 91, 92).

"The parasites of monitor lizards so far recorded have been referred to five genera, viz. *Duthiersia, Scyphocephalus* (both of which are bothriocephalids), *Pancerina, Palaia* and *Ichthyotaenia* (including *Acanthotaenia*). The name *Acanthotaenia,* whether necessary or not, was apparently given by Linstow under a misconception of the structure of the worm, of which he gave an account under the name of *Acanthotaenia shipleyi nov. gen. et sp.* (1903). In my opinion it was probably by reason of not having seen the peripherally situated yolk glands and of having wrongly termed the ovaries yolk glands that von Linstow created the genus, rather than by virtue of the densely set spinelets upon the holdfast, though the latter clearly suggested the name. Two worms from another species of *Varanus* had previously (in 1900) been described by von Ratz as members of the genus *Ichthyotaenia*; and this name is retained by Schwarz (1908) who, however, was apparently unacquainted with Linstow's paper which is not quoted in his list of literature. Finally, at about the same time as Schwarz, T. H. Johnston (1909d) described under the name of *Acanthotaenia* a fourth species from *Varanus varius.* So far as I am aware this exhausts the species of *Ichthyotaenia* which have been recorded from lizards of the genus *Varanus.*

"It appears to me probable that *Palaia varani*, a new species and genus described by Shipley (1900) from *Varanus indicus* is also to be referred to this genus *Ichthyotaenia*. It is true that Johnston in his memoir upon *Ichthyotaenia (Acanthotaenia) tidswelli* is not of that opinion; there are, however, certain reasons which seem to be favorable to its inclusion within the present genus.

"(1) Shipley did not know of Ratz's memoirs which appeared contemporaneously.

"(2) The only taeniid parasites of *Varanus* are *Ichthyotaenia* and *Pancerina*.

"(3) Eggs of *Palaia* clump together, individual eggs being adherent, a characteristic of reptilian members of *Ichthyotaenia*.

"(4) *Pancerina* is placed by systematists in the neighbourhood of *Oöchoristica* to which Shipley thought *Palaia* was allied." Beddard (1913a).

Beddard went on to describe three species of *Ichthyotaenia* from *Varanus varius* and to suggest that the ichthyotaeniids of *Varanus* only might be separated from *Ichthyotaenia* proper under Linstow's name *Acanthotaenia*. The genus should be distinguishable by the minute spines covering holdfast and anterior segments, by the restriction of parenchymal longitudinal musculature to the anterior region of the body, and by the large size of the rostellar region, which is apt to be insignificant in ichthyotaeniids from snakes.

Woodland (1925d), however, refused to recognize the genus, on the grounds that spinosity occurs also in *Gangesia*. Meggitt (1927b) merged the genus with *Crepidobothrium*, while Baylis (1929a) accepted the genus. According to Baylis: "The fact, however, remains that there is a series of forms, chiefly parasitic in species of *Varanus*, having the same character in common, viz. a covering of minute spines extending all over the holdfast and usually over the whole or at least the anterior part of the body and it is convenient to speak of them as 'Acanthotaenia.'"

Harwood (1933) also, dismissing the objections of Woodland, recognized the generic status of *Acanthotaenia* and defined the genus as follows: Having the characters of the family. Holdfast with four suckers and a conical rostellum which lacks hooks. Numerous spinelets present on the holdfast and often on the body. No fold of tissue on the holdfast. Testes in one or in two fields. Yolk glands lateral. Parasites of reptiles, mainly *Varanus spp.* Type species, *Acanthotaenia shipleyi* Linstow, 1903.

We accept the genus here as comprising a number of forms, chiefly parasitic in varanid lizards, which agree in having minute spines over the holdfast and usually over at least the anterior segments. Three species-groups may be distinguished:

1. Testes 80 or more .... GROUP I
   Testes 50–80 .... GROUP II
   Testes fewer than 50 2
2. External segmentation distinct, testes 30–38 ...... *A. saccifera* (GROUP III)
   External segmentation indistinct, testes 42 .... *A. biroi* (GROUP III)

GROUP I comprises:

striata Johnston, 1914; *tidswelli* Johnston, 1909; and *varia* Beddard, 1913, all from Australian monitor lizards; possibly also "*Proteocephalus sandgroundi*" of Carter (1943) from a Dutch East Indian monitor, although its holdfast is unknown; and *woodlandi* Moghe, 1926, from an Indian monitor.

GROUP II comprises:

articulata Rudin, 1917; *continua* Rudin, 1917; and *nilotica* Beddard, 1913, from African monitors; *gallardi* Johnston, 1911; *gracilis* Beddard, 1913; and *varia* Nybelin, 1917, from Australian monitors, the last named species, according to Woodland (1925d), being specifically distinct from Beddard's *varia* and requiring renaming, a conclusion which was opposed, however, by Baer (1927d); *beddardi* Woodland, 1925d; and *shipleyi* Linstow, 1903c, from Indian monitors.

GROUP III comprises:

saccifera Ratz, 1900 and *biroi* Ratz, 1900, both from Australian monitors. According to Baer (1927d):

"There seems no doubt as to the identity of *P. niloticus* and *P. articulatus.* The slight differences in the measurements are due to specific variability. The distribution of the testes is identical in both species and the average diameter of a single testis is nearly the same. We therefore consider *P. articulatus* (Rudin, 1917) as a synonym of *P. niloticus* (Beddard, 1913a). On comparing *P. niloticus* with *P. continuus*, the latter is found to differ from the former only in a few details, i.e., mainly in the size of the strobila, the testes being larger and more numerous, and the cirrus pouch being smaller. Are these differences sufficient to distinguish the species? Provisionally, *P. continuus* may be considered a good species until more material has been examined, although it may well be but a *forma major* of *P. niloticus.* With regard to the Indian species, i.e., *P. beddardi* (Woodland, 1925), *P. shipleyi* (Linstow, 1903) and *P. woodlandi* (Moghe, 1926a), *P. shipleyi* was described by Linstow (1903) from a single specimen with undeveloped uterus. His description is totally insufficient and renders any comparison difficult, yet we feel convinced that further study will show that *P. woodlandi* (Moghe, 1926) is synonymous with *P. shipleyi*; *P. beddardi*, on the other hand, although closely related to the preceding species, seems to present sufficient specific details to justify its systematic position. Therefore the Indian and African monitors harbour very closely related species of the same genus of tapeworms. Further study on more ample material will no doubt prove that the Indian and African monitors harbour the same species of parasites.

"The four species described from Australian monitors, namely *biroi, saccifera, tidswelli* and *varius* are also closely related, although it is impossible to compare them fully because *biroi, saccifera* and *tidswelli* are insufficiently known. We are however convinced that when more material has been examined similar results to those above described will be obtained and that the number of purported species of proteocephalids from Australian monitors will be much reduced."

Ophiotaenia La Rue

With the holdfast globose, without spines, flattened dorsally, with apex conical without apical depression or apical sucker but with a vestigial structure embedded within it. Suckers oval, deep, and muscular. Internal features as in *Proteocephalus* but with the testes typically in two separated fields. Genotype, *perspicua* La Rue, 1911.

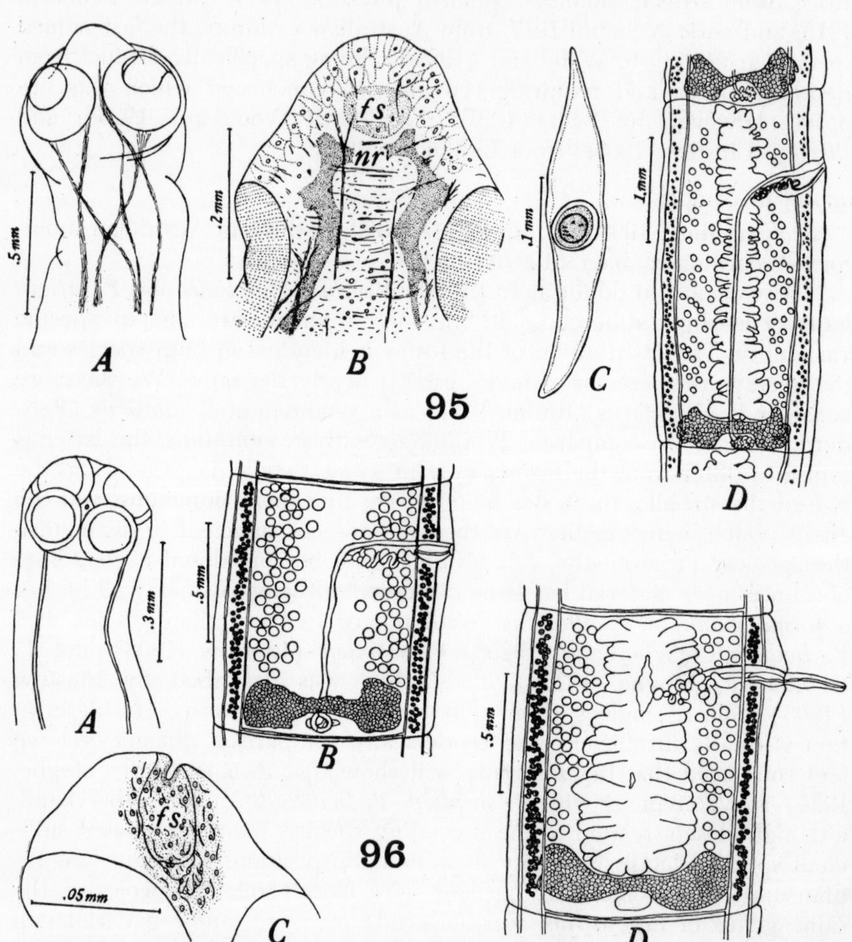

FIG. 95. *Ophiotaenia alternans*. After Riser, 1942. A. Holdfast. B. Holdfast in longitudinal section showing vestigial fifth sucker (*fs*) and nerve ring (*nr*). C. Eggs as removed from living proglottis. D. Gravid proglottis, ventral view. FIG. 96. *Ophiotaenia saphena*. After Osler, 1931. A. Holdfast. B. Mature proglottis, ventral view. C. Longitudinal section of holdfast to show vestigial fifth sucker (*fs*) with basement membrane, nuclei, muscle fibers, tubular openings. The partial outlines of other two suckers are shown for reference. D. Ruptured gravid proglottis, ventral view.

As a taxonomic unit this genus has had a checkered career. Established by La Rue (1911) for a form from a water snake, *Natrix rhombifer*, in Illinois, North America, the genus was increased by La Rue (1914a) by the addition of eleven species. Rudin (1917) accepted the genus and added eight further species. Woodland (1925d) merged it with the genus *Proteocephalus*. Meggitt (1927b) merged it with *Crepidobothrium*. Harwood (1933) regarded it as a subgenus of *Proteocephalus*. As Harwood stated:

"The case of *Ophiotaenia* is much the same as that for *Acanthotaenia* except that it is much weaker. The *Ophiotaenia* group consists of a large number of cestodes which are almost certainly monophyletic in origin. The only workable distinction between the *Ophiotaenia* group and the rest of the genus *Proteocephalus* is the division of the testes into two fields. The appearance of the same character in *Gangesia* and *Acanthotaenia* need not cause any consternation, as it may have been inherited from a common ancestor, and those two genera are sufficiently well marked by their own peculiar characters. But in a number of *Ophiotaenia* species, particularly in those which are parasites of Amphibia, the division is incomplete, while in a number of the *Proteocephalus* species, particularly those from siluroid fishes, there is a more or less distinct division of the testis field. So perfect is the gradation here that any division line must be so finely drawn that it will inevitably lead to considerable confusion. Yet so large are both groups that the preservation of some distinction is certainly desirable. Accordingly, I have assigned subgeneric rank to *Ophiotaenia* and have more or less arbitrarily disposed of the intermediate forms."

Here, we shall accept *Ophiotaenia* as a useful generic grouping for the two-field-testes proteocephalans of amphibians and reptiles. The genus is a large one, probably quite as large as *Proteocephalus*, and we shall recognize ten species-groups.

KEY TO SPECIES-GROUPS

1. Testes more than 100 2
   Testes fewer than 100 7
2. Cirrus pouch half or more of segment width 3
   Cirrus pouch one-third or less of segment width 4
3. Testes 100–120, uterine branches 20 on each side .... GROUP I
   Testes 60–120, uterine branches 27–33 on each side .... GROUP II
4. Testes more than 200 5
   Testes fewer than 200 6
5. Uterine branches 80 on each side .... GROUP III
   Uterine branches 30–50 on each side .... GROUP IV
   Uterine branches 1–30 on each side .... GROUP V
6. Uterine branches more than 25 on each side .... GROUP VI
   Uterine branches fewer than 25 on each side .... GROUP VII
7. Cirrus pouch half or more of the segment width 8
   Cirrus pouch one-third or less of the segment width .... GROUP VIII
8. Apical sucker present .... GROUP IX
   Apical sucker lacking .... GROUP X

NOTES ON SPECIES-GROUPS

GROUP I, with the testes exceeding 100, the cirrus pouch half or more of the segment width, and 20 uterine branches on each side, comprises:

One species only, *racemosa* Rudolphi, 1819. The species is of doubtful validity, Rudolphi's material—from a collection of material made by Natterer in Brazil from a variety of snakes—representing perhaps any one of, or even a composite of, the species now known as *marenzelleri, grandis, trimeresuri*, and *calmetti*. The same objection of course applies to both Diesing's (1850) and Schwarz's (1908) re-examination and re-description of the Natterer collection.

GROUP II, with the testes exceeding 100, the cirrus pouch half or more of the segment width, and 27–33 uterine branches on each side, comprises:

One species only, *san bernardinensis* Rudin, 1917 from *Helicops leprieuri*, Paraguay, South America.

GROUP III, with the testes exceeding 200, the cirrus pouch one-third or less of the segment width, and the uterine branches 80 on each side, comprises two species:

zschokkei Rudin, 1917 in *Naja haje*, South Africa.

phillipsi Burt, 1937 in the green pit viper, *Trimeresurus trigonocephalus*, Ceylon.

GROUP IV, with the testes exceeding 200, the cirrus pouch one-third or less of the segment width, and the uterine branches 30–50 on each side, comprises:

adiposa Rudin, 1917 in *Bitis arietans*, Cameroons, Africa.

faranciae MacCallum, 1921 in *Farancia abacura*, New York Zoological Gardens and Texas.

grandis La Rue, 1911 in *Agkistrodon piscivorus*, North America.

theileri Rudin, 1917 in *Naja haje*, South Africa.

mjöbergi Nybelin, 1917.

GROUP V, with the testes exceeding 200, the cirrus pouch one-third or less of the segment width, and the uterine branches less than 30 on each side, comprises:

fragile Essex, 1929 in *Ictalurus punctatus* (channel catfish), Illinois, North America.

lenha Woodland, 1933 in *Platystomatichthys sturio*, Brazil.

longmani Johnston, 1916.

marenzelleri Barrois, 1898 in *Agkistrodon piscivorus*, southern North America.

paraguayensis Rudin, 1917 in *Coluber sp.* Paraguay, South America.

perspicua La Rue, 1911 in *Tropidonotus fasciatus*, North America.

punica Cholodkovsky, 1908 reported by its discoverer from a dog in Tunis; by Southwell and Adler (1923) from a snake, *Causus rhombeatus*, Sierra Leone; and by Southwell (1930) from the Malayan palm civet, *Paradoxurus hermaphroditus*, in the Zoological Gardens of Calcutta.

testudo Magath, 1924 in *Amyda spinifera* (Chelonia), Minnesota, North America.

GROUP VI, with the testes fewer than 200, the cirrus pouch one-third or less of the segment width, and the uterine branches more than 25 on each side, comprises:

adiposa Rudin, 1917 in *Bitis arietans*, South Africa.
agkistrodontis Harwood, 1933 in *Agkistrodon piscivorus*, Texas.
alternans Riser, 1942 in *Amphiuma tridactylum*, Tennessee, North America.
amphiumae Zeliff, 1932 in *Amphiuma tridactylum*, Louisiana, North America.
calmetti Barrois, 1898 in *Lachesis lanceolatus*, Brazil and Martinique.
elapsoideae Sandground, 1928 in *Elapsoides guentheri*, Tanganyika.
filaroides La Rue, 1909 in *Ambystoma tigrinum*, North America.
gabonica Beddard, 1913 in *Bitis gabonica*, Africa.
japonensis Yamaguti, 1935 in *Elaphe quadrivirgata* and *Natrix tigrina*, Japan.
loennbergii Fuhrmann, 1895 in *Necturus maculosus*, North America.
magna Hannum, 1925 in *Rana catesbiana*, North America.
nankingensis Hsü, 1935 in *Zaocys dhumnades dhumnades*, Nanking, China.
perspicua La Rue, 1911 in *Tropidonotus fasciatus*, North America.
ranarum Iwata and Matuda, 1938 in *Rana nigromaculata*, Japan.
rhabdophidis Burt, 1937 in *Rhabdophis stolata*, Ceylon.
russelli Beddard, 1913 in *Vipera russelli*, India.
theileri Rudin, 1917 in *Naja haje*, South Africa.
trimeresuri Parona, 1896 in *Lachesis sumatrans*, East Indies.
viperis Beddard, 1913 in *Lachesis alternans*, India.

GROUP VII, with the testes fewer than 200, the cirrus pouch one-third or less of the segment width, and the uterine branches fewer than 25 on each side, comprises:

amphiboluri Nybelin, 1917.
crotaphopeltis Sandground, 1928 in *Crotaphopeltis tierneri*, Tanganyika, Africa.
cryptobranchi La Rue, 1914 in *Cryptobranchus alleghenienisis*, Pennsylvania, North America.
fragile Essex, 1929 in *Ictalurus punctatus*, Illinois, North America.
longmani Johnston, 1916.
marenzelleri Barrois, 1898 in *Agkistrodon piscivorus*, North America.
naiae Beddard, 1913 in *Naia tripudians*, India.
olor Ingles, 1936 in *Rana aurora*, California.
perspicua La Rue, 1911 in *Tropidonotus fasciatus*, North America.
ranae Yamaguti, 1938 in *Rana nigromaculata*, Japan.
saphena Osler, 1931 in *Rana clamitans*, Michigan.
synodontis Woodland, 1925 in *Synodontis schall* (siluroid fish), Anglo-Egyptian Sudan.

testudo Magath, 1924 in *Amyda spinifera*, Minnesota.
tigrinus Woodland, 1925 in *Rana tigrina*, Allahabad, India.
trimeresuri Parona, 1898 in *Lachesis sumatrans*, East Indies.

GROUP VIII, with the testes fewer than 100 and the cirrus pouch one-third or less of the segment width, comprises:

agkistrodontis Harwood, 1933 in *Agkistrodon piscivorus*, Texas.
amphiumae Zeliff, 1932 in *Amphiuma tridactylum*, Louisiana.
congolense Southwell and Lake, 1939 in *Boodon olivaceus* and *B. lineatus*, Belgian Congo.
fima Meggitt, 1927 in *Rhabdophis stolata*, Burma.
fixa Meggitt, 1927 in *Rhabdophis stolata*, Burma.
hylae Johnston, 1912 in *Hyla aurea*, Australia.
mönnigi Fuhrmann, 1924 in an unidentified snake in Burma.
nattereri Parona, 1901 in *Coluber sp*. Italy.
saphena Osler, 1931 in *Rana clamitans*, Michigan.
schulzei Hungerbühler, 1910 in *Rana adspersa*, South Africa.
striata Johnston, 1914 in *Lialis burtonii*, Australia.
tigrinus Woodland, 1925 in *Rana tigrina*, Allahabad, India.

GROUP IX, with the testes fewer than 100, the cirrus pouch about one-half the segment width, and an apical sucker present, comprises:

hylae Johnston, 1912 in *Hyla aurea*, Australia.
hyalina Rudin, 1917 in snakes from Brazil.
macrobothria Rudin, 1917 in *Elaps corallinus*, Brazil.

GROUP X, with the testes fewer than 100, the cirrus pouch about half the segment width, but with the apical sucker lacking, comprises:

schulzei Hungerbühler, 1910 in *Rana adspersa*, South Africa.
flava Rudin, 1917 in a snake from Brazil.

INCERTAE SEDIS:

armillaria Rudolphi, 1810 in *Alca alca*, Greenland.
bivitellatus Woodland, 1937 in *Tilapis sp*., Sierra Leone.
lactea Leidy, 1855 in *Tropidonotus sipedon*, North America.
pigmentata Linstow, 1908 in *Psammodytes pulverulentus* (fish).
Proteocephalus sp. Harwood, 1932 from *Anolis carolinensis*, Texas.
Proteocephalus sp. Harwood, 1932 from *Terrapene carolina triunguis*, Texas.

NOTES ON NORTH AMERICAN OPHIOTAENIIDS

IN FISHES:

1. *fragile* Essex. 45–80 mm. long; holdfast small, globose, without apical sucker; neck 5–10 mm. long; testes 150–230; cirrus pouch ⅙ to ⅕ of the segment width; everted cirrus unarmed, of great length, half or more of the segment width; genital aperture in second fourth or first third of segment margin; uterine branches 14–24 on each side; vagina anterior *or* posterior to the cirrus pouch; in channel catfish (*Ictalurus punctatus*), Illinois, North America; ref. Essex (1929a).

IN CAUDATE AMPHIBIA:

1. *alternans* Riser, 1942. 293–346 mm. long; holdfast end tetragonal or pyramidal with an apical prominence containing a vestigial apical sucker without an external opening; other suckers directed anteriad; genital pores irregularly alternating, in the anterior third, fourth, fifth, or sixth of the segment margin; testes 100–120, present throughout the entire breadth of the mature segment, anterior to the ovary, limited laterally by the osmoregulatory ducts; vagina usually anterior to the cirrus pouch but frequently posterior to it or crossing over it to become posterior; cirrus pouch 310–424 μ long, with a ratio to the segment width of 1:3; uterine branches 69–125 on each side; eggs spindle-shaped, with second membrane oval rather than spherical; in *Amphiuma tridactylum*, Tennessee, North America; ref. Riser (1942) (Figure 95).

2. *amphiumae* Zeliff, 1932. Up to 250 mm. in length; holdfast end apically flattened, without apical sucker; genital pores irregularly alternating, each in the anterior fifth of the segment margin; testes about 50–70 in each field, on both sides of the uterus, with a few approaching the middle line; vagina always anterior to the cirrus pouch; cirrus pouch 320–490 μ long, with a ratio to the segment width of about 1:3; 50–65 uterine branches on each side; eggs oval, very small, with a narrow granular zone between the first and second membranes; in *Amphiuma tridactylum*, Louisiana, North America; ref. Zeliff (1932).

3. *cryptobranchi* La Rue, 1914. Holdfast end globose with rounded apex, flattened dorso-ventrally, without furrows, rostellum, spines, or hooks; suckers shallow, oval, prominent, large; no apical sucker apparent; genital pores irregularly alternating, each in the first fourth of the segment margin; testes 107–160, distributed in two broad lateral fields; vagina anterior *or* posterior to the cirrus pouch; cirrus pouch fourth to sixth of the segment width, 239 × 119 μ; uterine branches 15, 18, 19, or 20 on each side; uterine egg spheroidal, with two membranes with clear space between; third membrane so closely adherent to the egg cell as to be indistinguishable; in *Cryptobranchus allegheniensis*, Pennsylvania, North America; ref. La Rue (1914b).

4. *filaroides* La Rue, 1909. 80–110 mm. long; holdfast end elliptical, with conical apex, suckers circular, directed laterad, no true apical sucker but represented by a submerged mass of tissue without external connection; genital pores irregularly alternating, each at the end of the first fifth of the segment margin; testes 70–114, in two lateral fields tending to unite anteriorly; vagina always anterior to the cirrus pouch; cirrus pouch about 220 μ long with a ratio to the segment width of about 1:4; uterine branches 25–35 on each side; eggs as in *cryptobranchi*; in *Ambystoma tigrinum*, Nebraska, North America; refs. La Rue (1909, 1914a) (Figure 59).

5. *loennbergii* Fuhrmann, 1895. Up to 170–190 mm. long; holdfast end flattened dorso-ventrally, globose, suckers oval, directed laterad, no apical sucker; neck about 2 mm. long; genital pores irregularly alternating, each at the end of the first third or first two-fifths of the segment

margin; testes 90–160, in two lateral fields but extending somewhat into the median zone; vagina anterior *or* posterior to the cirrus pouch; cirrus pouch short and broad, 185–290 μ long, with a ratio to the segment width of 1:4 to 1:5; uterine branches 25–40 on each side; in *Necturus maculosus*, middle United States; refs. Fuhrmann (1895b), La Rue (1909, 1911, 1914a), Beddard (1913a), Johnston (1914a), Pearse (1924a), Canavan (1928b), Stunkard (1932b), Rankin (1937).

IN SALIENT AMPHIBIA:

1. *magna* Hannum, 1925. 600 × 1.3 mm.; holdfast end globose, dorsoventrally flattened with distinct dorso-ventral and lateral furrows between the suckers that give it a pronounced tetragonal appearance; no true apex; no rostellum or apical sucker; suckers prominent, spherical, protruding; neck practically nonexistent; genital pores irregularly alternating, each at junction of first and second thirds of segment margin; testes 100–125, in two broad fields; vagina slightly posterior to the cirrus pouch; cirrus pouch 300 μ, approximately one-sixth the segment width; uterine branches 40–50 on each side; in *Rana catesbiana*, Oklahoma, North America; refs. Hannum (1925), Harwood (1932) (Figure 98).

2. *olor* Ingles, 1936. Combined length of two specimens 184 mm.; holdfast end ovoid, without apical sucker; suckers globular, cuplike, di-

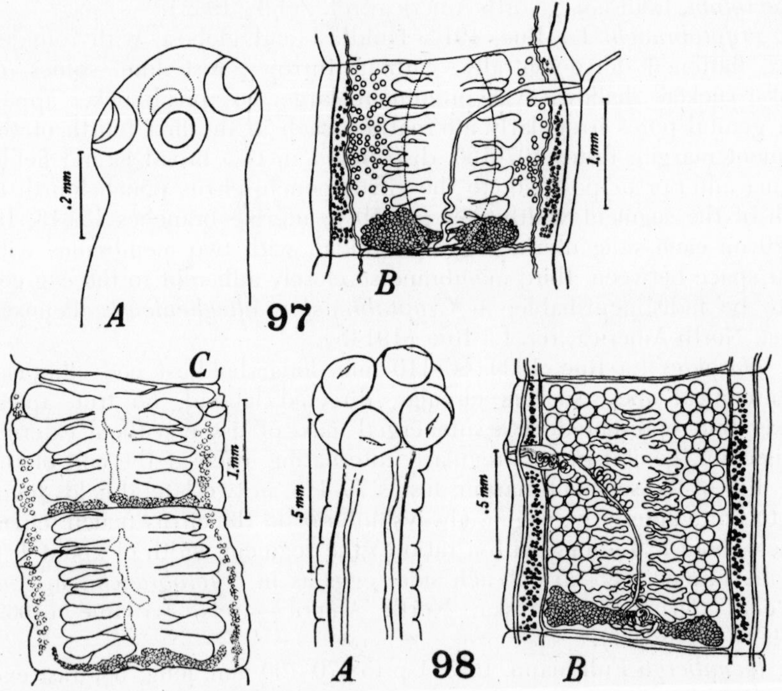

FIG. 97. *Ophiotaenia olor*. After Ingles, 1936. A. Holdfast. B. Mature proglottis. C. Gravid proglottis. FIG. 98. *Ophiotaenia magna*. After Hannum, 1925. A. Holdfast. B. Mature proglottis.

rected outward and upward; neck very long; genital pores each in first ⅙ of segment margin; testes 110–132 in lateral fields; vagina usually anterior to the cirrus pouch; cirrus pouch with a ratio to segment width of 1:9; uterine branches 10–18 on each side; in *Rana aurora*, Berkeley, California, North America; ref. Ingles (1936) (Figure 97).

3. *saphena* Osler, 1931. Up to 280 mm. long; holdfast end ovoid, with a degenerate apical sucker present as an elongated saclike organ surrounded by a basement membrane and filled with a mass of nuclei and scattered fibers, but having a small tubular cavity which connects with the exterior; other suckers prominent, cuplike; neck long and slender, 5–7 per cent of total length; genital pores irregularly alternating, each at the end of the first third of the segment margin; testes 88–120, in lateral fields; vagina usually anterior to the cirrus pouch, occasionally posterior or ventral to it; cirrus pouch with a ratio to the segment width of 1:6; uterine branches 14–18 on each side; in *Rana clamitans*, Michigan, North America; refs. Osler (1931), Thomas (1931, 1934a) (Figure 96).

IN SNAKES:

1. *agkistrodontis* Harwood, 1933. Holdfast end without trace of rostellum or apical sucker; neck very long; no trace of parenchymal muscles; genital pores each between posterior limits of first fifth and first fourth of segment margin; testes 90–110 in two fields, meeting anterior to the genital pore; vagina either anterior *or* posterior to the cirrus pouch, sometimes dorsal to it; cirrus pouch with a ratio to segment width of 1:3 to 1:4; uterine branches 25–30 on each side; in *Agkistrodon piscivorus*, Texas, North America; ref. Harwood (1933).

2. *faranciae* MacCallum, 1921. Holdfast end with a vestigial apical sucker; genital pores each between posterior end of first sixth and first third of segment margin; vagina usually posterior to cirrus pouch; cirrus pouch about fourth of the segment width; testes 390–420, uterine branches 30–50 on each side; in *Farancia abacura*, New York City Zoological Gardens, and Texas; refs. MacCallum (1921), Harwood (1932).

3. *grandis* La Rue, 1911. Up to 200 mm. long; holdfast end large, without apical sucker or rostellum; suckers deeply muscular, nearly circular; neck long (5–8 mm. in a 200 mm. strobila); genital pores each near mid-margin of the segment; testes 200–250, in lateral fields; vagina anterior *or* posterior to cirrus pouch; cirrus pouch with a ratio to the segment width of 1:3 to 1:5; uterine branches 40–60 on each side; in *Agkistrodon piscivorus*, National Zoological Park, Washington, North America; refs. La Rue (1911, 1914a).

4. *marenzelleri* Barrois, 1898. Up to 400 mm. long; holdfast end large, globose, without rostellum or apical sucker; genital pores each about the middle of the segment margin; vagina usually posterior to the cirrus pouch; testes 150, 200, 240, in lateral fields; cirrus pouch about one-third the segment width; uterine branches 20–25 on each side; in *Agkistrodon piscivorus*, southern United States; refs. Barrois (1898), Schwarz (1908), La Rue (1911, 1914a).

5. *perspicua* La Rue, 1911 (= *Taenia lactea* Leidy). Up to 360 mm.

long; holdfast end flattened, conical, divided by grooves into quadrants; no apical sucker; neck long, 5–7 mm.; genital pores each near middle or at end of first third of segment margin; testes 150–215 in lateral fields; vagina posterior to cirrus pouch; cirrus pouch one-quarter to one-third of segment width; uterine branches 20–30 on each side; in *Natrix* (*Nerodia*) *rhombifera*, Illinois; refs. La Rue (1911, 1914a), Anderson (1935), Herde (1938), Thomas (1934b, 1941).

IN TURTLES:

1. *testudo* Magath, 1924. 300–500 mm. long; holdfast end small, globose, slightly flattened anteriorly; suckers circular; apical sucker lacking; neck narrow and long; genital pores each at junction of first and second sixth; vagina always anterior to cirrus pouch; testes 125–200 in two broad lateral fields; cirrus pouch 560 μ long with a ratio to segment width of about 1:3; uterine branches 15–20 on each side; in *Amyda spinifera*, Mississippi River, Minnesota; refs. Magath (1924, 1929b).

INCERTAE SEDIS:

1. *Proteocephalus sp.* Harwood, 1932. An immature specimen of this form was found in *Anolis carolinensis*; no description was given.
2. *Proteocephalus sp.* Harwood, 1933. A single specimen but without mature segments was recorded from *Terrapene carolina triunguis*; no description was given.

Crepidobothrium Monticelli, 1899

With the holdfast large and swollen, with vestigial end organ and each sucker large, having on its posterior margin a notch such that the sucker outline is somewhat heart-shaped or even horseshoe-shaped. Internal features typically proteocephaline. Genotype, *gerrardii* Baird, 1860.

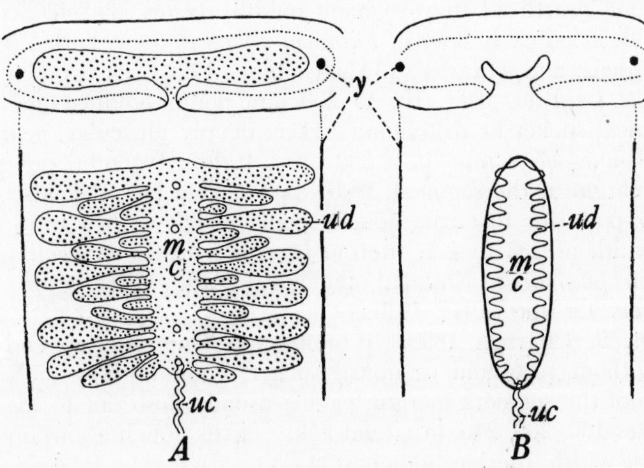

FIG. 99. Comparison of normal proteocephalid (A) and solenotaeniid (B) types of gravid uteri. After Woodland, 1925b. *mc*, median chamber of uterus; *uc*, uterine canal; *ud*, uterine diverticula; *y*, yolk glands.

The genotype was probably first seen by Diesing (1850) who recorded *Taenia racemosa* Rudolphi from a South American snake (Natterer collection). Diesing's material may have been any one of the forms now known as *marenzelleri, grandis, trimeresuri,* or *calmetti* (see above), so that *racemosa* cannot be accepted as the genotypic name.

Baird (1860, 1861) recorded, as *Tetrabothrium gerrardii,* a form from a South American boid snake (possibly *Boa constrictor*) collected by Edward Gerrard, and his specific description was accepted by Diesing (1864); by Lühe, Baird's form was assigned to the genus *Ichthyotaenia.* Monticelli (1899) re-examined Baird's type material in the British Museum and erected for it the genus *Crepidobothrium.* Shipley (1905) described, as *Taenia racemosa,* a form from the South American snake *Eunectes murina* (anaconda). Smith (1908), from the same host species, recorded *Taenia eunectes.* La Rue (1911) examined both Shipley's and Smith's type material and identified them with *Crepidobothrium gerrardii.* As such, it was accepted by Rudin (1917), but Nybelin (1917) merged within the genus the genera *Ophiotaenia, Ophidiotaenia,* and *Solenotaenia.*

Woodland (1925d) accepted *Crepidobothrium* as a subgeneric name: "A second large group, which may provisionally be labelled *Crepidobothrium* is that in which the holdfast is large or small, with a rostellum or without one, with or without an apical organ, and usually devoid of spinelets, with the testes usually to some extent, or entirely, segregated into two lateral fields, and with vaginal and cirrus apertures irregularly alternating as to which is anterior. This group is typically found in Ophidia but owing to the vagueness of the definition it will also include many Proteocephalids found in Amphibia, Siluroids and Chelonia, while others, evidently closely allied to the forms included, will be excluded. This group includes the forms recently described by MacCallum (1921) under the names of '*Tetrabothrium boae* (30 feet long),' '*T. lachesidis* (75 mm. long)' and '*T. brevis* (15 inches long).' The reason why this author labels these obvious Proteocephalids 'Tetrabothrius' is not apparent nor why he repeatedly states, in the year 1921, that 'the vagina curves towards the center to join the uterus' and regards the shell gland as a yolk gland. The other and very remarkable Cestodes described by this author are evidently Onchobothriidae, though labelled 'taenia.'

"In Amphibia, e.g., Fuhrmann's '*Ichthyotaenia*' *lönnbergii* conforms to the definition (although the testes are not completely separated into two fields) but La Rue's '*Ophiotaenia*' *filaroides* has the vaginal opening always anterior to the cirrus sac. Johnston's '*Ophiotaenia*' *hylae* has the testes in two fields but again the vagina is anterior to the cirrus, while in Hungerbühler's '*I.*' *schultzei* with testes in two fields the vagina is behind the cirrus. In my *P. tigrinus,* on the other hand, the testes are in one field (the vagina being usually anterior to the cirrus). In 'Ganoid' fishes the two species *P. sulcatus* and *P. pentastoma* both have the testes disposed to some extent into two fields but in both the vagina is posterior to the cirrus sac. In Siluroid fishes some proteocephalids have the testes in two fields and alternating vagina and cirrus apertures (*P.*

malapteruri and *P. synodontis* e.g.) but others have the testes in one field and either alternating vagina and cirrus (as in *P. solidum* syn. '*Corallobothrium*' and '*Gangesia*' spp.) or with the vagina anterior to the cirrus (*P. fossatus*) or posterior to the cirrus (as in *P. sulcatus* which is also found in a Siluroid—*Clarotes*). In Chelonia I have already pointed out that while '*O.*' *testudo* has the testes in two fields, '*Tetrabothrium*' *trionychinum* has the testes in one field (in both species the vagina is anterior to the cirrus). It is thus fairly evident that the characters of testis distribution and the position of the vagina relative to the cirrus sac are of very little use." Woodland (1925d).

Meggitt (1927b) accepted the genus *Crepidobothrium* and merged with it the genera *Acanthotaenia* and *Ophiotaenia*, thus giving to it 44 definite species and 9 doubtful ones. Magath (1924) at first placed his species *testudo* within the genus. Essex (1929) established *Crepidobothrium fragile* from *Ictalurus punctatus*. Meggitt (1940) added *nankingensis* Hsü (no holdfast known) from a water snake (*Homalopsis buccata*) in Burma. Zeliff (1932) added *amphiumae* from *Amphiuma tridactylum*. Dollfus (1932b) described as *C. gerrardii minus* a form from a collection made by Moniez, of doubtful authenticity (Figure 100). If, however, the term *Crepidobothrium* is reserved for notched-sucker forms from boid snakes, it is clear that the majority of the species assigned to it must be placed within *Ophiotaenia* and the genus regarded as containing only the one species *gerrardii*.

GENERA INQUIRENDA

Batrachotaenia Rudin, 1917

With variable segmentation, loose parenchyma, weak musculature. Vagina in constant relation with cirrus pouch. Testes in two fields. Established by Rudin for a heterogeneous group of Proteocephala parasitic in Amphibia and comprising *schultzei* Hungerbühler, *hylae* Johnston, *loennbergii* Fuhrmann, *filaroides* La Rue. These forms have been discussed above as species of *Ophiotaenia*.

Electrotaenia Nybelin, 1917

Established for the species *electricus* in *Malopterurus electricus*, Africa, and described as having a holdfast whose simply constructed rostellum carries several alternating rows of small hooks. Testis-free median field in anterior region of proglottis. Small bean-shaped cirrus pouch. Well-developed seminal vesicle. Large and muscular genital atrium. See *Gangesia*.

Manaosia Woodland, 1935

Rudolphiellinae or Monticelliinae. Holdfast large, containing large suckers embedded in its substance, each opening to the outside by a small aperture. No end organ. Genotype, *bracodemoca* from *Platystoma sp.*, Manaos, Brazil. Ref. Woodland (1935a) (Figure 102).

Palaia Shipley, 1900

Author's description: "The rostrum is absent and no hooks are present.

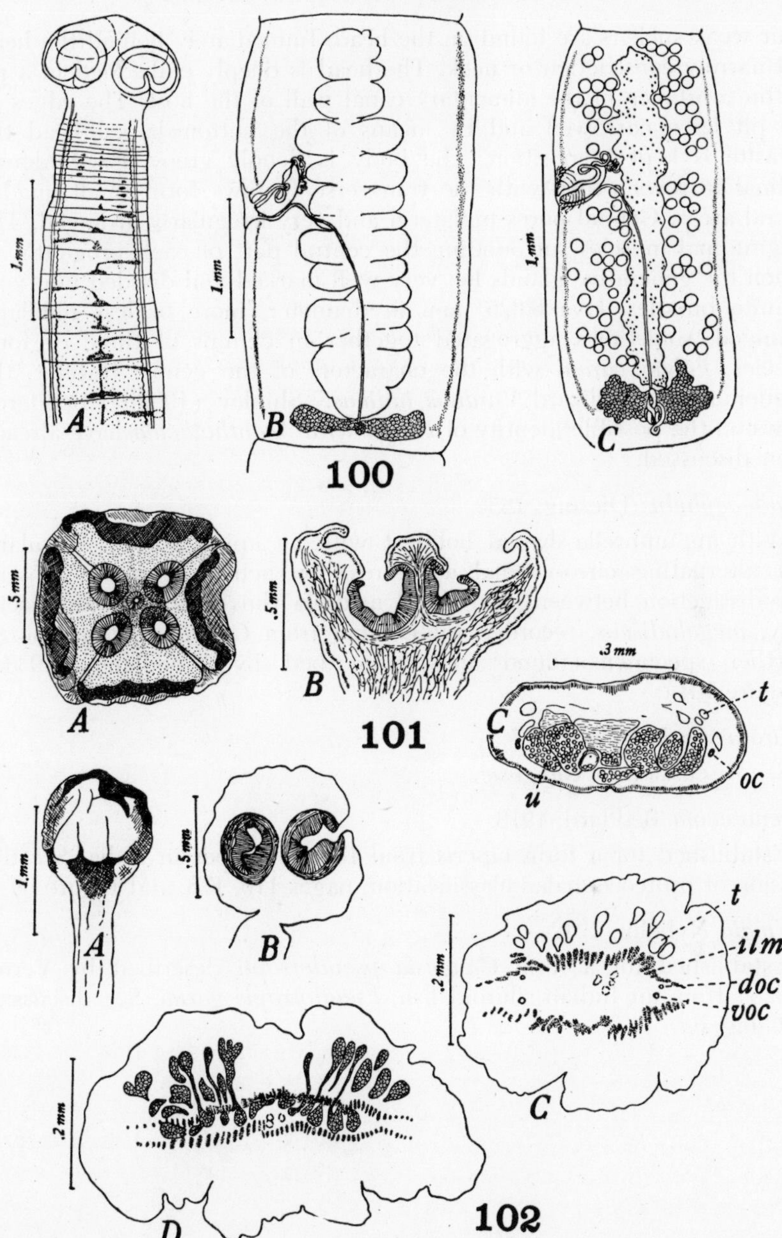

FIG. 100. *Crepidobothrium gerrardii minus.* After Dollfus, 1932b. A. Holdfast and beginning of body. B. Antepenultimate proglottis. C. Proglottis of advanced age. FIG. 101. *Sciadocephalus megalodiscus.* After Woodland, 1933a. A. Apical view of holdfast. B. Vertical section through 2 of the 4 suckers. C. Cross section of nearly gravid proglottis. FIG. 102. *Manaosia bracodemoca.* After Woodland, 1935a. A: Holdfast. B. Longitudinal section of holdfast. C. Cross section of proglottis anterior to ovary. D. Cross section of region of ovary. *doc,* dorsal osmoregulatory canal; *voc,* ventral osmoregulatory canal; *ilm,* inner longitudinal muscles; *t,* testes.

Four weak suckers are found on the head. Immediately behind the head is a narrow constriction or neck. The head is deeply embedded in a pit in the substance of the alimentary canal wall of the host. The edges of the pit have narrowed and by means of the button-shaped head the parasite is kept in position. The body is deeply grooved with longitudinal furrows which with the transverse furrows form small quadrilateral areas. Genital pores unilateral and very irregularly arranged. The longitudinal muscles surrounding the central part of each proglottis, in which the generative glands lie, very well marked and divided into very definite bundles. Ova 0.025 mm. in diameter, more or less regularly arranged, sometimes aggregated together in clumps of three or four. Species, *Palaia varani* with the characters of the genus. Habitat, the duodenum of the lizard *Varanus indicus*." Shipley (1900b). Beddard's views on the possible identity of *Palaia* with *Acanthotaenia* have already been discussed.

Sciadocephalus Diesing, 1850

With an umbrella-shaped holdfast with an apical sucker. Regularly (?) alternating cirro-vaginal apertures. Parenchymal muscles absent, any distinction between cortex and medulla thus lacking. One species only, *megalodiscus*, recorded by Diesing from *Cichla ocellaris*, Brazil. Further specimens found and redescribed by Woodland (1933a) (Figure 101).

Silurotaenia Nybelin, 1917

See discussion of *Gangesia*.

Solenotaenia Beddard, 1913

Established for a form *viperis* from Russell's viper in India. See discussion of proteocephalan classification, pages 176, 178, and Figure 99 B.

Vermaia Nybelin, 1942

Established for a form *Gangesia pseudotropii* described by Verma (1928) from an Indian siluroid fish, *Pseudotropis garua*. See discussion of *Gangesia*.

Order TETRAPHYLLIDEA

First use of the term "tetraphyllid," or at any rate of any word of similar etymological origin, must be credited to the famous Belgian pioneer in the study of tapeworms, Edouard van Beneden, who in 1849 suggested the word "Tetraphyllides" – later changed to "Tetraphylles" – as a group designation for six tapeworms which he recorded from selachians (i.e., sharks and rays) and which were peculiar in having four earlike or trumpetlike outgrowths of the holdfast end of the body. These outgrowths, according to Beneden, were extraordinarily mobile, contracting and expanding with great vigor and rapidity.

Beneden's term was adopted by Carus (1863), who used it for one of the five families among which he proposed to distribute the known tapeworms of his time, placing within the family thus designated the six forms that Beneden had recorded. Carus' term was adopted to some extent by Braun (1894–1900) for one of the orders among which he distributed the known tapeworms; but Braun's Tetraphyllidea included not only Beneden's forms but the family Lecanicephalidae of peculiar forms recorded by Linton (1889a), and the family Ichthyotaeniidae discussed in the section on Proteocephala.

This broadening of the conception of the limits of the group was carried further by Fuhrmann (1931), who recognized within it no fewer than seven families. Without embarking here upon any discussion of the validity of this view of Tetraphyllidea, we may state briefly that in the following pages the term will be used much as it was used by Beneden, the lecanicephalans and proteocephalans being treated as orders in their own right.

DESCRIPTION

Of the class Cestoda. Moderate-sized tapeworms whose holdfasts have four outgrowths – leaflike, trumpetlike, or earlike in shape – supplemented or not by true suckers. Body segments usually well marked. Terminal segments often becoming detached before the eggs are ripe and completing their development away from the rest of the body. Cirro-vaginal atrium opening on one margin. Parenchymal muscles so close to the subcuticle that there appears to be no boundary between cortical and medullary parenchyma. Testes entirely in front of ovary. Sperm duct in its descending portion running obliquely ventral to the vagina before entering the cirrus pouch. Vagina dorsal to the uterus and to the cirrus pouch, opening in front of the male opening. Ovary bilobed, posterior, each lobe two-layered so that in cross section the ovary appears X-shaped. Yolk glands in two lateral fields, widely separated in the mid-dorsal and mid-ventral regions. Uterus consisting of a small uterine duct, dorsal to the vagina, and a stemlike median uterine sac ventral to the vagina. Gravid uterus broad and occupying most of proglottis. Uterine pores preformed but delayed in appearance, comprising either a single pore or a slit or several tubular canals. Eggs within the uterus developing only as far as the oncosphere stage. Metacestode believed to be a plerocercoid within marine invertebrates. Adults parasitic in the gut of Selachii.

HISTORY

Under the term "Tetraphylles" Beneden (1849b, 1850a) established three groups of tapeworms. His Phyllobothriens comprised three forms with unarmed holdfasts—*Echeneibothrium, Phyllobothrium*, and *Anthobothrium*. His Phyllacanthiens consisted of three forms whose holdfasts bear hooklets—*Acanthobothrium, Onchobothrium*, and *Calliobothrium*. A third group, Phyllorhynchiens, was established for certain forms from selachians whose holdfasts have four threadlike, spiny tentacles. Beneden's first two groups are represented by the present families Phyllobothriidae and Onchobothriidae. His third group is regarded by most students of tapeworms today as a separate order, Trypanorhyncha, and will be so treated here.

Gradually there were added to Beneden's groups a number of other genera, many of them quite obviously belonging there, others quite obviously out of place. Discussion of the validity and the systematic position of these genera may be postponed, however. Braun (1896), whose classification has formed the basis of most later schemes of tapeworm classification, established Beneden's groups as the families Phyllobothriidae and Onchobothriidae, and this arrangement will be followed here.

RECOGNITION FEATURES

Apart from several aberrant forms—notably *Discobothrium* and *Balanobothrium*, whose affinities with Tetraphyllidea are dubious—a tetraphyllidean tapeworm is readily identifiable by the four outgrowths of its holdfast. In the past various terms have been given to these outgrowths. American writers commonly refer to them as "bothria," although Hart and Guberlet (1936) use the term "bothridia." European writers on the whole restrict the term "bothria" to the depressions of the holdfast surface found among Pseudophyllidea, and apply the term "bothridia" to outgrowths from the holdfasts of Tetraphyllidea and Trypanorhyncha. Beauchamp (1905) suggested the term "bothridia" as a general term both for depressions (exclusive of suckers) and for outgrowths, keeping the term "bothria" specifically for depressions and the term "phyllidea" specifically for outgrowths. Among recent writers, however, there is a growing tendency to refer to depressions as "bothria" and to outgrowths as "bothridia," unless such outgrowths are threadlike in nature, in which case they are better termed "tentacles." Similarly, any apical outgrowth of the holdfast is preferably termed a "rostellum."

There is little point in using the special term "myzorhynchus" for the apical outgrowth of a tetraphyllidean holdfast.

There is a great variety of shape among such bothridia. Since they are essentially organs of locomotion rather than of fixation and are extremely mobile in the living worm, their shapes after the worm is killed – unless special care is taken to ensure complete relaxation – will vary considerably, even among individuals of the same species. Among different genera, however, the bothridia may be either stalked or so slightly stalked as to appear sessile; they may be well separated, forming a cross with their stalks – the so-called "crossobothridiate" condition – or they may have their margins in contact with those of their neighbors. The concave surface of the bothridium may be so deep as to resemble the cavity of a cup, a boat, or even a vase; or it may be relatively shallow. The bothridial margin may be entire; it may be cut into lobes; or it may be greatly folded, curled, or crumpled so as to resemble a flower – the so-called "anthobothridiate" condition. Sometimes the concave surface is ridged, occasionally with ridges so large as to appear as partitions marking off the bothridial surface into compartments, commonly called "loculi." In other cases the bothridium may be so contracted marginally as to produce the effect of tiny loculi along the margins.

In many Tetraphyllidea a true sucker is present with each bothridium. Sometimes it is placed centrally, but more commonly it is anterior in position. When the bothridia are markedly crumpled or compartmented, the presence of such suckers is sometimes difficult to verify, although soaking of the whole holdfast in 95 per cent carbolic acid and judicious rolling of the worm between cover glass and slide will usually betray their presence if the suckers are there.

Internally, tetraphyllidean tapeworms are so uniform in their features that it is almost impossible to distinguish species or even genera if the holdfast is missing. Characteristic of tetraphyllidean anatomy are: (1) the position of the parenchymal muscles close to the subcuticle, thus providing no boundary between cortex and medulla; (2) the bilobed ovary, with each lobe divided horizontally so that in cross section the whole ovary appears like an X; (3) the position of the vagina dorsal to the uterine sac; (4) the arrangement of the yolk glands as two marginal bands well separated in the mid-dorsal and mid-ventral regions; (5) the preformed but delayed uterine aperture or apertures; and (6) the common, but not invariable, occurrence of hyperapolysis – the detachment of near-ripe segments and their progress to ripeness while detached from the body (Figures 103, 104).

While in no case is a complete tetraphyllidean life cycle known, there have been described at various times a number of larval forms – from cephalopod molluscs, marine teleostean fishes, and marine mammals – which in the consensus of opinion of those who have examined them are tetraphyllidean in nature. They may be listed as follows:

1. *Scolex pleuronectis* Mueller, 1788 (= *S. polymorphus* Rudolphi, 1819 = *S. delphini* Stossich, 1898). Under this term there has been re-

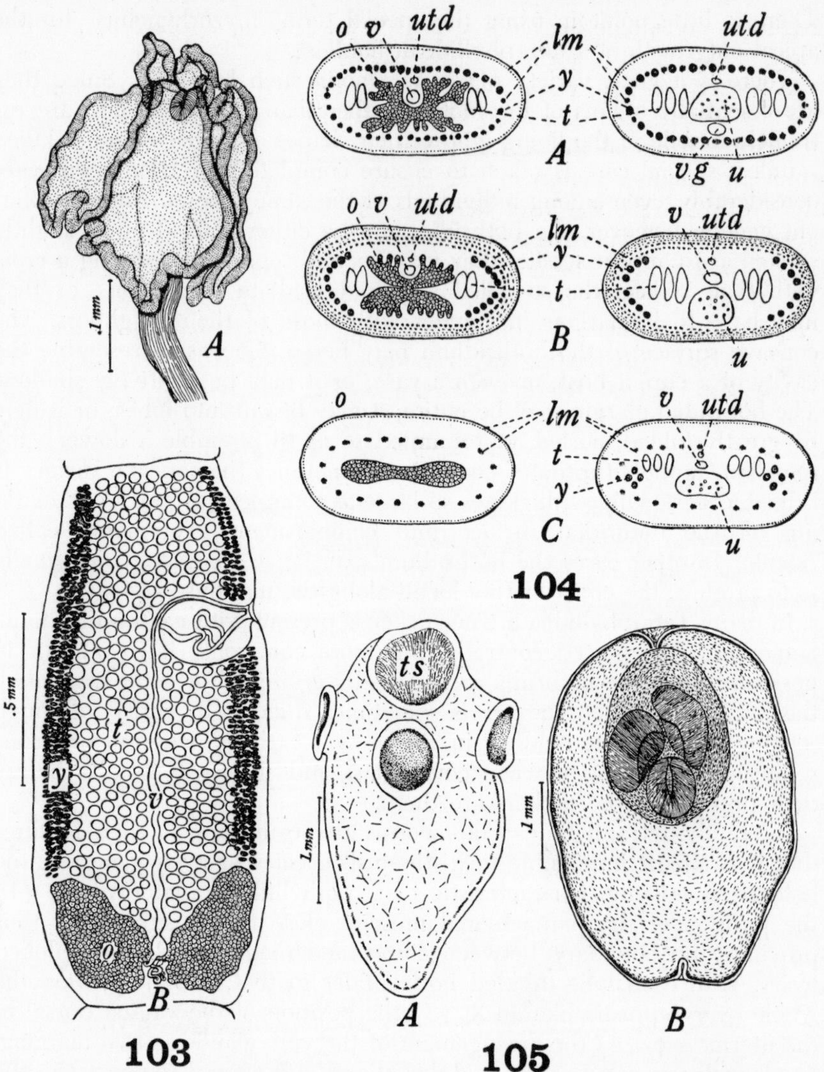

FIG. 103. *Phyllobothrium marginatum.* After Yamaguti, 1934. A. Holdfast. B. Mature proglottis, dorsal view. FIG. 104. Diagrams to illustrate the distinctions in cross sections of proglottides between Trypanorhyncha (A), Tetraphyllidea (B), and Proteocephala (C). After Woodland, 1927b. FIG. 105. *Scolex pleuronectis.* After Southwell, 1927. A. Holdfast evaginated. B. Holdfast invaginated. *lm*, longitudinal muscles; *o*, ovary; *t*, testes; *ts*, terminal sucker; *u*, uterus; *utd*, uterine duct; *v*, *vg*, vagina; *y*, yolk glands.

corded a variety of larvae, all apparently tetraphyllidean in being roughly conical in shape and having four bothridia with pleated margins placed on a broad, platformlike holdfast. In the innermost corner of each bothridium there is a sucker. The apex of the holdfast where the bothridia come together has a relatively low, moundlike rostellum whose tip is invaginated to form an apical sucker (Figure 105).

A variety of such forms has been recorded. Linton, for example, in various articles has described such forms from at least sixty species of teleostean fishes in the Atlantic waters of North America. They differ from one another mainly in the degree to which the apical sucker is developed, in the size and shape of the bothridia, in the presence or absence of cross partitions or "costae" on the bothridial surfaces, and in the presence or absence of patches of red pigment on the holdfast. Monticelli (1888b) fed such larvae to flounders (*Arnoglossus*) at Naples and recovered young specimens of *Calliobothrium filicollis*. Curtis (1911), in feeding experiments at Woods Hole, Massachusetts, where the infected teleost *Cyoscion regalis* was fed to a shark, *Carcharias littoralis*, obtained adult specimens of *Phoreiobothrium triloculatum*. It is probable, in fact, that these larvae represent a number of tetraphyllidean species.

2. *Phyllobothrium delphini* (Bosc, 1802) Gervais, 1870. This form was recorded by Bosc (as *Hydatis delphini*), by Rudolphi, 1810 (as *Cysticercus delphini*), and by many later observers. A recent account is that given by Southwell and Walker (1936) of material obtained from the belly muscles of the fur seal *Arctocephalus australis*. It is described as resembling a cysticercus (see Chapter II) with a bladder in which the holdfast and neck are completely inpocketed. When these are protruded, the larva resembles a stalked cherry, the bladder being 12–18 mm. in diameter by 6–10 mm. broad, the neck 12–14 mm. by 2–4 mm., and the holdfast about 2 mm. by 3 mm. The latter has four membranous bothridia whose margins are thickened and much puckered and crumpled. Each bothridium is roughly triangular in outline, owing to the pressure of its neighbors, and has at its apex a conspicuous, cup-shaped, muscular sucker, 200–350 μ in diameter. At the apex of the holdfast there is a broadly rounded rostellum, 120 μ high, in which there is a very distinct fifth sucker, also cup-shaped and muscular, 120–150 μ in diameter. It is believed that this sucker disappears completely before the adult stage is reached, for the latter is probably *Phyllobothrium tumidum* of the man-eater and mackerel sharks.

Adam (1938a) has discussed the various reports of cestode larvae from whales and finds that there are apparently two types, representing perhaps two species. From the toothed whale *Mesoplodion bidens* he obtained a form which would seem to be *Phyllobothrium delphini*, for the invaginated holdfast had four bothridia, each with an accessory sucker, and was at the end of a long filament which was an involution of the exterior membrane, whose cavity it completely filled.

3. *Monorygma grimaldi* (Moniez, 1889) Guiart, 1935 (= *Phyllobothrium grimaldi* Monticelli, 1889 = *Phyllobothrium chamassonii* Linton, 1905) is also a bladderlike form with an extremely long, almost hairlike neck and a very small holdfast. Linton recorded it from *Lagenorhynchus acutus*, Guiart (1935b) from the abdominal cavity of a dolphin.

4. *Plerocercoides portieri* Guiart, 1935 would seem to be more like a plerocercus than a cysticercus – that is to say, wormlike with an inpocketed holdfast. Guiart found his form in *Phoca sp.* (seal), Spitzbergen, and believed it to be pseudophyllidean rather than tetraphyllidean.

5. *Phyllobothrium loliginis* (Leidy, 1887) from the cephalopod *Ommastrephes illecebrosa* has been recorded by Linton (1897a) in "the stomachs of squids," and by Dollfus (1929a) from the stomach of *Loligo loligo* at Arcachon, France. Linton (1922c) believed the adult form to be *Phyllobothrium tumidum* in lamnid sharks (*Isurus, Carcharodon*).

6. *Diplobothrium pruvoti* Guiart, 1933 from *Loligo vulgaris*, Arcachon, is a 30–35 mm. larva with four hemispherical bothridia whose margins are very thick and infolded. The apical area of the holdfast is crosslike, with one arm of the cross longer than the other and with all four arms bluntly triangular with bluntly rounded ends. In the center of the cross, there is a rudimentary structure believed by Guiart to be glandular in nature. He believed the adult form to be *Diplobothrium simile* Beneden in *Lamna cornubica*, a tapeworm regarded by Southwell, however, as cyclophyllidean.

7. *Dinobothrium sp.* (= *Thysanocephalum* Linton, 1897), from *Ommastrephes illecebrosa*, has two pairs of flattened, shallow bothridia arranged back to back, each with an anteriorly placed accessory sucker (Figure 114).

The separation of the unarmed Tetraphyllidea, as Phyllobothriidae, from the armed forms, as Onchobothriidae, may not be desirable taxonomically speaking. However, such an arrangement is common and certainly convenient, and it will be used here.

Family PHYLLOBOTHRIIDAE Braun, 1900

DESCRIPTION

Of the order Tetraphyllidea. With the holdfast unarmed but having four stalked or sessile bothridia, which may be simple, shallow-surfaced structures or may be complexly folded, crumpled, or subdivided into compartments, and may each have an accessory sucker. Neck conspicuous or so short as to appear absent. Genital apertures marginal, unilateral, or regularly or irregularly alternating from side to side. Eggs commonly spindle-shaped. Mature segments generally leave the body and become gravid after separation. Type genus, *Phyllobothrium*.

HISTORY

Beneden's tribe, Phyllobothriens, contained originally three closely similar genera – *Phyllobothrium, Anthobothrium*, and *Echeneibothrium* – all established by Beneden himself. The symmetry of this arrangement was destroyed, however, by his admission of a form, *Discobothrium*, whose relatively enormous rostellum, apical sucker, and suckerlike bothridia were quite out of line with the original family characterization. Though accepted by Braun as a subgenus of *Echeneibothrium*, this form is relegated by modern students – though with some doubt – to the order Lecanicephala.

Further genera added to Phyllobothriidae since Beneden's establishment of the family have been: *Monorygma* Diesing, 1863; *Orygmatobothrium* Diesing, 1863; *Trilocularia* Olsson, 1867; *Dinobothrium* Beneden, 1889; *Crossobothrium* Linton, 1889; *Tritaphros* Loennberg, 1889; *Spongiobothrium* Linton, 1889; *Pelichnibothrium* Monticelli, 1889; *Diplobothrium* Beneden, 1889; *Rhinebothrium* Linton, 1889; *Anthocephalum* Linton, 1890; *Calyptrobothrium* Monticelli, 1893; *Staurobothrium* Shipley and Hornell, 1905; *Myzophyllobothrium* Shipley and Hornell, 1906; *Rhoptrobothrium* Shipley and Hornell, 1906; *Tiarobothrium* Shipley and Hornell, 1906; *Carpobothrium* Shipley and Hornell, 1906; *Eniochobothrium* Shipley and Hornell, 1906; *Aocobothrium* Mola, 1907; *Cyathocotyle* Mola, 1908; *Polipobothrium* Mola, 1908; *Bilocularia* Obersteiner, 1914; *Oriana* Leiper and Atkinson, 1915; *Pithophorus* Southwell, 1924; *Scyphophyllidium* Woodland, 1927; and *Myzophorus* Woodland, 1934.

Southwell (1925b) reduced the twenty-five genera recorded up to that date to eight, and later (1930) to five. The distinctiveness of *Anthobothrium* from *Phyllobothrium* is generally accepted by modern students. The observations of Woodland (1927b) have established the generic distinctiveness of *Dinobothrium*, and those of Yamaguti (1934) have established that of *Pelichnibothrium*. Accepting also the addition of *Scyphophyllidium* and *Myzophorus*, we shall recognize here eleven genera, the preliminary separation of which may be made as follows:

KEY TO GENERA

1. Holdfast consisting of a central pillar ending in a rounded prominence and bearing four ordinary suckers near the extremity .... *Myzophorus*
   Holdfast with four spherical, almost sessile, suckerlike bothridia .... *Scyphophyllidium*
   Holdfast with bothridia globular or cylindrical, open anteriorly and posteriorly .... *Pithophorus*
   Holdfast with bothridia not as above 2
2. Holdfast with apex prolonged as a muscular, nonretractile rostellum carrying four accessory suckers .... *Myzophyllobothrium*
   Holdfast with an apical sucker and four accessory suckers, each lying directly in front of the anterior border of the bothridia .... *Pelichnibothrium*
   Holdfast without such rostellum or apical sucker 3
3. Adherent surface of each bothridium transversely ridged .... *Echeneibothrium*
   Adherent surface of bothridia not thus ridged 4
4. Anterior end of each bothridium flat, circular, or cylindrical, carrying two opposed semicircular flaps; rest of bothridium having small marginal compartments; no accessory suckers in the bothridia .... *Carpobothrium*
   Bothridial surfaces simple, relatively smooth or complexly crumpled but never carrying terminal flaps 5
5. Bothridia usually stalked, well separated from each other, without accessory suckers .... *Anthobothrium*
   Bothridia commonly in contact, variable in complexity, each with one or more suckers 6
6. Holdfast relatively enormous; bothridia shallow, oval, scooplike, each with

a thickened shelflike anterior region .... *Dinobothrium*
Holdfast not unusually large; bothridia commonly in contact, with their marginal areas greatly crumpled .... *Phyllobothrium*
Bothridia shallow, oval, each with two accessory suckers, one situated anteriorly, the other situated in the center of the bothridial surface .... *Orygmatobothrium*

NOTES ON GENERA

Myzophorus Woodland, 1934

With four typical proteocephalan suckers, a unilaminate ovary, and an almost proteocephalan layer of parenchymal muscle bundles. However, due to the general distribution of the longitudinal muscle fibers, the crescentic arrangement of the yolk glands, and the late appearance of the uterine aperture, the genus must be referred to Phyllobothriidae. Genotype, *admonticellia* Woodland, 1934a, from a Brazilian siluroid fish, *Pirinampus sp.* Ref. Woodland (1934a).

Woodland later (1935b) emended the definition to include forms with any kind of suckers and with bodies with only a quarter of their length composed of gravid proglottides. The genus thus became merely a temporary assemblage of sucker-possessing phyllobothriids other than those belonging to the genus *Scyphophyllidium.* To the genus he added the species *pirarara* from *Phractocephalus hemiliopterus, dorad* from *Brachyplatystoma rousseauxii,* and *sudobim* from *Pseudoplatystoma fasciatum,* all from Brazil and all parasitic in fresh-water siluroid fishes.

Scyphophyllidium Woodland, 1927

Forms of "probably considerable" size. Holdfast with four globose bothridia ("resemblent à des ventouses de ténia pediculée," according to Beneden), with fairly thick walls, deep cavities, and irregularly slitlike mouths. Bothridia practically sessile. Rostellum absent. Neck very long, exceeding 30 mm. Genital apertures opening on the anterior third of the segment margins, irregularly alternating. Segments all broader than long. Internal features typically tetraphyllidean, but the cirrus and vagina are *ventral* to the nerve cord. Genotype, *giganteum* Beneden, 1858 (Figure 106).

The genotype was established by Beneden (as *Anthobothrium giganteum*) for a form from *Galeus canis* in European waters. Woodland (1927b) recorded and redescribed it from *Galeus vulgaris,* English Channel. No other tetraphyllidean is known with the bothridia modified as suckers and the rostellum lacking, except *Myzophorus.* Southwell (1925b) regarded as synonymous with this form: *Anthobothrium elegantissimum* Loennberg, 1889; *A. rugosum* Shipley and Hornell, 1906; *Phyllobothrium pammicrum* Shipley and Hornell, 1906; and *Anthobothrium floraformis* Southwell, 1912. Shipley and Hornell's *rugosum* was a foot long and had baglike suckers with puckered margins.

Pithophorus Southwell, 1925

With a holdfast with four globular, rarely cylindrical, stalked or sessile bothridia, each hollow and open both anteriorly and posteriorly.

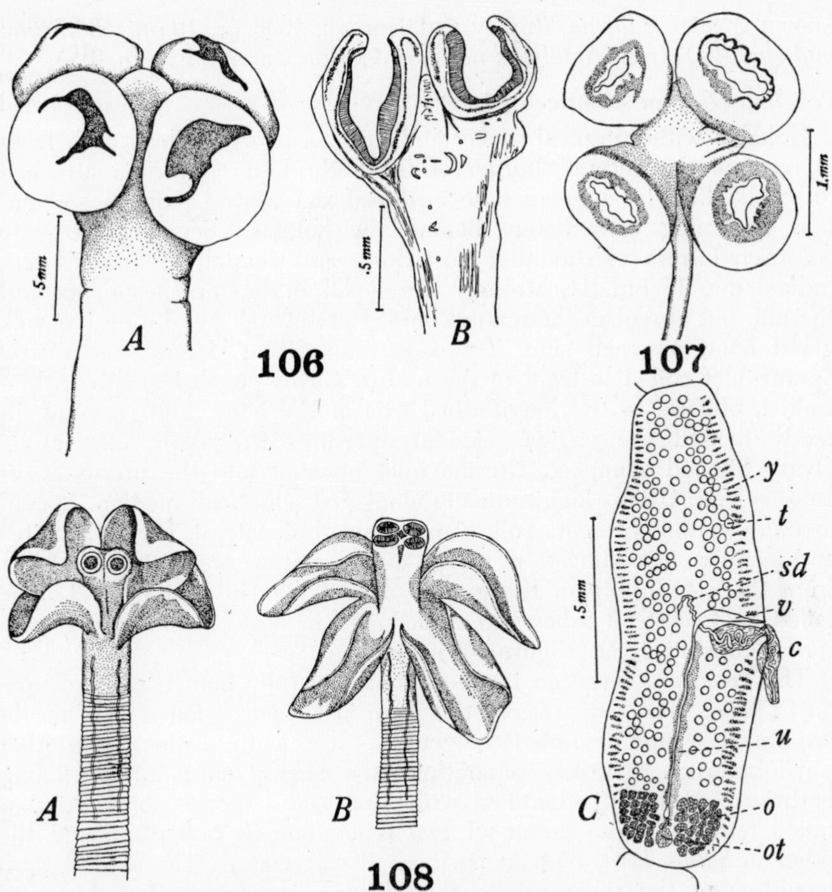

FIG. 106. *Scyphophyllidium giganteum.* After Woodland, 1927b. A. Holdfast. B. Holdfast in longitudinal section. FIG. 107. *Pithophorus tetraglobus,* holdfast. After Southwell, 1925b. FIG. 108. *Myzophyllobothrium rubrum.* After Southwell, 1925b. A and B. Views of holdfast. C. Entire segment. *c,* cirrus; *o,* ovary; *ot,* ootype; *sd,* sperm duct; *t,* testes; *u,* uterus; *v,* vagina; *y,* yolk glands.

Accessory suckers lacking. Rostellum present. Other features typically tetraphyllidean. Genotype, *tetraglobus* Southwell, 1911 (Figure 107).

The genotype was established (as *Orygmatobothrium tetraglobus*) by Southwell (1911a) for a form in *Rhynchobatis djeddensis* in Ceylon waters. An undetermined form recorded by Linton (1909) in Florida waters may belong to this genus.

Myzophyllobothrium Shipley and Hornell, 1906, emended Southwell, 1925b

Long forms up to 80 mm. Holdfast with a prominent rostellum which carries four suckers. Bothridia sessile or stalked, somewhat leaflike, with thickened, folded margins. Internal structure typically tetraphyllidean. Testes 140–180. Genital apertures mid-marginal. Genotype and only known species, *rubrum* Shipley and Hornell, 1906 (=*Rhoptrobothrium myliobatidis*), from *Aetobatis narinari*, Ceylon waters (Figure 108).

Pelichnibothrium Monticelli, 1889

Holdfast with an apical sucker and four accessory suckers, each lying in front of the anterior border of the bothridium. Bothridia attached to the holdfast by a broad base in dorsal and ventral pairs. Segmentation beginning immediately behind the holdfast. Segments strongly constricted from one another posteriorly and euapolytic. Inner longitudinal muscle bundles strongly developed in the first segments and the tail, but absent in the mature ones. Nerve trunk just inside the yolk gland band on each side. Testes very numerous, lateral, medullary. Sperm duct coiled in front of the uterus. Cirrus pouch elongated, thin-walled, oblique to the longitudinal axis of the body, and opening directly behind the vagina. Genital apertures irregularly alternating. Ovary bilobed, compact. Uterine duct opening into the uterus at its anterior end. Uterus longitudinally elongated, elliptical, median. Receptaculum seminis present. Yolk glands numerous, lateral, between cortex and medulla, extending from end to end in mature segments but absent from the anterior tip of the gravid ones. Adults in selachians. Larvae tailed, in teleostean fishes and cephalopod molluscs. Genotype, *speciosum* Monticelli, 1889 (Figure 109).

The generic description is given unusually fully here because Yamaguti (1934), who rediscovered this form in *Prionace glauca* from northern Pacific waters, regarded the genus as sufficiently distinct from other phyllobothriids to justify separation as a distinct subfamily, Pelichnibothriinae. Yamaguti identified with Monticelli's species some peculiar tailed tetraphyllidean larvae of two types, one in *Loligo sp.* and the other in *Salmo keta*, both in northern Pacific waters. The second form would seem the same as *Pelichnibothrium caudatum* Zschokke and Heitz, 1914 and *Phyllobothrium salmonis* Fujita, 1922. Yamaguti preferred to regard them all as representing the only known species of *Pelichnibothrium*—namely, *speciosum* Monticelli.

Echeneibothrium Beneden, 1850 (=*Rhinebothrium* Linton=*Tiarobothrium* Shipley and Hornell)

With the bothridia sessile or stalked, varying greatly in shape but characterized by having the adherent surfaces divided by ridges—either transverse ridges only, or one or two longitudinal ridges with transverse ridges in addition—the surface thus recalling the modified dorsal fin of the sucking-fish or remora (*Echeneis*). Genotype, *minimum* Beneden, 1850.

All descriptive accounts of echeneibothriid tapeworms agree that the bothridial surfaces have a single or double series of somewhat rectangular compartments. Southwell (1925b) speaks of these as being separated by "grooves"; most authors, however, speak of "ridges," "septa," or "costae." Southwell reduced the twenty species recognized at that date to five. Woodland (1927b) doubted the advisability of this and believed

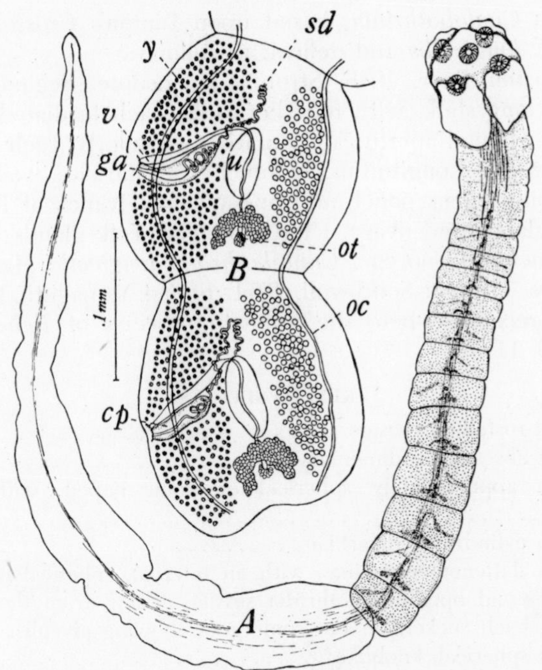

FIG. 109. *Pelichnibothrium speciosum*. After Yamaguti, 1934. A. Young worm, 22 mm. long. B. Mature segments, ventral view. *cp*, cirrus pouch; *ga*, genital aperture; *oc*, osmoregulatory canal; *ot*, ootype; *sd*, sperm duct; *u*, uterus; *v*, vagina; *y*, yolk glands.

the whole twenty might be distinct species. Certainly, he argued, the two species *affine* and *variabile* – regarded by Southwell as synonymous with *tumidulum* – "are about as distinct as any two species of one genus can be." Woodland added two further species, Yamaguti (1934) added another, and Hart (1936b) another.

Since the above was written, Linton's genus *Rhinebothrium* has been redescribed by Baer (1948) as follows:

Rhinebothrium Linton, 1890, emended Baer, 1948. Strobila feebly craspedote, segments apolytic. Holdfast with four stalked bothridia whose surfaces are divided into secondary loculi. Myzorhynchus lacking. Cephalic stalk sometimes present. Genital apertures irregularly alternating, each opening into a genital atrium. Vagina crossing cirrus pouch and opening in advance of it. Testes distributed between ovary and yolk glands, none between cirrus pouch and ovary of poral side. Uterus tubular, median. Yolk glands lateral. Genotype, *Rhinebothrium flexile* Linton, 1890.

Baer recognizes six species – *flexile* Linton, *burgeri n.sp.*, *maccallumi* Linton, *palombii n.sp.*, *rankini n.sp.*, and *shipleyi* Southwell. The species *insignis* Southwell, 1911 and *tobijei* Yamaguti, 1934, included here as species of *Anthobothrium*, are placed by Baer in a newly erected genus that he calls *Caulobothrium,* based upon Linton's *Crossobothrium laciniatum* var. *longicollis* and defined as follows:

Caulobothrium Baer, 1948. Strobila craspedote. Segments apolytic. Holdfast on long stalk, with four bothridia, each loculated. Myzorhynchus lacking. Genital apertures alternating irregularly, each opening into a genital atrium. Longitudinal parenchymal muscles well developed. Vagina crossing cirrus pouch and opening in advance of it. Testes between yolk glands and ovary. Uterus tubular. Yolk glands lateral. Eggs without filaments. Genotype, *Caulobothrium longicolle* (Linton, 1890). Other species, *insignia* Southwell, 1911; *tobijei* Yamaguti, 1934.

We shall recognize here the following species of *Echeneibothrium* (Figures 110, 111):

KEY TO SPECIES

1. Prominent rostellum present 2
   Rostellum absent or rudimentary 6
2. Rostellum approximately spherical or dome-shaped, with a terminal opening 3
   Rostellum cylindrical, pillarlike 5
3. Rostellum flattened, domelike, with an internal, spherical muscular mass and a terminal opening; bothridia sessile, arising from the sides of the rostellum, each suckerlike, but sometimes showing alveoli .... *fallax*
   Rostellum spherical, knoblike 4
4. Rostellum approximately spherical, its internal muscular mass irregular in shape and its terminal opening conspicuous; bothridia stalked, variable in shape, usually showing a number of compartments .... *variabile*
   Rostellum much as above but containing a terminal cavity with a terminal pore; bothridia quite suckerlike, each stalked, their walls showing traces of septa .... *julievansium*
5. Rostellum an extensible truncated pillar, its extreme end a thick pad covered with a circular fold of terminal subcuticle save for a small central opening; when retracted, this pad is suckerlike; bothridia stalked with the concave adherent surfaces subdivided by temporary lateral ridges into 15 or 17 loculi .... *maculatum*
   Rostellum presumably as above, cylindrical, 700 μ long by 120 μ broad, with a terminal pore, but merely described as "very distinct"; adherent faces of bothridia each divided by transverse ridges into 10 loculi .... *myzorhynchum*
6. Each bothridium Y-shaped, with the anterior half cleft longitudinally .... *trifidum*
   Bothridia not thus cleft 7
7. Each bothridium divided by a transverse hinge into equal anterior and posterior regions .... *flexile*
   Bothridia not thus hinged 8
8. Adherent surfaces of the bothridia divided by transverse ridges into one row of loculi 10
   Bothridial surfaces with more than one row of loculi 9
9. Bothridial surfaces divided into two rows of loculi by longitudinal median ridges and transverse ridges .... *tumidulum*

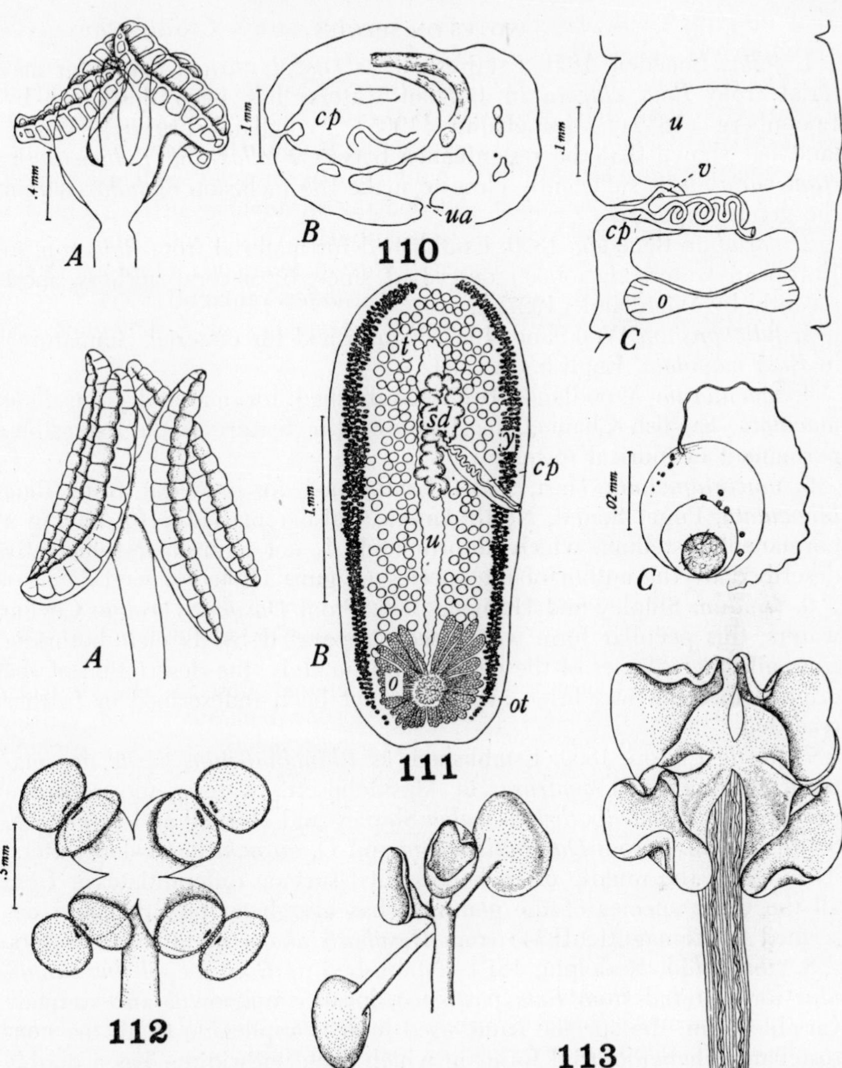

FIG. 110. *Echeneibothrium myzorhynchum.* After Hart, 1936b. A. Holdfast. B. Cross section of segment through uterine aperture. C. Semidiagrammatic view of segment. FIG. 111. *Echeneibothrium tobijei.* After Yamaguti, 1934. A. Holdfast. B. Isolated segment. C. Filamented egg. FIG. 112. *Carpobothrium chiloscyllium,* holdfast. After Southwell, 1925b. FIG. 113. *Anthobothrium cornucopia,* two views of living holdfast. After Southwell, 1925b. *cp,* cirrus pouch; *o,* ovary; *ot,* ootype; *sd,* sperm duct; *t,* testes; *u,* uterus; *ua,* uterine aperture; *v,* vagina; *y,* yolk glands.

Bothridial surfaces divided into three rows of loculi by two longitudinal ridges each and numerous transverse ridges .... *cancellatum*

10. Loculi 8–10 in number .... *minimum*

Loculi 16 in number .... *tobijei*

NOTES ON SPECIES

1. *fallax* Beneden, 1871. Established, as *Discobothrium fallax*, for material from *Raia clavata* in Belgian waters; has been described by Loennberg (1889a), Beauchamp (1905), Woodland (1927b). Woodland has shown that the resemblance between *fallax* and *Echeneibothrium variabile* is sufficiently close to make the inclusion of *fallax* within the genus imperative.

2. *variabile* Beneden, 1850. Established for material from *Raia spp.* in European waters; has been described since by several authors, most recently by Woodland (1927b).

3. *julievansium* Woodland, 1927. Established for material (immature) in *Raia maculata*, English Channel.

4. *maculatum* Woodland, 1927. Established for material from *Raia maculata*, English Channel; most noteworthy feature is the extensible, permanent cylindrical rostellum.

5. *myzorhynchum* Hart, 1936. Established for material from *Raia binoculata*, Puget Sound, North America; also remarkable for having a permanent rostellum, which unfortunately is not figured or sufficiently described by the author of the species (Figure 110).

6. *trifidum* Shipley and Hornell, 1906. From *Dasybatis walga*, Ceylon waters; this peculiar form would seem separated by its cleft bothridia from all other species of the genus; unfortunately, the description of the original material was brief, and it has not been redescribed or further recorded.

7. *flexile* Linton, 1890. Established, as *Rhinebothrium flexile*, for material from *Trygon centrura*, in Massachusetts waters, and recorded probably as *Echeneibothrium walga* Shipley and Hornell and *E. insignia* Southwell, 1911 from *Dasybatis walga* and *D. uarnaki* in Ceylon waters; its hinge in the middle of each bothridial surface differentiates it from all the other species of the genus; it has also been recorded and described by Yamaguti (1934) from *Dasybatis akajei* in Japanese waters.

8. *tumidulum* Rudolphi, 1819. Established as *Bothriocephalus tumidulus* for material from *Raia pastinaca*, locality unknown; an extremely variable form; the specific name used here is applicable to all the non-rostellate echeneibothriid forms in which each bothridium has a double series of loculi.

9. *cancellatum* Linton, 1890. Established, as *Rhinebothrium cancellatum*, for material from *Rhinoptera quadriloba* in Massachusetts waters and probably recorded, as *Echeneibothrium javanicum* Shipley and Hornell, 1906, from *Dasybatis walga* in Ceylon waters; in the present state of our knowledge, all echeneibothriids with more than two series of loculi may be placed within this species.

10. *minimum* Beneden, 1850. Established for material from *Trygon (Raia) pastinaca* in Belgian waters; probably recorded as *Tiarobothrium javanicum* Shipley and Hornell, 1906; *Rhinebothrium shipleyi* Southwell, 1911; *Anthobothrium ceylonicum* Southwell, 1912; the single series of 8 or 10 loculi in each bothridium would seem characteristic. Yamaguti

(1934), on the basis of material from *Dasybatis akajei* in Japanese waters, believed however that Southwell's *shipleyi* is a valid species, differing constantly from *minimum* in the number of segments and in the dimensions of the terminal segments.

11. *tobijei* Yamaguti, 1934. Established for material from *Myliobatis tobijei* in Japanese waters; similar in most respects to *minimum*, but the greater number of loculi serves to distinguish it (Figure 111).

Carpobothrium Shipley and Hornell, 1906, emended Southwell, 1925b

With each bothridium ending in a flattened, circular area from which project two opposing processes, one of them obcordate (reversed heart shape) in outline. Body coiled, with little or no neck. Cuticle very wrinkled. Genotype and only known species, *chiloscylii* Shipley and Hornell, 1906, established for a minute form found in *Chiloscyllium indicum* in Ceylon waters (Figure 112).

Southwell also recorded this form from *Rhynchobatis djeddensis* and *Urogymnus asperrimus* in the same area, and (1925b) gave a fuller and emended description. He described the body as being segmented and the holdfast as having four Y-shaped bothridia; the proximal portion of each bothridium is somewhat cylindrical (Southwell's figure suggests that "conical" would be a better term); and from its distal extremity two flaps arise, each having an entire margin. The periphery of each flap is marked by a single row of minute compartments which runs along the margin of that face of the bothridium which opposes the neighboring bothridium in each pair. Where the two flaps come off, there is a pair of very conspicuous muscle-pads on each flap. There is no rostellum, and accessory suckers are lacking.

Anthobothrium Beneden, 1850 (= *Spongiobothrium* Linton, 1889a = *Polipobothrium* Mola, 1908)

In Beneden's opinion the genus comprised those Phyllobothriens whose bothridia were hollow in the center, having the shape of a flower vase, or which stretched out like rounded disks placed on a protractile stalk. The bothridial edges were not crisped like a lettuce leaf and did not have parallel grooves. His genotype was *cornucopia* Beneden, from *Galeus canis* (Figure 113).

As emended by Southwell (1925b), the genus comprises phyllobothriids whose bothridial surfaces are not subdivided into compartments; in which the bothridial margins are entire or crenulate; and which lack accessory suckers. Southwell (1930) merged the genus with *Phyllobothrium* on the grounds that the presence or absence of accessory suckers is difficult to establish, but Yamaguti (1934) argued strongly for retaining the original generic grouping.

Apparently under certain conditions of expansion, the bothridial surfaces may give the appearance of being compartmented. Rees (1943), describing *Anthobothrium auriculatum*, found in the expanded bothridium an inner and an outer marginal ridge connected by transverse ridges to form a row "of rather indefinite loculi. They can hardly be described as loculi as the intervening walls are formed from longitudinal muscles passing up from the peduncle. In the contracted bothridium the floor of the 'funnel' is now a raised cushion, traversed by grooves which are the contracted muscular ridges." (See Figure 6.)

The following species of *Anthobothrium* may be recognized:

KEY TO SPECIES

1. Worms with body twisted round the longitudinal axis .... *tortum*
   Worms not thus twisted 2
2. Posterior borders of segments with four tongue-shaped lappets 3
   Posterior borders of segments entire 4
3. Relatively large forms, 150–200 mm. long .... *cornucopia*
   Relatively small forms, 16–25 mm. long .... *laciniatum*
4. Bothridia ill defined, flattened, with ragged margins .... *panjadi*
   Bothridia well defined 5
   Bothridia resembling four-leaved clover leaves .... *dipsadomorphi*
   Bothridia fleshy, sometimes funnel-shaped, with frilled margins; genital pores mid-marginal .... *pulvinatum*
   Bothridia not like four-leaved clover leaves; genital pores in posterior half of segment margin .... *auriculatum*
   Bothridia circular, almost sessile, membranous, with thickened borders .... *parvum*
5. Each bothridium hinged in its transverse axis .... *lintoni*
   Bothridia simple, leaflike, not hinged .... *variabile*

Incertae sedis: piramutab Woodland, 1933; *pristis* Woodland, 1934; *karuatayi* Woodland, 1934.

To the species listed in the key above may be added *hickmanni* Crowcroft, 1947 from the spiral valve of *Narcine tasmaniensis* in Tasmanian waters. It differs from most species of the genus in the simplicity of its holdfast and seems most nearly related to *variable* Linton (=*Echeneibothrium simplex* Shipley and Hornell, 1906), except in possession of a myzorhynchus.

NOTES ON SPECIES

1. *tortum* Linstow, 1904. Established for a peculiar form from a seal, *Phoca barbata.* The worm had its anterior end embedded in the stomach wall of the seal, and its body was twisted in spiral fashion; the holdfast was described by Shipley (1905), who re-examined it, as having four cushions and a central or apical mass of convoluted ridges. Practically nothing is known of its internal anatomy, and its relationship to phyllobothriids must be regarded for the time being as *sub judice.*

2. *cornucopia* Beneden, 1850. Established for material from *Galeus canis, Mustelus vulgaris,* in Belgian waters; a full description was given by Zschokke (1888c) and further points have been added by Woodland (1927b). One point of interest made by the latter writer is that the uterine aperture and the uterus proper are almost exactly of the "Solenotaenia" type described by Beddard (1913c) in a proteocephalan (*q.v.*). "In other words the uterus proper arises as a narrow median tube which later spreads a little to each side of the median line and then,

instead of extending throughout the medulla by developing lateral diverticula as in most Tetraphyllidea, unites its ventral wall along its entire length (i.e., from just in front of the ovary to near the anterior limit of the proglottis) with the ventral subcuticula (previously attenuated for the purpose) and opens to the exterior, thus liberating the eggs as fast as they arrive by the uterine duct. Thus the eggs are never stored in the uterus and the uterine aperture is not a mere dehiscence as is sometimes supposed." Woodland (1927b). The specific name *cornucopia* refers to the very characteristic hornlike or trumpetlike appearance of the relaxed bothridium.

3. *laciniatum* Linton, 1890. Established for material from *Carcharias obscurus*, Massachusetts waters; with trumpetlike bothridia and laciniated segment borders. Southwell (1925b) believed it to be identical with *cornucopia*, but Yamaguti (1934), redescribing material from *Scoliodon wahlbeemi* in Japanese waters, believed with Linton that the constantly smaller size of this form justified separation from *cornucopia*.

4. *panjadi* Shipley and Hornell, 1909 (=*Anthobothrium crispum* Shipley and Hornell, 1906). Established for material from *Myliobatis maculata* in Ceylon waters; described as having very short-stalked bothridia, much crumpled, fringed, frilled, and subdivided, the subdivisions extending nearly to the stalks and giving the appearance of six or eight bothridia; neck very long; genital pores in anterior thirds of segment margins; further details of the anatomy were given by Southwell (1925b) from material taken in the same area from *Aetiobatis narinari*.

5. *dipsadomorphi* Shipley, 1900. Established, as *Phyllobothrium dipsadomorphi*, from material from "a Malaga snake" (*Dipsadomorphus irregularis*); the bothridia described as heart-shaped lappets with well-marked rims from which a few radial ridges surround the lappets; the whole anterior end recalls a four-leaved clover as each lappet is indented on its outer edge. The form must be regarded as *sub judice*.

6. *pulvinatum* Linton, 1890 (=*Phyllobothrium blakei* Shipley and Hornell, 1906). Established for material from *Trygon centrura* in Massachusetts waters; characteristic are the fleshy, frilled bothridia, the mid-marginal genital apertures, the long neck, spiny cirrus, and the arrangement of the genitalia.

7. *auriculatum* Rudolphi, 1819 (=*Bothriocephalus auriculatus* Rudolphi, 1819). This is often described as an imperfectly known or even as a dubious form, but it has recently (1943) been described in detail by Rees from material taken from *Raja batis* in western Ireland waters. It seems to be a perfectly valid species, characterized by the dimensions of various parts of the body; by the position of the genital apertures (the deep tubular genital atrium in each segment lying transversely just behind the middle of the lateral margin and passing dorsal to the lateral nerve cord); by the auriculate (earlike) bothridia, each provided with marginal loculi or pseudo-loculi; and by the small conical (when contracted) or club-shaped (when expanded) rostellum (Figures 6, 11).

8. *parvum* Yamaguti, 1934. Established for material from *Alopias vulpinus* in Japanese waters; characteristic are the circular, membranous

bothridia with nonloculate margins and the very long neck. Otherwise the worm is similar to *lintoni.*

9. *lintoni* Southwell, 1911. Established, as *Spongiobothrium lintoni,* from *Rhynchobatis djeddensis* in Ceylon waters; peculiar in having the bothridia transversely hinged and in their having marginal loculi.

10. *variabile* Linton, 1889 (= *Spongiobothrium variabile* Linton, 1889 = *Echeneibothrium simplex* Shipley and Hornell, 1906 = *Polipobothrium vaccarii* Mola, 1908). Established for material from *Trygon centrura* in Massachusetts waters; the simple, leaflike, marginally loculated bothridia are characteristic; has been recorded and redescribed by Southwell (1925b) for material from *Trygon kuhli* in Ceylon waters, the identification being based upon the shape of the bothridia and the enormous genital atrium in the posterior half of each segment.

11, 12, 13. The three species described by Woodland – *piramutab, pristis,* and *karuatayi* – are peculiar in being found in fresh-water fishes, namely, siluroid fishes of the Amazon drainage system of Brazil. *Pristis* is a typical phyllobothriid, with a holdfast with bothridia, a single zone of longitudinal muscle fibers or bundles of fibers more or less coextensive with the subcuticle and not providing a boundary between medullary and cortical parenchyma, and in having the yolk glands, in a cross section of the segment, appearing as two lateral semicircles. On the other hand, the ovary does not appear X-shaped in cross section, there is no uterine duct, and the holdfast does not resemble that of any other anthobothriid.

The other two species would seem to be as much proteocephalan as tetraphyllidean. "It is difficult to assign this tapeworm to its correct systematic position [i.e., A. *karuatayi*]. The scolex is apparently as much proteocephalid as phyllobothriid (judging by types found in certain Zygobothriinae and Monticelliinae; see Woodland 1933a) and the same remark applies to the arrangement of the vitellaria (also found in certain Zygobothriinae and Monticelliinae). The unilaminar ovary is of the proteocephalid type. On the other hand, the disposition of the few longitudinal muscle fibres which are present (not forming a boundary between cortex and medulla) is phyllobothriid in character and we now know that true Phyllobothriidae are to be found in freshwater Silurids (e.g. *Anthobothrium pristis*). A somewhat similar case is that of *Anthobothrium piramutab* which I have described (Woodland, 1933b) from the Amazon (i.e., freshwater) Siluroid, *Brachyplatystoma vaillanti.* In this case the longitudinal muscle system is evidently of the phyllobothriid type, and the ovary is also unilaminar. The truth appears to be that these two species belong to a group more or less intermediate in character between Phyllobothriidae and Proteocephalidae, but it will not be possible to define this group until we possess more examples. In the meantime I assume that the phyllobothriid characters predominate over the proteocephalid, and I provisionally refer both species to the genus *Anthobothrium,* the only genus, as defined by Southwell (1929c) capable of receiving them." Woodland (1934b).

Dinobothrium Beneden, 1889, emended Sproston, 1948

With a somewhat cuboidal holdfast without hooks. Bothridia adpressed to the axis of the holdfast. Each with margin entire and without a sphincter and each fused anteriorly to a transverse crest at whose ends are pairs of reflexed bifid lobes with broad points. On the crest, above each bothridium, one or more suckers or pseudo-suckers, or both. Yolk glands spreading through the segment in the early, female phase of segment development but restricted later to narrow marginal bands. Vagina and sperm duct voluminous and acting as sperm reservoirs. Cirrus spiny. Eggs not filamented. Genotype, *septaria* Beneden, 1889. Other species: *keilini* Sproston, 1948; *planum* Linton, 1922; *paciferum* Sproston, 1948.

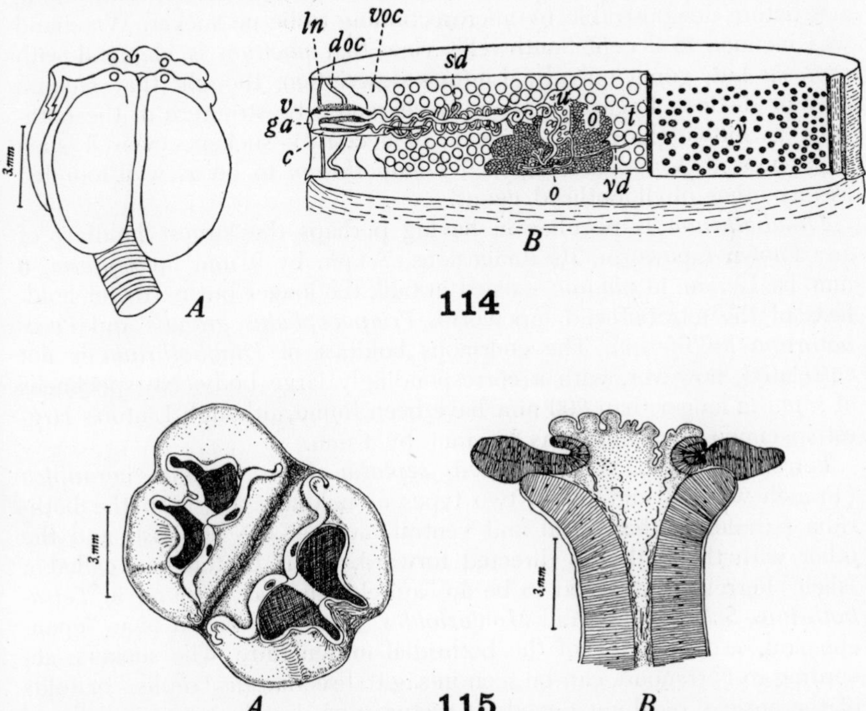

FIG. 114. *Dinobothrium planum*. After Linton, 1922c. A. Holdfast. B. Stereogram of mature proglottis. FIG. 115. *Dinobothrium septaria*. After Perrenoud, 1931. A. Holdfast, apical view. B. Holdfast, sagittal section. *c*, cirrus; *doc*, dorsal osmoregulatory canal; *ga*, genital aperture; *ln*, longitudinal nerve cord; *o*, ovary; *ot*, ootype; *sd*, sperm duct; *t*, testes; *u*, uterus; *v*, vagina; *voc*, ventral osmoregulatory canal; *y*, yolk glands; *yd*, yolk duct.

Beneden did not define his genus but merely described, briefly and insufficiently, an immature worm which he referred to it. The first definition of the genus was given by Linton (1922), who recorded a form apparently identical with Beneden's material from the shark *Carcharodon carcharias* in Massachusetts waters; Beneden's material, it may be noted, was taken from a mackerel shark (*Lamna cornubica*) in Belgian waters. In addition to the species *septaria*, Linton believed his material to contain two other specifically distinct forms of *Dinobothrium* which he described and designated *plicitum* and *planum*. To Southwell (1925b), Linton's statement that the shelflike ridge above each bothridium carried a small sucker was evidence that these forms belonged within the genus *Phyllobothrium*, and he grouped all three under the term *Phyllobothrium septaria*.

Woodland (1927b) recorded and redescribed the species *septaria* from *Lamna cornubica* in the English Channel, but he failed to find the suckers mentioned by Linton. He believed the latter observer to have been misled by a slight depression on the ridge above each bothridium, a structure demonstrable by microsectioning to be no sucker. Woodland was inclined to accept Southwell's view that *plicitum* is identical with *septaria* but, going only by Linton's description, thought that *planum* may be distinct. Regarding the very characteristic structure of the bothridia as outweighing the presence of accessory suckers, even if such were present, Woodland believed *Dinobothrium* to be as well-founded as any other phyllobothriid genus.

Dinobothrium is peculiar in having perhaps the largest holdfast of any known tapeworm. Its dimensions, 7 mm. by 9 mm. in *septaria*, 8 mm. by 10 mm. in *planum*, exceed in bulk the longer but narrower holdfasts of the tetrabothriid tapeworms *Priapocephalus grandis* and *Parabothrium bulbiferum*. The enormous holdfast of *Dinobothrium* is not correlated, however, with a correspondingly large body. No specimens of *septaria* longer than 200 mm. have been found, although Linton's largest specimen of *planum* was 825 mm. by 4 mm.

Perrenoud (1931) redescribed *septaria* from *Lamna cornubica* (French waters) and found two types of holdfast, one with the bothridia parallel to the dorsal and ventral faces of the holdfast, and the other with the bothridia directed forward. What Linton had called a "shelf" Perrenoud asserted to be an "auricle" such as is found in *Tetrabothrium*, *Schizometra*, and *Moniezioides*. That is to say, it is an "épanchement," a thickening of the bothridial musculature. The suckers, according to Perrenoud, can be seen in sagittal sections as "replis," or folds of the auricle, recalling Beneden's picturesque description of "swallows' nests cemented to a wall." Although their cavities are shallow and probably weak in adherent function, they seem to be a constant character of *septaria* and probably of *planum* also. Although at variance with Woodland's views on a number of points, Perrenoud agreed with him that *septaria* and *plicitum* are identical, *septaria* and *planum* distinct.

Sproston (1948) studied a range of English Channel material and based upon it a redefinition of *Dinobothrium*. She accepted the species *septaria* and *planum* and added two further species, *keilini* from *Carcharinus glaucus* and *paciferum* from *Cetorhinus maximus*.

Phyllobothrium Beneden, 1849

With the bothridia stalked or sessile, their adherent surfaces simple, complexly curled, or folded, their margins entire or complexly frilled or bearing minute, suckerlike organs. An accessory sucker commonly but not invariably present in each bothridium. A neck present or absent. Genotype, *lactuca* Beneden, 1850 (Figure 116).

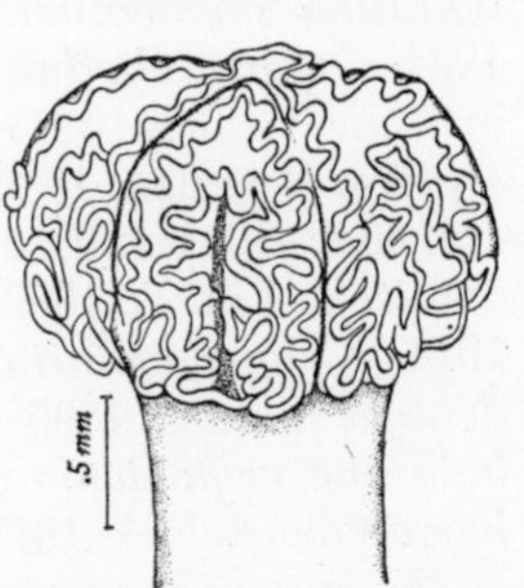

FIG. 116. *Phyllobothrium lactuca,* holdfast. After Beneden, 1850b.

Beneden's original generic description was very brief. "The four bothridia are sessile, cut out on the external surface of the head, and enjoying a very great mobility; they are curled and folded like the leaves of a lettuce." Nor have any later definitions, of Braun (1900), Linton (1924a), or Southwell (1925b, 1930), been much more satisfactory. It seems almost impossible to find characteristics which are peculiar to this genus alone, and which occur in every species of it. In the present state of our knowledge, it must be regarded as a lumber room of forms which cannot be fitted into other phyllobothriid genera.

To Beneden's original genus there have been assigned at one time or another the following species: *auricula* Beneden, 1858; *blakei* Shipley and Hornell, 1906; *brassicae* Beneden, 1870; *compacta* Southwell and Prashad, 1920; *crispatissimum* Monticelli, 1889; *dagnalli* Southwell, 1927; *dasybati* Yamaguti, 1934; *delphini* Gervais, 1885; *dipsadomorphi* Shipley, 1900; *dohrnii* Oerley, 1885; *fallax* Beneden, 1870; *foliatum* Linton, 1890; *gracile* Wedl, 1855; *inchoatum* Leidy, 1891; *ketae* Canavan, 1928; *lactuca* Beneden, 1850; *loliginis* Leidy, 1887; *magnum* Hart, 1936; *marginatum* Yamaguti, 1934; *minutum* Shipley and Hornell, 1906; *microsomum* Southwell and Hilmy, 1929; *pammicrum* Shipley and Hornell, 1906; *radioductum* Kay, 1942; *thridax* Beneden, 1850; *tumidum* Linton, 1922; *unilaterale* Southwell, 1925; *vagans* Haswell, 1902; and *variabile* Beneden, 1850.

In the opinion of Southwell (1925b), the majority of the above species are synonymous with *lactuca* Beneden, 1850. In addition to the above, Southwell placed in his emended *Phyllobothrium* the species listed below, which had previously been assigned to other genera. Some of them he merely removed from the genus to which they had been assigned. Others he regarded as belonging to genera which themselves are synonymous with *Phyllobothrium*.

These species are: *Anthobothrium auriculatum* Diesing, 1863; *Anthobothrium gracile* Linton, 1890; *Anthobothrium musteli* Beneden, 1860, *ex parte*; *Anthobothrium perfectum* Beneden, 1853; *Monorygma chlamy-*

doselachi Loennberg, 1898; *Monorygma dentatum* Linstow, 1907; *Monorygma elegans* Monticelli, 1890; *Monorygma galeocerdonis* MacCallum, 1921; *Monorygma gracile* Olsson, 1869–70; *Monorygma rotundum* Klaptocz, 1906; *Orygmatobothrium angustum* Linton, 1889; *Orygmatobothrium crenulatum* Linton, 1897; *Orygmatobothrium forte* Linton, 1924; *Orygmatobothrium paulum* Linton, 1889; *Orygmatobothrium velamentum* Yoshida, 1917; *Trilocularia gracilis* Olsson, 1867; *Dinobothrium septaria* Beneden, 1889; *Crossobothrium angustum* Linton, 1889; *Crossobothrium campanulatum* Klaptocz, 1906; *Crossobothrium laciniatum* var. *longicolle* Linton, 1889; *Pelichnibothrium caudatum* Zschokke and Heitz, 1914; *Calyptrobothrium minus* Linton, 1890; *Calyptrobothrium occidentalis* Linton, 1890; *Calyptrobothrium riggi* Monticelli, 1893; *Rhinebothrium ceylonicum* Shipley and Hornell, 1906; *Bilocularia hyperapolytica* Obersteiner, 1917, *ex parte*; *Phanobothrium monticelli* Mola, 1907.

The species recognized here will be apparent from the following key. In using such a key it must be remembered that because of their mobility, bothridia vary greatly in shape at any moment, even between individuals of the same species after fixation. Any distinction based upon differences in holdfast shape must be used with caution. The true identity of any species of *Phyllobothrium* can only be surmised after the material has been compared fully and carefully with the original and later descriptions of the whole anatomy of the worm. However, a key such as the following is useful to some extent in enabling provisional identification to be made.

KEY TO SPECIES

1. Bothridia relatively short-stalked or sessile, so that they are more or less in contact marginally with their neighbors 2
   Bothridia relatively long-stalked, so that they are separate from one another (crossobothridiate condition) or, if short-stalked, are still separate marginally 5
2. Bothridia simple, i.e., shallow, oval structures with their margins somewhat thickened but not cut up, infolded, or compartmented 3
   Bothridia with the margins conspicuously folded or crumpled, giving the holdfast end of the body a compact but crumpled appearance . . . . *lactuca, radioductum*
3. Holdfast end relatively large, about 4 × 2 mm., with the bothridia 2.5 mm. long, each provided with a very prominent accessory sucker . . . . . . *magnum*
   Neither holdfast end nor bothridial suckers unusually large 4
4. Each accessory sucker small, placed in the anterior region of the bothridium . . . . *marginatum, prionacis, dasybati, unilaterale*
   Each accessory sucker large, placed in the center of the bothridium . . . . *longicolle*
5. Margins of the bothridium entire, i.e., not lobed, infolded, or cut up 6
   Margins of the bothridia lobed, infolded, or cut up 8
6. Accessory sucker of each bothridium central . . . . *minutum*
   Accessory sucker of each bothridium anterior 7
7. Bothridia cuplike or boatlike . . . . *floriforme, microsomum, dohrnii, perfectum, chlamydoselachi, paulum*

Bothridia vaselike . . . . *gracile*
Bothridia leaflike, each accessory sucker horseshoe-shaped . . . . *riggii*
Bothridia with accessory suckers very prominent and large, with the rest of the bothridium having a septum such that the bothridium appears three-compartmented . . . . *acanthiae-vulgaris*
8. Bothridia with margins fringed by small compartments . . *foliatum, centrurum*
Bothridia without marginal compartments 9
9. Bothridia relatively smooth and thin . . . . *tumidum, rotundum, thridax, ketae*
Bothridia with surfaces ridged, folded, or laciniated . . *foliatum, dagnallium*

NOTES ON SPECIES

1. *lactuca* Beneden, 1850. This species, genotype of the genus, although actually one of the commonest of phyllobothriids, has not been described in detail either from European or from American material. Beneden's description was brief and stated that the near-gravid segments break free from the body; Southwell (1925b), describing what he believed to be this form, from *Galeocerdo tigrinus* in Ceylon waters, also stated that the near-gravid segments break free. Yoshida (1917), on the other hand, describing this species very fully from material in *Cynias manazo* from Japanese waters, and Woodland (1927b), describing such material from *Mustelus vulgaris* – Beneden's host source – in the English Channel, both stated definitely that gravid segments do *not* break free from the body; the latter author suggested that Beneden may have been misled by the presence of free segments of *Calliobothrium verticillatum* which occur commonly with *Phyllobothrium lactuca* in *Mustelus vulgaris.*

Characteristic of the species is the large, almost globular holdfast with its four very large, sessile bothridia whose margins are curled and crumpled in a fashion compared by Beneden with the leaves of a lettuce. The accessory suckers are small and difficult to see. Whether or not they are ever absent is uncertain. Synonymous with *lactuca* in Southwell's opinion are *P. crispatissimum* Monticelli, 1889; *P. inchoatum* Leidy 1891; *Rhinebothrium ceylonicum* Shipley and Hornell, 1906; and *P. compactum* Southwell and Prashad, 1920.

2. *radioductum* Kay, 1942. With bothridia sessile, each with an anterior accessory sucker and with margins thickened, crumpled; each bothridium sheathed with a thin cuticle, that of the upper surface minutely spinose, that of the lower surface smooth and thrown into loose folds; neck about one-fourth of the total length; genital apertures irregularly alternating and mid-marginal; testes 100 or more; lining of ejaculatory duct spinose; ovary bilobed, bilaminate; vagina with terminal portion thickened and muscular, dorsal to secondary uterus; dorsal and ventral osmoregulatory canals equal in diameter. In the bothridia the osmoregulatory system is complex. Parasitic in *Raia binoculata*, Puget Sound, North America; ref. Kay (1942) (Figure 118).

3. *magnum* Hart, 1936. Established for material from *Somniosus microcephalus* in Puget Sound, North America; Hart believed his species closely related to *perfectum* Beneden but definitely separated by the

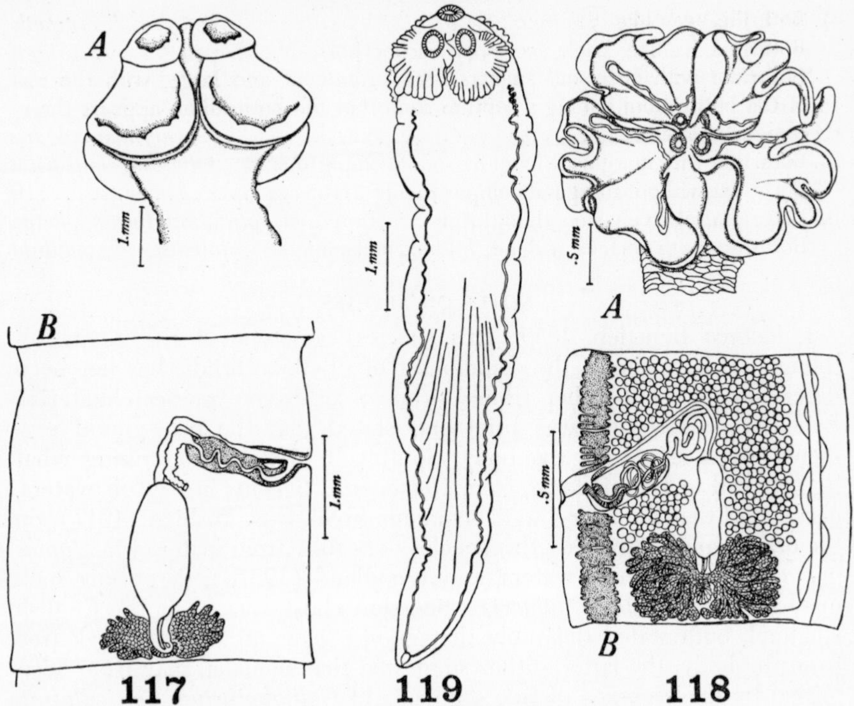

FIG. 117. *Phyllobothrium magnum.* After Hart, 1936b. A. Holdfast. B. Semidiagrammatic view of proglottis. FIG. 118. *Phyllobothrium radioductum.* After Kay, 1942. A. Holdfast. B. Nearly mature proglottis. FIG. 119. *Phyllobothrium* plerocercoid (*P. tumidulum*?). After Dollfus, 1929a.

size of its holdfast, the size and relationships of the proglottides, the manner in which the vagina opens, the location of the opening of the uterine duct into the uterus, the location of the sperm duct, the type, shape, and size of the ovary, and the shape of the eggs; ref. Hart (1936b) (Figure 117).

4, 5, 6. *marginatum, prionacis,* and *dasybati.* These species were established by Yamaguti (1934) from material in *Squatina japonica, Prionace glaucum,* and *Dasybatis okajei,* respectively, in Japanese waters; there is a strong similarity between the three forms, but certain internal differences – notably the testis numbers – support Yamaguti's view that the species are distinct. Close to these forms must be placed *unilaterale,* a new name suggested by Southwell (1925b) for Zschokke's *Phyllobothrium thridax.* The genital apertures are described as unilateral, however, as are those of *dasybati,* whereas those of Yamaguti's other two species are irregularly alternating. How much value can be given to this character has yet to be determined.

7. *longicolle* Molin, 1858. This species was established, as *Monorygma longicolle,* for material in *Scyllium stellare*; Molin's description was very brief. The large, centrally placed bothridial sucker also occurs in *minutum* Shipley and Hornell, 1906 from Ceylon waters, but the latter

species is much smaller and has the bothridia well separated from one another.

8. *floriforme* Southwell, 1912. Established as *Anthobothrium floraformis* by Southwell (1912) from *Carcharias bleekeri* and *Carcharias sp.*, Ceylon waters; the bothridia like shallow cups, without accessory suckers; ref. Southwell (1930).

9. *microsomum* Southwell and Hilmy, 1929. From *Ginglystoma concolor* in Ceylon waters; very minute, 2.2–2.4 mm. long with 6 or 7 segments; the bothridia boat-shaped, without accessory suckers; it may have been an immature form; ref. Southwell (1930).

10. *dohrnii* Oerley, 1885. Recorded from *Heptanchus cinereus*, European waters; has boat-shaped, extremely mobile bothridia, oval and simple, with anteriorly placed accessory suckers; has no neck; has fingerlike outgrowths from the posterior borders of the segments. Such features are shown also by *Crossobothrium laciniatum* Linton, 1889a; *Crossobothrium campanulatum* Klaptocz, 1906; and *Orygmatobothrium velamentum* Yoshida, 1917. Southwell (1925b) regarded these forms as synonymous with *dohrnii.* Woodland (1927b), however, believed Yoshida's form to be synonymous with Beneden's *Anthobothrium musteli.*

11. *perfectum* Beneden, 1853. Established, as *Anthobothrium perfectum,* from *Scimnus glacialis* and by Diesing (1863) as *Monorygma perfectum*; has deep, sauceboat-shaped bothridia, each with an anterior accessory sucker; has a neck and a rostellum. Southwell (1925b) did not regard the possession of neck and rostellum as sufficiently important to justify the separation of *Monorygma* from *Phyllobothrium* and submerged the identity of *Monorygma* in *Phyllobothrium,* placing the species *elegans* Monticelli, 1890 and *dentatum* Linstow, 1907 as synonyms of *perfectum,* and the species *gracile* Olsson, 1869 as a synonym of *acanthiae-vulgaris.*

12. *chlamydoselachi* (= *Monorygma chlamydoselachi* Loennberg, 1898). According to its author, this species is distinguishable from *perfectum* by the position of the genital aperture at the junction of the middle and posterior thirds of the segment margin; otherwise, its resemblance to *perfectum* seems suspiciously close; the original host was *Chlamydoselachus anguineus.*

13. *paulum* (= *Orygmatobothrium paulum* Linton, 1897b = *O. crenulatum* Linton, 1897b). A very small form (9 mm.) with each bothridium having *two* accessory suckers – an anterior, small and shallow one, and a posterior, larger and deeper one; the two suckers are confluent, whereas in true species of *Orygmatobothrium* the second accessory sucker is not formed from the whole bothridium (less the anterior sucker) but lies centrally on the bothridial surface; the original host was *Galeocerdo tigrinus* in Massachusetts waters.

14. *gracile* Wedl, 1855. From *Torpedo marmorata* and *Squatina angelus,* in European waters; has four vase-shaped bothridia with undulating crinkly margins. Southwell (1925b) regarded *Anthobothrium auriculatum* of Diesing (1863a) and Zschokke (1888c) as synonymous with this species.

15. *riggii* (= *Calyptrobothrium riggii* Monticelli, 1893). From *Torpedo marmorata*, Mediterranean waters; described as having bothridia like hoods, jutting out from the corners of the holdfast end; placed anteriorly on each bothridium is a large and powerful accessory sucker, resembling in shape a horseshoe; synonymous with this form, according to Southwell (1925b), are *Calyptrobothrium occidentale* Linton, 1890 and *C. minus* Linton, 1907a, from *Torpedo occidentalis* in Massachusetts waters; and *Bilocularia hyperapolytic* Obersteiner, 1914 from *Centrophorus granulosus* at Naples. The description of the latter form may have been based upon *Monorygma perfectum* and *Calyptrobothrium riggii.*

16. *foliatum* Linton, 1890. Each bothridium rather flat, shaped like a quarter-circle, thin, and leaflike, with one face smooth and the other face ridged with raylike projections; each bothridium has a prominent accessory sucker. Linton spoke of each bothridium as having a distinct row of compartments along its margin, but Southwell and Prashad (1920) neither mentioned nor figured such compartments. Linton's material was taken from *Trygon centrura* and *Carcharinus obscurus* in American waters, Southwell's and Prashad's from *Rhynchobatis djeddensis* in Ceylon waters.

17. *centrurum* Southwell, 1925, new name for *Anthocephalum gracile* Linton, 1890 and *Anthobothrium gracile* Linton, 1890. Figured by Linton as having the margin of each bothridium indented by numerous short grooves which, in an extended bothridium, might give the appearance of compartments; i.e., the margin is crenulate rather than truly compartmented; each bothridium has an accessory sucker. The species clearly seems to belong to *Phyllobothrium* rather than to *Anthobothrium,* and since Linton's specific name is preoccupied for a *Phyllobothrium* species (*gracile* Wedl, 1855), Southwell would seem justified in assigning a new specific name to Linton's form.

18. *tumidum* Linton, 1922. Figured by its author as having four thin bothridia with greatly cut-up margins, prominent accessory suckers, and a short domelike rostellum. Southwell (1927) identified material from *Hemigaleus balfouri* in Ceylon waters with this description; this species has also been recorded by Shuler (1938) from Dry Tortugas, Florida, North America.

19. *rotundum* Klaptocz, 1906. Recorded by its author as *Monorygma rotundum* as an immature specimen in *Notidanus griseus*, Adriatic Sea; it must be regarded as a dubious species. The bothridia were figured as very thin, leaflike, subcircular structures, each with a prominent accessory sucker.

20. *thridax* Beneden, 1850. Described at the same time its author described *lactuca.* In 1888 Zschokke described under the same name a form with unilateral genital pores in the anterior marginal quarters and with ruffle-margined bothridia; this form Southwell (1925b) regarded as a distinct species and gave it the name *unilaterale.*

21. *ketae* Canavan, 1928. Recorded from *Onchorhynchus ketae*, Alaskan waters; its larval form is common in *Onchorhynchus spp.* (see Wardle, 1932a). Despite its peculiar distribution, *ketae* seems to be a

perfectly valid species, with four stalked bothridia whose anterior marginal regions are pinched in somewhat, the posterior marginal regions curled and folded; each bothridium has an accessory sucker; there is also a terminal, vestigial, suckerlike structure. In many of its features it recalls *unilaterale.*

22, 23. *foliatum* and *dagnallium* Southwell, 1927 (= *dagnalli* Southwell, 1930). Of the two species whose bothridia are stalked and ridged, folded, or laciniated, *foliatum* is included because of the doubt as to whether its bothridial margins are or are not compartmented. The other species, *dagnallium,* was recorded from *Rhynchobatis ancylostomus, Chiloscyllium indicum,* and *Galeocerdo tigrinus* in Ceylon waters. It has somewhat peculiar bothridia, described by Southwell as recalling fully opened roses, as each bothridium is apparently divided into two, then folded upon itself; the bothridial margins are armed with small spines; four minute accessory suckers are present; in many respects this form recalls *Anthobothrium laciniatum* Linton, 1890, *A. pulvinatum* Linton, 1890, and *Phyllobothrium tumidum* Linton, 1922, perhaps resembling *tumidum* most of all though differing from it in larger size, in the mid-marginal position of the genital apertures (which are in the anterior third of the segment margin in *tumidum*), and in the absence of post-cirral testes on the poral side. However, apart from the presence of accessory suckers, it seems close to *Anthobothrium pulvinatum* and may be synonymous with it.

Orygmatobothrium Diesing, 1863

With *two* accessory suckers in each bothridium, one anterior, the other central, on the bothridial surface. Established to accommodate Beneden's *Anthobothrium musteli.* Beneden's material, however, according to Woodland (1927b), comprised in all probability three distinct forms: (1) the species described in detail by Yoshida (1917b) as *Orygmatobothrium velamentum,* from *Cynias manazo* in Japanese waters; (2) the species described by Zschokke (1888c) as *Anthobothrium* (*Orygmatobothrium*) *musteli* from *Mustelus spp.*; and (3) a species identical or closely similar to that described by Linton (1889a) under the term *Orygmatobothrium* (later *Crossobothrium*) *angustum,* from *Carcharias obscurus* in American Atlantic waters, and by Yoshida (1917b) as *Crossobothrium angustum* from *Triakis scyllium* in Japanese waters.

Woodland, on the basis of an examination of extensive material from Beneden's original host type, *Mustelus vulgaris,* from the English Channel, believed that Yoshida's *velamentum* corresponded exactly with Beneden's *Anthobothrium musteli,* but that Zschokke's form differed from it entirely in the shape of the bothridia, in the genital apertures being *behind* the middle of each segment margin instead of in front of it, in having two pairs of osmoregulatory canals, etc. Woodland suggested for Zschokke's material the term *Orygmatobothrium zschokkei.*

A number of species have been placed within the genus *Orygmatobothrium,* but Southwell (1925b) regarded them all as either dubious or

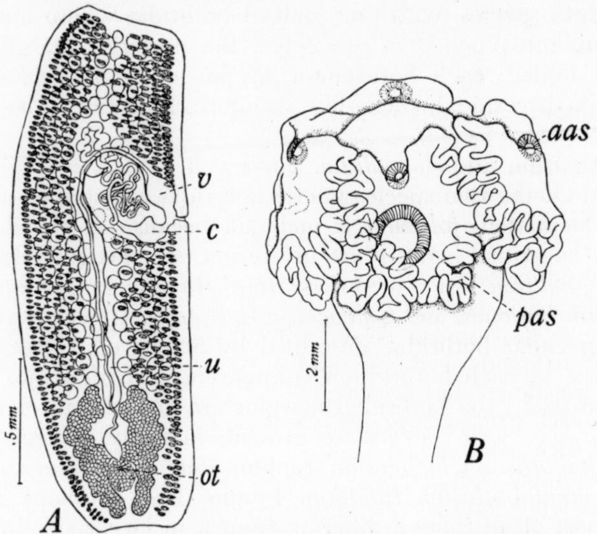

FIG. 120. *Orygmatobothrium plicatum.* After Yamaguti, 1934. A. Mature segments. B. Holdfast. *aas*, anterior accessory sucker; *c*, cirrus; *ot*, ootype; *pas*, posterior accessory sucker; *u*, uterus; *v*, vagina.

synonymous. Yamaguti's form, *plicatum* (1934), from a skate in Toyama Bay, Japan, may be a distinct and valid species, however (Figure 120).

The genotypic name *versatile* given by Diesing must be reserved as a general term for any larval form of *Orygmatobothrium*. It would thus replace *wyatti* Leiper and Atkinson, 1914, which seems to have been a larval orygmatobothriid.

Family ONCHOBOTHRIIDAE Braun, 1900

DESCRIPTION

Of the order Tetraphyllidea. With the holdfast armed with four pairs of hooks. Four sessile or only slightly stalked bothridia present. Accessory suckers present or lacking. Genital apertures regularly or irregularly alternating. Life cycle practically unknown. Type genus, *Onchobothrium* Blainville, 1828.

HISTORY

Beneden's tribe of Phyllacanthiens contained the three present onchobothriid genera – *Acanthobothrium, Onchobothrium,* and *Calliobothrium* – the first and third of which were founded by Beneden himself, the second by Blainville. This second genus was selected by Braun (1894–1900) as the type genus of his new family Onchobothriidae. Woodland (1927b) preferred to merge the families Onchobothriidae and Phyllobothriidae as one family Phyllobothriidae *sens. nov.* within his order Tetraphyllidea. Pintner (1927) also merged the two into one family, Tetraphyllidae. Southwell (1930) returned to the scheme of two families recognized by Braun.

The thirteen genera recognized here may be separated in preliminary fashion as follows:

KEY TO GENERA

1. Bothridia undivided, each with one pair of hooks .... *Pedibothrium*
   Bothridia divided by one or two transverse partitions 2
2. Each bothridium with one partition and two compartments 3
   Each bothridium with two partitions and three compartments 6
3. Each bothridium with one pair of forked, slender hooks on its anterior margins; the posterior compartments circular, suckerlike .... *Uncibilocularis*
   Each bothridium with one pair of simple or U-shaped but not forked hooks, latero-marginal in position 4
4. A pseudo-holdfast present behind the true holdfast, much frilled, dividing the neck into anterior and posterior regions .... *Thysanocephalum*
   No such pseudo-holdfast present 5
5. Hooks of each pair equal in size .... *Spiniloculus*
   Hooks of each pair unequal in size .... *Yorkeria*
6. Each bothridium with *two* pairs of hooks .... *Calliobothrium*
   Each bothridium with *one* pair of hooks 7
7. All the hooks simple and unforked .... *Onchobothrium*
   All the hooks forked 8
8. All the hooks two-pronged .... *Acanthobothrium*
   One hook of each pair two-pronged, the other hook three-pronged .... *Platybothrium*

To the above genera should be added *Acrobothrium* Baer, 1948, defined below. *Incertae sedis: Balanobothrium, Cylindrophorus, Ceratobothrium, Tetracampos.*

NOTES ON GENERA

Pedibothrium Linton, 1909, emended Southwell, 1925b

With four simple, undivided, somewhat leaflike bothridia, each armed with one pair of hooks, shaped like a rose thorn or two-pronged. Body ribbonlike, recalling that of *Taenia*. Neck present. Genotype, *globicephalum* Linton, 1909.

Five species of this genus are known:

1. Hooks shaped like a rose thorn .... *hutsoni*
   Hooks two-pronged 2
2. Inner prong of each hook straight .... *brevispine*
   Inner prong of each hook curved 3
3. Total hook length 35 μ .... *globicephalum*
   Total hook length 150–212 μ; worms with 10–30 segments ...... *longispine*

Incertae sedis: pinguicollum.

The species *globicephalum, brevispine,* and *longispine* were all recorded by Linton (1909) from the nurse shark, *Ginglistoma cirratum*, at Dry Tortugas, Florida, North America. Shuler (1938) also recorded *brevispine* and *longispine* from the same host species and locality. The species *hutsoni* Southwell, 1911 was recorded from *Ginglistoma concolor* in Ceylon waters. The species *pinguicollum* was established by Sleggs (1927) on material from an unidentified skate in Californian waters. Sleggs placed the species within the genus *Onchobothrium*, but its true generic position was established by Hart (1936b), who obtained material from *Raja binoculata* in Puget Sound. Neither Sleggs nor Hart, however, described the hooks sufficiently to permit inclusion of this species in the key given above.

Uncibilocularis Southwell, 1925

With each bothridium two-compartmented and armed on its anterior margin with one pair of simple or two-pronged hooks. Accessory suckers present or lacking. Genotype, *trygonis* Shipley and Hornell, 1906 (Figure 122).

The genotype was established, as *Prosthecobothrium trygonis*, by Shipley and Hornell (1906) on material from *Trygon sephen* and *Trygon walga* in Ceylon waters. Diesing's *Prosthecobothrium*, however, was

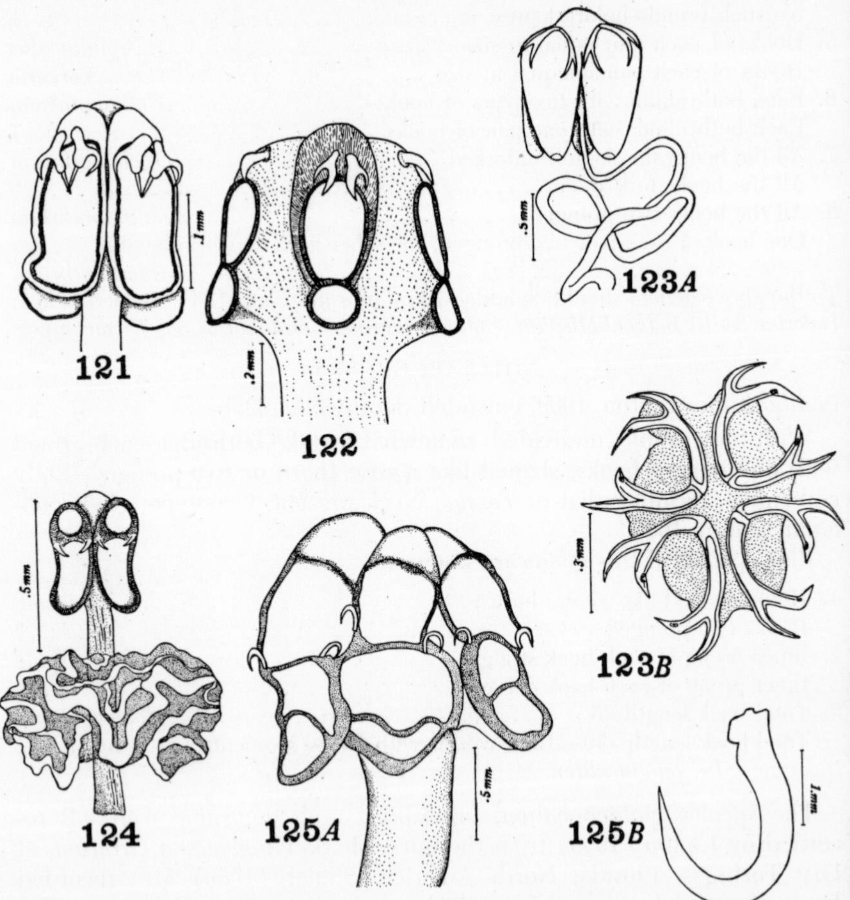

FIG. 121. *Pedibothrium brevispine*, holdfast. After Southwell, 1925b. FIG. 122. *Uncibilocularis trygonis*, holdfast. After Southwell, 1925b. FIG. 123. *Uncibilocularis mandleyi*. After Southwell, 1927. A. Holdfast and neck. B. Holdfast in apical view. FIG. 124. *Thysanocephalum thysanocephalum*, holdfast and pseudo-holdfast. After Southwell, 1925b. FIG. 125. *Spiniloculus mavensis*. After Southwell, 1925b. A. Holdfast. B. Single hook.

based upon an observation by Beneden that *dujardinii*, the genotype, had two-compartmented bothridia, which is apparently an error. Later observers believe that three compartments are present, unless the species varies or unless one compartment is so small that it cannot always be seen. In the opinion of Southwell (1925b), the name *Prosthecobothrium* should be discarded, and in place of it he suggested the generic term *Uncibilocularis* for those onchobothriids in which each bothridium is divided by a single transverse partition and in which the hooks are two-pronged. A second species, *mandleyi* Southwell, 1927, was recorded from *Hemigaleus balfouri* in Ceylon waters, differing from the genotype in size and shape of hooks (Figure 123).

Thysanocephalum Linton, 1889, emended Southwell, 1925

With the holdfast small or even lacking. Bothridia sessile, each divided into two compartments and armed with simple hooks which are prolongations of the posterior corners of the anterior compartments. Pseudo-holdfast present. Genital apertures in the posterior halves of the segment margins. Genotype, *thysanocephalum* Linton, 1889 (Figure 124).

This form was first described by Linton (1889a) as *Phyllobothrium thysanocephalum* from *Galeocerdo tigrinus*, Massachusetts waters; but later (1891b) he renamed it *Thysanocephalum crispum*. The term *Thysanocephalum*, not being preoccupied, must be retained in accordance with the International Rules. *Myzocephalus narinari* Shipley and Hornell, 1906 would seem to be synonymous with Linton's form.

The holdfast is very small, 350–380 μ long, with four, small, sessile bothridia, each biloculate. At the posterior corners of each anterior compartment there is a solid, pointed spine, there thus being two spines per bothridium. Then comes the first part of the neck, 200–250 μ by 90 μ, and then a massive, fleshy collar, ruffed and frilled, recalling somewhat the holdfast of *Phyllobothrium lactuca*. This pseudo-holdfast is followed by the rest of the neck, 480 mm. according to Linton. A more detailed study, particularly of the proglottis, has been made by Davis (1926) with material from *Galeocerdo arcticus* in Massachusetts waters. A second species from this same host, but in Florida waters, was added by Chandler (1942) as *Thysanocephalum rugosum*. Though strikingly similar to the genotype, Chandler's material lacked holdfasts and differed in general size and shape, in proportions of the segments, and particularly in having the cuticle marked by chitinous reticulations about 5–7 μ thick, enclosing irregular spaces and giving a very characteristic scaly appearance.

Spiniloculus Southwell, 1925

With each bothridium divided by two transverse partitions into three compartments, and the postero-lateral corners of the anterior compartments each provided with a U-shaped hook, the inner limb of which is longer than the outer. Genotype, *mavensis* Southwell, 1925 (Figure 125). The genotype and only known species was recorded by Southwell (1925b) from *Mustelus sp.*, Brisbane, Australia.

Yorkeria Southwell, 1927

With the bothridia oval or circular, each divided into two compartments, one very large, the other very small. Each bothridium with a pair of U-shaped hooks, unequal in size, one being placed near each lateral end of the partition. Genital apertures mid-marginal, irregularly alternating. Genotype, *parva* Southwell, 1927 (Figure 126).

The genotype and only known species was recorded from *Chiloscyllium indicum* in Ceylon waters. It is peculiar in having the bothridia in pairs, each pair at the end of a stout stalk, the two stalks uniting into a common trunk in Y- or T-fashion. In the original description the bothridia were described as undivided, but in a later description (1930), based upon more material, the bothridia were described as being quite definitely divided by a partition into two unequal compartments, the distal one being much the smaller. The whole surface of the holdfast is covered with innumerable small spines, each 10 μ long; and each bothridium is armed with a pair of U-shaped hooks, these being very unequal in size and placed one near the lateral end of each partition.

Calliobothrium Beneden, 1850

With bothridia having three compartments each and two pairs of simple, unforked hooks. Genotype, *verticillatum* Rudolphi, 1819.

The four known species may be distinguished as follows:

1. Small forms, less than 10 segments . . . . *eschrichtii*
   Large forms with numerous segments 2
2. Hooks of each pair similar . . . . *nodosum*
   Hooks of each pair dissimilar 3
3. Posterior segment borders not laciniated . . . . *leuckartii*
   Posterior segment borders markedly laciniated . . . . *verticillatum*

NOTES ON SPECIES

1. *Calliobothrium eschrichtii* Beneden, 1849 (= *Onchobothrium elegans* Diesing, 1854). Established, as *Acanthobothrium eschrichtii*, from *Mustelus vulgaris* in Belgian waters. It has also been recorded by Linton (1891a), by Yoshida (1917b), and by Southwell (1925b, 1930). It is a small form, 4–5 mm. long, the hooks 100 μ long.

2. *nodosum* Yoshida, 1917. From *Cynias manazo* in Japanese waters; has three accessory suckers per bothridium, is 1 mm. thick, has two pairs of simple hooks per bothridium, and shows a peculiar laciniation of the posterior segment borders.

3. *leuckartii* Beneden, 1850. Recorded by numerous observers from *Mustelus laevis, Mustelus vulgaris, Scyllium canicula*; synonymous with it are *Acanthobothrium leuckartii* Beneden, 1849b; *Onchobothrium heteracanthum* Diesing, 1854; *Calliobothrium eschrichtii* Beneden 1850a, Johnstone 1907. It is identifiable by the dissimilar shape of the two hooks of each pair, coupled with the absence of posterior border laciniations; by the genital pore being in the posterior third of the segment margin; and by the uterine pore being slitlike, in the mid-ventral line just in front of the middle of the segment.

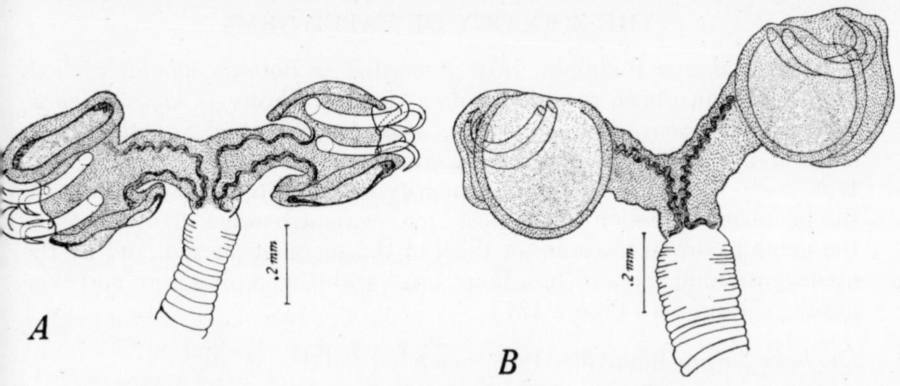

FIG. 126. *Yorkeria parva*. After Southwell, 1927. A. Holdfast in apical view. B. Holdfast in lateral view.

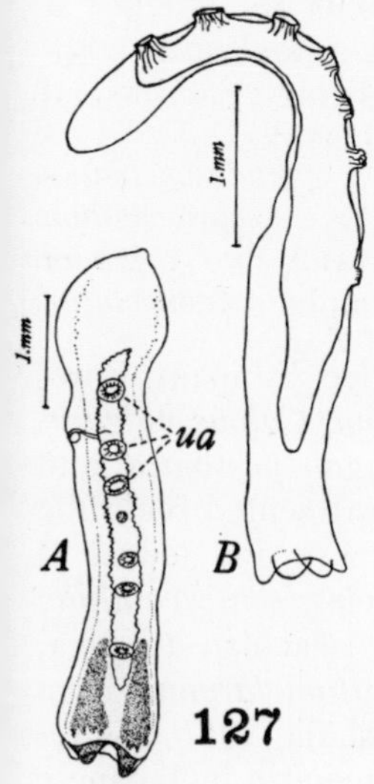

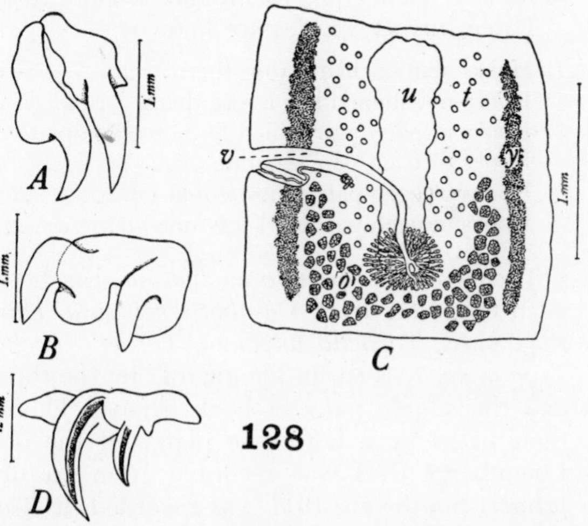

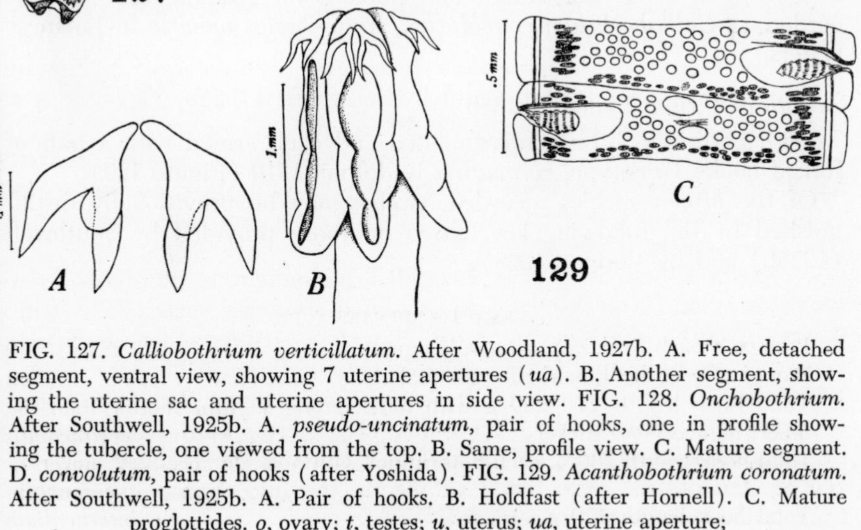

FIG. 127. *Calliobothrium verticillatum*. After Woodland, 1927b. A. Free, detached segment, ventral view, showing 7 uterine apertures (*ua*). B. Another segment, showing the uterine sac and uterine apertures in side view. FIG. 128. *Onchobothrium*. After Southwell, 1925b. A. *pseudo-uncinatum*, pair of hooks, one in profile showing the tubercle, one viewed from the top. B. Same, profile view. C. Mature segment. D. *convolutum*, pair of hooks (after Yoshida). FIG. 129. *Acanthobothrium coronatum*. After Southwell, 1925b. A. Pair of hooks. B. Holdfast (after Hornell). C. Mature proglottides. *o*, ovary; *t*, testes; *u*, uterus; *ua*, uterine aperture; *v*, vagina; *y*, yolk glands.

4. *verticillatum* Rudolphi, 1819. Recorded as *Bothriocephalus verticillatum*; has since been recorded from a variety of hosts – *Galeus vulgaris, Hexanchus griseus, Mustelus canis, Mustelus equestris, Squatina angelus,* and, as a larva, from the crab *Carcinus maenas,* in European waters. It is easily identified by the dissimilarity of the two hooks of each pair, the peculiar laciniation of the posterior segment borders, the position of the genital pore in the anterior third of the segment margin, and by the oviduct running forward to a point level with the genital pore and then joining the uterus (Figure 127).

Onchobothrium Blainville, 1828, emended Southwell, 1925

With each bothridium three-compartmented and armed anteriorly with two simple hooks which bear secondary tuberclelike or hairlike processes. Genotype, *pseudo-uncinatum* Rudolphi (Figure 128).

Three further species are known:

1. Hooks shaped like a rose thorn 2
   Hooks not shaped like a rose thorn 3
2. Hooks of each pair joined by horseshoe plate . . . . *pseudo-uncinatum*
   Hooks of each pair separate . . . . *schizacanthum*
3. Hooks of each pair almost equal . . . . *farmeri*
   Hooks of each pair markedly unequal . . . . *convolutum*

The genotype, *pseudo-uncinatum,* has been recorded by many European observers from *Dasybatis centrura, Dasyatis sayi, Galeus vulgaris, Raja batis, Torpedo uncinata, Torpedo ocellata, Trygon pastinaca,* and *Trygon sp.* It is easily identifiable by the three-compartmented bothridia and the simple pairs of hooks shaped like a rose thorn and joined at their bases by a horseshoe plate. Of the other species, *schizacanthum* Loennberg, 1893 was recorded from an unknown selachian in Java; *farmeri* Southwell, 1911 was recorded, as *Calliobothrium farmeri,* from *Trygon kuhli* in Ceylon waters; and *convolutum* Yoshida, 1917 was recorded, as *Calliobothrium convolutum,* from *Cynias manazo* in Japanese waters.

Acanthobothrium Beneden, 1850

With bothridia three-compartmented and each armed with a pair of forked hooks. Genotype, *coronatum* Rudolphi, 1819 (Figure 129).

Of the fifteen species recorded, twelve may be provisionally distinguished by the following key, based on those provided by Southwell (1925b) and by Verma (1928):

KEY TO SPECIES

1. Prongs of each hook *approximately* equal 2
   Prongs of each hook markedly unequal 3
2. Total hook length 270–290 μ with outer prong *slightly* shorter than the inner; no accessory suckers . . . . *cestraciontis*
   Total hook length 230 μ, each bothridium with a single accessory sucker . . . . *coronatum*
   Total hook length 170 μ . . . . *intermedium*

Total hook length 140–170 μ, each bothridium with three accessory suckers .... *ijimae*
Total hook length 130 μ, no accessory suckers .... *dasybati*
3. Outer prong of each hook markedly *shorter* than the inner prong 4
Outer prong of each hook a little *longer* than the inner prong .... *crassicolle*
4. Worms with more than 200 segments 5
Worms with fewer than 40 segments 6
5. Total hook length about 400 μ .... *macracanthum*
Total hook length about 200 μ .... *herdmani*
Total hook length about 100 μ .... *uncinatum*
6. Seminal vesicle distinct and voluminous; segments fewer than 25 (18–25), testes about 50 per segment .... *semnovesiculum*
Seminal vesicle indistinct or lacking 7
7. Segments fewer than 12, testes about 20 per segment .... *dujardinii*
Segments more than 30, testes about 45 per segment .... *benedenii*

Incertae sedis: heterodonti, ponticum, aetiobatis.

NOTES ON SPECIES

1. *cestraciontis* Yamaguti, 1934. Established for material from *Cestracion japonicus* in Japanese waters; forms up to 282 mm. long with several hundred segments; holdfast without accessory suckers; hooks 270–290 μ long, the inner prong with the basal tubercle being 160 μ long, the outer prong a little shorter.

2. *coronatum* Rudolphi, 1819. The genotype has been recorded frequently and has an imposing array of synonyms (see Southwell, 1925b). Of interest is its ventral uterine pore, a feature known also in some other onchobothriids; Pintner, and again Braun, were of the opinion that these are not true uterine pores, not being constant in position, but arise through pressure of the uterus against a cortex weakened by atrophy. Southwell (1925b) recorded *coronatum* from *Trygon kuhli* in Ceylon waters; Linton (1916) recorded it as *Onchobothrium tortum* from *Aetiobatis narinari* in Florida waters; Hornell (1912) recorded it as *Prosthecobothrium urogymni* from *Urogymnus asperrimus* in Ceylon waters (Figure 129).

3. *intermedium* Perrenoud, 1931. From *Trygon pastinaca*, New Zealand; apparently differs from *coronatum* only in dimensional characters, such as smaller hook length.

4. *ijimae* Yoshida, 1917 (= *Acanthobothrium coronatum* Johnstone, 1906, not Rudolphi, 1819 = *Acanthobothrium coronatum* Linton, 1901, not Rudolphi, 1819 = *Taenia incognita* MacCallum, 1921). The only acanthobothriid with three accessory suckers to each bothridium, this species was recorded by Yoshida from Japanese material, by Southwell (1925b) in *Raja spp.* (Irish Sea and North Sea), in *Narcine timleyi* and *Chiloscyllium sp.* in southern India and Ceylon waters; it has also been recorded and figured by Linton (1901) from Massachusetts material.

5. *dasybati* Yamaguti, 1934. From *Dasybatis akajei* in Japanese waters; recalls *cestraciontis* in lack of accessory suckers, but differs in shape and size of hooks, in characters of body, etc.

6. *crassicolle* Wedl, 1855 (= *A. filicolle* Zschokke, 1888 = *A. filicolle* var. *filicolle* Beauchamp, 1905). Recorded from *Trygon pastinaca* in European waters; also recorded from the same host species by Linstow (1878a), Carus (1884), Oerley (1885a), and Zschokke (1887b). Southwell (1925b), for Zschokke's material, gives the total hook length as 180 μ, inner prong length 90–95 μ, outer prong length 101–108 μ.

7. *macracanthum* Southwell, 1925. New name for *Prosthecobothrium trygonis* Shipley and Hornell, 1906 – or rather for a single worm found among a collection so labeled by Hornell; an obvious acanthobothriid, it differs however from other known species by the unusual size of its hooks, whose total length is 490 μ, with inner prong 300 μ and outer prong 235–245 μ; the original host was presumably *Urogymnus asperrimus* in Ceylon waters.

8. *herdmani* Southwell, 1912. From *Dasybatis kuhli* in Ceylon waters; with total hook length of 200 μ, inner prong 126 μ, outer prong 90–96 μ.

9. *uncinatum* Rudolphi, 1819. Original host uncertain; has been recorded by several observers from European waters; recorded by Southwell (1925b) also from *Trygon kuhli* in Ceylon waters; this author gives the total hook length as 90–100 μ, inner prong 55–64 μ, outer prong 36–44 μ. The only other species with an outer prong much shorter than the inner is *benedenii*, which has much fewer segments.

10. *semnovesiculum* Verma, 1928. Recorded from *Trygon sephen*, Ganges and Jumna rivers, India; in body dimensions approaches *crassicolle, benedenii*, and *dujardinii* but differs from these in the nonspiny character of its neck, in the voluminous convoluted seminal vesicle, number of segments, and size of hooks; total hook length 85–100 μ, inner prong longer than the outer.

11. *dujardinii* Beneden, 1849. This minute form has been recorded frequently from European waters, mainly in *Raja maculata*, and has been recorded by Linton (1901) as *Acanthobothrium brevissime* from Dry Tortugas, Florida.

12. *benedenii* Loennberg, 1889 (= *A. paulum* Linton, 1890 = *A. filicolle* var. *benedenii* Beauchamp, 1905). Also apparently common in European waters in species of *Raja* and in American Atlantic waters in *Pastinachus centrourus*.

13. *heterodonti* Drummond, 1927. Recorded from *Heterodontus philippi* off the coast of Victoria, Australia; is said to have accessory suckers, a characteristic hook shape, and certain minor characteristics of the genitalia.

14. *ponticum* Borcea, 1934. Recorded from *Raja clavata*, Black Sea. We have been unable to consult the Rumanian publication in which its description appears.

15. *aetiobatis* Shipley, 1900 (= *Calliobothrium aetiobatis* Shipley, 1900). Recorded from *Aetiobatis narinari*, western Pacific waters; Southwell (1925b) suggested an identity with the form described by Yoshida (1917b) as *ijimai*, but Shipley's description was too scanty to justify the abolition of Yoshida's species in favor of *aetiobatis*.

Baer (1948) has revised the species of this genus. Minimizing the value attached by Southwell and by Dollfus to hook dimensions, this author prefers to use as distinguishing characters the total length of body, the number of testes, and the lengths of hook handle, internal prong, and external prong, as compared with total hook length. His identification key is as follows:

KEY TO SPECIES OF ACANTHOBOTHRIUM, AFTER BAER

1. Worms parasitic in sharks 2
   Worms parasitic in rays 4
2. Total length less than 100 mm.; L = 30–80; T = 80–110; C = 93, 109, 130/216 .... *coronatum*
   Total length more than 100 mm. 3
3. L = 340; T = 120–150; C = 230, 250, 300/600 .... *heterodonti*
   L = 282; T = fewer than 120; C = 99, 143, 160/270–290 ... *cestracionis*
4. Length more than 150 mm.; L = 210; T = 42–53; C = 220, 300, 235–245/490 .... *macracanthum*
   Length less than 150 mm. 5
5. Testes 80–140 per segment 6
   Testes 60 or fewer per segment 8
6. Total hook length below 150 μ; L = 52; T = 90–110; C = 53, 95.4, 75–78/130 .... *dasybati*
   Total hook length above 150 μ 7
7. L = 63; T = ca. 100; C = 97, 126, 90–96/200 .... *herdmanni*
   L =80; T = 100–140; C = 100–126, 115–133, 69–94/180–220 .... *crassicollis*
8. Total hook length above 130 μ 9
   Total hook length below 130 μ 12
9. Cephalic stalk reaching half the total length; L = 6–8; T = 30–40; C = 51, 103.5, 94.5/170 .... *filicolle*
   Cephalic stalk not reaching half the total length 10
10. Bothridia with “appendices”; L = 0.6–2.0; T = 20–30; C = 39–44, 123–130, 100–126/207 .... *dujardini*
    Bothridia without “appendices” 11
11. L = 3–4; T = 24–30; C = 56, 123.5, 119.5/138–160 .... *benedeni*
    L = 11; T = 40–45; C = 79–104, 144–151; 108–144/216 .... *paulum*
12. L = 12–15; T = 50–55; C = 46–62, 90.81/129 .... *woodsholei*
    L = 29; T = 35–40; C = 58, 77–78, 47/127 .... *zschokkei*

L = total length in mm.; T = number of testes; C = hook handle, internal prong, external prong/total hook length, all in microns.

NOTES ON THE SPECIES OF THE ABOVE KEY

1. *coronatum* Rudolphi, 1819. Recorded by Baer from *Scyllium stellare* and *Mustelus laevis* at Naples; by Zschokke in *Scyllium cuniculi* at Naples; also in *Acanthias vulgaris, Squatina angelus*, and *Torpedo narce*. Specimens 30–50 mm. long with maximum breadth of 2 mm.; strobila of 200 segments; holdfast 800 μ to 1,000 μ long, with four apical suckers; further anatomical details as given in key; see Baer (1948).

2. *heterodonti* Drummond, 1927. Not redescribed by Baer.

3. *cestracionis* Yamaguti, 1934. Not redescribed by Baer.

4. *macracanthum* Southwell, 1925. Not redescribed by Baer.

5. *dasybati* Yamaguti, 1934. Not redescribed by Baer.

6. *herdmanni* Southwell, 1911. Regarded by Baer as identical with *coronatum* Southwell, 1925, not Rudolphi, 1819.

7. *crassicolle* Wedl, 1855. Identical according to Baer with *intermedium* Perrenoud, 1931, in part, and with *ponticum* Borcea, 1934.

8. *filicolle* Zschokke, 1887. Identical according to Baer with *paulum* Linton, 1924, not Linton, 1890.

9. *dujardini* Beneden, 1849 (*dujardinii* of Southwell). Identical according to Baer with *Prosthecobothrium dujardini* (Beneden) Diesing, 1863.

10. *benedeni* Loennberg, 1889 (*benedenii* of Southwell). Identical according to Baer with *filicolle* var. *benedeni* Beauchamp, 1905; *semnovesiculum* Verma, 1928; and *dujardini* Borcea, 1934, not Beneden, 1850.

11. *paulum* Linton, 1890. Redescribed by Baer.

12. *woodsholei* Baer, 1948. New name for *coronatum* Linton, 1901, not Rudolphi, 1819.

13. *zschokkei* Baer, 1948. New name for *Onchobothrium (Calliobothrium) uncinatum* Zschokke, 1888, not Rudolphi, 1819; and *Acanthobothrium ijimae* Yoshida, 1917.

Species inquirendae according to Baer are *Acanthobothrium ijimae* Southwell, 1925, not Yoshida, 1917, and *Acanthobothrium coronatum* Yoshida, 1917, not Rudolphi, 1819.

The species *Acanthobothrium intermedium* Perrenoud, 1931, *in part*, is taken from *intermedium* Perrenoud *proper* and made the genotype of a new genus defined as follows:

Acrobothrium Baer, 1948

Holdfast with four triloculated bothridia, each surmounted by a muscular pad bearing an apical sucker. One pair of hooks with wide bases and very unequal prongs between each pad and bothridium. Body weakly craspedote. Gravid segments not apolytic. Longitudinal musculature strongly developed in two layers, the innermost formed of large isolated bundles. Testes in two lateral fields, continuous. Genital ducts passing between the osmoregulatory canals. Yolk glands lateral and outside of the canals. Uterus discharging by a splitting of the ventral segment wall. Genotype, *musculosum* Baer, 1948, with the characteristics of the genus.

Platybothrium Linton, 1890, emended Southwell, 1925

With the bothridia arranged in pairs, their surfaces triloculate, each with a pair of hooks in which one member of the pair is two-pronged, the other three-pronged. Genotype, *cervinum* Linton, 1890.

Three species are known:

1. *cervinum* Linton, 1890. Recorded from *Carcharias obscurus* in Massachusetts waters; with the hindermost compartments of the bothridia indistinct; the spines on the neck small, 15 μ, and numerous; and the two hooks of each pair connected by a basal bar.

2. *parvum* Linton, 1901. Recorded from *Carcharias milberti, Isurus tigris, Sphyrna zygaena* in Massachusetts waters; with the hindermost bothridial compartments distinct; the spines on the neck large, 30 μ, and few; and the two hooks of each pair connected by a basal bar.

3. *hypoprioni* Potter, 1937. Recorded from *Hypoprion brevirostris* in Florida waters; with the hindermost bothridial compartments indistinct; the spines on the neck small, 14–17 μ; and no basal bars connecting the hooks of the pairs (Figure 130).

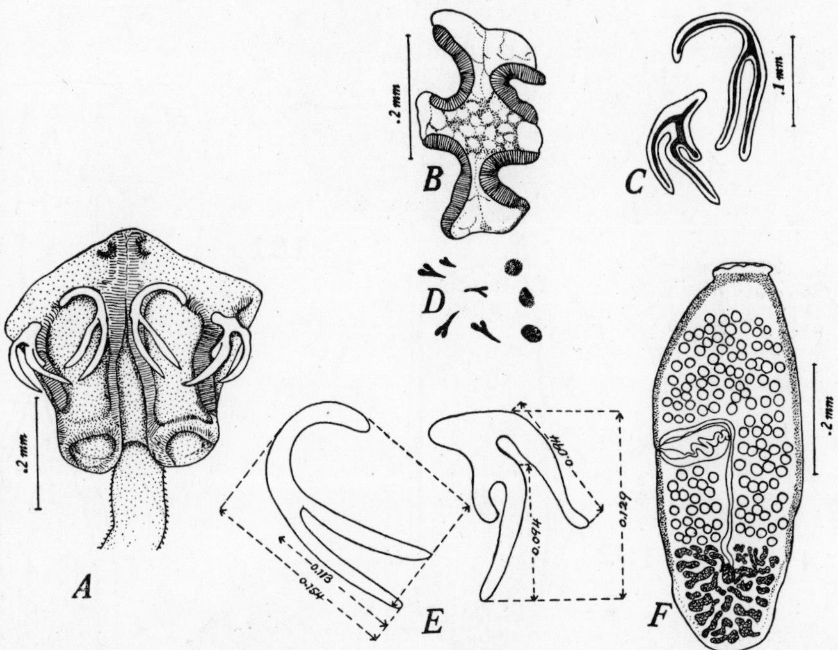

FIG. 130. *Platybothrium hypoprioni.* After Potter, 1937. A. Holdfast. B. Cross section through the bothridia. C. The two types of large hooks. D. Spines from neck region. E. Pair of large hooks showing dimensions in millimeters. F. Mature proglottis.

Balanobothrium Hornell, 1912

Holdfast acorn-shaped, with bulbous anterior portion surrounded at its base by a cuplike, membranous collar. Four pairs of very minute two-pronged hooks placed equidistantly on the upper circumference of the bulbous region. Above each pair of hooks a minute sucker. Neck very short. Body with short, wide, thick proglottides. Genotype, *tenax* Hornell, 1912 (Figure 131).

The genotype was established for material from *Stegostoma tigrinus*, Bay of Bengal and Ceylon Pearl Banks; a further species was added by Southwell (1925b) under the name of *parvum* from *Dasybatis sp.* and *Galeocerdo arcticus*, Ceylon Pearl Banks. The systematic position of this remarkable form has always been uncertain. The morphology of the holdfast, as described by Hornell, would seem to justify his establish-

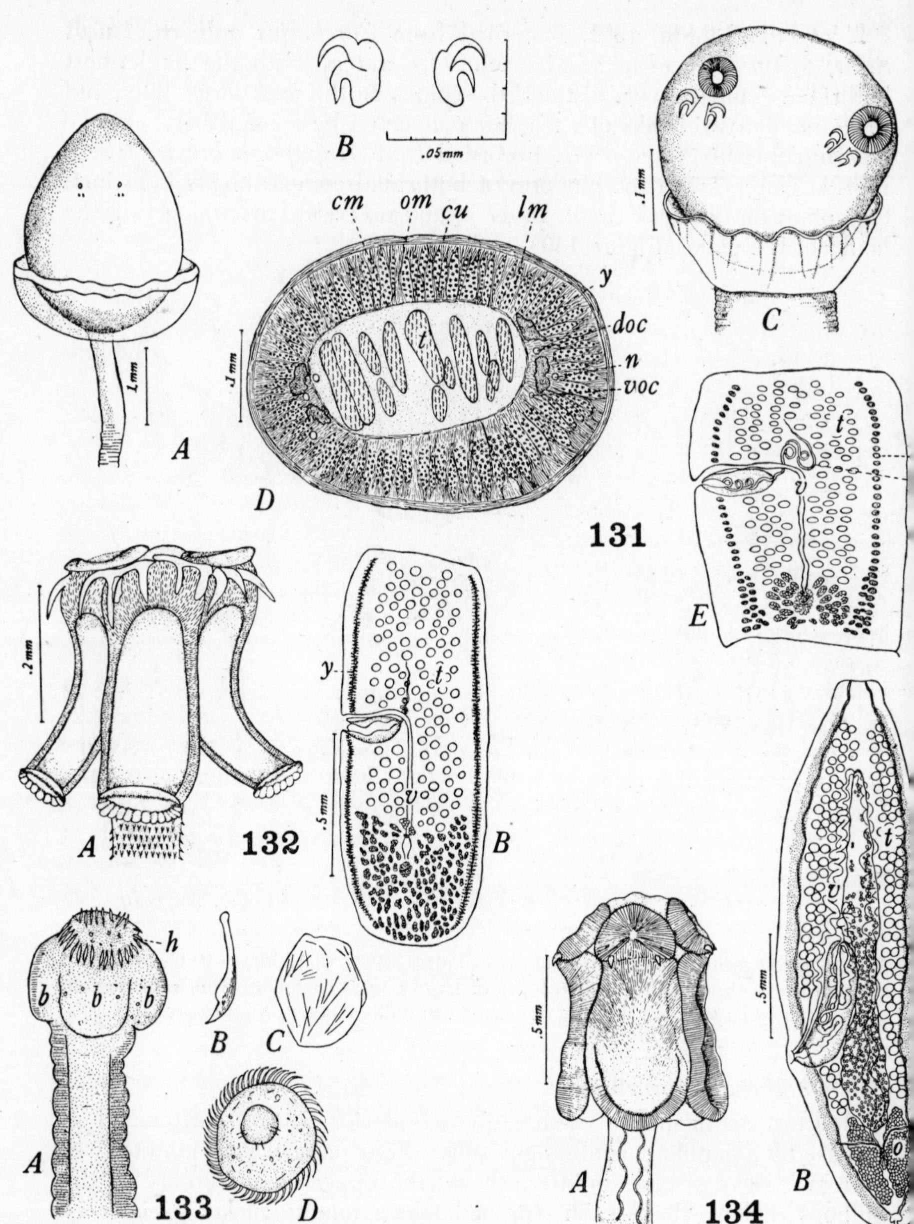

FIG. 131. *Balanobothrium.* After Southwell, 1925b. A. *tenax,* holdfast. B. *tenax,* pair hooks. C. *parvum,* holdfast. D. *parvum,* cross section of immature segment. E. *parvum,* mat segment. FIG. 132. *Cylindrophorus lasium.* After Southwell, 1925b. A. Holdfast. B. Mat segment. FIG. 133. *Tetracampos ciliotheca.* After Southwell, 1925b. A. Holdfast. B. Isolat hook. C. External egg shell. D. Internal ciliated egg shell enclosing embryo. FIG. 1 *Ceratobothrium xanthocephalum.* After Yamaguti, 1934. A. Holdfast. B. Gravid segme *b,* bothridia; *cm,* circular muscles; *cu,* cuticle; *doc,* dorsal osmoregulatory canal; *h,* hoo *lm,* longitudinal muscles; *n,* nerve cord; *o,* ovary; *om,* oblique muscles; *sd,* sperm duct; testes; *v,* vagina; *voc,* ventral osmoregulatory canal; *y,* yolk glands.

ment for it of a new genus, with a new species *tenax* as the genotype. He described the holdfast as comprising a bulbous head, subconical, encircled at its base by a bothridial collar; and he noted that in life the bulbous head is embedded, or enclosed, by a saclike growth of the gut mucosa. Southwell (1925b), describing two specimens found in *Trygon walga* on the Ceylon Pearl Banks, found this mucosal growth to hang freely in the lumen of the host intestine, enclosing tightly that portion of the holdfast between the globular region and the collar. On the basis of a detailed study of these specimens, Southwell placed the form within Cyclophyllidea, because it has four suckers, and in his new suborder Multivitellata of that order, because the yolk glands are paired. Within the suborder, he placed it in the family Lecanicephalidae, because the holdfast is made up of two regions.

Pintner (1928b), in his study of Linton's family Lecanicephalidae, argued from Hornell's and Southwell's descriptions that *Balanobothrium* must be excluded either from Lecanicephalidae or from Cephalobothriidae, even though its holdfast is formed of two regions. "Die kleinen Saugnäpfe und Hakenpaare bestimmen den eiförmigen Vorderteil als den eigentlichen Kopf von *Balanobothrium*, der Kragenteil aber ist ein Velum. Es sind also hier die beiden Kopfabschnitte nicht mit denen der Gamobothriidae gleichwertig." In consequence, he erected for the genus a new family, Balanobothriidae.

Perrenoud (1931) believed that Pintner was misled by the descriptions of Hornell and Southwell, who believed the collar to be membranous. On the other hand, his remarkable study of *Disculiceps* may have led him to interpret this collar as a velum, homologous with that of *Disculiceps*, particularly as this latter genus attaches itself to the host gut wall in a fashion curiously similar to that of *Balanobothrium*. "Das Tier ist stets so eingebohrst dass nur die Hinterfläche des später zu erwähnenden Kragenstückes in gleicher Ebene mit der Magenschleimhaut zu sehen ist." The two worms have identical methods of fixation, in fact, thus rendering superfluous the usual organs of fixation – the absence of suckers in *Disculiceps* and the smallness of the hooks in *Balanobothrium* seem correlated with this fact – and the holdfast is enclosed and surrounded by the gut mucosa of the host.

The descriptions of Hornell and Southwell seem to rest upon an error. Fuhrmann (1931), studying Southwell's cotypes, demonstrated that so far as the holdfast is concerned, *Balanobothrium* is a typical onchobothriid. "Die Familie ist zu streichen, denn in Wirkheit ist diese Form ein typischer Vertreter der Onchobothriidae und in der Nähe von *Pedibothrium* zu stellen, denn hinter den vier kleinen Saugnäpfchen und den Haken finden sich sehr flache Bothridien, die übersehen wurden und deren hinterer breiter und freier Rand verschmolzn so den obenerwähnten Kragen oder Velum vortäuscht."

Perrenoud (1931), studying the internal anatomy, found that in general it agreed with the indices furnished by the holdfast. In his opinion, nothing in the morphology justifies the creation of a special family to contain the genus. Summarizing the observations of Hornell, Southwell,

Fuhrmann, and himself, Perrenoud suggested the following generic definition of *Balanobothrium*:

Of the family Onchobothriidae. With four flattened bothridia, each sessile and not compartmented. Anterior bothridial borders each with one pair of composite hooks whose shape recalls the letter F. In front of each pair of hooks, a small accessory sucker. Genital pores unilateral, irregularly alternating. Testes in front of the ovary. Ovary two-winged. Yolk glands lateral. Uterus with lateral branches, discharging the eggs through a true uterine aperture.

The generic characters are obviously those of a tetraphyllidean of the family Onchobothriidae. *Balanobothrium* differs from *Pedibothrium*, the only other onchobothriid with nontubular and undivided bothridia, in the following respects: (1) it has an accessory sucker in front of each pair of hooks; (2) the bothridia are less free and mobile; (3) the hooks of *Pedibothrium* are fixed *upon* the bothridium, but in *Balanobothrium* they are placed above and to a certain distance *outside* the bothridium; (4) the longitudinal muscles of *Pedibothrium* are in a single layer, while in *Balanobothrium* they are extraordinarily developed, the bundles extending in several concentric layers from the medulla almost to the subcuticle; and (5) the cuticle of *Pedibothrium* is only 4 μ thick, while that of *Balanobothrium* is 10 μ thick.

Cylindrophorus Deising, 1863

Originally described as having four large and tubular bothridia, each suckerlike when contracted. On each bothridium a pair of hooks, one hook having two unequal prongs, the other having three unequal prongs. Neck long, its hinder region completely covered with spines. Genotype, *typicus* Diesing, 1863 in *Carcharias rondoletii* (Figure 132).

Linton (1889a) placed a tapeworm from *Carcharias obscurus* close to *Cylindrophorus* "because of its tubular bothridia"; but he erected for it a new genus, *Phoreiobothrium* – of which it formed the genotype *lasium* – because his form had a well-marked accessory sucker in front of each bothridium. Later he added the species *triloculatum, pectinatum,* and *exceptum.*

Southwell (1927) believed the genera *Cylindrophorus* and *Phoreiobothrium* to be identical and united them, retaining the name *Cylindrophorus* and recognizing five species – *typicus* Diesing, 1863 (= *Tetrabothrium carcharias-rondoletii* Wagener, 1854); *lasium* Linton, 1889a (= *Phoreiobothrium lasium*); *triloculatus* Linton, 1909 (= *Phoreiobothrium triloculatum*); *pectinatum* Linton, 1924 (= *Phoreiobothrium pectinatum*); and *exceptum* Linton, 1924 (= *Phoreiobothrium exceptum*). Whether or not he was right cannot be decided because Wagener's figures of *Tetrabothrium carcharias-rondoletii* are too poor to give a true indication, and no description accompanied the figures. If it could be proved that in this genus the bothridia are not really tubular, Linton's species would have to be placed within *Phoreiobothrium.*

Perrenoud (1931), studying *C. triloculatus*, found the bothridia neither cylindrical, tubular, nor hollow. At the level of the hooks, the bothridia are U-shaped in cross section; at a lower level they are practically flat; but a section through the lower portion of the bothridium, where the three compartments occur, gives the appearance of being a section of a flattened tube. This would seem to be an effect produced by the razor cutting the bothridium at first distally, then, more proximally, the row of three compartments; this is seen, of course, only at the base of the bothridium. Perrenoud suggested the retention of the name *Phoreiobothrium*. Shuler (1938), recording the species *lasium* from *Hypoprion brevirostris* in Florida waters, also argued that *Cylindrophorus* and *Phoreiobothrium* should be regarded as distinct genera.

Ceratobothrium Monticelli, 1892

With the bothridia large, sessile, undivided, each having an accessory sucker furnished on the posterior border with two projecting horns. Neck moderately long. Genital apertures marginal and irregularly alternating. Genotype, *xanthocephalum* Monticelli, 1892d (Figure 134).

Southwell (1925b) identified Linton's (1901) *Thysanocephalum ridiculum* with this form. Yamaguti recorded and described in detail a form from *Isurus glaucus* in Japanese waters which he identified with Monticelli's species (Yamaguti, 1934). The holdfast was large, 920 μ long by 660 μ broad, had four muscular bothridia each divided into an anterior compartment 270×330 μ and a posterior compartment 750×450 μ. The hornlike appendages projecting from the postero-lateral edges of each anterior compartment are not true hooks but consist mainly of circular muscle fibers.

Tetracampos Wedl, 1861

A genus not defined by Wedl but described by Braun (1894–1900) as having four bothridia and a rostellum in the form of a cupola, on which are four groups of nine hooks. The hooks are of unequal length, slightly curved, ending in a claw; the longest hook is in the middle, the shortest are at the sides of the group. Neck of average length. Four osmoregulatory canals per segment. Genital pores surficial (i.e., on one of the flat surfaces). Eggs thin-shelled, containing ciliated oncospheres. Genotype, *ciliotheca* Wedl, 1861 from *Heterobranchus anguillaris*, Egypt (Figure 133).

It is doubtful whether the possession of bothridia or pseudo-bothridia and simple hooks justifies the inclusion of this form within Onchobothriidae. Southwell (1925b) believed the so-called bothridia to be really suckers and the four groups of hooks to be remnants of a former hook-circle, in which case the worm might well belong "to the order Cyclophyllidea." Unfortunately, Wedl's material is no longer available, but Woodland (1925b) argued forcibly, on the basis of Wedl's figures and specific description, that this form was a bothriocephalid.

Order DISCULICEPITIDEA

DESCRIPTION

Of the class Cestoda. Relatively large tapeworms with the holdfast having neither bothridia, suckers, nor hooks, but consisting of a large, cushionlike pad followed by a collarlike region, the whole being embedded within the intestinal mucosa of the host. Body craspedote and anapolytic. Individual segments approximately square. Special granulations of the cuticle present. Cirro-vaginal atrium displaced ventrally. Vaginal aperture anterior to that of the cirrus pouch. Ovary voluminous, at the extreme posterior end of the segment, occupying its full width. Testes numerous. Yolk glands (see remarks below). Osmoregulatory system in the form of a net. Uterus lobed, greatly thickening the gravid segment. Uterine aperture lacking. Life cycle unknown. Adults in selachians. One family, Disculicepitidae; one genus, *Disculiceps* Joyeux and Baer, 1935; one species, *pileatum* Linton, 1890; all with the characteristics of the order (Figure 135).

HISTORY

Although from a taxonomic viewpoint there are objections to founding an order upon a single species, the form in question differs so greatly from all other known tapeworms that there seems little option in the matter.

The genus *Discocephalum* was established by Linton (1890) for a single species, *pileatum* Linton, 1890, found by him in *Carcharias obscurus* in Massachusetts waters (Figure 135).

"Head, a transversely flattened apical disk, entire, or with a single lateral notch, followed by a much smaller, globular, inflated, cervical mass, with botryoidal or corrugated surface, yellowish in colour, and separated from the apical disk by a narrow, orange-coloured band; unsegmented part of the body narrower than the head, merging into the segmented body. Anterior segments very short, much crowded; subsequent segments longer than broad; mature segments irregularly squarish, very changeable in living specimen. Strobila flat, increasing in breadth uniformly to the beginning of mature segments, beyond which point it is somewhat narrower.

"Genital apertures marginal, a little in front of middle, male and female approximate. Cirrus long and slender, vagina opening in front of cirrus. Length (maximum), 530 mm.; diameter of anterior disk 3 to 5 mm.; greatest breadth of body 3 to 5 mm. *Habitat: Carcharias obscurus*, spiral valve. Wood's Hole, Massachusetts, July 19, 1886. One adult, three young." Linton (1890).

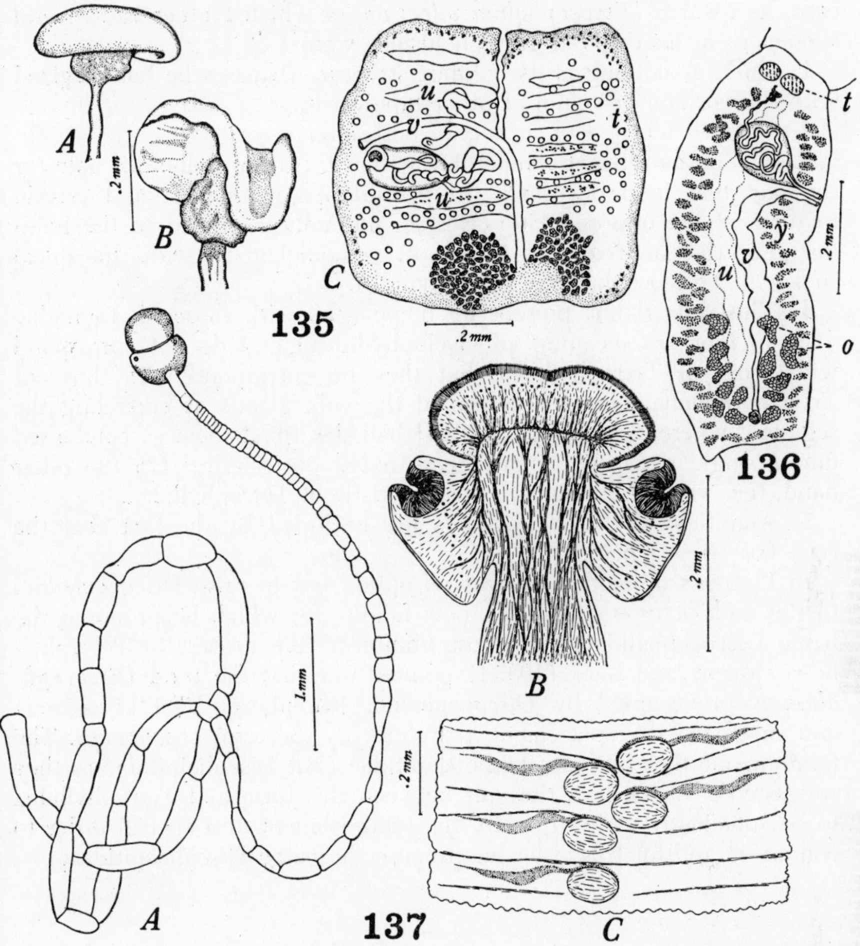

FIG. 135. *Disculiceps*. After Southwell, 1925b. A and B. Views of holdfast. C. Mature segment. FIG. 136. *Lecanicephalum peltatum*, mature segment. After Southwell, 1925b. FIG. 137. *Tetragonocephalum*. After Shipley and Hornell, 1906. A. Entire worm. B. Section of holdfast showing spinules and muscles. C. Immature proglottides. *o*, ovary; *t*, testes; *u*, uterus; *v*, vagina; *y*, yolk glands.

Linton (1890) proposed to place this genus—with *Lecanicephalum* Linton, 1890 and *Tylocephalum* Linton, 1890—in a family to be named Gamobothriidae, whose characters, however, he failed to define. A close study of Gamobothriidae by Pintner (1928b) led him to assert that the only character common to the members of the family was the possession of a holdfast which had two regions: (1) an anterior region having more or less the nature of a rostellum or an apical sucker, and (2) a posterior region which presented the appearance of a cushion or velum. To be of significance, however, the two regions should be homologous among all three genera of the family, and this does not seem to be the case. As regards *Discocephalum pileatum*, of which Pintner had several specimens at his disposal, his conclusions were:

1. There is nothing in its holdfast structure that can be homologized with the cushion or velum of other tapeworms.
2. There is no trace of suckers or bothridia.
3. The cushion is not comparable with a taeniid rostellum, if only for the fact that in it one finds the central nervous system and certain features of the osmoregulatory system normally restricted to the holdfast. For the same reasons it cannot be homologized with the apical sucker of Proteocephala or Tetraphyllidea.
4. The yolk glands present no homologies with those of Taeniidae (i.e., in Pintner's meaning, of Cyclophyllidea) and do not correspond with those of Tetraphyllidea; but they do correspond with those of Trypanorhyncha. (Pintner described the yolk glands as encircling the segment, whereas Southwell [1925b] had described them as condensed into a single mass and apparently situated posteriorly.) On the other hand, the "vaginal crossing" is characteristic of Tetraphyllidea.
5. Affinities with Cyclophyllidea are excluded by the fact that the type host is selachian.

In Pintner's opinion there was no option but to raise *Discocephalum* to the rank of type genus of a new family, for which he proposed the name Discocephalidae and whose affinities were nearest to Tetraphyllidea. Joyeux and Baer (1935d) pointed out that the term *Discocephalum* is preoccupied by *Discocephalum* Ehrenberg, 1809 (Protozoa) and suggested its replacement, therefore, by the term *Disculiceps.* The family name thus becomes Disculicepitidae (not Disculicipitidae as they suggested). We believe the gulf between this form and Tetraphyllidea to be sufficiently wide to justify the establishment of a special order to contain it, and for this order we propose the name Disculicepitidea.

Order LECANICEPHALA

DESCRIPTION

Of the class Cestoda. With the holdfast lacking bothridia but subdivided by a horizontal groove into an anterior region – dome-shaped, or flattened antero-posteriorly, or in the form of a deep, cuplike sucker, or even cut into retractile tentacles – and a posterior region, which is commonly cushionlike and has four suckers but which, again, may be collarlike or in the form of tentacles. Yolk glands usually in two lateral bands. Life cycle unknown. Adults in selachians.

HISTORY

The earliest recognition that lecanicephalans stand apart from other tapeworms of selachians was the establishment, already mentioned, of Linton's family Gamobothriidae. As there was no such genus as *Gamobothrium*, Linton's term was clearly inadmissible and was changed by Braun (1894–1900) to Lecanicephalidae. This family was placed within the order Tetraphyllidea along with Phyllobothriidae, Onchobothriidae, and Ichthyotaeniidae. The family was somewhat scantily defined as comprising tapeworms whose bothridia are fused into a globe-shaped structure, in which accessory suckers may or may not be present; whose neck is short, long, or even absent; whose genital pores are marginal; and which occur in elasmobranch fishes.

Gradually there were relegated to this convenient lumber room for unplaceable forms – tetraphyllidean in the Braunian sense but without bothridia or suckers – a number of genera which were mainly throw-outs from Phyllobothriidae. Among these were *Discobothrium* Beneden, 1870; *Polypocephalus* Braun, 1878; *Adelobothrium* Shipley, 1900; *Calycobothrium* Southwell, 1911; *Balanobothrium* Hornell, 1912; *Parataenia* Linton, 1889; *Prosobothrium* Cohn, 1902; *Tetragonocephalum* Shipley and Hornell, 1905; *Staurobothrium* Shipley and Hornell, 1905; *Kystocephalus* Shipley and Hornell, 1906; *Anthemobothrium* Shipley and Hornell, 1906; *Aphanobothrium* Seurat, 1906; *Thysanobothrium* Shipley and Hornell, 1905; *Eniochobothrium* Shipley and Hornell, 1906; *Hornellobothrium* Shipley and Hornell, 1906; *Phanobothrium* Mola, 1907; and *Cyclobothrium* Southwell, 1911. Many of these genera came from that welter of hastily recorded and carelessly described material that resulted from attempts to establish the pearl-provoking parasites of the Ceylon pearl oyster (1902–12) and which has done so much to foul our understanding of Tetraphyllidea and Trypanorhyncha.

Confusion was worse confounded when in 1925 there was published Southwell's scheme for relegating the lecanicephalids and the forms we have called Proteocephala to Braun's order Cyclophyllidea. In Southwell's opinion, the possession of suckers on the holdfast end of the body outweighed the undoubted affinities of these forms with Phyllobothriidae, notably in the similarities of genitalia arrangement, and the fact that whereas Cyclophyllidea are almost exclusively parasites of reptiles, birds, and mammals, the lecanicephalids are parasites of sharks and rays. The difficulty that the yolk glands of Lecanicephala and Proteocephala are represented by scattered follicles and not, as in true Cyclophyllidea, by a compact structure was met by Southwell by the establishment of two suborders of Cyclophyllidea – Multivitellata, to include Lecanicephala and Proteocephala and having scattered yolk glands; and Univitellata, comprising the remaining Cyclophyllidea and having a single, compact yolk gland. Seven genera were assigned to Multivitellata: *Balanobothrium, Calycobothrium, Polypocephalus, Cephalobothrium, Tylocephalium, Lecanicephalum,* and *Adelobothrium.* However, to a subgrouping *A*, not defined in status or characteristics, were assigned *Diplobothrium* Beneden, 1889 and *Eniochobothrium* Shipley and Hornell, 1906.

To the suborder Univitellata he assigned *Phanobothrium* Mola, 1907, a form in which Mola's description implies the presence of a single, compact yolk gland posterior to the ovary. By establishing a further order, Heterophyllidea, Southwell was able to bring into his scheme those lecanicephalan forms that lacked suckers – *Echinobothrium* Beneden, 1849; *Discocephalum* Linton, 1890; and *Diagonobothrium* Shipley and Hornell, 1906. Intermediate in character between Cyclophyllidea and Tetraphyllidea and so doomed to stand forlornly outside the Southwell scheme were the genera *Staurobothrium, Discobothrium,* and *Prosobothrium.*

This chaotic scheme was universally rejected by students of tapeworms, but it did at any rate focus attention upon what had been hitherto a somewhat unpopular group. Woodland (1927b), reviewing Tetraphyllidea (in the broad or Braunian sense) as a whole, suggested that further study might place within Phyllobothriidae the genera *Lecanicephalum, Cephalobothrium, Balanobothrium, Polypocephalus,* and *Calycobothrium*; that other forms, notably *Adelobothrium aetiobatidis* Shipley, *Tylocephalum marsupium* Linton, and *T. dierama* Shipley and Hornell show points of resemblance with Trypanorhyncha; and that the genera *Tylocephalum* and *Phanerobothrium,* until they have been further studied, must be regarded as of uncertain position in any scheme of classification.

Pintner reviewed (1928b) Lecanicephalidae of Braun and, as we have already mentioned, separated the genus *Discocephalum* to become the type genus of a new family. The remaining genera he divided between two families for which he suggested the terms "Lecanicephalidae" and "Cephalobothriidae." Perrenoud (1931), also surveying these forms, supported and adopted Pintner's scheme. It is this Pintner-Perrenoud scheme that will be followed here.

Family Lecanicephalidae Braun, 1900, emended Pintner, 1928

DESCRIPTION

Of the order Lecanicephala. With the anterior region of the holdfast muscular and either suckerlike or in the form of retractile tentacles. Posterior region carrying four suckers. Body segments relatively few, weakly craspedote or actually noncraspedote, generally cylindrical, rapidly attaining an extraordinary length. Pronounced cirro-vaginal atrium present. No crossing of the cirrus pouch by the vagina. Segments maturing rapidly and apolytic when gravid. Uterus constricted by the deep cirro-vaginal atrium so as to appear somewhat like a longitudinally oriented dumbbell. Type genus, *Lecanicephalum* Linton, 1890. Other genera: *Tetragonocephalum* Shipley and Hornell, 1905; *Parataenia* Linton, 1890.

NOTES ON GENERA

Lecanicephalum Linton, 1890

With the holdfast flattened, appearing as two cakelike disks, the anterior disk having a ruffed margin, the posterior disk carrying four suckers. Cirro-vaginal atria lacking. Genotype and only species, *peltatum* Linton, 1890 (Figure 136).

The genotype was established for material from a ray, *Pastinachus centrourus*, in New England waters. Additional descriptive details were added by Southwell (1925b) from material in *Pristis cuspidatus, Trygon kuhli*, and *Pteroplata micrura* in Ceylon waters. Reference should be made to a very complete description of *Lecanicephalum peltatum* published by Baer (1948).

Tetragonocephalum Shipley and Hornell, 1905

With the holdfast acornlike, the anterior region deeply domed, the posterior region a subquadrate cushion with a sucker at each corner. Cirro-vaginal atria deep and cuplike. Gravid uteri somewhat dumbbell-like. Genotype, *trygonis* Shipley and Hornell, 1905 (Figure 137).

The genotype *trygonis* (= *Tylocephalum trygonis* Southwell, 1925 = *Tetragonocephalum uarnaki* Shipley and Hornell, 1906) was recorded from *Trygon walga* in Ceylon waters and has been redescribed in detail by Southwell (1925b). Pintner recognized two additional species of the genus – *minutum* Southwell, 1925 from *Urogymnus sp.* in Ceylon waters, with fewer segments and more testes; and *similis* Pintner, 1928.

Parataenia Linton, 1890

With the anterior portion of the holdfast represented by a crown of sixteen retractile tentacles, and its posterior portion by a subglobular mass carrying four suckers. Cirro-vaginal atria lacking. Cirrus pouches large, pushing inward the poral sides of the uterine sacs. Yolk glands in lateral bands. Ovaries posterior, U-shaped. Testes described by Southwell as numbering only four per segment, but figured as around fifty, anteriorly placed and scattered. Genotype and only species, *medusiae* Linton, 1889 (Figure 138).

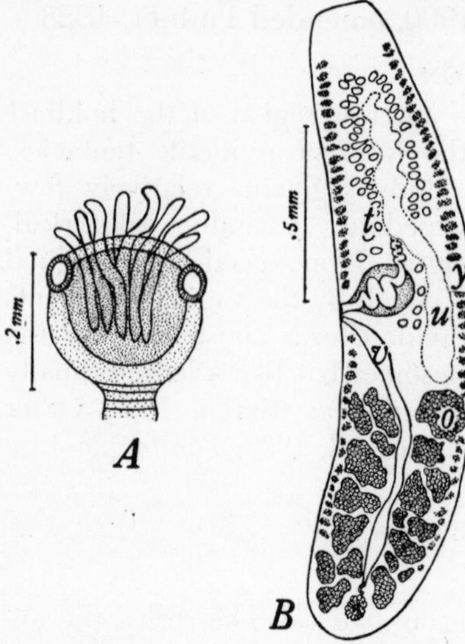

FIG. 138. *Parataenia medusiae.* After Southwell, 1925b. A. Holdfast. B. Mature proglottis. *o*, ovary; *t*, testes; *u*, uterus; *v*, vagina; *y*, yolk glands.

A very complete account of this curious little worm has been published by Baer (1948a) under the term *Parataenia medusia* Linton, 1889. The genus *Parataenia*, in Baer's opinion, has *two* species – *medusia*, with strobila short, weakly muscular, comprising a restricted number of noncraspedote, nonapolytic segments; and *elongata* Southwell, 1912, with strobila of large size, strongly muscular, comprising a large number of craspedote, apolytic segments. The generic description is therefore amended by Baer as follows:

Parataenia Linton, 1889. Strobila more or less cylindrical. Segments craspedote or noncraspedote and in each case apolytic. Holdfast more or less spherical, with four small suckers. At its apex a pear-shaped depression containing 14 to 16 evaginable tentacles which anchor the parasite to the host gut mucosa. Genital atria well marked, irregularly alternating. Cirrus pouch opening in advance of vagina. Testes few. Uterus extending forward in front of and in rear of the ovary. Yolk glands formed of large follicles; few, rare, or absent on the poral side, in front of the cirrus pouch. Genotype, *medusia* Linton, 1889.

The genotype was established for a 6-mm. worm of fifteen segments found in *Pastinachus centrourus* in Massachusetts waters. Southwell (1925b), after re-examining Linton's material, placed the species in the genus *Polypocephalus* Braun, 1878; but Pintner (1928b) accepted Linton's genus and placed it, although with some doubt, within Lecanicephalidae.

Family Cephalobothridae Pintner, 1928

DESCRIPTION

Of the order Lecanicephala. With the anterior region of the holdfast represented by a powerful protractile sucker, glandular or not, or by a group of retractile tentacles which may be featherlike. Posterior region of the holdfast subquadrate, with four suckers spaced symmetrically. Body segments numerous, oval in cross section, craspedote, scarcely elongated. Maturation of the segments slow. Uteri saclike. Cirro-vaginal atria lacking. Cirrus pouch and vagina crossing in some species. Vaginae dilated as seminal receptacles. Yolk glands in lateral bands. Type genus, *Cephalobothrium* Shipley and Hornell, 1906. Other genera: *Hexacanalis* Perrenoud, 1931; *Tylocephalum* Linton, 1890; *Polypocephalus* Braun, 1878; *Adelobothrium* Shipley, 1900; *Anthemobothrium* Shipley and Hornell, 1906; *Staurobothrium* Shipley and Hornell, 1905.

NOTES ON GENERA

Cephalobothrium Shipley and Hornell, 1906

With the anterior holdfast region represented by a large, circular sucker whose margin forms the rim of a cuplike posterior region. Equidistant, in the flattened rim of the sucker, are four, somewhat small, somewhat cup-shaped suckers. The median large sucker can be evaginated as a domelike projection. Genotype, *aetiobatidis* Shipley and Hornell, 1906 (Figure 139).

The genotype was established by Shipley and Hornell for a single specimen taken from *Aetiobatis narinari* in Ceylon waters.

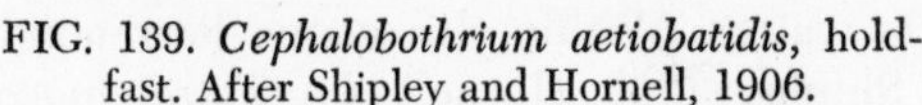

FIG. 139. *Cephalobothrium aetiobatidis*, holdfast. After Shipley and Hornell, 1906.

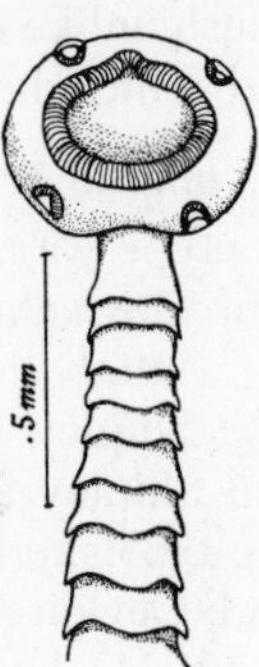

Hexacanalis Perrenoud, 1931

With the holdfast provided with an apical, protractile, but nonglandular sucker. Holdfast quadrangular in cross section. Majority of segments wider than long. Cirro-vaginal atria lacking. No vaginal crossing. Osmoregulatory system of six principal trunks, abundantly ramifying and anastomosing. Genotype, *abruptus* Southwell, 1911 (Figure 140).

The genotype was recorded (as *Cephalobothrium abruptum, C. variabile*) by Southwell (1911a) from *Pteroplata micrura* in Ceylon waters. It was redescribed by Perrenoud (1931) from cross sections of material taken in the same locality.

Tylocephalum Linton, 1890

With the anterior holdfast region uniformly muscular, either domelike, conical, or flattened, or concave and suckerlike. Posterior holdfast

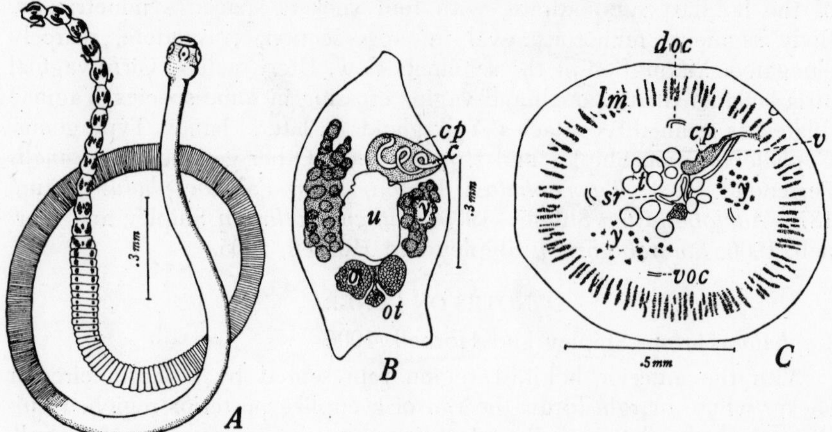

FIG. 140. *Hexacanalis abruptus.* After Southwell, 1925b. A. Entire worm. B. Entire mature segment. C. Cross section of immature segment. *c*, cirrus; *cp*, cirrus pouch; *doc*, dorsal osmoregulatory canal; *lm*, longitudinal muscles; *o*, ovary; *ot*, ootype; *sr*, seminal receptacle; *t*, testes; *u*, uterus; *v*, vagina; *voc*, ventral osmoregulatory canal; *y*, yolk glands.

region a cushionlike collar within which the anterior region can be withdrawn and which bears four suckers. Other features as for the family.

Genotype, *pingue* Linton, 1890.

The genotype was poorly described from material taken in *Rhinoptera bomasus* in Massachusetts waters. Within this genus Perrenoud placed tentatively *aetiobatidis* Shipley and Hornell (= *Tetragonocephalum aetiobatidis* Shipley and Hornell, 1905); *dierama* Shipley and Hornell, 1906; *kuhli* Shipley and Hornell, 1906; *ludificans* Jameson, 1912; *yorkei* Southwell, 1925; and *translucens* Shipley and Hornell, 1906 – all from Indian and Ceylon waters and possibly to some extent synonymous. Yamaguti (1934) has added *squatina* from *Squatina japonica* in Japanese waters (Figures 141, 142). In a rediscussion of *Tylocephalum*, Baer (1948) recognizes nine species: *pingue* Linton, *trygonis* Shipley and Hornell, *aetiobatidis* Shipley and Hornell, *dierama* Shipley and Hornell, *kuhli* Shipley and Hornell, *uarnak* Shipley and Hornell, *yorkei* Southwell, *minutum* Southwell, and *marsupium* Linton, not accepting *ludificans* Jameson, *minus* Jameson, and *margaritifera* Seurat.

Polypocephalus Braun, 1878

With the posterior holdfast region represented by a saclike cavity into which glands appear to open, and bearing four suckers. Anterior holdfast region represented by sixteen unarmed tentacles around the rim of the cavity. Genotype, *radiatus* Braun, 1878 (Figure 143).

The genotype was established for material from *Rhinobatis granulosus*; it is probably synonymous with *Parataenia elongatus* Southwell, 1912 and *Thysanobothrium uarnakense* Shipley and Hornell, 1906.

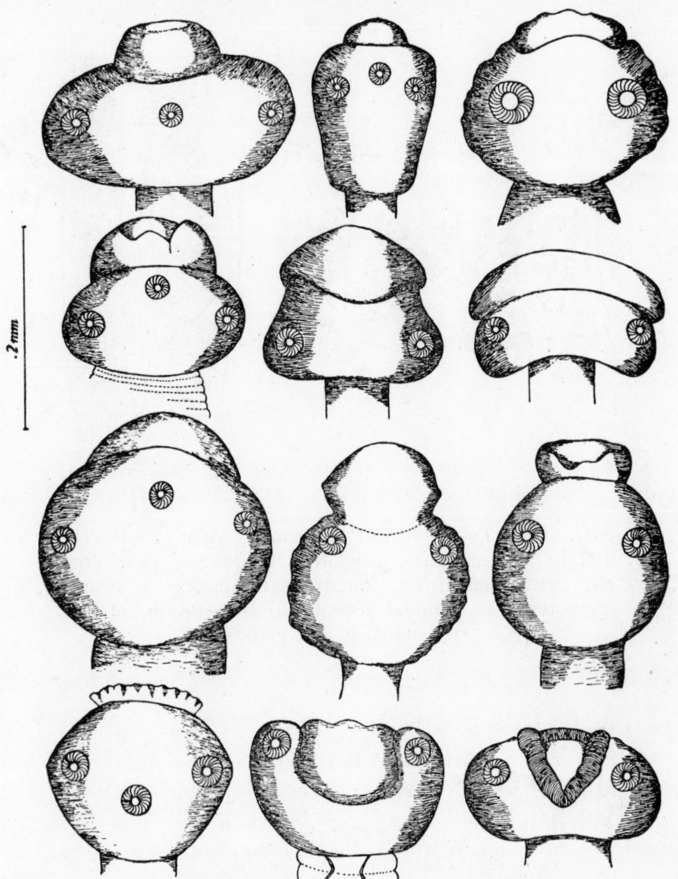

FIG. 141. *Tylocephalum dierama*, showing variations in shape of holdfast. After Southwell, 1925b.

Adelobothrium Shipley, 1900

With the anterior holdfast region conically rounded, the posterior holdfast region membranous and collarlike, bearing four suckers. Genotype, *aetiobatidis* Shipley, 1900 (Figure 144).

The genotype was recorded from *Aetiobatis narinari*, Loyalty Islands (Pacific waters). It was recorded and redescribed by Southwell (1925b) from material in *Rhynchobatis djeddensis*, Ceylon waters. Linton (1916) described under the name of *Tylocephalum marsupium* a form from *Aetiobatis (Stoasodon) narinari* in Florida waters which Shipley believed to be identical with *Adelobothrium aetiobatidis*. Fuhrmann (1931) and Perrenoud (1931) believed it to be distinct. It may belong to Lecanicephalidae.

Anthemobothrium Shipley and Hornell, 1906

With the holdfast almost spherical, its anterior region represented by

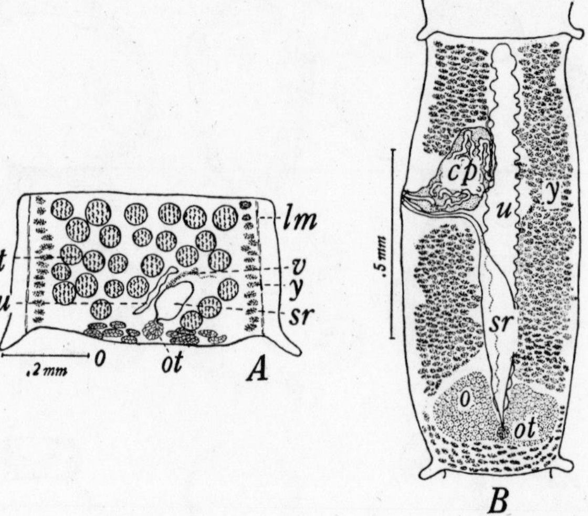

FIG. 142. *Tylocephalum dierama*. After Southwell, 1925b. A. Immature proglottis. B. Mature proglottis. *cp*, cirrus pouch; *lm*, longitudinal muscles; *o*, ovary; *ot*, ootype; *sr*, seminal receptacle; *t*, testes; *u*, uterus; *v*, vagina; *y*, yolk glands.

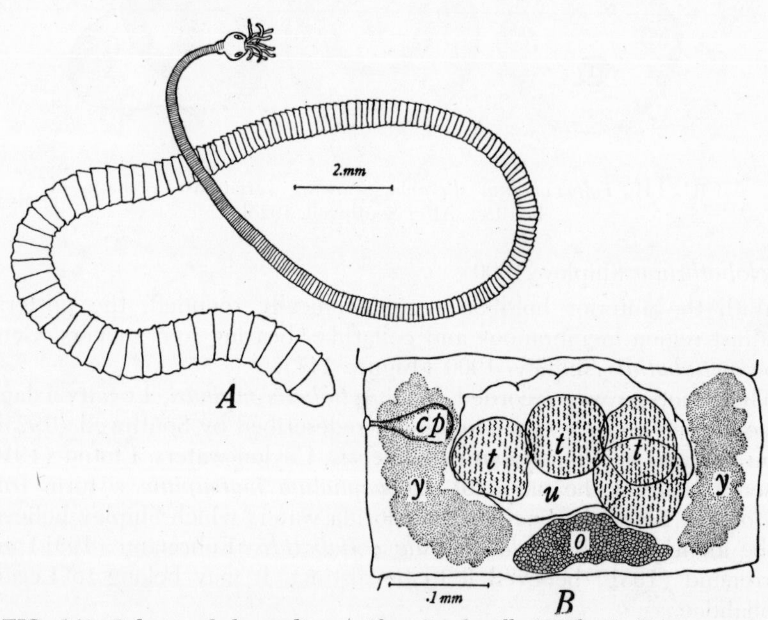

FIG. 143. *Polypocephalus radiatus*. After Southwell, 1925b. A. Entire worm. B. Mature segment. *cp*, cirrus pouch; *o*, ovary; *t*, testes; *u*, uterus; *y*, yolk glands.

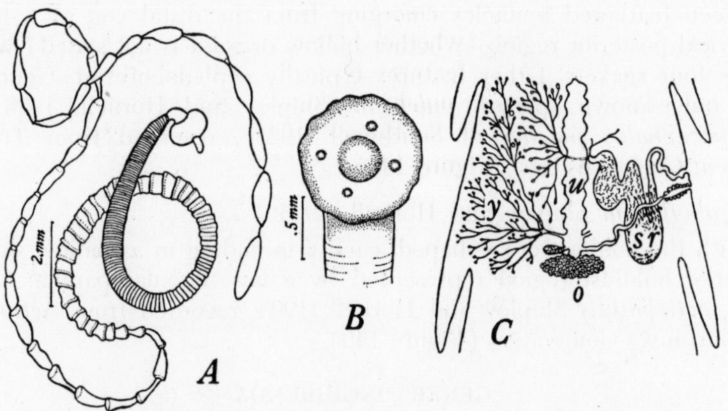

FIG. 144. *Adelobothrium aetiobatidis*. After Shipley, 1900b. A. Entire worm. B. Holdfast. C. Genitalia. o, ovary; *sr*, seminal receptacle; *u*, uterus; *y*, yolk glands.

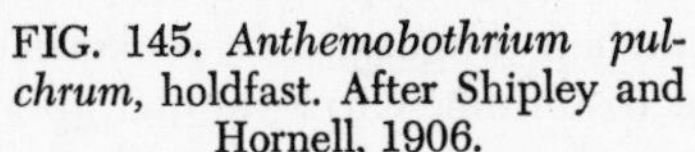

FIG. 145. *Anthemobothrium pulchrum*, holdfast. After Shipley and Hornell, 1906.

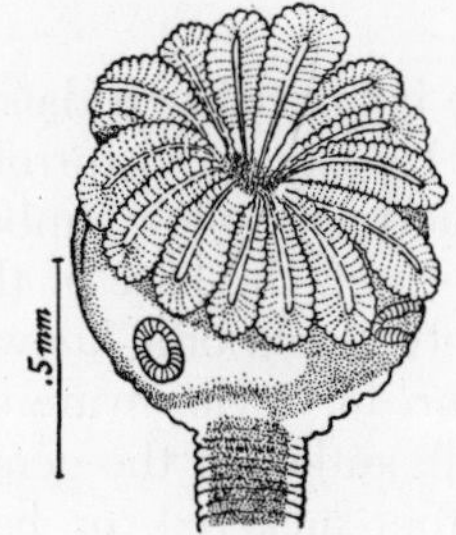

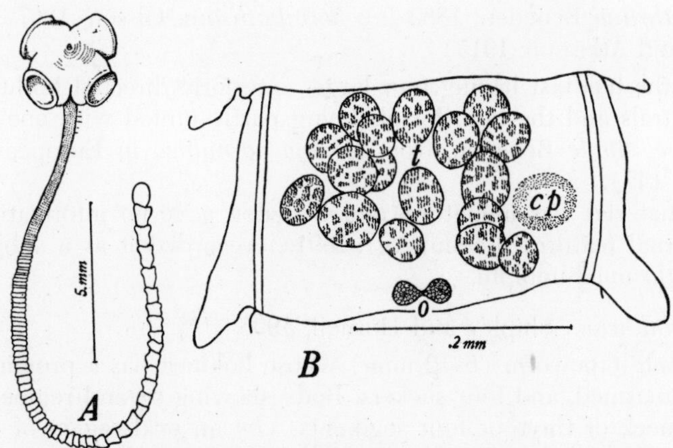

FIG. 146. *Staurobothrium aetiobatidis*. After Shipley and Hornell, 1906. A. Entire worm. B. Mature proglottis. *cp*, cirrus pouch; *o*, ovary; *t*, testes.

fourteen feathered tentacles emerging from the distal end of a hemispherical posterior region (whether hollow or solid is not stated) which bears four suckers. Other features typically cephalobothriid. Genotype and only known species, *pulchrum* Shipley and Hornell, 1906 (= *Polypocephalus pulcher* of Southwell, 1925), recorded from *Trygon sephen*, Ceylon waters (Figure 145).

Staurobothrium Shipley and Hornell, 1905

With the holdfast cross-shaped, each arm ending in a shallow sucker. Anterior holdfast region represented by a low, circular papilla. Genotype, *aetiobatidis* Shipley and Hornell, 1905, recorded from *Aetiobatis narinari* in Ceylon waters (Figure 146).

GENERA INQUIRENDA

There are a number of forms which cannot be fitted within the order Lecanicephala – nor within Tetraphyllidea or Disculicepitidea – but which nevertheless seem to have affinities with these orders.

Calycobothrium Stiles, 1912 (= *Cyclobothrium* Southwell, 1911, preoccupied)

With the holdfast like a daisy, with a central domelike rostellum bearing four (?) suckers and surrounded externally and posteriorly by a frill of about fourteen hollow, unbranched, fingerlike or suckerlike tentacles which arise from the base of the rostellum. Cirro-vaginal apertures marginal. Genotype and only known species, *typicum*, described from *Aetiobatis narinari* in Ceylon waters.

Southwell, author of the genotype, believed this form to be cyclophyllidean, if four-suckered, or heterophyllidean, if two-suckered. In general features, however, it would seem to be cephalobothriid.

Diplobothrium Beneden, 1889 (= *Tetrabothrium* Olsson, 1867 = *Oriana* Leiper and Atkinson, 1915)

With the holdfast having four large, anteriorly directed bothridia, the two ventrals and the two dorsals being partly united with one another. Genotype, *simile* Beneden, from *Lamna cornubica* in European waters (Figure 147).

The material was immature, and Beneden gave no information as to the internal features. Loennberg (1891a) regarded it as a subgenus of *Tetrabothrium* Rudolphi.

Eniochobothrium Shipley and Hornell, 1906

A minute tapeworm (6–12 mm.) whose holdfast has a prominent rostellum, unarmed, and four suckers. Body showing several regions: (*a*) a narrow neck of three or four segments; (*b*) an oval region of eighteen segments, linear, increasing in breadth to the tenth segment, then diminishing, overlapping like "a many caped cloak"; and (*c*) a second very narrow region of six to eight segments, rapidly maturing and becoming very large, the last one or two being as large as the rest of the body. Genital apertures marginal and alternating. Cirrus and cirrus

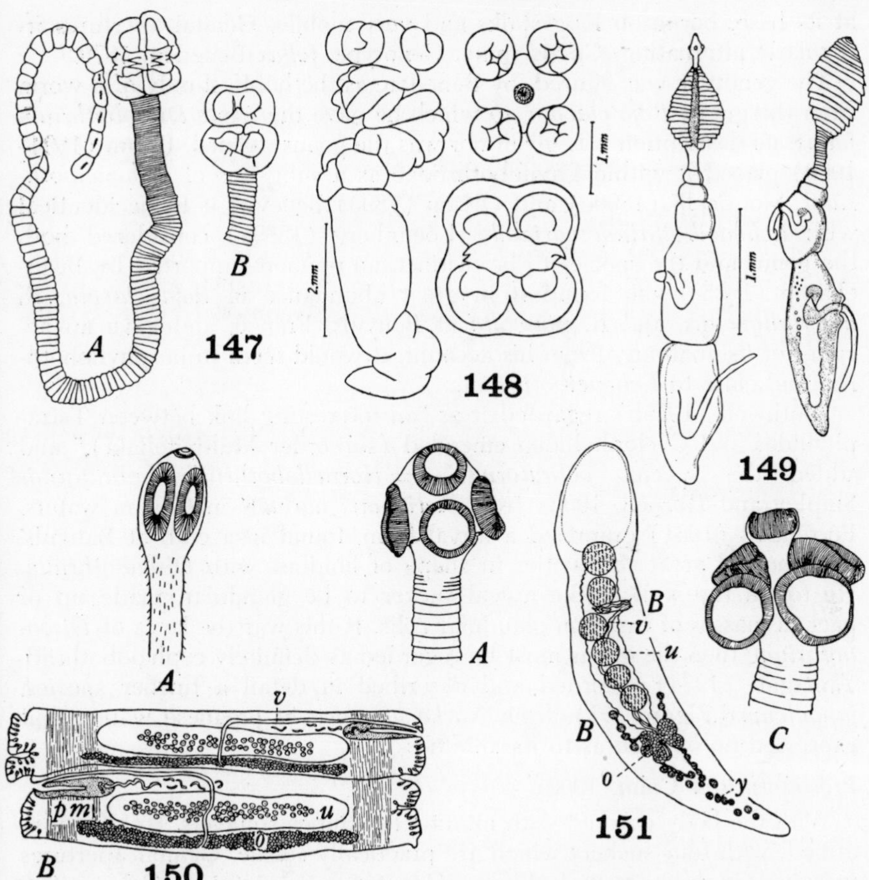

FIG. 147. *Diplobothrium simile.* After Beneden, 1889. Magnification unknown. A. Entire worm. B. Holdfast. FIG. 148. Diplobothriid plerocercoids. After Guiart, 1933. FIG. 149. *Eniochobothrium gracile,* entire worm. After Shipley and Hornell, 1906. FIG. 150. *Phanobothrium monticellii.* After Mola, 1907f. Magnification unknown. A. Holdfast. B. Two gravid segments. FIG. 151. *Discobothrium japonicum.* After Yamaguti, 1934. A. Holdfast. B. Free gravid segment. C. Extended holdfast. *o,* ovary; *pm,* parenchymal muscles; *u,* uterus; *v,* vagina; *y,* yolk glands.

pouch very large. Cirrus with a broad band of chitinous spicules. Genotype and only known species, *gracile* Shipley and Hornell, 1906 from *Rhinoptera javanica* in Ceylon waters (Figure 149).

Phanobothrium Mola, 1907

With a holdfast having four protrusible suckers and an apical accessory sucker. Holdfast and neck armed with minute spines. Genital apertures marginal. Yolk gland a single mass near the ovary. Adults in selachians. Genotype and only species, *monticellii* Mola, 1907 (Figure 150).

Discobothrium Beneden, 1870 (=*Hornellobothrium* Shipley and Hornell, 1906)

With holdfast large, with an enormous apical sucker. Four bothridia at its base, borne on long stalks and very mobile. Genital apertures irregularly alternating. Cirrus spiny. Genotype, *fallax* Beneden, 1870.

The genotype was figured, by Beneden, as the holdfast only of a worm from the gut of *Raja clavata*, to which he gave the name *Discobothrium fallax*; no description was given nor was the genus defined. Braun (1894–1900) placed it within Phyllobothriidae as a subgenus of *Echeneibothrium.* Monticelli (1890c) and Olsson (1893) believed it to be identical with *Echeneibothrium variabile.* Loennberg (1889a) considered both the genus and the species to be distinct, an opinion supported by Beauchamp (1905) who found it in great abundance in *Raja clavata, R. macrorhynchus,* and *R. punctata* at Banyuls, France, and gave an account of its anatomy. From his account, it would seem to be phyllobothriid and close to *Echeneibothrium.*

Southwell (1925b) regarded it as "an interesting link between Tetraphyllidea and Cyclophyllidea emended (sub-order Multivitellata)," and added the species *cobraformis* (= *Hornellobothrium cobraformis* Shipley and Hornell, 1906) from *Aetiobatis narinari* in Ceylon waters. Perrenoud (1931) examined a larval form, found in a crab at Banyuls, that showed great similarities in shape of holdfast with *Discobothrium.* He found the wall of the apical sucker to be glandular, made up of packed masses of fusiform glandular cells. If this was the larva of *Discobothrium,* then the genus must be regarded as definitely cephalobothriid. Yamaguti (1934) recorded and described in detail a further species, *japonicum* (Figure 151), from *Narke japonica* in Japanese waters, but expressed no opinion as to its affinities.

Prosobothrium Cohn, 1902

With the body covered with minute, deciduous spinelets. Holdfast unarmed, with four suckers which are practically sessile. Genital apertures marginal. Adults in selachians. Genotype, *armigerum* Cohn, 1902 (Figure 152) from *Carcharias rondoletii.* A further species, *japonicum* (Figure 153), has been recorded and described in detail by Yamaguti (1934) from *Prionace glauca* in Japanese waters.

Echinobothrium Beneden, 1849

With a holdfast having two large, simple, boat-shaped bothridia. Anterior to each bothridium, a group of large hooks. Region following holdfast (the "Kopfstiel") provided with longitudinal rows of hooks. Genital apertures on body ventral surface. No uterine pores. Genotype, *typus* Beneden, 1849 from *Raja clavata* in European waters (Figure 154).

Beneden did not define his genus at the time of its establishment but did give a brief description of the genotype. In 1858 he defined the genus as having a double rostellum with hooks, two big, very mobile bothridia, and a spiny neck, and gave a fuller description of *typus.* Wagener (1854) referred to this species a form which Diesing (1863a) preferred to distinguish as *Echinobothrium affine.* Southwell (1911) described the genotype, as *Echinobothrium boisii,* from *Aetiobatis narinari* in Ceylon waters. Pintner (1889) revised the genus and added two new species, *musteli* and *brachysoma.* Shipley and Hornell (1906) added the species *rhinoptera,* and Southwell (1925b) added *longicolle.*

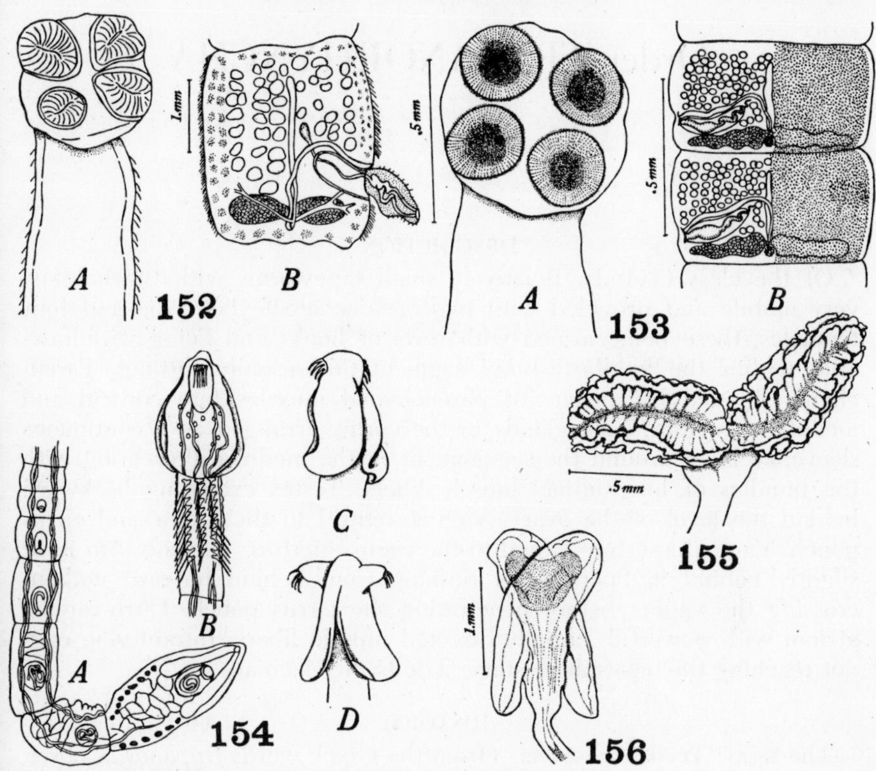

IG. 152. *Prosobothrium armigerum.* After Cohn, 1902. A. Holdfast. B. Mature segment vith everted cirrus. FIG. 153. *Prosobothrium japonicum.* After Yamaguti, 1934. A. Holdfast. . Mature segment, testes and yolk glands shown unilaterally. FIG. 154. *Echinobothrium pus.* After Beneden, 1849b. A and B. Entire worms. C and D. Holdfast. FIG. 155. *illersium owenium,* holdfast. After Southwell, 1927. FIG. 156. *Diagonobothrium asymmetrum,* holdfast. After Shipley and Hornell, 1906.

Pillersium Southwell, 1927

With holdfast having two unarmed, undivided bothridia extending laterally at an angle to the neck, their posterior surfaces smooth, their margins and anterior surfaces puckered and folded. Accessory suckers lacking. Neck very long. Body unknown. Genotype, *owenium* Southwell, 1927 from *Urogymnus asperrimus,* in Ceylon waters (Figure 155).

Diagonobothrium Shipley and Hornell, 1906

With the holdfast having a large, apical sucker and two earlike bothridia which run down right and left of the holdfast. One edge of each bothridium runs forward obliquely to lose itself in the crinkled membrane which surrounds the apical sucker. One edge only on each side thus prolonged and the two prolongations crossing one another at about a right angle, thus making the holdfast asymmetrical. Internal anatomy not known. Genotype, *asymmetrum* Shipley and Hornell, 1906 from *Myliobatis maculata* in Ceylon waters (Figure 156).

Order TRYPANORHYNCHA

DESCRIPTION

Of the class Cestoda. Relatively small tapeworms with the holdfast very mobile and provided with two or four sessile bothridia and four tentacles, these being armed with rows of hooks and being withdrawable within the holdfast. Body segmentation usually distinct. Parenchyma divided by a zone of parenchymal muscles into cortical and medullary regions. Yolk glands in the cortex arranged as a continuous sleevelike layer around the segment, or in the medulla alternating with the bundles of longitudinal muscle fibers. Testes extending backward behind the level of the ovary. Vagina ventral to the uterus and cirrus pouch. Vaginal aperture lateral to the cirrus aperture, or ventral to it, or slightly behind it. Sperm duct running from behind forward without crossing the vagina before penetrating the cirrus pouch. Cirro-vaginal atrium with powerful, radially directed muscle fibers. Intrauterine eggs not reaching the oncosphere stage. Adults in selachians.

HISTORY

The term "Trypanorhyncha" (from the Greek words *trypanos*, a borer, and *rhynchos*, a snout) was coined by Diesing (1863a) for three genera of tapeworms from selachians, namely, *Rhynchobothrium* Blainville, 1828; *Tetrarhynchobothrium* Diesing, 1854; and *Syndesmobothrium* Diesing, 1854, all of which had sessile bothridia and protrusible armed tentacles. However, even at this date, a number of obviously *larval* trypanorhynchans had been recorded, described, and even assigned to hypothetical genera; and the problem of devising a scheme of classification which would take account of these larval forms as well of adult forms was not satisfactorily solved by Diesing, nor, for that matter, has it been satisfactorily solved since.

The first such larva to be recorded taxonomically was *Tentacularia* of Bosc (1797). This was followed by *Tetrarhynchus* Rudolphi, 1809; *Hepatoxylon* Bosc, 1811; *Floriceps* Cuvier, 1817; *Gymnorhynchus* Rudolphi, 1819; *Anthocephalus* Rudolphi, 1819; and *Dibothriorhynchus* Blainville, 1824. We may note that Rudolphi's *Tetrarhynchus* was merely the taxonomic record of a number of larval forms that had been described by Redi (1684) and for which Rudolphi – ignoring the earlier suggestion by Gmelin (1790) that they be grouped as *Echinorhynchus argentinae* (Redi having found his forms in the viscera of the teleostean fish *Argentina sphyraena*) – coined the term *Tetrarhynchus elongatus*. In 1819 he recorded similar worms from the host form as *Tetrarhynchus argentinae*. *Tentacularia coryphaenae*, however, was founded upon material observed by Bosc himself. The first adult form to be recorded would seem to have been Rudolphi's *Rhynchobothrium*, 1819.

These early finds were scantily described and poorly figured (see Figure 157), and it has always been difficult to apply their descriptions to the forms discovered in later years. Taxonomically speaking, Trypanorhyncha have been the most chaotic and confused of tapeworm groups. However, Dollfus (1942) has done for the students of the group what Lühe and Fuhrmann did for students of Pseudophyllidea and

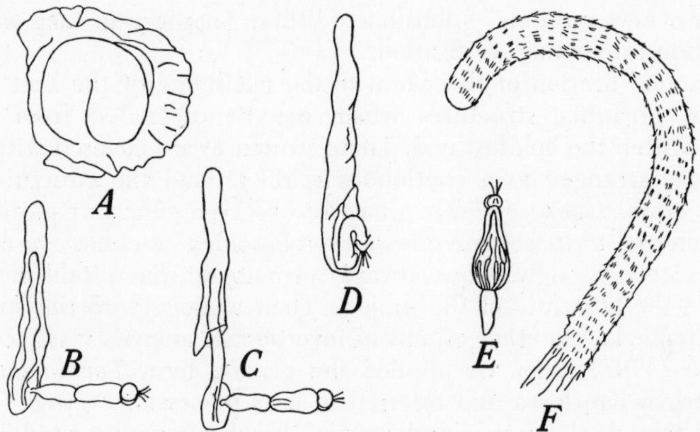

FIG. 157. Early figures of a trypanorhynchan larva, "*Anthocephalus elongatus*" (= the modern *Floriceps saccatus*). After Rudolphi, 1819, as reproduced by Guiart, 1935a. A. External appearance of the encysted larva. B and C. Remains of the cyst attached to the everted larva. D. Larva detached from the cyst. E. Holdfast of the larva showing tentacle bulbs. F. Armature of a tentacle.

Cyclophyllidea, respectively, and what La Rue (1914a) did for students of Proteocephala. That is to say, he has provided a clear-cut survey of the order and brought some degree of organization out of the confusion that prevailed previously. In the following account we shall follow mainly the views of this observer.

There would seem little to be gained here by conducting the reader upon a detailed tour through the jungles of trypanorhynchan synonymity and homonymity, or the classificatory scheme of this writer or that writer. Much of the earlier taxonomic history can be better discussed in the accounts of the respective genera which will follow, and in any case the detailed history of trypanorhynchans has been very thoroughly and admirably described by Southwell (1929c). An enormous literature has accumulated around these tapeworms, but apart from the contributions of the French writers Vaullegeard and Dollfus and the Austrian writer Pintner, most of it, to speak charitably, is worse than useless, since it has merely served to clog the path of more conscientious workers. The contributions of the three writers mentioned will become apparent during the course of this narrative.

RECOGNITION FEATURES

A trypanorhynchan tapeworm is readily identifiable as such by the nature of the holdfast end of the body, which is relatively long and cylindrical and carries two or four cuplike or oval bothridia, which project only slightly above the surface of the body and recall slightly the bothridia of Tetraphyllidea. These bothridia are very mobile, shortening and elongating rhythmically, ". . . their anterior extremities being pushed forward and fixed to the object over which the worm is moving; the posterior extremities are then drawn forward and the worm fixes itself in a new position." Johnstone (1912). They are in fact organs of locomotion rather than of fixation.

The actual fixation of the worm to the gut lining of the host is done by four threadlike structures which can be protruded from tubular sheaths within the holdfast end. These structures are covered with thornlike hooks arranged as a continuous spiral around the structure, or in oblique rows. Goeze (1782), an early observer of a trypanorhynchan larva, referred to these structures as "proboscides," a clumsy term which unfortunately, as ugly terms always seem to do, has established itself firmly in the literature of the subject. Their analogy with the structures called "tentacles" in other groups of invertebrate animals was recognized by Bosc (1797) when he applied the generic term *Tentacularia* to a trypanorhynchan larva and referred to it as possessing "retractile tentacles." Although the term "proboscides" has been perpetuated by later parasitologists, there seems to be no advantage in cluttering the terminology of tapeworm study unnecessarily, and these structures will be referred to in the following pages as "tentacles."

The protrusion of these tentacles from the holdfast end of the body is carried out in essentially the same way as is the protrusion of the proboscis in nemertine and acanthocephalan worms. Each tentacle is a tube. Its base widens out within the tapeworm body as a so-called "bulb."

"Each proboscis consists of a sheath continuous from the tip of the organ to its insertion in the proboscis bulb. The sheath consists of two parts—proximal and distal. The proximal part or posterior part is an integral part of the tissues of the scolex, is non-evaginable and is unarmed. The distal part is evaginable and is beset with hooks and spines on its internal surface. When it is invaginated it lies within the proximal part, but when it is evaginated the surfaces are reversed so that the hooks lie on its outer surface.

"The sheath of the proboscis is, in life, a clear, hyaline, tubular structure. The evaginable part consists of one uniform, structureless layer in which is inserted the hooks and spines. The part which lies within the scolex, and is non-evaginable consists of two concentric laminae differing slightly in staining reaction. These layers are indistinctly separated from each other after fixation and the external one may exhibit an apparent vacuolisation. There are no muscle fibres in the sheath but here and there one may see scattered nuclei; . . . The bulb is nearly circular in transverse section and consists of an outer wall of a cuticular nature which is continuous with the wall of the sheath and with that of the proboscis; of an inner wall, also continuous with the sheath; and of an intermediate layer of muscle fibres. This muscular part takes up by far the greater part of the thickness of the wall of the bulb: it is not of uniform thickness and fails entirely at the part of the wall nearest to the integument of the scolex and just here the cuticular outer part of the wall of the bulb is greatly thickened and forms the place of origin and insertion of the muscle fibres composing the intermediate layer. The diameter of the bulb [the writer is speaking of *Grillotia erinaceus*] is only about one-third of the total thickness of the latter, and the lumen itself is not quite circular in transverse section.

"The muscle fibres included in this intermediate part of the bulb wall are arranged in two series which run obliquely round, being inserted at either end into the thickened cuticular external wall. They continually decussate with each other, crossing at an angle of about 45°. They are not arranged in bundles or laminae but lie quite loosely from each other except at certain places where the fibres appear to be twisted round each other. Obviously the effect of the contraction of these muscles will be to reduce the diameter of the bulbs so to exert pressure on the fluid contained in the lumina of the sheaths." Johnstone (1912).

Extrusion of the tentacles is not, however, due directly to muscular contraction. The lumina of the sheaths and bulbs are filled with fluid, and the protrusion of the tentacles is due to an increase in the pressure of the fluid. The lumina of sheath and bulb are continuous, so that when the bulb is squeezed by its musculature the fluid in the sheath presses upon the part of the wall just where it is invaginated inward.

The withdrawal of the tentacles, however, is due directly to muscular contraction. The retractor muscle of each tentacle is a compact bundle of smooth muscle fibers which originates in the extreme posterior end of the bulb and is inserted in the internal wall of the tentacle at its extreme tip. That is to say, the muscle fibers run axially through the sheaths and bulbs and are quite free from the latter except at their ends. They must be able to contract to one-third of their lengths.

The above description refers mainly to *Grillotia erinaceus* (Beneden), but it applies with fair accuracy to trypanorhynchans in general. However, a few notes from the description given by Dollfus (1942) may be appended.

Dollfus speaks of the cavity of the extended tentacle as the "rhynchodeum." It is continuous with the cavity of the sheath and bulb. However, when the tentacle is withdrawn, this cavity disappears, and to the space between retracted tentacle and wall of sheath he gives the name "rhynchocoel." Histologically, the wall of the tentacle comprises, according to this writer: (*a*) a non-nucleated cuticle, in which the hooks are inserted; (*b*) a thin layer of longitudinal fibers; and (*c*) a cellular layer with very small nuclei, perhaps representing an atrophied epithelium. At its base the external wall of the tentacle is continuous with the outer cuticle of the body of the worm, or, according to the position of the tentacular pore, with the external cuticle of the corresponding bothridium; but there is a brief separation, and it has never been demonstrated that the cuticle of the tentacle is a modification of that of the body.

The layers of the sheath wall are not merely continuations of those of the tentacle wall; their structure is different. The sheath wall comprises two layers – internally, a pavement epithelium of polygonal cells with large nuclei; outside this, a non-nucleated layer, homogeneous and transparent, probably secreted by the epithelium. The sheaths are surrounded by the parenchyma and are bound to it by processes from the parenchymal cells. The sheaths may be straight or may have a corkscrew twist; the spiral is not continuous throughout the sheath length but at one level becomes reversed. Generally the sheaths are longer than the tentacles, and the latter when invaginated do not completely extend to the bottom of the sheath except in a few forms.

The bulb muscle fibers are in six layers, layers 2, 4, and 6 being crossed diagonally by layers 1, 3, and 5. The fibers are striated, are square or rectangular in transverse sections, and have a cavity extending the whole length of the fiber. The muscle layers may be disposed in "shells," each shell separated from its neighbors by a non-nucleated membrane. *Grillotia erinaceus*, described above, is exceptional in this respect. In the simplest cases, there is one layer of fibers to each shell. In *Tentacularia coryphaenae* Bosc (= *Stenobothrium macrobothrium* Rudolphi) on the other hand, Pintner (1925a) counted approximately 18 layers of muscle fibers in the outermost shell, then 22, 13, 12, and 10 for the following shells, and 1–2 only in the innermost shell. Usually within each shell the fibers run all in the same direction, whatever the number of layers, except in the family Tentaculariidae.

The bulbs are not directly in contact with the parenchyma but are often surrounded by a sort of fibrous skeleton formed by condensation of the parenchyma. They are held in place by special intrinsic bulb muscles running from the bulb wall to the inner surface of the surrounding skeletal sheath.

"The rhyncheal apparatus (bulb, sheath, tentacle) of each tentacle is completely closed and filled with a somewhat turbid fluid. Evagination of the tentacle is brought about by the contraction of the bulb which, by increasing the pressure of the fluid within the sheath, presses upon the tentacle which then evaginates. Invagination of the tentacle is caused by the contraction of the retractor muscle which is inserted, on the one hand to the distal extremity of the tentacle cavity, on the other hand to the wall of the bulb cavity (at a level which varies according to species and genus) or to the wall of the proximal part of the sheath, immediately in front of the bulb, as for example in Hepatoxylidae. When the tentacle is invaginated it reaches, or does not reach, according to species, the proximal end of the sheath; rarely does the tentacle when invaginated reach as far as the bulb-cavity. In certain species, when invagination is complete, the retractor muscle forms loose loops floating in the liquid of the bulb cavity.

"The four tentacles invaginate or evaginate independently of one another; a single tentacle can invaginate or evaginate, partly or completely, without the invagination or the evagination of the others being effected. It is never the distal portion of the tentacle that evaginates first. Evagination begins with the armed portion of the base; is continued by the metabasal portion; then the distal portion; finally, if evagination is pushed to the maximum, which rarely happens, the unarmed pro-basal region may appear outside the sheath, its wall in direct continuity with the surface of the holdfast." Dollfus (1942).

We will postpone for the moment a discussion of the hooks of the tentacles and survey briefly other features of the trypanorhynchan holdfast. The organs of locomotion are the bothridia, comparable to those of Tetraphyllidea; that is to say, they are muscular projections from the holdfast surface. They may be in pairs, one pair dorsal, the other ventral; or the members of a pair may fuse completely or partially, suggesting that the worm has only one dorsal and one ventral bothridium. The shape varies, but commonly is oval or ear-shaped. The bothridia may be completely sessile, without free margins, or may project sufficiently from the holdfast surface to have the lateral and posterior parts of the margin free. In one family, Pterobothriidae, the margins are almost wholly free, the bothridia being short-stalked, the members of each pair united only by a slight membrane. When at rest, the bothridial margin has a regular, even contour, but when the bothridia are in movement they are extremely mobile, the margins undulating continually, changing shape incessantly, extending and withdrawing. The surfaces of the bothridia are not always completely smooth, but they are never armed with hooks. In describing the bothridial shape, writers use such terms as "oval," "patelliform" (like a shallow, almost square plate), "cordiform" (conventionally heart-shaped), "reversed cordiform," and "elongated."

An understanding of the arrangement of the hooks on the tentacles is essential to the student of trypanorhynchan classification. The question has been discussed in great detail by Dollfus (1942) and we give here in abbreviated form the main points of his discussion.

Let us imagine the evaginated tentacle as a cylinder. Imagine further a cross section of this cylinder as if it were a clock face. Then the region from nine o'clock to three o'clock is the *bothridial surface*; that from three o'clock to nine o'clock is the *antibothridial surface*. Again, the region from twelve o'clock to six o'clock is the *external surface*; that from six o'clock to twelve o'clock is the *internal surface*. Or, by analogy with a human limb, the surfaces may be termed posterior, anterior, lateral, and medial, respectively.

The shape of the individual hook is somewhat like a rose thorn (Figure 175 B). In the figure, *t* and *h* represent the toe and the heel of the base. The length is the distance from the toe to the point of the hook; the height is the perpendicular distance from the prolongation of the base line to the point of the hook; other measurements are the length of the base and the distance from heel to point.

Dollfus recognizes three types of oncotaxy (hook arrangement) – the homeoacanthous, poeciloacanthous, and heteroacanthous types. In the homeoacanthous arrangement (Figures 161, 162) the hooks are approximately alike in size and shape and are arranged over the metabasal region of the tentacle in continuous spiral rows; or they may be arranged in quincunxes – that is to say, in sets of five, one hook in the center and one at each corner of an imaginary square.

In the poeciloacanthous arrangement, the hooks are not all of the same type. Along the external surface of the tentacle runs a band of small hooks, or a single row or double row of large hooks, forming what Dollfus calls a "chainette" and Pintner a "Kettlein." In a double row, each hook has a basal wing – a projection from one side or the other – alternately right and left along the line of hooks; and the points of the hooks do not point in the same direction, but alternately a little to the right and a little to the left of the middle line. In a single row, each hook has two wings, so as to appear like an open V. Thus in the example figured (Figure 167, *Floriceps saccatus*), the chainette consists of a single line of large, winged hooks (marked A in diagram key) each flanked by a small satellite hook (marked *a, a′* in diagram key). From the middle line of the opposite surface (internal surface), there run around the antibothridial and bothridial surfaces, to end between consecutive satellites, oblique lines of hooks usually numbered 1, 2, 3, 4, 5, 6, and 7 and 1′, 2′, 3′, 4′, 5′, 6′, and 7′. The arrangement will be comprehended better by studying the figure.

In the heteroacanthous arrangement, there is no chainette (Figures 170, 175), but when the tentacle is viewed from the external surface, one sees a sequence of oblique rows of hooks which have started on the opposite (internal) surface and crossed alternately around the bothridial and antibothridial surfaces. On the external surface each antibothridial row makes, as it were, an inverted V with the bothridial row.

There are, however, two forms of the heteroacanthous arrangement. In the "homeomorphous" type, the hooks are approximately alike in size and shape. In the "heteromorphous" type – the commonest arrangement – the hooks change abruptly in size and shape as they pass from internal to external surfaces. Both homeomorphous and heteromorphous are collectively termed "typical heteroacanthous." The members of the families Eutetrarhynchidae and Gilquinidae are of this type. In the family Otobothriidae, there is seen an oncotaxy which may be termed "atypical heteroacanthous." The hook rows which start from the internal surface do not reach the external surface. Instead, starting from the external surface there are different hook rows of small hooks; for each hook row that starts from the internal surface, there may be several rows that start from the external surface.

The holdfast of the trypanorhynchan consists of several regions. Pintner (1913) recognized four such regions (Figure 164). First there is the bothridial region (*pars bothridialis scolecis* of Pintner) which extends from the holdfast tip to the level of the posterior bothridial borders; it is thus the region which carries the organs of locomotion. It is followed by the stalk or neck (*Kopfstiel* of Pintner) of the holdfast, in which is found the rhyncheal apparatus – the four tentacles in their four sheaths and the four tentacle bulbs. The region traversed by the tentacle sheaths is the vaginal region (*pars vaginalis scolecis*). The region occupied by the tentacle bulbs is the bulbosal region (*pars bulbosa scolecis*). The holdfast extends as far back as the growth zone of the body, the region where new segments are produced. If this growth zone lies at some distance behind the bulbosal region, or if the stalk of the holdfast forms, behind the bulbs, a circular fold or velum around the growth zone, there can be distinguished a postbulbosal region (*pars postbulbosa scolecis*).

When the body has not yet developed, as in the plerocercus larva, the growth zone lies between the holdfast proper and the blastocyst – the bladderlike end of the larva; but as the growth zone is not always marked off externally from the holdfast, it is convenient to use a single term, "metabothridial region," for the holdfast *plus* the growth zone – that is to say, for the whole region between bothridia and blastocyst. When the growth zone forms before the adult condition is reached, a forerunner of the future body in the form of a posterior prolongation, ribboned or subcylindrical but not proglottised, may occur. Such a structure, whether very short or very long, is conveniently called the "appendix."

Strictly speaking, the holdfast ends and the body begins at the growth zone. This region is marked in some cases by a groove, but in many forms no boundary is apparent externally. Internally, there may be a condensation of the parenchyma to mark this region, but commonly it is necessary to resort to cross-sectioning or to special staining (methyl green–acid fuchsin in aqueous solution) which stains the holdfast parenchyma red and the growth zone green. By such methods it can be shown that in some forms the holdfast ends at the level of the bulbs.

In many species practically no indication of the posterior limit of the holdfast can be obtained, but in others there is a very active growth zone between the holdfast and the blastocyst – the so-called appendix – which may be very long. This appendix shows neither proglottisation nor genital apertures, but longitudinal nerve trunks and ventral and dorsal osmoregulatory canals occur within it. Often, too, the internal muscle zone – both longitudinal and circular fibers – is developed. In the postplerocercus stage, the appendix in many forms continues to grow, and at its posterior end, after the blastocyst has dropped off, there is formed by invagination a bladder – the bladder of the pygidium, or first formed adult proglottis. Whether in all forms the appendix becomes wholly transformed into the body, or whether part of it is broken down and digested in the final host, is as yet uncertain.

The body begins at the growth zone. Its anterior border may be hidden by the velum or overlap of the holdfast. It may not be indicated by any external sign, but the holdfast may continue to grow insensibly into the body. The actual area of growth may coincide with the first segment, or there may be between it and the first segment an unsegmented region or "neck," short or long, narrow or broad. At first the new segments are wider than long, and in many forms they remain so. In others they become square and finally rectangular, longer than wide. When the posterior border of each segment overlaps the anterior border of the following segment, the proglottis is craspedote. According to species, proglottides approaching maturity, or which have attained maturity, or which are gravid, automatically detach themselves or do not detach themselves from the body. If they so detach themselves, the body is apolytic. If they do not detach themselves, it is anapolytic.

In anapolysis the pygidium or first formed segment, which carries the common osmoregulatory aperture, stays always as the last segment of the body. This is the case with the genera *Sphyriocephalus*, *Hepatoxylon*, *Nybelinia*, and *Tentacularia*; and with the species *Gymnorhynchus horridus*, *Dasyrhynchus variouncinnatus*, *Gilquinia squali*, and *Eutetrarhynchus ruficollis*, for example. Among apolytic forms several types are known. The most common occurrence is for the gravid proglottis to come away from the body after the uterus has filled with eggs, a condition termed "euapolysis." In "hyperapolysis" the proglottis detaches itself before the eggs have appeared in the uterus.

It is not necessary to go into the details of the internal anatomy, since in most respects Trypanorhyncha follow the general type of structure discussed in Chapter I. The genitalia, on the whole, have the arrangement described for Tetraphyllidea, but some points of difference may be noted (Figure 158). Unlike the condition in Tetraphyllidea, there is

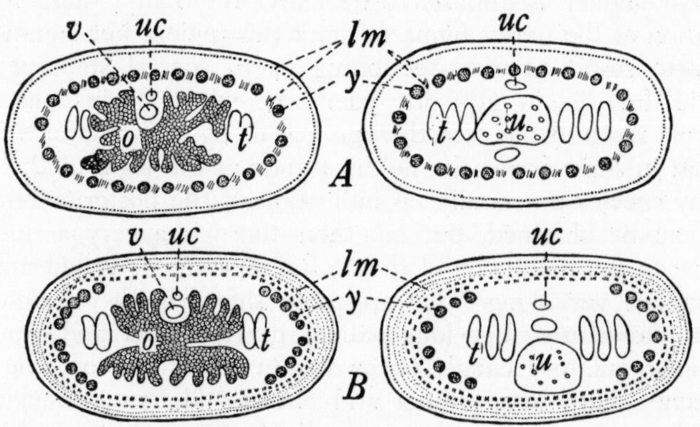

FIG. 158. Comparison of internal features of trypanorhynchan (A) and tetraphyllidean (B) tapeworms. After Woodland, 1927b. *lm*, longitudinal muscles; *o*, ovary; *t*, testes; *u*, uterus; *uc*, uterine canal; *v*, vagina; *y*, yolk glands.

a very definite zone of longitudinal muscle fibers lying approximately between the proglottis center and the proglottis circumference, thus demarcating a region of medullary parenchyma – within the zone – from an area of cortical parenchyma – outside it. Only rarely (in some species of *Gilquinia* and *Aporhynchus*) is this boundary rudimentary or lacking. Within this medullary region lie all the reproductive organs except the yolk glands.

The yolk glands form a continuous layer over the whole of the proglottis, lying as a rule between the subcuticle and the parenchymal muscle zone, but in some cases (e.g., *Grillotia erinaceus*) they lie among the muscle bundles or partly among them, partly outside them, and partly to the inside of them. Where the muscle zone is not developed (as in a few species, notably, of *Gilquinia* and *Aporhynchus*), the yolk glands may be regarded as forming the boundary between cortex and medulla.

The chief differences between Trypanorhyncha and Tetraphyllidea in the arrangement of the genitalia are (Figure 158): (1) the continuous, sleevelike distribution of the yolk glands of the trypanorhynchan, in contrast with the two separate fields of yolk glands in the tetraphyllidean; (2) the extension of the testes into the region behind the ovary; (3) the position of the vagina, ventral to the uterus and cirrus pouch; (4) the opening of the vagina ventral to or slightly behind that of the cirrus pouch; (5) the sperm duct passing from behind forward, without crossing the vagina before penetrating the cirrus pouch; (6) the muscular cirro-vaginal atrium; and (7) the delayed development of the intrauterine eggs which, in contrast with the condition in Tetraphyllidea, do not reach the oncosphere stage while within the uterus.

The eggs escape to the outside through an opening in the ventral proglottis wall. This opening may be *preformed*, or at any rate preindicated on the proglottis surface by an invagination which runs inward to meet a corresponding outpocketing of the uterine wall, long before the uterus receives eggs. In other cases the preformation may be incomplete, there being no invagination of the proglottis wall but an outpocketing of the uterine wall appearing before the eggs fill the uterus. This outpocketing grows outward to a predetermined place in the proglottis wall and there bursts through to the outside. Pintner's uterine aperture formation by *involution* is of this nature. A third condition is found in which neither outer wall nor uterine wall shows any preindication of the place where the tear or split in the proglottis wall will later occur.

Very few trypanorhynchans appear to have operculated eggs, such as have been observed in *Grillotia erinaceus*; even the closely related *Grillotia heptanchi* has not, carrying in fact a short filament at one pole of the egg. The life cycle of *Grillotia erinaceus*, the only trypanorhynchan whose complete life cycle has been elucidated (by Ruszkowski, 1932c) must not be taken as fully representing the condition in Trypanorhyncha generally until more information is available. In this case, there is a surprising resemblance to the life cycle features of certain pseudophyllidean tapeworms, the operculated egg liberating a ciliated coracidium which is ingested by copepod Crustacea (*Acartia longiramus, Pseudocalanus elongatus, Paracalanus parvum*, or *Temora longicornis*) and becomes a typical procercoid complete with a cercomer. Reference should be made to the articles of Ruszkowski (1932c, 1934) or to the brief summary of Ruszkowski's findings given by Dollfus (1942).

However, in contrast with Pseudophyllidea and with the orders already discussed – Tetraphyllidea, etc. – the later larval stage of a trypanorhynchan is a plerocercus and not a plerocercoid. The difference

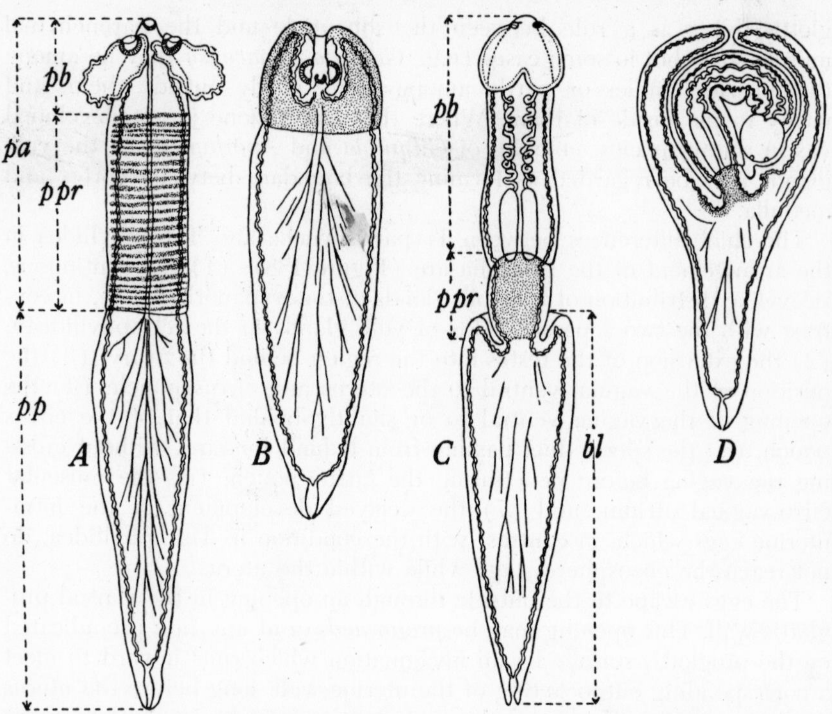

FIG. 159. Comparison of tetraphyllidean and trypanorhynchan larval forms. After Dollfus, 1942. A. Tetraphyllidean plerocercoid, extended. B. Same, with anterior end invaginated. C. Trypanorhynchan plerocercoid, extended. D. Same with holdfast withdrawn within the receptaculum of the blastocyst. *bl*, blastocyst; *pa*, pars antica; *pb*, pars bothridialis plus pedunculus scolecis; *pp*, pars postica; *ppr*, pars proliferus.

between the two may be illustrated by a comparison between the larval stages of a phyllobothriid and a trypanorhynchan (Figure 159).

In the plerocercoid of the phyllobothriid there can be distinguished an anterior region (*pars antica*) and a posterior region (*pars postica*). The anterior region comprises the bothridia, apical sucker or rostellum, if such be present, the stalk of the holdfast, and the growth zone. In most cases the stalk is included within the length of the bothridial region (*pars bothridialis*), but in some species it is longer than that region. At its posterior end the stalk passes into the growth zone, which is sometimes very long. Stalk plus growth zone may be termed the "metabothridial region"; it is thick, strongly muscular, its parenchyma dense. Its posterior limit is commonly indicated by a groove or a constriction; behind the groove is the posterior region, thinner, more translucent, and less muscular. At its extremity is the common osmoregulatory canal. When, as is usually the case, the plerocercoid is invaginated, it is only the bothridial region and its stalk which is withdrawn within the metabothridial part. The retractor muscle that performs this withdrawal sprays out into slender bundles which are inserted in the subcuticle of the posterior region.

In the trypanorhynchan, similarly, there is a bothridial region, but without any apical sucker or rostellum. The stalk is represented by the vaginal, bulbosal, and postbulbosal regions already mentioned. Following the stalk, as in Tetraphyllidea, there is a growth zone (*pars proliferus*). The posterior region, however, is represented by a bladderlike structure, the blastocyst. Rarely is the trypanorhynchan larva truly invaginated. Where such seems to be the case, it is not true invagination but a sinking-in, as it were, of the bothridial and metabothridial regions into a depression of the blastocyst surface (see Figure 159 D).

A trypanorhynchan larva which has lost its bladder is not therefore comparable with a plerocercoid. Its body or appendix is simply a growth development from the growth zone, and its terminal osmoregulatory duct is not the same thing as that of the tetraphyllidean, but corresponds with that in the first formed segment or pygidium of the latter.

Most writers on the group, following Diesing (1854), distinguish – as Thecophora – those trypanorhynchan larvae *with* blastocysts, and – as Atheca – those *without* blastocysts. Strictly speaking, the latter are post-

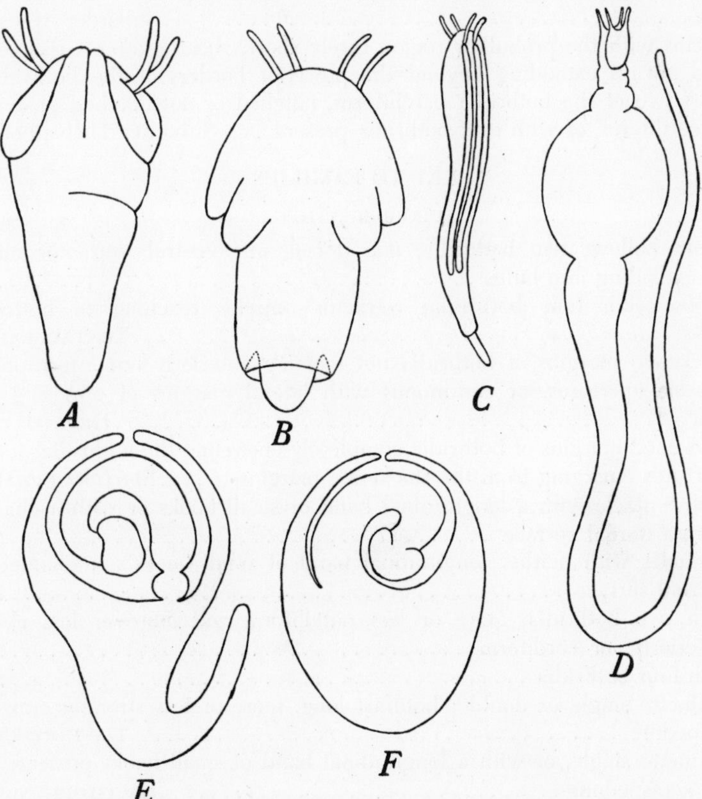

FIG. 160. Trypanorhynchan larval types. After Guiart, 1927. A. *Sphyriocephalus* and probably *Gilquinia*. B. *Nybelinia*. C. *Tentacularia*. D. *Gymnorhynchus*. E. *Lacistorhynchus*. F. *Eutetrarhynchus* and *Christianella*.

larval; they are forms whose blastocysts are greatly reduced or precociously degenerate. While the blastocyst form of most athecous forms is not known, Dollfus has described it for *Nybelinia* and *Tentacularia.* Such athecous forms seem able, in some cases at any rate, to *re-encapsulate*—that is to say, to pass from the gut of an unsuitable host into its body cavity, there to become enclosed by a bladderlike structure formed as an irritation product of the host tissues.

CLASSIFICATION

We shall use here the scheme of classification proposed by Dollfus (1942) which, while not complete—since he has included within it only those genera whose affinities he could definitely recognize—is by far the most workable of the many schemes put forward. This scheme recognizes two suborders—Atheca, with seven families, and Thecophora, with three.

I. Forms with the prebulbar region usually short; sheaths short, rarely corkscrewlike, not extending or extending only slightly beyond the level of the posterior borders of the bothridia; bothridia rarely patelliform or cordiform .... Suborder Atheca (1)

II. Forms with the prebulbar region rarely short; sheaths often corkscrewlike and always extending beyond the posterior borders of the bothridia; at least two of the bothridia patelliform, notched or not notched posteriorly, or cordiform, or with four bothridia present .... Suborder Thecophora (7)

KEY TO FAMILIES

SUBORDER ATHECA

1. Hooks hollow; two bothridia, one dorsal, one ventral; retractor muscles not extending into bulbs 2
   Hooks solid; four bothridia; retractor muscles reaching to bottom of bulbs .... TENTACULARIIDAE
2. Thickened margins of bothridia not meeting anteriorly but interrupted by tentacle apertures, or continuous with lateral margins of opposing bothridia .... HEPATOXYLIDAE
   Thickened margins of bothridia completely encircling the bothridia; tentacle apertures emerging from the thickened margins ...... SPHYRIOCEPHALIDAE
3. Each tentacle with a longitudinal band of small hooks or with a chainette on its external surface 4
   Tentacles with neither longitudinal band of small hooks nor chainette on external surface 7
4. With two bothridia, more or less patelliform and more or less notched posteriorly, or cordiform 5
   With four bothridia 6
5. Chainette single or double; holdfast long, more or less strongly or weakly craspedote .... DASYRHYNCHIDAE
   Chainette single, or with a longitudinal band of small hooks present; holdfast acraspedote .... LACISTORHYNCHIDAE
6. One pair of bothridia on each dorsal and ventral face; posterior and outer bothridial margins free of the holdfast; anterior margin fusing with anterior end of holdfast; holdfast not craspedote or only weakly so .... GYMNORHYNCHIDAE

The four bothridia with margins completely free from the holdfast, arranged in pairs in front of the extreme anterior end of the holdfast; holdfast acraspedote . . . . PTEROBOTHRIIDAE

SUBORDER THECOPHORA

7. Two bothridia, more or less patelliform, with posterior margins free and strongly notched or not notched; without eversible sensory fossettes; bulbs long; holdfast acraspedote . . . . EUTETRARHYNCHIDAE
Two bothridia, more or less patelliform, with posterior margins lightly notched or not; in the lateral margins or in the posterior margins of each bothridium two eversible sensory fossettes . . . . OTOBOTHRIIDAE
Four bothridia, one pair to each face, their internal anterior marginal regions fused with holdfast . . . . GILQUINIIDAE

Family TENTACULARIIDAE Poche, 1926, emended Dollfus, 1930 (=RUFFERIDAE Guiart, 1927; NYBELINIDAE Guiart, 1931)

DESCRIPTION

Of the order Trypanorhyncha. With holdfast strongly craspedote. Tentacles somewhat short and slender. Armature homeoacanthous, of solid hooks, closely similar, equally spaced. Tentacle sheaths never corkscrewlike or sinuous. Bulbs briefly ellipsoidal or banana-shaped, each comprising six shells of muscle fibers. Body anapolytic with segments wider than long. Cirro-vaginal atrium not quite marginal but displaced slightly toward the ventral surface; never in the posterior half of the segment margin. Postlarval stage reached by degeneration of blastocyst, lying in a capsule formed by the host tissues, or, if free from this capsule, lying freely in the host body cavity. Larval and postlarval stages encapsulated in muscles, gut wall, body cavity of various teleostean fishes and cephalopods, more rarely of gastropods and marine chelonians. Adults in gut of various selachians. Two genera:

1. Bothridia very narrow and long, without free posterior borders. Bulbs in anterior half of bothridial region. Yolk glands in medullary parenchyma, within zone of internal longitudinal muscles . . . . *Tentacularia*
2. Bothridia fairly wide, with posterior borders free. Bulbs in posterior half of bothridial region or completely or partly posterior to it. Yolk glands either in cortex or partly among longitudinal muscles or in medulla . . . . *Nybelinia*

Tentacularia Bosc, 1797 (=*Pierretia* Guiart, 1927; *Stenobothrium* Diesing, 1850; *Abothros* Welch, 1876)

With the characters given above. Recognizable by the long subcylindrical holdfast whose four long and parallel bothridia are completely separated from each other, without free posterior borders, and occupy the total length of the holdfast except for the velum, which is always present and well developed. Bulbs short and banana-shaped, in the anterior half of the bothridial region. Appendix of postlarva always well developed. Body absolutely acraspedote and anapolytic, flat, with segments never longer than half their width. Yolk glands in medulla. Genotype, *coryphaenae* Bosc, 1802 (Figure 161).

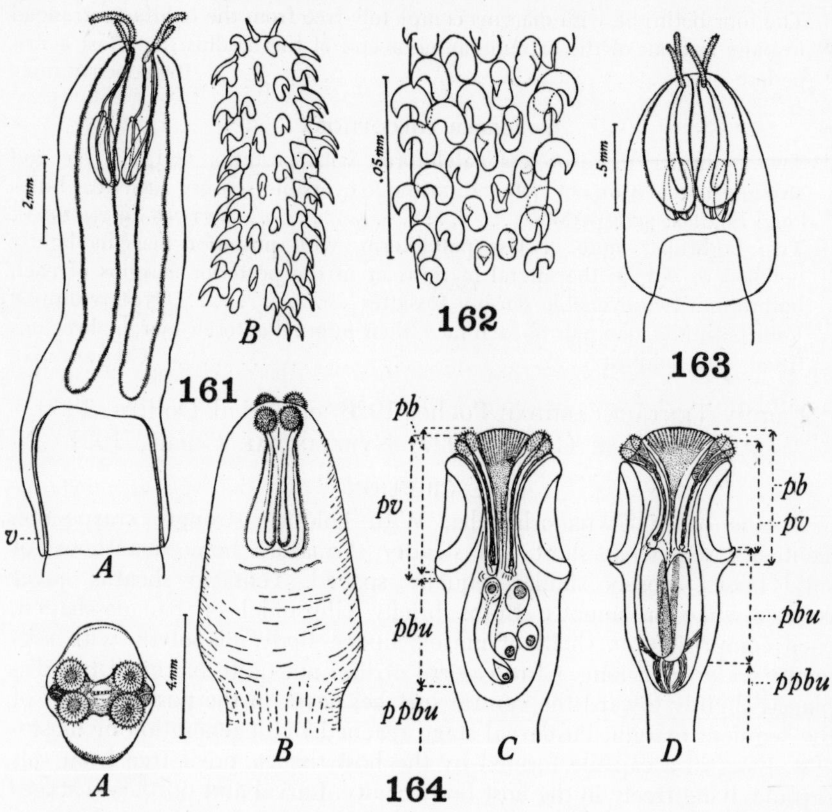

FIG. 161. *Tentacularia coryphaenae*. After Yamaguti, 1934. A. Holdfast. B. Hooks at apex of tentacles. FIG. 162. *Nybelinia lingualis*, proximal part of a completely evaginated tentacle. After Dollfus, 1942. FIG. 163. *Nybelinia pintneri*, holdfast in surficial view. After Yamaguti, 1934. FIG. 164. *Hepatoxylon trichiuri*, postlarva. After Dollfus, 1942. A and B. External views of holdfast. C and D. Nearly sagittal sections of holdfast. *pb*, pars bothridialis; *pbu*, pars bulbosa; *ppbu*, pars postbulbosa; *pv*, pars vaginalis; *v*, velum.

The genotype, *coryphaenae* Bosc, 1802, up to now the only species described, was established for a postlarva found in a fish, *Coryphaena sp.* Bosc's material was identical, possibly, with material described earlier (Goeze, 1782) as *Echinorhynchus quadrirostris* from *Salmo*; this is Dollfus' opinion, but until it can be proved the name *coryphaenae* must stand.

It is common as a larva, and especially as a postlarva, in many teleostean fishes, always occurring encysted and encapsulated if a larva, and encapsulated or free in the body cavity if a postlarva. When the holdfast is completely formed, the blastocyst which envelops it degenerates rapidly; and if the adventitious cyst (the product of host reaction) is not too thick, the holdfast, plus appendix, breaks away from it and becomes free in the host body cavity, fixed by its tentacles to the viscera. Linton (1900), for example, reported finding 30 specimens attached firmly to the stomach mucosa of a *Galeocerdo tigrinus* in Massachusetts waters.

Nybelinia Poche, 1926 (=*Aspidorhynchus* Molin, 1858, preoccupied; *Rufferia* Guiart, 1927; *Acoleorhynchus* Poche, 1926; *Stenobothrium* Diesing of Pintner, 1913; *Congeria* Guiart, 1935)

With the characters given above. Holdfast short, with bothridia paired on dorsal and ventral faces, each more or less triangular or kidney-shaped in outline, with posterior and outer margins free. Holdfast always with a well-developed overlap (velum) over the beginning of the body or the appendix. Body absolutely acraspedote or craspedote according to subgenus, anapolytic, flattened, with the segments wider than long or never longer than twice their width. Yolk glands cortical *or* medullary. Genotype, *lingualis* Cuvier, 1817.

Dollfus recognizes two subgenera:

1. *Nybelinia* Poche, 1926. With the segments acraspedote; genotype, *lingualis* Cuvier, 1817; with the additional species *aequidentata* Shipley and Hornell, 1906; *bisulcata* Linton, 1889; *herdmani* Shipley and Hornell, 1906; *lamonteae* Nigrelli, 1938; *lingualis* Cuvier, 1817; *narinari* McCallum, 1917; *peridaeus* Shipley and Hornell, 1906; *pintneri* Yamaguti, 1934; *robusta* Linton, 1889; *surmenicola* Okada, 1929; *tenuis* Linton, 1890.
2. *Syngenes* Dollfus, 1930. With the segments craspedote; genotype, *syngenes* Pintner, 1928; other species, *palliata* Linton, 1904.

For the specific characters of these species and for information as to their occurrence, reference should be made to Dollfus (1942). Broadly speaking, *lingualis* occurs in European Atlantic waters, in North American Atlantic waters, and in the Mediterranean Sea; *bisulcata, robusta, tenuis, lamonteae,* and *narinari,* occur in North American Atlantic waters; *aequidentata, herdmani,* and *peridaeus* are Indian Ocean forms; and *pintneri* and *surmenicola* are Pacific Ocean forms. Wardle (1932a) reported the postlarva of *surmenicola* as particularly common embedded in the stomach mucosa of *Ophiodon spp.* in British Columbia waters; *syngenes* is known at present only by specimens collected by Dr. Sixten Bock in *Cestracion zygaena* in American Atlantic waters and in the Bonin Islands; Chandler (1942b) has reported the species from Florida waters.

Family Hepatoxylidae Dollfus, 1940 (=Coenomorphinae Loennberg, 1889; Dibothriorhynchidae Ariola, 1899; Diplogonimidae Guiart, 1931)

DESCRIPTION

Of the order Trypanorhyncha. With the holdfast large, thick, muscular, acraspedote. Bothridia two in number, not projecting nor occupying the whole width of the holdfast, deeply embedded in the substance of the holdfast, more or less oval in outline, longer than wide, with lateral margins tending to approach, thus diminishing the bothridial mouth to a longitudinal slit. Bothridial margins reinforced by a padlike or cushion-like thickening (*bourrelet*) which does not completely surround the bothridium but is incomplete anteriorly, leaving a gap in which lies the aperture of the tentacle corresponding with the bothridium. The anterior portions of the lateral bourrelets may run over the holdfast tip to join those of the opposite bothridium. Tentacles short, globular, claviform or conically truncated, scarcely or not flexible, with large hollow hooks, almost all similar in shape, homeoacanthous, arranged in quincunxes. Tentacle sheaths short, arched, never sinuous or corkscrewlike. Retractor muscles not entering the bulbs but inserted on a protuberance of the proximal end of the sheath. Sheath joined to bulb by a short, narrow canal.

Body anapolytic, muscular, with segments always wider than long; more or less weakly craspedote. Genitalia double, with two uteri and two preformed uterine apertures. Copulatory apparatus with tubular cirrus, muscular, invaginating into terminal portion of sperm duct which is modified as an ejaculatory duct. A proximal seminal vesicle present, receiving proximal end of sperm duct, but no accessory vesicle (*Cirrusmotionsblase*) present.

Plerocercus larval stage unknown. Postlarva with a more or less long appendix, generally free in the body cavity of the host and fixed by its tentacles to the cavity wall or penetrating more or less deeply into the liver or gut wall or muscles; in various teleostean fishes and selachians. Adults found in the gut of large selachians. Type genus and only known genus, *Hepatoxylon* Bosc, 1811.

Hepatoxylon Bosc, 1811 (= *Dibothriorhynchus* Ducrotay and Blainville, 1828; *Tetrantaris* Templeton, 1836; *Coenomorphus* Loennberg, 1899; *Diplogonimus* Guiart, 1931)

With the characters of the family. Genotype, *trichiuri* Holten, 1802 (Figure 164). The genotype was established by H. S. Holten, 1802, as *Echinorhynchus trichiuri*, for a postlarva – known to naturalists for nearly a century and a half as a common parasite in teleostean fishes – most commonly found in the body cavity fixed and suspended by its tentacles and by the bothridia of one side, or embedded partly in the liver, ovary, muscles, heart, etc. Few adults are known. The most detailed description is that by Loennberg (1899). Yamaguti (1934) also gave a detailed description of several specimens from the stomach of *Isurus glaucus* in Japanese waters. This species is apparently large for a trypanorhynchan. Loennberg's largest specimen was 400 mm. long. Yamaguti's largest was 100 mm. A specimen in the Copenhagen Museum examined by Dollfus was 136.5 mm. long with a holdfast 12 mm. by 6 mm.

Hepatoxylon megacephalum was first described by Rudolphi (1819) as *Tetrarhynchus megacephalus*. It is known only as a postlarva. It much resembles *trichiuri* but is shorter, the tentacles conical rather than globular, the hooks shorter (150 μ as contrasted with 180–260 μ in *trichiuri*), the holdfast projecting somewhat below the level of the posterior bothridial margins. The adult has not yet been described. Monticelli (1893) recorded an adult tetrarhynchan found at Spezia (Italy) in *Carcharodon carcharias* that might have been this form, and some adults in the Berlin Museum – collected by Parona from the same host species in Mediterranean waters and mentioned by Pintner (1930c) – may belong here.

Family Sphyriocephalidae Pintner, 1913 (= Bouchardidae Guiart, 1927; Sphyriocephalinae Pintner, 1930)

DESCRIPTION

Of the order Trypanorhyncha. With the holdfast thick, muscular, squat, with well-marked velum. Bothridial region thicker than wide, giving the holdfast in profile the form of a mallet (hence the family name). On each dorsal and ventral face a large bothridium, circular or subcircular, never a longitudinal slit; with large, thickened rim (bourrelet) completely encircling it. Bothridial cavity deep, with longitudinal median ridge. Bothridia inclined toward each other roofwise. Tentacles cylindrical, slightly swollen at their bases, of medium length, emerging from the bothridial cavities within the internal margins of the bourrelets and curving outward somewhat in the fashion of ox horns. The hooks hollow, homeoacanthous, in quincunxes, almost all of the same size and shape. Tentacle sheaths short. Bulbs short, oriented transversely, the retractor muscles not penetrating into the bulbs.

Body thick, craspedote, anapolytic, with numerous segments. Distal region of sperm duct differentiated as a thick-walled, muscular ejaculatory duct, within whose dilated end portion the cirrus is invaginated, projecting as a cone or tube with the end carrying the aperture free within the dilatation; the whole surrounded by a muscular mass. No accessory seminal vesicle (*Cirrusmotionsblase*). Uterine pore preformed, displaced to poral side of middle line. Egg shell with an outgrowth at each pole. Plerocercus larva with the blastocyst unknown. Postlarva known from various teleostean fishes and selachians. Adults in various selachians. One genus only, *Sphyriocephalus* Pintner, 1913 (= *Bouchardia* Guiart, 1927; *Sphyriocephala* Pintner, 1929) with the characters of the family and genotype, *viridis* Wagener, 1854.

The genotype was established as *Tetrarhynchus viridis*, a large tapeworm 314 mm. long, from *Scymnorhinus licha* in Mediterranean waters. It has been recorded by Pintner (1930c) from a range of selachians and also by Guiart (1935b). *Sphyriocephalus tergestinus* Pintner, 1913 was recorded in *Vulpecula marina* (= *Alopecias vulpes*), and by Yamaguti (1934) in *Isurus glaucus*, in Japanese waters. As a postlarva it has been noted by Pintner (1913) and Dollfus (1930) in *Lepidopus argenteus* and *L. caudatus* in Mediterranean waters (Figure 165).

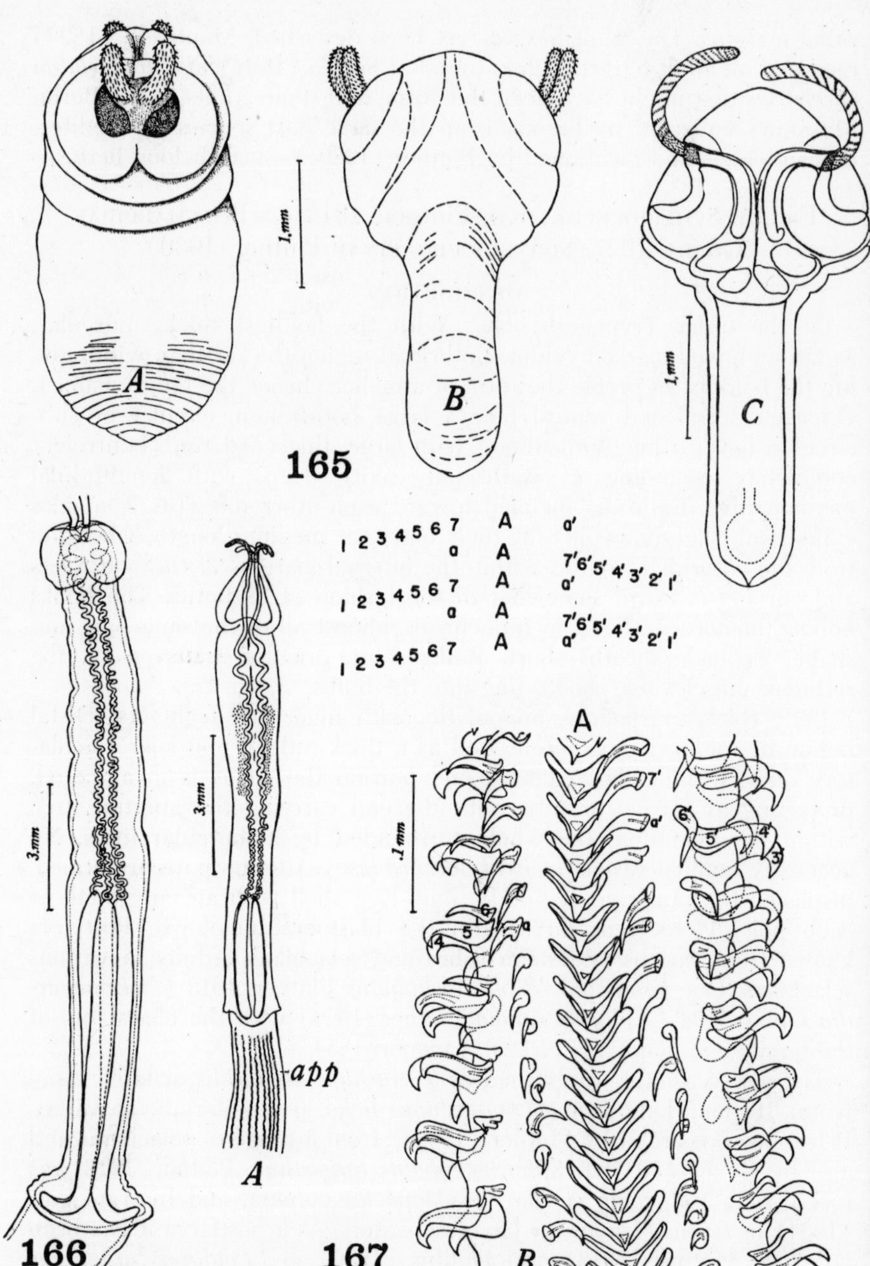

FIG. 165. *Sphyriocephalus tergestinus*, postlarva. After Dollfus, 1942. A. Surficial view B. Marginal view. C. Section, nearly sagittal. FIG. 166. *Dasyrhynchus talismani*, holdfast After Dollfus, 1942. FIG. 167. *Floriceps saccatus*. After Dollfus, 1942. A. Anterior portion of larva from *Mola mola*, showing appendix (*app*). B. Armature of first tentacle, lateral view in region of the 15th–31st elements of the chainette (see p. 292 for explanation).

Family DASYRHYNCHIDAE Dollfus, 1935 (= DASYRHYNCHIDAE Guiart, 1935)

DESCRIPTION

Of the order Trypanorhyncha. With holdfast very long and weakly craspedote. Bothridia two, patelliform or cordiform, each with posterior marginal notch. Vaginal region long with tentacle sheaths corkscrewlike or regularly sinuous. Frontal glands generally numerous in part of the vaginal region. Bulbs short or long, according to genus. Postbulbosal region short or lacking. Retractor muscles inserted in height of bulbar cavities. Tentacles poeciloacanthous, always with chainette in middle of external surface, at least over part of tentacle, and with principal rows of hooks alternating from one face of the tentacle to the other. On one part or other of the chainette there may be either intercalary rows of small hooks or intermediate groups of three hooks.

Body acraspedote, anapolytic, with segments becoming longer than wide. Genital apertures toward middle of segment margins or at beginning of last third. Yolk glands outside or inside of longitudinal muscle zone. Uterine pores not preformed, very close to anterior borders of segments. Eggs without polar filaments. Plerocercus larva with holdfast and appendix continuing to grow in length while within the blastocyst; parasitic in teleostean fishes. Adults in selachians. Two subfamilies:

1. Bulbs at least fifteen times as long as wide; elements of the chainette each with a basal wing and arranged in two files, or with a basal plate and arranged in one row; outside the chainette, one to four rows of intercalary hooks; a special basal armature present .... DASYRHYNCHINAE Dollfus
2. Bulbs six times as long as wide; elements of chainette always in one file, with or without basal wings, according to genus; outside the chainette, satellite hooks; no rows of intercalary hooks; no special basal armature .... CALLITETRARHYNCHINAE Dollfus

The family Dasyrhynchidae was proposed almost at the same time by Guiart and by Dollfus. Guiart recognized as genera *Dasyrhynchus* Pintner and *Floriceps* Cuvier, regarding the latter genus as *Callitetrarhynchus* of Pintner. Dollfus, however, regarded *Floriceps* and *Callitetrarhynchus* as distinct genera.

Dasyrhynchus Pintner, 1928 (= *Sbesterium* Dollfus, 1929)

With the characters of Dasyrhynchinae. Holdfast very long with basal region enlarged and weakly craspedote. Bothridia two, reverse heart-shaped, with strong posterior marginal notches. Vaginal region of holdfast long with tentacle sheaths sinuous or spiral. Tentacles with chainette of one or two rows according to species, and intercalary rows of small hooks. Other characteristics as given for the family. Genotype, *vario-uncinnatus* Pintner, 1913.

Dollfus (1942) recognized three species:

1. With a double chainette 2
   With a single chainette 3
2. With four rows of intercalary hooks on each tentacle ..... *vario-uncinnatus*

With two rows of intercalary hooks on each tentacle .... *giganteus*
3. With one row of intercalary hooks on each tentacle .... *talismani*

The genotype was established, as *Halsiorhynchus vario-uncinnatus*, by Pintner (1913) for a specimen in the Berlin Museum labeled as collected from a selachian in New Guinea waters. It was recorded by Linton (1924a), as *Tentacularia insignis*, as an adult in *Carcharinus milberti* and *C. commersoni* at Woods Hole, Massachusetts; by Shuler (1938), as *Tentacularia insignis*, in *Hypoprion brevirostris* in Florida waters; and by Chandler (1942b), as *Dasyrhynchus insigne*, from *Carcharias platyodon* in Florida waters. For European records reference should be made to Dollfus (1942).

Of the other species, *giganteus* Diesing, 1850 is known only from a plerocercus recorded, as *Anthocephalus giganteus*, from beneath the skin of a Brazilian carangiform fish in the Natterer collection. The remaining species, *talismani* Dollfus, 1935, was established for material from the Talisman expedition, collected from *Galeus glaucus* in West African waters. It has been described in great detail by its author (Dollfus, 1942) (Figure 166).

Floriceps Cuvier, 1817

With the characters of Callitetrarhynchinae. Bothridia reverse heart-shaped. Bulbs 5–8 times as long as wide. Tentacles with satellite hooks flanking the chainette. Chainette hooks each two-winged. No special basal armature on the tentacles. Genotype and only known species, *saccatus* Cuvier, 1817 (Figure 167).

The genotype *saccatus* (= *Anthocephalus elongatus* Rudolphi, 1819) was recorded as a plerocercus larva in the fish *Mola mola*, and has been recorded since by many observers as a plerocercus in this same host form. The adult was recorded by Linton (1909), as *Rhynchobothrium ingens*; by Linton again (1921) as *Dasyrhynchus ingens*, in both cases from *Carcharinus obscurus* in American Atlantic waters. Dollfus (1935) found Cuvier's type material to contain two distinct forms for which he suggested the names *Dasyrhynchus ingens* (Linton, 1921) and *Gymnorhynchus horridus* Goodsir, 1841, rejecting the names *Floriceps* and *Anthocephalus*. His family Floricipitidae became Gymnorhynchidae, and *G. horridus* became the genotype of a new subgenus *Molicola*. Later, however (1942), he revived the term *Floriceps* for *D. ingens* but retained *Molicola* as a subgenus of *Gymnorhynchus*. As a plerocercus, *Floriceps saccatus* is usually found encysted in the liver (beneath the capsule), in the peritoneum or the mesenteries, or beneath the serous covering of the gut, but not in the muscles.

Callitetrarhynchus Pintner, 1931 (= *Anthocephalus* Rudolphi, 1819; *Callotetrarhynchus* Pintner, 1931; *Lintoniella* Yamaguti, 1934 *nec. Lintoniella* Woodland, 1927)

With the characters of Callitetrarhynchinae. Bothridia patelliform. Bulbs 3–6 times as long as broad. Tentacles with chainette hooks spaced, wingless. Satellite hooks present. No basal armature. Genotype and only known species, *gracilis* Rudolphi (Figure 168).

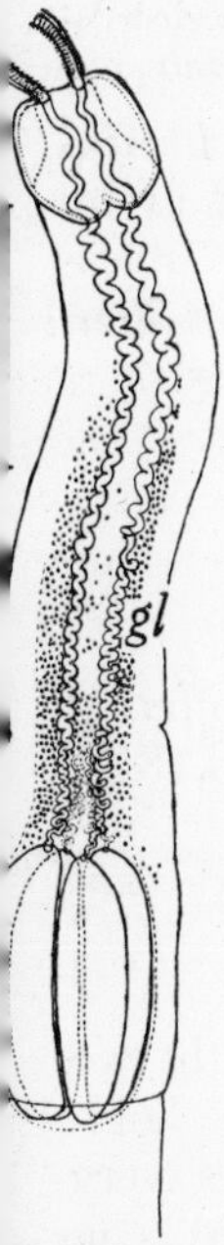

168

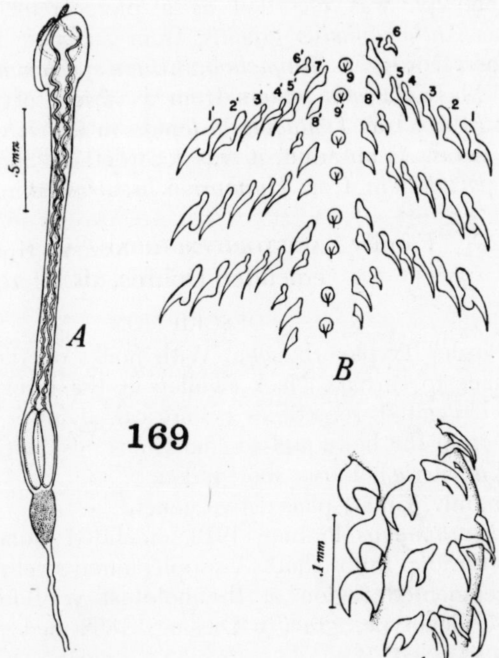

169

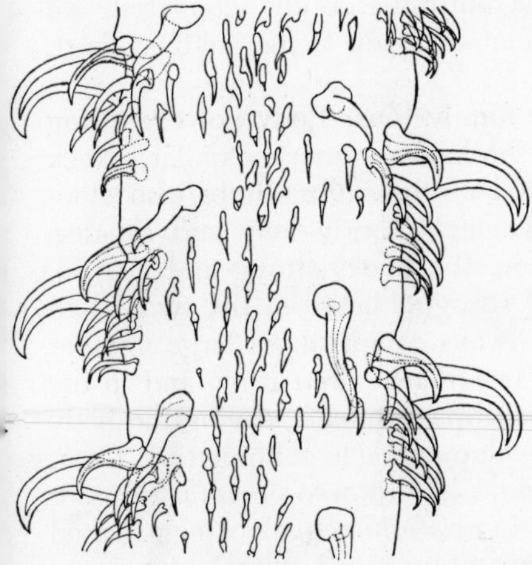

170

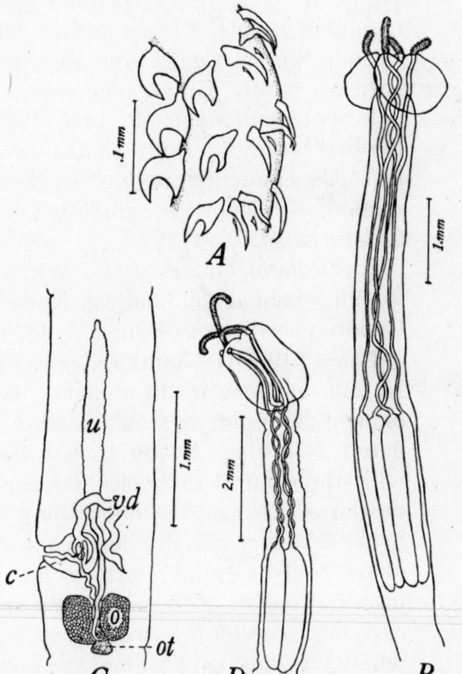

171

IG. 168. *Callitetrarhynchus gracilis,* holdfast of a plerocercus. Note that the frontal glands *gl*) are absent from the first quarter of the pars vaginalis. After Dollfus, 1942. FIG. 169. *acistorhynchus tenuis.* After Dollfus, 1942. A. An individual with the beginning of the body liform. B. Metabasal armature of a tentacle. Hooks 9 and 9′ indicate the middle line of the xternal face, hooks 1 and 1′ indicate that of the internal face. FIG. 170. *Grillotia erinaceus,* ıetabasal armature of a tentacle, external face. Bothridial face to the left. After Dollfus, 1942. IG. 171. *Grillotia* species. After Hart, 1936a. A. *musculara,* mid-portion of a tentacle. B. *musculara,* holdfast. C. *musculara,* proglottis. D. *heptanchi,* holdfast.
c, cirrus; *o,* ovary; *ot,* ootype; *u,* uterus; *vd,* vaginal duct.

The genotype was recorded as a plerocercus larva by Rudolphi (1819), as *Anthocephalus gracilis*, from *Scomber rocheus*. As a larva also it was recorded as *Rhynchobothrium speciosum* by Linton (1897–1924) in Massachusetts waters from a variety of teleosteans, and by Chandler (1935a) as *Tentacularia lepida* in *Galeichthys felis* at Galveston Bay, Texas. As an adult, it was recorded by Shuler (1938), as *Tentacularia pseudodera*, from *Hypoprion brevirostris* in Florida waters.

Family Lacistorhynchidae Guiart, 1927, emended Dollfus, 1935

DESCRIPTION

Of the order Trypanorhyncha. With hooks on the tentacles differing from surface to surface. Neck swollen at the level of the bulbs. Ripe segments elongated, sometimes cylindrical; living a long time after detachment from the body and so sometimes misidentified as cestodarians (genus *Wageneria*). Larva short-tailed.

In his family, Guiart placed two genera:

1. *Lacistorhynchus* Pintner, 1913, emended Guiart, 1927. With two bilobed bothridia. Bulbs short. A supplemental swelling behind the holdfast. Unsegmented region of the holdfast very long. Segments very numerous. Genotype, *gracilis* Diesing, 1863 *nec.* Rudolphi, 1819, in *Galeus canis.*

2. *Grillotia* Guiart, 1927. With four bothridia. Bulbs elongated. No swelling behind the holdfast. Nonsegmented region of the holdfast short. Genotype, *erinaceus* Beneden, 1858.

Later (1935b) Guiart redefined the family thus: Body not exceeding 15 cm. in length. In general, two bothridia almost circular. Neck elongated, slightly swollen in the region of the bulbs. Bulbs also elongated, 5–7 times longer than wide. Tentacles fairly long and slender, with three kinds of hooks: on one face, the hooks strong and curved; on the other face, the hooks long and straight; between the two, small hooks. Neck of variable length. Body always comprising a large number of segments. Genital apertures lateral, irregularly alternating, and in the posterior halves of the segment margins. Ripe segments leaving the body early and continuing to increase in development (hyperapolytic). Commonly showing longitudinal parallel ridges like those on certain fruits or on *Beroe* (Ctenophora). Larva stocky (*Lacistorhynchus*) or egg-shaped (*Grillotia*), with a cephalic invagination at one end. Principal genera: *Lacistorhynchus, Diesingella*, and *Grillotia.*

Dollfus (1942), with some doubt, retained *Lacistorhynchus* and *Grillotia* within the one family despite the great differences in tentacle armature, *Lacistorhynchus* having a chainette of the callitetrarhynchid type, widely different from the condition in *Grillotia.* The two genera, however, he made type genera of separate subfamilies, Lacistorhynchinae and Grillotiinae. While reluctant to pronounce an opinion upon the status of *Diesingella,* he suggested it might be placed within Eutetrarhynchinae.

Subfamily Lacistorhynchinae Joyeux and Baer, 1934, emended Dollfus, 1942

DESCRIPTION

Of the order Trypanorhyncha. Small, weak forms with two bothridia, each notched posteriorly. Vaginal region longer than bothridial region. Bulbosal region equal to, or a little longer than, bothridial region. Retractor muscles weak, inserted slightly in front of middle of bulb length. Tentacles when completely invaginated far from reaching the bulbs. Holdfast never craspedote, whether of the plerocercus or of the adult. Postbulbosal region formed by union of two parts, the anterior one belonging to body of holdfast, the posterior one generally larger, often globular, constituted by growth zone of holdfast and homologous with appendix of plerocercus. Tentacle armature comprising a basal region, slightly swollen, carrying a group of large billhook-shaped hooks (*serpe à bec*) sharply recurved, but without any areas of microhooks. Above this, the tentacle carries obliquely transverse rows of hooks arranged in ascending half-turns, those of one face alternating with those of the other face, each half-turn comprising eight hooks, the largest of which is nearest to the mid-line of the internal surface. At the end of each half-turn is a ninth hook. These ninth hooks are all in one line, recalling the arrangement called a chainette. The elements of this chainette are not particularly close to one another, and all their points have the same posterior direction. All the hooks are hollow. Cuticle of holdfast and body with small spines which in places become scales or small papillae.

Body completely noncraspedote; hyperapolytic or euapolytic; very long and threadlike when fully extended; segments rapidly becoming longer than wide. Genital apertures always behind the middle of the segment margins, each in a fairly deep notch limited anteriorly and posteriorly by a sphincter muscle (*ventouse*). Eggs regularly ovoid in shape, without polar filaments, set free before becoming embryonated. Procercus larva occurring encysted in various fishes. The blastocyst with a posterior prolongation of variable length. The external cyst (host reaction cyst) typically swollen anteriorly, with a cylindrical prolongation posteriorly. With one genus, *Lacistorhynchus* Pintner, 1913.

In their subfamily, Joyeux and Baer (1934a) placed five genera: *Callitetrarhynchus* Pintner, 1931; *Grillotia* Guiart, 1927; *Lacistorhynchus* Pintner, 1913; *Oncomegas* Dollfus, 1929; and *Otobothrium* Linton, 1890. They placed this subfamily, with Eutetrarhynchinae Joyeux and Baer, 1934 (in which they brought together *Christianella* Guiart, 1931; *Diesingella* Guiart, 1931; *Eutetrarhynchus* Pintner, 1913; and *Tetrarhynchobothrium* Diesing, 1850), in the family Eutetrarhynchidae Guiart, 1927. Here we shall follow Dollfus (1942) in rejecting this conception of a family containing both poeciloacanthous and heteroacanthous forms.

Lacistorhynchus Pintner, 1913

With the characters of Lacistorhynchinae. Tentacles each with a simple chainette of the callitetrarhynchid type; never with groups of small interpolated hooks between the obliquely transverse consecutive rows of principal hooks. Genotype and only known species, *tenuis* Beneden, 1858 (Figure 169).

The larva of this form, by reason of the characteristic shape of its cyst and its common occurrence in edible fishes of European waters, has long been known to helminthologists from Deslongchamps (1824) to the present day. The adult was recorded and described for the first time by Beneden (1858–1861) who found it in *Galeus canis* at Ostend, Belgium. Later records and descriptions were made by many European observers (see Dollfus, 1942). It was repeatedly recorded in North American Atlantic waters by Linton as a plerocercus encysted in teleosteans and in selachians, and, as an adult, in *Squalus acanthias, Mustelus canis,* and *Vulpecula marina.*

Subfamily Grillotiinae Dollfus, 1942

DESCRIPTION

Of the order Trypanorhyncha. With the holdfast acraspedote, the bothridia patelliform, each slightly indented posteriorly. Vaginal region always longer than the bothridial region. Tentacles heteroacanthous, armed with obliquely transverse half-turns of principal hooks, 4–6 hooks in each half-turn, increasing gradually in size from internal to external surfaces. No hooks along the middle line of the internal surface. Midline of external surface with a longitudinal band of small hooks. Between each two consecutive principal rows an interpolating group of small hooks confluent with the longitudinal band of the external surface. Base of each tentacle armed or not, according to species, with a special armature of a field of small hooks on the external surface extending more or less over the bothridial and antibothridial surfaces. Tentacle sheaths very sinuous but not regularly corkscrewlike. Bulbosal region shorter than vaginal region. Retractor muscles inserted within bulbar cavities. Postbulbosal region short.

Body euapolytic, with unsegmented neck, short or lacking, completely noncraspedote or craspedote according to species; segments becoming longer than wide. Genital apertures at the beginning of the last thirds or last fourths of the segment margins. Yolk glands sometimes within, sometimes outside, the longitudinal muscles. Eggs oval or ellipsoidal, without or with a short polar filament, according to species. Plerocercus encysted in peritoneum of body cavity or in muscles of various fishes, principally teleosteans. Reaction capsule oval or pyriform, stalked or not, but never with anterior swelling and tail. One genus, *Grillotia* Guiart, 1927.

Grillotia Guiart, 1927 (=*Heterotetrarhynchus* Pintner, 1929)

With the characters of Grillotiinae. A very homogeneous genus whose species are difficult to distinguish. Genotype, *erinaceus* Beneden, 1858 (Figure 170).

Dollfus (1942) recognized the following species:

KEY TO SPECIES

1. More than eight hooks per row .... *paralica*
   Fewer than eight hooks per row 2
2. Basal armature present 3
   Basal armature lacking 4
3. Basal armature of small hooks on the external face and large hooks on the internal face; four hooks per principal row; insertion of retractor muscles posterior .... *erinaceus*
   Basal armature reduced, with small hooks on the external face but no large hooks on the internal face; four hooks per principal row; insertion of retractor muscles posterior .... *musculara*
4. Six hooks per principal row; insertion of retractor muscles median or submedian .... *Kahl's species*
   Six hooks per principal row; insertion of retractor muscles anterior .... *heptanchi*

To this list may be added *acanthoscolex* Rees, 1944; *smaris-gora* (Wagener, 1854), added to the genus by Dollfus (1946); and *pastinacae* Dollfus, 1946, placed by its author as the type species of a subgenus *Progrillotia.*

The genotype is a common type of parasite in fishes of Atlantic waters, and the literature about it is extensive. It was the subject of a monographic study by Johnstone (1912). Its life cycle has been described by Ruszkowski (1932c). It was recorded, both as larva and as adult (as *Rhynchobothrium imparispine*), by Linton on several occasions from hosts in Massachusetts coastal waters. The adult is apparently commoner in skates and rays than in dogfishes and sharks (see Wardle, 1932a).

The species *perelica* Shuler, 1938 was recorded as an adult from *Hypoprion brevirostris* in Florida waters; *musculara* Hart, 1936 was recorded (as *Tentacularia musculara*) in *Hexanchus griseus* in Puget Sound; and Kahl's species (*Grillotia sp.* Kahl, 1937) was an unnamed plerocercus encysted in the muscles of *Sebastodes marinus* in Norwegian waters. The species *heptanchi* Vaullegeard, 1899 was established (as *Tetrarhynchus heptanchi*) for a form which had been formerly described by various authors under such names as *Bothriocephalus corollatus, Tetrarhynchus corollatus,* and *Rhynchobothrium erinaceus.* It appears to be a parasite typically of seven- and six-gilled sharks (*Heptanchus, Hexanchus*). It was recorded by Wardle (1933) as *Grillotia erinaceus* from *Hexanchus caurinus* in British Columbian waters; and as *Tentacularia megabothridia* by Hart (1936a) in *Hexanchus griseus* from Puget Sound. Rees (1944) has recorded a species, *acanthoscolex*, in *Hexanchus griseus* in British waters.

Family GYMNORHYNCHIDAE Dollfus, 1935 (=VAULLEGEARDIDAE Guiart, 1927; FLORICIPITIDAE Dollfus, 1929)

DESCRIPTION

Of the order Trypanorhyncha. With the holdfast noncraspedote. Two pairs of bothridia whose posterior and outer margins are free of the holdfast, the anterior margins fusing with it. Bothridial region always a little shorter than the vaginal region. Bulbosal region longer than bothridial region. Bulbs more than three times as long as wide. Postbulbosal region becoming very long after breaking from blastocyst, in the form of an appendix.

Tentacles poeciloacanthous, naked at their bases; above the naked portion, the armature shows on the internal surface a group of long, more or less falciform hooks; above these, the hooks are arranged in obliquely transverse rows, ascending, each forming a half-turn of the tentacle; the half-turns alternate from one face to the other; each begins close to the middle line of the internal surface and ends close to the middle line of the external surface. The two first hooks of each row are macrohooks, shaped like rose thorns, their bases having an anterior and a posterior projection; the following hooks are long and narrow, less robust, with reduced bases. The middle line of the external surface carries either a double chainette (subgenus *Gymnorhynchus*) or a longitudinal band of very small hooks (subgenus *Molicola*). There are never any small hooks interpolated between the oblique rows.

Plerocercus with large blastocyst, globular, ellipsoidal, or pear-shaped, with a very long tail. Holdfast still in the blastocyst, partly retracted, partly invaginated. Encysted in pelagic teleostean fishes. Adult in large selachians. One genus, *Gymnorhynchus* Rudolphi, 1819 with two subgenera, *Gymnorhynchus* – with genotype *gigas* Cuvier, 1817 – and *Molicola* – with genotype *horridus* Goodsir, 1841.

The species *gigas* Cuvier, 1817, with a double chainette, is common as a plerocercus in the muscles of *Brama rayi*, or more rarely, in *Xiphias gladius*. It is a remarkable form with a relatively enormous blastocyst from which the holdfast may be fully extended; it is not known as an adult and has never been recorded in American waters (Figure 172).

The species *horridus* Goodsir, 1841 (established as *Molicola horridus* by Dollfus, 1935) is a fairly common parasite of *Mola mola* and has been recorded as such in American waters by Linton (as *Tetrarhynchus elongatus*) on several occasions. It has not been recorded as an adult in American waters unless Linton's (1924a) "*Rhynchobothrium incinatum*" from *Vulpecula marina* in Massachusetts waters was such.

Family Pterobothriidae Pintner, 1931

DESCRIPTION

Of the order Trypanorhyncha. With four bothridia each on a short, mobile stalk, so that the four appear crosswise in front of the apex of the subcylindrical holdfast. The bothridia move as pairs, outward or inward, i.e., toward the long axis of the body; the stalks of one or the other face united by a basal membrane. Body of holdfast subcylindrical, narrower than bothridial region, swollen slightly in vicinity of bulbs. Tentacles poeciloacanthous, of three different types: in the first and second types, there is no chainette on the external surface but a longitudinal band of small hooks; in the first type, the shape of the principal hooks is com-

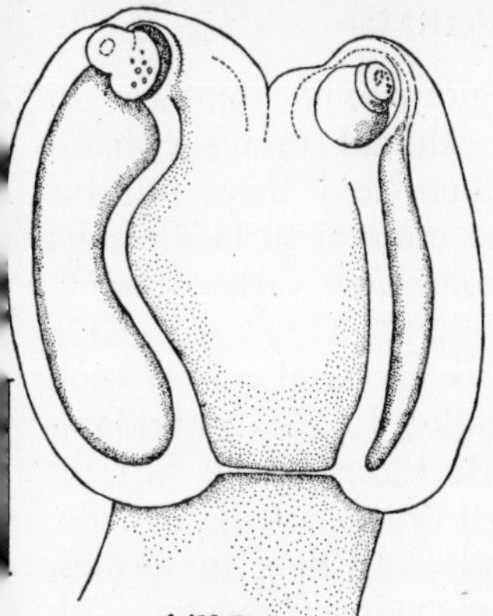

172

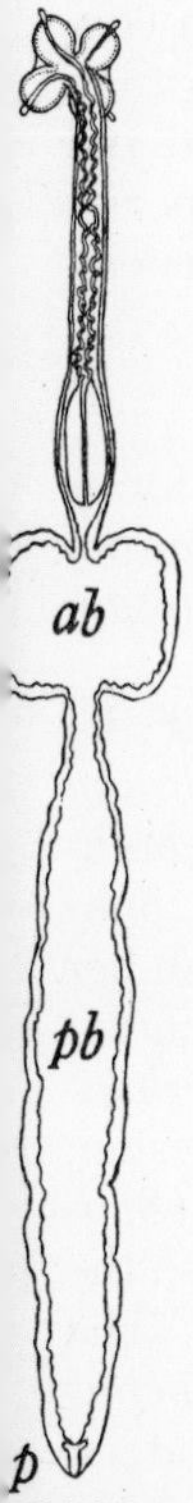

173

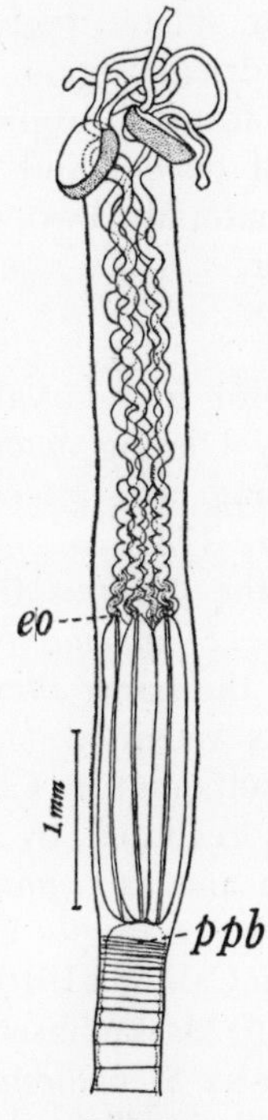

174

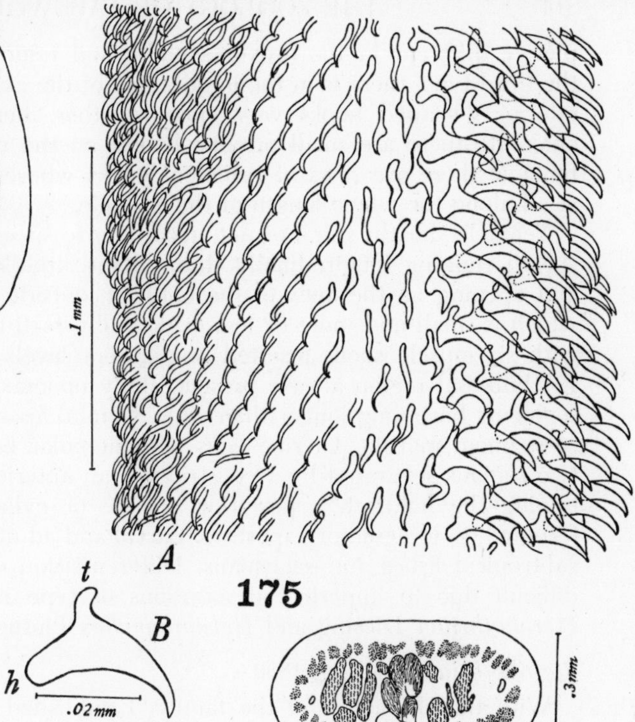

175

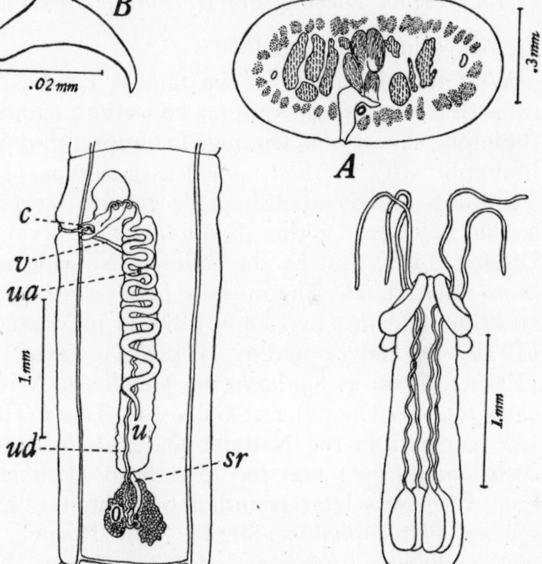

176

IG. 172. *Gymnorhynchus gigas*, holdfast. After Dollfus, 1942. FIG. 173. *Pterobothrium* ierocercus showing anterior region of blastocyst (*ab*), posterior region of same (*pb*), and rminal osmoregulatory aperture (*tp*). After Dollfus, 1942. FIG. 174. *Eutetrarhynchus lineaus*, holdfast. After Dollfus, 1942. FIG. 175. *Eutetrarhynchus ruficollis*. After Dollfus, 1942. Armature of tentacle, bothridial face. B. Large tentacle hook showing toe (*t*), heel (*h*), nd point. FIG. 176. *Gilquinia squali*. After Hart, 1936a. A. Cross section through uterine perture. B. Segment. C. Holdfast. *c*, cirrus; *eo*, enigmatic prebulbar organ; *o*, ovary; *ppb*, pars postbulbosa; *sr*, seminal receptacle; *u*, uterus; *ua*, uterine aperture; *ud*, uterine duct; *v*, vagina.

pletely different in the proximal and distal regions of the tentacle; in the third type, there is in the middle line of the external surface a chainette of V-shaped hooks very close together; here and there on this chainette there are small satellite hooks; on the internal surface of the tentacle there are rows of principal hooks whose shape varies scarcely at all along the whole length of the tentacle.

Tentacle sheaths spiral or not, according to species; distal part of each sheath running longitudinally through the middle of each bothridium and opening on the apex of the holdfast, outside the adherent surface, which is small and more or less oval. Bulbs 4–10 times as long as wide, with six muscle shells inserted at different levels according to species. Postbulbosal region always present. Body noncraspedote, apolytic, with segments becoming longer than wide. Genital apertures in posterior half of segment margin. Uterine eggs without polar filaments. Blastocyst of two regions separated by a constriction, an anterior, dilated region containing the holdfast, a posterior, saclike or cylindrical region with a terminal osmoregulatory aperture. Larval and adult forms in tropical and subtropical fishes and selachians. Differentiation of genera and species difficult due to imperfect descriptions of type material. Two genera, *Pterobothrium* Diesing and *Halsiorhynchus* Pintner.

Pterobothrium Diesing, 1850

With the characters of the family. Established for four larval forms from Brazilian fishes, Natterer collection, named by Diesing *macrourum* Rudolphi, *crassicolle* Diesing, *heteracanthum* Diesing, and *interruptum* Rudolphi, with the first named as genotype (Figure 173).

Diesing (1855) abolished his generic term on the grounds that the larvae belonged within *Synbothrium* Diesing (= *Syndesmobothrium* Diesing, 1855), but by the Rules of Nomenclature the name *Pterobothrium* must stand. The species *heteracanthum* was recorded (as *Synbothrium filicolle*) by Linton (1897a) in Massachusetts and by Chandler (1935a) in Galveston Bay, Texas. The adult was recorded by Linton (1905a), again as *Synbothrium filicolle*, in Virginia and as *Gymnorhynchus gigas* by Chandler at Galveston, Texas. The species *fragile* Diesing, 1850 came from the Natterer material; *lintoni* MacCallum, 1916 (*Synbothrium lintoni*) was recorded from *Dasybatis* in Massachusetts; the same form was later recorded by Linton (1924a) as *S. malleum.* The species *platycephalum* Shipley and Hornell, 1906 (= *Tetrarhynchus platycephalus*) was recorded from *Trygon walga* in Ceylon waters; *tangoli* MacCallum, 1921 (= *Rhynchobothrium tangoli*) was found encysted in the peritoneum of a scombriform fish in Borneo waters; *minimum* Linstow, 1904 occurs in dasybatid selachians in India waters.

Halsiorhynchus Pintner, 1913

With the characters of the family. Tentacle hook arrangement of the third type. One species, *macrocephalus* Shipley and Hornell, 1906, known only as an adult from three species of selachians in Ceylon waters.

Family Eutetrarhynchidae Guiart, 1927, emended Dollfus, 1942

DESCRIPTION

Of the order Trypanorhyncha. With two bothridia each more or less patelliform. Posterior bothridial margins free and strongly notched even to giving the appearance of four bothridia. Always without sensorial fossettes. Tentacles heteroacanthous. Bulbs at least three times as long as wide. Holdfast acraspedote. Testes not extending between ovary and posterior border of segment. Plerocercus in decapod Crustacea or in lamellibranch Mollusca. One subfamily, Eutetrarhynchinae, with four genera – *Eutetrarhynchus* Pintner, 1913; *Christianella* Guiart, 1931; *Prochristianella* Dollfus, 1946; and *Parachristianella* Dollfus, 1946.

Joyeux and Baer established a second subfamily, Lacistorhynchinae, but, as previously mentioned, such a union of heteroacanthous and poeciloacanthous forms within the one family was rejected by Dollfus (1942), whose arrangement we follow.

Eutetrarhynchus Pintner, 1913

With the characters of the family. Established for a form, *ruficollis* Eysenhardt, 1829, common in *Mustelus spp.* in European, Atlantic, and Mediterranean waters. Dollfus recognized four species:

1. With bulbs not more than half total length of holdfast 2
   With bulbs always more than half total length of holdfast 3
2. Bulbs a little more than one-quarter of the holdfast length; segments becoming more than three times as long as wide .... *lineatus*
   Bulbs a little less than half the holdfast length .... *carayoni*
3. Segments becoming three times or less longer than wide ..... *leucomelanus*
   Segments becoming only as long as wide .... *ruficollis*

Eutetrarhynchus ruficollis (Figure 175) is a common trypanorhynchan in selachians of European waters, its larval stage occurring in decapod Crustacea; the literature about it is extensive and reference should be made to Dollfus (1942). *Eutetrarhynchus lineatus* Linton, 1909 (Figure 174) was summarily described from immature material from *Ginglystoma cirratum* at Dry Tortugas, Florida and is also mentioned, without description, by Shuler (1938), who transferred it to the genus *Tentacularia* to which it obviously does not belong. *Eutetrarhynchus carayoni* Dollfus, 1942 is known only from a plerocercus in *Clibanarius misanthropus,* Arcachon, France. *Eutetrarhynchus leucomelanus* Shipley and Hornell, 1906 was recorded (as *Tentacularia leucomelana*) from *Dasybatis sephen, Rhynchobatis djeddensis,* and *Dasybatis kuhli,* Ceylon waters.

Christianella Guiart, 1931 (= *Armandia* Guiart, 1927)

Small-sized forms. Two bothridia, each elongated, sometimes circular in outline, with posterior borders strongly notched so as to give each bothridium the appearance of being double. Tentacles very long, heteroacanthous, with similar hooks arranged in spiral half-turns, not in continuous rows, each starting obliquely from the middle line of the internal surface. Genotype, *minuta* Beneden, 1849.

The genotype was established (as *Rhynchobothrium minutum*) for an adult in *Squatina sp.* in Belgian waters. Another species, *trygon-brucco* Wagener, 1854 (= *Tetrarhynchus trygon-brucco* Wagener, 1854), from *Trygon brucco* in Mediterranean waters is recognized by Dollfus.

Prochristianella Dollfus, 1946

Heteracantha typica with two bothridia, long bulbs, very long and slender tentacles with basal enlargement armed with special hooks; metabasal armature consisting chiefly or entirely of small falciform or spiniform hooks. In the type species, each obliquely ascending row in the proximal region of the metabasal armature begins with small hooks; the first hooks, those nearest to the middle of the internal face, are small and short; the following ones, on the bothridial and antibothridial faces, are much longer; and the last ones, on the internal face, are again short and small. In the distal direction the armature changes gradually; the ascending rows become less oblique, the number of hooks diminishing in each half-turn, the hooks of the series 1(1′), 2(2′) becoming greater, like those at the end of the half-turn toward the middle of the external face. In the second species, the shape of the hooks is homogeneous along the whole length of the metabasal armature. Genotype, *trygonicola* Dollfus, 1946 from gut of *Trygon pastinaca*, Concarneau. A second species may be represented by *Rhynchobothrium tenuispine* Linton, 1890 in *Trygon centroura*, Massachusetts waters.

Parachristianella Dollfus, 1946

Heteracantha typica with two bothridia and heteromorphic armature. In the proximal metabasal armature each obliquely ascending row of hooks starts from the middle of the internal face as a large triangular hook with a recurved point; the second hook has its insertion base lower but is again a large hook; the following hooks diminish gradually in size over the surface of the tentacle and the last ones of each half-turn, on the external face of the tentacle, are small. Genotype, *trygonis* Dollfus, 1946 from *Trygon pastinaca*, Concarneau.

Family Gilquiniidae Dollfus, 1942

DESCRIPTION

Of the order Trypanorhyncha. With four well-separated, ear-shaped or oval-patelliform bothridia whose inner margins are fused with the holdfast; the two on the dorsal face and the two on the ventral face forming pairs occupying the total width of those faces. Holdfast acraspedote, delimited from the body by a constriction. Body acraspedote, apolytic or anapolytic, with fewer than sixty segments. Longitudinal muscles greatly reduced. Copulatory apparatus in cirrus pouch receiving at the proximal end from the dorsal side a small seminal vesicle and continued into the interior of the segment as a large contractile accessory bladder. Testes reaching to the posterior border of the segment.

Ovary two-winged. Uterus not reaching anteriorly beyond the level of the accessory bladder. Uterine apertures not preformed. Two subfamilies, Gilquiniinae and Aporhynchinae, the former with its rhyncheal apparatus complete, the latter with the rhyncheal apparatus absent or vestigial; each with one genus only.

Gilquinia Guiart, 1927

With the characters of Gilquiniinae. Genotype, *squali* Fabricius, 1794 (Figure 176).

The genotype is common in *Squalus acanthias* in Atlantic and Mediterranean waters, and the literature concerning it is extensive. It was recorded by Wardle (1932a) in *Squalus sucklii* in British Columbian waters and by Hart and Guberlet (1936b), as *Tetrarhynchus anteropus*, in the same host species in Puget Sound. The plerocercus was recorded by Ekbaum (1932) in *Citharichthys stigmaeus* in British Columbian waters. The normal larval host, however, is probably crustacean. Another species, *nannocephala* Pintner, 1930 (= *Tetrarhynchobothrium nannocephalum*) from the Sixten Bock Expedition material, is recognized by Dollfus.

Aporhynchus Nybelin, 1918

With the characters of Aporhynchinae. Genotype, *norvegicum* Olsson, 1868.

Established (as *Tetrabothrium norvegicum*) from adult material in *Etmopterus spinax* in Norwegian and Portuguese waters, the form was rediscovered by Loennberg (1890b) and redescribed by Nybelin (1918b). Apart from the vestigial rhyncheal apparatus, it differs little from *Gilquinia*. The peculiar holdfast has been described in detail by Rees (1941b).

Family Otobothriidae Dollfus, 1942

DESCRIPTION

Of the order Trypanorhyncha. With two bothridia, each patelliform, subcircular or a little longer than wide, with or without posterior notches; somewhat inclined toward each other roofwise. On the external and posterior free margins a bourrelet, sometimes weak and of variable width. In the thickness of the bourrelet, there occur symmetrically on each face two ciliated depressions (retractile organs). Stalk of holdfast relatively short, cylindrical or subcylindrical. Tentacles shorter than sheaths. Armature heteroacanthous, rows of large hooks ascending obliquely from the middle line of the internal face and alternating with one another; more numerous rows of small hooks alternating, beginning from the middle line of the external face; never any chainette. Body acraspedote, apolytic. Holdfast of plerocercus with appendix short and oval, according to genus, with very long, ribbonlike prolongation. Three genera: *Otobothrium, Diplootobothrium*, and *Poecilancistrium*.

Otobothrium Linton, 1890

Established for *Otobothrium crenacolle*, recorded as a larva by Linton in a wide range of fishes in Massachusetts waters and as an adult in *Carcharinus obscurus, Carcharinus platyodon, Scoliodon terrae-novae,* and *Sphyraena zygaena* at Beaufort, North Carolina, and Woods Hole, Massachusetts (Figure 177). Dollfus recognized two subgenera:

1. *Otobothrium.* With short bulbs; retractor muscles inserted at the entrance to the bulbs; armature comprising more than one row of small hooks for each row of large hooks. With the species *crenacolle* Linton; *curtum* Linton, 1909; *pronosomum* Stossich, 1900; *balli* Southwell, 1929; *insigne* Linton, 1903; *penetrans* Linton, 1907.

2. *Pseudotobothrium.* With long bulbs, 5–8 times as long as wide; retractor muscles inserted toward the anterior quarters of the bulb cavities; armature with as many rows of small hooks as of large hooks. With the species *magnum* Southwell, 1924; *linstowi* Southwell, 1912; *dipsacum* Linton, 1897.

Diplootobothrium Chandler, 1942

With long bulbs, 7–8 times as long as wide. Retractor muscles inserted near the upper ends of the bulbs. Hooks arranged in diagonal rows of 9 or 10 large, recurved hooks shaped like a rose thorn, reaching about two-thirds to three-fourths the distance around the tentacle, the intervening area being occupied by small hooks more or less irregularly arranged. Segments with double genitalia. Genotype, *springeri* Chandler, 1942, adult in *Platysqualus tudes,* Florida waters. The larval stage may be *Otobothrium robustum,* established by Chandler (1935b) for larval material from Galveston Bay, Texas (Figure 178).

Poecilancistrium Dollfus, 1930

Established for an encysted larval stage in the muscles of tropical and subtropical teleostean fishes. Encysted capsule and blastocyst showing an anterior swollen region and a very long tail. Genotype, *caryophyllum* Diesing, 1850 (Figure 179). In the same genus Dollfus would place *robustum* Chandler, 1935 from *Cynoscion nebulosus,* Galveston Bay, Texas (but see above); *gangeticum* Shipley and Hornell, 1906; and *ilisha* Southwell and Prashad, 1918.

Within the family Otobothriidae, Dollfus (1942) was inclined to place a form, *Bombicirhynchus sphyraenaicus* Pintner, 1930, established for a single encysted plerocercus in the abdominal cavity of *Sphyraena commersoni* in Ceylon waters. No sensorial fossettes were observed, but in other features the form seems to be otobothriid.

Incertae sedis

1. The group *microbothrium-pillersi.* In this group Dollfus places (*a*) *Rhynchobothrium sp.* of Southwell, 1912 based on larvae encysted in four teleostean species in Ceylon waters; (*b*) *Tentacularia pillersi* Southwell, 1929 based on numerous cysts round the vertebral column of *Cossyphus axillaris* (labrid fish) in Indian waters; (*c*) *Rhynchobothrium microbothrium* MacCallum, 1917 encysted in the thyroid gland of *Neomaenis analis* (lutianid fish), New York Aquarium; (*d*) *Tetrarhynchus*

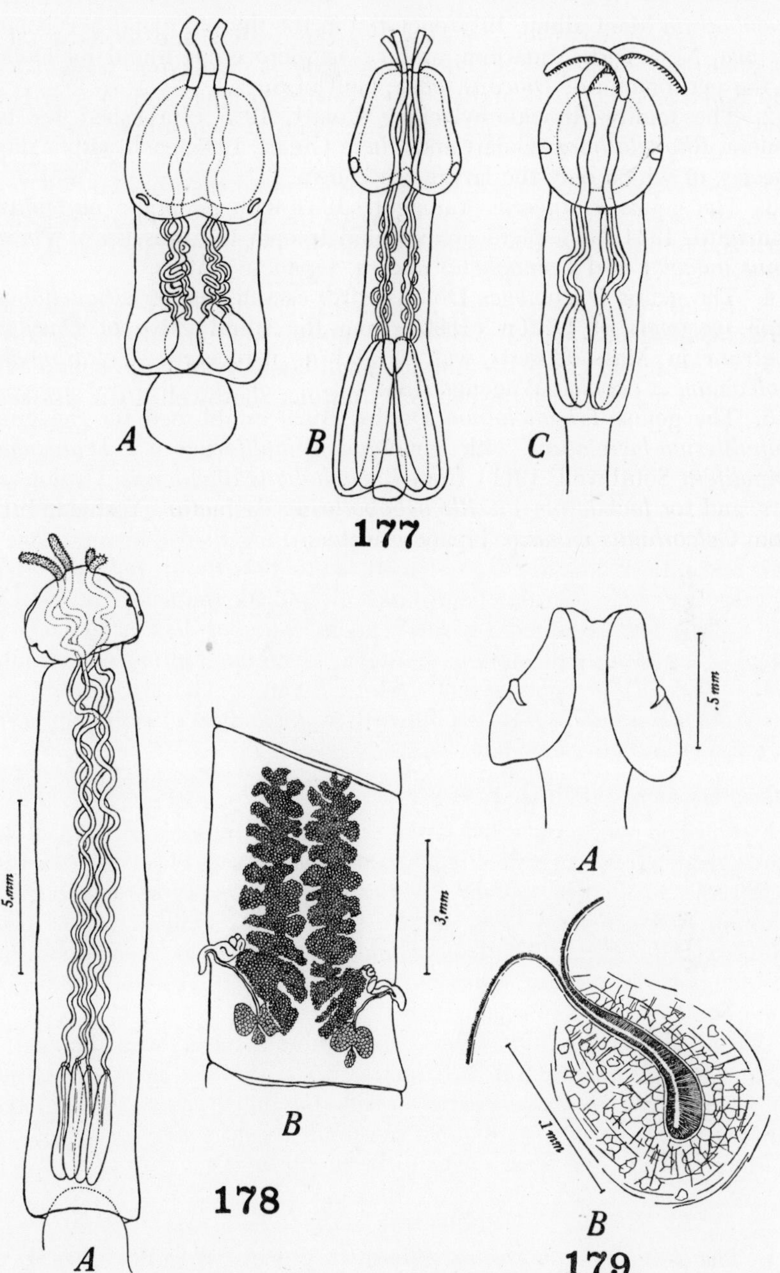

FIG. 177. *Otobothrium*, holdfasts. After Dollfus, 1942. A. *Otobothrium* type. B. *Pseudotobothrium* type. C. *Poecilancistrium* type. FIG. 178. *Diplootobothrium springeri*. After Chandler, 1942b. A. Holdfast. B. Ripe segment, yolk glands omitted. FIG. 179. *Poecilancistrium caryophyllum*. After Pintner, 1934a. A. Holdfast with retractile organs. B. Magnified retractile organ.

brevibothria MacCallum, 1917 encysted in the thyroid gland of *Neomaenis aya*, New York Aquarium; and (*e*) a plerocercus found by Dollfus in the peritoneum of *Diacops sebae*, Gulf of Suez.

2. The family Rhopalothylacidae Guiart, 1935 established for two genera, *Rhopalothyrax* Guiart and *Clujia* Guiart, 1935, each with a single species, of which only the larvae are known.

3. The genus *Pintnerella* Yamaguti, 1934 with genotype *musculicola* Yamaguti, 1934 for a plerocercus found free in the muscles of *Pagrosomus unicolor* and *Epinephelus akaara*, Japanese waters.

4. The genus *Oncomegas* Dollfus, 1929 established for *Rhynchobothrium wageneri* of Linton (1890) from the spiral valve of *Dasybatis centrura* in Massachusetts waters, and a plerocercus, *Tetrarhynchus scolecinum* = *cepolae* Wagener, 1854.

5. The genus *Trigonolobum* Dollfus, 1929 established for the group *spinuliferum-laciniatum* with genotype *spinuliferum* (= *Tentacularia spinulifera* Southwell, 1911) from *Rhynchobatis djeddensis*, Ceylon waters, and for *laciniatum* (= *Rhynchobothrium lacinatum* Yoshida, 1917) from *Galeorhinus manazo*, Japanese waters.

Order CYCLOPHYLLIDEA

DESCRIPTION

Of the class Cestoda. Tapeworms ranging in length from a few millimeters to thirty meters or more. Holdfast varying in detail but provided typically with four suckers, large and prominent. Apical end commonly projecting as a domelike or fingerlike rostellum which may or may not be armed with hooks or spines and may or may not be withdrawable within the holdfast. Body segmentation usually well marked, with the new segments originating from a growth zone between the holdfast and the body. Segments commonly much wider than long, with the posterior borders overlapping the anterior borders of the following segments, leaving the body when gravid. Genital apertures on one or both margins. Testes in the medullary parenchyma. Ovary a fan of lobes, or a dumbbell of two spherical lobes. Yolk gland typically single, compact, postovarian, in the medulla. Gravid uterus varying in shape between genera: a median tube with lateral branches; or a transverse tube; or a tubular network; sometimes breaking down into compartments (egg capsules); sometimes replaced entirely by parenchymatous structures (parenchymatous capsules, pouches, or organs). Uterine apertures lacking, the eggs escaping by marginal splitting of the segments or by general disintegration of the gravid segments. Eggs not operculated. Larva commonly some type of bladder worm in a vertebrate intermediate host, or a cysticercoid in an arthropod host; or, if solid, with the holdfast not withdrawn within the body. Adults parasitic in amphibians (though rarely), in reptiles, birds, and mammals.

HISTORY

The origin of the term "Cyclophyllidea" is disputed. Meggitt (1924) gave the credit to Carus, although it does not appear as a name for any of the five groups of tapeworms proposed by that writer in 1863. Sprehn (1932) ascribed the term to Beneden, although again it does not appear in that writer's classification of 1850. It was definitely used by Braun (1894–1900) to indicate an order synonymous with Zwicke's Taenioidea of 1841, and it has been used by most later writers on tapeworms. It was rejected, however, by Poche (1926), who substituted the term "Taeniidea"; by Pintner (1926), who placed cyclophyllidean forms within a single family, Taeniidae; and by Southwell (1930), who preferred to place them within a superfamily, Taenioidea, of the order Eucestoda.

Those tapeworms, now regarded as cyclophyllidean, which were recorded during the period 1750–1850 were placed in that ragbag of miscellaneous forms, the genus *Taenia* of Linnaeus, 1758 (= *Halysis* and *Alyselminthus* of Zeder, 1800). The gradual steps in the breakdown of this unwieldy group are outlined below.

1845. Dujardin pointed out that the genus *Taenia* included seven different types, distinguished by features of the holdfast and by the position of the genital apertures; but to those types he assigned no subgeneric names.

1858. Weinland separated from *Taenia* the genera *Hymenolepis* and *Dilepis. Hymenolepis* was established for some fragmentary material from an infant in Boston, North America, for which—upon the basis of a detailed description of the external features and the reproductive system, in which Weinland stressed the occurrence of three transparent membranes around the embryo, the unilateral distribution of the genital apertures, and the transverse, saclike uterus—the generic and specific terminology *Hymenolepis flavopunctata* was suggested.

Since 1888, when Grassi showed that Weinland's form was synonymous with Rudolphi's *Taenia diminuta*, the accepted name for this well-known parasite of humans has been *Hymenolepis diminuta.* The term *Hymenolepis* refers to the transparent nature of the embryonic membranes. Weinland also established two subgenera of *Hymenolepis*—*Lepidotrias*, for a form occurring in rats and now usually known as *Hymenolepis fraterna*, and *Dilepis*, for a form in passeriform birds, now commonly called *Dilepis undula.*

To the current assemblage of taeniid forms, Weinland gave the family name of Taeniodea—changed by Ludwig (1886) to Taeniidae—and recognized two subfamilies, Sclerolepidota—corresponding to the present-day Taeniidae—and Malacolepidota, in which he placed *Hymenolepis, Dilepis, Alyselminthus* of Zeder (= *Dipylidium caninum*), and *Proteocephalus.* Recognition of Weinland's genera came slowly. As late as 1873, Joseph Leidy was still using the generic name *Taenia* for hymenolepid forms.

1885–88. Zschokke, however, recognized Weinland's *Hymenolepis* and placed within it fourteen species of tapeworms from mammals.

1891. R. Blanchard also recognized the genus and published a detailed description of *Hymenolepis diminuta.* Blanchard further suggested that a large group of taeniid species in herbivorous mammals, which lack completely either rostellum or holdfast hooks or spines, should be separated as a subfamily (of Ludwig's Taeniidae) under the term Anoplocephalinae, with three genera—*Anoplocephala, Bertia*, and *Moniezia.*

1892. Railliet proposed to distribute the hymenolepid forms of birds between two genera, *Drepanidotaenia* and *Dicranotaenia.*

1896. Stiles proposed the subfamily term "Dipylidiinae" for Weinland's Malacolepidota.

1899. Ariola, in a revised classification of tapeworms, distinguished among Cotylina—a group corresponding to the present Cyclophyllidea—two tribes: Mesoporinae, with genital apertures on one flat surface, comprising the present family Mesocestoididae; and Pleuroporinae, with genital apertures on one margin, comprising the families (Ariola's terms) Ichthyotaeniidae, Anoplotaeniidae, Hymenolepidae, Taeniidae, and Echinocotylidae. Unfortunately Ariola failed to indicate the genera he proposed for each tribe.

By the beginning of the present century, a mass of information concerning the internal features of taeniid tapeworms had accumulated, and it became possible to differentiate more genera than could previously be separated on external features alone.

1894–1900. The new knowledge was reflected in the scheme of tapeworm classification proposed by Braun for Bronn's *Klassen und Ordnungen des Thierreichs.* Placing all those tapeworms with a four-suckered holdfast and a single, compact yolk gland into a single family Taeniidae, Braun recognized the variety of internal structure prevalent among them by establishing ten subfamilies. Thus, Blanchard's genera with spiny sucker margins were given subfamily rank as Davaineinae. The hymenolepidid forms were placed within a subfamily Dipylidiinae. A number of forms which lack vaginal apertures were separated as Acoleinae, a term suggested by Fuhrmann; and so forth.

1906. Greater weight was given to structural variation among taeniid tapeworms, however, by Stiles, who suggested the recognition of these forms as a superfamily, Taenioidea, and the elevation to family rank of Braun's subfamilies, with the termination *-idae* replacing *-inae.*

1907–8. One of the most stimulating contributions to an understanding of cyclophyllidean relationships was Fuhrmann's essay—*Die Systematik der Ordnung der Cyclophyllidea* (1907a), followed by the scarcely less important *Die Cestoden der Vögel* (1908c). Bringing to the analysis of taeniid tapeworms a wealth of new data, Fuhrmann raised Blanchard's Anoplocephalinae to family rank, and added to it eleven genera. The hymenolepid forms with vaginal pores were assigned to the families Acoleinidae and Amabilinidae. The other hymenolepids were distributed among three families—Dilepinidae, Hymenolepinidae, and Fimbriariidae. Upon the suggestion of Railliet and Henry (1909), the grammatically preferable terms "Hymenolepididae" and "Dilepididae" were adopted later by Fuhrmann, and the terms "Acoleidae" and "Amabiliidae," suggested by Ransom (1909), were adopted also in place of those used in the article of 1907.

Fuhrmann's scheme has withstood the strain that is placed upon all schemes of classification by the discovery of new forms, and it is used still, with little modification, by European authors. North American writers, however, have tended to follow the later scheme offered by Ransom (1909) which united Ariola's Hymenolepidae and Echinocotylidae and Fuhrmann's Dilepinidae in one large family Hymenolepididae.

Among later emendations of the Fuhrmann scheme have been the addition by Poche (1926) of a family, Diploposthidae, for certain hymenolepid genera with double genitalia; of a family, Biuterinidae, by Meggitt (1927c) for certain forms with triangular rostellar hooks; and the addition of a family, Dioicocestidae, by Southwell (1930) for certain forms with separate sexes.

In a later edition of his monograph on the taeniid tapeworms of birds,

Fuhrmann (1932) retained substantially the scheme of classification of the earlier edition, but adopted the family terms Dilepididae, Hymenolepididae, Acoleidae, and Amabiliidae, and reduced the family Fimbriariidae to subfamily status within Hymenolepididae. This later scheme will be followed in the following pages.

RECOGNITION FEATURES

If we could exclude from Cyclophyllidea the families Tetrabothriidae and Mesocestoididae, the order would appear as a closely knit group of forms readily identifiable among tapeworms by the four suckers of the holdfast, the marginal genital apertures, the single and compact postovarian yolk gland of each segment, and the lack of uterine apertures. However, the inclusion of tetrabothriid and mesocestoidid forms, apparently unavoidable in the present state of our knowledge, prevents such a compact definition and restricts the definition of cyclophyllideans to sucker-bearing tapeworms with one or at most two yolk glands.

The division of the order into families is made chiefly upon the following characteristics: (1) the absence or presence of a rostellum; (2) the retractibility or nonretractibility of the rostellum when present; (3) the shape of the hooks on the rostellum; (4) the position of the genital apertures; (5) the position and number of yolk glands; (6) the number and arrangement of testes; (7) the presence or absence of vaginal apertures; (8) the nature of the gravid uterus; and (9) the nature of the embryonic envelopes.

A preliminary separation of the fourteen families recognized here may be made as follows:

KEY TO FAMILIES

1. No rostellum * 2
   Rostellum present 6
2. Genital apertures median, on ventral surface .... MESOCESTOIDIDAE
   Genital apertures on one or the other margin 3
3. Yolk gland in front of ovary .... TETRABOTHRIIDAE
   Yolk gland behind ovary 4
4. Segmentation weak, apparent only in posterior region of body; body cylindrical; testes never more than two; parasites of reptiles and amphibians .... NEMATOTAENIIDAE
   Segmentation well marked throughout body 5
5. Gravid segments usually much wider than long; yolk gland usually compact, rounded; gravid uterus a transverse tube, or a network of tubes, or represented by compartments, or replaced by paruterine organs; adult in mammals, birds, reptiles but not in amphibians .. ANOPLOCEPHALIDAE
   Gravid segments usually much longer than wide; both ovary and yolk gland multilobed, often fanlike, in the anterior third of the segment; testes mainly or wholly postovarian; gravid uterus with a median stem and numerous pairs of irregularly shaped lateral lobes, extending almost

*A number of genera which lack rostella are known from families whose members are otherwise rostellate. Such are *Anoplotaenia* and *Taeniarhynchus* (Taeniidae); some species of *Hymenolepis* (Hymenolepididae); *Cotylorhipis, Anonchotaenia, Metroliasthes, Rhabdometra* (Dilepididae); and *Shipleyia* (Dioicocestidae).

the full length of the segment .... CATENOTAENIIDAE

6. Rostellum permanently extruded, armed usually with two circles of hooks; gravid uterus with a median stem and lateral branches ...... TAENIIDAE
   Rostellum withdrawable within the holdfast 7
7. One set of genitalia per segment 8
   Two sets of genitalia per segment 9, 11, 12, 13
8. Vaginal apertures present 9
   Vaginal apertures lacking 12
9. Rostellar hooks T-shaped; sucker margins spinose; rostellum with a double or triple circle of hooks; genitalia occasionally double; gravid uterus replaced by parenchymatous pouches .... DAVAINEIDAE
   Rostellar hooks not T-shaped; sucker margins not spinose 10
10. Rostellar hooks triangular .... BIUTERINIDAE
    Rostellar hooks thornlike 11
11. Testes rarely more than four in number .... HYMENOLEPIDIDAE
    Testes numerous .... DILEPIDIDAE
12. Vagina present but functioning as a seminal receptacle ...... ACOLEIDAE
    Vagina absent; replaced in function by an accessory canal which opens to the exterior .... AMABILIIDAE
13. Sexes separate .... DIOICOCESTIDAE
    Hermaphroditic forms .... DIPLOPOSTHIDAE

The Russian author Spasski (1948a) has described briefly a remarkable form, generically and specifically termed *Skrjabinochora sobolevi*, which lacks a uterus or any uterine derivatives at all stages of development, and which Spasski regards as representative of a new cyclophyllidean family, Skrjabinochoridae. We have been unable to consult the original article so cannot comment upon this family.

Family MESOCESTOIDIDAE Perrier, 1897

DESCRIPTION

Of the order Cyclophyllidea. Small to medium-sized forms. Holdfast with four prominent suckers but without rostellum. Genital apertures median and on the ventral surface of the body. Eggs occurring within a thick-walled, posterior paruterine organ. Adults in birds and mammals. Type genus and only genus, *Mesocestoides* Vaillant, 1863. Perrier established the family for this genus, *Mesocestoides*, and its position among Cyclophyllidea has never been questioned by later authors.

Mesocestoides Vaillant, 1863

With the holdfast lacking rostellum or homologous structure and with four unarmed suckers. Cirro-vaginal atrium opening on middle line of ventral segment surface and receiving both male and female ducts. No uterine pore. Genitalia single per segment. Ovary and yolk gland double and in posterior portion of segment. Testes numerous, lateral or medial to the osmoregulatory canals. Cirrus pouch oval, almost on the middle line of the segment. No apparent seminal vesicle. Uterus a blind tube winding along the middle line of the segment. Ripe eggs with oncospheres and massed in a true paruterine organ formed independently of the uterus. Second larval stage a tetrathyridium parasitic in various ver-

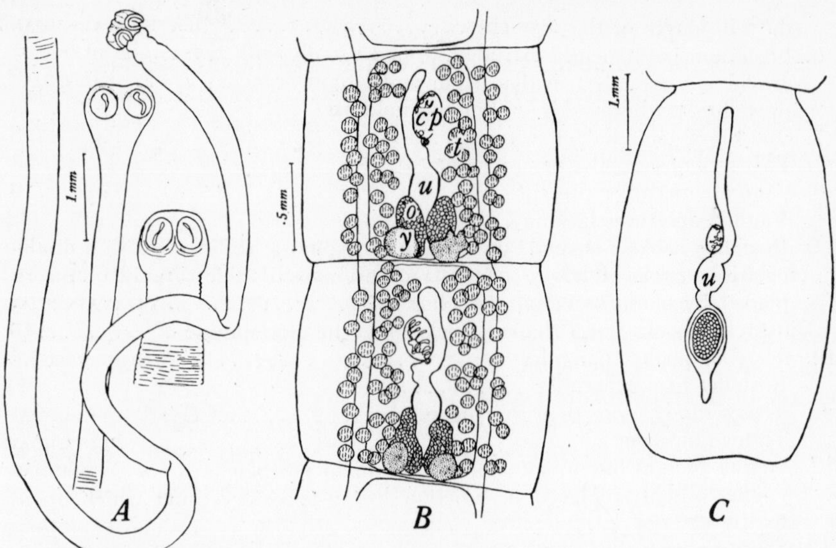

FIG. 180. *Mesocestoides lineatus f. lineata.* After Witenberg, 1934. A. Various shapes of holdfast. B. Mature segments. C. Gravid segment. *cp*, cirrus pouch; *o*, ovary; *t*, testes; *u*, uterus; *y*, yolk glands.

tebrate hosts. Adults parasitic in mammals and birds. Genotype, *ambiguus* Vaillant, 1863 *sp. inq.*

Characteristic of *Mesocestoides* is the apparent mixture of pseudophyllidean and cyclophyllidean characters, especially the combination of four-suckered holdfast with surficial genital apertures. However, as stressed by Cameron (1925), the mixture is more apparent than real, the typical cyclophyllidean internal organs having turned through a right angle. Male and female ducts open into the common cirro-vaginal atrium, and not independently to the surface. There are no uterine apertures and the eggs are typically cyclophyllidean in character. There are, however, *two* yolk glands.

Hamann (1885) and Mühling (1898) believed the ootype and its Mehlis' glands to be represented by a zone of intensely staining cells from which the paruterine organ appears to originate. This view was supported by Mueller (1928), but Chandler (1946c), in *Mesocestoides latus*, found a typical ootype and Mehlis' gland complex, though in a somewhat unusual position, on the oviduct just after it leaves the ovaries, proximal to the entrance of the common yolk duct. Chandler (*op. cit.*) observed further, despite the opinions of earlier workers, a distinct system of efferent sperm ducts linking up the testes with the sperm duct.

Most noteworthy of Chandler's observations, however, was his belief that the so-called egg capsule or uterine capsule, stated by all earlier observers to be formed from the posterior region of the uterus, is a true paruterine organ, originating independently of the uterus, between it and the ovary in the median line of the proglottis, as a solid mass of intensely stainable cells, and secondarily establishing a broad connection with the uterus at a point behind the entrance of the uterine duct.

Actually, as Chandler (1947) later admitted, Byrd and Ward (1943) had described the true nature of the egg capsule and the relationships of the various components of the female reproductive system. The structure which Chandler regarded as the ootype and which he believed to be surrounded by Mehlis' glands is in reality an oocapt, the Mehlis' glands surrounding the uterine duct in the usual position just beyond the junction of uterine duct and common yolk duct, as Fuhrmann figures. Byrd and Ward believe the genital-pore surface of the proglottis to be dorsal, since it is on the opposite surface from that nearer to the ovaries. This view must be accepted if the position of ovaries is taken as lying nearer to the tapeworm's ventral surface.

Long considered to be the larval stage of *Mesocestoides* is a form, *Tetrathyridium* (= *Cysticercus dithyridium* of Villot, 1883), commonly found in reptiles and birds. *Tetrathyridium* Rudolphi, 1819 is not a generic name but a collective term for a group of tapeworm larvae which have been described under such names as *Cephalocotyleum* Diesing, 1850; *Cysticercus* Zeder, 1800; *Dithyridium* Rudolphi, 1819; *Dubium* Rudolphi, 1819; *Plerocercoides* Neumann, 1892; *Plerocercus* Braun, 1883; *Petathyrus* Cobbold, 1860; *Piestocystis* Diesing, 1850; *Slossia* Meggitt, 1931; *Tetrathyridium perdicis saxatilis* Rudolphi, 1819; and *Tetrathyrus* Creplin, 1839.

The tetrathyridium larva has a remarkably contractile body, threadlike with knoblike thickenings here and there when extended, 2–5 mm. long in reptiles and up to 70 mm. long in mammals. It is flat, semitransparent, anteriorly wide and posteriorly tapering when contracted, and only 10–20 mm. long in mammals. The holdfast is invaginated, has four unarmed suckers, and is devoid of rostellum or homologous structures. Such larvae occur free in serous cavities or encysted in various regions of the host's body. Unencysted forms may be found in the peritoneal cavity of mammals, in the lungs of birds, sometimes in hundreds. Markowski (1933b) regarded the encysted and free tetrathyridia as analogous with the cysticercus and the plerocercus types of other tapeworm larvae.

The identity of tetrathyridia with *Mesocestoides* has been established beyond doubt from feeding experiments carried out by Skrjabin and Schultz (1926), Henry (1927), Schultz (1927), Schwartz (1927c), Joyeux and Baer (1932, 1935d), Markowski (1933b, 1934), Joyeux, Baer, and Martin (1933b), Witenberg (1934), Srivastava (1939), and Carta (1939a). It seems fairly certain, however, that the tetrathyridium is the *second* of two larval stages. It develops not from an oncosphere but from an earlier larval stage unknown to us.

The genus *Mesocestoides* was founded by Vaillant (1863) for material, which he named *ambiguus*, from a genet (*Genetta genetta genetta*) in the western Mediterranean area. His description was vague and it is not possible to identify the form he had in mind. To the genus, other species were soon added by Railliet and others – such species as *alaudae* Stossich, 1896 from *Alauda arvensis* (field lark), Europe and Northern

Asia; *angustatus* Rudolphi, 1819 from *Meles taxus* (badger), Europe; *candelabrarius* Goeze, 1782 from an owl (*Strix aluco*), Europe; *cateniformis vulpis* Gmelin, 1790 from foxes in Europe; *chrysaeti* Viborg, 1795 from *Aquila chrysaetos* (golden eagle), Europe; *imbutiformis* Polonio, 1860 from a goose in Italy; *lagopodis* Rudolphi, 1810 from *Alopex lagopus* (blue fox), Europe; *lineatus* Goeze, 1782 from *Felis sylvestris* (wild cat), Europe; *litteratus* Batsch, 1786 from a "fox," in Europe; *longistriatus* Setti, 1897 from a wild cat in Erythraea; *macrocephalus* Creplin, 1825 from *Anguilla vulgaris* (European eel); *magellanicus* Monticelli, 1889, host not stated; *margaritifera* Creplin, 1829 from "birds of prey," Europe; *michaelseni* Loennberg, 1896 from *Cerdocyon azarae* (crab-eating dog), Brazil; *perlatus* Goeze, 1782 from a hawk, *Falco buteo*, Europe; *pseudocucumerina* Bailliet, 1863 from a dog; *tenuis* Creplin, 1829 from "birds of prey"; *utriculifera* Walter, 1866, from *Vulpes vulpes* (common fox) in Europe.

Hoeppli (1925) added *corti* from *Mus musculus* (house mouse) in Colorado; Cameron (1925) added *bassarisci* MacCallum, 1921 from *Bassariscus astutus* (raccoon-fox) in Mexico; *caestus n.sp.* from the Cape ratel (*Mellivora ratel*), Northeast Africa (but in London Zoological Gardens). Mueller (1927) added *latus n.sp.* from *Mephitis minnesota* (skunk) in Minnesota; *variabilis n.sp.* from *Urocyon cinereo-argenetatus californicus* (gray fox), *Spilogale phenax phenax* (little spotted skunk), and *Mephitis occidentalis occidentalis* (skunk), all in California; the forms from the skunk Mueller distinguished as var. *major*. Meggitt (1928) added *elongatus* from a "wolf" in Egypt and (1931) *tenuis n.sp.* (not *tenuis* Creplin) from a dog in Burma. Joyeux and Baer (1932) obtained, by feeding tetrathyridia to a cat in Marseilles, an adult *Mesocestoides* which they identified with Vaillant's genotype *ambiguus*.

The first serious attack upon the validity of the species mentioned above came from Witenberg (1934). This writer placed twenty-four alleged species as *species inquirenda*, including Vaillant's genotype. He recognized three species only: the two from birds – *charadrii* Fuhrmann, 1909, recorded twice in *Tringa minuta*, Egypt; and *perlatus* Goeze, 1782 – and the common dog-fox form *lineatus*, of which, however, he recognized three morphae – *caesta, lineata*, and *litterata*. The species and morphae were differentiated mainly on the shape of the segments and the distribution of the testes.

Joyeux and Baer (1935d) reiterated their belief that *ambiguus* is a valid species distinguishable from *lineatus* by having 25–32 testes per segment (*lineatus* has 55–63 testes according to Joyeux and Baer; 29–60 according to Witenberg); by the size of the cirrus pouch (230–250 μ in *ambiguus*; 365–385 μ in *lineatus*); and by the absence from *ambiguus* of subcuticular muscles.

Among later contributions Coatney (1936) recorded *lineatus* from dog and raccoon in North America; Morgan and Waller (1940) recorded over 300 immature *Mesocestoides*, probably *M. lineatus*, in a raccoon (*Procyon lotor lotor*) in Iowa, U.S.A. Chandler (1942c) recorded *Mesocestoides manteri n.sp.* from a lynx (*Lynx rufus*) in Nebraska,

U.S.A., and redescribed *latus* Mueller and *variabilis* Mueller. Further (1942e), this same observer recorded the first case of human infection, identifying *M. variabilis* in a child in Texas. Byrd and Ward (1943) redescribed in considerable detail Mueller's *variabilis* from an opossum (*Didelphys virginiana*) in Mississippi. Chandler (1944a) recorded *kirbyi n.sp.* from *Canis latrans* (coyote) in California and (1946) recorded observations upon a specimen of *latus.*

While it is possible that all the alleged species of *Mesocestoides* from mammalian hosts are in reality morphae of one highly variable species, such an assumption cannot be taken for granted in the present state of our knowledge. In the meantime, the following species – discussed in alphabetical order – may be recognized.

NOTES ON SPECIES

1. *ambiguus* Vaillant, 1863. From *Genetta genetta,* North Africa; with the characters given for the genus; total length 16–360 mm.; holdfast with diameter of 700 μ; suckers 250–275 μ in diameter; neck 7 mm. long; first segments wider than long, increasing in length until the mature segments are almost square; following segments longer than wide, the last ones cucurbitiform or barrel-shaped, 1 mm. long by 1.4 mm. wide; genital apertures on ventral surface, a little in front of center, vaginal aperture anterior, cirral aperture posterior; cirrus pouch 130–230 μ long by 90–110 μ wide; testes 25–30, almost spherical, 40–50 μ in diameter, placed mainly in the area bounded by the lateral osmoregulatory canals; ovary and yolk gland bilobed, in posterior region of segment; paruterine organ thick-walled, ovoid, 500–600 μ long by 359–400 μ wide; eggs 35–42 μ long by 22–30 μ wide; oncosphere 20 μ, very active; adults in Viverridae, circum-Mediterranean countries.

This form was reared by Joyeux and Baer (1932) by feeding cats with tetrathyridia from snakes – *Elaphe scalaris, Zemenis hippocrepis* – in southern France and Tunisia. The development was somewhat irregular in rate because the cat is not a normal host. In one case, ripe segments appeared in the host after 56 days; in other cases, only ten-millimeter-long specimens, barely segmented, were found after 145 days. These observers reported the ability of tetrathyridia to penetrate the host gut wall and to re-encyst in serous cavities, regenerating the posterior, tail-like part of the body that was lost during passage through the host gut.

2. *bassarisci* MacCallum, 1921. From *Bassariscus astutus* (raccoon-fox) in Mexico; small forms with few segments; mature segments indistinctly divided from one another; neck smooth and unstriated for about one-quarter of the worm's length; testes comparatively few in number, all between the osmoregulatory canals.

3. *caestus* Cameron, 1925. From *Mellivora ratel* (Cape ratel), London Zoo; over 800 mm. long by 2 mm. broad; holdfast about 500 μ long by 450 μ broad; neck about 3.5 mm.; early segments broader than long; gravid segments barrel-shaped; genital apertures ventral, at junction of anterior and middle thirds; atrium discoid; cirrus pouch antero-dorsal; testes about 60, 50 μ in diameter, lying on both sides of each osmoregu-

latory canal but never invading the central area; ovary dumbbell-shaped; vagina very large and convoluted; uterus a thin-walled tube, large and voluminous, becoming dumbbell-shaped, the anterior "bell" later disappearing, the posterior "bell" becoming replaced by a paruterine organ; eggs 20 μ in diameter. Cameron stressed as recognition characters the great length, the serrated margins of the nongravid segments, which are broader than long, the cucumber-seed shape of gravid segments, the large transverse osmoregulatory vessel in each segment, and the dumbbell shape of the semigravid uterus.

4. *charadrii* Fuhrmann, 1910. From *Limonites* (= *Tringa*) *minuta* in Egypt; found on three occasions; up to 50 mm. long, with testes mostly lateral to the osmoregulatory canals; ovary and yolk gland in the shape of irregular sacs and not, as in other species, bilobed.

5. *corti* Hoeppli, 1925. From *Mus musculus* (house mouse), Colorado; average length (100 specimens) 40–80 mm.; holdfast with large suckers with rims incomplete posteriorly; neck 1–2 mm. long; first segments twice as wide as long, even the 100th segment being wider than long; end segments barrel-shaped, others round, ovoid, or bell-shaped; genital apertures median and slightly anterior; ratio of cirrus pouch length to segment thickness 1:2.5; testes 36–60, on both sides of each osmoregulatory canal, ovoid, 26 by 34 μ; ovary of two spherical or ovoid connected structures; close to each ovarian lobe and ventral to it, a yolk gland more or less spherical and slightly smaller than the ovarian structure; paruterine organ thick-walled and apparently identical with that described for *lineatus*; eggs 19 by 24 μ.

"In internal structure there is no characteristic difference between *M. litteratus* and *M. corti*. They differ, however, in the length of the neck, the size of the mature segments, and the size of the eggs. Besides this, *M. corti* is a parasite of a rodent, whereas *M. litteratus* is described from the dog and the fox." Hoeppli (1925).

6. *kirbyi* Chandler, 1944. From *Canis latrans* (coyote), California; 190–300 mm. long by 1.7–2.0 mm. wide; holdfast 350–470 μ wide and 360–440 μ long; suckers 230–300 μ long and 130–150 μ wide with slitlike openings, 170–200 μ long; calcareous corpuscles few and scattered; mature segments nearly as long as wide when relaxed; gravid segments strikingly bell-shaped, 2.2–4.0 mm. long and 1.1–1.5 mm. wide, the anterior borders only 200–500 μ wide; testes 100–120, 45–65 μ in diameter; cirrus pouch 180–210 μ long and 130–150 μ wide; ovarian lobes each 120–170 μ long by 65–85 μ wide, almost contiguous; yolk glands ventral and slightly posterior to the ovarian lobes, each 50–70 μ in diameter; uterus curving around cirrus pouch and ending in a club-shaped enlargement anterior to it; paruterine organ carrot-shaped, with thick fibrous walls, 450–560 μ in diameter with egg mass 280–320 μ in diameter. The species differs from all previously described forms in the large number of testes and, from all but *M. lineatus*, in the large size of cirrus pouch; it differs also from all except *M. manteri* in the bell shape of the gravid segments. Except for the large number of testes it shows a strong resemblance to *M. lineatus*.

7. *latus* Mueller, 1927. From *Mephitis minnesotae* (skunk) in Minnesota (Mueller, 1927) and *Didelphis virginiana* (opossum) in Texas (Chandler, 1946c); lengths of four specimens reported by Chandler as 34.5, 76, 106, and 112 cm., thus exceeding the greatest length previously reported for this species (50 cm.) by Mueller (1930). The 76-cm. specimen had about 800 segments; holdfast blunt and not set off from the neck; mature segments about 1.4–1.8 mm. wide and 0.45–0.7 mm. long; segments becoming approximately square at about the 600th. End segments of the longest worm which were almost fully ripe were 3.4 mm. long and 1.6 mm. wide. This worm, as pointed out by Mueller, lacks calcareous corpuscles and becomes very clear in microscopic preparation as compared with other species; ovarian lobes and yolk glands almost in a transverse line, yolk glands outermost; internal organs greatly crowded posteriorly; longitudinal osmoregulatory canals very much compressed by testes and narrower and straighter than in *M. corti*, transverse commissures almost obliterated. Webster (1949a), in an interesting description of attempts to determine the intermediate hosts of this form, has added further details of adult anatomy and has discussed the probable life cycle.

8. *lineatus* Goeze, 1782 (= *Taenia lineata* Goeze, 1782; *Halysis lineata* Zeder, 1803; *Taenia canis lagopodis* Rudolphi, 1810; *Taenia pseudocucumerina* Bailliet, 1866; *T. pseudo-elliptica* Bailliet, 1866; *Ptychopsis lineata* Hamann, 1885; *Mesocestoides lineatus* var. *lineata* Witenberg, 1934). From dog, cat, jackal, and other wild carnivores, Europe, western Asia (Palestine), Africa; from 30 cm. to 2.5 meters long; holdfast massive, anteriorly truncated with slight apical depression; 600–900 μ in diameter; suckers elongated, oval; neck very short; first intersegmental boundaries indistinct; the following segments square; the end segments barrel-shaped, 4–6 mm. long by 2–3 mm. wide; genital apertures ventral, median, cirrus aperture close to vaginal aperture; cirrus pouch 150–230 μ long by 100 μ wide; testes 54–58, relatively large, 50 μ diameter, on each side of osmoregulatory canals; ovary and yolk gland bilobed, in posterior region of segment; paruterine organ ovoid, 400–550 μ diameter; eggs ovoid with two thin membranes, 40–60 μ long by 34–43 μ wide.

Life cycle imperfectly known. Witenberg believed three hosts to be necessary — a first intermediate host, probably a coprophagous insect; a second intermediate host, probably a vertebrate; and a final host, which is a mammal. The second larva is believed to be *Tetrathyridium bailleti* Railliet, 1885 (= *T. elongatum* Blumberg, 1882), a slender worm, very extensible, 1–2 cm. long but sometimes as long as 35 cm.; the anterior region — white, opaque, irregularly wrinkled, and 1.5–3.0 mm. long — has at its tip a longitudinal slit which is the aperture of an invagination in which lies the holdfast; the latter, difficult to evaginate artificially, has neither rostellum nor hooks but four elliptical suckers darker than the rest of the body, with slitlike openings and measuring 500–600 μ in diameter; anterior region followed by a narrower region, tail-like, about 1 mm. wide; small specimens may have the tail so short as to appear cordiform; body filled with calcareous corpuscles.

The first experiments to support the view of Moniez (1880a) that *Tetrathyridium* is the larval form of *Mesocestoides* were made by Neumann (1896), who obtained adult *Mesocestoides* from dogs fed with *Tetrathyridium.* Confirmatory experiments were made by Skrjabin and Schultz (1926), Henry (1927), Schwartz (1927), and Witenberg (1934).

9. *litteratus* Batsch, 1786 (= *Taenia litterata* Batsch, 1786; *Mesocestoides lineatus* var. *litterata* Witenberg, 1934). From dogs, cats, foxes, Europe; 30–130 mm. long, never as long as *lineatus*; holdfast 550–600 μ in diameter, about 500 μ in length; four very muscular suckers, 40 μ thick, 250–280 μ diameter, with openings about 160 μ long; neck very short, 400–500 μ long; segments rapidly becoming mature; end segments elliptical, maximum width 100 μ; genital apertures median and ventral; cirrus pouch as in *lineatus*; testes 30–45, ellipsoidal, 50–70 μ diameter, distributed irregularly; eggs 25–35 μ diameter; only intermediate hosts known are fowl and several wild birds, several Corvidae particularly. Experiments of Markowski (1934) suggest *Tetrathyridium variabilis* as second larval stage, a form 2–4 mm. long by 1.5–2.0 mm. wide, sometimes longer than wide, sometimes wider than long, very thick, the body transversely wrinkled, a slitlike depression at each end; anterior slit containing invaginated holdfast. Markowski found in the gut of a magpie whose lungs contained this tetrathyridium the remains of the scarabaeid beetle *Geotrupes.*

10. *manteri* Chandler, 1942. From *Lynx rufus*, Nebraska; 9–16 mm. long by 1–1.25 mm. wide; with 25–55 segments; holdfast 420–490 μ in diameter and 285–350 μ in length, set off from the neck inconspicuously or not at all; suckers in two pairs, dorsal and ventral, 175–210 μ long by 155–180 μ wide; with strong muscles; slits antero-posterior; neck 315–500 μ broad at junction with holdfast, almost immediately becoming as broad as holdfast; segments becoming fully mature at 16th to 20th; mature segments 700 μ wide by 485 μ long to 900 μ wide and 175 μ long; usually only one gravid segment, bell-shaped, its border with preceding segment only 265–350 μ broad; testes about 30–45, closely crowded in area bounded by osmoregulatory canals, 4 or 5 lateral to each canal, spherical, 48 μ by 48 μ to 50 μ by 60 μ; cirrus pouch 88–110 μ in diameter, antero-dorsal, 88–140 μ long; with much coiled sperm duct; persisting even in gravid segments; ovarian lobes 90–110 μ long by 70–110 μ broad; yolk glands smaller than ovarian lobes and ventral to them; uterus appearing first in a few segments after sexual maturity is reached, bending around cirrus pouch first on one side then on the other, ending just short of anterior border; later expanding and filling with eggs to form a series of saclike bodies, one large body anterior to cirrus pouch; posterior body becoming replaced by posteriorly formed paruterine organ; latter slightly longer than broad; egg mass 245–275 μ broad by 220–260 μ long.

11. *perlatus* Goeze, 1782 (= *Taenia chrysaeti* Viborg, 1795; *T. margaritifera* Creplin, 1829; *Halysis perlata* Goeze, 1782; *Taenia tenuis* Creplin, 1829). Recorded in species of *Aquila, Buteo, Falco, Circaetus,*

Milvus and possibly peculiar to birds of prey; anatomy substantially as for *lineatus*; living specimens slightly pink posteriorly; body margins serrated, each segment being trapezoidal.

12. *tenuis* Meggitt, 1931. From a dog in Burma; 150 mm. by 900 μ; holdfast lacking in type material; genital apertures antero-central; testes 14–18 on each side, in two separated rows lateral with respect to osmoregulatory canals; paruterine organ 460–490 μ long by 300–340 μ wide; eggs 35–44 μ long by 30–35 μ wide.

13. *variabilis* Mueller, 1927. From *Urocyon cinereo-argenteus, Spilogale phenax phenax*, and *Mephitis occidentalis occidentalis* in California; found by Chandler in raccoons (*Procyon lotor*) in Texas; by Byrd and Ward (1943) in opossum (*Didelphis virginiana*) in Mississippi; and by Chandler (1942f) in a child in Texas; detailed description of the mature segment given by Byrd and Ward; with the characters of the genus; 50–300 mm. or more long; Chandler (1942d) obtained from a raccoon two complete specimens each 200 mm. by 1.25–1.50 mm.; their holdfasts measured 320 and 380 μ in diameter; anatomy in general similar to that of *latus* but the holdfast is smaller, the calcareous corpuscles are more numerous, the muscles thicker, the paruterine organ bowl-like around a central mass of eggs. Byrd and Ward believed the genital apertures of this species – and presumably of mesocestoidids in general – to be really *dorsal* and not ventral in position.

Family Tetrabothriidae Linton, 1891, emended Fuhrmann, 1907

DESCRIPTION

Of the order Cyclophyllidea. With the holdfast lacking rostellum or hooks and rectangular in shape. Suckers large, oval, commonly with muscular outgrowths from their margins structurally identical with the suckers. Suckers in exceptional cases lacking completely. Genital apertures unilateral on left margin of body. Genital atria deep and muscular. Cirrus pouches small, globular, each connected with genital atrium by a *canalis masculinus*. Testes fairly numerous. Yolk gland in front of, or partly beneath, the ovary. Uterus saclike, often lobed, with or without dorsally situated aperture or apertures. Eggs with three membranes. Type genus, *Tetrabothrius* Rudolphi, 1819.

HISTORY

The term "Tetrabothriidae," as a name for a family of tapeworms, was used originally by Linton (1891a) as an etymological correction of the earlier term "Tetrabothria" of Rudolphi and Diesing. As used by Linton, Monticelli (1892b), Perrier (1897b), Pintner (1896b), Benham (1901), and even Baylis (1926a), however, the term covered in addition to *Tetrabothrius* a number of forms now considered to be Tetraphyllidea. Braun (1894–1900), however, used the term as a subfamily designation (of Taeniidae), with *Tetrabothrius* as the only genus. This subfamily was raised by Fuhrmann (1907a) to family rank.

Nybelin (1922) added to the family his newly established genera

Chaetophallus and *Priapocephalus* and argued strongly for the inclusion of the family within Pseudophyllidea on the grounds that: (1) the anteriorly situated yolk gland is a condensation of the follicular yolk glands of the pseudophyllidean arrangement, transition between the two arrangements being shown by *Priapocephalus* (Tetrabothriidae) and *Parabothrium* (Pseudophyllidea); (2) the four-sucker arrangement in Tetrabothriidae is derivable from the two-bothria arrangement of Abothriinae (Pseudophyllidea) by longitudinal division, the appendages of the suckers representing the terminal plate of the pseudophyllidean; and (3) the rudimentary aperture of the tetrabothriid uterus represents a final stage in a gradual degeneration of the pseudophyllidean arrangement.

Nybelin's view was accepted by Poche (1926), who placed the family in a tribe, Tetrabothriodae, of his order Bothriocephalidea. It was strongly opposed, however, both by Meggitt (1928) and by Fuhrmann (1932). As Meggitt said, after analyzing and dismissing Nybelin's arguments:

"To accept the hypothesis of Nybelin, a hypothesis not substantiated by reference to facts, that four suckers can be homologised with two bothridia, auricular appendages with a terminal scolex plate, and a compact vitelline gland with a follicular sheath, would abolish the present classification of the Cestoda without the suggestion of any substitute. It is easier to assume the displacement of a vitelline gland from a posterior through a ventral, to an anterior position; a variability of the scolex within the family, as shown by *Priapocephalus, Tetrabothrius* and *Anophryocephalus*; and a uterine pore vestigial, but not to the point of complete disappearance as in the remainder of Cyclophyllidea. Tetrabothriidae are therefore considered as belonging to that order."

Fuhrmann stated:

"This interesting group of cestodes was placed by Nybelin (1922) in the order Pseudophyllidea near to Amphicotylidae although Tetrabothriidae have four well-marked suckers. He based his opinion upon the presence of an uterine pore (*Porotaenia*) and on the fact that in the aberrant genus *Priapocephalus* the yolk gland is not compact but somewhat follicular and the yolk duct in one species of this genus divides into several branches. Nybelin's opinion, supported by Poche (1926), is without any doubt erroneous for the uterine apertures of Amphicotylidae and Tetrabothriidae are not homologous structures; in the first family, it is, as in Pseudophyllidea, generally, placed ventrally, while in the latter family it is always dorsal. As regards yolk glands, these in Tetrabothriidae are exceptional among Cyclophyllidea in being situated *anterior* to the ovary while in Amphicotylidae there are *two* such glands as against the single one of Tetrabothriidae, each broken up into follicles. If the possession of a branching yolk duct has any phylogenetic value, it suggests an origin rather from Tetraphyllidea than from Pseudophyllidea. Such a view is corroborated by the marked resemblance of the holdfast of *Tetrabothrius* to that of Tetraphyllidea. Its organs of fixation recall certain features of bothridia. It has in fact suckers which are not characteristic of Cyclophyllidea in being deeply sunk into the parenchyma of the holdfast but which are attached rather to the surface of it, as in the majority of Tetraphyllidean bothridia.

"Any transformation of two pseudobothridia (bothria) into four suckers, highly differentiated, as seems possible to Nybelin and Poche, seems to us completely excluded. On the other hand, neither Cyclophyllidea nor Tetraphyllidea, as is admitted generally, have evolved from Pseudophyllidea; on the contrary these latter forms represent probably a lateral evolution from Trypanorhyncha which, like Pseudophyllidea, have in general two pseudobothridia.

"Nybelin notes, as his third argument, the resemblance of the eggs of *Abothrium* and *Parabothrium* to those of *Tetrabothrius.* The eggs of *Abothrium* and *Parabothrium*, however, are pseudophyllidean eggs with a shell, very thin it is true, while those of *Tetrabothrius* are cyclophyllidean eggs, with three envelopes and a single yolk cell, as against the several yolk cells of the others. There can then be no question of placing Tetrabothriidae in Pseudophyllidea. They constitute probably the most primitive family of Cyclophyllidea and their possible origin must be sought for among Tetraphyllidea." Fuhrmann (1932).

Baylis (1922a) added to the family the genus *Anophryocephalus*, emphasizing the affinities of this form with *Dinobothrium* and suggesting the inclusion of that genus also within the family. It is significant that by most authors *Dinobothrium* is accepted as a tetraphyllidean.

Szpotanska (1925) studied the tetrabothriids of procellariform birds and added to the family a new genus, *Porotaenia.* This genus was abolished by Johnston (1935) as being a synonym of *Chaetophallus.* Nybelin (1931) established the genus *Neotetrabothrius* and added it to Tetrabothriidae. Baer (1932b) added *Strobilocephalus* and *Trigonocotyle.* Yamaguti (1940) added *Paratetrabothrius.*

RECOGNITION FEATURES

While, speaking generally, tetrabothriid tapeworms are recognizable by their host distribution, by having four suckers, lateral genital apertures, antero-ovarian and single yolk glands, and a saclike uterus, they nevertheless show puzzling variability. The best discussion of the question is probably that of Baer (1932b) in his study of the tapeworms of whales. His views on Tetrabothriidae are worthy of extended quotation.

"The family Tetrabothriidae comprises today (i.e., 1932) seven genera, *Tetrabothrius* Rudolphi, 1819: *Chaetophallus* Nybelin, 1916: *Anophryocephalus* Baylis, 1922: *Priapocephalus* Nybelin, 1922: *Porotaenia* Szpotanska, 1917: *Strobilocercus n.gen.* and *Trigonocotyle n.gen.*

"If one compares one with another the scolex of these different genera, it is clear that several types can be recognized. In *Anophryocephalus* the four suckers are oval and have no traces of appendices or auricles; in *Trigonocotyle*, each sucker has three small muscular appendices and in *Tetrabothrius, Porotaenia* and *Chaetophallus* the suckers have each an auricle bound to the summit of the scolex by a sort of membrane forming a little *avant-toit* [i.e., like the eaves of a roof]. In *Strobilocephalus* the suckers are small and deeply embedded in the basal region of the scolex, the apical portion of the scolex being strongly developed and almost spherical [see Figure 181]. Finally, in *Priapocephalus* the suckers have completely disappeared and the apical region of the scolex has reached a maximum of development. We may suppose then, as we shall see later, and as our diagram [Figure 181] indicates, that the type *Anophryocephalus* has given origin to two series of genera, one characterised by a progressive development of the suckers (*Trigonocotyle, Tetrabothrius, Porotaenia, Chaetophallus*), the other on the contrary by a reduction of the suckers and by the progressive development of the apical region of the scolex (*Strobilocephalus, Priapocephalus*).

"From a morphological point of view, we may note likewise that the

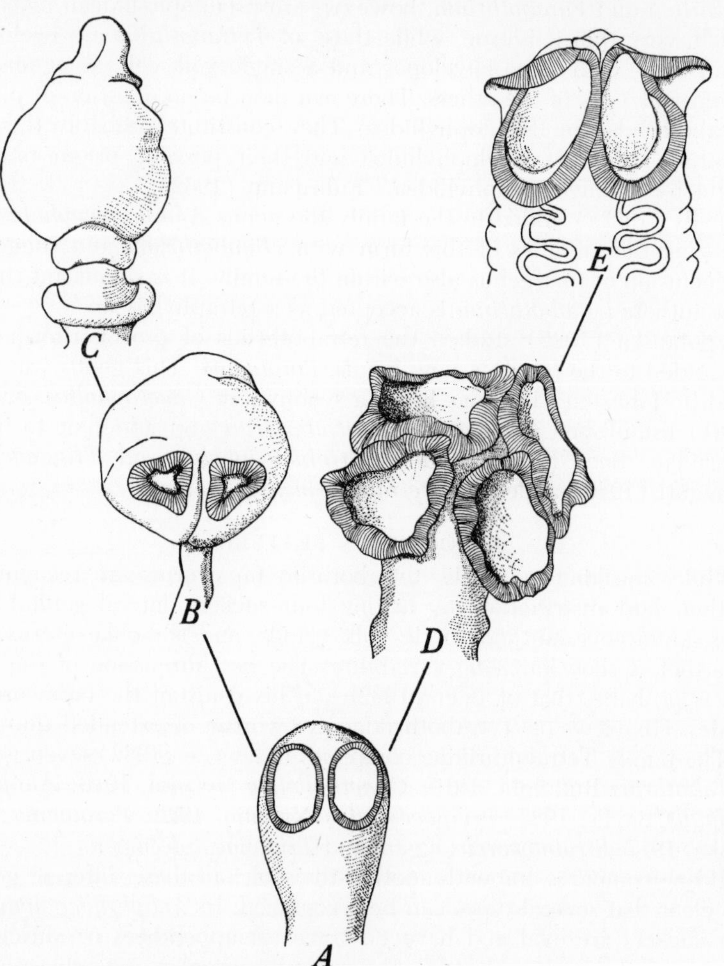

FIG. 181. Tetrabothriid genera. After Baer, 1932a. A. *Anophryocephalus*. B. *Strobilocephalus*. C. *Priapocephalus*. D. *Trigonocotyle*. E. *Tetrabothrius*, *Porotaenia*, and *Chaetophallus*.

muscular genital atrium shows some degree of evolution. Poorly developed in *Anophryocephalus*, it becomes less marked in *Strobilocephalus*, and has disappeared completely from *Priapocephalus*. On the other hand, the genital atrium is well developed in *Trigonocotyle* and reaches a maximum of complexity in *Tetrabothrius* and *Porotaenia*, and *Chaetophallus*, the most evolved stage. It would seem that the cirrus-pouch evolved along similar lines, for it is weakly muscular and oval in *Priapocephalus*, then becomes more characteristic of the classic type in *Anophryocephalus*, and become altogether typical in *Tetrabothrius, Porotaenia* and *Chaetophallus*.

"We have sought to compare this evolution of tetrabothriids with that of their vertebrate hosts. *Chaetophallus, Porotaenia*, and the very large majority of species of *Tetrabothrius* are found exclusively in aquatic, especially marine, birds. The other four genera, as well as three species of *Tetrabothrius*, are parasites of marine mammals—pinnipeds and cetaceans.

"Palaeontological information on marine mammals is scanty, yet it would seem according to Abel (in Weber, 1928) that Pinnipedia are geologically older than Cetacea. It is generally admitted that Pinnipedia, and probably Cetacea, have evolved from terrestrial mammals which became secondarily marine. As regards Pinnipedia, the ancestral stock according to Abel, is the same that gave origin to Ursidae and Canidae.

"The genus *Anophryocephalus* is found only in Pinnipedia; it shows the simplest type of suckers; the other genera are found in Cetacea, indifferently in Mystacoceti and Odontoceti. How can it be explained, then, that the majority of species of the genera *Tetrabothrius, Porotaenia*, and *Chaetophallus* are found exclusively in birds, vertebrates which phylogenetically are much older than mammals? Studying the different tetrabothriids of birds one is struck by the small number of specific characters. Today about 47 species of the genus *Tetrabothrius* occur, but it is very difficult to distinguish one from another. One gets sharply the impression that the tetrabothriids of birds are actively evolving; their specific characters show the instability characteristic of parasites recently acquired by their hosts. The conclusion may be drawn that Tetrabothriidae have been harboured by birds only a relatively short time and that they are really parasites of mammals which are becoming adapted to such birds as have alimentary habits similar to that of the mammalian hosts. Particularly in this case, Pinnipedia and Cetacea have food habits analogous to those of Lariformes, Procellariformes, Pelicaniformes, Alciformes and Colymbiformes, habitual hosts of Tetrabothriidae. The same argument may be raised to explain the occurrence in predatory birds of tapeworms characteristic of mammals, such genera as *Taenia, Dipylidium* and *Mesocestoides*.

"In making use of the hypothesis given above, consideration must be given to the position occupied by Tetrabothriidae in schemes of tapeworm classification. Nybelin (1922, 1928) placed Tetrabothriidae in the order Pseudophyllidea. Baylis (1926a) followed his example, but placed *Tetrabothrius* close to *Dinobothrium*, a shark tapeworm which, as Perrenoud (1931) demonstrated, is a typical tetraphyllidean. Pintner (1896a) supposed the auricles of the tetrabothriid to be vestigial bothridia. These arguments were refuted by Fuhrmann (1899, 1931) who considered the family Tetrabothriidae as very primitive Cyclophyllidea. Let us consider further the arguments of these authors.

"Nybelin compared Tetrabothriidae with the family Amphicotylidae. Basing his arguments upon his own researches and upon those of Spätlich (1909) the Swedish author considered the suckers of Tetrabothriidae not as true suckers, such as one finds in Cyclophyllidea, but as tetraphyllidean bothridia. The existence of an uterine pore in some species of Tetrabothriidae is analogous to what one finds in Amphicotylidae and notably in *Abothrium gadi.* On the other hand, *Priapocephalus* has the yolk gland follicular as in *Parabothrium*, not compact as in other tetabrothriids. Finally, more recently (1928) the same author found that in *Priapocephalus minor* the yolk duct subdivides into several branches, from which he concludes that there is here a reminiscence of an ancestral follicular yolk gland similar to the condition in Pseudophyllidea.

"Reviewing the arguments of Nybelin, Fuhrmann could not admit that the suckers of tetrabothriids were derived from the two bothria of Pseudophyllidea. On the other hand, the uterine pore is found in Tetrabothriidae on the dorsal surface, while is it always ventral in Amphicotylidae. Finally, the eggs of Tetrabothriidae are of cyclophyllidean type, for there is only one yolk cell in the egg, whereas in Pseudophyllidea the number of yolk cells in the egg is always considerable. Contrary to the opinion of Nybelin, Fuhrmann considered the Amphicotylidae as primitive pseudophyllideans.

"Taking into account the arguments advanced above, it must be admitted that *Anophryocephalus*, parasitic in Pinnipedia, has a primitive type of scolex, four oval suckers without appendices. We had hoped to find in *Priapocephalus* a *scolex deformatus* and thus support Nybelin's hypothesis but as we have demonstrated above the structure of the scolex of this genus is a structure *sui generis*, not having anatomically anything in common with any *scolex deformatus* of Pseudophyllidea. It must be admitted then that the most primitive type of tetrabothriid has four suckers. Now, as Fuhrmann (1931) has demonstrated, and as we have already argued above, it is impossible to derive suckers from bothria. In this particular case the scolex characters are more important for placing a family in one order than in another. Besides, in adopting the phylogenetic scheme of Cestoda maintained by Fuhrmann, Pseudophyllidea and Cyclophyllidea must be considered as having arisen from a common tetraphyllidean ancestral stock. One may admit then a double possibility, whether it be convergence of characters, whether it be a return to ancestral characters, to explain certain anatomical similarities between Tetrabothriidae and Amphicotylidae.

"If on the other hand, one admits the palaeontological hypothesis that Pinnipedia, and perhaps also Cetacea have come from terrestrial groups which secondarily became marine, we must seek the origins of Tetrabothriidae among cestodes which may have given rise on the one hand to the Taeniidae of Carnivora and on the other hand to those of Pinnipedia.

"We know in fact that Carnivora, Pinnipedia and Cetacea harbour numerous cestodes belonging to the order Pseudophyllidea and particularly to the family Diphyllobothriidae whose genus *Diphyllobothrium* should, by this fact, go far back to the Miocene. Now the great majority of Pseudophyllidea are harboured by vertebrates living in water or having easy access to it. Thus the palaeontological hypothesis supports the zoological hypothesis as to the origin of tetrabothriids from Pseudophyllidea. If now we apply the same reasoning to Cyclophyllidea of Carnivora we find in these a family of tapeworms whose structure has set them somewhat apart from other Cyclophyllidea, namely Mesocestoididae with the single genus *Mesocestoides.* We regard this genus as very ancient, its anatomical features, aberrant for Cyclophyllidea, showing very great stability resulting doubtless from precocious isolation. The fact that its life-cycle requires two intermediate hosts would seem to support this way of envisaging the problem. Comparing the scolex of *Mesocestoides* with that of *Anophryocephalus*, one is struck by the great resemblance. It is possible that *Mesocestoides* and *Anophryocephalus* represent two neighbouring branches, both very ancient, and Fuhrmann (1931) was right in considering tetrabothriids as primitive Cyclophyllidea.

"From an anatomical standpoint great difficulties arise in attempting to derive tetrabothriids from present day forms. In all tetrabothriids the yolk gland is situated *in front of the ovary*, and in those species which we consider to be the most primitive, it lies also ventral to the ovary. It is easy by a flight of imagination to picture the yolk glands of *Proteocephalus* for example condensing on the ventral face of the ovary and in front of it, but we know of no intermediate forms that can justify such a supposition. In conclusion, all that can be said is that Tetrabothriidae represent a very old family of Cyclophyllidea whose members were harboured originally by mammals but which in course of time have adapted themselves to birds." Baer (1932b).

CLASSIFICATION

Nine genera of Tetrabothriidae will be recognized here. They may be distinguished as follows:

KEY TO GENERA

1. Holdfast with four suckers 2
   Holdfast represented by a conical structure with a collarlike basal portion, lacking suckers . . . . *Priapocephalus*
2. Suckers small; presucker region of holdfast enormously developed so that the suckers appear to be sunk into the base of the holdfast . . . . *Strobilocephalus*
   Suckers relatively large; presucker region not unusually swollen or enlarged 3
3. Suckers without appendices . . . . *Anophryocephalus*

Suckers with appendices 4
4. Suckers roughly triangular in outline with each corner prolonged as a small fleshy outgrowth ....*Trigonocotyle*
Suckers oval or round, each with an antero-lateral outgrowth projecting from its margin like the eaves of a roof 5
5. Genital atrium weakly muscular; canalis masculinus short; cirrus with long bristles ....*Chaetophallus*
Genital atrium deep and muscular 6
6. With uterine apertures opening dorsally ....*Porotaenia*
Without uterine apertures 7
7. Testes entirely postovarian; yolk gland *behind* the ovary. .*Paratetrabothrius*
Testes mainly located behind the ovary but to some extent at the sides of and in front of it; yolk gland *in front of* the ovary 8
8. Vagina and sperm duct uniting to enter the genital atrium as a canalis communis ....*Neotetrabothrius*
Vagina and sperm duct opening separately into the genital atrium ....*Tetrabothrius*

NOTES ON GENERA

Priapocephalus Nybelin, 1922

With the holdfast conical or egg-shaped and lacking suckers. Basal region of holdfast collarlike. Genital atrium shallow, weakly muscular. Canalis masculinus lacking. Cirrus with short bristles. Yolk gland relatively small and inclined to be follicular. Uterus with several dorsally situated and rudimentary apertures. Genotype, *grandis* Nybelin, 1922 (Figure 181 C).

The genotype was recorded from whales, *Balaenoptera intermedia* and *B. borealis* in antarctic waters. Nybelin (1928) added a further species, *minor*, also from *B. borealis*. The genus is characterized by its holdfast (see figure) which shows no trace of suckers and is embedded in the gut wall of the host, thus recalling the condition seen in some pseudophyllidean tapeworms of fishes, notably *Abothrium gadi, Parabothrium bulbiferus*, and *Fistulicola plicatus*; but in these forms the young tapeworm has two definite bothria which, as the holdfast becomes embedded, become a holdfast deformatus. Such is not the case with *Priapocephalus.*

Strobilocephalus Baer, 1932 (=*Strobilocephala* Guiart, 1935)

With the holdfast carrying four small suckers and the presucker region enormously developed so that the suckers appear as if embedded in the base of the holdfast. Medium-sized forms with genital apertures unilateral. Genital ducts running between poral osmoregulatory canals and ventral to poral nerve trunk. Testes few but large, lying in the dorsal and ventral medullary regions. Canalis masculinis opening on the dorsal face of the genital atrium. Distal portion of vagina with a thick wall and a dorso-ventral curvature. Yolk gland ventral to the ovary. Uterus crossing laterally the osmoregulatory canals and having a rudimentary opening in the last segments. Genotype and only known species. *triangularis* Diesing, 1850.

The genotype (= *Tetrabothrius triangulare* Diesing, 1850; *Prostheco-cotyle triangulare* Fuhrmann, 1899; *Tetrabothrius triangulare* Fuhrmann, 1904) was recorded, and has since been recorded, from toothed whales – *Hyperoodon rostratus, Lagenorhynchus acutus,* and *Delphinus sp.* in Atlantic waters. Possibly to this genus should be added the species *forsteri* Krefft, 1873 from *Delphinus forsteri* in Australian waters; *diplosoma* Guiart, 1935 from *Delphinus delphis* in Mediterranean waters; and *pachysoma* Guiart, 1935 from a dolphin off Cape Ferrat – all three relegated by Guiart to a genus *Prosthecocotyla (sic).*

Anophryocephalus Baylis, 1922

With suckers without appendices. Genital apertures unilateral and dextral. Genital atrium with a small, rounded muscular chamber ventral to the vagina. Testes 30, mainly dorsal. Genotype and only known species, *anophrys* Baylis, 1922b from a seal (*Phoca hispida*).

Trigonocotyle Baer, 1932

With the holdfast having four large, circular suckers, each with three small, fleshy appendices arranged at the corners of a triangle. Medium-sized forms. Genital ducts passing between the poral osmoregulatory canals. Genital pores unilateral. Genital atrium strongly muscular. Testes few but large, in dorsal region of segment. Cirrus pouch small. Vagina thick-walled, not forming seminal receptacle. Ovary bilobed, in posterior half of segment, behind the yolk gland. Uterus a transverse tube, not extending over the osmoregulatory canals laterally. Genotype and only known species, *monticellii* Linton, 1923.

The genotype was recorded, as *Prosthecocotyle monticellii,* from a whale, *Globicephalus melas,* in American waters. Guiart (1935b) recorded it from *Globicephalus melaena* in French waters.

Chaetophallus Nybelin, 1916

With the holdfast typically tetrabothriid (i.e., like *Tetrabothrius*). Genital atrium weakly muscular but deep. Canalis masculinus present but relatively short. Cirrus and canalis with dense, long bristles. Yolk gland small but compact. Rudimentary uterine aperture present in some individuals in terminal segments. Genotype, *robustus* Nybelin, 1916.

The genotype was recorded from a procellariiform bird, *Thalassogeron chlororhynchus.* Other species are *umbrellus* Fuhrmann, 1899 in *Diomedea sp.* and *Phoebetria fuliginosa* (Procellariiformes); and *setigerus* Fuhrmann, 1921 in *Phoebetria fuliginosa.*

Porotaenia Szpotanska, 1917

With holdfast and internal anatomy similar to that of *Tetrabothrius* but with a uterine aperture on the dorsal surface of each segment. Genotype, *setigera* Szpotanska, 1917.

Szpotanska, in his study of the tetrabothriids of Procellariiformes (1925), contrary to the Rules of Nomenclature, changed a certain number of the specific names he had given in his preliminary note of 1917 and did not indicate the hosts of his forms; thus *setigera,* 1917 became *siedleckii*, 1925; *kowalewskii*, 1917 became *macrocirrosa*, 1925; *fragilis*, 1917 became *fragilis* var. *capensis*, 1925; while *fragilis* var. *exulans*, 1917 became *fragilis*, 1925.

Fuhrmann (1932) accepted as valid the species *brevis* Szpotanska, 1917; *fragilis* Szpotanska, 1917; *fragilis* var. *exulans* Szpotanska, 1917; *fuhrmanni* Szpotanska, 1917; *kowalewskii* Szpotanska, 1917; *longissima* Szpotanska, 1917; and *setigera* Szpotanska, 1917. Johnston (1935), reviewing the genus, made it synonymous in part with *Chaetophallus*, in part with *Tetrabothrius*. Thus *Porotaenia setigera* Szp., 1917 (= *siedleckii* Szp., 1925; *Chaetophallus musculosus* var. *fuliginosus* Szp.; *Chaetophallus setigerus* Fuhrmann, 1921) became *Chaetophallus setigera* (Szpotanska, 1919); *Porotaenia fragilis* Szp., 1917 became *Tetrabothrius fragilis* (Szp.); *Porotaenia kowalewskii* Szp., became *Tetrabothrius kowalewskii* (Szp.).

Paratetrabothrius Yamaguti, 1940

With the holdfast typically tetrabothriid (as in *Tetrabothrius*). Inner longitudinal musculature strongly developed, in two distinct layers. Testes entirely postero-dorsal to the ovary. Ovary multilobate, in anterior medulla. Yolk gland median, immediately behind the ovary. Seminal receptacle distinct. Uterus filling the segment when fully gravid. Male and female genital ducts between dorsal and ventral osmoregulatory canals. Genital atrium suckerlike. Genital apertures unilateral. Genotype, *orientalis* Yamaguti, 1940.

The genotype was recorded from *Colymbus arcticus pacificus* in Japanese waters. Yamaguti would add to the genus the species *Tetrabothrius lobatus* von Linstow, 1905, also from *Colymbus*.

Neotetrabothrius Nybelin, 1931

With a typical tetrabothriid holdfast. Large forms, strongly flattened dorso-ventrally. Genital ducts ventral to the poral osmoregulatory canals. Genital atrium deep and muscular. Canalis masculinus joining vagina to form a canalis communis which opens at the tip of a genital papilla in the genital atrium. Cirrus with very short bristles. Yolk gland small and compact. Rudimentary uterine aperture occasionally present in end segments, sometimes breaking through to the outside. Genotype, *pellucidus* Nybelin, 1929. Additional species, *eudyptidis* Loennberg, 1896. Both from penguins (Sphenisciformes).

Tetrabothrius Rudolphi, 1819 (= *Tetrabothrium* Diesing, 1856; *Amphoterocotyle* Diesing, 1863; *Prosthecocotyle* Monticelli, 1892; *Bothridiotaenia* Loennberg, 1896; *Tetrabothrium* Fuhrmann, 1932)

With suckers having antero-lateral outgrowth from their margins. Genital atrium very deep and muscular. With a canalis masculinus running to a globular cirrus pouch. Testes surrounding female genitalia. Ovary multilobed. Uterus saclike, often lobed, with opening of a median canal directed toward the dorsal surface of the segment. Genotype, *macrocephalus* Rudolphi, 1819.

The genus is a large one. Fuhrmann (1932) recorded 45 species from birds. Baer (1932b) recorded *affinis* Loennberg, 1891; *forsteri* Krefft, 1871; *ruudi* Nybelin, 1929; and *wilsoni* Leiper and Atkinson, 1914, all from whales. To Fuhrmann's list must be added *lari* Yamaguti, 1935, mainly in fish-eating birds; *rostratulae* Yamaguti, 1940 from charadriiform birds; and *perfidum* Joyeux and Baer, 1934a from *Colymbus cristatus* and *C. aurita* in France.

Family NEMATOTAENIIDAE Lühe, 1910

DESCRIPTION

Of the order Cyclophyllidea. Small forms with holdfast nonrostellate and body cylindrical and mainly unsegmented. Genital apertures alternating irregularly from one margin to the other. Testes only one or two in number. Gravid uterus forming egg capsules, each with one or several eggs. Egg capsules enclosed within paruterine organs, multiple and separate from each other. Adults in Amphibia and Reptilia. Type genus, *Nematotaenia* Lühe, 1899.

HISTORY

The type genus was established by Lühe (1899c) for a form that had previously been recorded in European toads by Goeze (1782) under the term *Taenia dispar*. Lühe, however, provided no description of his suggested genus until 1910, when he made it the type of a new family, Nematotaeniidae. In the meantime both Fuhrmann (1908c) and Ransom (1909) had placed *Nematotaenia* within the subfamily Paruterininae of the family Hymenolepididae. Jewell (1916) described another nematotaeniid form, *Cylindrotaenia*, in North America and established for it a new subfamily, Cylindrotaeniinae, of the family Dilepididae. Fuhrmann (1932) preferred to accept Lühe's suggestion, and later students of nematotaeniid forms have accepted the family Nematotaeniidae.

RECOGNITION FEATURES

Nematotaeniids are readily distinguishable from other tapeworms by their cylindrical body shape, nonrostellate holdfast, restriction of body segmentation to the posterior region, apparent simplicity of genitalia, and arrangement of paruterine organs. In gravid segments there are few or no traces of the original transverse, tubular uterus. The embryonated eggs lie in ones or twos or more within capsules formed by the breakdown of the uterus, and these capsules lie within hollow, pear-shaped spaces in the parenchyma. The number and arrangement of these so-called paruterine organs distinguish the four known genera—*Nematotaenia, Cylindrotaenia, Distoichometra,* and *Baerietta.*

In *Nematotaenia*, according to Hsü (1935), the uterus appears at first as a simple transverse sac which breaks up into capsules each containing one egg; all the capsules are grouped in the vicinity of the cirrus pouch and extend backward in two rows, one dorsal and one ventral, in such a way that a sagittal section of a ripe segment shows the uterine capsules arranged in horseshoe fashion. The beginnings of the paruterine organs appear in the neighborhood of the uterus. The embryonic rudiment divides, each part dividing again into several parts. Each of these parts appears as a hollow spherical or ovoid structure which extends backward toward the center of the segment and encloses within its basal portion several uterine capsules. In the gravid segment, therefore, there appear two rows of paruterine organs, all separate from one another at their bases (Figure 183). Into the terminal portions of the paruterine organs the uterine capsules then pass, and the basal portions atrophy.

A similar origin of paruterine organs is seen in the other genera, but in *Distoichometra* the basal portions of the organs remain united with one another so that two parallel rows of paruterine organs appear, united more or less by their bases, which form a single cavity.

The four genera of Nematotaeniidae may be distinguished as follows:

Nematotaenia Lühe, 1910

With testes two in number. Paruterine organs numerous, each containing several uterine capsules, and arranged in two parallel rows separate from one another. Genotype, *dispar* Goeze, 1782 (Figure 183).

Nematotaenia dispar (= *T. dispar* Goeze, 1782; *T. dispar salamandrae* Froelich, 1789; *T. bufonis* Gmelin, 1790; *Halysis obvoluta* Zeder, 1803; *Proteocephalus dispar* Weinland, 1858) has been recorded in Europe from *Bufo bufo, Bufo viridis, Hyla arborea, Pelobates fuscus, Rana esculenta, Rana temporaria, Salamandra atra, Salamandra salamandra*; in Africa from *Bufo mauritanicus, Bufo sarticus, Rana madagascariensis*; in North America from *Bufo americana, Bufo terrestris, Rana pipiens, Acris gryllus, Necturus maculosa*; in India from *Bufo melanostictus* and *Bufo sp.* The North American records are dubious and have not been confirmed by any modern writer. The synonymity and manner of paruterine organ formation have been discussed by Hsü (1935).

Nematotaenia dispar was the only known species of the genus until Lopez-Neyra (1944) established *Nematotaenia tarentolae* for a form occurring in the northern Mediterranean lizards *Tarentola mauritanica* and *Platydactylus guttatus* and which he believed to be the form regarded by Rudolphi (1809) as Goeze's *Taenia dispar*. According to Lopez-Neyra, this form can be distinguished from *dispar* by the size of the holdfast and suckers, by the small extent of the cirrus pouch, and by the presence of single eggs in the uterine capsules of the gravid segment. Soler (1945) established *Nematotaenia lopezneyra* for a form from *Bufo sp.* in the same area. This species, while resembling to some extent the species *jägerskiöldi* assigned by Hsü (1935) to *Baerietta*, does not agree with the characters of this genus.

Cylindrotaenia Jewell, 1919

With one testis only per segment. Paruterine organs two, each with three uterine capsules and united basally. Genotype, *americana* Jewell, 1916 (Figure 184).

The genotype (= *Cylindrotaenia americanum* Trowbridge and Hefley, 1934) has been recorded in the United States from *Acris gryllus,*

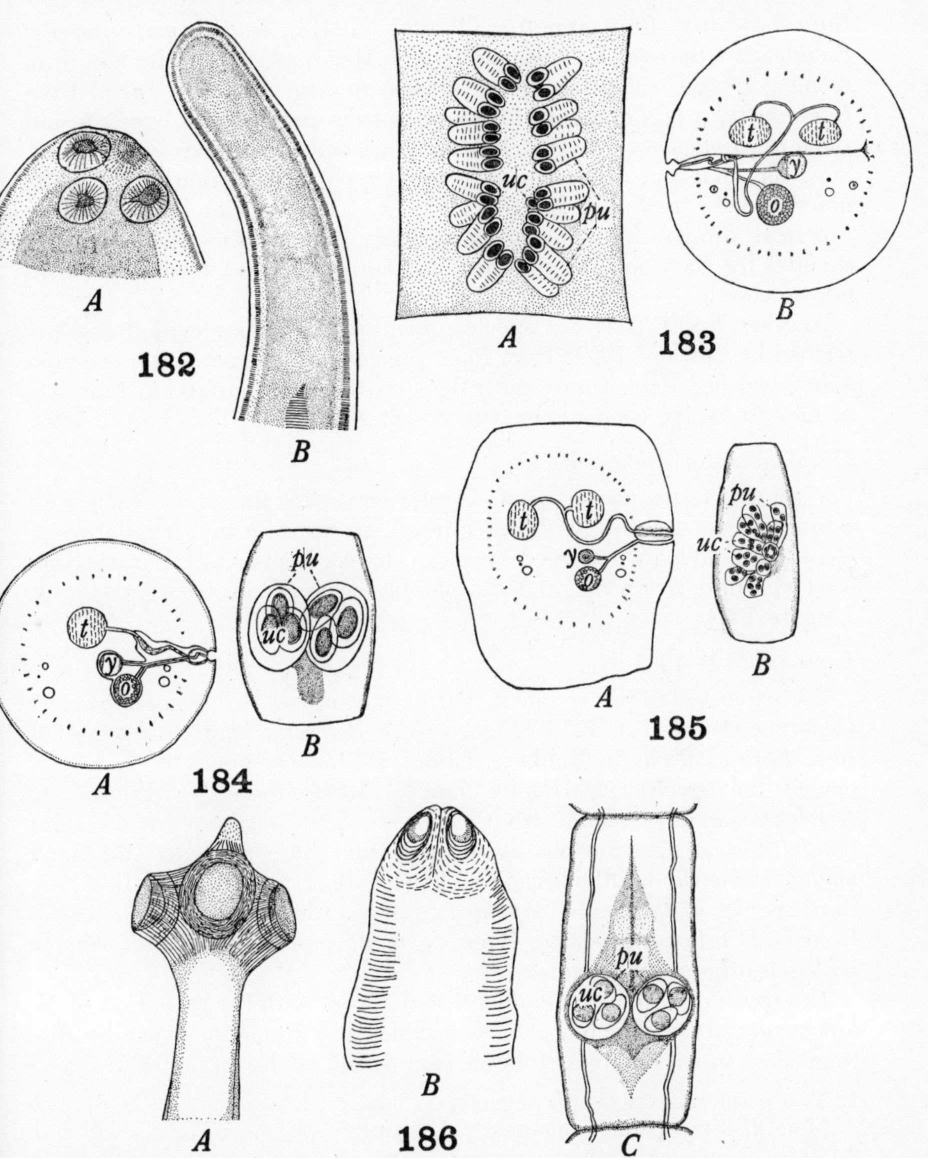

FIG. 182. *Baerietta baeri,* holdfast (A) and anterior region (B). After Hsü, 1935. FIG. 183. *Nematotaenia dispar.* A. Gravid segment showing arrangement of paruterine organs (*pu*) in parallel rows. After Hsü, 1935. B. Cross section of mature segment. After Fuhrmann, 1932. FIG. 184. *Cylindrotaenia americana.* After Jewell, 1916. A. Cross section of mature segment showing single testis (*t*), ovary (*o*), and yolk gland (*y*). B. Ripe segment. FIG. 185. *Distoichometra bufonis.* After Dickey, 1921. A. Cross section. B. Ripe segment. FIG. 186. *Cylindrotaenia quadrijugosa.* After Lawler, 1939. A and B. Holdfast. C. Gravid segment.
o, ovary; *pu*, paruterine organs; *t*, testes; *uc*, uterine capsules; *y*, yolk gland.

Bufo terrestris, Bufo canorus (Walton, 1941); from *Hyla squirella, Pseudacris triseriata, Leiopisma laterale* (Harwood, 1932), the last form being a reptile, and from *Rana pipiens*; in Argentina and Brazil from *Leptodactylus ocellatus*; in Mozambique from *Arthroleptes ogoensis* and *Rana acquiplicalata* (Joyeux, 1924b). Harwood (1932) has pointed out, however, that the discrepancies from Jewell's description that Joyeux noted are so great that specific identity of the African form with the American form seems unlikely, particularly since a form which was discovered by Harwood in an American reptile matched Jewell's description so closely.

Another North American species, *quadrijugosa*, was recorded and described by Lawler (1939) from *Rana pipiens* in Michigan. It differs from *americana* in having transverse ridges on the body surface in four sets of nine to twelve each, along with two paruterine organs (Figure 186).

Distoichometra Dickey, 1921

With two testes per segment. Paruterine organs numerous, each with 3 to 6 uterine capsules, with bases fused, arranged in two parallel rows. Genotypė and only recorded species, *bufonis* Dickey, 1921 from *Bufo fowleri, Bufo terrestris*, and *Scaphiopus sp.*, all in Georgia, U.S.A. (Figure 185).

Baerietta Hsü, 1935

With two testes per segment. Paruterine organs two, united basally. Genotype, *baeri* Hsü, 1935 (Figure 182). *Baerietta baeri* was recorded from *Bufo asiaticus* in Nanking, China. Within the genus Hsü also included the species *jägerskiöldi* Janicki, 1926 (formerly recorded as *Nematotaenia jägerskiöldi* from *Bufo regularis* in Egypt, from *Bufo pantherinus* in French Somaliland, and from *Bufo regularis* and *Rana madagascariensis* in Rhodesia; see Joyeux, Baer, and Martin, 1936). A third species of the genus, *japonica*, was recorded by Yamaguti (1938) from *Hyla arborea japonica, Rana esculenta japonica*, and *Polypedates schlegeli arborea* in Japan.

The species of Nematotaeniidae listed above, with the exception of *N. lopezneyra* about which we have insufficient information, may be distinguished provisionally as follows (key based on Lawler, 1939):

1. Two paruterine organs per segment 2
   More than two paruterine organs per segment 4
2. 20 to 25 eggs per paruterine organ ....
   ....*Baerietta baeri, B. jägerskiöldi, B. japonica* *
   8 or fewer eggs per paruterine organ 3
3. Cuticular ridges on body ....*Cylindrotaenia quadrijugosa*
   Cuticular ridges lacking ....*Cylindrotaenia americana*
4. Paruterine organs in two rows of 4 to 6 each ......*Distoichometra bufonis*
   Paruterine organs scattered, 13 to 30 present ......*Nematotaenia dispar* (more than one egg per capsule), *N. tarentolae* (one egg per capsule)

* *B. baeri* and *B. jägerskiöldi* are distinguished by the dimensions of the holdfast, suckers, and cirrus pouch and by the course of the sperm duct. *B. japonica* resembles *baeri* in number of testes and paruterine organs but differs in egg size.

Observations upon the life cycle of *Cylindrotaenia americana* were reported by Joyeux (1924c). He found no stages between oncosphere and cysticercoid and believed that there is no intermediate host.

Family ANOPLOCEPHALIDAE Cholodkovsky, 1902, emended Fuhrmann, 1907

DESCRIPTION

Of the order Cyclophyllidea. Medium to large forms with nonrostellate holdfast and depressed, well-segmented body. Testes numerous. Uterus varying in shape between genera. Eggs commonly with a characteristic embryonic membrane drawn out into a pair of cross-tapered processes. Larva a cysticercoid in, so far as is known, oribatid mites. Adults parasitic in mammals, to a lesser extent in birds and reptiles. Type genus, *Anoplocephala* E. Blanchard, 1848.

HISTORY

Two tapeworm genera, *Bertia* and *Moniezia*, were established by R. Blanchard (1891b) for material in the old group *Taenia* and set aside with *Anoplocephala* E. Blanchard, 1848 as a subfamily (of Taeniidae) under the term "Anoplocephalinae." Cholodkovsky (1902) separated the group entirely from Taeniidae under the family term "Anoplocephalidae." Fuhrmann (1907a) redefined the family and added to it a number of genera which he distributed among three subfamilies – Anoplocephalinae, Linstowinae, and Thysanosominae – according to the nature of the egg-holding mechanism. Gough (1911) contributed a detailed morphological study of the thysanosomine genus *Stilesia* and established a fourth subfamily, Avitellinae, to contain this genus and the genus *Avitellina*, both of which lack yolk glands and ootypes. However, Baer (1927a), in a monograph of the family, restored these forms to Thysanosominae.

Among other prominent contributions to the zoology of Anoplocephalidae may be mentioned Skrjabin's (1933) general systematic review of the family; Douthitt's survey (1915) of North American forms; the studies of Southwell (1929b) on thysanosomine forms; of Woodland (1927a, 1928a) and again of Southwell (1929b) on avitelline forms; of Theiler (1924) and Taylor (1928) on *Moniezia*; of Meggitt (1934b), Hsü (1935), Loewen (1940), Hughes (1940b) on *Oochoristica*; of Hussey (1941) on *Aporina*; of Arnold (1938) on the Anoplocephalidae of rabbits; of Southwell (1921a), Stunkard (1926), and Sandground (1933) on those of rhinoceroses; and the contributions of Stunkard (1937–40), discussed below, toward an understanding of the anoplocephalid life cycle.

RECOGNITION FEATURES

An anoplocephalid tapeworm is usually readily recognized by a number of features. The holdfast is uniformly similar throughout the family, being small, globular, with four relatively large suckers whose rims lie flush with the surface, and completely lack anything in the nature of accessory suckers, rostellum, spines, hooks, bothridia, and so forth. In one genus, *Moniezioides*, a pair of muscular outgrowths juts out from the front margin of each sucker and in front of the sucker there is a group of glandular cells of unknown function. In several species of *Anoplocephala* the rear margin of the holdfast has four lobelike outgrowths—usually termed "lappets"—two of them reaching over the dorsal surface of the body, two over the ventral surface. In the genus *Baeriella*, the region of the holdfast surface between the suckers is deeply grooved so as to give the appearance of a cross-shaped groove on the tip.

The mature segment, as a rule, is conspicuously wider than long and, after microtechnical preparation, shows a characteristic picture. A dorsal and a ventral pair of osmoregulatory canals are present, connected in some forms by a network of transverse vessels. Either in the center, or slightly off center, is the conspicuous ovary, a deeply lobed structure with the lobes arranged like the sticks of a fan. The lobes may radiate in all directions in the horizontal plane from the point of emergence of the oviduct, as in the species of *Anoplocephala*. The handle of the fan is represented by a short, muscular oviduct; this is joined by the vagina, and the common duct (*fertilization duct*) thus produced proceeds further until joined by the yolk duct coming from a single, compact yolk gland which lies behind the ovary. The union of fertilization duct and yolk duct produces a short, wide, tubular ootype from which a short, slightly twisted uterine passage leads to the uterus proper (Figure 187). The Y-shaped junction of fertilization duct, yolk duct, and uterine passage is surrounded by the lobes of Mehlis' gland.

The proximal third of the vagina, the third nearest to the ovary, is dilated as a seminal receptacle, filled usually with seminal fluid and visible as a white spot in the living segment. The distal region of the vagina is muscular and may be posterior, dorsal, or even ventral to the corresponding male duct; its mouth lies within a cirro-vaginal atrium and has its own sphincter muscle. The vaginal aperture and vagina may be posterior to the cirrus pouch (*Aporina, Andrya*), the primitive position among tapeworms, or posterior and somewhat dorsal (*Bertiella*), or directly ventral (*Anoplocephala*). In *Aporina* the vagina and the cirrus pouch open into a common genital passage. In many anoplocephalids, the vagina atrophies after the segments have been fertilized.

The testes are usually numerous, spheroid or ovoid in shape, scattered through the medullary parenchyma between the osmoregulatory canals or forming a narrow band that crosses the medulla, either anteriorly or posteriorly to the ovary; or the testes may be in one or two groups.

The sperm duct runs nearly straight to the cirro-vaginal atrium; its end portion forms the muscular, spiny cirrus or copulatory organ and is enclosed within a pear-shaped cirrus pouch. Before entering this pouch the duct may be dilated as an external seminal vesicle, and after entering the pouch may again be dilated as an internal seminal vesicle. The sperm duct is almost always surrounded by transparent cells which in some forms are grouped as so-called "prostate glands."

In the gravid segments the most conspicuous feature is provided by

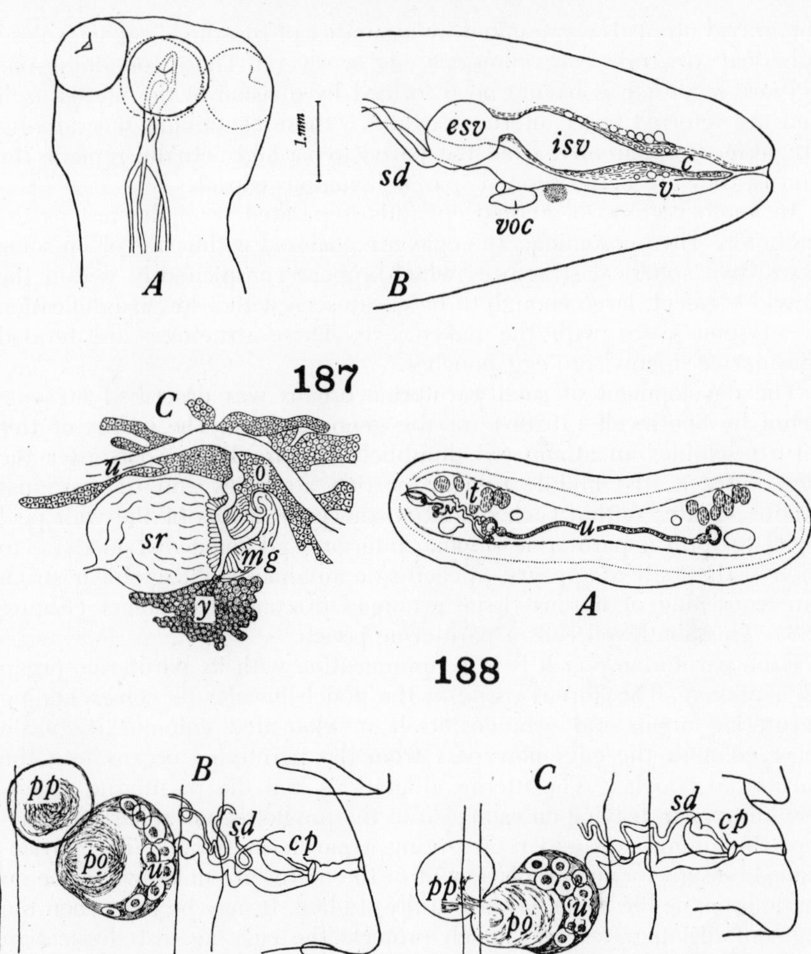

FIG. 187. *Aporina delafondi.* After Hussey, 1941. A. Holdfast. B. End region of genital ducts. C. Female genital complex. FIG. 188. *Stilesia hepatica.* After Southwell, 1929b. A. Cross section of segment. B. Section to show paruterine organs. C. Section to show duct connecting the two paruterine structures. *c*, cirrus; *cp*, cirrus pouch; *esv*, external seminal vesicle; *isv*, internal seminal vesicle; *mg*, Mehlis' glands; *o*, ovary; *po*, paruterine organ; *pp*, paruterine pouches; *sd*, sperm duct; *sr*, seminal receptacle; *t*, testes; *u*, uterus; *v*, vagina; *voc*, ventral osmoregulatory canal; *y*, yolk gland.

the mechanism for holding the developing eggs. This, in most cases, is a persistent uterus which, beginning as a simple transverse tube or as a tubular network, appears – when bloated with eggs – as a transverse sac giving off outpocketings from the front and rear borders. This structure nearly fills the whole of the segment and tends to obliterate the other elements of the reproductive system. In *Moniezia*, however, the meshlike appearance of the uterus persists even when the structure is gravid.

In a number of forms, however, grouped as the subfamily Linstowinae, the gravid uterus is represented by a number of so-called "egg capsules," spherical structures containing one egg or several. Those containing one egg are regarded as having been formed by division of the uterus itself and are referred to as "uterine capsules"; those containing several eggs are formed, apparently, from the parenchyma and actually replace the uterus; they are better termed "parenchymatous capsules."

In another group of anoplocephalids, separated from the rest as the subfamily Thysanosominae, the eggs are enclosed within one or, in some cases, two spherical structures which appear conspicuously within the gravid segment, large enough to be easily seen with a low magnification or in some cases with the naked eye. These structures are termed "paruterine organs" or "egg pouches."

The development of such paruterine organs was described in some detail by Southwell (1929b) for the genus *Stilesia.* The uterus of this form resembles an attenuated dumbbell (Figure 188). Soon after the eggs enter it, the middle tubular portion atrophies and the terminal "knobs" dilate. Within each dilatation the inner layers of the wall peel away to form a paruterine organ. Anterior, and somewhat median, to each of these, there appears on each side an almost solid globular structure consisting of fibrous tissue arranged in concentric layers (Figure 188). This Southwell calls a paruterine pouch.

Each paruterine pouch is in communication with its paruterine organ by a passage. The fibrous tissue of the pouch invades its corresponding paruterine organ and arranges itself in elongated columns. Between these columns the eggs now pass from the paruterine organs into the paruterine pouches. The uterine dilatations and the paruterine organs now disappear, leaving on each side of the proglottis one spherical structure containing eggs and representing a paruterine pouch. The physiological reasons for such replacement of the uterus are unknown, since no thysanosomine life cycle has been fully studied. It may be that when the segment disintegrates, the pouch protects the eggs against dessication until such time as the pouch and contained eggs are ingested by the appropriate intermediate host.

The ripe egg of the anoplocephalid has, so to speak, three shells. There is an outer vitelline membrane; a middle, relatively thick, albuminous layer; and an innermost, chitinous membrane prolonged at one point as a pair of tapering, cross-tipped, filamentous projections, the "pyriform apparatus." The possible function of this pyriform apparatus has stimulated several flights of fancy. One popular explanation, before Stunkard established the part played by oribatid mites in the life cycle of anoplocephalids, was that the pyriform apparatus enabled the eggs to be windborne indirectly into the nostrils of the mammalian definitive host.

The life cycle of the anoplocephalid type of tapeworm remained an enigma despite intensive investigations by many workers until the publication of the first of a series of articles (1937–41) by the American zoologist H. W. Stunkard. This observer showed that in the case of *Moniezia, Bertiella,* and *Cittotaenia,* at any rate, the intermediate hosts are free-living, soil-dwelling mites (Oribatidae), a wide range of such mites being incriminated. In the life cycle of *Cittotaenia ctenoides*, for example, a common parasite of European wild rabbits, there is in the early egg no shell but a boundary membrane within which is an eccentrically placed bladder, attached to the inner surface of the boundary membrane and suspended in a fluid matrix; inside this bladder is the oncosphere. Later this bladder develops a pair of long, tapering, hornlike structures, the pyriform apparatus, and outside the boundary membrane a shell is formed as a series of concentric lamellae, secreted presumably by the uterine wall.

The embryonated eggs leave the segment through slits in the marginal walls and are eaten by oribatid mites. Stunkard (1941) incriminated a long list of species of such mites. The oncosphere tears its way into the hemocoel of the mite, and mainly through active multiplication of 10–14 germinal cells, it slowly gains in size. At the end of four weeks it is spherical and immobile, its hooks functionless—just a mass of cells with an irregularly shaped cavity, on one side of which lie the hooks. By the eighth week it is pear-shaped. By the twelfth week it has a tail-like cercomer, carrying the hooks. During the twelfth to the fifteenth weeks it becomes a typical cysticercoid larva, its spherical body containing a formed holdfast, its cercomer now a mere fibrous appendage. Swallowed by a rabbit, the cysticercoid takes about eleven weeks to become an adult, egg-producing tapeworm (Figure 43).

A similar life cycle characterizes *Moniezia expansa* of the lamb. Eggs and proglottides appear in the droppings 25–35 days after the lambs have been placed on pasture in May (in North America). This suggests that the infected oribatid mites overwinter from October to May (Hawkins, 1948). The mites concerned are *Galumna nigra, G. emarginata, G. obvious, G. virginiensis, Scheloribates laevigatus, Protoscheloribates seghetti, Peloribates curtipilus, Oribatula minuta* in North Amerca (see Krull, 1939; Kates and Runkel, 1948); *Galumna obvious, Scheloribates laevigatus* in Europe (see Potemkina, 1941, 1944a). A similar life cycle characterizes *Bertiella studeri* (Stunkard, 1940a) and *Anoplocephala perfoliata* (Bashkirova, 1941). Such a life cycle probably characterizes all Anoplocephalidae.

CLASSIFICATION

Fuhrmann (1932) recognized three subfamilies of Anoplocephalidae—Anoplocephalinae, Linstowinae, and Thysanosominae. Skrjabin (1933) proposed to separate a fourth subfamily, Stylesiinae, from Thysanosominae on the basis of testis arrangement. We shall follow here the somewhat simpler scheme of Fuhrmann.

Subfamily Anoplocephalinae Blanchard, 1891, emended Fuhrmann, 1932

DESCRIPTION

Of the family Anoplocephalidae. The uterus persists in the gravid segment as a transverse sac, with front and rear outpocketings, or as a tubular net. Vagina and sperm duct crossing dorsally the poral osmoregulatory canals and nerve cord. Vagina soon atrophying and disappearing from the aging segment. The genera contained within this subfamily may be distinguished in preliminary fashion as follows:

KEY TO GENERA

1. Gravid uterus a trilobed sac . . . . *Triuterina*
   Gravid uterus a transverse tube or sac or a tubular network 2
2. Gravid uterus a tubular network 3
   Gravid uterus a transverse sac or tube 7
3. One set of reproductive organs per segment 4
   Two sets of reproductive organs per segment 5
4. Vagina posterior to the cirrus pouch . . . . *Andrya*
   Vagina anterior to the cirrus pouch . . . . *Monoecocestus*
5. No interproglottidal glands . . . . *Fuhrmannella*
   Interproglottidal glands present 6
6. Stalked prostate gland present; genital aperture in posterior quarter of segment margin . . . . *Diandrya*
   No stalked prostate gland; genital aperture mid-marginal . . . . *Moniezia*
7. One set of reproductive organs per segment 8
   Two sets of reproductive organs per segment 17
8. Ovary almost as wide as the medulla . . . . *Anoplocephala*
   Ovary considerably narrower than medulla 9
9. Ovary median or only slightly poral in position 10
   Ovary decidedly poral or aporal in position 13
10. Testes in a continuous transverse band anterior to the ovary . . . . *Taufikia*
    Testes not forming a continuous transverse band 11
11. Testes divided by the ovary into poral and antiporal groups 12
    Testes scattered through the medulla; uterus horseshoe-shaped . . . . *Hemiparonia*
12. Genital aperture absent from mature and gravid segments . . . . . . *Aporina*
    Genital pore present . . . . *Killigrewia*
13. Ovary in antiporal half of segment . . . . *Parabertiella*
    Ovary in poral half of segment 14
14. Testes occupying full width of medulla . . . . *Pseudanoplocephala*
    Testes not occupying whole width of medulla 15
15. Testes in antiporal half of segment . . . . *Paranoplocephala*
    Testes scattered through the medulla 16
16. Suckers more or less stalked; cirrus pouch well developed; uterus a transverse tube crossing both osmoregulatory canals ventrally . . . . . *Prototaenia*
    Suckers sessile; cirrus pouch weak; uterus a tube not crossing the osmoregulatory canals . . . . *Bertiella*
17. Testes in a continuous band across the medulla 18
    Testes in two groups or scattered through medulla 19
18. Testes in a band in front of the ovary; tip of holdfast cross-shaped by reason of deep cruciate indentation between suckers; eggs with pyriform apparatus . . . . *Baeriella*
    Testis band behind the ovary; each sucker with two muscular projections from the margin; eggs without pyriform apparatus . . . . *Moniezioides*
19. Testes in two groups, each in front of the ovary 20
    Testes scattered through the medulla 21
20. Cirrus pouch large; two tubular or saclike uteri per segment; eggs with pyriform apparatus . . . . *Hepatotaenia*

Cirrus pouch small; gravid uterus a single, lobed sac; eggs without a pyriform apparatus .... *Progamotaenia*

21. Gravid uterus a horseshoe-shaped but lobed sac; eggs with a rudimentary pyriform apparatus or without one .... *Paronia*

Gravid uterus a transverse tube; eggs with a pyriform apparatus .... *Cittotaenia*

Incertae sedis: Triplotaenia, Baeria.

Hansen (1948) has recently established a new genus *Schizorchis,* with genotype *S. ochotonae,* from material in the pika or rock rabbit, *Ochotona princeps figginsi* in Colorado. The genus is differentiated from *Monoecocestus (Schizotaenia),* which it closely resembles, and from *Cittotaenia* by its unarmed cirrus.

NOTES ON GENERA

Triuterina Fuhrmann, 1921

With gravid uterus a trilobed sac. Small, muscular forms with genital apertures alternating irregularly. Genital ducts running between the poral osmoregulatory canals and dorsal to the nerve cord. Testes very numerous, scattered through the medulla, most numerous in the antiporal half of the segment. Female genitalia in the poral half of the segment. Uterus of three parts, a median and two latero-posterior regions. Eggs without pyriform apparatus. Adults in parrots. Genotype and only known species, *anoplocephaloides* Fuhrmann, 1902 from *Psittacus erythraeus*, equatorial Africa.

Andrya Railliet, 1893

With vagina posterior to cirrus pouch. Medium to large forms with extremely linear segmentation. Genital apertures unilateral *or* alternating. Testes numerous, in front of antiporal side of ovary, tending to extend dorsally across the antiporal osmoregulatory canal and nerve trunk. Genital ducts dorsal to poral osmoregulatory canals and nerve trunk. Cirrus pouch small, with internal seminal vesicle. Stalked prostate gland usually present or, if absent, replaced by an external seminal vesicle. Female genitalia in poral half of segment. Uterus at first netlike, later becoming saclike and lobed. Eggs with well-developed pyriform apparatus. Adults in rodents. Genotype, *rhopalocephala* Riehm, 1881.

Douthitt (1915) regarded *Andrya* as being nearer to the ancestral anoplocephalid than any other genus, notably in the median position of the ovary, the postcirral position of the vagina and vaginal aperture, the generalized distribution of the testes, the primitive, unmodified sperm duct, and the little modified reticulate uterus. He recognized six species—*rhopalocephala* Riehm, 1881 from *Lepus timidus* (European hare) in Germany; *cuniculi* R. Blanchard, 1891 from *Lepus timidus* and *Oryctolagus cuniculi* in France; *macrocephala* Douthitt, 1915 from *Geomys bursarius* (pocket gopher) in Minnesota; *translucida* Douthitt, 1915 also from *Geomys bursarius* (Baer, 1927a, regarded these two forms as synonymous); *primordialis* Douthitt, 1915 from *Tamiasciurus hudsonicus* (red squirrel) in Colorado (Joyeux, 1923a, recorded a variety of this species, as *gundii*, from a South African mouse *Clethrionomys dactylus gundi*); and *communis* Douthitt, 1915 from *Clethrionomys gapperi galei* (red-backed mouse) and *Tamiasciurus hudsonicus* in Colorado. This last form Baer (1927a) considered synonymous with *primordialis*.

To the above list may be added *africana* Baer, 1933 from *Tatera lobengulae* in Rhodesia; *caucasica* Kirschenblatt, 1938 from *Microtus socialis satunini* in Georgia, Russia; *neotomae* Voge, 1946 from *Neotoma fuscipes* in California; *sciuri* Rausch, 1947 from *Glaucomys sabrinus macrotis* (northern flying squirrel) in Wisconsin; *microti* Hansen, 1947 from *Microtus ochrogaster* in Nebraska; and *ondatrae* Rausch, 1948 from *Ondarta z. zibethica* (muskrat) in Ohio.

Kirschenblatt (1938) separated the genus into two subgenera:

1. *Andrya s. str.* Prostate gland present; vas deferens without vesicula seminalis externa; testes mainly in anterior region of segment; osmoregulatory canals well developed; comprising *rhopalocephala, cuniculi, primordialis,* and *primordialis gundii.*

2. *Aprostatandrya.* Prostate gland absent; vas deferens with vesicula seminalis externa; testes in anterior and posterior, or only in posterior, region of segment; ventral osmoregulatory canals not unusually developed; comprising *macrocephala, caucasica, africana,* and *monodi* Joyeux and Baer.

Following Rausch (1948b), the North American forms may be distinguished as follows:

1. Testes confined to the area between the longitudinal canals 2
   Testes overlapping the longitudinal canals 3
2. Testes 60 to 74 in number; prostate gland absent; ventral canals not enlarged .... *neotomae* Voge, 1946
3. Testes overlapping longitudinal canals on both sides 4
   Overlapping aporally only 5
4. Testes 100 to 110 in number; prostate gland absent; ventral canals not enlarged .... *sciuri* Rausch, 1947
   Testes 75 to 95 in number, extending on both sides to lateral margins of ventral canals; prostate glands absent; ventral canals somewhat enlarged .... *ondatrae* Rausch, 1948
5. Testes 28 to 35, prostate gland present (?), ventral canals not enlarged.... .... *microti* Hansen, 1947
   Testes 75 to 95, prostate gland present, ventral canals not enlarged........ .... *primordialis* Douthitt, 1915
   Testes 43 to 57, prostate gland absent, ventral canals enlarged .... *macrocephala* Douthitt, 1915

With regard to *microti*, Rausch believes that its morphological and distributional similarity to *caucasica* justifies consideration of possible specific identity. We may note, also, that a recent (1949a) survey by Rausch and Schiller of the extent of morphological variation among specimens of *Andrya macrocephala* has induced some feelings of doubt as to the value of the distribution and number of testes and the size of the ventral osmoregulatory canals as characters for the differentiation of *Andrya* species. Average egg diameter, however, would seem to be a sufficiently stable character. The survey suggested that *microti, ondatrae,* and probably *caucasica* are merely synonyms of *macrocephala.*

Monoecocestus Beddard, 1914 (= *Schizotaenia* Janicki, 1904)

Medium-sized forms with linear segments. Genital apertures unilateral and dextral or irregularly alternating. Testes numerous, postero-median, reaching porad. Cirrus pouch well developed. Cirrus spiny. Vagina anterior to cirrus pouch. Ovary median or porad. Uterus a degenerate network. Eggs with a pyriform apparatus. Adults in mammals. Genotype, *decrescens* Diesing, 1856.

Janicki's term *Schizotaenia* is invalid, having been used earlier for a myriapod. Diesing's material (*Taenia decrescens*) was obtained from a peccary (*Dicotyles*) in South America. Janicki (1904a) added a further species, *hagmanni,* from the capybara (*Hydrochaerus*). Baer (1927a) believed the two species to be identical, despite the wide difference in host distribution. Stiles (1895b) established *americana* (*Schizotaenia*) from a porcupine (*Erethizon*). Douthitt (1915) established *variabilis* also from a porcupine. Both species are valid according to Chandler (1936), who disagreed with Baer's (1927) argument that *variabilis* is synonymous with *Monoecocestus erethizontis* Beddard, 1914d. Rather, Chandler believed, Beddard's form is synonymous with *americana* (see also Olsen, 1939b). Douthitt also established *anoplocephaloides* from *Geomys breviceps.* A fourth North American species, *sigmodontis,* was recorded by Chandler and Suttles (1922) from the cotton rat *Sigmodon.*

The North American species of *Monoecocestus* may be distinguished provisionally as follows:

1. Testes in a continuous band of approximately uniform thickness, posterior to the ovary; or in two groups, separated by the yolk gland; ovary median or on the poral side of the middle line 2
   Testes in a continuous band which is much thicker in one half or the other of the segment 3
2. Testes in two groups separated by the yolk gland . . . . *anoplocephaloides*
   Testes in two or three continuous rows across the medulla; form 30–60 mm. long by 3.0–4.5 mm. wide; with the ovary median . . . . *americanus* (Figure 190)
   As above, but 33–42 mm. long by 7.5–9.5 mm. broad; with ovary between mid-line and genital aperture, the worm appearing to have a double row of ovaries . . . . *variabilis*
3. Testes mainly in the poral half of the segment; ovary also poral . . . . *erethizontis*
   Testes mainly in the antiporal half of the segment; ovary median . . . . *sigmodontis*

Fuhrmannella Baer, 1925

With segments wider than long. Genitalia double per segment. Genital ducts dorsal to the osmoregulatory canals and nerve trunks. Interproglottidal glands lacking. Testes occupying the median field between the ovaries but also to some extent on the poral sides of them. Uterus netlike, forming a sort of tunnel, antero-dorso-ventral; in old segments evaginations of the uterus passing between the longitudinal muscles; all

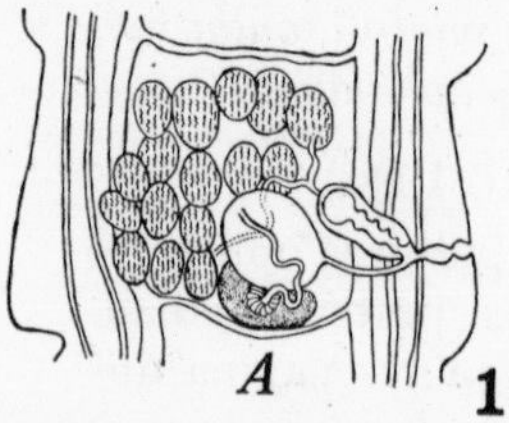

189

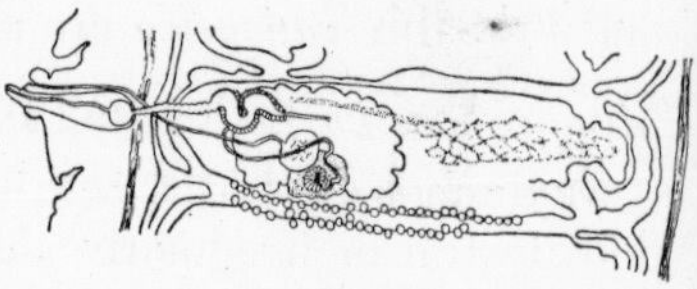

190

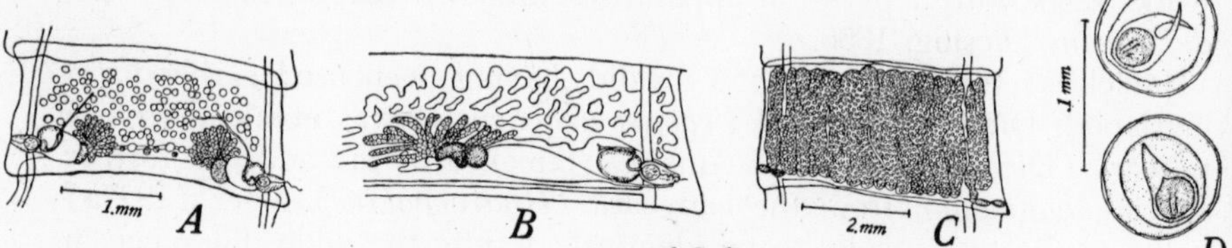

191

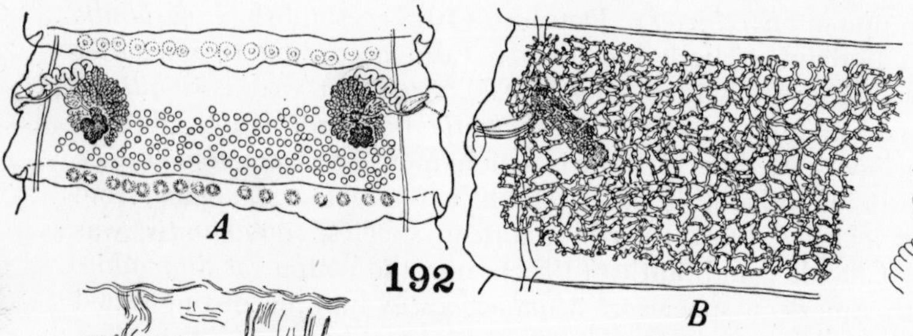

192

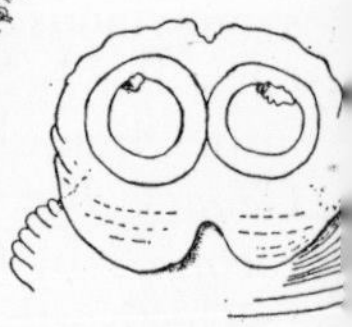

193

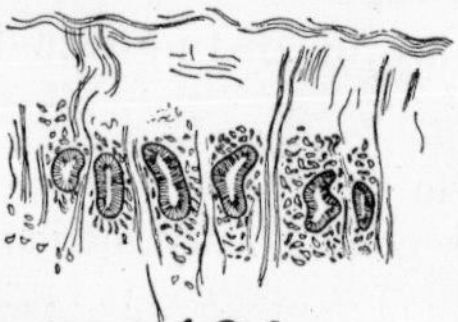

194

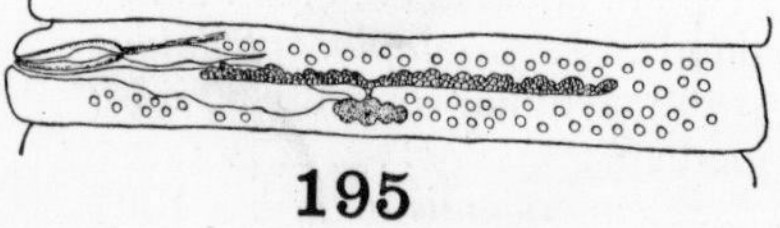

195

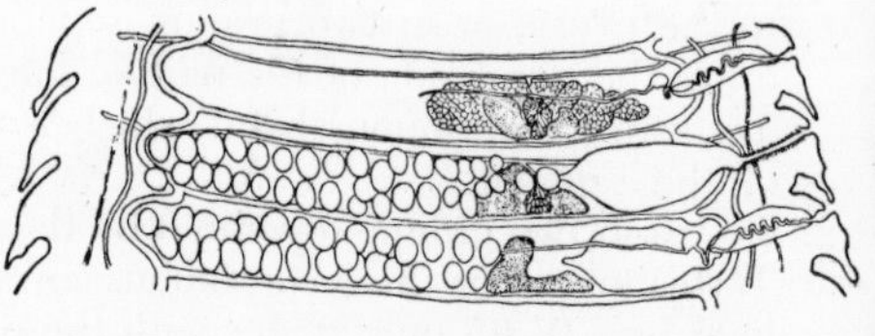

196

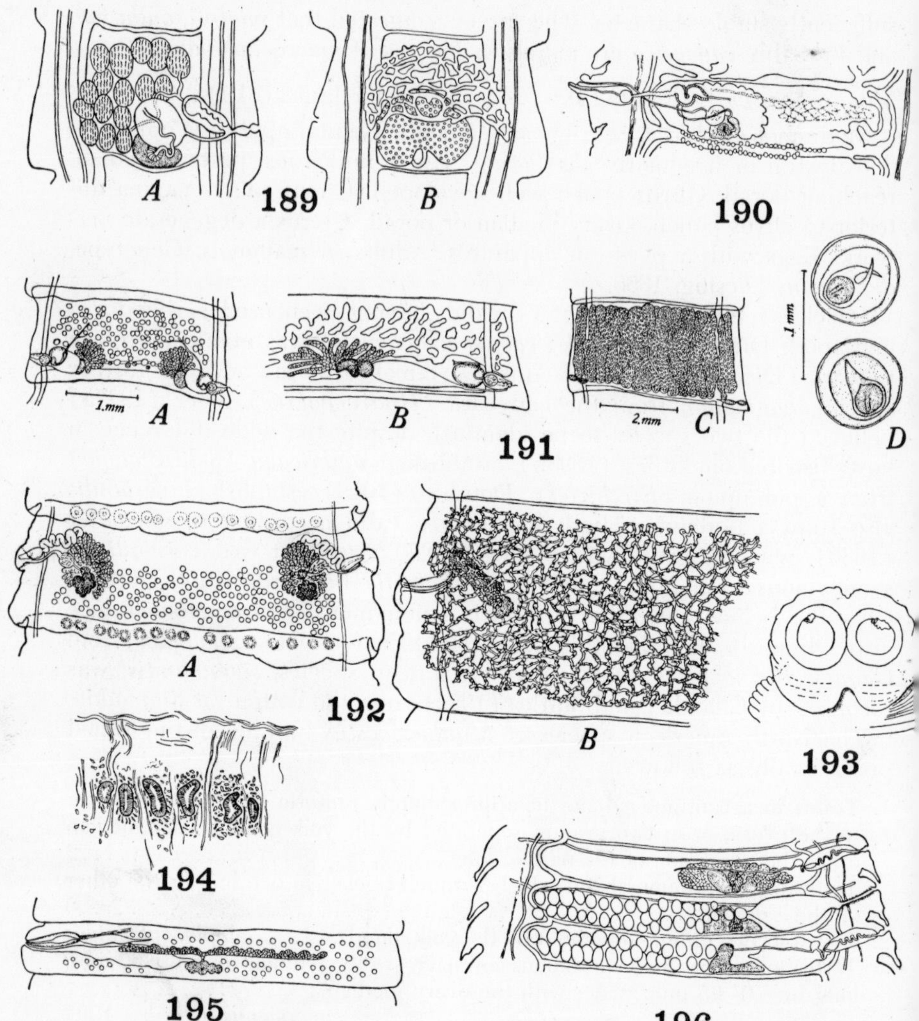

FIG. 189. *Andrya primordialis.* A. Mature segment. B. Gravid segment. After Douthitt, 191 FIG. 190. *Monoecocestus americanus,* mature segment. After Douthitt, 1915. FIG. 19 *Diandrya composita.* After Darrah, 1930. A. Mature segment. B. Semigravid segment showi formation of uterus just before breaking down of ovary; testes omitted. C. Gravid segme D. Eggs. FIG. 192. *Moniezia expansa.* After Fuhrmann, 1932. A. Mature segment. B. Grav segment. FIG. 193. *Anoplocephala perfoliata,* holdfast. After Baer, 1927a. FIG. 194. *Moniez monardi,* cross section of segment through interproglottidal glands. After Fuhrmann, 1933 FIG. 195. *Anoplocephala spatula,* mature segment. After Fuhrmann, 1932. FIG. 196. *Paranoplocephala mamillana,* mature segments. After Douthitt, 1915.

the segments finally becoming bloated with eggs. Eggs with pyriform apparatus. Adults in rodents. Genotype and only known species, *transvaalensis* Baer, 1925d in *Otomys bisulcatus* (a water rat), South Africa.

Diandrya Darrah, 1930

With double genitalia per segment. Medium-sized forms. Genital ducts dorsal to osmoregulatory canals and nerve trunks. Stalked prostate gland present. Interproglottidal glands may be present. Testes numerous, in single field across the segment, between the osmoregulatory canals. Uterus a network. Eggs with well-developed pyriform apparatus. Adults in rodents. Genotype and only known species, *composita* Darrah, 1930 in *Marmota flaviventris* (yellow-bellied woodchuck) Wyoming (Figure 191).

Moniezia R. Blanchard, 1891

With double genitalia per segment. Large forms. Genital ducts dorsal to osmoregulatory canals and nerve trunks. Vagina ventral to cirrus pouch on one side, dorsal to it on the other. Testes small, numerous, scattered through medulla. Uterus single, a network of tubes crossing the osmoregulatory canals dorsally, becoming saclike when egg-filled. Eggs with pyriform apparatus. Interproglottidal glands present or lacking. Larva a cysticercoid in oribatid mites. Adults mainly in ruminant mammals. Genotype, *expansa* Rudolphi, 1810 (Figure 192).

R. Blanchard established the genus for all the double-pored anoplocephalids then known, namely, thirteen species in ruminant mammals, four in rodents, and one in a marsupial. Stiles and Hassall (1893) divided these forms into three groups: a *planissima* group in which the interproglottidal glands form a line across the segment; an *expansa* group in which these glands are grouped in rosettes as round, blind sacs; and a *denticulata* group in which these glands are lacking. Theiler (1924) reduced the number of valid species to three – *expansa, benedeni* (= *planissima*), and *denticulata* – to which Baer (1927a) insisted on adding three more – *trigonophora, rugosa*, and *conjugens*. Taylor (1928) again reduced the number of valid species to three, namely:

1. *Moniezia expansa* Rudolphi, 1810 (= *oblongiceps* Stiles and Hassall, 1893; *trigonophora* Stiles and Hassall, 1892; *minima* Marotel, 1912; *nullicollis* Moniez, 1891). With the interproglottidal glands grouped as round, blind sacs, thus giving a rosette appearance to each group of glands; the species is common in lambs almost everywhere where sheep are reared on a large scale (Figure 192).

2. *Moniezia benedeni* Moniez, 1879 (= *planissima* Stiles and Hassall, 1893; *translucida* Jenkins, 1923; *alba* Perroncito, 1879; *triangularis* Marotel, 1913; *crassicollis* Sauter, 1917; *parva* Sauter, 1917; *neumanni* Moniez, 1891; *pellucida* Blei, 1922; *amphibia* Linstow, 1901; *chappuisi* Baer, 1923a). With the interproglottidal glands arranged in a short, transverse row just in front of the posterior border of each segment; a cosmopolitan form, common in nearly all stock-raising areas, but probably commoner in calves than in lambs.

3. *Moniezia pallida* Mönnig, 1926. With the uterus extending ventrally as well as dorsally over the osmoregulatory canals but with the interproglottidal glands arranged as in *benedeni*; in horses in South Africa.

A fourth species was established by Fuhrmann (1933b) under the name *monardi* for a form from an antelope (*Redunca amadirum*) in Angola, West Africa. Similar in most respects to *expansa*, notably in the arrangement of the interproglottidal glands, Fuhrmann believed sufficient differences to be present to warrant specific differentiation (Figure 194). Yet another species, *mattami*, has been recorded by Baylis (1934d) from the wart hog (*Phacochaerus aethiopicus*) in Uganda. It bears a close resemblance to *benedeni* but differs in lacking interproglottidal glands and in the vagina being tortuous instead of straight.

Anoplocephala E. Blanchard, 1848

Large, well-segmented forms with markedly linear segmentation. Genital apertures unilateral. Testes numerous, scattered through the medulla. Ovary with marked poral and antiporal wings, filling nearly the whole medullary width. Gravid uterus large, saclike, and lobed. Eggs with well-developed pyriform apparatus. Adults in perissodactyl mammals. Genotype, *perfoliata* Goeze, 1782 (Figure 193).

Of the nine species accepted here, *perfoliata* Goeze, 1782 and *magna* Abildgaard, 1789 are common in asses and horses all over the world. The two forms are not always sharply distinguishable. Typically, *perfoliata* is small (30–70 by 12 mm.), has a holdfast somewhat cuboid with four backwardly directed projections from the posterior border, two of these lappets being dorsal, two ventral; the testes are few. *Magna*, on the other hand, is larger (350 by 25 mm.), has a spherical holdfast usually without lappets, and has 400–500 testes as against the 200 of *perfoliata*. *Anoplocephala manubriata* Railliet, Henry, and Bauche, 1914 occurs in the Asiatic elephant; *rhodesiensis* Yorke and Southwell, 1921 in the zebras of East Africa; *spatula* Linstow, 1901e in the African hyraxes (*Heterohyrax, Procavia*) (Figure 195).

The anoplocephalids of rhinoceroses have been the subject of considerable discussion; see Peters (1871), Murie (1870), Blanchard (1891a), MacCallum and MacCallum (1912), Deiner (1912), Southwell (1921a), Stunkard (1926), Baer (1927), and Sandground (1933). Two species may be recognized – *gigantea* Peters, 1856 (= *Plagiotaenia gigantea* Peters, 1871; *latissima* Deiner, 1912; *vulgaris* Southwell, 1921; *longa* Stunkard, 1926); and *diminuta* Sandground, 1933 from *Rhinoceros sondaicus*.

Anoplocephala gorillae Nybelin, 1927 was recorded from the mountain gorilla, *Gorilla beringei*, of central Africa. *Anoplocephala genettae* Ortlepp, 1937 was recorded from *Genetta rubiginosa* in South Africa.

Taufikia Woodland, 1928 (= *Gidhaia* Johri, 1934; *Parvirostrum* Fuhrmann, 1908; *sensu* Southwell, 1930)

Medium-sized forms with only one pair of osmoregulatory canals. Genital ducts passing *between* the poral canal and nerve trunk. Genital apertures alternating irregularly. Cirrus pouch small, with an internal seminal vesicle. External seminal vesicle surrounded by glandular cells. Testes in two lateral fields joining in the anterior region of the segment. Female genitalia in the poral half of the segment. Uterus appearing early, as a small trilobed sac, later filling almost the whole medulla and extending laterally over the osmoregulatory canals. Eggs without pyriform apparatus. Adults in birds of prey. Genotype, *edmondi* Woodland, 1928 in *Gyps rüppeli,* Northeast Africa.

Lopez-Neyra (1935a) transferred to this genus Southwell's *Parvirostrum magnisomum* and moved the genus from Anoplocephalinae to Dilepidinae; synonymous with it in his opinion is *Gidhaia indica* of Johri (1934).

Hemiparonia Baer, 1925

Medium-sized forms. Genital apertures unilateral. Genital ducts dorsal to the poral osmoregulatory canal. Testes numerous, in a single field overlapping the osmoregulatory canals. Cirrus pouch well developed. Ovary and yolk gland median. Uterus a tubular horseshoe, with the convexity anterior. Eggs without (?) pyriform apparatus. In birds. Genotype, *cacatuae* Maplestone, 1922.

The genotype was established, as *Schizotaenia cacatuae*, for material from a cockatoo (*Cacatua galerita*) in Australia. A second species, *merotomocheta*, was added by Woodland (1930a), also from an Australian cockatoo, *Cacatua leadbeateri.*

Aporina Fuhrmann, 1902

Medium-sized forms, commonly without genital apertures. Testes in a continuous band across the segment. Cirrus pouch and cirro-vaginal atrium degenerate or atrophied. Ovary median or slightly poral. Gravid uterus a transverse, lobed sac. Eggs without pyriform apparatus. Adult in birds. Genotype, *alba* Fuhrmann, 1902d.

The genotype was established for material from a Brazilian parakeet, *Pyrrhura sp.*, and had no genital apertures. Actually, of the three species known, the genotype *alba* has no genital apertures; *fuhrmanni* Skrjabin, 1915 (host unknown) has genital apertures; and *delafondi* Railliet, 1892a – a parasite of pigeons and doves which has been redescribed in detail by the American observer Hussey (1941) – has a cirro-vaginal atrium in each mature segment which communicates by a very narrow passage, distinguishable only with difficulty, with the outside (Figure 187).

Killigrewia Meggitt, 1927

Identical in most respects with the preceding genus but with the testis band broken into two groups by the ovary. Gravid uterus, while extending laterally across the osmoregulatory canals, does not run forward at each end as a blind branch parallel and close to the osmoregulatory canal, as is the case in *Aporina.* Genotype, *frivola* Meggitt, 1927d.

The close similarity between *Killigrewia* and *Aporina* is undeniable, and Fuhrmann (1932) regarded the two forms as identical. The distinctiveness has been argued, however, both by Johri (1934) and Yamaguti (1935a, 1940). The latter author has added to Meggitt's species *frivola* and *pamelae*—from an unknown Egyptian host and from *Turturoena sharpi*, Egypt, respectively—the species *oenopeliae* Yamaguti, 1935 (from *Oenopelias transquebarica humilis*) and *streptopeliae* Yamaguti, 1935 (from *Pycnotus sinensis formosa* and *Streptolia orientalis orientalis*) in Formosa. Meggitt also added to his genus the species *Bertiella aberrata* of Nybelin (1917), a form placed by Baer (1927a) in the genus *Prototaenia.*

Parabertiella Nybelin, 1917

Small forms with stalked suckers. Genital apertures alternating irregularly. Genital ducts dorsal to the poral osmoregulatory canals and nerve trunk. Cirrus pouch large. Cirrus spiny. Testes in a single field in the anterior half of the segment. Ovary and yolk gland in the antiporal half of the segment. Uterus a transverse tube overlapping the osmoregulatory canals of each side. Eggs with a pyriform apparatus. Genotype and only known species, *campanulata* Nybelin, 1917a in *Pseudochirus lemuroides* (marsupial) in Australia.

Pseudanoplocephala Baylis, 1927

With one set of genitalia per segment and genital apertures unilateral. One pair only of osmoregulatory canals. Genital ducts passing dorsally over the poral osmoregulatory canal and nerve trunk. Vagina ventral to the cirrus pouch. Testes occupying the full width of the medulla but more numerous porally. Female organs median. Uterus saclike with numerous outgrowths. Eggs without pyriform apparatus. Genotype and only known species, *crawfordi* Baylis, 1927b from a wild boar (*Sus cristatus*) in Ceylon.

Paranoplocephala Lühe, 1910 (= *Anoplocephaloides* Baer, 1923)

Medium-sized forms with unilateral or with irregularly alternating genital apertures. Testes numerous, antiporal to the ovary. Ovary poral. Gravid uterus a transverse, lobed sac. Eggs with a pyriform apparatus. Adults in rodents and perissodactyl mammals. Genotype, *omphalodes* Hermann, 1793.

In some respects this is an unsatisfactory genus. From rodents there have been recorded *omphalodes* Hermann, 1793 (*Microtus agrestis, Arvicola terrestris*, Europe); *transversaria* Krabbe, 1879 (*Marmota marmota,* northern Eurasia); *wimerosa* Moniez, 1880 (*Lepus timidus, Oryctolagus cuniculus,* Europe); *blanchardi* Moniez, 1891 (*Microtus agrestis, Microtus arvalis, Microtus nivialis,* Europe); *borealis* Douthitt, 1915 (*Microtus spp.,* North America); *infrequens* Douthitt, 1915 (*Geomys bursarius, Clethrionomys spp., Microtus spp.,* North America); *variabilis* Douthitt, 1915 (*Microtus spp.,* North America); *acanthocirrosa* Baer, 1924 (*Otomys irroratus,* South Africa); *brevis* Kirschenblatt, 1938 (*Microtus spp.,* Transcaucasia, Russia); and *troeschi* Rausch, 1946 (*Micro-*

tus cranicus, Michigan). On the other hand, *mamillana* Mehlis, 1831 has been recorded, though rarely, from horses in various parts of the world and also from a South American tapir (Figure 196).

The three North American species are distinguished by Rausch and Schiller (1949a) as follows:

1. Testes extend beyond aporal ventral longitudinal osmoregulatory canal . . 2
   Testes do not extend beyond the aporal canal . . . . *infrequens*
2. Testes from 60 to 80 in number; size large; ratio of length to width of mature segments about 1:12 . . . . *variabilis*
   Testes from 38 to 50 in number; size small; ratio of length to width of mature segments about 1:4 . . . . *borealis*

Baer (1949) would also place within *Paranoplocephala* the species *isomydis* Setti, 1892 (= *Taenia isomydis* Setti, 1892), recorded by Setti from the rodent *Isomys abyssinicus* of northeast Africa.

Prototaenia Baer, 1927 (= *Bertiella* Stiles and Hassall)

Variably sized forms with suckers more or less stalked and musculature well developed. Genital apertures alternating irregularly. Genital ducts dorsal to the poral osmoregulatory canals and nerve trunk. Cirrus pouch well developed and cirrus armed. Testes numerous, scattered through the whole width of the medulla. Female organs in the poral half of the segment. Uterus a transverse tube, becoming saclike and overlapping ventrally the osmoregulatory canals. Eggs with more or less well-developed pyriform apparatus. Adults in marsupials and insectivores. Genotype, *elongata* Bourquin, 1905.

Baer established the genus for those species of *Bertiella* found in marsupials and insectivores. Although close to *Bertiella*, the genus differs in the very great development of the cirrus pouch; in the powerful parenchymal musculature; in the fact that the uterus overlaps ventrally the osmoregulatory canals; and in having the dorsal osmoregulatory canals lying on the inner side of the ventral ones.

The genotype, *elongata* Bourquin, 1905, was established for a form from *Galeopithecus volans*, southern Asia. Other species are: *aberrata* Nybelin, 1917 from *Pseudochirus herbetensis*, Australia; *edulis* Zschokke, 1899 from *Phalanger ursinus*, Celebes; *obesa* Zschokke, 1898 from *Phascolarctus cinereus*, Australia; *pellucida* Nybelin, 1917 from *Pseudochirus lemuroides*, Australia; *plastica* Sluiter, 1896 from *Galeopithecus volans*, southern Asia; *pseudochiri* Nybelin, 1917 from *Pseudochirus herbetensis*, Australia; *rigida* Janicki, 1906b from *Phalangista sp.*, New Guinea; *sarasinorum* Zschokke, 1899 from *Phalanger ursinus*, Celebes; *undulata* Nybelin, 1917 from *Pseudochirus lemuroides*, Australia.

Baylis (1934c) suppressed Baer's genus and added its ten species to *Bertiella*, adding further the species *kapul* from the spotted cuscus (*Phalanger maculatus krämeri*) on Manus Island, Admiralty Group, and *anapolytica* from a rodent, *Rattus rattus brevicaudatus* at Buitenzorg, Java.

Bertiella Stiles and Hassall, 1902

Medium-sized forms with well-marked segmentation and a short neck. Genital pores alternating irregularly. One set of genitalia per segment. Testes numerous, scattered through the medulla in the area bounded by the osmoregulatory canals. Cirrus pouch well developed, with an internal seminal vesicle. Vagina surrounded by a layer of glandular cells. Gravid uterus a transverse tube, not overlapping the osmoregulatory canals, discharging when gravid through marginal slits or craters on the proglottis surface. Eggs with well-developed pyriform apparatus. Genotype and only species, *studeri* Blanchard, 1891a in Primates (Figure 197).

The term *Bertiella* replaced Blanchard's term *Bertia* which had been used earlier for another zoological form. Blanchard established his genus for two forms, *studeri* from chimpanzees, and *satyri* from orangutans. In 1913 he recorded *satyri* also from a child in Mauritius, and since then *Bertiella* has been found eleven or twelve times in humans, as well as in other Primates. Blanchard recognized no fewer than eighteen species of the genus. Chandler (1925a), in a key to the species occurring in humans, recognized only six such. Cram (1928b) accepted only three species as occurring in humans, nineteen as occurring in other mammals. Baer (1927a) went further still and restricted the whole genus to two species, occurring only in Primates – *studeri* in the Eastern Hemisphere, and *mucronata* in the Western Hemisphere. The species *satyri, conferta, polyorchis*, and *cercopitheci* he regarded as synonyms of *studeri*, whose range of primate hosts was thus widened to include *Homo sapiens, Simia satyrus, Anthropithecus troglodytes, Hylobates hoolock, Cercopithecus pygerythraeus, Cercopithecus schmidti, Cynomolgus sinicus*, and *Cynomolgus fascicularis.*

Meggitt (1927d) was unable to differentiate *mucronata* from *cercopitheci*, but established a further species, *fallax* (Figure 198), for a form from a capuchin monkey (originally South American) in the Cairo Zoological Gardens. Cameron (1929) doubted whether any differences occurred between *mucronata* and *studeri*. We shall take the view here that the genus contains only one species, *studeri,* widely distributed among Primates.

Baer (1940a), discussing the origin of human tapeworms, suggested that *studeri* is perhaps the only tapeworm to have been acquired by prehistoric man before the Ice Age.

"It has subsequently become localized in sub-tropical climates although such climates do not appear to be necessary for the completion of the life-cycle. Stunkard (1939c) has shown that ordinary free-living mites such as are found in northern Europe can be infected experimentally with larvae when fed mature ova. Our pre-hominian and even our hominian ancestors could consequently have acquired their tapeworm infection long before they became hunters or fishermen. The actual status of the problem of host-specificity urges us to state that in all probability *B. studeri* is the only original tapeworm acquired by man through evolution. The scarcity of this species today as a human para-

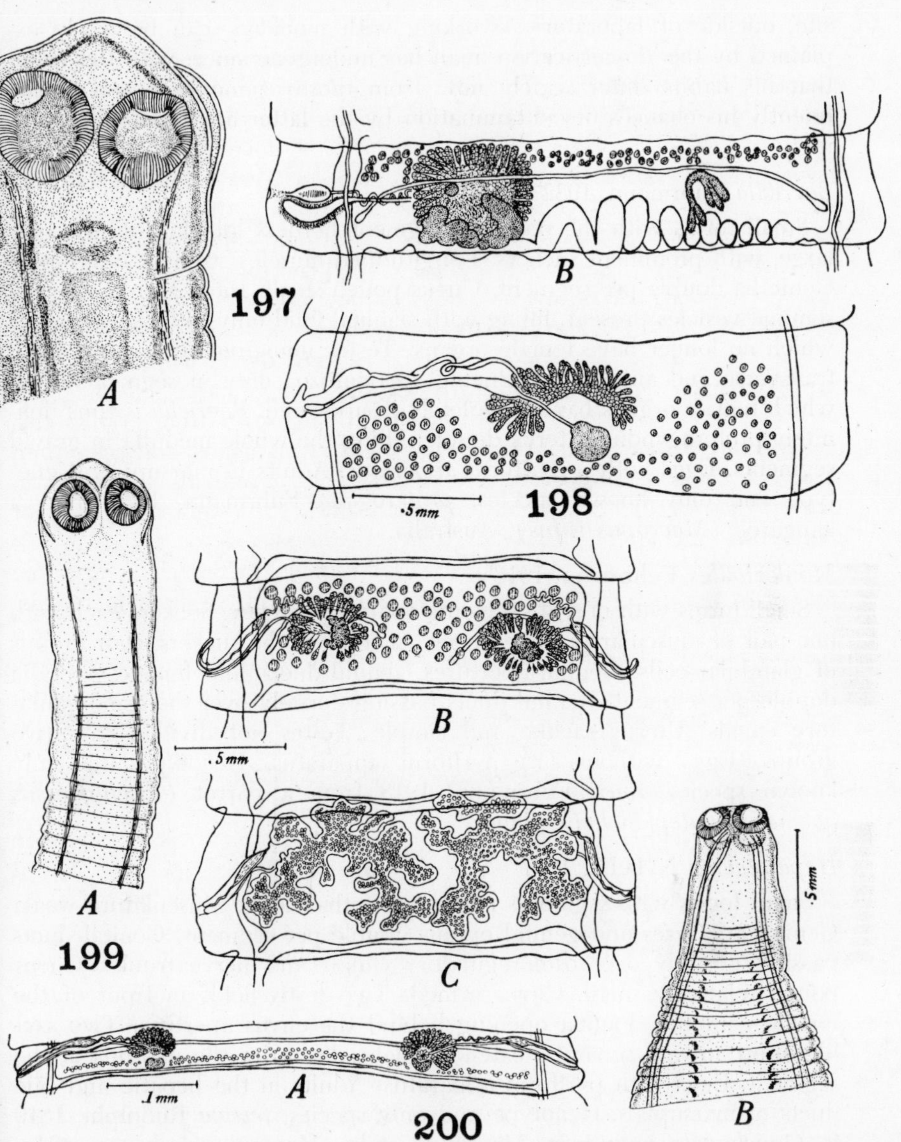

G. 197. *Bertiella studeri*. After Stunkard, 1940a. A. Holdfast. B. Mature segment. FIG. 198. *rtiella fallax*, mature segment. After Meggitt, 1927d. FIG. 199. *Paronia pycnonoti*. After maguti, 1935a. A. Holdfast. B. Mature segment, ventral. C. Gravid segment, ventral. G. 200. *Cittotaenia pectinata americana*. After Arnold, 1938. A. Mature segment. B. Holdfast.

site, outside of laboratories working with monkeys, can be easily explained by the 'domestication' man has undergone since, with the result that his habits differ widely now from those of monkeys and consequently his chances of contamination by the latter are reduced accordingly."

Baeriella Fuhrmann, 1932

Small forms with the posterior segment borders lobed. Holdfast very large, with prominent suckers. Longitudinal muscles strongly developed. Genitalia double per segment. Cirrus pouch small. Internal and external seminal vesicles present, filling with seminal fluid only in those segments which no longer have female organs. Testes numerous in a single field, transverse and anterior, producing spermatozoa only in segments from which female organs have completely disappeared. *Baeriella* is thus definitely proterogynous. Uterus double, filling the whole medulla in gravid segments. Eggs with a pyriform apparatus. Adults in marsupials. Genotype and only known species, *proterogyna* Fuhrmann, 1932 from a kangaroo (*Macropus rufus*), Australia.

Moniezioides Fuhrmann, 1918

Small forms with gravid segments relatively narrow. Suckers each with one pair of muscular protuberances. In front of the suckers, four groups of glandular cells. Genital apertures, genital ducts, and female genitalia double per segment. Genital ducts passing dorsally over the osmoregulatory canals. Uterus saclike and simple. Testes not divided into two groups. Eggs without (?) pyriform apparatus. Genotype and only known species, *rouxi* Fuhrmann, 1918 from a parrot (*Trichoglossus haematodes deplanchei*), Timor.

Hepatotaenia Nybelin, 1917

Small forms with segments much wider than long. Musculature weak. Genital apertures and genital organs double per segment. Genital ducts passing dorsally over osmoregulatory canals and nerve trunks. Cirrus pouch relatively small. Cirrus armed. Two testis fields in front of the female genitalia. Vagina opening behind the cirrus aperture. Two saclike uteri, always separate, extending laterally up to the margins of the segment. Eggs with pyriform apparatus. Adults in the hepatic and bile ducts of marsupials. Genotype and only species, *festiva* Rudolphi, 1819 in *Onychogale unguifera, Macropus agilis, Macropus derbyanus, Macropus giganteus, Macropus robustus*, Australia.

Progamotaenia Nybelin, 1917

Small forms with double genitalia per segment. Genital ducts passing dorsal over osmoregulatory canals and nerve trunks. Cirrus pouch large. Cirrus strongly armed. Testes in two distinct fields in anterior region of segment. Vagina atrophying after copulation. Uterus at first simple or double, forming in gravid segments a *single* lobed sac. Eggs without pyriform apparatus. Adults in marsupials. Genotype, *bancrofti* Johnston. 1912.

The genotype was based upon material from *Onychogale unguifera*, *Onychogale frenata*, Australia. Other species are: *diaphana* Zschokke, 1907 from *Phascolomys ursinus*, Australia; *lagorchestis* Lewis, 1914 from *Lagorchestes conspicillatus*, Australia; and *zschokkei* Janicki, 1906 from *Macropus sp.*, New Guinea. Baer (1927a) included also *Hepatotaenia festiva*, but Fuhrmann (1932) disagreed and argued for the distinctiveness of this form.

Paronia Diamare, 1900

Medium-sized forms with double genitalia per segment. Testes very numerous and in one continuous field. Gravid uterus a branched horseshoe. Pyriform apparatus of the egg rudimentary or lacking. Adults in birds. Genotype, *carrinoi* Diamare, 1900.

Of this characteristic form, formerly placed within the genus *Moniezia* (see Douthitt, 1915), Baer (1927a) recognized five species: *carrinoi* Diamare, 1900a from an Australian parakeet; *ambigua* Fuhrmann, 1902c from a Brazilian parakeet; *beauforti* Janicki, 1906 from a New Guinea parakeet; *columbae* Fuhrmann, 1904b from southern Asiatic pigeons; and *variabilis* Fuhrmann, 1904b from South American rhamphastiform birds. To these must be added *pycnonoti* Yamaguti, 1935 from *Pycnotus sinensis formosae* in Formosa (Figure 199); *coryllidis* Burt, 1939 and *biuterina* Burt, 1939 in *Coryllus beryllinus*, Ceylon; *calcaruterina* Burt, 1939 from *Molpestes haemorrhous*, Ceylon; *bockii* Schmelz, 1941 from *Megalema virens* and *Cyanops ramsayi*, Siam; and *zavattarii* Fuhrmann and Baer, 1943 from *Colius striatus erlangeri*, Abyssinia.

Cittotaenia Riehm, 1881

Medium-sized forms with double genitalia per segment. Testes scattered through the medulla. Gravid uterus a transverse tube, double or single. Adults in rabbits and birds. Genotype, *denticulata* Rudolphi, 1804.

The genus was established for two double-apertured tapeworms found in European rabbits; for the subsequent history of the genus reference should be made to Stiles (1896), Douthitt (1915), Baer (1927a), and Arnold (1938). Baer recognized as valid species: *pectinata* Goeze, 1782 in rabbits, Europe and North America; *denticulata* Rudolphi, 1804 in *Oryctolagus cuniculus*, the common European rabbit; *ctenoides* Railliet, 1890, also in *Oryctolagus cuniculus*; *praecoquis* Stiles, 1895 from the pocket gopher, *Geomys bursarius*, North America; *avicola* Fuhrmann, 1897 from a duck (*Anas sp.*) in Switzerland; *kuvaria* Shipley, 1900 from wild pigeons, Oceania; *psittaca* Fuhrmann, 1904b from a parrot, *Stringops habroptilus*, New Zealand and Australia; *rhea* Fuhrmann, 1904b from *Rhea americana*, South America; and *africana* Joyeux and Baer, 1927a in the African bird *Bucorax*.

Arnold (1938), studying the anoplocephaline tapeworms of North American rabbits, recognized: *perplexa* Stiles, 1895, common in *Sylvilagus nuttalli pinetis*, *S. floridanus mallurus*, and *S. floridanus acer*, Colorado, Maryland, Oklahoma; *pectinata-americana* Douthitt, 1915 in

Lepus californicus melanotis and *L. americanus*, Nebraska, Kansas, and western Canada; *variabilis* Stiles, 1895 in *Sylvilagus floridanus mallurus*, *S. floridanus acer*, and *S. palustris*, New York State, Maryland, Kansas, and Pennsylvania. To the cittotaeniids of birds H. E. Davis (1944) added *sandgroundi* from *Dendrocygna javanica* in Java, but later (1947) transferred the species to the genus *Diplogynia*.

The cittotaeniids of North American rabbits may be distinguished as follows:

KEY TO SPECIES IN NORTH AMERICAN RABBITS

1. Cirrus pouch crossing poral osmoregulatory canal 2
   Cirrus pouch not crossing the osmoregulatory canal 4
2. Cirrus pouch barely crossing the osmoregulatory canal and with maximum length of 0.64 mm.; maximum body length 100 mm. . . . . *perplexa*
   Cirrus pouch extending well over the osmoregulatory canal; long-bodied forms 3
3. Cirrus pouch with maximum length of 1.03 mm. upward; up to 190 segments; body length up to 300 mm. . . . . *pectinata*
   Cirrus pouch with maximum length of 1.8 mm.; more than 360 segments; body length up to 220 mm. . . . . *pectinata americana*
4. Maximum number of segments 300; first appearance of the female genital ducts between 17th and 40th segments; earliest indication of male genital primordia and ducts from 35th to 60th and 36th to 70th segments, respectively . . . . *denticulata*
   Maximum number of segments 750; first appearance of the female genital ducts between 45th and 50th segments; first appearance of male genital primordia and ducts, from 75th to 100th and 76th to 105th segments, respectively . . . . *ctenoides*
   Maximum number of segments 750; first appearance of the female genital ducts between 95th and 105th segments; male genital primordia and ducts originating at 125th to 175th segments, respectively; well-defined neck present . . . . *variabilis*

Triplotaenia Boas, 1902

Unsegmented tapeworms with *double* holdfast, single testis, and 4–5 cirrus pouches per segment. Genital apertures unilateral. Uterus saclike. Eggs with pyriform apparatus. Genotype, *mirabilis* Boas, 1902.

The genotype of this curious form was obtained from a marsupial (*Petrogale penicillata*) in eastern Australia. Janicki (1904a) and Baer (1927a) regarded the form as a monster, but Fuhrmann (1932) recognized it as a valid anoplocephalid species, pointing out that four specimens were found in one host individual and fragments of a specimen in another.

Baeria Moghe, 1933

Anoplocephaline in most respects but peculiar in having, along with a spherical, persistent uterus, a paruterine organ. It thus seems to provide a link between anoplocephaline and thysanosomine forms. Genotype and only known species, *orbiuterina* Moghe, 1933 from *Turdoides somervillei*, near Nagpur, India.

Subfamily Linstowinae Fuhrmann, 1907

DESCRIPTION

Of the family Anoplocephalidae. In which the gravid uterus breaks down to uterine capsules each containing one egg, or is represented by parenchymatous capsules each containing several eggs. Seven genera, distinguishable as follows:

KEY TO GENERA

1. Gravid uterus represented by uterine capsules 2
   Gravid uterus represented by parenchymatous capsules 5
2. Two sets of genitalia per segment ....*Pancerina*
   One set of genitalia per segment 3
3. Genital ducts ventral to the osmoregulatory canals ....*Linstowia*
   Genital ducts *between* or *dorsal to* the osmoregulatory canals 4
4. Genital apertures unilateral; adults in birds ....*Multicapsiferina*
   Genital apertures alternating irregularly; genital ducts *between* or *dorsal to* the osmoregulatory canals; in reptiles and mammals.......................
   ....*Oochoristica, Diochetos*
5. Genital ducts passing *between* the osmoregulatory canals; ovary poral in position; in rodents and hyraxes ....*Inermicapsifer*
   Genital ducts *dorsal* to the osmoregulatory canals; ovary median; in lemurs
   ....*Thysanotaenia*

NOTES ON GENERA

Pancerina Fuhrmann, 1899

Medium-sized forms with two sets of genitalia per segment. Genital ducts running between the osmoregulatory canals of each side and dorsal to the nerve trunks. Testes in two groups, surrounding the female organs. Two independent uteri, breaking down to uterine capsules each containing one egg and extending laterally through the segment. Adults in reptiles. Genotype and only species, *varanii* Stossich, 1895.

Fuhrmann's generic term replaces *Panceria* Stossich, which is preoccupied by a sponge. The genus and species were established for a form from *Varanus griseus*, South Africa.

Linstowia Zschokke, 1899

Medium-sized forms with the suckers more or less stalked. Genital apertures alternating irregularly. Genital ducts ventral to the poral osmoregulatory canal and nerve trunk. Four longitudinal osmoregulatory canals. Cirrus pouch well developed. Testes numerous, in a single field dorsal to the female organs. Female organs median in position. Uterus a transverse tube breaking down into uterine capsules each containing one egg. Pyriform apparatus lacking in the egg. Adults in monotremes and marsupials. Genotype, *echidnae* Thompson, 1893.

The genus was established for two species of tapeworms – *Taenia semoni* Zschokke, 1896 in a marsupial, and *Taenia echidnae* Thompson, in a monotreme. Other species were added by Zschokke and by Janicki. To reduce the difficulty of distinguishing this genus from the allied *Oochoristica*, Baer (1927a) established two subgenera:

1. *s.g. Linstowia.* With the characters of the genus; cirrus pouch well developed and reaching the middle line of the segment; testes very numerous and occupying the whole dorsal face of the segment between the osmoregulatory canals; distinguishable from *Oochoristica* by the suckers which are prominent and separated by deep grooves giving a pseudo-stalked effect. With two species, *echidnae* Thompson, 1893 in *Echidna aculeata* (monotreme) and *Isoodon obesula* (marsupial), Australia; and *semoni* Zschokke, 1896 in *Isoodon obesula,* Australia, with a variety, *acanthocirrosa,* in *Perameles macrura,* Australia (see Nybelin, 1917).

2. *s.g. Paralinstowia.* With the characters of the genus; with the cirrus pouch small, not reaching even the poral osmoregulatory canals; testes fewer than in *s.g. Linstowia,* occupying all the dorsal face of the median medullary parenchyma; distinguishable from *Oochoristica* by the course of the genital ducts and the arrangement of the testes. With two species, *brasiliensis* Janicki, 1904 in *Didelphis americana* and *D. bistriata,* Brazil; and *jheringi* Zschokke, 1904b in *Didelphis americana,* Brazil.

It may be noted that *Linstowia (Linstowia) echidnae* has been redescribed by T. Kerr (1935) from *Tachyglossus setosa.*

Multicapsiferina Fuhrmann, 1921 (=*Linstowia* Zschokke of Fuhrmann, 1901; *Zschokkea* Fuhrmann, 1902 *nec.* Könicke, 1892; *Zschokkeella* Ransom, 1909 *nec.* Auerbach, 1909)

Medium-sized forms with the genital apertures unilateral. Dorsal osmoregulatory canals lying to the outer side of the ventral canals and united with them by a network of secondary canals. Genital ducts passing between the canals and dorsal to the nerve trunk on the poral side. Cirrus pouch weak. Testes scattered through the medulla. Female organs between the ventral and dorsal osmoregulatory canals. Uterus breaking down to uterine capsules each containing one egg. Genotype and only known species, *linstowi* Parona, 1885 in the guinea fowl, *Numida.*

Oochoristica Lühe, 1898

Medium-sized forms with gravid segments commonly longer than wide. Genital apertures alternating irregularly. Genital ducts passing between the osmoregulatory canals *or* dorsal to them. Testes numerous but sometimes reduced to fewer than ten. Ovary and yolk gland median. Gravid uterus a transverse tube breaking down to uterine capsules each with a single egg. Adults in reptiles and mammals. Genotype, *tuberculata* Rudolphi, 1819.

The species of *Oochoristica* are difficult to distinguish. For discussions of specific characterization and synonymity, reference may be made to Baer (1927a), Harwood (1932), Dollfus (1932c), Meggitt (1934b), Hsü (1935), Steelman (1939a), Hughes (1940b), Loewen (1940), and Stunkard and Lynch (1944).

The North American forms may be distinguished by the following data:

IN LIZARDS:

1. *anniellae* Stunkard and Lynch, 1944. With body length up to 15

mm. and breadth 0.37–0.57 mm.; holdfast 370–400 μ diameter; suckers 100–124 by 153–173 μ; seminal receptacle lacking; genital aperture in anterior fourth of segment margin; course of genital ducts not stated; cirrus pouch 186–378 μ when extended, reaching to the middle line of the segment; testes 60–70, postovarian, 200–340 μ in diameter; ovary bilobed, 110–120 μ in width; yolk gland comparable in size with the ovary; egg 42–58 μ; its inner capsule 17–23 μ; size of oncosphere not stated; in *Anniella pulchra nigra.*

2. *anolis* Harwood, 1932. Dimensions 70 by 1 mm.; holdfast 350 μ; suckers 160 by 300 μ; neck 2 by 0.35 mm.; seminal receptacle small; genital aperture at first fourth of segment margin; genital ducts between poral osmoregulatory canals; cirrus pouch reaching slightly over the poral osmoregulatory canal, 145–160 by 90–110 μ; testes 20–35, postovarian, 300 μ in diameter; ovary bilobed, 350 μ wide; yolk gland 350 μ wide; egg 64 μ; oncosphere 40 μ; in *Anolis carolinensis.*

3. *bivitellolobata* Loewen, 1940. Dimensions 15–150 by 1.32 mm.; holdfast 396 μ; suckers 140 μ; neck 425 by 460 μ; seminal receptacle lacking; genital apertures alternating irregularly, each one-seventh to one-quarter of the segment margin from the anterior border; genital ducts running between the osmoregulatory canals of the poral side; cirrus pouch 75 by 165 μ, reaching between the poral osmoregulatory canals nearly to the middle line of the segment; testes 48–106, postovarian, 30–92 μ in diameter; ovary bilobed, 240 μ wide; yolk gland also bilobed, the two lobes nearly as large as those of the ovary; this character of the yolk gland is unique among species of *Oochoristica* and suggested the specific name; egg 53 μ; oncosphere 30 μ; in *Cnemidophorus sexlineatus* (Figure 203).

4. *eumecis* Harwood, 1932. Dimensions 103 by 1.2 mm.; holdfast 500 μ; suckers 220 by 260 μ; neck 2 by 0.35 mm.; genital aperture at first quarter of segment margin; genital ducts between the poral osmoregulatory canals; cirrus pouch crossing the poral canals, 180–260 by 60–70 μ; ovary bilobed, 400 μ wide; testes 40–50, posterior and lateral to the ovary; egg 42 μ in diameter; oncosphere 20 μ in diameter; in *Eumeces fasciatus.*

5. *parvovaria* Steelman, 1939. Dimensions 5–22 by 0.61–0.81 mm. with 5–7 segments; holdfast 320–380 μ; suckers 110–130 μ; genital apertures alternating irregularly, each at first quarter of segment margin; genital ducts between the poral osmoregulatory canals; cirrus pouch crossing the poral canals almost to the middle line of the segment, 220–270 by 110–130 μ in dimensions; testes 52–87, each 23–33 μ in diameter, mostly postovarian, mostly in two lateral fields; egg 49–71 μ; oncosphere 26–46 μ; in *Phrynosoma cornutum* (Figure 205).

6. *phrynosomatis* Harwood, 1932. Dimensions 55–70 by 1 mm.; holdfast 400–600 μ; genital aperture at first third of segment margin; genital ducts between poral osmoregulatory canals; cirrus pouch 220–300 by 130–180 μ, reaching well over the poral canals; testes 125–180, almost all postovarian and mostly in two lateral fields; ovary 250 μ wide; egg 55 μ; oncosphere 30 μ; first formed segment sterile; in *Phrynosoma cornutum.*

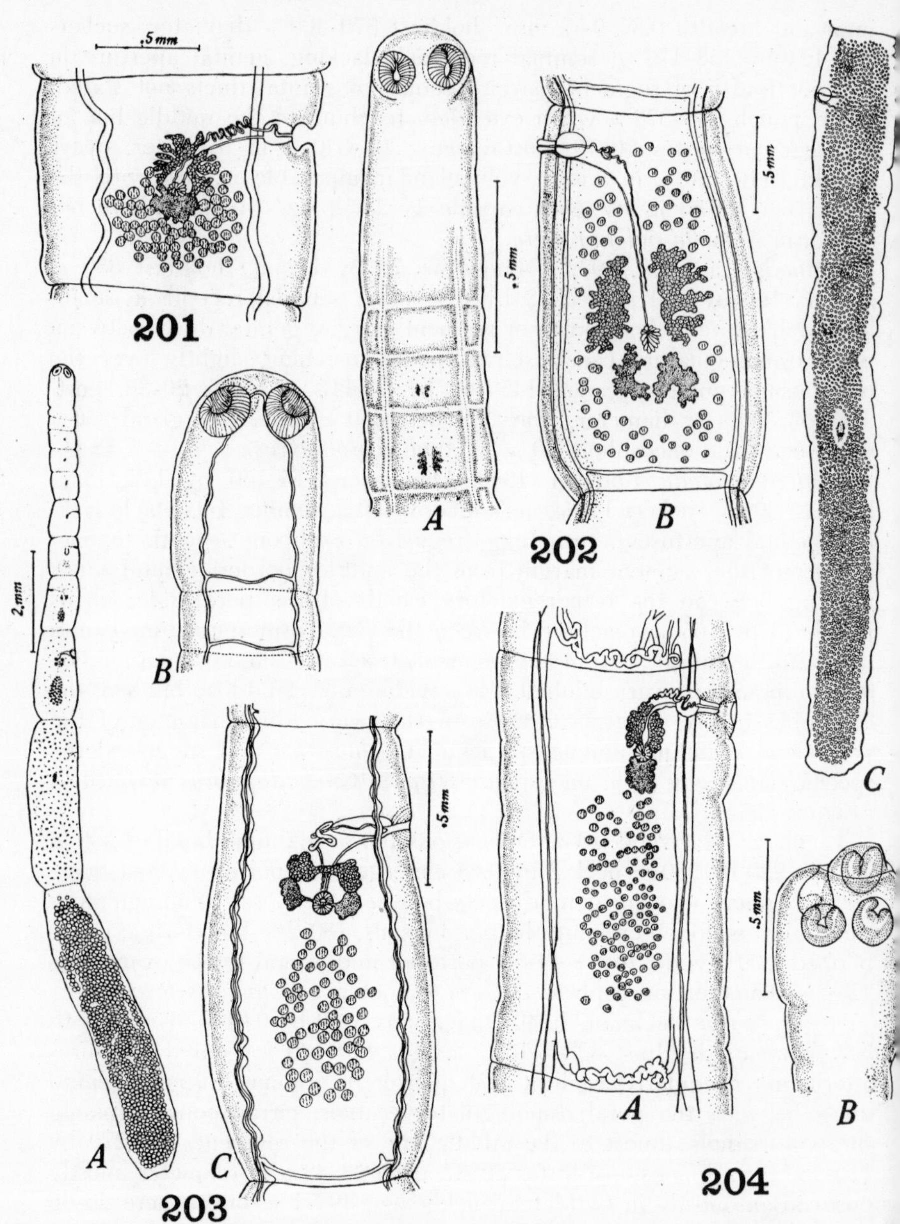

FIG. 201. *Oochoristica osheroffi*, mature segment. After Meggitt, 1934b. FIG. 202 *Oochoristica taborensis*. After Loewen, 1934. A. Holdfast and neck. B. Immature segment C. Gravid segment showing distribution of the eggs. FIG. 203. *Oochoristica bivitellolobata* After Loewen, 1940. A. Entire worm. B. Holdfast. C. Mature segment. FIG. 204. *Oochoristica gracewileyae*. After Loewen, 1940. A. Mature segment. B. Holdfast.

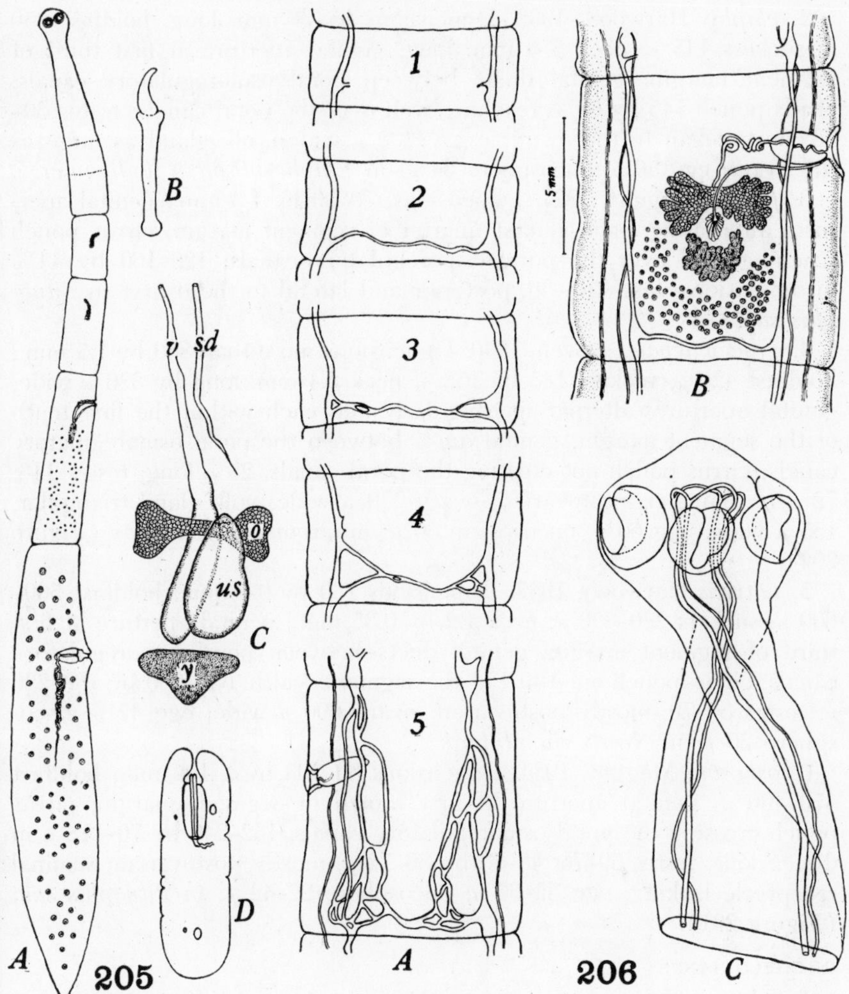

FIG. 205. *Oochoristica parvovaria.* After Steelman, 1939b. A. Entire worm. B. Hooklet of oncosphere. C. Reproductive complex. *o*, ovary; *sd*, sperm duct; *us*, uterine sac; *v*, vagina; *y*, yolk gland. D. Gravid segment, cross section. FIG. 206. *Oochoristica whitentoni.* After Steelman, 1939a. A. Series of older segments to show gradual development of the transverse osmoregulatory canals and associated network. The last segment is mature. B. Typical fully mature segment, ventral view, osmoregulatory plexus omitted. C. Holdfast, neck accidentally twisted.

IN SNAKES:

1. *americana* Harwood, 1932. Dimensions (immature) 40 by 0.85 mm.; holdfast 500 μ wide; suckers 160 μ wide; neck 3 mm. long; genital aperture at first third of segment margin; genital ducts between the poral osmoregulatory canals; cirrus pouch 200 by 90 μ, crossing the poral canals; testes 35–40, postmedian to the ovary; ovary 350 μ wide; dimensions of egg and oncosphere not stated; in *Farancia abacura.*

2. *elaphis* Harwood, 1932. Dimensions 65–75 mm. long; holdfast 350 μ; suckers 145 μ; neck 5–6 mm. long; genital aperture at first third of segment margin; genital ducts between poral osmoregulatory canals; cirrus pouch 145 by 68 μ, reaching well over the poral canals; testes 30–53, postmedian to the ovary; ovary 300 μ wide; yolk gland as large as the ovary; egg 50 μ; oncosphere 34 μ; in *Elaphe obsoleta lindheimer.*

3. *fibrata* Meggitt, 1927. Dimensions, 70–90 by 1.3 mm.; genital apertures alternating, each at first quarter of segment margin; cirrus pouch reaching well over the poral osmoregulatory canals; 120–160 by 44 μ in dimensions; testes 35–36, posterior and lateral to the ovary; in *Pityophis sayi.*

4. *gracewileyae* Loewen, 1940. Dimensions more than 850 by 1.5 mm.; holdfast 426 μ; suckers 145 by 152 μ; neck 2.4 mm. long by 326 μ wide; genital apertures alternating irregularly and each within the first tenth of the segment margin; genital ducts between the poral osmoregulatory canals; cirrus pouch not crossing the poral canals, 25 μ long; testes 113, 72 μ in diameter, postovarian; ovary 230 μ wide; yolk gland triangular, 155 μ wide; egg 60 μ; oncosphere 30 μ; in *Crotalus atrox atrox* (Figure 204).

5. *natricis* Harwood, 1932. Dimensions 130 by 0.8 mm.; holdfast 500–600 μ; suckers 220–300 μ; neck 1.2 by 0.35 mm.; genital aperture at first third of segment margin; genital ducts between poral osmoregulatory canals; cirrus pouch one-third of the segment width, 650–900 by 180–220 μ; testes 50–70, mostly postovarian; ovary 600 μ wide; egg 42 μ; oncosphere 20 μ; in *Natrix rhombifera.*

6. *osheroffi* Meggitt, 1934. Dimensions 60–205 by 1–1.4 mm.; holdfast 370–400 μ; genital aperture at first fourth of segment margin; cirrus pouch crossing the poral osmoregulatory canals, 132–240 by 70–118 μ in dimensions; testes 59–76, 48–80 by 36–72 μ, mostly postovarian; seminal receptacle lacking; egg 32–60 μ; oncosphere 22–42 μ; in *Pityophis sayi* (Figure 201).

IN CHELONIANS:

1. *whitentoni* Steelman, 1939. 275 mm. long; holdfast 360–440 μ; suckers 150–180 μ; genital apertures alternating irregularly, each in the first third of the segment margin; genital ducts between the poral osmoregulatory canals, 130–230 μ by 70–120 μ; ovary 130–360 μ wide; testes 100–150, posterior and lateral to the ovary; eggs not observed; in *Terrapene triunguis* (Figure 206).

IN CARNIVORA:

1. *mephitis* Skinker, 1935. Dimensions 11–25 by 1.3 mm. with 40–70 segments; genital apertures unilateral; genital ducts dorsal to the poral osmoregulatory canals; cirrus pouch spheroidal, crossing the poral canals, 55–65 μ long; testes 44–77, posterior and lateral to the ovary; ovary 192 by 192 μ; yolk gland 92 μ; seminal receptacle 145–185 by 43–50 μ; egg 30 μ; in *Mephitis elongata.*

2. *oklahomensis* Peery, 1939. Dimensions 29–114 by 0.9–1.47 mm.; holdfast 508–705 μ; suckers 222–296 by 195–225 μ; genital apertures uni-

lateral; genital ducts alternating irregularly; dorsal to and between the poral canals; cirrus pouch crossing the poral canals, 68–85 μ in diameter; testes 37–46, lateral, posterior and ventral to the ovary; ovary 211–318 μ wide; yolk gland 85–125 μ wide; seminal receptacle 94–134 by 40–45 μ; oncosphere 36–47 μ; in *Spilogale interrupta* (Figure 207).

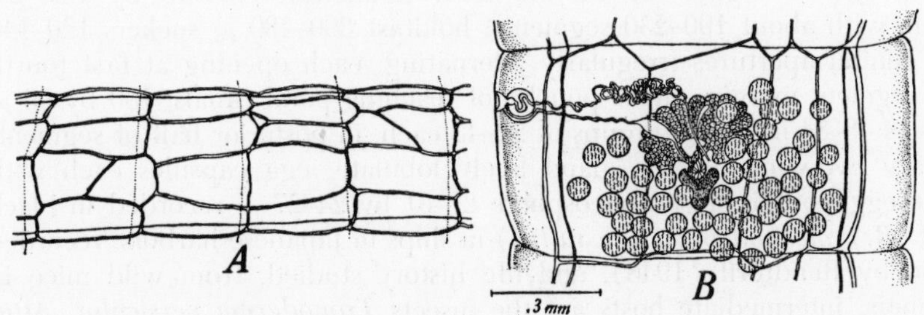

FIG. 207. *Oochoristica oklahomensis.* After Peery, 1939. A. Pattern of osmoregulatory canals in 4 consecutive segments, front end to left. B. Mature segment.

3. *procyonis* Chandler, 1942. Dimensions 8–23 by 0.9–1.6 mm.; holdfast 300–375 μ wide by 150–200 μ long; suckers small, 90–100 μ in diameter; neck very short, 100–200 μ distant from holdfast; genital apertures alternating irregularly, each between first seventh and first fifth of segment margin; genital ducts dorsal to the poral osmoregulatory canals; cirrus pouch well over the poral canals, 110–130 μ long; testes 48–63, 30 by 40 μ, mostly posterior and lateral to the ovary; ovary large, much branched, roughly kidney-shaped, 375–530 μ wide; yolk gland 175–195 μ wide; seminal receptacle 60–80 μ long; oncosphere 25–28 by 30–34 μ; in *Procyon lotor lotor* (Figure 208).

IN CHIROPTERA:

1. *taborensis* Loewen, 1934. Dimensions 8.9 by 1.4 mm. with about 31 segments; holdfast 320–370 μ; suckers 128–132 by 142–156 μ; genital apertures alternating irregularly, each at first seventh of segment mar-

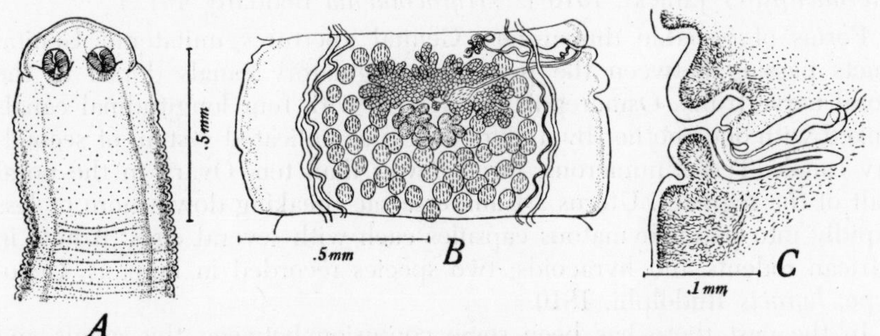

FIG. 208. *Oochoristica procyonis.* After Chandler, 1942a. A. Holdfast. B. Mature segment. C. Genital atrium and cirrus pouch region.

gin; cirrus pouch well across the poral osmoregulatory canals, 140–153 by 122–123 μ; testes about 75, anterior and posterior to the ovary; ovary distinctly bilobed; yolk gland distinctly bilobed; egg 33 by 39 μ; oncosphere 25 μ; in *Lasiurus borealis borealis* (Figure 202).

IN RODENTIA:

1. *ratti* Yamaguti and Miyata, 1937. Dimensions 65–75 by 1.35–2.0 mm. with about 190–230 segments; holdfast 390–480 μ; suckers 120–140 μ; genital apertures irregularly alternating; each opening at first fourth of segment margin; cirrus pouch not reaching poral canals, 150 by 60 μ; testes 48–84 in lateral groups of 22–43 each, in posterior half of segment; ovary two-winged; yolk gland finely lobulate; egg capsules each with one egg, containing an oncosphere 27–31 by 24–27 μ; recorded in black rat (*R. r. alexandrinus, R. r. rattus*) in ships in Japanese harbors; recorded also by Rendtorff (1948), and life history studied, from wild mice in Illinois; intermediate hosts are the insects *Trogoderma versicolor, Attagenus picens, Anthrenus verbasci, Tribolium confusum, T. ferrugineum, Tenebroides mauritanicus, Plodia interpunctella.*

Diochetos Harwood, 1932

With relatively few, elongated segments. Mature segments two to six times as long as broad. Genital apertures alternating irregularly. Genital ducts dorsal to the single lateral osmoregulatory canal. Dorsal osmoregulatory canals and secondary ramifications usually absent except at the ends of young worms. Testes very numerous with a tendency to be arranged in two lateral fields. Ovary median and very small. About the anterior two-fifths of the mature segment not occupied by genitalia. Uterus breaking down into capsules, evenly distributed but sparse in number, each containing one egg. Adults in lizards of the genus *Phrynosoma.* The diagnosis is based on a single species and will doubtless have to be modified if other species are discovered. Genotype, *phrynosomatis* Harwood, 1932.

Harwood based his generic and specific descriptions upon material from *Phrynosoma cornutum* in Texas. Baer (1935) believed Harwood's genus to be synonymous with *Oochoristica.*

Inermicapsifer Janicki, 1910 (= *Hyracotaenia* Beddard, 1912)

Forms of variable dimensions. Genital apertures unilateral. Genital ducts passing between the poral osmoregulatory canals dorsal to the poral nerve trunk. Osmoregulatory system with four longitudinal canals linked with one another by a more or less complicated system of secondary canals. Testes numerous, rarely fewer than ten. Ovary in the poral half of the segment. Uterus a transverse sac breaking down more or less rapidly into parenchymatous capsules each with several eggs. Adults in African rodents and hyracoids; two species recorded in humans. Genotype, *hyracis* Rudolphi, 1810.

In the past there has been some confusion between this genus and *Zschokkeella* Ransom, 1909. Douthitt (1915) was inclined to include the two within one genus although he did not commit himself to naming the genus he had in mind.

"Within two years Beddard has actually placed one cestode (whose latest name is *Zschokkeella gambianum*) in three genera, representing two subfamilies; and there is no assurance that the present disposition is final. Since Beddard has proved his worth as an investigator by his researches in other fields one might expect better things in the future; but, as yet, he has dwelt at great length upon the significance of the size and appearance of the sucker and scolex, the presence or absence of a neck, and other such features; he has failed to tell, in any instance, whether the genital ducts cross the excretory ducts dorsally or ventrally or pass between them; at least several hours were spent in search in his voluminous articles without finding any information on this point. Bischoff (1912) has likewise contributed considerably towards a state of confusion in this group. He has added to the genus *Inermicapsifer* several species without giving, apparently, any adequate study to each. The few facts that he gives are not sufficient in most cases to show that the species exist; and if they do exist, there is no evidence in many cases that they should be placed in the *Inermicapsifer* group rather than in some allied group.

"In the present condition of affairs there are no characters except trivial, unimportant ones upon which to separate the so-called genera *Zschokkeella, Inermicapsifer, Thysanotaenia*, and *Hyracotaenia* from each other. My own opinion is that they all belong in one genus, with the exception of *Zschokkeella remota* and *Thysanotaenia lemuris* which seem to belong elsewhere." Douthitt (1915).

Ransom (1909), however, stated definitely that the genotype of his suggested genus was Parona's *linstowi*. As this species was selected by Fuhrmann (1902c) as the genotype of his genus *Zschokkea*, a name which he later (1921) found to have been used previously for a mite and which he therefore abandoned in favor of the term *Multicapsiferina*, it is clear that *Zschokkeella* is a synonym of *Multicapsiferina*. Southwell and Maplestone (1921) were wrong, therefore, in suggesting the suppression of the term *Inermicapsifer* in favor of *Zschokkeella*. Nor was Baer (1924a, 1926a) correct in suggesting that *Multicapsiferina* should give place to *Inermicapsifer* in nomenclature, whether or not the two are regarded as identical. Later (1927a) Baer changed his viewpoint and stated his belief that the two genera are distinct.

Baer (1927a) recognized as valid species of *Inermicapsifer* the following: *hyracis* Rudolphi, 1810; *aberratus* Baer, 1924; *apospasmation* Bischoff, 1912; *arvicanthidis* Kofend, 1917; *guineensis* Graham, 1908; *interpositus* Janicki, 1910; *lopas* Bischoff, 1912; *norhalli* Baer, 1924; *pagenstecheri* Setti, 1897; *prionodes* Bischoff, 1912; and *settii* Janicki, 1910. Later (1933) Baer added *tanganyikae*.

All the above species are African and occur in rodents or hyracoids. Two species of *Inermicapsifer* have been recorded as parasites of man, namely, in order of record, *I. cubensis*, described by Kouri in Cuba in

1938, and *I. arvicanthidis* (Kofend, 1917), a form already known from African rodents and recovered by Baylis (1949) from a native child in Kenya. Kouri named his form *Raillietina cubensis* and we owe its correct systematic identification to Baer, who examined the material presented by Kouri before the Third International Congress of Microbiology at New York in 1939. For a general account of this worm reference should be made to Kouri and Rappaport (1940), Stunkard (1940c), Kouri (1944), Ortiz (1945), and particularly to Baer, Kouri, and Sotolongo (1949). The last named authors summarize the status of this worm as follows:

"A detailed anatomical study of *Inermicapsifer cubensis*, based on the original material deposited in the School of Tropical Medicine in Havana shows that we are dealing with a single, well defined species of this genus. Over one hundred cases have been recorded so far from the western parts of the island. It is very likely, however, that this parasite will be found in other parts of Cuba, as well as in Porto Rico and Venezuela. Children of the age of 1–5 years and 9–11 years are most frequently infested. All cases except two have been recorded from white children. It is probable that parasitism is accidental and that the normal host will be found amongst the Cuban fauna. No systematic research has been made so far with this end in view. Among native rodents, 'Jutias' (*Capromys pilorides* and *C. prehensilis*) apparently do not harbour this worm. Inermicapsiferiasis is discovered by finding the ripe segments singly, in the faeces. These cannot, however, be distinguished from those of *Raillietina*, the presence of which, in the West Indies, is quite possible. It is always necessary to recover the scolex and to examine it for the presence of the peculiar hooks of this genus." Baer, Kouri, and Sotolongo (1949).

While admitting that *cubensis* shows a close resemblance to the African form *arvicanthidis*, Baer, Kouri, and Sotolongo (1949) believed that differences in the size of the cirrus pouch and number of egg capsules were sufficiently constant to separate the two species. Baylis (1949), however, comparing the metromorphic characters of several specimens of *arvicanthidis* with those given for *cubensis*, could find no valid differences between the two forms. Fain (1950), on the basis of a detailed examination of African material, believes *cubensis* to be identical with *arvicanthidis*.

In view of the interest of this genus to practitioners of tropical medicine, the following key to the species of *Inermicapsifer* given by Joyeux and Baer (1949b) is presented.

1. Testes in aporal half of segment .... *aberratus* Baer
   Testes in both halves of segment 2
2. Testes in two distinct groups on each side of ovary 3
   Testes distributed uniformly behind ovary 4
3. Genital atrium in posterior third of segment .... *settii* Janicki
   Genital atrium in middle of segment .... *leporis* Ortlepp
4. Genital pores in front of or at the middle of the segment margin 5
   Genital pores behind middle of segment margin 9

5. Length reaching or exceeding 180 mm. 6
   Length not exceeding 40 mm. 8
6. Testes 90–130; cirrus pouch 140–160 μ long . . . . *guineensis* Graham
   Testes 28–55; cirrus pouch 150 μ long 7
7. Testes 30–35; cirrus pouch 140–150 μ long; egg capsules with 12–15 eggs . . . . *arvicanthidis* Kofend
   Testes 28–32; cirrus pouch 90–126 μ long; capsules with 4–7 eggs . . . . *cubensis* Kouri
8. Testes 20–36 . . . . *apospasmation* Bischoff
   Testes 50–80 . . . . *interpositus* Janicki
9. Fewer than 60 testes per segment 10
   More than 60 testes per segment 12
10. Testes 27–30; cirrus pouch 250 μ long . . . . *norhalli* Baer
    Testes 40–50; cirrus pouch 120–200 μ long 11
11. Testes arranged in two groups united by a row behind the ovary . . . . *lopas* Bischoff
    Testes scattered over whole dorsal region of segment . . *prionodes* Bischoff
12. Testes 120–200 over whole width of segment as well as in front of ovary 13
    Testes 90–140 over whole width of segment with one row behind the ovary . . . . *hyracis* Rudolphi
13. Testes 120–180; cirrus pouch 270 μ long . . . . *pagenstecheri* Setti
    Testes 180–200; cirrus pouch 330–370 μ long . . . . *tanganyikae* Baer

Thysanotaenia Beddard, 1911

Medium-sized forms. Genital apertures unilateral. Genital ducts dorsal to the poral osmoregulatory canals and nerve trunk. Cirrus pouch well developed. Testes numerous, behind and on both sides of the female organs. Ovary and yolk gland median. Uterus breaking down to parenchymatous capsules, each with several eggs. Genotype, *lemuris* Beddard, 1911b in *Lemur varius, Lemur macao*, Madagascar; a second species, *incognita* Meggitt, 1927c, was found in *Macropus ruficollis* (kangaroo) in the zoological gardens of Rangoon, Burma.

Subfamily THYSANOSOMINAE Fuhrmann, 1907

DESCRIPTION

Of the family Anoplocephalidae. The gravid uterus disappears and is replaced in function by fibrous "paruterine pouches" into which the eggs pass. Seven genera, distinguishable as follows:

KEY TO GENERA

1. Yolk gland and ootype present 2
   Yolk gland and ootype lacking 3
2. Large forms, with weakly segmented bodies; uterus a transverse tube, replaced in gravid segments by 8–12 paruterine pouches each with several eggs; adults parasitic in ruminant mammals . . . . *Ascotaenia*
   Large forms, with the uterus in the form of an undulating tube almost filling the whole segment but replaced in gravid segments by very numerous paruterine pouches each with several eggs; adults in ruminant mammals . . . . *Helictometra*
3. Posterior border of each segment with a fringe of outgrowths; adults in the

liver ducts of ruminant mammals .... *Thysanosoma*
Posterior segment borders not fringed 4

4. Testes in a single row, occupying when fully developed the anterior two-thirds of the segment; uterus a transverse sac behind the degenerated testes, flanked anteriorly by poorly developed paruterine organs .... *Wyominia*
Testes in two lateral bands, each band not subdivided by the osmoregulatory canal of its side; uterus an attenuated dumbbell, replaced in gravid segments by two paruterine pouches each situated laterally; adults in ruminant mammals .... *Stilesia*
Testes in two lateral bands, each band subdivided by the enormous osmoregulatory canal of its side; testes few; a single median paruterine pouch 5
5. Each enormous osmoregulatory canal flanked by a very narrow dorsal one; longitudinal muscles in a double layer; glandular region of vagina longer than the cirrus pouch; vagina alternately dorsal and ventral to the cirrus pouch .... *Avitellina*
One pair of osmoregulatory canals only, the dilated ventral ones; longitudinal muscles in a single layer; glandular region of vagina shorter than, or only as long as, the cirrus pouch; vagina always ventral to the cirrus pouch .... *Anootypus*

NOTES ON GENERA

Ascotaenia Baer, 1927

Large forms with weak segmentation and irregularly alternating genital apertures. Genital ducts dorsal to the poral osmoregulatory canals. Testes on both sides of the female glands. Female glands in poral half of segment. Yolk gland only slightly developed. Uterus a transverse tube becoming sacciform, replaced by 8–10 paruterine pouches each containing several eggs. Genotype and only known species, *pygargi* Cholodkovsky, 1902 (= *Thysanosoma pygargi*) in *Capreolus pygargi*, Siberia.

Helictometra Baer, 1927

Large forms with genital apertures alternating irregularly. Genital ducts passing between the poral osmoregulatory canals and dorsal to the nerve trunk. Testes outside the osmoregulatory canals, in lateral fields. Female glands in the poral half of the segment. Yolk gland and rudimentary ootype present. Uterus an undulating tube, filling almost all the segment, replaced by very numerous paruterine pouches each with several eggs. Genotype, *giardi* Moniez, 1879 (= *Taenia giardi*) in *Bos taurus, Aepyceros malampus, Ovis aries, Taurotragus oryx, Tragelaphus scriptus, Bubalis caama, Sus scrofa dom*, Europe, Asia, Africa. Under the name of *Thysaniezia ovilla* its life cycle has been studied by Potemkina (1944b) in Russia.

Thysanosoma Diesing, 1835

Medium-sized forms with posterior segment borders fringed with outgrowths. Genitalia double per segment. Genital ducts passing between the osmoregulatory canals and dorsal to the nerve trunks. Testes very numerous, occupying all the posterior half of the segment between the two ovaries. No yolk glands or ootypes. Uterus a *single* undulating tube, whose eggs pass into numerous paruterine pouches. Adults in the liver ducts of ruminant mammals. Genotype and only known species, *actinioides* Diesing, 1835, a cosmopolitan parasite in stock-raising countries.

Wyominia Scott, 1941

With posterior segment borders not fringed. Genital ducts passing between the osmoregulatory canals. Two sets of genitalia per segment. Testes 40–52 in a single row occupying the anterior two-thirds of the segment. Uterus a transverse sac lying posterior to the degenerated testes and bordered anteriorly by poorly developed paruterine organs. The genus is distinguished from *Thysanosoma*, the closest related genus, by the lack of border fringes, the number of testes, the unarmed cirrus, the location of the genital apertures (male aperture on the anterior outer border of the segment, female aperture posterior, dorsal, and somewhat median to the position of the male pore), by the position of the uterus posterior to the testes, and by the poorly developed paruterine organs. Genotype and only known species, *tetoni* Scott, 1941 in *Ovis canadensis canadensis*, Wyoming, in the bile ducts of liver, gall bladder, small intestine.

Stilesia Railliet, 1893

Long, narrow forms with weak segmentation and irregularly alternating genital apertures. Genital ducts passing between the poral osmoregulatory canals and dorsal to the poral nerve trunk. One set of genitalia per segment. Testes few, in lateral fields. Ovary in poral half of segment. Yolk gland and ootype lacking. Uterus a long, transverse, dumbbell-shaped tube. Two paruterine organs. Parasitic in ruminant mammals. Genotype, *globipunctata* Rivolta, 1874.

Stilesia, according to Baer (1927a), has three species: *globipunctata* Rivolta, 1874 in sheep and goats in Europe; *hepatica* Wolffhügel, 1903 in cattle, buffaloes, antelopes in Africa and Asia; and *vittata* Railliet, 1896b in the dromedary in East Africa. Leiper (1935) added *okapi* from the okapi in Africa, but Baer (1950a) believes this form to be merely a variety (var. *okapi*) of *globipunctata*.

Southwell (1929b), in a study of *Stilesia hepatica*, surveyed the genera of Thysanosominae and described *Stilesia* and *Avitellina*. Within the latter genus he included *Hexastichorchis* Blei, 1921 and *Anootypus* Woodland, 1928. His key to the identification of thysanosomine genera was as follows:

1. With double genitalia per segment .... *Thysanosoma*
   With single genitalia per segment 2
2. With one paruterine pouch per segment .... *Avitellina*
   With more than one paruterine pouch per segment 3
3. With two paruterine pouches .... *Stilesia*
   With many paruterine pouches 4
4. Testes bounded laterally by the osmoregulatory canals .... *Ascotaenia*
   Testes in two fields, one lateral to the osmoregulatory canals on each side .... *Helictometra*

Fuhrmann (1932), however, accepted *Avitellina* and *Anootypus* as separate genera.

Avitellina Gough, 1911 (= *Hexastichorchis* Blei, 1921)

Large forms with narrow bodies and segmentation scarcely apparent except in the last segments, which are cylindrical. Genital apertures alternating irregularly. Genital ducts dorsal to the poral osmoregulatory canals and nerve trunk. Testes few, situated close to the right and left segment margins and divided into two groups on each side by the voluminous osmoregulatory canals and nerve trunk. Ovary in the poral half of the segment. Yolk gland and ootype lacking. Uterus a median sac bearing a paruterine pouch which eventually receives the eggs. Parasites of ruminant mammals. Genotype, *centripunctata* Rivolta, 1874.

Until the article by Woodland (1927a), the genotype was the only known species of the genus. Woodland added four species – *sudanea, lahorea, chalmersi*, and *goughi* – and redescribed the genotype from the type material. Southwell (1929b) added the species formerly ascribed to *Hexastichorchis* Blei, 1921 and *Anootypus* Woodland – namely, *pintneri* Blei, 1921; *edifontaina* Woodland, 1928; and *ricardi* Woodland, 1928. Nagaty (1929) added *southwelli* and *aegyptica*; Fuhrmann (1931) added *monardi*; Woodland (1935d) added *sandgroundi*; Bhalerao (1936) reviewed the genus and added *woodlandi* and *tatia*. Bhalerao recognized the following species:

KEY TO SPECIES

1. Cirrus pouch longer than vulva * 2
   Cirrus pouch shorter than vulva 3
2. Cirrus pouch at most twice as long as vulva; outer column of testes 1–2 testes deep .... *tatia*
   Cirrus pouch three or more times as long as vulva; outer column of testes 3–4 testes deep .... *woodlandi*
3. Dorsal osmoregulatory canals internal to the ventrals 5
   Dorsal osmoregulatory canals external to the ventrals 4
4. Some testes lateral to the dorsal osmoregulatory canals .... *pintneri*
   No testes lateral to the dorsal osmoregulatory canals .... *aegyptica*
5. Outer column of testes as a rule one testis deep 6
   Outer column of testes as a rule more than one testis deep 7
6. Mature paruterine organs kidney-shaped .... *sudanea*
   Mature paruterine organs snail-shaped .... *lahorea*
7. Mature paruterine organs banana-shaped .... *goughi*
   Mature paruterine organs pear- or sac-shaped 8
8. A row of testes external to the nerve cord .... *southwelli*
   No testes external to the nerve cord 9
9. Outer column of testes about two testes deep; genital apertures situated each on a thickening .... *chalmersi*
   Outer column of testes 2–3 testes deep; genital apertures not on a thickening .... *centripunctata*

* Bhalerao used the term "vulva" for the terminal portion of the vagina, surrounded by glandular cells.

The genotype, *centripunctata*, has been recorded from sheep, goats, antelopes, and buffaloes in Europe, southern Asia, and Africa, but not in India. Of the other species, *tatia, woodlandi, lahorea*, and *southwelli* are

Indian, from sheep and goats; *sudanea, chalmersi,* and *goughi* are African, also from sheep and goats.

Anootypus Woodland, 1928

Similar in most respects to the preceding genus but lacking dorsal osmoregulatory canals, having a single layer of longitudinal muscles, and having the cirrus pouch dorsal to the vagina. Genotype, *edifontainus* Woodland, 1928.

The genotype and a second species, *ricardi* Woodland, 1928, occur in most African antelopes; a third species, *monardi* Fuhrmann, 1933, occurs in the antelope, *Taurotragus oryx,* in Angola, West Africa.

Family CATENOTAENIIDAE n. fam.

DESCRIPTION

Of the order Cyclophyllidea. With the holdfast carrying in young worms a functional apical sucker which disappears as the worm matures. Osmoregulatory system with ramifications and secondary anastomoses. Genital apertures alternating irregularly. Genital ducts generally dorsal to the poral osmoregulatory canals. External and internal seminal vesicles lacking. Vagina surrounded by a sleeve of glandular cells, greatly elongated, folded upon itself, ending in a seminal receptacle. Testes behind, rarely at the sides of, the ovary. Ovary branched, with two voluminous lobes, dorsal and ventral. Yolk gland similarly branched, in poral half of segment. Uterus with a median stem and lateral branches. Eggs small. Larva a merocercoid in tyroglyphid mites. Adults in rodents. Type genus, *Catenotaenia* Janicki, 1904.

Catenotaenia Janicki, 1904

With the characters of the family. Genotype, *pusilla* Goeze, 1782, recorded originally from a house mouse (*Mus musculus*) in Germany and since recorded from *Mus musculus* – wild and albino – *Mus wageneri albellus, Apodemus sylvaticus, Rattus rattus, Rattus norvegicus, Evotomys glareolus, Microtus agrestis,* and *Microtus arvalis,* in Europe, North America, and Japan. It seems to be widespread among rodents in the Northern Hemisphere. In laboratory mice its distribution is sporadic, some colonies remaining free from infestation, others showing strong infestation.

Catenotaenia pusilla has been the subject of a monographic study by Joyeux and Baer (1945), based upon material from laboratory mice. The study included a detailed account of the life cycle. In view of the extreme interest of this genus, from the standpoint of tapeworm evolution, a summary of Joyeux and Baer's findings may be given here.

The egg development corresponds closely with that described for *Taenia* by Beneden (1881), St. Remy (1901a), and Janicki (1907). One point, however, that has not previously been noted in cestode development is shown by stage B of Figure 46. The future embryo is seen as a cellular mass whose numerous nuclei do not all possess the same shape and structure. There may be seen, in addition to three pairs of large nuclei, numerous nuclei which are smaller and stain very intensely. These disappear during the course of development, and no particular function can be ascribed to them. Their regularity of size and shape preclude the possibility that they may be remnants of yolk.

At the beginning of envelope development, the embryo is central in position. Gradually it becomes displaced more and more until finally it lies at one of the poles of the middle envelope. While the three nuclei of the external envelope disappear rapidly, those of the middle envelope persist long after the embryophore has been formed. Neither staining with hemalum-eosin nor with Feulgen-Lichtgrün will demonstrate the cell limits in the interior of the embryo.

The intermediate host of *Catenotaenia pusilla* is a mite, *Glyciphagus domesticus*, or rather the adult and deutonymph stages of this mite, for larval mites have the mid-gut and hind-gut occluded and cannot be infected. Figure 47 shows that at 8 days the larva, in the hemocoel of the mite, is a mass of large cells, $69 \times 50\ \mu$ in diameter. As development proceeds, the embryonic hooks disappear. The developing larva is very active, though enclosed within a thin-walled cyst. While within this cyst, the larva proceeds to develop a large apical sucker. As differentiation of the larval tissues proceeds, the sucker-bearing region becomes withdrawn within the rest of the body. The wall of the cyst begins to thicken and to restrict larval mobility. At this stage, 15 days after the eggs were ingested by the mite, the larva is infective to rodents. It measures 95–103 by 80 μ, the invaginated apical sucker being 46 μ in diameter.

When placed in an extract of mouse mucosa, the cyst wall dissolves, the apical sucker is evaginated, and a constriction appears to divide the larval body in hourglass fashion. Into the anterior part of this hourglass there pass calcareous corpuscles from all parts of the body. In the host, the liberated larva fixes itself to the mucosa by the apical sucker. At first there are no other suckers. The lateral suckers begin to show themselves as clusters of nuclei, however. As they gradually take form, the apical sucker begins to disappear, and finally it vanishes, leaving no trace (Figure 48).

The catenotaeniid larva is thus a plerocercoid larva, with a solid body, a formed holdfast, and a terminal osmoregulatory bladder. But all such larvae previously described have a holdfast identical with that of the adult worm, a holdfast which in fact *is* that of the adult worm. The early plerocercoid of *Catenotaenia pusilla*, however, does not have the four suckers characteristic of the adult worm. It is an incomplete larval type. Joyeux and Baer suggested for it the term "merocercoid larva." It recalls somewhat in its structure a larval form – described by Shipley and Hornell (1904) in the pearl oyster of Ceylon waters and in the nuclear portions of pearls – whose adult form is probably a lecanicephalan parasite of rays. In the same category may be placed also some larval forms described under the term *Merocercus* by Hornell and by Willey (see Southwell and Prashad, 1918c) from *Placuna placenta* (a lamellibranch mollusc). These latter larval forms show a form of endogenous multiplication, the mechanism of which remains obscure.

Southwell (1921e) has described also, from a medusa, larval forms which present some analogy with the catenotaeniid larva described above. Larval forms described by Wagener (1854) from fishes in the Mediterranean Sea and termed *scolices bothriis simplicibus* also approach somewhat the forms described above. On the other hand, the reabsorption of the apical sucker, which is so well developed in the larva yet so lacking in the adult, has been observed also in several species of Proteocephala parasitic in fishes and reptiles. But these forms always possess, as larvae, four lateral suckers in addition to the apical sucker. It may be noted, though, that Herde (1938) has observed in the larva of *Ophiotaenia perspicua* an apical organ which appears in development before the suckers, as early in fact as the procercoid stage.

On the basis of their studies, Joyeux and Baer offered a new view as to the systematic position of *Catenotaenia.*

"Does the presence of cestode larvae in Tyroglyphidae indicate a new acquisition? Up to now, only Oribatidae have been found harbouring spontaneously cysticercoids of Anoplocephalidae; they have also been infected experimentally (Stunkard, 1938, 1940, 1941). If, for reasons of systematic convenience, we united today Tyroglyphidae with Oribatidae as a sub-order Sarcoptiformes, that does not necessarily imply that close bonds exist between the two tapeworm groups. The anoplocephalid larvae described by Stunkard are of the cysticercoid type. Their embryonic development is slow and they are not fully formed even at the end of three months. In *Catenotaenia,* as we have seen, the larva is a merocercoid whose development is passed through in fifteen days. Nevertheless it is possible to envisage possible affinities between *Catenotaenia* and Anoplocephalidae. The larval differences between the two do not provide an unsurmountable obstacle to such a view. We know for example in Taeniidae two species, *T. crassiceps* and *T. polyacantha,* both parasitic in foxes, yet having, one a cysticercus larva in rodents, the other a plerocercus larva in rodents.

"The genus *Catenotaenia* has been placed by some writers in the family Taeniidae (Meggitt, 1924), by others in Dilepididae (Fuhrmann, 1932; Joyeux and Baer, 1936). The shape of the gravid uterus recalls the arrangement of that organ in Taeniidae. On the other hand, the arrangement of the genitalia, and in particular the pre-testis position of the ovary, recalls Dilepididae. Among Taeniidae, alone among known species, *T. saginata* Goeze possesses an unarmed scolex and an apical organ. The latter structure, very well developed in the larva, has been observed by several authors and in particular by Moniez (1880) who compared it, correctly in our opinion, with the armed, muscular rostellum of the other species of Taeniidae. *T. saginata* is nevertheless a typical species of Taeniidae which has doubtless undergone a mutation provoking a loss of hooks, only the rostellum persisting.

"It is exceptional to find among Dilepididae, genera with an unarmed scolex or a weakly developed muscular rostellum; such occur mainly in the sub-family *Paruterininae* whose anatomical features are very different from *Catenotaenia.* In the family Anoplocephalidae on the contrary an absence of rostellum and a possession of an unarmed scolex are fundamental characteristics without any exception. The arrangement of the longitudinal muscles of the strobila, the arrangement of the osmoregulatory system, ramifying more or less according to species, and the arrangement of the genitalia fit *Catenotaenia* perfectly into this family. In the majority of Anoplocephalidae the segments are always wider than long but in the genus *Oochoristica* the adult segments are generally square and the gravid segments longer than wide. The structure of the young uterus of *Catenotaenia* is not duplicated in any known genus of Cyclophyllidea. Nevertheless this does not exclude this genus from Anoplocephalidae, and in particular from *Anoplocephalinae,* in which the uterus may be tubular, sac-like or net-like. The structure of the egg and the reduced size of the oncosphere seems also to link *Catenotaenia* with Anoplocephalidae in which the embryophore does not necessarily have a pyriform apparatus.

"One of us (Baer, 1927) has suggested that Anoplocephalidae may have originated from the family Ichthyotaeniidae, parasites of fishes and reptiles. The presence of an apical sucker in the larval *Catenotaenia* supports such an hypothesis since such an organ appears also in Ichthyotaeniidae whose life cycle is known.

"The arguments presented above appear sufficient to us to justify inclusion of *Catenotaenia* in the family Anoplocephalidae and in particular in the sub-family *Anoplocephalinae.* It is more than probable that we shall have to modify our present conception of cyclophyllidean classification when more life cycles are known. At present any classification cannot be otherwise than provisional." Joyeux and Baer (1945).

To the present writers, it would seem that in *Catenotaenia* we have a form for which strong arguments can be raised for and against inclusion in either Taeniidae, Anoplocephalidae, or Dilepididae. It would seem in fact to stand closer to the ancestral stock from which these three families divergently evolved. Under the circumstances we felt it justifiable to establish for this genus a separate family, Catenotaeniidae, with the one genus *Catenotaenia.*

Joyeux and Baer (1945) recognized eight species of *Catenotaenia,* to which may be added the species recorded by McIntosh (1941) as *linsdalei* from the pocket gopher (*Thomomys bottae bottae*) in California. These species may be separated provisionally by the following key based upon one offered by Joyeux and Baer (1945):

KEY TO SPECIES

1. Testes entirely post-ovarian 2
   Testes both post-ovarian and latero-ovarian 4
2. Vagina short and straight 3
   Vagina very long and coiled upon itself . . . . *geosciuri*
3. Testes 70–100; uterus with 9–13 branches on each side . . . . *pusilla*

Testes 130; uterus with 40–50 branches on each side . . . . *linsdalei*
Testes 140–180; uterus with 35–40 branches on each side . . . . . . *dendritica*

4. Testes in two groups on each side; osmoregulatory system normal . . . . *oranensis*
Testes in two groups united behind the ovary; osmoregulatory system ramifying . . . . *lobota*

Incertae sedis, for lack of sufficient information: *symmetrica, rhombidis, ris.*

NOTES ON SPECIES

1. *geosciuri* Ortlepp, 1938. Up to 93 mm. long; holdfast 270–348 μ in diameter (Ortlepp, 1938c), 380–400 μ (Fuhrmann and Baer, 1943a); suckers 87–128 μ in diameter (Ortlepp), 160 μ in diameter (Fuhrmann and Baer); osmoregulatory system without secondary ramifications; testes postovarian, about 200 in number; cirrus pouch 200–250 μ by 110–

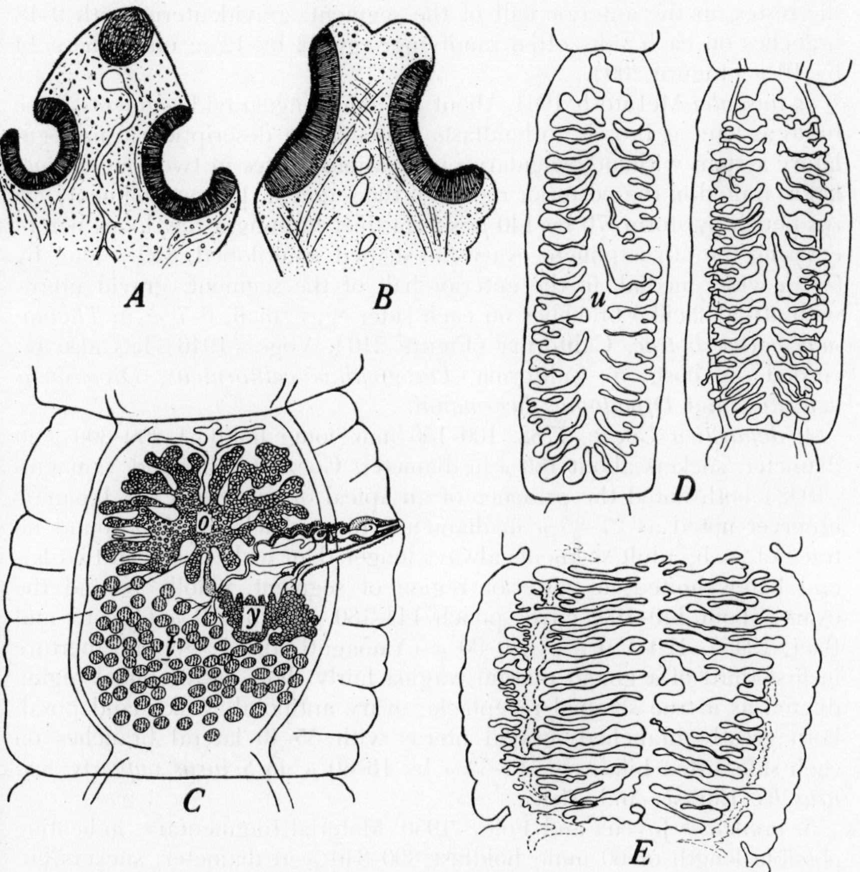

FIG. 209. *Catenotaenia pusilla.* After Joyeux and Baer, 1945. A. Section of holdfast of young worm showing remains of apical organ. B. Similar section of holdfast of adult lacking all trace of apical organ. C. Mature segment. *o*, ovary; *t*, testes; *y*, yolk gland. D. Gravid segments showing different shapes of uterus (*u*). E. Horizontal section of contracted segment showing diverticula of uterus passing over the osmoregulatory canal.

130 μ (Ortlepp), 216–260 μ by 108 μ (Fuhrmann and Baer); sperm duct dilated within the cirrus pouch but not forming a true internal seminal vesicle; ovary almost entirely in the antiporal half of the segment; yolk gland in the poral half; vagina very long, coiled several times upon itself; uterus with 12–18 branches on each side; the branches almost all bifid; eggs 23–25 μ; oncosphere 14–15 by 11 μ; in *Geosciurus capensis, Xerus rutilus stephanicus, Euxerus erythropus*, Africa; a species apparently adapted to African ground squirrels and in some ways parallel with *dendritica* of Eur-African arboreal squirrels.

2. *pusilla* Goeze, 1782. Hosts already listed; in Northern Hemisphere; 30–160 mm. long; holdfast 230–300 μ in diameter; suckers circular, 72–115 μ in diameter; osmoregulatory system without secondary ramifications; testes postovarian, 70–100 in number; cirrus pouch 144–180 μ by 72–90 μ; female genitalia characteristic of the genus, wholly in front of the testes, in the anterior half of the segment; gravid uterus with 9–13 branches on each side, often ramifying; egg 22 by 12 μ; oncosphere 14 by 10 μ (Figure 209).

3. *linsdalei* McIntosh, 1941. About 135 mm. long; gravid segments three times as long as broad; no holdfasts available for description; osmoregulatory system without secondary ramifications; testes in two longitudinal fields, united in the posterior region of the segment, 130 per segment; cirrus pouch pyriform, 70 by 140 μ; sperm duct forming a few loops before entering the cirrus pouch; ovary fan-shaped, multilobed, 350 μ long by 500 μ wide, medial, in the anterior half of the segment; gravid uterus with 40–50 saclike branches on each side; eggs small, 6–7 μ; in *Thomomys bottae bottae*, California (Figure 210). Voge (1946) has also recorded, as hosts in California, *Perognathus californicus, Dipodomys venustus*, and *Dipodomys heermanni*.

4. *dendritica* Goeze, 1782. 100–150 mm. long; holdfast 290–300 μ in diameter; suckers about 150 μ in diameter; Goeze (1782) and Yamaguti (1942) both noted the presence of an apical organ which the Japanese observer noted as 27–35 μ in diameter; Riggenbach (1895a) found no trace of such; adult segments always longer than wide; testes in two lateral bands united in posterior region of segment, wholly behind the ovary, about 140–190; cirrus pouch 144–180 μ by 54–79 μ (Joyeux and Baer, 1945), 120–180 μ by 70–90 μ (Yamaguti, 1941); genital aperture in first third of segment margin; vagina fairly short, its proximal region dilated as a true seminal receptacle; ovary antiporal; yolk gland poral; both greatly branched; gravid uterus with 35–40 lateral branches on each side, often bifid; egg 18–33 μ by 16–30 μ; in *Sciurus vulgaris, Sciurus lis*, Eurasia and Africa.

5. *oranensis* Joyeux and Foley, 1930. Material fragmentary, indicating possible length of 60 mm.; holdfast 300–340 μ in diameter; suckers circular or oval, 110–150 μ in diameter; osmoregulatory system without ramifications; testes in two lateral fields without any commissure, to the number of 180, the antiporal group with 100, the poral group with 80; cirrus pouch 120 μ by 35 μ; yolk gland surrounded on almost three sides by the ovary, only the poral side being free; gravid uterus with a very

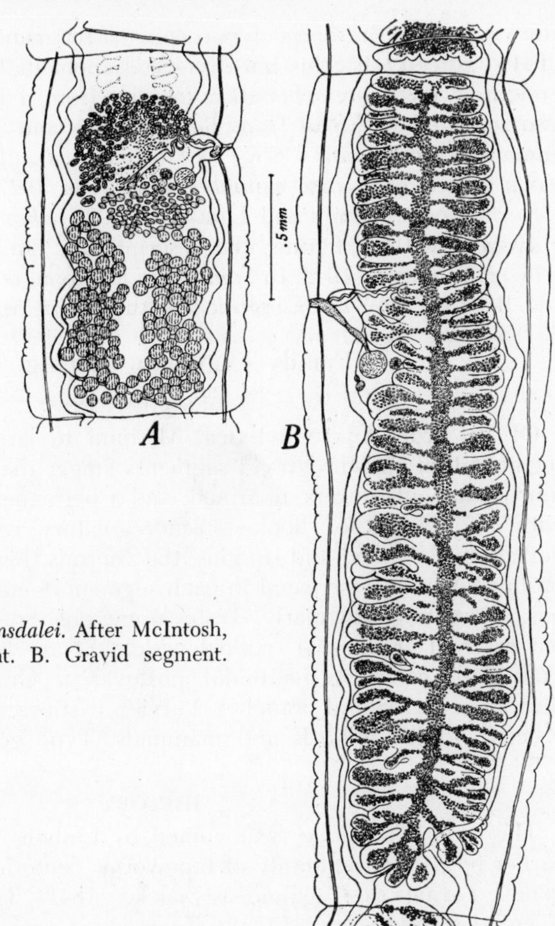

FIG. 210. *Catenotaenia linsdalei.* After McIntosh, 1941. A. Mature segment. B. Gravid segment.

short median stem, placed in the anterior quarter of the segment; lateral branches few, ramifying, directed posteriad; ripe eggs unknown but embryo without hooks measured 10 μ by 8 μ; in *Meriones shawi shawi*, Algeria.

6. *lobata* Baer, 1925. From 12–140 mm. long; holdfast 300–700 μ in diameter; suckers circular, 120–200 μ; osmoregulatory system with numerous secondary ramifications forming a network; testes behind and at the sides of the ovary, about 200 in all; cirrus pouch 150–170 μ by 60 μ; female genitalia normal; gravid uterus with 10–15 branches, often bifid; eggs not known; in *Apodemus sylvaticus, Rattus marungensis, Mastomys erythroleucus, Mastomys coucha microdon, Taterona kempi, Evotomys glareolus*, Europe and Africa; a common Eur-African species in rodents.

7. *symmetrica* Baylis, 1927. From *Rattus rattus* in India; transferred by Meggitt and Subramanian (1927) to *Oochoristica*, due to the lack of

uterus and the presence of parenchymatous capsules; Joyeux and Baer (1945) agreed with this but disagreed about its being synonymous with Beddard's (1916) *Oochoristica lemuris* from a lemur; the species was also recorded in Japan from *Rattus rattus* and *Rattus alexandrinus* by Yamaguti and Miyata (1937) as *Oochoristica ratti*, a name thus synonymous with *Oochoristica symmetrica* (Baylis, 1927c).

8. *rhombidis* Schulz and Landa, 1934. In *Rhombys opimus*; described in Russian without figures; the description is not available to us.

9. *ris* Yamaguti, 1942. In *Sciurus lie* in Japan; considered by Fuhrmann and Baer (1943a) to be identical with *dendritica*.

Family Taeniidae Ludwig, 1886

DESCRIPTION

Of the order Cyclophyllidea. Medium to large forms with marked segmentation and the gravid segments longer than broad. Holdfast with four prominent suckers, unarmed, and a permanently extruded rostellum with two circles of hooks. Osmoregulatory canals conspicuous, the dorsals thick-walled and sinuous, the ventrals thin-walled and straight; a prominent transverse canal in each segment. Genital apertures conspicuous, alternating irregularly. Testes numerous. Sperm duct sinuous, without external or internal seminal vesicle. Ovary bilobed. Vagina curved. Yolk gland compact, pyramidal, postovarian. Gravid uterus with a median stem and lateral branches. Larva a cysticercus, coenurus, or echinococcus. Adults in birds and mammals. Type genus, *Taenia* Linnaeus, 1758.

HISTORY

The term "Taeniidae" was coined by Ludwig (1886) to replace such earlier terms for the family of tapeworms centering round Linnaeus' old genus *Taenia* as Taenioidea Zwicke, 1841; Taeniadae Baird, 1853; Taeniodea Goldberg, 1855; and Taeniadea Carus, 1863. Formerly a large family, it has gradually been so whittled down by the transfer of genera and species to other families that today it is a relatively small family of eleven genera.

RECOGNITION FEATURES

Taeniid genera make up a fairly compact group of forms readily identifiable, as a rule, by the combination of four characters – four suckers, nonretractable rostellum, compact, postovarian yolk gland, and median, stemmed, laterally branched gravid uterus. The apex of the holdfast is bluntly domed and may be homologized with the retractable rostellum of other Cyclophyllidea, although many authors prefer to apply to it the term "rostrum" and to assume that a true rostellum is lacking. The suckers are large, their rims commonly prominent but not armed with spines or hooks. On the rostellum, however, there are usually two concentric circles of hooks constituting a so-called "crown." One circle consists of relatively large hooks, the other of relatively small hooks. Large hooks and small hooks may alternate, thus giving somewhat the effect of a single circle of large and small hooks alternately.

The shape of the hooks, while not peculiar to Taeniidae, being found also among hymenolepidid and dilepidid tapeworms, is very characteristic. It may be described as like a rose thorn, with a curved, flattened blade rising from a wide, concave base which is sunk into the rostellar surface. Or, again, it may be compared with a shallow sickle, the blade being strongly curved, the handle straight and thick, and a knoblike guard occurring at the junction of handle and blade (Figure 233).

Observations upon the development of the taeniid hook have been made by Clapham and Peters (1941) and Clapham (1942a). The hooks are formed during larval development and make no further growth after the larva reaches the definitive host.

"The two types of hook do not arise in precisely similar circumstances. In immature scolices it can be seen that the large hooks develop from at least two centres of chitinization. The blade and the guard portion appear early and the handle is added afterwards from a second centre and gradually grows forward to meet the blade. Thus there is a stage, which can be seen quite frequently, in which the large and the small hooks appear to form a single circlet, each hook being of approximately the same size and shape. Alternate hooks, however, have a wedge of chitin in close proximity. As this grows forward, the blade also grows to complete its normal size until the fully developed hook is apparent. All the intermediate stages from a very small wedge of handle chitin to full union have been seen.

"Further evidence that this is the normal method of development is afforded by certain monstrous forms. A fairly high percentage of such forms have been observed in coenuri that have developed in unusual hosts, e.g., *Coenurus cerebralis* in man, and *Coenurus serialis* in a variety of odd hosts. On many occasions the large hook has developed without its attendant handle; in others, no blades or guards of either sized hooks have developed, though the handles of the large ones are present. This suggests that some cause has operated to abolish either the blades and guards of all the hooks, or the handles of the large ones. This further suggests that the blade and guard of the large hook, and the entire small hook, arise from a common ring of chitinization, and the handles of the large hooks arise from a distinct one.

"There was seen a young scolex in which the armature appeared as wedges of chitin of a roughly triangular shape, regularly arranged round the rostellum. It may be that this was a stage in the early development of the armature, but as no intermediate stages have been seen, it cannot be certain. These observations bring to mind the case of the species *Taenia monostephanos*. This was first reported by von Linstow in 1905 who first regarded it as a specimen of *Taenia laticollis* and later as a distinct species, on the ground that it had only a single crown of hooks and those of an atypical shape. They have a much reduced handle, the result being like that of a rose thorn. If this is a normal state then the material must represent a distinct species and one not entirely typical of the genus *Taenia*. It is however possible that von Linstow was dealing with an immature form in which the handle was represented by small masses of chitin still not fused with the main portion of the hooks. The fact that he described 19 hooks – an odd number – is not a real difficulty for specimens frequently lose one or more hooks during handling." Clapham (1942a).

Although the number, size, and shape of the rostellar hooks are characters frequently used in distinguishing taeniid species, such a practice is not entirely satisfactory. The hooks are readily lost when taeniid material is preserved and handled. Further, no uniform system of measuring the hooks has been devised.

Meggitt (1927e) suggested a standardized method of expressing the shape and size of hymenolepidid hooks which can be applied also to the hooks of taeniids. The base *ab* (see Figure 264) of the hook is taken as unity and the other measurements are expressed as decimal fractions of this; *eh* is a tangent drawn parallel to *ab* and touching the hook at its highest point *h*; *fc*, *gb*, and *kl* are three perpendiculars drawn from *ab* to the two ends *g* and *f* of the hook and to the inside, *k*, of the curve *fg*. With the points *a*, *g*, *h*, and *k* fixed, the approximate shape of the hook is determined. The various formulas may then be compared or the hook itself reconstructed. The shape is represented by a formula of five values, in millimeters, representing respectively *ab*, *bl*, *bc*, *cf*, and *de*.

Clapham (1942b), using hook measurements to distinguish species of *Multiceps*, found the small hooks to have little or no diagnostic value. She measured the handle, the dorsal edge of the blade, and the ventral edge of the blade, and stressed the importance of measuring a large number of hooks and of examining the measurements statistically.

In the mature segment of a taeniid there is to be seen a clear median area occupied by the ovary – dumbbell-shaped or appearing as two separated spherical bodies – and the median stem of the uterus; to each side of this clear area there is a dense band of spherical or ovoid testes. Behind the ovary are the conspicuous ootype and the somewhat pyramidal yolk gland. These, together with the much convoluted sperm duct – not differentiating as a rule into external and internal seminal vesicles – the simple, curved vagina, and the tumid-lipped cirro-vaginal atrium, make up a picture readily identifiable as that of a taeniid tapeworm segment. From the gravid segment, the male and female genitalia have usually disappeared, the whole medullary area being filled with the tortuously branching side pockets of the median uterine stem.

The egg is at first thin-shelled, but the shell soon disappears, leaving the oncosphere enveloped by a thick, radially striated embryophore. Eggs are liberated through the ruptured anterior borders of the apolysed segments. The general features of the embryology and life cycle have already been discussed (Chapter II). Further details may be postponed to the descriptions of individual genera.

The genera may be distinguished in preliminary fashion as follows:

KEY TO GENERA

1. Segments fewer than five in number; gravid uterus with short, wide, unbranching side lobes; yolk gland globular; bladder worm with secondary

bladders containing many holdfasts .... *Echinococcus*
Segments more than five in number; uterine branches distinct and commonly subdividing; yolk gland elongated or pyramidal; bladder worm never with secondary bladders 2

2. Holdfast without hooks 3
Holdfast with one circle of hooks .... *Fossor*
Holdfast with two circles of hooks 5
3. Cirrus pouch nearly spherical; testes numerous, surrounding the uterine stem and female genitalia; uterus with a median saclike stem and numerous lateral ramifications .... *Anoplotaenia*
Cirrus pouch pear-shaped; testes not extending behind the ovary 4
4. Testes in two lateral groups, of which the poral group is the larger, extending to the sides of, or in front of, but never in rear of, the ovary; gravid uterus with a median stem and fingerlike side branches which fill the whole medulla .... *Paracladotaenia*
Testes very numerous, scattered throughout the medullary except behind the ovary; uterine stem with 15–30 pairs of dichotomously branching side branches .... *Taeniarhynchus*
5. Small forms with unilateral genital apertures; large seminal receptacle; gravid uterus with very short and wide median stem and two pairs of saclike side branches which when egg-filled nearly fill the whole segment; with certain peculiarities of the holdfast .... *Dasyurotaenia*
Medium to large forms with the characteristics of the family 6
6. Rostellar hooks small, less than 50 μ long; testes in two lateral groups or bands, on either side of the ovary, not meeting, or meeting, behind it; no internal seminal vesicle; gravid uterus with simple saclike or simple forklike lateral lobes from a median stem .... *Cladotaenia*
Rostellar hooks large, greater than 50 μ and often several hundred microns long; testes distributed indiscriminately through the medulla but absent from the region behind the ovary; uterine side pockets sub-branches 7
7. Segmentation of the body beginning immediately behind the holdfast; larva a strobilocercus .... *Hydatigera*
A distinct "neck" between holdfast and first segment 8
8. Rostellar hooks large, each with a sinuous handle; vagina with a reflexed loop near the poral osmoregulatory canals; larva a coenurus .... *Multiceps*
Handle of the large hooks not sinuous; vagina without a loop; larva a cysticercus .... *Taenia*

Spasski (1948b) has established a new genus and species, *Insinuarotaenia schikhobalovi*, for a taeniid from the badger *Meles meles*. Characteristic of the new form is a peculiar muscular structure in front of the suckers which he names the *organon permearum* and which is used as the main organ of adherence. We have been unable to consult the original paper.

NOTES ON GENERA

Echinococcus Rudolphi, 1801

Small forms with not more than four or five segments, of which only the last one is gravid at one time. Holdfast with a double crown of hooks. Genital apertures alternating irregularly. Muscular vaginal sphincter present. Larva an echinococcus. Genotype, *granulosus* Batsch, 1786.

The genus was established by Rudolphi (1801) for a bladder worm that had been recorded by Goeze (1782) as *Taenia visceralis socialis granulosa* in the sheep. This form was renamed by Batsch (1786) in accordance with the binomial system as *Hydatigena granulosa*. Gmelin (1790) changed the name to *Taenia granulosa*. For its further synonymity, reference should be made to Meggitt (1924a).

The adult form was recorded first by Siebold (1853), as *Taenia echinococcus*. Experimental confirmation that Goeze's bladder worm was the larva of Siebold's form was made by Beneden (1887) or, as some assert, by Leuckart (1863). *Echinococcus granulosus* (Figures 213, 215) has been recorded in the adult stage from a range of Canidae and from certain Felidae (although in catlike carnivores there seems doubt as to

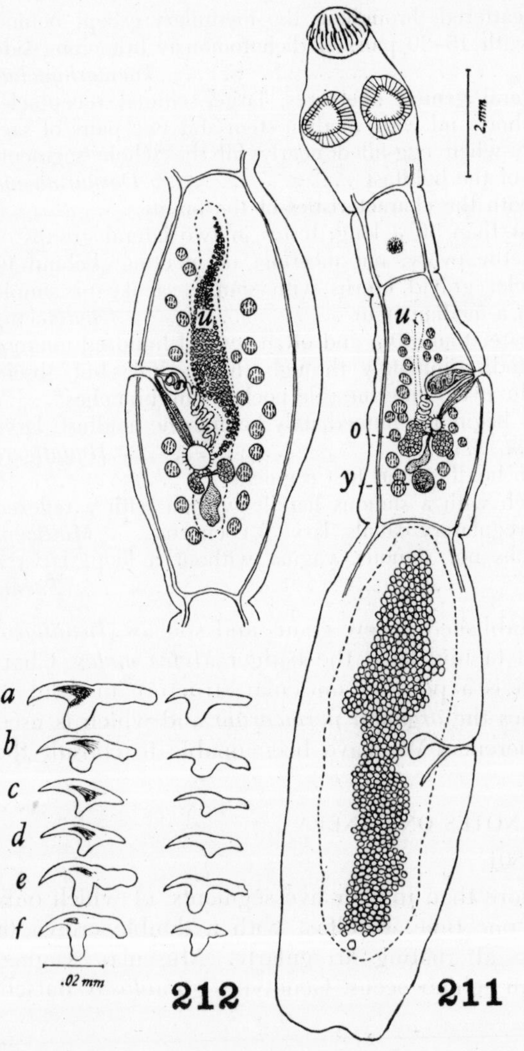

FIG. 211. *Echinococcus oligarthrus*, entire worm. After Cameron, 1926. The single gravid segment is drawn from another specimen to show the transitional stage between maturity and gravidity. *o*, ovary; *u*, uterus; *y*, yolk gland. FIG. 212. Echinococcid hooks. After Cameron, 1926. *a*, *oligarthrus*; *b*, *granulosus*; *c* and *d*, mature hooks from a hydatid in a horse, England; *e*, *Echinococcus* from *Lycaon capensis*, South Africa; *f*, *Echinococcus* from *Canis lupus*, Macedonia.

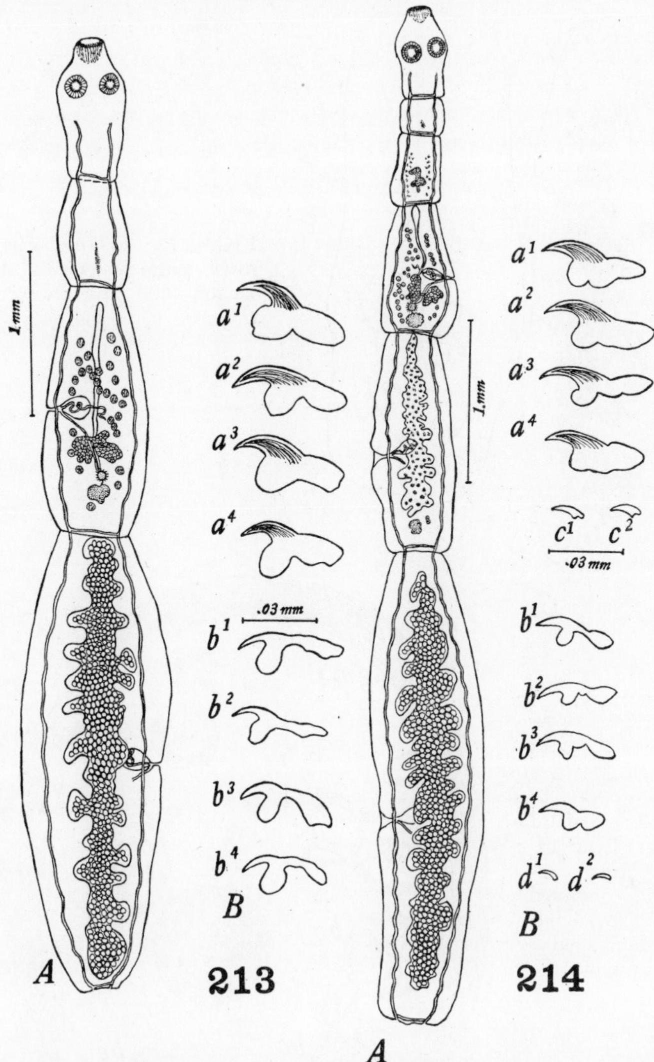

FIG. 213. *Echinococcus granulosus*. After Ortlepp, 1934. A. Entire worm. B. Hooks. a^1–a^4 from anterior row; b^1–b^4 from posterior row.
FIG. 214. *Echinococcus lycaontis*. After Ortlepp, 1934. A. Entire worm. B. Hooks. a^1–a^4 from anterior row; b^1–b^4 from the 2nd row; c^1–c^2 from the 3rd row; d^1–d^2 from the 4th row.

whether the worm can attain maturity). In its larval stage it is known from a wide range of mammalian hosts (see Hall, 1919).

Another species, *Echinococcus oligarthrus* (Figure 211), was described by Diesing (1863b) – as *Taenia oligarthra* – from *Felis concolor* (puma); was studied by Lühe (1910b); and in later years was redescribed by Cameron (1926) from material collected from *Felis jaguarondi* (jaguar). Its hydatid stage, in Cameron's opinion, is the form

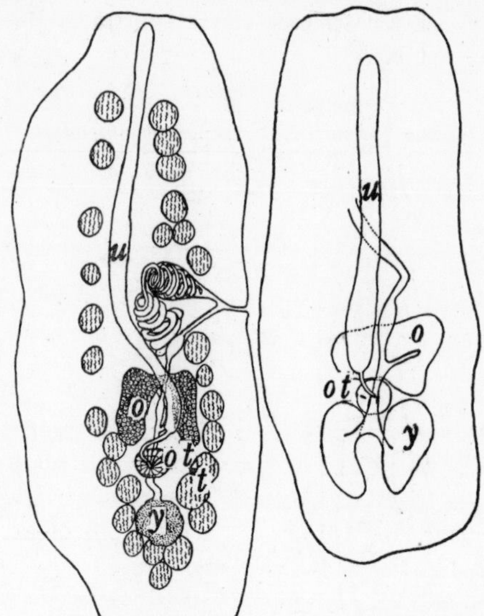

FIG. 215. *Echinococcus granulosus*, mature segments. After Erlanger, 1890. *o*, ovary; *ot*, ootype; *t*, testes; *u*, uterus; *y*, yolk gland.

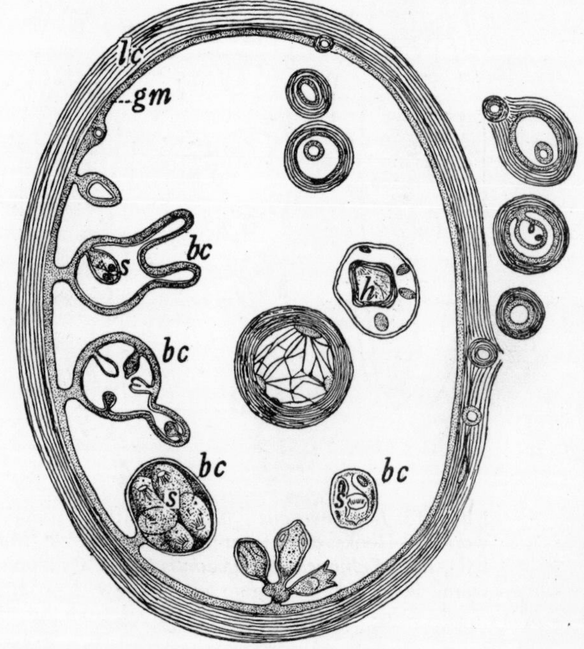

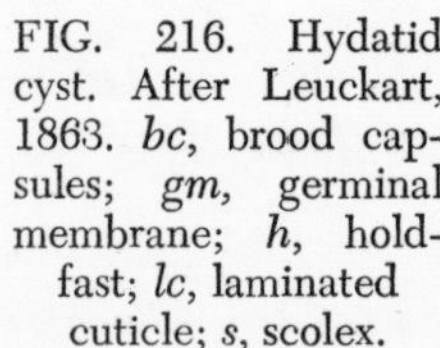
FIG. 216. Hydatid cyst. After Leuckart, 1863. *bc*, brood capsules; *gm*, germinal membrane; *h*, holdfast; *lc*, laminated cuticle; *s*, scolex.

described by Brumpt and Joyeux (1924) as *Echinococcus cruzi* from the agouti (*Dasyprocta agouti*) in Brazil. Cameron (*op. cit.*) recorded also the species *minimus* from *Canis lupus* (wolf) in Macedonia, and the species *longimanubrius* from the Cape hunting dog (*Lycaon capensis*) in South Africa. Ortlepp (1934) added to the genus the species *cameroni* from *Vulpes vulpes* (fox) in England, and *lycaontis* from *Lycaon pictus* in South Africa (Figure 214).

The principal measurements of the above species are summarized by Ortlepp (1934) in the accompanying table.

	granulosus	*oligarthrus*	*minimus*	*longi-manubrius*	*cameroni*	*lycaontis*
Length	5–8 mm.	1.7–2.5 mm.	?	?	5–7 mm.	4–7 mm.
Segments ...	3–4	3	?	?	4–5	4–7
Testes	35–53	20–33	?	?	50–60	40–50
Hooks	30–36	36–40	?	?	28–32	68–72 (34–36 large)
Large hooks..	42–49	45 μ	32 μ	35 μ	35–38 μ	40–45 μ
Small hooks..	32–42 μ	32 μ	20 μ	30 μ	30–33 μ	28–32 μ

Echinococcus granulosus has long been the subject of medical and veterinary interest owing to its frequent occurrence as a bladder worm in humans and domesticated animals, the large size to which the bladder worm may grow, and the danger thus threatened to the host. The picture of its life cycle, despite intensive investigation, is far from clear. The facts available have been presented fairly by Brumpt (1936).

Hydatid disease, as infestation with echinococcid larval stages is termed, may appear in two forms – *locular hydatidosis* and *alveolar hydatidosis.* The simplest is unilocular hydatidosis, in which a fluid-filled bladder, ranging in size from a millimeter in diameter to the diameter of a child's head, may grow and develop in the lungs, liver, abdominal cavity, kidney, pelvis, spleen, brain, etc., of the intermediate host.

Whether the oncosphere reaches its final position via the lymphatic system or via the portal venous system is uncertain. Although relatively large, 20–25 μ, the oncosphere can pass along any blood vessel through which a red cell can pass. At the end of one month after entering the host, nodules one millimeter in diameter appear beneath the serous covering of the liver, each enclosing an echinococcid 250–350 μ in diameter. At the end of two months, the oncosphere has become bladderlike and has doubled in volume. At the end of five months – in the hog – the bladder is about one centimeter in diameter but has developed as yet no internal buds. These appear several months later.

The fully formed hydatid is then a fluid-filled bladder which is attached to the host tissue by an *adventitious membrane*, an inflammatory product of host irritation, and is usually difficult or impossible to dislodge. Within the adventitious membrane the bladder wall comprises a *laminated cuticle*, non-nucleated, apparently chitinous in nature; and, to the inside of this, a *germinal membrane*, granular, nucleated, 10–25 μ thick. Within the bladder itself there is a water-clear fluid, 1,005–1,015 in density, with a freezing point of 0.53° C.; the fluid is not coagulable by heat or acids. It contains traces of albumin, of something akin to casein, sodium chloride (5–8 g. per liter), sodium sulphate, sodium phosphate, sodium and calcium succinates, traces of sugar, and inositol. The fluid is sterile, although when removed it can serve as an ideal medium for microorganism culture. It contains something in the nature of a toxalbumin, responsible probably for the "shock effect" upon hosts in which the hydatid has burst or been punctured.

Projecting into the cavity of the bladder from the germinal membrane are internal buds — bladderlike "brood capsules" — with walls continuous with the germinal membrane. The brood capsules may be acephalous (without holdfasts), but in a matter of months or years their internal surfaces give off "buds," each with a cavity lined by a thin internal cuticle. Within these buds holdfasts develop, ten to thirty per bud. These holdfasts are invaginated and appear as ovoid masses. Commonly, the ripe brood capsules break away from the germinal membrane to form a sediment, the so-called "hydatid sand" which is suspended freely in the fluid of the hydatid. In the hydatid sand in human hydatids — though rarely in those of domesticated animals, which do not live long enough to permit time for such development — there commonly occur also miniature replicas of the parent bladder — so-called "endogenous daughter cysts" — complete with laminated cuticle, germinal membrane, and brood capsules (Figure 216).

The origin of such cysts is disputed. Early observers (Davaine, Leuckart, Moniez) believed them to be derived from islets of germinal tissue within the laminated cuticle. Later observers (Bremser, Siebold, Wagener, Naunyn) derived them from the brood capsules. Recent observers such as Dévé and Coutelen believed such cysts to develop from holdfasts liberated from the brood capsules.

Islet tissue in the cuticle is probably responsible, however, for the similar daughter cysts that may develop on the outer surface of the parent hydatid. Such clusters of hydatids are common in domesticated animals, but rare in humans. The rupture of a parent bladder, either spontaneously or through surgical interference, may allow the diffusion of daughter cysts to other parts of the body and provoke a secondary hydatidosis, notably of bladders attached to the peritoneum or in the lungs, or even in the liver.

The term "multilocular hydatidosis" is more commonly applied, not to the condition where the hydatid is represented by a cluster of daughter bladders, but to a condition frequently seen in the livers of infested cattle where the hydatid is represented by a mass of small, sterile bladders, each not exceeding a centimeter in diameter, separated from each other by fibrous tissue.

Hydatidosis may terminate naturally, after a number of years, by the death of the holdfasts, the absorption of the fluid by the host tissues, and the conversion of the bladder walls by host reaction into a vitreous mass. Penetration of microorganisms between the cuticle and germinal membrane may bring about the death and suppuration of the hydatid, with the appearance in the host of abscesslike symptoms. Spontaneous rupture of a large hydatid, if located in a part of the body where escape of the contents to the exterior is possible, may bring about spontaneous healing of the disease. More commonly, such rupture produces severe shock to the host and the possibility of widespread secondary hydatidosis in other regions of the body.

The diagnosis of hydatidosis is difficult. Roentgenology is of little value. Surgical exploration is dangerous. In recent years attention has been given to the possibilities of serological methods of diagnosis—by precipitins, by complement fixation, by intradermal reactions. The literature on the subject is voluminous and any detailed analysis would be out of place here; reference should be made to the summaries put forward by Kellaway and Fairley (1932), Fairley and Kellaway (1933), and Graña (1944–48).

The most successful method of diagnosing the presence of the adult in dogs is by fecal examination, following administration of 0.002 to 0.003 grams of arecoline hydrobromide per kilogram of body weight, followed by male fern in a dose of about 0.2–0.3 grams per kilogram of body weight (see Nosik, 1940).

Diagnosis of the presence of the bladder worm in humans may be made upon the results of (*a*) examination of hydatid material from the suspect; (*b*) the determination of the degree of eosinophilia; (*c*) the Casoni or intradermal test; and (*d*) the complement-fixation test of the suspect's serum in the presence of hydatid antigen. The presence of laminated membrane, holdfasts, or hooks in the sputum, urine, feces, or other discharges gives positive information. Diagnostic puncture is of course dangerous, due to the risk of anaphylaxis, of secondary echinococcosis, or of rupture of bladder fluid into the bronchial passages.

Kellaway and Fairley found an eosinophilia of more than 300 eosinophiles per cubic millimeter in 50 per cent of cases shown by operation to be infected, and in about one-third of the cases the eosinophilia exceeded 500 per cubic millimeter. The cause of such eosinophilia is not certain; but Graña and Oehninger (1944) obtained from hydatid cuticle an insoluble protein, giving both protein and carbohydrate reactions, not dissolved by either pepsin or trypsin, stainable by Best's carmine, which when introduced into rabbits provoked an intense eosinophilia.

The intradermal (Casoni) test requires special care in its technique and in the interpretation of its results. The reagent usually is pooled hydatid fluid from uncomplicated cysts of sheep, fluid containing holdfasts being selected. Sterility of the fluid is insured by filtration. Its antigenic properties are retained for many months even at room temperature. It is injected intradermally into the skin of the outer half of the upper arm in amounts sufficient to raise a white area approximately one centimeter in diameter. Usually about 0.25 cc. are required. For a control, a similar amount of normal saline (0.9 per cent) is injected a few centimeters from the site of the first injection, and the skin of the other arm, or of the forearm, is stroked moderately freely with a blunt instrument (the stroke test).

In the typical immediate reaction, the control wheal fades rapidly while that from the hydatid fluid increases and usually shows pseudopodial outrunners. A zone of erythema surrounds the wheal, which reaches maximum size within half an hour, then fades quickly. The greatest diameter of the wheal is measured from the extremity of one outrunner, and a second measurement is taken approximately at right angles to the first one. The response is considered positive when the wheal measures at least 2.4 cm. in one diameter or 2.2 in both diameters.

Doubtful cases are those with both diameters between 2.0–2.2 cm. Diameters less than 2.0 cm. are negative (Kellaway and Fairley, 1932).

The normal reaction to the stroke test is a red line confined to the area of pressure, followed within half a minute by a spreading flush. Swelling and wheal formation over the stroke line are characteristic of factitious urticaria. When this condition is present, an immediate reaction to the intradermal test has no significance.

Further investigation is required to interpret the significance of doubtful or positive reactions. The possibility must always be considered of present or past infections of the host with other tapeworms. If such be proved, a positive intradermal reaction must be disregarded. Thus Chung and T'ung, using both hydatid fluid and cysticercus fluid, found that both hydatidosis and cysticercosis patients have positive reactions with either fluid. A positive intradermal reaction also occurred with patients suffering from intestinal taeniid infestation. Some positive results were given also by sufferers from syphilis and kala azar (Chung and T'ung, 1939). Kellaway and Fairley, in Australia, found about 75 per cent of infested cases gave a positive reaction. Among uninfested subjects, about 5 per cent of the reactions are positive.

A delayed reaction may take place in the form of an area of erythema with subjacent induration. It may disappear in 12 hours or persist 24 hours. It is usually read at 18–24 hours after injection. Positive reactions are infiltration and edema in an area at least 4 cm. in diameter, and an absence of induration in the vicinity of control injections. Such a delayed reaction occurs in more than 50 per cent of infected patients.

In the complement-fixation test (technique of N. H. Fairley), positive reactions are denoted by the signs P+, P++, and P+++ to denote fixation by the serum of the suspect, in the presence of hydatid antigen, of 3, 4½, and 6 or more minimal hemolytic doses of complement, respectively. Positive results are claimed in 50–60 per cent of hydatid cases. Complement fixation is especially useful in diagnosing recurrent or residual cysts in cases who have already undergone operations, for whom the skin test is useless.

Graña (1944), working in Uruguay, has developed what he terms a "triple response test." He recommends the intradermal injection of 2 cc. of hydatid fluid daily for 5 days. The triple response is then as follows: (1) a local and general eosinophilia; (2) a positive complement fixation may be expected to develop within 24, 48, or 96 hours after the first injection; this reaction is most constant and specific from the 5th to the 10th day after the last injection; and (3) agglutination of sheep red cells is very marked. In the latter respect, suspected sera before antigen injection of the suspect will agglutinate at 2- to 8-fold dilutions, whereas after antigen injection the sera will agglutinate at 32- to 2,000-fold dilutions.

The danger of larval echinococcids to the host results mainly from the mechanical pressure exerted by the growing cysts upon the surrounding tissues. In order of preference – or accidental location – the principal host locations are the liver (50–69 per cent), kidneys (3.5–8.9 per cent), cranial cavity (7.9 per cent), lungs (7.4–11.9 per cent), abdominal cavity (6.12–7.85 per cent), and skin and muscles (1.10–8.37 per cent). These figures are for humans only and are taken from a table compiled by Brumpt (1936). No medicinal treatment has proved effective. Treatment can only be surgical, by removal or by drainage, and is always risky.

Locular hydatidosis, although in a sense cosmopolitan, is fortunately endemic in few world areas. Iceland, with its numerous sheep and dogs, used to be a classic center for infestation in Europe. To a much less extent, hydatidosis has been seen in Germany, Russia, Bulgaria, Hungary, Britain, and France. In Asia, it has been noted in Arabia, Turkestan, and Indochina. In Africa hydatidosis is common in Algeria, Tunisia, and Morocco; it has been noted in Egypt and in Abyssinia (with the dromedary as intermediate host). Australia, particularly the state of Victoria, has much of it. It is common in Argentina and Uruguay. In North America it was known at one time in western Canada among first generation Icelanders, but is now rare. Magath (1936) reviewed 482 human cases reported for Canada and the United States between 1822 and 1936, mostly in immigrants. Riley (1933, 1939a, 1939b), stressing the long period of latency – in some cases as long as 30 years – the rarity with which medical records of it are reported, and the difficulty of diagnosis, believed that human hydatidosis may be less rare than has been supposed. It is by no means rare in sheep, hogs, and cattle, and is relatively common, according to this observer, in the lungs of moose in Minnesota, the adult carriers probably being wolves and coyotes.

The alveolar form of hydatidosis is known mainly from Bavaria and Tyrol, in the form of a malignant tumor of the liver – and occasionally elsewhere – characterized by the appearance of a spongelike mass of fibrous-walled cavities containing gelatinous material. First recorded in 1852, its true nature was elucidated by Virchow in 1856. The restricted geographical distribution of the infestation has induced suppositions that the adult worm – which has been reared by several observers in dogs – is specifically distinct from *granulosus*; but the zoological evidence to that effect is not convincing, and it is noteworthy that no investigator has succeeded in provoking alveolar hydatidosis in experimental animals. The belief in the occurrence of two morphae of *Echinococcus granulosus* – namely, *cysticus* and *alveolaris* – is based of course upon presumed differences in geographical distribution and on a presumed absence of transitional forms.

Against this view, Dévé (1933a) claimed that such transitional forms do occur. Posselt (1934), however, in a survey of four cases of alveolar hydatidosis, was unable to find intermediate forms between the larval forms provocative of the two types of hydatidosis. In favor of a distinct *Echinococcus multilocularis* as causative of this type of hydatidosis is its extreme rarity elsewhere – only one case of this type having been noted in such endemic areas of locular hydatidosis as Argentina and Australia.

The life cycle of the alveolar form is not fully known. The investigations of Melnikow in Russia suggested that the larva, instead of being bladderlike, is a nucleated plasmodium which spreads by buds which break away from plasmodial prolongations of the original larval surface.

The complete infestation appears as a huge tumor, greater than a human head, without definite boundaries – thus unlike the multilocular form of hydatidosis in cattle. The tumor is of a solid, cartilagelike consistency, has a central cavity formed by necrosis, and in cross section shows numerous cavities recalling those in a slice of bread. Commonly the central cavity is like a large pocket filled with a grayish green mass – hemin crystals, cholesterol, calcareous corpuscles, fat globules, etc. Each subcavity is lined by germinal membrane, outside of which is a laminated cuticle. Supporting the cavity walls is a meshlike stroma of a fibroid nature. The tumor grows by protoplasmic extensions from its surface, which later cuticularize and give rise to further cavities. Within the subcavities occur brood capsules containing holdfasts.

Clinical diagnosis of alveolar hydatidosis is difficult since the liver enlargement, jaundice, ascites, enlarged spleen, and collateral venous circulation may suggest nonparasitic cirrhosis. Even at autopsy, the parasitic nature of the tumor may be easily overlooked and a diagnosis of carcinoma arrived at. Any form of medicinal or surgical treatment appears impossible. The tumor cannot be drained; it cannot be removed; partial hepatectomy has been tried, however, with some degree of success.

In addition to the endemic area of alveolar hydatidosis that comprises Bavaria, Würtemberg, Tyrol, and northern Switzerland, another area has been reported in Siberia.

Fossor Honess, 1937

Small forms, 39–46 mm. by 2.9–3.0 mm. with 183–264 segments. Holdfast 577–838 μ long by 666–818 μ wide. Rostellum 262–308 μ in diameter with 22–25 hooks in a *single* circle, each hook 83–99 μ long. Suckers facing sideways, 192–239 μ in basal diameter, with mouths 77–127 μ in diameter. Neck 1.33–2.39 mm. Genital apertures alternating irregularly, each mid-marginal. Genital papilla with a diameter of 473 μ. Cirrus

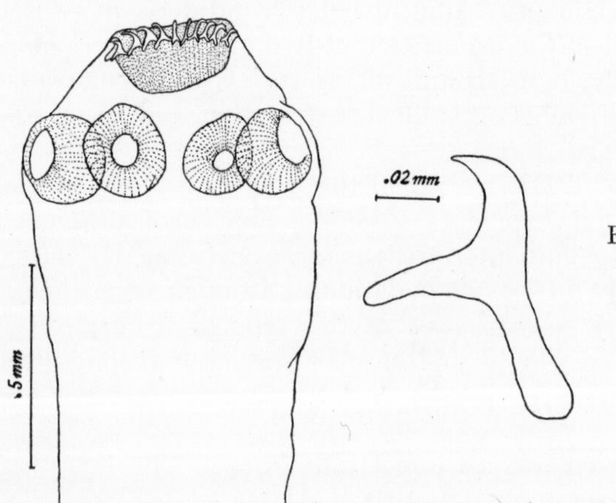

FIG. 217. *Fossor angertrudae*, holdfast and single hook. After Honess, 1937.

pouch 281 by 137 μ. Testes numerous. Ootype ovoid. Gravid uterus with 11–23 lateral branches on each side. Genotype and only known species, *angertrudae* Honess, 1937 in *Taxidea taxus taxus* (badger), Wyoming (Figure 217).

The genus and the species were based upon four specimens, each having only one circle of rostellar hooks and each showing no scar tissue or other indication that another circle had been present. Only one other taeniid with a single circle of hooks has been recorded – namely, *Taenia monostephanos* Linstow, 1905 – from a lynx (*Lynx lynx*) in Russia, and this has been regarded by most authors as a teratological or as a traumatic form of double-crowned *Taenia sp.* Until further specimens of Honess' form are recorded, the genus *Fossor* must be regarded as *sub judice.*

Anoplotaenia Beddard, 1911, emended Baer, 1925

Small-sized tapeworms. Holdfast unarmed. Suckers large. Genital apertures alternating irregularly. Genital ducts passing between the poral osmoregulatory canals, and dorsal to the poral nerve trunk. Testes in a single field, interrupted dorsally to the coils of the sperm duct and to the ovary and yolk gland. One row of testes behind the latter organ. Cirrus pouch spherical, opening into a highly differentiated genital atrium which has a powerful sphincter muscle perforated by the vagina. Uterus a median stem with numerous lateral outgrowths. In marsupials. Genotype and only known species, *dasyuri* Beddard, 1911.

The genus and genotype were established for material from *Sarcophilus satanicus* (Tasmanian devil) in the London Zoological Gardens. Beddard, after a somewhat lengthy discussion, placed his form within the subfamily Anoplocephalinae of Anoplocephalidae because the holdfast is unarmed and because the host is a marsupial. Meggitt (1924a), basing his argument upon Beddard's error of interpretation, considered the genus to be synonymous with *Oochoristica* because the uterus breaks down and the eggs are scattered in the parenchyma; and he listed it accordingly. Baer (1925c) re-examined Beddard's material and concluded that the lack of holdfast armature was not a good reason for assigning the genus to Anoplocephalidae, since unarmed forms are known among Taeniidae, Hymenolepididae, and Dilepididae. On the other hand, the uterus of *Anoplotaenia* is very similar to that of *Taenia sensu strictu.*

The holdfast end of *Anoplotaenia* is somewhat peculiar – 860 μ in diameter, with four large, oval suckers, 480 by 290 μ in diameter, and no trace of a rostellum. The rim of each sucker is interrupted middorsally by a circular, pitlike structure, which, oddly, is not mentioned by either Baer or Beddard. Another remarkable feature is the extraordinarily powerful sphincter muscle that surrounds not the exit of the cirro-vaginal atrium, but the exit, at the bottom of it, of the cirrus sac, and is pierced laterally to permit the passage of the vagina into the atrium. This sphincter is shallow, bowl-like, the walls having numerous radial fibers. Baer suggests that the function of the sphincter is to permit interproglottidal fertilization; but it is a little difficult to understand how this can be, for one would think that contraction of the sphincter would cause contraction of the vaginal portion running through it.

Paracladotaenia Yamaguti, 1935

With an unarmed rostellum. Neck present. Segments imbricate, broader than long throughout. Inner longitudinal muscles composed of separate bundles. Osmoregulatory canals with a valve, central to the cirrus sac and vagina. Genital apertures alternating irregularly. Testes numerous, in two submedian fields. A conspicuous internal seminal vesicle present. Ovary bipartite, well developed. Yolk gland distinctly bilobed in fully mature segments. Vagina opening directly behind the cirrus, with a small seminal receptacle. Uterus with a median stem and digitiform lateral pouches, occupying the entire medulla when fully gravid. Egg shell rigid, without radially striated embryophore. Adult parasitic in birds. Genotype and only recorded species, *acciptris* Yamaguti, 1935 from *Accipiter virgatus gularis*, Formosa (Figure 218).

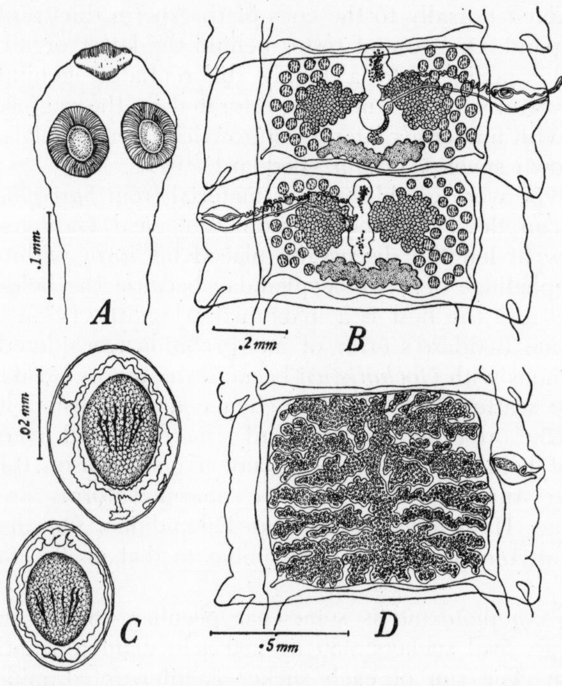

FIG. 218. *Paracladotaenia acciptris*. After Yamaguti, 1935a. A. Holdfast. B. Mature segments, dorsal. C. Eggs. D. Gravid segment, dorsal.

Yamaguti's generic diagnosis is given fully here because there seems to be some doubt as to the validity of this genus. While admitting a general resemblance to *Cladotaenia* Cohn, Yamaguti believed his genus to differ in the absence of rostellar hooks, the separation of the testes in two distinct lateral groups, the presence of a distinct internal seminal vesicle, the extent of the uterine stem, etc. The absence of rostellar hooks in a taeniid cannot be determined, however, from a single specimen.

One of the forms established by Ortlepp (1938a) as a species of *Cladotaenia* had only one rostellar hook remaining. Meggitt (1933) established *Cladotaenia feuta* for a form with no rostellar hooks. The separation of the testes into lateral bands is seen also in some species of *Cladotaenia*. Until a revision of the known species of *Cladotaenia* has been made, Yamaguti's genus must be regarded as *sub judice*.

Taeniarhynchus Weinland, 1858

With the holdfast end lacking both rostellum and hooks. Characteristics otherwise typically taeniid. Adult in humans. Larva a cysticercus, in Bovidae. Genotype, *saginatus* Goeze, 1782.

The genotype, a long-known and cosmopolitan parasite of humans, is readily distinguished from the other taeniid of humans, *Taenia solium*, by the lack of rostellum and hooks; the larger size (4–12 meters); the greater number of segments (about 2,000); the extreme irregularity of the alternating genital apertures; the lack of a vaginal sphincter; the dichotomously branching and more numerous uterine branches (15–50); the tendency of the gravid segments to be separate, rather than in chains, and to force their way through the anal sphincter of the host by their own muscular powers of mobility; and by the restriction of the cysticercus larva to Bovidae.

The life cycle and biology of this form have been fully described in zoological, medical, and veterinary texts and scarcely need description here. A description of the egg was given by Skvortsov (1942). In areas where the two forms coexist, *Taeniarhynchus saginatus* is decidedly commoner than *Taenia solium*, due perhaps to the smaller size and fewer numbers of the former's larvae (*Cysticercus bovis*), which allow infestation to pass unnoticed in any perfunctory meat-inspection technique unless such inspection is concentrated upon the jaw muscles, heart wall, or diaphragm.

Taeniarhynchus confusus Guyer, 1898 (= *Taenia confusa*) has been reported three times from humans in the southern United States and may be a form introduced originally by the slave trade from Africa (it appears identical with the form *bremneri*, described by Stephens, from man in northern Nigeria). Chandler (1920), who described *confusus* in some detail, was of the opinion that it may be commoner than the records suggest, since it could be readily overlooked as a specimen of *saginatus*.

Contrasted with *saginatus*, *confusus* shows a sharp distinction between the holdfast and the neck, the former being decidedly oblong in shape, with the suckers grouped in a pair on each side. We may note, too, the delicate cuticle and weak musculature; sparse calcareous bodies; small testes, 105–125 μ in diameter; small cirro-vaginal atrium with a short, pluglike papilla nearly filling it; the vagina with a distinct seminal receptacle, preceded by a short, constricted, thick-walled portion, and with cilia pointing *toward* the genital atrium; the ootype oval, traversed by the vaginal canal and connected with the uterus by a *separate egg canal* which opens into the uterus dorsally. The ovaries are large, kidney-shaped; the yolk gland triangular, unpaired, wedged between the ovarian lobes; the gravid uterus with a median stem and 14–18 irregularly ramifying branches, frequently constricted at the points of emergence from the median stem and swollen at their tips. The eggs are oval, 33 by 42 μ, with two short filaments attached to the thin outer shell. See Ward (1896), Guyer (1898), Stephens (1908), Chandler (1920). Anderson (1934), however, has shown *confusus* and *saginatus* to be linked by intergradations of every specific character and has expressed the belief that *confusus* is merely a variety of *saginatus* (Figures 219, 220).

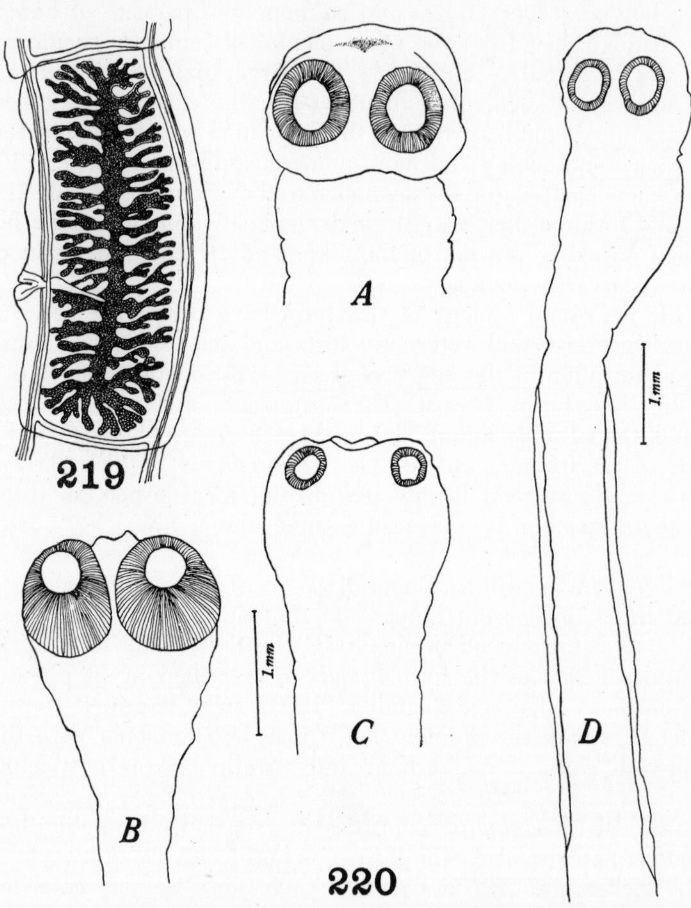

FIG. 219. *Taeniarhynchus saginatus*, gravid segment. After Stiles, 1906.
FIG. 220. *Taeniarhynchus saginatus*. A. Holdfast of specimen of "*Taenia confusa*." After Chandler, 1920. B and C. Holdfasts of *Taeniarhynchus saginatus* in different stages of contraction. After Leuckart, 1886a. D. Holdfast and neck of *Taeniarhynchus saginatus* showing "marginal elytra." After Anderson, 1934.

Dasyurotaenia Beddard, 1912, emended Baer, 1925

Small but stout forms without rostellum but with holdfast immense, carrying four small suckers of which two are armed with hooks. Segments very short and muscular, having four to six layers of longitudinal muscle bundles. Only a single, greatly hypertrophied osmoregulatory canal (ventral?) on each side, divided into a series of compartments, one per segment, by septa. Genital apertures unilateral. Testes numerous, chiefly lateral, anterior, and dorsal. Ovary bipartite, median and posterior. A large seminal receptacle present. Uterus described by Beddard as saclike, persistent, filling nearly the whole gravid segment; by Baer as having a median stem and very long, club-shaped lateral branches. Eggs thin-shelled, the embryophore thin and not striated. Genotype, *robusta* Beddard, 1912 from *Dasyurus ursinus* (Tasmanian devil), London Zoological Gardens (Figure 221).

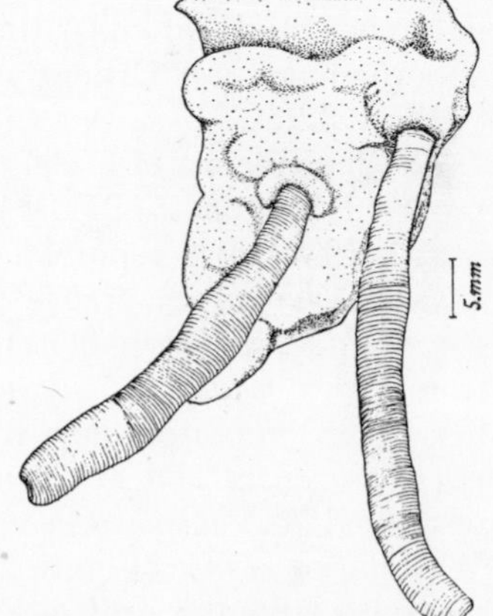

FIG. 221. *Dasyurotaenia robusta*, two entire worms *in situ*. After Beddard, 1912c.

Peculiar are the hypertrophied holdfast, completely embedded in a cystlike cavity in the host gut wall; the extraordinarily thick musculature; and the division of the ventral osmoregulatory canal by separate valves in each segment. The four-suckered holdfast was described by Beddard as having two external and two internal suckers. Baer was unable to confirm this, having no holdfast available, but thought that Beddard misinterpreted his sections and that the "two inner suckers armed with hooks" of Beddard's description represented in reality a rostellum armed with a double crown of hooks. The affinities of the genus with Taeniidae are obviously doubtful.

Cladotaenia Cohn, 1901

With a small rostellum armed with a double crown of hooks. Genital apertures alternating irregularly. Testes numerous, in two lateral fields, meeting or not behind the ovary. Internal seminal vesicle lacking. Gravid uterus typically taeniid, but with the median stem not extending into the anterior and posterior quarters of the segment. Parasites of birds. Genotype, *cylindracea* Bloch, 1782.

The genus was established for *Taenia globifera* Batsch, 1786, which is now generally believed to be a synonym of *Taenia cylindracea* Bloch, 1782. McIntosh (1940), however, believed Bloch's material to have been a dipylidiine form, possibly belonging to the genus *Diplopylidium*, and that Batsch's material may have been *T. globifera*, as redescribed by Morell (1895). McIntosh therefore accepted ten species of *Cladotaenia* as valid: *globifera* Batsch, 1786; *armigera* Volz, 1900; *mirsoevi* Skrjabin and Popoff, 1924; *secunda* Meggitt, 1928; *fania* Meggitt, 1933; *feuta* Meggitt, 1933; *circi* Yamaguti, 1935; *freani* Ortlepp, 1938; *vulturi* Ortlepp, 1938; and *foxi* McIntosh, 1940.

To these may be added: *melierax* Woodland, 1929 (= *Rhabdometra melierax* Woodland, 1929a), redescribed and reassigned by Fuhrmann and Baer (1943); and the additional species noted below. Ortlepp was inclined to assign his two species to Yamaguti's genus *Paracladotaenia* if further study of the latter should show the lack of hooks to be an abnormal feature; Ortlepp's *vulturi* had only one small hook adherent to the holdfast.

The first record of a cladotaeniid in North America was of *globifera*, reported by Jones (1930) from *Circus hudsonius* and *Asio flammeus*. Scott (1930) also reported *Cladotaenia sp.* from the liver of a rodent, *Cynomys leucurus* (prairie dog), and experimentally from *Buteo regalis* (= *Archibuteo ferrugineus*). Erickson (1938) reported *Cladotaenia sp.* from *Peromyscus maniculatus* (Labrador white-footed mouse), and Penner (1938) reported such from *Accipiter cooperi*, *Peromyscus leucopus novoboracensis*, and *Microtus pinetorum scalopsoides*. McIntosh (1940) described *foxi n.sp.* from a duck hawk (*Falco peregrinus anatum*) at Washington, D.C. (Figure 222) and obtained cysticerci by feeding segments to laboratory mice. F. L. Schmidt (1940) recorded *oklahomensis* from *Buteo jamaicensis* in Oklahoma. Reference should be made to the original descriptions of these species.

Crozier (1946), adding to the known species *banghami* from *Haliaeetus leucocephalus* in Ohio, recognizes twelve species of *Cladotaenia*: *globifera* Batsch, 1786; *armigera* Volz, 1900; *mirsoevi* Skrjabin and Popoff, 1924 (the only species recorded from a mammal); *secunda* Meggitt, 1928; *feuta* Meggitt, 1933; *fania* Meggitt, 1933; *circi* Yamaguti, 1935; *freani* Ortlepp, 1938; *vulturi* Ortlepp, 1938; *foxi* McIntosh, 1940; *oklahomensis* Schmidt, 1940; and *banghami* Crozier, 1946.

Hydatigera Lamarck, 1816 (= *Reditaenia* Sambon, 1924)

With the rostellum columnar with a double crown of hooks. Suckers prominent, at the base of the rostellum, and directed forward and outward. Neck apparently lacking, segmentation beginning immediately behind the posterior border of the suckers. Other features typically taeniid. Larva typically a strobilocercus with extruded holdfast and segmented body ending in a small bladder. Genotype, *taeniaeformis* Batsch, 1786.

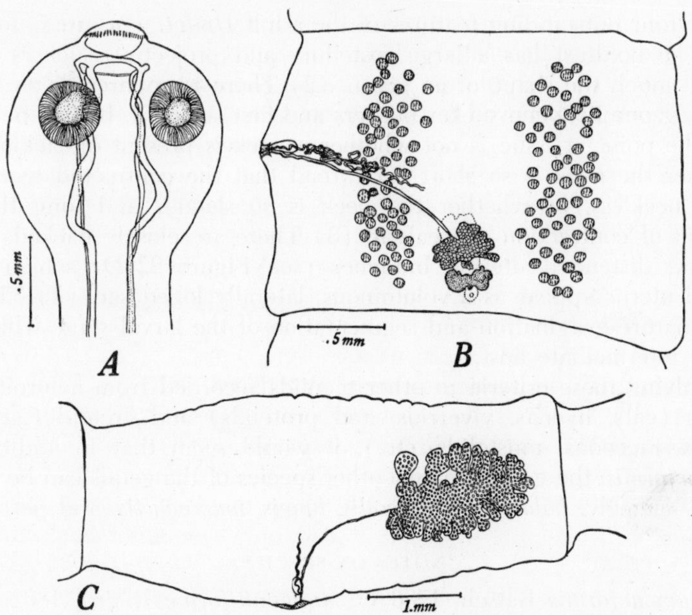

FIG. 222. *Cladotaenia foxi*. After McIntosh, 1940. A. Holdfast. B. Mature segment. C. Gravid segment.

The establishment of genera, indistinguishable as adults, upon features of the larval stages has much to commend it, but there is much to be said against it too (see Cameron, 1926). The recognition of the taeniid genera *Echinococcus, Hydatigera, Multiceps*, and *Taenia* on such grounds has long been the practice among American parasitologists. This practice opens up the question as to whether, in the absence of any practicable method of counting chromosomes, the specific and generic units of zoological classification shall be based upon readily recognizable characteristics of the *adult* animal, or upon features of the life cycle and of the biology, a procedure which while eminently desirable is rarely attainable. Without taking sides in the argument, we shall follow in this matter the current American practice.

The genus *Hydatigera* was established for a larval form (*Cysticercus fasciolaris*) recorded by Rudolphi (1808) from the livers of rodents. It was a form which had been recorded even earlier under such names as *Vermis vesicularis muris* Hartmann, 1695; *Fasciola muris hepatica* Roederer, 1762; *Taenia hydatigena* Pallas, 1766, *ex parte*; and *Taenia vesicularis taeniaeformis* Bloch, 1782. Reference to this form has been made previously (Chapter III) in connection with the experiments of Miller upon host resistance. Fairly common and widespread among rodents, especially rats and mice, this larva is peculiar in having a relatively small bladder, between which and the extruded holdfast there is a long, segmented body. The term "strobilocercus" of Sambon (1924) is commonly used for such a taeniid larval form.

The four outstanding features of the adult *Hydatigera* are as follows: (1) The holdfast has a large rostellum and projecting suckers which give it much the shape of an acorn. (2) There is apparently no unsegmented zone between sucker borders and first segment. It may be noted that the point at issue is not whether a neck is present or lacking, but whether the neck is so short and broad that the contracted worm appears neckless, or whether the neck is so slender and long that no amount of contraction conceals it. (3) There are closely packed, parallel, and distended uterine branches (see Figure 223D) which make gravid uterus appear as a voluminous, laterally lobed sac. (4) There is a premature evagination and segmentation of the larval stage while still in the intermediate host.

Applying these criteria to other taeniids recorded from aeluroid Carnivora (cats, hyenas, viverrids, and protelids) and arctoid Carnivora (bears, raccoons, mustelids, etc.), it would seem that in addition to *taeniaeformis*, the genotype, five other species of the genus can be recognized—namely, *balaniceps, laticollis, lyncis, macrocystis*, and *parva.*

NOTES ON SPECIES

1. *taeniaeformis* Batsch, 1786 (= *ammonitiformes* Baird, 1862; *collobrevissimo* Bloch, 1780; *crassicollis* Rudolphi, 1810; *fasciolaris* Rudolphi, 1808; *foinae* E. Blanchard, 1848; *felina* Goeze, 1782; *felis* Gmelin, 1790; *globulata* Goeze, 1782; *infantis* Bacigalupo, 1922; *intermedia* Rudolphi, 1810; *moniliformis* Batsch, 1786; *semiteres* Baird, 1862; *serrata* Goeze, 1782; *servata* Diesing, 1850). With the characters of the genus; rostellum with 26–52 large hooks, 380–420 μ long; the small hooks are 250–279 μ long; body from 150–600 mm. long by 5–6 mm. wide; anterior segments short, the following ones cuneiform, the end segments elongated; genital apertures mid-marginal; dorsal osmoregulatory canals sinuous, thick-walled; ventral ones straight, thin-walled. In the figures given by Hall (1919) (see Figure 223 C) two dorsal and two ventral canals are shown on each side; Hall speaks of the transverse osmoregulatory canal as "a single tube in the median portion of the strobila," possibly a misprint for segment, and forking at each end so as to surround the dorsal canal. Testes numerous; cirrus pouch slender, 430–475 μ in mature segments, 300–345 μ in gravid segments; ovary appearing as two spherical bodies, the poral one somewhat smaller than the antiporal one; yolk gland conspicuous, elongated, parallel with the posterior segment border; gravid uterus voluminous, obliterating the remaining genitalia, its middle stem when fully formed having 16–18 side branches which are notably close together and parallel to one another, showing little tendency to sub-branch or fork, but rather tending to become distended at their tips so that the distended uterus recalls a much-lobed sac; eggs spherical, 31–37 μ in diameter; larva a strobilocercus in the livers of rodents; adult a common and cosmopolitan parasite of the domestic cat, but recorded also from a range of Felidae and Mustelidae; the identity of the larval and adult forms appears to have been established by Batsch (1786) (Figures 223, 224).

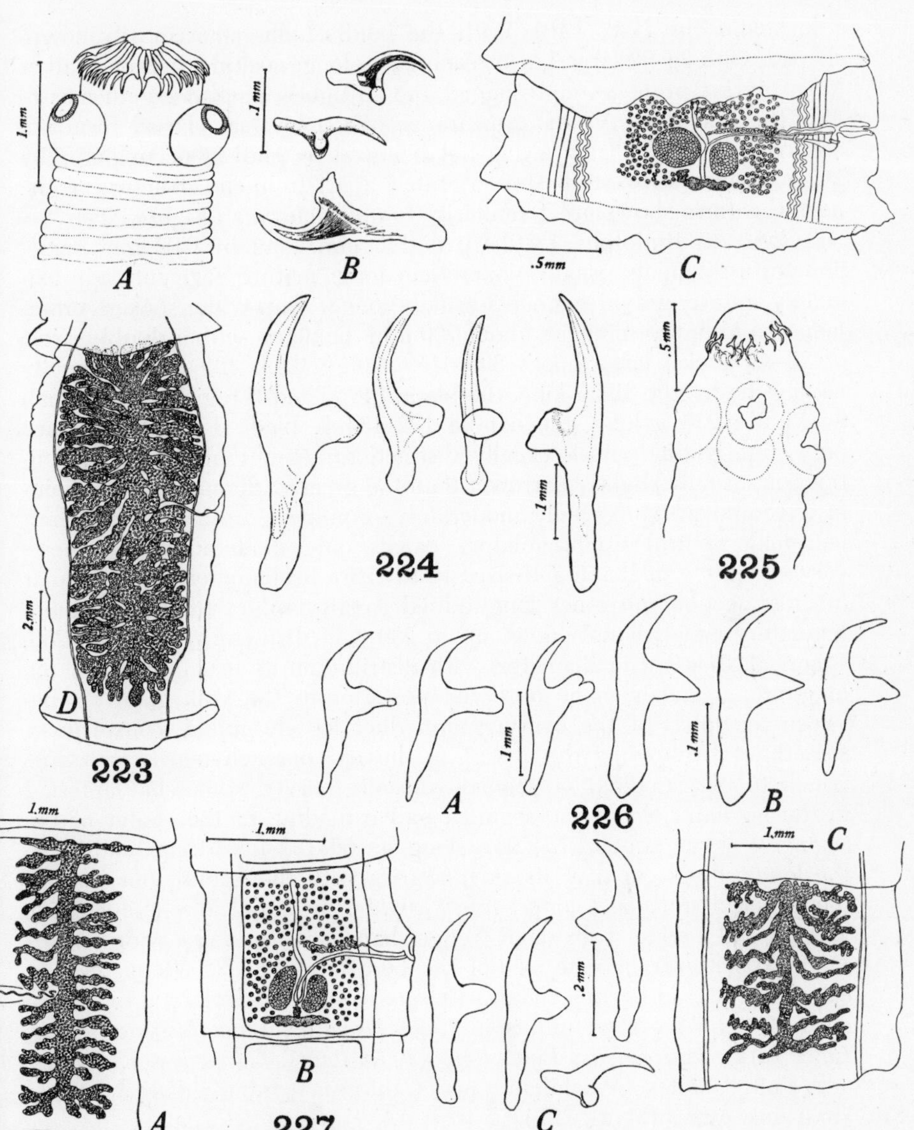

IG. 223. *Hydatigera taeniaeformis*. After Hall, 1919. A. Holdfast. B. Large and small hooks. . Mature segment. D. Gravid segment. FIG. 224. *Hydatigera taeniaeformis*, hooks. After ollfus, 1938. FIG. 225. *Hydatigera balaniceps*, holdfast. After Hall, 1910a. FIG. 226. *Hydatig-ra lyncis*. After Skinker, 1935d. A. Small hooks showing bifid condition. B. Lateral view of arge and small hooks. C. Gravid segment. FIG. 227. *Hydatigera laticollis*. After Skinker, 1935d. A. Gravid segment. B. Mature segment. C. Hooks.

2. *balaniceps* Hall, 1910. With the holdfast characteristically acorn-shaped, with 28–32 large hooks, each 145 μ long; neck distinct and rather long; uterine branches club-shaped and so tightly packed together as to give the gravid uterus the appearance of a lobed sac; larval form not observed; recorded from a dog but believed by Hall to occur naturally in lynxes in southwestern United States; apart from the structure of the neck this form shows great similarity to *taeniaeformis* (Figure 225).

3. *laticollis* Rudolphi, 1819. Up to 140 mm. long by 0.32 mm. wide; immature segments usually wider than long; mature segments approximately square; gravid segments usually longer than wide; suckers prominent; rostellum prominent, about 700 μ in diameter, with a double circle of 38–42 hooks; large hooks 390–415 μ long; hook 400 μ long usually having the handle 195 μ long, the blade 146 μ, and the guard 73 μ; small hooks 214–238 μ long, the handle 122–134 μ, blade 134–140 μ, guard only slightly bifid; neck usually distinct, sometimes obscured by contraction, usually slightly narrower than the greatest diameter of the holdfast; genital apertures only moderately prominent, approximately midmarginal; ventral osmoregulatory canals only moderately prominent, varying widely in shape and size, up to 125 μ in diameter when circular in cross section; no other longitudinal canals visible; transverse osmoregulatory canals conspicuous, up to 230 μ in diameter; testes 180–250, spherical, 37–49 μ in diameter, with distribution as usual, between the longitudinal canals; none observed posterior to the yolk gland or between the lobes of the ovary; sperm duct loosely coiled, conspicuous, sometimes occupying the entire medullary parenchyma from cirrus pouch to median field of segment, usually curved somewhat anteriad in the median field of the segment and extending to the center of the segment; cirrus pouch 275–293 μ long by 66–131 μ wide, extending to the longitudinal canal of its side; ovaries with the aporal lobe usually the larger, about 360 μ long by 180 μ wide, the poral lobe about 295 μ long by 180 μ wide; yolk gland wedge-shaped, 595 to 655 μ wide (measured along the transverse axis of the body) by 60–120 μ long, usually extending laterad beyond the ovaries; uterus with 10–15 lateral branches; eggs 40 μ by 28–32 μ; adults in *Lynx fasciatus, Lynx fasciatus rufus, Lynx rufus californicus, Lynx lynx* (*Felis lynx*), *Canis lestes*, Europe and United States (Washington and California); intermediate host and larva unknown (Figure 227).

This species was recorded originally from a European lynx (*Lynx lynx*). Rudolphi's material was re-examined by Diesing (1850), Leuckart (1856), Lühe (1910b), and additional material was described by Stiles and Hassall (1894) from *Lynx canadensis* in North America, by Joyeux and Baer (1935d) from *Viverra genetta* in southeastern France, and by Skinker (1935d) – whose specific description is given above – from *Lynx fasciatus, Lynx lynx*, and *Canis lestes*, both European and North American. Its identity with, or its distinction from, *taeniaeformis* is still *sub judice*. Hall (1919) believed the form to be merely an immature *taeniaeformis*. Some observers have been inclined to stress the absence of a vaginal sphincter from *laticollis* and the presence of one in *taeniae-*

formis. Skinker (1935d) claimed that the two species are readily separated by even casual examination on the basis of the difference in shape of the large hooks and the striking difference in the size of the body in mature specimens; the guard of the hooks of *taeniaeformis* is much more prominent than in *laticollis*, and the body of *taeniaeformis* is much longer and wider than that of *laticollis*.

4. *lyncis* Skinker, 1935. Up to 640 mm. long by 11 mm. maximum width; holdfast usually wider than first segment, 620–1,000 μ wide; suckers conspicuous, round, 165–205 μ in diameter; rostellum 250–400 μ in diameter with a double crown of 36–46 hooks; large hooks 220–258 μ long, handle 110–151 μ long, widest portion at distal end, blade 79–85 μ long, guard conspicuous, 55–70 μ long; small hooks 159–208 μ long, handle 79–122 μ, blade 61–73 μ, with guard distinctly bifid and 43–63 μ long; rostellum sometimes protruding one and one-half times the length of the rest of the holdfast; neck usually short, segmentation usually beginning 540 μ to 1.4 mm. posterior to the suckers; genital apertures inconspicuous, approximately mid-marginal; ventral longitudinal osmoregulatory canals 700–800 μ from margin of segment; transverse canals conspicuous; testes distributed as usual between the osmoregulatory canals but with a few in the space between ovaries and yolk gland, 200–500 altogether; testes usually overlapping lateral regions of yolk gland; several behind the yolk gland but rarely behind the ovary; 60–95 μ in diameter; cirrus pouch 200–375 μ long, 70–110 μ wide; ovaries varying in shape, typically forming two rounded masses; yolk gland usually linear, occasionally triangular, usually not extending beyond the lobes of the ovary; vagina posterior to the cirrus pouch; seminal receptacle 125–170 μ long by 50–61 μ wide; uterus developing side pocketings which become reduced to more delicate lateral branches, 4–10 on each side; eggs 25 μ by 28–35 μ; larva with large, terminal, bulblike bladder about 8 mm. long by 6.5 mm. wide, and transversely striated; body of larva about 11 mm. long and 2.5 maximum width; adults in *Lynx rufus rufus*, *L. r. californicus*, *L. r. fasciatus*, *L. r. uinta*, *Felis concolor azteca*, *F. c. hippolestes*, *F. c. oregonensis*; larvae in *Odocoileus columbianus scaphiatus*, *O. hemionus hemionus*, and *O. virginianus macrourus*, in lungs and pericardium, and possibly in the rodent *Peromyscus maniculatus nubriterrae* (attached to liver), United States (Figure 226).

5. *macrocystis* Diesing, 1850. With a prominent rostellum with 60–74 hooks; large hooks arranged alternately nearer to the center of the rostellum and farther from it, each 320–355 μ long, forming in effect two circles of large hooks; neck short and broad; uterine branches 8–15 pairs, relatively short and themselves branching; larva (in *Sylvilagus brasiliensis*) resembling that of *taeniaeformis*; possibly more than one species represented in Diesing's material; Skinker believed (1935d) that some forms may have been specimens of *laticollis*; hosts *Felis tigrina*, *Felis jaguaroundi*, Brazil; *Lynx rufus*, *Lynx baileyi*, United States. The forms recorded by Stiles and Hassall (1894) as *laticollis* from *Lynx canadensis* were identified by Skinker (1935d) as *macrocystis*.

6. *parva* Baer, 1926. Up to 55 mm. long; body very muscular; holdfast

1 mm. in diameter; suckers 200 μ wide; rostellum powerful, 600 μ in diameter, with a double circle of 44 hooks, 361 μ long, base 228 μ, curvature of blade not pronounced, guard with a small protuberance; small hooks 228 μ long, base 141 μ; neck short, 200 μ long by 1.6 mm. wide; cuticle very thick, 29 μ; immediately beneath it two layers of circular muscles and beneath these two to three layers of longitudinal muscles; subcuticle very distinct and 50 μ thick; parenchymal muscles extraordinarily developed; longitudinal fibers in two layers, in lateral fields of the cortical parenchyma; internal to the longitudinals is a thick layer of transverse fibers; calcareous corpuscles very abundant; testes 500, in two to three layers in the dorsal region of the medulla, dorso-ventral diameter 100 μ; sperm duct without seminal vesicles; very coiled; surrounded by so-called prostatic cells; cirrus pouch very long, 440 μ, its wall composed chiefly of longitudinal muscle fibers which form on its distal portion two powerful retractor muscles embedded in the transverse musculature; cirrus pouch opening into a very deep, funnel-like genital atrium whose inner lining is corrugated; ovary bilobed, the poral lobe smaller than the antiporal; yolk gland well developed; uterus with 7–12 pairs of lateral branches; embryophore 27 by 33 μ; adults in *Genetta ludia*, Transvaal, South Africa.

Multiceps Goeze, 1782

With the characters of the family. Each large rostellar hook *usually* has a sinuous handle. The vagina *usually* has a reflex loop in the vicinity of the osmoregulatory canal of that side. Larva a coenurus. Genotype, *multiceps* Leske, 1780.

This genus has always been difficult to distinguish from *Taenia* when in the adult stage, the only morphological differences, apparently, being *Multiceps'* possession of a coenurus larva, sinuous large-hook handles, and of *usually* looped vaginae. The species of the genus also have always been difficult to separate, and several attempts have been made to establish such distinctions by statistical examination of the hook dimensions (see Bhaduri and Maplestone, 1940; Clapham and Peters, 1941; Clapham, 1942b; and Crusz, 1944).

Clapham (1942b) studied the total size and proportions of the large hooks of fourteen alleged species of *Multiceps* and concluded: (1) that the genus contains not more than six species, these being *multiceps, radians, twitchelli, gaigeri, macracantha*, and *otomys*; (2) that *Multiceps multiceps* comprises the species formerly termed *multiceps, serialis, glomeratus, packi, spalacis, clavifer, polytuberculosus, lemuris*, and *ramosus*, and is characterized by having a large-hook length varying from 110–175 μ with a mean of 137.738 and a standard deviation of 4.3486; a ventral blade length (see remarks earlier in this section upon Clapham's methods of measurement) varying from 43–73 μ with a mean of 58.907 and a standard deviation of 3.794; and a dorsal blade length varying from 70–120 μ with a mean of 101.241 μ and a standard deviation of 3.03; (3) that *Multiceps multiceps* is of wide geographical and biological distribution and may contain several different *strains* which establish themselves in different hosts where they adopt an individual form and behave in their own characteristic way; (4) that the coenurus may occur in the central nervous system, the intermuscular connective tissue, the abdominal cavity, the thoracic sheath, and the pericardial sheath of the intermediate hosts.

NOTES ON SPECIES

Since Clapham's somewhat drastic reduction of recognized species is not accepted by all authors, some notes may be given here upon the forms she thinks are synonymous with *multiceps*.

1. *Multiceps multiceps* (Leske, 1780) (= *Taenia socialis* Bloch, 1780; *Taenia coenurus* Küchenmeister, 1853; *Cystotaenia coenurus* Leuckart, 1863; *Multiceps multiceps* Hall, 1910). A cosmopolitan parasite of dogs, foxes, jackals. Its coenurid stage (= *Polycephalus multiceps* Leske, 1780) has been recorded from the brains of humans, horses, cattle, sheep – in which it is particularly common – goats, pigs, and rabbits; it occurs infrequently in other regions of the body. In sheep the cysts may occur in the brain or in the lumbar region of the spinal cord. If they are scattered in numbers through the brain, the victim shows symptoms of blindness and acute encephalitis; if the parasite is located as a single or double egg-sized cyst in the cerebral hemisphere of one side, the animal shows the syndrome termed "gid" (English), "Wirbling" (German), or "tournoiement" (French), the animal walking in circles, staggering, and showing giddiness. Similar cases have been recorded, though rarely, in humans. Reference may be made to veterinary and parasitological texts for detailed descriptions of the disease.

The adult *multiceps* is described by Neveu Lemaire (1936) as 400 mm. by 1 mm. in dimensions with the holdfast pear-shaped, 800 μ wide, carrying a rostellum with a double circle of 22–32 hooks; the larger hooks measure 150–170 μ in length, the smaller ones 90–130 μ; the large-hook handle has a slightly sinuous shape and is as long as the blade; the guard is heart-shaped; neck distinctly narrower than the holdfast and fairly long; first segments narrow, 15–20 cm. from the holdfast, becoming square; gravid segments 8–12 mm. long by 3–5 mm. wide; genital apertures alternating irregularly; testes 200 per segment; uterus when gravid with a median stem and 9–26 branches on each side, parallel, only slightly ramifying; embryophores almost spherical, 31–36 μ in diameter; coenurus up to the size of a hen's egg, with several hundred contained holdfasts; the coenurus takes two to three months to attain full size; the adult worm has a prepatent period of three or four weeks.

2. *Multiceps serialis* (Gervais, 1847) (= *Taenia coenuri cuniculi* Diesing, 1864; *Multiceps serialis* Meggitt, 1924). Also cosmopolitan in dogs, foxes, jackals, but has its coenurus stage chiefly in rodents, especially rabbits. Examined critically by Clapham (1942b), its larval form – *Coenurus serialis* – showed no significant differences in hook dimensions whether from a gelada baboon (*Theropithecus gelada*), a porcupine (*Hystric longicauda*), from *Myopotamus sp.*, from rats in Accra and Nigeria, from a gerbil (*Gerbillus hirtipes*), from mice in London, or

from English rabbits. The large hooks ranged in length from 110 μ to 175 μ, with a mean of 136.06 μ and a standard deviation of 3.448; the smaller ones measured 68–120 μ. The ventral blade lengths of the larger hooks were 43–64 μ, with a mean of 57.3916 μ and a standard deviation of 2.34; the dorsal blade lengths varied from 70 μ to 114 μ, with a mean of 99.618 μ and a standard deviation of 3.13.

Crusz (1944), using Clapham's system of measurements on three coenurids from rabbits (*Lepus nigricollis singhala*) in Ceylon, measured 935 hooks and found the mean ventral blade length of the larger hooks to be 78.2 μ; of the smaller hooks to be 60.2 μ and 58.5 μ, respectively; the dorsal blade lengths (large hooks) with means of 116.9 μ and 110.5 μ, respectively (two coenuri); and total large-hook lengths to be 135–137 μ.

The adult form is described by Neveu Lemaire (1936) as 200–720 mm. long; the holdfast spherical, somewhat tetragonal, 850 μ to 1.3 mm. wide, with a double crown of 26–32 hooks with undulating handles; neck narrower than the holdfast and relatively long; segments resembling those of *multiceps*, the terminal ones 8–16 mm. long by 3 to 5 mm. broad; testes numerous; gravid uterus with 20–25 pairs of branches; embryophores 34 μ long by 27 μ wide.

The coenurus stage is a bladder up to the size of a hen's egg, peculiar in being able to bud off daughter bladders either internally, floating in the bladder liquid, or externally, attached by stalks. It is normally a parasite of the intermuscular connective tissue of rabbits and hares. In Primates it is rare. Sandground (1937) listed the literature on the subject and recorded five cases in Primates other than man and two in humans. Elek and Finkelstein (1939) have described in detail the pathology of a multiple infestation of *Multiceps serialis* in a baboon (*Theropithecus gelada*).

3. *Multiceps glomeratus* (Railliet and Henry, 1915). Recorded by these authors from a gerbil (*Gerbillus hirtipes*) in Tunis and by Turner and Leiper (1919) from a man in West Africa; adult form unknown; both specimens apparently immature, with the rostellar hooks imperfectly chitinized.

4. *Multiceps packi* Christenson, 1929. Reared in a dog from a coenurus in northern hares (*Lepus americanus phaenotus*) in Minnesota; 360–600 mm. long with 150–200 segments; anterior portion of body with serrated margins; posterior segments elongated, often tapering at both ends; holdfast with 26–32 hooks. Baylis (1932b) pointed out that the hook dimensions – total large-hook length 145–150 μ, small-hook lengths 96–100 μ – are indistinguishable from those of *serialis*. Christenson stressed the inequality of the ovarian lobes, the bending of the sperm duct at the lateral osmoregulatory canal to form an obtuse angle, and the extension of the testes as far back as the yolk gland (Figure 228).

5. *Multiceps spalacis* Joyeux, 1923. Recorded as a larva from *Tachyoryctes splendens* in Abyssinia; length of large hooks 162–170 μ, of small hooks 125–130 μ.

6. *Multiceps clavifer* Pagenstecher, 1877. Recorded by Pagenstecher

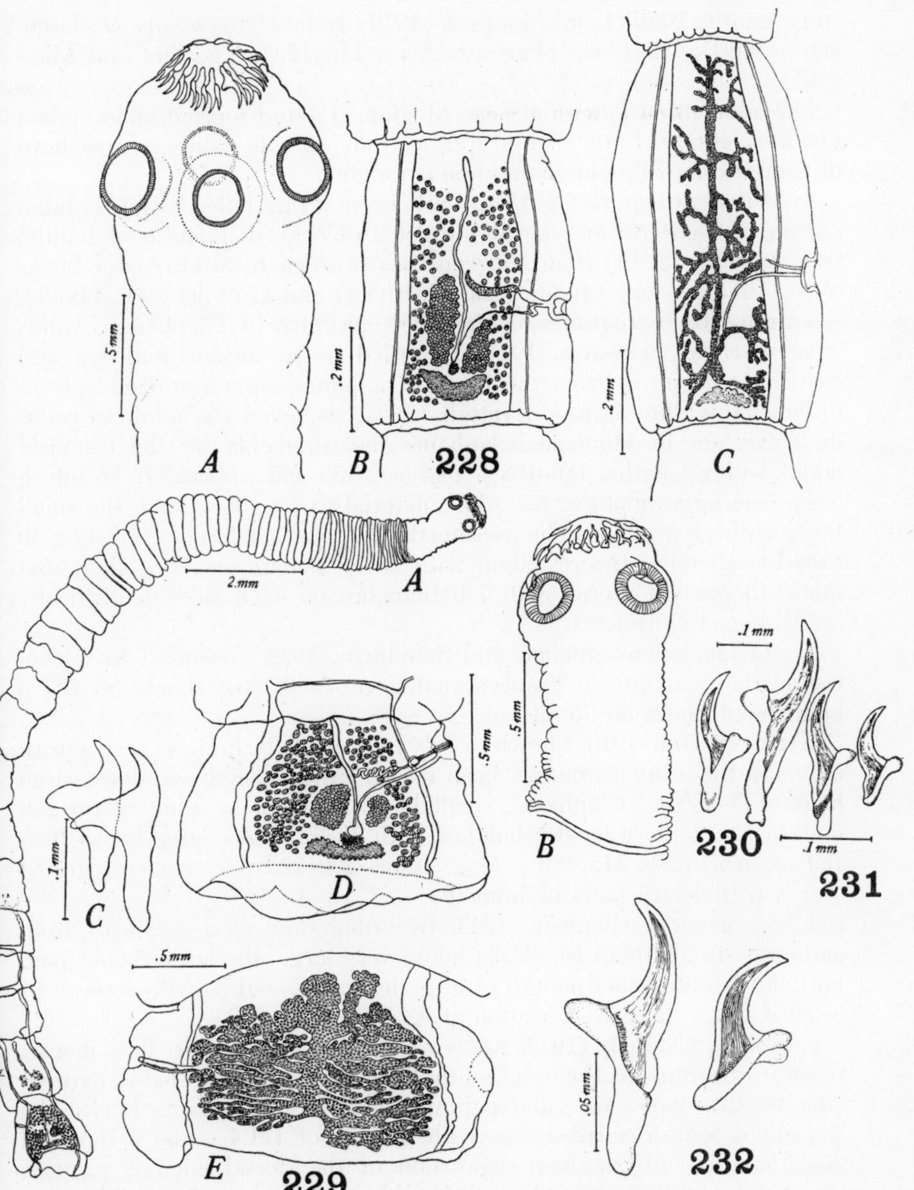

IG. 228. *Multiceps packi.* After Christenson, 1929. A. Holdfast. B. Mature segment. C. ravid segment. FIG. 229. *Multiceps twitchelli.* After McIntosh, 1938. A. Anterior region of orm. B. Holdfast. C. Hooks. D. Mature segment. E. Gravid segment. FIG. 230. Hooks of *ulticeps macracantha.* After Clapham, 1942. FIG. 231. *Multiceps otomys,* hooks. After Clapham, 1942. FIG. 232. *Multiceps glomeratus,* hooks. After Clapham and Peters, 1941.

and again by Railliet and Mouguet (1919) from *Myopotamus sp.*; large-hook lengths 122–130 μ (Pagenstecher), 114–120 μ (Railliet and Mouguet).

7. *Multiceps polytuberculosus* Megnin, 1880. From a tame jerboa (*Jaculus saggitta*); the hooks appear from Megnin's drawings to have measured only 70 μ (large) and 50 μ (small).

8. *Multiceps lemuris* Cobbold, 1861. From a ring-tailed lemur, London Zoological Gardens; may be identical with *Coenurus ramosus* of Railliet and Marrulaz (1919) from *Macacus sinicus*; in each case the large hooks were 110–132 μ long (Railliet and Marrulaz) and 125 μ long (Cobbold).

Turning to other species of *Multiceps*, accepted by Clapham as valid:

1. *twitchelli* Schwartz, 1924. Recorded as a curious budding and branching coenurus from the lungs of a porcupine (*Erethizon epixanthum myops*) in Alaska. McIntosh (1938) believed the adult to occur in wolverines in Montana. Clapham's measurements for the coenurid hooks were: lengths, 189–198 μ (large), 155–163 μ (small). McIntosh found the large hooks of his adult material to be 195 μ long, the small hooks to be 155 μ long. The presumed adult was small, not exceeding 50 mm. by 2.5 mm.; the rostellum with 30–36 hooks; the neck short and thick; the gravid uterus with 7–9 branches on each side, dendritically branching (Figure 229).

2. *radians* Joyeux, Richet, and Schulman, 1922. Recorded as a coenurus from a mouse in France; small form, with large hooks 85–105 μ long, small hooks 58–75 μ.

3. *gaigeri* Hall, 1916. Known mainly from goats in India as a coenurus, although the adult worm has been reared experimentally in dogs; large hooks 145–180 μ (Clapham), small hooks 103–160 μ; adult worm 250 mm. to 1.82 mm. in length; holdfast with 28–32 hooks; large hooks 160–180 μ, small ones 115–150 μ long; testes 200–225 per segment; gravid uterus with 12–15 pairs of branches.

4. *macracantha* Clapham, 1942. Recorded only as a coenurus from white rats in Southern Rhodesia; hooks very large, the larger hooks having bifid handles; total length of large hooks 377–391 μ, with a mean of 379.2 μ and a standard deviation of 5.431 (Figure 230).

5. *otomys* Clapham, 1942. Known only from a coenurus in a mouse, *Otomys erroratus*, at Pretoria, South Africa; it is distinguishable particularly by the shape, size, and curious markings of the large hooks; the large-hook length is 162–182 μ, with a mean of 171.4 μ and a standard deviation of 2.497; a deep depression of the dorsal edge is present; the guard is set at an angle with the blade and tapered to a blunt tip (Figure 231).

6. *brauni* Setti, 1897 (= *brachysoma* Setti, 1899). From a dog in Eritrea, northeast Africa; with the rostellum weak, the neck short and broad; holdfast with 30 hooks, 95–140 μ long (large), 70–90 μ (small); intermediate host *Gerbillus pyramidum*; Hamilton (1940) regarded his form *Taenia laruei*, from a coyote in Oklahoma, as showing many resemblances to *brauni*.

SPECIES INQUIRENDA

1. *crassiceps* Zeder, 1800. Body length 120–220 mm.; holdfast 750 μ broad by 900 μ long, with 32–34 hooks, 186 μ (large), 135 μ (small); adult recorded from a fox, *Vulpes vulpes*, in Europe; larval stage a mass of small bladders beneath the skin of rodents (*Citellus citellus, Cricetus cricetus, Microtus arvalis, Microtus terrestris, Mus musculus, Scirusus vulgaris*) and in the European mole (*Talpa europaea*). Southwell and Kirshner (1937a) described from a rat (*Mastomys erythroleucus*) in Sierra Leone a polycephalic cestode larva which consisted of a small, spherical bladder about 10 mm. in diameter from which radiated twelve segmented bodies, each having at its tip four suckers and a double crown of 44 hooks, 22 large ones (380–400 μ in length) and 22 small ones (220–240 μ in length). These authors believed their form to be a larval *Hydatigera taeniaeformis*, but they pointed out that the only other polycephalic larva on record was Setti's form recorded above as *brauni*, which has been accepted by some authors as a larval form of *crassiceps*.

Taenia Linnaeus, 1758, *s.str.*, emended Stiles and Hassall, 1926

Relatively large forms with the characters of the family. Rostellum distinct but not massive; armed with a double crown of hooks. Handles of the large hooks usually not sinuous. Neck usually distinct. Vagina straight or curved in the vicinity of the poral canals but without any reflexed loop at this point. Body with ten to several hundred segments. Larval stage a cysticercus, with only one holdfast, in herbivorous mammals and omnivorous mammals, occasionally in humans. Adults in carnivorous mammals including humans. Genotype, *solium* Linnaeus, 1758.

Apparently *Taenia solium* was erroneously selected as genotype of the genus *Taenia*, however, and if the International Rules of Zoological Nomenclature were strictly applied *Dibothriocephalus latus* should be the genotype of *Taenia*. Accordingly, the plenary powers of the Inter-

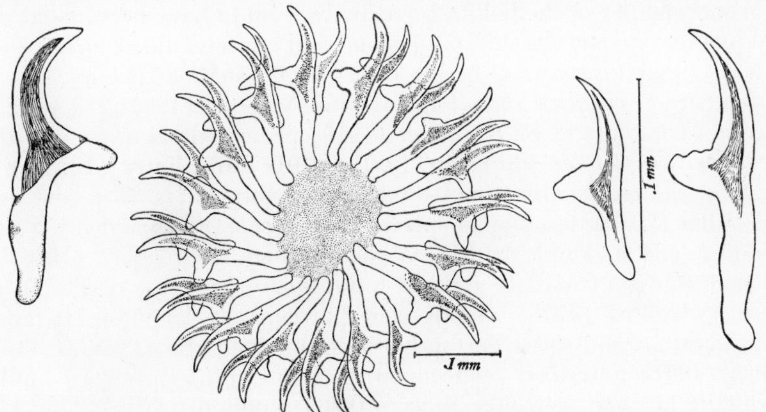

FIG. 233. Typical taeniid hooks. After Clapham and Peters, 1941, and Dollfus, 1944.

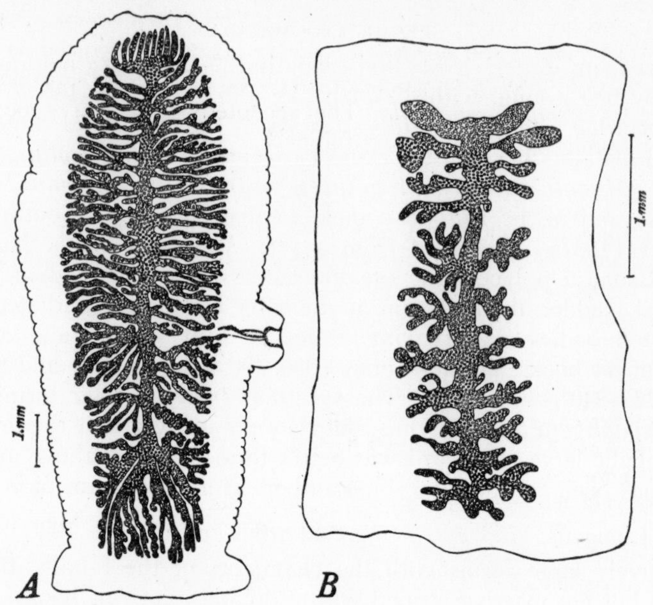

FIG. 234. Typical taeniid gravid segments. A. *Taenia ovis*. After Ransom, 1913b. B. *Taenia taxidiensis*. After Skinker, 1935d.

national Commission have been invoked to suspend the rules for *Taenia* for the purpose of fixing irrevocably *Taenia solium* as type of this genus (see Hemming, 1947).

The generic term *Taenia* may be used for any taeniid that has a double crown of rostellar hooks and has a cysticercus larval stage; if the type of larva is unknown, it is almost impossible to say with certainty whether a double-crowned taeniid species belongs to *Hydatigera, Multiceps*, or *Taenia*.

Abnormalities of the holdfast and body seem to have been noted more frequently among species of *Taenia* and closely allied genera than among other tapeworms. Braun (1894–1900) summarized to that date the recorded cases of forked tapeworms. Vigener (1903) recorded the cases of triradiate taeniids. Barker (1910) presented cases of polyradiate specimens of *Taenia pisiformis*. Foster (1916) and Faust (1925) listed most of the recorded cases of tapeworm abnormalities. In recent years, Chandler (1930) described a specimen of *Taenia pisiformis* with a single holdfast and a double body; Dobrovolny and Dobrovolny (1935) described thirteen triradiate and one tetraradiate specimens of *Taenia pisiformis*; Dollfus (1938) described a polycephalic larva of *Hydatigera taeniaeformis* and surveyed the literature on such abnormalities; Roudabush (1941) described a specimen of *Taenia pisiformis* with multiple genitalia in some segments; Kuntz (1943) reported two fully developed strobilocerci of *Hydatigera taeniaeformis* attached to a single bladder.

As used in the earlier literature, the genus *Taenia* was far removed from present-day conceptions. Hughes (*The Taeniae of Yesterday*, 1941a) listed 1,600–1,700 forms which were formerly regarded as species of *Taenia*. Today the genus contains about twenty accepted species and about thirty *species inquirenda*. The accepted species may be distinguished in preliminary fashion as follows:

KEY TO SPECIES

1. Larger hooks 300–400 μ in length . . . . *rileyi*
   Larger hooks less than 300 μ in length 2
2. Larger hooks 225–300 μ in length 3
   Larger hooks 100–255 μ in length 4
   Larger hooks less than 100 μ in length 7
3. Uterine branches fewer than 10 pairs . . . . *bubesei, regis*
   Uterine branches 8–14 pairs . . . . *pisiformis*
4. Uterine branches fewer than 10 pairs 5
   Uterine branches more than 10 pairs 6
5. Testes more than 500 in number . . . . *hydatigena*
   Testes fewer than 500 in number . . . . *krabbei, solium, acinonyxi, ingwei, jakhalsi*
   Testis number unknown . . . . *erythraea*
6. Testes more than 500 in number . . . . *laruei, gonyamei*
   Testes fewer than 500 in number . . . . *ovis, krabbei, hlosei, hyaenae*
   Testis number unknown . . . . *cervi*
7. Hook length 79–99 μ; testes 200–300 . . . . *taxidiensis*
   Hook length 16 μ; testes 90–125 . . . . *tenuicollis*

Incertae sedis (hooks unknown; testes 200–250; uterine branches 8–10 pairs): *pungutchui.*

NOTES ON SPECIES

1. *rileyi* Loewen, 1929. 310 mm.; holdfast with 32 hooks; larger hooks 340–386 μ; smaller hooks 212–220 μ; testes 450–550; uterine branches 7–11 pairs; adult in *Lynx canadensis*, Minnesota; larval stages unknown (Figure 239).

2. *bubesei* Ortlepp, 1938. 450–550 mm.; holdfast with 42–46 hooks; larger hooks 235–273 μ, smaller hooks 130–180 μ; testes 500–600; uterine branches 3–7 pairs; in lions (*Felis leo krugeri*), South Africa.

3. *regis* Baer, 1923. 160 mm.; holdfast with 32 hooks; larger hooks 290 μ; smaller hooks 190 μ; testes 200; uterine branches 2–3 pairs; in lions (*Felis leo krugeri*), South Africa.

4. *pisiformis* Bloch, 1780 (for synonymity see Hall, 1919; Neveu Lemaire, 1936). 30–200 mm.; holdfast with 34–48 hooks; larger hooks 225–294 μ; smaller hooks 132–177 μ; testes 400–500; uterine branches 8–14 pairs; in *Canis familiaris, Thos spp., Felis catus, Panthera pardus*, etc.; cosmopolitan; larval stage in rabbits and hares (Figure 235).

5. *hydatigena* Pallas, 1766 (for synonymity see Stiles and Stevenson, 1905; Stiles and Hassall, 1912; Meggitt, 1924a; Hall, 1919; Neveu Lemaire, 1936; Stiles and Baker, 1935). 750–5,000 mm.; holdfast with 22–44 hooks; larger hooks 170–220 μ; smaller hooks 110–160 μ; testes 600–700; uterine branches 5–10 pairs; adult in *Canis familiaris, Canis lupus*,

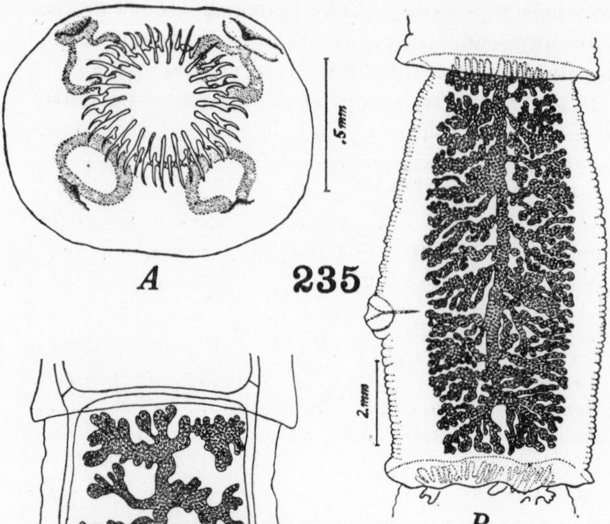

235

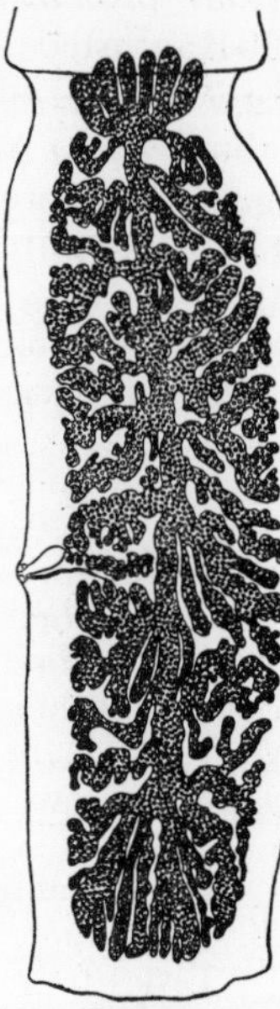

236

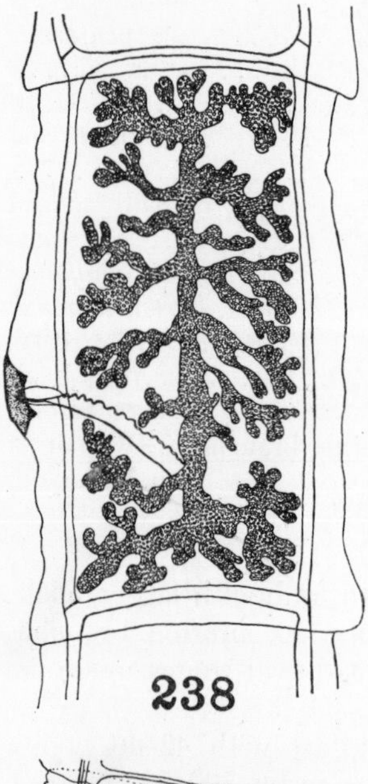

238

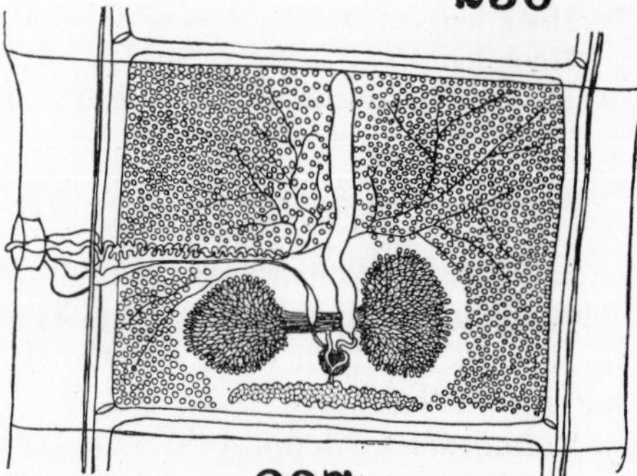

237

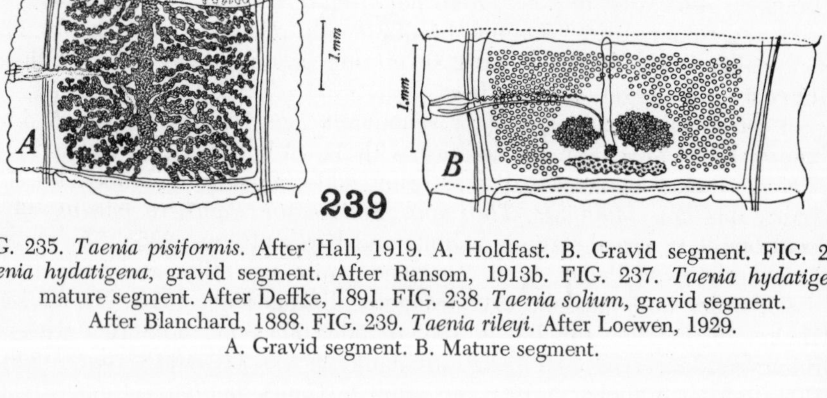

239

FIG. 235. *Taenia pisiformis*. After Hall, 1919. A. Holdfast. B. Gravid segment. FIG. 23 *Taenia hydatigena*, gravid segment. After Ransom, 1913b. FIG. 237. *Taenia hydatigen* mature segment. After Deffke, 1891. FIG. 238. *Taenia solium*, gravid segment. After Blanchard, 1888. FIG. 239. *Taenia rileyi*. After Loewen, 1929. A. Gravid segment. B. Mature segment.

Thos mesomelas; larval stage in a wide range of rodents, ungulates, etc.; bladder worm large, up to 50 mm. in diameter or, rarely, the size of a hen's egg; cosmopolitan (Figures 236, 237).

6. *krabbei* Moniez, 1879. About 200 mm.; holdfast with 25–34 hooks; larger hooks 148–170 μ; smaller hooks 35–120 μ; testes 260; uterine branches 9–10 pairs according to Moniez (quoted by Neveu Lemaire, 1936; Ortlepp, 1938b), 20–24 pairs according to Cram (1926b); adult in dogs, wolves; larva (*Cysticercus tarandi*) in reindeer. Cram (1926), who redescribed this species from material collected by Ransom, mentioned as the most striking feature of the mature segments the compact appearance of the internal organs, all of them much compressed and elongated in the transverse axis of the segment. Cram mentioned as a further peculiarity the occurrence of two vaginal sphincters, but Christiansen (1932) found a similar arrangement in *cervi.* This latter author, describing *Cysticercus tarandi*, found these larvae compact, without trace of bladder or bladder fluid, with the larger hooks 144–148 μ, the smaller hooks 111–114 μ. Though regarded usually as a purely European form, the larval *krabbei* occurs in Alaska in reindeer, and Shaw, Simms, and Muth (1934) recorded it in deer in Oregon, an observation confirmed by rearing fifty-five mature *Taenia krabbei* in dogs. Rollings (1945) has found specimens of *krabbei* in the bobcat (*Lynx rufus rufus*) in Minnesota. Pushmenov (1945), by feeding cysticerci from reindeer to puppies, obtained typical *krabbei* from muscle cysticerci; but from liver cysticerci, he obtained a form he regards as distinct and names *Taenia parenchymatosa.* He describes it as a slender worm, reaching 94 mm. in length and having 30 hooks arranged in two circles, the hooks measuring 0.23–0.24 mm. and 0.13–0.16 mm., respectively.

7. *solium* Linnaeus, 1758 (for synonymity see Brumpt, 1936). 2,000–8,000 mm.; holdfast with 25–50 hooks; larger hooks 160–180 μ; smaller hooks 110–140 μ; testes 150–200; uterine branches 7–10 pairs; adult in humans; larval stage (*Cysticercus cellulosae*) in swine; occasionally in other mammals including humans; cosmopolitan (Figure 238). The literature on the distribution, biology, and pathogenicity of this form is relatively enormous. Reference may be made to Brumpt (1936) for an exhaustive summary of such literature. A comprehensive study of cysticercosis in domesticated animals has been published by Viljoen (1937). The subject of cerebral cysticercosis in humans has been discussed in particular by Antonow (1932), Heilmann (1932), Morenas (1933), Menon and Veliath (1940), and Gaehtgens (1943).

8. *acinonyxi* Ortlepp, 1938. 350 mm.; holdfast with 38 hooks; larger hooks 196–223 μ long; smaller hooks 128–136 μ; testes 250–300; uterine branches 8–10 pairs; in the cheetah (*Acinonyx jubatus jubatus*), South Africa.

9. *ingwei* Ortlepp, 1938. 270 mm.; holdfast with 32–34 hooks; larger hooks 197–202 μ; smaller hooks 148–151 μ; testes 400–500; uterine branches 6–10 pairs; eggs oval, pitted, 35–38 by 28 μ; in leopards (*Panthera pardus*), South Africa.

10. *jakhalsi* Ortlepp, 1938. 550 mm.; holdfast with 30–32 hooks; larger

hooks 195–220 μ; smaller hooks 131–142 μ; testes 400–500; uterine branches 6–10 pairs; in jackals (*Thos mesomelas*), South Africa.

11. *erythraea* Setti, 1897. 140–170 mm.; holdfast with 20 hooks; larger hooks 185 μ; smaller hooks 95 μ; testis number unknown; uterine branches 6–14 pairs; in jackals (*Thos mesomelas*), Abyssinia.

12. *laruei* Hamilton, 1940. Body length unknown; holdfast with 28 hooks; larger hooks about 125 μ; smaller hooks about 90 μ; testes 500–550; uterine branches 13–15 pairs; in coyote, *Canis sp.*, Oklahoma.

13. *gonyamai* Ortlepp, 1938. Up to 520 mm.; holdfast with 32–38 hooks; larger hooks 188–209 μ; smaller hooks 122–143 μ; testes 500–600; uterine branches 14–18 pairs; in lions (*Felis leo krugeri*), South Africa.

14. *ovis* Cobbold, 1860 (for synonymity see Neveu Lemaire, 1936). 450–1,000 mm.; holdfast with 24–36 hooks; larger hooks 156–188 μ; smaller hooks 96–128 μ; testes 300; uterine branches 20–25 pairs; in dogs; larval stage in *Ovis aries, Capra hircus*; cosmopolitan (Figure 234). One distinctive feature of this species according to Hall (1919) is the crossing of the ovary by the vagina on its way from the segment margin to the interovarian field.

15. *hlosei* Ortlepp, 1938. 450 by 9 mm.; holdfast with 36–40 hooks; larger hooks 209–218 μ; smaller hooks 142–151 μ; testes about 400; uterine branches 20–30 pairs; in cheetah (*Acinonyx jubatus jubatus*), South Africa.

16. *hyaenae* Baer, 1926. 300 mm.; holdfast with 32–38 hooks; larger hooks 196–223 μ; smaller hooks 124–156 μ; testes 300; uterine branches up to 26 pairs; in *Hyaena brunnea*, South Africa.

17. *cervi* Christiansen, 1932. 2,000–2,500 mm.; holdfast with 26–32 hooks; larger hooks 160–174 μ; smaller hooks 96–123 μ; testis number not stated; uterine branches 10–12 pairs; in dogs and foxes; larva a cysticercus well known in Europe in the muscles of roe deer, *Cervus capreolus*. This form shows a great similarity to *ovis*, but the *ovis* adult is smaller and its gravid uterus has 20–30 pairs of branches.

18. *pungutchui* Ortlepp, 1938. Possibly reaching 700 mm.; holdfast and hook number unknown; testes 200–250; uterine branches 8–10 pairs; in jackal (*Thos mesomelas*), South Africa.

19. *taxidiensis* Skinker, 1935. Redescribed by Skinker (1947); 480 mm. long; holdfast averaging 570 μ in diameter, with 20–27 hooks in *single* circle, each 79–99 μ long; average hook length 90 μ; handle and guard nearly equal in length, former averaging 54 μ and latter 46 μ, both about 16 μ wide at base, tapering toward end to about 10 μ; blade strongly arched; testes 200–300 in number, ovoid, 70–90 μ; uterine branches averaging 10 on each side; eggs spherical, 31 μ average diameter; shell pitted; embryo averaging 20 μ in diameter; in *Taxidea taxus*, Montana, Wisconsin; intermediate host unknown, believed to be a ground squirrel (Figure 234).

20. *tenuicollis* Rudolphi, 1819. Size relatively small, length of known specimens from North America not exceeding 70 mm.; holdfast with about 48 hooks usually lost during preservation, all similar in size and

shape, about 15–16 μ long; testes 90–125 in number; uterine branches 10–19 each side; adult in mustelid Carnivora; intermediate host a rodent.

"Most of the synonyms listed have been queried for the reason that Rudolphi (1819) listed *Taenia putorii* and *T. mustelae vulgaris* as synonyms of *T. tenuicollis* and for each of them he listed several synonyms. Examination of the literature to show any valid name which might have priority over *tenuicollis* leads finally to *T. pusilla* and *T. serrata*, both published by Goeze (1782). Of these, *pusilla* receives priority on the basis of pagination. However, the hosts of *T. pusilla* were rats and mice whereas Rudolphi gave *Mustela vulgaris* as the host of *Taenia tenuicollis*; furthermore, the original description of *T. pusilla* gave no characters adequate for specific identification. The present writer accepts *tenuicollis* Rudolphi, 1819 as a name for this species." Skinker (1935b).

This form is frequently confused with *intermedia* Rudolphi, 1810, but Rudolphi described *intermedia* as having a double circle of powerful, small hooks, in contrast to the lack of hooks in *tenuicollis*. Skinker assumed that the hooks that Rudolphi would have described as powerful were relatively large, while the hooks of the size (15–16 μ) of those of *tenuicollis* may have escaped his notice or have been lost. Skinker believed the form described by Cameron (1933) as *intermedia* to have been *tenuicollis*, but believed what he described as *tenuicollis* to have been some other form. Both Cameron (1933) and Baer (1932a) considered *Taenia brevicollis* as a synonym of *tenuicollis*, but Rudolphi (1819) stated that the first named form was like *intermedia*, from which he separated it on account of the branched ovary—the ovary of *tenuicollis* being described by him as unbranched. Skinker believed *intermedia* to be a valid species but preferred to regard *brevicollis* as a *species inquirenda* rather than as a synonym of *tenuicollis* or *intermedia*.

The features of European and North American *tenuicollis* material may be contrasted as follows:

A. European *tenuicollis* (Thienemann, 1906, etc.). 12–147 mm. by 2 mm.; neck 1.9–2.2 mm. long; holdfast 260–550 μ wide; hooks 36–72; hook lengths, 16–24 μ large, 13–21 μ small; genital papilla prominent, anterior to middle of segment margin; osmoregulatory canals conspicuous; testes 60–114; testis size 42–67 by 37–52 μ; uterine branches 12–18 pairs; eggs 20–23 by 24–28 μ; definitive hosts, *Mustela nivalis, Mustela erminea*; intermediate hosts, *Cricetus cricetus, Talpa europaea, Microtus agrestis, Microtus agrestis arvalis, Apodemus sylvaticus, Clethrionomys glareolus, C. rufocampus.*

B. North American *tenuicollis* (Skinker, 1935). Up to 70 mm. in length by 2.4 mm. in width; neck 28 μ to 1,000 μ long; holdfast 237–303 μ wide; hooks about 42; hook lengths 15–16 μ large and small; genital papilla prominent, anterior to middle of segment margin; osmoregulatory canals prominent; testes 90–125, 39–55 μ in diameter; uterine branches 10–19 pairs; eggs 17–20 μ; definitive host, *Mustela vison* (mink); intermediate hosts, *Ondatra zibethica, Ondatra spatulata* (muskrats).

Joyeux and Baer (1936d) suggested avoiding the confusion caused by use of the term *tenuicollis* by using as a *nomen novum* the term *joyeuxiana* for *tenuicollis* Rudolphi, 1810, which they believed to have been *hydatigena*.

INQUIRENDA AND DUBIA

Synonymous generically with *Taenia* are: *Taeniola* Pallas, 1760; *Hydatigena* Goeze, 1782; *Megacephalos* Goeze, 1782; *Finna* Werner, 1786; *Haeruca* Gmelin, 1790; *Hydatula* Abildgaard, 1790; *Hydatis* Blumenbach, 1797; *Alyselminthus* Zeder, 1800; *Cysticercus* Zeder, 1800; *Hygroma* Schrank, 1802; *Halysis* Zeder, 1803; *Polycephalus* Zeder, 1803; *Psychiosoma* Brera, 1809; *Goeziana* Rudolphi, 1810; *Fischiosoma* Chiaje, 1835; *Trachelocampylus* Fredault, 1847; *Acanthotrias* Weinland, 1858; *Cystotaenia* Leuckart, 1863; and *Neotenia* Sodero, 1886 (see Meggitt, 1924a). Most European authors would also regard *Multiceps* Goeze, 1782; *Hydatigera* Lamarck, 1816; and *Taeniarhynchus* Weinland, 1858 as synonyms of *Taenia*.

Of the large number of species accredited to the genus at one time or another, many have been relegated to dilepidid and hymenolepidid genera, or to other taeniid genera. Others have been shown to be synonymous with accepted species of *Taenia*. Thus, synonymous wholly or partly with *Taenia hydatigena* are the following: *Lumbricus hydropicus* Tyson, 1691; *Taenia solium* Linnaeus, 1758, *ex parte*; *Taenia hydatoidea* Pallas, 1760; *Taenia cucurbitina* Pallas, 1766, *ex parte*; *Hydra hydatula* Linnaeus, 1767; *Vermis vesicularis eremita* Bloch, 1780; *Hydatigena orbicularis* Goeze, 1782; *Hydatigena vesicularis* Goeze, 1782; *Taenia cateniformis* Goeze, 1782, *ex parte*; *Taenia cateniformis lupi* Goeze, 1782; *Hydatis animata* Maratti, 1776; *Taenia hydatigena orbicularis* Goeze, 1782; *Taenia serrata* Goeze, 1782; *Cysticercus taeniae-marginatae* Goeze, 1786; *Fischiosoma globosa* Batsch, 1786; *Hydatigena oblonga* Batsch, 1786; *Taenia marginata* Batsch, 1786; *Taenia lupina* Schrank, 1788; *Hydatis apri* Gmelin, 1790; *Hydatis bovina* Gmelin, 1790; *Hydatis caprina* Gmelin, 1790; *Hydatula cervorum* Gmelin, 1790; *Hydatula hepatis* Gmelin, 1790; *Hydatula liensis* Gmelin, 1790; *Hydatula peritonai* Gmelin, 1790; *Hydatula pulmonis* Gmelin, 1790; *Hydatula solitaria* Viborg, 1790; *Hydatula saigae* Gmelin, 1790; *Psychiosoma globosa* Gmelin, 1790; *Taenia apri* Gmelin, 1790, *ex parte*; *Taenia bovina* Gmelin, 1790; *Taenia ovilla* Gmelin, 1790; *Taenia simiae* Gmelin, 1790; *Hydatis solitaria* Viborg, 1795; *Hydatigena ferrarum* Bosc, 1802; *Cysticercus clavatus* Zeder, 1803; *Halysis marginata* Zeder, 1803; *Halysis putorii* Zeder, 1803; *Cysticercus lineatus* Laennec, 1804; *Cysticercus fistularia* Rudolphi, 1805; *Cysticercus hepaticus* Brera, 1809; *Cysticercus tenuicollis* Rudolphi, 1810; *Cysticercus visceralis hominis* Rudolphi, 1810; *Cysticercus visceralis simiae* Rudolphi, 1810; *Cysticercus talpae* Rudolphi, 1819, *ex parte*; *Taenia hydatigenum suum* Laennec, 1812; *Cysticercus vesicae hominis* Diesing, 1850; *Cysticercus tenuicollis hominis* Eschricht, 1853; *Cysticercus hominis dubius* Diesing, 1854; *Cysticercus hypopudaei* Leuckart, 1856; *Taenia marginata ex cysticerco tenuicolli* Küchenmeister, 1857; *Cysticercus phacochoeri-aethiopici* Cobbold, 1861; *Cysticercus potamochoeri penicillati* Cobbold, 1861; *Taenia cysticercus* Molin, 1862; *Taenia cynica* Boircier, 1859; *Cystotaenia marginata* Leuckart, 1863; *Taenia visceralis treutleri* Slavikowski, 1879; *Taenia cysticerci tenuicollis* Leuckart, 1886.

Synonymous wholly or in part with *Taenia ovis* are: *Cysticercus ovis* Cobbold, 1869; *Cysticercus cellulosae* of Küchenmeister and Zurn, 1878; *Cysticercus ovipariens* Maddox, 1873; *Cysticercus tenuicollis* of Chatin, in Railliet, 1885; *Cysticercus oviparus* Leuckart, 1886.

Synonymous wholly or in part with *Taenia pisiformis* are: *Lumbricus latus* Tyson, 1682, *ex parte*; *Vermis cucurbitinus a cane excretus* Clericus, 1715; *Taenia cucurbitina* Pallas, 1766, *ex parte*; *Vermis vesicularis pisiformis* Bloch, 1780; *Taenia canina* Bloch, 1782, *ex parte*; *Taenia caninum solium* Werner, 1782; *Hydatigena utriculenta* Goeze, 1782; *Hydatigena pisiformis* Goeze, 1782; *Cystotaenia pisiformis, Cystotaenia serrata, Halysis serrata, Hydatigena cordata, Hydatigena pisiformis, Hydatigena utricularis*, all of Batsch, 1786; *Taenia cucurbitina canis* Batsch, 1786; *Vesicaria pisiformis* Schrank, 1788; *Taenia serrata canis* Gmelin, 1790; *Taenia serrata canis domestici et vulpis* Rudolphi, 1793; *Cysticercus pisiformis* Zeder, 1803; *Monostomum leporis* Kuhn, 1830; *Hydatigena hepatis murinae* Dujardin, 1845; *Taenia serrata vera* Küchenmeister, 1855; *Taenia serrata monostephana* Diesing, 1863; *Taenia novella* Neumann, 1896; *Taenia utricularis* Hall, 1912.

Synonymous wholly or in part with *Taenia solium* are: *Taenia degener* Spigelius, 1618; *Taenia de la seconde espèce* Andry, 1718, *ex parte*; *Taenia secunda plata* Ernst, 1743; *Taenia articuli demittens* Dyonis, 1749; *Taenia osculis marginalibus solitarius* Dubois, 1751; *Taenia cucurbitina* Pallas, 1766, *ex parte*; *Taenia finna* Gmelin, 1780; *Taenia cucurbitina pellucida* Goeze, 1782; *Taenia cucurbitina plana pellucida* Goeze, 1782; *Taenia vulgaris* Werner, 1782; *Vesicaria lobata* Fabricius, 1783; *Taenia hydatigena* Fischer, 1788; *Taenia solitaria* Leske, 1784; *Taenia dentata* Gmelin, 1790; *Taenia albopunctata* Treutler, 1793; *Hydatula albopunctata* Treutler, 1793; *Vermes hygroma humana* Schrank, 1793; *Taenia hydatigena anomala* Steinbach, 1802; *Taenia cellulosae* Bosc, 1802; *Taenia armata hominis* Brera, 1802; *Taenia armata umana* Brera, 1802; *Halysis solium* Zeder, 1803; *Finna hepatica* Brera, 1809; *Taenia humana armata* Rudolphi, 1810; *Cysticercus dicystis* Laennec, 1804; *Cysticercus fischerianus* Laennec, 1804; *Cysticercus aortae* Notarjanni, 1818; *Cysticercus canis* Rudolphi, 1819; *Taenia armata* Pruneyre, 1823; *Finna cysticercus* Chiaje, 1825; *Taenia fenestrata* Chiaje, 1825; *Taenia hydatigena suilla* Fischer, in Chiaje, 1825; *Taenia longiannulata* Andral, 1831; *Cysticercus telae cellulosae* Zwicke, 1841; *Vesicaria lobata suillae* Diesing, 1850; *Taenia monroi, Taenia tenuis, Taenia variabilis, Taenia lata*, all of Leach, in Baird, 1853; *Taenia pyriformis, Taenia scalariformis* Notta, 1855; *Taenia secunda* Küchenmeister, 1855; *Taenia hamoloculata* Küchenmeister, 1855; *Taenia acanthotrias* Weinland, 1858; *Taenia serrata* Nicklas, 1858; *Taenia solium hominis* Küchenmeister, 1860; *Taenia communis* Moquin-Tandon, 1861; *Taenia hydatigena eremita* Werner, 1861; *Cysticercus turbinatus* Koeberle, 1861; *Cysticercus melanocephalus*

Koeberle, 1861; *Cysticercus mulosus, Cysticercus solium, Cysticercus suis*, in Cobbold, 1869; *Cysticercus botryoides* Haller, 1874; *Taenia tenella* Cobbold, 1874; *Taenia solium fenestrata* Cohn, 1876; *Taenia solium minor* Asmunde, 1885; *Taenia solium scalariforme* Notta, 1885; *Hydatis cysticerci-cellulosae* Walley, 1891; *Taenia grandis saginata* Dolley, 1894; *Taenia officinalis* Bos, 1894.

There still remain many forms whose descriptions, scanty as they are, suggest an affinity with *Taenia* rather than with any other tapeworm genus. Too scantily known even to justify comment are: *Cysticercus alpacae* Moniez, 1880 from the alpaca; *Taenia barroisii* Moniez, 1880 in *Talpa europaea*, Europe; *blanchardi* Mola, 1907 from *Talpa europaea*, Italy; *brachydera* Diesing, 1854 from *Epimys norvegicus*, Ireland (probably *Hymenolepis microstoma*); *crassiscolex* Linstow, 1890 from *Sorex araneus*, Europe; *crassipora* Rudolphi, 1819 from *Viverra narica*, Brazil; *foinae* Blanchard, 1848 from *Martes foina*, Europe; *hyperborea* Linstow, 1905 from *Alopex lagopus*, arctic Europe; *imbricata* Diesing, 1854 from *Mus musculus*, Europe; *muris ratti* Creplin, 1825 from *Epimys rattus*, Europe; *mustelae* Gmelin, 1790 from *Martes martes, Putorius putorius, Mustela nivalis*, Europe; *neglecta* Diesing, 1850 from *Crocidura russula, Neomys fodiens, Sorex araneus*, Europe; *obtusata* Rudolphi, 1819 from a range of bat species in Europe; *oligarthra* Diesing, 1863 from *Felis concolor*, Brazil; *omissa* Lühe, 1910 from *Felis concolor*, South America; *opuntioides* Rudolphi, 1819 from *Canis lupus*, Berlin; *ovata* Molin, 1858 from *Vulpes vulpes, Alopex lagopus*, Europe; *platydera* Gervais, 1847 from *Genetta genetta*, southern France and Tunisia; *saccifera* Mehlis in Creplin, 1845 from *Neomys fodiens*, in Europe; *secunda* Olsson, 1893 from *Meles meles*, Europe; *strobile* Beneden, 1873 from *Myotis mystacinus*, Europe; *umbonata* Molin, 1858 from *Epimys rattus, Mus musculus*, Europe (probably *Catenotaenia pusilla*); *ursina* Linstow, 1893 from *Ursus arctos*, Copenhagen; *ursimaritimi* Rudolphi, 1810 from *Ursus maritimus*, Paris; *vespertilionis-auriti* Rudolphi, 1819 from *Plecotus auritus* in Europe.

Somewhat better known are the following:

1. *antarcticae* Fuhrmann, 1922. 250 mm.; holdfast with 28–34 hooks; larger hooks 144–156 μ; smaller hooks 92–102 μ; testes 500; uterine branches 13–15 pairs; eggs 20 μ; in dogs, Antarctica.

2. *bremneri* Stephens, 1908. Dimensions of body and number of testes not stated; holdfast without hooks; uterine branches 22–24 pairs; eggs 30–39 μ; in man, Nigeria. Brumpt (1936) regarded this form as *Taeniarhynchus saginatus*.

3. *brevicollis* Rudolphi, 1819. From *Mustela erminea*. Cameron (1933) and Baer (1932a) regarded this form as synonymous with *tenuicollis* Rudolphi, 1819, but Rudolphi described it as having a *branching* ovary whereas he described *tenuicollis* as having an *unbranching* ovary. Skinker (1935b) preferred to place it as a *species inquirenda*.

4. *infantis* Bacigalupo, 1922. 300 mm.; holdfast with 35–40 hooks, 260–410 μ long; genital apertures alternating irregularly; eggs 35–40 μ.

The form differs from *Taenia solium* only in the size of the hooks, and since it was taken from a five-year-old child, it might be thought identical with *solium.* Joyeux and Baer (1929a), however, believed it to be a specimen of *Hydatigera taeniaeformis.*

5. *intermedia* Rudolphi, 1810. In *Martes martes, Martes foina, Putorius putorius,* in Europe. Cameron (1933) described from *Mustela erminea* and *Mustela nivalis* in Scotland a form he believed to be identical with this species. He described it as having a short, broad rostellum with 36–40 small hooks, 20 μ long; a short, broad neck; 16–20 pairs of uterine branches. Skinker (1935b) believed Cameron's form to have been *tenuicollis* Rudolphi, 1819 but believed *intermedia* to be a valid species.

6. *macrocystis* Diesing, 1850. 120 mm.; holdfast with 60–74 hooks; larger hooks 320–365 μ, smaller hooks 180–200 μ; testes "relatively few"; uterine branches 8–15 pairs; eggs 34 by 48 μ; in the jaguar, South America (see discussion of *Hydatigera laticollis*).

7. *multiformis* Hölldobler, 1937 (as *Cysticercus multiformis*). From the subcutaneous tissue of a fox in Germany; occurring as a mass of cysts of various sizes showing varying degrees of budding, usually from the pole opposite to the holdfast; the latter has four suckers and a single (*sic*) crown of hooks; the author suggested affinities with *Echinococcus.*

8. *monostephanos* Linstow, 1905. Only 145 μ long; holdfast with *one* circle of 29 hooks, 190–210 μ long; testes not estimated; uterine branches numerous; eggs 36 by 29 μ; in a lynx in Russia.

9. *nilotica* Krabbe, 1869. Established for a tapeworm in a charadriiform bird in Egypt. Leuckart (1879) placed within this species a proliferating bladder worm found by Metchnikow in an oligochaete worm at Odessa. Krabbe described his form very briefly, having only immature specimens measuring 4 mm. long, without genitalia, and having a crown of 12 hooks measuring 62–72 μ.

10. *novella* Neumann, 1896. From domestic cats; 6–33 mm. long; holdfast pear-shaped, about 1.2 mm. wide, carrying 40–42 hooks; larger hooks 250–260 μ long; smaller hooks 150–155 μ long; suckers prominent. Lühe (1910) identified this form with *laticollis,* but Hall (1919) argued that the possession of a distinct neck and the shape, size, and number of rostellar hooks are all features which relate it to *Taenia pisiformis.* The internal anatomy is imperfectly known.

11. *parva* Baer, 1925. 55 mm. long; holdfast with 44 hooks; larger hooks 300 μ long; smaller hooks 228 μ; testes 500; uterine branches 9–14 pairs; eggs 27 by 23 μ; in *Genetta ludia,* South Africa. This form would seem close to *Hydatigera laticollis,* especially in the number, size, and shape of its hooks and in the lack of a vaginal sphincter; but is distinguishable mainly by the very special development of the longitudinal musculature.

12. *philippina* Garrison, 1907. 800–100 mm. long; holdfast without hooks; testis number not stated; uterine branches 15–30 pairs; eggs 26 by 35 μ; in humans, Philippine Islands. Accepted by most authors as synonymous with *Taeniarhynchus saginatus.*

13. *polyacantha* Leuckart, 1856. 120 mm. long; holdfast with 62 hooks; larger hooks 58 μ; smaller hooks 34 μ; testes not estimated; uterine branches 8 pairs; eggs 22 by 28 μ; in *Vulpes alopex*, Europe.

14. *retracta* Linstow, 1904. 550 mm. long; holdfast with 34 hooks; larger hooks 308 μ; smaller hooks 211 μ; testis number not given; uterine branches immature; eggs unknown; in *Vulpes ferrilatus*, Tibet.

15. *triserrata* Meggitt, 1928. 250 mm. long; holdfast with *three* circles of hooks, number not given; first circle, hooks 210 μ long; second circle, 160 μ; third circle, 120 μ; testis number not given; uterine branches not estimated; eggs 32 by 27 μ; in *Felis sp.*, Paraguay.

Family Davaineidae Fuhrmann, 1907

DESCRIPTION

Of the order Cyclophyllidea. Small to medium-sized tapeworms with a retractable rostellum having two or three circles of T-shaped hooks. Suckers with spiny margins. Genitalia usually single per segment but occasionally double. Genital apertures single or double, unilateral, alternating regularly or irregularly. Gravid uterus replaced in function by parenchymatous egg pouches. Adults in birds and mammals. Type genus, *Davainea* Blanchard and Railliet, 1891.

HISTORY

The genus *Davainea*, named in honor of the French parasitologist Casimir Joseph Davaine, was established by R. Blanchard and Railliet, 1891 for a number of tapeworm species included formerly within the genus *Taenia*. The description of the genus was based upon the species *proglottina* Davaine.

Davainea was made the type genus of a family Davaineidae by Fuhrmann (1907a). In 1920 this same author pruned the unwieldy genus, which by this time contained 113 species, by establishing the genera *Davaineoides*, *Houttuynia*, and *Raillietina*. The last named genus was further subdivided into four subgenera – *Ransomia, Paroniella, Johnstonia*, and *Skrjabinia*. The subgenus *Johnstonia* was later abolished on the grounds that its type species, *echinobothrida*, belonged in its characteristics with *Ransomia*. The other species of *Johnstonia* were united under a new generic term, *Fuhrmannetta*, with *crassula* as type species. The generic term *Ransomia* was also abandoned, in favor of the term *Raillietina*, following Article 30 of the International Rules, according to which a subgenus containing the type species of the genus must receive the same name as the genus.

RECOGNITION FEATURES

The typical davaineid tapeworm is small, 20–80 mm. long, and is markedly segmented (Figure 240). The segments are wider than long except toward the end of the body, where they may be relatively long or barrel-shaped. The holdfast is small, somewhat cuboidal in shape, less than half a millimeter in breadth or length. The suckers are relatively large, circular or oval in outline, with their margins armed with con-

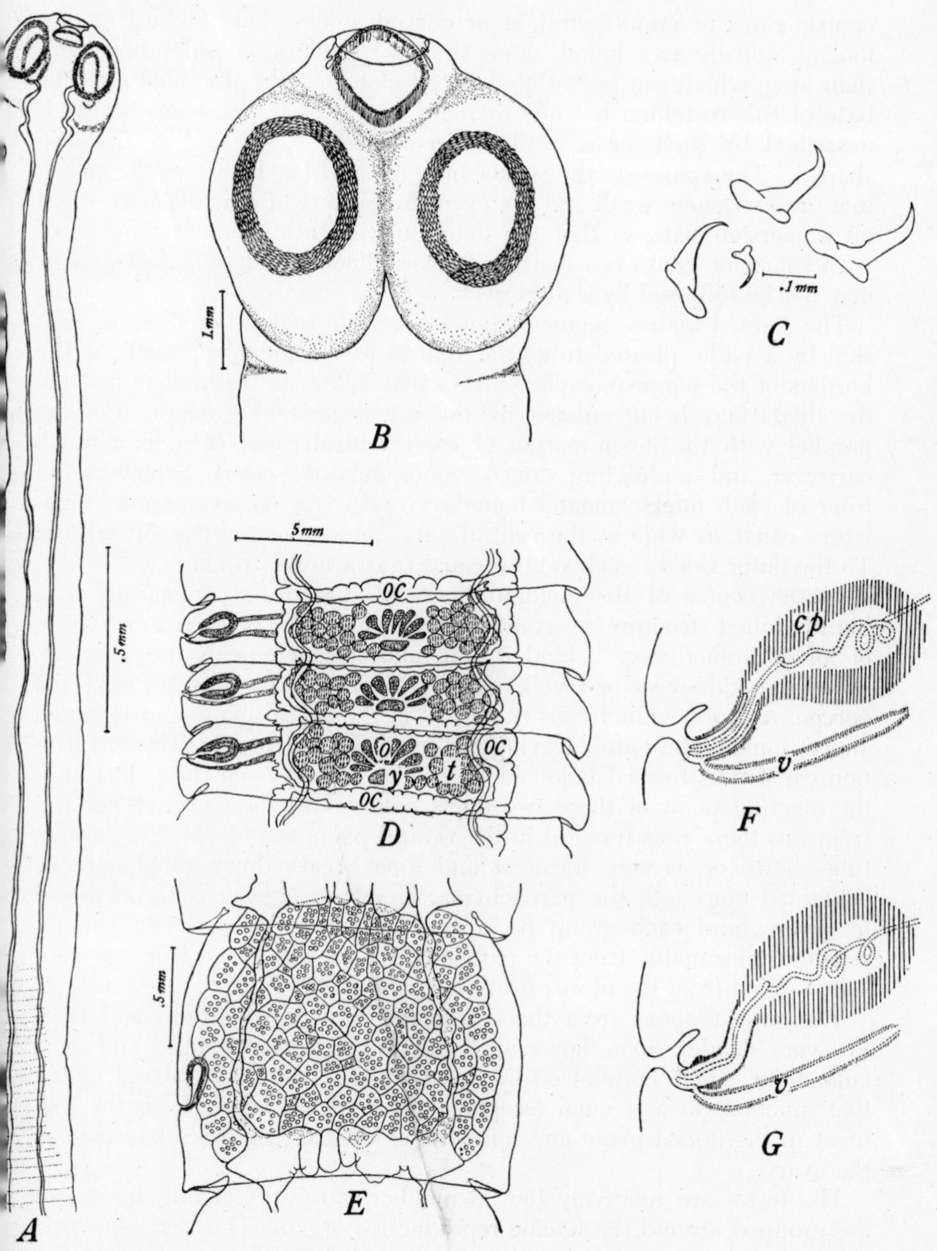

G. 240. *Raillietina echinobothrida.* After Lang, 1929. A. Holdfast and neck. B. Enlarged ldfast. C. Sucker rim hooks. D. Mature segment. E. Gravid segment. F. Cirrus pouch (*cp*) with canalis masculinus. G. Cirrus pouch with neck region. *o*, ovary; *oc*, osmoregulatory canals; *t*, testes; *v*, vagina; *y*, yolk gland.

centric rings of minute straight or curved spines. The holdfast is prolonged apically as a broad, dome-shaped rostellum, considerably wider than long, which can be withdrawn completely within the holdfast. The base of this rostellum has one or more circles of hooks whose shape is described by such terms as "hammer-shaped," "T-shaped," or "pickax-shaped." The spines on the sucker margins and the hooks on the rostellum are extremely small and tax even the powers of magnification of an oil immersion lens, so that the determination of the exact number of such spines or hooks is a matter of some difficulty. The holdfast may or may not be followed by a short neck.

The stained mature segment shows a middle region bounded on each side by a wide, pleated tube, the ventral osmoregulatory canal. At the borders of the segment, each ventral canal dilates in bladderlike fashion, the dilatations being crossed by the intersegmental grooves. Running parallel with the inner margin of each ventral canal there is a much narrower and undulating dorsal osmoregulatory canal. Somewhat in front of each intersegmental boundary there is a transverse osmoregulatory canal, as wide as the ventral one, connecting the two dilatations. To the outer side of each ventral canal runs a nerve trunk.

In the center of the median space lies the ovary, appearing as a bluntly lobed structure, or as a fan of narrow lobes, or even as a rosette of lobes. Immediately behind it, and almost touching, is the compact, somewhat kidney-shaped yolk gland. Dorsal to this may be seen the ootype. A short oviduct runs backward in the dorsal plane and is joined almost immediately after leaving the ovary by the vagina. The fertilization canal thus formed is joined shortly by a duct from the yolk gland; the meeting point of these two ducts enlarges to form an ootype, and from this there runs forward in the ventral plane the uterus. The uterine tube, however, is very transient and soon breaks down to liberate its contained eggs into the parenchyma. Here the eggs become arranged in groups, and each group becomes enclosed within an "egg pouch," secreted presumably from the parenchyma and not, like a true egg capsule, formed from the uterus itself.

The vagina opens from the marginal cirro-vaginal atrium and is at first very slender. Soon, however, it dilates into a thick-walled and muscular tube, which is followed by a thin-walled, somewhat dilated region that functions as a seminal receptacle. The vagina now crosses the segment in the dorsal plane and joins the oviduct on the dorsal surface of the ovary.

The testes are relatively few in number, rarely exceeding sixty, and are grouped around the female reproductive organs. The vasa efferentia unite near the center of the segment, near the dorsal surface, to form a sperm duct. This follows a much convoluted course to the cirrus pouch, which it enters to become, after a few coils, the muscular cirrus. The cirrus pouch is unusually large, pear-shaped, its basal portion surrounded by a prominent layer of longitudinal muscle fibers; its narrower portion – variously termed the "neck," "Halsteil," "canalis masculinus," or "atrium genitale masculinus" – has a thick layer of circular muscle fibers. The neck opens into the cirro-vaginal atrium, just anterior to the vaginal aperture. The cirro-vaginal atrium opens to the exterior by the cirro-vaginal or genital aperture on one margin of the segment.

In a transverse section of the mature segment, the region within which lie the reproductive organs and nerve cords is seen to be enclosed within a thin band of circular muscle fibers, outside of which is a layer of bundles of longitudinal muscle fibers, round or oval in cross section. Outside these, again, there is a layer of transverse muscle fibers, and outside these, a second layer of bundles of longitudinal muscle fibers. Between the outermost muscle layer and the cuticle there are scattered bundles of longitudinal fibers and isolated fibers.

In the gravid segment, the parenchyma may appear almost entirely filled by a transverse, lobed, saclike uterus which seems filled with eggs. Commonly, however, an area of denser parenchyma, lying close to the uterus, receives the ripe eggs as they pass from the disintegrating uterus; or, in many cases, the uterus does not reach full development but disintegrates early, the ripe eggs appearing within so-called "egg pouches" formed from this dense area of parenchyma, this *paruterine organ*. Except for the uterus or egg pouches, and occasionally the cirrus pouch, the reproductive organs disappear entirely from gravid segments.

Although the life cycle of the majority of davaineid tapeworms is unknown, such information as is available suggests that the larval davaineid is a cysticercoid, and that the intermediate host is an insect. Considerable information to this effect is available from the observations of Ackert (1918), Cram and Jones (1929), Lang (1929), Jones (1930–32), Wetzel (1933, 1934), Ackert and Reid (1936), Reid, Ackert, and Case (1938), Harwood (1938), and Wisseman (1945) on *Raillietina (Skrjabinia) cesticillus*. This particular davaineid lives habitually in the upper third of the small intestine of the domestic fowl, its holdfast end embedded in the gut mucosa a short distance below the entrance of the pancreatic and bile ducts. The segments mature in a few days, become gravid in about two weeks, and break away and pass from the host.

During a continuous 18-months' observation of the course of infestation in an individual fowl, Harwood found that segment elimination declined. The decline was not gradual, however, but marked by periods of intense segment elimination, between which were periods when no segments, or few segments, were eliminatd. At the beginning of a cycle, the segments were large and well-filled with eggs, but gradually they became smaller, contained fewer eggs, and a few sterile segments were eliminated. This phase of the cycle ended abruptly with the appearance of chains of obviously unripe segments, and for a time the bird eliminated few or no segments. The phase of low elimination rate lasted from a few days to several weeks.

The gravid segments show considerable powers of movement and travel to the outer surface of the fecal mass. This movement, according to Ackert, is not a phototropism. According to Wetzel, observing another davaineid, the majority of the gravid segments are voided during late afternoon, and such appears to be the case also in *cesticillus*.

Each gravid segment contains about 300 oncospheres. Each oncosphere is ovoid or spherical in shape, 74–84 μ in diameter, clear and hyaline, its six hooks arranged in pairs. It is apparently enclosed by five successive membranes (Figure 241). Of these, the innermost may not

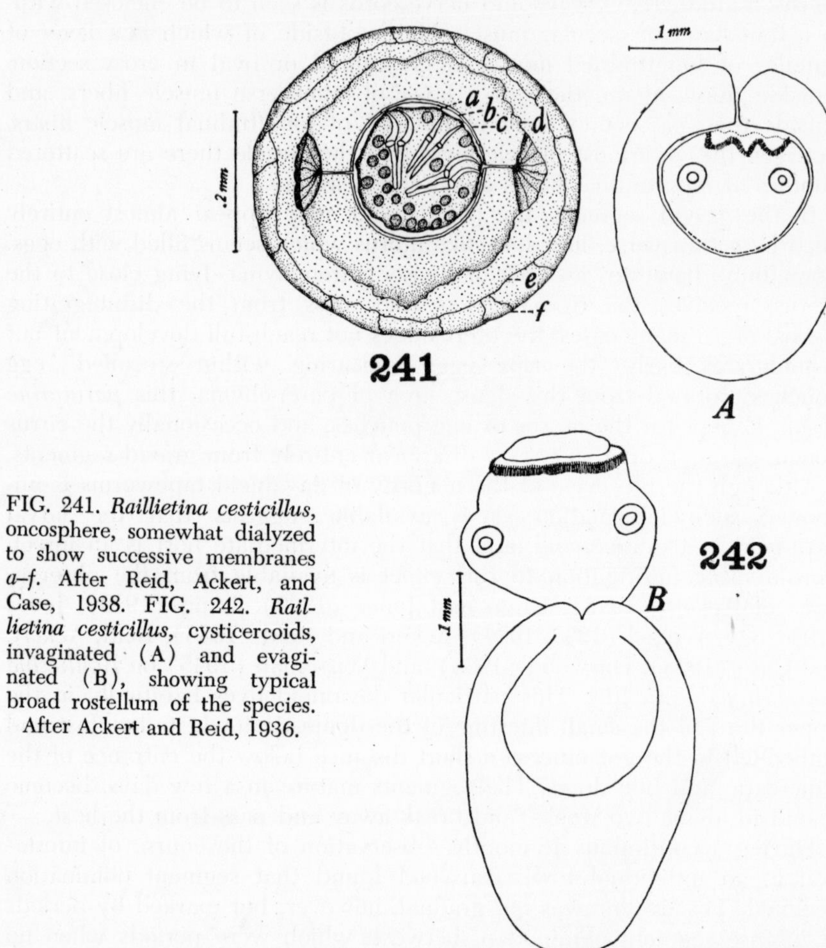

FIG. 241. *Raillietina cesticillus*, oncosphere, somewhat dialyzed to show successive membranes *a–f*. After Reid, Ackert, and Case, 1938. FIG. 242. *Raillietina cesticillus*, cysticercoids, invaginated (A) and evaginated (B), showing typical broad rostellum of the species. After Ackert and Reid, 1936.

be a true membrane but a surface coagulation; Ackert compares it with the hyaline membrane of an amoeba. The second and the third membranes are close together so as to form, as it were, an inner capsule; the second and the fourth membranes are connected by two small tubular structures – the "filaments" of Ransom (1905) and Guberlet (1916a) – so attached to the fourth membrane as to draw it inward in funnel fashion (Figure 241). The space between the two outermost membranes (*e* and *f*) is crossed by short membranes representing, according to Ackert, the former uterine wall.

The natural intermediate hosts of *Raillietina cesticillus* are probably carabid beetles (subfamily Harpalinae). At any rate, Wetzel in Germany has reported such cysticercoids in species of *Calathus, Amara, Pterostichus, Bradycellus*, and *Harpalus*, and in North America they have been reported from *Anisotarsus, Choeridium, Cratacanthus, Calathus, Stenolaphus, Stenocellus*, and *Amara*, but also, it may be noted, from *Aphodius* and houseflies.

The cysticercoid (Figure 242) is egg-shaped, 373–415 by 264–288 μ, with an invaginated holdfast at the broader end. The point of invagination is marked by a groove extending into a central cavity. When placed in water, the cysticercoid often protrudes the holdfast, which then appears exactly like that of the adult worm. In amarid beetles kept in an environmental temperature varying between 15° and 43° centigrade, the cysticercoids take 18 days to become fully formed. When such infected beetles are fed to chickens, gravid segments of the worm pass from the birds after 11–13 days.

CLASSIFICATION

Following Fuhrmann, we shall recognize here three subfamilies of Davaineidae – Ophryocotylinae, Davaineinae, and Idiogeninae.

Subfamily Ophryocotylinae Fuhrmann, 1907

DESCRIPTION

Of the family Davaineidae. With a very broad rostellum armed with a double circle of very small and very numerous hooks. Uterus saclike, slightly lobed, persistent in gravid segments. Adults parasitic in birds. Two genera, distinguishable as follows:

1. Rostellum unusually wide, with a great number of hooks arranged in two wavy circles; suckers circular with spines on the anterior part of the margins only; genital apertures alternating irregularly; gravid uterus saclike, slightly lobed . . . . *Ophryocotyle*
2. Rostellum not unusually wide, with hooks on rostellum arranged in two circles; suckers with spines all around the margins; genital apertures unilateral . . . . *Ophryocotyloides*

Ophryocotyle Friis, 1870

With an unusually broad rostellum which under certain conditions of contraction may be represented by several pits. A double circle of very small and very numerous hammer-shaped hooks. Suckers armed with concentric rows of small hooks on anterior margins only. Genital apertures alternating irregularly. Gravid uterus saclike and lobed. Genotype, *proteus* Friis, 1870 (Figure 243).

The genotype was established for material from gulls in Europe. It was recorded by Linton (1927) from *Larus atricilla* and *Larus argentatus* at Woods Hole, Massachusetts. He described the rostellum as "a broad terminal sucker with strong muscular walls and with a scalloped border which is armed with very numerous spines, nearly straight with abruptly curved tips, closely placed in a sinuous row following the scalloped border." The genus appears restricted to birds. Other species recorded are: *insignis* Loennberg, 1890 in charadriiform birds; *zeylanica*

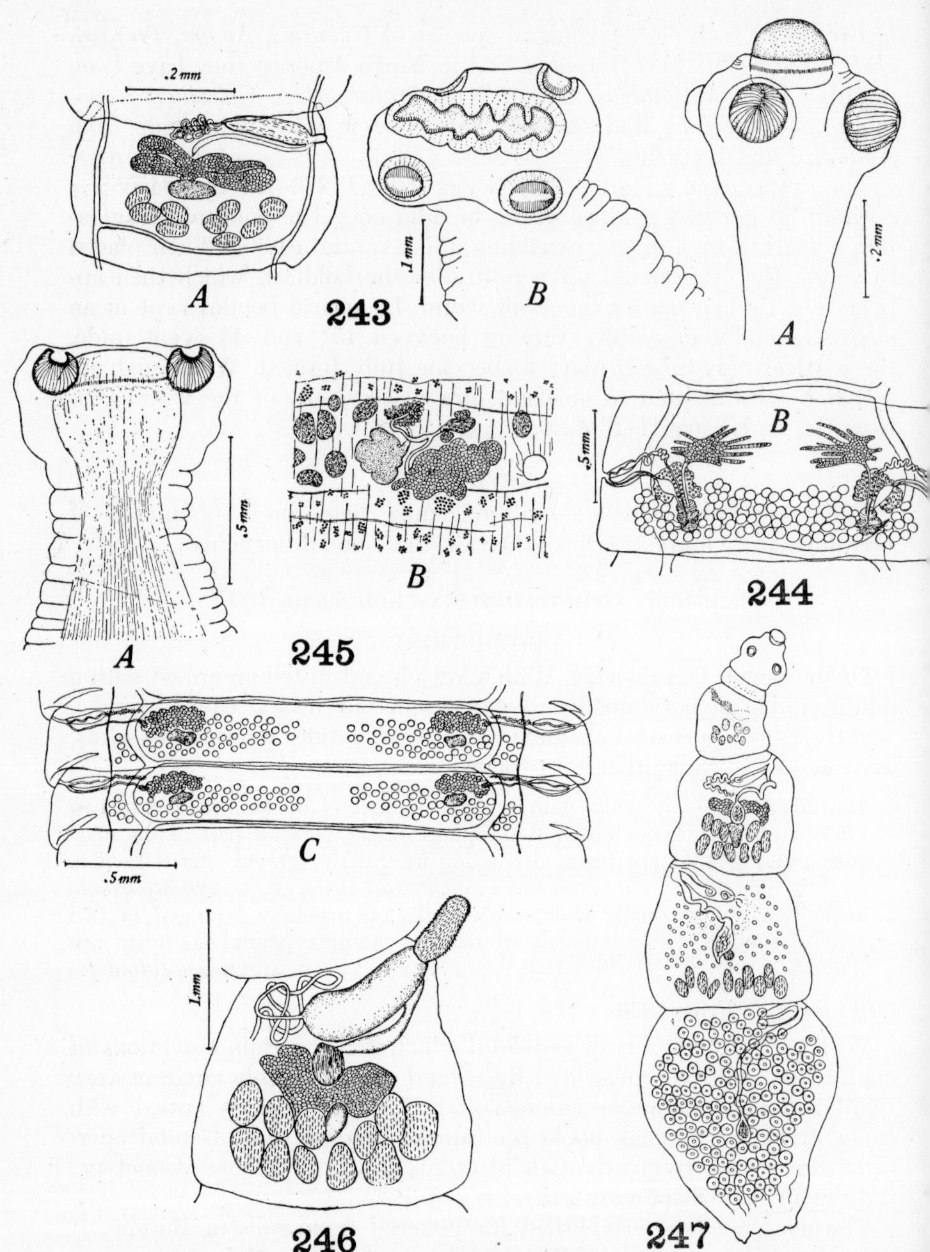

FIG. 243. *Ophryocotyle proteus*. After Linton, 1927. A. Mature segment. B. Holdfa
FIG. 244. *Cotugnia polytelidis*. After Burt, 1940b. A. Holdfast. B. Mature segment. FIG. 2
Cotugnia taiwanensis. After Yamaguti, 1935a. A. Holdfast. B. Transverse section of matu
segment showing ovarian complex. C. Mature segments. FIG. 246. *Davainea proglottina*, mature segment. After Meggitt, 1926a. FIG. 247. *Davainea proglottina*, entire worm. After Fuhrmann, 1920a.

Linstow, 1906 in bucerotiform birds; *herodiae* Fuhrmann, 1909 in ardeiform birds; *lacazii* Villot, 1875 in lariform birds; *turdina* Cholodkovsky, 1913 in passeriform birds; *alaskensis* Webster, 1949, in shore birds.

Ophryocotyloides Fuhrmann, 1920

With a typical davaineid holdfast but with unilateral genital apertures. Genotype, *uniuterina* Fuhrmann, 1908.

The genotype was recorded from passeriform birds and has a persistent uterus combined with a typical davaineid holdfast. Other species since recorded are: *pinguis* Fuhrmann, 1904 from bucerotiform birds; *meggitti* Moghe, 1933 from *Corvus splendens*, Nagpur, India; *monacanthis* Moghe and Inamdar, 1934 from *Dendrocitta rufa*, Nagpur, India; and *bhaleraoi* Inamdar, 1944 from *Cinnyris zeylonicus*, India.

Subfamily Davaineinae Braun, 1900

DESCRIPTION

Of the family Davaineidae. With degenerate spines on the sucker margins arranged in several circles. Uterus replaced in gravid segments by egg pouches containing one or several oncospheres. Adult in mammals and birds. Type genus, *Davainea*.

KEY TO GENERA

1. Each segment with double genitalia .... *Cotugnia*
   Each segment with single genitalia 2
2. One oncosphere per egg pouch 3
   Several oncospheres per egg pouch 6
3. Cirrus pouch crossing the poral osmoregulatory canals 4
   Cirrus pouch rarely crossing the poral canals and in such cases having the genital apertures lateral or alternating irregularly 5
4. Very small forms with few segments, neck lacking, suckers small. . *Davainea*
   Medium to large forms with segments wide but short, testes 90–150, osmoregulatory canals 6–20 .... *Davaineoides*
5. Genital apertures unilateral .... *Raillietina (Paroniella)*
   Genital apertures alternating irregularly .... *Raillietina (Skrjabinia)*
6. Cirrus pouch not reaching the poral canals 7
   Cirrus pouch crossing or reaching the poral canals 8
7. Genital apertures unilateral .... *Raillietina (Raillietina)*
   Genital apertures alternating irregularly .... *Raillietina (Fuhrmannetta)*
8. Rostellum usually very prominent with two circles of large hooks followed by several rows of spines; sucker margins not armed; adult in ratite birds .... *Houttuynia*
   Rostellum not unusually prominent but with three circles of hooks; dorsal osmoregulatory canals lacking; ventral ones large; genital apertures unilateral; female organs markedly poral in position; adults in gallinaceous birds .... *Porogynia*

The use of genital-aperture position in the generic discrimination of Davaineinae has been opposed by Lopez-Neyra (1929b, 1932a, 1934), who pointed out that in a single specimen of *Raillietina echinobothrida* the genital apertures may be unilateral for one stretch of segments, may alternate irregularly for another stretch, or that unilateral series may occur alternately on one side or the other. The Spanish parasitologist proposed to replace Blanchard's *Davainea* by six genera, namely: *Davainea* Blanchard, 1891, emend. Lopez-Neyra, 1929; *Idiogenoides* Lopez-Neyra, 1929; *Meggittia* Lopez-Neyra, 1929; *Kotlania* Lopez-Neyra, 1929; *Brumptiella* Lopez-Neyra, 1929; and *Ophryocotyloides* Fuhrmann, 1920. The scheme was severely criticized both by Baer (1931a) and by Fuhrmann (1932) and has not found general acceptance by students of the group.

NOTES ON GENERA

Cotugnia Diamare, 1893

With two sets of genitalia per segment. With segments linear except the last ones. Parenchymal muscles with several layers of longitudinal fibers alternating with transverse fibers. Female organs at the margins of the medullary parenchyma. Genital ducts dorsal to the osmoregulatory canals and nerve trunks. Testes occupying the middle zone of the medulla but crossing laterally over the canals. Often arranged as two groups. Eggs dispersed in parenchymatous capsules, one egg per capsule. Genotype, *digonopora* Pasquale, 1890.

This genus, the only davaineid genus with double genitalia per segment, is a parasite of tropical pigeons and parrots. About 26 species are known. Reference should be made to Meggitt (1915, 1924d, 1927b), Fuhrmann (1932), Moghe (1933), Johri (1934), Yamaguti (1935a), Joyeux, Baer, and Martin (1936), Tubangui and Masilungan (1937), Burt (1940b), and Weerekoon (1944) (see Figures 244, 245).

Davainea R. Blanchard, 1891

With few segments and small suckers. Holdfast typically davaineid. Neck lacking. Parenchymal muscles weak. Genital apertures alternating regularly, rarely unilateral. Cirrus pouch voluminous, conspicuously crossing the poral osmoregulatory canals. Parenchymatous egg pouches each with a single oncosphere. Genotype, *proglottina* Davaine, 1860 (Figures 246, 247).

The genotype is a common, cosmopolitan parasite of domestic fowls. Its distribution, life cycle, and intermediate hosts have been discussed in detail by Wetzel (1932). Reference may be made also to Ransom (1909), Fuhrmann (1932), Wetzel (1933), E. L. Taylor (1933), Bayon (1933), and Kotland (1925). The intermediate hosts are gastropod Mollusca – the limacid species *Agriolimax agrestis, Limax cinereus, Limax flavus*; the arionid species *Arion empiricorum, Arion hortensis, Arion circumscriptus, Arion intermedius*; and the helicid species *Gepaea nemoralis*. Other *Davainea* species are *minuta* Cohn, 1901; *himantopodis* Johnston, 1911; *nana* Fuhrmann, 1912; *paucisegmentata* Fuhrmann, 1909; *tetraoensis* Fuhrmann, 1919; *tragopani* Southwell, 1922; *andrei* Fuhrmann, 1933; and *baeri* Schmelz, 1941, all small forms and all from charadriiform and galliform birds except *baeri*, which is from a piciform bird.

Davaineoides Fuhrmann, 1920

This genus was separated from *Davainea* for Skrjabin's form *Davainea vigintovasus* of fowls on the ground of larger size, 6–20 osmoregulatory canals, and irregularly alternating genital apertures. Meggitt (1927d) offered reasons for regarding this genus as synonymous with *Raillietina.*

Raillietina Fuhrmann, 1920

With numerous segments and small cirrus pouch. Holdfast with a double circle of hammer-shaped hooks. Sucker margins with several circles of small, degenerate hooks. Genital apertures unilateral or alternating irregularly, never, according to Fuhrmann, alternating *regularly.* Testes numerous. Parenchymatous pouches with one or several eggs, the pouches often grouped and surrounded by modified parenchyma. Genotype, *tetragona* Molin, 1858.

The genus was established for a number of species of *Davainea* in which the cirrus pouch does not in the majority of cases reach the poral osmoregulatory canals, and in which the genital apertures are unilateral (subgenus *Paroniella*) or alternating irregularly (subgenus *Skrjabinia*) in those forms with one oncosphere per parenchymatous pouch; and unilateral (subgenus *Raillietina*) or alternating irregularly (subgenus *Fuhrmannetta*) in those forms with several oncospheres per parenchymatous pouch. The genus is a large one. Hughes and Schultz (1942) listed 225 species but did not, unfortunately, attempt the admittedly difficult task of providing an identification key.

The North American species are as follows:

1. *bakeri* Chandler, 1942. Subgenus *Raillietina*; 60 by 1.2 mm.; holdfast 250–375 μ in diameter with a double crown of about 66 hooks, appearing almost as a single circle since alternate hooks are only about 2 μ out of line; each hook about 20–22 μ long and about 13 μ across the hammerlike head; suckers 80–100 μ in diameter, with a plug of tissue filling most of the cups and provided with minute spines, 4–5 μ long, in at least two circles; the spines are readily lost in preservation; cirrus pouch not reaching the poral canals; testes 30–40; ovary slightly poral; egg pouches 80–90 in number, each with 6–9 oncospheres, occasionally 10; in *Sciurus niger-rufiventer*, southeast Texas. In the small number of testes, small cirrus pouch, and small number of egg pouches, the species most nearly resembles *Raillietina loechesalavezi* Dollfus, 1939–40, described from a specimen in a child in Cuba (Figure 249).

2. *centrocerci* Simon, 1937. Subgenus *Skrjabinia*; 135–450 by 1.5–3.0 mm.; holdfast 413 μ long by 431 μ wide, with a double crown of 198–205 hooks; suckers with several circles of hooks, each 15 μ long; cirrus pouch reaching nearly halfway to the poral canals; testes 63–118; ovary slightly poral; eggs singly in pouches, number of pouches not stated; in sage grouse (*Centrocercus urophasianus*), Wyoming.

Simon provided a key to the species of *Raillietina (Skrjabinia)* which is worthy of quotation:

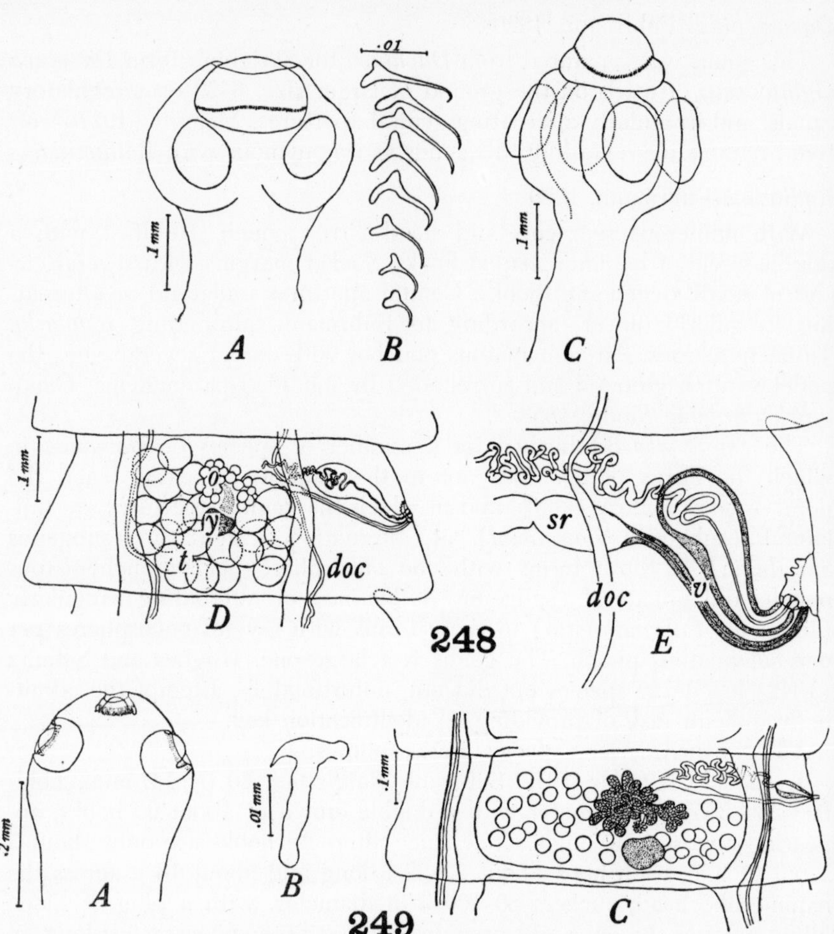

FIG. 248. *Raillietina* (*Paroniella*) *centuri.* After Rigney, 1943. A. Holdfast with rostellum retracted. B. Sucker margin hooks. C. Holdfast with rostellum protruded. D. Submature segment, ventral view. E. Details of reproductive tract, dorsal view. *doc*, dorsal osmoregulatory canal; *o*, ovary; *sr*, seminal receptacle; *t*, testes; *v*, vagina; *y*, yolk gland. FIG. 249. *Raillietina* (*Raillietina*) *bakeri.* After Chandler, 1942a. A. Holdfast. B. Rostellar hook. C. Mature segment.

1. Testes more than 60 .... *centrocerci*
2. Testes 40–60
   A. Testes more than 45; hooks 110 .... *joyeuxi*
   B. Testes 40–45, hooks 120–130 .... *bolivari*
   C. Testes 40, hooks 200 .... *polyuterina*
3. Testes numbering 30
   A. Forms about 22 mm. long .... *microcotyle*
   B. Forms 60–70 mm. long .... *columbae*
4. Testes 15–30
   A. Forms up to 130 mm.; hooks 200 or 400–500 .... *cesticillus*
   B. Forms 4–14 mm.; hooks 500 .... *ransomi*
   C. Forms up to 17 mm.; hooks 70–90 .... *lavieri*

D. Forms up to 185 mm.; hooks 220 . . . . *retusa*
5. Testes fewer than 20
A. Hooks 200 or 800 . . . . *circumvallata*
B. Hooks 150 or fewer . . . . *cryptocotyle*
C. Hooks 500 . . . . *ransomi*

Not included, for lack of data are: (*a*) *maroteli*; length 60–80 mm.; width 2.0–2.5 mm.; rostellar hooks 400–450; length of hooks 12–13 μ; and (*b*) *magnicornata*; length 15–20 mm.; width 0.4–0.5 mm.; rostellar hooks 200; length of hooks 9 μ; diameter of holdfast 80–100 μ; diameter of suckers 38 μ.

References to the above species are: *centrocerci* (Simon, 1937); *joyeuxi* (Lopez-Neyra, 1929b); *bolivari* (Lopez-Neyra, 1929b); *polyuterina* (Fuhrmann, 1908c); *microcotyle* (Skrjabin, 1914b); *columbae* (= *bonini* Megnin, 1899) (Fuhrmann, 1909); *cesticillus* (Molin, 1858); *ransomi* (Williams, 1931); *lavieri* (Joyeux and Baer, 1928a); *retusa* (Clerc, 1903); *circumvallata* (Krabbe, 1869); *cryptocotyle* (Baer, 1925b); *maroteli* (Neveu Lemaire, 1912); *magnicornata* (Fuhrmann, 1908c); see Simon (1937) for bibliographical details.

3. *centuri* Rigney, 1943. Subgenus *Paroniella*; 60–70 mm. by about 1 mm. wide; holdfast with approximately 130 hooks, anterior row 15–16 μ long, posterior row 11–12 μ long; suckers with several circles of prominent spines ranging in length from 14 μ in the outermost row to 6 μ in the innermost row; cirrus pouch not reaching the poral canals; genital apertures unilateral and dextral in two of the specimens observed; in the third specimen they were 119 left, 25 right, 40 left, 11 right, 22 left, 4 right, and 1 left; testes 21–31; ovary median, one-third of the segment width; egg pouches widely distributed, one oncosphere per egg pouch; in red-bellied woodpecker (*Centurus carolinus*), Oklahoma (Figure 248).

4. *cesticillus* Molin, 1858. Subgenus *Skrjabinia*; 9–130 mm. by 1.5–3.0 mm.; holdfast 300–600 μ with 400–500 hooks, each 7–12 μ long; suckers small, not prominent, *unarmed*; neck lacking; genital apertures alternating irregularly, each in anterior third of segment margin; cirrus pouch 120–150 μ, barely reaching the poral canals; testes 18–30; egg pouches 70–85 μ diameter, each with one oncosphere; a cosmopolitan parasite of domestic poultry, turkeys, pheasants, guinea fowl. Intermediate hosts are *Musca domestica* and various beetles (see earlier discussion); a very detailed study of the immature stages has been published by Wisseman (1945) (Figures 241, 242, 250).

5. *colinia* Webster, 1944. Subgenus *Raillietina*; 60–90 mm.; holdfast with 100–108 hooks, 11.3 to 12.2 μ; suckers with four to five rows of hooks, each 7–9 μ long; genital apertures unilateral, on left side; cirrus pouch not reaching the poral canals; testes 29–40; ovary bilobed, slightly poral; egg pouches 124–136 μ, each containing 4–6 oncospheres; in bob-white quail (*Colinus virgianus*), Texas.

6. *comitata* Ransom, 1909. Subgenus *Raillietina*; 44–55 mm. by 1.16 mm.; holdfast 250–320 μ long by 250–290 μ broad, minutely spinose, with a crown of about 80 hooks arranged in a single circle, each 11–13 μ

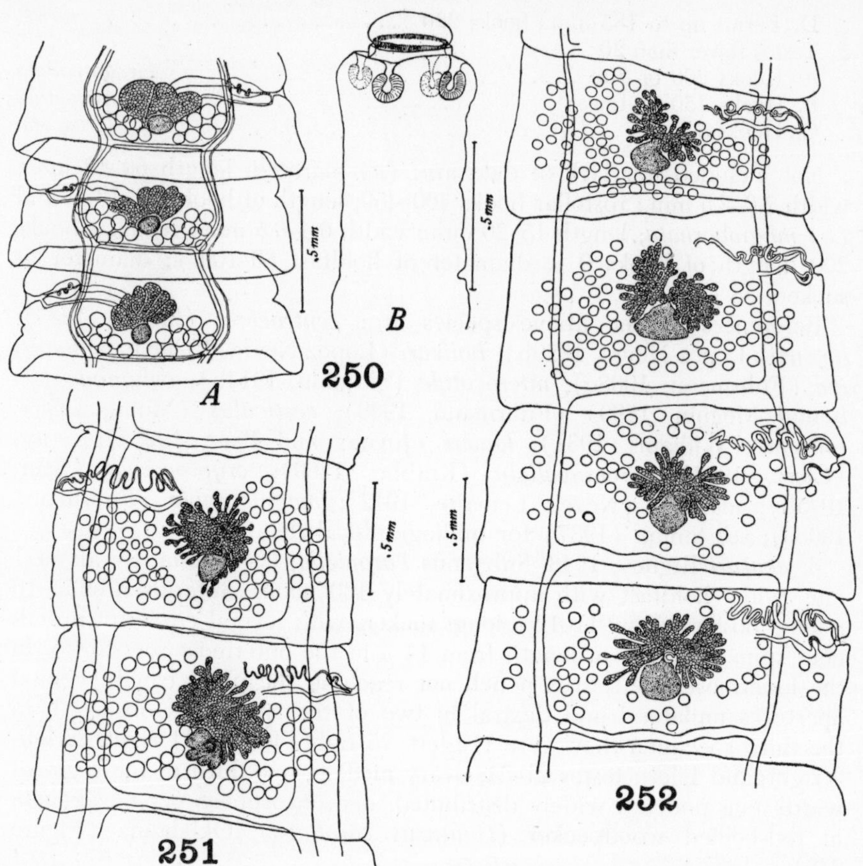

FIG. 250. *Raillietina* (*Skrjabinia*) *cesticillus*. After Lang, 1929. A. Mature segments. B. Holdfast. FIG. 251. *Raillietina* (*Fuhrmannetta*) *leoni*, mature segments. After Dollfus, 1940. FIG. 252. *Raillietina equatoriensis*, mature segments with unilateral genital apertures and tendency for the ovary to separate as two lobes. After Dollfus, 1940.

long; genital apertures unilateral, on left side; cirrus pouch reaching about halfway to the poral canals; testes 30–35; ovary median, compact, lobulated, 200 μ wide; egg pouches 40–50 in surficial view, each with 6–12 eggs; in woodpeckers (*Colaptes auratus, Melanerpes erythrocephalus*), Iowa, Nebraska, Maryland.

7. *echinobothrida* Megnin, 1881. Subgenus *Raillietina*; 250 by 1–4 mm.; holdfast 250–400 μ diameter with a double crown of 200–250 hooks, each 10–13 μ long; suckers with 8–10 circles of small, degenerate spines; neck lacking; genital apertures unilateral, at times alternating irregularly; cirrus pouch reaching about one-third of the distance to the poral canals; testes 20–30; egg pouches 90–150, each with 8–12 eggs; in fowl, pheasant, turkey, cosmopolitan; life cycle unknown (Figure 240).

8. *klebergi* Webster, 1947. Subgenus *Raillietina*; 34–50 by 0.7–1.1 mm.; holdfast 195–273 μ in diameter with double crown of 66–76 hooks,

each 10–13 μ long; suckers with 4–5 circles of small hooks, less than one micron in length; neck as broad, or almost so, as holdfast even when fully extended; genital apertures unilateral on left side; cirrus pouch almost reaching poral canal; testes 29 to 39 in number, almost surrounding the ovary; egg pouches each with 6 to 12 eggs; in bobwhite quail (*Colinus virginianus texanus*), Texas; life cycle unknown.

9. *magninumida* Jones, 1930. Subgenus *Paroniella*; 100–150 mm. by 1.3 mm.; holdfast 160–210 μ diameter with 50–160 hooks, in two circles, each 8–10 μ long; suckers with at least ten circles of small spines; cirrus pouch large, 280–350 μ long; testes variable in number, usually 13–18; one egg per egg pouch; in turkey, guinea fowl, Washington, D.C.

10. *minuta* Webster, 1947. Subgenus *Paroniella*; 24 to 34 mm. by 0.4 mm.; holdfast unknown; genital apertures unilateral on right side; cirrus pouch reaching halfway to poral canal; testes 14 to 22 in number, situated on all sides of ovary; egg pouches 50 to 100, each with one egg; in bobwhite quail (*Colinus virginianus texanus*), Texas; life cycle unknown.

11. *ransomi* Williams, 1931. Subgenus *Skrjabinia*; 4–14 mm. by 650 μ to 1,000 μ wide; holdfast 237–290 μ with a double crown of 500–550 hooks, alternating, the larger being 11–12 μ long, the smaller being 8–9 μ long; suckers *unarmed*; neck short; genital apertures alternating irregularly; cirrus pouch 140–160 μ; testes 15–25; egg pouches each with one egg; in wild turkey (*Meleagris gallopavo silvestris*), Philadelphia Zoological Gardens.

12. *retractilis* Stiles, 1925. Subgenus *Paroniella*; 105 mm. or more by 3 mm. with about 1,000 segments; holdfast with a double crown of hooks, 40–60 per circle, 12 μ long; suckers with 75 diagonal rows of hooks, 5–20 in each row, 500–700 hooks per sucker; neck short or lacking; osmoregulatory canals distinct, ventrals lateral to dorsals; genital apertures unilateral; cirrus pouch small, 120 by 60 μ; eggs 80 μ in diameter, one per egg pouch; in cottontail rabbit (*Lepus zonai*), Nevada.

13. *rhynchota* Ransom, 1909. Subgenus *Paroniella*; 50–60 by 1 mm.; holdfast minutely spinose with a crown of alternating long and short hooks, about 400 in number; large hooks 18 μ long, small hooks 14 μ long; crown rosettiform with eight lobes; suckers armed with numerous hooklets of varying size, up to 10 μ, arranged in diagonal rows, 16–18 hooklets per row; genital apertures unilateral on left margin; cirrus pouch slightly more than halfway between margin and poral canals; testes about 24; ovary median, compact, lobed, 250–320 μ wide; egg pouches with one egg each; in woodpeckers (*Colaptes auratus, Melanerpes erythrocephalus*), Nebraska, Iowa, Maryland.

14. *stilesiella* Hughes, 1941. Subgenus *Fuhrmannetta*; *nomen novum* for *Taenia salmoni* Braun, 1896; 86 by 3 mm.; about 450 segments; holdfast with double crown of hooks, 60 per circle, 20 μ long; suckers with about 750 marginal hooks, 10 μ or less; neck thin, short; genital apertures alternating irregularly; testes about 200; cirrus pouch small and muscular, 144 by 44 μ; egg pouches with 3–15 eggs each; in *Lepus melanotis, L. sylvaticus*, Texas, Maryland.

15. *tetragona* Molin, 1858. Subgenus *Raillietina*; 10–250 by 1–4 mm.; holdfast with a double crown of 100 hooks, each 6–8 μ long; sucker margins with 8–10 rows of small spines; neck short; genital apertures unilateral, opening mid-marginally; cirrus pouch short, 75–100 μ; testes 20–30; egg pouches 50–100, each containing 6–12 eggs; in fowl, peacock, guinea fowl, cosmopolitan. Ackert (1919) demonstrated that the intermediate host is the housefly, *Musca domestica*.

16. *variabilis* Leigh, 1941. Subgenus *Skrjabinia*; 47–272 mm. by 0.6–2.8 mm.; holdfast 239–279 μ in diameter with a crown of hammer-shaped hooks, 240–272 in number, in two circles; length of first circle hooks 17–19 μ; of second circle hooks, 15–16 μ; cirrus pouch extending from one-half to all the way to the poral canals; testes 33–82; egg pouches each with a single egg; in prairie chicken (*Tympanuchus americanus*), Illinois. Among a wide range of specimens, Leigh found the size of the complete gravid forms, the number and size of the testes, and the size and extent of the cirrus pouch to vary within wide limits. On the other hand, the number, shape, and size of the rostellar hooks and the size and appearance of the egg pouches, oncospheres, and oncospheric hooks were relatively constant throughout the material.

17. *williamsi* Fuhrmann, 1932 (=*Davainea fuhrmanni* Williams, 1931; *Raillietina* [*Raillietina*] *williamsi* Fuhrmann, 1932). Subgenus *Raillietina*; 143–367 by 3.5–4.25 mm.; holdfast 382–535 μ with a double crown of 155 hooks, the largest being 37.6–39 μ, the smallest being 33.5–34 μ; suckers with 12–13 marginal circles of spines, 9–12 μ long; genital apertures unilateral; cirrus pouch 122–145 μ long; testes 25–35; egg pouches 75–100, each with 8–13 eggs; in wild turkey (*Meleagris gallopavo silvestris*), Philadelphia Zoological Gardens.

For detailed descriptions of raillietinids which occur or are likely to occur in domesticated birds, reference should be made to Neveu Lemaire (1936).

Nine species of *Raillietina* have been recorded from humans: *R. (R.) davainei* Dollfus, 1940 from material found by Davaine in 1877 in Madagascar; *demariensis* Daniels, 1895 from British Guiana; *luisaleoni* Dollfus, 1939, *brumpti* Dollfus, 1939, *equatoriensis* Dollfus, 1939, *quitensis* Leon, 1895, *leoni* Dollfus, 1939, all from Ecuador; *loechesalavezi* Dollfus, 1940 and *kouridovali* Dollfus, 1940, both from Cuba (see Dollfus, 1939, 1940). Joyeux and Baer (1940a) were inclined to regard all the New World forms as of one species, *demariensis*. Lopez-Neyra (1943) reviewed the whole field of human infestation with *Raillietina spp.* in tropical areas (Figures 251, 252). The species *cubensis*, added to *Raillietina* by Kouri (1939), is now generally accepted as being *Inermicapsifer cubensis* (Kouri, 1939) Stunkard, 1941 (see Chitwood, McIntosh, and Price, 1946).

Houttuynia Fuhrmann, 1920

Large forms with very prominent rostellum armed with two circles of large hooks behind which are numerous rows of small spines. Suckers unarmed. Genital apertures unilateral. Cirrus pouch long. Testes very

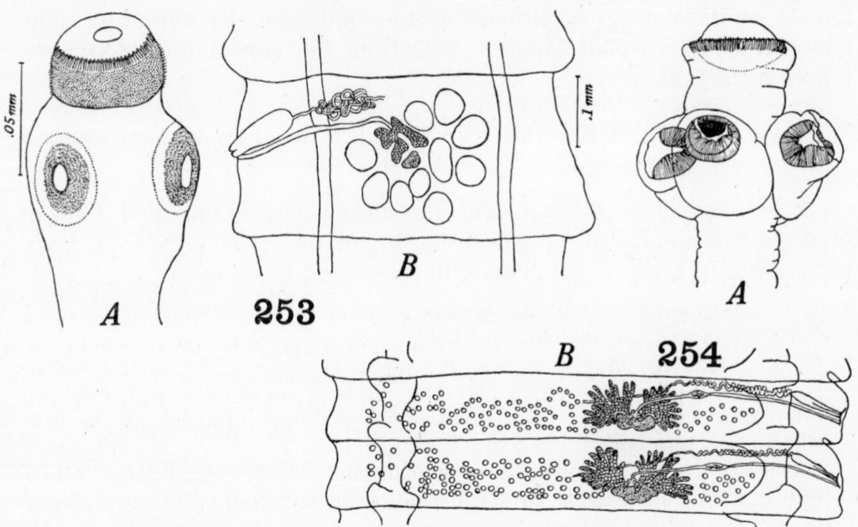

FIG. 253. *Houttuynia torquata.* After Meggitt, 1924d. A. Holdfast showing spiny collar and rostellar hooks. B. Mature segment. FIG. 254. *Houttuynia struthionis.* After Fuhrmann, 1920a. A. Holdfast. B. Two segments with genitalia well developed.

numerous. Ovary and yolk gland in the poral half of the segment. Egg pouches each with several eggs. Parasitic in struthioniform and rheiform birds (Ratitae). Genotype, *struthionis* Houttuyn, 1773 (Figure 254).

A variety of the genotype, var. *neogaea*, was recorded by Baer (1928) from the South American ostrich (Rhea). The genotype, so far as is known, is restricted to ostriches (*Struthio camelus, S. australis, S. massaicus, S. molybdophanes*) in Africa.

In view of the restricted occurrence of a spiny collar among davaineids, Meggitt (1924d) suggested that the genus be redefined by the exclusion of certain features – large cirrus pouch, numerous testes, poral female genitalia, egg pouches with several eggs – to permit the inclusion of *Davainea beddardi* Meggitt, 1921; *Davainea frontina* (Dujardin, 1845); *Davainea linstowi* Meggitt, 1921; and *Davainea torquata* Meggitt, 1924 (Figure 253), all of which have a collar of spines behind the rostellum. Johri (1933), on the other hand, maintained that no valid differences can be shown to exist between the genera *Raillietina* and *Houttuynia*, and although if such is the case the latter name has priority, he suggested that the International Rules be waived and the name *Raillietina* retained to avoid confusion.

Porogynia Railliet and Henry, 1909

With *three* circles of hooks. Segments much wider than long. Parenchymal musculature greatly developed. Dorsal osmoregulatory canals lacking; the ventral ones hypertrophied. Genital apertures unilateral. Ovary and yolk gland on the poral side of the segment, the latter to the inside of the ovary. Testes in a simple layer on the antiporal side of the female genitalia. Eggs in parenchymatous pouches. Genotype and only known species, *paronai* Moniez, 1892 from the guinea fowl (*Numida ptilorhyncha*), Europe.

Subfamily Idiogeninae Fuhrmann, 1932

DESCRIPTION

Of the family Davaineidae. With the sucker margins unarmed. Gravid uterus supplemented by a paruterine organ into which the ripe eggs pass. Adult in birds. Four genera, distinguished as follows:

1. With 10–12 circles of rostellar hooks . . . . *Sphyronchotaenia*
   With not more than two circles of hooks 2
2. Cirrus pouch reaching well over the poral canals; gravid uterus a horseshoe, with a paruterine organ like a longitudinal sac in front of it; holdfast often degenerate and replaced by a pseudo-holdfast formed from the first segments of the body . . . . *Idiogenes*
   Cirrus sac barely crossing the poral canals; holdfast typically davaineid; gravid uterus a sac with the paruterine organ as a transverse sac in front of it 3
3. Sucker margins armed with circles of spines . . . . *Chapmania*
   Sucker margins unarmed . . . . *Schistometra*

NOTES ON GENERA

Sphyronchotaenia Ransom, 1911

With 10–12 circles of rostellar hooks and the sucker margins unarmed. Paruterine organ in front of the uterus. Genotype and only recorded species, *uncinata* Ransom, 1911 from an African bustard, *Neotis caffra* (Figure 258).

Idiogenes Krabbe, 1867

With the holdfast commonly degenerate and replaced in function by a modification of the anterior segments. Genital apertures unilateral. Uterus an inverted U with a voluminous paruterine organ in front of it. Genotype, *otidis* Krabbe, 1867.

The genus contains ten species and one subspecies, namely: *bucorvi* Joyeux, Baer, and Martin, 1936 from *Bucorvus abyssinicus*, Africa; *buteonis* Schultz, 1939 (Figure 255), a form with a typical davaineid holdfast, from Swainson's hawk (*Buteo swainsoni*), Oklahoma; *flagellum* Goeze, 1782 from the Egyptian kite, *Milvus aegyptica*; *furtiva* Meggitt, 1933 from *Falco peregrinus*, Egypt; *grandiporus* Cholodkovsky, 1905 from *Tetrax tetrax*, Siberia; *horridus* Fuhrmann, 1908 from a Brazilian crane, *Cariama cristata*; *horridus* var. *africanus* Hungerbühler, 1910 from an unidentified African bird of prey; *korvi* Ortlepp, 1938 from *Choriotis korvi*, South Africa; *nana* Fuhrmann, 1925 from the Eurasian bustard *Tetrax tetrax*; *otidis* Krabbe, 1867 from *Houbara undulata*, *Tetrax tetrax*, *Trachelotis senegalensis* (Old World Otidiformes); *travassosi* Ortlepp, 1938 from *Milvus migrans*, South Africa.

Chapmania Monticelli, 1893

With holdfast and genitalia as in *Raillietina*. Body thick and muscular.

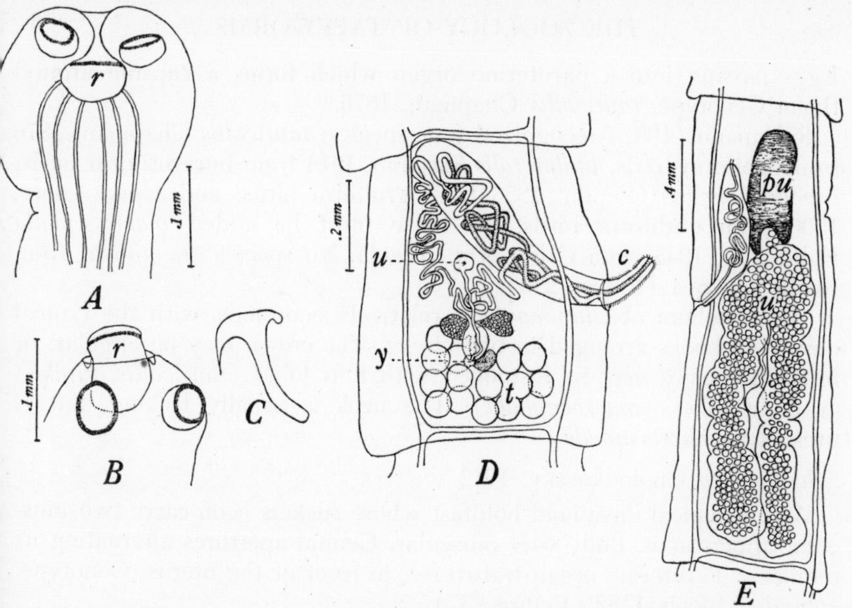

IG. 255. *Idiogenes buteonis.* After Schultz, 1939b. A. Holdfast with rostellum (r) etracted. B. Same with rostellum partly protruded. C. A rostellar hook. D. Mature segment, ventral view. c, cirrus; t, testes; u, uterus; y, yolk gland. E. Gravid segment showing paruterine organ (pu) and uterus (u).

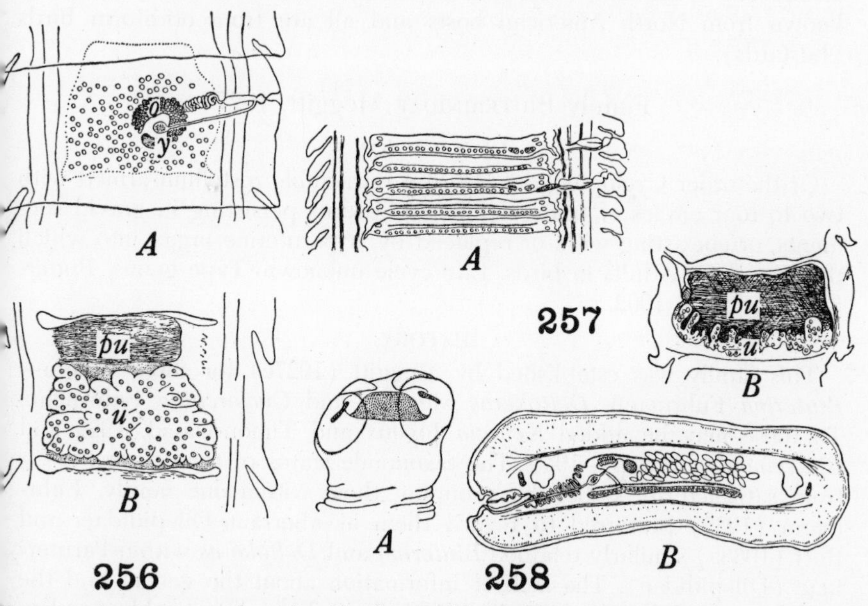

G. 256. *Chapmania tapika.* After Skrjabin, 1914a. A. Young segment with genitalia well eloped. B. Segment with uterus (u) and paruterine organ (pu). FIG. 257. *Schistotra conoideis.* After Skrjabin, 1914a. A. Horizontal section of five young segments. B. avid segment with uterus (u) and paruterine organ (pu). FIG. 258. *Sphyronchotaenia inata.* After Ransom, 1911. A. Holdfast. B. Transverse section of a mature segment.

Eggs passing into a paruterine organ which forms a capsule around them. Genotype, *tauricollis* Chapman, 1876.

Fuhrmann (1932) recognized four species: *tauricollis* Chapman, 1876 from rheiform birds; *unilateralis* Skrjabin, 1914 from bucerotiform birds; *brachyrhynchus* Creplin, 1853 from gruiform birds; and *tapika* Clerc, 1906 from otidiform birds. To these must be added *macrocephala* Fuhrmann, 1943 from *Otis caffra*, Angola. No species are known from North America (Figure 256).

The rostellum of *Chapmania* is relatively enormous, with the typical davaineid hooks arranged in two circles. The crown may be circular, or in some species may be festooned with four lobes (*tauricollis, tapika*) or eight lobes (*macrocephala*). The neck is usually lacking, but is present in *macrocephala*.

Schistometra Cholodkovsky, 1912

With a typical davaineid holdfast whose suckers each carry two muscular appendages. Body very muscular. Genital apertures alternating irregularly. Paruterine organ transverse, in front of the uterus. Genotype, *conoideis* Bloch, 1782 (Figure 257).

Fuhrmann (1932) regarded this genus as identical with the later proposed generic forms *Otidotaenia* Beddard, 1912 and *Paraschistometra* Woodland, 1930. Of the three species known – *conoideis* Bloch, 1782; *macqueeni* Woodland, 1930; and *wettsteini* Weithofer, 1916 – none are known from North American hosts and all are from otidiform birds (bustards).

Family Biuterinidae Meggitt, 1927

DESCRIPTION

Of the order Cyclophyllidea. With a retractable rostellum armed with two to four circles of triangular hooks. Uterus persisting in gravid segments, or coexisting with, or replaced by, a paruterine organ into which the eggs pass. Adults in birds. Life cycle unknown. Type genus, *Biuterina* Fuhrmann, 1902.

HISTORY

This family was established by Meggitt (1927c) for three genera – *Biuterina* Fuhrmann, *Deltokeras* Meggitt, and *Cyclorchida* Fuhrmann. To these may be added *Neyraia* Joyeux and Timon-David, 1934 and *Biuterinoides* Ortlepp, 1940. The taxonomic status of these forms is far from satisfactorily settled by grouping them within one family. Fuhrmann (1932) preferred to regard them as aberrant Dilepididae, and Burt (1938a) similarly retained *Biuterina* and *Deltokeras* within Paruterinae (Dilepididae). The lack of information about the genera and the apparent variability of their characteristics makes impracticable any key for their provisional separation.

NOTES ON GENERA

Biuterina Fuhrmann, 1902

With a double crown of triangular hooks. Gravid uterus coexisting with a paruterine organ of variable shape which receives the eggs and forms a capsule around them. Genotype, *clavulus* Linstow, 1888.

According to Meggitt (1927), the former genus *Sphaeruterina* Johnston, 1914 is synonymous with *Biuterina*. About 16 species are known, mainly from passeriform birds. Ransom (1909) recorded in North America the species *longiceps* Rudolphi, 1819 from *Cairina moschata*; *passerina* Fuhrmann, 1908 from *Alauda arvensis*; and *trapezoides* Fuhrmann, 1908 from *Molothus ater*.

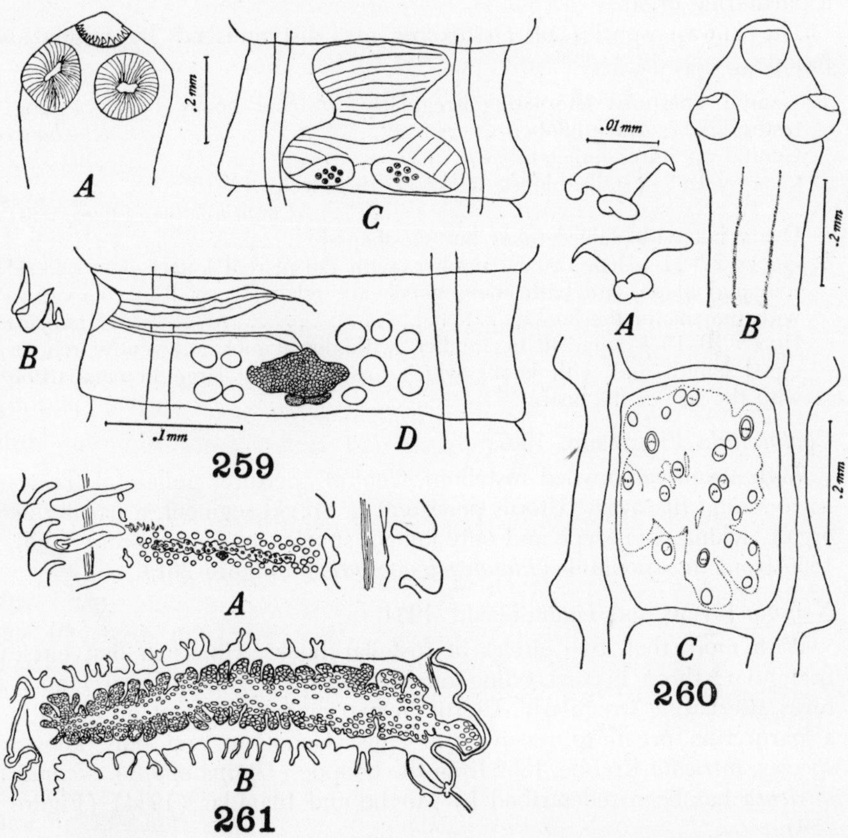

FIG. 259. *Neyraia intricata.* After Moghe and Inamdar, 1934. A. Holdfast. B. Rostellar hooks. C. Gravid segment. D. Mature segment. FIG. 260. *Deltokeras multilobatus.* After Olsen, 1930. A. Rostellar hooks. B. Holdfast. C. Frontal section of gravid segment showing uterus with paruterine tissue. FIG. 261. *Cyclorchida omalancristrota.* After Skrjabin, 1914e. A. Horizontal section of a mature segment. B. Same, of a gravid segment.

Deltokeras Meggitt, 1927

With a double-crowned rostellum. Gravid uterus persistent and saclike, a paruterine organ appearing in some species, not appearing in others. Adult in tropical passeriform birds. Genotype, *ornitheios* Meggitt, 1927.

Meggitt believed that *ornitheios* lacked a paruterine organ. Joyeux,

Gendre, and Baer (1928), for the species *camylometra*, and Hsü (1935), for the species *delachauxi*, however, reported a thickening of the parenchyma surrounding the uterus and believed this to be a paruterine organ. Similar traces of paruterine tissue have been demonstrated also by Olsen (1930) in the species *multilobatus* from a bird of paradise in the New York Zoological Gardens. In respect to the paruterine organ, therefore, *Deltokeras* would seem to hold an intermediate position between *Cyclorchida* without a paruterine organ and *Biuterina* and *Neyraia* with a paruterine organ.

The known species of *Deltokeras* are distinguished by Olsen as follows:

1. Genital apertures alternating irregularly; rostellar hooks 14–15 μ long; testes 15–17; ovary bilobed .... *delachauxi*
   Genital apertures unilateral 2
2. Ovary with 8–9 stalked lobes; hooks 17–19 μ; testes 12–16 .... *multilobatus* (Figure 260)
   Ovary not with stalked lobes but sac-shaped 3
3. Hooks 27–31 μ long, 80 in number, with dorsal root longer than ventral root and blade, and with knobs which are relatively small in comparison with the size of the hooks .... *ornitheios*
   Hooks 10–15 μ long, 46 in number, with dorsal root and ventral root of equal length and with knobs which are extremely large in comparison with the size of the hooks .... *campylometra*

Cyclorchida Fuhrmann, 1907

With a double-crowned rostellum. Genital apertures unilateral. Testes surrounding the ovary. Uterus persistent in gravid segment, a paruterine organ lacking. Genotype and only known species, *omalancristrota* Wedl, 1855 from the spoonbill (*Platalea leucorodia*) (Figure 261).

Neyraia Joyeux and Timon-David, 1934

With more than two circles of rostellar hooks. Hooks in first circle triangular; those in succeeding circles more elongated. Genital apertures alternating irregularly. Uterus in two masses, in front of which is a paruterine organ to receive the eggs. Genotype and only known species, *intricata* Krabbe, 1882 from the hoopoe (*Upupa epops*). *Neyraia intricata* has been redescribed by Moghe and Inamdar (1934) (Figure 259).

Biuterinoides Ortlepp, 1940

With four circles of rostellar hooks. Body length 47–100 or more millimeters. Posterior rostellar hooks triangular and up to 410 μ long. Hooks of second, third, and fourth circles pear-shaped and smaller. Total hook number about 80. Genital apertures alternating irregularly, each in the anterior third of the segment margin. Cirrus pouch reaching and even crossing the poral canals. Testes about 10. Paruterine organ at first hourglass-shaped, later becoming columnar. Uterus giving rise to two apparently separate egg capsules containing up to about 40 eggs. Genotype, *upupai* Ortlepp, 1940 in *Upupa africana*. Ortlepp suggested the addition to his genus of Krabbe's *Taenia intricata*, 1882, from *Upupa* also. Comparison of Ortlepp's material with *Neyraia* will probably show synonymic identity.

Family Hymenolepididae Railliet and Henry, 1909

DESCRIPTION

Of the order Cyclophyllidea. Small to medium-sized tapeworms with the holdfast provided with a retractable rostellum armed with a single circle of eight or ten thorn-shaped hooks. Genitalia single per segment. Genital apertures unilateral. Testes large, rarely exceeding four. Gravid uterus a transverse tube. Type genus, *Hymenolepis* Weinland, 1858.

HISTORY

As noted earlier in this section, the genus *Hymenolepis*, upon whose characteristics the family was founded, was established by Weinland (1858) for a form *flavopunctata* which is now, in accordance with the rules of zoological nomenclature, known as *Hymenolepis diminuta* (Rudolphi, 1819). The family term "Hymenolepididae" owes its origin to Railliet and Henry (1909), who suggested it as a correction of Fuhrmann's suggested term "Hymenolepinidae."

Various attempts to break down the vast genus *Hymenolepis* into more manageable groups of species have not met with universal acceptance. Hughes (1941b), in a survey of the genus, recognized some 328 valid species, and the genus is growing rapidly. One of the earliest such attempts was the division of *Hymenolepis* by Cohn (1901) into two subgenera: (1) *Hymenolepis*, with more than 10 rostellar hooks or with the rostellum rudimentary and unarmed; and (2) *Drepanidotaenia*, with 8–10 rostellar hooks. The main objections to Cohn's subgenera are the great similarity between them in internal structure, and the practical difficulty of dividing accurately a group of species on the basis of number of hooks or shape of hooks.

Clerc (1902) suggested as breakdown features the number of testes, those forms with three or more testes per segment to be termed *Hymenolepis*, those with two testes to be termed *Diorchis*, and those with one testis to be termed *Monorchis*. The latter name was later (1903) dropped in favor of the name *Aploparaksis*. On the grounds of etymological accuracy Mayhew (1925) changed the spelling of this name to "*Haploparaxis*," but such a change is contrary to the International Rules and Clerc's original form must be retained. Cohn (1904a) and Fuhrmann (1906b) took into consideration the positions of ovary and testes relative to each other, and the latter author established the genus *Oligorchis* for those hymenolepidids with four testes.

Mayhew (1925), surveying the avian species of Hymenolepididae, used the generic terms *Haploparaxis* (= *Aploparaksis* Clerc) for the one-testis forms; *Diorchis* Clerc for the two-testis forms; *Oligorchis* Fuhrmann for the four-testis forms; and distributed the three-testis forms among six genera, namely: *Hymenolepis*, with the testes in a transverse row; *Weinlandia*, with the testes arranged at the points of a triangle, one anterior and two posterior, or one poral and two antiporal;

Wardium, with the testes variable in position in different segments of the same body (Figure 262); *Echinorhynchotaenia*, with the genital ducts passing *between* the poral osmoregulatory canals; *Hymenofimbria*, with 10 osmoregulatory canals; and *Fimbriaria*, with 3–11 osmoregulatory canals (as against 4 in other genera), with a small holdfast or a large pseudo-holdfast (Figure 263). Tseng Shen (1932a) added to Mayhew's scheme the genus *Fuhrmanniella* for hymenolepidid species in which the three testes are arranged at the points of an inverted triangle.

Fuhrmann (1932), while admitting the merits of Mayhew's scheme in handling the unwieldy group of three-testis hymenolepidids, was unable, though regretfully, to accept the genera *Wardium, Weinlandia*, and *Fuhrmanniella*, since they were based upon a characteristic which may alter with the state of contraction of the preserved material. Further, the type genus and species of the family, *Hymenolepis diminuta*, shows even greater variability in distribution of testes than does the type species *macrostrobilodes*, upon which Mayhew based his *Wardium*. If *Wardium* were accepted, the terms *Hymenolepis* and Hymenolepididae would be thrown into the discard in favor of *Wardium* and Wardiidae, and the present confusion would be intensified. The genus *Echinorhynchotaenia*, according to Fuhrmann, its author, is better placed in the family Dilepididae, despite its anatomical resemblances with *Hymenolepis*, because the armature of the rostellum and the passage of the genital ducts between the osmoregulatory canals exclude it from the *Hymenolepis* group.

The scheme proposed by Fuhrmann (1932), and accepted with a few slight amendments by the majority of later writers, postulated two subfamilies – (1) Hymenolepidinae, with the genera *Chitinolepis, Diorchis, Diplogynia, Diploposthe, Drepanidotaenia, Echinocotyle, Haploparaxis, Hymenofimbria, Hymenolepis*, and *Oligorchis*; and (2) Fimbriariinae, with the genera *Fimbriaria* and *Fimbriaroides*. To this scheme, Joyeux and Baer (1935) added a third subfamily, Pseudhymenolepinae, for the genus *Pseudhymenolepis*.

In the following pages, while keeping substantially to the Fuhrmann-Joyeux-Baer scheme, we shall consider the genera *Diploposthe* and *Diplogynia* as belonging to Poche's family Diploposthidae, and to the genera listed above we shall add *Pseudoligorchis* Johri.

RECOGNITION FEATURES

The hymenolepidid holdfast end is spherical or conoidal, rarely exceeding half a millimeter in diameter, and has four prominent suckers whose margins are not armed with spines (see Figure 265). The apex of the holdfast end is bluntly pointed and may be referred to as a "rostrum." Within this rostrum there is an oval sac whose walls contain a layer of longitudinal muscle fibers and one of oblique muscle fibers. This sac is the "rostellar sheath" or "rostellar sac." There can be protruded from it, or conversely, there can be withdrawn within it, a club-shaped structure, hollow in some forms, solid in others, for which the term "rostellum" should be reserved. Arranged around the bulbous tip of this

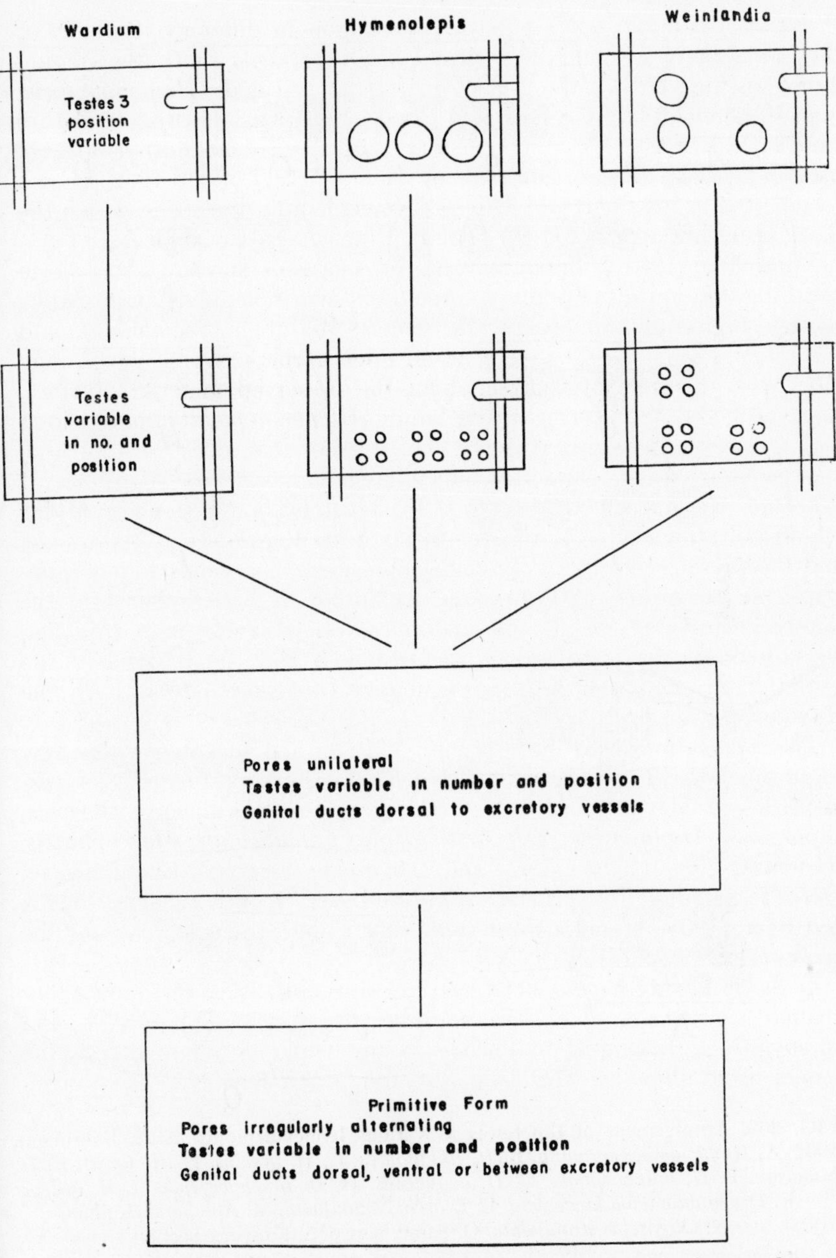

FIG. 262. Phylogenetic relationships between *Wardium*, *Hymenolepis*, and *Weinlandia*. After Mayhew, 1925.

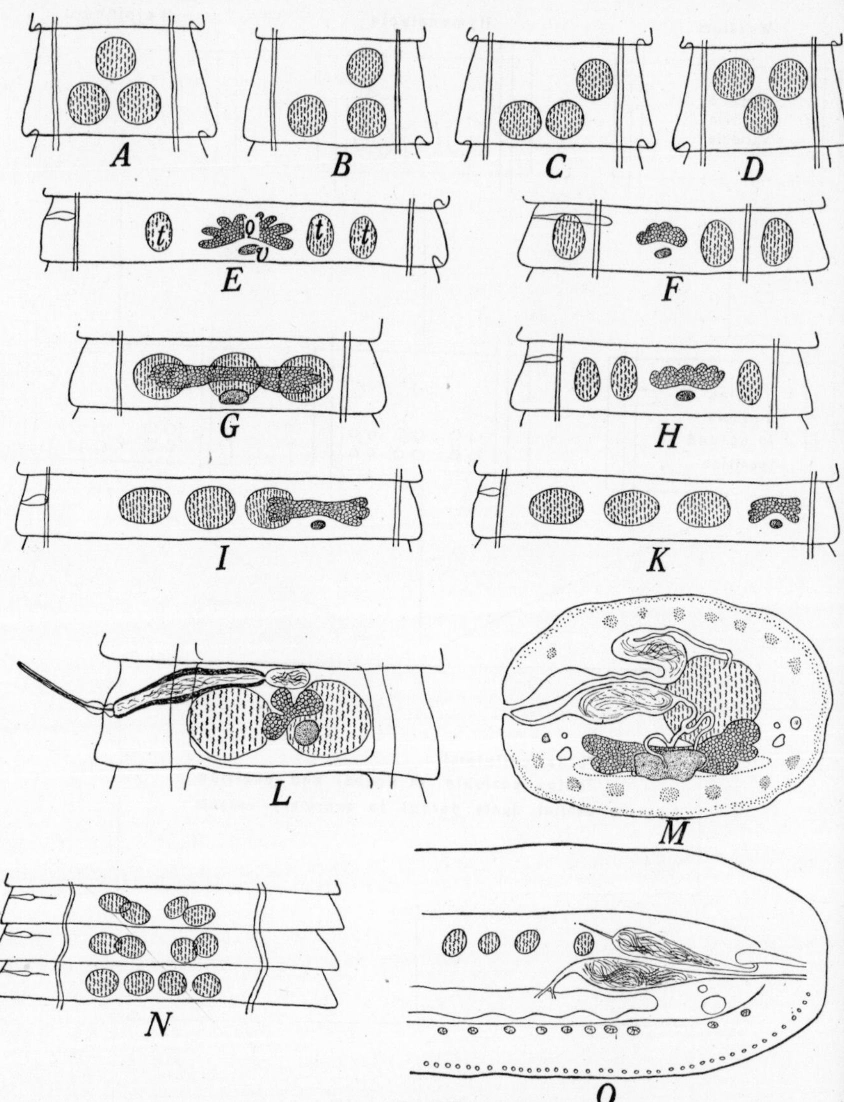

FIG. 263. Arrangement of the testes in various hymenolepidids. After Fuhrmann, 1932. A. *Hymenolepis coronula*. B. *H. linguloides*. C. *H. gracilis*. D. *H. fausti*. E. *H. bisaccata*. F. *H. microcephala*. G. *H. aequabilis*. H. *H. brachycephala*. I. *H. ardeae*. K. *Drepanidotaenia lanceolata*. L. *Diorchis acuminata*. M. *Aploparaksis filum*. N. *Oligorchis strangulata*. O. Same, part of a transverse section.

rostellum, there is commonly a single circle of 8 or 10 or more thorn-shaped hooks.

The shape of the hymenolepidid hook, while very characteristic, is not peculiar to this family. Similarly shaped hooks are found also in Taeniidae and Dilepididae. The hook may be described as a flattened blade arising from a wide, concave base (Figure 264). Skrjabin and

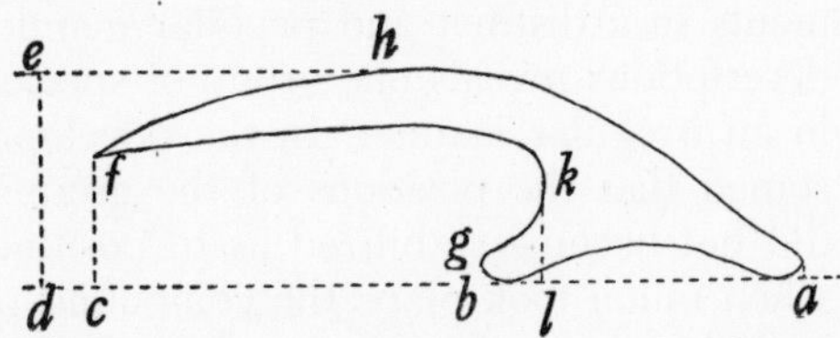

FIG. 264. Typical hymenolepidid hook. After Meggitt, 1927c. For explanation of letters see p. 390.

Matevosyn (1942b) term the blade an *acies* and the base a *radix*, and recognize in the base a *manubrium* and a *processus radici*. They use the morphological peculiarities of these parts and the correlations between their respective dimensions to establish a number of morphological types.

Meggitt's scheme for classifying the hooks of Hymenolepididae has been referred to earlier (see the section on Taeniidae). There can be no doubt that the hooks provide valuable systematic characters for the differentiation of species, since their numbers, shapes, and dimensions appear to be fairly constant for each species while differing markedly between species. Supplementing the hooks as a valuable systematic character is the arrangement of the genitalia.

Following the holdfast is a short "neck." The body segments are markedly wider than long. Along one margin of the body, usually the left-hand margin, runs a line of genital apertures, each placed usually in the anterior half of the segment margin.

In the stained and mounted segment, the middle field is occupied largely by one to four large testes. The arrangement of these testes varies considerably between genera and species, as shown in Figure 263. The arrangement appears to be relatively constant within the species although there are some – notably *diminuta* – in which the testis arrangement shows great variability. Mayhew (1925) suggested that the ancestral *Hymenolepis* may have had at least six, and possibly as many as twelve, testes; that its genital apertures alternated from side to side; and that its genital ducts ran dorsal or ventral to the poral osmoregulatory canals.

"The first forms with fixed characters, which diverged from this, most probably had the genital ducts dorsal to the excretory canals and the pores unilateral. The most distinctive morphological feature to appear next probably was in connection with the testes. It seems quite possible that the several testes first became localized in groups in definite locations in the proglottid. As an illustration let us assume that there were twelve testes and that these became localized along the posterior border of the proglottid in groups of four or that two groups came to be found along the posterior border and the other in front of the posterior antiporal group. The next stage was seen in the union of these testes in those respective positions. In this manner it becomes apparent that the groups of species which have similar patterns of testis arrangement are fundamentally related and that this relationship goes back to their common origin. They are thus separated from the species having other arrangements in a distinct and peculiar manner. The study of material and of descriptions reveals one group of species which have the testes arranged in an irregular manner. In the development of this group it may be assumed that the positions of the groups of testes in the ancestral form did not become stabilized as to position in the proglottid, consequently when union took place the compound organ retained this characteristic, and this group of present day species presents a variable pattern of testes arrangement." Mayhew (1925).

The cirro-vaginal atrium is cup-shaped or bell-shaped and may have, opening from it on its dorsal surface, an "accessory sac," which in some species appears to lodge the swollen apex of the cirrus. The sperm duct is differentiated into an external seminal vesicle, often considerable in size, and an internal seminal vesicle, which lies within the cirrus pouch and occupies at least the aporal half of it. The two seminal vesicles are connected by a narrow and sinuous duct. From the internal seminal vesicle the sperm duct continues as the looped ejaculatory duct to join the cirrus. The cirrus is commonly only slightly protrusible, may be finely spinose, and may have a "cirrus whip," a very long and slender tubular filament which extends through the lumen of the cirrus and somewhat beyond it. The cirrus pouch itself is commonly long, often extending to the middle of the segment or nearly to the aporal osmoregulatory canal.

The ovary is irregularly and coarsely lobed, transversely elongated, and situated ventral to the male organs and midway between the two ventral osmoregulatory canals. In some cases, however, it may lie to one side of the segment sufficiently to divide the testes into poral and antiporal groups. The yolk gland is postero-median to the ovary, and potato-shaped. The proximal region of the vagina is conspicuously dilated as a seminal receptacle, the remainder of it forming a slender tube parallel with the sperm duct, running between the cirro-vaginal atrium and the seminal receptacle.

A transverse section of the mature segment shows a conspicuous layer of parenchymal longitudinal muscle bundles. The osmoregulatory canals on each side consist of a narrow, thick-walled canal (dorsal) and a wide, thin-walled canal (ventral); the two wide canals are connected in the first formed segment to discharge through a common terminal pore. As a rule, no transverse canals are to be seen. The gravid segment is occupied almost wholly by the gravid uterus, which appears as a transverse sac and may be divided by septa into irregular lobes.

Although a hymenolepidid tapeworm (*Hymenolepis nana*) was the subject of the classical investigations of Grassi (1887) on the development of the cysticercoid type of tapeworm larva, the embryology of the family as a whole is still incompletely understood. The observations of Grassi have been confirmed and elaborated by numerous later workers, notably, in recent years, Scott (1923), Woodland (1924a, 1924b), Joyeux (1925), Bacigalupo (1928a, 1928b, 1928c, 1928d, 1928e, 1929, 1932), Shorb (1933), Brumpt (1933), Hunninen (1935a, 1935b, 1935c), Chandler (1939, 1940), Hearin (1941), and Larsh (1943a, 1943b, 1943c, 1943d, 1944a, 1944b, 1944c, 1944d, 1945a, 1945b, 1945c). The general features of the life cycle of *Hymenolepis nana* may be noted briefly as indicating to some extent the general lines of the hymenolepidid life cycle story.

There is considerable evidence in favor of the existence of at least three strains or races of *Hymenolepis nana*, anatomically indistinguishable but possibly physiologically distinct. There is a human strain, *Hymenolepis nana s. s.*; a rat strain, called by Shorb the W strain; and a mouse strain, called by Shorb the M strain. The rat and mouse strains constitute what observers in the past have called *Hymenolepis nana* var. *fraterna*. Even within this rat-mouse strain, Larsh (1943a, 1943b, 1943c, 1943d) found physiological differences in worms from mice of different localities, as indicated by the percentage of eggs which gave rise to cysticercoids. The *Taenia murina* of Dujardin (1845) was possibly one or the other of these rodent strains. It may be noted that the bulk of observational and experimental work upon the life cycle of this tapeworm have been carried out with the rodent strains. The three strains are interchangeable in regard to their hosts, although rats appear to show some resistance toward infection with the human strain and are distinctly refractory to the mouse strain. It may be stated at the outset that *Hymenolepis nana* is peculiar among tapeworms in that an intermediate host can be dispensed with, and eggs swallowed by a definitive host give rise to cysticercoids which complete their life cycle in the same host.

The ripe egg is elliptical, the outer membrane 40–50 μ, the inner membrane 29–30 μ. At each pole of the inner membrane there is a rounded projection provided with filamentous appendages. The egg contains a fully developed oncosphere and is infective from the moment it leaves the host. Grassi and Rovelli (1892) believed that the oncosphere was liberated from the ingested egg by the action of the gastric and pancreatic juices of the host upon the egg membranes, but later observers have cast doubt upon this view and prefer to believe that the oncosphere tears its way through the membranes by its own exertions. After leaving the egg membranes, the oncosphere in the majority of cases bores into a villus and within 30–40 hours after initial infection has reached the tunica propria of the villus, though not as yet showing any development of suckers or rostellar hooks. Grassi and Rovelli believed the latter to appear at 80–90 hours, but Hunninen observed rostellar hooks as early as 50 hours after initial infection. At 93–96 hours the cysticercoid is fully formed, and breaks out from the villus at between 102 and 144 hours (Hunninen, 1935a, 1935b, 1935c). The fully formed cysticercoid is pear-shaped, tailless, with four conspicuous suckers and an invaginated rostellum. Hunninen found in rats and mice that 91 and 86 per cent, respectively, of the cysticercoids occur in the first half of the small intestine (Figures 266–68).

There is some difference of opinion among observers as to the length of the prepatent period – the period that elapses between initial infection and the appearance of ripe eggs in the feces of the host. Earlier experimenters, working before concentration methods for egg recovery were widely used, estimated the prepatent period at 14–30 days. Shorb (1933) found the prepatent period to be 11–16 days for the W strain in rats, and 15 days and over for the M strain in mice. Hunninen (1935a, 1935b, 1935c) found the prepatent period for the M strain in mice to vary from 14 to 25 days, with 15 days as the commonest value.

The majority of the adult worms are found in the last four centimeters of the small intestine of the host (Hunninen, 1935a, 1935b, 1935c). The patent or egg-producing period of the adult *Hymenolepis nana* is 1–11 days, and after the 13th day the loss of worms from the host gut is rapid and constant (Shorb, 1933).

Although direct infection by ingestion of ripe eggs is possibly the commonest method by which humans, rats, or mice become infected with *Hymenolepis nana*, it may not be the original method. Bacigalupo (1928–31) in Argentina found that cysticercoids will develop in a number of insects and can be transferred by them to the definitive host. In particular, fleas (*Xenopsylla cheopis, Ctenocephalus canis, Pulex irritans*) and to a lesser extent the mealworm beetles, *Tenebrio molitor* and *Tenebrio obscurus*, can serve as intermediate hosts.

Among other hymenolepidids whose life histories have been investigated, the intervention of an arthropod host seems to be the rule rather than the exception. In *Hymenolepis diminuta*, a habitual parasite of rats and mice, the tailed cysticercoid (*Cercocystis*) has been found occurring naturally in the caterpillar of the flour moth, *Asopia farinalis*; in an earwig, *Anisolabis annulipes*; in beetles, *Akis spinosa, Scaurus striatus, Dermestes peruvianus* larva, *Ulosonia parvicornis* adult; and in fleas, *Ceratophyllus fasciatus, Xenopsylla cheopis*. The commonest intermediate host is probably the larva of *Asopia farinalis*.

Hymenolepis brachycephala of charadriiform birds has its cysticercoid in *Cyclops spp. Hymenolepis cantaniana* of galliform birds uses scarabaeid beetle larvae and possibly larvae of the stable fly, *Stomoxys. Hymenolepis collaris* of anseriform birds uses *Diaptomus, Cyclops, Cypris*, and *Gammarus. Hymenolepis coronula* of anseriform birds uses Cypridae. *Hymenolepis gracilis* of anseriform and gruiform birds uses copepod and ostracod Crustacea. *Drepanidotaenia lanceolata* of anseriform birds uses *Cyclops* and *Diaptomus*; and so on. The list could be extended considerably.

Subfamily Hymenolepidinae Perrier, 1897

DESCRIPTION

Of the family Hymenolepididae. With the characters of the family. Holdfast distinct, usually with a retractable rostellum armed with hooks.

Genital apertures unilateral. Genital ducts dorsal to the poral osmoregulatory canals. Testes rarely more than four in number. Sperm duct short, with a very large external seminal vesicle. Uterus a transverse sac. Egg with three membranes. With eight genera, distinguished as follows:

KEY TO GENERA

1. Rostellum unarmed 2
   Rostellum usually armed, testes usually 4 or fewer 3
2. Rostellum rudimentary, testes 8–10 in a transverse row; egg with outermost membrane thick . . . . *Chitinolepis*
   Rostellum present but unarmed; testes 7–12, grouped laterally and posteriorly around the ovary; outermost egg membrane delicate . . *Pseudoligorchis*
3. Testes 4 in number . . . . *Oligorchis*
   Testes fewer than 4 in number 4
4. Testes 3 in number 5
   Testes fewer than 3 7
5. Holdfast small; rostellar hooks 8; testes poral in position, in a transverse row; ovary and yolk gland antiporal in position . . . . *Drepanidotaenia*
   Holdfast medium to large; rostellar hooks 8, 10, or more; testes in a transverse row or at the points of an imaginary triangle but never entirely poral 6
6. Suckers wide and shallow, their margins armed with small hooks; rostellum with 10 hooks . . . . *Echinocotyle*
   Suckers moderately wide and deep without marginal hooks; rostellar hooks 8, 10, or more . . . . *Hymenolepis*
7. Testes 2 in number; rostellar hooks 10 . . . . *Diorchis*
   Testes 1 in number; rostellar hooks 10 . . . . *Aploparaksis*

NOTES ON GENERA

Chitinolepis Baylis, 1926

With the rostellum rudimentary and unarmed. Testes nine to twelve, in a transverse row interrupted by the ovary. Ovary median, lobed, well developed. Seminal receptacle present. Cirrus pouch relatively short for a hymenolepidid but having an internal and an external seminal vesicle. Gravid uterus a transverse sac as wide as the segment. Genotype and only known species, *mjoebergi* Baylis, 1923.

The genotype was established for a form from *Rattus sabanus* in Sarawak, East Indies. Its position is somewhat dubious for it satisfies neither the criteria for Hymenolepididae nor yet those for Dilepididae, although Meggitt and Subramanian (1927) preferred to place it within the latter family.

Pseudoligorchis Johri, 1934

With the rostellum believed to be unarmed. Genital apertures unilateral. Genital ducts running *between* the poral osmoregulatory canals. Testes numerous, grouped around the female genitalia. Uterus irregularly lobed and saclike. Genotype, *magnireceptaculata* Johri, 1934.

This is another somewhat unsatisfactory form, credited by its discoverer to Hymenolepididae. It was established for material from a bat in Lucknow, India. Johri also placed within his genus the species *Oligorchis paucitesticulata* Fuhrmann, 1913, a form with seven to eleven testes, whose affinities with *Oligorchis* are admittedly doubtful. The species *paucitesticulata* (Southwell and Lake, 1939, preferred the termination *-us* for oligorchid species) is known, however, only from the Eurasian plover, *Vanellus vanellus*, which would seem to make unlikely any close affinity with Johri's form.

Oligorchis Fuhrmann, 1906

With the rostellum armed and – if we except *paucitesticulata* and *kwangensis* – with only four testes. Otherwise typically hymenolepidid. Genotype, *strangulata* Fuhrmann, 1906.

The essential characters of *Oligorchis* are (1) its restriction to birds; (2) the double layer of parenchymal longitudinal muscles; (3) the presence of both external and internal seminal vesicles; and (4) the four testes.

The genotype was established for material from an acciptriform bird, *Elanoides furcatus*, in Brazil, and it is one of the only two hymenolepidid tapeworms recorded from this order of birds. Fuhrmann also placed in the genus the species *paucitesticulata* (see above); *longivaginosus* Mayhew, 1925 from the white pelican (*Pelicanus erythrorhynchos*) of Yellowstone Park, United States; and *toxometra* Joyeux and Baer, 1928a from a West African snipe (*Gallinago*). The species *delachauxi* Fuhrmann, 1909 and *yorkei* Kotlan, 1923, credited by Mayhew to this genus, were removed to Dilepididae (genus *Dilepis*). Joyeux and Baer (1935d) would place *delauchauxi* (= *Dilepis scolecina* Joyeux, Gendre, and Baer, 1928) in the dilepidid genus *Paradilepis*. To Fuhrmann's list of oligorchid species may be added *hierticos* Johri, 1937 from an acciptriform in India, and *kwangensis* Southwell and Lake, 1939 from *Galachrysia nuchalis nuchalis* (Charadriiformes), Belgian Congo (Figure 269).

Drepanidotaenia Railliet, 1892

With eight rostellar hooks on a small holdfast. Testes three, in the poral half of the segment. Ovary and yolk gland antiporal. Genotype, *lanceolata* Bloch, 1782.

The genotype is a common parasite of domesticated ducks and geese in Europe and North America and of a number of wild anseriform birds. The life cycle was described by the Polish zoologist Ruszkowski (1932a), who found the intermediate host to be *Cyclops strenuus*. Two additional species have been added to the genus by Szpotanska (1932), namely *bisacculina* and *curiosa*, both from the Australian anseriform bird *Chenopsis atrata*.

Echinocotyle Blanchard, 1891

With ten rostellar hooks. Suckers wide and shallow, with margins armed with minute hooks. Three testes. Otherwise typically hymenolepidid. Genotype, *rosseteri* Blanchard, 1891.

The genotype was recorded from *Anas boschas* in Europe and was listed by Mayhew (1925) as *species inquirenda*. Fuhrmann (1932) added to the genus the species *nitida* Krabbe, 1869; *nitidulans* Krabbe,

1882; *tenuis* Clerc, 1906 – placed by Mayhew in the genus *Weinlandia*; and *uralensis* Clerc, 1902 – regarded by Mayhew as *species inquirenda*; all from charadriiform birds; and *dolosa* Joyeux and Baer, 1928 from the West African passeriform bird *Spermestes cuculatus*.

Hymenolepis Weinland, 1858

With the characters of the family. Rostellum usually armed with a single circle of hooks. Three testes, variable in arrangement. Cirrus pouch usually large, with an external and an internal seminal vesicle and an accessory sac. A large seminal receptacle usually present. Genotype, *diminuta* Rudolphi, 1819.

The rostellum of *Hymenolepis* commonly carries a single circle of eight or ten hooks but some species are unarmed and others may have between thirty and forty hooks. The testes are arranged either at the three points of an imaginary triangle or in a straight line, but combinations of these arrangements may occur. The cirrus pouch is long, commonly extending over the poral osmoregulatory canals as far as the middle line of the segment, or, as in the species *macracanthos*, extending right to the antiporal margin of the segment and producing a prominent protuberance there. In the majority of hymenolepid species the cirrus pouch has, at the end nearer to the genital atrium, a pocket commonly lined by spines; this is the "accessory sac" (see Figure 265 A and B, *as.*).

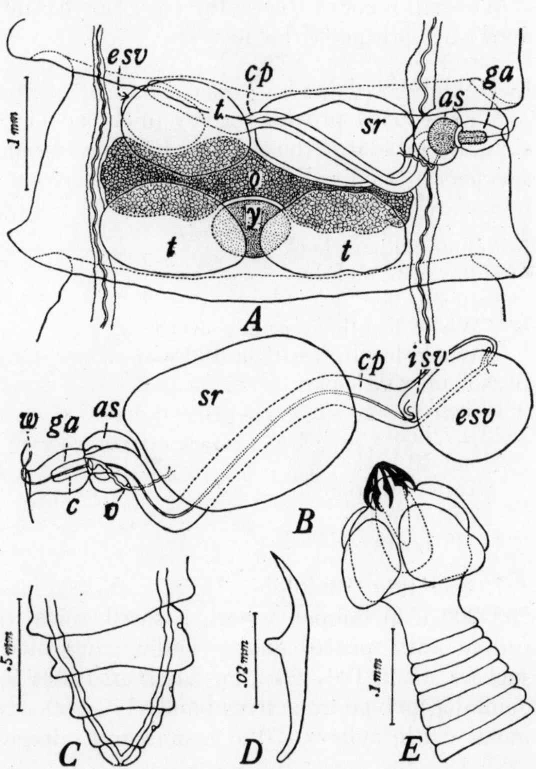

FIG. 265. *Hymenolepis filumferens*. After Brock, 1942. A. Mature segment, dorsal view. B. Reproductive tracts, ventral. C. Posterior end showing sterile first-formed segment. D. Rostellar hook. E. Holdfast. *as*, accessory sac; *c*, cirrus; *cp*, cirrus pouch; *esv*, external seminal vesicle; *ga*, genital atrium; *isv*, internal seminal vesicle; *o*, ovary; *sr*, seminal receptacle; *t*, testes; *v*, vagina; *w*, cirrus whip; *y*, yolk gland.

When the cirrus is everted, the sac is everted too, and may appear as a spiny, knoblike protuberance from the base of the cirrus.

The internal seminal vesicle is large, sometimes occupying the posterior or innermost half of the cirrus pouch. The part of the ejaculatory duct between the internal seminal vesicle and cirrus that lies nearer to the cirrus may be lined by chitin and may be everted with the cirrus so as to appear as a chitinous tube – the "cirrus stylet" or "cirrus whip" – running through the cirrus lumen and projecting beyond the cirrus tip to a length as long again as the cirrus (Figure 265 B, *w.*).

For a discussion of the synonymity and the range of species of this widely distributed and unwieldy genus, reference should be made to Fuhrmann (1924a, 1932), Hughes (1940a, 1941b), Polk (1942a, 1942b), T. I. Davies (1938a, 1939, 1945a, 1945b), and Joyeux and Baer (1950b). Fuhrmann (1924a) recognized 206 species, of which 134 had been recorded in Europe. Hughes (1940a, 1941b) listed 328 species and subspecies. Two of these, according to Schultz (1940b), belong to *Diorchis* and two others (Polk, 1942a) to *Dilepis*. H. E. Davis (1945a), despite these deductions, raised the number of *Hymenolepis* species to 336 by new species described by Baer (1940a), Brock (1942), Burt (1940a), Johri (1941), Lopez-Neyra (1941b), Polk (1942b, 1942c), Schmelz (1941), and Vigueras (1941a, 1941b). Davis (1945b) added to these the species *furcouterina* from a Celebesian black-bellied snakebird.

We shall recognize here forty-six North American species, whose characteristics are noted below.

IN MAMMALS:

Macy (1931) provided a key to the species in bats. Hübscher (1937) similarly tabulated the six known species from bats and the twenty-seven species reported to that date from Insectivora, except for *capensis*, whose hooks are unknown.

Rostellum without hooks
  Testes in triangle . . . . *diminuta*
  Testes in line
    Whole length exceeding 100 mm. . . . . *scalopi, citelli*
    Whole length less than 100 mm. . . . . *anthocephalus*
Rostellum with hooks
  10 hooks . . . . *evaginata, ondatrae*
  22–27 hooks . . . . *nana*
  About 36 hooks
    Testes in triangle . . . . *bacillaris*
    Testes in line . . . . *christensoni, gertschi*
  41–48 hooks . . . . *roudabushi*

1. *diminuta* Rudolphi, 1819. 200–300 mm. by 3–4 mm.; holdfast 299–300 μ in diameter, with a small apical depression which lodges a rudimentary, pear-shaped rostellum, unarmed and scarcely protrusible; suckers small, 100–120 μ in diameter; testes in line, one poral to female genitalia, two aporal; cirrus pouch 170–380 μ by 50–80 μ, 1/10 to 1/12 of segment width; eggs 60–70 μ; in rats and mice; cosmopolitan. A tapeworm

occasionally recorded in children, contracted by the consumption of insufficiently cooked breadstuffs, made from flour infested with grain insects (see Riley and Shannon, 1922).

2. *scalopi* Schultz, 1939. 100–200 mm. by 3 mm.; with about 1,000 segments; holdfast 170–232 μ; suckers 80–110 μ, not spinose; rostellum 78–117 μ, without hooks; testes in a triangle; cirrus pouch 125 μ by 45 μ extending over the poral canals; cirrus not spinose; eggs 57–65 μ; oncospheres 27–30 μ; in *Scalopus aquaticus* (prairie mole), Michigan.

3. *citelli* McLeod, 1933. 150 by 2.8 mm.; holdfast 245 μ wide by 157 μ dorso-ventrally; rostellum indefinite, triangular, 38 μ long, without hooks; testes in triangle; cirrus pouch fusiform, 157 μ long; eggs 78–86 by 59–65 μ; in ground squirrels (*Citellus spp.*) Manitoba, Canada (Figure 274).

4. *anthocephalus* Van Gundy, 1935. 40–100 mm. by 0.3 to 0.65 mm.; holdfast 250–389 μ; vestigial rostellum devoid of hooks; three pyriform testes, two posterior, one anterior, position variable but never in a straight line; cirrus pouch one-third the segment width; seminal receptacle and accessory sac lacking; cirrus spinose; ovary three-lobed; eggs 47 by 30 μ; oncospheres with hooks 12 μ long; in the mole shrew (*Blarina brevicauda*), Michigan.

5. *evaginata* Barker and Andrews, 1915. 200–400 mm. by 2.3 mm.; holdfast 320 μ; suckers 90–110 μ; ten hooks, each 7 by 4 μ; ovary bilobed; eggs 20 by 16 μ; in *Ondatra zibethica* (muskrat), Nebraska.

6. *ondatrae* Rider and Macy, 1947. 80 mm. by 1.25 mm.; holdfast 250–280 μ; rostellum elongate, 120–190 μ in length by 40–67 μ in width; with single circle of 8–10 hooks; testes in triangle, one poral, one aporal, the third medial; cirrus pouch reaching to mid-line or beyond with prominent external seminal vesicle; cirrus spinose; ovary smoothly oval or slightly trilobate; eggs 30–35 by 40–45 μ; in muskrat (*Ondatra zibethica occipitalis*), Oregon.

7. *nana* Siebold, 1853. 50–60 mm. by 0.5 to 1.0 mm.; holdfast 300–400 μ; rostellum short, 50–80 μ, with 20–27 hooks (22–27 according to some authors); hooks 16–18 μ long; testes in line; cirrus pouch 50–70 by 20–25 μ; eggs 50–53 by 37–41 μ; oncospheres 24–25 by 21–27 μ; in humans, rats, mice; cosmopolitan (Figures 266–68).

The life cycle of *nana* has been discussed earlier in this section. This species is unevenly distributed in North America and is most commonly found in school children in the mountain districts of the southeastern United States, where its incidence may be as high as 9 to 10 per cent. Infection probably comes through consumption of fresh feces. Sunkes and Sellers (1937) found, among 7,249 cases of tapeworm infestation in thirteen southern states, 7,149 due to *Hymenolepis nana* and representing an incidence of approximately 0.75 per cent of 927,625 fecal examinations. Gordadze, Kamalova, and Bugianishvili (1944) in southeastern Georgia (U.S.S.R.) found only twelve persons out of 1,209 infected with *nana*. Gorodilova (1944), however, found among children in an orphanage and in a sanitorium an incidence ranging from 16.3 to 58.3 per cent,

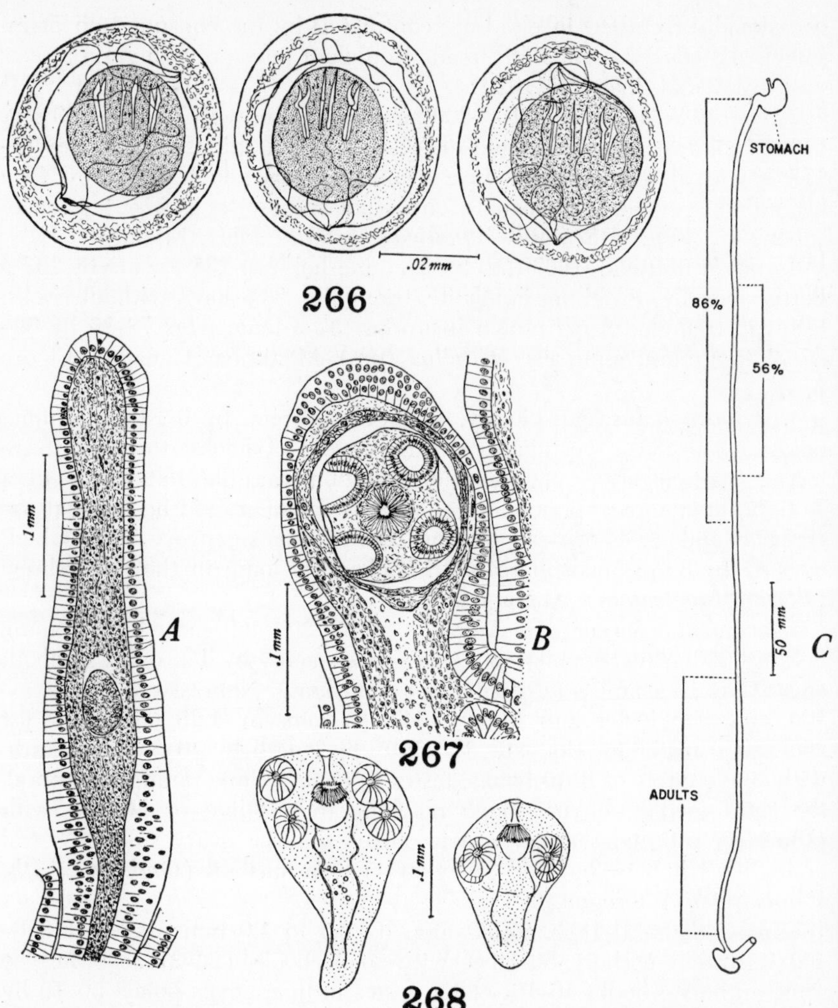

FIG. 266. *Hymenolepis nana*, eggs showing polar filaments. After Brumpt, 1936. FIG. 267. *Hymenolepis nana* var. *fraterna*, cysticercoid-host relationships. After Hunninen, 1935c. A. 30-hour cysticercoid within an intestinal villus. B. 93-hour cysticercoid within an intestinal villus of a 2½-months-old mouse. C. Percentage distribution of cysticercoids in small intestine of 2½-months-old mouse. FIG. 268. *Hymenolepis nana* var. *fraterna*, holdfasts of young individuals. After Brumpt, 1936.

infection being mainly through fecal contamination of food. Stunkard (1945) drew attention to the common occurrence of *nana* in the Syrian hamster (*Cricetus auratus*) commonly used as a laboratory animal.

8. *bacillaris* Goeze, 1782. 150 by 2.4 mm.; rostellum with 36 hooks, each 20 μ in length; testes in triangle; cirrus pouch 120 μ; eggs 71–81 by 58 μ; in Insectivora; recorded in North America by Leidy (1855).

9. *christensoni* Macy, 1931. 39 by 1.5 mm.; holdfast 320 μ; suckers 110 μ; rostellum 130 by 140 μ with 35–41 hooks, each 33–38 μ long; testes

in straight line; cirrus pouch 110 by 40 μ; eggs 50 μ; in *Myotis lucifugus* (mouse-eared bat), Minnesota.

10. *gertschi* Macy, 1947. About 55 mm. by 0.65 mm. wide; holdfast about 0.4 mm. wide; suckers 80–100 μ; 35–41 hooks; testes in transverse row, close together; cirrus pouch 90–120 μ long, crossing poral canal; eggs 27 by 32 μ; in Northwest Coast bat (*Myotis californicus caurinus*), Oregon.

11. *roudabushi* Macy and Rausch, 1946. 40–70 mm. by 1.5 mm.; holdfast 0.26–0.31 mm.; suckers 70–80 μ; 41–48 hooks; testes in line; cirrus pouch crossing poral canal; external seminal vesicle large, reaching to mid-line; cirrus not spinose; eggs 25–30 μ; in bats (*Eptesicus fuscus, Nycticeius humeralis, Lasionycteris noctivagans*), Ohio.

IN DUCKS:

Rostellum without hooks .... *dafilae, megalops*
Rostellum with 8 or 10 hooks
  Testes in triangle .... *collaris, filumferens, cyrtoides*
  Testes in line .... *compressa, cuneata, lintoni, tritesticulata*
Rostellum with more than 10 hooks
  Testes in triangle ..*introversa, macrostrobiloides, parvisaccata, sacciperium*
  Testes in line .... *anceps, coronula*
Rostellum unknown .... *mastigopraedita, stolli*

1. *dafilae* Polk, 1942. 35–40 by 1 mm.; holdfast 105–120 μ; suckers ellipsoidal, 77 by 46 μ; rostellum 115 by 33 μ, without hooks; testes in triangle; cirrus pouch 280 by 84 μ, extending nearly to the middle of the segment; cirrus spinose, with a cirrus whip 72.6 μ long and 6.6 μ in diameter, projecting 16 μ beyond the cirrus tip; ovary bilobed; accessory sac present; eggs 27 μ; oncospheres 17 μ; in pintail duck (*Dafila acuta tzitsihoa*) (Figure 272).

2. *megalops* Nitsch, 1828. 34–54 by 0.75 mm.; holdfast 400–600 μ; rostellum without hooks; testes in triangle; cirrus pouch 300 by 60 μ; ovary bilobed; cirrus whip lacking; eggs 47.6 μ; oncospheres 32 μ; cosmopolitan in domestic duck, Barbary duck, various wild ducks; recorded in North America by Ransom (1902).

3. *collaris* Batsch, 1786. 160 by 2 mm.; holdfast 200–250 μ; suckers 13 by 60 μ; rostellum with 10 hooks, 51–61 μ long; testes in triangle; cirrus pouch 500 by 40 μ; cirrus and accessory sac spinose; a cirrus whip present; eggs 75 by 40 μ; oncosphere 35–44 μ; cosmopolitan in a wide range of anseriform birds; see Stiles (1896); Fuhrmann (1908c, 1932); Joyeux and Baer (1936d).

4. *filumferens* Brock, 1942. 26 by 0.7 mm.; holdfast 140–143 by 156.5–170 μ; suckers 83–100 by 65–73 μ; rostellum 116.5 by 63.6 μ, with 8 hooks, 42–47.6 μ long; testes in triangle; cirrus pouch 23–33 μ in diameter; cirrus spiny; cirrus whip present; ovary irregularly elongated; eggs not observed; in *Anas discors*, Oklahoma (Figure 265).

5. *cyrtoides* Mayhew, 1925. 3–10 mm.; holdfast 150 μ; suckers 70 μ; rostellum 80 by 60 μ with 8 hooks, 65–79 μ long; testes in triangle; eggs 28–35 by 19–23 μ; oncosphere 21–30 μ by 14 μ; in *Erismatura jamaicensis*, Illinois.

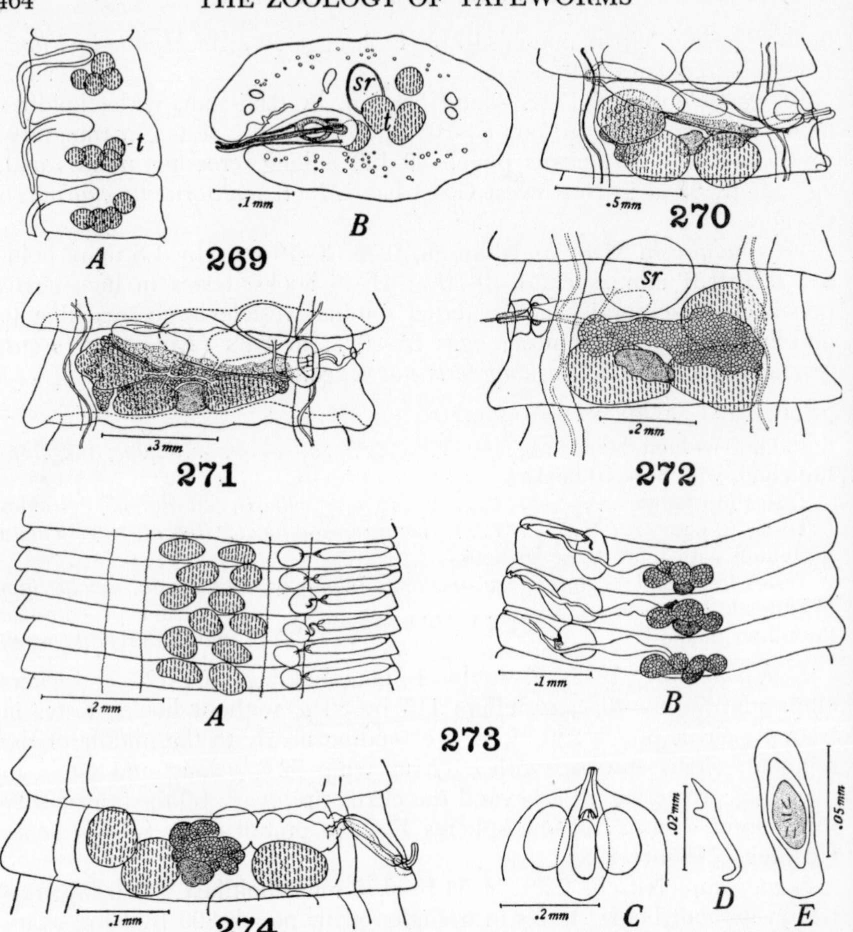

FIG. 269. *Oligorchis longivaginosis.* After Mayhew, 1925. A. Three successive segments showing variations in testis arrangement. B. Locations of organs in cross section (*sr*, seminal receptacle; *t*, testes). FIG. 270. *Hymenolepis mastigopraedita*, mature segment, dorsal view. After Polk, 1942b. FIG. 271. *Hymenolepis stolli*, mature segment. After Brock, 1941. FIG. 272. *Hymenolepis dafilae*, mature segment (*sr*, seminal receptacle). After Polk, 1942c. FIG. 273. *Diorchis nyrocae.* After Long and Wiggins, 1939. A. Successive segments showing male genitalia. B. Successive segments showing female genitalia. C. Holdfast with rostellum retracted. D. Rostellar hook. E. Mature egg. FIG. 274. *Hymenolepis citelli*, mature segment. After McLeod, 1933.

6. *compressa* Linton, 1892. 40 by 0.6 mm.; holdfast 250 μ; suckers 75 by 11 μ; rostellum 220 μ with 10 hooks, 55–58 μ long; testes in line; cirrus pouch 110–130 μ by 90–100 μ; neither accessory sac nor cirrus whip; cosmopolitan in a wide range of anseriform birds.

7. *cuneata* Mayhew, 1925. 40 by 3–4 mm.; holdfast 350 μ; suckers 150 μ; rostellum with 6–8 hooks, 102–115 μ long; testes in line; no cirrus whip reported; cirrus pouch 1 mm.; ovary with 15–20 lobes; from "a wild duck," Nebraska.

8. *lintoni* Lopez-Neyra, 1932. 13 by 0.53 mm.; holdfast 260 μ; suckers 75 μ; rostellum with 8 hooks, 90 μ long; testes in line; oncosphere 18 μ; in merganser (*Mergus serrator*), Massachusetts; see Linton (1927), Lopez-Neyra (1932b).

9. *tritesticulata* Fuhrmann, 1907. 10–250 mm. by 1.5 mm.; holdfast 170–320 μ; suckers 140 μ; rostellum with 10 hooks, 32–39 μ long; cirrus pouch 280 μ; cirrus spiny, without a whip; accessory sac present; eggs 45 μ; oncosphere 18 μ; in a wide range of anseriform birds; recorded in North America by Linton (1927).

10. *introversa* Mayhew, 1925. 50–80 by 1.5–2.0 mm.; holdfast 200 μ; suckers 80 μ; rostellum 50 by 70 μ, with 20 hooks, 17–20 μ long; testes in triangle; in *Anas spp.* Illinois.

11. *macrostrobiloides* Mayhew, 1925. 150 by 2.0–2.5 mm.; holdfast 125 μ; suckers 70 μ; rostellum 60 by 50 μ, with 20–21 hooks, 15–16 μ in length; testes in triangle; cirrus pouch crossing the poral osmoregulatory canals; eggs 23–30 by 17–28 μ; oncosphere 17–25 by 10–16 μ; in *Anas rubripes*, Illinois.

12. *parvisaccata* Shepard, 1943. 93 by 2.8 mm. up to 110 mm.; holdfast 141–157 μ in diameter; suckers 44 μ and 46 μ in two specimens; rostellum with 14–17 hooks, each about 11 μ long; testes in triangle; cirrus pouch 308–351 μ by 94–102 μ, clearly overlapping the poral canals; eggs not described; in pintail duck (*Dafila acuta tzitsihoa*), Oklahoma.

13. *sacciperium* Mayhew, 1925. 320 by 2 mm.; holdfast 200 μ; suckers 60 μ; rostellum 25 by 60 μ, with 18–22 hooks, 14–17 μ long; testes in triangle; cirrus pouch 300 μ; cirrus not spiny; without whip; egg 40 μ; oncosphere 16–32 by 13–18 μ; in *Nyroca marila*, Illinois.

14. *anceps* Linton, 1927. 295 by 4 mm.; holdfast 130–220 μ; suckers 75 μ; about 18 hooks, each 12 μ long; testes coarsely lobed, in line; cirrus pouch 280 by 56 μ; ovary lobed; yolk gland trilobed; in *Mergus serrator*, Massachusetts.

15. *coronula* Dujardin, 1845. 125–190 by 3 mm.; holdfast 198–220 μ; suckers 65–69 μ; rostellum 50–60 by 80–90 μ, with 24–26 hooks, 12–17 μ long; testes in line; cirrus pouch 300 μ; cirrus and accessory sac spinose; no cirrus whip; ovary deeply lobed; yolk gland massive and slightly lobed; widely distributed in anseriform birds; see Stiles (1896). Kingscote (1931) recorded an enzootic among ducks in Ontario due to this worm.

16. *mastigopraedita* Polk, 1942. 57–68 by 1.5 mm.; holdfast unknown; testes in triangle, one poral, two antiporal in rather characteristic arrangement, two of them being posteriorly located on opposite sides of the median line, with the third antero-sinistrad from them, all on a level dorsal to the osmoregulatory canals and ovary; cirrus pouch 770 by 90 μ, extending obliquely across the segment even into the next segment; cirrus spinose, with a cirrus whip; accessory sac prominent; ovary irregularly lobed; in pintail duck (*Dafila acuta tzitsihoa*), Oklahoma (Figure 270).

17. *stolli* Brock, 1941. 75 by 1.87 mm.; holdfast unknown; testes on a level dorsal to the female organs and rather uniformly arranged in a

triangle, two of them on opposite sides of the median line, with the third antero-sinistrad from them; cirrus pouch 308–504 μ by 97–127 μ, rather straight; cirrus spinose, with a whip; accessory sac large; ovary irregularly bilobed; eggs 30–45 μ in diameter; oncospheres 27–33 by 18–24 μ; in pintail duck (*Dafila acuta tzitsihoa*), Oklahoma (Figure 271). Comparison of the original descriptions of *mastigopraedita* and *stolli* suggest specific identity, but until such a conclusion is admitted by either author opinion must be reserved.

IN GULLS:

1. *ductilis* Linton, 1927. 18–25 mm. by 0.5 mm.; holdfast 240 μ; suckers 120 by 110 μ; rostellum much longer than the holdfast, with 10 hooks, each 39 μ long; testes in line; cirrus pouch 170 by 24 μ; cirrus not spinose; no cirrus whip; eggs 36 μ; in *Larus argentatus, Larus marinus*, Massachusetts.

2. *fryei* Mayhew, 1925. 115 by 0.8 mm.; holdfast 106 μ; with 10 hooks, each 17–19 μ long; testis arrangement variable; cirrus not spinose; no cirrus whip; cirrus pouch extending to the middle line; eggs 37–52 by 26–49 μ; oncosphere 28–40 by 23–40 μ; in *Larus glaucescens*, Washington State.

3. *lateralis* Mayhew, 1925. 250 by 1.6 mm.; holdfast 160 μ; suckers 75 μ; hooks 8, each 26–30 μ long; testes in triangle, all poral; cirrus pouch reaching the middle line; cirrus spinose; no cirrus whip; eggs 16–21 by 12–16 μ; oncospheres 10–16 by 11–12 μ; in *Larus glaucescens*, Washington State.

4. *neoarctica* Davies, 1938. 45 by 0.45 mm.; holdfast 140–170 μ; rostellar sac 117 by 58 μ; rostellum 64 by 64 μ, with 10 hooks, each 21–23 μ long; suckers 70 μ; cirrus pouch 360 by 32 μ; testes in triangle; cirrus spiny, very long (400 μ when everted), without whip; ovary bilobed, with lobes subdivided; vagina much convoluted; in *Larus argentatus, Larus maritimus*, Massachusetts; recorded as *Hymenolepis fusus* Krabbe by Linton (1927).

IN HERONS:

1. *ardeae* Fuhrmann, 1906. 123 by 3 mm.; holdfast 350 μ; suckers 80–90 μ; hooks 10, each 45 μ long; cirrus spinose, without whip; cirrus pouch 280 by 70 μ; testes crowded, in line, all poral to the ovary; ovary lobed; eggs 27 by 21 μ; in *Butorides striatus, Butorides virescens*, Massachusetts, by Linton (1927).

IN DIVERS AND GREBES:

1. *lintonella* Fuhrmann, 1932. *Nomen novum* for forms described by Linton (1927) as *Hymenolepis pachycephala*; length not given; holdfast 240 μ; suckers 100 by 90 μ; rostellum 290 μ long with 10 hooks, each 45 μ long; in *Colymbus grisegena*, Massachusetts.

2. *lobulata* Mayhew, 1925. 60–85 by 2.0–2.5 mm.; holdfast 600 μ; suckers 250 μ; rostellum 200 μ with a terminal enlargement 100 μ wide having marginal lobes, one for each hook; 8–11 hooks, 14–17 μ long;

testes in line; cirrus pouch crossing the poral canals; eggs 18–28 μ; oncospheres 7–12 μ; in *Podilymbus podiceps*, Michigan.

3. *rostellata* Abildgaard, 1790. 80–190 by 2 mm.; holdfast 370–560 μ; 10 hooks, 48–52 μ long; cirrus pouch extending aporally; eggs 27 μ; in *Colymbus grisegena*, Massachusetts, by Linton (1927).

4. *woodsholei* Fuhrmann, 1932. *Nomen novum* for specimens identified by Linton (1927) as *Hymenolepis podicipina* Szymanski; 60 by 0.4 mm.; holdfast 180–210 μ; suckers 80 μ; rostellum 80 μ, with 10 hooks, 30 μ long; in *Colymbus auritus, Colymbus grisegena*, Massachusetts.

We may note at this point that Joyeux and Baer (1950b), in a survey of the *Hymenolepis* species parasitic in grebes, reject *rostellata* on the grounds that it was established on material of doubtful purity and substitute for it a new species, *pseudorostellata*, founded upon Rudolphian material in the Vienna Museum. They reject also *lintonella*, as being a synonym of *Tatria biremis* Kowalewsky, 1904, and fail to mention *woodsholei*. They recognize only the following six species:

1. Blade *(manche)* of hooks shorter than base *(garde)*; hooks 14–17 μ long.... .... *H. lobulata* Mayhew
   Blade of hooks longer or as long as the base 2
2. Blade of hooks more or less equal to base 3
   Blade of hooks longer than base; hooks 29–38 μ long; cirrus pouch 176–280 μ .... *H. furcigera* (Krabbe)
3. Hook length below 30 μ 4
   Hook length above 30 μ 5
4. Cirrus pouch 184–225 μ; ratio to segment width 1:1.2 . . *H. capillaris* (Rud.)
   Cirrus pouch 80–100 μ; ratio to segment width 1:4.5 .... *H. capillaroides* Fuhrmann
5. Hooks 39–41 μ long; cirrus pouch 115–210 μ ...... *H. japonica* Yamaguti
   Hooks 49–57 μ; cirrus pouch 160–200 μ .... *H. multistriata* (Rud.)

IN POULTRY AND GAME BIRDS:

With rostellum unarmed .... *cantaniana, carioca*
With rostellum armed .... *microps*

1. *cantaniana* Polonio, 1860. 2–12 by 0.4 mm.; holdfast 120–160 μ; suckers 60–70 μ; rostellar sac 50–80 μ by 25–35 μ; no hooks; testes in variable arrangement; cirrus pouch 65–95 by 18–25 μ; eggs 45–60 by 35 μ; in galliform birds; larva of *Urocystis* type in scarabaeid larvae; cosmopolitan; first recorded in North America by Ransom (1909) (Figure 275).

2. *carioca* de Magalhaes, 1898. 30–80 by 0.5–0.7 mm.; holdfast 120–160 μ; suckers 70–90 μ; rostellar sac 110 by 30 μ; no hooks; testes in triangle; cirrus pouch 120–175 by 15 μ; eggs 55 by 40–45 μ; in galliform birds; larvae in Coleoptera; cosmopolitan; recorded in North America by Ransom (1909).

3. *microps* Diesing, 1850. 20–30 by 0.5 mm.; holdfast 16 μ; suckers 54 μ; hooks numerous, 16 μ long; testes in triangle; cirrus pouch 115–200 by 33 μ, reaching the middle line; eggs 70 μ; oncospheres 40 by 20 μ; in galliform birds; recorded by Jones (1935).

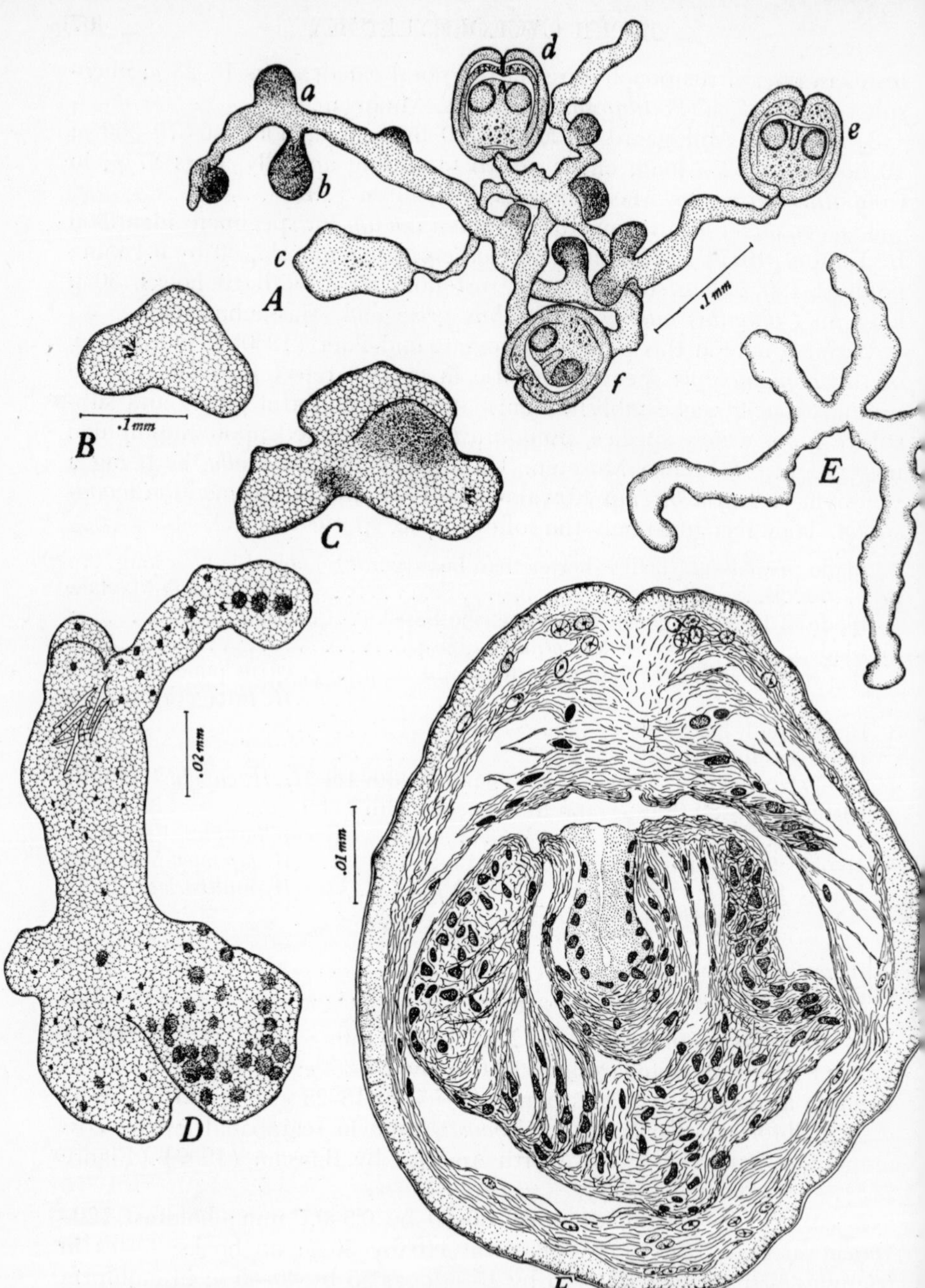

FIG. 275. Life cycle of *Hymenolepis cantaniana*. After Jones and Alicata, 1935. A. Larva from the beetle *Ataenius cognatus*. *a*, *b*, and *c*, developing cysticercoids; *d*, *e*, and *f*, apparently mature cysticercoids still attached to branching larval tissue. B to F. Larvae from *Ataenius cognatus*. B and C. 24 hours after initial infection. D. Young larva from a natural infection. E. Branching larva 8 days after initial infection. F. Completely formed cysticercoid, sectioned material.

IN PASSERIFORM BIRDS:

1. *corvi* Mayhew, 1925. 62 by 0.8 mm.; holdfast dimensions not given; suckers 80 μ; 8–10 hooks, 33–36 μ long; testes in triangle; cirrus pouch crossing poral canals; in *Corvus*, Illinois.

2. *farciminosa* Goeze, 1782. 120 by 1 mm.; holdfast with 10 hooks, 20–32 μ long; testes in triangle; cirrus pouch 120 μ; oncosphere 80 by 60 μ; recorded by Cannon (1939) in *Sturnus vulgaris*, Quebec, Canada.

3. *microcirrosa* Mayhew, 1925. 30–36 by 2 mm.; holdfast 1 mm.; rostellum 20 μ with 10 hooks, 12 μ long; testes in triangle; cirrus pouch crossing poral canals; cirrus not spinose; eggs 42–54 by 31–45 μ; oncospheres 31–35 by 21–38 μ; in *Turdus migratorius*, Illinois.

4. *passeris* Gmelin, 1790. 50–60 mm.; holdfast with rostellum retracted 0.256 mm. diameter; with rostellum protruded, 0.234 mm.; rostellum 53 μ in diameter, 85 μ in length; rostellar sac 228 μ; suckers 100 μ diameter; 10 hooks; testes in triangle; cirrus pouch 172 by 64 μ; cirrus not spinose; ovary large, markedly bilobed; oncospheres 79 μ; in *Passer domesticus*, Indiana; ref. Kintner (1938).

5. *planestici* Mayhew, 1925. 10–35 by 0.5–1.5 mm.; holdfast 200 μ; with 10 hooks, 14 μ long; testes in triangle; cirrus pouch crossing poral canals; eggs 42–56 by 28–42 μ; oncospheres 28–40 by 19–30 μ; in *Acridotheres tristis, Turdus migratorius*, Illinois.

6. *variabilis* Mayhew, 1925. 20–30 by 1 mm. with about 250 segments; holdfast 200 μ; suckers 80 μ; rostellum 20 μ; hook number not determined; hooks 20–22 μ long; testis arrangement variable; cirrus pouch one-third the segment width; in *Corvus brachyrhynchus*, Illinois.

Diorchis Clerc, 1903

With the holdfast bearing ten hooks. Longitudinal parenchymal muscles in two layers, the innermost comprising four dorsal and four ventral bundles. Testes two in number. Gravid uterus saclike, filling the whole medullary area. Genotype, *acuminata* Clerc, 1902.

The genotype was recorded (as *Drepanidotaenia acuminata*) from European anseriform birds (*Chaulelasmus streperus, Fuligula affinis, Mareca penelope, Nettion crecca*). Mayhew (1929) surveyed the genus and recognized ten species, seven of which he accepted as North American. Moghe and Inamdar (1934) added *magnicirrosa* from India. Johri (1939) added *alvedea* and *chalcophapsi* from India. Long and Wiggins (1939) added *nyrocae* from North America and recognized sixteen species of the genus. Schultz (1940b) surveyed the genus and listed twenty-three species, of which nine were North American. Jones (1944a, 1944b) added *reynoldsi* and *ralli* from North American hosts.

The eleven North American species have the following characteristics (see Figure 276):

1. *americana* Ransom, 1909. 100 by 1.5–2.0 mm.; holdfast 160 by 250 μ; suckers 100–120 μ; spinose; rostellar hooks 10, 65 μ long; testes 100–130 μ, 2 in number; ovary trilobed; yolk gland not lobed; uterus reaching slightly over the osmoregulatory canals; cirrus pouch 250–300 by 30–40 μ, reaching slightly beyond the middle line of the segment; cirrus 100 by

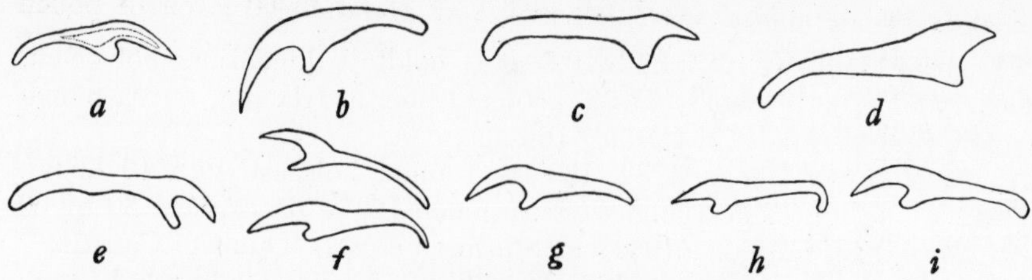

FIG. 276. *Diorchis spp.*, hooks. After Schultz, 1940b. *a, americana*; *b, bulbodes*; *c, microcirrosa*; *d, kodonodes*; *e, excentrica*; *f, longibursa*; *g, spinata*; *h, wigginsi*; *i, ransomi.*

1.5–2.0 μ; genital apertures unilateral, on the right margin; recorded by Ransom from *Fulica americana.*

2. *bulbodes* Mayhew, 1929. 60–70 by 0.7–0.8 mm.; a neck present; holdfast 200 μ wide; rostellum 200 μ long; hooks 65–70 μ long; ovary multilobed; uterus extending over the osmoregulatory canals; cirrus pouch reaching to the middle line; cirrus pyriform, stout, coarsely spinose; in *Anas platyrhynchos*, Louisiana.

3. *excentrica* Mayhew, 1925. 25–52 by 1.4 mm.; neck 190 μ; holdfast 175 μ wide; rostellum 75 by 70 μ; hooks 26–31 μ; aporal testis slightly poral to the ovary; ovary slightly aporal to the middle line, slightly lobed; cirrus pouch extending slightly over the poral osmoregulatory canal; cirrus large, conspicuous, spinose; in ruddy duck (*Erismatura jamaicensis*), Illinois.

4. *kodonodes* Mayhew, 1929. 156 by 1.5 mm.; rostellar hooks 17 μ; ovary with one to three lobes; uterus extending over the osmoregulatory canals; cirrus pouch reaching three-quarters across the segment; in *Querquedula discors*, Louisiana.

5. *longibursa* Steelman, 1939. 86.5 by 1.15 mm.; neck 880 μ long; suckers 115 μ; holdfast 240 μ; hooks 37 μ; ovary trilobed, 135–225 μ wide; testes 63–101 μ in diameter; cirrus pouch extending slightly over the poral canals; cirrus 200 by 7.5 μ with spinose basal bulb; in *Fulica americana,* Oklahoma.

6. *microcirrosa* Mayhew, 1929. 25–33 by 0.75 mm.; neck short; holdfast 250 μ; hooks 29–32 μ long; ovary median, shape variable; cirrus pouch reaching the middle line; cirrus 12–15 by 5 μ; genital apertures in the anterior fourth of the margin; in *Querquedula discors,* North Dakota.

7. *ralli* Jones, 1943. 50 by 0.7 mm.; holdfast 320 by 400 μ; suckers 125–140 μ, unarmed; rostellar hooks in a single circle, each hook 770 μ long; testes 150–250 μ in diameter; one aporal, the other poral to the ovary and yolk gland; vagina simple, not coiled, spinose, or dilated; cirrus pouch 250 by 65 μ; cirrus small, unarmed, 150 by 10 μ; oncospheric hooks dimorphic, two stout and four slender; in *Rallus elegans,* Virginia.

8. *ransomi* Schultz, 1940. *Nomen novum* for specimens identified as *Diorchis acuminata* by Ransom (1909); 35 by 0.65 mm.; holdfast 165 by 225–235 μ; rostellum 100 by 50 μ; suckers 80 μ, spinose all over; hooks

38 μ; testes 100–130 μ; ovary trilobed; yolk gland 45–60 μ; cirrus pouch reaching the middle line; cirrus 150 by 6–8 μ with a basal bulb, 14–16 μ, not spinose; in *Fulica americana*, Nebraska.

9. *reynoldsi* Jones, 1944. 7–10 by 0.15 to 0.30 mm.; holdfast 250 by 225 μ; rostellum small, about 70 by 150 μ when extended; rostellum in the form of a terminal sucker whose rim carries about 100 minute hooks; cirrus pouch 50–100 μ long; cirrus small, spinose, 12–15 μ; testes dorsal and poral to the ovary; vagina coiled tightly sixteen times in middle region; ovary somewhat bilobed, dorso-posterior to the compact yolk gland; in shrew, *Blarina brevicauda*, Virginia.

10. *spinata* Mayhew, 1929. 80–122 by 1.3 mm.; holdfast 250 μ; hooks 46–48 μ; ovary slightly lobed; cirrus pouch reaching across half to three-quarters of the segment width; cirrus conspicuous, 150 by 20 μ; in *Chaulelasmus streperus*, Louisiana.

11. *wigginsi* Schultz, 1940. *Nomen novum* for *Diorchis nyrocae* Long and Wiggins, 1935; 150–280 by 1 mm.; holdfast 289–348 μ; rostellum 210–252 by 98–112 μ; suckers 149 by 99 μ, spinose on margins; rostellar hooks 27 μ long; ovary trilobed, small; cirrus pouch 100–200 by 21–33 μ; cirrus not mentioned or figured; in *Nyroca valisneria*, Oklahoma (Figure 273).

Aploparaksis Clerc, 1903 (= *Monorchis* Clerc, 1902; *Haploparaxis* Clerc, 1903; *Haploparaksis*, Neslobinsky, 1911; *Skorikowia* Linstow, 1905)

Typically hymenolepidid in all details of structure but with only one testis. Genotype, *filum* Goeze, 1782.

Fuhrmann (1932) recognized five species from anseriform birds, eight from charadriiform birds, three from lariform birds, one from a passeriform bird. Yamaguti (1935) added *japonensis, scolopaci*, and *clerci* from Japanese hosts. Johri (1935) added *kamayuta* from Burma. Kintner (1938) proposed the name *linstowi* for *Aploparaksis fringillarum* Linstow. Joyeux and Baer (1939b) added *parafilum* from a charadriiform bird.

Ransom (1909) listed, as occurring in North America: *birulai* Linstow, 1905 in *Somateria spectabilis*; *brachyphallos* Krabbe, 1869 in *Aegialitis histicula, Calidris leucophaea, Pisobia damacensis, Pelidna alpina, Arquatella maritima*, and *Tringo canutus*; *cirrosa* Krabbe, 1869 in *Larus canus, Larus minutus*, and *Sterna hirundo*; *crassirostris* Krabbe, 1869 in *Haematopus ostralegus, Squatarola squatarola, Aegialitis histicula, Machetes pugnax, Pisobia damacensis, Pelidna alpina, Gallinago gallinago, Scolopax rusticola*, and *Lobipes lobatus*; *diminuens* Linstow, 1905 in *Phalaropus fulicarius*; *dujardinii* Krabbe, 1869 in *Sturnus vulgaris* and *Turdus musicus*; *filum* Goeze, 1782 in a wide range of charadriiform birds; *furcigera* Rudolphi, 1819 in *Nettion crecca* and *Anas platyrhynchos*; *penetrans* Clerc, 1902 in *Pisobia damacensis* and *Gallinago gallinago*; and *pubescens* Krabbe, 1882 in *Helodromas ochropus* and *Scolopax rusticola*. It may be noted that the main diagnostic features of the three closely related species *filum, clerci*, and *brachyphallos* have been discussed in detail by Davies (1940) from material in Wales.

Subfamily Fimbriariinae Wolffhügel, 1899, emended Webster, 1943

DESCRIPTION

Of the family Hymenolepididae. With a pseudo-holdfast. True holdfast small, with ten rostellar hooks. Body with or without distinct segmentation. Longitudinal osmoregulatory canals six to eleven. Inner layer of longitudinal muscles well developed. Outer layer rudimentary or absent. Testes three in number. Cirrus spinose. Genital apertures unilateral. Ovary reticulate and transversely elongated. Uterus reticulate. Type genus, *Fimbriaria* Froelich, 1802.

HISTORY

Wolffhügel (1898b) established a family, Fimbriariidae, upon a peculiar tapeworm from birds first recorded as *Taenia fasciolaria* by Pallas (1781) and as *Taenia malleus* by Goeze (1782). Froelich (1802) changed the generic name to *Fimbriaria*, with Goeze's term *malleus* used for the type species. Later (1894–1900) Wolffhügel's group was placed by Braun as a subfamily (of Taeniidae), but Lühe (1910a) restored it to family rank to include two species – *Fimbriaria fasciolaris* (Pallas) (= *Taenia malleus* Goeze), and *Fimbriaria plana*, a form which had been added to the genus by Linstow (1905a). Skrjabin (1914e) added to the family the new genus *Hymenofimbria*.

Lopez-Neyra (1931d), reviewing the family, stated his belief that *Fimbriaria* and *Hymenofimbria* must be regarded as monstrosities, synonymous respectively with *Diorchis* and *Hymenolepis*. He held that *Fimbriaria fasciolaris* is a degenerate form of *Diorchis acuminata*, whose pseudo-holdfast may appear anywhere along the worm even in regions swollen with eggs. Fuhrmann (1932) strongly criticized this review, believing that the Spanish author had been misled by badly preserved material of *Diorchis acuminata*. Fuhrmann placed Fimbriariinae as a subfamily of Hymenolepididae with two genera, *Fimbriaria* and *Fimbriaroides*. Wolffhügel (1936), in a detailed re-examination of his family, identified Linstow's species *plana* with *fasciolaris* and recognized species belonging to four genera – *Profimbriaria, Fimbriariella, Fimbriaroides*, and *Fimbriaria*.

Webster (1943) surveyed the subfamily, emended the subfamily and generic definitions, and rejected *Profimbriaria* on the grounds that it had been established for specimens (*Acanthocirrus multicanalus* Baczynska, 1914) which lacked holdfasts, pseudo-holdfasts, and gravid segments, and which had not been examined by Wolffhügel. He followed Baer (1937b) in placing *Cladogynia* – a form showing some similarities with Fimbriariinae – in Dilepididae, and followed Wolffhügel in rejecting *Hymenofimbria* Skrjabin, 1914.

NOTES ON GENERA

Fimbriaria Froelich, 1802, emended Webster, 1943

With a well-developed pseudo-holdfast containing no genital primordia. External segmentation lacking and internal segmentation obscure.

Longitudinal osmoregulatory canals six, in pairs in the medulla. Outer layer of longitudinal muscles lacking. Testes ovoid. Yolk gland slightly lobed. Ovary nonmetameric, reticulate (Wolffhügel claimed that at first the ovary is metameric, but both Fuhrmann and Webster denied this). Uterus a nonmetameric reticulum (at first metameric, according to Wolffhügel, never metameric according to both Fuhrmann and Webster). Genotype and only known species, *fasciolaris* Pallas, 1781 (Figure 277).

The genotype is a fairly common and cosmopolitan parasite of do-

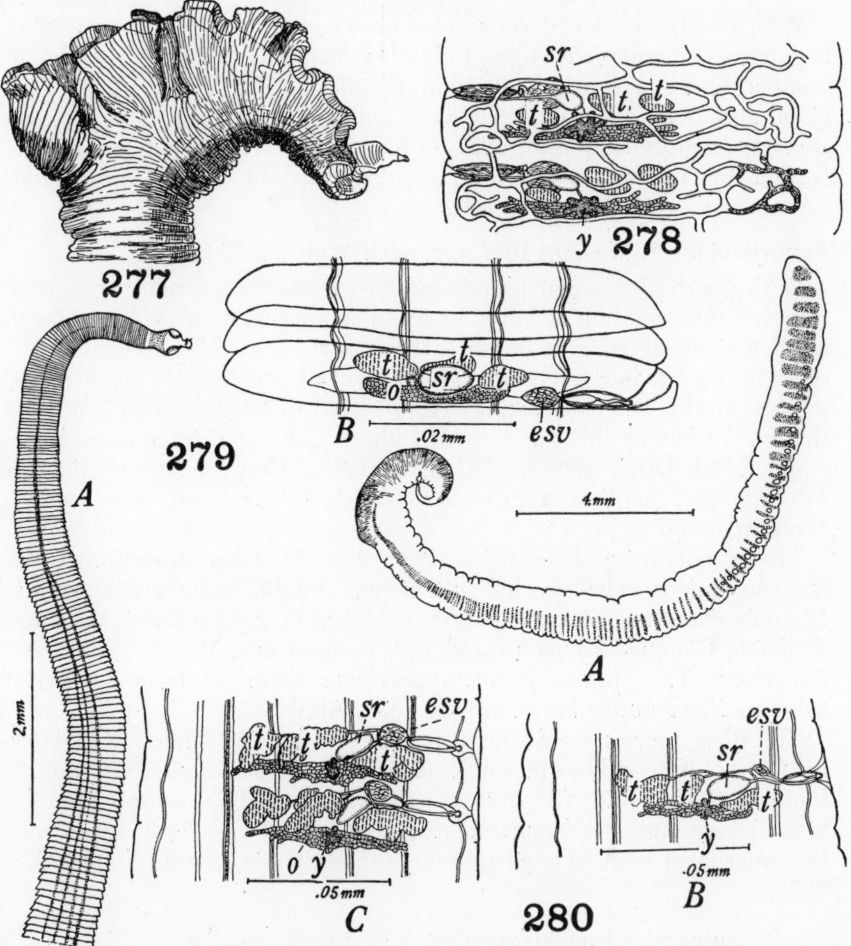

FIG. 277. *Fimbriaria fasciolaris,* holdfast and pseudo-holdfast. After Wolffhügel, 1900a. FIG. 278. *Fimbriaroides intermedia,* two segments showing genitalia and common reticulate uterus. After Fuhrmann, 1913a. FIG. 279. *Fimbriariella falciformes.* After Webster, 1943. A. Anterior region of the worm. B. Mature segment. FIG. 280. *Fimbriaroides* species. After Webster, 1943. A. Entire specimen of *F. haematopodis.* B. Mature segment of same. C. Mature segment of *F. lintoni. esv,* external seminal vesicle; *o, ovary; sr,* seminal receptacle; *t,* testes; *y,* yolk gland.

mestic and wild anseriform birds, its intermediate hosts being copepod Crustacea (*Diaptomus spp., Cyclops spp.*). In North America, Linton recorded it in *Mergus serrator* in Massachusetts; Wardle (1933) recorded it in *Mergus americanus* in British Columbia; Webster (1943) recorded it in *Anas rubripes*, New York State, and in *Haematopus bachmani* at Sitka, Alaska – an unusual host, perhaps, although Wolffhügel recorded it from a charadriiform bird (*Erolia maritima*) and four times from domestic fowls. For a detailed description, reference should be made to Wolffhügel (1898b, 1899a, 1936).

Fimbriariella Wolffhügel, 1936, emended Webster, 1943

With poorly developed pseudo-holdfast containing genital primordia. Segmentation complete. Longitudinal osmoregulatory canals eight in number. Outer layer of longitudinal muscles lacking. Testes lobate. Yolk gland also lobate. Uterus saclike, later netlike. Genotype and only known species, *falciformis* Linton, 1927 (Figure 279). The genotype was recorded by Linton, as *Fimbriaria falciformis*, in *Melanitta deglandi* (Anseriformes) in Massachusetts.

Fimbriaroides Fuhrmann, 1932, emended Webster, 1943

With poorly developed pseudo-holdfast containing genital primordia. External segmentation lacking but internal segmentation evident. Osmoregulatory canals nine or eleven – three in the cortical parenchyma, six or eight in pairs in the medulla. Outer layer of parenchymal longitudinal muscles rudimentary or lacking. Testes ovoid or lobate. Yolk gland star-shaped. Uterus originating as a reticulum. Genotype, *intermedia* Fuhrmann, 1913. Other species, *lintoni* Webster, 1943, *nomen novum* for *Fimbriaroides falciformis* Fuhrmann, 1932, in part; and *haematopodis* Webster, 1943.

The genotype was recorded from the Eurasian anseriform bird *Oedemia nigra*. The species *lintoni* was established for material in Linton's collection of material from *Melanitta perspicillata, Melanitta deglandi, Clangula hyemalis*, and *Fulica americana*, Woods Hole, Massachusetts. The species *haematopodis* was recorded from an oyster catcher, *Haematopus bachmani*, at Sitka, Alaska.

The three species are distinguished by Webster as follows: (1) *intermedia*: holdfast unknown; single layer of 140–150 longitudinal muscle bundles; testes ovoid; (2) *lintoni*: single layer of 80–90 muscle bundles; testes lobate; and (3) *haematopodis*: longitudinal muscles in two layers, the inner layer with 44 to 61 muscle bundles; testes lobate (Figures 278, 280).

Subfamily Pseudhymenolepinae Joyeux and Baer, 1935

DESCRIPTION

Of the family Hymenolepididae. With a single circle of hooks. Body strongly hyperapolytic, the segments detaching themselves before the appearance of the genital apertures. Three testes per segment. Female genitalia in front of the testes. Uterus breaking down into capsules each containing one egg. Adult in mammals. Type genus, *Pseudhymenolepis* Joyeux and Baer, 1935.

Pseudhymenolepis Joyeux and Baer, 1935

With the characteristics of the subfamily. Genotype and only known species, *radonica* Joyeux and Baer, 1935.

The genotype was found in a shrew, *Crocidura russula*, Haute Savoie, France: holdfast 112–130 μ in diameter; four suckers, circular, 47–54 μ in diameter; rostellum 90 μ long with a single circle of 14 hooks, each 21 μ long, with slightly bifid guards. This holdfast was probably seen by Dujardin (1845), who established for it the species *Taenia pistillum*. The mature segments, which break away and ripen away from the body, were also seen by Dujardin, who established for them the generic term *Proglottis*. This term, having been used as a collective term, cannot be used as a generic one.

Joyeux and Baer described the mature segments as resembling those of a *Hymenolepis* species, with three testes in a triangle, two anterior and one posterior, about 30 μ in diameter. Cirrus pouch 58–72 μ long by 11–14 μ in diameter, opening in the anterior fourth of the segment margin. A small external seminal vesicle and a large internal seminal vesicle present. Vagina opening behind the cirrus pouch and ending in a large seminal receptacle. Ovary horseshoe-shaped with the convexity anterior, multilobed. Yolk gland behind the ovary. Female genitalia in front of the testes.

All these characteristics could be those of a *Hymenolepis* species, but the uterus, instead of being saclike and persistent, breaks down immediately into egg-bearing capsules, each with a single egg and filling the entire medullary parenchyma. On this account, Joyeux and Baer established the new subfamily. The specific name refers to the fact that Dujardin made the first discovery at Rennes.

Family Dilepididae Railliet and Henry, 1909, emended Lincicome, 1939

DESCRIPTION

Of the order Cyclophyllidea. Small to medium-sized tapeworms with the holdfast having four suckers, which may or may not be armed with spines, and a retractable rostellum. Rarely, the rostellum is lacking, degenerate, or unarmed. Commonly, however, it has one, two, or several circles of rose-thorn hooks. Genitalia single or double per segment. Genital apertures unilateral, or alternating either regularly or irregularly. Testes usually more than four in number and commonly numerous. Gravid uterus a transverse, lobed sac, or replaced in function by a paruterine organ or by egg capsules containing one or more eggs. Parasitic in birds and mammals. Type genus, *Dilepis* Weinland, 1858.

HISTORY

The genus *Dilepis* was established by Weinland for *Taenia undula* Schrank, 1788 (= *Taenia angulata* Rudolphi, 1810), a parasite of passeriform birds in Eurasia and North America. As stated previously, Fuhrmann (1907a) made *Dilepis* the type genus of a family, Dilepinidae, a name which later was changed, on the suggestion of Railliet and Henry, to Dilepididae. Fuhrmann recognized three subfamilies of his family—Dilepininae, Dipylidiinae, and Paruterininae. For those cyclophyllidean parasites of birds which had one circle only of rostellar hooks and four testes or fewer he established, as we have seen, a separate family, Hymenolepinidae (later changed in name to Hymenolepididae).

In the meantime, considerable confusion for later workers was caused by a scheme put forward by Ransom (1909), in which Fuhrmann's two families were united as Hymenolepididae with *Hymenolepis* as type genus; further, making confusion worse confounded, Ransom fused Fuhrmann's subfamilies, Dilepininae and Dipylidiinae, into one subfamily, *Dipylidiinae.* Ransom thus recognized as subfamilies of his Hymenolepididae the groupings Hymenolepidinae, Dipylidiinae, and Paruterininae. The term "Dilepididae," when used in the following pages, must be understood, therefore, as referring to *Fuhrmann's grouping*, with some genera removed and some new ones added, however.

RECOGNITION FEATURES

The many points of resemblance between dilepidid and hymenolepidid tapeworms will be obvious from the definitions of the two families already given. Dilepidid forms differ from hymenolepidid forms mainly in the greater variability of arrangement of the rostellar hooks and the reproductive organs.

The rostellum may be absent, or it may be present but unarmed; but both conditions are uncommon. Commonly, the rostellum is prominent and has hooks scattered uniformly over its surface; or it may have one circle or two circles of such hooks, shaped like a rose thorn. Some authors prefer to speak of single crowns and double crowns of hooks, as the case may be. Whatever terms we give to the respective arrangements, it is still difficult to be certain in many cases that there is one circular row or two circular rows of rostellar hooks. The hooks of the second row may tend to crowd into the spaces between the hooks of the first row, so that unless there is a difference in hook length or hook shape between the two rows, their distinction is difficult. It is not uncommon to find one author describing the rostellum of a dilepidid species as single-crowned, while another author describes it as double-crowned.

"There seems to be no clear line of demarcation between forms with single and double rows of hooks. In the case of the species described here [i.e., *Monopylidium chandleri*], for instance, where all the hooks are of the same size and shape, but in which the alternate ones are set at slightly different levels on the rostellum, it is merely a matter of opinion whether or not they should be considered as being arranged in one or two rows." Moghe (1925).

"The number of rows of rostellar hooks affords a ready distinction in many cases where the difference in the sizes of the two rows of hooks and the levels of their insertions are sufficiently great; in others, these differences are so small as to be practically non-existent, e.g. *Anomotaenia platyrhyncha* (Krabbe, 1869): 'Uncinulorum 28 corona duplex, quorum anteriores longit. 0.027–0.028 mm., posteriores 0.025–0.026 mm.' and *Anomotaenia ericetorum*: 'Uncinulorum 32 corona duplex, quorum anteriores longit. 0.035 mm., posteriores 0.034 mm.'" Meggitt (1927).

With regard to the reproductive organs, the commonest arrangement is to find the central medullary parenchyma occupied by a cluster of female organs which comprise: (*a*) a transverse, irregularly rounded yolk gland; (*b*) a pear-shaped ootype, immediately in front of the yolk gland; and (*c*) a swollen, baglike, seminal receptacle to which, from the marginal cirro-vaginal atrium, there runs the vagina. On either side of this central complex and in front of the yolk gland and ootype, there is a group of scattered ovarian follicles, sometimes condensed into a lobed mass.

The testes lie usually behind and a little to each side of the female organs, but sometimes they are partly in front of them, or partly behind them, or even completely in front of them. The extremely convoluted sperm duct, and the vagina with it, may lie either dorsal to or between the poral osmoregulatory canals. In the young segment, the uterus is usually a short-stemmed T whose crossbar represents the uterus proper, while the short stem is the uterine duct. The uterus may persist in the gravid segment as a transverse sac, lobed or laterally branched, sometimes spherical or even longitudinal. In dipylidiine forms, however, the uterus disintegrates and is replaced in function by spaces in the parenchyma which contain one or more eggs. In paruterinine forms, the gravid uterus persists but the eggs pass from it into a paruterine organ, a dense area of medullary parenchyma, lying close to it.

While the complete life cycle is known for only a few dilepidid forms, such information as is available suggests a close resemblance between dilepidid and hymenolepidid life cycles. The larval stage is some form of cysticercoid, and the intermediate host is commonly an insect, adult or larval. Comment upon the details of such life cycles may be postponed, however, to the discussions of individual genera.

Subfamily Dilepidinae Fuhrmann, 1907

DESCRIPTION

Of the family Dilepididae. With the characters of the family but with the uterus saclike, persistent, more or less lobed or branched; in rare cases ring-shaped or reticulate.

The thirty-five recorded genera may be distinguished provisionally as follows:

KEY TO GENERA

1. Holdfast unknown; otherwise typically dilepidine, with testes in front of female organs; recorded once, from a vulture in India .... *Gidhaia*
   Holdfast known; with or without rostellum 2
2. Rostellum lacking; sucker margins spinose, arranged like the sticks of a fan .... *Cotylorhipis*

Rostellum present, armed or unarmed 3
3. Rostellum unarmed or *believed* unarmed 4
Rostellum armed with hooks 5
4. Rostellum unarmed, rudimentary; genital apertures alternating irregularly; cirro-vaginal atrium very deep; testes numerous ....*Unciunia*
Rostellum prominent, believed hookless; genital apertures unilateral, each with a sphincter muscle; testes five only ....*Pentorchis*
5. Rostellum with hooks distributed uniformly over surface; testes three ....*Echinorhynchotaenia*
Rostellum with hooks in circles 6
6. One row of hooks 7
Two or more rows of hooks 18
7. Hook row wavy or zigzag 8
Hook row circular 9
8. The zigzag row showing little regularity, the hooks originating at four or more levels; testes close to posterior segment border ....*Angularella*
The zigzag row more or less regular, the hooks originating definitely at three levels; testes extending dorsal to female organs, and on the poral side approaching the anterior segment border ....*Pseudangularia*
9. Testes fewer than seven 10
Testes more than seven 11
10. Testes seven or fewer, surrounding the female organs; cirrus pouch present ....*Clelandia*
Testes three; cirrus pouch lacking, replaced by complicated copulatory mechanism ....*Cladogynia*
11. Genital apertures unilateral 12
Genital apertures alternating 15
12. Genital atrium very deep and muscular ....*Valipora*
Genital atrium not unusually deep 13
13. Genital atrium subdorsal, the segments being subspherical in cross section ....*Trichocephaloidis*
Genital atrium marginal, the segments oval in cross section 14
14. Gravid uterus saclike; testes mainly behind female organs ....*Lateriporus*
Gravid uterus netlike, crossing osmoregulatory canals; testes few, 10–12, lateral, 6 or 7 on the antiporal side, 2 or 3 on the poral side of the female organs ....*Pseudandrya*
15. Genital apertures alternating *regularly*; testes twelve or more, close to posterior segment border ....*Amoebotaenia, Bakererpes*
Genital apertures alternating *irregularly* 16
16. Female organs near posterior segment border; testes in two groups, one on each side of female organs ....*Laterorchites*
Female organs approximately central 17
17. Gravid uterus saclike ....*Paricterotaenia*
Gravid uterus netlike ....*Krimi*
18. Genital apertures unilateral 19
Genital apertures alternating 20
19. Genital ducts dorsal to poral canals .....*Dilepis, Paradilepis, Proorchida*
Genital ducts between poral canals ....*Ophiovalipora, Dendrouterina, Gryporhynchus*
20. Genital apertures alternating *regularly* 21
Genital apertures alternating *irregularly* 22
21. Testes behind female organs; uterus strongly lobed ....*Liga*
Testes behind and before the female organs but also scattered dorsally

through the parenchyma; gravid uterus ringlike, surrounding the female organs . . . . *Cyclustera*

22. Testes in two groups, one before and one behind the female organs . . . . *Bancroftiella*

   Testes either entirely behind or to the sides of the female organs 23

23. Testes *behind* the female organs . . . . *Anomotaenia, Chitinorecta, Parvitaenia, Proparuterina*

   Testes *at the sides of* the female organs . . . . *Laterotaenia, Parorchites, Parvirostrum, Vitta*

NOTES ON GENERA

Gidhaia Johri, 1934

With the holdfast unknown. Segmentation distinct. Genital apertures alternating irregularly, each in the anterior half of the segment margin. Cirrus pouch very small, flask-shaped, 206 by 125 μ, not reaching the poral canals. Genital ducts dorsal to the poral canals. Testes 32–40, mainly in front of the female organs but with poral and antiporal groups on each side of them; stretching the full width of the medulla. Female organs central. Gravid uterus transversely elongated, with lateral extremities greatly subdivided. Genotype, *indica* Johri, 1934.

The genus and its genotype were established for material from a vulture, *Gyps indica*, at Lucknow, India. Despite the lack of a holdfast, the species was definitely identifiable as dilepidine and was sufficiently different, in Johri's opinion, from other known dilepidines to justify generic separation. Johri suggested also the inclusion of *Parvirostrum magnisomum* Southwell in this genus. Lopez-Neyra (1935a) regarded *Gidhaia* as synonymous with *Taufikia*, which genus he removed from Anoplocephalidae to Dilepididae, transferring to it Southwell's *Parvirostrum magnisomum*.

Cotylorhipis Blanchard, 1909

Without rostellum but with peculiar suckers, weakly muscular with membranous rims that can be extended in umbrella fashion due to the presence of long hooks arranged like the ribs of an umbrella or the sticks of a fan. Genital apertures alternating irregularly, each in the anterior angle of the segment margin. Genotype, *furnarii* Del Pont, 1906 (Figure 281).

This peculiar form is known only from Del Pont's scanty description of material from an Argentine passeriform bird, *Furnaria rufus*. No other species has been added.

Unciunia Skrjabin, 1914

The only rostellate but unarmed dilepidine known. Small, with rudimentary, hookless rostellum. Genital apertures alternating irregularly. Genital atria very deep. Basal collar of spines around cirrus, plus a single, strong, chitinous hook. Testes numerous, mainly behind ovary. Yolk gland transversely elongated and central. Uterus saclike, divided by septa into compartments. Genotype, *trichocirrosa* Skrjabin, 1914 (Figure 285).

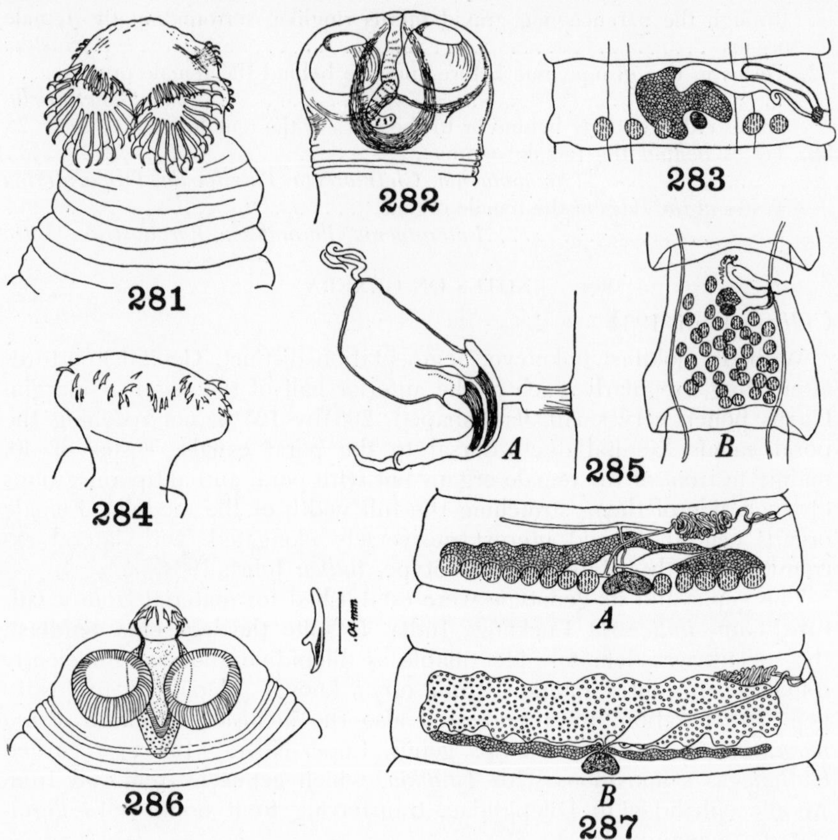

FIG. 281. *Cotylorhipis furnarii*, holdfast. After Blanchard, 1909. FIG. 282. *Echinorhynchotaenia tritesticulata*, holdfast. After Fuhrmann, 1910a. FIG. 283. *Pentorchis arkteios*, mature segment showing five testes. After Meggitt, 1927c. FIG. 284. *Angularella beema*, holdfast. After Clerc, 1906. FIG. 285. *Unciunia trichocirrosa*. After Skrjabin, 1914c. A. Genital ducts and genital atrium. B. Mature segment. FIG. 286. *Amoebotaenia setosa*, holdfast. After Burt, 1940a. FIG. 287. *Amoebotaenia sphenoides*. After Mönnig, 1928. A. Mature segment. B. Gravid segment.

The genotypic material came from an acciptriform bird, *Polyborus sp.*, in Paraguay. Woodland (1928b) added to the genus the species *sudanea* from a guinea fowl, *Numida ptilorhyncha*, in the Egyptian Sudan, but Baylis (1934b) believed the species identical with *Octopetalum longicirrosum* Baer, 1925, a paruterinine form. Moghe (1933) added *acapillicirrosa* from *Anas platyrhyncha* (domesticated) at Nagpur, India. Ortlepp (1938a) added *travassosi* from the kite, *Milvus migrans*, South Africa.

Pentorchis Meggitt, 1927

With the rostellum believed to be unarmed. Genital apertures unilateral, each with a sphincter muscle. Testes only five in number, placed close to the posterior segment border, and partly outside the osmoregulatory canals. Seminal receptacle well developed. Uterus saclike. Genotype, *arkteios* Meggitt, 1927 (Figure 283).

The genotype was recorded from a Malayan sun bear (*Ursus malayensis*) in Rangoon, Burma. Despite the uncertainty as to whether rostellar hooks are present or lacking, this form would seem definitely dilepidine in its lack of external seminal vesicle; yet the few testes, unilateral genital apertures, and short, broad segments suggest Hymenolepididae. Its poverty of testes link it with *Clelandia* (see below).

Echinorhynchotaenia Fuhrmann, 1909

With the rostellum in the form of a flat, rigid, very slender, chitinoid rod, armed only at the tip with very minute spines (see Southwell and Lake, 1939). Genital apertures unilateral. Genital ducts between the poral canals. Cirrus with both external and internal seminal vesicles. Testes few (3). Uterus saclike and lobed. Genotype, *tritesticulata* Fuhrmann, 1909 (Figure 282).

The genotypic material came from a pelican, *Plota rufa*, in Syria and North Africa. Southwell and Lake (1939) recorded it also from *Anhinga rufa rufa* in the Belgian Congo. A second species, *nana*, was recorded by Maplestone and Southwell (1922c) from the black swan (*Chenopsis atrata*) in Queensland, Australia. In most respects *Echinorhynchotaenia* would seem to be hymenolepidid rather than dilepidid in its affinities, and Szpotanska (1932) renamed the Maplestone-Southwell form *Hymenolepis southwelli*.

Angularella Strand, 1928 (= *Angularia* Clerc, 1906, preoccupied)

With the rostellum having an anterior disklike region, bearing a zigzag row of hooks, and a posterior globular region. Genital apertures alternating irregularly. Genital ducts dorsal to the poral canals. Testes numerous and close to the posterior border of the segment. Genotype, *beema* Clerc, 1906 (Figure 284).

The genotype occurs in hirundinid birds (swallows, martins) – *Clivicola riparia* and *Hirundo rustica* in Europe and Asia, and *Riparia riparia* (bank swallow) in North America (Ransom, 1909). Yamaguti (1940) added *taiwensis* from *Hirundo daucica striolata* and *ripariae* from *Riparia paludicola chinensis*, both in Formosa. The zigzag appearance of the crown is due to the hooks' originating at different levels, there being at least four such levels according to the interpretation placed by Burt (1938a) on Clerc's figure.

Pseudangularia Burt, 1938

With three rows of rostellar hooks giving the appearance of a zigzag crown. Genital apertures irregularly alternating. Genital ducts dorsal to the poral canals. Testes numerous, posterior and dorsal to the female organs. Internal and external seminal vesicles present. Vagina dilated, dorsal to the cirrus. Vagino-receptacular aperture surrounded by a dumbbell-shaped body interpreted by Burt as a double vaginal sphincter muscle. Uterus saclike and lobed. Genotype, *thompsoni* Burt, 1933.

The genotype was recorded from the Indian edible-nest swiftlet (*Col-*

localia unicolor unicolor) in Ceylon. A further species, *triplacantha* Burt, 1938, was also recorded from the same host species.

Clelandia Johnston, 1909

With a single crown of rostellar hooks. Genital apertures unilateral. Testes few, surrounding the female organs. Cirrus strongly spiny at the base. Uterus saclike. Genotype, *parva* Johnston, 1909 from a heron, *Xenorhynchus asiaticus*, Australasia.

Cladogynia Baer, 1937

With a single crown of hooks. Genital apertures unilateral. Genital ducts dorsal to the poral canals. Testes few (3). Neither external nor internal seminal vesicles. Cirrus pouch lacking, replaced by a copulatory apparatus formed of a strongly muscular ejaculatory duct to which runs a chitinous dart contained in a pocket which opens on a papilla into the genital atrium. Female glands very strongly branched. Ovary occupying the whole ventral face of the medulla, branching strongly and crossing the osmoregulatory canals ventrally. Uterus a fine network, dorsal to the ovary and, like it, crossing the osmoregulatory canals. Eventually the walls of the network coalesce under the pressure of the contained eggs. Genotype and only known species, *phoeniconaiadis* Hudson, 1934, recorded as *Hymenolepis phoeniconaiadis* from an African flamingo.

Valipora Linton, 1927

With a single crown of rostellar hooks. Genital apertures unilateral. Genital ducts between the poral canals. Genital atrium deep and muscular. Testes mainly behind the female organs. Gravid uterus saclike and strongly lobed. Genotype, *mutabilis* Linton, 1927 (Figure 288).

The genotype was recorded from the night heron (*Nycticorax nycticorax naevius*). A further species was recorded, as *parvispine*, by Linton from the common loon (*Gavia immer*); both in Massachusetts (Figure 289).

Trichocephaloidis Sinitzin, 1896

With a single crown of rostellar hooks. Segments subspherical in cross section so that the genital apertures appear dorso-lateral. Genital apertures unilateral. Genital ducts dorsal to the poral canals. Testes few, mainly in the posterior half of each segment. Terminal portion of the vagina dilated and dorsal to the cirrus pouch. Uterus saclike, with relatively few eggs. Genotype, *megalocephala* Krabbe, 1869 (Figure 290).

The genotype was recorded from a charadriiform bird, *Totanus calidris*, in Europe. Other species recorded are *birostrata* Clerc, 1906 and *charadrii* Lavroff, 1908 from Charadriiformes. Ransom (1909) reported *megalocephala* from a range of North American charadriiform birds.

Lateriporus Fuhrmann, 1907

With a single crown of hooks. Genital apertures unilateral. Genital ducts dorsal to the poral canals. Testes mainly behind the female organs. Gravid uterus saclike. Genotype, *teres* Krabbe, 1869.

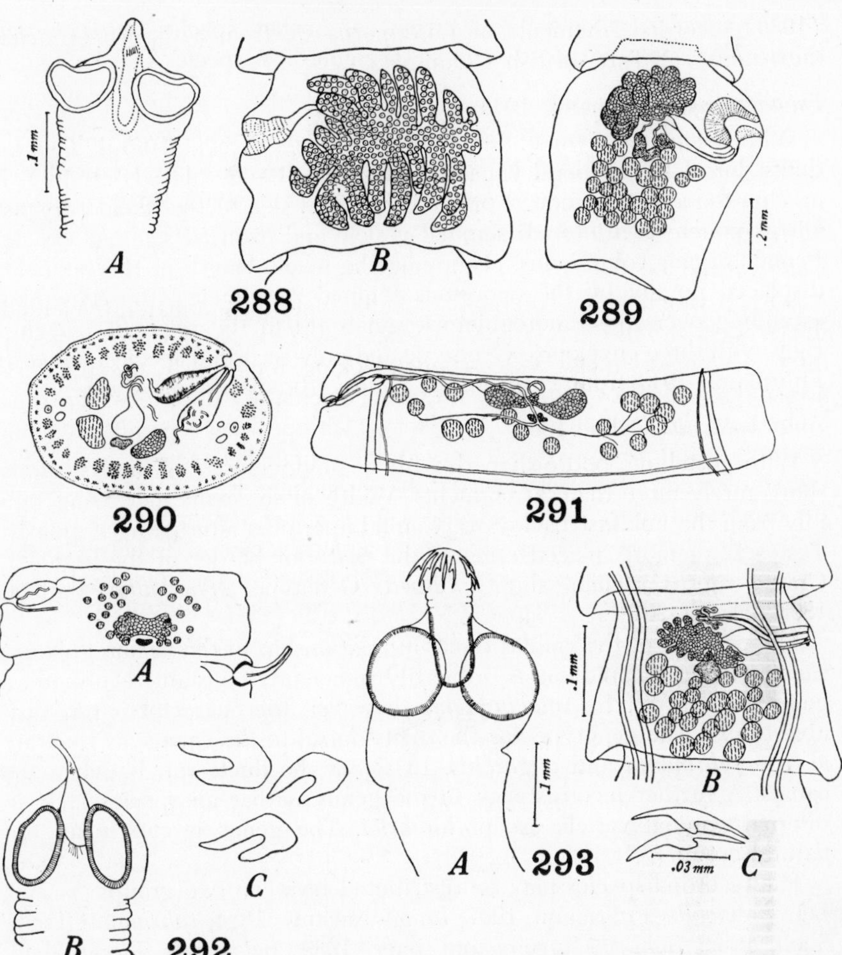

FIG. 288. *Valipora mutabilis.* After Linton, 1927. A. Holdfast. B. Gravid segment. FIG. 289. *Valipora parvispine*, mature segment. After Linton, 1927. FIG. 290. *Trichocephaloidis megalocephala*, cross section of a mature segment. After Clerc, 1902. FIG. 291. *Lateriporus biuterinus*, mature segment. After Fuhrmann, 1908c. FIG. 292. *Laterorchites bilateralis.* After Fuhrmann, 1908c. A. Mature segment. B. Holdfast. C. Rostellar hooks. FIG. 293. *Paricterotaenia cirrospinosa.* After Patwardhan, 1935. A. Holdfast. B. Mature segment. C. Rostellar hooks.

Ten species of *Lateriporus* have been recorded, mainly from ardeiform, anseriform, corsciiform, and lariform birds, but Southwell (1925c) recorded *fuhrmanni* from "a large, grey eagle" in northern Nigeria. Ransom (1909) reported the genotype from North American *Somateria mollissima, Harelda hyemalis*; and reported *biuterinus* from *Oidemia fusca, Cairina moschata, Dendrocygna autumnalis* (Figure 291). *Lateriporus geographicus* was recorded by Cooper (1921) from *Somateria v-nigra* at Bernard Harbour, N.W.T. (arctic Canada). Wardle

(1933) recorded fragments of *Lateriporus sp.* from a dipper (*Cinclus mexicanus*) at Taft, British Columbia.

Pseudandrya Fuhrmann, 1943

With a single crown of hooks. Genital apertures unilateral. Genital ducts dorsal to the poral canals. Testes few, 10–12, placed laterally, 6 or 7 on the antiporal side, 2 or 3 on the poral side of the female organs. Cirrus pouch with internal seminal vesicle and external seminal vesicle. Female organs voluminous, occupying the whole length of the segment, displaced porally by the enormous seminal receptacle. Uterus netlike, extending over the osmoregulatory canals up to the segment margins. Eggs with three envelopes. Genotype and only recorded species, *monardi* Fuhrmann, 1943 from *Paracynictis selousi*, Angola, West Africa.

Amoebotaenia Cohn, 1900

With rostellum bottle-shaped with a single crown of hooks. Body short, rarely more than 30 segments. Width of segments increasing rapidly from the holdfast backward. Genital apertures alternating regularly. Testes 12 or more, placed close to the posterior border of the segment. Gravid uterus saclike, slightly lobed. Genotype, *sphenoides* Railliet, 1892 (Figure 287).

The position of the genital ducts in relationship to the osmoregulatory canals among Dilepidinae is ordinarily sufficiently constant to provide a generic character. In *Amoebotaenia*, however, the character is too variable to use. The genotype has the ducts *dorsal* to the canals, as they are also in *fuhrmanni* and *oligorchis*. In *setosa* the ducts run between the canals. A further inconsistency in the genus is that all species lack an internal seminal vesicle except *lumbrici*. The genus is clearly an unnatural group.

The recorded species may be distributed between two groups:

1. *brevicollis* Fuhrmann, 1907; *brevis* Linstow, 1884; *fuhrmanni* Tseng Shen, 1932; *lumbrici* Joyeux and Baer, 1939; *pekinensis* Tseng Shen, 1932; *setosa* Burt, 1940; and *vanelli* Fuhrmann, 1907; all from charadriiform birds. Of these, *brevicollis, lumbrici, pekinensis, setosa*, and *vanelli* all possess 16 rostellar hooks and are distinguished only by size, number of segments, size of hooks, size of cirrus pouch, number of testes, size of testes, and size of oncospheres (see Burt, 1940a) (Figure 286).

2. *sphenoides* Railliet, 1892 in the domestic fowl in Australia, Brazil, India, Burma, Japan, western Europe, Italy, North America; and *oligorchis* (5 or 6 testes only) in the fowl in Japan (see Yamaguti, 1935). The anatomy of *sphenoides* has been described in detail by Meggitt (1914b). Its cysticercoid larva is believed to occur naturally in earthworms (*Allolobophora foetida, Pheretima peguana*). In Canada, Baker (1932) recorded *sphenoides* in fowls in Quebec.

Bakererpes Rausch, 1947

With a single crown of rostellar hooks. Genital apertures regularly alternating. Genital atrium large, surrounded by large muscular area and provided with spines. Cirrus pouch very large, extending across entire width of mature segment; relatively smaller in other segments. Cirrus spined. Vagina separated into parts by narrow constriction. Genital ducts passing between osmoregulatory canals. Rostellum well developed, armed with few hooks in single row. Testes numerous, posterior and lateral to ovary and yolk gland. Uterus develops sacculations which later break down, becoming single large sac in gravid segment. Small, weakly muscled cestodes with few segments, parasitic in birds. Genotype, *fragilis* Rausch, 1947.

The genotype has ten hooks and about eight segments and was recorded by Rausch from the eastern nighthawk (*Chordeiles minor minor*) in Ohio. Another species, *addisi*, was described from the same host in Texas by Webster (1948); it has twelve segments, eight rostellar hooks, and the ovary has several lobes rather than two as in *fragilis*.

Laterorchites Fuhrmann, 1932

With a single crown of rostellar hooks. Genital apertures alternating irregularly. Cirrus pouch with an external seminal vesicle but lacking an internal one. Cirrus spiny. Testes numerous, in two groups, one group on each side of the female organs. Female organs close to the posterior border of the segment. Gravid uterus saclike. Genotype and only known species, *bilateralis* Fuhrmann, 1908 from a grebe, *Podicipes dominicus* in Central America (Figure 292).

Paricterotaenia Fuhrmann, 1932

With a single crown of rostellar hooks. Genital apertures alternating irregularly. Genital ducts between the poral canals. Testes numerous, placed behind the female organs. Uterus saclike. Genotype, *porosa* Rudolphi, 1810.

Most of the species now regarded as paricterotaeniid were placed originally by Fuhrmann (1907a) in Railliet's genus *Choanotaenia*, but were separated from that genus by Railliet and Henry (1909) under the generic grouping *Icterotaenia*, and by Lühe (1910a) – presumably in ignorance of Railliet and Henry's suggestion – under the generic name *Parachoanotaenia*. However, the genotype chosen by Railliet and Henry for *Icterotaenia* was shown both by Cohn and by Skrjabin to be a composite of forms belonging, according to Fuhrmann (1932), to the genus *Anomotaenia*. Fuhrmann therefore suggested the establishment of a new generic term and a new genotype.

As defined by Fuhrmann (1932), the genus was a fairly large one, comprising about 40 species all from birds. Patwardhan (1935) added *cirrospinosa* from a "snipe" in India (Figure 293). Burt (1940a) redescribed *Taenia coronata* Creplin, 1829 and placed it within this genus, adding also from Ceylon material a species *tringa*.

The North American paricterotaeniids unfortunately have not been reviewed. Ransom (1909), under the generic name *Choanotaenia*, reported the species *borealis, coronata, dodecacantha, inversa, laevigata, paradoxa, parina, porosa, stellifera*, and *sternina*; under the generic name *Monopylidium*, the species *macracantha*; and under *Anomotaenia*, the species *aegyptica* and *borealis*; all from North American hosts. Cooper

(1921) reported *passerellae*; Linton (1927) reported *ransomi*. Webster (1948) has recorded from the eastern nighthawk (*Chordeiles minor minor*) in Texas the species *pauciannulata* Fuhrmann, 1908, known previously only from *Podager nacunda* in Brazil. A survey of this genus among North American hosts is urgently needed.

Krimi Burt, 1944

With a single crown of rostellar hooks. Small forms with few segments. Genital apertures alternating irregularly. Genital ducts between the poral canals. Testes numerous and posterior. Uterus netlike and persistent. Genotype, *chrysolaptis* Burt, 1944 from *Chrysolaptes guttacristatus stricklandi* (Layard's woodpecker), Ceylon.

Dilepis Weinland, 1858

With a double crown of rostellar hooks. Genital apertures unilateral. Genital ducts dorsal to the poral canals. Testes numerous, behind the markedly bilobed ovary and irregularly rounded yolk gland. Gravid uterus saclike and lobed. Genotype, *undula* Schrank, 1788 (Figure 295).

The genus was established for *Taenia undula* Schrank, 1788 (= *Taenia angulata* Rudolphi, 1810), a common parasite of passeriform

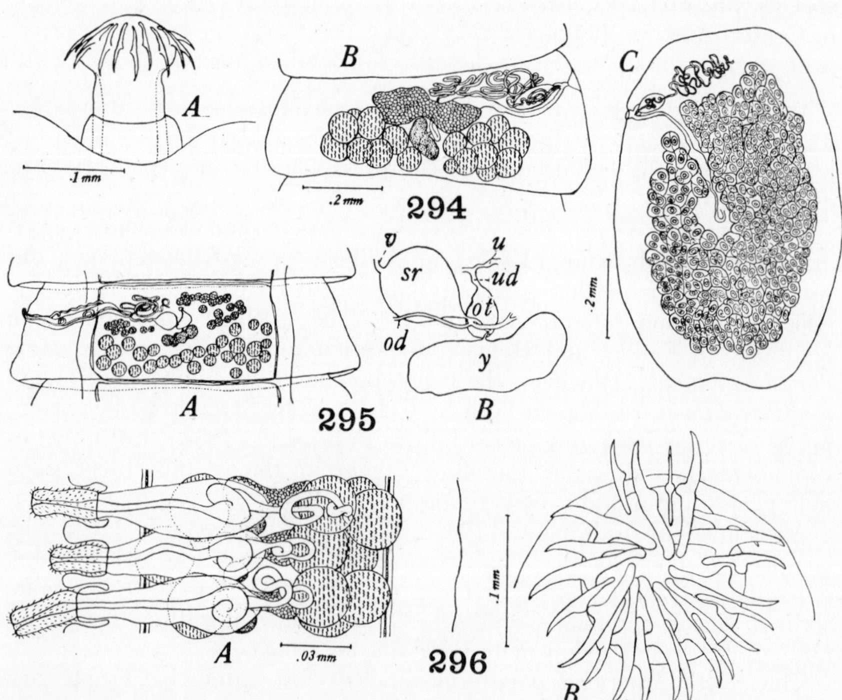

FIG. 294. *Liga brasiliensis*. After Ransom, 1909. A. Holdfast with rostellum extended. B. Mature segment. C. Gravid segment. FIG. 295. *Dilepis undula*. After Davies, 1935. A. Mature segment. B. Female genitalia. *od*, oviduct; *ot*, ootype; *sr*, seminal receptacle; *u*, uterus; *ud*, uterine duct; *v*, vagina; *y*, yolk gland. FIG. 296. *Paradilepis brevis*. After Burt, 1940a. A. Mature segments. B. Apex of holdfast.

birds in Europe, Asia, and North America. Its characteristics have been fully described by Nitsche (1873), Volz (1900), Rosseter (1906a), and Davies (1935). Other species attributed to the genus have been check-listed by Polk (1942a), who recognized 45 species as valid. Of these the following are North American: *hilli* Polk, 1941 in ciconiiform birds, Oklahoma; *transfuga* Krabbe, 1869, also in ciconiiform birds; and *undula* Schrank, 1788, recorded by Chapin (1926) in Washington, D.C. (as *Southwellia ransomi*) from *Turdus migratorius* (see Figure 307).

Paradilepis Hsü, 1935

With a double crown of rostellar hooks. Genital apertures are unilateral. Genital ducts are dorsal to the poral canals. Testes are few (4). Cirrus pouch is without an external seminal vesicle. Genotype, *duboisi* Hsü, 1935.

The genotype was found in a cormorant, *Phalacrocorax capillatus*, at Peiping. Hsü also placed within the genus the species *scolecina* Rudolphi, 1819. However, Joyeux and Baer (1935) believed *duboisi* to be identical with *scolecina*, in which case *scolecina* should be the genotype. These authors described this form as embedded deeply in the host gut wall, the holdfast enclosed in a saclike diverticulum of the gut wall in such a way that specimens collected are commonly without holdfasts. A similar habit is shown by *Oligorchis delachauxi* of Fuhrmann, and close comparison showed *delachauxi* (from African specimens of *Phalacrocorax africanus*) to be identical with *Dilepis scolecina* Joyeux and Baer *nec.* Rudolphi, 1819.

Yamaguti (1940) not only obtained the adult form of *Paradilepis scolecina* from *Phalacrocorax carbo hanedae* in Japan but also obtained its cysticercoid from *Gnathopogon elonagus caerulescens.* Joyeux and Baer (1935d) recognized as valid species of *Paradilepis* the following: *scolecina* Rudolphi, 1819; *delachauxi* Fuhrmann, 1909; *macracantha* Joyeux and Baer, 1935; and probably *longivaginosus* Mayhew, 1925 (= *Oligorchis*). To these, Burt (1940a) added *brevis* from *Phalacrocorax fascicollis* in Ceylon (Figure 296).

Joyeux and Baer (1950a) have added to the genus the species *urceus* Wedl, 1855. This is the form described previously under the names *Dilepis urceus* (Wedl) Fuhrmann, 1908; *Hymenolepis urceus* (Wedl) Meggitt, 1927; *Hymenolepis multihamata* Meggitt, 1927; *Oligorchis hieraticos* Johri, 1934; and *Meggittiella multihamata* (Meggitt) Lopez-Neyra, 1942. Surveying the genus *Paradilepis* as a whole, Joyeux and Baer accept six valid species:

1. *Paradilepis delachauxi* (Fuhrmann, 1909b) = *Dilepis scolecina* Joyeux and Baer, 1928 not Rudolphi, 1819; *Paradilepis lepidocolpos* Burt, 1936. Hosts: *Haliaëtor africanus* (Gm.), *Haliaëtor niger* (Vieill.).
2. *Paradilepis kempi* (Southwell, 1921d) = *Dilepis kempi* Southwell, 1921; *Hymenolepis kempi* (Southwell) Mayhew, 1925; *Oligorchis burmaensis* Johri, 1941; *Meggittiella kempi* (Southwell) Lopez-Neyra, 1942. Hosts: *Haliaëtor pygmaeus* (Pall.), *Haliaëtor niger* (Vieill.).
3. *Paradilepis macracantha* Joyeux and Baer, 1936 = *Dilepis dela-*

chauxi Joyeux and Baer, 1928 not Fuhrmann, 1909. Host: *Haliaëtor africanus* (Gm.).

4. *Paradilepis scolecina* (Rudolphi, 1819) = *Paradilepis duboisi* Hsü, 1935; *Paradilepis brevis* Burt, 1940. Hosts: *Phalacrocorax carbo* L., *Ph. capillatus* (Temm. and Schleg.), *Ph. fuscicollis* Stephens, *Haliaëtor africanus* (Gm.).

5. *Paradilepis simoni* Rausch, 1949. Host: *Pandion haliaetus carolinensis* (Gm.).

6. *Paradilepis urceus* (Wedl, 1855) = *Dilepis urceus* (Wedl) Fuhrmann, 1908; *Hymenolepis urceus* (Wedl) Meggitt, 1927; *Hymenolepis multihamata* Meggitt, 1927; *Oligorchis hieraticos* Johri, 1934; *Meggittiella multihamata* (Meggitt) Lopez-Neyra, 1942. Hosts: *Platalea leucorodia* L., *Plegadibis falcinellus* (L.), *Milvus cinellus* (L.), *Milvus migrans aegyptius* (Gm.), *Milvus migrans govinda* Sykes.

Joyeux and Baer (1950a) suggest the following key to the species of *Paradilepis*:

1. Length of strobila not exceeding 10 mm. 2
   Length of strobila exceeding 10 mm. 3
2. Number of testes usually 3, exceptionally 4 . . . . *urceus*
   Number of testes usually 4 . . . . *scolecina*
3. Large hooks more than 300 μ in length . . . . *macracantha*
   Large hooks less than 300 μ in length 4
4. Number of rostellar hooks 20–22 5
   Number of rostellar hooks 36 . . . . *simoni*
5. Small hooks 135 μ in length; 3 testes . . . . *kempi*
   Small hooks 80–87 μ in length; 5 testes . . . . *delachauxi*

Proorchida Fuhrmann, 1908

With a double crown of rostellar hooks. Genital apertures unilateral. Genital ducts dorsal to the poral canals. Testes in front of the female organs. Gravid uterus saclike, believed strongly lobed. Genotype, *lobata* Fuhrmann, 1909 from an ardeiform bird *Cancroma cochlearis* in Columbia, Brazil, Guiana (South America).

Ophiovalipora Hsü, 1935

With a double crown of rostellar hooks. Genital apertures unilateral. Genital ducts between the poral canals. Testes numerous, dorsal to the female organs and almost surrounding them except on the poral side. Gravid uterus saclike, lobed, filling the whole medulla. Ventral osmoregulatory canal normal in position in the poral half of the segment, dorsal to the true dorsal canal in the antiporal half of the segment. Genotype, *houdemeri* Hsü, 1935 from a snake, *Elaphe carinata*, in Nanking, China, the only dilepidid form recorded from other than a bird or mammal.

Dendrouterina Fuhrmann, 1912, emended Olsen, 1937

With a double crown of rostellar hooks. Large osmoregulatory canal dorsal on one side of the segment and ventral on the other. Genital apertures unilateral. Genital ducts between the poral canals. Cirrus armed. Testes few to numerous, posterior to, or posterior and lateral to, the ovary. Uterus present in young segments, a simple, transversely elongated sac, or horseshoe-shaped, the latter shape forming a reticulum which extends laterally over the osmoregulatory canals. Genotype, *herodiae* Fuhrmann, 1912.

The genotype was recorded from the little egret (*Herodias garzetta*) in Africa. Johnston (1916a) believed the genus to be identical with *Bancroftiella* Johnston, 1911, but both Meggitt (1924a) and Olsen (1937a, 1937b) believed the two forms to be distinct. Olsen stressed the fact that the testes in *Bancroftiella* are divided between two fields, an anterior and a posterior, separated by the ovary, while in *Dendrouterina* they form a single group posterior and lateral to the ovary. Further, in *Bancroftiella* the ventral osmoregulatory canals are large, the dorsal ones small; in *Dendrouterina* the ventral poral canal is large, the dorsal one small; the ventral antiporal canal is small, the dorsal one large. Olsen also found the genital apertures unilateral in *Dendrouterina*, but alternating in *Bancroftiella.*

The life cycle of dendrouterinid species is unknown. Olsen (1939) found minute cysticercoids with hooklets characteristic in size and shape of *Dendrouterina nycticoracis* in the gall bladder of the fish *Ameiurus melas* in Minnesota, suggesting that a water flea is probably the first intermediate host.

To the genus Meggitt (1933) added the species *fovae* from the Indian tree-pie (*Dendrocitta rufa*), a passeriform bird. Olsen (1937a, 1937b) added *nycticoracis* from *Nycticorax nycticorax hoaetli* in Minnesota, and *lintoni* from *Butorides virescens* in Massachusetts. He distinguished the four known species as follows:

1. Testes small, numerous (44); mature uterus horseshoe-shaped, with numerous branches; cirrus pouch short . . . . *herodiae*
   Testes large, not more than 15 2
2. Seventy hooks on the rostellum; cirrus pouch short and thick, extending mesad to the poral canals; testes 11–15 . . . . *fovae*
   Hooks not more than 20; cirrus pouch long and slender, extending mesad to the middle line of the segment 3
3. Small hooks, 10–13 μ – i.e., about one-third the length of the large ones with the end of the shaft bent sharply ventrad; testes 9 to 10; longitudinal parenchymal muscle bundles about 95 in number. . *nycticoracis* (Figure 297)
   Small hooks 18 μ long, more than one-half the length of the large ones with the entire shaft bent sharply dorsad; testes 7 to 8; longitudinal muscle bundles 50 in number . . . . *lintoni*

Recently Rausch (1948a, 1949a) has added the species *botauri n. sp.* from *Botaurus l. lentiginosus* and *Ixobrychus e. exilis* in Ohio. This new form has a well-developed holdfast about 165 μ in diameter, with a short rostellum carrying 2 rows of hooks, 18 in number. Revising the genus, Rausch would transfer *lintoni* and *nycticoracis* to the genus *Dilepis*, leaving only *herodiae* (genotype) and *botauri.* The species *botauri* differs from *herodiae* in the formation of the uterus and in having more testes.

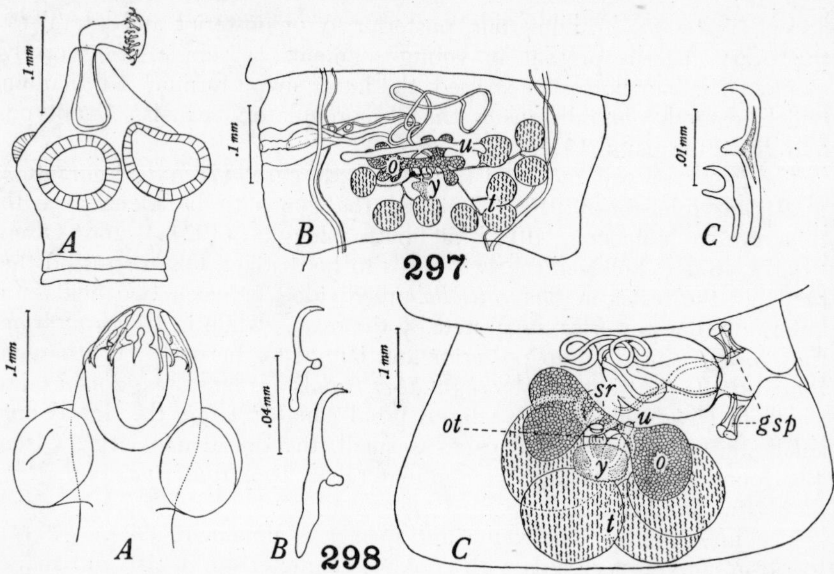

FIG. 297. *Dendrouterina nycticoracis*. After Olsen, 1939a. A. Holdfast. B. Mature segment. C. Rostellar hooks. FIG. 298. *Gryporhynchus tetrorchis*. After Hill, 1941. A. Holdfast. B. Rostellar hooks, front and rear rows. C. Mature segment. *gsp*, genital spines; *o*, ovary; *ot*, ootype; *sr*, seminal receptacle; *t*, testes; *u*, uterus; *y*, yolk gland.

Gryporhynchus Nordmann, 1832 (=*Acanthocirrus* Fuhrmann, 1907, Ransom, 1909)

With a double crown of rostellar hooks. Genital apertures unilateral. Genital ducts between the poral canals. Cirrus with one or two pairs of hooks at its base, placed in special pockets. Testes few. Gravid uterus saclike. Genotype, *pusillus* Nordmann, 1832.

The genotype (=*Taenia macropeos* Wedl, 1855) was recorded from a southeastern Asiatic heron, *Ardeola grayi*. Another species, *cheilancristota* Wedl, 1855, was added to the genus by Ransom (1909). A third species, *macrorostratus* Fuhrmann, 1903 from the passeriform bird *Anthus pratensis* (Africa, Europe), was also added by Ransom (1909). The first record from the Western Hemisphere was apparently the species *tetrorchis* (Figure 298) established by Hill (1941) for material from the great blue heron (*Ardea herodias herodias*) in Oklahoma. This North American species is distinctive in having only four testes, in its relatively shorter cirrus pouch (75 by 45 μ), in the U shape of the gravid uterus, and in its New World distribution. Further, it is considerably larger than *pusillus*, considerably smaller than *cheilancristota*, and distinct from *macrorostratus* in having four instead of two genital spines.

Liga Weinland, 1857

With a double crown of hooks. Small forms with few segments. Genital apertures alternating *regularly*. Genital ducts dorsal to the poral canals. Testes behind the female organs. Gravid uterus strongly lobed.

Some species have minute spines on the sucker margins (see Dollfus, 1934b). Genotype, *brasiliensis* Parona, 1901 (Figure 294).

Liga was established by Weinland for a form which he called *Liga punctata*, found by him in the golden-winged woodpecker (*Colaptes auratus*) in North America. What appears to have been this form was recorded later by Parona (1901) as *Fuhrmannia brasiliensis* in a species of woodpecker (*Picus*) in Brazil. The identity of Parona's form with that of Weinland was established by Ransom (1909), who obtained material agreeing with Weinland's somewhat meager description from a golden-winged woodpecker in Maryland. The specific name *punctata* having been pre-empted by Rudolphi (1802) for a form now referred to as *Bothriocephalus scorpii*, Weinland's term is a homonym and must be replaced by the next available name, which is *brasiliensis* Parona.

The genus has been surveyed by Szpotanska (1931b). Five species are recognized: *alternans* Cohn, 1900 and *facile* Meggitt, 1927 from charadriiform birds; *brasiliensis* Parona, 1901 from piciform birds; *frigida* Meggitt, 1927 from cypseliform birds; and *gallinulae* Beneden, 1858 from the Old World ralliform bird, *Gallinula chloropus*.

Cyclustera Fuhrmann, 1901

With a double crown of rostellar hooks. Genital apertures alternating irregularly. Genital ducts between the poral canals. Sperm duct and vagina joining to form a muscular common genital canal. Testes dorsal throughout the medulla. Uterus ringlike, surrounding the female organs. Genotype, *capito* Rudolphi, 1819.

The genotype was recorded (as *Taenia capito* Rudolphi, 1819) from a heron, *Pseudotantalus ibis*, in Madagascar. A second species, *fuhrmanni* Clerc, 1906, was recorded from a bittern, *Botaurus stellaris*, in Russia.

Bancroftiella Johnston, 1911

With a double crown of hooks. Genital apertures alternating *irregularly*. Genital ducts between the poral canals. Testes numerous, in two groups, one in front of, one behind, the female organs. Uterus saclike, with its cavity subdivided by numerous septa. Genotype, *tenuis* Johnston, 1911.

The genotype was recorded from a kangaroo (*Macropus ualabatus*) in Victoria, Australia. Johnston added a second species, *ardeae*, from a heron, *Nycticorax sp.*; a third species, *glandularia* Fuhrmann, 1905, also came from an Australasian heron, *Herodias timorensis*. Meggitt (1933) added a fourth species, *forna*, from the charadriiform bird *Tringa hypoleuca* in the Calcutta Zoo.

Anomotaenia Cohn, 1900

With a double crown of hooks. Genital apertures alternating irregularly. Genital ducts between the poral canals. Testes mainly behind the female organs. Uterus saclike. Genotype, *microrhyncha* Krabbe, 1869.

The genus is a large one. Fuhrmann (1932) recognized 64 species. Joyeux and Timon-David (1934a) added *passerum* from *Turdus merula*;

Yamaguti (1935) added *nycticoracis* from a heron *Nycticorax nycticorax nycticorax* in Japan; Davies (1938b) added *gallinaginis* from a snipe in Wales (Figure 299).

Ransom (1909) recorded the following species as occurring in North America:

1. In alciform birds: *campylacantha* Krabbe, 1869 in *Cepphus grylle*; *micracantha* Krabbe, 1869 in *Pagophila alba, Rissa tridactyla, Larus hyperboreus, Larus marinus, Larus canis, Cepphus grylle*; *sociabilis* Ransom, 1909 in *Uria troile*; and *tordae* Fabricius, 1780 in *Uria troile, Alca torda.*

2. In charadriiform birds: *arionis* Siebold, 1850 in *Totanus melanoleucus, Totanus flavipes, Helodromas ochropus*; *bacilligera* Krabbe, 1869 in *Gallinago gallinago, Scolopax rusticola*; *cingulata* Linstow, 1905 in *Pelidna alpina*; *citrus* Krabbe, 1869 in *Gallinago gallinago*; *clavigera* Krabbe, 1869 in *Arenaria interpres, Pisobia damacensis, Pelidna alpina, Tringa canutus*; *ericetorum* Krabbe, 1869 in *Charadrius apricarius*; *globulus* Wedl, 1856 in *Helodromas ochropus, Machetes pugnax*; *microphallos* Krabbe, 1869 in *Vanellus vanellus, Pisobia damacensis*; *microrhyncha* Krabbe, 1869 in *Charadrius apricarius, Aegialitis histicula, Aegialitis dubia, Machetes pugnax*; *nymphaea* Schrank, 1790 in *Numenius borealis, Numenius phaeopus, Bartramia longicauda*; and *platyrhyncha* Krabbe, 1869 in *Totanus totanus, Pisobia damacensis.*

3. In cypseliform birds: *cyathiformis* Froehlich, 1791 in *Riparia riparia.*

4. In lariform birds: *larina* Krabbe, 1869 in *Rissa tridactyla, Larus hyperboreus*; *micracantha* in *Rissa tridactyla, Larus hyperboreus, Larus maritima, Larus canis.*

5. In passeriform birds: *borealis* Krabbe, 1869 in *Motacilla alba, Plectrophenax nivalis*; *constricta* Molin, 1858 in *Turdus musicus, Pica pica, Corvus ossifraga, Corvus brachyrhynchus, Corvus corax*; *hirundina* Fuhrmann, 1907 in *Riparia riparia*; and *trigonocephala* Krabbe, 1869 in *Saxicola oenanthe.*

6. In ralliform birds: *pyriformis* Wedl, 1869 in *Crex crex.*

Chitinorecta Meggitt, 1927

With a double crown of rostellar hooks. Body short. Genital apertures alternating irregularly. Genital ducts between the poral canals. Testes partly cortical. Ovary strongly lobed. Uterus deeply lobed. Genotype, *agnosta* Meggitt, 1927.

The host was given as a "Spornkubitz" (presumably the charadriiform bird *Holopterus spinosus*) in Egypt. The extension of the testes and ovary into the cortex would seem to set this peculiar form apart from all known dilepidids.

Parvitaenia Burt, 1940

With a double crown of rostellar hooks. Genital apertures alternating irregularly. An extremely small form (1.1 to 1.7 by 0.15 to 0.17 mm.), perhaps the smallest tapeworm to be recorded from birds. Testes few (7–9), posterior to the female organs but tending to extend to the side

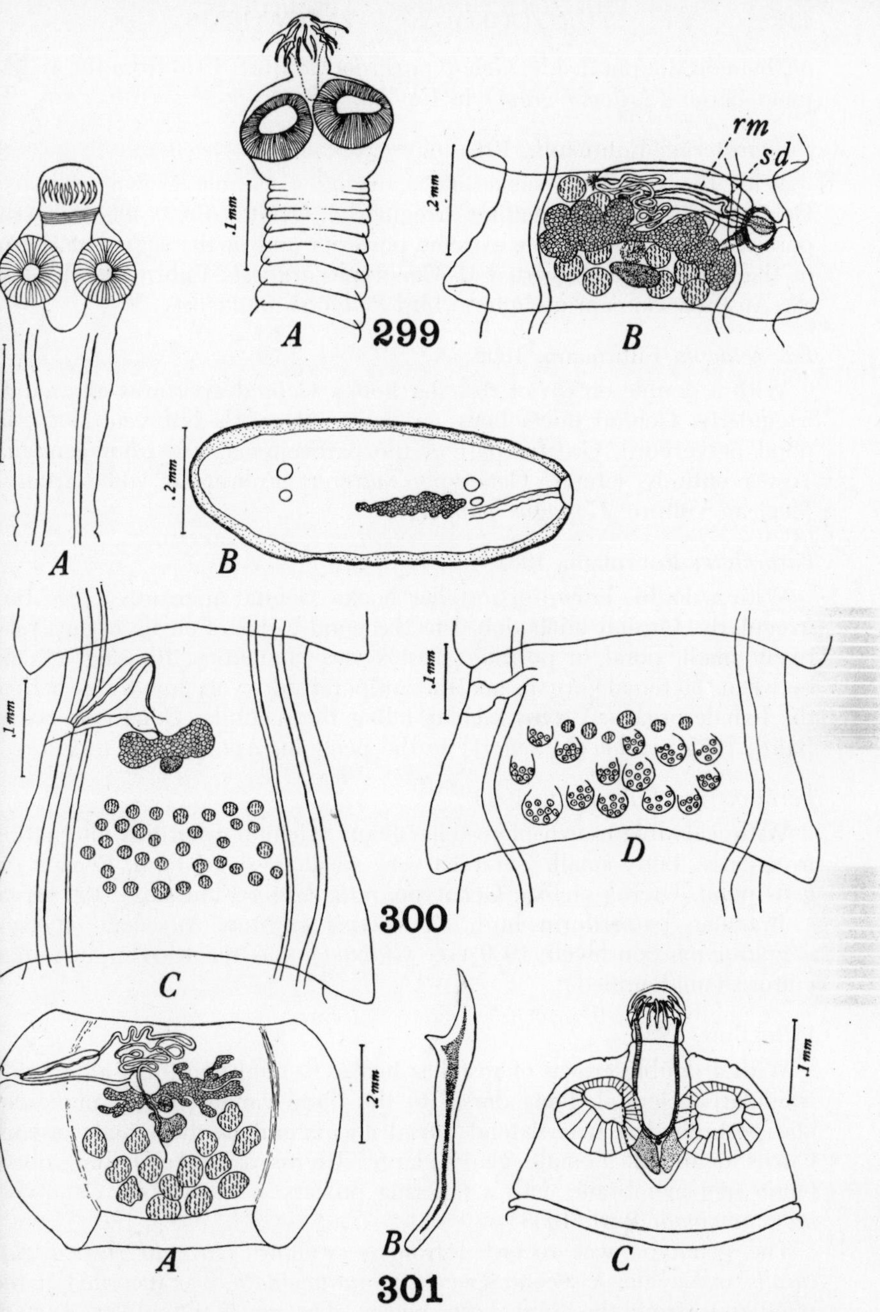

[F]IG. 299. *Anomotaenia nycticoracis.* After Yamaguti, 1935a. A. Holdfast. B. Mature [se]gment, dorsal. *rm*, retractor muscle of cirrus; *sd*, sperm duct. FIG. 300. *Similuncinus [do]tani-ochropodos.* After Inamdar, 1934. A. Holdfast. B. Cross section of mature seg[m]ent. C. Mature segment. D. Gravid segment. FIG. 301. *Choanotaenia iolae.* After Lincicome, 1939. A. Mature segment. B. Rostellar hook. C. Holdfast.

of them on the poral side. Genotype, *ardeolae* Burt, 1940 from the India pond heron (*Ardeola grayi*) in Ceylon.

Proparuterina Fuhrmann, 1911

With the rostellum suckerlike, carrying a double crown of hook Genital apertures alternating irregularly. Genital ducts between th poral canals. Testes at the extreme posterior end of the segment. Uteru in the shape of an inverted U. Genotype, *aruensis* Fuhrmann, 1911 i the Australasian caprimulgiform bird *Podergus papuensis.*

Laterotaenia Fuhrmann, 1906

With a double crown of rostellar hooks. Genital apertures alternatin irregularly. Genital ducts between the poral canals but ventral to th poral nerve cord. Greater part of the parenchyma free from genitali Testes entirely lateral. Genotype, *nattereri* Fuhrmann, 1906 from Mexican vulture, *Gypagus pappa.*

Parorchites Fuhrmann, 1932

With a double crown of rostellar hooks. Genital apertures alternatin irregularly. Genital ducts dorsal to the poral canals. Female organs rela tively small, poral in position. Testes very numerous, forming a ban between the female organs and the antiporal side; very few testes behin the female organs. Uterus saclike, filling the medulla. Genotype, *zeder* Baird, 1853 (=*Taenia zederi*) in the penguin, *Aptenodytes forsteri.*

Parvirostrum Fuhrmann, 1909

With a double crown of rostellar hooks. Genital apertures alternatin irregularly. Body small. Genitalia very small. Testes lateral. Female or gans poral. Uterus saclike. Genotype, *reticulatum* Fuhrmann, 1908 from a Brazilian passeriform bird, *Dendrornis elegans.* A second species *magnisomum* Southwell, 1930 (see *Gidhaia*), was recorded in an India vulture (unidentified).

Vitta Burt, 1938

With a double crown of rostellar hooks. Genital apertures alternatin irregularly. Genital ducts dorsal to the poral canals. Testes numerou and posterior but may extend dorsal and lateral to the female organs Cirrus unarmed. Female glands large. Uterus sac-shaped and lobed Outer egg membrane with a tapering process at each pole. Genotype *magniuncinata* Burt, 1938.

The genotype was recorded from a swallow, *Hirundo rustica gut turalis*, in Ceylon. A second species, *minutiuncinata*, was recorded at th same time from the same host species. The genus resembles *Anomo taenia* in most respects but differs in the relation of the genital duct to the poral canals. The author (Burt) suggested that further examina tion of species of *Anomotaenia* may show that some of them should b placed in his new genus.

Subfamily Dipylidiinae Stiles, 1896

DESCRIPTION

Of the family Dilepididae. With the characters of the family but with he gravid uterus represented by egg capsules containing one or several ggs. With thirteen genera, distinguishable provisionally as follows:

KEY TO GENERA

. Rostellum *believed* unarmed 2
Rostellum with one or more crowns 3
. Genital apertures unilateral .... *Eugonodaeum*
Genital apertures alternating regularly or irregularly . . *Pseudochoanotaenia*
. Rostellum with one crown 4
Rostellum with more than one crown 5
. Genital apertures unilateral . . . . *Similuncinus, Aleurotaenia, Malika* in part
Genital apertures alternating irregularly .... *Choanotaenia* in part, *Kowalewskiella, Onderstepoortia*
. Rostellum with two crowns 6
Rostellum with several crowns . . . . *Diplopylidium, Dipylidium, Joyeuxiella*
. Genital apertures unilateral .... *Southwellia, Malika* in part
Genital apertures alternating irregularly . . . . *Choanotaenia* in part, *Panuwa*

Witenberg (1932) restricted the subfamily to those genera (*Diplo-ylidium, Dipylidium, Joyeuxiella*) which had double genitalia per seg-nent and placed the remainder in a new subfamily, Monopylidiinae, ased upon *Monopylidium* Fuhrmann. Fuhrmann (1932) objected that he practice of separating, among Cyclophyllidea, those genera with louble genitalia from those with single, or those with a special arrange-nent of rostellar hooks from those with the common hymenolepidid or lilepidid arrangement, merely established a confusing number of sub-amilies of no particular value to the systematist. In any case, the term Monopylidiinae" for such a new subfamily is disqualified because Fuhr-nann, author of the generic name *Monopylidium*, discarded it as being ynonymous with *Choanotaenia*.

NOTES ON GENERA

ugonodaeum Beddard, 1913

With the rostellum believed to be hookless. Genital apertures uni-ateral. Genital ducts between the poral canals. Cirrus pouch volumin-us. Cirrus unarmed. Testes few, behind the female organs. Female rgans poral. Egg capsules each with one egg. Genotype, *oedicnemi* eddard, 1913.

The genotype was based upon material from a South American haradriiform bird, *Oedicnemus bistriatus*. Johri (1934) added the spe-ies *ganjeum* from *Acridotheres tristis*, and *testifrontosa* from *Gallinago oelestis*, both in Lucknow, India. In Johri's species, the gravid uterus ersists and the egg capsules are formed within it, the uterus expanding o hold them and stretching over the ventral canals. Johri was unable o establish any differences between his species and the three accepted species of *Unciunia* (Dilepidinae) and took the view that *Unciunia* i synonymous with *Eugonodaeum.*

Pseudochoanotaenia Burt, 1938

With the rostellum believed hookless. Genital apertures alternatin regularly or irregularly. Genital ducts between the poral canals. Cirru pouch large but without any internal seminal vesicle. Testes about 14 behind the female organs. Latter central. Uterus transient, appearin first as a reticulum and, after receiving the eggs, becoming constricte between them to form uterine egg capsules each with a single egg Genotype, *collocaliae* Burt, 1938 in the Indian edible-nest swiftlet, *Col localia unicolor unicolor*, in Ceylon.

Similuncinus Johnston, 1909

With a single crown of rostellar hooks. Genital apertures unilateral Testes behind the female organs. Uterus at first a tube behind the testes later surrounding the entire genitalia before breaking down to a reticu lum and thence into egg capsules. Genotype, *dacelonis* Johnston, 1909

Johnston's material was obtained from an Australian kingfisher, *Dacel gigas.* A further species, *totani-ochropodos* (Figure 300) was added b Inamdar (1934) from the green sandpiper, *Totanus ochropus,* at Nag pur, India.

Aleurotaenia Cameron, 1928

With a single crown of rostellar hooks. Genital apertures unilateral Testes lateral and posterior to the female organs. Uterus saclike, break ing down into egg capsules, each with one egg. Genotype, *planicipiti* Cameron, 1928.

The genotypic material was collected by Cameron from a rusty tige cat (*Felis planiceps*) in Trinidad, West Indies. Woodland (1929b) be lieved *Aleurotaenia* to differ from Johnston's *Similuncinus* – taken fron the Australian "laughing jackass" – merely in the number and shape o the rostellar hooks (12 in *Aleurotaenia* against 36 in *Similuncinus*), i the number of testes, in the position of the coils of the sperm duct, i the presence or absence of seminal vesicles, and in the shapes of ovar and yolk gland. Despite such differences – which would seem importan enough to the general student of tapeworm taxonomy – Woodlan asserted that Cameron's form must lapse into synonymity with *Similuncinus.*

"Personally, I think that if we allow such relatively trivial difference as those to serve for generic distinction, classification will soon arrive a a state of hopeless confusion . . . it is true that 'Aleurotaenia' is fron a mammal and *Similuncinus* from a bird and these two cestodes ma have had a very divergent origin and therefore in reality be supergenerically distinct, but classification from the systematist's standpoint cannot, in the absence of positive evidence, take possible convergence of characters into account in its definitions." Woodland (*op. cit.*).

It seems to the present writers, looking at the matter from the standpoint of the general zoologist, that Cameron's characters are by no means trivial, correlated as they are with such vast differences in geographical and host distribution; that similar triviality of characters can be shown repeatedly to be correlated with deep physiological and life cycle differences; that the phenomenon of convergence of morphological characters is one that cannot by any means be ignored by the systematist; and that the addition of further genera and species to animal groups is no more productive of confusion than is the addition of new words to the vocabulary of a language; rather, is it productive of greater clarity.

Malika Woodland, 1929

With a single crown of rostellar hooks. Genital apertures unilateral. Every segment except the last much wider than long. Genital ducts between the poral canals. Ovary poral. Yolk gland median. Uterus breaking down to capsules each with several eggs. Genotype, *oedicnemus* Woodland, 1928.

The genotype host was a stone curlew (*Oedicnemus scolopax*) at Allahabad, India. Other species have been added to the genus from the same geographical area: *pittae* Inamdar, 1933 (Figure 308) from *Pitta brachyura*, Nagpur; *kalawewaensis* Burt, 1940 from *Burhinus indicus*, Ceylon; *himantopodis* Burt, 1940 from *Himantopus himantopus himantopus*, Ceylon; *zeylanica* Burt, 1940 from *Burhinus oedicnemus*, Ceylon.

In this matter, Woodland's criticism of *Aleurotaenia*, quoted above, recoils on the critic, since *Malika* would seem to differ from *Southwellia* Moghe, 1925 – a genus occurring in galliform birds in India – mainly in whether we regard the number of rows of rostellar hooks in *Malika* as one or two; and apparently such a decision is difficult to make in species of *Malika*. However, there is also some difference in testis distribution between the two genera, sufficient in the reluctant opinion of Burt (1940a) to justify retaining *Malika* as a valid genus.

Choanotaenia Railliet, 1896

With a single crown of rostellar hooks. Suckers armed or not with cuticular spines. Genital apertures alternating irregularly. Genital ducts between the poral canals. Seminal vesicles lacking. Testes numerous, behind and to the sides of the female organs. Uterus saclike or strongly lobed, breaking down eventually into egg capsules each with a single egg. Genotype, *infundibulum* Bloch, 1779.

The genus is a large one and one of the most difficult of all cyclophyllidean genera to delimit. It has long been the subject of much taxonomic confusion. The picture has been lightened considerably in recent years, however, through the studies of Meggitt (1927e), Fuhrmann (1932), Inamdar (1934), Stunkard and Milford (1937), Kintner (1938), Joyeux and Baer (1939b), and Burt (1940a). A historical review of the genus has been published by Stunkard and Milford (1937).

Railliet (1896a) – Joyeux and Baer (1939b) give the date as 1893 – established the genus with *infundibulum* Bloch, 1779 (= *Taenia infundibuliformis* Goeze, 1782) as genotype. Now *infundibulum* is a common and well-recorded tapeworm that has been described repeatedly from domestic poultry: 50–200 mm. long; holdfast small, rounded or conoidal bearing minute surface spines; suckers prominent, elongated anteroposteriorly, 180–210 μ by 135–175 μ in dimensions, also with surface spines; neck short; anterior segments short, funnel-shaped when older posterior segments 1.5 to 2.5 mm. broad by 1.5 to 3.0 mm. long with convex margins; the rostellum, 60–70 μ in diameter, has a single circle of hooks, 16–20 in number, 25–30 μ long; testes 25–40 or more in number in posterior half of segment, behind and at the sides of the large yolk gland; cirrus pouch ovoid, 75–95 μ in long diameter; cirrus 50–65 μ long armed with spines.

However, due to the fact that the segments leave the body before they are completely gravid, there has always been some doubt as to whether the saclike uterus persists in the form of a mass of compartments or whether it definitely breaks up and is replaced by egg capsules. Ransom, Cohn, and Meggitt accepted the former view, which would assign the genus to Dilepidinae; Crety, Clerc, Joyeux, and Baer have held the latter view, placing the genus among Dipylidiinae.

We may add that *Choanotaenia infundibulum* was one of the earliest of dilepidid tapeworms to be investigated embryologically, and from Grassi and Rovelli (1889a) to Horsfall and Jones (1937) a succession of observers has established the ability of a wide range of insects to serve as intermediate hosts, and the occurrence of a simple, tailless cysticercoid, with or without an external membrane, to act as infective agent. In the grasshopper, *Melanoplus femur-rubrum*, at 75–90° Fahrenheit 17–20 days is the minimum period of development for the cysticercoids to reach an infective stage. In the beetle, *Aphodius granarius*, at 60–75° Fahrenheit 48 days are required (see Horsfall and Jones, 1937).

There would seem to be some doubt as to the correct version of the specific name of the genotype. Meggitt (1927e) and Inamdar (1934) speak of *Choanotaenia infundibuliformis* (Goeze, 1782), but Fuhrmann (1932), Sprehn (1932), Neveu Lemaire (1936), Stunkard and Milford (1937), and Lincicome (1939) speak of *Choanotaenia infundibulum* (Bloch, 1779), which would seem on grounds of priority of nomenclature to be preferable.

So long as *Choanotaenia* was believed to have the uterus persistent, it was regarded as a single-crowned dilepidine, the double-crowned forms of similar morphology being allotted to the genus *Anomotaenia*. Fuhrmann (1899c) established the genus *Monopylidium* for single-crowned *or* double-crowned forms whose morphology was similar to that of *Choanotaenia* or *Anomotaenia* but whose uterus was replaced when gravid by egg capsules. To this new genus Fuhrmann moved the species *infundibulum*, genotype of *Choanotaenia*, suggesting that in its place Zeder's species *galbulae* be adopted. But such a procedure violates the principles of the International Code of Zoological Nomenclature.

"Although Fuhrmann (1907a, 1908c) and Clerc (1903) recognize *Monopylidium* and *Choanotaenia* as distinct genera, they would place *Ch. infundibuliformis*, the type of *Choanotaenia*, in *Monopylidium*, and

Fuhrmann (1908c) has selected *Choanotaenia galbulae* (Zeder, 1803) as a new type for *Choanotaenia*. This arrangement, as has been pointed out by Railliet and Henry (1909) is in violation of the law of priority of the International Code of Zoological Nomenclature, inasmuch as a type once fixed cannot be changed. *Monopylidium* must fall into synonymy if *Ch. infundibuliformis* (type of *Choanotaenia*) is made congeneric with *Monopylidium musculosum* (type of *Monopylidium*), *Choanotaenia* (1893) [*sic*] being of date prior to that of *Monopylidium* (1899). [*Choanotaenia* was actually established in 1896.] If as Clerc and Fuhrmann believe, *Ch. infundibuliformis* and *M. musculosum* should go into the same genus, that genus must be known as *Choanotaenia*, not as *Monopylidium*. Such action would leave the genus *Choanotaenia* of Fuhrmann (not Railliet) without a name and it would become necessary to re-name the genus. This, Railliet and Henry (1909) have done, proposing the name *Icterotaenia* for the species *galbulae, porosa, parina*, etc. Until however a more careful comparative study of the various species of *Monopylidium* and of *Choanotaenia*, especially the type species of the two genera, has been made, I believe it justifiable to recognize both these generic names, notwithstanding this necessitates the separation of *Choanotaenia infundibuliformis* and *Monopylidium musculosum* which Clerc and Fuhrmann would place together. I am inclined to doubt that the uterus of the former species breaks down into egg capsules as Clerc (1903) has stated. My own observations support those of Cohn (1901) who affirms that the uterus is persistent and possesses an irregularly lobulated cavity, incompletely subdivided by infoldings from the wall. If this is true, and if no later development of egg capsules occurs, *Choanotaenia infundibuliformis* differs from *Monopylidium*, in which the uterus is said to break down into egg capsules, and it is therefore possible to recognize both *Choanotaenia* and *Monopylidium*, changing but slightly Fuhrmann's arrangement of species." Ransom (1909).

It may be noted, in view of the doubt as to whether the gravid uterus of *Choanotaenia* persists or breaks down into egg capsules, that Stunkard and Milford (1937), examining material from the house sparrow (*Passer domesticus*) in Alabama which they tentatively identified as *Choanotaenia passerina*, reported that the uterus was initially saclike, later anastomosing, and finally dividing into small compartments, corresponding rather closely to the description given by Ransom (1909) for this stage and structure in *C. infundibulum.*

"In the anastomosing condition the uterus was observed to ramify over the segment, occupying any portion medial to the dorsal excretory vessels. At the interstices of the channels, one or a few eggs or developing embryos were observed. The uterus persists as a thin-walled structure, and while embryos appear to be free in the parenchyma when observed under ordinary magnification, observations of frontal sections with oil immersion lenses make apparent the folded condition of the uterine wall . . . the possibility of interpreting a transitional uterus in a posterior segment of a member of the genus *Choanotaenia* as that of a member of *Paricterotaenia* appears admissible." Stunkard and Milford (1937).

Kintner (1938), however, also observing *Choanotaenia passerina* (from sparrows in Indiana), believed the uterus to break down finally into distinct egg capsules, although he admitted that the nature of the uterus may depend upon the age of the proglottis, being successively sacciform, lobated, and finally dispersed as distinct egg capsules. Burt (1940a), studying a range of species of *Choanotaenia* in Singhalese charadriiform birds, always spoke of the uterus being *transient*, the eggs coming to lie in egg capsules or, in some cases, coming to lie in the parenchyma, no definite egg capsules being formed. Fuhrmann (1943) placed provisionally in *Choanotaenia* a form, *upupae*, from *Upupa africana* which differs in having the uterus in the form of a very distinct net, which, as in other species, disappears wholly from the gravid segment. The majority of choanotaeniids have a saclike or strongly lobed uterus which breaks down to uterine capsules; or, as in *Ch. crateriformis* (Goeze) and *Ch. musculosa* (Fuhrmann), the uterus is in the form of a narrow tube which breaks down to uterine capsules.

For the "nameless" *Choanotaenia* Fuhrmann then, Railliet and Henry (1909) – as Ransom stated – established the generic term *Icterotaenia*, with *galbulae* as genotype. Lühe (1910), ignorant of or deliberately ignoring the suggestion of the French authors, established the generic term *Parachoanotaenia* but did not designate any genotype. Thus Lühe's genus is clearly a homonym of *Icterotaenia* and was rightly suppressed by Fuhrmann (1932). However, the investigations of Skrjabin and of Cohn have clearly demonstrated, in Fuhrmann's opinion, that *galbulae* belongs to the genus *Anomotaenia*; and so the term *Icterotaenia* becomes invalid. Fuhrmann replaced it, therefore, by the generic term *Paricterotaenia*, with *porosa* as genotype. His final conclusion (1932) was that *Choanotaenia* is a dipylidiine; that its species appear single-crowned or double-crowned according to the extent of differentiation of the hooks; and that the generic terms *Monopylidium* Fuhrmann, *Prochoanotaenia* Meggitt, *Multitesticulata* Meggitt, and *Viscoia* Mola are homonymic and should be discarded.

The species of *Choanotaenia* fall into two groups: (1) those species in which the hooks appear all alike and all at the same level, so that the rostellum appears to be single-crowned; and (2) those species in which the hooks appear alternately large and small, or in which every alternate hook appears to originate at a slightly lower level than its neighbors, so that the rostellum appears to be double-crowned. The distinction is not always easy to establish, however, so that the same species may appear in both groups.

"In sections of the scolex of Alabama specimens the hooks have a circular arrangement on the retracted rostellum; they are uniform in length and are disposed in a single row. In whole mounts, when the rostellum is partially retracted, the hooks often manifest an irregular or alternating arrangement, probably the result of unequal muscular tension, and this condition simulates a double row." Stunkard and Milford (1937) *in re Ch. passerina.*

Recorded as single-crowned are the species: *arctica* Baylis, 1919; *burhini* Burt, 1940; *cayennensis* var. *scolopacis* Joyeux and Baer, 1939; *chandleri* Moghe, 1925; *cingulifera* Krabbe, 1869; *coronata* Creplin, 1829; *glareolae* Burt, 1940; *gondwana* Inamdar, 1934; *infundibulum* Bloch, 1779; *iolae* Lincicome, 1939 (Figure 301); *joyeuxi* Tseng Shen, 1933; *lobipluviae* Burt, 1940; *magnihamata* Burt, 1940; *marchali* Mola, 1907; *meliphagidarum* Johnston, 1911; *microsoma* Southwell, 1922; *numenii* Owen, 1946; *parina* Dujardin, 1845; *passerina* Fuhrmann, 1908; *stagnatilidis* Burt, 1940; *tringae* Joyeux, Baer, and Martin, 1937; *triganciensis* Joyeux and Baer, 1939.

Recorded as double-crowned are the species: *cayennensis* Fuhrmann, 1907; *cayennensis* var. *africana* Joyeux and Baer, 1928; *chandleri* Moghe, 1925; *cingulifera* Krabbe, 1869; *crateriformis* Goeze, 1782; *dispar* Burt, 1940; *fieldingi* Maplestone and Southwell, 1923; *guiarti* Tseng Shen, 1932; *manipurensis* Patwardhan, 1935; *macracantha* Fuhrmann, 1907; *musculosa* Fuhrmann, 1896; *platycephala* Rudolphi, 1810; *polyorchis* Klaptocz, 1908; *rostrata* Fuhrmann, 1918; *secunda* Fuhrmann, 1907; *southwelli* Fuhrmann, 1932; *stercoraria* Baylis, 1919; *taylori* Johnston, 1912; *unicoronata* Fuhrmann, 1908.

Distributed among host groups, the above species may be arranged as follows: in Acciptriformes: *polyorchis*; in Alcediformes: *rostrata*; in Charadriiformes (as listed by Joyeux and Baer, 1939): *arctica, burhini, cayennensis, cayennensis* var. *africana, cayennensis* var. *scolopacis, chandleri, cingulifera, dispar, glareolae, guiarti, joyeuxi, lobipluviae, macracantha, magnihamata, manipurensis, numenii, rostellata, secunda, southwelli, stagnatilidis*: *triganciensis, tringae*; in Galliformes: *infundibulum*, in Lariformes: *stercoraria*; in Passeriformes: *fieldingi, gondwana, iolae, meliphagidarum, microsoma, musculosa, parina, passerina, platycephala, taylori, unicoronata*; in Piciformes: *crateriformis*; in Ralliformes: *marchali.*

Recorded from North America are the species: *cingulifera* (in *Aegialitis dubia, Totanus totanus, Machetes pugnax, Pisobia damacensis*); *coronata* (in *Aegialitis nivosa*); *infundibulum* (in *Gallus gallus domesticus, Phasianus colchicus, Coturnix coturnix*); *iolae* (in *Planesticus planesticus migratorius*); *musculosa* (in *Sturna vulgaris*); *numenii* (in *Numenius americanus americanus*); *parina* (in *Passer domesticus, Passer montanus*); *passerina* (in *Passer domesticus*); *rostellata* (in *Himantopus mexicanus*).

Kowalewskiella Baczynska, 1914

With a crown of small hooks. Segments much longer than wide. Genital apertures alternating irregularly. Genital ducts between the poral canals. Testes in front of and also behind the female organs. Uterus saclike, breaking down to egg capsules each with a single egg. Genotype, *longiannulata* Baczynska, 1914.

Baczynska's material came from Old World Charadriiformes (*Totanus glareola*). On the strength of his description of the gravid uterus as sac-like, the form was formerly regarded as dilepidine (see Fuhrmann, 1932). Meggitt (1927e), however, redescribing the species, found the uterus of gravid segments to be represented by egg capsules each with a single egg.

Onderstepoortia Ortlepp, 1938

With a single crown of hooks. Genital apertures alternating irregularly. Testes numerous (120–150) and surrounding the female organs except on the poral side. Ovary slightly poral and crescentic. Seminal receptacle large. Uterus breaking down to egg capsules each with a single egg. Genotype, *taeniaeformis* Ortlepp, 1938, from a stone curlew, *Burhinus capensis capensis* in South Africa.

Diplopylidium Beddard, 1913

With several circles of rostellar hooks of which only the last circle consists of rose-thorn hooks. Genital apertures in the first third of the segment margins. Two sets of genitalia per segment. Cirrus pouches pear-shaped, large, reaching almost to the middle line of the segment. Testes few, placed mainly behind the female organs. Vagina crossing the cirrus pouch on each side to open in front of the cirrus. Ovaries each with two faintly lobed wings. Yolk glands compact and often kidney-shaped. Egg capsules each with a single egg. Larva a cysticercoid in reptiles. Adults in mammals and birds. Genotype, *genettae* Beddard, 1913.

Synonymous with this genus, in the opinion of Meggitt (1927e), is *Progynotaenia* Skrjabin, 1914 and Lopez-Neyra, 1927. Fuhrmann (1932) regarded *Progynopylidium* Skrjabin, 1924 and *Dipylidium* Leuckart, 1863, in part, as also synonymous with it. Beddard's original description being scanty and the type material having apparently been lost, Lopez-Neyra (1928) suggested that the generic name be changed to *Progynopylidium* with *nolleri* Skrjabin, 1914 as genotype, a suggestion which, while eminently sensible, conflicts with the International Rules of Zoological Nomenclature.

Meggitt (1927e) recognized ten species: *columbae* Fuhrmann, 1908; *fabulosum* Meggitt, 1927; *fortunatum* Meggitt, 1927; *genettae* Beddard, 1913; *monoophorum* Lühe, 1898; *nolleri* Skrjabin, 1924; *quinquecoronatum* Lopez-Neyra and Muñoz-Medina, 1921; *trinchesei* Diamare, 1892; *triseriale* Lühe, 1898; and *zschokkei* Hungerbühler, 1910. To these may be added *avicolae* Fuhrmann, 1906.

Witenberg (1932) was inclined to restrict the recognized species to five, namely: *acanthotreta* Parona, 1887, established for a cysticercoid in a snake, *Coluber viridiflavus*, in Italy (according to Witenberg this form is identical with *trinchesei* Diamare, *triseriale* Lühe, and *quinquecoronatum* Lopez-Neyra and Muñoz-Medina); *avicolae* Fuhrmann, 1906; *monoophorum* Lühe, 1898; *nolleri* Skrjabin, 1924 (= *monoophoroides* Lopez-Neyra); and *zschokkei* Hungerbühler, 1910. Popov (1935) recorded *Diplopylidium skrjabini* after feeding cysticercoids from the peritoneum of a lizard, *Gymnodactylus caspus*, to young cats. It would seem to differ from *nolleri* mainly in the size of the holdfast and suckers, and in color.

The three species found in dogs and cats – *acanthotreta, nolleri,* and *skrjabini* – have the following characteristics (see Neveu Lemaire, 1936):

1. *acanthotreta* Parona, 1886 (= *Cysticercus acanthotreta* Parona, 1886; *Dipylidium trinchesei* Diamare, 1893; *D. triseriale* Lühe, 1898; *D. quinquecoronatum* Lopez-Neyra and Muñoz-Medina, 1921; *Diplopylidium fabulosum* Meggitt, 1927). 40–122 mm. long by 1.5 mm. broad; holdfast 400 μ in diameter; rostellum 160–200 μ in diameter with 3–5 circles of hooks, 18–24 per circle; hook lengths, first circle, 62–73 μ; second circle, 52–60 μ; third circle, 26–36 μ; fourth circle, 16–24 μ; fifth circle, 11–16 μ; neck as wide as holdfast; segments 8–50; testes 30–60, 30–70 μ in diameter; cirrus pouch 160–310 μ; egg capsules 57–83 μ; eggs 40–50 μ.

2. *nolleri* Skrjabin, 1924 (= *Dipylidium trinchesei* of Lopez-Neyra and Muñoz-Medina, 1921; *Progynopylidium nolleri* Skrjabin, 1924; *Progynopylidium monoophoroides* Lopez-Neyra, 1928). 9–120 mm. long by 1 mm. wide; holdfast 240–500 μ in diameter; rostellum 110–230 μ in diameter with three or sometimes four circles of hooks, 20–22 hooks per circle; hook lengths of first circle 42–54 μ; second circle, 34–46 μ; third circle, 11–20 μ; fourth circle, 7–19 μ; neck narrower than holdfast; segments 25–120; testes 15–40, each 44–62 μ in diameter; cirrus pouch 140–190 μ; egg capsules 70–170 μ; eggs 30 μ (Figure 303).

3. *skrjabini* Popov, 1935. 430–510 mm. long; holdfast 158–160 μ in diameter; rostellum 90 μ with four circles of hooks, 11 hooks per circle; hook lengths, first circle, 42 μ; second circle, 19 μ; third circle, 12 μ; fourth circle, 7 μ; neck 83 μ; segments 56–60; testes 12, each 15–18 μ in diameter; cirrus pouch 182 by 60 μ; egg capsules 80–83 μ; eggs 36–43 μ.

Such observations as have been made upon the life cycle of *Diplopylidium* suggest that the intermediate hosts are reptiles or batrachians and that the larval stages are cysticercoids or dithyridia. Meggitt (1927e) believed that most four-suckered larval tapeworms in reptiles are of this genus or of *Dipylidium*.

Lopez-Neyra (1928), changing the generic name to *Progynopylidium*, distinguished the species as follows:

KEY TO SPECIES

1. Ovaries ovoid, with a single lobe corresponding to the middle lobe of other forms; three crowns of hooks, 36, 30, 20 μ long, respectively; testes 25–29, 40 μ in diameter; cirrus pouch pear-shaped, curved, 150 by 50 μ; genital aperture in first fifth of segment margin; eggs 41 μ in diameter; uterine capsules restricted to area between osmoregulatory canals; in *Civettictis civetta* and *Genetta afra*, Tunisia . . . . *monoophorum*
   Ovaries slightly bilobed 2

2. Very small forms 6 mm. long, with 28 segments; rostellum with two crowns of hooks, 34 per circle, lengths not given; genital aperture in first fourth of segment margin; testes numerous; egg dimensions not given; in *Genetta dongolana*, London Zoo .... *genettae*
Forms 10 mm. in length or longer 3
3. Hooks of first circle more than 60 μ long 4
Hooks of first circle less than 60 μ long 7
4. Uterine capsules between osmoregulatory canals 5
Uterine capsules crossing osmoregulatory canals 6
5. Rostellum with 78–85 hooks in four circles; hooks 62, 58–60, 31, and 15 μ, respectively; neck short; genital aperture in first third or first fourth of segment margin; testes 41, ovarian lobes spherical; total body length 25 mm.; in cats, Naples, Alexandria .... *trinchesei*
Rostellum with four circles of hooks, 70, 45–50, 30–33, and 24 μ long, respectively; genital aperture in first fourth of segment margin; cirrus pouch 217–280 by 35–50 μ; testes 36–39; total length 10 mm.; in cat, Gizeh, Egypt .... *fabulosum*
6. Rostellum with three circles of hooks, 63–68, 52–56, and 38–42 μ, respectively; genital aperture in first third or fourth; cirrus pouch 280 by 50–60 μ; testes 39–44; egg capsules 60 by 56 μ; eggs 37 μ; body length 15–25 mm.; in *Civettictus civetta* and *Genetta afra*, Tunisia ...... *triseriale*
Rostellum with five, rarely four, circles of hooks, 70–78, 56–60, 36–41, 22–30, and 13–17 μ, respectively; genital aperture in first fourth or fifth; cirrus pouch 150 by 50 μ; testes 48–64, each 46 μ in diameter; egg capsules 58–63 μ; eggs 38–41 μ; body length 32–60 mm.; in cats, Granada and Almeria, Spain .... *quinquecoronatum*
7. Uterine capsules lying inside the area bounded by the osmoregulatory canals 8
Uterine capsules spreading over the canals 9
8. Rostellum 200–230 μ in diameter, with 3–4 circles of 100 hooks, 48–53 μ in first circle to 10 μ in last; holdfast 450–500 μ in diameter; genital aperture in first fifth or seventh; cirrus pouch dimensions not stated; testes 12–16; uterine capsules 70–90 μ; body length 40–55 mm.; last segments brown in color; in cats, Russian Turkestan .... *nolleri*
Rostellum 110–114 μ in diameter, with 3–4 circles of hooks, 51–56, 34–40, 27–30, and 12–14 μ, respectively; holdfast 215–310 μ; genital aperture in first fifth or sixth; cirrus pouch 125 by 40 μ; testes 20–25; eggs 45–48 μ; capsules 68–70 μ by 78–82 μ; segments with characteristic oblique surfaces; last segments blood-red in color; body length 25–75 mm.; in cats, Granada and Almeria, Spain .... *monoophoroides*
Hooks 45–48 μ (only four known); genital apertures in first seventh of segment margins; testes ?; eggs 30 μ; capsules 90 μ; cirrus pouches not visible in gravid segments; body length several centimeters; in *Columba sp.*, Egypt .... *columbae*
9. Rostellum with three circles of hooks, 45, 30, and 17 μ, respectively; genital apertures in first fourth of segment margins; cirrus pouches 185 by 65 μ; testes 30; capsules 20–40 μ; body length 120 mm.; in *Cynictis penicillata* (bushy-tailed Meerkat), South Africa .... *zschokkei*
Rostellum with one (?) row of hooks only, 23 in number, 28 μ in length (possibly the final row); genital apertures between the first and second fourths; cirrus pouches 230–300 μ; testes numerous; eggs 32 μ in diameter; body length 150 mm.; in *Gyps kolbi* (vulture), South Africa ...... *avicola*

Dipylidium Leuckart, 1863, emended Lopez-Neyra, 1928, Venard, 1938

With the rostellum muscular, retractile, armed with rose-thorn hooks which appear to be arranged in transverse circular rows. Testes numerous, occupying most of the area between the osmoregulatory canals. Vaginae opening behind the cirri into the genital atria. Genital apertures each slightly behind the middle of the segment margin. Uterus netlike in mature segments, breaking down to capsules each with several eggs. Genotype, *caninum* Linnaeus, 1758 (Figure 302).

In contrast with *Diplopylidium*, the testes in this genus are numerous and denser in front of the female organs than behind them. The ovaries are distinctly bilobed. Each vagina is ventral and posterior to the corresponding cirrus pouch. Each capsule contains several eggs.

Dipylidium is a well-known and cosmopolitan parasite of dogs and cats and, occasionally, of children. It has long been an object of study by many investigators; see Melnikow (1869), Schiefferdecker (1875), Steudener (1877), Moniez (1881), Sonsino (1889a), Grassi (1888a, 1888b), Grassi and Rovelli (1889a, 1889b, 1892), Brandt (1888), Diamare (1893b), Setti (1895), Ransom (1909), Galli Valero (1911), Joyeux (1916), Millzner (1926), Schwartz (1927b), Lewis (1927a), Gulati (1929), Witenberg (1932), Chen (1934), Venard and Ellis (1933), Venard (1938), and Stewart (1939).

Twenty species have been assigned to this genus at one time or another: *buencaminoi* Tubangui, 1925; *caninum* Linnaeus, 1758; *carracidoi* Lopez-Neyra, 1928; *catus* Gulati, 1929; *columbae* Fuhrmann, 1908; *compactum* Millzner, 1926; *crassum* Millzner, 1926; *diffusum* Millzner, 1926; *dongolense* Beddard, 1913; *genettae* Gervais, 1847; *gervaisi* Setti, 1895; *gracile* Millzner, 1926; *halli* Tubangui, 1925; *longulum* Millzner, 1926; *monticelli* Diamare, 1893; *oerlyi* Ratz, 1900; *otocyonis* Joyeux, Baer, and Martin, 1936; *porimamillanum* Lopez-Neyra, 1928; *sexcoronatum* Ratz, 1900; and *walkeri* Sondhi, 1923.

Millzner (1926), examining 28 dogs and 30 cats in the vicinity of Oakland, California, found 89 per cent of the dogs to contain species of *Dipylidium*. Of 385 worms, only three were *caninum* and only one was *sexcoronatum*; the remainder belonged, in Millzner's opinion, to two new species, *crassum* and *gracile*. Among the 30 cats, 83 per cent contained *Dipylidium*. Of 845 worms found, 24 were *sexcoronatum*, the others belonging to four new species—*gracile, compactum, diffusum,* and *longulum*. Of these, *gracile* was found also in dogs. No *caninum* was found in the cats.

Lopez-Neyra (1928) reviewed the genus, redefined it, and accepted thirteen species, distinguishable as follows:

KEY TO SPECIES

1. Eggs very small, 8 μ in diameter; rostellum with 4–5 alternating crowns of hooks 7 μ in length for the first row, smaller for the later rows; testes 150–180 per segment; cirrus pouch 114 by 38 μ, reaching the osmoregulatory canals; uterine capsules with 3–12 eggs each; total length 30 mm.;

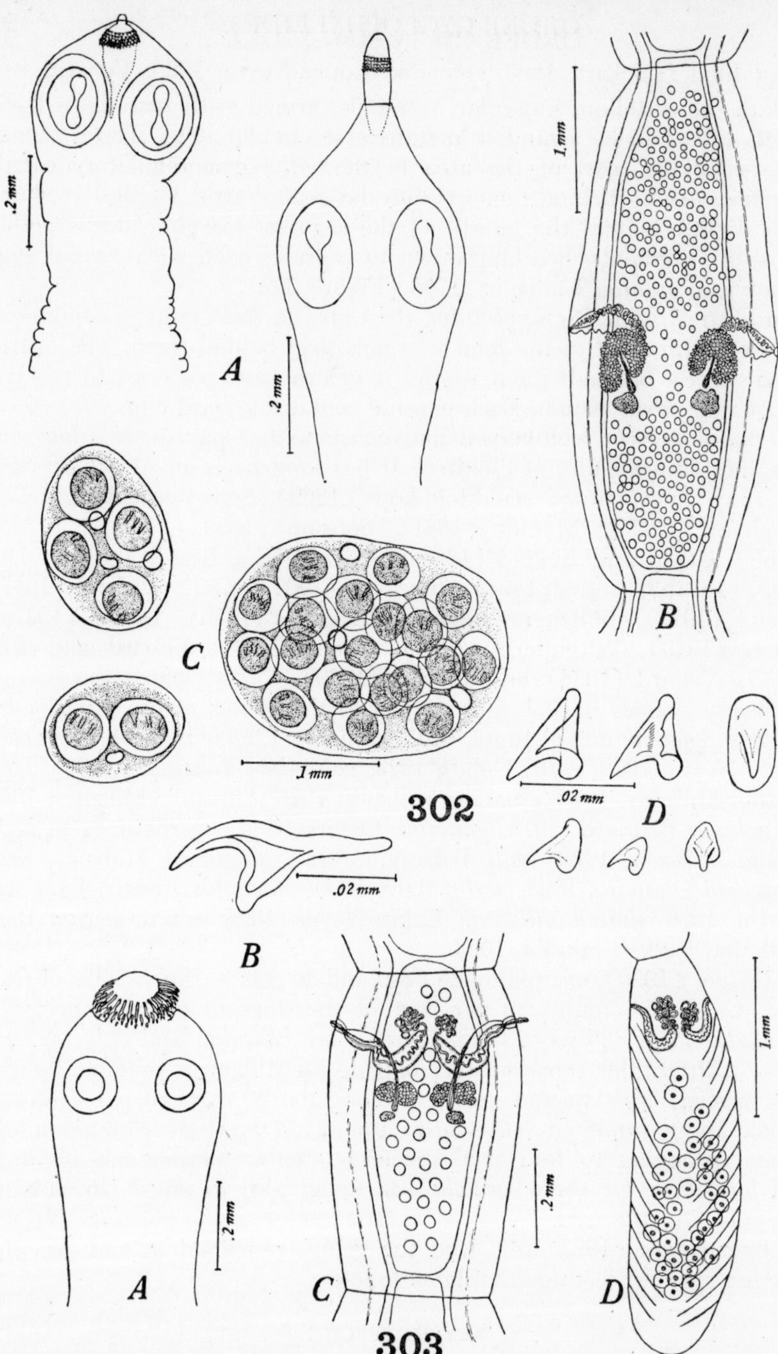

FIG. 302. *Dipylidium caninum*. After Witenberg, 1932. A. Holdfast in various stages of contraction. B. Mature segment. C. Eggs within uterine capsules. D. Rostellar hooks. FIG. 303. *Diplopylidium nolleri*. After Witenberg, 1932. A. Holdfast. B. Rostellar hook. C. Mature segment. D. Gravid segment.

in dogs in Manila . . . . *buencaminoi* Tubangui
Eggs 25 μ or more 2

2. Rostellum conical, with 3–4 rows of hooks 12–15 μ long in the first row and 5–6 μ in the later rows; testes 100–200; vagina without seminal receptacle; cirrus pouch not crossing the osmoregulatory canals; uterine capsules in a single layer, each containing 5–30 eggs 40–50 μ in diameter; total length 150 mm., rarely 800 mm.; in dog, cat, *Felis sylvestris, F. maniculata, F. libyca, Canis mesomelas, C. aureus, Homo sapiens, Zibethailurus viverrina*; cosmopolitan . . . . *caninum* Linnaeus
Rostellum with more than 3–4 crowns of hooks 3

3. Rostellum club-shaped, with 8 transverse rows of hooks 13 μ in length in the first rows and 5 μ in the last; testes 100–150; cirrus pouch 250–320 by 60 μ briefly crossing the osmoregulatory canals; genital apertures somewhat prominent; uterine capsules each with 4–7 eggs of 25 μ diameter; total length more than 30 mm.; in cats, Manila . . . . *halli* Tubangui
Rostellum conical and not bluntly club-shaped 4

4. Genital apertures prominent, projecting 5
Genital apertures not prominent, generally depressed 6

5. Genital apertures only slightly prominent, on muscular papillae (mammelons) 125 μ in diameter by 50–60 μ high; rostellum with 6–7 crowns of hooks, 14 μ long in the first rows, 5–6 μ in the later rows (Lopez-Neyra probably implies a gradation from 14 μ to 5 μ); testes 300–320; cirrus pouch 260–300 by 55–60 μ, reaching the osmoregulatory canals; eggs 36–40 μ, thick-shelled (10–12 μ); total length 130–140 mm.; in dog and cat, Granada, Spain . . . . *porimamillanum* Lopez-Neyra
Genital apertures prominent but not "mammelonated"; rarely more than 5 rows of hooks, 10 μ in length in first rows and 4 μ in later rows; testes 150–170; cirrus pouch 225 by 65 μ; eggs 35 μ; total length 300 mm.; in dogs, California . . . . *crassum* Millzner

6. Hooks in first row less than 10 μ long 7
Hooks in first row more than 10 μ long 8

7. Rostellum with 5–7 rows of hooks, 8 μ in first row, 5 μ in later rows; testes 200–250, 70 μ in diameter; cirrus pouches 235 by 75 μ, crossing the osmoregulatory canals; eggs 30 μ; body length 40–200 mm.; in dogs and cats, California . . . . *gracile* Millzner
Rostellum with 5 rows of hooks, 7 μ in first row, 5 μ in later rows; testes 180–240, 60 μ in diameter; cirrus pouches 275 by 75 μ, reaching but rarely crossing the canals; eggs 40 μ; body length 50–120 mm.; in cats, California . . . . *longulum* Millzner
Rostellum with 6, rarely 7 or 8, rows of hooks, 9 μ in first row, 5 μ in later rows; testes 160–250, 70 μ in diameter; cirrus pouches 225 by 70 μ; uterine capsules not reticulated; eggs 33 μ; body length 70–150 mm.; in cats, California . . . . *diffusum* Millzner

8. Rostellum constantly with 5 rows of hooks 9
Rostellum with 6–7 rows of hooks 10

9. Suckers oval, 110–125 by 100 μ, scarcely prominent, with opening ellipsoidal; rostellar hooks from 12–12.5 to 4.6 μ; testes 110–156, according to Ratz's drawings; 90–100 μ diameter; cirrus pouches 250 by 70 μ, crossing the canals; genital pores depressed; uterine capsules with 2–12 eggs; eggs 25–28 μ; some gravid segments pear-shaped; body length 50–110 mm.; in cats and dogs, Budapest, Punjab (India), Almeria (Spain) . . . . *oerlyi* v. Ratz
Suckers ellipsoidal, prominent, 190–220 μ long by 150–160 μ broad, with

narrow openings, elongated or characteristically linear; rostellar hooks 14–16 μ to 5.5–7 μ; testes 260–306; genital apertures in deep atria; cirrus pouches 280–350 by 60–65 μ, long and slender, just crossing the canals; uterine capsules with 1–8 eggs 26–30 μ in diameter; gravid segments not pear-shaped; body length 120–150 mm.; in cats, Granada and Madrid (Spain) .... *carracidoi* Lopez-Neyra

10. Cirrus pouches not reaching the canals, 118 by 56 μ; rostellum with 6–7 rows of hooks, 12 μ to 2 μ; testes 225, 72–90 μ in diameter, some lying outside the osmoregulatory canals; uterine capsules in a single layer in the parenchyma of the medulla and not reticulated; eggs 35 μ with shell 4 μ; body length 100–280 mm.; in dogs, Punjab, India ..*walkeri* Sondhi
Cirrus pouches reaching the canals 11
11. Eggs 25–26 μ in diameter with embryos 20 μ enclosed in polygonal uterine capsules arranged in 2 or 3 layers, forming in the gravid segments a very characteristic mesh; rostellum with 6 rows of hooks, 12–13 μ (11 μ according to Millzner) down to 4–5 μ in length; cirrus pouches 220–290 by 50–60 μ; testes 130–190; body length 100–230 mm.; in cats, cosmopolitan .... *sexcoronatum* v. Ratz
Eggs 36 μ in diameter; rostellum with 6 rows of hooks ranging in length from 15 to 9 μ; testes 140–200, 65 μ in diameter; cirrus pouches 245 by 60 μ; uterine capsules not reticulated; body length 50–150 mm.; in cats, California .... *compactum* Millzner

Witenberg (1932) reduced the number of species to one, *caninum*, which he regarded as including *sexcoronatum, oerlyi, walkeri, carracidoi,* and *porimamillanum*. Into the genus *Joyeuxiella* he removed *fuhrmanni, rossicum, chyzeri*, and *fortunatum*. Into the genus *Diplopylidium* went *quinquecoronatum, trinchesei*, and *triseriale*.

A more conservative viewpoint was that of Venard (1938) who, after critically examining the genus, reduced the number of valid species to three, separable as follows:

1. Rostellar hooks less than 16 μ long 2
Rostellar hooks in four rows, those of the first three rows 42–26 μ long .... *otocyonis*
2. Eggs 35–60 μ in diameter .... *caninum*
Eggs 8 μ in diameter .... *buencaminoi*

The species *caninum* is cosmopolitan; *buencaminoi* was recorded by Tubangui (1925) from a dog in Manila, Philippine Islands. The latter is a small form, not over 30 mm. long; the largest rostellar hooks are 7 μ long; the egg diameter is only 8 μ. In all respects except this extraordinarily small egg, the form is identical with *caninum*. The species *otocyonis* was recorded by Joyeux, Baer, and Martin (1936) from *Otocyon megalictis* in Somaliland, N.E. Africa.

For a detailed account of the biology, morphology, and life cycle of *caninum* reference should be made to Neveu Lemaire (1936) and to Venard (1938). Stewart (1939) rejected the view that *sexcoronatum* is synonymous with *caninum* (see Witenberg, 1932; Neveu Lemaire, 1936; Venard, 1938) and took the stand that fundamental differences between species of the same genus are physiological and not necessarily expressed morphologically. He claimed that despite the overlapping of characters shown by the two species in question, physiological differences have been demonstrated. Zimmermann (1937) was unable to infect the dog louse, *Trichodectes canis*, the intermediate host for *sexcoronatum*, with *caninum*, whose normal intermediate hosts seem to be the flea species *Ctenocephalides felis* and *C. canis*. Stewart himself found that while isoamylorthocresol is a highly efficient anthelmintic against *caninum* in dogs, it has no effect upon *sexcoronatum*.

Joyeuxiella Fuhrmann, 1935 (=*Joyeuxia* Lopez-Neyra, 1927, preoccupied)

Of medium or small size. Holdfast with a retractile, conical, or cylindrical rostellum armed with several rows of small hooks, less than 20 μ long, shaped like a rose thorn, with discoid bases. Suckers unarmed. Genitalia double and symmetrical per segment. Two genital apertures per segment, in the anterior half of each margin. Testes fewer than 100 (Lopez-Neyra called them "few"; Witenberg called them "numerous"). Ovaries bilobed, compact, ramifying. Vaginae opening behind the cirrus pouches. Uterus reticulate, breaking down to egg capsules each containing a single egg. Genotype, *chyzeri* Ratz, 1897 (not *pasqualei* Diamare as Neveu Lemaire stated).

Joyeuxiella is obviously similar in most respects to *Dipylidium*, but has fewer rostellar hooks and testes and has only one egg per uterine capsule. The generic name *Joyeuxia* which was proposed by Lopez-Neyra (1927) had been used previously (for a sponge) and is inadmissible. *Joyeuxiella* is a *nomen novum* proposed by Fuhrmann (1935a).

Lopez-Neyra (1927c, 1928) placed ten species within the proposed genus and distinguished them as follows:

KEY TO SPECIES

1. Cephalic invagination armed with hooks entirely like those of the rostellum; later when evaginated showing up to 25 crowns of hooks, from 16 μ in length down to 5 μ; body length 70 mm.; in *Fennecus zerda* (fennec fox) and domestic cat, Egypt, Tunis .... *echinorhynchoides* Sonsino, 1899
   Cephalic invagination unarmed 2
2. Rostellum with four crowns of very small hooks 2 μ in length; body length 5–6 mm. with 22–26 segments; in *Genetta dongolana*, London Zoo .... *dongolense* Beddard, 1913
   Rostellum with at least eight crowns of hooks 3
3. Body small, not reaching 100 mm. 4
   Body slightly exceeding 100 mm. 6
4. Rostellum with 60 hooks of medium length arranged in 8–12 crowns; testes 80 per segment; genital apertures in anterior fourths of segment margins or anterior sixth; body length 10–40 mm.; in *Genetta tigrina*, Eritrea, Africa .... *gervaisi* Setti, 1896
   Rostellum with 11 crowns of hooks, lengths not stated; genital apertures in anterior part of segment but approaching mid-margins; cirrus pouches 90–130 by 30–50 μ, reaching the osmoregulatory canals; testes 55; egg dimensions not stated; cirrus armed; body length 20–30 mm. by 0.56 mm.; in *Felis sylvatica*, Egypt .... *aegyptica* Meggitt, 1927
   Rostellum with 14–18 crowns of hooks 5
5. Rostellum with 14–16 crowns of hooks of lengths not stated; testes 40–50;

cirrus pouches large, reaching the anterior border of the segment; body length 30 mm.; in *Zibethailurus serval, Felis caffra,* South Africa .... *fuhrmanni* Baer, 1924

Rostellum with 16–18 crowns of hooks, of lengths not stated; cirrus pouches large, 105–150 μ; body length 15–60 mm.; in *Felis capensis phillipsi,* Sudan .... *J. sp.* Kofend, 1917

6. Rostellum conical with 12–14 crowns of hooks 7
   Rostellum cylindrical with 15–16 crowns of hooks 8
7. Rostellum with 12–14 crowns of hooks, 14–15 μ high and 10–12 μ long in first rows, and 6 by 5 μ in later rows (16 to 8 μ according to Meggitt); holdfast 320–450 μ in diameter; testes 55–110 (45–50 μ in diameter according to Ratz's figures, 20–30 μ according to Meggitt's figures); cirrus pouches rarely reaching the osmoregulatory canals, 200–210 by 70 μ; eggs 40 μ in capsules of 55–50 μ; body length 120–170 mm.; in cats, Budapest, Granada (Spain), Egypt ....*chyzeri* Ratz, 1897
   Rostellum with 12–13 crowns of hooks, 15–12.5 μ long; holdfast 710 μ in diameter; testes 145; cirrus pouches 215–250 μ by 62–100 μ, crossing the osmoregulatory canals; each uterine capsule, according to Skrjabin, measuring 30–25 by 17 μ and enclosing *several* eggs of diameter not stated; total length 168 mm.; in dogs and cats, Don Province of Russia ....*rossicum* Skrjabin, 1923
8. Rostellum with 16 crowns of hooks, 7–8 μ in first row, smaller in later rows; cirrus pouches small, not reaching the osmoregulatory canals; female apertures level with male apertures; testes 56 (according to Diamare's drawings); egg dimensions unknown; body length 200 mm.; in cats, Alexandria ....*pasqualei* Diamare, 1893
   Rostellum with 16 crowns of hooks, 11–12 μ in first rows down to 6 μ in later rows; testes 80–100; cirrus pouches 200 by 90 μ, just crossing the osmoregulatory canals; female apertures below male apertures; eggs 35–40 μ; body length 190–300 mm.; in cats and dogs, Granada, Spain ....*pasqualaeiformis* Lopez-Neyra, 1928

Witenberg (1932), however, reduced the number of valid species of *Joyeuxiella* to two—namely, *pasqualei* and *echinorhynchoides*—asserting that the species *gervaisi* and *dongolense* were too insufficiently described to permit an opinion, and that the species *fuhrmanni, aegyptica, rossicum, pasqualaeiformis, chyzeri,* and Kofend's species are identical with *pasqualei.* Meggitt's *fortunatum* was established upon a holdfast of *Joyeuxiella pasqualei* and segments of *Diplopylidium acanthotreta.* Witenberg distinguished the two valid species as follows:

1. 14–16 rows of rostellar hooks with bases wider than blades; egg capsules medial and lateral to the osmoregulatory canals ....*pasqualei*
2. 23–24 rows of rostellar hooks, with bases shorter than blades; egg capsules medial entirely to the osmoregulatory canals ....*echinorhynchoides*

Ortlepp (1933) considered *Joyeuxiella fuhrmanni* to be distinct from *Joyeuxiella pasqualei,* since in the former species the testes extend in a zone in front of the sperm ducts which are removed from the anterior segment border. Neveu Lemaire (1936), accepting the views of Witenberg, described the two species in some detail. Their characteristics may be summarized as follows:

1. *pasqualei* Diamare, 1893 (=*Dipylidium chyzeri* Ratz, 1897; *D.*

rossicum Skrjabin, 1922; *D. fuhrmanni* Baer, 1924; *Joyeuxia aegyptica* Meggitt, 1927; *Joyeuxia pasqualei* Lopez-Neyra, 1927; *Joyeuxia pasqualaeiformis* Lopez-Neyra, 1927). Body lengths 65–500 mm.; holdfast flattened dorso-ventrally, 400–500 μ wide, 200–300 μ deep; rostellum retractile, conical or cylindrical when evaginated, 100–160 μ long by 80–120 μ broad; with 14–18 crowns of hooks, shaped like a rose thorn, ranging in length from 11–16 μ in first rows to 6–10 μ in last; neck in extended specimens narrower than holdfast and eight times as long; segments numbering 70–359; testes 40–100, 40–70 μ in diameter; cirrus pouches elliptical, 180–330 μ long; genital apertures prominent, between first third and first half of segment margins; egg capsules 53–76 μ in diameter, each with a single egg 34–50 μ in diameter. Definitive hosts: dog, wolf, cat, *Felis caffra, F. sylvatica, Zibethailurus serval.* Intermediate hosts: various reptiles—*Lacerta viridis, L. muralis, Tarentola mauritanica, Hemidactylus turcicus, Varanus griseus, Acanthodactylus syriacus, Trapelus ruderatus, Stellio vulgaris, Zamenis carbonaria, Z. dahli, Ailurophis fallax*; and a small mammal, *Crocidura suaveolens suaveolens.*

Part of the life cycle has been elucidated by Lopez-Neyra and Muñoz-Medina (1921), Parrot and Joyeux (1920), and Witenberg (1932). The latter investigator attempted to obtain the first larval stages in houseflies (*Musca domestica*) following the suggestion of Lopez-Neyra (1927c), but without success. Distribution: Europe (Hungary, Spain, Italy, South Russia), Africa (Egypt, Algeria, Belgian Congo) (Figure 304).

2. *echinorhynchoides* Sonsino, 1889 (=*Taenia echinorhynchoides* Sonsino, 1889; *Dipylidium echinorhynchoides* Lühe, 1894; *Joyeuxia echinorhynchoides* Lopez-Neyra, 1927). Body length 30–250 mm.; holdfast globular, cuneiform or rhomboidal, 250–670 μ wide by 350–440 μ thick; rostellum when evaginated cylindrical, wider at base than tip, the latter showing a constriction and a terminal enlargement 310–540 μ long and 110–150 μ in diameter; with 23–25 crowns of hooks, ranging in lengths from 19–26 μ in anterior rows to 9–11 μ in posterior rows; neck always very short, 2–4 times as long as holdfast; segments 90–250; testes 30–120, 40–80 μ in diameter; cirrus pouches oval, elongated, 110–420 μ long; genital apertures opening in depressions between first third and first half of segment margins; ovaries lobed; egg capsules 60–70 μ in diameter with one egg in each, 30–40 μ in diameter. Definitive hosts: *Canis rostrata, C. nilotica, C. aureus, Vulpes sp., Fennecus zerda*; experimentally in dogs and cats. Intermediate hosts: various reptiles—*Stellio vulgaris, Scincus officinalis, Ptyodactylus hasselquisti, Psammophis moniliger, Zamenis carbonaria, Z. ravergieri, Z. dahli, Coelopeltis monspessulana, Ailurophis phallax* in Palestine; *Zamenis viridiflavus, Seps chalcides* in Italy. Distribution: Italy, Egypt, Palestine (Figure 305).

Concluding our discussion of the multiple-crowned dipylidiines, it may be noted that according to Witenberg (1932), *Dipylidium* requires a *bloodsucking* insect as intermediate host, whereas *Joyeuxiella* and *Diplopylidium* require a *coprophagous* insect as first intermediate host, and a reptile or a small mammal as second intermediate host.

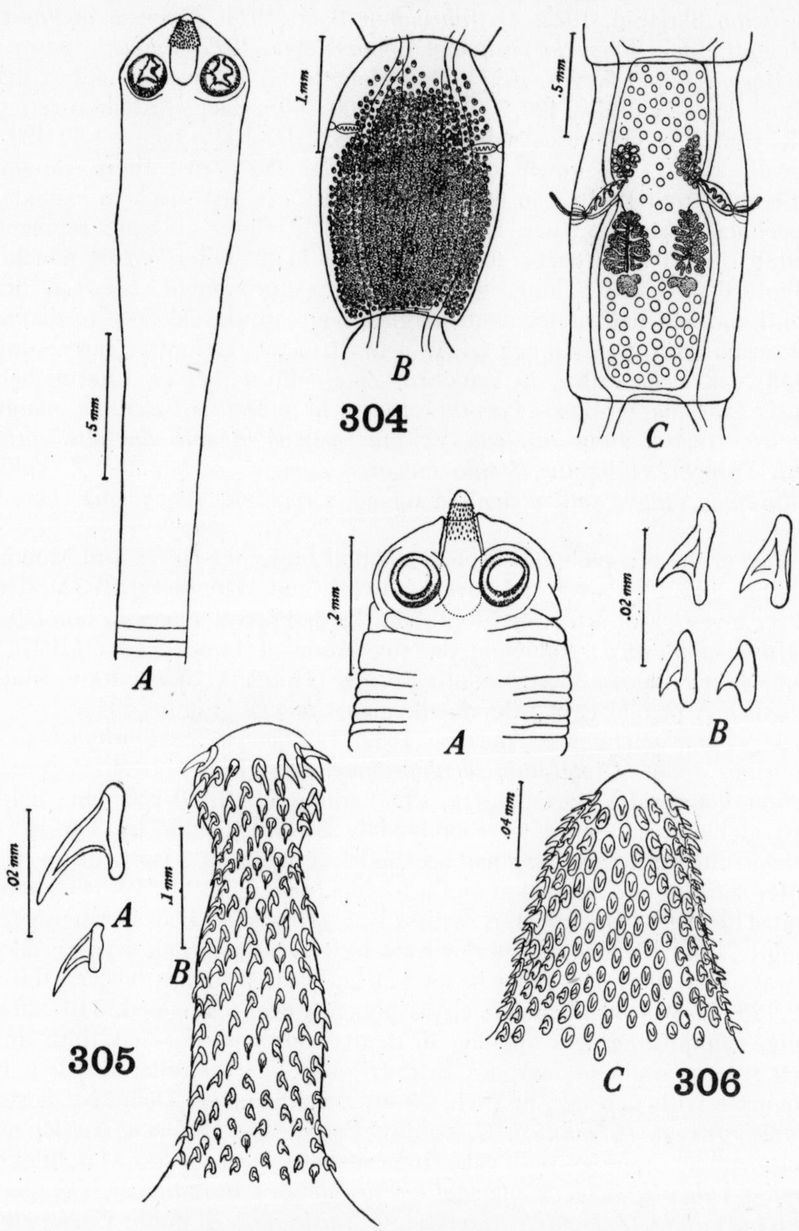

FIG. 304. *Joyeuxiella pasqualei.* After Witenberg, 1932. A. Holdfast. B. Gravid segment. C. Mature segment. FIG. 305. *Joyeuxiella echinorhynchoides.* A. Rostellar hooks. B. Rostellum. FIG. 306. *Joyeuxiella sp.* of Kofend. After Witenberg, 1932. A. Holdfast. B. Rostellar hooks. C. Rostellum.

Southwellia Moghe, 1925

With a double crown of 120 large hooks; neck very short; genital apertures unilateral, each close to the anterior segment border; testes numerous and surrounding the female organs; cirrus pouch voluminous; egg capsules each with 5–9 eggs; genotype, *gallinarum* Southwell, 1921. The genus was established for *Monopylidium gallinarum* Southwell, 1921 from the domestic fowl in India. A second species *ransomi* was recorded by Chapin (1926) in *Turdus migratorius* at Washington, D.C. (U.S.A.) (Figure 307).

Panuwa Burt, 1940

With a double crown of hooks. Genital apertures alternating irregu-

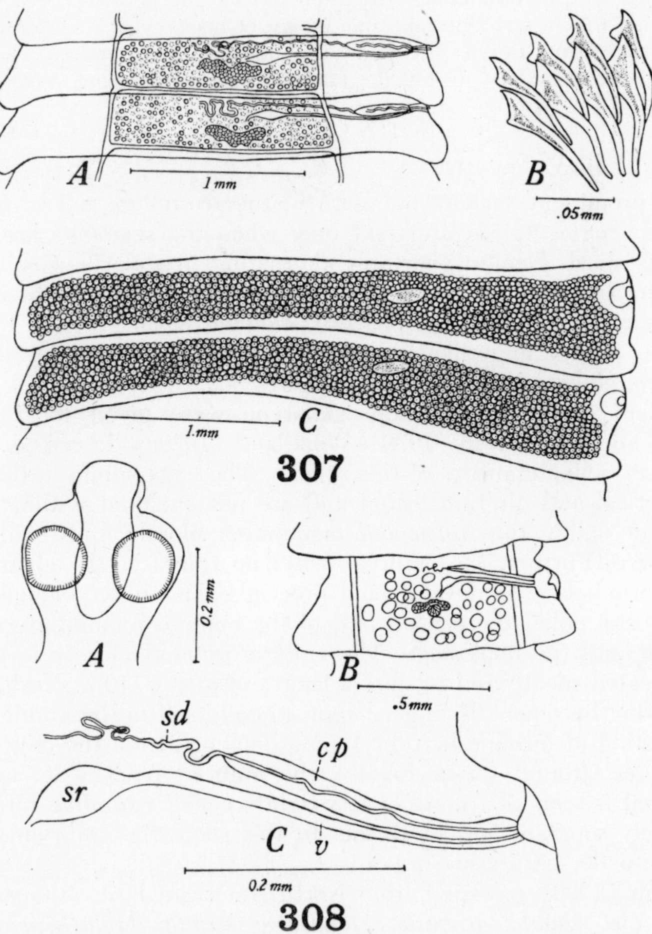

FIG. 307. *Southwellia ransomi.* After Chapin, 1926. A. Mature segments. B. Rostellar hooks. C. Gravid segments. FIG. 308. *Malika pittae.* After Inamdar, 1933. A. Holdfast. B. Mature segment. C. Cirrus pouch (*cp*), sperm duct (*sd*), seminal receptacle (*sr*), and vagina (*v*).

larly. Genital ducts dorsal to the poral canals. Testes numerous, behind the female organs. Egg capsules each with a single egg. Genotype, *lobivanelli* Burt, 1940 from the Indian red-wattled lapwing, *Lobivanellus indicus indicus* in Ceylon.

Subfamily Paruterininae Fuhrmann, 1907

DESCRIPTION

Of the family Dilepididae. With the characters of the family but having in each gravid segment a paruterine organ to receive the eggs. With ten genera distinguishable provisionally as follows:

1. Holdfast lacking rostellum and hooks ....*Anonchotaenia, Metroliasthes, Octopetalum, Rhabdometra*
2. Holdfast with a rudimentary rostellum but lacking hooks ......*Ascometra*
3. Holdfast with a rostellum and one crown of hooks ....*Zosteropicola*
4. Holdfast with a double-crowned rostellum ....*Culcitella, Paruterina, Sphaeruterina, Notopentorchis*

NOTES ON GENERA

Anonchotaenia Cohn, 1900

With prominent suckers but with neither rostellum nor armature of any kind. Segmentation apparent only when the segments are mature. Segments short. Genital apertures alternating irregularly. Genital ducts ventral to the poral canals. Ovary and yolk gland ovoid, without lobulation. Uterus small, ovoid or spherical, showing when gravid a few eggs; joined to it is a fingerlike paruterine organ which receives the eggs. Genotype, *globata* Linstow, 1879 (Figures 309, 310).

Excellent descriptions of the genotype were given by Fuhrmann (1908b) and by Ransom (1909). Woodland (1929a) described in detail the nematodelike embryos of this species. The eggs, while in the uterus, are spherical and multinucleated and are not enclosed within ordinary shells, but within thin *nucleated* membranes closely appressed against the embryo. Further, the embryo shows no traces of the characteristic oncospheric hooks. As development proceeds, the embryo elongates from two opposite poles, the central part of the embryo remaining greater in diameter until the final stage. The embryo remains closely invested by the nucleated sheath and reaches a length of about 110 μ. Next, the embryo having become still longer begins to coil itself in the middle region, the investing membrane here becoming detached from the coils to form a loose sac around them. Finally, the embryo reaches its maximum length and is seen as a more or less tightly coiled wormlike form inside an entirely separate and loose sac. In this stage the embryonated egg passes into the paruterine organ.

Ransom (1909) recorded from North American hosts *Anonchotaenia globata* (in *Alauda arvensis, Dendroica striata, Melospiza melodia, Passer domesticus, Passer montanus, Aegiothus linaria, Loxia curvirostra*); *Anonchotaenia longiovata* Fuhrmann (in *Plegadis guarauna*); and *Anonchotaenia macrocephala* Fuhrmann (in *Progne subis*).

The history of the genus and species and their recorded hosts have

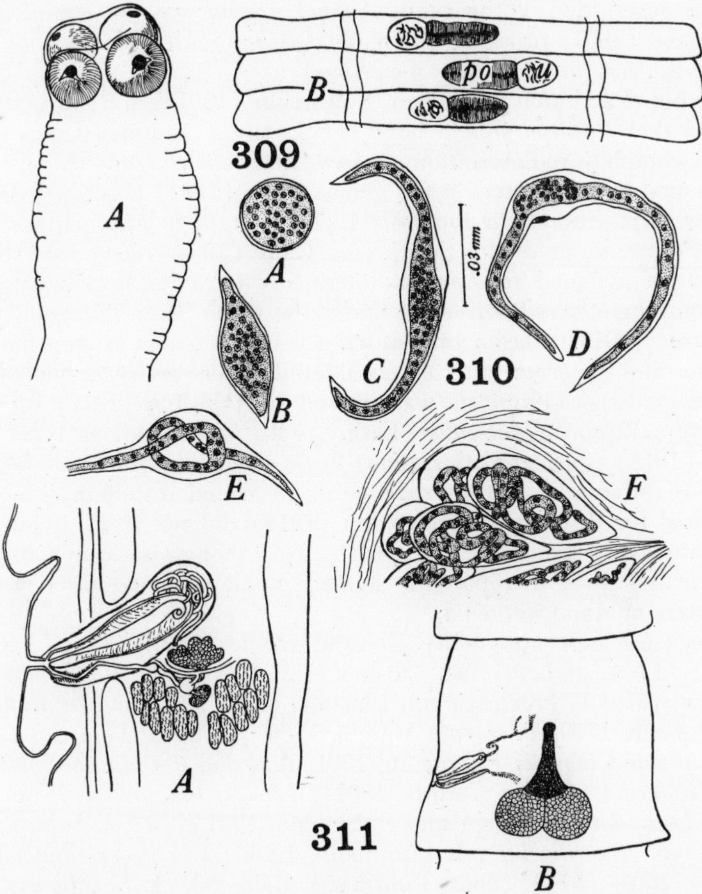

FIG. 309. *Anonchotaenia globata.* After Fuhrmann, 1908c. A. Holdfast. B. Gravid segments. *po*, paruterine organ; *u*, uterus. FIG. 310. *Anonchotaenia globata*, nematodiform embryos. After Woodland, 1929a. A. Young spherical embryo from uterus with investing nucleated membrane. B. Embryo beginning to elongate. C. Elongated embryo with middle region dilated. D. Same. E. With middle region beginning to coil. F. Coiled, fully grown embryos in capsules, formed by nucleated membranes, within paruterine organ. FIG. 311. *Metroliasthes lucida.* After Ransom, 1900. A. Mature segment. B. Gravid segment.

been surveyed by Rausch and Morgan (1947), from whom we quote the following:

"The genus *Anonchotaenia* was proposed by Cohn (1900a) for a cestode from *Parus c. caeruleus*, with *A. clava* as the type species. Von Linstow (1879) described *Taenia Rudolphiana* (syn. *T. Loxiae recurvirostrae* Blumenbach, 1779), *T. globata* and *T. breviceps*, which Fuhrmann (1908) recognized to be synonymous with *A. clava.* Fuhrmann also selected *A. globata* as the most suitable for the type species.

"The description of the genus *Anonchotaenia* was not complete, and Fuhrmann (1901) proposed the name *Anurina* with *A. longiovata* as the type. *Anurina inermis* was mentioned as a further species, but no qualifying description was given. Fuhrmann (1901), in a correction, indicated that *Anurina* should have been written *Amerina*. Cohn (1901) gave a complete re-description of *Anonchotaenia clava*, which definitely established the characters of the genus. Clerc (1902) described *Amerina inermis n.sp.* from *Sitta uralensis* Licht., but in a later paper (1903) gives Fuhrmann credit for the species. Clerc (1903) recognized that the species he assigned to *Amerina inermis* was an undescribed species, and consequently redescribed it under the name *Anonchotaenia bobica*. Diamare (1901) makes a brief reference to the genus as *Anurina*. Both *Anurina* and *Amerina* must be considered synonyms of *Anonchotaenia*.

"The genus *Zosteropicola* was erected by Johnston (1912) for a cestode from *Zosterops lateralis* (Lath.), with *Z. clelandi* as type. Fuhrmann (1918) considered this genus to be identical with *Anonchotaenia*, and was dubious as to the existence of an armed rostellum, which was described for *Z. clelandi*. Fuhrmann (1918) did not think it justifiable to create a new genus for this species, even though an armed rostellum might exist, since it apparently agreed in all other respects with the characters of *Anonchotaenia*.

"There are now apparently 15 valid species in the genus *Anonchotaenia*: (1) *A. globata* (von Linstow, 1870) (syn. *T. Rudolphiana* von Linstow, 1879; *T. breviceps* von Linstow, 1879; *T. Loxiae recurvirostrae* Blumenbach, 1779; *T. clavata* Marchi, 1869; *Anonchotaenia clava* Cohn, 1900; *Anurina inermis* Fuhrmann, 1901; *Amerina inermis inermis* Clerc, 1902; *Amerina alaudae* Cerutti, 1901); (2) *A. longiovata* (Fuhrmann, 1901) (syn. *Anurina longiovata* Fuhrmann, 1901); (3) *A. bobica* Clerc, 1903 (syn. *Amerina inermis* Fuhrmann, 1901); (4) *A. oriolina* Cholodkowsky, 1905; (5) *A. conica* Fuhrmann, 1908; (6) *A. brasiliensis* Fuhrmann, 1908; (7) *A. macrocephala* Fuhrmann, 1908; (8) *A. trochili* Fuhrmann, 1908; (9) *A. arhyncha* Fuhrmann, 1918; (10) *A. piriformis* Fuhrmann, 1918; (11) *A. dendrocitta* (Woodland, 1929) (syn. *Rhabdometra dendrocitta* Woodland, 1929); (12) *A. sbesteriometra* Joyeux and Baer, 1935; (13) *A. rostellata* Rodgers, 1941; (14) *A. castellanii* Fuhrmann and Baer, 1943; (15) *A. quiscali n.sp.*"

The majority of anonchotaeniids recorded from North American birds belong to the species *globata*, a somewhat variable form. Rodgers (1941) and Rausch and Morgan (1947) found *rostellata* in the cardinal bird. Rausch and Morgan (1947) erected the species *quiscali* for material from grackles.

KEY TO SPECIES OF ANONCHOTAENIA (after Rausch and Morgan, 1947)

1. Testes 15 to 16 in number 2
   Testes fewer than 15 3
2. Testes 16; in double row .... *conica*
   Testes about 15, unevenly distributed .... *oriolina*
3. Testes 10 to 13 4
   Testes 8 to 10 7

Testes 8 or fewer 8
4. Prostate gland present 5
Prostate gland lacking 6
5. Testes 12; prostate gland surrounding sperm duct . . . . *piriformis*
6. Genital ducts ventral to osmoregulatory canals; testes 10 to 13; uterus and paruterine organ relatively small . . . . *macrocephala*
Genital ducts between osmoregulatory canals; testes 10 to 12. . *dendrocitta*
7. Testes in two lateral groups, 10 in number; paruterine organ anterior to uterus . . . . *bobica*
Testes not in lateral groups, 8 to 10 in number; cirrus pouch 70 to 80 μ long . . . . *longiovata*
Well-developed sphincter muscle at mouth of cirrus pouch; testes 9 or 10 . . . . *castellanii*
No special development of sphincter muscle; uterus double; testes 9 . . . . *rostellata*
No special development of sphincter muscle; uterus single; testes 9 . . . . *quiscali*
8. Testes 6 to 8; cirrus pouch 70 to 72 μ long . . . . *brasiliensis*
Testes 7; cirrus pouch 80 to 90 μ long . . . . *arhyncha*
Testes 6 or fewer 9
9. Testes 4 or 6; cirrus pouch 108 by 18 μ . . . . *sbesteriometra*
Testes 4 or 5 (but not otherwise as above) 10
10. Testes 5; cirrus pouch 70 to 80 μ by 25 μ . . . . *globata*
Testes 4; cirrus pouch reaching osmoregulatory canal . . . . *trochili*

Metroliasthes Ransom, 1900

Without rostellum. Genital apertures alternating irregularly. Genital ducts running between poral canals. Testes numerous (20 to 40), in posterior region of segment. Cirrus pouch cylindrical, crossing the poral canals. Cirrus armed with long spines. Ovary central, with anterior border lobed, posterior border concave. Gravid uterus appearing as two more or less fused sacs lying side by side in the posterior region of the segment. Paruterine organ developing as a conical fibrous structure anterior to the uterus. Eggs passing out of the uterus into the paruterine organ which serves as a heavy-walled egg capsule, prominent in gravid segments as an opaque whitish or yellowish mass. Eggs ovoid, with three membranes. Genotype, *lucida* Ransom, 1900 (Figures 311, 312).

The genotype and only known species is a common parasite of galliform birds (*Meleagris gallopavo, M. gallopavo sylvestris, Gallus gallus, Numida meleagris, Numida sp., Caccabis rufa*, and *Coturnix rufa*) but is most common in turkeys. It has been reported from North America, Europe, Africa, India, and Australia, but is probably originally and naturally a parasite of the American wild turkey. The life history of this species has been studied in some detail by Jones (1936a) who developed the parasite in turkeys and guinea fowl by feeding them cysticercoids from grasshoppers (*Melanoplus spp., Chorthippus curtipennis, Paroxya clavuliger*). The time necessary for the development of the infective cysticercoids in insects varies from fifteen days in July (Washington, D.C.) to six weeks or more during winter at room temperatures. The adult worm requires a prepatent period of approximately three weeks.

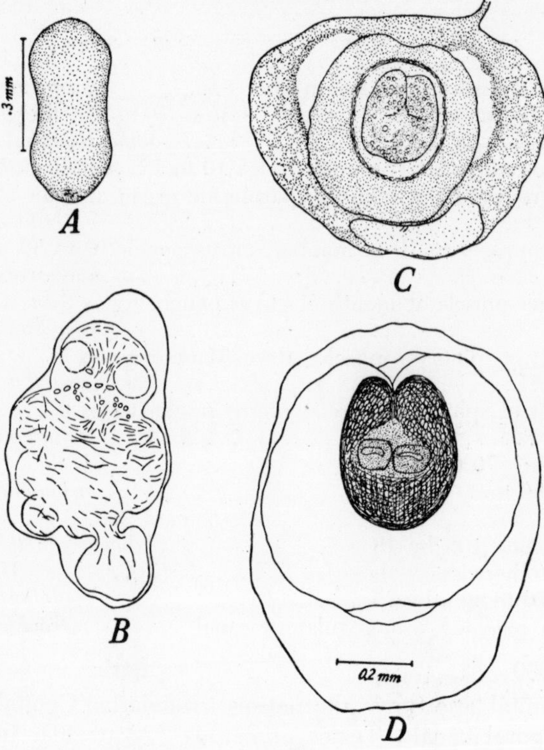

FIG. 312. *Metroliasthes lucida*, life cycle stages. After Jones, 1936a. A. Young, elongated larva with embryonic hooks. B. Larva beginning to invaginate, at 7 to 9 days. C. Completely invaginated larva, caudal appendages with adventitious membrane. D. Infective cysticercoid.

Octopetalum Baylis, 1914

Without rostellum. Suckers covered almost completely by lobelike appendices from their anterior margins and each having a deep median incision. Genital apertures alternating irregularly. Testes surrounding the female organs. Yolk gland dorsal and lateral to the ovary. Paruterine organ anterior to the uterus. Eggs with three envelopes. Genotype, *gutterae* Baylis, 1914.

The genotype was recorded, and has since been recorded again, from the galliform birds *Numida ptilorhyncha* (N.E. Africa) and *Guttera edouardi* (S. Africa). A second species, *longicirrosum* (Figure 313), was added by Baer (1925d) from the same host species. Woodland's *Unciunia sudanea* (1928) has been recorded by Baylis (1934b) as synonymous with Baer's species. Gwynn and Hamilton (1935) recorded from a red locust (*Nomadacris septemfasciata*) in Nigeria a cysticercoid with an unarmed holdfast and lappets overhanging the orifices of the suckers, recalling the adult holdfast of *Octopetalum*.

Rhabdometra Cholodkovsky, 1906

Rostellum rudimentary. Genital apertures alternating irregularly. Genital ducts between the poral canals. Testes mainly posterior. Uterus with a paruterine organ anterior to it and extending nearly to the anterior segment border. Genotype, *tomica* Cholodkovsky, 1906.

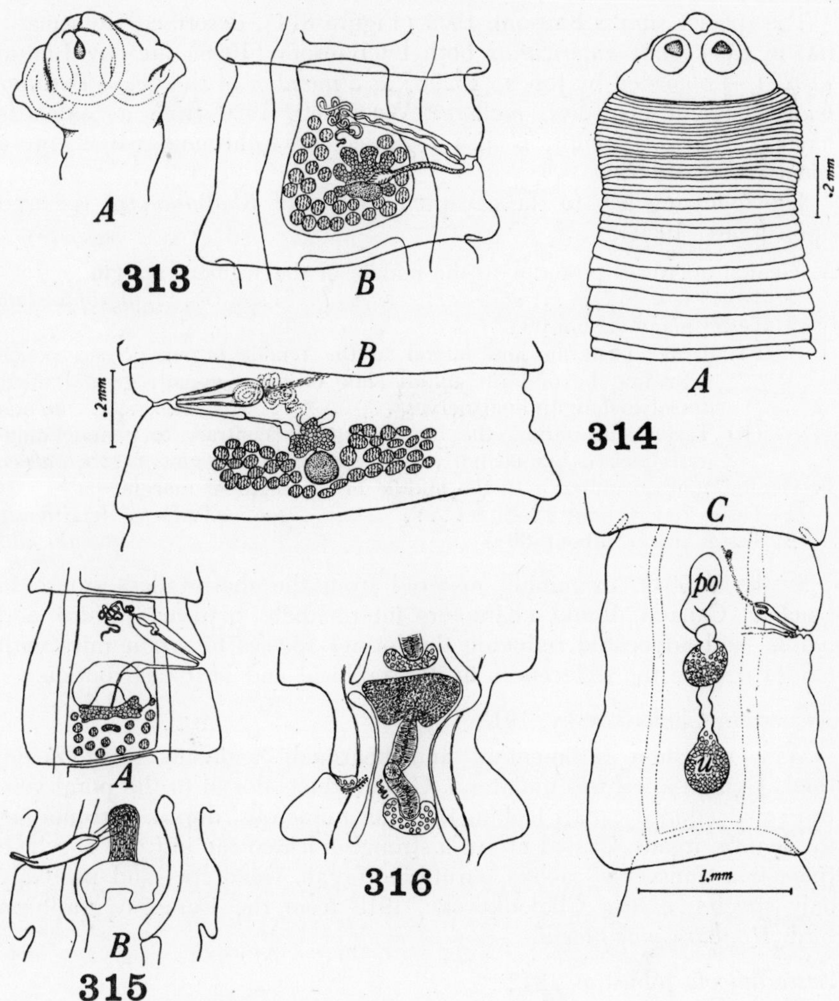

FIG. 313. *Octopetalum longicirrosum.* After Baer, 1925d. A. Holdfast. B. Mature segment. FIG. 314. *Rhabdometra similis.* After Ransom, 1909. A. Holdfast. B. Mature segment. C. Gravid segment. *po,* paruterine organ; *u,* uterus. FIG. 315. *Paruterina angustata.* After Fuhrmann, 1906a. A. Mature segment. B. Gravid segment. FIG. 316. *Sphaeruterina punctata,* gravid segment. After Fuhrmann, 1918.

The genotype was recorded from a galliform bird, *Lyrurus tetrix,* in Russia. Other species recorded are: *cylindrica* Beddard, 1914 from the North African galliform, *Caccabis melanocephalus*; *dendrocitta* Woodland, 1929 from *Dendrocitta rufa* in India; *nigropunctata* Crety, 1890 from *Coturnix coturnix*; *nullicollis* Ransom, 1909 from *Centrocercus urophasianus, Pedioecetes phasianellus columbianus,* Colorado, and by Simon (1940) from *Centrocercus urophasianus,* Wyoming; *numida* Fuhrmann, 1909 from the Sudanese guinea fowl, *Numida ptilorhyncha*; and *odiosa* Leidy, 1897 from *Colinus virgianus,* Florida, U.S.A.

The species *similis* Ransom, 1909 (Figure 314), described from material in *Coccygeus americanus* both by Ransom (1909) and by Linton (1927), is regarded by Jones (1929b) as a member of the genus *Paruterina.* Woodland's species, *melierax* Woodland, 1929 from a Sudanese hawk (*Melierax gabar*), is also regarded by Fuhrmann (1932) as a species of *Paruterina.*

The following key to the accepted species of *Rhabdometra* is based upon Jones (1929):

A. Genital apertures posterior to the middle of the segment margin
  1. Testes few (12) ....*nigropunctata*
  2. Testes many (about 60)
    (a) Testes posterior and lateral to the female organs; cirrus pouch extending beyond the middle line of the segment; genital ducts dorsal to longitudinal nerves ....*numida*
    (b) Testes surrounding the female organs (contrary to generic diagnosis); cirrus pouch not reaching midline of segment ..*cylindrica*

B. Genital aperture anterior to the middle of the segment margin
  1. Testes few (about 12–30) ....*tomica, odiosa, dendrocitta*
  2. Testes many (about 60) ....*nullicollis*

Swales (1934), examining material from the sharp-tailed grouse in Quebec, Canada, found characters intermediate between *tomica* and *odiosa,* and advocated reducing the former species to synonymity with *odiosa* despite the differences in geographical and host distribution.

Ascometra Cholodkovsky, 1913

With rostellum rudimentary and unarmed. Segments short, wide, thick. Genital apertures unilateral. Genital ducts dorsal to the poral ventral canal (dorsal canals lacking). Testes numerous, dorsal, surrounding the female organs. Gravid uterus a strongly pleated sac in front of which there is a transverse, saclike paruterine organ. Genotype, and probably only species, *vestita* Cholodkovsky, 1913 from the Eurasian otidiform bird, *Houbara macqueeni.*

Zosteropicola Johnston, 1912

With the rostellum with a single crown. Other features apparently identical with those of *Anonchotaenia* (*q.v.*). That is to say, the genital apertures alternate more or less regularly. The genital ducts are ventral to the poral canals and nerve cord. Testes few and arranged in a transverse row. Paruterine organ in front of the uterus and somewhat rounded. Genotype, *clelandi* Johnston, 1912 from an Australian passeriform bird, *Zosterops lateralis.*

Culcitella Fuhrmann, 1906

With a double crown of hooks. Genital apertures unilateral *or* alternating irregularly. Genital ducts between the poral canals. Testes mainly behind the ovary, numerous. Uterus a transverse sac with a paruterine organ in front of it. Genotype, *rapacicola* Fuhrmann, 1906 from a South American hawk, *Asturina nitida.* Also recorded: *bresslaui* Fuhrmann,

1927; *crassa* Fuhrmann, 1906; *fuhrmanni* Southwell, 1925; all from acciptriform birds.

Paruterina Fuhrmann, 1906

Rostellum with a double crown of hooks. Genital apertures unilateral *or* irregularly alternating. Testes mainly in rear of ovary. Uterus horseshoe-shaped with a paruterine organ anterior to it. Genotype, *candelabraria* Goeze, 1782.

The genotype is known from a range of Old World strigiform birds and from the North American owl, *Asio flammens.* Fuhrmann (1932) listed 12 species of the genus, to which may be added *septotesticulata* Moghe and Inamdar, 1934; *purpurata* Joyeux and Timon-David, 1934; and *meggitti* Joyeux, Baer, and Martin. Besides *candelabraria*, another North American species is *similis* Ransom, 1909 in *Coccygus americanus* (Figure 314). Rausch (1948c) has redescribed *candelabraria* from the great horned owl, *Bubo virginianus*, and the barred owl, *Strix v. veria*, in the north central United States.

Sphaeruterina Johnston, 1914

Rostellum with a double crown of hooks. Genital apertures alternating irregularly. Genital ducts between poral canals. Testes few, in rear of ovary. Uterus somewhat rounded. Paruterine organ with a distinct anterior dilatation. Genotype, *punctata* Johnston, 1914 from the New Caledonian passeriform bird, *Pachycephala xantherythraea* (Figure 316).

Also recorded are the species *fuhrmanni* Baczynska, 1914 from the Brazilian jaccamariform bird, *Bucco sp.*; and *longiceps* Rudolphi, 1819 from the South American passeriform bird, *Cassicus affinis.* This latter species was recorded by Ransom (1909) as *Biuterina longiceps* from *Cairina moschata* (?) in North America.

Notopentorchis Burt, 1938

Rostellum with double crown of hooks. Genital apertures alternating irregularly. Genital ducts ventral to the poral canals and nerve. Testes few, dorsal. Uterus saclike, becoming spherical, with a paruterine organ developing anterior to it. Genotype, *collocaliae* Burt, 1938 from the Indian edible-nest swiftlet, *Collocalia unicolor unicolor*, Ceylon.

Family Acoleidae Ransom, 1909

DESCRIPTION

Of the order Cyclophyllidea. With a small holdfast provided with an armed rostellum. Segments very muscular, with two layers of longitudinal muscles alternating with three layers of transverse muscles. Female genital apertures lacking, not replaced in function by accessory apertures. Adults in birds. Type genus, *Acoleus* Fuhrmann, 1899.

HISTORY

The family has had a checkered career. Established in 1907 by Fuhrmann under the name Acoleinidae to hold a form, *Acoleus armatus* (=

Taenia vaginata Rudolphi, 1819), the name was emended by Ransom (1909) for grammatical exactitude to Acoleidae. As accepted by Ransom, the family comprised the genera *Acoleus* Fuhrmann, 1899; *Gyrocoelia* Fuhrmann, 1899; *Diplophallus* Fuhrmann, 1900; *Dioicocestus* Fuhrmann, 1900; and *Shipleya* Fuhrmann, 1908. Fuhrmann later added *Progynotaenia* (1909) and *Proterogynotaenia* (1911).

Meggitt (1924a) added *Monecocestus* Beddard, 1914; *Urocystidium* Beddard, 1912; and *Diploposthe* Jacobi, 1896. Poche (1926a) established for the last-named form a separate family, Diploposthidae, to which Southwell and Hilmy (1929b) added the genera *Diplophallus* and *Dioicocestus*, redefining the family Acoleidae in terms almost identical with the definition given above.

Fuhrmann (1932) asserted that of Meggitt's three additions, *Monecocestus* is synonymous with *Schizotaenia* Janicki and is an anoplocephalid. He asserted further his belief that Beddard's *Urocystidium* was a larval taeniid and that *Diploposthe* is a hymenolepidid. He retained within the family Acoleidae the genera *Acoleus, Dioecocestus* (Fuhrmann's spelling), *Diplophallus, Gyrocoelia, Leptotaenia, Progynotaenia, Proterogynotaenia*, and *Shipleyia* (*sic*; *Shipleyia* is etymologically correct but by the International Rules synonymous with *Shipleya* Fuhrmann, 1908). Later (1936a) the genera *Progynotaenia* and *Proterogynotaenia* were removed by Fuhrmann to a newly established family, Progynotaeniidae, and the remaining Acoleidae were distributed between two subfamilies —Acoleinae, for forms without vaginal apertures, and Dioecocestinae (*sic*), for separately sexed forms which possess vaginal apertures.

Burt (1939) restored Dioicocestinae to family rank as Dioicocestidae, and added to them the genera *Dioicocestus, Infula, Shipleya*, and *Gyrocoelia*, retaining within the family Acoleidae only the genera *Acoleus* and *Diplophallus*. We shall take the view here that Acoleidae contains only one valid genus, *Acoleus*, leaving the status of the other genera mentioned for later discussion.

Acoleus Fuhrmann, 1899

With the characters of the family. Rostellar armature not clearly understood. Male apertures alternating regularly. Vaginal apertures lacking. Vagina represented in each segment by a large seminal receptacle. One set of genitalia per segment. Sperm duct ventral to the poral canals. Testes numerous, in a band across the segment. Uterus a transverse, lobed sac which when gravid almost fills the segment. Genotype, *vaginatus* Rudolphi, 1819 (Figure 317).

The genotype is known from several charadriiform birds: from the South American *Belonopterus cayennensis*; from *Himantopus himantopus* (Europe, Asia, Africa); *Himantopus mexicanus* (United States, Central and South America); *Himantopus spinosus* (Europe and Africa). Also recorded are the species *crassus* Fuhrmann, 1900 from the Brazilian charadriiform *Tringa sp.*; *hedleyi* Johnston, 1910 from the Australian charadriiform *Himantopus leucocephalus*; and *longispiculus* Stossich, 1895 from the Eurasian ralliform bird *Zapornia parva.*

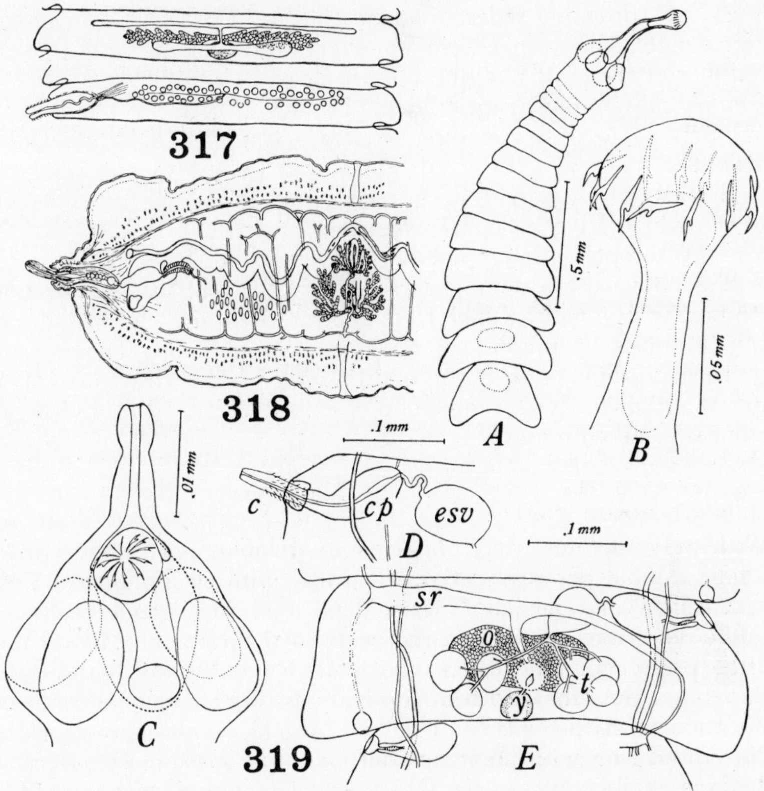

FIG. 317. *Acoleus vaginatus*, two mature segments. After Fuhrmann, 1900b. FIG. 318. *Amabilia lamelligera*, portion of a cross section of a segment. After Clausen, 1915. FIG. 319. *Tatria duodecacantha*. After Schultz, 1940a. A. Whole worm. B. Everted rostellum. C. Holdfast with retracted rostellum. D. Cirrus pouch (*cp*) with protruded cirrus (*c*). *esv*, external seminal vesicle. E. Mature segment. *o*, ovary; *sr*, seminal receptacle; *t*, testes; *y*, yolk gland.

Family Amabiliidae Ransom, 1909

DESCRIPTION

Of the order Cyclophyllidea. Small forms with an armed rostellum. Segments of the body with marginal extensions upon which the male genital apertures open. Vaginal apertures lacking but sometimes replaced in function by centrally situated accessory apertures. Eggs with a thin, transparent shell. Type genus, *Amabilia* Diamare, 1893.

HISTORY

Amabiliinae, as a subfamily of Taeniidae, was established by Braun (1894–1900) for a peculiar tapeworm from the Old World flamingo, *Phoenicopterus ruber*, recorded originally by Owen (1832) as *Taenia lamelligera* and placed later by Diamare (1893a) in a new genus *Ama-*

bilia. It was probably redescribed by Linstow (1906a) as *Aphanobothrium catenata*. The specific term *lamelligera* refers of course to the lateral extensions of the body margins.

Braun's subfamily was raised by Fuhrmann (1907a) to family rank as Amabilinidae, to comprise three genera – *Amabilia, Schistotaenia*, and *Tatria*. The name was corrected by Ransom (1909) to Amabiliidae. Although this family serves as a convenient grouping for these three genera – which have marginal extensions and which lack vaginal apertures – its acceptance must not be allowed to imply close genetic relationships between the three genera. The fact is that the classification of all those Cyclophyllidea which have aberrant features – forms indiscriminately grouped at present as Acoleidae, Amabiliidae, Dioicocestidae, and Diploposthidae – is quite unsatisfactory. The discovery of new material and a closer re-examination of existing material may change the present scheme entirely.

NOTES ON GENERA

Amabilia Diamare, 1893

With the rostellum armed. Segments with marginal extensions. Male genitalia double per segment. Cirri armed with strong spines. Female organs single and median. Ovary dendritic. Yolk gland postovarian, strongly dendritic, larger than the ovary. Vagina opening into a dorso-ventral osmoregulatory canal which itself opens on both segment surfaces and puts the two transverse canals of each segment into communication with the outside. Uterus a cagelike network formed by a dorso-ventral ring with numerous dorso-ventral anastomoses. Eggs with a fusiform shell. Adults in the Old World flamingo. Genotype and only known species, *lamelligera* Owen, 1832 (Figure 318).

Schistotaenia Cohn, 1900

Small forms with marginal extensions or outgrowths. Holdfast partly spinose, with rostellum very long and armed with a single crown of hooks of taeniid type. Male genital apertures alternating irregularly. Testes numerous, extending the whole width of the segment. Vagina and vaginal aperture lacking, replaced in function by a dorso-ventral canal opening on both surfaces. Genotype, *macrorhynchus* Rudolphi, 1810, recorded by several observers (see Krabbe, 1869; Cohn, 1900c; Clerc, 1907) from the arctic grebes, *Colymbus auritus* and *C. dominicus*.

Chandler (1948a) has added to the genus the species *macrocirrus* Chandler, 1948 from the pied-billed grebe (*Podilymbus podiceps*) in Ohio; and *tenuicirrus* Chandler, 1948 from the same host, from the horned grebe (*Colymbus auritus*), and from the crow (*Corvus brachyrhynchus*) in Minnesota, Michigan, Ohio, and Illinois. Baer (1940a), it may be noted, has recorded *scolopendra* in Antigua.

Chandler distinguishes the four species of *Schistotaenia* as follows:

1. Hooks with relatively short blade, the hook length being only 2 to 5 μ less than the base; Old World form . . . . *macrorhynchus*
2. Hooks with relatively long blade, the hook length being 15 to 30 μ greater

than the base 3

3. Holdfast less than 0.5 mm. in diameter, 20 hooks; testes 16–22 per segment; South American . . . . *scolopendra*
   Holdfast 0.75 mm. or more in diameter, 22–26 hooks; testes more than 40 per segment; North American 4
4. Cirrus over 3 mm. long, 50 μ broad at base; body less than 15 mm. long, markedly attenuated posteriorly . . . . *macrocirrus*
   Cirrus about 1.5 mm. long, 30 μ broad at base; body up to 30 mm. long with lateral margins nearly parallel most of length . . . . *tenuicirrus*

Tatria Kowalewski, 1904

Very small forms, with the marginal outgrowths very conspicuous. Rostellum very long, with a single crown of a few large hooks. Rostellar surface, holdfast surface, and suckers all finely spinose. One set of genitalia per segment. Male apertures alternating regularly. Cirrus pouch large. Cirrus spinose. Testes few (7 in genotype). Distal end of vagina, instead of opening to the outside, turning back into the following segment to open into the seminal receptacle, there being consequently a continuous sperm passage from segment to segment. Vaginal apertures lacking but in each segment an accessory vagina, present on the opposite side of the segment from the cirrus pouch, sometimes opening to the exterior. Adult in grebes. Genotype, *biremis kowalewski*, 1904.

Fuhrmann (1932) recognized four species: *acanthorhyncha* Wedl, 1855 (from *Colymbus grisegena, C. dominicus, C. fluviatilis, Colymbus ruficollis japonicus*); *appendiculata* Fuhrmann, 1908 (from *Colymbus dominicus*); *biremis* Kowalewski, 1904 (from *Colymbus auritus*); and *decacantha* Fuhrmann, 1913 (from *Colymbus auritus* and *Colymbus cristata*).

Tatria acanthorhyncha was described in detail by Yamaguti (1940) from Japanese material. Observations upon its life cycle have been published by Mrazek (1927), who found the larval stages in the larvae of various species of dragonfly (*Agrion*), a fact previously observed (and the larva figured) by Linstow. The advanced larva has a typical *Tatria acanthorhyncha* holdfast, a necklike region, and a bladder. The whole is enclosed by a double-walled envelope within which the larva can turn freely. The bladderlike portion of the larva seems morphologically to be the first segment. The double-walled envelope seems to represent in its anterior region the wall of the usual cysticercoid body, the posterior region representing the tail-like portion of the cysticercoid in which, in this case, the developing holdfast has invaginated.

Olsen (1939c) and Schultz (1940a), independently, recorded a fifth species, *duodecacantha* Olsen, 1939 from the pied-billed grebe (*Podilymbus podiceps podiceps*) in Iowa (Olsen) and Oklahoma (Schultz) (Figure 319). Both authors provided keys to the known species of *Tatria*. We give Schultz's key as being the more recent:

1. With 10 rostellar hooks 2
   With 12 rostellar hooks . . . . *duodecacantha*
   With 14 rostellar hooks 4
2. Rostellar hooks less than 30 μ long 3

Rostellar hooks 44–50 μ long . . . . *biremis*
3. Guard of rostellar hook longer than handle . . . . *decacantha*
Guard of rostellar hook shorter than handle . . . . *appendiculata*
4. With 7 testes . . . . *acanthorhyncha*
With 11–13 testes or "testis lobes" . . . . *fuhrmanni*

Detailed descriptions of *acanthorhyncha, biremis*, and *decacantha* have been given by Joyeux and Baer (1936d).

Family Dioicocestidae Southwell, 1930, emended Burt, 1939

DESCRIPTION

Of the order Cyclophyllidea. In which the sexes may be separate, some worms containing only male organs, others only female organs. Type genus, *Dioicocestus* Fuhrmann, 1900.

HISTORY

The family was established by Southwell (1930) for Fuhrmann's genus *Dioicocestus*, the only tapeworm with separate sexes known at the time. Since then, however, Burt (1939) has described another separately sexed form under the generic term *Infula* and has given reasons for his belief that the genera *Shipleya* and *Gyrocoelia*, formerly regarded as Acoleidae, have separate sexes and should go into this family.

NOTES ON GENERA

Dioicocestus Fuhrmann, 1900 (= *Dioecocestus* Fuhrmann, 1932)

With characteristics recalling Acoleidae but with separate male and female forms, the males being more slender than the females and having two sets of reproductive organs per segment. Females with one set of reproductive organs per segment, and with the vagina in each segment close to the segment margin and alternating irregularly from segment to segment. Uterus saclike, strongly lobed. Adults in birds. Genotype, *paronai* Fuhrmann, 1900.

Fuhrmann always refused to recognize this form as anything but an acoleid. Of the seven species recorded, all except one (the genotype), which is from a heron, are from grebes, these species being *acotylus* Fuhrmann, 1904 (Figure 320 C, D, and E); *aspera* Mehlis, 1834 (Figure 320 A); *fuhrmanni* Linton, 1925; *novae-guineae* Fuhrmann, 1914 (Figure 320 B); and *novae-hollandiae* Krefft, 1871. Linton (1925) recorded *fuhrmanni* from *Colymbus auritus* and *C. holboelli* at Woods Hole, Massachusetts.

Infula Burt, 1939

With an unarmed rostellum. Male and female worms each with a single set of reproductive organs per segment. Yolk glands postovarian. Genital apertures alternating. Vagina cirruslike in structure. Uterus ringlike, with numerous outgrowths when fully developed and with dorsal and ventral apertures in the middle line of the posterior region of the segment. Adults in birds. Genotype and only known species, *burhini*

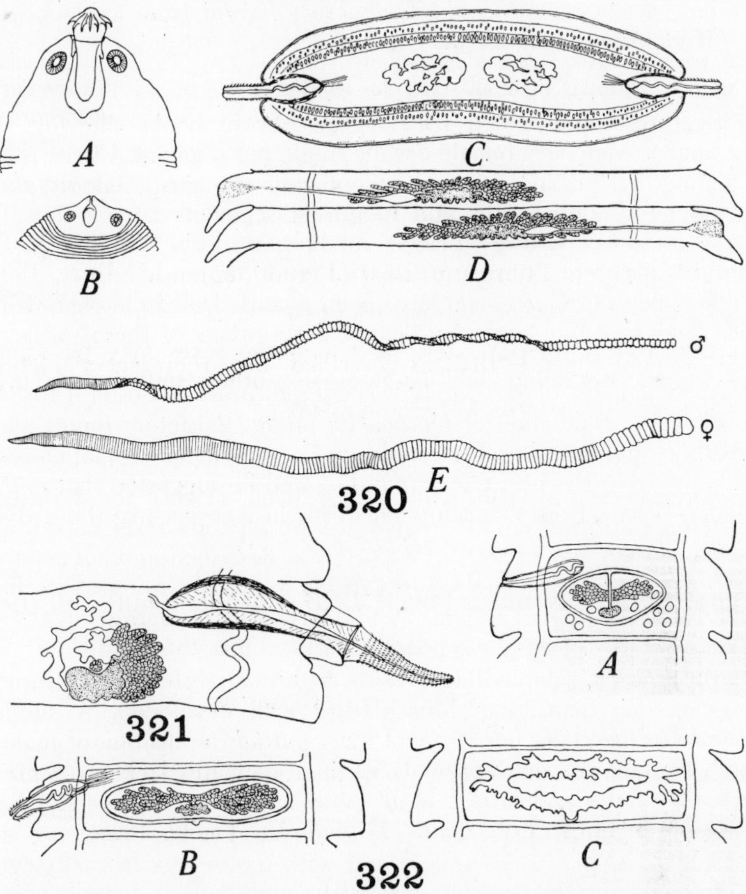

FIG. 320. *Dioicocestus* species. After Fuhrmann, 1932. A. *aspera*, holdfast. B. *novae-guineae*, holdfast. C. *acotylus*, transverse section of a segment of a male worm. D. *acotylus*, horizontal section of segments of a female worm. E. *acotylus*, male and female specimens. FIG. 321. *Shipleya inermis*, part of a horizontal section of a segment. After Fuhrmann, 1932. FIG. 322. *Gyrocoelia perversa*. After Fuhrmann, 1899b. A, B, and C. Three segments of different ages.

Burt, 1939 from charadriiform birds (*Burhinus oedicnemus indicus, Himantopus himantopus himantopus*) in Ceylon.

Shipleya Fuhrmann, 1908 (= *Shipleyia* Fuhrmann, 1932)

With the holdfast unarmed and lacking rostellum. Genital apertures alternating regularly. Seminal receptacle very small. Yolk glands dorsal to the ovary. Uterus ringlike with numerous outgrowths. Adults in birds. Genotype, *inermis* Fuhrmann, 1908 from a Brazilian charadriiform bird, *Gallinago gigantea* (Figure 321).

Burt (1939) gave reasons for assuming that *Shipleya inermis*, as described by Fuhrmann, was the female of a separately sexed species.

Inamdar (1942) recorded *Shipleyia* (*sic*) *farrani* from a black-winged stilt (*Himantopus himantopus*) in India.

Gyrocoelia Fuhrmann, 1900

With a rostellum armed with zigzag row of hooks showing six or eight angles. Male and female organs single per segment. Cirrus pouches alternating irregularly. Seminal receptacle very small. Uterus ringlike with numerous outgrowths and in gravid segments having dorsal and ventral uterine apertures placed medio-posteriorly. Adults in birds. Genotype, *perversa* Fuhrmann, 1899 (Figure 322).

Eight species of *Gyrocoelia* have been recorded, all from charadriiform birds. Analyzing the somewhat scanty descriptions of these forms, Burt (1939) argued cogently that, as described, they represent a mixture of males and females of separately sexed tapeworms. Webster (1943), on examining the type slide of *Gyrocoelia milligani* Linton, found another species, belonging to another family, to be present (*Progynotaenia sp.*), both being from the bird *Crocethia alba*; and he suggested that *milligani* of Baer (1940a) from *Oxyechus vociferus* in Antigua may be a distinct species.

Family Diploposthidae Poche, 1926, emended Southwell, 1929

DESCRIPTION

Of the order Cyclophyllidea. With an armed rostellum. Mature segments broader than long. Musculature well developed. A single or double set of genitalia per segment, or a *partial* duplication of male and female genitalia in each segment. Vaginal apertures lacking or present. Cirrus very large and armed with spines. Uterus a transverse, sinuous sac. Adults in birds. Type genus, *Diploposthe* Jacobi, 1896.

HISTORY

The family was established by Poche (1926a) for Jacobi's form on account of its double vaginae. Southwell and Hilmy (1929b) added two other genera, *Diplophallus* and *Jardugia*, with double vaginae, and redefined the family. We believe that in this family should be placed also the genus *Diplogynia* recorded by Baer (1925a).

NOTES ON GENERA

Diploposthe Jacobi, 1896

With male organs duplicated in each segment. Testes 3–7, postovarian. Female organs single per segment but with two vaginae present. Vaginal aperture present. Uterus a transverse, sinuous sac. Genotype, *laevis* Bloch, 1782, recorded from a range of anseriform birds (Figure 323).

Matevosyan (1942) suggested that *laevis* is a composite of three species. The original *laevis* had ten rostellar hooks, each 21 μ long and of characteristic shape, and had three testes per segment. Specimens with 14–17 testes he proposed to separate as *Diploposthe skrjabini*, while other specimens possessing only six testes he proposed to separate also,

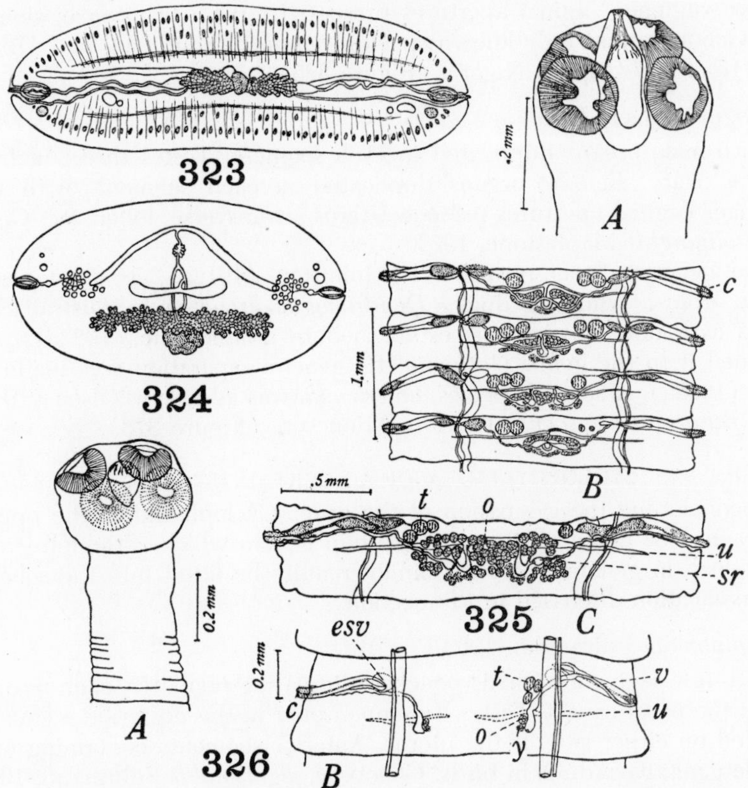

FIG. 323. *Diploposthe laevis*, cross section of mature segment. After Jacobi, 1897a. FIG. 324. *Diplophallus polymorphus*, cross section of mature segment. After Wolffhügel, 1898a. FIG. 325. *Jardugia paradoxa*. After Southwell and Hilmy, 1929b. A. Holdfast. B. 4 segments with mature male genitalia. C. Segment with mature female genitalia. FIG. 326. *Diplogynia americana*. After Olsen, 1940. A. Holdfast. B. Mature segment. *c*, cirrus; *esv*, external seminal vesicle; *o*, ovary; *sr*, seminal receptacle; *t*, testes; *u*, uterus; *v*, vagina; *y*, yolk gland.

deferring the naming of this third type, however, until more material was available.

Diplophallus Fuhrmann, 1900

With male organs duplicated in each segment. Testes about 100, in two lateral fields. Female organs single per segment but with two vaginae. Vaginal apertures lacking. Uterus a transverse, sinuous sac. Genotype and only known species, *polymorphus* Rudolphi, 1819 from the charadriiform bird *Himantopus himantopus*, Europe and Africa (Figure 324).

Jardugia Southwell and Hilmy, 1929

With the male organs single or duplicated in each segment. Testes 3–5, in front of the ovary. Female organs single or duplicated, with one or two vaginae. Vaginal apertures present. Uterus a transverse, sinuous sac. Genotype and only known species, *paradoxa* Southwell and Hilmy, 1929 from *Ardea sp.* in Nigeria (Figure 325).

Diplogynia Baer, 1925

With male organs duplicated in each segment. Testes three, in front of the ovary. Female organs duplicated in each segment, with two vaginae. Vaginal apertures present. Uterus a transverse, lobed sac. Genotype, *oligorchis* Maplestone, 1922.

The genotype was recorded by Johnston (1912a), as *Diploposthe laevis*, from a whistling duck (*Dendrocygna arcuata*) in Australia. Its status as a new species was established by Maplestone (1922a), who assigned it to the genus *Cotugnia*. Its generic separation was made by Baer (1925a). A second species, *americana*, was added by Olsen (1940) from *Butorides virescens virescens*, Minnesota (Figure 326).

CYCLOPHYLLIDEA OF UNCERTAIN STATUS

In concluding the discussion of the order Cyclophyllidea, the opportunity may be taken of discussing certain genera which, although cyclophyllidean in general features, cannot readily be fitted into the scheme of classification discussed in this section.

Progynotaenia Fuhrmann, 1909

With few segments. Cirrus pouches alternating regularly, each passing under the poral canals. Testes developed only in the posterior segments, situated on either side of the uterus. Anterior segments containing only female genitalia. Adults in birds. Genotype, *jägerskiöldi* Fuhrmann, 1909.

The genotype was recorded from a charadriiform bird, *Pluvianus aegypticus*, in Egypt. Fuhrmann (1932) recognized six additional species, all from charadriiform birds, including a form which had been recorded by Linton (1927) as *Gyrocoelia milligani* from *Crocethia alba* at Cape Lookout, North Carolina. Joyeux and Baer (1939b), accepting these species, distinguished them as follows:

1. *evaginata* Fuhrmann, 1909. With 60 rostellar hooks (20 according to Meggitt, 1928) of 18 μ length, in broken line.
2. *flaccida* Meggitt, 1928. With 28 hooks 31–34 μ in length, in double crown.
3. *foetida* Meggitt, 1928. With 20 rostellar hooks 46–51 μ in length.
4. *jägerskiöldi* Fuhrmann, 1909. With 34 rostellar hooks of 52 μ in single crown.
5. *milligani* Linton, 1927. With hooks not described, but cirrus pouch longer than in other forms.
6. *pauciannulata* Baczynska, 1911. With 19 rostellar hooks 44 μ in length.
7. *odhneri* Nybelin, 1914. With 12 rostellar hooks 59–63 μ in length in single crown.

Baer (1940a), however, resurveyed the genus and restricted the number of species to three, namely: *evaginata* Fuhrmann, 1909 (=*pauciannulata* Baczynska, 1914 in part) (Figure 327); *odhneri* Nybelin, 1914 (=*pauciannulata* Baczynska, 1914 in part, and *foetida* Meggitt, 1928); and *jägerskiöldi* Fuhrmann, 1909.

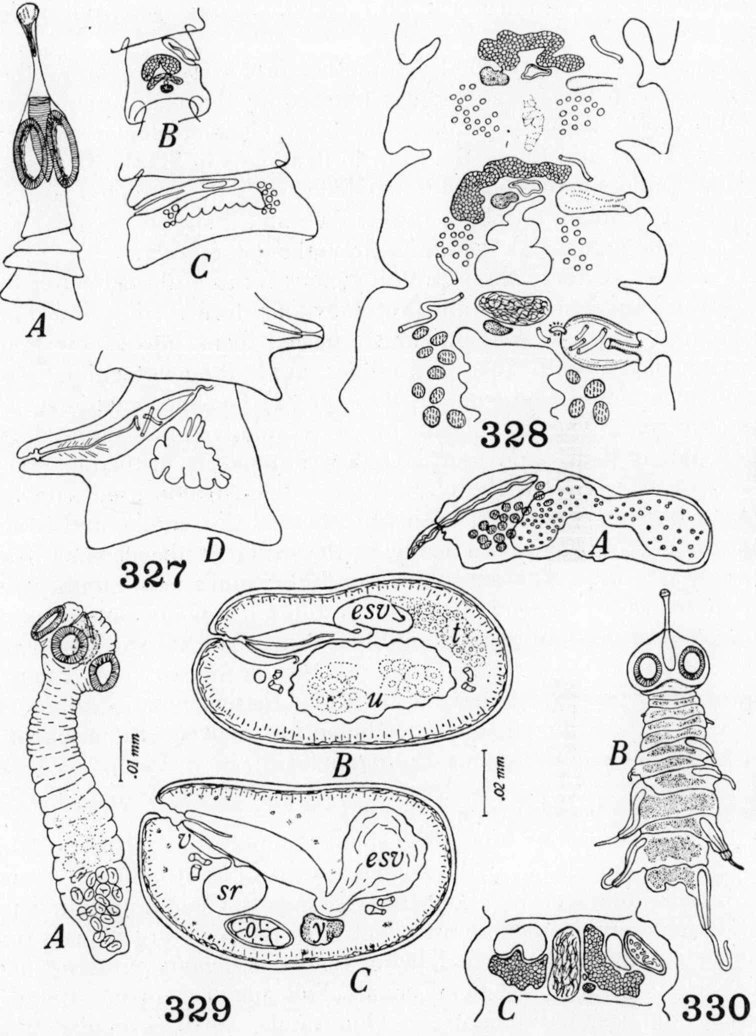

FIG. 327. *Progynotaenia evaginata.* After Fuhrmann, 1909b. A. Holdfast. B, C, and D. Segments of different ages. FIG. 328. *Proterogynotaenia rouxi*, horizontal section of three segments. After Fuhrmann, 1911. FIG. 329. *Protogynella blarinae.* After A. W. Jones, 1943. A. Whole worm. B. Cross section of mature male region. C. Cross section of mature female region. *esv*, external seminal vesicle; *o*, ovary; *sr*, seminal receptacle; *t*, testes; *u*, uterus; *v*, vagina; *y*, yolk gland. FIG. 330. *Leptotaenia ischnorhyncha.* After Cohn, 1899. A. Cross section of mature segment. B. Whole worm. C. Gravid segment.

Proterogynotaenia Fuhrmann, 1911

Small forms with the rostellum armed with a double crown of hooks. Cirrus pouches alternating irregularly, passing between the poral canals. Testes present only in the posterior segments which have a fully formed uterus. Genotype and only known species, *rouxi* Fuhrmann, 1911 from the cosmopolitan charadriiform bird *Ochthodromus geoffroyi* (Figure 328).

Fuhrmann (1936a) recorded yet another proterogynous form – that is to say, one with the female organs anteceding the male organs – from the Old World flamingo, under the term *Gynandrotaenia stammeri.* Stammer (1936) also found the form in flamingos in Silesia. It possesses a peculiar projection of the holdfast which bears the retracted rostellum and which Fuhrmann termed a "proscolex"; and it shows a regular alternation of male and female genitalia throughout the body.

On the basis of these three proterogynous forms Fuhrmann felt justified (1936a) in removing all proterogynous forms from the family Acoleidae, in which he had previously placed them, into a new family, Progynotaeniidae, with two subfamilies – (1) Progynotaeniinae, with *Progynotaenia* and *Proterogynotaenia*; and (2) Gynandrotaeniinae, with *Gynandrotaenia.* The establishment of a family upon physiological grounds rather than upon morphological grounds is justifiable enough if it is demonstrable that the physiological phenomenon used as a basis of discrimination is restricted to the members of this family, and is not a phenomenon occurring sporadically in the order or the class of which the family is a unit. The acceptance of Fuhrmann's new family would seem, therefore, to depend upon the results of a wider survey of the phenomenon of proterogyny among tapeworms than has yet been made. Should additional knowledge lead to the acceptance of Progynotaeniidae, other genera may have to be placed therein, notably *Diplogynia* – placed at present among Diploposthidae but believed by Olsen to be proterogynous – and the genus *Protogynella.*

Protogynella Jones, 1943

Small forms (0.75 mm. long), the smallest tapeworms recorded. Holdfast spherical, unarmed, with saclike, protrusible rostellum. A neck region present, followed by about thirty segments. Genital apertures unilateral. Female organs median and ventral to the male organs and functioning before them, the animal being thus *functionally* proterogynous. Genital ducts dorsal to the poral canals. Yolk gland compact, aporal to the ovary and seminal receptacle. One single, small, irregular testis. Uterus pocketlike, filling the gravid segment except in the vicinity of the testis. Genotype, *blarinae* Jones, 1943 from the short-tailed shrew (*Blarina brevicauda*), Virginia (Figure 329).

Leptotaenia Cohn, 1901

With the rostellum armed with a single crown of hooks. Neck lacking. Body small, 12–15 segments. Male genital apertures alternating regularly. Genitalia slightly proterogynous. Cirrus very long and armed.

Testes only on the poral side. Vagina lacking. Ovary occupying the full width of the medulla. Yolk gland median and arranged longitudinally. Seminal receptacle median and longitudinal, almost the full length of the segment. Uterus saclike, filling the whole medulla. Genotype and only known species, *ischnorhyncha* Lühe, 1898 from the flamingo *Phoenicopterus antiquorum* (Figure 330). Fuhrmann (1932), while placing the genus among Acoleidae, suggested that further examination might show it to be amabiliid.

Copeosoma Sinitsin, 1896

Holdfast with a voluminous rostellum. Genital organs discharging at the summit of a papilla. Genital apertures alternating irregularly in young segments and situated on the ventral surface; in gravid segments situated laterally. Genotype, *papillosum* Sinitsin, 1896 from the charadriiform bird, *Limonites damacensis*, Siberia.

Tetracisdicotyla Fuhrmann, 1907 (= *Tetracisdicotyle* Fuhrmann, 1907)

With a holdfast lacking rostellum. With four large suckers each with a peculiar muscular organ. Body segmentation indistinct. Genital apertures alternating irregularly. Cirrus pouches large. Testes numerous. Genotype, *macroscolecina* Fuhrmann, 1907 from the South American heron, *Butorides virescens*.

Order APORIDEA

DESCRIPTION

Of the class Cestoda. Small forms, up to 13 mm. in length. Holdfast of simple hymenolepidid type but lacking suckers, or provided with an elaborate, glandular rostellum and relatively enormous suckers. External segmentation lacking. Proglottisation lacking in one genus, present in the other. Testes and ovaries without ducts or other communication with the outside. Ootypes lacking. Yolk glands present or, doubtfully, lacking. Ovaries cortical, forming a sleeve around the testes. Adults protandrously hermaphroditic, some forms without female organs at all. With one family, Nematoparataeniidae, with the characters of the order.

HISTORY

This order was established by Fuhrmann (1933) for two species of *Nematoparataenia* Maplestone and Southwell, a genus for which Poche (1926a) had established the family Nematoparataeniidae.

"Poche, relying upon the very incomplete description of the species described by Maplestone and Southwell, established the new family of Nematoparataeniidae with a diagnosis which takes up half a page of text but which has scarcely anything in it that corresponds with reality. The only character of value mentioned by Maplestone and Southwell (lacking however from their generic description) is ignored because Poche would not admit that genital apertures might be lacking.

"Poche even expressed doubts as to whether *Nematoparataenia paradoxa* was a tapeworm at all. Unjustifiable doubts, for the holdfasts of the two species resemble holdfasts of Cyclophyllidea, as does also the arrangement of the muscles, the osmoregulatory system, and the eggs with their double embryonic envelope and six-hooked oncospheres; all these features are typical of cestodes. On the other hand, the reproductive system is aberrant, and if we do not wish to reduce the diagnosis of the order Cyclophyllidea merely to characters of the holdfast, taking away from such diagnosis any reference to the plan of the genitalia, it seems necessary to establish a new order. Our description of *Nematoparataenia southwelli* shows that the genitalia, apart from being hermaphroditic, have no resemblance with those of other cestode orders. For this reason we propose to place the two species of *Nematoparataenia* in the new order Aporidea with the characters of the genus and the family." Fuhrmann (1933c).

Wolffhügel (1938) preferred to group these forms – together with his newly established genus *Gastrotaenia* – as a suborder (Heterocyclophyllidea) of the order Cyclophyllidea, the remaining cyclophyllideans comprising the suborder Eucyclophyllidea. He objected to the term Aporidea on the grounds that Fuhrmann had previously used the term *Aporina* for an anoplocephalid genus.

It may be stressed, however, that the name of a zoological order is not founded necessarily upon the name of any genus within it. There are, for example, no such genera as *Cyclophyllidium* or *Pseudophyllidium*. The present writers therefore support the suggestion of Fuhrmann. However, since Fuhrmann's definition – based upon *Nematoparataenia* only – requires emendation, we have substituted for it a definition which is substantially that given by Wolffhügel for Heterocyclophyllidea.

NOTES ON GENERA

Nematoparataenia Maplestone and Southwell, 1922, emended Fuhrmann, 1933

Small forms up to 3.5 mm. long. Holdfast relatively enormous, with four very prominent suckers whose apertures face forward, and an enormous cushionlike rostellum, usually completely evaginated, armed with an undulating circle of about 1,000 minute hooks recalling those of certain Hymenolepididae. Body cylindrical, with a short anterior sterile re-

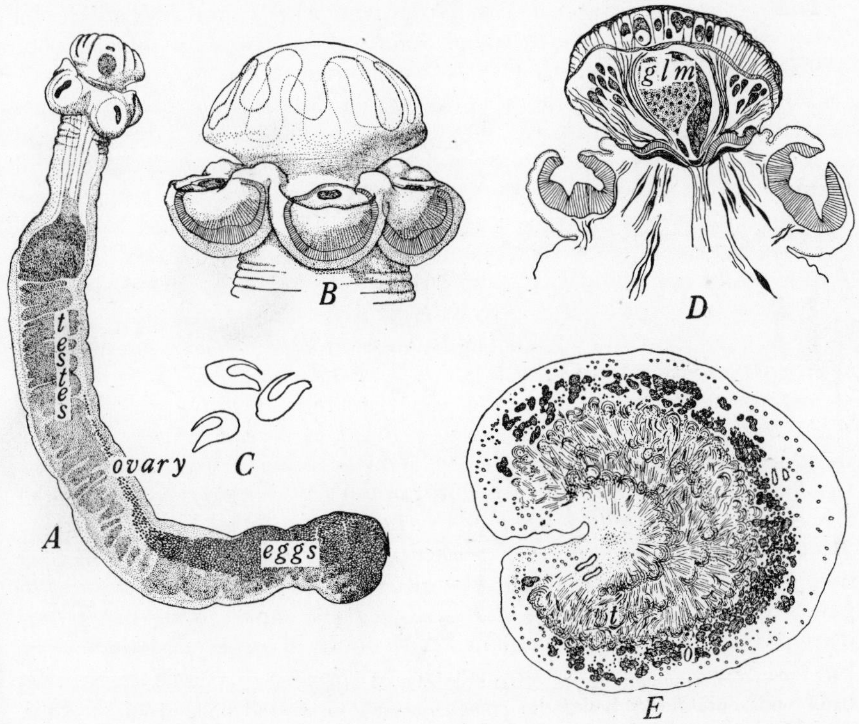

FIG. 331. *Nematoparataenia southwelli*. After Fuhrmann, 1933c. A. Lateral view of a single adult showing region of testes, ovary, and eggs. B. Holdfast. C. Rostellar hooks. D. Longitudinal section of holdfast (*glm*, glandular mass). E. Cross section of body showing follicular peripheral ovaries (*o*) surrounding the testes (*t*).

gion and a longer sexual region which has on one side a deep gutter. External segmentation and internal proglottisation not evident. Genitalia filling almost completely the medullary parenchyma. Male and female organs follicular, without ducts and without genital apertures. Testis tissue occupying the internal parenchyma the full length of the sexual region as a compact mass, fan-shaped in cross section. Female organs in the form of a sleeve of very small follicles surrounding the male organs. Eggs each with a double envelope, in clusters of 10–14 within membranous bladders, within which they are fertilized by wandering sperm cells and within which they undergo development. Life cycle unknown. Genotype, *paradoxa* Maplestone and Southwell, 1922 from the black swan, *Chenopsis atrata*, Australia. Second species, *southwelli* Fuhrmann, 1933 in the swan, *Cygnus olor*, Sweden (Figure 331).

Wolffhügel (1938) suggested that the cushionlike rostellum is nutri-

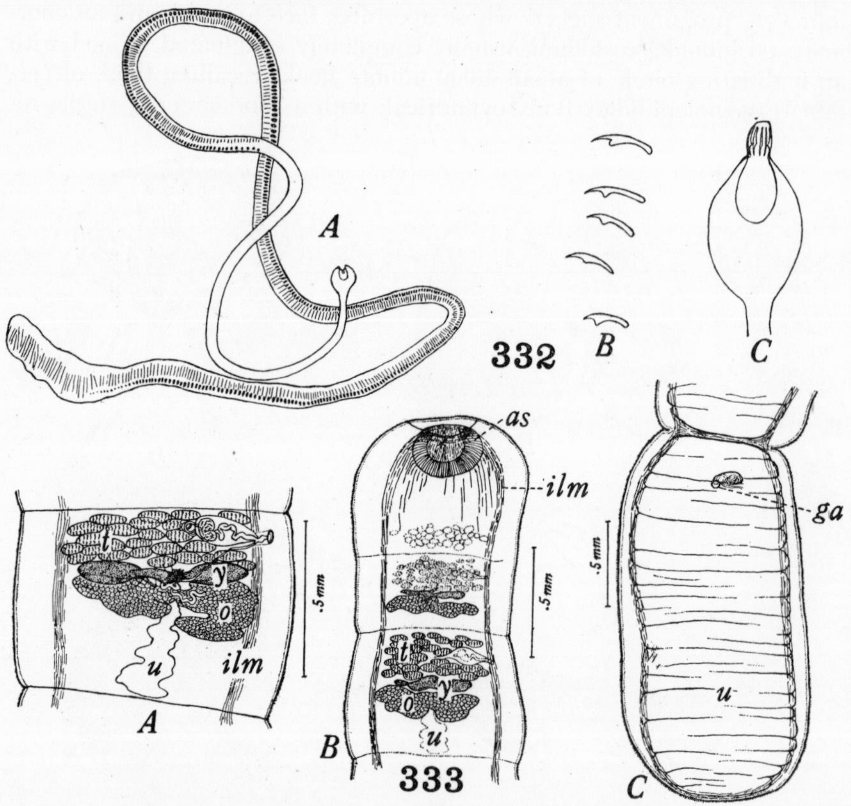

FIG. 332. *Gastrotaenia cygni.* After Wolffhügel, 1938. A. Entire worm, the right band with dark flecks being the *anlage* of the ovaries and yolk glands, the left, cross-hatched band indicating the *anlage* of the testes. B. Rostellar hooks. C. Holdfast. FIG. 333. *Nippotaenia chaenogobii.* After Yamaguti, 1939. A. Mature segment. B. Anterior region of the worm, ventral view. C. Gravid terminal segment. *as*, anterior sucker; *ga*, genital aperture; *ilm*, internal longitudinal muscles; *o*, ovary; *t*, testes; *u*, uterus; *y*, yolk gland.

tive in function, and that the forwardly directed suckers hold the holdfast firmly against the host gut mucosa and through alternately contracting and expanding movements of the rostellum attract a current of blood and mucus into the glandular cells within it. These he assumed to be of three types – proteolytic, acid-producing, and blood-coagulating. A similar function, he suggested, may be possessed by the swollen but rostellumless holdfast of *Hymenolepis megalops* (for which he suggested the generic term *Cloacotaenia*) in the cloaca of anseriform birds, and by the "proscolex" of Fuhrmann's *Gynandrotaenia stammeri* from the flamingo.

Gastrotaenia Wolffhügel, 1938

Small forms, up to 13.5 mm. in length. Holdfast hymenolepidid in type, but without suckers, having a single circle of ten hooks on the rostellum. External segmentation lacking but proglottisation evident. Anterior region of the body without reproductive organs. Longitudinal muscles weak. Fertile region of the body cylindrical. Two dorsal osmoregulatory canals connected metamerically by transverse canals; two ventral osmoregulatory canals connected by a netlike anastomosis. Ovaries as in *Nematoparataenia* but with yolk glands in close proximity. Testes arranged metamerically, horseshoe-shaped when mature. Genotype, *cygni* Wolffhügel, 1938 from *Cygnus melanocoryphus* in Uruguay, South America (Figure 332). Wolffhügel would place within his genus Cram's (1926a) cestode larva from the gizzard of a duck and Taylor's (1934) "*Fimbriaria fasciolaris*" from a swan.

Order NIPPOTAENIIDEA

DESCRIPTION

Of the class Cestoda. With the body nearly cylindrical and holdfast with a single well-developed sucker, but with no other organs of fixation. Neck short, fused with holdfast. Segments few, each with one set of genitalia. Yolk gland compact, bipartite. Osmoregulatory canals numerous, cross-connected. Adults in fishes. One family known, Nippotaeniidae.

HISTORY

The order was established by the Japanese zoologist Satyu Yamaguti (1939) for a form taken from a fresh-water fish (*Chaenogobius*) in Japan. In his opinion the possession of a very powerful apical sucker, the arrangement of the reproductive organs, of the osmoregulatory system, etc., fully justified the establishment for it not merely of a new family but of a new order. In its general features, especially in the character of the yolk glands, it recalls Cyclophyllidea more closely than any other tapeworm group; but in the arrangement of the osmoregulatory system it bears a decided resemblance to the order Caryophyllidea.

Family Nippotaeniidae Yamaguti, 1939

DESCRIPTION

Of the order Nippotaeniidea. With the characters of the order. Relatively small forms with lateral genital apertures. Testes numerous, in the anterior region of the medulla. Cirrus pouch present. Ovary central or antero-central. Yolk gland immediately in front of the ovary. Uterus extending longitudinally in the medulla, developing a number of secondary outgrowths when gravid; without uterine aperture. Eggs with a six-hooked embryo. Type genus, *Nippotaenia*.

Nippotaenia Yamaguti, 1939

With the characters of the family. Body round or oval in cross section, completely covered with minute spines. Holdfast rounded in front, with a globular apical sucker. Neck containing genital primordia and somewhat narrower than the holdfast. Segments increasing in length posteriorly, with parallel or slightly convex margins; terminal gravid segments easily detachable. Inner longitudinal muscle fibers not in bundles but forming a definite sheath attached to a sphincterlike anterior end of the apical sucker. Longitudinal osmoregulatory canals numerous in the cortex but scanty in the medulla. Poral nerve cord ventral to the cirrus pouch and vagina. Testes restricted to the medulla, placed between the anterior end of the segment and the yolk gland. Sperm duct convoluted.

Cirrus pouch thin-walled, situated for the most part in the medullary parenchyma, containing the cirrus and a convoluted ejaculatory duct whose proximal portion may serve as an internal seminal vesicle.

Genital atrium appearing as a direct continuation of the vagina, opening indifferently on right or left segment margin near its anterior end. Ovary consisting of two symmetrical lateral wings and a ventral isthmus, from whose mid-dorsal surface the oviduct originates. A feebly muscular oocapt present. Yolk gland composed of two symmetrical lateral lobes, each of which rests upon the corresponding part of the ovary. Yolk reservoir transversely elongate, immediately in front of the ovarian isthmus. Vagina divided into two regions, a distal wide region directly continuous with the genital atrium, running inward along the posterior margin of the cirrus pouch; and a proximal region, narrow, running inward and backward and joining the germiduct without forming a seminal receptacle. Uterus extending in the central and dorsal medulla from the posterior border of the segment into the testis zone in mature segments, but occupying the entire medulla when fully developed. Eggs three-shelled; outer shell delicate and large; middle one rather rigid and small; innermost one thin and membranous. Adults in fresh-water fishes. Genotype, *chaenogobii* from *Chaenogobius annularis urotaenia*, Japan (Figure 333).

Yamaguti and Mijata (1940) recorded a second species, *Nippotaenia mogurndae* from the fish *Mogurnda obscura* in Japan. Achmerov (1941) described and figured *Amurotaenia perccotti n.g. n.sp.* from the fish *Perccottus glehni* in Russia and placed this new genus within Nippotaeniidea. The generic description is not available to us, but apparently it differs from *Nippotaenia* mainly in the single terminal sucker being larger and better developed.

Order CARYOPHYLLIDEA

Like the order Spathebothridia, discussed in the following section, tapeworms of the order Caryophyllidea are small, unsegmented forms whose genital apertures and uterine apertures open on the same flat surface of the body, the uterine apertures of each set of reproductive organs opening between those of the male and female organs. There is never a common cirro-vaginal atrium. The holdfast may be completely undifferentiated from the body or may show vaguely demarcated grooves or depressions, but true suckers or true bothria are not found. The eggs are operculated and are nonembryonated when laid. These forms have been recorded only from fishes. They would seem to be neotenic larvae, possibly neotenic procercoids.

DESCRIPTION

Of the class Cestoda. Small forms possessing only one set of reproductive organs. Holdfast undifferentiated, or with grooves sometimes sufficiently broad to simulate bothria. Genital aperture and uterine aperture opening on the ventral surface of the body. Uterus and vagina commonly discharging into a common utero-vaginal canal or into a utero-vaginal atrium. Yolk glands cortical or medullary, or partly cortical and partly medullary, according to family. Adults in mormyrid, silurid, catastomid, and cyprinid fishes, but with one genus parasitic in freshwater annelid worms.

HISTORY

There is no unanimity of opinion among students of tapeworms as to the systematic position of the monozootic tapeworms – that is to say, of those tapeworms with only one set of reproductive organs – that are discussed here. On the contention of Loennberg (1897) that the monozootic condition is secondary and has originated from a polyzootic or multigenitalial condition, they are usually admitted to the order Pseudophyllidea, either as a separate family – Caryophyllaeidae – or, following Nybelin (1922), as a subfamily of Cyathocephalidae. Woodland (1923b), studying a number of newly discovered caryophyllidean forms, removed the group from Pseudophyllidea and placed them in the class Cestodaria of flatworms as a separate order, thus removing them from tapeworms proper. Hunter (1927b), however, reviewing the known caryophyllidean forms of that date, preferred to retain them within Pseudophyllidea as an independent family. The very detailed studies made by Wisniewski (1930) upon the caryophyllidean genus *Archigetes* definitely established the tapeworm nature of these forms.

We shall take the view here that the monozootic condition is a character sufficiently fundamental to justify separating these forms as a separate order, Caryophyllidea, characterized by: (1) monozooty; (2) lack of external segmentation; (3) presence of genital apertures on the same flat surface (ventral) as the uterine aperture; (4) occurrence of the uterine aperture between the male and female apertures; and (5) the tendency of the uterus and vagina to open at the bottom of a utero-vaginal depression. However, it must be admitted that only the first characteristic really separates these forms from Cyathocephalidae.

CLASSIFICATION

Following Hunter (1927b) we shall recognize four families (corresponding with Hunter's subfamilies), distinguished as follows:

1. Genital apertures opening on the anterior half of the ventral surface .... WENYONIDAE
   Genital apertures opening on the posterior half of the ventral surface 2
2. Yolk glands medullary .... CARYOPHYLLAEIDAE
   Yolk glands cortical 3
3. Yolk glands wholly cortical .... LYTOCESTIDAE
   Yolk glands partly cortical .... CAPINGENTIDAE

Family WENYONIDAE n. fam. (= WENYONINAE Hunter, 1927)

DESCRIPTION

Of the order Caryophyllidea. Small forms with the holdfast either undifferentiated or with numerous longitudinal grooves. Genital apertures on the anterior half of the ventral surface. Utero-vaginal atrium present. Ovary medullary, follicular, H-shaped. Uterus long, at least equal in length to the testis field. Type and only genus, *Wenyonia* Woodland, 1923.

Wenyonia virilis Woodland, 1923, the genotype, is up to 52.5 mm. long and has an arrow-shaped holdfast end with 13–26 longitudinal grooves on it; *acuminata* Woodland, 1923, 17.5–34.5 mm. long, is nematodiform, with the holdfast end undifferentiated; and *minuta* Woodland, 1923 is only about 3.5 mm. long, with a flattened body with bluntly pointed ends. The species *longicauda* Woodland, 1937, 25 by 1.53 mm. in size, has the holdfast somewhat *Proteocephalus*-like but without suckers, and a tapewormlike body, pseudo-segmented with longitudinal and transverse cuticular grooves but not truly segmented. All the species were taken from African siluroid fishes (*Synodontis schall*, *S. membranaceus*, *Chrysichthys auratus* in the Egyptian Sudan; *Synodontis gambiensis* in Sierra Leone) (Figure 334).

Family CARYOPHYLLAEIDAE Leuckart, 1878

DESCRIPTION

Of the order Caryophyllidea. Small forms with the holdfast end varying in shape. Genital apertures on the last fourth of the ventral surface. Utero-vaginal atrium present but without a sphincter muscle. Longitudinal parenchymal muscles in two layers. Yolk glands medullary. Type genus, *Caryophyllaeus* O. F. Mueller, 1787.

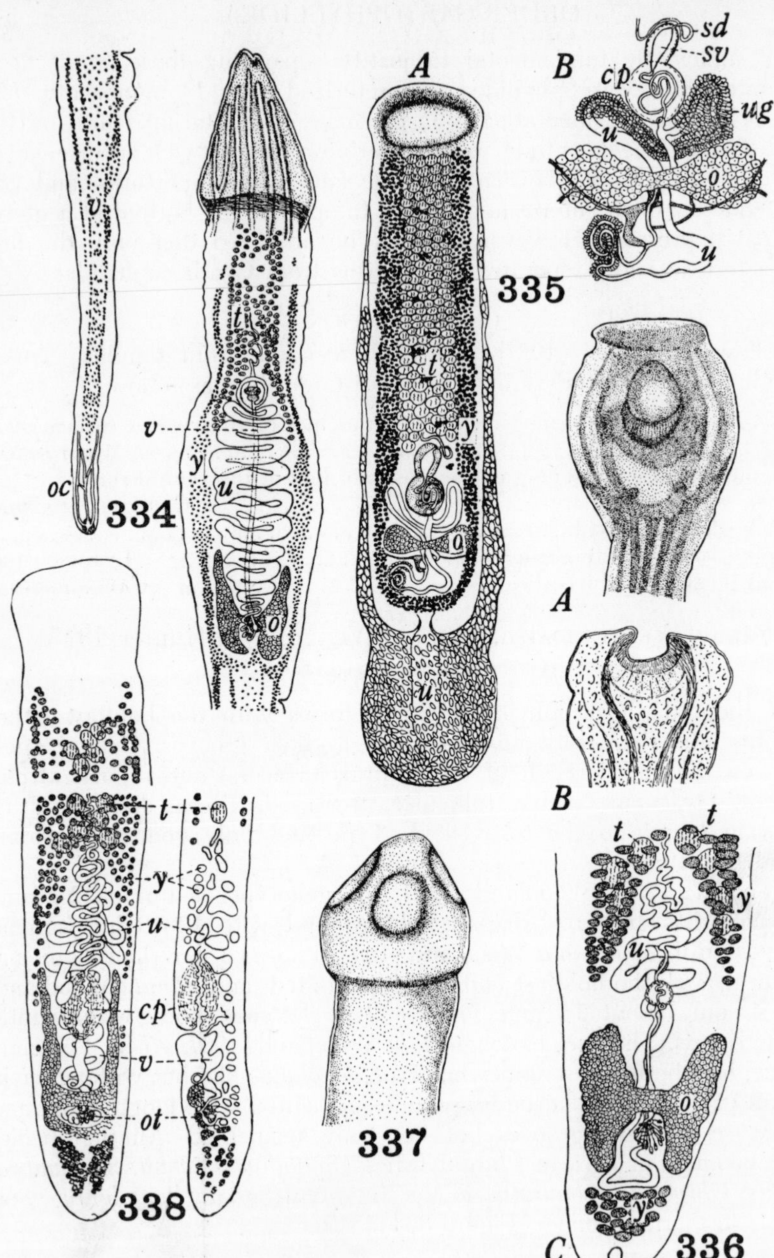

FIG. 334. *Wenyonia virilis*, whole worm. After Woodland, 1923b. FIG. 335. *Archigetes cryptobothrius*. After Wisniewski, 1930. A. Whole worm. B. Female genitalia. FIG. 336. *Biacetabulum infrequens*. After Hunter, 1927b. A. Holdfast end. B. Sagittal section of holdfast end. C. Female reproductive organs. FIG. 337. *Biacetabulum meridianum*, holdfast. After Hunter, 1927b. FIG. 338. *Caryophyllaeides fennica*, whole worm and lower half in sagittal section. After Nybelin, 1922. *cp*, cirrus pouch; *o*, ovary; *oc*, osmoregulatory canals; *ot*, ootype; *sd*, sperm duct; *sv*, seminal vesicle; *t*, testes; *u*, uterus; *ug*, uterine glands; *v*, vagina; *y*, yolk glands.

The family was erected by Leuckart (1878). For its subsequent taxonomic history reference should be made to Hunter (1927b). We recognize seven genera:

KEY TO GENERA

1. Uterine coils in front of cirrus pouch 2
   Uterine coils never in front of cirrus pouch 5
2. In fishes 3
   In fresh-water annelid worms (Tubificidae) ....*Archigetes*
3. Ovary H-shaped 4
   Ovary shaped like inverted A; holdfast undifferentiated; cirrus pouch opening into utero-vaginal atrium ....*Caryophyllaeides*
4. Holdfast with a pair of saucerlike depressions; external seminal vesicle present ....*Biacetabulum*
   Holdfast poorly defined, with three pairs of shallow pseudo-bothrial depressions; cirrus pouch opening ahead of utero-vaginal atrium ....*Hypocaryophyllaeus*
5. Holdfast with terminal introvert; hexagonal in shape, with six weak, shallow grooves; cirrus pouch and utero-vaginal canal opening together on last fourth of ventral surface into a shallow eversible atrium ...*Monobothrium*
   Holdfast end of the body without terminal introvert 6
6. Holdfast end of the body broad or curled, without pseudo-bothrial depressions; cirrus pouch discharging into a shallow, noneversible atrium; no external seminal vesicle present ....*Caryophyllaeus*
   Holdfast end of the body well defined, with three pairs of pseudo-bothrial depressions; an external seminal vesicle present ....*Glaridacris*

NOTES ON GENERA

Archigetes Leuckart, 1878

With the holdfast well defined, hexagonal in shape, with two pseudobothrial depressions. Cirrus pouch opening into the utero-vaginal atrium. Ovary H-shaped. Uterine coils extending anterior to the cirrus pouch. Sperm duct with an external seminal vesicle. Adults parasitic in the body cavity of Tubificidae (Annelida). Genotype, *sieboldii* Leuckart, 1878. Other species, *brachyurus* Mrazek, 1908; *cryptobothrius* Wisniewski, 1929 (Figure 335).

The genotype was first recorded by Udekem (1855) in *Tubifex tubifex* and *Nais proboscidea* (Annelida) and was regarded as a larval tapeworm. The form in *Nais* may in fact have been a larval stage of some species of *Caryophyllaeus*, but the form in *Tubifex* has been considered by later authorities – notably Leuckart, Mrazek, Braun, and Nybelin – to have been some other form. In 1868 Ratzel found what he believed to be developmental stages of *Caryophyllaeus appendiculatus* (his term). Leuckart (1869) found similar forms and also regarded them as larval forms of *Caryophyllaeus*, but, in his opinion, of *Caryophyllaeus mutabilis* (= *C. laticeps*). Later observations (1878), however, suggested to him that since these forms were sexually mature, here was no larval stage of *Caryophyllaeus* but an adult worm, for which he suggested the generic term *Archigetes* and the specific term *sieboldii*. These forms he regarded as identical with Ratzel's material.

Grüber (1881) accepted Leuckart's view, but Braun and Mrazek, while agreeing that these worms were adult forms, preferred to retain Ratzel's term *appendiculatus.* Mrazek (1897, 1908), after a careful, detailed study, recognized a second species, *brachyurus.* Nybelin (1922) came to the conclusion that Ratzel's material and Leuckart's material were not identical but differed in certain details of the holdfast end and osmoregulatory system. Some features of Ratzel's form suggest, in fact, that it was a larva of *Caryophyllaeus.*

A third species of *Archigetes,* namely *cryptobothrius,* was added by Wisniewski (1928). This author contributed the most detailed study yet attempted of the morphology and life history of the genus (Wisniewski, 1930). His conclusions, briefly stated, are that *Archigetes* is a distinct genus whose whole life cycle is spent in oligochaete worms; that it is a neotenic procercoid; and that host infection occurs through ingestion of tapeworm eggs, no free-swimming embryo being liberated. Wisniewski recognized three species — *sieboldii, brachyurus,* and *cryptobothrius.*

Szidat (1938), restudying three larval tapeworms of the *Archigetes* type, suggested that *Archigetes sieboldii* should be placed within Hunter's genus *Biacetabulum* and that the adult of *Archigetes brachyurus,* when found, will probably be seen to correspond with a form found by him in the fish *Gobio fluviatilis,* a form intermediate in characters between the genera *Biacetabulum* and *Glaridacris* and to which he assigned the name *Brachyurus gobii.*

Caryophyllaeides Nybelin, 1922

With the ovary shaped like an inverted A. The cirrus pouch opening into the utero-vaginal atrium. Uterine coils extending in front of the cirrus pouch. Genotype, *fennica* Schneider, 1902 (Figure 338).

Both the genotype and a second species, *skrjabini* Popoff, occur in rutilid fishes (*Leuciscus erythrophthalmus* and *L. idus* in Finland; *L. rutilus* in Sweden). The life cycle is unknown, but *Nais proboscidea* is suspected to be the intermediate host.

Biacetabulum Hunter, 1927

With a well-defined holdfast provided with a pair of pseudo-bothrial depressions. Cirrus pouch opening into the utero-vaginal atrium as in preceding genus. Ovary H-shaped. Coils of the uterus extending in front of cirrus pouch. Genotype, *infrequens* Hunter, 1927 (Figure 336).

The genotype was recorded from the catostomid fish *Moxostoma anisurum* in Illinois. Other species are *meridianum* Hunter, 1927 (Figure 337) from the catostomid fish *Erimyzon sucetta* in North Carolina, differing from the genotype in the more specialized nature of the pseudobothrial depressions, in having 65–95 testes (cf. 420–440 in *infrequens*), and in several other points; and *giganteum* Hunter, 1927, from the catostomid fish *Ictiobus bubalus* in Mississippi, differing from the genotype in having six indentations on the holdfast end, in size, in number of testes, etc.

Hypocaryophyllaeus Hunter, 1927

With three pairs of shallow, poorly defined depressions on the holdfast end. Cirrus pouch opening independently into a shallow, non-eversible atrium. Ovary H-shaped. Uterine coils extending anterior to the cirrus pouch. Genotype and only recorded species, *paratarius* Hunter, 1927 from the catostomid fishes *Carpiodes carpio, C. velifer, Ictiobus cyprinella* in Illinois and Iowa (Figure 339).

Monobothrium Diesing, 1863

With the holdfast end oval in cross section and having six shallow,

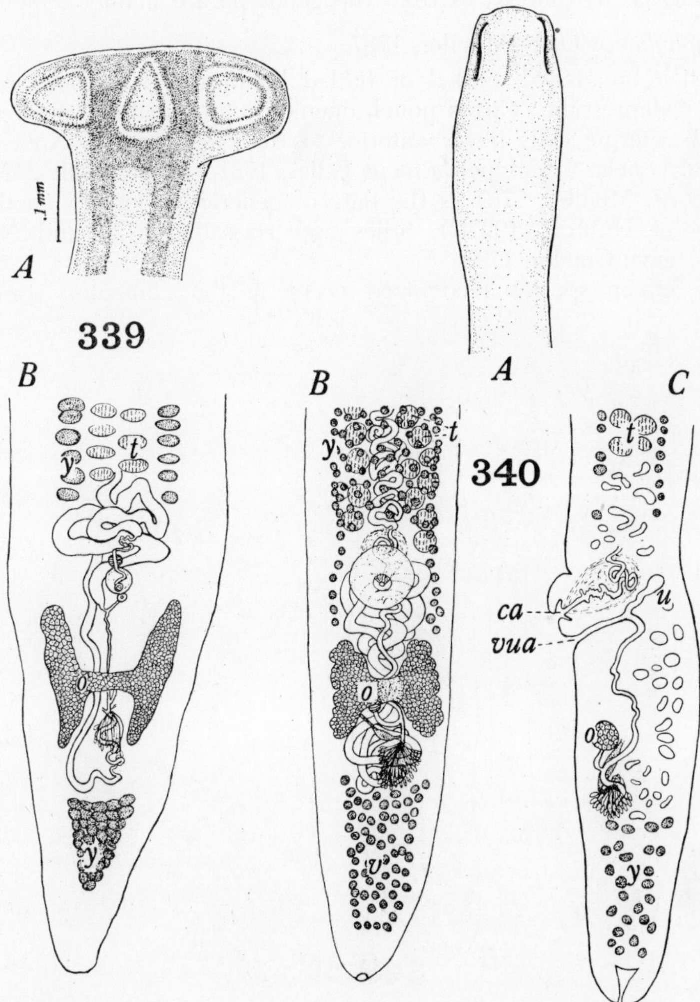

FIG. 339. *Hypocaryophyllaeus paratarius.* After Hunter, 1927b. A. Holdfast end. B. Reproductive system. FIG. 340. *Monobothrium wageneri.* After Nybelin, 1922. A. Holdfast end. B. Reproductive system, ventral view. C. Same in sagittal view. *ca*, cirrus aperture; *o*, ovary; *t*, testes; *u*, uterus; *v*, vagina; *vua*, vagino-uterine aperture; *y*, yolk glands.

longitudinal grooves and a terminal, funnel-like introvert. Cirrus pouch and utero-vaginal canal opening together into a shallow atrium, but having the external openings separated by a bulky, ringlike pad (male genital papilla). Ovary H-shaped. Uterine coils never anterior to the cirrus pouch. Genotype, *wageneri* Nybelin, 1922 (Figure 340).

The genotype *wageneri* (= *M. tuba* Siebold, 1853) occurs in the cyprinid fish *Tinca tinca*, northern Italy. A second species, *ingens* Hunter, 1927, occurs in *Ictiobus cyprinella* in Minnesota, in pits in the gut mucosa; its differences from the genotype are mainly dimensional.

Caryophyllaeus O. F. Mueller, 1787

With a broadened, curled or folded holdfast end, without pseudobothrial depressions. Cirrus pouch opening into a shallow, noneversible atrium. Uterine coils never anterior to the cirrus pouch. No external seminal vesicle. Genotype, *laticeps* Pallas, 1781 (Figures 341, 342). We give O. F. Mueller, 1787 as the date of generic authorship on the authority of Hunter (1927b). Stiles and Hassall (1912) and Nybelin (1922) gave Gmelin, 1790.

The fifteen species recognized occur in the alimentary tracts of

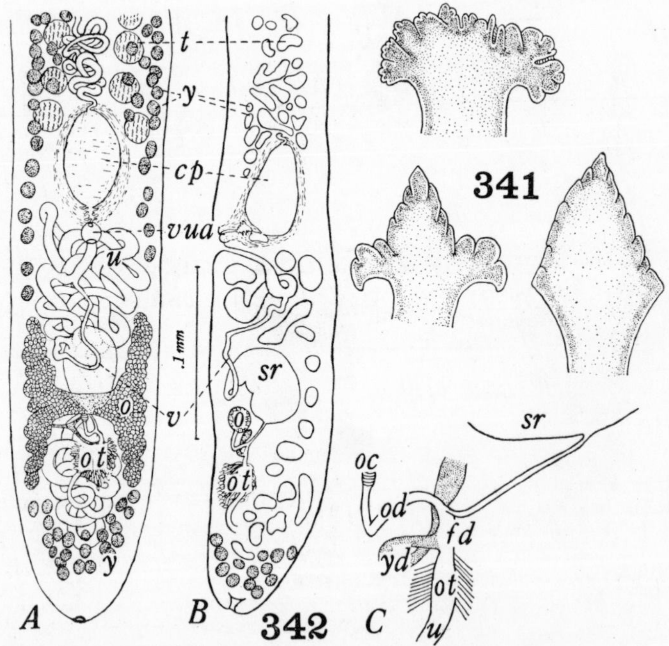

FIG. 341. *Caryophyllaeus laticeps*, shapes of holdfast end. After Benham, 1901. FIG. 342. *Caryophyllaeus laticeps*. After Nybelin, 1922. A. Reproductive system, ventral view. B. Same in sagittal view. C. Female reproductive organs. *cp*, cirrus pouch; *fd*, fertilization duct; *o*, ovary; *oc*, oocapt; *od*, oviduct; *ot*, ootype; *sr*, seminal receptacle; *t*, testes; *u*, uterus; *v*, vagina; *vua*, vagino-uterine aperture; *y*, yolk glands; *yd*, yolk duct.

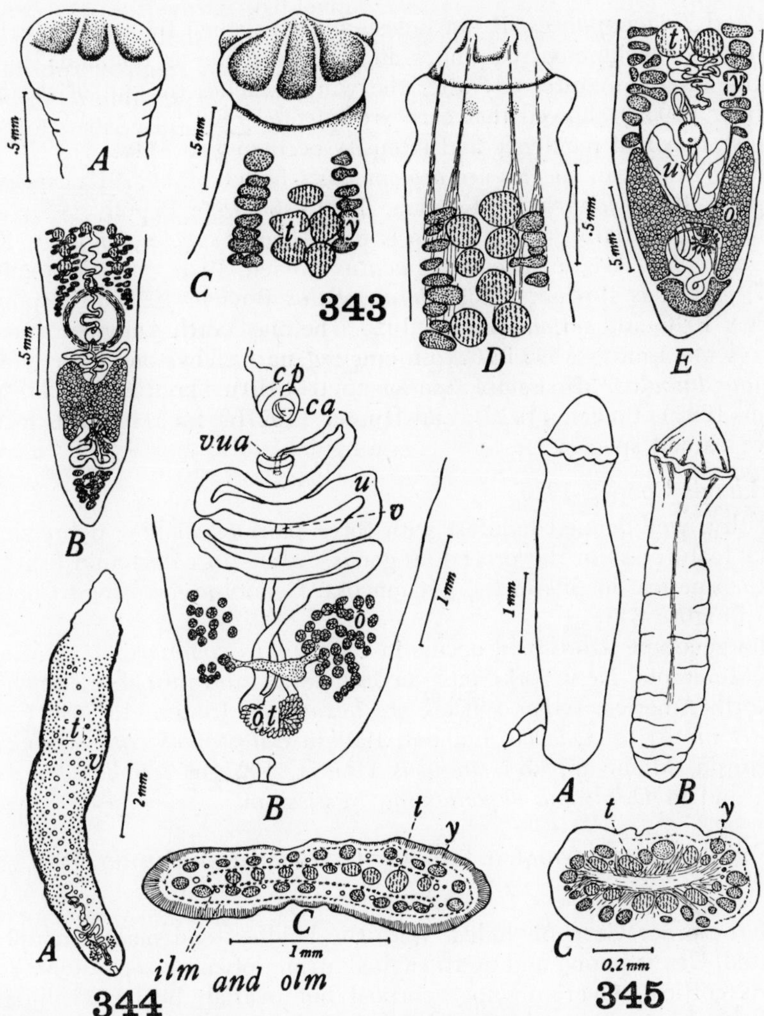

FIG. 343. *Glaridacris* species. After Hunter, 1927b. A. *catostomi*, holdfast end. B. *catostomi*, reproductive organs. C. *hexacotyle*, holdfast end. D. *confusus*, holdfast end. E. *confusus*, reproductive organs. FIG. 344. *Lytocestus indicus*. After Moghe, 1931. A. Whole worm, ventral view. B. Reproductive system, ventral view. C. Cross section through the testis region. FIG. 345. *Balanotaenia bancrofti*. After Johnston, 1924. A and B. Whole worms. C. Cross section of middle region. *ca*, cirrus aperture; *cp*, cirrus pouch; *ilm* and *olm*, inner and outer longitudinal muscles; *o*, ovary; *ot*, ootype; *t*, testes; *u*, uterus; *v*, vagina; *vua*, vagino-uterine aperture; *y*, yolk glands.

cyprinid and catostomid fishes. The genotype *laticeps* (= *mutabilis* Rudolphi 1802) is common in *Abramis brama* in northern Europe. According to Sekulowicz (1932), its intermediate hosts are the tubificid worms *Tubifex tubifex* and *Tubifex barbatus*; the larval stage is a procercoid with a cercomer, and its infective stage recalls those of *Dibothrioceph-*

alus and *Triaenophorus*. If not ingested at this stage by a cyprinid fish, the larval development continues and the cercomer is retained. Reproductive organs mature only after the worm reaches the gut of the fish. Wunder (1939) showed that carp are infected only between April and August, maximal incidence and intensity occurring in May.

Other European species are *armeniacus* Cholodkovsky, 1915; *caspiacus* Klopina, 1919; *fimbriceps* Klopina, 1919; *skrjabini* Popoff, 1924; and *syrdarjensis* Skrjabin, 1913. There is one African species, *niloticus* Kulmatycki, 1924. Asiatic species are *acutus* Bovien, 1926; *gotoi* Motomura, 1927; *javanicus* Bovien, 1926; *microcephalus* Bovien, 1926; *oxycephalus* Bovien, 1926; and *serialis* Bovien, 1926. The one North American species is *terebrans* Linton, 1893 in *Catostomus ardens*, Yellowstone Park, and in *Ictiobus bubalus*, Mississippi. See Klopina (1919), Skrjabin (1913), Nybelin (1922), Bovien (1926), and Hunter (1927b) for references to the above named species.

Glaridacris Cooper, 1920

With a well-defined holdfast with three pairs of shallow depressions. Other features as in the preceding genus. Adults in catostomid fishes in North America, in pits in the gut mucosa. Genotype, *catostomi* Cooper, 1920 (Figure 343).

The genotype, *catostomi*, occurs in *Catostomus commersonii* in Michigan, Minnesota, New York State, Saskatchewan, and probably elsewhere in North America. Other species are *hexacotyle* Linton, 1897 in *Catostomus sp.*, Arizona; *laruei* Lamont, 1921 in *Catostomus commersonii* in Wisconsin, Michigan; and *confusus* Hunter, 1927 in *Ictiobus bubalus*, Iowa and in *Dorosoma cepadianum*, Mississippi.

Family LYTOCESTIDAE n. fam. (= LYTOCESTINAE Hunter, 1927)

DESCRIPTION

Of the order Caryophyllidea. With the holdfast end mainly undifferentiated. Cirrus pouch and utero-vaginal atrium opening separately. Yolk glands cortical. Ovarian wings cortical but ovarian bridge medullary. Adults in mormyrid and siluroid fishes. Type genus, *Lytocestus* Cohn, 1908.

The seven genera recognized here may be distinguished as follows:

KEY TO GENERA

1. Holdfast end of body undifferentiated 2
   Holdfast end of body with pseudo-bothrial depressions 4
2. No postovarian yolk glands 3
   Postovarian yolk glands present . . . . *Lytocestoides*
   Both preovarian and postovarian yolk glands present . . . . *Khawia*
3. Inner longitudinal muscles in two parallel sheets between the testes . . . . *Balanotaenia*
   Inner longitudinal muscles in a ring around the testes . . . . *Lytocestus*
4. Yolk glands in the form of two lateral crescents . . . . *Stocksia*
   Yolk glands as a ring around the testes 5
5. Uterine coils reaching nearly as far forward as the testes; holdfast end

globular with a terminal pseudo-bothrium . . . . *Djombangia*
Uterine coils reaching less than the length of the testis field; holdfast end with longitudinal furrows and terminal introvert . . . . *Monobothrioides*

NOTES ON GENERA

Lytocestoides Baylis, 1928

With a short, conical anterior end devoid of depressions. Postovarian yolk glands present. Genotype and only known species, *tanganyikae* Baylis, 1928 in the digestive tract of a fish (probably *Alestes sp.*) in Tanganyika, Africa.

Khawia Hsü, 1935

With a rounded, undifferentiated anterior end. Yolk glands both anterior and posterior to the ovary. Adults in cyprinid fishes in China and Japan. Genotype, *sinensis* Hsü, 1935; other species, *japonensis* Yamaguti, 1934.

Balanotaenia Johnston, 1924

With the anterior end showing muscular ridges or a "frill" when contracted, otherwise undifferentiated. Inner longitudinal muscles in two parallel sheets between the testes. In the Australian siluroid fish *Tandanus tandanus*, Queensland. Genotype, *bancrofti* Johnston, 1924 (Figure 345).

Lytocestus Cohn, 1908

With the anterior end undifferentiated and not broader than the body. Inner longitudinal muscles in a ring around the testes. In mormyrid and siluroid fishes. Genotype, *adhaerens* Cohn, 1908 in Hong Kong. Other species, *filiformis* Woodland, 1923 in the Egyptian Sudan; and *indicus* Moghe, 1925 in India (Figure 344).

Stocksia Woodland, 1937

With the holdfast end flat, pointed, having a narrow longitudinal groove on each flat surface. Inner longitudinal muscles in two well-marked rings of bundles. Yolk glands in two lateral crescents. Uterus extending anterior to the ovary. Only two main osmoregulatory canals present. Genotype and only known species, *pujehuni* from the siluroid fish *Clarias lazera*, Sierra Leone, Africa.

Djombangia Bovien, 1926

With the holdfast end globular and with a terminal introvert. Uterine coils reaching nearly as far forward as the testes. Parasitic in *Clarias sp.* Genotype and only known species, *penetrans* Bovien, 1926 from Java.

Monobothrioides Fuhrmann and Baer, 1925

With the holdfast end showing numerous furrows and having a terminal introvert. Uterine coils extending less than half the length of the testis field. In African siluroid fishes. Genotype, *cunningtoni* Fuhrmann and Baer, 1925, Tanganyika. Other species, *chalmersius* Woodland, 1924, Egyptian Sudan. Woodland (1937b), criticizing the characters by which

Hunter (1927b) separated *Lytocestus* from *Monobothrioides*, would place also within the latter genus the species *filiformis* Woodland, 1923 and *indicus* Moghe, 1925 (see *Lytocestus*).

Family Capingentidae n. fam. (= Capingentinae Hunter, 1927)

DESCRIPTION

Of the order Caryophyllidea. Resembling in most respects Lytocestidae. Yolk glands, however, cortical only for one-third to one-half of their bulk, the remainder lying in the medulla. Type genus, *Capingens* Hunter, 1927. The three genera recognized may be distinguished as follows:

1. Holdfast end of body large, one-fifth or more of the body length; one pair of depressions recalling bothria; postovarian yolk glands present .... *Capingens*
   Holdfast end of body less than one-fifth of the body length; no postovarian yolk glands 2
2. Holdfast end with three pairs of depressions; ovary U-shaped . . *Spartoides*
   Holdfast end undifferentiated; ovary H-shaped .... *Pseudolytocestus*

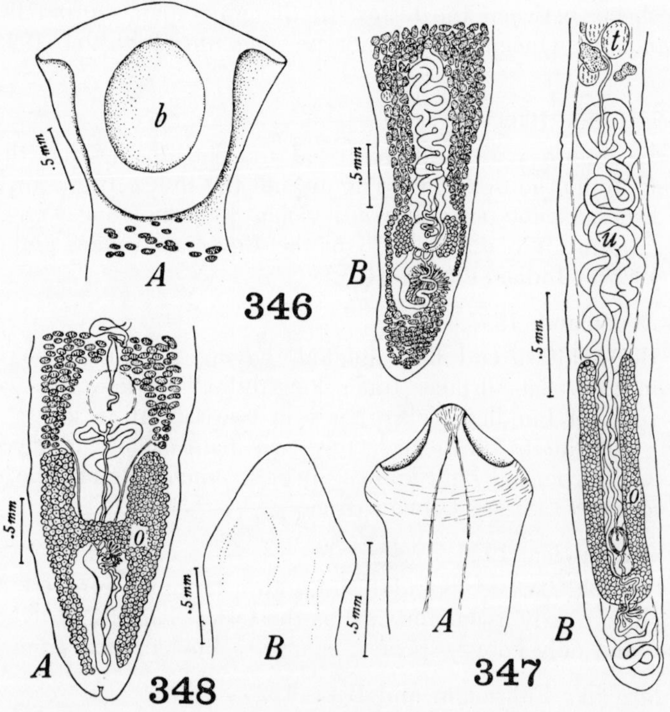

FIG. 346. *Capingens singularis.* After Hunter, 1927b. A. Holdfast end. B. Reproductive organs. FIG. 347. *Spartoides wardi.* After Hunter, 1927b. A. Holdfast end. B. Reproductive organs. FIG. 348. *Pseudolytocestus differtus.* After Hunter, 1927b. A. Reproductive organs. B. Holdfast. *b*, pseudo-bothrium; *o*, ovary; *t*, testes; *u*, uterus.

NOTES ON GENERA

Capingens Hunter, 1927

With the characters given in the key. In the *stomach* of catostomid fishes. Genotype and only known species, *singularis* Hunter, 1927 in *Carpiodes carpio*, Illinois, and *Ictiobus urus*, Minnesota (Figure 346).

Spartoides Hunter, 1927

With the characters given in the key. Genotype and only known species, *wardi* Hunter, 1927 in *Carpiodes carpio*, Illinois and Iowa, *Carpiodes thompsoni*, Minnesota, and *Ictiobus cyprinella*, Minnesota (Figure 347).

Pseudolytocestus Hunter, 1927

With the characters given in the key. Genotype and only known species, *differtus* Hunter, 1927 in the intestine of *Ictiobus bubalus*, Minnesota (Figure 348).

Order SPATHEBOTHRIDEA

DESCRIPTION

Of the class Cestoda. Small forms with the holdfast end varying in degree of differentiation but never having true bothria or suckers. Body showing proglottisation but not external segmentation or apolysis. Genital apertures on the ventral surface. Uterine aperture of each genital complex opening *between* the male and the female apertures. Testes medullary, in two lateral bands. Ovary median, markedly bilobed, with the lateral lobes denser than the bridge, or rosettiform. Ootype surrounded by well-defined shell glands. Uterus tubular, sinuate, without local expansions. Uterine glands usually prominent. Eggs thick-shelled, operculate, but apparently not liberating ciliated embryos. Adult form apparently a neotenic procercoid, sexually functional in fishes. Adults mainly in ancient, and probably primitive, groups of fishes.

HISTORY

The order is established for certain genera formerly included within Pseudophyllidea. There is, however, no evidence that their organs of adherence are derived from bothria. We base the order upon the genus *Spathebothrium* because we regard the lack of a differentiated holdfast end in that genus as a more primitive character than the differentiated holdfast end of the other genera.

We shall recognize three families, which may be distinguished provisionally as follows:

1. Holdfast end completely undifferentiated externally . . . . SPATHEBOTHRIIDAE
   Holdfast end with organs of adherence 2
2. Holdfast end with a cuplike or funnel-like structure . . CYATHOCEPHALIDAE
   Holdfast end with two spherical, hollow structures fitting saddle-fashion from the dorsal to the ventral surfaces of the body and opening each by a forwardly directed aperture . . . . DIPLOCOTYLIDAE

Family SPATHEBOTHRIIDAE n. fam.
(= SPATHEBOTHRIINAE Yamaguti, 1934)

DESCRIPTION

Of the order Spathebothridea. Small forms with a bluntly tapering anterior end and a sharply tapering posterior end, and with the anterior end completely undifferentiated. Longitudinal parenchymal muscles lacking. Genital apertures alternating irregularly from one flat surface to the other. Vaginal aperture behind the cirrus aperture. Uterine aperture at the same level as the vaginal aperture but lateral to it. No utero-vaginal depression. Reproductive organs serially repeated, up to thirty-six sets. Testes arranged in two lateral bands extending through the whole body. Ovary rosettiform, with a central opening. Uterus a much-convoluted tube. Eggs spindle-shaped, operculated, 40 by 20 μ. Life cycle unknown. Type genus and only known genus, *Spathebothrium* Linton, 1922 with one species, *simplex* Linton, 1922 from the teleostean fish *Liparis liparis* in North American Atlantic waters (Figure 349).

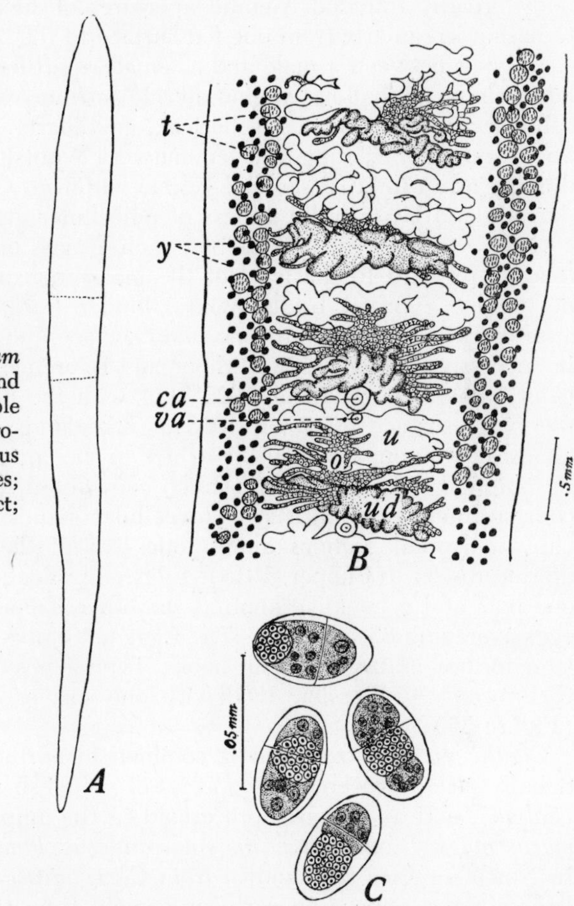

FIG. 349. *Spathebothrium simplex.* After Hart and Guberlet, 1936. A. Whole worm. B. 4 successive proglottides. C. Eggs. *ca*, cirrus aperture; *o*, ovary; *t*, testes; *u*, uterus; *ud*, uterine duct; *va*, vaginal aperture; *y*, yolk glands.

Linton did not assign his genus to any known family but did oppose its inclusion within the order Pseudophyllidea. Poche (1926a) and Fuhrmann (1931), on the basis of Linton's description, placed the form within Cyathocephalidae. Yamaguti (1934), describing material from *Crystallias matshushima* in Japanese waters, established for the genus the subfamily Spathebothriinae (of Cyathocephalidae). Hart and Guberlet (1936), studying material from *Liparis fucensis* in North American Pacific waters (Puget Sound), believed the lack of holdfast organs to be sufficient grounds for establishing a new superfamily, Spathebothrioidea, of tapeworms.

Family CYATHOCEPHALIDAE Nybelin, 1922, emended

DESCRIPTION

Of the order Spathebothridea. Small forms, up to 33 mm. by 3 mm. Body flat, completely unsegmented but proglottised, having 20–45 sets of reproductive organs. Holdfast end provided with a chitinous, funnel-like structure whose margin rolls outward slightly. Opposite end of the body broadly rounded. Genital apertures of successive proglottides alternating irregularly from one flat surface to the other. Uterine apertures each lying between a male and a female aperture and opening with the latter into a shallow vagino-uterine atrium whose aperture has a sphincter muscle. Testes spherical, medullary, in two lateral bands. Sperm duct not dilating as a seminal vesicle outside the cirrus pouch but dilating as an internal seminal vesicle within it. Cirrus pouch enveloped dorsally and laterally by a mass of unicellular glands.

Ovary with two winglike lobes, each a mass of tubules, and each extending forward to the level of the male aperture; the two wings connected by a broad bridge whose hinder border is lobulated. Ovary approximating first toward one body surface and then toward the other in successive proglottides, without any reference to the position of the genital aperture (Nybelin, 1922) but with the bridge always nearer to the poral surface (Cooper, 1918). Yolk glands numerous, forming an almost continuous layer 70–90 μ thick in the cortex and tending to mask the internal organs. Uterus a much convoluted tube, with the proximal coils surrounded by a mass of unicellular glands "so extensive as to occupy in frontal sections almost one half of the posterior half of the uterine rosette" (Cooper, 1918). Eggs ellipsoidal, with an operculum at one pole and a hooklike knob at the other. Dimensions of the extruded eggs averaging 35–50 by 28–37 μ. Eggs not embryonated when laid. The later formed embryo without hooks. Type genus and only known genus, *Cyathocephalus* Kessler, 1868 with one species, *truncatus* Pallas, 1781 (Figure 350).

Cyathocephalus truncatus is common in northern Europe as a functionally sexual procercoid in species of whitefish (*Coregonus*) and trout (*Salmo*), and as an early procercoid in the amphipod Crustacea *Gammarus pulex, Rivulogammarus spinicaudatus, Pontogammarus bosniacus.* In North America it is known from *Coregonus clupeaformis* and *Salvelinus alpinus*, and as an early procercoid from the amphipodan *Pontoporeia affinis.*

Cooper (1918), studying material from Lakes Huron and Michigan, believed the American form to differ from European material on a number of points and established for it the species *americanus.* Nybelin (1922), re-examining European material but not American material, suggested that *americanus* was identical with *truncatus*, and that Cooper's points of difference were merely differences from Kraemer's admittedly inadequate description (1892). One of the differences – the alleged absence from *americanus* of a sphincter muscle around the vagino-uterine aperture – was shown by Wardle (1932b) to be invalid. The two forms appear to be identical.

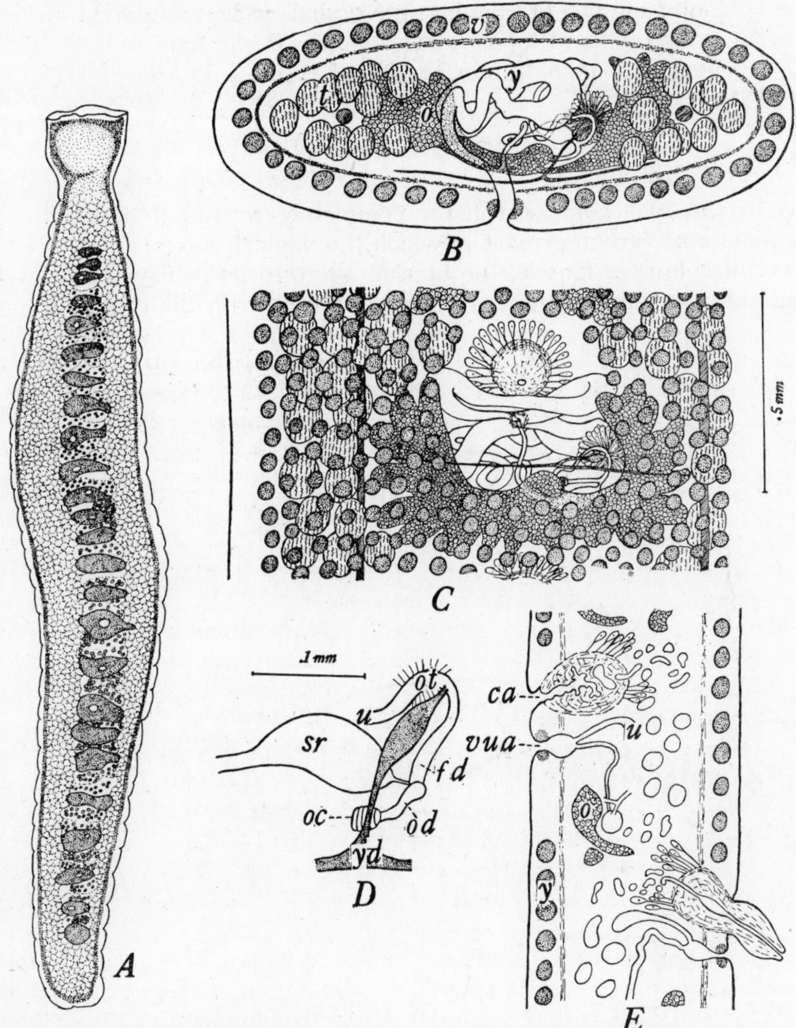

FIG. 350. *Cyathocephalus truncatus.* A. Whole worm. After Wisniewski, 1933. B. Cross section of mature proglottis (*v*, yolk glands; *y*, vagina). C. Mature proglottis, ventral view. D. Female reproductive organs. E. Reproductive system in sagittal view. B to E after Nybelin, 1922. *ca*, cirrus aperture; *fd*, fertilization duct; *o*, ovary; *oc*, oocapt; *od*, oviduct; *ot*, ootype; *sr*, seminal receptacle; *t*, testes; *u*, uterus; *vua*, vagino-uterine aperture; *y*, yolk glands; *yd*, yolk duct.

Family Diplocotylidae n. fam.

DESCRIPTION

Of the order Spathebothridea. Small to medium-sized forms. Holdfast end with one or two spherical, hollow structures whose apertures face forward. Number of sets of reproductive organs large. Uterine aperture narrowly in front of the vaginal aperture, both enclosed within a common sphincter muscle, or opening into a shallow vagino-uterine atrium. Ovarian bridge without lobules. Type genus, *Diplocotyle* Krabbe, 1874. Other genera, *Didymobothrium* Nybelin, 1922 and *Bothrimonus* Duvernoy, 1842.

NOTES ON GENERA

Diplocotyle Krabbe, 1874

With the two holdfast spheres completely separated internally. A vagino-uterine atrium present in which the vaginal aperture has its own powerful sphincter muscle, the uterine aperture its own weakly developed sphincter muscle. Ovarian bridge narrow, with the ovarian wings

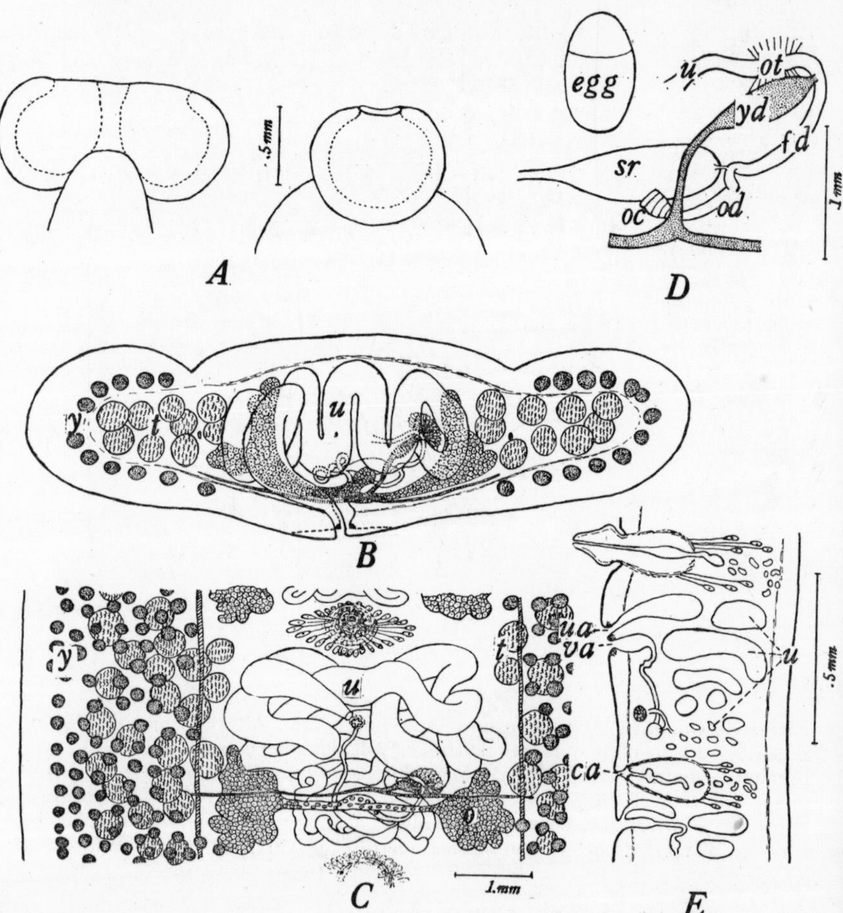

FIG. 351. *Diplocotyle olrikii.* After Nybelin, 1922. A. Views of holdfast end. B. Cross section of mature proglottis. C. Mature proglottis, ventral view. D. Reproductive organs and egg. E. Reproductive organs in sagittal view. *ca*, cirrus aperture; *fd*, fertilization duct; *o*, ovary; *oc*, oocapt; *od*, oviduct; *ot*, ootype; *sr*, seminal receptacle; *t*, testes; *u*, uterus; *ua*, uterine aperture; *va*, vaginal aperture; *y*, yolk glands; *yd*, yolk duct.

not enclosing the distal uterine coils. Genotype and only known species, *olrikii* Krabbe, 1874 (Figure 351).

The genotype has been recorded from *Salmo carpio* and *Salmo alpinus* in Iceland; in *S. alpinus* and *Artediellus incinatus* in Greenland; in *Salvelinus alpinus, S. fontinalis, Leucichthys artedi, Coregonus clupeaformis, Myoxocephalus quadricornis* in northern Canada (Wardle, 1932b). Doguel and Volkova (1946) described plerocercoids of *Diplocotyle*, found in *Gammarus locusta* at Kharlovsk, U.S.S.R., as of large size and containing up to 140 genitalia which had reached adult size and development but lacked embryonated eggs in the uteri.

Didymobothrium Nybelin, 1922

With the cavities of the holdfast spheres *partly* fused. Genotype and only species, *rudolphi* Monticelli, 1890 from *Solea vulgaris* and *Solea impar*.

Bothrimonus Duvernoy, 1842

With the cavities of the holdfast spheres *completely* fused. Genotype, *sturionis* Duvernoy, 1842.

The genotype was recorded from a sturgeon, *Acipenser sturionis*, in North America and has not been rediscovered. Duvernoy's description is too scanty to enable any other differences from *Diplocotyle* to be stated. Cooper (1918) preferred to regard the two forms as identical,

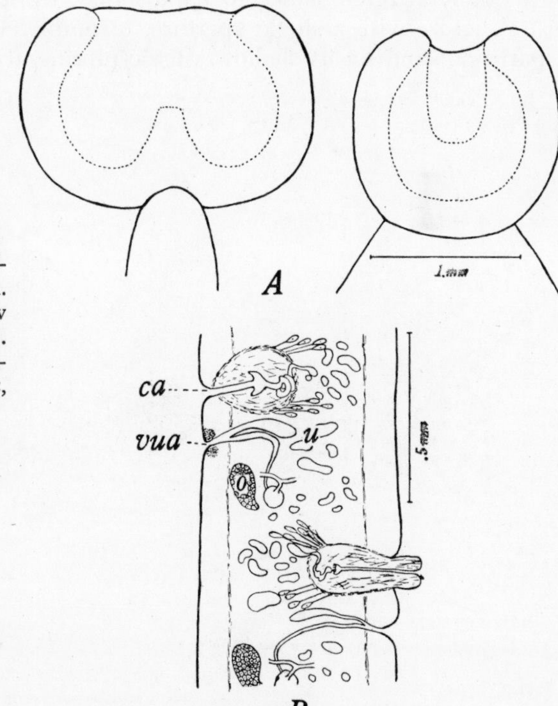

FIG. 352. *Bothrimonus fallax*. After Nybelin, 1922. A. Holdfast end, marginal view (left), surficial view (right). B. Sagittal view of two consecutive proglottides. *ca*, cirrus aperture; *o*, ovary; *u*, uterus; *vua*, vagino-uterine aperture.

under the older term *Bothrimonus*, and to recognize as valid species: *sturionis* Duvernoy, 1842 from *Acipenser oxyrhynchus* (=*Acipenser sturio* L.); *olrikii* Krabbe, 1874; *fallax* Lühe, 1900 from *Acipenser ruthenus* in Rumania, which has been redescribed by Nybelin from *Acipenser stellatus* of the Caspian Sea (Figure 352); *nylandicus* Schneider, 1902 from *Pleuronectes limanda* and *P. platessa* in Finnish waters; *cohaerens* Linstow, 1903 from *Pleuronectes flesus* in the Baltic Sea; *pachycephalus* Linstow, 1904 also from *P. flesus*; and *intermedius* Cooper, 1918 from *Pseudopleuronectes americanus* in eastern Canadian waters.

An examination of a large number of specimens of *Diplocotyle* from salmonoid fishes of northern Canada by one of the present writers gave no indication that contracted specimens may show a single holdfast aperture, as Cooper and Schneider suggested; and until an opportunity occurs for examining material from Canadian sturgeon species we prefer to retain the generic term *Bothrimonus* for the species *sturionis* and *fallax*, while retaining the term *Diplocotyle* for the species *olrikii*. The species *nylandicus, cohaerens*, and *intermedius* we prefer to regard as synonyms of *olrikii* from abnormal hosts (pleuronectid fishes); *pachycephalus* and *caspicus* (Cholodkovsky, 1916) we regard as synonyms of *fallax*. Linstow's *serrata*, from an antelope, *Strepsiceros kudu*, was almost certainly an anoplocephalid tapeworm.

Should *Bothrimonus* be found again, it should be readily recognizable by its general resemblance to *Diplocotyle*; by its single spherical holdfast structure with a single aperture, incompletely divided internally by a partition; and by its shallow vagino-uterine atrium.

Order PSEUDOPHYLLIDEA

DESCRIPTION

Of the class Cestoda. Tapeworms ranging from a few millimeters to thirty meters or more in length. Holdfast somewhat variable in appearance; typically with a dorsal and a ventral bothrium, but sometimes lacking bothria or having only weak mid-dorsal and mid-ventral grooves representing them. Neck conspicuous or so short as to appear lacking in contracted specimens. Segmentation usually well marked but often weak or lacking. Segments anapolytic, commonly acraspedote, commonly linear. Parenchymal musculature powerful. Genital apertures surficial in some families, marginal in others. Usually only one set of reproductive organs per segment but two sets per segment not infrequently found. Testes follicular, scattered, numerous. Ovary bilobed, medullary. Yolk glands follicular, scattered, numerous, cortical. Gravid uterus most commonly tubular and sinuous, sometimes partly tubular, partly saccular; rarely, wholly saccular. Permanent uterine aperture present, always surficial and ventral. Eggs commonly but not invariably operculated, often liberating a ciliated embryo. Life cycle with a procercoid larval stage and a plerocercoid larval stage in different hosts. Adults mainly parasitic in fishes.

HISTORY

The earliest pseudophyllidean tapeworm to be scientifically recorded was probably the so-called "fish tapeworm" of humans, *Dibothriocephalus latus*, which appeared in *Systema Naturae* of Linnaeus (1758) as *Taenia lata*. Within the hundred years following that date, five pseudophyllidean genera were established: *Ligula* Bloch, 1782; *Triaenophorus* Rudolphi, 1793; *Bothriocephalus* Rudolphi, 1808; *Schistocephalus* Creplin, 1829; and *Diphyllobothrium* Cobbold, 1858. In 1863 Carus coined the term "Pseudophyllidea" for one of the five families among which he proposed to distribute all the known genera of tapeworms. In this family he placed the four genera *Ligula, Triaenophorus, Schistocephalus,* and *Bothriocephalus*. During the following thirty years or so, other pseudophyllidean forms were discovered and genera were established for them: *Abothrium* Beneden, 1870; *Duthiersia* Perrier, 1873; *Ptychobothrium* Loennberg, 1889; *Pyramicocephalus* Monticelli, 1890; and *Dibothriocephalus* Lühe, 1899.

By the 1890's, attempts were being made to bring these forms within some satisfactory system of grouping, but the attempts were frustrated by the vagueness of the data upon which the earlier genera had been founded, such data referring mainly to the shape and size of the holdfast and to the position of the genital apertures. Increasing attention, therefore, began to be paid to internal features, and analytical attacks based upon the internal anatomy were made—notably upon Rudolphi's *Bothriocephalus* by Loennberg (1890b), R. Blanchard (1894), and Ariola (1900).

The most notable contributions to the subject of pseudophyllidean classification around the turn of the century were those of Max Lühe (1899a, 1899b, 1900a, 1900b, 1900c, 1901, 1902c, 1910a), who argued for a broader basis of classification and laid down a classical, comprehensive definition of pseudophyllidean tapeworms, which he regarded as comprehensible within the single family Bothriocephalidae. This definition, somewhat freely translated, is as follows:

"Bothriocephalidae are polyzootic tapeworms which, in contrast with the so-called 'Tetrabothriids' of other authors, and the Taeniadae, show a development of the reproductive organs from before backward only in the anterior portion of the chain of segments. Behind this region there are a number of segments in which the reproductive organs reach maturity more or less synchronously. The segments are usually broader than long but occasionally the reverse condition occurs. The external segmentation may be obscure or incomplete; in rare cases it is lacking, as in *Triaenophorus* or in the posterior body region of *Ligula*. The holdfast may be unarmed or armed and varies extraordinarily in shape. As a rule it has two surficial bothria. In some species, marginal bothria are said to occur, but I believe such observations may have to be corrected, as has been done for *Bothriocephalus crassiceps* Rud. and *Bothriocephalus latus*. The bothria, however, in some cases, show great modification, or may be rudimentary, or may be lacking and replaced in function by an unpaired apical organ of adherence.

"The reproductive organs of each segment are usually in a single set, rarely doubled. A surficial and ventral uterine aperture is always present. The ovary, whose bilobed nature is not always apparent, lies close to the posterior border of the segment, and in a segment with a single set of reproductive organs is placed in the middle line, rarely nearer to one or the other margin unless that margin carries the genital apertures. An oviductal sphincter muscle is always present. The yolk glands are numerous but vary in position. The testes also are numerous, usually not massed together like yolk glands but in two bands which are more or less separate from one another. The sperm duct always undulates." Lühe (1899a).

Lühe divided the family Bothriocephalidae into five subfamilies: Triaenophorinae, Ptychobothriinae, Dibothriocephalinae, Ligulinae, and Cyathocephalinae. Modern practice, it may be noted, is to name one subfamily of a family, usually the largest or the oldest, after the family. Thus Lühe should have called one of his subfamilies "Bothriocephalinae."

In its original form Lühe's scheme was adopted substantially by Braun (in "Bronn's Thierreich," 1894–1900). However, in 1902 Lühe discarded his earlier scheme, adopted Carus' term "Pseudophyllidea" as the name for an order, and recognized only two families of this order, namely

Dibothriocephalidae (a term he changed later to "Diphyllobothriidae") and Ptychobothriidae. Later he added a third family, Amphitretidae, a term changed later to "Acanthophallidae."

This second scheme of Lühe's remained the basis of most later schemes of pseudophyllidean grouping. It was adopted by Cooper (1918), who added yet another subfamily, Marsipometrinae, to the already overweighted Dibothriocephalidae; by Nybelin (1922), who raised Lühe's subfamilies to the rank of families and adopted Schumacher's term "Echinophallidae" in place of the term "Acanthophallidae"; and by Joyeux, Du Noyer, and Baer (1931a). It was rejected, however, by Poche (1926a), who preferred to revive Diesing's old term "Bothriocephalidea" as a name for the order to which these tapeworms belong, although Poche retained the family names of the Lühe-Nybelin scheme and added to them the families Lüheellidae Baer (1942b) and Tetrabothriidae Fuhrmann (1908).

The Italian authority Mola, in a somewhat confusing treatment (1929b), preferred to emend the order Pseudophyllidea by keeping only two families, Ligulidae (with two subfamilies, Ligulinae and Tricuspidariinae) and Bothriocephalidae (with subfamilies Monogoninae and Diplogoninae). Monogoninae was to comprise the genera *Anchistrocephalus, Schistocephalus, Pyramicocephalus,* and *Bothriotaenia.* Diplogoninae was to comprise the one genus *Diplogonoporus.* A separate order was established, as Monophyllidea, for the families Cyathocephalidae and Discocephalidae, and another order, Diphyllidea, for the families Dibothriophyllidae (*sic*) (with subfamilies Amphicotylinae, Solenophorinae, Lecanicephalinae, Bothrimoninae, and Dittocephalinae) and Dibothriacanthidae (*sic*). Mola's scheme, like that of the earlier Italian observer Ariola, showed a lack of appreciation of the advances made in the zoology of tapeworms during the preceding forty years, and a bland indifference to the recommendations of the International Committee on Zoological Nomenclature. The scheme has not to our knowledge been seriously considered by any later writer.

RECOGNITION FEATURES

Among pseudophyllidean tapeworms there are very considerable differences in the shape of the holdfast and in the nature of the organs of adherence upon it. Nybelin (1922) suggested that the original type of pseudophyllidean holdfast is represented by that found today in the genera *Triaenophorus* and *Eubothrium*, where each bothrium is a shallow, circular widening of a former median groove, with no rim projecting above the surface of the holdfast. He suggested that an elongation of such a bothrium during evolution would produce the oval type seen in *Bothriocephalus*; that the approximation of the edges of such an oval bothrium would produce the deep, slitlike type of bothrium seen in *Dibothriocephalus*; that an elongation and crumpling of the rear portion of the edges of the slit type would lead to the type of bothrium shaped like an arrowhead or like the conventional heart, found in many genera, whereas a fusion of the bothrial edges from behind forward would change an elongated type of bothrium into the small, cup-shaped structure characteristic of *Clestobothrium*; and finally, that the fusion of a pair of cup-shaped bothria would produce the funnel-like terminal organ of *Cyathocephalus*.

Nybelin's speculations, while of great interest, rested upon the assumption that pseudophyllidean tapeworms have evolved from a compact ancestral group. The assumption is completely unproven and is by no means likely. It is possible that these forms are not primitive, as most authors have assumed, but that they represent a scattering of neotenic larval forms which evolved at various times from a proteocephalan-tetraphyllidean stock, at a time before a true holdfast had appeared among tapeworms; and that these forms developed, as an adaptation to gut-dwelling life, what may be called a "pseudo-holdfast" to serve as a *temporary* organ of attachment between shifts of position.

The boundary between this pseudo-holdfast and the rest of the body is rarely clearly defined, as is to be expected if it has evolved from the anterior region of the body. Where definitely delimited bothria are present, which is not always the case, the rear margins of such bothria serve to indicate such a boundary.

The body of the pseudophyllidean may lack all evidence of external segmentation, or may show segmentation for only part of its length; or again, the body may be markedly segmented. Whatever the condition, the mature and gravid segments are anapolytic, showing no tendency to leave the body and complete development or undergo egg discharge elsewhere. Such anapolysis seems to be a fundamental characteristic of Pseudophyllidea in general. In *Dibothriocephalus latus*, notably, and probably in some other long-bodied forms, those segments whose eggs have been discharged may break from the body and leave the host as strips of egg-free segments. This phenomenon is a pseudo-apolysis and must not be regarded as true apolysis.

Nybelin believed, however, that true apolysis does occur occasionally in Pseudophyllidea, notably in the genera *Abothrium* and *Parabothrium*. In these genera he had never seen a primary terminal segment, and what looked like the last segment was somewhat sharply marked off from its neighbor. However, in view of the absence of apolysis from Pseudophyllidea generally, Nybelin's observations require confirmation.

The absence of apolysis may be correlated with (1) the absence of internal boundaries between the successive sets of reproductive organs; (2) the limitation in longitudinal growth of the body brought about by the switching of growth material, which in other tapeworms goes to form new segments, to the acceleration of sexual maturity – always a characteristic of neoteny; and (3) the absence, or at any rate the apparent absence – for the histology of tapeworms is far from being adequately understood – of a defined growth zone between the holdfast and the rest of the body.

In the majority of Pseudophyllidea, in sharp contrast with such groups of tapeworms as Cyclophyllidea, there seem to be no sharply marked internal divisions between successive groups of reproductive organs.

Only in *Bathybothrium, Abothrium,* and *Parabothrium,* those forms in which Nybelin suspected the occurrence of apolysis, has any sharp boundary between successive genitalia been demonstrated. In a number of forms, notably in *Dibothriocephalus* and related genera, some sort of boundary between successive proglottides may be found, but it is less clearly evident than in the genera mentioned above, and often the yolk glands do not take part in such separation. In the genus *Bothriocephalus* a similarly weak boundary is to be found between the so-called "double proglottides." Among other pseudophyllidean genera any internal boundaries between successive proglottides seem to be lacking completely.

Growth occurs *diffusely* in the young pseudophyllidean by active multiplication of parenchymal cells. In some forms, such as *Ligula, Triaenophorus,* and *Schistocephalus,* such growth seems to cease before the tapeworm reaches its final host. In other forms, such as *Dibothriocephalus* and *Eubothrium,* once the worm has reached the final host, the growth processes lead to a simultaneous proglottisation—that is to say, to a simultaneous appearance of sets of reproductive organs in metameric succession along the body, developing at the same rate. There may be also a similar synchronicity of external segmentation so that a *primary segmentation* is produced. In *Bothriocephalus* such primary segmentation does not always coincide with primary proglottisation, one primary segment often enclosing two primary proglottides. After primary segmentation has appeared, further segments—in *Dibothriocephalus latus* at any rate—may originate from a zone of cellular activity situated between the holdfast and the first of the primary segments; but in *Bothriocephalus,* again, the diffuse method of segment formation persists and the double proglottides may each separate into two externally marked segments. Whether the segments that are formed later in *Bothriocephalus* still originate from a growth zone, as in *Dibothriocephalus,* is uncertain.

In view of the many uncertainties as to the correct interpretation of pseudophyllidean phenomena, Nybelin's views upon growth and segmentation, although far from being in accord with those of the present writers, are worthy of extended quotation. We translate freely:

"As regards the growth processes of the worm, it is almost superfluous to point out that they stand in close relationship with apolysis, or conversely anapolysis, since the growth of anapolytic worms must naturally be restricted while that of apolytic worms may be unrestricted through the whole life of the individual. In some forms a restriction of growth occurs even before they pass into the definitive host, as for example in *Cyathocephalus, Ligula, Schistocephalus,* and in most cases in *Triaenophorus*; in others, growth begins only in the final host and the reproductive organs appear only after the worm is fully grown, as for example in *Eubothrium rugosum* and other eubothriid species. The same phenomenon occurs apparently in *Anchistrocephalus microcephalus.* I have many times observed meter-long specimens of this species which had no trace of reproductive organs.

"It is now of interest to establish that these forms with restricted growth are those in which I asserted the absence of histologically distinguishable growth zones in contrast with apolytic forms which have such structures. It is essential, therefore, to correlate these two observations. At first I believed that the growth zone, which is nothing but an aggregation of parenchymal cells in active division, can be no longer recognized as such after the growth of the worm is completed but must be present during growth. However, cross sections of triaenophorid larvae and of very young specimens of *Eubothrium crassum* convinced me that this is not the case. A histologically demonstrable zone was no more to be found in them than in full-grown individuals. There must exist, in fact, in anapolytic forms *diffuse longitudinal growth*, whereas growth in apolytic worms appears to take place chiefly in the foremost portion of the worm, thus producing the effect of a special growth zone. Above all, this growth zone cannot occur in the region of the fixation organs, as in that case these would sooner or later be pushed farther away from the end of the body. Anything in any way related to the fixation organs must be separated from the growth zone and must lie in front of it.

"Pintner, in his definition of the holdfast, is undoubtedly correct so far as forms with unrestricted growth and possession of a growth zone are concerned. Where such are lacking, it appears to me that the boundary of the holdfast can only be arrived at by determining the extent of the fixation organs.

"It is further worthy of note that anapolysis, or apolysis, of the pseudophyllidean worm is correlated also with the absence of, or presence of, internal separation of the genitalia. Where proglottides are cast off singly, or in short or long sections, it is of importance that the internal organization of the worm not be broken or torn irreparably. By an internal division between genitalia or, as in the *Bothriocephalus* species, between groups of such, any such damage is prevented and the break is prepared for occurrence at predetermined places. The formation of a transverse muscle structure, as in *Abothrium* and *Parabothrium*, or an interproglottidal zone, as in many Cyclophyllidea, may indicate either a precocious scar formation before separation, or a reminiscence of potential autotomy. On this view, the occurrence of internal division or of proglottis formation in anapolytic worms would be quite meaningless, and it does not occur in these forms.

"In this connection some space may be devoted to the meaning of apolysis. Generally it is regarded as an adaptation for egg distribution in forms without uterine openings. This is certainly plausible in many cases, as for example in the *Taenias* of man and in other cestodes. Possibly the same explanation holds good for Abothriinae among Pseudophyllidea. This explanation, nevertheless, is not altogether sufficient, especially for those cases where a uterine aperture is present through which eggs pass gradually to the outside, as for example in *Dibothriocephalus latus*. Braun has previously noted this circumstance and found a happy explanation. 'When in such cases definitely formed segments are cast off, it may be correlated with an inability of the species concerned to exceed a definite though varying length and number of segments rather than correlated with the necessity of permitting the expected brood an exit from the host.' ('Bronn's Thierreich,' p. 1226).

"This gradual disintegration of single segments or groups of segments is thus not comparable biologically with apolysis in *Taenias*. In order to express this fact terminologically, this type of apolysis might be termed 'pseudapolysis' to distinguish it from apolysis in the strict sense, which is an adaptation for egg distribution.

"The phenomena of euapolysis and hyperapolysis might be regarded as a gradual disintegration or simply as an arrangement for egg distribution, but they must have originated for other reasons. These phenomena occur almost exclusively among the cestodes of sharks and rays and among these are found only in fragile worms; thus, the *Acanthobothrium* species are euapolytic or hyperapolytic while the closely related but muscular body of *Onchobothrium uncinatum* (Rud.) is simply apolytic; the fragile body of *Trilocularia gracilis* (Olsson) is hyperapolytic while the powerful body of *Monorygma perfectum* (Ben.) is apolytic; and so on.

"Now the parasites of Selachii are provided as a rule with specially powerful attachment organs developed in correlation with the nature of the host gut contents. It appears very plausible that violent pressure must also influence the structure of the body. Muscular forms are able to withstand such pressure, but long or fragile forms undergo the risk of being wholly or partly torn loose and carried to the outside before they are sexually ripe. There are two conceivable ways in which this danger might be minimized. In the first place, sexual maturity might be arrived at quickly so that the whole worm consists of a few segments among which only one or two are ripe simultaneously, as is the case with *Echinobothrium affine* Dies.; or, secondly, the proglottides might break away early from the worm and wedge themselves in the recesses of the spiral valve, or even attach themselves by special structures to the gut wall, as for example in *Trilocularia*. On account of their relative minuteness the proglottides are thus protected against the pressure of the gut contents.

"We may distinguish, therefore, among cestodes four different types of body—the anapolytic, pseudapolytic, simple apolytic, and the euapolytic to hyperapolytic types. The relation of these types to one another is in my opinion as follows: If multiplication of genitalia, like multiplication of rediae and cercariae in Trematoda, is a result of parasitism which on account of the great mortality of the young is useful or even necessary to individual forms, it follows that unrestricted growth, with the resulting enhanced possibilities of egg production, is a further step in this direction. We may then regard restricted growth as a primitive condition from which unrestricted growth has evolved. As to the circumstances which have induced this evolution, it is difficult to say. According to such facts as are available, there appears to be a direct correlation between anapolysis and annualism, and apolysis appears to be correlated with perennialism. It appears to me that unrestricted growth is an adaptation to perennialism.

"Then, however, the question arises as to how perennialism came into existence. The parasites of warm-blooded hosts may be considered as quite independent of fluctuations of external temperature and living under fairly constant conditions of life. That this is not always the case, however, seems shown by the case of the fish parasites *Eubothrium* and *Parabothrium.* I am inclined with Schauinsland to take into consideration certain biological relationships of host and intermediate host as influential factors.

"However that may be, unrestricted growth results as noted above, in the gradual dissolution of the oldest parts and the appearance of this phenomenon termed pseudapolysis. It is possible that this dying-off allows eggs to reach the outside and so renders the uterine apertures superfluous, pseudapolysis thus passing into true apolysis. Likewise it may be suggested that the extreme phenomena of euapolysis and hyperapolysis have gradually evolved out of simple apolysis." Nybelin (1922).

Each gravid segment of a pseudophyllidean has a permanent uterine aperture which opens on one of the flat surfaces of the segment. So characteristic of Pseudophyllidea is this permanent uterine aperture that even a fragment of tapeworm body in which permanent uterine apertures can be distinguished can safely be relegated to this group. Whether the surface on which the uterine aperture opens should be regarded as dorsal or ventral is disputable. Most authorities follow the convention laid down by Eschricht (1841) who, in describing *Dibothriocephalus latus*, termed the surface bearing the genital apertures the *ventral* surface. However, the positions of the male and female genital apertures among tapeworms in general vary greatly, being sometimes marginal and sometimes surficial, and in the latter case either on the same surface as the uterine aperture or on the opposite surface to it. The position of the uterine aperture, if present, is therefore a better indication of the ventral surface. Where it is absent, as in the majority of tapeworms, the ventral surface will be that surface to which the *female* reproductive organs approximate.

CLASSIFICATION

We shall use in the following pages what is substantially the Lühe-Nybelin scheme, accepting the view that the dibothriate tapeworms may be grouped within the order Pseudophyllidea and among the following seven families:

KEY TO FAMILIES

1. Genital aperture or apertures opening on one flat surface of the segment. . 2
   Genital aperture or apertures opening on one margin of the segment 5
2. Genital aperture or apertures on the *same* surface as the uterine aperture. 3
   Genital aperture or apertures on the *opposite* surface to the uterine aperture 4
3. Small forms; holdfast of the plerocercoid and of the primary segmented adult club-shaped with four protrusible tentacles; replaced in the secondary

segmented adult by a rectangular pseudo-holdfast which resembles the first formed segment but has a dorsal and a ventral shallow bothrium; cirrus minutely spiny; uterus with a proximal coiled region and a distal saclike region .... HAPLOBOTHRIIDAE
Large forms; holdfast variable in shape but never with tentacles; uterus tubular throughout; cirrus smooth .... DIBOTHRIOCEPHALIDAE

4. Holdfast with bluntly rounded apex; bothria slitlike, deep, with inrolled margins; proximal region of uterus tubular, sinuous; distal region of uterus saclike, sharply differentiated; uterus opening on one side of the middle line of the segment surface; eggs thin-shelled, without opercula, each containing an embryo when laid .... PTYCHOBOTHRIIDAE
Holdfast with four-lobed, fleshy apex and long, oval, shallow bothria; uterus as above; eggs with opercula, not containing embryos when laid.... .... BOTHRIOCEPHALIDAE

5. Small fleshy forms; unsegmented but with lobelike outgrowths from the posterior border of each anterior proglottis; bothria shallow, oval depressions; uterine aperture between middle line of segment surface and poral margin of segment; cirrus very distinctly protrusible and armed at its base with recurved spines; eggs with opercula but not containing embryos when laid .... ECHINOPHALLIDAE
Relatively large forms, usually well segmented; cirrus not conspicuously protrusible nor armed with spines 6

6. Segmented *or* unsegmented forms; holdfast cuboidal, with shallow, rounded bothria and an apex commonly armed with hooks; uterus tubular; uterine aperture surficial, on ventral surface of segment, anterior to the level of the genital apertures (which are on the opposite surface); eggs with opercula, not containing embryos when laid .... TRIAENOPHORIDAE
Segmented forms; holdfast subspherical, with relatively deep, circular bothria and a bilobed apex which is not armed; uterus saclike with its aperture rudimentary and surficial, either dorsally *or* ventrally; eggs without opercula but containing embryos when laid .... AMPHICOTYLIDAE

Bacigalupo (1945) has established an additional family of Pseudophyllidea upon the characteristics of a single specimen of tapeworm that was evacuated by a Polish immigrant to Argentina. The proglottides are described as resembling those of a *Taenia*, the holdfast as being unarmed, and the bothria as anchor-shaped and two in number. The specimen was made the type of a new genus and species, *Diancyrobothrium taenioides* Bacigalupo, 1945, and of a new pseudophyllidean family, Diancyrobothriidae. For the present the status of this family must be considered *sub judice*.

Family HAPLOBOTHRIIDAE Meggitt, 1924

DESCRIPTION

Of the order Pseudophyllidea. Small, slender worms up to 110 mm. long. Mature worm formed by subdivision of the segments of a primary worm whose holdfast is a cylindrical structure, somewhat club-shaped, with four protrusible tentacles. Holdfast of the mature worm merely the slightly modified foremost segment, without tentacles but with a shallow dorsal depression and a shallow ventral depression, both analogous presumably with the bothria of other Pseudophyllidea. An elongated neck present in the primary worm. Segments of the primary worm long and narrow. Segmentation of the secondary worm beginning immediately behind the holdfast but being complete only in the anterior region of the worm. One set only of reproductive organs per segment. Genital apertures in the middle of the ventral surface of the segment. Yolk glands medullary in position, as are also the testes, both sets of organs lying to the inner side of the nerve trunks. Testes arranged in lateral bands by the median osmoregulatory canal and the genital organs in the middle line. Sperm duct enlarged to form a large, nonmuscular external seminal vesicle. Cirrus armed with short spines. Seminal receptacle moderate in size, sharply marked off from the vagina. Uterus comprising a much-coiled proximal duct and a large uterine sac. Type genus, *Haplobothrium* Cooper, 1914.

HISTORY

The term "Haplobothriinae" was coined by Cooper (1917) for a new subfamily of Dibothriocephalidae which he proposed to establish for a peculiar tapeworm, named by him *Haplobothrium globuliforme*, that he had found in the primitive North American fresh-water fish *Amia calva*. Meggitt (1924a) raised the subfamily to the rank of a family. No further genera or species have been added.

RECOGNITION FEATURES

The outstanding feature of *Haplobothrium* is of course the supposed resemblance of its primary holdfast to that of members of the order Trypanorhyncha (Figure 353). The primary segmented worm is small, not exceeding 70 mm. in length. Its holdfast is cylindrical, somewhat club-shaped. From the apex protrude four tentacles which can be withdrawn into four muscular cavities within the holdfast end or, conversely, can be protruded from them. These tentacles recall somewhat those of trypanorhynchids, since each is covered with minute spines; but they are stumpier, more tapering, than trypanorhynchid tentacles, and when thrust forth splay outward so as to lie each at right angles to the long axis of the worm.

Each tentacle consists of a permanently protruded basal portion covered by minute spines, and a tubular portion that can be protruded or withdrawn. From Cooper's description it is not clear just how this protrusion or withdrawal of the smooth tubular portion is effected, since he implies that the edge of the solid, stumpy basal portion is continuous with the wall of the muscular cavity internal to it. There seems nothing to correspond with the tentacle sheath of the trypanorhynchan unless the basal stump so corresponds. Cooper believed that *Haplobothrium* throws some light upon the manner in which protrusible tentacles may have arisen.

"In discussing the homologies of the proboscides of the Trypanorhyncha, Benham (1901) said: 'It appears more probable that each proboscis has been developed by the deepening and modification of an accessory sucker of some Tetraphyllidean as its relation to the bothridia and its mode of development closely agree with these structures. Functionally, too, it is a perfection of the armature plus the accessory sucker of three forms (Acanthocephala, Nemertini and Taenioidea) while there is no doubt that the phyllidea of the orders are identical.'

"The fact [Cooper continues] that here the walls of the bulbs, since they are composed of an outer layer of longitudinal muscles, a middle layer of circular muscles, and an inner layer of cuticle, are not only comparable but directly continuous with the cuticle and cuticular muscles of the body wall, and in the reverse order, would seem to lend support to this view. Simple invagination of the external layers of the body wall, in development, would account for these structures, while the proboscis with its retractor muscles might well be formed by the modification of the external layers of an accessory sucker." Cooper (1918).

The division of the primary worm into segments is foreshadowed when it is only 4 to 5 mm. long by faint transverse lines, presumably feeble aggregations of nuclei, across the flat surfaces at regular intervals in the hinder region of the body. These primary segments lengthen as the worm grows and the lines between them deepen into grooves. When this primary segmented worm is about 10 mm. long, its rearmost segment, itself about 1.5 mm. long, begins to show faint transverse lines decreasing in intensity from before backward. A similar appearance is seen on the surface of the last segment but one and later on the last segment but two, and so on. The faint lines deepen into grooves, and each transversely grooved segment falls in its turn from the primary worm and grows into a secondarily segmented worm. In the secondary worm thus formed from a shed segment of the primary worm, segmentation becomes more and more marked from before backward. The most anterior segment, though remaining similar to the others in general shape, develops a dorsal and a ventral depression and assumes the function of a holdfast. The posterior border of each of the first twenty-five segments of this secondary worm is bluntly bilobed, dorsally and ventrally, to form what Cooper called "auricular appendages."

"The scolex is quite small, simple externally, and with the unaided eye can scarcely be distinguished from the first joint. It is shaped roughly like a rectangular solid, hollowed out laterally to form simple depressions and dorso-ventrally to form the shallow bothria or organs of attachment. The summit is somewhat prolonged as a low, pyramidally shaped disk, quite comparable to that ('Scheitelplatte') found in the members of the subfamily Triaenophorinae Lühe, 1899. The opposite end of the scolex is modified to form two pairs of auricular appendages closely resembling internally as well as externally those of the foremost joints." Cooper (1914a).

Such an apolysis of terminal segments certainly recalls the similar phenomenon in Trypanorhyncha, and several authors, notably Southwell (1930) and Fuhrmann (1931), have maintained that *Haplobothrium* is an aberrant trypanorhynchan, perhaps a neotenic trypanorhynchan larva. The internal anatomy, however, of the gravid segment is decidedly pseudophyllidean. The genital apertures are surficial, median and ventral, as in the members of Dibothriocephalidae. The bothria, though weakly represented, recall in nature those of Bothriocephalidae. The uterus, comprising a much-coiled uterine duct and a large uterine dilatation, also recalls that of Bothriocephalidae. The spinose cirrus recalls Echinophallidae. The minute spininess of the tip of the holdfast of the secondary worm recalls certain Triaenophoridae. The observations of Meinkoth (1947) definitely show the life cycle to be pseudophyllidean in type.

On the other hand, definitely nonpseudophyllidean is the medullary position of the yolk glands, follicular though they be.

The most authoritative pronouncement upon the status of *Haplobothrium* is that of Dollfus (1942):

"Several helminthologists, Fuhrmann (1931) among them, admit into the tetrarhynchs as an aberrant form, *Haplobothrium globuliforme* A. R. Cooper, 1914. This species, found in the pyloric region (duodenum) of *Amia calva* L. (ganoid) has been recorded from various places in North America and has been described by Cooper (1914a, 1915b, 1917, 1918) who has established for it the subfamily Haplobothriinae Cooper, later become the family Haplobothriidae Meggitt.

"The holdfast carries neither bothria nor bothridia nor suckers; there are four tentacles of simple structure comprising an invaginable portion, unarmed, and a basal enlargement, always extruded, not invaginable, carrying small spines. There are no sheaths, the tentacles being immediately preceded by bulbs which reach anteriorly the surface of the holdfast; they comprise a layer of longitudinal muscles, internal to which is a layer of circular muscles. The interior of the bulbs is occupied by parenchyma traversed by 10–14 retractor muscles. Behind the bulbs, in the parenchyma of the stalk of the holdfast, there are numerous frontal glands.

"The genital apertures are on the same surface, ventral, median, and very anterior; the vaginal aperture is immediately posterior to that of the cirrus pouch; a genital atrium is scarcely apparent and there is no common genital canal. The uterine aperture forms slowly by involution, almost at the level of the posterior end of the uterus, a little way in front of the level of the ovary. The testes are fairly numerous and some are to be found behind the ovary; they are separated into two fields by a medio-dorsal osmoregulatory canal. The cirrus pouch has two seminal vesicles, external and internal; the sperm duct is dorsal to the uterus and the vagina ventral to the uterus. The yolk glands comprise a small number of very large follicles which, in the anterior region of the proglottis, extend across the whole face but in the posterior region are restricted to the sides. The eggs are like those of Pseudophyllidea, with opercula and coracidia. There are two longitudinal ventral osmoregulatory canals but only one dorsal osmoregulatory canal. Secondary worms are formed, each with a secondary holdfast (pseudo-holdfast) provided with weak bothria. The six or seven first segments are craspedote, the remainder are acraspedote.

"In what respects is *Haplobothrium* related to Trypanorhyncha? To that question I reply: *Haplobothrium* is not related to Trypanorhyncha. There are evidently some characteristics which occur also in Trypanorhyncha; the testes extend behind the ovary, the longitudinal muscles separate the cortical from the medullary parenchyma, the sperm duct is dorsal and the vagina is ventral in relation to the uterus; but these are characteristics which one finds also in Pseudophyllidea, and the arrangement of the medio-ventral genital apertures is a pseudophyllidean arrangement. The anatomical features do not justify any relegation of *Haplobothrium* to Trypanorhyncha.

"O. Fuhrmann (1931) believed the trypanorhynchan nature of *Haplobothrium* was proved by the larva found by Essex (1928b, 1929c) a larva with unarmed tentacles found encysted in the liver, close to the surface, of *Ameiurus nebulosus* in the Mississippi (Minnesota). *Amia calva* presumably becomes infected by ingesting *Ameiurus*. This larva, according to Fuhrmann, is not a plerocercoid as in Dibothriocephalidae but a plerocercus in which the tentacle-carrying holdfast is followed by a bladder (*blastocyst*) with a receiving cavity for the retracted holdfast such as is known among Trypanorhyncha but unknown elsewhere among Pseudophyllidea. According to Essex's description the larva that he observed encysted in the *Ameiurus* liver (but unfortunately did not figure) seems closer to the plerocercus of Trypanorhyncha than to the plerocercoid of Dibothriocephalidae, but we are far from knowing if all Pseudophyllidea have the same sort of plerocercoid as have Dibothriocephalidae and we do not know whether or not there occurs among Pseudophyllidea a larval type whose *pars antica scolecis* is retracted, at least in part, within an invagination of the *pars metabothridialis scolecis* as is the case among Tetraphyllidea and in Proteocephala, which are in some respects intermediate between Tetraphyllidea and Pseudophyllidea. Without undervalueing the validity of Fuhrmann's argument, it does not convince me; firstly, because we know the post-embryonic development and larval stages of only a few Pseudophyllidea, which does not permit a generalization, and secondly because *Haplobothrium* being an aberrant form, its post-embryonic development may be aberrant as compared with Pseudophyllidea as a whole, without any implication of affinity with Trypanorhyncha.

"But, it may be objected, there are the tentacles. To that I reply, they are not tentacles of a trypanorhynchan; their structure is entirely different, even in the bulbs. It is not merely tentacles that characterize a trypanorhynchan, for in *Aporhynchus* they have disappeared leaving only a few vestiges but nevertheless the anatomy of the worm is that of a trypanorhynchan, as Nybelin (1918b) has clearly shown. Franz Poche (1924) has seen in the tentacles of *Haplobothrium* a phylogenetic stage in the evolution of trypanorhynchan tentacles conforming to the classical but purely hypothetical scheme of Pintner (1896a) according to which each tentacle results from the transformation of an accessory sucker situated at the apex of a bothridium as in many Tetraphyllidea. That Pintner's hypothesis may explain the origin of the tentacles of *Haplobothrium* is possible; but as regards Trypanorhyncha, ingenious as is this hypothesis, and in spite of Pintner's efforts to reconcile it with the facts of ontogeny, it seems to me almost certain that what we know of the manner of development of the tentacular apparatus of Trypanorhyncha is not in agreement with it.

"To me, *Haplobothrium* is an isolated form, derived from Pseudophyllidea; it has evolved independently and its tentacles do not imply any affinity with Trypanorhyncha; in that I agree fully with Woodland (1927b); I believe that Cooper was not far from the truth when he placed *Haplobothrium* in the family Diphyllobothriidae of Lühe. Nybelin (1922) is not of that opinion, believing that in certain features of its structure (position of testes and yolk glands in the medullary parenchyma, formation of the uterus, nature of the holdfast) *Haplobothrium* is distant from any known forms of Pseudophyllidea. The case of the tentacles of *Haplobothrium* seems to me to be a phenomenon of convergence analogous with that of *Rhopalias* Stiles and Hassall, 1898 (= *Rhopalophorus* Diesing, 1850) in distomid Trematoda. In *Rhopalias* there are two evaginable tentacles each armed with hooks and each having a retractor muscle and a bulb; as in *Haplobothrium* there is no sheath and the tentacular apparatus is even a little simpler than in *Haplobothrium* and closer to Pintner's scheme." Dollfus (1942).

Support for the views of Dollfus has come from observations made by Meinkoth (1947) upon material gathered in Michigan. This observer points out that the egg of *H. globuliforme* is typically pseudophyllidean, comprising an ovoid, operculate shell within which is a coracidium. This coracidium is an oncosphere bearing a ciliated embryophore. Unlike other pseudophyllidean oncospheres, however, the coracidium is ready to hatch and does so as soon as it reaches fresh water. Secondly, this swimming coracidium serves to attract the attention of the first intermediate host, a copepod, which devours it. There develops within the copepod a procercoid closely similar to that of other pseudophyllideans. No sign of holdfast characters is apparent in procercoids up to 24 days old. When ingested by a fish, this procercoid develops into a plerocercoid with the typical haplobothriid holdfast. The whole life cycle opposes the assignation of this tapeworm to Trypanorhyncha.

Family Dibothriocephalidae Lühe, 1902

DESCRIPTION

Of the order Pseudophyllidea. Medium to large-sized tapeworms with the holdfast somewhat variable in shape, commonly compressed, with the bothria surficial. Neck region long and distinct or so short as to appear absent from contracted specimens. Segmentation usually distinct. Genital apertures surficial and ventral, opening directly and independently to the outside or opening by way of a common cirro-vaginal atrium. An external seminal vesicle present, sometimes wholly or partly fused with the cirrus pouch. Ovary medullary and ventral, two-winged, in the last quarter of the proglottis. Yolk glands small and numerous, cortical in position, usually in two bands which meet in front of the genital apertures. Uterus a spiral tube opening to the outside behind the vaginal aperture. Eggs operculated, not embryonated when laid but liberating later a ciliated embryo. Procercoid larval stage in fishes, amphibians, reptiles, birds, and mammals. Adults mainly parasitic in fishes but sometimes in reptiles, birds, and mammals. Type genus, *Dibothriocephalus* Lühe, 1899.

HISTORY

The family was established by Lühe to contain a number of forms similar in structure to a common and long-known tapeworm of humans that up to 1899 had been termed zoologically *Bothriocephalus latus* Bremser. In that year, however, Lühe renamed this tapeworm *Dibothriocephalus latus* and named his new family accordingly. In 1910 Lühe became convinced that this form was identical generically with a tapeworm that Cobbold (1858) had described from toothed whales under the term *Diphyllobothrium stemmacephalum.* The generic name was therefore changed by Lühe to *Diphyllobothrium*, and the name of the family became Diphyllobothriidae.

In view of Cobbold's extremely inadequate description of his genus, many students of tapeworms have refused to adopt the change made by Lühe. Most European workers consistently refuse to do so, but the terms *Diphyllobothrium* and Diphyllobothriidae have become firmly established in American parasitological literature.

In the following pages we shall offer an opinion based upon descriptions by Eric Cohn (1912), Yamaguti (1935b), and Hsü (1935) of tapeworm material from toothed whales, material which these authors assumed to be identical generically with Cobbold's *Diphyllobothrium.* It is our opinion that any generic identity of Cobbold's genus *Diphyllobothrium* with Lühe's genus *Dibothriocephalus* is unproven and, in view of the anatomical and physiological differences between their respective hosts, is unlikely. We shall therefore retain Lühe's earlier terms *Dibothriocephalus* and Dibothriocephalidae.

RECOGNITION FEATURES

The features by which a dibothriocephalid tapeworm may be recognized are essentially those which characterize *Dibothriocephalus latus.* No other tapeworm has been the subject of so much description, and little is to be gained here by repeating the details of description elaborated by such writers as Sommer and Landois (1872), Schauinsland (1885), Essex (1927b), Magath (1929a), Hans Vogel (1929a, 1929b, 1929c, 1930), Joyeux, Du Noyer, and Baer (1931b), Wardle (1932b, 1934, 1935b), and Wardle and McColl (1937).

Surveying the group as a whole, however, we shall find many departures from the structural pattern seen in *Dibothriocephalus latus.* Thus, for example, the holdfast is not necessarily always spoon-shaped, almond-shaped, or olive-shaped. The bothria may be, instead of slits, mere grooves continuous with one another over the tip of the holdfast, representing either continuations of the mid-surficial grooves or possibly, if doubtfully, in some forms continuations of the mid-marginal grooves;

or they may be relatively wide, keyholelike apertures. Or again the bothria may be funnel-like with frilled lips; or they may even appear as open-ended tubes or as shallow lateral depressions of the holdfast surface.

The male and female ducts may open *separately* on the surface of the segment and not into a common cirro-vaginal atrium. The uterine whorls may appear as a central rosette of loops instead of as a series of laterally arranged loops; or the uterus may be so dilated by egg pressure as to appear as one or as two saclike structures.

However, there is little to be gained in taxonomic convenience by using these departures from *Dibothriocephalus latus* to establish separate families within a common superfamily grouping, or even as a basis for establishing subfamilies of Dibothriocephalidae. Until more dibothriocephalid life cycles have been studied it is preferable to accept the family Dibothriocephalidae as a convenient receptacle for all pseudophyllidean worms which (1) have the uterine and genital apertures on the ventral surface, (2) have a tubular and convoluted uterus, and (3) have the bothria essentially slitlike or groovelike. Eighteen genera may be admitted to the family, two of them, however, of doubtful validity. A preliminary distinction may be made as follows:

KEY TO GENERA

1. Bothria rudimentary 2
   Bothria well defined, as saucerlike depressions or as slits or as open-ended tubes 6
2. Holdfast with a well-developed suckerlike structure, behind which and well back are two shallow rudimentary bothria; vaginal aperture without a sphincter muscle; uterus with 2–3 loops on each side, of which only one enlarges to hold the eggs; adults in varanid lizards. . . . *Scyphocephalus*
   Holdfast crossed at its tip by a groove 3
3. Apical groove apparently continuous with the mid-marginal grooves of the body; holdfast surficially triangular; body unsegmented but deeply cross-wrinkled . . . . *Pyramicocephalus*
   Apical groove apparently continuous with the mid-surficial grooves of the body; holdfast bluntly pointed; body unsegmented but cross-wrinkled . . 4
4. Each proglottis with two sets of reproductive organs . . . . *Digramma*
   Each proglottis with one set of reproductive organs 5
5. Testes centrally situated in the proglottis . . . . *Ligula*
   Testes in two lateral bands . . . . *Braunia*
6. Bothria in the form of open-ended tubes . . . . *Bothridium*
   Bothria never tubular 7
7. Bothria in the form of two slits separated by a partition 8
   Bothria in the form of saucerlike depressions 15
8. Bothrial slits funnel-like, with their margins fringed or scalloped, the two giving the holdfast the appearance of a fan; adults in varanid lizards . . . . *Duthiersia*
   Bothrial slits relatively simple 9
9. Parenchyma of the holdfast with numerous unicellular glands which discharge on the outer and inner surfaces of the bothrial slits 10
   Parenchyma of the holdfast without unicellular glands 11
10. Cirrus pouch connected with the cirro-vaginal atrium by a canal . . . . . .

. . . . *Adenocephalus*
Cirrus pouch opening directly to the cirro-vaginal atrium . . *Glandicephalus*

11. Holdfast heart-shaped or broadly oval in marginal outline with bothrial slits deep; neck short, commonly hidden in contracted specimens; body strongly muscular; adults in sea mammals (Pinnipedia, Cetacea) 12
Holdfast finger-shaped, spoon-shaped, club-shaped, but rarely heart-shaped in marginal outline; neck prominent; body only weakly muscular; adults in land mammals (Carnivora, Primates) and in fish-eating birds . . 14

12. Very large forms up to or exceeding 2,500 mm. in length by 15 mm. in breadth; holdfast compressed, small, broadly oval in marginal outline; uterine loops numerous, parallel, close together, not rosettelike in arrangement; adults in toothed whales . . . . *Diphyllobothrium*
Small to large forms with holdfast conventionally heart-shaped in marginal outline; segments short and broad, often with two sets of reproductive organs per segment; uterine loops few and tending to be loosely rosettelike 13

13. Relatively large forms with bothrial slits deep; segments short and broad, with two sets of reproductive organs per segment; uterine loops few and rosettelike in arrangement; adults in whalebone whales . . *Diplogonoporus*
Relatively short and broad forms with holdfast typically heart-shaped in marginal outline, oval or triangular in surficial outline; bothrial slits deep and keyholelike; reproductive organs usually in one set per segment but sometimes in two sets; uterus with 4–8 loops on each side, usually parallel and close together but sometimes loose and rosettelike; end loop greatly distended; eggs with rounded ends; adults in seals, sea lions, walruses, occasionally in humans and dogs . . . . *Cordicephalus*

14. Small to medium-sized, weakly muscular forms with holdfast small, compressed, spoon-shaped or finger-shaped in marginal outline; bothrial slits broad and shallow and fading indefinitely into the mid-dorsal and mid-ventral furrows of the body; neck long and slender; cirrus and vagina opening separately on the body surface; uterus a close spiral of closely appressed coils, never rosettelike in arrangement; eggs pointed at each end; adults in catlike Carnivora . . . . *Spirometra*
Relatively large, slender, weakly muscular forms with holdfast compressed, elongated, olive-shaped, spoon-shaped, club-shaped in marginal outline; bothrial slits narrow, deep; neck long and slender; cirrus and vagina opening into a cirro-vaginal atrium; uterus with 4–8 loops on each side, rosettelike in arrangement; eggs with rounded ends; adults in doglike Carnivora and fish-eating birds . . . . *Dibothriocephalus*

15. Bothria very shallow, dorsal and ventral in position, connected by a groove over the apex of the holdfast; adults in birds . . . . *Schistocephalus*
Bothria apparently lateral in position and not connected by an apical groove; adults in South African clawed frogs . . . . *Cephalochlamys*

NOTES ON GENERA

Scyphocephalus Riggenbach, 1898

With one pair of rudimentary bothria occupying only the basal quarter of the holdfast, the rest being taken up by a deep apical accessory organ which gives the holdfast what Riggenbach called a "beaker-like appearance." Neck region apparently not seen. Reproductive organs corresponding in every respect with those of *Duthiersia* but having only two or three uterine coils of which only the most anterior one serves to hold the eggs. No vaginal sphincter muscle. Genotype and only known species, *bisulcatus* Riggenbach, 1898.

Both genus and species were established for material from a varanid lizard; this, plus the marked similarity between the reproductive system and that of *Duthiersia* suggests strongly that an aberrant specimen of *Duthiersia* was in question.

Pyramicocephalus Monticelli, 1890 (= *Alyselminthus* Zeder, 1800; *Halysis* Zeder, 1803; *Tetrabothrium* Rudolphi, 1808; *Bothriocephalus* Rudolphi, 1808)

With the holdfast triangular in surficial outline, the bothria represented by a deep groove across the tip continuous with the mid-marginal grooves. Body subrectangular in cross section, unsegmented but deeply wrinkled. Internal structure recalling that of *Cordicephalus*. Genotype and only recorded species, *anthocephalus* Fabricius, 1780 (Figure 354).

The genotype was established by Fabricius for material from a seal in Greenland waters. It has been recorded since by many observers, mainly from the bearded seal (*Erignathus barbatus*) in Greenland waters under such specific names as *phocae* Mueller, 1780; *lanceolato-lobatus* Zeder, 1800; *anthocephalus* Rudolphi, 1810; *anthocephalus* Baird, 1853; and *anthocephalum* Diesing, 1854. Cooper (1921) recorded it also from *Erignathus* in arctic Canadian waters, and Wardle (1932b) recorded the larval form from a tommycod (*Gadus ogac*) in the same area. The plerocercoid stage is distinct enough to justify the establishment of this genus, but most of the alleged adults were probably species of *Cordicephalus* (cf. Figure 354, B and C, after Ariola).

Digramma Cholodkovsky, 1915

With the bothria represented by a short dorso-ventral groove with tumid lips running over the tip of the anterior end. Each flat body surface with two shallow, parallel grooves, 3–5 mm. apart; between them on the ventral side there is a median groove. Each proglottis with two sets of reproductive organs, each with a cirro-vaginal aperture in the nearer ventro-lateral groove, and a uterine aperture somewhat lateral to it. Genotype, *alternans* Rudolphi, 1810 (Figure 355).

The genotype (= *Ligula alternans* Rudolphi) was established for adult material from a gull, *Larus tridactylus*, in Europe and recorded again by Creplin (1839) as larval material from a goldfish (*Cyprinus carassius*) in Germany. Yamaguti (1935) redescribed similar material in Japan, also from a goldfish. Joyeux and Baer (1929a) identified with this form a larva recorded by Leon (1907b) from man in Rumania (as *Diplogonoporus brauni*). We believe *Digramma* to be merely an uncommon diplogonadic morpha of *Ligula*.

Ligula Bloch, 1782

Large, fleshy worms up to 280 mm. in average length by 8 mm. in average breadth, with the anterior portion of the body segmented for 15–20 proglottides and the rest of the body unsegmented but transversely wrinkled. Anterior end of the body bluntly pointed, with the

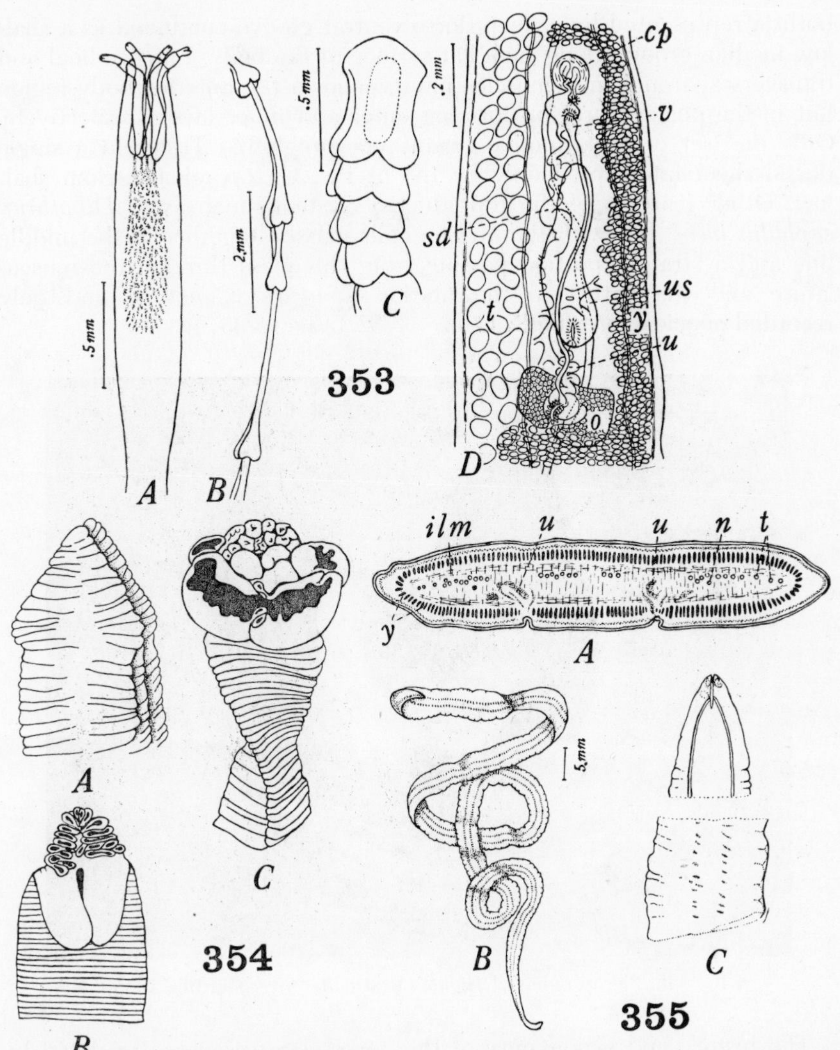

FIG. 353. *Haplobothrium globuliforme.* After Cooper, 1914a, 1918. A. Holdfast of primary segmented worm. B. 12th, 13th, and 14th segments of same. C. Holdfast and first 3 segments of secondary segmented worm. D. Mature proglottis. *cp*, cirrus pouch; *o*, ovary; *sd*, sperm duct; *t*, testes; *u*, uterus; *us*, uterine sac; *v*, vagina; *y*, yolk glands. FIG. 354. *Pyramicocephalus anthocephalus.* A. Holdfast of plerocercoid. After Wardle, 1932b. B and C. Holdfasts of adults. After Ariola, 1900. FIG. 355. *Digramma alternans.* After Yamaguti, 1934. A. Cross section of larval form. *ilm*, inner longitudinal muscles; *n*, nerve cord; *t*, testes; *u*, *anlage* of uterus; *y*, yolk glands. B. *Digramma brauni*, larval worm. After Leon, 1908. C. Anterior end of adult worm. After Leon, 1908.

bothria represented by a deep dorso-ventral groove continued as a shallow median groove along each flat surface of the body. Longitudinal and transverse parenchymal muscles intertwined in the anterior body region but in the posterior region forming outer and inner layers respectively. Only one set of reproductive organs per proglottis. Testes in a single dorsal sheet interrupted only by the uterus. Cirro-vaginal atrium shallow. Other features of the reproductive system much as in *Dibothriocephalus latus,* but with the uterine coils massed together in the middle line and a straight portion passing from this mass through the musculature and the cortex to the uterine aperture. Genotype and only recorded species, *intestinalis* Goeze, 1782 (Figure 357).

FIG. 356. Plerocercoids of *Ligula intestinalis.* After Wardle, 1935b.

The history and synonymity of this form were discussed in detail by Cooper (1918). It is a common tapeworm which has been recorded repeatedly from the alimentary tract of diving and wading birds in Europe, but in North America it is known only from mergansers (*Mergus spp.*). The plerocercoid larva (Figure 356), however, is common in both Europe and North America as a large unsegmented worm, 20 to 600 mm. long, closely resembling the sexual form but with the anterior end blunter, the bothrial groove less evident, and the segmentation lacking completely. It is a common parasite in the body cavity of fresh-water fishes (in Canada in *Catostomus, Notropis, Micropterus, Gasterosteus, Salmo, Perca*). Although so common in fishes, the worm is found relatively rarely in fish-eating birds since its adult life in the bird host is very short.

Joyeux and Baer (1936a, 1938b) infected domesticated ducks and herring gulls with ligulid plerocercoids from tench; the worms were sexually functional in two to three days, losing, before becoming so, the posterior half of the body. Their longevity in the bird was a matter of a few days at most. For fourteen days after losing the worms the bird was resistant to further infection, but after twenty to thirty days was readily infectible again.

It is customary to refer all ligulid larvae whatever their size to *Ligula intestinalis*, but the possibility of this species representing a group of morphologically similar but physiologically distinct forms must always be considered.

Braunia Leon, 1908

With the ovary branching and central in position, and the testes in two separate lateral bands. A form recorded only once, from a man at Jassy in Rumania, as *Braunia jassyensis*. Its resemblance to *Ligula* is very close.

Bothridium Blainville, 1824 (= *Prodicoelia* La Blond, 1836; *Solenophorus* Creplin, 1839)

Moderate-sized forms up to 500 mm. long by 6 mm. broad, with numerous short segments and a large distinct holdfast whose bothria are represented by two tubes with small, slitlike ends, provided fore and aft with sphincter muscles. Vagina opening immediately behind the cirrus pouch into a cirro-vaginal atrium whose aperture lies at the junction of the first and middle thirds of the ventral surface of the segment. Testes in two lateral bands, behind the cirrus pouch. Seminal receptacle of the vagina large and thick-walled. Ovary V-shaped, with the apex of the V directed dorsally, surrounded by the testes. Yolk glands lying between an inner and an outer zone of longitudinal parenchymal muscles. Uterus in the form of a uterine passage and a uterus proper, the latter consisting of two sacs connected by a narrow canal; no uterine rosette. Life cycle in snakes. Adult in boid snakes. Genotype and only known species, *pithonis* Blainville, 1824 (= *ditrema* La Blond, 1836; *laticeps* Duvernoy, 1833; *megalocephalus* Creplin, 1839; *grandis* Creplin, 1839) (Figure 358).

The inclusion of this genus among Dibothriocephalidae is not altogether satisfactory and rests mainly upon the early anatomical descriptions provided by Roboz (1882), Monticelli and Crety (1891), and Lühe (1900a). A re-examination based upon further material, and supported by a study of the life cycle, might suggest that this form is worthy of relegation to a separate family.

Solomon (1932) described and figured the development of *Bothridium pithonis* as far as the procercoid stage from eggs obtained from adult worms in a specimen of *Python molurus*. These eggs hatched in one to three days, according to room temperature, and the coracidia thus liberated readily infected the copepod *Cyclops viridis*, a single example of this crustacean harboring afterward as many as fifteen procercoids. The procercoid develops an elongated cercomer within fourteen days, but by the twentieth day has lost it.

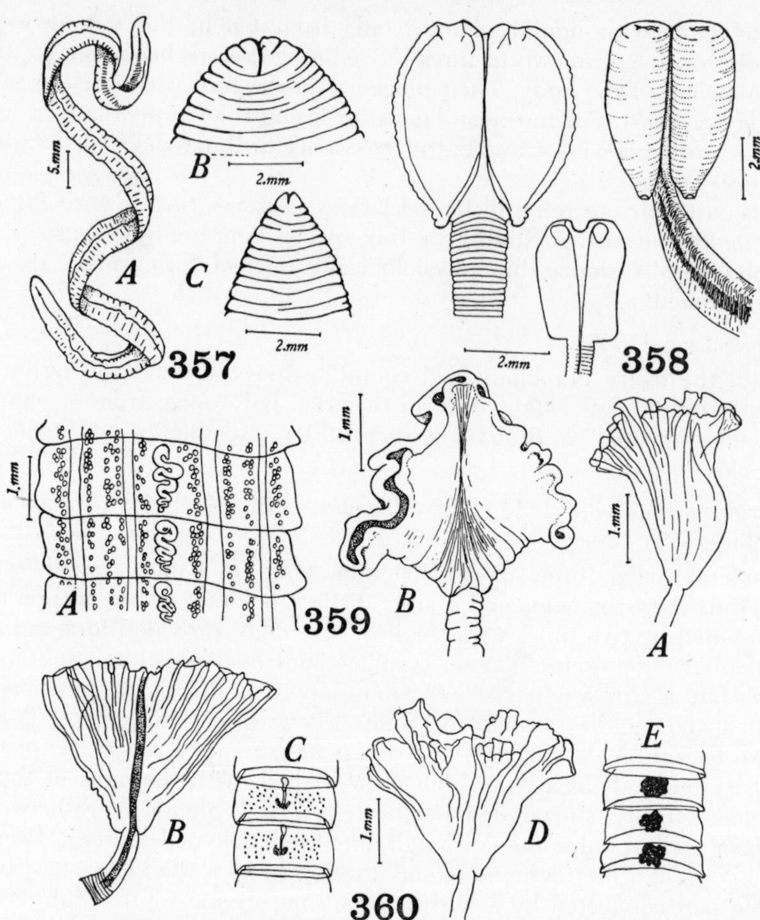

FIG. 357. *Ligula intestinalis.* A. Whole worm. After Neveu Lemaire, 1936. B. Anterior end of larval stage. C. Anterior end of adult. Both after Cooper, 1918. FIG. 358. *Bothridium pithonis,* views of holdfast. After Southwell, 1928b, and Joyeux, Du Noyer, and Baer, 1931b. FIG. 359. *Duthiersia fimbriata.* After Southwell, 1928b. A. Mature segments. B. Holdfast. FIG. 360. *Duthiersia expansa.* After Woodland, 1938. A, B, and D. Holdfasts. C. Young proglottides. E. Gravid proglottides.

Duthiersia Perrier, 1873

Small worms not exceeding 200 mm. in length. Holdfast compressed, broadly fan-shaped, triangular or nearly circular in marginal outline and suggesting a flattened funnel whose stem is the worm's body. Each bothrium funnel-like, not extending below half the length of the holdfast, with margins frilled, scalloped, or crenulated. Posterior bothrial apertures present on the side of the body in Asiatic forms but absent from African forms. Neck short, apparently lacking in contracted specimens. Surface of the body commonly smooth. Yolk glands placed to the outside of the longitudinal parenchymal muscles and in lateral bands. Vaginal aperture with a sphincter muscle, opening just behind the cirrus pouch. Uterus tubular, laterally looped, rosettelike. Adults in varanid lizards in southeastern Asia and in Africa. Genotype, *expansa* Perrier, 1873 from *Varanus indicus*, Moluccas (Figures 359, 360).

Woodland (1938) divided the genus into seven species, five of them new: *sarawakensis n.sp.*, *venusta n.sp.*, and *crassa n.sp.* from Asiatic material; *elegans* Perrier, 1873, *robusta n.sp.*, and *latissima n.sp.* from African material; these in addition, of course, to the genotype. Later (1941), however, he expressed the opinion that all the African species – lacking posterior bothrial apertures – should be considered as identical with *Duthiersia fimbriata* Diesing, 1854, and all the Asiatic species – which possess posterior bothrial apertures – as identical with *Duthiersia expansa* Perrier, 1873. The validity of *sarawakensis* was left undecided.

Adenocephalus Nybelin, 1931

With the parenchyma of the holdfast rich in unicellular glands and with the cirrus pouch connected with the cirro-vaginal atrium by a short canal. Holdfast narrowly oval in surficial (bothrial) view, broadly oval in marginal view, with the bothria keyholelike, somewhat undulating, deep. Neck very short. Segmentation well marked, with the segments relatively long. Cirro-vaginal aperture of each segment at the junction of the first and second fifths of the ventral surface. Vaginal aperture behind the cirrus aperture and some distance from it. Uterine aperture central, to right or to left of the middle line. Testes extending continuously from segment to segment in lateral bands, uniting, except for the area around the genitalia, behind the genital complex; in a single layer but with individual follicles displaced to lie among the muscle bundles. External seminal vesicle dorsal to the cirrus pouch. Cirrus pouch pear-shaped, 300–320 μ in length, typically dibothriocephalid. Body surface immediately above the cirrus pouch sinking inward in trench fashion. Hinder end of cirrus pouch extending into the dorsal longitudinal muscles. Cirrus opening into the cirro-vaginal atrium by a cloacal canal which opens upon a papilla. Ovary strongly bilobed. Yolk glands numerous, small, forming an unbroken half-cylinder between the subcuticula and the longitudinal muscles. Adult worms in sea lions. Genotype, *pacificus* Nybelin, 1931 (Figure 361).

Nybelin believed his genus sufficiently separated from *Glandicephalus* (see below) by features of host distribution, musculature, and genitalia. His material was taken from *Arctocephalus australis* (southern sea lion) in southern Pacific waters. Within the genus Nybelin placed also, as the species *septentrionalis*, a form that had previously been recorded by Stiles and Hassall (1899) as *Bothriocephalus sp.* from *Callorhinus ursinus* in the Pribilof Islands. He pointed out, too, that Cholodkovsky (1914) found in the same host species (*Callorhinus ursinus*) a form he recorded as *Clestobothrium glacialis*, which may have been Stiles and Hassall's form. Wardle, McLeod, and Stewart (1947), examining what they believed to be Stiles and Hassall's form, could find no trace of intra-holdfast glands and regarded this form as *Cordicephalus arctocephalinus*.

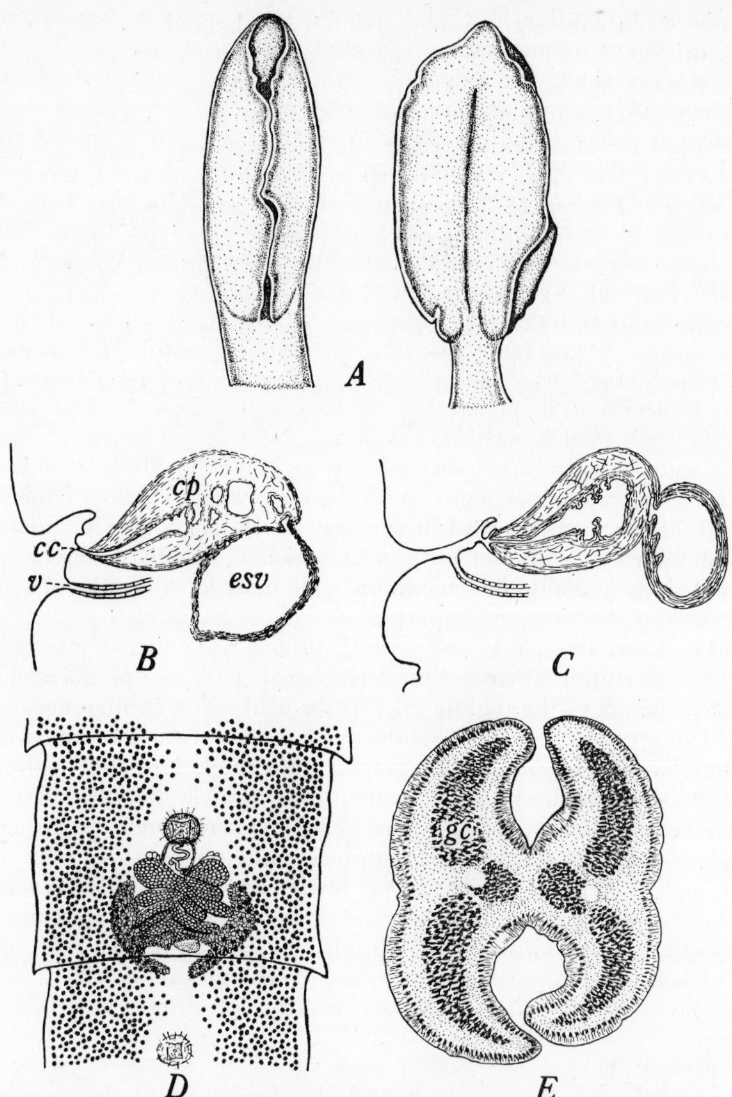

FIG. 361. *Adenocephalus pacificus.* After Nybelin, 1931. A. Marginal and surficial views of the holdfast. B. Genital atrium and cirrus pouch. *cc*, cloacal canal; *cp*, cirrus pouch; *esv*, external seminal vesicle; *v*, vagina. C. Genital atrium and cirrus pouch of *Adenocephalus septentrionalis.* D. Gravid segment of *Adenocephalus pacificus.* E. Cross section of the holdfast of *Adenocephalus pacificus* showing the intraholdfast glands (*gc*).

Glandicephalus Fuhrmann, 1921

With the parenchyma of the holdfast rich in unicellular glands but with the cirrus pouch opening directly into the cirro-vaginal atrium. Holdfast fingerlike, bluntly rounded apically. Bothria relatively wide, with lips well separated anteriorly, overlapping somewhat posteriorly, each bothrial lip ending in a small lobe. Neck very short. Segmentation beginning almost immediately behind the posterior bothrial borders. Segments short, thick, markedly craspedote. Anterior region of the body almost circular in cross section, flattened oval in the posterior region. Parenchymal muscles abnormally thick, comprising 6–8 layers of longitudinal muscle bundles between which are sheaths of transverse fibers. Medullary parenchyma greatly reduced in consequence. Osmoregulatory system with 10 to 12 dorsal, and as many ventral, longitudinal canals linked by a richly branching network, and two medullary canals, with a marked covering layer of longitudinal and circular muscle fibers, and a number of dorsal and ventral branch canals which originate within the muscle layers. Testes lying mainly between the longitudinal muscles. Cirrus pouch long and muscular, opening directly into the cirro-vaginal atrium. Ovary ventral, penetrated by muscle bundles so as to appear reticulate. Yolk glands cortical, as a single layer in the winglike expansions of each segment. Vagina opening posterior to the cirrus pouch, median or slightly left or right of the middle line. Uterus strongly serpentine, median, wholly medullary, its lateral loops narrow and surrounded by gland cells; eggs in single file within the uterus. Adult worms in seals of Antarctica. Genotype, *antarcticus* Baird, 1853 (Figure 362).

Baird's material was obtained from *Ommatophoca rossi* (Ross's seal). With it, Fuhrmann identified material previously examined and described by Shipley (1907) and by Rennie and Reid (1912) under the terms *Dibothrium antarcticum* Diesing; *Diplogonoporus antarcticus* Zschokke; *Dibothriocephalus antarcticus* Shipley; and *Diphyllobothrium antarcticum* Railliet and Henry.

Agreeing with *Adenocephalus* and *Glandicephalus* in having intraholdfast glands is *Dibothriocephalus wilsoni* Shipley, 1907 from *Ommatophoca rossi* and *Ogmorhinus leptonyx* (leopard seal) in antarctic waters. The scanty descriptions of previous writers were amplified by Fuhrmann (1921) from a re-examination of Shipley's material. Fuhrmann's description, freely translated, is as follows:

Dibothriocephalus wilsoni Shipley, 1907

Small tapeworms, 2 to 10 mm. long by 1.0 to 1.7 mm. broad, with holdfast ovoid, 450–550 μ long by 350–400 μ broad and having simple, slitlike bothria; holdfast parenchyma with numerous unicellular glands discharging into bothrial cavities. Neck apparently lacking (contracted specimens). Body segmentation well marked, with 8 to 13 segments which increase rapidly in length and breadth from before backward until the last segment is as long as wide. Genital apertures in the midventral line at the junction of the first and second fourths of the segment surface. Osmoregulatory system with 14 straight cortical canals lying dorsally and ventrally, and two medullary canals. Testes numerous, small, on either side of the other reproductive organs, with an unbroken line of 18 in front of the cirrus pouch. Cirrus pouch short and thick, strongly muscular, 100–114 μ long, provided with a dorsal external semi-

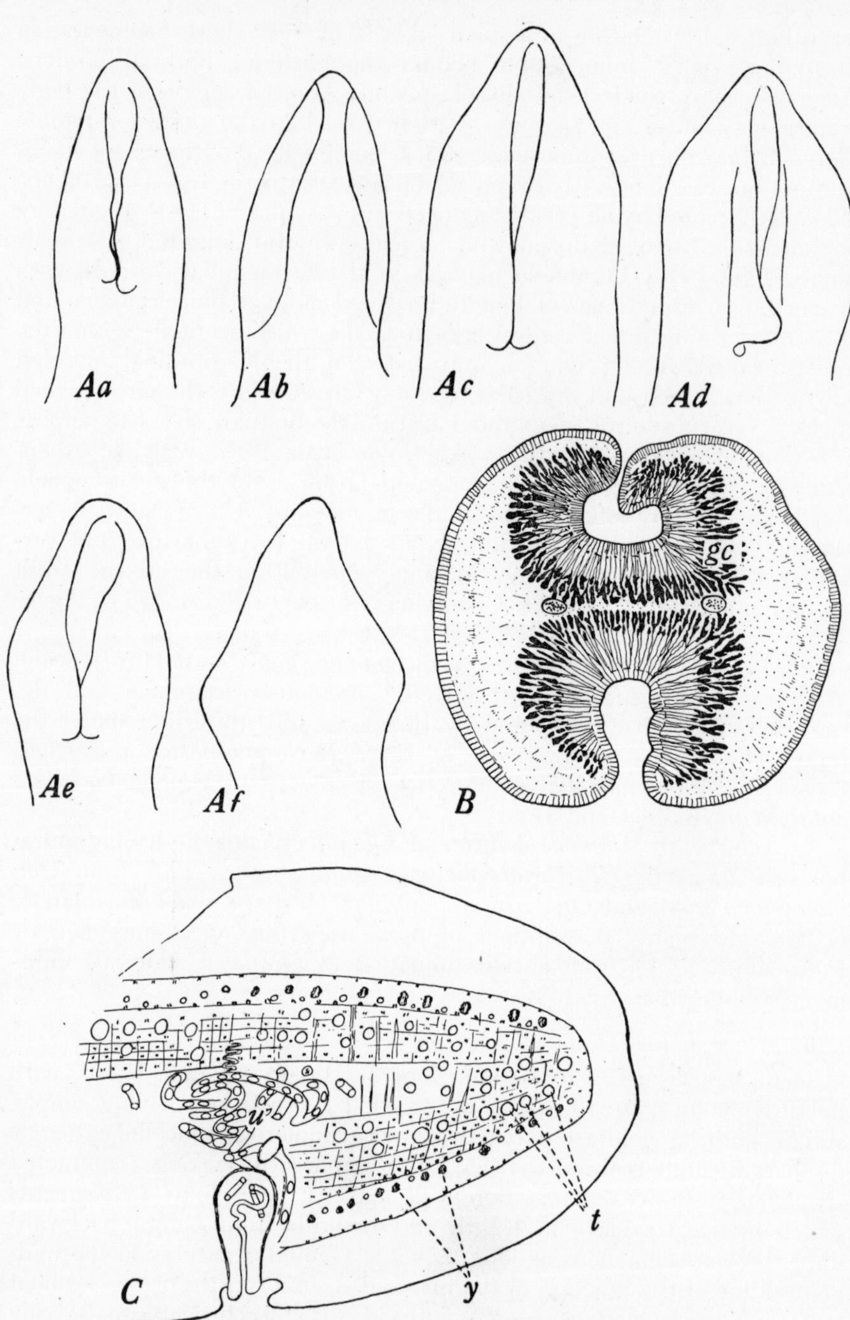

FIG. 362. *Glandicephalus antarcticus*. After Fuhrmann, 1920b. A*a* to A*f*. Outlines of holdfast. B. Cross section of holdfast to show the intraholdfast glands (*gc*). C. Part of a cross section of a segment through the genital aperture. *t*, testes; *u*, uterus; *y*, yolk glands.

nal vesicle and a small internal seminal vesicle. Ovary broad, very slightly lobed, 360–400 μ wide, placed in the hinder region of the segment. Yolk glands interrupted dorsally and ventrally but distributed laterally throughout the segment. Uterus with several loops, the terminal one distended with eggs. Eggs 48–60 μ by 32–36 μ. Adult worms recorded from *Ommatophoca rossi, Ogmorhinus leptonyx, Leptonychotes weddelli*, all antarctic seals.

Until further material is available the exact status of this form must remain doubtful. Apart from the presence of holdfast glands, it would fit very well into the genus *Cordicephalus* described below.

Diphyllobothrium Cobbold, 1858

Very large forms, up to and even exceeding 2,500 mm. in length by 15 mm. in breadth, with the body thick and muscular. Holdfast small, compressed, not exceeding one millimeter either way, with marginal surfaces broader than long and bluntly pointed apically. Bothrial slits shallow, their lips projecting somewhat above the holdfast surface so as to give the bothria a pseudo-tubular appearance and when contracted thrown into festoons. Neck short, up to one millimeter long. Dorsal and ventral body surfaces each with 8 to 10 longitudinal furrows. One set of reproductive organs per segment. Cirro-vaginal atrium shallow, its aperture on the second fourth of the ventral segment surface and surrounded by an oval field of papillae. Uterine aperture conspicuous, behind the cirro-vaginal aperture and well separated from it. Testes in a single layer on either side of the uterine field. External seminal vesicle postero-dorsal to the cirrus pouch and very muscular. Gravid uterus with lateral loops parallel and close together, not rosettelike in arrangement. Adults in toothed whales. Life cycle unknown. Genotype, *stemmacephalum* Cobbold, 1858.

There has been some confusion by previous authors as to the correct date when Cobbold established his genus. We are indebted for the following ruling to Dr. William A. Riley of the University of Minnesota (personal communication):

"On referring to the *Trans. Linn. Soc. London*, Vol. 22, I find that Cobbold's paper, 'Observations on Entozoa,' in which he describes *Diphyllobothrium stemmacephalum* from *Delphinus phocaena*, was read December 3, 1857. Though the volume is dated 1859, the papers are grouped in the index in four parts, dated in such a way as to indicate that they were published separately. The 'Part' in which Cobbold's paper appeared was dated early in 1858. Marschall, and following him, Scudder, date the publication 1859, but all the subsequent nomenclators say 1858, as does Stiles, who was a stickler for accuracy."

Two species of the genus are recognized:

1. *stemmacephalum* Cobbold, 1858. With the holdfast triangular in outline, 160 μ long by 240 μ wide; longitudinal parenchymal muscles two and one-half times as thick as the transverse muscles; cirrus pouch 320–370 μ by 160–270 μ; 12 to 18 uterine loops on each side; eggs 55 by 40 μ; adult worms in *Delphinus phocaena*, northern Atlantic waters; refs. Cob-

bold (1858), Cohn (1912), Borcea (1935b), Stunkard (1948) (Figure 363 A and B). Stunkard (1948) re-examined Cobbold's original material and found the uterus to have 6–9, usually 8, loops on each side, and the eggs to measure 65–70 μ by 40–50 μ.

2. *fuhrmanni* Hsü, 1935. With the holdfast elongated in outline, 520 by 240 μ; longitudinal parenchymal muscles five to six times as thick as the transverse muscles; cirrus pouch 640 by 260 μ; 7 to 9 uterine loops on each side; eggs 63–66 by 45–47 μ; adult worms in *Delphinus dus-*

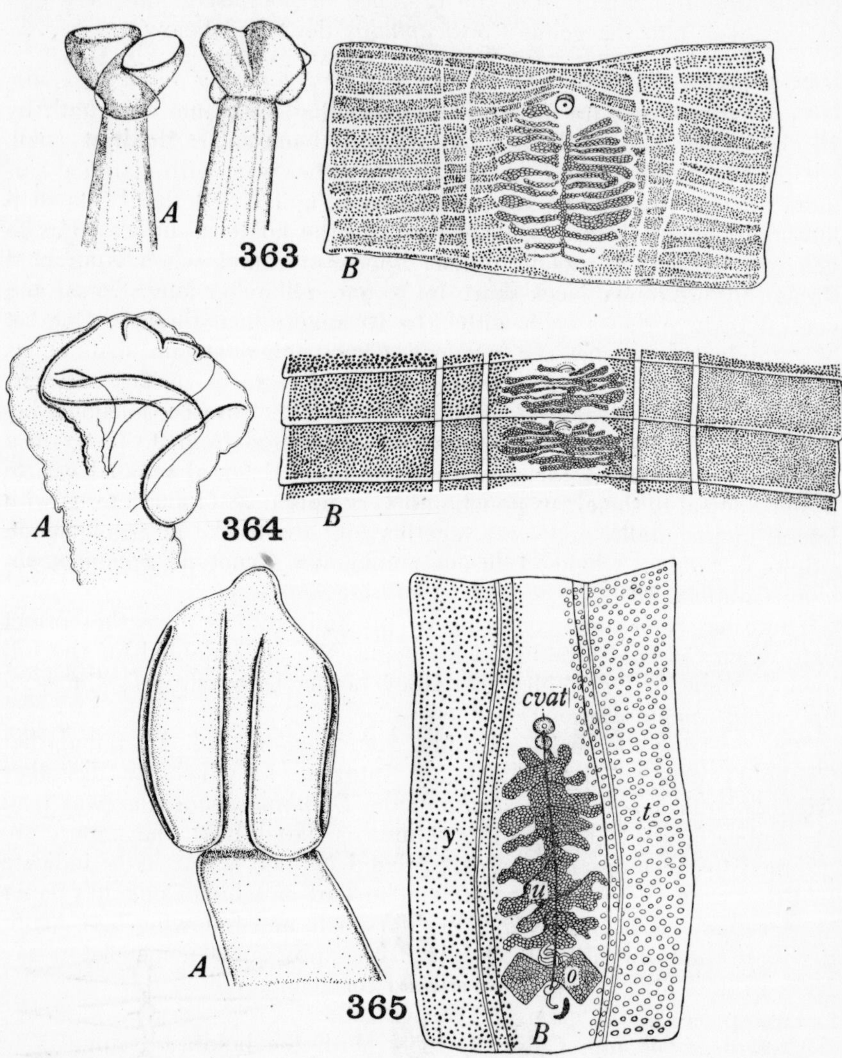

FIG. 363. *Diphyllobothrium stemmacephalum.* After E. Cohn, 1912. A. Holdfast. B. Gravid segment. FIG. 364. Yamaguti's "*Diphyllobothrium stemmacephalum.*" After Yamaguti, 1935b. A. Holdfast. B. Gravid segments. FIG. 365. *Diphyllobothrium fuhrmanni.* After Hsü, 1935. A. Holdfast. B. Gravid segment. *cvat*, cirro-vaginal atrium; *o*, ovary; *t*, testes; *u*, uterus; *y*, yolk glands.

sumieri and *Neomeris phocaenoides* in Sino-Japanese waters; refs. Yamaguti (1935b), Hsü (1935) (Figures 364, 365). Stunkard (1948) regards Yamaguti's and Hsü's forms as specifically distinct and believes the worms described by the Japanese observer to have been *stemmacephalum* or a closely related species.

As stated previously, the generic term *Diphyllobothrium* was adopted by Lühe (1910a) in place of his previous term *Dibothriocephalus.* In the Lühe sense, the term covered a cumbersome group of about 70 species, many of which were of doubtful validity. It comprised forms from toothed whales, seals, sea lions, carnivorous land mammals, and fish-eating birds. Several species were recorded from humans and one even from a snake. It was always an unsatisfactory genus to define and analyze, and the evaluation of those forms from seals and sea lions continually recorded by successive arctic and antarctic expeditions was particularly difficult.

It would seem doubtful on biological grounds that so restricted a group as a genus, especially from a class of parasites so notoriously narrow in choice of hosts as are tapeworms, should be equally adaptable to the wide variations of anatomy and physiology represented by such a wide range of host forms. In view, therefore, of the redescriptions of the genus *Diphyllobothrium* Cobbold published by Cohn (1912), Borcea (1935b), Yamaguti (1935b), Hsü (1935), Stunkard (1948), and the analyses of the dibothriocephalids of pinnipede mammals published by Wardle, McLeod, and Stewart (1947) and Stunkard (1948), we feel justified in discarding Lühe's interpretation of the generic limits of *Diphyllobothrium* and restricting that term to the dibothriocephalid tapeworms of toothed whales, distributing the other species formerly included within *Diphyllobothrium* among the genera *Diplogonoporus, Cordicephalus, Spirometra,* and *Dibothriocephalus.*

Diplogonoporus Loennberg, 1892 (= *Krabbea* Blanchard, 1894)

Relatively large forms with the holdfast recalling that of *Cordicephalus.* Bothria deep and slitlike. Segments very short and broad. Two sets of reproductive organs per segment. Uterine loops few and rosettelike in their arrangement. Adult worms in whalebone whales. Genotype, *balaenopterae* Loennberg, 1891 (Figure 366).

Five species of this genus were formerly recognized, namely: *balaenopterae* Loennberg, 1891 from *Balaenoptera borealis* in Scandinavian

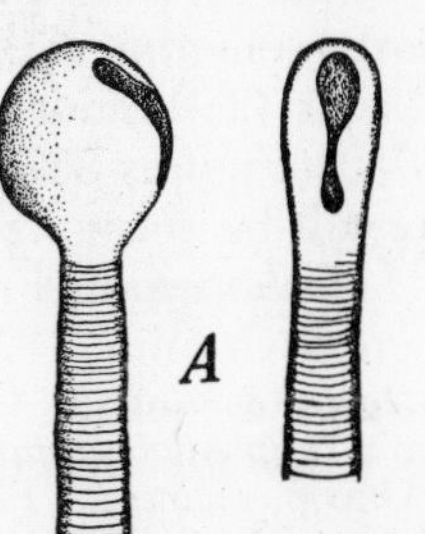

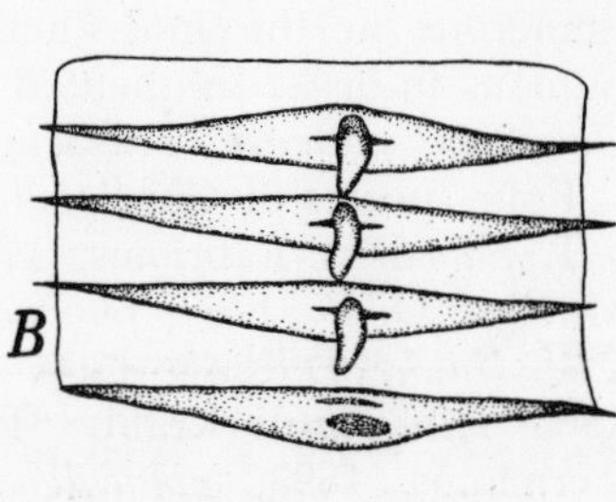

FIG. 366. *Diplogonoporus balaenopterae.* After Loennberg, 1892a. A. Holdfast. B. Mature segments with evaginated cirri.

waters; *fasciatus* Krabbe, 1865; *variabilis* Krabbe, 1865; *tetrapterus* Siebold, 1848, all from seals in northern Atlantic waters; and *grandis* Blanchard, 1894 from man in Japan. All were poorly described and wretchedly figured (cf. Figure 366). Baer (1932b) regarded *variabilis* as synonymous with *tetrapterus*, and the latter as a species of Lühe's *Diphyllobothrium*. The remaining species he distinguished by the number of uterine loops and the dimensions of the eggs, *balaenopterae* having 4–5 loops on each side and eggs 67 by 42 μ in size, *fasciatus* having 2–4 loops and eggs 45–50 μ long, and *grandis* having 1–2 loops and eggs 63 μ long. We regard these species, other than *balaenopterae*, as belonging to the genus *Cordicephalus*.

Cordicephalus Wardle, McLeod, and Stewart, 1947 (= *Diplogonoporus* Loennberg, 1892, in part; *Krabbea* R. Blanchard, 1894; *Dibothriocephalus* Lühe, 1899, in part; *Diphyllobothrium* Lühe, 1910, in part)

Short, thick-bodied forms with the holdfast typically heart-shaped, broadly oval, or even triangular in marginal outline, lanceolate to broadly oval in surficial outline. Bothrial slits gaping, with prominent lips, commonly wider anteriorly so as to appear in outline like a keyhole or a reversed triangle. Glandular tissue lacking from the parenchyma within the holdfast. Neck short, wide, commonly overlapped by the holdfast. Body commonly broadening rapidly from the neck backward, with the margins markedly serrated. Segments conspicuously short and craspedote, each with the cirro-vaginal aperture in the first third of the ventral surface. Parenchymal musculature well developed, appearing in cross sections as a continuous, conspicuous band equal to or one-half of the medullary thickness.

One set *or* two sets of reproductive organs per segment. Testes relatively few, large, spheroidal, appearing in cross sections in single or double layer to the number of 15 follicles on each side of the uterus. Cirrus pouch in length two-thirds of the medullary thickness, with the protruding cirrus apically lobed and the external seminal vesicle dorsal and well developed. Ovary with two flattened lobes. Yolk glands in a cortical band, usually interrupted dorsally and ventrally opposite the distended uterus by gaps one-tenth to one-sixth of the segment width. Uterus with 4–8 loops on each side, closely appressed and somewhat parallel but often loosely rosettelike in arrangement. Eggs with rounded ends. Life cycle unknown. Plerocercoids of northern forms known from marine salmonoid fishes. Adult worms in seals and sea lions, often very numerous in the individual host; sometimes in walruses, dogs, and humans in areas frequented by seals (Labrador, Japan, Transbaikalia). Genotype, *phocarus* Fabricius, 1780 (Figures 367–70).

Four species of *Cordicephalus* will be recognized here:

1. *phocarus* Fabricius, 1780 (= *phocarum* Fabricius, 1780; *phocae* Mueller, O. F., 1780; *phocae foetida* Creplin, 1825; *tetrapterus* Siebold, 1848; *hians* Diesing, 1860; *cordatus* Leuckart, 1863; *elegans* Krabbe, 1865; *lanceolatus* Krabbe, 1865; *variabilis* Krabbe, 1865; *schistocheilos* Germanos, 1895; *polycalceolus* Ariola, 1896; *römeri* Zschokke, 1903;

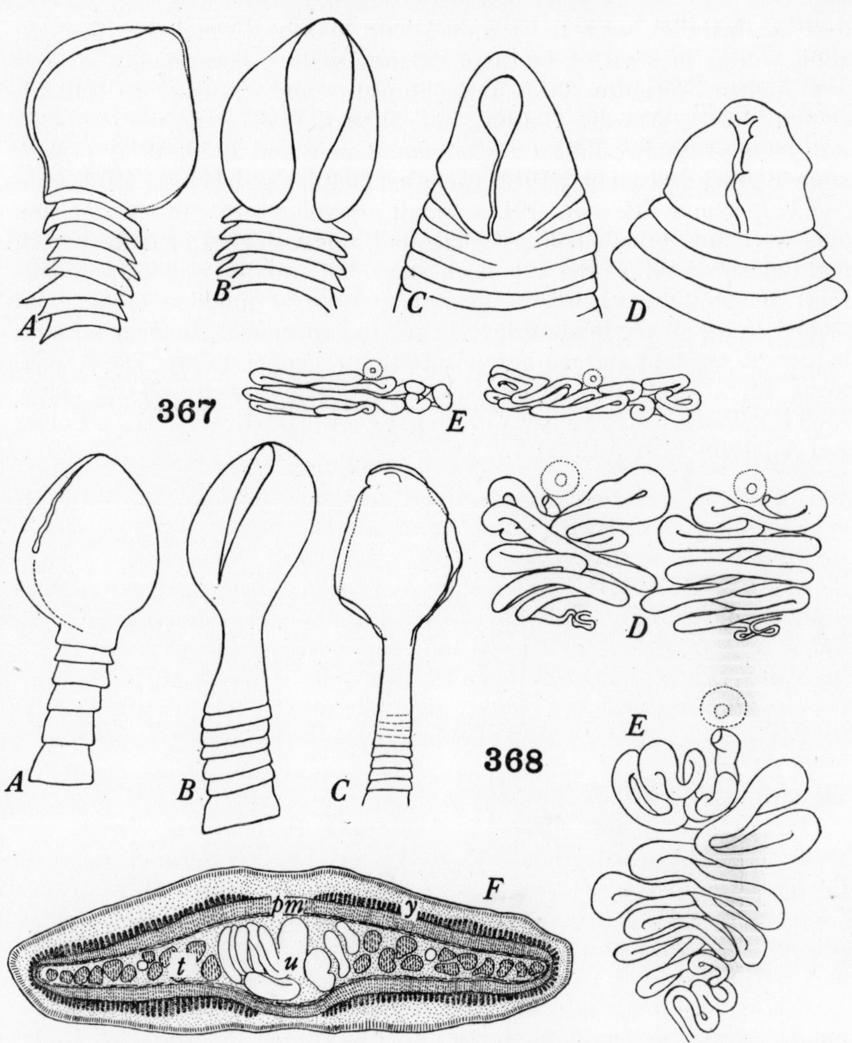

FIG. 367. *Cordicephalus phocarus.* After Wardle, McLeod, and Stewart, 1947. A to D. Holdfast outlines. E. Uteri of diplogonadic type. FIG. 368. *Cordicephalus arctocephalinus.* After Wardle, McLeod, and Stewart, 1947. A to C. Holdfast outlines. D. Uteri of diplogonadic type. E. Uterus of monogonadic type. F. Cross section of gravid segment of monogonadic type. *pm*, parenchymal muscles; *t*, testes; *u*, uterus; *y*, yolk glands.

macrophallus Linstow, 1905; *coniceps* Linstow, 1905; *minus* Cholodkovsky, 1916). With the holdfast typically heart-shaped or triangular in marginal outline; body broadening rapidly from the holdfast backward with margins markedly serrated; segments markedly craspedote; genital aperture or apertures at junction of first and second thirds of the ventral segment surface; commonly concealed in contracted segments by the overlap of the preceding segment; uterine loops 3 or 4 on each side, close together, parallel, with the terminal loop greatly distended with eggs; adult worms in seals of northern Atlantic waters, occasionally in dogs and humans (Figure 367); refs. Stunkard and Schoenborn (1936), Lyster (1940), Wardle, McLeod, and Stewart (1947).

2. *tectus* Linstow, 1892 (=*scoticum* Rennie and Reid, 1912; *perfoliatum* Railliet and Henry, 1912; *clavatum* Railliet and Henry, 1912; *lashleyi* Leiper and Atkinson, 1914). Small muscular forms up to 220 mm. long by 7 mm. broad; holdfast elongated, finger-shaped or club-shaped; bothrial slits keyhole-shaped; neck short but usually visible; segments short, moderately craspedote; genital aperture at junction of first and second thirds of segment surface in relaxed specimens, or near anterior border of segment surface in contracted specimens; uterine loops "relatively few"; adult worms in seals of antarctic waters; refs. Linstow (1892c), Railliet and Henry (1912b), Rennie and Reid (1912), Leiper and Atkinson (1914, 1915).

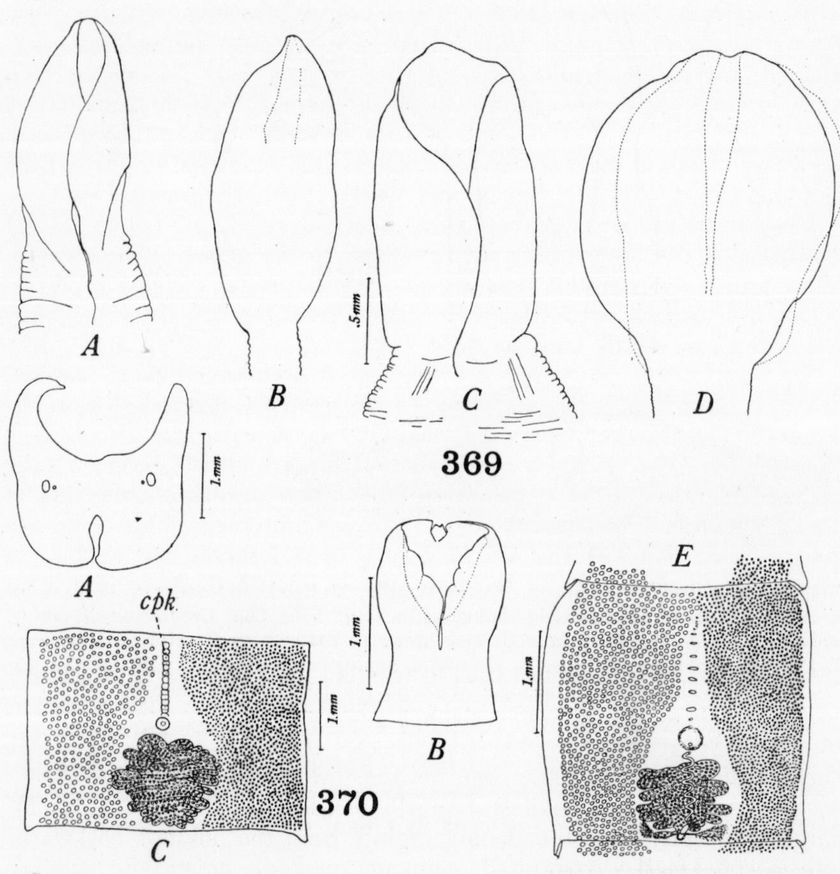

FIG. 369. "*Diphyllobothrium arctocephalinus*" of Johnston, 1937. After Johnston, 1937. A to D. Holdfast outlines. E. Gravid segment. FIG. 370. "*Diphyllobothrium arctocephali*" of Drummond, 1937. After Drummond, 1937. A. Cross section of the holdfast. B. Holdfast. C. Gravid segment showing cuticular puckerings (*cpk*).

3. *arctocephalinus* Johnston, 1937 (=*arctocephali* Drummond, 1937; *septentrionalis* Nybelin, 1931; *glacialis* Cholodkovsky, 1914; *grandis* R. Blanchard, 1894). Relatively long and slender forms with the holdfast up to 2 mm. long, heart-shaped in marginal outline, oval in surficial outline; bothrial slits narrowly triangular, broader anteriorly than posteriorly; neck short but visible; segments mainly rectangular, moderately craspedote; genital aperture or apertures antero-central (in relaxed segments) or at junction of first and second thirds of the ventral segment surface (in contracted segments); one set of reproductive organs per segment, occasionally two sets; uterus with 4–5 loops on each side, loosely arranged, somewhat rosettelike; uterus mainly or entirely behind the cirrus pouch; adult worms in sea lions (*Callorhinus ursinus, Arctocephalus australis, Arctocephalus forsteri, Arctocephalus tasmanicus*) in Alaskan and Australasian waters; refs. Johnston (1937), Drummond (1937), Wardle, McLeod, and Stewart (1947) (Figure 368).

4. *quadratus* Linstow, 1893 (=*resimum* Railliet and Henry, 1912; *coatsi* Rennie and Reid, 1912). Small forms with the holdfast egg-shaped; parenchymal muscles weak; uterus with 6 or 7 loops on each side, becoming distended terminally; genital aperture at junction of first and second fifths of ventral segment surface; adult worms in *Ogmorhinus leptonyx* (leopard seal) in antarctic waters; refs. Linstow (1892c), Railliet and Henry (1912b), Rennie and Reid (1912), Fuhrmann (1921a).

The "relatively weak parenchymal musculature" (Fuhrmann) throws doubt upon the admissibility of this form to the genus *Cordicephalus*. Fuhrmann's redescription was based upon Linstow's original material which may or may not in this respect have been typical. The other characteristics are clearly cordicephalid.

Stunkard (1947) surveyed a collection of pseudophyllidean material from Alaskan pinnipedes and rejected the genus *Cordicephalus* on the grounds that (1) the name is a synonym of *Pyramicocephalus* (although no such synonym is given by Stiles and Hassall, 1912), and (2) the species included in the genus constitute a heterogeneous collection of forms which lack real morphological unity. Limitations of space do not permit us to deal with this article as fully as it deserves, but we believe the morphological unity of the four species described above is evident from their descriptions. Stunkard agrees with us that *arctocephalinus* of Johnston (Figure 369) and *arctocephali* of Drummond (Figure 370) are identical, but reserves decision as to whether they occur in northern Pacific sea lions. Other material from *Callorhinus ursinus* in Alaskan waters he believed to be *Diplogonoporus* and "may be identical with *D. tetrapterus* (Siebold, 1848), *D. variabilis* (Krabbe, 1865) or *D. fasciatus* (Krabbe, 1865)." His material from *Eumetopias jubata* he believed resembled *Diplogonoporus fasciatus*, but final decision was reserved.

Spirometra Mueller, 1937

Small to medium-sized forms, weakly muscular, with the holdfast small, compressed, spoon-shaped or finger-shaped in marginal outline. Bothria slitlike but broad and shallow, and fading indefinitely into the mid-dorsal and mid-ventral furrows of the body. Neck long and slender. Cirrus and vagina opening independently upon a slight swelling of the ventral segment surface caused by the underlying cirrus pouch. Cirrus pouch composite, its dorsal portion representing the external seminal vesicle of other genera. Uterus a simple spiral of closely appressed coils, rarely rosettelike in arrangement. Eggs pointed at each end. Adult worms occurring mainly in catlike Carnivora, occasionally in dogs and humans. Genotype, *erinacei-europaei* Rudolphi, 1819.

The genus was established by Mueller (1937b) but the name had been used earlier (Faust, Campbell, and Kellogg, 1929). Within this group there have been placed at one time or another the following forms: *Dubium erinacei-europaei* Rudolphi, 1819; *Bothriocephalis felis* Creplin, 1825; *Bothriocephalus maculatus* Leuckart, 1848; *Dibothrium decipiens* Diesing, 1850; *Dibothrium serratum* Diesing, 1850; *Ligula reptans* Diesing, 1850; *Sparganum reptans* Diesing, 1854; *Sparganum affine* Diesing, 1854; *Sparganum erinacei-europaei* Diesing, 1854; *Ligula ranarum* Gastaldi, 1854; *Bothriocephalus sulcatus* Molin, 1858; *Sparganum ellipticum* Molin, 1858; *Ligula pancerii* Polonio, 1860; *Bothriocephalus decipiens* Bailliet, 1866; *Ligula mansoni* Cobbold, 1882; *Bothriocephalus liguloides* Leuckart, 1886; *Bothriocephalus mansoni* R. Blanchard, 1888; *Dibothrium mansoni* Ariola, 1900; *Sparganum mansoni* Stiles and Taylor, 1902; *Sparganum proliferum* Ijima, 1905; *Plerocercoides mansoni* Guiart, 1910; *Sparganum raillieti* Ratz, 1912; and *Sparganum philippinensis* Tubangui, 1924.

Under the generic term *Diphyllobothrium* the following spirometrid species have been described: *decipiens* Gedoelst, 1911; *raillieti* Ratz, 1913; *longicolle* Parodi and Widakowich, 1917; *tangalongi* MacCallum, 1921; *pretoriensis* Baer, 1924; *reptans* Meggitt, 1924; *ranarum* Meggitt, 1925; *bresslauei* Baer, 1927; *gracile* Baer, 1927; *mansoni* Joyeux and Houdemer, 1927; *felis* Southwell, 1928; *houghtoni* Faust, Campbell, and Kellogg, 1929; *erinacei* Faust, Campbell, and Kellogg, 1929; *okumurai* Faust, Campbell, and Kellogg, 1929; *serpentis* Yamaguti, 1935; *mansonoides* Mueller, 1935; and *urichi* Cameron, 1936.

Many of the forms listed above were larval, as is indicated by such generic names as *Sparganum, Dubium, Ligula,* and *Plerocercoides.* The term *Sparganum,* now commonly used for the larval stage of any species of *Spirometra,* was proposed by Diesing (1854) as a generic name for any unidentified pseudophyllidean larva. Thus he assigned the name to a larval form that Rudolphi (1819) had found encysted in the intercostal muscles of a European hedgehog (*Erinaceus europaeus*) and had named *Dubium erinacei-europaei.* Diesing *assumed* on the basis of Rudolphi's scanty description that the form was pseudophyllidean.

Now there is not to our knowledge any record of this form having been found again – no record, let us say, of any pseudophyllidean larva occurring and being noticed repeatedly in European hedgehogs. Faust, Campbell, and Kellogg (1929) admittedly found sparganid larvae to occur commonly in hedgehogs in China (*Erinaceus dealbatus*), reared such larvae to maturity, and assigned to the undoubted *Spirometra* species thus obtained the Rudolphian specific name, *erinacei*, thus making an assumption even greater than that of Diesing. Iwata (1934) in Japan went even further in suggesting that *all* spirometrids of the Sino-Japanese area, whatever their hosts, were forms of *erinacei*. Joyeux, Houdemer, and Baer (1934) also accepted Faust's view but believed that in Indochina the species *mansoni* is distinct from *erinacei*. The French parasitologist Brumpt (1936) believed that Rudolphi's *erinacei-europaei* had actually been found again by numerous European observers but recorded under such names as *Ligula ranarum* Gastaldi, 1858; *Sparganum ellipticum* Molin, 1858; *Sparganum lanceolatum* Molin, 1858; *Ligula pancerii* Polonio, 1860; and *Sparganum raillieti* Ratz, 1912. On the basis of this quite unjustified assumption, Brumpt provided a specific description of the adult *erinacei-europaei* which was substantially the description published by Ratz (1913) of the form he had obtained by rearing in cats and dogs his *Sparganum raillieti*.

Before attempting to decide between the merits of Faust's *erinacei* and Brumpt's *erinacei* as contenders for the honor of being Rudolphi's *erinacei-europaei*, it must be noted that (1) there is no known method of distinguishing specifically one sparganid larva from another except by rearing the two to maturity in a possible final host such as a cat; and (2) the host range of any sparganid larva, to judge from laboratory experience, is a wide one. A form found in a frog or snake can pass quite readily from the gut of the bird or mammal to which it is fed and appear in the muscles of the new host still as a sparganid. A sparganid in the muscles of a skinned and split frog used as an eye poultice in Indochina can pass quite readily into the eyeball of the human victim and cause the condition known as ocular sparganosis. Only when the bird or mammal is the appropriate final host will the sparganid larva remain in the host gut, discard the posterior region of its body, and attain proglottisation and sexual maturity.

There is therefore no justification for supposing that a sparganid occurring in Chinese hedgehogs in the 1920's is specifically identical with one that occurred in European hedgehogs a century earlier, or that sparganids found in Italian frogs, Burmese frogs, and Hungarian hogs are identical with those described so perfunctorily by Rudolphi in 1819, unless we are prepared to believe that there is only the one species of *Spirometra* all over the world.

The fact of the matter is that we do not know and shall never know just what Rudolphi described. It may not have been a spirometrid at all. The name *erinacei* should disappear from the literature of the subject. To designate *erinacei* Rudolphi as the genotype of *Spirometra*, as Mueller (1937b) did, was unfortunate. We believe that the genotype should be the form of *mansoni* described by Joyeux and Houdemer (1928), the first spirometrid adult to be reared experimentally from a known and described sparganid larva.

If from the list of recorded spirometrid forms given above we subtract those known only as sparganids, the remainder can be distributed between two groups (Figure 371). Just how we designate these groups is

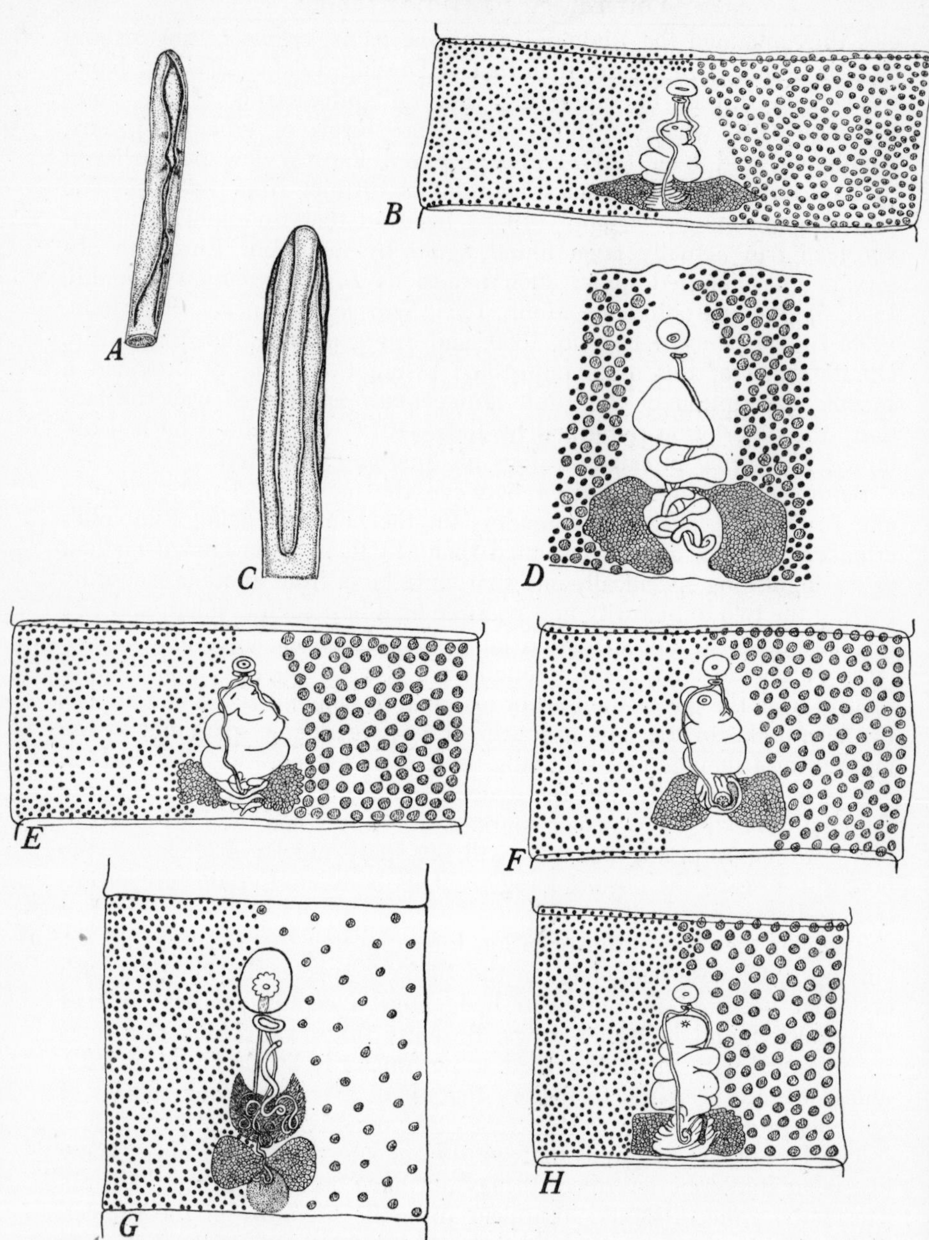

FIG. 371. *Spirometra* species. A. *mansoni*, holdfast. After Joyeux, 1927c. B. *mansoni*, mature segment. After Faust, Campbell, and Kellogg, 1929. C. *reptans*, holdfast. After Meggitt, 1924e. D. *reptans*, mature segment. After Meggitt, 1924e. E. *ranarum*, mature segment. After Faust, Campbell, and Kellogg, 1929. F. *decipiens*, mature segment. After Faust, Campbell, and Kellogg, 1929. G. *felis*, mature segment. After Southwell, 1928a. H. *houghtoni*, mature segment. After Faust, Campbell, and Kellogg, 1929.

immaterial. For convenience here, we shall use the first specific name, in alphabetical order, of each group. The two groups are as follows:

1. The *bresslauei* group. Spirometrids in which the lateral zones of testes and yolk glands, respectively, meet in the region of the segment that lies in front of the genital apertures: *bresslauei* Baer, 1927; *decipiens* of Faust, Campbell, and Kellogg (1929); *erinacei* of Faust, Campbell, and Kellogg (1929); *felis* of Southwell (1928b); *gracile* Baer, 1927; *houghtoni* Faust, Campbell, and Kellogg, 1929; *mansoni* of Joyeux and Houdemer (1927b); *mansonoides* Mueller, 1935; *reptans* of Joyeux and Houdemer (1928); *serpentis* Yamaguti, 1935; and *urichi* Cameron, 1936.

2. The *okumurai* group. Spirometrids in which there is no union of lateral testis zones or lateral yolk gland zones in the region in front of the genital apertures: *okumurai* Faust, Campbell, and Kellogg, 1929; *pretoriensis* Baer, 1924; *raillieti* Ratz, 1913 (= *erinacei* Brumpt, 1936); *ranarum* of Meggitt (1925); and *reptans* of Meggitt (1924e).

The species *tangalongi* MacCallum, 1921 for lack of specific details cannot be assigned to either group.

To what extent the union of testis and yolk gland zones in front of the genital apertures is a character constant within the species cannot be said with certainty. Joyeux and Houdemer (1928) made observations upon what they believed to be the adult form of Cobbold's *Ligula mansoni.* They believed that all conditions between complete union and complete separation of testis and yolk gland zones were to be found. It is not clear from their description, however, whether such variation occurs also among the segments of individual worms.

The salient features of the members of the *bresslauei* group are as follows:

NOTES ON SPECIES OF THE BRESSLAUEI GROUP

1. *bresslauei* Baer, 1927. Established for a tapeworm from an opossum in Brazil; length 270 mm., breadth 8 mm.; holdfast typically spirometrid; cuticle of body surface very thin, not exceeding 16 μ in thickness; longitudinal parenchymal muscles powerful, very irregularly arranged in bundles; transverse muscles scarcely developed; osmoregulatory system with four medullary canals connected by an anastomosing network in the cortex; 750 testes in two lateral zones which unite in the region in front of the genital apertures; about 12–20 testes visible on each side in a cross section of the segment behind the genital apertures; external seminal vesicle thick-walled, dorsal to the cirrus pouch; ovary H-shaped; yolk glands forming an almost continuous cortical sheet interrupted only mid-dorsally and mid-ventrally by the reproductive organs; uterus with four loops on each side; uterine aperture lying behind the vaginal aperture, irregularly right or left of the middle line; eggs 65 by 29 μ. The position of the genital apertures was not indicated, but Baer's figure suggests that the male aperture lies slightly behind the junction of the first and second sixths of the ventral segment surface, and the female aperture lies close behind it. Adult worm found in an opossum, *Didelphys aurita,* in Brazil, the first case of a dibothriocephalid tapeworm to be

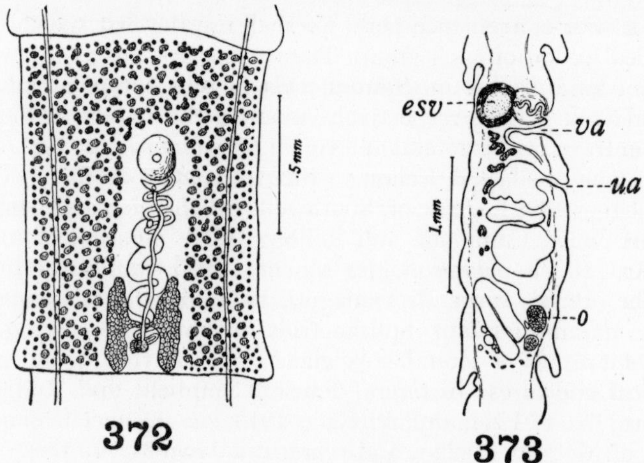

FIG. 372. *Spirometra gracile,* single segment. After Baer, 1927e. FIG. 373. *Spirometra bresslauei,* single segment. After Baer, 1927e. *esv,* external seminal vesicle; *o,* ovary; *ua,* uterine aperture; *va,* vaginal aperture.

recorded from a marsupial except for Ariola's (1900) *Bothriocephalus didelphidis* (Figure 373).

2. *decipiens* of Faust, Campbell, and Kellogg (1929). Established by Diesing (1850) as *Dibothrium decipiens* for an adult worm from an unidentified catlike animal in Brazil. By present-day standards his description was inadequately brief. Lühe (1899a) published a somewhat fuller description of the Diesing material in the Zoological Museum of Vienna. Further notes upon it were contributed by Ariola (1900). Its generic identity with Lühe's *Diphyllobothrium* was asserted by Gedoelst (1911). Further information was added by Boehm (1921). The first alleged rediscovery of this form was made by Chandler (1925b) from a domestic cat and a clouded leopard (*Felis nebulosa*) in the Calcutta Zoological Gardens. Wolffhügel and Vogelsang (1926) reared in dogs what they believed to be this form by feeding spargana from frogs (*Leptodactylus ocellatus*) in Uruguay. Joyeux and Houdemer (1927b) described samples of the Diesing material and verified Chandler's statement that "the yolk glands and testes are evenly scattered throughout the lateral portion of the segments and across the middle portion anteriorly but leave a conspicuous clear central area surrounding the uterus and genital openings; that the female genital aperture lies nearer to the uterine aperture than to the male aperture; and that the uterine coils increase in amplitude from behind forward."

Faust, Campbell, and Kellogg (1929), in China, found what they believed to be *decipiens* in a wild cat (Peking), a leopard (Peking), and a dog (Amoy), and obtained the same form experimentally by feeding sparganids from tree frogs (*Microhyla sowerbyi*) to dogs. They found no outstanding differences between their material and other spirometrid forms, but believed that the general features of the mature segment, taken as a whole, are distinctive. Their description therefore is worthy of extended quotation:

"Ovarian lobes highly reticulated; rather large ootype situated in the mid-ventral line some little distance in front of the posterior margin of the segment. On the right side, a long slightly coiled duct may be traced forward along the uterine mass to the crescentic vaginal opening. On the left of the ootype is the retort-shaped receptaculum seminalis with a short duct which joins the vagina just behind its entrance into the ootype. Around the ootype is a tightly coiled and twisted mass, the inner part of the uterus, arising from the anterior side of the ootype and enlarging in its anterior face into the outer uterine mass. This outer mass consists of four or at most five piled coils rounded out with eggs. The subterminal coil is the broadest while the terminal one is subspherical in contour. The uterine pore, with a conspicuous sphincter, is far ventral in position under the bulge of the terminal uterine coil. There is a conspicuous gap between the most anterior uterine mass and the other genital openings. These latter, the vaginal pore and the male genital pore, are situated close to one another, the former being crescentic in outline with a definite muscular margin, and the latter being a delicate lenticular object with rather weak muscular elements situated on the elevation produced by the mass of the cirrus and its surrounding tissues. In some specimens, such as those fixed in aceto-sublimate whilst still alive, the entire cirrus complex is introverted within the cirrus sac. In other cases it is partly everted. In still others it may be completely exserted so that the male pore is found with difficulty. The cirrus is strongly muscular, is elongated conoidal in shape, and is covered with a heavy integumentary thickening which is wrinkled into a number of irregular annulations when the organ is partly everted.

"On the inner dorsal aspect of the cirrus there are numerous prostate glands surrounding the chamber. From its dorsal aspect there is introduced the vas deferens which may be traced distad along the left side of the terminal ball of the uterus, where it is found to bifurcate into the two vasa efferentia. The lateral fields of each mature proglottis are studded with irregularly polygonal testes, which lie in the dorsal plane, and with minute vitellaria which are situated ventrad. The number of each varies considerably in different specimens, depending primarily on the maturity of the proglottis. Although each of these two types of glands meets in the mid-anterior line there is always a free conoidal area surrounding the median genital organs. The eggs of *Diphyllobothrium decipiens*, unlike those of *D. latum*, are elliptical rather than broadly oval, and the operculum is more conical. They range in size from 56.5 to 60.1 microns in length by 34.2 to 36.2 microns in transverse diameter. The procercoids develop experimentally in numerous species of *Cyclops* while frogs and snakes commonly serve as the second intermediate hosts." Faust, Campbell, and Kellogg (1929) (Figure 371 F).

3. *erinacei* of Faust, Campbell, and Kellogg (1929). Tapeworms 600–750 mm. long by 8 mm. broad; holdfast spoon-shaped; gravid segments about one and one-half times as broad as long; male genital aperture at

junction of first and second thirds of the ventral segment surface; vaginal aperture a broad, crescentic slit just behind the male aperture; uterine aperture approximately central, some little distance behind the anterior margin of the terminal, subspherical coil of the uterus; ovary completely dendritic; testes and yolk glands forming broad lateral fields on each side of the female genitalia, the fields broadly united in the anterior sixth of the segment; uterus of 5 to 7 piled coils, the inner mass of 3 to 4 loosely piled coils behind the outer pile, and one convoluted coil which ascends under the posterior two outer coils; eggs ellipsoidal, 57–61 by 33–36.3 μ; a form reared in dogs in China by Faust, Campbell, and Kellogg (1929) from sparganid larvae from the Chinese hedgehog (*Erinaceus dealbatus*) and believed by these authors to be identical with Rudolphi's *erinacei-europaei.*

Pullar (1946) and Bearup (1948) found this form to be common in cats and foxes in Australia. The procercoid stage is found in the copepod Crustacea *Mesocyclops obsoletus, Cyclops australis,* and *Leptocyclops agilis.* The sparganid occurs in snakes and lizards.

4. *felis* of Southwell (1928b). Up to 250 mm. long by 8.8 mm. broad; genital apertures near the anterior border; testes numerous and extending over the dorsal surface of the segment except in the middle line; uterus figured as a rosette of loose coils; eggs 60 by 30 μ; other features as for *Spirometra* generally. The species was established, as *Bothriocephalus felis,* by Creplin (1825) for two small specimens found in a cat. Southwell claimed its rediscovery in *Felis tigris* and *Felis pardus,* Calcutta Zoological Gardens. Creplin's description was so inadequate that it is impossible to prove the identity of Southwell's form with Creplin's material (Figure 371 G).

5. *gracile* Baer, 1927. One of the smallest spirometrids recorded, being only 70 to 80 mm. long by 1 mm. broad; with 100 segments, all longer than broad; holdfast described as typically spirometrid and 500 μ long by 200 μ broad; positions of genital apertures not given; from Baer's figure the male aperture seems to lie at the junction of the first and second thirds of the ventral surface of the segment, with the female aperture well to its rear; 250 testes in a continuous dorsal layer interrupted only by the median genitalia; external seminal vesicle large and muscular with its long axis at right angles to the long axis of the cirrus pouch; vagina opening behind the male aperture within a little atrium; uterus scarcely undulating, with four to five bends on each side of the middle line; eggs 57 by 27 μ; an obviously immature specimen from *Felis macrura,* Brazil (Figure 372).

6. *houghtoni* Faust, Campbell, and Kellogg, 1929. The species was established for an adult worm found in man in Shanghai; it was believed at first to be a specimen of *mansoni* but later was distinguished from this form by Faust and his co-workers by having 4 to 6 uterine coils, the posterior one slightly broader, the terminal one hemispherical with its aperture in the mid-ventral line of the segment surface; the inner uterine mass comprised a large number of densely packed and convoluted coils; the ovary extended as far back as the posterior border of the segment

and was squarish in outline; the ootype lay in the midst of the uterine coils; egg dimensions were 57–62 by 35.2–37.4 μ (Figure 371 H).

7. *mansoni* of Joyeux and Houdemer (1928). The specific name was invented by Cobbold (1883) for twelve sparganid larvae found by Patrick Manson at Amoy in China during an autopsy on a Chinese male, the worms occurring in the subperitoneal fascia. There seems to be some room for opinion as to the credit that should be given for the specific name. Dr. William A. Riley, in a personal communication to the present writers, states:

"Regarding *mansoni*, Cobbold in 1883 made no mention of Manson's use of the name in 1882. If there was no description of the species, the use of the name in 1882 would not establish the species. If there was at that time enough of a description to merit recognition, the species would be *mansoni* Manson, 1882. In short, Cobbold's suggestion of a name for a species which he intended to describe had no more standing than a manuscript name."

There can be no doubt that the first description and use of the name *mansoni*, for an *adult* spirometrid, was published by Joyeux and Houdemer (1928). We believe, therefore, that *mansoni* Cobbold, 1883 should be treated as a dead name and that the specific name should be *mansoni* Joyeux and Houdemer, 1928. We believe further that in view of the doubt concerning the validity of Rudolphi's *erinacei-europaei*, the genotype of *Spirometra* should be *mansoni* Joyeux and Houdemer, 1928.

The occurrence of sparganid larvae in humans in Japan has been noted by many observers from 1882 to recent years. Similar reports have come from British East Africa, British Guiana, Texas, Australia, even from Holland. The common occurrence of sparganids in the eye (ocular sparganosis) of humans in Indochina has been reported by many French medical authors. Further cases have been reported from China since 1927. All the sparganid larvae thus found in humans have been regarded as identical with Cobbold's *Ligula mansoni*. Yoshida (1917a) obtained adult worms by feeding dogs with man-infesting sparganids and published notes on what he termed *Bothriocephalus liguloides*. Joyeux and Houdemer (1928), however, as stated above, must be given credit for the first detailed description of "*Diphyllobothrium mansoni*" based upon rearings in dogs of sparganids from a wide range of Indochinese animals.

Despite the suspicion of many observers, notably of Kobayashi (1931) and of Iwata (1934), that *mansoni* may not be a specific entity, there is today a tendency to regard any spirometrid reared in dogs from sparganids found in mammalian tissues as *mansoni*.

The characteristics of this species would seem to be as follows:

A. It is a typical spirometrid tapeworm, rearable in dogs and cats from sparganid larvae of an unbranched type found in humans.

B. The male and female genital apertures are approximately central or slightly in front of center (Joyeux and Houdemer said the third eighth of the ventral surface of the segment) and placed close together. The male aperture is small and circular, the female aperture a transverse slit. The uterine aperture is also a transverse slit, 50 to 120 μ behind the female aperture. The latter is always closer to the male aperture than to the uterine aperture (cf. *decipiens*).

C. The holdfast is fingerlike, scarcely wider than the neck, almost quadrangular in cross section. The bothria are shallow, fading out posteriorly into the neck, their lips mobile and tending somewhat to overlap.

D. The testes number 320 to 540 and form a continuous sheet interrupted only by the central genitalia.

E. The uterus is somewhat variable in shape between one segment and another. The outer region has four transverse coils (Mueller), three large coils (Joyeux and Houdemer), four and one-half coils (Faust), three coils on either side (Sprehn, Brumpt), or as many as seven coils of irregular disposition and length (Mueller). The coils tend to decrease in bulk as the uterine aperture is approached. There is no specialized and muscular terminal portion.

F. The eggs measure 52 to 76 μ by 31 to 44 μ.

The other features of *mansoni* described by various observers would seem to be in the main common to other spirometrids (Figure 371 A and B). The identification with *mansoni* of the branched type of sparganid occasionally found in humans and named by Ijima (1905) *Sparganum proliferum* is *sub judice*.

8. *mansonoides* Mueller, 1935. Established for a form found in cats in New York State and subsequently reared from spargana occurring in snakes (*Natrix*) in Florida and from spargana reared in mice by oral infection with procercoid-bearing *Cyclops sp.* Close comparison with *mansoni* material shows points of constant difference in uterus and vagina; characteristic is the large terminal uterine coil, like a letter U placed on its side, the anterior limb constricted in the middle so as to mark off a terminal chamber or egg ejector. The vagina of *mansonoides* passes in a posterior direction from the vestibule in an approximately straight path to the median line, whereas the vagina of *mansoni* is thrown into lateral undulations of considerable magnitude. The other features seem common to both speices. The true host of *mansonoides* is probably *Lynx rufus* (see McIntosh, 1937; Mueller, 1937c) (Figure 374).

9. *reptans* of Joyeux and Houdemer (1928). The species was established by Diesing (1850) as *Ligula reptans* for a sparganid. Meggitt (1924e) identified with this form a sparganid in Burmese frogs that he reared to maturity in dogs. Joyeux and Houdemer (1928) identified with it a form in the domestic cat and clouded leopard. Comparing their material with co-types of Meggitt's material, they found points of disagreement with his description. In their material and the co-types the lateral zones of testes converged and met in the anterior region of the segment, but the lateral zones of yolk glands did not, despite Meggitt's statement which is contradicted by his figure (Figure 371 D). The egg dimensions were 53–57 by 27–28 μ (Meggitt's figures were 53–59 by 36–40 μ). The vaginal aperture may lie somewhat out of line with the male and uterine apertures, as Meggitt stated, but in some segments all three apertures

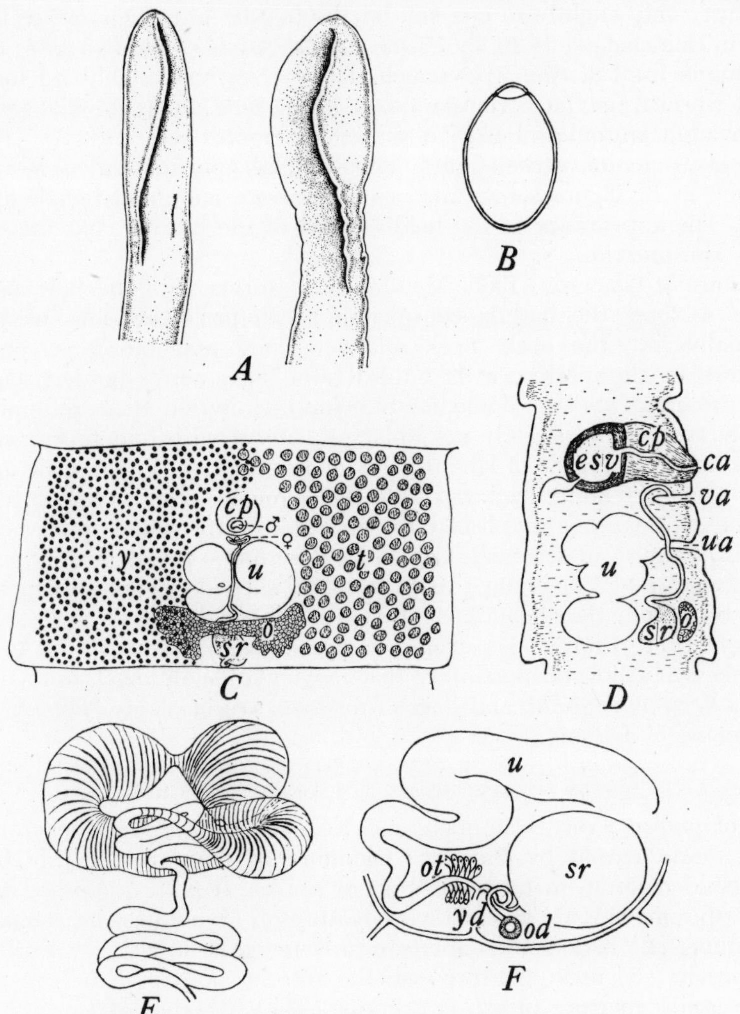

FIG. 374. *Spirometra mansonoides*. After Mueller, 1935, 1937b. A. Holdfast. B. Egg. C. Mature segment. D. Sagittal section of a segment. E. Uterus, dorsal view. F. Female reproductive organs. *ca*, cirrus aperture; *cp*, cirrus pouch; *esv*, external seminal vesicle; *o*, ovary; *od*, oviduct; *ot*, ootype; *sr*, seminal receptacle; *t*, testes; *u*, uterus; *ua*, uterine aperture; *va*, vaginal aperture; *y*, yolk gland; *yd*, yolk duct.

are in one straight line. In other features these authors agreed with Meggitt's description.

10. *serpentis* Yamaguti, 1935. 115 mm. long by 4 mm. broad; holdfast about 1 mm. long with well-developed bothria; testes 210–230 in number in lateral bands uniting in front of the cirrus pouch; seminal vesicle 100 to 125 μ broad; cirrus pouch 160 to 230 μ broad; ovary 270 to 850 μ; uterine coils 4–6; uterine aperture definitely posterior to the cirro-vaginal

aperture, only slightly to one side of the middle line; eggs ovoid, light brown, thin-shelled, 54–61 by 33–42 μ; yolk glands of the two sides continuous in front of the cirrus pouch. The species was established for an adult worm from the Formosan cobra (*Naja naja atra*), the first record of an adult spirometrid from a snake. Yamaguti's references to "atrial aperture," "genital atrium," and "cirro-vaginal aperture" are somewhat obscure as his figure shows apparently separate male and female apertures. The appearance of the holdfast and of the uterine coils are definitely spirometrid.

11. *urichi* Cameron, 1936. Medium-sized forms with the holdfast as broad as long, the bothria conspicuous, with projecting lips, merging gradually into the neck; neck relatively long and broad, in profile quadrate; male aperture at first third from the anterior border; female aperture crescentic and immediately behind it; uterine aperture approximately central and slightly medio-lateral; uterus with four to five coils; testes and yolk glands in lateral fields uniting in front of the male aperture; ovary extending backward into the segment behind; eggs 55 by 30 μ. The species was established for an adult worm found in an ocelot (*Felis pardalis*) in Trinidad. Cameron's description recalls that given by Wolffhügel and Vogelsang (1926) of their alleged *decipiens*, which, it may be noted, they identified also with *longicolle* Parodi and Widakowich, 1917, a form taken from a jaguar (*Felis jaguarondi*) in Argentina. It is not beyond possibility that *longicolle*, Wolffhügel and Vogelsang's *decipiens*, *urichi*, and Baer's *bresslauei* are in reality "*Dibothrium decipiens*" of Diesing.

NOTES ON SPECIES OF THE OKUMURAI GROUP

1. *okumurai* Faust, Campbell, and Kellogg, 1929. Established for an adult worm reared by Professor Okumura in dogs, presumably from sparganid material in Japanese frogs or snakes. It is distinguished from other spirometrids by the following features: (1) holdfast heart-shaped in outline; (2) male genital aperture surrounded by a large, oval sphincter muscle; (3) male aperture near the anterior border of the segment; (4) vaginal aperture broad, crescentic, a short distance in front of the anterior uterine mass; (5) testes and yolk glands as lateral bands running as far forward as the genital apertures but never arching inward to meet in front of them; (6) an inner uterine mass (by the term "inner" Faust and his collaborators imply the region commonly termed by other authors "proximal") consisting of a rosette of small tubules; an outer (i.e., distal) portion of the uterine mass comprising three or four spirally wound coils of which the posterior two or three are broad and the anterior terminal one is spherical; (7) eggs ranging in size from 63.8 to 68.2 μ in length, by 31.9 to 34.1 μ in transverse diameter. The other features described in some detail by the authors of the species differ scarcely at all from those of spirometrids in general.

2. *pretoriensis* Baer, 1924. With the holdfast unknown; position of genital apertures not stated; testes and yolk glands in separate lateral bands not approximating; uterus with a single coil, distending under egg

pressure so as to appear as two sacs (no figure was given but the author's description states: "l'uterus forme une seule boucle de chaque côte de la ligne mediane; cette boucle se distend sous le pression des oeufs en donnant l'aspect de deux sacs"); eggs 61 by 34 μ; other features as for spirometrids generally. The species was established for an adult worm from a South African wild canine, *Otocyon megalotis.* It was regarded at first, since it lacks an external seminal vesicle, as representing a new genus, *Lüheella*, and new family, Lüheellidae, of Pseudophyllidea, but later it was named *Diphyllobothrium pretoriensis* (Joyeux and Houdemer, 1928).

3. *raillieti* Ratz, 1913 (= *erinacei-europaei* of Brumpt, 1936). Worms averaging 520 mm. in length by 7 mm. broad; holdfast lancet-shaped or finger-shaped, 850 μ long by 510 μ wide, with bothria that run the full length of the holdfast and have conspicuous lips; neck region 12 mm. long, tapering in breadth from 300 μ behind the bothria to 800 μ at the first interproglottidal groove; all the segments decidedly linear; ventral surface of the body showing a median ridge formed by the somewhat raised underlying cirrus pouches; middle point of each elevation about one-sixth of the segment length from the anterior segment border; on the anterior slope of each elevation is the circular male aperture, on the posterior slope is the crescentic female aperture; about 200 μ behind this is the uterine aperture; testes 300–500; uterus with 6 or 7 distal coils; eggs 62–72 by 37–45 μ. The species was established for worms reared in dogs from sparganid larvae found in hogs in Hungary and Serbia (Ratz, 1912; Kotlan, 1923a). Meijer and Sahar (1934) believed they had obtained the same form by rearing sparganids from swine in Sumatra. Both these authors, as well as Kotlan, believed that such sparganids are not transmissible to humans. Similar in general features to *mansoni*, this form is distinguishable by the nonapproximation of testes and yolk glands.

4. *ranarum* of Meggitt, 1925. Up to 1,130 mm. in length by 5 mm. in breadth; holdfast 1.4–1.7 mm. long by 0.37–0.41 mm. broad; all the segments either broader than long or square; male genital aperture almost at the anterior border of the segment and median; female aperture slightly lateral to it; testes in two bands, 100–110 in each band, not uniting anteriorly; uterine coils 3 to 5; uterus extending laterally to the genital apertures; a terminal uterine enlargement present; eggs 58–67 by 34–36 μ. The species was established by Gastaldi (1854) for a sparganid in Italian frogs. The name was adopted by Meggitt for a sparganid common in Burmese frogs, which when reared in dogs produced an adult worm that he named *Diphyllobothrium ranarum* (Gastaldi, 1854). We identify Meggitt with the specific name here because we cannot accept this assumed coincidence of Burmese and Italian forms merely upon the basis of a common host of the larval stage (Figure 371 E). Further comments upon this form were made by Faust, Campbell, and Kellogg (1929):

"The larval (sparganum) stage of this worm was first described by Gastaldi (1854) from *Rana esculenta* presumably obtained in Italy. In 1924 Meggitt reported the presence of spargana in the stomach wall of

Rana tigrina from Rangoon and the following year large numbers of the same worm from the same host. Some of the specimens were fed to a dog which was autopsied fifty-eight days later and found to be parasitised with adult diphyllobothriids, which this investigator described as *Diphyllobothrium ranarum*.

"It is impossible to decide whether or not Meggitt's larva was of the same species as Gastaldi's but in view of the recognizable characters of Meggitt's adult worm obtained from experimental feeding, the name has become available for spargana which develop into this adult species of diphyllobothriid. Following Meggitt, Joyeux and Baer (1927c) in studying the complete life cycle of this species found both *Rana esculenta* and *Tropidonotus natrix* to be favorable hosts for the sparganum stage while the cat proved to be suitable for the development of the adult worm which they have described and figured in detail. The present writers [i.e., Faust, Campbell, and Kellogg] have studied material from natural infections of the cat and dog in Peking, of the dog in Amoy and Canton, and from experimental feeding of spargana obtained from *Canis procyonides* from Foochow. In view of Joyeux and Baer's (1927c) careful detailed description of this species it is only necessary to summarize the characters which serve to differentiate this species. There are only three and one-half or four outer coils of the uterus, of which the posterior two are considerably broader and more dilated than the terminal one. The inner coils are more or less rosetted and are not markedly separate from the outer ones. The ovaries are highly dendritic. Testes and vitellaria closely approximate the lateral margins of the two lower coils of the outer uterine complex but do not usually meet in the anterior median line. The vaginal and male genital pores are one behind the other in the mid plane, some distance anterior to the terminal uterine coil. Both the vagina and vas deferens are more or less convoluted between their openings and their approximation of the uterus. The eggs are similar in shape to those of *Diphyllobothrium decipiens* and measure 57 to 60 by 34.2 to 35.3 microns." Faust, Campbell, and Kellogg (1929).

5. *reptans* of Meggitt (1924e). Body dimensions 1,000 mm. in length by 9 mm. in breadth; holdfast elongated, finger-shaped, 800 by 40 μ, with the bothria long and shallow with indistinct lips, and fading anteriorly and posteriorly into the holdfast; neck long; all the segments linear; genital apertures in the anterior sixth of the ventral surface of the segment; testes 144 to 220, in two separate bands, slightly converging anteriorly; yolk glands also in separate lateral bands but converging and meeting anteriorly in front of the genital apertures; uterus not described but figured as having four loose coils behind the ovarian bridge and two such coils in front of it, the terminal coil being greatly enlarged; eggs 53 to 59 by 36 to 40 μ; other features as in spirometrids generally.

The species was established by Diesing (1850) as *Ligula reptans* for a larval form. Meggitt (1924e) believed the name to be valid for sparganids of reptiles in particular and gave a long list of amphibians, reptiles, birds, and mammals from which he believed *Sparganum reptans* had been recorded. Accepting a larva which occurs commonly in Burmese boid snakes as identical with Diesing's *reptans*, Meggitt reared in dogs from this sparganid the adult worm he regarded as *Diphyllobothrium reptans* (Diesing, 1850) (Figure 371 C and D).

The species *tangalongi* was established by MacCallum (1921) for a form from *Viverra tangalonga* (spotted civet) in Borneo. It would seem notable for its small eggs, the dimensions of which are only 40 by 20 μ. The description given is too scanty to permit conclusions as to its relationship with other spirometrids.

Dibothriocephalus Lühe, 1899

Relatively long, slender, weakly muscular forms with the holdfast long and compressed, olive-shaped, spoon-shaped, club-shaped in marginal outline according to the age and extent of contraction of the worm, narrowly oval or lancetlike in surficial (bothrial) outline. Bothrial slits deep, narrow, without projecting lips. Neck long and slender. Body only weakly craspedote and serrated. Segmentation well marked. Primary segmented worm without neck and with the segments one and one-half to two times longer than broad and the end segment bluntly rounded. Secondary segmented worms with the segments at first linear, then quadrate, then under ample nutritive conditions becoming linear again, with breadths three or four times the lengths. Gravid, exhausted segments leaving the worm (pseudapolysis). Genital and uterine apertures in the first third of the ventral segment surface. Parenchymal longitudinal muscles relatively weak, comprising two layers of loosely packed bundles not exceeding five times the thickness of the weak transverse muscles. Relative thicknesses of the successive body layers in a cross section of a mature segment: cuticle 1.5; subcuticle 7.0; cortex 14.0; longitudinal muscle zone 7.0; transverse muscle zone 1.5; medulla 40.0; all in percentages of the segment thickness measured dorso-ventrally in the median line.

One set of reproductive organs per segment, rarely two sets. Cirrovaginal atrium and aperture conspicuous. Testes 10 to 15 on each side of the genitalia in a cross section of the segment, in a single row. Cirrus pouch simple, with an external seminal vesicle not part of the cirrus pouch and postero-dorsal to it. Ovarian lobes large, giving the ovary a butterfly or dumbbell shape. Vagina relatively straight. Uterus with 4 to 8 loops on each side, the loops somewhat crowded and twisted, pointing forward or backward in rosettelike fashion. Eggs with rounded ends. Coracidium swimming with a slow rolling motion. First intermediate host a species of the copepod crustacean *Diaptomus*. Second intermediate host a fresh-water fish. Adults in fish-eating mammals and birds. Genotype, *latus* Linnaeus, 1758.

Presumably valid species of this much-discussed genus are: from mammals, *latus* Linnaeus, 1758; *laruei* Vergeer, 1942; *theileri* Baer, 1925; and *trinitatis* Cameron, 1936; from birds, *canadensis* Cooper, 1921; *cordiceps* Leidy, 1871; *dendriticus* Nitzsch, 1824; and *oblongatus* Thomas, 1946. Their distinguishing characteristics vary so widely that no satisfactory key to their separation can be constructed.

Definitely *species inquirenda* are: from mammals, *americanus* Hall and Wigdor, 1918; *fuscus* Krabbe, 1865; *minus* Cholodkovsky, 1916; *nenzi* Petrov, 1938; *parvus* Stephens, 1908; *similis* Krabbe, 1865; *skrjabini* Plotnikov, 1932; *strictus* Talysin, 1932; *taenioides* Leon, 1916; and *tungussicus* Podjapolska and Gnedina, 1932; from birds, *ditremus* Creplin, 1825; *exile* Linton, 1892; and *fissiceps* Creplin, 1829.

NOTES ON SPECIES

1. *latus* Linnaeus, 1758. Established, as *Taenia lata*, for a form first described by Thaddeus Dunus of Locarno in 1592 under the name *Lumbricus latus.* Under such vernacular names as "fish tapeworm," "broad tapeworm," and "Russian tapeworm" it is a relatively common parasite of humans in certain areas. The specific characters of *latus* have been described by a great many writers and therefore need not be discussed in detail here. The following description applies particularly to Canadian material (see Wardle and McColl, 1937) (Figure 375).

FIG. 375. *Dibothriocephalus latus,* holdfast (left), gravid segments (middle), enlarged gravid segments (right). Photographs of Canadian material. After Wardle, 1935b.

Holdfast lancet-shaped, spoon-shaped, or more frequently club-shaped in marginal outline, 1.3 to 2.4 mm. long by 0.625 to 1.0 mm. broad, both shape and dimensions varying with the state of contraction; neck region varying in mature specimens (from dogs) between 1.4 and 2.6 mm. in length, the posterior limit being difficult to fix with precision; first body segments appearing simultaneously along the whole worm, thus producing a primary strobila, when the worm is 25 to 72 hours in the final host; the primary segments "long," the lengths one and one-half to two times the breadths, the segments markedly craspedote, the end segment bluntly rounded along its posterior border.

In superinfested animals such primary segmented worms may persist for several months, but usually within three weeks after the entrance of the plerocercoid larva into the mammalian host secondary segments begin to appear in the neck region, at first linear, three to four times as wide as long. Secondarily segmented worms in superinfested hosts may show strips of long, craspedote segments of the primary type interrupting a sequence of quadrate segments; eventually the new linear secondary segments become quadrate, only appearing linear throughout the body when the worm is contracted by preservation in hypertonic reagents.

Dorso-ventral dimensions of the internal structures, expressed as percentages of the segment thickness are: for the cuticle 0.34 to 2.8 (thickest in specimens from dogs), subcuticle 3.0 to 11.1, cortex 11.0 to 23.5, yolk glands 9.4 to 13.6, muscle zone 9.6 to 22.0 (thinnest in specimens from dogs), medulla 17.6 to 33.2, testes 14.0 to 24.6, cirrus pouch (percentage of *maximum* segment thickness) 0.50 to 0.57. Position of cirro-vaginal aperture, measured from its center to the anterior border of the segment, varying between 0.134 to 0.209 per cent of the segment length. Uterine loop counts varying from 3.4 to 4.9 on either side, with a mean value of 4.3 for the anterior loops, and from 1.1 to 3.4 with a mean value of 2.0 for the posterior loops (in material from humans); 5.3 to 8.0 for the anterior loops, 1.3 to 3.9 for the posterior loops (in material from dogs). Circum-cloacal papillae absent or only faintly visible in human material, prominent in canine material. On the whole, Canadian material shows a somewhat closer resemblance to Japanese material than to European.

It may be added that the use of uterine loop counts as a taxonomic character is not altogether satisfactory. In the primary "long" type of segment, when it persists in mature worms, the anterior loop count is approximately eight on either side of the middle line, the posterior loop count approximately three or four on each side. The later quadrate segments, however, show in their loop counts a lower number, and the loops, due to the intrinsic pressure of the increasing number of eggs and the extrinsic pressure of the muscular medullary margin, lose their parallel alignment and lie at an angle to the central area so that a rosettelike arrangement is produced. This is especially marked in the posterior uterine region. The bends of the loops become bloated with eggs and in mounted specimens may produce the appearance of a linear series of egg sacs on either side of the middle line. The two most anterior bends are particularly enlarged. Continued egg pressure brings about a corkscrewlike torsion of some of the anterior loops (see Figure 29) or a sub-looping, so that in a flattened preparation they may appear forked. Russian material shows this pseudo-forking to a marked degree; Canadian material shows more of the torsion effect. If a fork be counted as two loops, then the loop counts of European material will appear greater than those of Canadian material. In all cases the loop count is difficult to estimate with accuracy, and the values found vary within wide limits.

The life cycle of *Dibothriocephalus latus* has been discussed previously (see Chapter II), but the following observations upon the distribution of this form may be noted. The adult worm has been recorded from a wide variety of mammalian hosts: from humans, dogs (*Canis familiaris, C. azarae, C. cinereo-argentatus, C. occidentalis*), cats (*Felis domestica, F. concolor, F. mellivora, F. hernandesii, F. macroura, F. pardus, F. mitis*), mongoose (*Herpestes leucurus*), walrus (*Odobaena rosmarus*), seals and sea lions (*Leptonyx monachus, Phoca barbata, Phoca hispida, Phoca vitulina, Phocaena phocaena*), bears (*Thalarctos maritimus, Ursus americanus, Ursus horribilis*), foxes (*Vulpes fulva*), and mink (*Mustela vison*).

Many of these records, notably those from Pinnipedia, are doubtless cases of misidentification; others are cases of accidental host infection. In North America, if the worm is really indigenous and not a form introduced by immigrants, the normal host is probably the brown bear (*Ursus americanus*). Specimens from bears have been recorded from localities so far apart as Alaska, Wyoming, and Michigan.

The plerocercoid stage has been recorded from a long list of fresh-water fish species, though here again there is doubt as to whether all the species thus recorded have been *latus*; but it has never been recorded from a truly marine fish. In northern Russia, Petruschevsky (1931) found the most favored hosts, and the frequencies of infection among them, to be: *Acerina cernua* (ruffe or pope) 98 per cent, *Lota lota* (burbot) 91.6 per cent, *Esox lucius* (pike) 88.8 per cent, *Perca fluviatilis* (fresh-water perch) 53.8 per cent, and *Anguilla anguilla* (fresh-water eel) 27.7 per cent. Individual infection was high, averaging in *Lota* 338.6 larvae per fish, distributed chiefly among the muscles, and in *Esox* 152 larvae per fish, distributed chiefly over the lining of the body cavity.

In North America, on the contrary, only four species of fishes have been found, by rearing tests of the actual larvae, to harbor the plerocercoids of *Dibothriocephalus latus*, namely: *Esox lucius* (northern pike), *Stizostedion vitreum* (pickerel, walleyed pike, pike perch), *Stizostedion canadense* (sauger), and *Perca flavescens* (yellow perch). The number of larvae per fish is also low, running from 1.2 per individual (*Stizostedion canadense*) to 2.3 per individual (*Esox lucius*) (see Vergeer, 1929a; Wardle, 1932e, 1935b). Occasional specimens of a nonencysted dibothriocephalid larva have been recorded in species of Pacific salmon (*Oncorhynchus*) but confirmatory rearing tests were not made (see Ward, 1930; Wardle, 1932a). A dibothriocephalid larva similar to that of *latus* occurs also in Lakes Winnipeg and Ontario in the burbot (*Lota lota*) but *encysted* in the wall of the stomach and pyloric caeca. The nature of the host and the encystment habit preclude it from identification with *latus*; Vergeer (1942) provisionally named it *Sparganum pseudosegmentatum*.

Dibothriocephalus latus was probably one of the earliest of human parasites to attract attention. There is no evidence, however, that it was known to the early civilizations of the Mediterranean and Mesopotamian regions. The *elminthes plateae* of the Greek writers Hippocrates and Theophrastes, and the *Taenia, Tinea*, and *Taeniola* of Pliny and other Latin writers referred almost certainly to the beef tapeworm, *Taeniarhynchus saginatus*. North of the Alps, however, particularly in Switzerland and in central and Baltic Europe and Asia, the fish tapeworm has probably been familiar to man from the earliest times. The first recognizable description of it was that by Thaddeus Dunus of Locarno in

1592 under the name of *Lumbricus latus*. Plater, in his *Opus praxeos medicae*, published in 1602, distinguished under the term *Taenia secunda plateri* the fish tapeworm from other forms occurring in man. Linnaeus (1758) designated it *Taenia lata* in contrast with *Taenia vulgaris*, a term comprising the beef tapeworm and the pork tapeworm.

At the present day, the adult worm is endemic in circum-Baltic Europe, Siberia, Switzerland, Palestine, Japan, Uganda, North America (Michigan, Minnesota, Manitoba), and possibly in the Philippine Islands. Plerocercoids have been recorded in perch (39 per cent) from Lake Gardice, County Leitrim, Ireland, by Harris and Hickey (1945), their identity with *latus* being confirmed by rearing in dogs.

The North American form of *latus* may represent an infestation introduced by immigrants from northern Europe superimposed upon an older infestation that came in via the Bering Straits. There is evidence of its occurrence in humans and dogs as far north as Aklavik at the mouth of the Mackenzie River (see Saunders, 1949).

For discussions of the frequencies of infection and the topographical distribution within these areas, reference should be made to Ward (1930), Wardle (1935b), Brumpt (1936), and to the bibliographical references given by these writers.

Extensive surveys carried out between 1925 and 1940 in Russia, in addition to providing very detailed information as to the strikingly high incidence of *D. latus* among humans in certain districts, uncovered the presence in man and dogs of a number of other dibothriocephalid species which were believed by their investigators to be specifically distinct from *latus*. These species were *minus, nentsi* (or *nentzi*), *skrjabini, strictus*, and *tungussicus*.

2. *laruei* Vergeer, 1942. Worms 112 mm. long by 2.103 mm. broad; holdfast ellipsoidal, more acute anteriorly than posteriorly, 1.677 by 0.859 mm.; bothria extending only two-thirds of the holdfast length from the tip; neck 1.59 by 0.33 mm.; maximum number of segments 280, progressing from linear to rectangular in shape; cirro-vaginal atrium medial, at junction of first and second thirds of the ventral segment surface; uterine aperture shortly behind the cirro-vaginal aperture and in a separate depression; cirro-vaginal aperture surrounded by a field of cuticular papillae (suggested by Vergeer to have some use during intersegmental copulation); osmoregulatory canals 8 to 10 in the cortex, 2 in the medulla; testes 225 to 400, continuous from segment to segment; external seminal vesicle club-shaped, thick-walled; cirrus pouch cylindrical; yolk glands in a single, closely packed layer in the cortex, continuous from segment to segment; uterus with 7 or 8 loops on either side, the most anterior pair of loops lying lateral to the cirrus pouch; eggs ellipsoidal, 43 to 52 by 32 to 33 μ; plerocercoids elongated, cylindrical or slightly depressed, tapering from the holdfast end backward; holdfast end ellipsoidal, bothria deep, total length of body 2 to 26 mm.; found in small, spherical cysts applied closely to the peritoneum of the stomach outer surface; recorded from all five of the Great Lakes and

from Lake Nipigon, Ontario, in species of *Leucichthys* (lake herring, tullibee), mainly *artedi*; reared with some difficulty in dogs, but not rearable in gulls (Figure 376).

3. *theileri* Baer, 1925. Worms 350 to 400 mm. long by 3 mm. wide; holdfast typically dibothriocephalid, 53 to 86 by 25 to 30 μ; longitudinal muscles well developed; transverse muscles weak; testes large, in a single sheet arranged as two lateral zones uniting in the anterior part of the

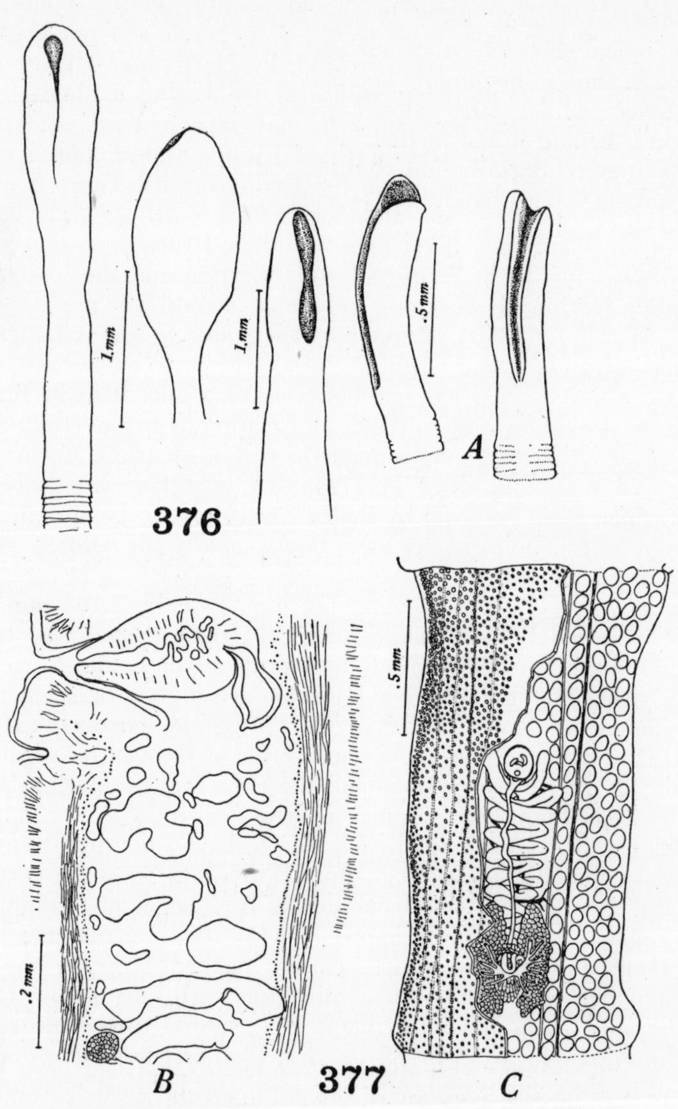

FIG. 376. *Dibothriocephalus laruei*, 3 outlines of holdfast. After Vergeer, 1942. FIG. 377. *Dibothriocephalus oblongatus*. After Thomas, 1946. A. Holdfast. B. Sagittal section of a segment. C. Mature segment.

segment by a single row; vagina and cirrus pouch opening at the base of a deep cirro-vaginal atrium; position of cirro-vaginal aperture not stated; uterus with a broad central stem, three branches on one side, four on the other; eggs 57 by 34 μ. The species was established for a number of specimens taken from South African Felidae (*Zibethailurus serval, Felis caffra*). Baer regarded this form as close to *Spirometra raillieti* Ratz, but the general features would seem to be dibothriocephalid rather than spirometrid.

4. *trinitatis* Cameron, 1936. Worms less than 100 mm. long; holdfast bluntly conical; bothria on dorsal and lateral (*sic*) surfaces; neck absent; segmentation beginning immediately behind the bothria; gravid segments rectangular; cirro-vaginal aperture almost central; uterine aperture shortly behind it and medial; uterine loops few (3 to 4), described as being directed dorsally and ventrally rather than laterally; testes and yolk glands in lateral bands, testes meeting in front of the cirro-vaginal aperture and posterior to the ovary, yolk glands only meeting behind the ovary; eggs oval, 58 by 28 to 30 μ. The species was established for a number of specimens from a crab-eating raccoon (*Procyon cancrivora*) in Trinidad, West Indies.

5. *canadensis* Cooper, 1921. Worms 235 mm. or more in length by 6.5 mm. in breadth; holdfast small, elongated, rectangular in outline both surficially and marginally except for the rounded apex, 0.84 mm. long by 0.37 mm. wide at base and 0.46 mm. in thickness in the middle; bothria long and narrow, not sharply separated posteriorly from the body surface; neck 0.7 mm. long; gravid segments linear; cirro-vaginal atrium at the junction of the first and second thirds of the ventral segment surface; testes at least 150 in number, in a single sheet continuous from segment to segment and from side to side except where interrupted by the female genitalia; external seminal vesicle spheroidal, thick-walled, muscular, and postero-dorsal to the cirrus pouch; yolk glands crowded together, continuous from segment to segment; uterine loops rosettelike in arrangement, circular or elliptical in surficial view, 8 to 10 coils on either side, the most anterior pair passing forward on each side of the cirrus pouch; uterine aperture central; eggs ellipsoidal, 56 to 59 μ by 37 to 39 μ with a knob at the end opposite to that bearing the operculum. The species was established for material from the northern raven (*Corvus corax principalis*) at Bernard Harbour, arctic Canada.

6. *cordiceps* Leidy, 1871. Established, as *Dibothrium cordiceps*, for a larval form found in *Salvelinus fontinalis* (brook trout), Wyoming; the name was used by Linton (1891c) for similar larvae from *Salmo mykiss* and *Salvelinus fontinalis* and for adult tapeworms from *Pelicanus erythrorhynchus* from the same locality as Leidy's material. The adult form was described by Ward (1918) as 2 meters long by 7.5 mm. broad, in maximum dimensions, with the holdfast heart-shaped, 2 mm. long by 0.6 to 0.8 mm. broad; neck short; genital aperture median, ventral, distinct; testes in lateral fields; vagina with a seminal receptacle near the distal end; ovary posterior, ventral, transverse to the main axis; shell gland dorsal, near the ovary and posterior to it; uterus in lateral coils

approaching the form of a rosette; eggs 70 by 35 μ. The description would fit almost any species of *Dibothriocephalus.*

7. *dendriticus* Nitzsch, 1824. Established for material from gulls (*Larus ridibundus, Larus canis, Rissa tridactyla*) in northern Europe; described by Lühe (1910a) as being up to 43 mm. long by 7 mm. broad; with up to 300 segments, testes 470, uterus with 8 or 9 lateral loops giving the appearance of a "dendritic figure." Baylis (1945) recorded what he regarded as this species from birds in Wales and Ireland, but pointed out that individuals obtained by rearing plerocercoids in birds may have fewer testes and duplicated cirrus pouches and uteri as compared with naturally occurring forms. Hickey and Harris (1947) also recorded this species in Ireland, the greater activity of the plerocercoids with a rise in temperature producing during the summer months a peritonitis in trout in the river Liffey. Adult worms were found in three species of gulls. Procercoid stages occurred in the copepod Crustacea *Diaptomus gracilis* and *Cyclops strenuus abyssorum.* Plerocercoid stages occurred in sticklebacks (*Gasterosteus aculeatus*) which were fed upon by the trout.

8. *oblongatus* Thomas, 1946. Established, as *Diphyllobothrium oblongatum,* for material from young gulls and Caspian terns in northern Lake Michigan. The present writers have material of this form from gulls in western Canada so that the species may be common across North America. We therefore quote the author's description of the species in full:

Small cream-colored worms when alive; in length from 28 to 57 cm.; mature segments in posterior third of the worm longer than broad, 3 to 7 mm. by 1.75 to 2 mm.; maximum thickness 0.419 mm. Tandem duplication of the reproductive organs frequent; largest number of segments 455; holdfast finger-shaped, 1.75 by 0.44 mm.; bothria deep, extending the full length of the holdfast, open at the summit; neck short, 1.09 by 0.7 mm.; transverse striations extending a short distance before segmentation begins; genital aperture 44 μ in diameter, median, circular, in a papillose area 1.2 by 0.962 mm.; uterine aperture median, circular, papillose, posterior to the genital aperture by an average distance of 166 μ; uterine loops in a loose spiral extending from the genital complex anteriorly to the cirrus pouch, with a lateral loop on either side of this organ; anterior loops 7 to 8; walls thick; posterior loops 3 to 4, narrow, thin-walled; yolk glands ovoidal, averaging 15 by 16 μ in diameter, numbering approximately 2,884, scattered in a single layer, in two fields joined anteriorly and posteriorly; yolk ducts numerous, anastomosing to form antlerlike connections with the oviduct; testes ovoid, average diameter 87 by 131 μ, numbering 264–318, in a single medullary layer scattered between two fields, each lateral to the ovary and joined in the anterior and posterior regions of the segment; ovary bilobed, compact, with lobes bean-shaped, 875 to 970 μ long by 175 to 262 μ wide, joined in front by an isthmus 131–149 by 149–157 μ; ovarian lobes meeting occasionally at their posterior tips; cirrus 87 μ at its base, when everted 140 μ long; cirrus pouch pear-shaped, 175 to 201 by 306 μ, median, about 1.14 to 1.0 mm. from the anterior border of the segment and weakly muscular; sperm duct extending from the apex of the ovarian lobes in a loose spiral right and left of the middle line to join the thick-walled, pear-shaped seminal vesicle, 70 to 96 μ in diameter, which is situated posterior to and at the base of the cirrus pouch; vagina median, slightly spiral, irregularly alternating to the right and left of the uterine aperture and the oviduct; vaginal aperture oval, opening into a common genital atrium; seminal receptacle sleevelike, 219 to 230 μ long by 79 to 96 μ in diameter; ootype empty, measuring 17 to 23 μ in diameter, thick-walled, oocapt present; osmoregulatory ducts in the cortex, numerous and anastomosing, in the medulla two, lateral to the uterine coils, continuous from segment to segment; main nerve trunks two, 44 to 53 μ wide, lateral to the main osmoregulatory canals by the width of one or two testes and 393 to 437 μ from the lateral margins of the segment; Mehlis' gland diffuse, large, 219 to 306 μ wide by 115 to 306 μ long and 206 to 306 μ thick, extending ventrally into the longitudinal muscles neither above the isthmus nor posteriorly beyond the ovarian lobes; muscles: hypodermal circular and longitudinal fibers weak; medullary transverse fibers few and weak; cortical glands numerous, in a layer 43 to 65 μ thick [Thomas apparently means by this term the subcuticular cells; their alleged glandular nature is at present not proven]; eggs ovoid, amber colored, measuring on the average 61 by 39 μ; with the operculum slightly tangential and apical boss obscure; undeveloped when laid; coracidium free-swimming; procercoid in *Diaptomus oregoniensis*; plerocercoid encysted on the mesenteries and stomach wall of lake herring (Coregonidae) *Leucichthys artedi*, Lakes Michigan, Huron, Nipigon; adult worm in gulls (Figure 377).

9. *americanus* Hall and Wigdor, 1918. Established for four immature worms taken from a dog in Detroit, United States. It is generally regarded by North American writers as synonymous with *latus*.

10. *fuscus* Krabbe, 1865. Established for a tapeworm from a dog in Iceland. Krabbe's description was poor and his figures of holdfast and gravid segment suggest strongly that his form was *latus*; Sprehn (1932), however, listed it as a valid species of *Diphyllobothrium* Lühe.

11. *minus* Cholodkovsky, 1916. Established for a single specimen from man in Transbaikalia, but it was recovered and redescribed in some detail by Talysin (1930) from the same area. The length of Cholodkovsky's specimen was 100 mm. Talysin found dimensions of 100 to 265 mm. by a maximum breadth of 7 to 11 mm.; anterior third of the body bluish-white shading to bright yellow; rest of the body brown; body markedly depressed, with the margins serrated; holdfast not sharply differentiated from the body, 0.8 to 1.7 mm. long by 0.5 to 1.0 mm. in basal diameter, conical, apically rounded, oval in marginal outline, triangular in surficial outline; bothria deep, with the lips in the middle region projecting and overlapping, fading out posteriorly as a shallow groove dorsally and ventrally which extends over the first 25 to 30 segments; neck absent; segmentation beginning shortly behind the bothria; about 200 segments, increasing rapidly in breadth but with the lengths remaining relatively constant, one-twelfth to two-ninths of the breadth; position of the genital

apertures not given; ovary foreshortened antero-posteriorly, drawn out laterally; vagina with several undulations; uterus mainly in the posterior half of the segment, behind the genital aperture, with its loops parallel to the posterior segment border and not grouped rosettelike; uterine aperture approximately central; number of loops not stated; eggs spherical to ovoid, 58 to 72 μ by 41 to 49 μ with an average of 64 by 44 μ, commonly with a little spine at one pole or the other. It is our opinion that this form was *Cordicephalus phocarus* (Fabricius, 1780).

12 and 13. *nenzi* Petrov, 1938, and *skrjabini* Plotnikov, 1932. Both recorded by Petrov (1938) from humans in the Nenzi area of northern Siberia, *skrjabini* being a rediscovery. We have no information beyond a brief abstract (*Helminthological Abstracts*, 1938).

14. *parvus* Stephens, 1908. Established for a specimen obviously of a primary segmented worm from man in Australia. The general concensus of opinion among students of this and similar forms – such as the alleged *parvus* described by Fain (1947) from jackals in Belgian Congo – is that such forms are merely immature primary specimens of *Dibothriocephalus latus*. The same comment may be applied to *similis* Krabbe, 1865 from a dog in Iceland.

15. *strictus* Talysin, 1932. Established for two small worms, 470 and 195 mm. respectively, obtained by vermifugation of humans in the vicinity of Lake Baikal. They were figured as possessing some segments with two sets of reproductive organs arranged tandem; *strictus* agrees with the form *taenioides* described by Leon (1916) in Rumania and usually regarded by authorities as an immature specimen of *latus*.

16. *tungussicus* Podjapolska and Gnedina, 1932. Established for 477 specimens of a worm obtained by vermifugation of humans in the Yenesei district of Siberia. The specimens ranged in size from 600 mm. in length by 3.5 mm. in breadth down to much smaller specimens, with a maximum of 502 segments, mainly linear in shape. This form seems to differ from *latus* mainly in having a bean-shaped ovary and in having a maximum of four uterine loops on each side of the middle line.

17. *ditremus* Creplin, 1825. Established for a form from fish-eating birds (*Urinator arcticus, Urinator stellatus, Mergus merganser, Mergus serrator, Larus argentatus*) in northern Europe. It was described by Lühe (1910a) as ranging up to 13 mm. by 2.5 mm. in dimensions with the holdfast flattened, egg-shaped, and about 1.2 mm. long by 1.0 mm. broad and 0.5 mm. thick; segments up to 110; testes 380 to 390 and about 110 μ in diameter, with about 24 testes in the middle line and two-thirds of the segment length between the cirrus pouch and the segment in front; cirrus pouch about 282 μ long and 164 μ in diameter; about 3,000 yolk glands of 90 μ by 54 μ diameter, arranged not only in lateral zones but in the anterior and posterior regions of the segment; uterine loops 7 on each side. Baylis (1945) has identified with this scanty description a tapeworm from a cormorant in Ireland.

18. *exile* Linton, 1892. Established for material from *Larus californicus*. The specimen was immature, 153 mm. long, the holdfast spoon-shaped and measuring 1.5 mm. long by 0.6 mm. wide and 0.2 mm. thick;

the neck was long and slender. Other details given are applicable to any species of this genus.

19. *fissiceps* Creplin, 1829. Established for a single specimen taken from *Sterna hirundo* in Europe and described as 80 to 150 mm. long by 5 mm. broad, with an elongated holdfast, no neck, segments at first linear, later becoming rectangular.

Schistocephalus Creplin, 1829

With the body ovo-lanceolate in outline, broadly depressed, fragile, with distinct segmentation and up to 200 mm. in length by 5 to 8 mm. in breadth. Holdfast not clearly differentiated from the body but represented by a triangular area with a basal diameter of 1.2 mm. and a length of 0.8 mm., on each flat surface of which is a shallow depression representing a bothrium but inconspicuous in stained, cleared specimens; each depression interrupting posteriorly the boundary between the holdfast segment and the following segment; the two depressions connected by a short groove passing dorso-ventrally over the tip of the holdfast region. Body with maximum breadth, in specimens in the writers' possession, at the junction of the first and second thirds, that is to say, in the region of segments 40 to 44 in a worm of 125 segments. Mid-ventral line of the body rounded, mid-dorsal line grooved or shallowly concave. Segmentation complete, craspedote, with margins conspicuously serrated. Segments varying in length scarcely at all from a mean value of 0.8 mm. Reproductive organs visible even in unstained specimens, beginning early, in the 18th segment in a worm of 125 segments. Cirro-vaginal atrium extremely shallow and inconspicuous, median and ventral, in the anterior third of the segment. Cirrus pouch subspherical, 250 μ in transverse diameter, almost touching the anterior border of the segment. External seminal vesicle conspicuous, spherical, dorsal to the cirrus pouch, 150 μ in diameter. Vagina opening behind the posterior edge of the cirrus aperture and in the middle line. Uterine aperture posterior and lateral to the vaginal aperture, irregularly alternating from side to side. Testes in a single layer along the dorsal surface of the medulla, 400 to 500 per segment. Yolk glands cortical, very numerous, crowded, continuous from segment to segment and completely surrounding the segment except for an oval clear field in the center of the segment. Uterus tubular, alternating from side to side of the middle line. Intrauterine eggs 75 by 50 μ. Plerocercoid larva white, broad, depressed, the holdfast segment short with the tip rounder and blunter than in the adult worm. Mean body dimensions 40 by 6 mm., nearly half the length of the host fish. Segmentation complete, craspedote, but less so than in the adult worm. Mean segment length 0.5 to 0.6 mm. Genotype and only known species, *solidus* Creplin, 1829 (Figure 378).

The North American form of *Schistocephalus* is undoubtedly identical so far as anatomy is concerned with the form recorded repeatedly by European authors as adult in a wide range of water birds and as a plerocercoid in the body cavity of a wide range of fresh-water fishes. It was first recorded in North America by Linton (1897a) as a larva in

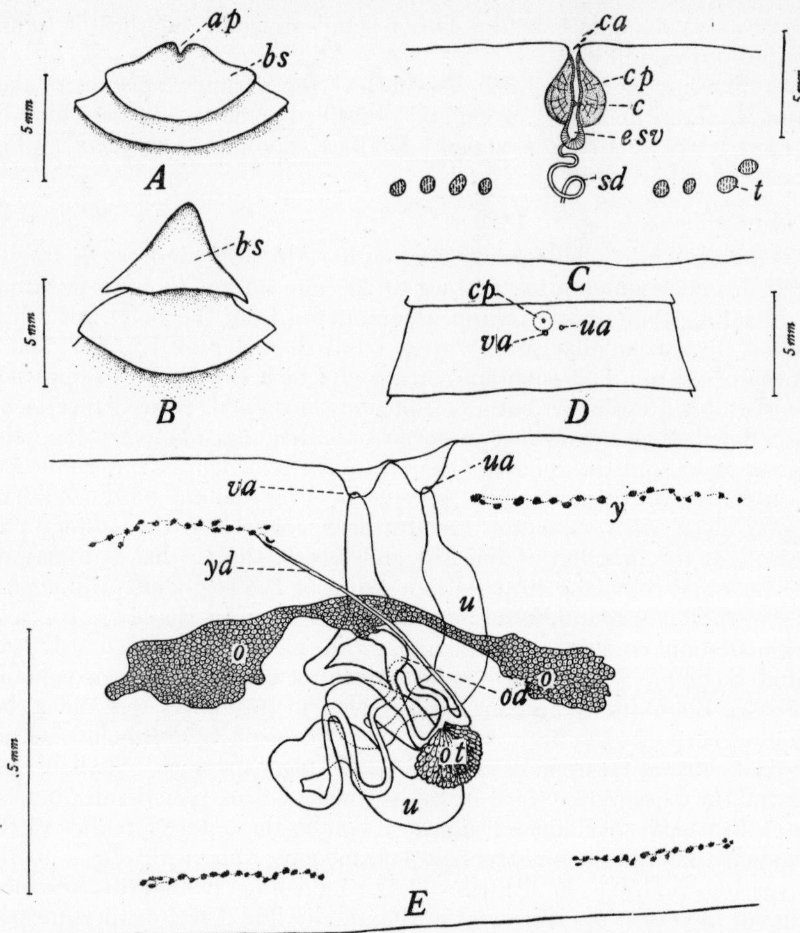

FIG. 378. *Schistocephalus solidus*. After Smyth, 1946. A. Bothrial end of plerocercoid. B. Bothrial end of adult. C. Male genitalia of plerocercoid. D. Arrangement of the genital apertures in a segment. E. Female genitalia of plerocercoid. *ap*, anterior pit; *bs*, bothrial segment; *c*, cirrus; *ca*, cirrus aperture; *cp*, cirrus pouch; *esv*, external seminal vesicle; *o*, ovary; *od*, oviduct; *ot*, ootype; *sd*, sperm duct; *t*, testes; *u*, uterus; *ua*, uterine aperture; *va*, vaginal aperture; *y*, yolk glands; *yd*, yolk duct.

Cottus bairdi in Montana. Later it was recorded by Cooper (1918) in *Gasterosteus bispinosus* at Chamcook Lake, New Brunswick; in *Uranidea formosa* at Port Credit, Ontario; and in *Pygosteus pungitius* at Bernard Harbour, arctic Canada; by Wardle (1933) in *Cottus sp.* at Shuswap Lake, British Columbia, and in *Salvelinus fontinalis* in various lakes of Quebec. The adult worm has been recorded in North America only by Cooper (1918) in *Lophodytes cucullus* in Nebraska, and by Wardle (1933) in *Mergus americanus*, British Columbia, and free on the shore of Nanaimo Lake, Vancouver Island.

Observations on the life cycle have been made by Callot and Desportes (1934) in the case of a fatal infestation of ducks (*Anas boschas*) in the vicinity of Paris. Up to 340 living schistocephalid adults could be found in a single duck. The eggs took three weeks to hatch, and *Cyclops viridis*, even in the nauplius stage, would readily ingest the coracidia, up to as many as 60 procercoids developing in an individual *Cyclops*. The plerocercoid hosts in the lake of the Bois de Boulogne were found to be *Gasterosteus aculeatus* and *Pygosteus pungitius*.

Cephalochlamys Blanchard, 1908 (= *Chlamydocephalus* Cohn, 1906)

With two shallow bothria asserted by Cohn to be lateral in position and separated by a mobile dorsal and ventral plate. Small forms. Two layers of longitudinal muscles. Genital aperture median, anterior to the uterine aperture, in the anterior half of the segment. Testes few (7–12) in two lateral fields. Ovary posterior, U-shaped. Yolk glands few, in two lateral fields of the cortex. Uterus a narrow, coiled canal extending nearly to the anterior border of the segment and lying between the two testis zones. Uterine aperture anterior and median. Eggs thin-shelled, not operculated. Genotype and only known species, *namaquensis* Cohn, 1906 from *Xenopus laevis*, a southwestern African frog (Figure 379).

The genus and species were established by Cohn (1906) as *Chlamydocephalus namaquensis*. The generic term, however, had previously been introduced into zoological nomenclature by Diesing in 1850 and again by Schmarda in 1859 and so was unacceptable for this form. R. Blanchard (1908) suggested, therefore, the generic term *Cephalochlamys*. Further notes on the species were published by Ortlepp (1926), Baylis (1934a), and Southwell and Kirshner (1937b). From these observers we gather that what Cohn believed to be lateral bothria are really large oval bothridia whose posterior halves stand away from the body and thus give the holdfast an arrowhead appearance. When somewhat warped by microtechnical preparation, these bothridia may give the appearance of being lateral, but actually they would seem to be dorsal and ventral. Definitely dibothriocephalid is the presence of a cirro-vaginal atrium placed on a slight elevation just behind the anterior border of the segment; the presence of an external seminal vesicle; and the long and tubular uterus. Definitely not dibothriocephalid, however, is the absence of any operculum in the egg. On the whole the dibothriocephalid affinities of *Cephalochlamys* must be regarded as doubtful. The form requires restudy in considerably more detail than has hitherto been the case.

Two other genera have been assigned on somewhat doubtful grounds by some authors to Dibothriocephalidae:

Lytocephalus Cohn, 1908

A dubious form described from a single specimen that was taken from a siluroid fish, *Clarias fuscus*, in Hong Kong, and named specifically *adhaerens*. It was assigned by Cohn to Dibothriocephalidae on account of the surficial position of the genital apertures, the cortical position of the yolk glands, and the coiled nature of the uterus. On the other hand,

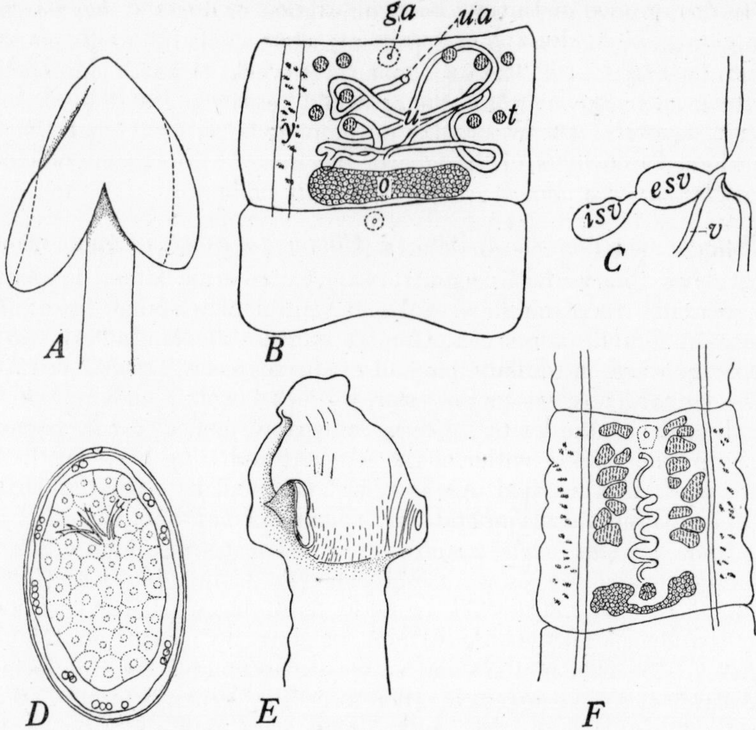

FIG. 379. *Cephalochlamys namaquensis*. A. Holdfast. B. Mature segment. C. Genital ducts. All after Ortlepp, 1926. *esv*, external seminal vesicle; *ga*, genital aperture; *isv*, internal seminal vesicle; *o*, ovary; *t*, testes; *u*, uterus; *ua*, uterine aperture; *v*, vagina; *y*, yolk glands. D. Egg. After Southwell and Kirshner, 1937b. E. Holdfast. F. Mature segment. Both after Cohn, 1906.

the nature of its host, the early apolysis of its segments, and the absence of preformed uterine apertures suggest closer affinities with Tetraphyllidea.

Dittocephalus Parona, 1887

Established for a form specifically named *linstowi* and taken from a shark, *Squalus sp.*, in the Mediterranean. It was described as having the anterior end of the body and the first three segments forked, each fork of the holdfast having a bothrium. The external segmentation was irregular. The genital apertures were surficial. Until this form has been rediscovered and redescribed it must be regarded as *sub judice.*

Family Ptychobothriidae Lühe, 1902, emended

DESCRIPTION

Of the order Pseudophyllidea. Medium-sized worms with the holdfast strongly compressed, bluntly rounded apically, with the marginal surfaces broad, somewhat triangular in outline. and each with a median longitudinal groove or furrow. Bothria surficial, dorsal and ventral, very deep, giving the holdfast in cross section an H shape. Bothrial lips very mobile, tending to roll inward. Neck apparently absent, segmentation beginning immediately behind the posterior borders of the bothria. Body showing complete and incomplete areas of segmentation. Segments not craspedote. Parenchymal longitudinal muscles in bundles. Cirrus pouch and vagina opening into a cirro-vaginal canal which in turn opens into a funnel-shaped cirro-vaginal atrium whose common genital aperture opens in the center of the *dorsal* surface. Testes medullary, dorsal, in two lateral zones. Ovary small, compact, near the posterior border of the segment. Seminal receptacle small. Yolk glands in two lateral zones, cortical in position. Gravid uterus comprising a sinuous uterine duct occupying almost the whole medullary parenchyma, and a sharply differentiated uterine sac which opens to the exterior on the *ventral* surface, just behind the anterior border of the segment and to one side of the median line. Eggs thin-shelled, without opercula, containing each a subglobular, hooked embryo when laid. Adult worms parasitic in marine teleostean fishes. Type genus, *Ptychobothrium* Loennberg, 1889.

HISTORY

The family was established by Lühe (1902c) with *Bothriocephalus* named as the type genus. As viewed by Lühe, the family contained a mixture of ptychobothriid, bothriocephalid, and amphicotylid forms and was described as containing tapeworms with shallow bothria, with the seminal vesicle lacking, with yolk glands cortical *or* medullary, with eggs without opercula (although those of *Bothriocephalus* are known to have such a structure), and with the genital apertures surficial *or* marginal. Nybelin (1922) separated those forms with marginal genital openings, which had been grouped by Lühe as a subfamily Amphicotylinae, as a separate family Amphicotylidae. We propose here to separate the bothriocephalid forms as a family Bothriocephalidae, thus reducing the family Ptychobothriidae to the four genera discussed below.

NOTES ON GENERA

Ptychobothrium Loennberg, 1889

With the holdfast spoon-shaped or elongated heart-shaped, compressed, without any terminal disk. Bothria well developed. Neck lacking. Segmentation incomplete. Testes lateral, near the dorsal boundary of the medulla. Cirrus pouch thin-walled, without prostate glands around its proximal end; opening with the vagina by a common cirro-vaginal duct at the base of the funnel-shaped cirro-vaginal atrium. Ovary compact, near the posterior border of the segment. Seminal receptacle small. Other characters as for the family generally. Genotype and only recorded species, *belones* Dujardin, 1845 (Figure 383).

Ptychobothrium belones was recorded by Dujardin (1845), as *Bothriocephalus belones*, from the marine fish *Belones acus* at Cette, France. Loennberg (1889a) made Dujardin's species the genotype of a new genus *Ptychobothrium*, mainly on the characters of the holdfast. It was recorded by Linton (1891a) as *Dibothrium restiforme* from *Tylosurus caribbaeus*, Woods Hole, Massachusetts. A detailed description was published by Janicki (1928a). It was recorded and again described by Yamaguti (1934) from material found in *Tylosurus schismatorhynchus* in Japanese waters. Shuler (1938) recorded it from *Strongylura notata* and *Tylosurus raphidoma* at Dry Tortugas, Florida.

Senga Dollfus, 1934

Small to medium-sized forms with the holdfast rectangular, tipped by a bilobed disk whose margin carries a row of hooks recalling somewhat those of Taeniidae, and divided into two half-circles by dorsal and ventral indentations of the disk margin, the two half-circles being connected by rudimentary hooks in the indented areas of the margin. Bothria shallow, oval, thick-lipped. Neck lacking. Body with segmentation incomplete, some segments corresponding to two proglottides. Segments few (fewer than 40), not craspedote, rectangular, anapolytic or pseudapolytic. Segments at first wider than long, then square, then longer than wide. Cirro-vaginal aperture dorsal, surficial, slightly behind the center of the segment surface. Male reproductive system not described. Ovary in the posterior half of the segment, not bilobed. Yolk glands cortical, in a single continuous layer around the segment. Uterus with a uterine duct passing from the region of the ovary almost to the anterior border of the segment, right or left of the cirro-vaginal aperture, and dilating into a uterine sac whose external aperture is ventral and median, just behind the anterior border of the segment. Eggs thin-shelled, not operculated, not embryonated when laid. Adult forms in fresh-water fishes (Labyrinthiformes, Cypriniformes) in Southeast Asia. Genotype, *besnardi* Dollfus, 1934 (Figure 380).

Of the three species recognized, *besnardi* Dollfus, 1934 came from a specimen of *Betta splendens*, the Siamese fighting fish, in an aquarium at Vincennes, France; *ophiocephaliana* Tseng, 1933 was recorded, as *Anchistrocephalus opicephalianus*, from *Ophiocephalus argus* at Tsinan, China, and identified with a form previously recorded by Southwell (1913b) as *Anchistrocephalus polyptera* from *Ophiocephalus striatus* (Labyrinthiformes) in Bengal, India; and *pycnomerus* Woodland, 1924 was recorded, as *Bothriocephalus pycnomerus*, from *Ophiocephalus marulius* at Allahabad, India. Although some details are obscure, Dollfus was inclined to place *pycnomerus* within the genus *Senga*.

Polyonchobothrium Diesing, 1863

Small to medium-sized forms with the holdfast approximately rectangular, the apex domed, with a circle of 32 hooks arranged in four quadrants. Body weakly segmented. Cirro-vaginal aperture dorsal, surficial, median, at the junction of the first and second fourths of the segment surface. Testes 12 on each side of the ovary. Yolk glands cortical, in two dorsal and two ventral bands. Eggs thin-shelled, not operculated. Adult worms in the African fishes *Polypterus spp.* and *Clarias spp.* Genotype, *polypteri* Leydig, 1853 (Figure 385).

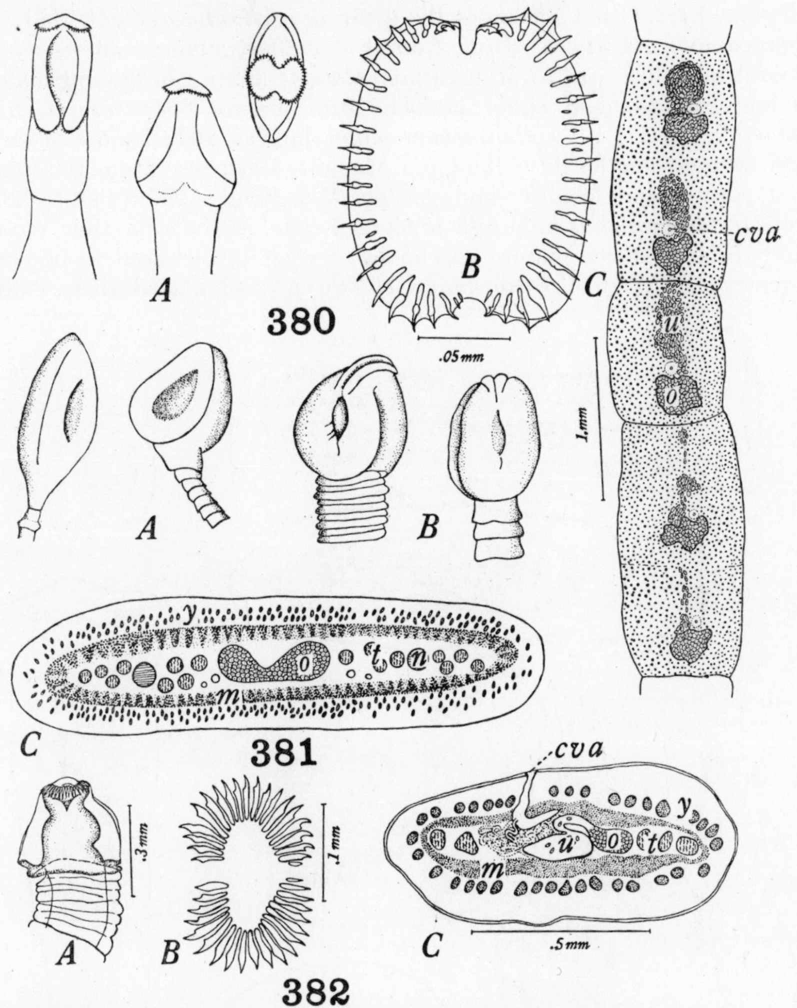

FIG. 380. *Senga besnardi.* After Dollfus, 1934c. A. Holdfast. B. Hooks from holdfast. C. Three segments (12, 13, and 14 externally, corresponding to proglottides 23, 24, 25, 26, and 27 at maturity), dorsal view (*cva,* cirro-vaginal atrium). FIG. 381. *Clestobothrium crassiceps.* After Wardle, 1935a. A. Holdfast, living. B. Holdfast, preserved. C. Cross section of mature segment. FIG. 382. *Polyonchobothrium gordoni.* After Woodland, 1937b. A. Holdfast with contracted crown, the hooks appearing as a continuous circle. B. End-on view of the crown of hooks. C. Cross section through the cirro-vaginal aperture (*cva*). *m,* parenchymal muscle zone; *n,* nerve cord; *o,* ovary; *t,* testes; *u,* uterus; *y,* yolk glands.

The genotype was recorded, as *Tetrabothrium polypteri,* from *Polyp terus bichir,* probably in the Nile Valley. Probable synonyms are: *Onchobothrium septicolle* Diesing, 1854; *Polyonchobothrium septicolle* Diesing, 1863; *Anchistrocephalus polypteri* Monticelli, 1900; *Rhynchobothrium polypteri* Klaptocz, 1906; and *Polyonchobothrium pseudopolypteri*

Meggitt, 1930. Other species of the genus are: *ciliotheca* Wedl, 1861 (as *Tetracampos ciliotheca*) from *Clarias anguillaris*, Nile Valley; *clarias* Woodland, 1925 (as *Clestobothrium clarias*) from *Clarias anguillaris*, Sudan; *cylindraceum major* Janicki, 1926 (Figure 384) from *Clarias anguillaris* in Egypt; *cylindraceum minor* Janicki, 1926 from this same host species and locality; *fulgidum* Meggitt, 1930, also from this same host species and locality; and *gordoni* Woodland, 1937 (Figure 382) from *Heterobranchus bidorsalis* in Sierra Leone. At the same time Woodland recorded three mature specimens of what he believed to be a rediscovery of Wedl's "*Tetracampos ciliotheca*" and placed them within

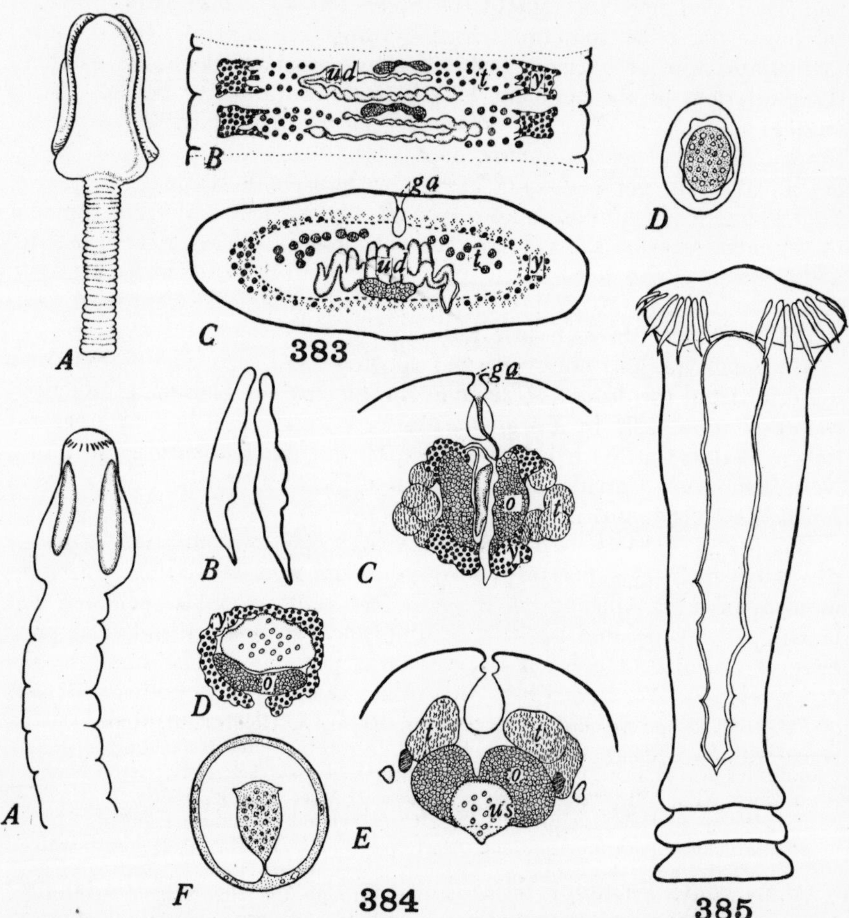

FIG. 383. *Ptychobothrium belones*. After Janicki, 1926. A. Holdfast. B. Immature segment. C. Cross section of an immature segment. D. Intrauterine egg. FIG. 384. *Polyonchobothrium cylindraceum*. After Janicki, 1926. A. Holdfast. B. Hooks from holdfast. C. Genitalia in cross section of a segment. D. Female genitalia in surficial view. E. Female genitalia in cross section with yolk glands omitted. F. Ripe egg in uterus. FIG. 385. *Polyonchobothrium polypteri*, holdfast. After Janicki, 1926. *ga*, genital aperture; *o*, ovary; *t*, testes; *ud*, uterine duct; *us*, uterine sac; *y*, yolk glands.

Polyonchobothrium as the species *ciliotheca*. He recorded also, but did not name, a second form of *Polyonchobothrium* from *Heterobranchus anguillaris*.

Clestobothrium Rudolphi, 1808

With the holdfast almost spherical, the bothria capacious with lips fused except for a small aperture at the anterior end; with the two bothrial apertures connected across the apex of the holdfast by a saddle-like groove. Body with margins serrated. Neck not visible. Segmentation apparently beginning behind the posterior borders of the bothria. Segmentation complete throughout the body, the segments in the posterior region of the body sometimes having transverse furrows, the so-called "articulatio spuriae." Cirro-vaginal aperture median, dorsal, one-half to three-quarters of the segment length from the anterior border. Cirro-vaginal aperture forming the outlet of a short cirro-vaginal canal (sometimes called the *hermaphrodite duct*). Testes medullary, in two lateral fields, 40 to 50 per segment. Vagina with a small seminal receptacle. Yolk glands cortical, continuous around the segment and from segment to segment. Uterine sac voluminous, elliptical. Uterine aperture median and ventral, closed until the uterine sac is greatly distended with eggs. Eggs ovoid, 75 by 40 μ, thin-shelled, without opercula. Genotype, *crassiceps* Rudolphi, 1808 (Figure 381).

The genotype and only recorded species, *crassiceps*, was founded on material from the hake (*Merluccius merluccius*) at Naples. It has been recorded repeatedly by European observers, was described in great detail by Cooper (1918) from material in *Merluccius bilinearis* at St. Johns, New Brunswick, Canada, and briefly described by Wardle (1935a) from *Merluccius productus* in British Columbia.

Woodland (1935c) recorded and described but did not name a ptychobothriid from *Plagioscion squamosissima*, a nonsiluroid fish common in the river Amazon off Manaos. The holdfast of his specimen was lacking, or represented perhaps by the tapering anterior end. The presence or absence of operculated eggs was not noted. The small saclike uterus suggested a bothriocephalid rather than a ptychobothriid. It was of interest in being the first ptychobothriid *or* bothriocephalid to be recorded from South America.

Family Bothriocephalidae E. Blanchard, 1849, emended

DESCRIPTION

Of the order Pseudophyllidea. Small to large forms with the holdfast elongated, somewhat rectangular, sometimes conical. Marginal surfaces truncatedly oval, surficial surfaces typically rectangular. Bothria elongatedly oval, tending to be deep and narrow in relaxed material, wide and shallow in contracted material. Apex of the holdfast flattened, bilobed, and disklike, indented on each surficial edge, the two indentations being connected by a furrow. Neck lacking. Body segmented throughout, the segments craspedote, the anterior ones wider than long, the middle ones square, the posterior ones rectangular, subdivided into secondary segments each equivalent to two proglottides. Each surficial surface with a median furrow. Marginal grooves indistinct. Cirro-vaginal aperture surficial, median, dorsal. Testes in two lateral zones, medullary, continuous from segment to segment. Ovary and ootype median. Vagina without seminal receptacle. Yolk glands cortical, continuous from segment to segment. Uterus with a winding uterine duct and a capacious, roughly spherical uterine sac opening on the surficial surface opposite to that which bears the genital aperture. Eggs provided with opercula. Adult worms in teleostean fishes. Type genus, *Bothriocephalus* Rudolphi, 1805, emended Lühe, 1899.

HISTORY

As established by E. Blanchard (1849), the group was almost equivalent to the modern order Pseudophyllidea, and this viewpoint persisted for fifty years. Later students of dibothriate tapeworms removed from Blanchard's Bothriocephalidae those forms with marginal genital apertures (Triaenophoridae, Amphicotylidae), those with the genital apertures surficial but close to the margin (Echinophallidae), and those in which the genital and uterine apertures were on the same surface (Dibothriocephalidae). Finally, as mentioned earlier, we have removed those forms which, while having the genital aperture and uterine aperture on opposite surfaces, differ from true Bothriocephalidae in having eggs without opercula (Ptychobothriidae). Bothriocephalidae will be regarded here, therefore, as Pseudophyllidea in which the genital aperture and the uterine aperture open medianly on opposite surfaces of the segment, and whose eggs have opercula. Five genera will be recognized.

KEY TO GENERA

1. Holdfast armed with hooks and markedly compressed .... *Onchodiscus*
   Holdfast unarmed and not markedly compressed 2
2. Holdfast with a bilobed apical disk; cirro-vaginal aperture median 3
   Holdfast without apical disk; cirro-vaginal aperture between middle line and margin of segment 4
3. Yolk glands cortical in position .... *Bothriocephalus*
   Yolk glands medullary in position .... *Taprobothrium*
4. Holdfast bluntly conical; yolk glands cortical ...... *Parabothriocephaloides*
   Holdfast apex rectangular; yolk glands medullary .... *Parabothriocephalus*

NOTES ON GENERA

Onchodiscus Yamaguti, 1934

With the holdfast strongly compressed and its apex disklike, armed with minute hooks along the margin. Bothrial lips much crenulated. Segmentation of the body complete. Neck lacking. Segments broader than long, bell-shaped, with a median indentation on the posterior border. Inner longitudinal muscle zone well developed. Two main osmoregulatory canals in the submedian region of the medulla. Testes in the lateral regions of the medulla. Cirrus pouch not very thick-walled; studded with strong muscle fibers. No prostatic cells. Cirrus protrusible, opening directly behind the vagina by a prominent genital cloaca in the mid-dorsal line, behind the center of the segment. Vagina greatly enlarged and muscular in its distal region. Ovary compact, lobulated, near the posterior border of the segment. No seminal receptacle. Uterine duct coiling forward in the median field. Uterine sac opening ventrally in the middle line by a longitudinally elongated aperture at about the center of the segment, sometimes enormously expanded and encroaching upon the ovary of the segment in front. Yolk glands very numerous, entirely cortical. Eggs thin-shelled, operculated, with unsegmented embryos when laid. Adult worms in marine fishes. Genotype and only known species, *sauridae* Yamaguti, 1934 (Figure 395), established for material from *Saurida argyrophanes* in Japanese waters.

Bothriocephalus Rudolphi, 1808, emended Lühe, 1899

With the holdfast elongated, somewhat depressed, with a bilobed apical disk whose bothrial edges are indented, the two indentations being connected by a groove. Marginal surfaces of the holdfast truncatedly oval, slightly concave. Surficial surfaces of the holdfast rectangular, each with an elongated bothrium wider anteriorly than posteriorly, narrow and deep when relaxed, wide and shallow when contracted. Neck lacking. Segmentation of the body complete, craspedote, anapolytic. Anterior segments funnel-like, median ones square, posterior ones rectangular, subdivided commonly into four secondary segments each representing two proglottides. Testes medullary, in lateral zones. Yolk glands continuous from segment to segment, as are the testes. Seminal receptacle lacking. Other features as for the family. Eggs thin-shelled, operculated, not embryonated when laid. Genotype, *scorpii* Mueller, 1776 (Figure 386).

This genus was formerly a convenient receptacle for unassigned pseudophyllidean forms, no fewer than 200 species having been at various times relegated to it. The genotype, *scorpii*, was established for material from *Cottus scorpio* in Danish waters and has been recorded by many later writers (see Hilmy, 1929). The species of *Bothriocephalus* are most difficult to distinguish from one another, and the brief descriptions given below of the North American forms should be supplemented by reference to the more detailed descriptions given by the authorities mentioned.

1. *claviceps* Goeze, 1782. Up to 540 mm. long by 2 to 3 mm. broad; holdfast small, elongated when relaxed, spherical when contracted, with the apical disk prominent; cirro-vaginal atrium funnel-like and central; testes spherical or subspherical, 58 by 64 μ, 50 to 60 per segment; sperm duct in loose coils close to the cirrus pouch; cirrus pouch ellipsoidal, 127 to 145 μ by 81 to 104 μ, thin-walled; ovary compact, about half a millimeter wide; yolk glands not in lateral zones, 450 to 720 in number; uterine duct voluminous; uterine sac transversely elongated, occupying one-third or more of the segment width, the apertures of the successive sacs forming a zigzag ventral row on the body surface; eggs 58 to 63 μ by 37 to 40 μ, *without* opercula (*sic*); species established for material from the common eel (*Anguilla vulgaris*) in Europe; recorded in eastern

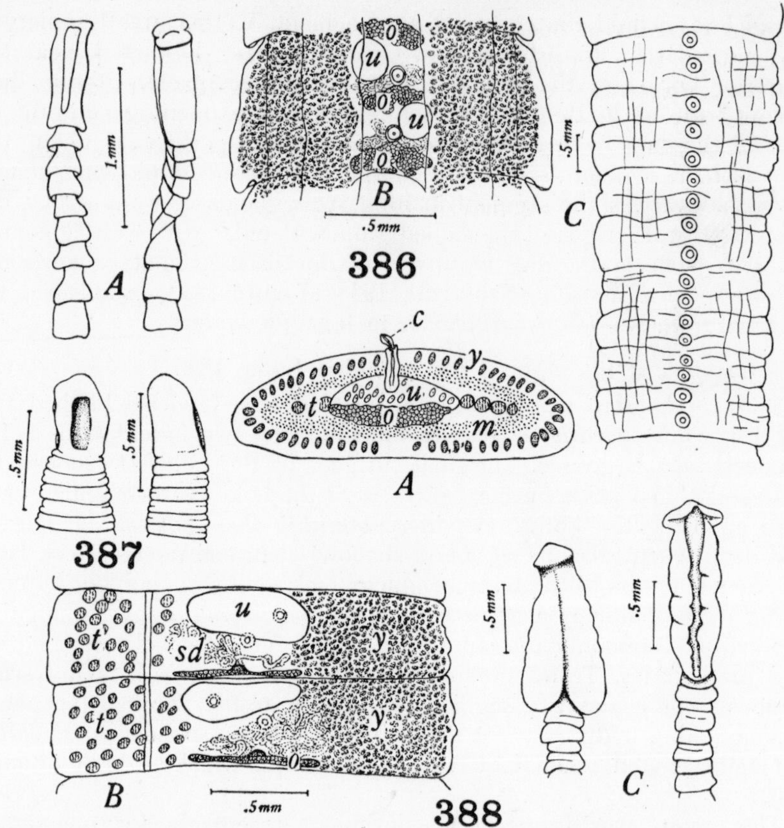

FIG. 386. *Bothriocephalus scorpii.* A. Holdfast. After Wardle, 1932a. B. Two consecutive segments. C. Outline of mature segments. Both after Cooper, 1918. FIG. 387. *Bothriocephalus claviceps,* holdfast. After Cooper, 1918. FIG. 388. *Bothriocephalus cuspidatus.* A. Cross section (diagrammatic) of mature segment. After Wardle, 1932b. B. Two mature segments. C. Holdfast. Both after Cooper, 1918. *c,* cirrus; *m,* longitudinal muscles; *o,* ovary; *sd,* sperm duct; *t,* testes; *u,* uterus; *y,* yolk glands.

North America by Cooper (1918) from *Anguilla rostrata, Eupomotis gibbosus, Gasterosteus bispinosus.*

2. *cuspidatus* Cooper, 1917. Rarely exceeding 150 mm. in length; holdfast rectangular, about one millimeter long by one-third of a millimeter wide; apical disk bilobed; apex bluntly rounded; genital apertures in the first third of the segment surface; cirrus pouch about one-half of the dorso-ventral thickness of the segment; cirrus conspicuous, commonly protruding; testes large, 60 to 70 μ in diameter, about 50 per segment, in two groups on each side separated by the lateral nerve trunk; sperm duct strongly coiled with invaginated cirrus straight; ovary irregular in shape, about one-quarter of the segment width; yolk glands large, ovoid, 90 to 100 μ in longest diameter, cortical in position, with mid-dorsal and mid-ventral gaps of one-third to one-fifth of the segment width but con-

tinuous ventrally at one point by a single row of follicles; intrauterine eggs 40 to 50 μ long; adult worms common in caeca of *Stizostedion vitreum, Stizostedion canadense, Amphiodon alosoides, Hiodon tergisus,* occasionally in *Esox lucius, Perca flavescens,* and sometimes, though rarely, in species of *Leucichthys*; recorded from all across Canada and the northern United States; refs. Cooper (1917, 1918), Wardle (1932b) (Figure 388). Life cycle described by Essex (1928a) (Figure 389).

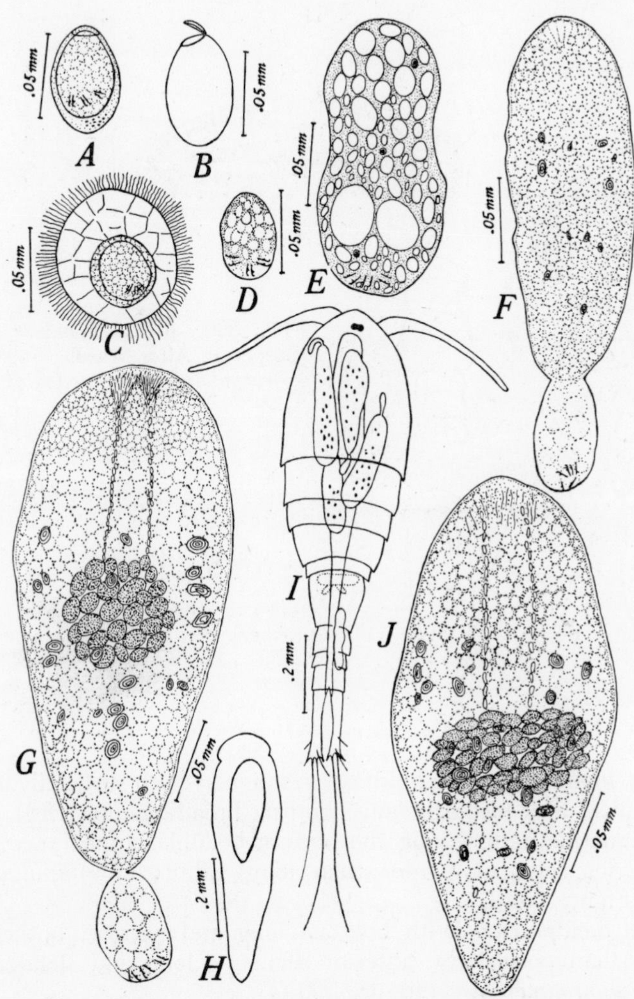

FIG. 389. *Bothriocephalus cuspidatus,* life cycle. After Essex, 1928a. A. Mature egg. B. Shell with operculum attached, after escape of the oncosphere. C. Coracidium. D. Procercoid 15 hours after exposure of *Cyclops* to coracidia. E. Procercoid about 30 days old. F. Procercoid at 7 days. G. Procercoid at 9 days. H. Plerocercoid from gut of *Stizostedion vitreum.* I. *Cyclops brevispinosus* 9 days after exposure to coracidia. J. Procercoid at 10–11 days.

With three subspecies:

(A) *s.s. cuspidatus*. With the holdfast subrectangular surficially, somewhat triangular marginally; apical disk conspicuous, well separated from the holdfast; bothria wide, deep, with lips irregular, sometimes wavy; first segments subtriangular, twice as long as broad, showing early subdivision into two secondary segments; middle segments subquadrate; posterior segments rectangular; adults in *Stizostedion* (Figure 390 A).

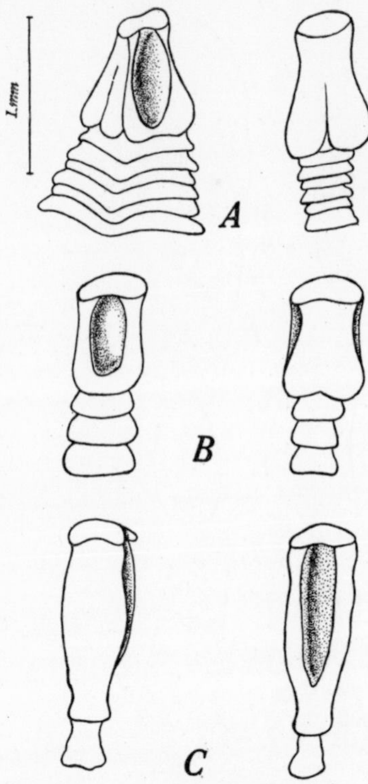

FIG. 390. *Bothriocephalus cuspidatus* subspecies. After Wardle, 1932b. A. *s.s. cuspidatus*. B. *s.s. hiodontos*. C. *s.s. luciopercae*.

(B) *s.s. hiodontos*. With holdfast rectangular both surficially and marginally; apical disk inconspicuous; bothria broad, shallow; first 15 to 20 segments subquadrate, giving the body a beadlike appearance; median and posterior segments wider than long; adults in *Amphiodon* and *Hiodon* (Figure 390 B).

(C) *s.s. luciopercae*. With holdfast long and narrow; bothria wider anteriorly than posteriorly; anterior segments long and slender; adults in *Stizostedion canadense* (Figure 390 C).

3. *formosus* Mueller and Van Cleave, 1932. Up to 30 mm. long by 1.3 mm. wide; holdfast club-shaped to cylindrical; apical disk lacking; holdfast 320 to 475 μ long by 130 to 230 μ wide; bothria long, wide, shallow, very weak and indistinctly delimited; first segments almost as wide as the holdfast; most of the primary segments showing one or more transverse divisions, but distinct partitions completely separating the second-

ary products of strobilation are frequently lacking, even in segments bearing mature eggs; segments variable in shape and size, commonly two to three times as broad as long; testes 30 to 45 per segment; yolk glands numerous, occupying the whole cortex; eggs 53 to 59 μ by 33 to 35 μ; adult worms in trout perch (*Percopsis omisco-maycus*), New York State. The form is readily distinguishable from *cuspidatus* in the opinion of its authors by the smaller size and the lack of apical disk; similar characteristics separate it from *claviceps*. Other North American bothriocephalids, except *rarus*, are marine.

4. *manubriformis* Linton, 1889 (=*laciniatum* Linton, 1898; *histiophorus* Shipley, 1909). Up to 220 mm. long by 5 mm. broad; holdfast 2 to 3.5 mm. long with a prominent apical disk, deeply notched on each margin and well marked off from the holdfast; bothria long and narrow; first segments wedgelike, with salient posterior borders which are distinctly emarginate; middle segments broadly wedge-shaped, less emarginate; posterior segments many times broader than long; cirro-vaginal atrium central or slightly to one side of center; testes 60 to 70 per segment; cirrus pouch long, cylindrical, with thick walls and cirrus usually withdrawn; vaginal aperture with bulbous sphincter; ovary irregularly branched; yolk glands very numerous; uterine duct voluminous; uterine sacs alternating irregularly, their apertures appearing as a double row, 1 mm. apart, along the ventral surface; eggs 58 by 34 μ; established as *Dibothrium manubriforme* from *Tetrapterus albidus*, Massachusetts; recorded also from *Histiophorus gladius, Tarpon atlanticus*, also from American waters. Recorded, as *Bothriocephalus histiophorus*, by Shipley (1901) from unidentified species of swordfish (*Histiophorus*) in Pacific waters. Ref. Cooper (1918), who re-examined and redescribed Linton's material in great detail (Figure 391).

5. *occidentalis* Linton, 1898. Up to 234 mm. long by 5 mm. broad; holdfast small, less than one and one-half millimeters long, club-shaped, constricted posteriorly, with conspicuous apical disk with rounded apex; bothria wide and shallow or narrow and deep according to the state of contraction of the worm; segment margins frilled or plicated in the posterior half of the body due to the great antero-posterior shortening of the median region of each segment; genital apertures consequently often hidden by the overlap of foreshortened segments; testes fewer than 100 per segment, in a single horizontal layer in the medulla; cirro-vaginal atrium short, tubular; ovary one-tenth of the segment width; vagina without bulbous sphincter muscle; yolk glands numerous, large, two-layered, surrounding the segment except for free mid-dorsal and mid-ventral gaps one-tenth of the segment wide; each yolk gland ovoid with its long axis dorso-ventral; ripe uterus (duct plus sac) forming a pear-shaped mass bulging through the longitudinal muscle layer, one-third of the segment width; the duct indistinguishable from the sac; uterine aperture just behind the anterior border of the segment, overlapped by the preceding segment; eggs with their longest diameters 60 to 70 μ; adult worm established as *Dibothrium occidentalis* from *Sebastodes sp.* (rock cod) in North American Pacific waters; rediscovered by Wardle

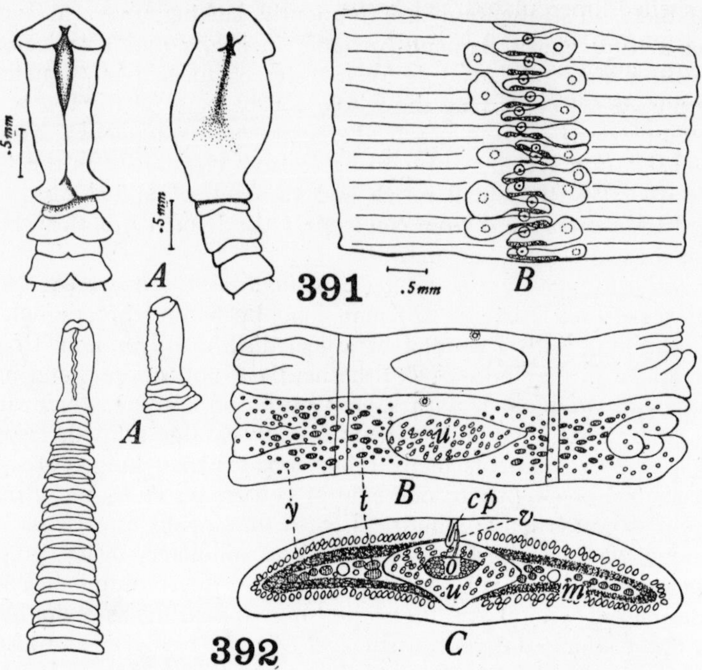

FIG. 391. *Bothriocephalus manubriformis.* After Cooper, 1918. A. Holdfast. B. Mature segments. FIG. 392. *Bothriocephalus occidentalis.* After Wardle, 1932a. A. Holdfast. B. Mature segments. C. Cross section of same. *cp*, cirrus pouch; *m*, longitudinal muscles; *o*, ovary; *t*, testes; *u*, uterus; *v*, vagina; *y*, yolk glands.

(1932a) in *Leptocottus armatus* and *Sebastodes sp.* (uncommon) in British Columbian waters; refs. Cooper (1918), Wardle (1932a).

Wardle's material agreed more closely with the Atlantic *manubriformis* than with *occidentalis* as described by Linton. Nevertheless, in view of the coincidence of hosts and locality between his material and *occidentalis* of Linton, it is fair to assume that the latter species was concerned. Possibly there exists a group of "manubriform species" of *Bothriocephalus* comprising *manubriformis, plicatus* Rudolphi, 1819, *histiophorus* Shipley, 1901, and *occidentalis*, all large cestodes characterized by having a club-shaped holdfast, a broad, frilled body, and a ripe uterine sac at least one-third of the segment width (Figure 392).

6. *rarus* Thomas, 1937. Small, delicate forms, 67 to 300 mm. long; holdfast 740 to 912 μ long, by 270 to 378 μ broad in the mid-region; neck lacking; holdfast with or without prominent apical disk according to the state of contraction; bothria shallow; segmentation beginning immediately behind the holdfast but sometimes not complete throughout the body; 60 to 250 segments at maturity; genital apertures nearly median; ovary compact, bilobed; uterine sac ventral, frequently globoidal; uterine duct median in corkscrew spirals; cirrus pouch dorsal, 10.8 by 184.4 μ long; cirrus vestigial; testes 34 to 62; yolk glands 210 to 250; eggs

thick-shelled, operculated, not embryonated when laid, 41 to 56 μ by 59 to 65 μ; procercoid larva in *Cyclops* species; plerocercoid larva in the gut of newts; adult worm also in the gut of newts (*Triturus viridescens*, vermilion spotted newt), Michigan; refs. Thomas (1937a, 1937b) (Figure 393).

7. *scorpii* Mueller, 1776. Up to 950 mm. long by 6 mm. broad; holdfast large, with prominent apical disk; bothria long, narrow; first segments wedgelike; cirro-vaginal apertures at the bottom of a longitudinal

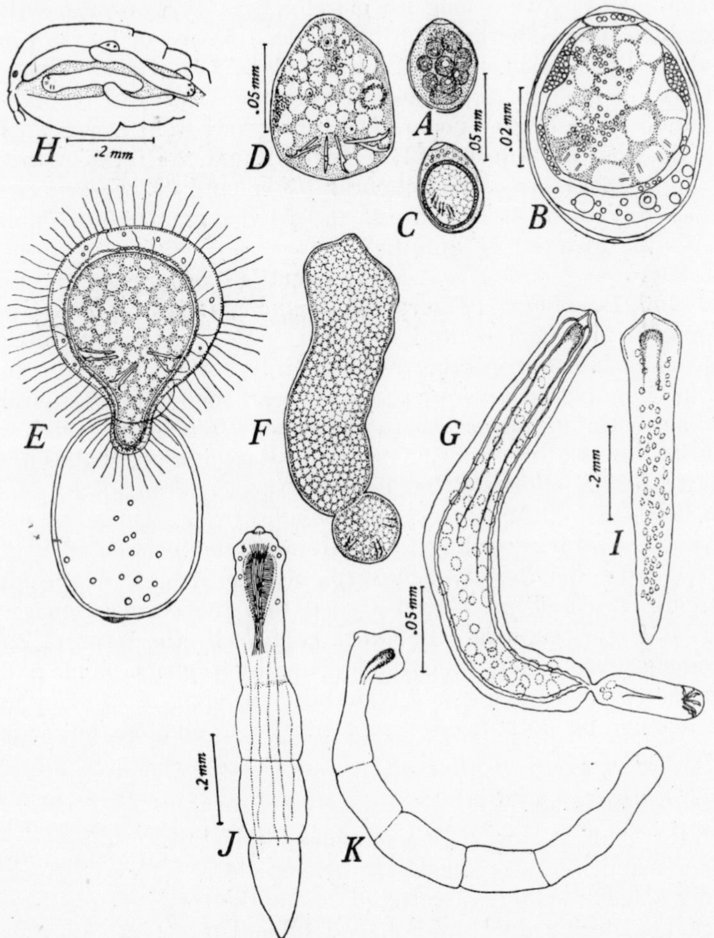

FIG. 393. *Bothriocephalus rarus*. After Thomas, 1937a. A. Egg shortly after being laid. B. Hooklets beginning to show on the oncosphere after 2 days' embryonic development. C. Embryo after 3 days at 75° F. D. Liberated oncosphere. E. Coracidium escaping from egg shell. F. Procercoid. G. Procercoid from the body cavity of *Cyclops vulgaris*. H. Procercoids in *Cyclops* after 7 days. I. Young tapeworm from a larval newt (experimental). J. Same as observed in natural infection. K. Young tapeworm attached to gut wall of host.

median furrow of the dorsal surface, each aperture on a low papilla; testes 30 to 60 per segment; cirrus sac at right angles to the dorsal surface, extending briefly into the medulla; ovary compact; yolk glands in two lateral weakly united zones; uterine duct voluminous; uterine sac spherical to flattened, one-sixth of the segment width, alternating irregularly from side to side; eggs 66 to 80 μ by 43 to 45 μ; adult worm established, as *Taenia scorpii* (= *Vermis multiembris rhombi* of Leeuwenhoek, 1722; *Bothriocephalus punctatus* Rudolphi, 1810; *Dibothrium punctatus* Diesing, 1850; *Bothriocephalus bipunctatus* Lühe, 1899a).

Cooper (1918) gave a long list of references by European writers to this common form. The first North American record of it was probably that of Leidy (1855) from "Platessa plana" (= *Pseudopleuronectes americanus* of modern terminology). For other American records reference should be made to Cooper. The first record from American Pacific waters was that of Wardle (1932a), who found the form in the shore fishes *Leptocottus armatus, Enophrys bison,* and *Hexagrammos decagrammus* of Vancouver Island, and indicated certain minor differences from Atlantic material (Figure 386).

In fishes from Japanese waters, Yamaguti (1934) recorded four species of *Bothriocephalus* (Figure 394): *japonicus* in *Anguilla japonica*; *scheilognathi* in *Scheilognathus rhombea*, with a holdfast recalling that of *Clestobothrium* but in other respects truly bothriocephalid; *opsalichthydis* in *Opsalichthys uncirostris*, with a heart-shaped holdfast and deep trenchlike bothria; and *sciaenae* in *Sciaena schlegeli*, which recalls *manubriformis*. All these specific names for the bothriocephalids are new.

Guiart (1935b) added to the genus the species *hirondellei* from *Syngnathus pelagicus* off the Azores; *tintinnabulus* from *Syngnathus phlegon*, off Monaco, a form according to Guiart with *nonoperculated* eggs; and *breviceps* from *Synaphrobranchus sp.* off the Azores, a species that seems close to *claviceps*. Guiart argued that the correct generic term should be "Bothriocephala," the Greek *kephala* by the Laws of Zoological Nomenclature being translatable only by *cephala*. Such a drastic change, however, involving as it would the changing of so many generic names, cannot be authorized except by the Committee on Zoological Nomenclature.

Taprobothrium Lühe, 1899

With the holdfast long, with a prominent apical disk. Bothria typically bothriocephalid. Body segmentation incomplete at intervals. Neck lacking. Yolk glands medullary, scattered among the testes. Seminal receptacle lacking. Uterine duct an S-shaped tube. Uterine sac varying with the extent of egg distension, opening to right or left of the middle line and approximately central. Cirro-vaginal aperture dorsal and central. Eggs distinctly operculated. Genotype and only known species, *japonensis* Lühe, 1899. The genotype was established for material from *Muraenesox cinereus* in Japanese waters; further descriptive details have been published by Yamaguti (1934) based upon material from this same host species (Figure 396).

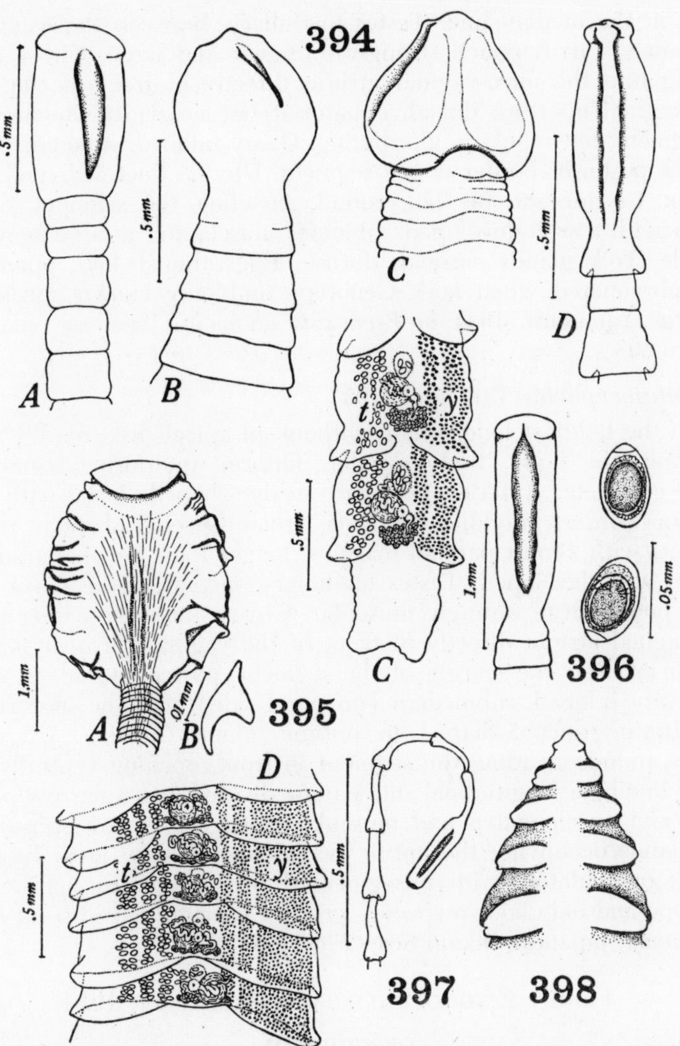

FIG. 394. Holdfasts of Japanese species of *Bothriocephalus*. After Yamaguti, 1934. A. *japonicus*. B. *scheilognathi*. C. *opsalichthydis*. D. *sciaenae*. FIG. 395. *Onchodiscus sauridae*. After Yamaguti, 1934. A. Holdfast. B. Marginal hook from terminal disk. C. End proglottides, dorsal view. D. Gravid segments. *t*, testes; *y*, yolk glands. FIG. 396. *Taprobothrium japonensis*, holdfast and eggs. After Yamaguti, 1934. FIG. 397. *Parabothriocephalus gracilis*, anterior region. After Yamaguti, 1934. FIG. 398. *Parabothriocephaloides segmentatus*, pseudo-holdfast. After Yamaguti, 1934.

Parabothriocephaloides Yamaguti, 1934

With the holdfast represented by a pseudo-holdfast, cone-shaped, with surficial depressions. Neck lacking. Body pointed at each end, broadest near the anterior end, with prominent posterior borders to the segments except in the median line. Testes medullary, between the osmoregulatory canals. Cirrus pouch strongly muscular and large. Cirrus spinose, opening into the cirro-vaginal atrium directly in front of the vagina. Cirro-vaginal aperture dorsal, equatorial but nearer to one margin of the segment, not regularly alternating. Ovary bilobed, submedian, poral, near the posterior border of the segment. Uterine duct S-shaped, almost median. Uterine sac median, round, invading the segment in front. Vagina with a well-developed sphincter muscle and a large seminal receptacle. Yolk glands cortical, diffuse. Eggs thin-shelled, operculated, not embryonated when laid. Genotype and only known species, *segmentatus* Yamaguti, 1934 in *Psenopsis anomala*, Japanese Inland Sea (Figure 398).

Parabothriocephalus Yamaguti, 1934

With the holdfast long, small, without an apical disk, readily detachable from the body. Body slender, filiform anteriorly. Segmentation almost complete. Anterior segments wedge-shaped, long, with salient posterior borders; middle segments broadly wedge-shaped; posterior segments with almost parallel margins, longer than broad. Parenchymal muscles well developed. Testes medullary, medial to the nerve trunks. Cirrus pouch large, strongly muscular. Cirrus spinose, opening into the cirro-vaginal atrium directly in front of the vagina. Cirro-vaginal aperture dorsal, near the margin of the segment, postequatorial, to right or left. Ovary bilobed, submedian (on poral side) near the posterior border. Uterine duct S-shaped in outline, almost median. Uterine sac median, round, invading the segment in front, opening ventrally in the middle line by a longitudinal slit. Vagina divided into a narrow proximal region and an elongated and muscular distal sac with a spinose base. Yolk glands occupying the entire available medullary area. Eggs thin-shelled, operculated, with unsegmented ova. Adults in marine fishes. Genotype and only known species, *gracilis* Yamaguti, 1934 from *Psenopsis anomala*, Japanese Inland Sea (Figure 397).

Family Echinophallidae Schumacher, 1914

DESCRIPTION

Of the order Pseudophyllidea. Short, fleshy forms with the margins of the body hypertrophied. Holdfast of young forms long, truncated apically, broadened posteriorly. With an inconspicuous apical disk and shallow, oval bothria. Mature forms with an approximately trapezoidal pseudo-holdfast with surficial depressions. Posterior borders of the first few segments projecting dorsally and ventrally as lobelike appendages which tend to broaden posteriorly into a collar. Farther back, the posterior segment borders divided dorsally and ventrally into tongue-shaped lappets, broader and shorter on the ventral side than on the dorsal side. Cirro-vaginal aperture dorsal, close to the margin. Testes medullary, medial to the ovary, mainly in the posterior half of the segment. Cirrus pouch large, muscular. Cirrus large, protrusible, conspicuously armed at its base with strong spines. Ovary strongly lobed, near the posterior border of the segment. Uterine duct strongly coiled medially to the cirrus pouch, leading into a uterine sac lying closer to the median line, weakly muscular; opening ventrally between the bundles of the inner longitudinal muscles, near the anterior border of the segment. Yolk glands numerous, filling almost the entire cortical parenchyma. Eggs elliptical, thin-shelled, operculated, with unsegmented ova. Type genus, *Echinophallus* Schumacher, 1914; other genus, *Atelemerus* Guiart, 1935.

Echinophallus Schumacher, 1914

With the characters of the family. Genotype, *wageneri* Monticelli, 1890. Three species recognized: *wageneri* Monticelli, 1890, and *settii* Ariola, 1895, both from the marine fish *Centrolophus pompilius*; and *japonicus* Yamaguti, 1934 from *Psenopsis anomala* in Japanese waters (Figure 399).

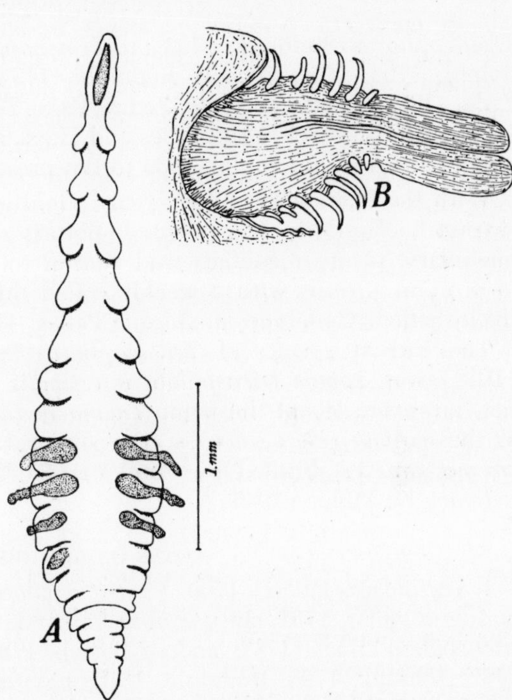

FIG. 399. *Echinophallus japonicus*. After Yamaguti, 1934. A. Young form with primary holdfast, ventral view. B. Extruded and armed cirrus.

Atelemerus Guiart, 1935

With a pseudo-holdfast shaped like a funnel and recalling that of *Cyathocephalus*, and with the body incompletely segmented. Two sets of reproductive organs per segment. Genital apertures dorsal and close to the segment margins. Uterine apertures ventral and anterior to the genital apertures. Cirrus spinose. Eggs without opercula (*sic*). Genotype and only known species, *acanthodes* from *Centrolophus pompilius* off the Azores.

Family Triaenophoridae Loennberg, 1889, emended (= Triaenophorinae Lühe, 1899)

DESCRIPTION

Of the order Pseudophyllidea. Medium-sized forms with the holdfast stout, subcuboidal or subpyramidal, with a broadly domed apex armed or not with hooks. Neck lacking. Genital apertures marginal, alternating irregularly from margin to margin of successive segments. Seminal receptacle small. One set of reproductive organs per segment. Uterus a much-coiled tube, enlarging only slightly as a uterine sac before opening surficially on the ventral surface of the segment in front of the level of the genital aperture. Eggs with opercula, liberating eventually a ciliated embryo. Type genus, *Triaenophorus* Rudolphi, 1793. Other genera, *Fistulicola* Lühe, 1899; *Anchistrocephalus* Monticelli, 1890; *Anonchocephalus* Lühe, 1902.

NOTES ON GENERA

Triaenophorus Rudolphi, 1793 (= *Triaenophorus vel Tricuspidaria* Rudolphi, 1793; *Tricuspidaria* Rudolphi, 1793; *Rhytelminthus, ex parte,* Zeder, 1800; *Rhytis, ex parte,* Zeder, 1803; *Tricuspidaria* Rudolphi, 1802, 1809, 1810; Lamarck, 1816; Stiles and Hassall, 1902; *Triaenophorus* of all other writers from Creplin, 1839 to the present day)

With the characters of the family. Holdfast armed with four trident-shaped hooks. Body unsegmented. Bothria circular and shallow. Testes medullary. Ovary medullary and ventral to the testes, somewhat poral in position. Uterus with a weakly coiled duct and a uterine sac. Eggs thick-shelled. Genotype, *nodulosus* Pallas, 1760.

The earliest species of *Triaenophorus* listed by Stiles and Hassall (1912) was *Taenia tricuspidata intestinalis* Bloch, 1779. Most authorities, however, accept the name *Taenia nodulosa* used by Pallas (1760) as the earliest reference to a triaenophorid species. A second species, *crassus,* was established by Forel (1868), and a third species, *stizostedionis,* by Miller (1945c).

NOTES ON SPECIES

1. *nodulosus* Pallas, 1760 (= *tricuspidata intestinalis* Bloch, 1779; *nodulosa* Pallas, 1781, not *nodulosa* Lamarck, 1816; *tricuspis* Pallas, 1781; *tricuspidata* Bloch, 1782; *nodosa* Batsch, 1786; Knoch, 1862, not Bloch, 1782; Schrank, 1798; Rudolphi, 1810; *piscium* Rudolphi, 1802; *tricuspis* Lamarck, 1819; *nodosus* Dujardin, 1845; *nodulus* Sramek, 1901; *tricuspidatus morpha microdentatus* Wardle, 1932b). Worms 100 to 300 mm. long (European material), 70 to 270 mm. long (Canadian material); holdfast (Figure 400 C) small, narrow, with the apical disk usually inconspicuous and the bothria shallow and somewhat vaguely outlined; length of holdfast 0.55 to 0.92 mm. (Cooper, 1918), 0.44 to 0.62 mm. (Miller, 1945c); width of apical disk 0.35 to 0.42 mm. (Cooper, 1918), 0.30 to 0.35 mm. (Miller, 1945c); width posteriorly 0.26 to 0.64 mm. (Cooper, 1918), 0.53 to 0.72 mm. (Miller, 1945c); hooks small, with

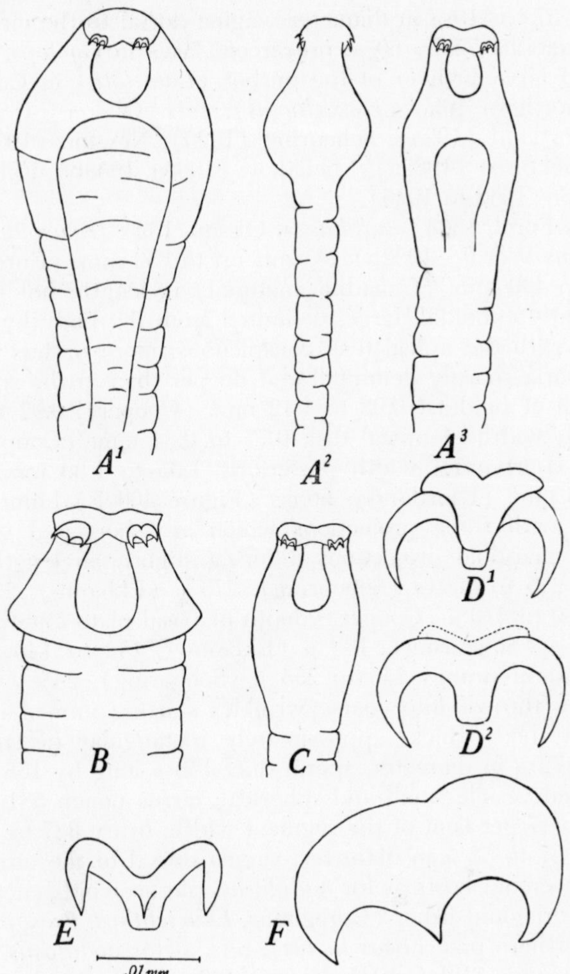

FIG. 400. *Triaenophorus* species. After Miller, 1945c. A¹–A³ and D¹–D². Holdfast and hook of *stizostedionis*. B and F. *crassus*. C and E. *nodulosus*.

shallow and remarkably curved basal plate with four projections (Figure 400 E), the lateral ones slender and deeply curved, the medial ones somewhat shorter; width of the basal plate 90 to 140 μ (Scheuring, 1929), 112 to 140 μ (Miller, 1943a), 130 to 190 μ (Cooper, 1918); depth of the basal plate antero-posteriorly 23 to 45 μ (Scheuring), 20 to 30 μ (Miller); length of the lateral (marginal) prong 45 to 75 μ (Scheuring); holdfast not sharply delimited from the body, the latter continuing as a thin filament for some distance before being thrown into wrinkles; testes 57 to 88 μ in diameter; sperm duct 400 μ long by 282 μ wide; internal seminal vesicle very large and broadly ovoid; cirrus pouch 739 to 968 μ long, 47 to 60 per cent of the segment width; ovary 202 to 238 μ wide;

yolk glands 57 to 110 μ in diameter; vagina dorsal to the cirrus; eggs 61 by 44 μ; coracidia 75 by 60 μ; procercoid larva in *Cyclops, Diaptomus*; plerocercoid larva in liver of the burbot (*Lota lota*) in Canada; adult worm in northern pike (*Esox lucius*); refs. Olsson (1893), Cooper (1918), Hjortland (1928), Scheuring (1929), Newton (1932), Wardle (1932b), Nicholson (1932a), Michajlow (1933a, 1933b), Ekbaum (1935, 1937), Miller (1943 to 1946).

2. *crassus* Forel, 1868 (= *robustus* Olsson, 1893; *tricuspidatus morpha megadentatus* Wardle, 1932b). Worms up to 650 mm. (European material), 130 to 400 mm. (Canadian material) in length; holdfast (Figure 400 B) bluntly cuboidal, large, delimited from the body by a collarlike thickening, with the apical disk conspicuous, more or less rectangular, and the bothria sharply delimited and deeper than in the species *nodulosus*; length of holdfast 0.98 to 1.12 mm. (Cooper), 0.92 to 1.29 mm. (Hjortland); width of apical disk 0.77 to 0.84 mm. (Cooper), 0.67 to 0.92 mm. (Hjortland); width posteriorly 1.05 to 1.30 mm. (Cooper), 0.92 to 1.38 mm. (Hjortland); hooks (Figure 400 F) blunt, with deep basal plate with three projections which are short and very slightly curved, the marginal projections differing slightly in length; width of basal plate 285 to 300 μ (Scheuring), 275 μ (Ekbaum), 255 to 300 μ (Miller), 280 to 310 μ (Cooper); depth of basal plate antero-posteriorly 125 to 135 μ (Scheuring), 138 μ (Ekbaum), 132 to 140 μ (Miller); length of lateral prongs 240 to 255 μ (Scheuring), 245 μ (Ekbaum); body surface thrown into coarse wrinkles starting immediately behind the holdfast; body thick, approximately rectangular in cross section; testes 64 to 72 μ in diameter; sperm duct 158 μ long by 158 μ wide; internal seminal vesicle small and spherical; cirrus pouch 581 to 739 μ in length, 40 to 47 per cent of the segment width; ovary 387 to 440 μ wide; yolk glands 37 to 53 μ in diameter; vagina dorsal to the cirrus; eggs 61 by 44 μ; procercoid hosts as for *nodulosus*; plerocercoids encysted in the muscles of coregonid fishes (*Coregonus, Leucichthys, Prosopium*); adult worms in northern pike (*Esox lucius*); refs. as for *nodulosus*.

3. *stizostedionis* Miller, 1945. Worms 120 to 380 mm. long by 2 to 4 mm. wide; holdfast broadly oval surficially, with bothria deep and conspicuous, circular, and 422 μ in diameter; apical disk distinct; holdfast dimensions, length 0.53 to 1.14 mm., width of apical disk 0.62 to 0.88 mm., width posteriorly 1.06 to 1.94 mm.; hooks characteristic, each with a narrow, curved basal plate with three prongs; median prong stout and embedded with the basal plate in the tissue of the holdfast; marginal prongs longer, curved, slender, and projecting above the holdfast surface; the fourth projection characteristic of *nodulosus* is lacking; each hook having on its mesial surface a somewhat Y-shaped protuberance (Figure 400 D) difficult to see unless the hook is dissected from the holdfast; hook measurements, width of basal plate 123 to 198 μ, depth antero-posteriorly 22 to 23 μ, lengths of marginal prongs 48 to 77 μ; reproductive organs much as in *crassus*; testes 62 to 114 μ in diameter; sperm duct long, strongly coiled, central, dilated within the cirrus pouch as a large, conspicuous internal seminal vesicle; sperm duct measure-

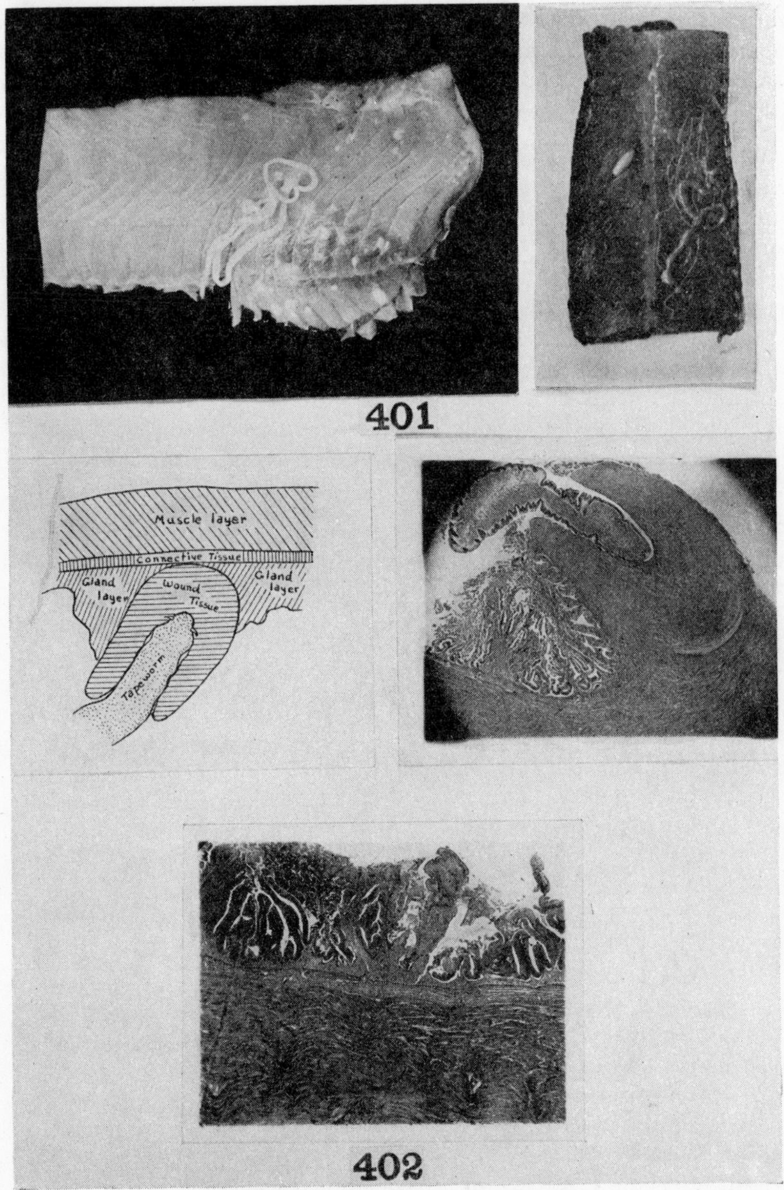

FIG. 401. Larvae of *Triaenophorus crassus in situ* (Wardle). FIG. 402. Attachment of adult *Triaenophorus nodulosus* to the host gut lining. (Photographs by courtesy of R. B. Miller.)

ments 264 μ long by 88 μ wide; cirrus pouch transversely elongated, averaging 616 μ in length, 32 to 37 per cent of the segment width; ovary bilobed, 317 to 387 μ wide; yolk glands numerous, 35 to 53 μ in diameter; vagina dorsal to the cirrus; eggs 56 by 40 μ; procercoids in *Cyclops bicuspidatus*; plerocercoids encysted in trout perch (*Percopsis omiscomaycus*); adult worms in pickerel, walleyed pike (*Stizostedion vitreum*) in Alberta, Canada; ref. Miller (1945c).

Fistulicola Lühe, 1899

With the holdfast arrow-shaped due to the projection of the posterior portions of the bothrial lips; unarmed; sometimes replaced by a pseudoholdfast. Neck lacking. Body segmentation pronounced; segments very short with leaflike marginal expansions. Cirrus pouch and vagina opening independently of one another on one or the other margin. Testes medullary, dorsal, continuous from side to side but not from segment to segment. Sperm duct strongly coiled. Seminal vesicles lacking. Ovary and ootype displaced ventrad or porad by the foreshortening of the segment and the great development of the uterus. Uterus a wide, strongly coiled canal. Eggs thick-shelled, believed to be operculated. Genotype and only known species, *plicatus* Rudolphi, 1819 from the swordfish (*Xiphias gladius*) in European and North American Atlantic waters. Refs. Linton (1901), Cooper (1918) (Figure 403).

Anchistrocephalus Monticelli, 1890 (= *Ancistrocephalus* Lühe, 1899)

With the holdfast compressed, armed with small hooks. No pseudo-

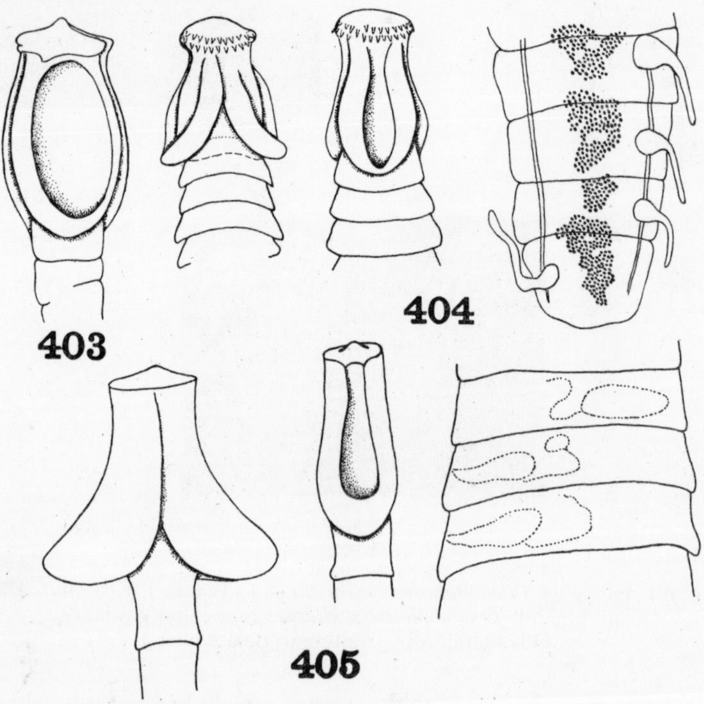

FIG. 403. *Fistulicola plicatus*, holdfast. After Wagener, 1854. FIG. 404. *Anchistrocephalus microcephalus*, holdfast and end segments. After Wagener, 1854. FIG. 405. *Anonchocephalus chilensis*, holdfast and segments. After Riggenbach, 1895b.

holdfast. Body smooth, ribbonlike, segmented, with the segments linear. Longitudinal nerve trunks central to the cirrus pouch and vagina and relatively distant from the segment margins. Cirro-vaginal apertures marginal. Testes completely internal to the nerve trunks, in two lateral zones which unite in the posterior region of the segment and approximate ventrad. Yolk glands medullary in two lateral zones, each to the outer side of a nerve trunk; a further layer of yolk glands present in the dorsal region of the cortex. Ovary depressed, lobulated, median or somewhat porad. Uterus a long, strongly coiled, relatively narrow canal, with its terminal portion enlarged somewhat and opening ventrally nearer to one margin, but not necessarily the poral margin. Eggs unknown. Genotype and only known species, *microcephalus* Rudolphi, 1819 (Figure 404).

The genotype was established, as *Bothriocephalus microcephalus*, for a form from the sunfish (*Orthagoriscus mola*) at Naples. Monticelli (1890a), in his analysis of Rudolphi's *Bothriocephalus*, established for the species the generic term *Anchistrocephalus*, which Lühe (1899a) erroneously transcribed as *Ancistrocephalus* and identified as triaenophorid. It has not to our knowledge been rediscovered or redescribed.

Anonchocephalus Lühe, 1902

With the holdfast unarmed, arrow-shaped. No pseudo-holdfast. Neck lacking. Body weak, ribbonlike, distinctly segmented with the segments mostly linear. Longitudinal nerve trunks ventral to the cirrus pouch and vagina and relatively distant from the segment margins. Testes in two lateral zones which unite posteriorly. Yolk glands also medullary, forming a layer ventral to the testes. Ovary poral. Uterus a long and strongly sinuate, relatively narrow canal, its terminal region enlarged and muscular, its aperture close to the middle line of the ventral surface of the segment. Eggs not clearly known. Genotype and only known species, *chilensis* Riggenbach, 1896 from *Genypterus chilensis*, Chile (Figure 405).

Family Amphicotylidae Nybelin, 1922, emended Beaver and Simer, 1940

DESCRIPTION

Of the order Pseudophyllidea. Small to medium-sized forms with the holdfast always unarmed, sometimes replaced by a holdfast deformatus or pseudo-holdfast. Bothria distinct, often shallow. Body segmentation distinct but often masked by secondary transverse folds of the cuticle. Body margins serrated or not. Neck lacking or present. Genital apertures marginal, commonly unilateral. Testes numerous, limited to the region between the nerve trunks (exception, *Amphicotyle heteropleura*). Poral nerve trunk dorsal to the cirrus pouch. Sperm duct strongly coiled, with its proximal portion wide and thin-walled, its distal portion narrow and thick-walled. External seminal vesicle lacking. Cirrus unarmed. Yolk glands in the medulla or in the innermost region of the cortex, variously distributed and developed. Uterus saclike or in the form of a lobulated sac, with a rudimentary aperture which is median and ventral (dorsal in *Amphicotyle heteropleura*). Eggs not operculated, with extremely thin shells. Embryonic development within the uterus. Adult worms in the gut of fishes. Three subfamilies: Amphicotylinae, Abothriinae, and Marsipometrinae.

HISTORY

Among the genera comprised within his subfamily Ptychobothriinae of Bothriocephalidae, Lühe (1899a) included, somewhat doubtfully, a form, *Amphicotyle typica*, that had been recorded by Diesing (1863b) from a sunfish (*Centrolophus pompilius*) and that was probably identical with an earlier recorded form, *Amphicotyle heteropleura*, also recorded by Diesing (1850) from this host species. In his later scheme, Lühe (1902c) made *Amphicotyle* the type genus of a separate subfamily, Amphicotylinae, of his family Ptychobothriidae, associating with it the genus *Abothrium* Beneden, 1871 and a newly established genus *Bathybothrium*. Nybelin (1922) raised this subfamily to family rank and recognized two subfamilies, Amphicotylinae and Abothriinae.

Another and earlier subfamily had been established by Cooper (1917, 1918) as Marsipometrinae for the genus *Marsipometra*. Neither Nybelin nor Fuhrmann (1931) were prepared to accept this, but Beaver and Simer (1940) restudied the genus *Marsipometra*, emended Nybelin's definition of Amphicotylidae to comprise this genus, and recognized the subfamily Marsipometrinae that Cooper had established for it.

Subfamily AMPHICOTYLINAE Lühe, 1900, emended Nybelin, 1922

DESCRIPTION

Of the family Amphicotylidae. With a clearly differentiated holdfast provided with an apical disk and with fairly deep, circular bothria. Body segmentation typically well marked, craspedote and anapolytic. Cirro-vaginal atrium marginal, irregularly alternating from one margin to the other in successive segments. Testes between the nerve cords. Sperm duct much coiled. External seminal vesicle lacking. Vagina with a well-marked seminal receptacle or merely enlarged in this region. Yolk glands cortical. Uterus saclike, opening on the ventral surface only when distended with eggs. Adult worms in fishes. Type genus, *Amphicotyle* Diesing, 1864. Other genera, *Eubothrium* Nybelin, 1922 and *Pseudobothrium* Guiart, 1935.

NOTES ON GENERA

Amphicotyle Diesing, 1864

With the bothria each provided with a partition marking off a posterior suckerlike region. Body unsegmented but transversely wrinkled, these wrinkles in young forms demarcating the proglottides but in older, mature forms added to by secondary wrinkles so that three to four such wrinkles correspond with each proglottis. Testes mainly to the outer side of the nerve trunks. Cirrus pouch very large and weakly muscular. Internal seminal vesicle lacking. Cirro-vaginal atrium small. Yolk glands very numerous, forming a sheath outside the longitudinal muscles.

Uterus simple, saclike, opening on the dorsal (*sic*) surface. Genotype and only known species, *heteropleura* Diesing, 1850.

Amphicotyle heteropleura is so nontypical, in many respects, of the family as a whole that we must regret that Lühe selected it as the type genus of his family. It was established by Diesing (1850), as *Dibothrium heteropleurum*, for material from a sunfish, *Centrolophus pompilius*. His description was inadequate and to our knowledge the form has not been redescribed.

Eubothrium Nybelin, 1922

With the bothria simple. Body segmentation usually distinct. A dorsal and a ventral median furrow along the surficial surfaces of the body. Testes exclusively between the nerve trunks. Cirrus pouch not unusually large or muscular. Vagina S-shaped, opening *anterior* to the cirrus pouch in the narrow but deep cirro-vaginal atrium. Seminal receptacle lacking but the vagina widened in that region. Ootype situated dorsally. Yolk glands cortical, in two crescentic lateral zones. Uterine aperture on the ventral surface of the segment. Genotype, *rugosum* Batsch, 1786; other species: *parvum* Nybelin, 1922; *fragile* Rudolphi, 1802; *crassum* Bloch, 1779; *crassoides* Nybelin, 1922; *salvelini* Schrank, 1790; *arcticum* Nybelin, 1922; and *oncorhynchi* Wardle, 1932; all in fishes.

NOTES ON SPECIES

1. *rugosum* Batsch, 1786. Worms 100 to 520 mm. long by 1.25 to 1.45 mm. wide (European material); 200 to 300 mm. long by 2.0 to 3.5 mm. wide (North American material); holdfast large, 0.75 to 1.32 mm. by 0.41 to 0.74 mm.; bothria shallow; apical disk small but distinct; testes in lateral zones connected by a single row of follicles between the successive sets of reproductive organs; sperm duct extending to the middle line, its distal portion about the length of the cirrus pouch; cirrus pouch bean-shaped, not quite reaching the poral nerve trunk; distal portion of the ejaculatory duct widening almost to the appearance of an internal seminal vesicle; ovary kidney-shaped, not lobed, almost wholly median, completely filling the medulla; its breadth about one-quarter of the segment width; yolk glands not especially numerous, relatively small, massed together almost entirely between the inner muscle bundles, partly in the medulla, with free median fields about one-quarter of the segment width; uterus a simple sac; adult worms in the burbot (*Lota lota*) (Figure 406).

Canadian material differs from European in lacking an internal seminal vesicle, a transitory character even among European forms, and in the common occurrence of a deformed holdfast. This *scolex deformatus* has been described in detail by Cooper (1918) and by Ekbaum (1933a). The deformity consists of a hypertrophy of the apical disk and anterior half of the holdfast to form a pyramidal, cushionlike pad which is embedded in the wall of the pyloric caecum of the fish in which the worm lies. Both normal and deformed types of holdfast may be found in the same fish and at the same stage of development.

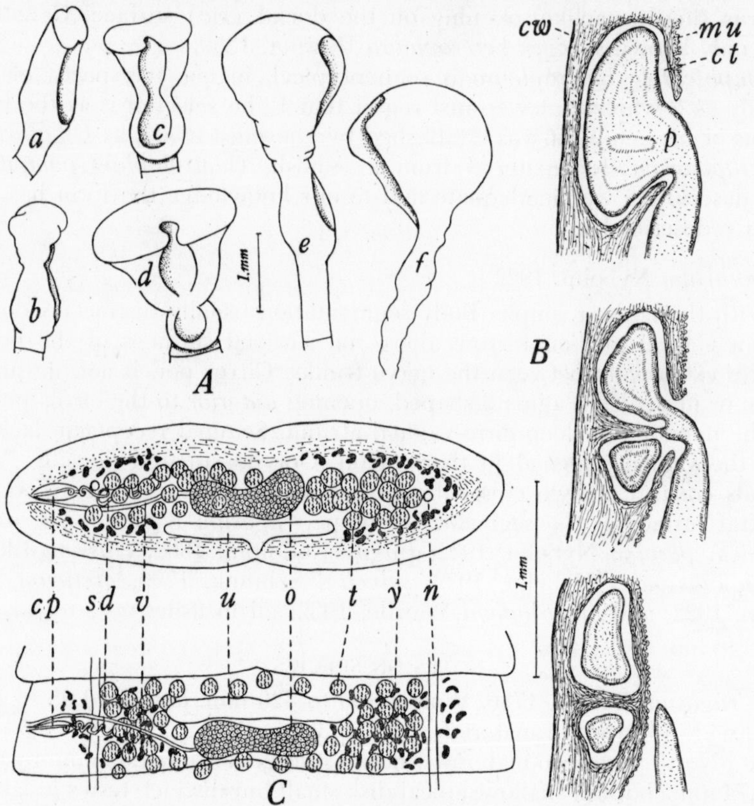

FIG. 406. *Eubothrium rugosum.* After Ekbaum, 1933a. A. Successive stages between the normal holdfast (*a*) and the deformed holdfast (*f*). B. Sections through the encysted holdfast. *ct*, cyst; *cw*, cyst wall; *mu*, mucosa of caecum; *p*, parasite. C. Sectional and surficial appearance of the mature segment. *cp*, cirrus pouch; *n*, nerve trunk; *o*, ovary; *sd*, sperm duct; *t*, testes; *u*, uterus; *v*, vagina; *y*, yolk glands.

"An interesting transition stage between the two types of specimens was shown by a 12 millimeter worm which was attached to the mucosa by one side only of the scolex. The side of the scolex which was attached to the host tissue showed remarkable hypertrophy, whilst the free side was entirely normal. The mucosa was destroyed at the point of contact but the typically round cavity usually produced in the mucosa had not developed. It may be concluded that as the cestode gradually burrows into the mucosa the latter gradually forms a round, nest-like cyst around the enlarged scolex of the cestode, this cavity having a round opening which fits closely round the neck of the worm. In many cases the host tissue actually fuses with the cestode tissue and in this case it is rarely possible to dissect an embedded scolex without injuring it. In addition to forms with the normal scolex and forms with a *scolex deformatus,* there occur forms which have lost their strobilae and which now protrude into the lumen of the caeca as structureless protrusions from the cyst. In other forms, where the disjunction has taken place closer to the scolex, the strobila does not protrude from the cyst and the scolex is distinguishable as a white nodule in the brownish cyst. It is possible that the fate of such worms is to be completely overgrown and enclosed within the cyst." Ekbaum (1933a).

2. *parvum* Nybelin, 1922. Forms 50 mm. long by 3 mm. wide, with the holdfast small, rounded, the bothria deep, the apical disk weak and slightly concave; testes in two sharply separated lateral zones, fairly numerous, each ellipsoid in shape; sperm duct extending almost to the aporal nerve trunk, the extension of its distal region less than the length of the cirrus pouch; cirrus pouch ovoid, narrowed distally, stretching internally over the poral nerve trunk; no internal seminal vesicle; withdrawn cirrus weakly coiled; ovary kidney-shaped, not lobed, inclined porad slightly from the middle line, filling dorso-ventrally almost the whole medulla, its breadth one-third of the segment width; yolk glands numerous, very large, exclusively outside the longitudinal muscle bundles, leaving free in the middle line only small dorsal and ventral gaps; follicles of successive sets of reproductive organs scarcely distinguishable; uterus a simple sac or slightly lobed; adult worms in *Mallotus villosus*, Norway.

3. *fragile* Rudolphi, 1802 (as *Taenia fragilis*). Worms 200 mm. long by 2.35 mm. wide; with the holdfast small, the bothria weak, the apical disk weak; lateral testis zones united by a single row of follicles between the successive sets of reproductive organs, each follicle fairly large, rounded; sperm duct reaching approximately to the middle line, its extension about equal to the length of the cirrus pouch; cirrus pouch longitudinally ovoid, reaching beyond the poral nerve trunk; internal seminal vesicle lacking; withdrawn cirrus weakly coiled; ovary kidney-shaped, finely lobed, in the middle line and filling the medulla dorso-ventrally, its breadth about one-quarter of the segment width; yolk glands very numerous, very small, mainly outside the longitudinal muscle bundles, the mid-dorsal and mid-ventral free fields narrow; follicles in successive sets of reproductive organs sharply separated; uterus a simple sac; adult worms in *Clupea finta*, European waters.

4. *crassum* Bloch, 1779 (= *Taenia crassa* Bloch, 1779; *Bothriocephalus infundibuliformis* Bellingham, 1844). Worms 120 to 600 mm. long by 2.5 to 5.6 mm. wide; with the holdfast large, the bothria relatively shallow, the apical disk distinct; lateral testis zones connected between the successive sets of reproductive organs by a single row of follicles; sperm duct extending almost to the middle line, the extension of its distal portion usually longer than the cirrus pouch; cirrus pouch ovoid, narrowed distally, reaching usually the poral nerve trunk; no internal seminal vesicle; withdrawn cirrus weakly coiled; ovary strongly lobed, directed slightly porad from the middle line, not completely filling the medulla dorso-ventrally; yolk glands numerous, fairly large, largely outside the longitudinal muscle bundles but to a slight extent between them; the mid-dorsal and mid-ventral free fields narrow; follicles of successive sets of reproductive organs sharply separated; uterus a simple sac or with

only slight lobes; adult worms in Atlantic salmon (*Salmo salar*) and trout (*Salmo trutta*), Europe and Canada, in the pyloric caeca (Figure 407). In the larval stage this species has been identified with a series of amphicotylid larvae from fishes, but without certainty. According to Rosen (1919), the procercoid stage in Europe occurs normally in *Cyclops strenuus* and *Cyclops serratulus*, and the plerocercoid stage in *Perca fluviatilis*.

5. *crassoides* Nybelin, 1922. Medium-sized forms, 300 to 400 mm. long by 4 mm. wide; with the holdfast large, the bothria fairly deep, the

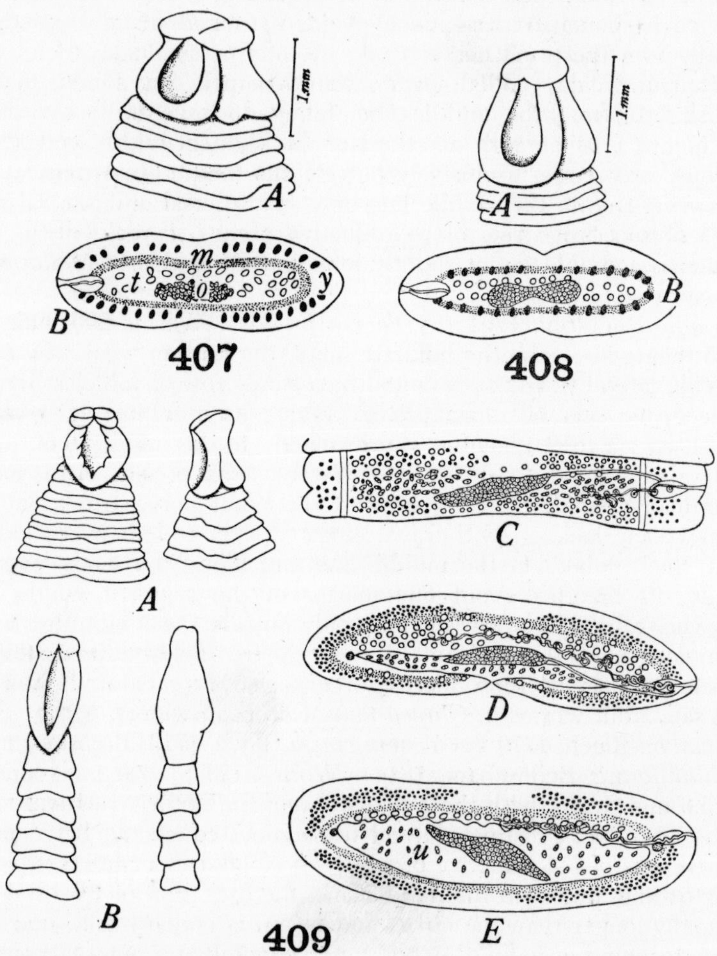

FIG. 407. *Eubothrium crassum*. After Wardle, 1932b. A. Holdfast. B. Cross section of mature segment. FIG. 408. *Eubothrium salvelini*. After Wardle, 1932b. A. Holdfast. B. Cross section of mature segment. FIG. 409. *Eubothrium oncorhynchi*. After Wardle, 1932a. A and B. The two types of holdfast. C. Mature segment, dorsal view. D. Cross section of same. E. Cross section of gravid segment. *m*, longitudinal muscle zone; *o*, ovary; *t*, testes; *u*, uterus; *y*, yolk glands.

apical disk strongly developed; lateral testis zones connected by a single row of follicles between the successive sets of reproductive organs, each follicle elliptical; sperm duct reaching to the middle line, its distal portion approximately the length of the cirrus pouch; cirrus pouch longitudinally ovoid, reaching to the poral nerve trunk; no internal seminal vesicle; withdrawn cirrus weakly coiled; ovary strongly lobed, extending porad from the middle line, almost filling the medulla dorso-ventrally, its breadth one-quarter of the segment width; yolk glands not numerous, small, exclusively between the longitudinal muscle bundles, the free median fields about one-quarter of the segment width, the follicles of successive segments sharply separated; uterus unknown; in the sturgeon (*Acipenser stellatus*), Astrakhan.

6. *salvelini* Schrank, 1790 (= *Taenia salvelini*). Up to 280 mm. in length by 2.25 mm. wide; with the holdfast fairly large, the bothria fairly deep, the apical disk weak; lateral testis zones connected by *several* rows of follicles between successive sets of reproductive organs, relatively numerous, rounded; sperm duct reaching to the middle line, its distal region less than the cirrus pouch length; cirrus pouch egg-shaped, long, reaching the poral nerve trunk; internal seminal vesicle lacking; withdrawn cirrus straight; ovary kidney-shaped, median, one-fifth to one-fourth of the segment width; yolk glands few, large, the majority between the longitudinal muscle bundles, the free median fields about one-fifth of the segment width, follicles of successive segments sharply separated; uterus a sac with strong lateral lobing; adult worms in *Salvelinus* (brook trout) Europe, Canada; *Cristivomer* (northern lake trout), Canada; *Oncorhynchus kennerlyi* and *Ptychocheilus oregonensis,* British Columbia (Figure 408).

7. *arcticum* Nybelin, 1922. Small forms, 60 mm. in length by 3.5 mm. wide; with the holdfast relatively large, scarcely separated from the body; apical disk weak but distinct; lateral testis zones sharply separated, the follicles relatively few, elliptical; sperm duct reaching to the middle line, its distal region a little shorter than the cirrus pouch length; cirrus pouch bean-shaped, crossing the poral nerve trunk; withdrawn cirrus straight; ovary kidney-shaped, not lobed, inclined porad, filling the medulla almost completely dorso-ventrally, its breadth one-third of that of the segment; yolk glands few but in great majority between the longitudinal muscle bundles, with single follicles partly or wholly in the medulla, free median fields one-eighth of the segment width dorsally, one-quarter of it ventrally; yolk glands of successive segments separate; uterus with lateral lobes; adult worms in *Lycodes pallidus*, Greenland.

8. *oncorhynchi* Wardle, 1932. Large forms, up to 600 mm. long by 5 mm. wide; with the holdfast small (less than 1 mm. long), the bothria deep, the apical disk conspicuously bilobed; body anapolytic, craspedote, the segments linear; lateral testis zones connected in each segment by one or two rows of follicles; sperm duct reaching from the cirrus pouch to a point midway between the middle line and the aporal nerve trunk; cirrus pouch pear-shaped, reaching to the poral nerve trunk; ovary compact, one-quarter to one-fifth of the segment width, not com-

pletely filling the medulla dorso-ventrally; yolk glands numerous, chiefly external to the longitudinal muscle bundles, the median free fields one-fifth of the segment width; uterus saclike, almost completely filling the medulla; adult worms in Pacific salmon (*Oncorhynchus*), Canadian Pacific waters (Figure 409).

This species, the common tapeworm of the Pacific salmon (*Oncorhynchus*), is obviously very close in its features to *crassum*, the common tapeworm of Atlantic salmon (*Salmo*), and must therefore be regarded as *species inquirenda*. Its oncorhynchid hosts may be four or five years old when caught, so that if the life cycle is like that of *Eubothrium crassum* this form must be perennial or else its intermediate hosts are marine. *Oncorhynchus tschawytscha* and *Oncorhynchus kisutch* feed largely upon herrings, and the assertion by Schneider (1902a) of the presence of eubothriid plerocercoids in Baltic Sea herrings is therefore of great interest. It may be added that an examination of 200 fingerling *Oncorhynchus nerka* from Cultus Lake, British Columbia, by one of the present writers, failed to yield any specimens of *Eubothrium*. The suggestion may be put forward that amphicotylid tapeworms are originally parasites of marine fishes which come into fresh waters to spawn and which frequently become landlocked and become purely fresh-water in habitat.

No injurious effects seem to be caused in the Pacific salmon by the presence of this relatively enormous parasite. Even a 600 mm. worm is folded so completely within one of the host's pyloric caeca that little of it projects into the gut lumen, and no case was observed among the several hundred fishes examined by the writer of any obstruction of the alimentary tract by this parasite. The adherent powers of the holdfast are so slight that it is doubtful whether the worm could counteract the active peristalsis of the host's gut musculature were it not able to fold itself within a pyloric caecum. On the other hand, specimens of cut-throat trout in Alberta were found to have the pyloric region of the gut solidly blocked by small eubothriid individuals, but as the material was post-mortem the occurrence of the cestodes in the gut lumen rather than in the caeca may have been abnormal. The chief function of the pyloric caeca of a fish is fat absorption, and although it is possible that eubothriid infection may interfere to some extent with this process, the interference must be slight, as infected fishes seem as healthy as uninfected ones.

Pseudobothrium Guiart, 1935

Small forms, 55 mm. long by 4 mm. wide; with the holdfast somewhat recalling that of *Fimbriaria* (Hymenolepididae). Gravid segments very linear, their posterior borders pleated. Genital apertures unilateral. Uterus filling the medullary parenchyma. In other respects this obviously contracted material would seem to have been intermediate between *Amphicotyle* and *Eubothrium*. Genotype and only recorded species, *grimaldii*, in *Thynnus alalonga* near the Azores.

Guiart stated that the anterior end of the worm showed no trace whatever of a holdfast, but no description of this anterior end was given. The segments, to judge by Guiart's figure, appear to be craspedote; each posterior segment border seems to have 10 to 12 pleats; a short horizontal groove midway along each margin of the segments suggests the beginnings of a secondary segment; the genital aperture appears to be *surficial* and very close to one margin. On the whole, the affinities of this form must be considered *sub judice*.

Subfamily Abothriinae Nybelin, 1922

DESCRIPTION

Of the family Amphicotylidae. With the holdfast weakly formed or deformed and lacking an apical disk. Body with a neck and with distinct segmentation, but the segments are acraspedote and probably apolytic. Testes exclusively within the area bounded laterally by the nerve trunks. Ejaculatory duct muscular, always dilated as an internal seminal vesicle. Withdrawn cirrus always straight, and not sharply demarcated from the ejaculatory duct. Ovary median, in the rear portion of the segment, filling the entire medulla from floor to roof, its aporal portion always larger than its poral portion. Female genital ducts in front of the ovary, the vagina and yolk duct entering the fertilization canal aporally, thus causing the vagina to curve characteristically over the other genital ducts. Yolk glands exclusively medullary. Uterine aperture ventral, not reaching the cuticle until after the beginning of egg production. Adult worms in teleostean fishes. Life cycle unknown. Type genus, *Abothrium* Beneden, 1871. Other genera, *Bathybothrium* Lühe, 1902 and *Parabothrium* Nybelin, 1922.

NOTES ON GENERA

Abothrium Beneden, 1871

With a *scolex deformatus*. Testes numerous, in lateral zones on either side of the ovary and uterus. Cirrus pouch bean-shaped, not unusually large. Sphincter vaginae lacking. Yolk glands between the testes. Uterus saclike, its medianly situated exit funnel not reaching the longitudinal muscles until after egg formation begins. Eggs with rounded ends, very thin-shelled. Adult worms in marine Gadidae (codfishes). Genotype and only known species, *gadi* Beneden, 1871 (Figure 410). Lühe used the generic term *Abothrium* not only for Beneden's form but for those forms which Nybelin later placed in his new genus *Eubothrium*. *Abothrium gadi* was redescribed by Nybelin (1922) from material from *Gadus callarias* and *Gadus aeglefinus* in Norwegian waters.

Bathybothrium Lühe, 1902

With a normal but relatively weakly constructed holdfast. Testes numerous, in an unbroken zone in front of and to the sides of the ovary and uterus. Cirrus pouch bean-shaped, not unusually large. Sphincter vaginae lacking. Yolk glands crowded in two lateral zones to the inner side of each nerve trunk. Uterus with marked lateral lobes, its aperture median or a little to the aporal side of median, already approaching the cuticle at the beginning of egg formation. Eggs with thin, longitudinally ovoid shells. Adult worms in cyprinid fishes. Genotype and only known species, *rectangulum* Bloch, 1778 (Figure 411).

Parabothrium Nybelin, 1922

With a *scolex deformatus.* Testes very numerous, in two clearly separated zones, on either side of the ovary and the uterus. Cirrus pouch unusually large, elongated, strongly muscular. Sphincter vaginae present. Yolk glands only in two zones in the rear portion of the segment, ventral to the testes, extending laterally to the nerve trunks. Uterus saclike, its medianly situated exit funnel extending over the longitudinal muscle bundles at the beginning of egg formation. Eggs with rounded, very thin shells. Adult worms in marine Gadidae. Genotype and only known species, *bulbiferum* Nybelin, 1922 (Figure 412).

Subfamily Marsipometrinae Cooper, 1917, emended Beaver and Simer, 1940

DESCRIPTION

Of the family Amphicotylidae. With a well-defined and persistent holdfast bearing two very definite and sometimes deep bothria. The middle region of the holdfast, which bears the bothria, often distinctly demarcated from the apical disk by shallow fissures or other circumferential markings. Body segmentation well marked. Body margins serrated or not. Neck present or lacking. Cirrus and vagina opening into a cirro-vaginal atrium which itself opens near the middle of the segment margin. Cirrus muscular, protrusible. Testes numerous, not continuous from segment to segment. Yolk glands restricted to the region of the longitudinal muscles or lying just within the medulla. Uterus saclike, with radial or lateral secondary pouching. Uterine aperture ventral, not reaching the cuticle until egg formation has begun (occasional exception, *Marsipometra hastata*) and never opening until the uterus is distended with eggs. Whole female genital complex anterior or ventral to the ovary, never behind it. Ootype near the floor of the medulla. Ovary large, kidney-shaped, extending from floor to roof of the medulla. Vagina well differentiated, extending from the dorsally situated seminal receptacle ventrad to join the oviduct near the floor of the medulla. Common yolk duct and adjacent ducts dilated as a yolk reservoir of somewhat variable shape; entrance into the fertilization duct immediately proximal to the ootype. Type genus, and only genus, *Marsipometra* Cooper, 1917.

Cooper's original definition was based upon *Marsipometra hastata* only. Beaver and Simer's definition is based upon *hastata* and two additional species. As these writers point out, the subfamily differs from both Amphicotylinae and Abothriinae in the character of the yolk glands, uterus, seminal receptacle, and body segmentation. Thus in Marsipometrinae the yolk glands are between the cortex and the medulla, in Amphicotylinae they are mostly in the cortex, and in Abothriinae mostly in the medulla. The uterus in Marsipometrinae is secondarily pouched, but merely saclike in the others. The vagina has a well-marked seminal

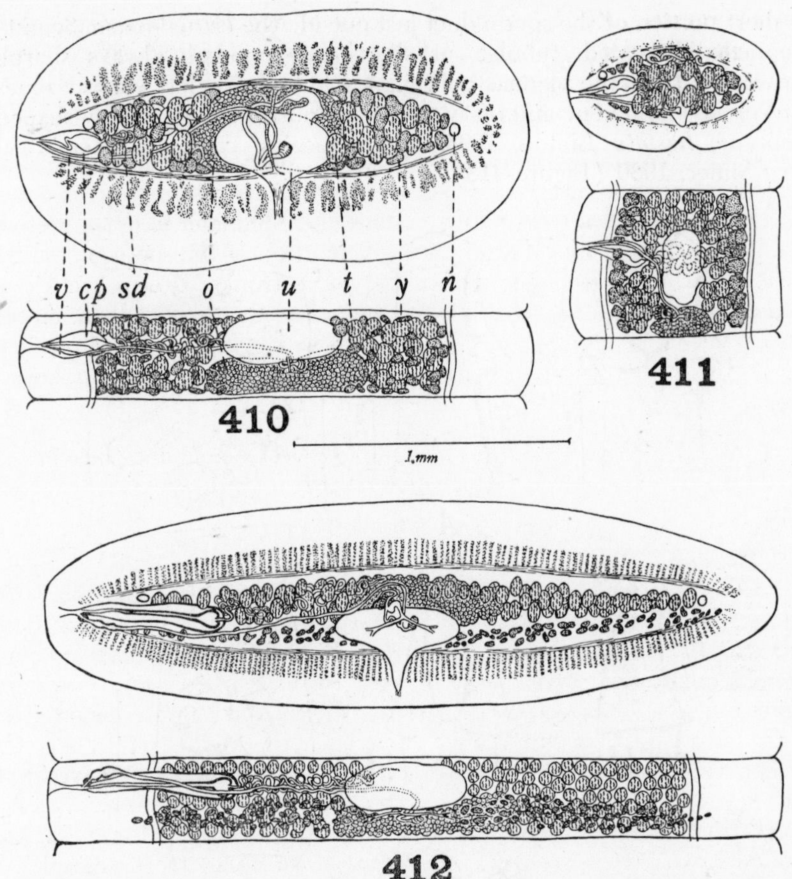

FIG. 410. *Abothrium gadi,* mature segment in surficial (ventral) and cross sectional views. After Nybelin, 1922. *cp,* cirrus pouch; *n,* nerve trunk; *o,* ovary; *sd,* sperm duct; *t,* testes; *u,* uterus; *v,* vagina; *y,* yolk glands. FIG. 411. *Bathybothrium rectangulum,* mature segment in surficial (ventral) and cross sectional views. After Nybelin, 1922. FIG. 412. *Parabothrium bulbiferum,* mature segment in surficial (ventral) and cross sectional views. After Nybelin, 1922.

receptacle in Marsipometrinae, a mere widening in the others. Body segmentation is pronounced and persistent in Marsipometrinae, but it is masked and complicated by secondary wrinkling in the others.

Marsipometra Cooper, 1917, emended Beaver and Simer, 1940

With the characters of the subfamily. Holdfast roughly pyramidal or arrow-shaped, with the apical disk narrower in diameter than the base of the holdfast. Neck with or without a zone of proliferation. Early segments wider than long, later becoming square or rectangular. Nerve trunks close to the segment margins, diffuse and inconspicuous in cross sections. Testes in two lateral zones, joined in front of the uterus and usually joined behind the ovary. A prostate gland present, placed along the short portion of the sperm duct just outside the cirrus pouch. Seminal receptacle elongated, tubular, or short and rounded, always sharply demarcated from the vagina. Yolk glands in right or left ventral zones, more or less confluent anteriorly and posteriorly. Ovary kidney-shaped. Genotype, *hastata* Linton, 1898. Other species, *confusa* Simer, 1930; *parva* Simer, 1930 (Figure 413).

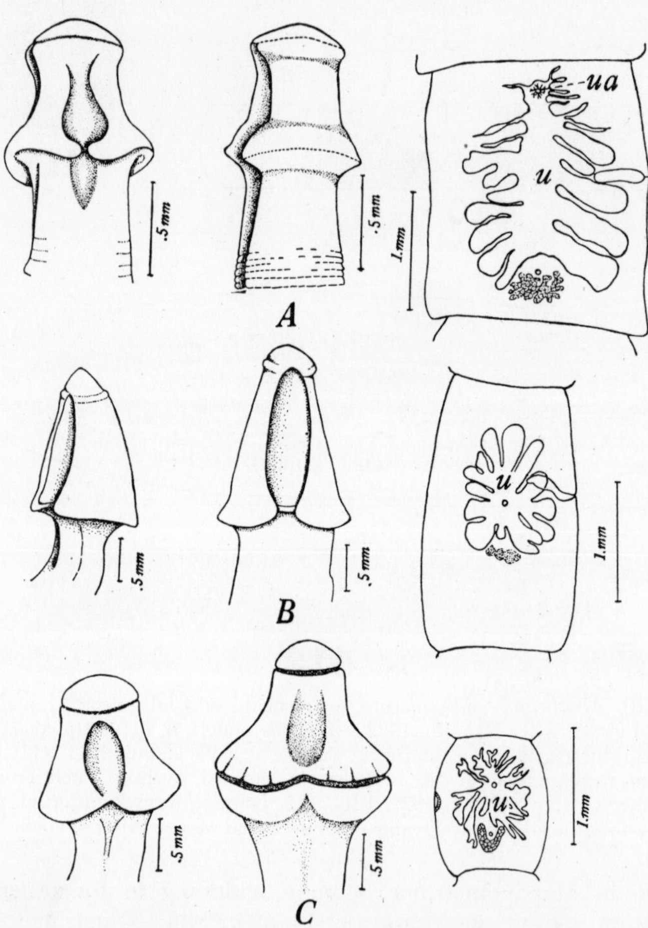

FIG. 413. *Marsipometra* species. After Beaver and Simer, 1940. A. *confusa*, holdfast and segment showing uterus (*u*), uterine aperture (*ua*), and ovary. B. *hastata*, similar views. C. *parva*, similar views.

The genotype was recorded, as *Dibothrium hastatum*, from the primitive fish *Polyodon spathula* of the Mississippi drainage system, and is apparently common in that host. The other species also came from that host species. For points of distinction, reference should be made to their authors.

Orders AMPHILINIDEA, GYROCOTYLIDEA, BIPOROPHYLLIDEA

The three orders named above, whose description will conclude this discussion of the zoology of tapeworms, are not strictly speaking tapeworms at all but Cestodaria, a term coined by the Italian zoologist Francesco Saverio Monticelli in 1892 for certain tapewormlike forms that were usually referred to in zoological textbooks as monozoic or monozootic tapeworms. Although these forms recall tapeworms (Cestoda) in being gut parasites of vertebrate animals, in having no alimentary organs, and in having parenchymal muscles, they as readily recall flukes (Trematoda) in the nature of their holdfast structures, their lack of segmentation and proglottisation – only one set of reproductive organs being present – and in having the cirrus, vagina, and uterus opening independently to the exterior. Monticelli's view that these forms should be regarded as distinct from Cestoda and Trematoda is, on the whole, accepted by current zoological opinion. We shall recognize here three orders.

Order AMPHILINIDEA

DESCRIPTION

Of the class Cestodaria. Forms with the body flattened, more or less elongated, rich in calcareous corpuscles but without surface spines or hooks. With one end of the body provided with a boring mechanism (variously termed *proboscis, boring muscle, anchor cells*) but without suckers or bothria. Opposite end of the body with the osmoregulatory aperture. With the cirrus and vaginal apertures either close together or separated only by a short interval and placed on or near the margin of the body at the end farthest away from the proboscis. Testes and uterus extending throughout the greater part of the body, the testes as two lateral zones lying external to the uterine coils but sometimes scattered. Vagina on the side of the ovary away from the proboscis. Uterus on the proboscis side of the ovary, with its aperture at the proboscis end of the body, and having three limbs arranged like a letter N when viewed from one surface. Two osmoregulatory canals opening by a common aperture at the end of the body farthest from the proboscis. Larval form with ten hooklets. With a single family, Amphilinidae Claus, 1879, with the characteristics of the order.

HISTORY

The genus *Amphilina,* upon which the family and the order are founded, was established by Wagener (1858) for a form recorded originally by Rudolphi (1891) as a trematode, under the name *Monostoma foliaceum.* Claus (1876) – not Braun (1883a) as Southwell (1928a) asserted – made this form the type genus of a family, Amphilinidae, to which Braun (1883a) added another genus, *Amphiptyches* Grube and Wagener, 1842. Poche (1922) gave the amphilinid forms the rank of an order, Amphilinidea, with two families, Amphilinidae and Schizochoeridae. Woodland (1923a) added *Amphilina paragonopora* from freshwater siluroid fishes of the river Ganges drainage system in India. Poche (1926a) made this form the representative of a new genus, *Gephyrolina,* and a new subfamily, Gephyrolininae, regarding its characters as intermediate between those of Amphilinidae and Schizochoeridae and in consequence suppressing the latter group as a family and accepting only the one family Amphilinidae, with four subfamilies – Amphilininae, Gigantolininae, Schizochoerinae, and Gephyrolininae. To these, Ihle and Ihle-Landenberg (1932) added a fifth subfamily, Kosterininae, a name which was changed by Johnston (1934), on grounds of priority of description, to Austramphilininae. Poche (1926a), it may be noted, placed the orders Amphilinidea and Gyrocotylidea together as a subclass, Amphilinoinei, of monozootic cestodes. Poche's subfamily arrangement was accepted by Fuhrmann (1931) but has not been accepted by all students of the group. Here we shall recognize only three of his subfamilies – Amphilininae, Gigantolininae, and Austramphilininae – of the one family, Amphilinidae.

RECOGNITION FEATURES

Detailed anatomical descriptions of *Amphilina* have been provided by Salensky (1874), Cohn (1904b), Hein (1904a), Pintner (1906), Monticelli (1893), Southwell (1915), and Woodland (1923a). In view of the unusual interest of this form to those who see in Cestodaria a link between tapeworms and flukes, some amplification of certain points in the definition of the order may be added here.

An amphilinid worm is usually ribbonlike, up to 15 inches in length, and cream or gray in color. Its usual habitat is the body cavity of a fish of the families Acipenseridae, Osteoglossidae, Haemulidae, Siluridae, or it may be found below the peritoneum or above the swim bladder; or it may even tunnel through the body wall to the outside. From two to eight individuals may be found in one fish. It owes its boring powers to a small, proboscislike mechanism which can be protruded from the anterior end of the body and withdrawn into it. It is a modification of the body wall in the form of a thick-walled, conical bulb whose wall, though resembling that of the body wall in general structure, lacks the circular and longitudinal muscle fibers but has very powerfully developed radially directed fibers and a serrated cuticle. The core, so to speak, of this "proboscis" is a relatively enormous bundle of muscle fibers which run back through the worm to its posterior end, the region of the ovary, there to be inserted in certain large cells, the "problematical cells" of Salensky, the "anchor cells" of Woodland. The latter writer regarded the function of this boring muscle as threefold: (1) to give a partial twist to the movement of the proboscis (the fibers being twisted anteriorly); (2) to act as a stout support for the anterior end of the body when the worm is boring; and (3) to drag the hinder part of the body through the perforation made by the proboscis. These three functions he thought accounted for the enormous size of the muscle. A true and distinct retractor muscle for the proboscis lies outside the boring muscle.

Amphilinids are ovoviviparous. The complete life cycle is unknown, but the observations of Salensky (1874) upon *Amphilina foliacea* and of Woodland (1923a) upon *Gephyrolina paragonopora* have thrown some light upon the probable course of development. Woodland described the fully formed egg cell as being enclosed with a quantity of yolk material within a relatively thin, irregularly ovoid shell, to one end of which a short filament is attached. According to Salensky, the egg is not operculated and its development resembles that of a tapeworm egg, an oval embryo issuing from it. Half of the embryo is ciliated and the opposite half carries ten hooks precisely like those on the cirrus in number and shape.

Woodland described the first limb of the uterus as containing eggs with two to twelve or more blastomeres, and eggs containing embryos consisting of a solid morula of cells within an investing membrane. The third limb of the uterus is filled with embryos, still within the egg shell, approximately ovoid in shape with a definite ectoderm, a cavity containing scattered round cells and a group of elongated large cells drawn out toward one end of the embryo – and compared by Woodland with the unicellular glands of trematode cercariae – as well as another group of elongated cells at the other end of the embryo which apparently form the characteristic ten hooks of the larva. The liberated larva is about 100 μ long and has the anterior end of the body – the end opposite to that which carries the hooks – somewhat drawn out. The gland cells are not visible, perhaps because they are distended with an unstainable secretion. No trace of cilia could be detected. Woodland believed such larvae are discharged through the uterine aperture after the adult worm has bored through the body wall of the fish to the outside. Larvae prematurely discharged within the host's body cavity, he believed, become surrounded by histolytic tissue derived from the host mesentery and are destroyed. In fishes infected with active *Gephyrolina* adults, enormous masses of tissue may be found attached to the mesenteries or free in the body cavity; they vary in size from a pinhead to three inches or more in length and originate apparently from small, spherical, multicellular masses, each about 30 μ in diameter, which are enclosed in capsules formed by the mesenteric issue. They give rise to active amphilinids, and within these masses all transitions can be observed between the multinucleate mass and the fully formed amphilinid. Occasionally they develop into sexual amphilinids inside the capsules, since individual worms containing full-grown larvae are occasionally met with inside large capsules.

The three subfamilies of Amphilinidae recognized here are characterized as follows:

Subfamily Amphilininae Poche, 1922

DESCRIPTION

Of the family Amphilinidae. With the characteristics of the family. Body flat, oval or ribbonlike in outline. Anterior end pointed or slightly truncated according to the state of contraction. Posterior end rounded, pointed, or emarginate. A small, protrusible proboscis present at the anterior end connected with a large boring muscle whose fibers end posteriorly in giant "anchor cells" situated in the parenchyma. Osmoregulatory system comprising two main longitudinal canals which open posteriorly by a common aperture and are connected by an anastomosis of narrower canals. Testes numerous. Ovary and openings of sperm duct and vagina posterior. Uterus a long convoluted tube with three limbs, N-shaped in ventral view, each limb extending the full length of the body, and opening anteriorly at the base of the proboscis on the opposite side to that on which the uterus originates. Type genus, *Amphilina* Wagener, 1858. Other genus, *Gephyrolina* Poche, 1926.

Amphilina Wagener, 1858

With the body oval or leaf-shaped in outline, the anterior end pointed. Dorsal surface more curved than the ventral surface. Adult worms in the body cavity of European species of the sturgeon (*Acipenser*). Genotype, *foliacea* Rudolphi, 1819 (Figure 414).

The genotype is a flat, leaf-shaped, creamy-white worm, 20 to 60 mm. long, with a bluntly pointed anterior end and a rounded or slightly concave posterior end. Looked at from the dorsal surface, the surface farthest from the ovary, the vagina lies behind the ovary and on the left side of the sperm duct and opens on the left side of the body about 2 mm. from the male aperture, which opens exactly in the middle of the indented posterior end. The cirrus is armed at its outer end with ten hooks. The testes are scattered. Other features of the internal anatomy will be apparent from Benham's diagram (Figure 414).

The species *neritina* Salensky, 1874, also from the European sturgeon, is gray-green in color, smaller in size than *foliacea* but in other respects apparently identical with it; its distinction from the genotype requires confirmation. The same may be said for *japonica,* established by Goto and Ishii (1936) for a form from a sturgeon (*Acipenser mikado*) in Japan, and for *bipunctata* Riser, 1948 from a sturgeon in Oregon and distinguished from *japonica,* according to its author, by size and shape of testes, ova, apical organ, and size of the *bulbus propulsorius.*

Gephyrolina Poche, 1926

With the anterior end pointed, the posterior end pointed or indented. Ribbonlike forms. Vagina to the right of the sperm duct in dorsal view and opening directly in the middle line toward the posterior end. Testes in lateral zones. No hooks on the cirrus. Genotype, *paragonopora* Woodland, 1923 from *Macrones acer* and *Macrones seenghala* (siluroid fishes) in the rivers Jumna and Ganges, India (Figure 415). If this genus is accepted, a further member would seem to be *liguloidea* Diesing, 1850 from *Arapsima gigas* in Brazil.

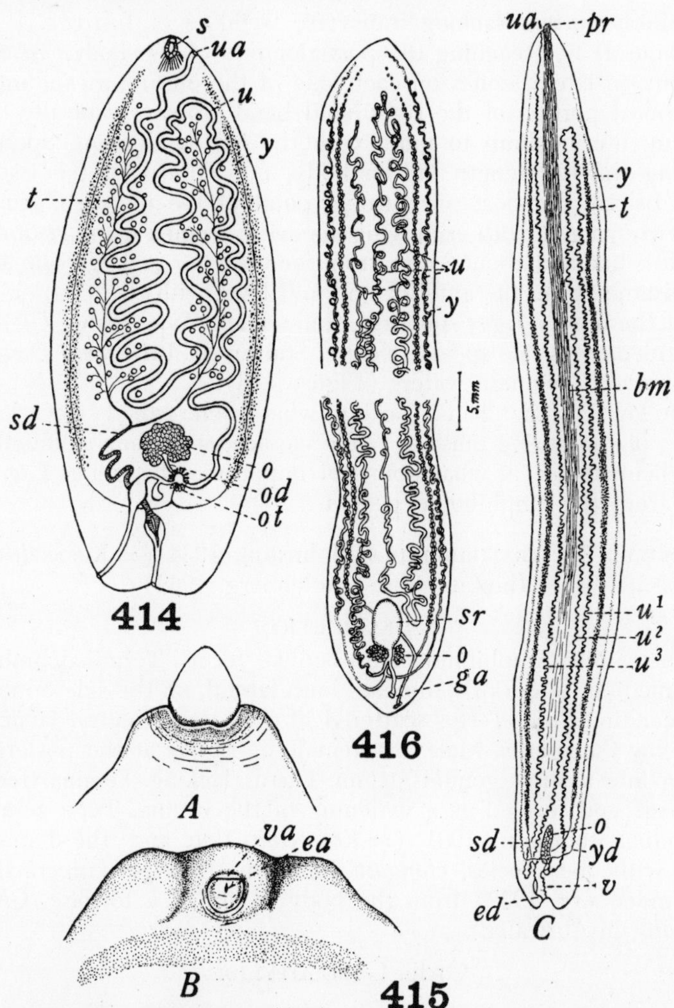

FIG. 414. *Amphilina foliacea*. After Benham, 1901. FIG. 415. *Gephyrolina paragonopora*. After Woodland, 1923a. A. Anterior end of a 280 mm. specimen showing evaginated proboscis. B. Posterior end of same specimen showing vaginal aperture (*va*) dorsal, and ejaculatory aperture (*ea*) at the end. C. Whole worm, surficial and dorsal view. FIG. 416. *Gigantolina magna*, anterior and posterior regions of entire worm. After Southwell, 1928a. *bm*, boring muscle; *ed*, ejaculatory duct; *ga*, genital aperture; *o*, ovary; *od*, oviduct; *ot*, ootype; *pr*, proboscis; *s*, sucker; *sd*, sperm duct; *sr*, seminal receptacle; *t*, testes; *u*, uterus; u^1, u^2, and u^3, proximal, middle, and distal regions of uterus; *ua*, uterine aperture; *v*, vagina; *y*, yolk glands; *yd*, yolk duct.

Subfamily Gigantolininae Poche, 1926

DESCRIPTION

Of the family Amphilinidae. With the characteristics of the family. Large forms, up to 381 mm. long when alive, with both ends narrow and round. Body surface lacking transverse wrinkles or furrows. With the boring muscle not reaching the posterior end of the body. Testes very numerous, in lateral zones on each side of the uterine ascending limbs, the rearmost portion of the right-hand band crossing ventrally the first ascending uterine limb to unite with the left-hand band. Sperm duct extending the full length of the body, not ramifying, the two ducts uniting behind the posterior turning point of the uterus. Cirrus short. Ovary two-winged, with each wing dendritic. Vagina opening dorsally in the middle line and about 3 mm. from the posterior end. Uterine aperture some distance from the anterior end and level with the anterior turning point of the uterus. Eggs spherical, thin-walled. Type genus, *Gigantolina* Poche, 1926, with one species, *magna* Southwell, 1915 from *Diagramma crassispinum*, Ceylonese waters (Figure 416).

We follow Woodland in regarding what Poche called "frontal glands" as fibers of the boring muscle. While we accept Poche's subfamily here, it is difficult to see in what points of importance his genus *Gigantolina* differs from the amphilinine genera.

Subfamily Austramphilininae Johnston, 1934 (= Kostermininae Ihle and Ihle-Landenberg, 1932)

DESCRIPTION

Of the family Amphilinidae. Ribbonlike forms. Terminal limb of the uterus median; posteriorly directed limb lateral, on the side opposite the first ascending limb. Testes scattered in dorsal and ventral layers above and below the uterus. Male and female apertures at the posterior end, opening into a short genital atrium. Cirrus lacking. Seminal receptacle very large and formed as a widening of the vagina. Type genus, *Austramphilina* Johnston, 1931 (= *Kosterina* Ihle and Ihle-Landenberg, 1932), with one species, *elongata* Johnston, 1931 (= *kuiperi* Ihle and Ihle-Landenberg, 1932) from the body cavity of a tortoise, *Chelodina longicollis*, in Australia.

Order Gyrocotylidea

DESCRIPTION

Of the class Cestodaria. Flattened, elongated forms with an anterior cuplike sucker and a posterior organ of attachment in the form of a sphincter muscle or a rosettelike structure. Uterine aperture and male genital aperture on the ventral body surface, female genital aperture on the dorsal body surface. Osmoregulatory system as a mesh of fine canals. Larval stage with ten hooks. Adult worms parasitic in Holocephali. With one family, Gyrocotylidae Benham, 1901, and two genera, *Gyrocotyle* Diesing, 1850 and *Gyrocotyloides* Fuhrmann, 1931.

HISTORY

Diesing (1850) invented the binomial term *Gyrocotyle rugosa* for a specimen in the Vienna Museum which he believed to be a trematode and whose origin was believed to have been an African antelope. With this form he identified specimens from a mollusk (*Mulinia edulis*) at Valparaiso. Wagener (1857) transferred to the genus a form that he had previously recorded, as *Amphiptyches urna* Grube and Wagener, 1852, from a chimaeroid fish, *Chimaera monstrosa*. By Benham (1901), *Gyrocotyle* was made type genus of a family Gyrocotylidae. Furhmann (1931) added another genus, *Gyrocotyloides,* for a form taken by Nybelin from *Chimaera monstrosa*. The validity of Fuhrmann's genus has been established by the detailed study published by Joyeux and Baer (1950c). We accept *Gyrocotyle* and *Gyrocotyloides,* therefore, as valid cestodarian genera, constituting the family Gyrocotylidae Benham, 1901 of the order Gyrocotylidea.

NOTES ON GENERA

Gyrocotyle Diesing, 1850

Of the order Gyrocotylidea and the family Gyrocotylidae. Body flat, elongated, devoid of calcareous corpuscles but possessing cuticular spines. Anterior end with an ovoid sucker, posterior end with a rosette. Cirrus and vaginal apertures adjacent but on opposite surfaces of the body. Testes situated anteriorly and to the outer sides of the median uterus. Uterine aperture anterior, on the ventral surface, in or close to the middle line, a short distance, but separate, from the vaginal aperture. Osmoregulatory system a close network of fine vessels devoid of longitudinal canals and not opening by a posterior bladder. Larva with ten hooks. Adult worms parasitic in Holocephali (chimaeroid fishes). Genotype and only species, *urna* Grube and Wagener, 1852.

Gyrocotyle urna has been described in detail by Grube and Wagener (1852), Braun (1889b), Spencer (1889), Monticelli (1889c, 1890b), Loennberg (1890a), Haswell (1902a), Kofoid and Watson (1910), Watson (1911), Ward (1912c), Dollfus (1923a), Wardle (1932a), and Lynch (1945). It is generally accepted as a parasite only of chimaeroid fishes (*Chimaera, Hydrolagus*). It occurs in pairs, representing twin survivors of a mass infection, exactly opposite to one another and attached to the mucosa of the anterior region of the large intestine of the chimaeroid host. A specimen in which complete muscular relaxation has been obtained by killing with hot acetic-sublimate fixative or hot Zenker's solution has the appearance shown in Figure 418. It is about (Wardle's specimens) 40 to 50 mm. long by 7 to 12 mm. broad, creamy-white in color, flattened; the posterior quarter of the body is narrow and tapering and carries an elaborately frilled organ of fixation, the "rosette organ," by which the parasite clings to the mucosa of the host gut.

This rosette has been compared by various observers with a carnation, a cabbage head, a circular tuft of folds, a crowded series of folds, a funnel with pleated walls, and so forth. Its appearance depends in fact upon

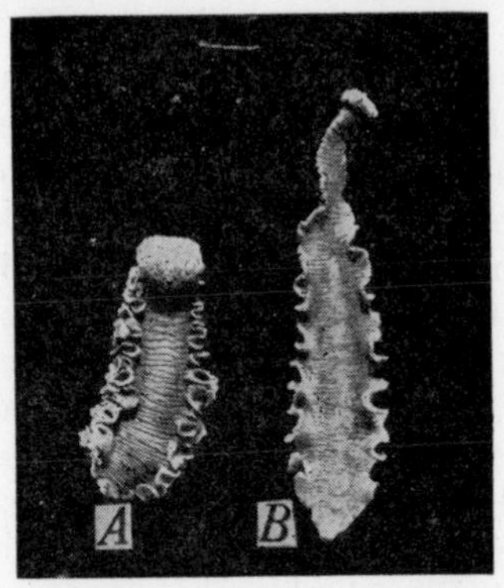

FIG. 417. Photograph of a pair of *Gyrocotyle urna* from *Hydrolagus colliei*. After Wardle, 1932a. A. Contracted. B. Expanded.

the degree of contraction of the worm. In fully relaxed specimens it appears as two distinct sets of folds, right and left of a median furrow which is continued as a "rosette canal" to end on the curved surface of the body as a minute pore. The folds are crowded together, each being thin, transparent, with little or no muscle tissue. The wall of the rosette canal has a highly developed layer of transverse muscle fibers and a weaker layer of longitudinal fibers.

Ward (1912c) stated: "The latter organ [the rosette] is clearly a

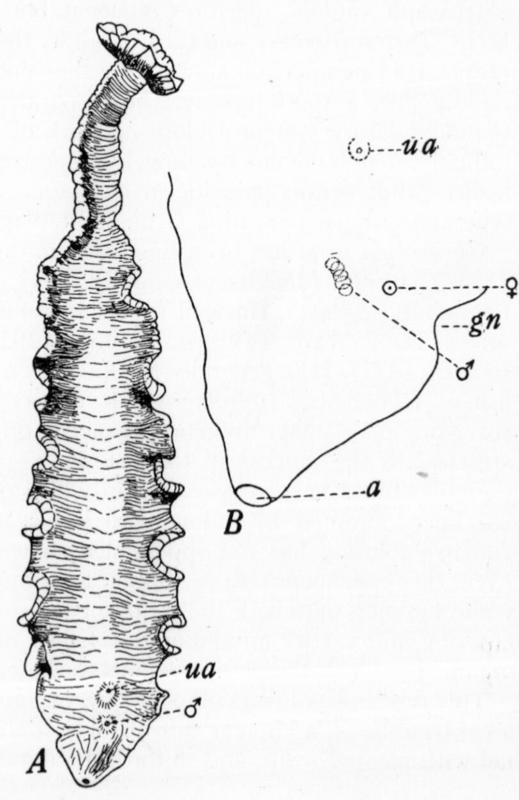

FIG. 418. *Gyrocotyle urna*. After Wardle, 1932a. A. Fully extended specimen, ventral view, to show the position of the uterine aperture (*ua*) and the male aperture (♂). B. Composite drawing of the acetabular end of 13 specimens to show comparatively stable position of the uterine aperture (*ua*) and female aperture (♀), and the variable position of the male aperture (♂). *a*, acetabulum; *gn*, genital notch.

terminal sucker of a compound laminated type analogous in structure to the folded suckers on the scolex of certain cestodes. The rosette is just what would be produced by excessive contraction of a long, thin-walled tube under the influence of longitudinal fibers inserted at various points along its course, while the funnel form represents a stage of contraction intermediate between the long tube form and the convoluted rosette form." The funnel plus its canal is the "Trichter" of German observers. That the rosette organ is homologous with the holdfast of true tapeworms is accepted by most students of the question. However, some variance of opinion exists as to whether it is to be regarded as anterior or posterior in position.

At the other end of the gyrocotylid is a less complicated structure, probably not used for fixation, and called variously "sucker," "acetabulum," "Kopfzapfen," "Cephalic cone," etc. It is a contractile structure with very muscular walls, a circular mobile rim, and a central, deep cavity. It may be of significance that this structure has the position occupied by the invaginated osmoregulatory aperture of many adult cestodes and larval cestodes, but no osmoregulatory aperture has been observed within it.

The body of *Gyrocotyle* is thick, flat, transversely wrinkled, and its margins are frilled. One surface is strongly convex—the ventral surface according to Watson (1911), the dorsal surface according to Ward (1912c)—and the other surface is flat. On the curved surface is the vaginal aperture, placed between the middle line and the "genital notch," an indentation on the right side (Figure 418). On the flat surface are the male aperture and the uterine aperture. The internal anatomy of *Gyrocotyle* has been described in considerable detail by Watson (1911) and need not be elaborated here. While not closely comparable with that of tapeworms, it is at any rate nearer to the tapeworm condition than it is to the trematode condition, particularly in its lack of alimentary organs and in the distribution of the internal muscles, the yolk glands, and the testes.

Gyrocotyle urna Grube and Wagener, 1852 seems to be the only valid species of the genus. It has been recorded from *Chimaera monstrosa* in Atlantic waters, *Chimaera ogilbyi* in Australian waters, and *Hydrolagus colliei* in northern Pacific waters. According to Watson (1911), the Pacific material differs from the typical *urna* in the relative positions of the male and female apertures, the latter in *Gyrocotyle urna* being closer to the margin and to the acetabular end of the body than is the male aperture, whereas in Pacific material the female and the male apertures are at the same level, although of course on opposite surfaces of the animal. Watson distinguished, among her Pacific specimens, forms with a simple, frilled rosette organ, which she regarded as a Pacific variety of *urna*, and forms with a complex rosette organ, which she regarded as a distinct species, *Gyrocotyle fimbriata*.

Now the validity of such presumably variable characteristics as the plication of the rosette organ and the relative positions of male and female apertures will depend upon the extent to which they vary, a question that can be decided only by the study of a much larger number of specimens than have so far been examined. Ward (1912c), after examining an unstated number of specimens, concluded that the plication of the rosette organ varies according to the degree of contraction or relaxation of the worm, a conclusion which an examination by Wardle (1932a) of 13 individuals from *Hydrolagus colliei* from British Columbian waters completely endorsed.

As regards the relative positions of the genital apertures, measurements made upon these 13 specimens suggested that the female aperture varied in position scarcely at all from a point on the curved surface approximately midway between the genital notch and the mid-dorsal line of the animal (Figure 418♀) and at a distance from the uterine aperture, although of course on the opposite surface, approximately equivalent to one-third of the distance between uterine aperture and acetabular extremity. The male pore (Figure 418♂), however, situated on the flat surface and nearer to the middle line than the female aperture, varied from a position on the acetabular side of the female aperture to a position on the uterine side of it. That is to say, the variations in position of the genital apertures from the condition described in *Gyrocotyle urna* were so slight that in spite of the wide geographical separation of the host fishes, the Pacific coast *Gyrocotyle* must on present evidence be regarded as identical with the Atlantic form. Lynch (1945) has redescribed material from the spiral valve of *Hydrolagus colliei* from Puget Sound and the Washington coast of the United States. He distinguished two forms of *urna* by the size of the acetabular spines.

Despite the attempt by Lynch to revive the species *rugosa* by offering a provisional diagnosis, this species in our opinion is definitely *species inquirenda.* As already stated, it was established by Diesing for material alleged to have come from an antelope in South Africa and from a mollusk in South America, a preposterous disparity of hosts. Monticelli (1890b) identified with Diesing's scanty description a specimen in the British Museum taken from a chimaeroid fish, *Callorhynchus antarcticus,* possibly the same form that had been recorded by Spencer (1889) from the mouth of that host species in New Zealand waters and identified with Wagener's *Amphiptyches urna.* Linstow (1901e) also used Diesing's description of *rugosa* to identify a form from a wild sheep (*Ovis bimangvatorum*) in South Africa.

Haswell (1902a) described *Gyrocotyle urna* (on Wagener's description), *Gyrocotyle rugosa* (Monticelli's description), and what he believed to be a new species, *Gyrocotyle nigrosetosa,* all from *Chimaera ogilbyi* in Australian waters. In *rugosa,* according to this observer, the male aperture is margino-ventral and the female aperture dorsal and to the left of the middle line, a little behind the level of the male pore. In *urna* the male aperture is close to the mid-ventral line and the female aperture dorsal and in front of the level of the male aperture. In *nigrosetosa* the male aperture and the female aperture are near the posterior end, on the left side of the body, the male aperture ventral and slightly left of the middle line, the female aperture dorsal and marginal. Hungerbühler

(1910), reviewing material collected from *Callorhynchus antarcticus* in South African waters, also recognized both *urna* and *rugosa*, the latter from Monticelli's description, which was not, of course, a description of *rugosa* at all.

The life cycle of *Gyrocotyle urna* is not completely known. Ruszkowski (1932b) incubated eggs taken from what he believed to be *Gyrocotyle urna* but which Joyeux and Baer (1950c) suggest may have been *Gyrocotyloides nybelini*. The eggs secrete a gelatinous capsule a few hours after liberation from the uterus. An operculum is present. In 5 to 7 days after leaving the uterus the yolk cells have fused; in 10 to 15 days the embryonic hooks have appeared; in 12 to 20 days the first embryonic movements are seen; and in 25 to 30 days a so-called "lycophore" leaves the egg, that is to say, a 10-hooked, uniformly ciliated larva. Infection experiments with the mollusks *Cardium*, *Mytilus*, and *Lima* were negative. Unfortunately ophiuroids, which form an important item of the chimaeroid diet, were not tried. It may be noted that Linstow (1903e) described as *Gyrocotyle medusarum* what may have been a gyrocotylid larva from a jellyfish, *Phyllorhiza rosacea*, in western Pacific waters. Ruszkowski also found in fish hosts larvae 3 to 5 mm. long in which the rosette was already formed, and observed that the ten hooks of the lycophore were grouped together precisely where the rosette had formed. The Polish observer homologized such larvae with procercoid larvae of Pseudophyllidea in which larval hooks are found always at the pole opposite to that where the holdfast appears. This observation would seem to settle the disputed question of the orientation of *Gyrocotyle* if, as Ruszkowski believes, the rosette organ is the *posterior* end of the worm and is not to be homologized with the holdfast of the true tapeworm.

Gyrocotyloides Fuhrmann, 1931, emended Joyeux and Baer, 1950

Of the order Gyrocotylidea and the family Gyrocotylidae. With the cuticle smooth, without cuticular spines. Body at posterior end cylindrical, contractile, ending in a powerful sphincter muscle. Median canal from this region opening on the dorsal surface, behind the ovary. Anterior end with a deep sucker, weakly muscular. Osmoregulatory system a network of longitudinal vessels which open on the dorsal surface by two apertures placed in the anterior half of the body. Testes very numerous, extending in front of the ovary to just short of the anterior sucker. Seminal vesicle long, turned on itself, prolonged as an ejaculatory canal which opens by way of a deep *masculine atrium* to the ventral surface, to the right of the middle line and in front of the vaginal aperture. Uterus very short, opening by a very large and elongated uterine sac on the ventral surface in the middle line. Vagina opening on the dorsal surface between the male aperture and the uterine pore. Eggs large, operculated, not embryonated when laid. Adult worms in *Chimaera monstrosa*. Genotype, *nybelini* Fuhrmann, 1931.

Fuhrmann's original description has been amplified in considerable detail by Joyeux and Baer (1950c) and the validity of the species established beyond doubt.

Order Biporophyllidea

DESCRIPTION

Of the class Cestodaria. With a flattened, elongated body containing calcareous corpuscles and having cuticular spinelets. With an anterior protrusible proboscis. Male and female genital apertures opening into a common atrium placed in the anterior half of the body. Testes scattered in front of the ovary. Uterus saclike with its aperture dorso-median, at or slightly behind the level of the common genital aperture. Osmoregulatory system comprising a network of vessels in the parenchyma and two longitudinal canals each opening to the outside by a simple dilated vesicle at the posterior end of the body. Nervous system comprising anterior and posterior nerve rings connected by two longitudinal cords. Adult worms in the gut of sharks. With one family, Biporophyllaeidae, with the characters of the order.

The order and its family are based on a single form, *Biporophyllaeus madrassensis* Subramanian, 1939 from a shark, *Chiloscyllium griseum* in Indian waters.

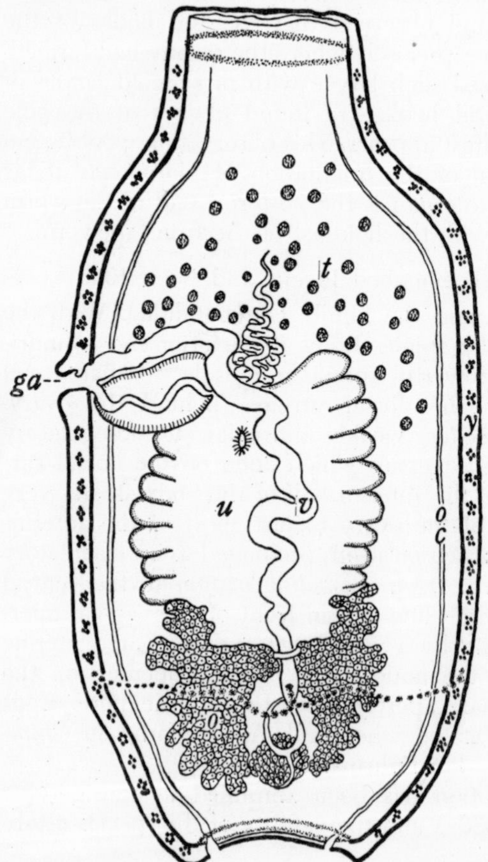

FIG. 419. *Biporophyllaeus madrassensis*. After Subramanian, 1939. *ga*, genital aperture; *o*, ovary; *oc*, osmoregulatory canal of one side; *t*, testes; *u*, uterus; *v*, vagina; *y*, yolk glands.

Biporophyllaeus Subramanian, 1939

With the characters of the order. Cuticular spines limited to the surface of the proboscis. Cirrus with a covering of spines and provided with a cirrus pouch. Vagina opening in front of the uterus. Ovary roughly H-shaped. Longitudinal extent of the uterus less than that of the region of the testes. Genotype, *madrassensis* Subramanian, 1939 (Figure 419).

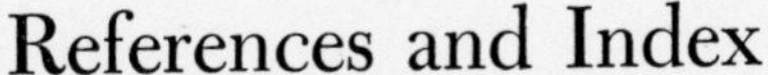

References and Index

References

The abbreviations used below are those of the "List of Periodicals Abstracted by Chemical Abstracts" (American Chemical Society, Ohio State University, Columbus, Ohio). In the few cases where the periodical quoted does not appear in that list, a similar system of title abbreviation is followed.

Abildgaard, P. C. 1789. In O. F. Mueller. Zoologicae Danicae. Havniae.

Abildgaard, P. C. 1790. Almindelige Betragtninger over Indvolde-Orme . . . Skrivter af Naturhistorie Selskabet, Kjobenhavn I, pp. 26–64.

Abildgaard, P. C. 1793. Allgemeine Betrachtung der Eingeweidewürmer . . . Schriften der naturforsch. Ges. Kopenhagen I, pp. 24–59.

Achmerov, A. K. 1941. *Amurotaenia perccotti* n. gen., n. sp. Vertreter einer neuen Cestoden-Ordnung. Compt. rend. acad. sci. U.R.S.S. *30,* 191–192.

Ackert, J. E. 1918. On the life-cycle of the fowl cestode, *Davainea cesticillus* (Molin). J. Parasitol. *5,* 41–43.

Ackert, J. E. 1919. On the life-history of *Davainea tetragona* (Molin), a fowl tapeworm. J. Parasitol. *6,* 28–34.

Ackert, J. E. 1942. Natural resistance to helminthic infections. J. Parasitol. 28, 1–24.

Ackert, J. E., and W. M. Reid. 1936. The cysticercoid of the fowl tapeworm, *Raillietina cesticillus.* Trans. Am. Microscop. Soc. *55,* 97–100.

Adam, W. 1938a. Sur une larve de cestode de *Mesoplodon bidens* (Sowerby). Bull. musée roy. hist. nat. Belg. *14* (15), 1–17.

Adam, W. 1938b. Notes sur les céphalopodes. IX. Sur la présence d'une larve de cestode (Tetrarhynchidae) dans la cavité palléale d'un *Octopus* des Iles Andamans. Bull. musée roy. hist. nat. Belg. *14* (35), 1–4.

Adams, A. R. D., and L. Webb. 1933. Two further cases of human infestation with *Bertiella studeri* (Blanchard, 1891) . . . Ann. Trop. Med. Parasitol. 27, 471–475.

Addis, C. J., Jr. 1946. Experiments on the relation between sex hormones and the growth of tapeworms *(Hymenolepis diminuta)* in rats. J. Parasitol. *32,* 574–580.

Addis, C. J., Jr., and A. C. Chandler. 1944. Studies on the vitamin requirement of tapeworms. J. Parasitol. *30,* 229–236.

Addis, C. J., Jr., and A. C. Chandler. 1946. Further studies on the vitamin requirement of tapeworms. J. Parasitol. *32,* 581–584.

Africa, C. M., and E. Y. Garcia. 1935. The occurrence of *Bertiella* in man, monkey and dog in the Philippines. Philippine J. Sci. *56,* 1–11.

Alicata, J. E. 1936. The amphipod, *Orchestia platensis,* an intermediate host of *Hymenolepis exigua,* a tapeworm of chickens in Hawaii. J. Parasitol. *22,* 515–516.

Alicata, J. E., and E. Chang. 1939. The life-history of *Hymenolepis exigua,* a cestode of poultry in Hawaii. J. Parasitol. *25,* 121–127.

Alicata, J. E., and M. F. Jones. 1933. The dung beetle, *Ataenius cognatus,* as the intermediate host of *Hymenolepis cantaniana.* J. Parasitol. *19,* 244.

Alt, H. L., and O. A. Tischer. 1931. Observations on the metabolism of the tapeworm, *Moniezia expansa.* Proc. Soc. Exp. Biol. Med. *29,* 222–224.

Anderson, M. G. 1934. The validity of *Taenia confusa* Ward, 1896. J. Parasitol. *20,* 207–212.

Anderson, M. G. 1935. Some intestinal parasites of *Natrix sepedon* Linn. With notes on the identity of *Ophiotaenia (Taenia) lactea* Leidy with *Ophiotaenia perspicua* La Rue. Ohio J. Sci. *35,* 78–80.

Ando, A., and S. Ito. 1921, 1922. A contribution to the study of *Dibothriocephalus latus.* Iji Shinbun, Tokyo, Nos. 1083, 1094.

Andry, N. 1700. De la génération des vers dans le corps de l'homme. 470 pp. Paris.

Antonow, A. 1932. Ueber die Art der Kapselbildung bei Hirncysticercose. Virchow's Arch. path. Anat. *285,* 485–493.

Ariola, V. 1896a. Sulla "Bothriotaenia plicata (Rud.)" e sul suo sviluppo. Atti soc. ligust. sci. nat. geogr. Genova *7,* 117–126.

Ariola, V. 1896b. Sopra alcuni Dibotrii nuovo o poco noti e sulla classificazione del gen. *Bothriocephalus.* Atti soc. ligust. sci. nat. geogr. Genova *7,* 261–282.

Ariola, V. 1899a. Osservazione sopra alcuni Dibotrii dei pesci. Atti soc. ligust. sci. nat. geogr. Genova *10,* 60–70.

Ariola, V. 1899b. Il gen. *Scyphocephalus* Rigg. e proposta di una nuova classificazione dei cestodi. Atti soc. ligust. sci. nat. geogr. Genova *10,* 160–167.

Ariola, V. 1900. Rivisione della famiglia Bothriocephalidae. Arch. Parasitol. *3,* 369–484.

Ariola, V. 1902a. Soni i cestodi polizoici? Atti soc. ligust. sci. nat. geogr. Genova *13,* 236–244.

Ariola, V. 1902b. La métamèrie et la théorie de la polyzoicité chez les cestodes. Rev. gen. sci. *13,* 471–476.

Ariola, V. 1902c. Ricerche anatamo-zoologiche sui cestodi parassiti del *Centrolophus pompilius.* Atti reale univ. Genova *17,* 117–170.

Arnold, J. G., Jr. 1938. A study of the anoplocephaline cestodes of North American rabbits. Zoologica *23,* 31–53.

Bacigalupo, J. 1926. *Hymenolepis diminuta*: su evolución. Semana Med. (Buenos Aires) *33,* 67–69.

Bacigalupo, J. 1927. *Hymenolepis intermedius* (nueva especie). Su evolución. Semana Med. (Buenos Aires) *34,* 239–240.

Bacigalupo, J. 1928a, 1928b, 1928c. Estudio sobre la evolución biológica de algunos parásitos del género *Hymenolepis* (Weinland, 1858). Semana Med. (Buenos Aires) *35,* 1249–1267, 1349–1366, 1428–1444.

Bacigalupo, J. 1928d. La evolución del *Hymenolepis nana.* Semana Med. (Buenos Aires) *35,* 200–201.

Bacigalupo, J. 1928e. *Hymenolepis microstoma* (Dujardin) chez *Mus musculus* (L.). Compt. rend. soc. biol. *99,* 2048–2057.

Bacigalupo, J. 1929. *Hymenolepis nana* (von Siebold, 1854) e *Hymenolepis fraterna* (Stiles, 1906). Rev. soc. Argentina biol. *5,* 599–604.

Bacigalupo, J. 1931a. El *Ctenocephalus canis* Curtis, en la évolution de la *Hymenolepis fraterna* Stiles. Semana Med. (Buenos Aires) *38,* 878–880.

Bacigalupo, J. 1931b. Evolution de l'*Hymenolepis fraterna* Stiles chez *Pulex irritans* L., *Xenopsylla cheops* Rothschild et *Ctenocephalus canis* Curtis. Ann. parasitol. humaine et comparée *9,* 339–343.

Bacigalupo, J. 1932. Algunas consideraciones sobre teniasis per *Hymenolepis nana.* Arch. Argentinos Enfermedades *7,* 359–364.

Bacigalupo, J. 1933. Quel est l'avenir du scolex échinococcique avalé par le lapin? Compt. rend. soc. biol. *114,* 89–92.

Bacigalupo, J. 1938. Nuevo huesped intermedierio de la *Hymenolepis diminuta* (Rudolphi, 1829), *Embia (Rhagadachir) argentina* Navas. Rev. med. trop. y parasitol. *4,* 45–47.

Bacigalupo, J. 1945. Diancyrobothriidae, neuva familia del ordan Seudophyllidea. Rev. soc. Argentina biol. *21,* 383–392.

Bacigalupo, J., and R. Rivero. 1948. Vaginal sphincter, new organ of *Echinococcus granulosus.* J. Parasitol. *34* Suppl., 25.

Baczynska, H. 1914. Etudes anatomiques et histologiques sur quelques nouvelles espèces de cestodes d'oiseaux. Bull. soc. sci. nat. Neuchâtel *40,* 187–239.

Baer, C. E. V. 1829. Ueber Linne's im Wassergefundenen Bandwürmer. Verhandl. Ges. nat. Freunde, Berlin I.

Baer, J. G. 1923a. Résultats zoologiques du voyage du Dr. P. A. Chappuis au Nil supèrieur, III. Helminthes. Rev. suisse zool. *30,* 337–352.

Baer, J. G. 1923b. Considérations sur le genre *Anoplocephala.* Bull. soc. sci. nat. Neuchâtel *48,* 3–16.

Baer, J. G. 1924a. On a cestode parasite of East African rock rabbits (*Procavia* sp.). J. Helm. *2*, 77–80.

Baer, J. G. 1924b. Contributions à la faune helminthologique Sud Africaine. Note préliminaire. Ann. parasitol. *2*, 239–247.

Baer, J. G. 1925a. Quelques cestodes d'oiseaux nouveaux et peu connus. Bull. soc. sci. nat. Neuchâtel *49*, 138–154.

Baer, J. G. 1925b. Sur quelques cestodes du Congo belge. Rev. suisse zool. *32*, 239–251.

Baer, J. G. 1925c. On some Cestoda described by Beddard, 1911–1920. Ann. Trop. Med. Parasitol. *19*, 1–22.

Baer, J. G. 1925d. Cestodes nouveaux du Sud-Ouest de l'Afrique. Rev. suisse zool. *31*, 529–548.

Baer, J. G. 1926a. Contribution to the helminth fauna of South Africa – mammalian cestodes. Union of South Africa Dept. Agr. 11th and 12th. Rep. Dir. Vet. Ed. Res. Pretoria, pp. 61–136.

Baer, J. G. 1926b. Cestodes de mammifères. Bull. soc. sci. nat. Neuchâtel *50*, 77–81.

Baer, J. G. 1927a. Monographie des cestodes de la famille des Anoplocephalides. Bull. biol. France et Belg. Suppl. 10. 241 pp. Paris.

Baer, J. G. 1927b. On a new species of *Hymenolepis* from a monkey. J. Parasitol. *14*, 48–50.

Baer, J. G. 1927c. Des cestodes adultes peuvent-ils vivre dans la cavité générale d'oiseaux? Ann. parasitol. humaine et comparée *5*, 337–340.

Baer, J. G. 1927d. Contributions to the anatomy of some reptilian cestodes. Parasitology *19*, 274–283.

Baer, J. G. 1927e. Die Cestoden der Säugetiere Brasiliens. Abhandl. Senkenbergischen Naturforsch. Ges. *40*, 377–386.

Baer, J. G. 1928. Notes sur les Ténias des autruches. Bull. soc. sci. nat. Neuchâtel *52*, 7–13.

Baer, J. G. 1931a. A propos d'une nouvelle classification des cestodes du genre *Davainea* R. Bl. s. l. Bull. soc. zool. France *55*, 44–57.

Baer, J. G. 1931b. Sur la position systématique du *Taenia muris-sylvatica* Rudolphi, 1819. Bull. soc. sci. nat. Neuchâtel *55*, 35–39.

Baer, J. G. 1932a. Contribution à faune helminthologique de Suisse. Rev. suisse zool. *39*, 1–57.

Baer, J. G. 1932b. Contribution à l'étude des cestodes de cétacés. Rev. suisse zool. *39*, 195–228.

Baer, J. G. 1933. Contribution à l'étude de la faune helminthologique africaine. Rev. suisse zool. *40*, 31–84.

Baer, J. G. 1935. Etude de quelques helminthes de lémuriens. Rev. suisse zool. *42*, 275–291.

Baer, J. G. 1937a. Un cestode nouveau parasite d'un poisson d'ornament. Bull. soc. nationale d'acclimation France, Année 84, pp. 168–173.

Baer, J. G. 1937b. Un genre nouveau de cestodes d'oiseaux. Bull. soc. sci. nat. Neuchâtel *62*, 149–156.

Baer, J. G. 1940a. Some avian tapeworms from Antigua. Parasitology *32*, 174–197.

Baer, J. G. 1940b. The origin of human tapeworms. J. Parasitol. *26*, 174–197.

Baer, J. G. 1941. L'existence aventureuse des vers solitaires. Leçon inaugurale prononcée par Jean G. Baer le 26 Novembre 1941 à son installation à la chaire de zoologie et d'anatomie comparée a l'Université de Neuchâtel.

Baer, J. G. 1945. La sparganose oculaire. Acta Tropica *2*, 155–157.

Baer, J. G. 1946a. Le parasitisme. 232 pp. Lausanne.

Baer, J. G. 1946b. Les helminthes parasites des vertébrés. Premier colloque franco-suisse, Besançon.

Baer, J. G. 1946c. La signification des générations larvaires chez les vers plats parasites. Rev. scientifique *84*, 263–272.

Baer, J. G. 1948. Contributions à l'étude des cestodes de sélaciens. I–IV. Bull. soc. sci. nat. Neuchâtel *71*, 63–122.

Baer, J. G. 1949. Contributions à la faune helminthologique africaine. Acta Tropica *6*, 41–45.

Baer, J. G. 1950a. Etude critique des helminthes parasites de l'okapi. Acta Tropica *7*, 164–186.

Baer, J. G. 1950b. Phylogénie et cycles, évolutifs des cestodes. Rev. suisse zool. *57*, 553–558.

Baer, J. G., and C. Joyeux. 1944. Réalisation expèrimentale d'un nouveau cycle évolutif de cestode de la souris blanche (note préliminaire). Actes soc. helv. sci. nat., pp. 133–134.

Baer, J. G., P. Kouri, and F. Sotolongo. 1949. Anatomie, position systematique et epidemologie de *Inermicapsifer cubensis* (Kouri, 1938) Kouri, 1940. Acta Tropica *6*, 120–130.

Bailliet, C. 1863. Recherches sur un cystique polycéphale du lapin. Mém. acad. imp. Toulouse *11*, 452–482.

Bailliet, C. 1866. Histoire naturelle des helminthes des principaux mammifères domestiques. Paris.

Baird, W. 1853. A catalogue of the species of entozoa or intestinal worms contained in the collection of the British Museum. 132 pp. London.

Baird, W. 1860. Descriptions of some new species of intestinal worms. Proc. Roy. Soc. London *28*, 446–448.

Baird, W. 1861. Descriptions of some new species of intestinal worms. Ann. Mag. Nat. Hist. 7.

Baird, W. 1862. Descriptions of two new species of cestode worms belonging to the genus *Taenia*. Proc. Zool. Soc. London, 1862, pp. 18–25.

Baker, A. D. 1932. Records of distribution of internal parasites of poultry in Quebec. Sci. Agr. *13*, 127–130.

Balss, H. H. 1908. Ueber die Entwicklung des Geschlechtsgänge bei Cestoden. Z. wiss. Zool. *91*, 226–296.

Baltzer, F. 1926. Vermännlichungen indifferenter Bonellia-larven durch Bonellia Extrakte. Rev. suisse zool. *33*.

Bangham, R. V. 1925–1941. Series of articles on the tapeworms of North American freshwater fishes in Ohio J. Sci. *25*, *41*; Trans. Am. Fish. Soc. *63*, *68*, *70*.

Bangham, R. V., and C. E. Venard. 1942. Studies on the parasites of Reelfoot Lake fishes. Tennessee Acad. Sci. *17*, 22–38.

Barbieri, C. 1909. Ueber eine neue Species der Gattung *Ichthyotaenia* und ihre Verbreitungsweise. Centralbl. Bakt. Parasitenk. *49*, 334–340.

Barker, F. 1910. Some new cases of trihedral *Taenia*. Science *31*, 837.

Barker, F. 1914. A contribution to the evolution of the cestode rostellum. Science *39*.

Barker, F. 1915. Parasites of American muskrats (*Fiber zibethicus*). J. Parasitol. *1*, 184–197.

Barker, F. 1916. Are polyradiate cestodes mutations? Anat. Rec. *11*, 507.

Barrois, T. 1898. Sur quelques Ichthyoténias parasites de serpents. Bull. soc. sci. agr. arts Lille 2.

Bartels, E. 1902. *Cysticercus fasciolaris*. Beiträge zur Anatomie, Entwicklung und Umwandlung in *Taenia crassicollis*. Zool. Jahrb. Anat. *16*, 511–570.

Bashkirova, E. Y. 1941. Etude biologique des *Anoplocephala perfoliata* Goeze, 1782. Vestnik Selskokhozyaustvennol Nauki. Veterinariya No. 2, 57–67.

Batsch, A. J. G. 1786. Naturgeschichte der Bandwurmgattung ueberhaupt und ihre Arten insbesondere . . . 298 pp. Halle.

Bavay, M. 1890. Sur la presénce du *Bothriocephalus latus* à Madagascar. Bull. soc. zool. France *15*, 134–135.

Baylis, H. A. 1914. On *Octopetalum*, a new genus of avian Cestodes. Ann. Mag. Nat. Hist. (Ser. 8) *14*, 414–420.

Baylis, H. A. 1915. A new cestode of the genus *Zschokkeella*. Ann. Mag. Nat. Hist. (Ser. 8) *16*, 40–49.

Baylis, H. A. 1919a. A collection of Entozoa, chiefly from birds, from the Murman Coast. Ann. Mag. Nat. Hist. (Ser. 9) *3*, 501–513.

Baylis, H. A. 1919b. On two new species of the cestode genus *Oochoristica* from lizards. Parasitology *11*, 405–414.

Baylis, H. A. 1920. Notes on some parasitic worms from East Africa. Ann. Mag. Nat. Hist. (Ser. 9) *9*, 292–295.

Baylis, H. A. 1922a. A new cestode . . . from Spitzbergen. Ann. Mag. Nat. Hist. (Ser. 9) 9, 421–497.

Baylis, H. A. 1922b. Observations on certain cestodes of rats . . . Parasitology *14*, 1–8.

Baylis, H. A. 1926a. Some tetrabothriid cestodes from whales of the genus *Balaenoptera*. J. Linnean Soc. London *36*, 161–172.

Baylis, H. A. 1926b. Some parasitic worms from Sarawak. Sarawak Museum J. No. 10, pp. 303–322.

Baylis, H. A. 1927a. Some parasites of whales. Nat. Hist. Mag. London *1*, 55–57.

Baylis, H. A. 1927b. On two adult cestodes from wild swine. Ann. Mag. Nat. Hist. (Ser. 9) *19*, 417–425.

Baylis, H. A. 1927c. The cestode genus *Catenotaenia*. Ann. Mag. Nat. Hist. (Ser. 9) *19*, 433–439.

Baylis, H. A. 1928a. Some parasitic worms . . . from Tanganyika. Ann. Mag. Nat. Hist. (Ser. 10) *1*, 552–562.

Baylis, H. A. 1928b. A new species of *Schizotaenia* from the capybara. Ann. Mag. Nat. Hist. (Ser. 10) *1*, 601–605.

Baylis, H. A. 1929a. On larval forms of *Acanthotaenia*. Ann. Mag. Nat. Hist. (Ser. 10) *10*.

Baylis, H. A. 1929b. Some new parasitic nematodes and cestodes from Java. Parasitology *21*, 25–65.

Baylis, H. A. 1932a. List of worms parasitic in Cetacea. Discovery Reports (Government Dependencies, Falkland Islands), Cambridge University Press, *6*, 393–418.

Baylis, H. A. 1932b. On a coenurus from man. Trans. Roy. Soc. Trop. Med. Hyg. *25*, 275–280.

Baylis, H. A. 1934a. Miscellaneous notes on parasitic worms. Ann. Mag. Nat. Hist. (Ser. 10) *13*, 223–228.

Baylis, H. A. 1934b. On a collection of cestodes and nematodes from small mammals in Tanganyika Territory. Ann. Mag. Nat. Hist. (Ser. 10) *13*, 338–353.

Baylis, H. A. 1934c. Two new species of the genus *Bertiella* . . . Ann. Mag. Nat. Hist. (Ser. 10) *14*, 412–421.

Baylis, H. A. 1934d. Notes on four cestodes. Ann. Mag. Nat. Hist. (Ser. 10) *14*, 587–594.

Baylis, H. A. 1934e. Some parasitic worms from Australia. Parasitology *26*, 129–132.

Baylis, H. A. 1935a. Some parasitic worms from muskrats in Great Britain. Ann. Mag. Nat. Hist. (Ser. 10) *15*, 543–549.

Baylis, H. A. 1935b. Note on the cestode *Moniezia (Fuhrmannella) transvaalensis* (Baer, 1925). Ann. Mag. Nat. Hist. (Ser. 10) *15*, 673–675.

Baylis, H. A. 1935c. The plerocercoid larva of *Bothridium*. Ann. Mag. Nat. Hist. (Ser. 10) *16*, 482–485.

Baylis, H. A. 1945. On the probable identity of a cestode of the genus *Diphyllobothrium* occurring in Wales and Eire. Ann. Trop. Med. Parasitol. *39*, 41–45.

Baylis, H. A. 1948. "Taenia exigua" Dujardin. Ann. Mag. Nat. Hist. (Ser. 11) *14*, 355–358.

Baylis, H. A. 1949. A new human cestode infection in Kenya, *Inermicapsifer arvicanthidis*, a parasite of rats. Trans. Roy. Soc. Trop. Med. Hyg. *42*, 531–542.

Bayon, H. P. 1927a. Parasites and malignant proliferations. J. Trop. Med. Hyg. London *30*, 73–80.

Bayon, H. P. 1927b. Carcinoma in apposition to *Cysticercus fasciolaris* in a mouse infected with cancer cells. Parasitology *19*, 328–332.

Bayon, H. P. 1933. Recent advances in our knowledge of poultry diseases. Vet. Rec. *13*, 655–669.

Bearup, A. J. 1948. Observations on the life-cycle of *Diphyllobothrium (Spirometra) erinacei* in Australia. Australian J. Sci. *10*, 183–184.

Beauchamp, P. M. de. 1905. Etude sur les cestodes des sélaciens. Arch. Parasitol. *9*, 463–539.

Beaver, P. C., and P. H. Simer. 1940. A re-study of the three existing species of the cestode genus *Marsipometra* Cooper (Amphicotylidae) from the spoonbill, *Polyodon spathula* (Wal.). Trans. Am. Microscop. Soc. *59*, 167–182.

Becker, E. R. 1933. Two observations on helminthes. Trans. Am. Microsop. Soc. 52, 361–362.

Becker, R. 1920. Ueber das Vorkommen von Bandwürmern beim Pferde. Berlin. u. München. tierärzt. Wochenschr.

Becker, R. 1921a. Die aussere Gestalt der Pferdebandwürmer. Centralbl. Bakt. Parasitenk. *87*, 110–118.

Becker, R. 1921b. Weitere Beträge zur Anatomie der Pferdebandwürmer. Centralbl. Bakt. Parasitenk. *87*, 216–227.

Becker, R. 1922. Der Genitalapparat der Pferdebandwürmer. Centralbl. Bakt. Parasitenk. *88*, 483–501.

Becker, R. 1923. Zur Nomenklatur der Pferdebandwürmer. Centralbl. Bakt. Parasitenk. *91*, 63–67.

Beddard, F. E. 1911–1916. Contributions to the anatomy and systematic arrangement of the Cestoidea. Proc. Zool. Soc. London, 1911–1916.

1911a. I. On some mammalian Cestoidea. Pp. 626–660.

1911b. II. On two new genera of Cestoides from mammals. Pp. 904–1018.

1912a. III. On a new genus of tapeworms (*Otidotaenia*) from the bustard (*Eupodotes kori*). Pp. 194–221.

1912b. IV. On a new species of *Inermicapsifer* from the hyrax and on the genera *Zschokkeella, Thysanotaenia* and *Hyracotaenia.* Pp. 576–607.

1912c. V. On a new genus (*Dasyurotaenia*) from the Tasmanian devil *Dasyurus ursinus,* the type of a new family. Pp. 677–695.

1912d. VI. On an asexual tapeworm from the rodent *Fiber zibethicus* showing a new form of asexual reproduction and on the supposed asexual form. Pp. 822–850.

1913a. VII. On six species of tapeworms from reptiles belonging to the genus *Ichthyotaenia* (s.l.). Pp. 4–36.

1913b. VIII. On some species of *Ichthyotaenia* and *Ophidotaenia.* Pp. 153–168.

1913c. IX. On a new genus of Ichthyotaeniids. Pp. 243–261.

1913d. X. On two new species of tapeworms from *Genetta dongolana.* Pp. 549–571.

1913e. XI. On a new tapeworm from *Oedicnemus.* Pp. 861–877.

1914a. XII. Further observations on the genus *Urocystidium.* Pp. 1–22.

1914b. XIII. On two new species belonging to the genera *Oochoristica* and *Linstowia.* Pp. 265–269.

1914c. XIV. On a new species of *Rhabdometra* and on paruterine organs in *Otidotaenia.* Pp. 859–887.

1914d. XV. On a new species and genus of the family Acoleidae. Pp. 1039–1055.

1915a. XVI. On certain points in the anatomy of the genus *Amabilia* and of *Dasyurotaenia.* Pp. 175–191.

1915b. XVII. On *Taenia tauricollis* of Chapman and on the genus *Chapmania.* Pp. 429–443.

1915c. XVIII. On *Taenia struthionis* (Parona) and allied forms. Pp. 589–601.

1916. XXII. On two new species of cestodes belonging to the genera *Linstowia* and *Cotugnia.* Pp. 695–706.

Beddard, F. E. 1917. On the scolex of the cestode genus *Duthiersia* . . . Proc. Zool. Soc. London, p. 73.

Beddard, F. E. 1920. On a new tentaculate cestode. Ann. Mag. Nat. Hist. (Ser. 9) 5, 203–207.

Beneden, P. J. van. 1849a. Sur le développement des Tétrarhynches. Bull. acad. roy. sci. Belg. *16*, 44–52.

Beneden, P. J. van. 1849b. Notice sur un nouveau genre d'helminthe cestoide. Bull. acad. roy. soc. sci. Belg. *16*, 182–193.

Beneden, P. J. van. 1849c, 1850a. Les helminthes cestoïdes considerés sous le rapport de leurs métamorphoses, de leur composition anatomique, et de leur classification. Bull. acad. roy. sci. Belg. *16*, 269–282; *17*, 102–108.

Beneden, P. J. van. 1850b. Recherches sur le faune littorale de Belgique; les vers cestoïdes. Mém. acad. roy. sci. Belg. *25*, 1–204.

Beneden, P. J. van. 1858–61. Mémoire sur les vers intestinaux. Suppl. to Compt. rend. acad. sci. Paris *2*, 1–376.

Beneden, P. J. van. 1870a. Recherches sur la composition et la signification de l'oeuf. Mém. acad. roy. sci. Belg. *38*.

Beneden, P. J. van. 1870b. Les poissons des côtes de Belge, leurs parasites et leurs commençeaux. Mém. acad. roy. sci. Belg. *38*, 1–120.

Beneden, P. J. van. 1881. Recherches sur le développement embryonnaire de quelques Ténias. Arch. Biol. Liège *2*, 183–210.

Beneden, P. J. van. 1889. Deux cestodes nouveaux de *Lamna cornubica*. Bull. acad. roy. sci. Belg. *17*.

Benedict, H. M. 1900. On the structure of two fish tapeworms of the genus *Proteocephalus* Weinland, 1858. J. Morph. *16*, 337–368.

Benham, W. B. 1900. The structure of the rostellum in two new species of tapeworm from *Apteryx*. Quart. J. Microscop. Sci. *43*, 83–96.

Benham, W. B. 1901. The Platyelmia and Nemertini. A treatise on zoology. E. R. Lankester. Pt. 4. 204 pp. London.

Beumer, H. 1919. Zur pathogenetischen Bedeutung der Ölsäure bei Anämien. Biochem. Z. *95*, 239–248.

Bhaduri, N. V., and P. A. Maplestone. 1940. Variations in *Taenia gaigeri* (Hall, 1919). Records of the Indian Museum *42*, 431–435.

Bhalerao, G. D. 1936. On some representatives of the cestode genus *Avitellina* from India. J. Helm. *14*, 141–162.

Birkeland, I. W. 1932. Bothriocephalus anemia: *Diphyllobothrium latus* and pernicious anemia. Medicine *11*.

Bischoff, C. R. 1912. Cestoden aus Hyrax. Zool. Anz. *39*, 751–758.

Bischoff, C. R. 1913. Cestoden aus Hyrax. Rev. suisse zool. *21*, 225–284.

Blainville, H. D. 1820. Entozoorum synopsis cui accedunt mantissa duplex et indices locupletissimi, auctore Carolo Asmund Rudolphi . . . Extrait par M. H. de Blainville, Journal du Physique, Paris, *40*, 229–234.

Blainville, H. D. 1824. Traité zoologique et physiologique sur les vers intestinaux de l'homme. 52 pp. Paris.

Blainville, H. D. 1828a. *Proteocephala*. Dictionnaire des sciences naturelles . . . par plusieurs professeurs du Jardin du Roi . . . *52*, 365–625.

Blainville, H. D. 1828b. Tentaculaire, *Tentacularia*. Dictionnaire des sciences naturelles . . . par plusieurs professeurs du Jardin du Roi . . . *53*, 94–95.

Blanchard, E. 1848. Deuxième ordre des intestinaux, les Parenchymateux. In Le règne animal . . . par Georges Cuvier. Paris.

Blanchard, E. 1849. Recherches sur l'organisation des vers. In Recherches anatomiques et zoologiques . . . par H. Milne Edwards, A. de Quatrefages, Emile Blanchard. Ann. sci. nat. zool. *10*, *11*, 321–364, 106–202.

Blanchard, R. 1888. Traité du zoologie médicale. Paris.

Blanchard, R. 1891a. Sur les helminthes des Primates anthropoïdes. Mém. soc. zool. France *4*, 186–196.

Blanchard, R. 1891b. Notions helminthologiques (2me sér.); sur les Téniadés à ventouses armées genres *Echinocotyle, Davainea, Ophriocotyle*. Mém. soc. zool. France *4*, 420–429.

Blanchard, R. 1891c. Histoire zoologique et médicale des Téniadés du genre *Hymenolepis* Weinland. 112 pp. Paris.

Blanchard, R. 1894. Notice sur les parasites de l'homme (3me sér.); sur le *Krabbea grandis* et rémarques sur la classification de Bothriocéphalines. Compt. rend. soc. biol. Paris *46*, 699–702.

Blanchard, R. 1908. Le genre *Chlamydocephalus* Cohn, 1906 remplacé par *Cephalochlamys* R. Bl. Arch. Parasitol. *12*, 334.

Blanchard, R. 1909. *Cotylorhipis furnarii*, nouveau genre de Téniadés. Arch. Parasitol. *13*, 477–482.

Blanchard, R. 1913. *Bertiella satyri* de l'orang utan . . . Bull. acad. méd. (Paris) 9, 286–296.

Blanchard, R. 1916. Tête de *Davainea madagascariensis*. Bull. soc. path. exotique Paris 9, 413.

Blanchard, R., and A. Railliet. 1891. In R. Blanchard, Histoire zoologique . . . du genre *Hymenolepis* Weinland. Paris.

Blei, R. 1921. Drei neue Schafszestoden. Centralbl. Bakt. Parasitenk. 87, 365–387.

Bloch, M. E. 1779. Beitrag zur Naturgeschichte der Würmer, welche in andern Thieren leben. Beschft. Berl. Ges. naturf. Fr. *4*, 534–561.

Bloch, M. E. 1782. Abhandlung von der Erzeugung der Eingeweidewürmer und den Mitteln wider disselben. 54 pp. Berlin.

Blochmann, F. 1892. Ueber Sommer's sogenannte "plasmatische Längsgefässe" bei *Taenia saginata* Goeze und *Taenia solium* L. Centralbl. Bakt. Parasitenk. *12*, 373–379.

Blochmann, F. 1895. Ueber freie Nervendigungen und Sinneszellen bei Bandwürmern. Biol. Zentr. *15*, 14–25.

Blochmann, F. 1896. Die Epithelfrage bei Cestoden und Trematoden. 12 pp. Hamburg.

Blochmann, F. 1897. Zur Epithelfrage bei Cestoden. Zool. Anz. *20*, 460–463.

Bloor, W. R. 1925. Plasma lipoids in experimental anemia. J. Biol. Chem. *63*, 1–15.

Bloor, W. R. 1936. The cholesterol content of muscle. J. Biol. Chem. *114*, 639–648.

Bloor, W. R., and D. J. MacPherson. 1917. The blood lipids in anemia. J. Biol. Chem. *31*, 75–95.

Boas, J. E. V. 1902. *Triplotaenia mirabilis.* Zool. Jahrb. Syst. *17*, 329–334.

Boehm, L. K. 1921. Beiträge zur Kenntnis tierischer Parasiten. Centralbl. Bakt. Parasitenk. *87*, 407–426.

Boehm, L. K. 1925. Ein neuer Bandwurm vom Huhn, *Raillietina (Davainea) grobbeni* n. sp. Z. wiss. Zool. *125*, 518–532.

Bonnet, C. 1762. Considérations sur les corps organisés. Amsterdam.

Bonsdorff, B. von. 1939–1943. *Diphyllobothrium latum* and pernicious anemia. Studies I–VI. Acta Medica Scandinavica *100–116*.

Borcea, L. 1933. Note sur *Tetrarhynchobothrium tenuicolle* Diesing. Ann. sci. univ. Jassy *17*, 565–567.

Borcea, L. 1934. Note préliminaire sur les cestodes des Elasmobranches ou Sélaciens de la Mer Noire. Ann. sci. univ. Jassy *19*, 345–369.

Borcea, L. 1935a. Nouvelle note sur *Acanthobothrium ponticum* L. Borcea. Ann. sci. univ. Jassy *20*, 480–481.

Borcea, L. 1935b. Sur la présence du cestode *Diphyllobothrium stemmacephalum* Cobbold comme parasite chez le marsouin, *Phocaena phocaena,* de la Mer Noire. Ann. sci. univ. Jassy *21*, 524–525.

Borrel, A. 1906. Tumeurs cancereuses et helminthes. Bull. acad. méd. (Paris) *56*, 141.

Borrel, A., and F. Larrousse. 1932. Forme anormale du *Cysticercus fasciolaris* et adenome hépatique chez le rat. Compt. rend. soc. biol. *109*, 225–227.

Bosc, L. A. G. 1797. Description des objets nouveaux d'histoire naturelle trouvés dans une traversée de Bordeaux a Charles-town. Bull. des sciences par la soc. philomatique, Paris, mai 1797, pp. 9–10.

Bosc, L. A. G. 1802. Histoire naturelle des vers . . . Vol. II. 300 pp. Paris.

Bosc, L. A. G. 1811. Sur des nouveaux genres des vers . . . Bull. des sciences par la soc. philomatique, Paris, *2*, 384–385.

Bosc, L. A. G. 1817. Hepatoxylon, *Hepatoxylon.* Nouveau dictionnaire d'hist. nat. appliquée aux arts . . . par une soc. de naturalistes et d'agriculteurs, Paris, *14*, 334–355.

Bosc, L. A. G. 1819a. Tentaculaire, *Tentacularia.* Nouveau dictionnaire d'hist. nat. appliquée aux arts . . . par une soc. de naturalistes et d'agriculteurs, Paris, *33*, 54–55.

Bosc, L. A. G. 1819b. Tetrarhynque, *Tetrarhynchus.* Nouveau dictionnaire d'hist. nat. appliquée aux arts . . . par une soc. de naturalistes et d'agriculteurs, Paris, *33*, 429.

Boughton, R. 1932. The influence of helminth parasites on the abundance of the snowshoe rabbit in western Canada. Can. J. Research 7, 524–547.

Bourquin, J. 1905. Cestodes de mammifères; le genre *Bertia.* Rev. suisse zool. *13*, 415–503.

Bourquin, J. 1906. Une nouveau Taenia (*Davainea*) chez les Prosimiens. Centralbl. Bakt. Parasitenk. *41*, 222.

Bovien, P. 1926. Caryophyllaeidae from Java. Medd. fra Dansk. naturh. Foren *82*, 167–181.

Brand, T. von. 1929. Stoffbestand und Stoffwechsel von *Moniezia expansa.* Verh. deutsch. zool. Ges. *33*; Suppl. Zool. Anz., pp. 64–66.

Brand, T. von. 1933. Untersuchungen ueber den Stoffbestand einiger Cestoden und den Stoffwechsel von *Moniezia expansa.* Z. vergleich. Physiol. *18*, 562–596.

Brand, T. von. 1938. The nature of the metabolic activities of intestinal helminths in their natural habitat: aerobiosis or anaerobiosis. Biodynamica *41*, 1–13.

Brand, T. von, F. Holtz, and H. Vogel. 1933. Experimentelle Verkalkung unter dem Einfluss des Calcinofaktors bei Befall mit tierischen Parasiten. Z. Parasitenk. *6*, 308–322.

Brand, T. von, and W. Weise. 1932. Beobachtungen ueber den Sauerstoffgehalt der Umwelt einiger Entoparasiten. Z. vergleich. Physiol. *18*, 339–346.

Brandt, B. B. 1936. Parasites of certain North Carolina salients. Ecological Monogr. *6*, 491–532.

Brandt, E. K. 1888. Zwei Fälle von *Taenia cucumerina* Rud. beim Menschen. Zool. Anz. *11*, 481–484.

Braun, M. 1882. Zur Frage des Zwischenwirts von *Bothriocephalus latus* Brem. Zool. Anz. *5*, 39–43.

Braun, M. 1883a. Die thierischen Parasiten des Menschen nebst einer Anleitung zur praktischen Beschäftigung mit der Helminthologie. 232 pp. Wurzburg.

Braun, M. 1883b. Zur Entwicklungsgeschichte des breiten Bandwurms (*Bothriocephalus latus* Brems.). 64 pp. Wurzburg.

Braun, M. 1888. Ueber parasitische Schnurwürmer. Centralbl. Bakt. Parasitenk. *3*, 16–19.

Braun, M. 1889a. Die embryonale Entwicklung der Cestoden. Centralbl. Bakt. Parasitenk. *5*.

Braun, M. 1889b. *Gyrocotyle, Amphiptyches* und Verwandte. Zusammenfassender Bericht. Centralbl. Bakt. Parasitenk. *6*, 436–441.

Braun, M. 1891. Helminthologische Mittheilungen. Centralbl. Bakt. Parasitenk. *9*, 52–56.

Braun, M. 1892. Verzeichniss von Eingeweidewürmern aus Mecklenburg. Archiv. des Vereins der Freunde der Naturgeschichte in Mecklenburg *45*. Gustrow.

Braun, M. 1894–1900. In H. G. Bronn, Klassen und Ordnungen des Thierreichs, Band IV, Vermes; Abtheilung I.b., Cestodes. Pp. i–vii + 927–1731. Leipzig.

Braun, M. 1896. Helminthologische Notizen. V. Ein prolieferender Cysticercus und die zugehörige Tänie. Zool. Anz. *19*, 417–420.

Braun, M. 1897. Zur Entwicklungsgeschichte des *Cysticercus longicollis* Rud. Zool. Anz. *20*, 1–2.

Braun, M. 1905. Notiz zur Entwicklung der *Taenia tenuicollis* Rud. Centralbl. Bakt. Parasitenk. *39*.

Bremser, J. G. 1811. Nachricht von einer betrachtlichen Sammlung thierischer Eingeweidewürmer. 31 pp. Vienna.

Bremser, J. G. 1819. Ueber lebende Würmer in lebenden Menschen. 284 pp. Vienna.

Bremser, J. G. 1824. Icones helminthum systema Rudolphii entozoologicum illustrantes. 12 pp. Vienna.

Bresslau, E. 1904. Beiträge zur Entwicklungsgeschichte der Turbellaria. Jenaische Z. *76*, 213–332.

Briganti, V. 1819. Descrizione delle ligule, che abitano nell' addomine de ciprini del lago di Palo in prov. di principato Citra. Atti reale accad. sci. Napoli *1*, 209–233.

Briganti, V. 1825. Ne novo vermium intestinalium genere, cui nomen *Balanoforus* descriptio. Atti reale accad. sci. Napoli *2*, 79–86.

Brock, M. E. 1941. *Hymenolepis stolli,* a new hymenolepidid cestode from the pintail duck. Wasmann Collector *4*, 35–37.

Brock, M. E. 1942. A new hymenolepidid tapeworm, *Hymenolepis filumferens,* from the blue winged teal. Trans. Am. Microscop. Soc. *61*, 180–185.

Brown, F. J. 1933. Life-history of the fowl tapeworm, *Davainea proglottina.* Nature *131*, 276–277.

Brumpt, E. 1933. Evolution de l'*Hymenolepis nana* var. *fraterna* . . . Arch. zool. exp. gen. *75*, 235–246.

Brumpt, E. 1934. Réproduction expérimentale du sarcoma hépatique du rat par le cysticerque du *Taenia taeniaeformis* (= *T. crassicollis*) du chat. Ann. parasitol. humaine et comparée *12*, 130–133.

Brumpt, E. 1936. Précis de parasitologie. 5th Edition. Paris.

Brumpt, E., and C. Joyeux. 1924. Un nouvel échinocoque, *Echinococcus cruzi*. Ann. parasitol. humaine et comparée *2*.

Bugge, G. 1902. Zur Kenntnis des Excretionsgefässesystem der Cestoden und Trematoden. Zool. Jahrb. Anat. *16*, 177–234.

Bull, H. B. 1937. Biochemistry of the lipids. New York.

Bullock, F. D., and M. R. Curtis. See Curtis and others.

Burge, W. E., and E. L. Burge. 1915. The protection of parasites in the digestive tract against the action of digestive enzymes. J. Parasitol. *1*, 179–183.

Burr, A. 1912. Zur Fortpflanzunggeschichte der Süsswasser Tricladen. Zool. Jahrb. Syst. *33*.

Burt, D. R. R. 1933. *Oochoristica lygostomatae* sp. n. . . . Ceylon J. Sci. *18*, 1–7.

Burt, D. R. R. 1937. Two new reptilian cestodes of the genus *Proteocephalus* (*Ophiotaenia*). Ceylon J. Sci. *20*, 157–179.

Burt, D. R. R. 1938a. New avian cestodes of the family Dilepididae from *Collocalia unicolor unicolor* . . . Ceylon J. Sci. *21*, 1–14.

Burt, D. R. R. 1938b. A new avian cestode, *Pseudochoanotaenia collocaliae* gen. et sp. nov. (Dipylidiinae) . . . Ceylon J. Sci. *21*, 15–20.

Burt, D. R. R. 1938c. New avian cestodes of the sub-family Dilepidinae from the eastern swallow (*Hirundo rustica gutturalis*) with descriptions of *Vitta magniuncinata* gen. et sp. nov. Ceylon J. Sci. *21*, 21–30.

Burt, D. R. R. 1939. Some new cestodes of the genus *Paronia*. Ceylon J. Sci. *21*, 209–218.

Burt, D. R. R. 1940a. Some new species of cestodes from Charadriiformes, Ardeiformes and Pelicaniformes in Ceylon. Ceylon J. Sci. *22*, 1–63.

Burt, D. R. R. 1940b. New avian cestodes of the family Davaineidae from Ceylon. Ceylon J. Sci. *22*, 65–77.

Burt, D. R. R. 1944a. A new avian cestode, *Krimi chrysocolaptis* . . . gen. et sp. nov. . . . Ceylon J. Sci. *22*, 162–164.

Burt, D. R. R. 1944b. New avian species of *Hymenolepis* from Ceylon. Ceylon J. Sci. *22*, 165–172.

Butning, P. 1927. Ueber den Mechanismus der Verwandlung des *Cysticercus cellulosae* in die *Taenia solium* und ueber die Wirkung der Verdauungssafte auf diesen Prozess. Z. Okol. Tiere, Berlin, *8*, 400–432.

Bychowsky, B. E. 1937. Ontogenetic and phylogenetic relationships of parasitic flatworms. Bull. acad. sci. U.R.S.S. classe sci. math. et nat. ser. biol., pp. 1353–1383.

Byrd, E. E., and J. W. Ward. 1943. Observations on the segmental anatomy of the tapeworm *Mesocestoides variabilis* Mueller from the opossum. J. Parasitol. *29*, 217–226.

Callot, J., and C. Desportes. 1934. Sur le cycle évolutif de *Schistocephalus solidus* (O. F. Mueller). Ann. parasitol. humaine et comparée *12*, 35–39.

Cameron, G. R. 1926. A note on the enzymes of the hydatid cyst. Australian J. Exp. Biol. Med. Sci. Adelaide *3*, 11–14.

Cameron, G. R., and A. S. Fitzpatrick. 1925. The hydatid cyst: the microchemical reactions of the hydatid cyst wall. Am. J. Path. *1*, 227–233.

Cameron, T. W. M. 1925. The cestode genus *Mesocestoides* Vaillant. J. Helm. *3*, 33–44.

Cameron, T. W. M. 1926. Observations on the genus *Echinococcus* Rudolphi, 1801. J. Helm. *4*, 13–22.

Cameron, T. W. M. 1927. Some modern conceptions of the hydatid. Proc. Roy. Soc. Med. *20*, 272–283.

Cameron, T. W. M. 1928. On some parasites of the rusty tiger cat (*Felis planiceps*). J. Helm. *6*, 87–98.

Cameron, T. W. M. 1929. A new record of the occurrence of a tapeworm of the genus *Bertiella* in man. J. Helm. *7*, 231–234.
Cameron, T. W. M. 1933. The internal parasites of land mammals in Scotland. Proc. Roy. Physical Soc. *22*, 133–154.
Cameron, T. W. M. 1936. Studies on the endoparasitic fauna of Trinidad. III. Some parasites of Trinidad carnivora. Can. J. Research *14*, 25–38.
Cameron, T. W. M. 1937. Concepts and mechanisms of resistance in helminthic infections. Can. J. Research *15*, 77–90.
Campbell, D. H. 1936. Active immunisation of albino rats with protein fractions from *Taenia taeniaeformis* and its larval form *Cysticercus fasciolaris*. Am. J. Hyg. *23*, 104–113.
Campbell, D. H. 1937. The immunological specificity of a polysaccharide fraction from some common parasitic helminths. J. Parasitol. *23*, 348–353.
Campbell, D. H. 1942. Experimental eosinophilia with keratin from *Ascaris suum* and other sources. J. Infectious Diseases *71*, 270–276.
Canavan, W. P. 1927. Notes on the actual appearance of a cestode shell gland. Parasitology *19*, 283.
Canavan, W. P. 1928a. A new species of *Phyllobothrium* van Ben. from an Alaska dog salmon, with a note on the occurrence of *Crossobothrium augustum* Linton in the thresher shark. J. Helm. *6*, 51–55.
Canavan, W. P. 1928b. Notes on the occurrence of *Ophiotaenia loennbergi* in Pennsylvania. J. Helm. *6*, 56.
Canavan, W. P. 1932. The spread of broad fish tapeworm of man. Science *75*, 270.
Canavan, W. P. 1933. A six suckered tapeworm, *Taenia hydatigena* (*Hydatigena* Pallas, 1776). J. Parasitol. *20*, 57.
Cannon, D. G. 1939. On the parasites of the small intestine of the European starling (*Sturnus vulgaris*) in Quebec. Canadian Field Naturalist *53*, 40–42.
Carta, A. 1939a. L'identificazione del ciclo evolutivo del *Mesocestoides lineatus* provata sperimentalmente. Riv. Parass. *3*, 65–81.
Carta, A. 1939b. Il *Tetrathyridium bailleti* pub riprodursi? Profilassi *12*, 71–73.
Carter, W. J. 1943. *Proteocephalus sandgroundi*, a new tetraphyllidean cestode from an East Indian monitor lizard. Trans. Am. Microscop. Soc. *62*, 301–305.
Carus, J. V. 1863. Räderthiere, Würmer, Echinodermata, Coelenterata und Protozoen. In Peters, Carus, and Gerstaecker, Handbuch der zoologie. Vol. II. Leipzig.
Carus, J. V. 1884. Prodromus Faunae Mediterraneae sive Descriptio Animalium maris mediterraneii incolarum . . . Part I. Cestodes, pp. 113–121. Stuttgart.
Castle, W. B., and G. R. Minot. 1936. Pathological and clinical description of the anemias. Oxford Univ. Press.
Chaloner, J. W. 1912. On the cestode parasites of trout with special reference to the plerocercoid disease of trout from Loch Morar. Report of British Association Sci. 1912, pp. 507–509.
Chance, M. R. A., and P. Dirnhuber. 1949. The water soluble vitamins of parasitic worms. Parasitology *39*, 300–301.
Chandler, A. C. 1920. A new record of *Taenia confusa* with additional notes on the morphology. J. Parasitol. *7*, 34–38.
Chandler, A. C. 1922. Species of *Hymenolepis* as human parasites. J. Am. Vet. Assoc. *78*, 636–639.
Chandler, A. C. 1923. Observations on the life-cycle of *Davainea proglottina* in the United States. Trans. Am. Microscop. Soc. *42*, 144–147.
Chandler, A. C. 1925a. New records of *Bertiella satyri* (Cestoda) in man and apes. Parasitology *17*, 421–425.
Chandler, A. C. 1925b. The helminthic parasites of cats in Calcutta . . . Indian J. Med. Research *13*.
Chandler, A. C. 1930. On a specimen of *Taenia pisiformis* with a completely double strobila. Trans. Am. Miscroscop. Soc. *49*, 168–173.
Chandler, A. C. 1932a. Susceptibility and resistance to helminth infections. J. Parasitol. *18*, 135–152.
Chandler, A. C. 1932b. Notes on the helminth parasites of the opossum (*Didelphys*

virginiana) in Southeast Texas, with descriptions of four new species. Proc. U. S. Nat. Mus. *81*, 1–15.

Chandler, A. C. 1935a. Parasites of fishes in Galveston Bay. Proc. U. S. Nat. Mus. *83*, 123–157.

Chandler, A. C. 1935b. A new tetrarhynchid larva from Galveston Bay. J. Parasitol. *21*, 214–215.

Chandler, A. C. 1936. The genus *Schizotaenia* in porcupines. J. Parasitol. *22*, 513.

Chandler, A. C. 1939. The effects of numbers and age of worms on the development of primary and secondary infections with *Hymenolepis diminuta* in rats . . . Am. J. Hyg. *29*, 105–114.

Chandler, A. C. 1940. Failure of artificial immunization to influence *Hymenolepis diminuta* infections in rats. Am. J. Hyg. *31*, 17–22.

Chandler, A. C. 1941. Helminths of muskrats in Southeast Texas. J. Parasitol. *27*, 183–184.

Chandler, A. C. 1942a. Helminths of tree squirrels in Southeast Texas. J. Parasitol. *28*, 135–140.

Chandler, A. C. 1942b. Some cestodes from Florida sharks. Proc. U. S. Nat. Mus. *92*, 25–31.

Chandler, A. C. 1942c. *Mesocestoides manteri* n. sp. from a lynx, with notes on other North American species of *Mesocestoides*. J. Parasitol. *28*, 227–231.

Chandler, A. C. 1942d. The helminths of raccoons in East Texas. J. Parasitol. *28*, 255–268.

Chandler, A. C. 1942e. First record of a case of human infection with tapeworms of the genus *Mesocestoides*. Am. J. Trop. Med. *22*, 493–496.

Chandler, A. C. 1942f. First case of human infection with *Mesocestoides*. Science *96*, 112.

Chandler, A. C. 1943. Studies on the nutrition of tapeworms. Am. J. Hyg. *37*, 121–130.

Chandler, A. C. 1944a. A new species of *Mesocestoides, M. kirbyi,* from *Canis latrans*. J. Parasitol. *30*, 273.

Chandler, A. C. 1944b. Introduction to parasitology, with special reference to the parasites of man. 7th Edition. x + 716 pp. New York and London.

Chandler, A. C. 1946a. The making of a parasitologist. J. Parasitol. *32*, 213–221.

Chandler, A. C. 1946b. Helminths of armadillos, *Dasypus novemcinctus,* in eastern Texas. J. Parasitol. *32*, 237–241.

Chandler, A. C. 1946c. Observations on the anatomy of *Mesocestoides*. J. Parasitol. *32*, 242–246.

Chandler, A. C. 1947. The anatomy of *Mesocestoides* – corrections. J. Parasitol. *33*, 444.

Chandler, A. C. 1948a. New species of the genus *Schistotaenia* with a key to the known species. Trans. Am. Microscop. Soc. *67*, 169–176.

Chandler, A. C. 1948b. Factors modifying host resistance to helminthic infections. Internat. Congr. Trop. Med. and Malaria (4th), Washington, D.C. May 10–18, 1948. Abstracts, Sect. VI, pp. 76–77.

Chandler, A. C. 1949. Introduction to parasitology, with special reference to the parasites of man. 8th Edition. xii + 756 pp. New York.

Chandler, A. C., and R. N. Chopra. 1928. Anthelminthics and their uses. Baltimore.

Chandler, A. C., and C. L. Suttles. 1922. A new rat tapeworm, *Schizotaenia sigmodontis,* from North America. J. Parasitol. *8*, 123–128.

Chapin, E. A. 1926. *Southwellia ransomi* n. sp. J. Parasitol. *13*, 29–33.

Chapman, H. C. 1876. Description of a new *Taenia* from *Rhea americana*. Proc. Acad. Nat. Sci. Philadelphia, p. 14.

Chapman, K. H. 1945. The connection between degree of rainfall and of infection of cattle by "Cysticercus bovis" Cobbold in Tanganyika Territory. J. South African Vet. Med. Assoc. *16*, 44–46.

Chapman, K. H. 1948. *Taenia* in man in South and East Africa . . . Ann. Mag. Nat. Hist. (Ser. 12) *1*, 506–528.

Chapman, P. A. 1935. Some helminth parasites from partridges and other English birds. J. Helm. *13*, 139–148.

Chen, H. T. 1933. A preliminary report on a survey of animal parasites of Canton, China. Lignan Sci. J. Canton *12*, 65–74.

Chen, H. T. 1934. Reactions of *Ctenocephalides felis* to *Dipylidium caninum*. Z. Parasitenk. *6*, 603–637.

Child, C. M. 1904–1911. Series of studies on gametogenesis, fertilisation and cleavage of the egg of *Moniezia expansa*. Biol. Bull. *12, 13, 18, 21*; Anat. Anz. *25, 29, 30*.

Child, C. M. 1924. Physiological foundations of behaviour. New York.

Child, C. M. 1926. The physiological gradients. Protoplasma 5.

Chitwood, B. G., A. McIntosh, and E. W. Price. 1946. Report of the committee on nomenclature. Authors of combinations of zoological names. J. Parasitol. 32, 519–520.

Cholodkovsky, N. 1895. Helminthologische Notizen. Centralbl. Bakt. Parasitenk. *18*, 10–12.

Cholodkovsky, N. 1902. Contributions à la connaissance des Tenias des ruminants. Arch. Parasitol. *6*, 145–148.

Cholodkovsky, N. 1905. Eine *Idiogenes* species mit wohlentwickeltem Scolex. Zool. Anz. *29*, 580–583.

Cholodkovsky, N. 1906. Cestodes nouveaux ou peu connus. 1me ser. Arch. Parasitol. *10*, 332–347.

Cholodkovsky, N. 1908. Ueber eine neue Tänie des Hundes. Zool. Anz. 33, 418–420.

Cholodkovsky, N. 1912. Explanatory catalogue of the collection of parasites of the Imperial Military Academy of Medicine. Part I. Tapeworms (Cyclophyllidea) (in Russian). 96 pp. St. Petersburg.

Cholodkovsky, N. 1913. Cestodes nouveaux ou peu connus. 2me ser. Ann. mus. acad. sci. imp. St. Petersburg *18*, 221–232.

Cholodkovsky, N. 1914. Cestodes nouveaux ou peu connus. 3me ser. Ann. mus. acad. sci. imp. St. Petersburg *19*, 516–523.

Cholodkovsky, N. 1915a. Notes helminthologiques. Ann. mus. acad. sci. imp. St. Petersburg *20*, 164–166.

Cholodkovsky, N. 1915b. Contributions to the knowledge of cestodes (Pseudophyllidea) of the Russian fauna (in Russian). Trav. soc. imp. nat. St. Petersburg *46*, 59.

Cholodkovsky, N. 1916. Sur un nouveau parasite de l'homme. Russian Zoology I, 235–237. Abstract by Leiper. Trop. Diseases Bull. *19* (1922), 669.

Christenson, R. O. 1929. A new cestode reared in the dog. *Multiceps packii* n. sp. J. Parasitol. *16*, 49–53.

Christenson, R. O. 1931. An analysis of the reputed pathogenicity of *Thysanosoma actinioides* in adult sheep. J. Agr. Research *42*.

Christiansen, M. 1927. Muskelfinnen beim Reh (*Cervus cap reolus*). Vidensk, Medd. naturh. Foren Kjob. *84*, 251–279.

Christiansen, M. 1932. Die Muskelfinnedes Rehes und deren Bandwurm (*Cysticercus et Taenia cervi n. sp. ad interim*). Z. wiss. Zool. *4*.

Chung, H. L., and T. T'ung. 1939. The non-specificity of the so-called specific biological tests for hydatid disease. Trans. Roy. Soc. Trop. Med. *32*, 697–706.

Clapham, P. A. 1933. Recent researches on helminth immunity. Imp. Bureau Agr. Parasitol. Publication.

Clapham, P. A. 1939a. On the presence of hooks on the rostellum of *Hymenolepis microps*. J. Helm. *17*, 21–24.

Clapham, P. A. 1939b. Some polyradiate specimens of *Taenia pisiformis* and *Dipylidium caninum*, with a bibliography of the abnormalities occurring among cestodes. J. Helm. *17*, 163–176.

Clapham, P. A. 1942a. On two new coenuri from Africa and a note on the development of the hooks. J. Helm. *20*, 25–31.

Clapham, P. A. 1942b. On identifying *Multiceps spp.* by measurement of the large hook. J. Helm. *20*, 31–40.

Clapham, P. A., and B. G. Peters. 1941. The differentiation of *Coenurus* species by hook measurements. J. Helm. *19*, 75–84.

Clarenburg, A. 1932. Onderzoekingen over de levensvatbarheid van *Cysticercus inermis*. Tijdschr. Diergeneeskunde *59*, 779–780, and in German, Z. Infektionsberichte *11*.

Claus, C. 1876. Grundzuge der Zoologie II Auft. Marburg and Leipzig.

Claus, C. 1885. Lehrbuch der Zoologie III Auft. Marburg and Leipzig.

Claus, C. 1889. Zur morphologischen und polygenetischen Beurtheilung des Bandwurmkorpers. Wiener Klin. Wochenschr. *2*, 697–700.

Clausen, E. 1915. Recherches anatomiques et histologiques sur quelques cestodes d'oiseaux. 111 pp. Thesis, Univ. Neuchâtel.

Cleland, J. B. 1918. Presidential address to the Royal Society of New South Wales. J. Roy. Soc. New South Wales, pp. 1–165.

Cleland, J. B. 1922. The parasites of Australian birds. Trans. Roy. Soc. South Australia *46*, 85–118.

Clerc, W. 1902. Contribution à l'étude de la faune helminthologique de l'Oural. Part I. Zool. Anz. *25*, 569–575. Part II. Zool. Anz. *25*, 650–664.

Clerc, W. 1903. Contribution à l'étude de la faune helminthologique de l'Oural. Part III. Rev. suisse zool. *11*, 241–368.

Clerc, W. 1904a. Quelques remarques à propos d'une critique. Zool. Anz. *28*, 243–245.

Clerk, W. 1904b. Courte notice sur mes excursions zoologiques en 1903 et 1904 (russes). Bull. soc. ouralienne sci. nat. *25*, 11 pp.

Clerc, W. 1906a, 1906b. Note sur les cestodes d'oiseaux de l'Oural. I. Centralbl. Bakt. Parasitenk. *42*, 433–436; II. Centralbl. Bakt. Parasitenk. *42*, 713–720.

Clerc, W. 1907. Notes sur les cestodes d'oiseaux de l'Oural. III. Centralbl. Bakt. Parasitenk. *43*, 703–708.

Clerc, W. 1910. Liste des oiseaux ouvert durant les excursions de 1905 dans la région de l'Oural . . . Bull. soc. ouralienne sci. nat. *30*, 91–98.

Clerc, W. 1930. Quelques données sur l'origine de l'unisexualité dans le genre *Dioicocestus*. Rev. suisse zool. *37*, 147–171.

Clerici (no initials). 1715. Historia naturalis et medica latorum lumbricorum intra hominem et alia animalia . . . Geneva.

Coatney, G. R. 1936. Some notes on cestodes from Nebraska. J. Parasitol. *22*, 409.

Cobbold, T. S. 1858. Observations on some Entozoa with notices of new species . . . Trans. Linnean Soc. London *22*, 155–172. (Read December 1857.)

Cobbold, T. S. 1859. On some new forms of Entozoa. Trans. Linnean Soc. London *22*, 363–366.

Cobbold, T. S. 1861. List of Entozoa . . . Proc. Zool. Soc. London *8*, 117–127.

Cobbold, T. S. 1862. Remarks on all the human entozoa. Proc. Zool. Soc. London.

Cobbold, T. S. 1864. Entozoa: An introduction to the study of helminthology. London.

Cobbold, T. S. 1866a. Catalogue of the specimens of Entozoa in the museum of the Royal College of Surgeons of England. London.

Cobbold, T. S. 1866b. New species of human tapeworm. Trans. Path. Soc. London *17*, 438–439.

Cobbold, T. S. 1869. Entozoa: A supplement to the Introduction to the study of helminthology. 1864. London.

Cobbold, T. S. 1879. Parasites: A treatise on the Entozoa of man and animals. 519 pp. London.

Cobbold, T. S. 1882. Human parasites . . . London.

Cobbold, T. S. 1883. Description of *Ligula mansoni*, a new human cestode. J. Linnean Soc. London *17*, 78–83.

Cohn, E. 1912. Ueber *Diphyllobothrium stemmacephalum* Cobbold. Inaugural Dissertation. 29 pp. Koenigsberg.

Cohn, L. 1898a. Untersuchungen ueber das centrale Nervensystem der Cestoden. Zool. Jahrb. Anat. *12*, 89–158.

Cohn, L. 1898b. Zur Anatomie der *Amabilia lamelligera* (Owen). Zool. Anz. *21*, 557–562.

Cohn, L. 1899. Zur Systematik der Vogeltaenien. Part I. Centralbl. Bakt. Parasitenk. *26*, 222–227. Part II. Zool. Anz. *22*, 405–408. Part III. Zool. Anz. *22*, 415–422.

Cohn, L. 1900a. Zur Kenntnis einiger Vogeltaenien. Zool. Anz. *23*, 91–98.

Cohn, L. 1900b. Zur Systematik der Vogeltaenien. Part IV. Centralbl. Bakt. Parasitenk. *27*, 325–328.

Cohn, L. 1900c. Zur Anatomie der Vogelcestoden. I. Z. wiss. Zool. *67*, 255–290.

Cohn, L. 1901. Zur Anatomie und Systematik der Vogelcestoden. Nova Acta Leop. Carol. Akad. *79*, 269–450.

Cohn, L. 1902. Zur Kenntnis des Genus *Wagenaria* Monticelli und anderen Cestoden. Centralbl. Bakt. Parasitenk. *33*, 53–60.

Cohn, L. 1903. Helminthologische Mittheilungen. Arch. Naturg. Jena *69*.

Cohn, L. 1904a. Helminthologische Mittheilungen. Arch. Naturg. Jena *70*, 243–248.

Cohn, L. 1904b. Zur Anatomie der *Amphilina foliacea* (Rud.). Z. wiss. Zool. *76*.

Cohn, L. 1906. Zur Anatomie zweier Cestoden. Centralbl. Bakt. Parasitenk. *40*, 362–367.

Cohn, L. 1907. Die Orientierung der Cestoden. Zool. Anz. *32*, 51–66.

Cohn, L. 1908a. Die Anatomie eines neuen Fischcestoden. Centralbl. Bakt. Parasitenk. *46*, 134–139.

Cook, S. F., and F. E. Sharman. 1930. The effect of acids and bases on the respiration of tapeworms. Physiol. Zool. *3*, 145–163.

Cooke, W. E., and E. Ponder. 1927. The polynuclear count. London.

Cooper, A. R. 1914a. On the systematic position of *Haplobothrium globuliforme* Cooper. Trans. Roy. Soc. Can. *8*, 1–5.

Cooper, A. R. 1914b. A new cestode from *Amia calva* L. Trans. Roy. Can. Inst. *10*, 81–119.

Cooper, A. R. 1915. Contributions to the life-history of *Proteocephalus ambloplitis*, a parasite of the black bass. Contrib. Can. Biol. Ottawa, 1911–1914. Fasc. 2, 177–194.

Cooper, A. R. 1917. A morphological study of bothriocephalid cestodes from fishes. J. Parasitol. *4*, 33–39.

Cooper, A. R. 1918. North American Pseudophyllidean cestodes from fishes. Illinois Biol. Monogr. *4*, 243 pp.

Cooper, A. R. 1920. *Glaridacris catostomi* n. g. n. sp., a cestodarian parasite. Trans. Am. Microscop. Soc. *39*, 5–24.

Cooper, A. R. 1921. Trematoda and Cestoda: Reports Can. Arctic Exped. 1913–1918. Parts G–H.

Cousi, D. 1933. La cysticercose bovine en Tunisie. Revue vet. et j. de médicine vet. et de zootech. *85*, 121–130.

Coutelen, F. 1926. Evolution vésiculaire du scolex échinococcique obtenu *in vitro*. Compt. rend. soc. biol. *94*.

Coutelen, F. 1927a. Essai de culture *in vitro* de scolex et hydatides échinococciques (*E. granulosus*). Ann. parasitol. humaine et comparée *5*, 1–19.

Coutelen, F. 1927b. Contribution à l'étude morphologique des scolex échinococcique. Ann. parasitol. humaine et comparée *5*, 243–244.

Coutelen, F. 1928. Contribution aux essais de culture *in vitro* d'embryos de filaires. Bull. soc. path. exotique Paris *21*, 313–322.

Coutelen, F. 1929. Essai de culture *in vitro* du cénure sérial: vésiculation des scolex. Compt. rend. soc. biol. Paris *100*, 619–621.

Coutelen, F. 1931. Recherches sur le système excréteur des hydatides échinococciques. Ann. parasitol. humaine et comparée *9*.

Coutelen, F. 1936. Four articles on the potentiality of birds as hosts of *Echinococcus* and on the migrations of echinococcid scolices in white mice. Compt. rend. soc. biol. *121*.

Cram, E. B. 1924. The presence of *Bertiella delafondi* in the pigeon (*Columba domestica*) in the United States. J. Parasitol. *11*, 115.

Cram, E. B. 1926a. Larval tapeworms in the gizzard of a duck. J. Parasitol. *12*, 178–179.

Cram, E. B. 1926b. Re-description of *Taenia krabbei* Moniez. J. Parasitol. *13*, 34–41.

Cram, E. B. 1928a. The present status of our knowledge of poultry parasitism. North Am. Veterinarian 9, 43–51.

Cram, E. B. 1928b. A species of the genus *Bertiella* in man and chimpanzee in Cuba. Am. J. Trop. Med. *8*.

Cram, E. B., and M. F. Jones. 1929. Observations on the life-histories of *Raillietina cesticillus* and of *Hymenolepis carioca*. North Am. Veterinarian *10*, 49–51.

Creplin, F. C. H. 1825. Observationes de Entozois. 86 pp. Gryphiswaldiae.

Creplin, F. C. H. 1829. Novae observationes de Entozois. 134 pp. Berolini.

Creplin, F. C. H. 1839. Article on Eingeweidewürmer, Binnenwürmer and Thierwürmer in J. J. Ersch and J. G. Gruber, Allg. Encykl. Wiss. u. Künstl. Part 32, 293–301. Leipzig.

Creplin, F. C. H. 1842. Helminthologisches aus dem Französischen Mitgetheilt. Floricep's neue Notizen aus dem Gebiet der Natur und Heilkunde *24*, No. 575. Weimar.

Creplin, F. C. H. 1846. Nachträge zu Gurit's Verzeichniss der Thiere bei welchen Entozoen gefunden worden sind. Arch. Naturgeschichte 12 Jahrg., Bd. 1, pp. 129–146.

Creplin, F. C. H. 1849. Zweiter Nachträge . . . Arch. Naturgeschichte 15 Jahrg., Bd. 1, pp. 52–80.

Creplin, F. C. H. 1851. Vierter Nachtrag . . . Arch. Naturgeschichte 17 Jahrg., Bd. 1, pp. 269–310.

Creplin, F. C. H. 1853. Eingeweidewürmer des *Dicholophus cristatus*. Abhandl. naturf. Ges. Halle *1*, 59–68.

Crety, C. 1890a. Cestodi della *Coturnix communis*. Boll. mus. zool. anat. comp. Torino *5*, 16 pp.

Crety, C. 1890b. Ricerchi anatomichi ed istologichi sul genere *Solenophorus* (Creplin). Atti reale accad. Lincei, Ser. IV, *6*.

Crety, C. 1890c. Sopra alcuni cisticherchi di una foca (*Monachus albiventer* Gray). Boll. soc. nat. Napoli *4*, 106–108.

Crowcroft, P. W. 1947. Note on *Anthobothrium hickmani*, a new cestode from the Tasmanian electric ray (*Narcine tasmaniensis* Richardson). Papers and Proceedings Royal Soc. Tasmania, 1946, pp. 1–4.

Crozier, B. U. 1946. A new taeniid cestode, *Cladotaenia banghami*. Trans. Am. Microscop. Soc. *65*, 222–227.

Crusz, H. 1944. Contributions to the helminthology of Ceylon. I. On *Multiceps serialis*. Ceylon J. Sci. *22*, 173–181.

Crusz, H. 1948a. On the transverse fission of *Cysticercus pisiformis* in experimentally infested rabbits, and the phylogenetic significance of asexual phenomena in cysticerci. J. Helm. *22*, 165–178.

Crusz, H. 1948b. Further studies on the development of *Cysticercus fasciolaris* and *Cysticercus pisiformis*, with special reference to the growth and sclerotization of the rostellar hooks. J. Helm. *22*, 179–198.

Culbertson, J. T. 1938. Recent contributions to the immunology of helminthic infections. Arch. Path. *25*, 85–117.

Curtice, C. 1890. The animal parasites of sheep. Special Report, U. S. Dept. Agr. Washington, D. C.

Curtice, C. 1892. Parasites: being a list of those infesting the domesticated animals and man in the United States. J. Comp. Med. and Vet. Arch. N. Y. *13*, 223–236.

Curtis, M. R., F. D. Bullock, and W. F. Dunning. 1920–1934. Articles on the provocation of liver sarcomas in rats by the larva of *H. taeniaeformis*. Am. J. Cancer *17*, *21*; J. Cancer Research *8*, *9*; Proc. N. Y. Path. Soc. *20*; Science *77*.

Curtis, W. C. 1888–1890. *Crossobothrium laciniatum* and developmental stimuli in the Cestoda. Biol. Bull. *5*, 125.

Curtis, W. C. 1911. The life-history of *Scolex polymorphus* of the Woods Hole region. J. Morph. *22*, 819.

Cushing, H. B., and H. L. Bacal. 1932. *Diphyllobothrium latum* (fish tapeworm) infestation in eastern Canada. Can. Med. J. *30*, 377–384.

Cuvier, G. 1817. Le règne animal distribué d'après son organization. 4 vols. Paris.

Daniels, C. W. 1895. *Taenia demerariensis.* British Guiana Med. Ann. Hospital Rep. 7.

Daniels, C. W. 1896. *Taenia demerariensis.* Lancet, No. 1455.

Daniels, C. W. 1913. Tropical medicine and hygiene. Part 2. Diseases due to the Metazoa . . . viii + 283 pp. London.

Darrah, J. H. 1930. A new anoplocephalid cestode from the woodchuck, *Marmota flaviventris.* Trans. Am. Microscop. Soc. *49,* 252–257.

Daubney, R. The life-cycle of *Moniezia expansa.* J. Parasitol. *19,* 5–11.

Davaine, C. 1860. Traité des Entozoaires et des maladies vermineuses de l'homme et des animaux domestiques. 838 pp. Paris.

Davaine, C. 1865. Sur une ligule (*Ligula minuta*) de la truite du lac du Genève. Compt. rend. soc. biol. Paris *4,* 87–88.

Davies, T. I. 1935. The anatomy of *Dilepis undula* (Schrank, 1798). Proc. Zool. Soc. London, pp. 717–722.

Davies, T. I. 1938a. A description of *Hymenolepis neoarctica* n. nom. syn. of *H. fusus* Linton, with a discussion on the synonymity of *Taenia fusus* Krabbe, 1869. Parasitology *30,* 339–343.

Davies, T. I. 1938b. On *Anomotaenia gallinaginis* n. sp. from the intestine of the common snipe, *Gallinago gallinago* (Linn.). Parasitology *30,* 344–346.

Davies, T. I. 1938c. Some factors governing the incidence of helminth parasites in the domestic duck. Welsh Journal Agriculture *14,* 280–287.

Davies, T. I. 1939. Four species of *Hymenolepis* Weinland parasitic in the oyster catcher, *Haematopus ostralegus* Linn. Parasitology *31,* 401–412.

Davies, T. I. 1940. Three closely related species of *Aploparaksis* Clerc, 1903. Parasitology *32,* 198–207.

Davies, T. I., and G. Rees. 1947. *Androepigynotaenia haematopodis* n. g. n. sp., a new protogynous tapeworm from the oyster catcher *Haematopus ostralegus occidentalis* Neumann. Parasitology *38,* 93–100.

Davis, H. E. 1944. *Cittotaenia sandgroundi,* a new anoplocephalid cestode from a Javanese tree duck. J. Parasitol. *30,* 241–244.

Davis, H. E. 1945a. A new hymenolepidid cestode, *Hymenolepis javanensis,* from an East Indian tree duck. Trans. Am. Microscop. Soc. *64,* 213–219.

Davis, H. E. 1945b. A new hymenolepidid cestode, *Hymenolepis furcouterina,* from a Celebesian black-bellied snakebird. Trans. Am. Microscop. Soc. *64,* 306–310.

Davis, H. E. 1947. The tapeworm "Cittotaenia sandgroundi" transferred to *Diplogynia.* Oklahoma Acad. Sci. *27,* 65–66.

Deffke, O. 1891. Die Entozoen des Hundes. Arch. wiss. u. prakt. Tierheilk. *17,* 1–60.

Deiner, E. 1912. Anatomie der *Anoplocephala latissima* (nom. nov.). Arb. zool. Inst. Wien *19,* 347–372.

Dence, W. A. 1940. The occurrence of "free-living" *Ligula* in Catlin Lake, Central Adirondacks. Copeia, 1940, p. 140.

Deschiens, R. 1948. Les substances toxiques vermineuses. Ann. inst. Pasteur *75,* 397–410.

Deslongchamps, E. 1824. Anthocéphale, Bothriocéphale, Floriceps . . . Encylopédie méthodique. Histoire naturelle des zoophytes 2. Paris.

Deuel, H. J., and others. 1936, 1937. The re-conversion of triglycerides to glycogen. J. Biol. Chem. *112,* 15–23; *117,* 119–129, 131–133.

Deusch, G. 1925. Zur spezifischen Diagnostik der menschlichen Echinokokkenerkräng ungen, insbesondere mittels der Intrakutanreaktion. Deut. med. Wochschr. *51,* 1319–1320.

Dévé, F. 1926. Evolution vésiculaire du scolex échinococcique obtenu *in vitro.* La culture artificielle du kyste hydatique. Compt. rend. soc. biol. *94,* 440–441.

Dévé, F. 1927. La cuticularisation des capsules proligères échinococciques. Ann. parasitol. humaine et comparée *5,* 310–328.

Dévé, F. 1933a. De l'éxistence de formes de transition entre l'échinococcose hydatique et l'échinococcose alvéolaire chez l'homme. Compt. rend. soc. biol. *113,* 223–224.

Dévé, F. 1933b. La souris blanche, animal réactif pour les inoculations échinococciques. Un essai de sérothérapie anti-échinococcique aspécifique. Compt. rend. soc. biol. *113*, 1443–1445.

Dévé, F. 1934a. Intermediate, transitional and pathological forms between hydatid echinococcus and alveolar echinococcus (Bavaro-Tyrolienne) in man. Australian and New Zealand J. Surgery *4*, 99–117.

Dévé, F. 1934b. Essai d'immunisation anti-échinococcique par injections sous-cutanées de membranes hydatiques broyées à l'état frais. Compt. rend. soc. biol. *115*, 1025–1026.

Dévé, F. 1935. Formes anatomo-pathologiques intermédiaires et formes de passage entre l'échinococcose hydatique et l'échinococcose alvéolaire (Bavaro-Tyrolienne) chez l'homme. Ann. anat. path. med. chirug. *10*, 1155–1178.

Dew, H. R. 1925a. The histogenesis of the hydatid parasite *(Taenia echinococcus)* in the pig. Med. J. Australia *12*, 101–110.

Dew, H. R. 1925b. Daughter cyst formation in hydatid disease. Med. J. Australia *12*, 497–505.

Dew, H. R. 1926. The mechanism of daughter cyst formation in hydatid disease. Med. J. Australia *13*, 451–466.

Dew, H. R. 1934. Hydatid disease of the brain. Surgery, Gynecology and Obstetrics *59*, 321–329.

Dew, H. R., C. H. Kellaway, and F. E. Williams. 1925. The intradermal reaction in hydatid disease and its clinical value. Med. J. Australia *12*, 471–478.

Diamare, V. 1892. Di un nuovo cestode del gen. *Dipylidium* Lt. Boll. soc. nat. Napoli *6*, 46–48.

Diamare, V. 1893a. Note su' cestodi. Boll. soc. nat. Napoli *7*, 9–13.

Diamare, V. 1893b. Il genere *Dipylidium* Lt. Atti reale accad. sci. Napoli *6*, 1–31.

Diamare, V. 1893c. La funzione dell' ovaria nella *Davainea tetragona* (Mol.). Rend. accad. sci. Napoli, pp. 8–12.

Diamare, V. 1897a. Anatomie der Genitalien des Genus *Amabilia mihi*. Centralbl. Bakt. Parasitenk. *21*, 862–872.

Diamare, V. 1897b. Die Genera *Amabilia* und *Diploposthe*. Centralbl. Bakt. Parasitenk. *22*, 98–99.

Diamare, V. 1898. Ueber die weiblicher Geschlechtsteile der *Davainea tetragona* (Molin), eine kurze Antwort an Herrn Dr. Holzberg. Centralbl. Bakt. Parasitenk. *24*, 480–483.

Diamare, V. 1899a. Ueber *Amabilia lamelligera* (Owen). Centralbl. Bakt. Parasitenk. *25*, 357–359.

Diamare, V. 1899b. Einige Bemerkungen zur Antwort an Herrn Dr. L. Cohn. Centralbl. Bakt. Parasitenk. *26*, 780–782.

Diamare, V. 1900a. *Paronia carrinoi* n. g. n. sp. di Taenioide a duplici organi genitali. Boll. mus. zool. anat. comp. Genova *91*, 8 pp.

Diamare, V. 1900b. *Paronia carrinoi* n. g. n. sp. von Taenioiden mit doppelten Geschlechtsorganen. Centralbl. Bakt. Parasitenk. *28*, 846–850.

Diamare, V. 1901. Zur Kenntnis der Vogelcestoden (Ueber *Paronia carrinoi* mihi). Centralbl. Bakt. Parasitenk. *30*, 369–373.

Dickey, L. D. 1921. A new amphibian cestode. J. Parasitol. *7*, 128–136.

Diesing, K. M. 1835. *Tropisurus* und *Thysanosoma*, zwei neue Gattungen von Binnenwürmern aus Brasiliens. Med. Jahrb. L. K. Oesterreichischen Staates, Wien, *16*, 83–116.

Diesing, K. M. 1850. Systema helminthum. Vol. I. i–xvi + 680 pp. Vienna.

Diesing, K. M. 1851. Systema helminthum. Vol. II. i–vi + 188 pp. + corrigenda. Vienna.

Diesing, K. M. 1854. Ueber eine naturgemässe Verteilung der Cephalocotyleen. Sitzber. Akad. Wiss. Wien Math. naturw. Klasse Abt. I. *13*, 555–616.

Diesing, K. M. 1855. Sechzehn Gattungen von Binnenwürmern und ihre Arte. Denkschr. Akad. Wiss. Wien Math. naturw. Klasse Abt. I. *9*, 171–185.

Diesing, K. M. 1856. Zwanzig Arten von Cephalocotyleen. Denkschr. Akad. Wiss. Wien Math. naturw. Klasse Abt. I. *12*, 23–38.

Diesing, K. M. 1863a. Revision der Cephalocotyleen. Abtheilung: Paramecocotyleen. Sitzber. Akad. Wiss. Wien Math. naturw. Klasse Abt. I. *48*, 200–345.

Diesing, K. M. 1863b. Revision der Cephalocotyleen. Abtheilung: Cyclocotyleen. Sitzber. Akad. Wiss. Wien Math. naturw. Klasse Abt. I. *49*, 357–430.

Diesing, K. M. 1864. Revision der Cephalocotyleen. Reprint. 74 pp. octavo. Wien.

Ditlevsen, H. 1914. Conspectus Faunae Groendlandicae. Meddelser om Groenland *23*, Kobenhavn.

Dobrovolny, C. G., and M. F. Dobrovolny. 1933. An unusual collection of polyradiate tapeworms from a dog. Trans. Kansas Acad. Sci. *36*, 214.

Dobrovolny, C. G., and M. F. Dobrovolny. 1935. Polyradiate tapeworms from a dog. Trans. Am. Microscop. Soc. *54*, 22–27.

Dobrovolny, C. G., and M. J. Harbaugh. 1934. *Cysticercus fasciolaris* from the red squirrel. Trans. Am. Microscop. Soc. *53*, 67.

Doguel, V. A., and M. M. Volkova. 1946. Sur le cycle vital du *Diplocotyle* (Cestoda, Pseudophyllidea). Compt. rend. acad. sci. U.R.S.S. *53*, 385–387.

Dollfus, R. Ph. 1923a. L'orientation morphologique des *Gyrocotyle* et des cestodes en général. Bull. soc. zool. France *48*, 203–242.

Dollfus, R. Ph. 1923b. Enumération des cestodes du plancton et des invertébrés marins. Ann. parasitol. humaine et comparée *1*, 276–300, 363–394.

Dollfus, R. Ph. 1926. Sur *Acanthobothrium crassicolle* K. Wedl, 1855. Bull. soc. zool. France *51*, 464–470.

Dollfus, R. Ph. 1929a. Addendum à mon "Enumération des cestodes du plancton et des invertébrés marins." Ann. parasitol. humaine et comparée *7*, 325–347.

Dollfus, R. Ph. 1929b. Sur les Tétrarhynques. I. Définition des genres. Bull. soc. zool. France *54*, 308–342.

Dollfus, R. Ph. 1930. Sur les Tétrarhynques (2me contribution. *Dibothriorhynchus, Sphyriocephala, Tentacularia, Nybelinia*). Mém. soc. zool. France *29*, 139–216.

Dollfus, R. Ph. 1931. Nouvelle addendum à mon "Enumération des cestodes du plancton et des invertébrés marins." Ann. parasitol. humaine et comparée *9*.

Dollfus, R. Ph. 1932a. Amoenitates helminthologicae. II. Qu'est-ce que *Corynesoma* Leuckart? Bull. soc. zool. France *56*, 410–419.

Dollfus, R. Ph. 1932b. Identification d'un cestode de la collection du laboratoire de parasitologie de la Faculté de Médicine de Paris. Bull. soc. zool. France *57*, 246–258.

Dollfus, R. Ph. 1932c. Mission saharienne Augieras-Draper, 1927–1928. Cestodes de reptiles. Bull. muséum hist. nat. (Paris) Ser. 2, *4*, 539–554.

Dollfus, R. Ph. 1934a. Sur une larve de Tétrarhynque enkystée chez un *Dentex macrophthalmus* Cuv. Travaux publiés par la station d'aquiculture et de pêche de Castiglione: année 1932. 2me fasc. Alger, 1934, pp. 123–133.

Dollfus, R. Ph. 1934b. Sur "Taenia gallinulae" P. J. van Beneden, 1858. Ann. parasitol. humaine et comparée *12*, 267–272.

Dollfus, R. Ph. 1934c. Sur un cestode pseudophyllide parasite de poisson d'ornement. Bull. soc. zool. France *59*, 476–490.

Dollfus, R. Ph. 1935. Sur quelques Tétrarhynques (notes préliminaires). Bull. soc. zool. France *60*, 353–357.

Dollfus, R. Ph. 1936. Cestodes des invertébrés marins et thalassoïdes. In C. Joyeux and J. G. Baer, Cestodes. Faune de France, Vol. 30, Paris 1936, pp. 508–539.

Dollfus, R. Ph. 1938. Sur un *Cysticercus fasciolaris* Rudolphi teratologique (Polycéphale). Ann. parasitol. humaine et comparée *16*, 133–141.

Dollfus, R. Ph. 1939. Cestodes du genre *Raillietina* récemment observés chez l'homme en Equateur. Bull. soc. path. exotique *32*, 660–665.

Dollfus, R. Ph. 1940. Cestodes du genre *Raillietina* trouvés chez l'homme en Amérique intertropicale. Ann. parasitol. humaine et comparée *17*, 542–562.

Dollfus, R. Ph. 1942. Etudes critiques sur les Tétrarhynques du Muséum de Paris. Archiv. muséum hist. nat. (Paris) *19*, 1–466.

Dollfus, R. Ph. 1944. Sur les cestodes de *Puma concolor* (L.). Bull. muséum hist. nat. (Paris) *16*, 316–320.

Dollfus, R. Ph. 1946. Notes diverses sur des tétrarhynques. Mém. muséum nat. hist. Paris *22*, 179–220.

Dollfus, R. Ph. 1948a. Coenurose de la cavité abdominale chez un écureuil (*Sciurus vulgaris* L.) à Richelieu (Indre-et-Loire). Ann. parasitol. humaine et comparée *22,* 143–147.

Dollfus, R. Ph. 1948b. Amoenitates helminthologicae. VI. *Raillietina* (*R.*) *kouridovali* R. Ph. Dollfus et *Inermicapsifer cubensis* (P. Kouri) P. Kouri. Ann. parasitol. humaine et comparée *22,* 277–278.

Dollfus, R. Ph., and J. Carayon. 1948. Larve de cestode chez un hémiptère hétéroptère. Ann. parasitol. humaine et comparée *22,* 276.

Donnadieu, A. L. 1877a. Contribution à l'histoire de la ligule. J. anat. physiol. *13,* 321–370.

Donnadieu, A. L. 1877b. Contribution sur le développement de la ligule de la tanche. Lyon Méd. *24,* 563–567.

Douthitt, H. 1915. Studies on the cestode family Anoplocephalidae. Illinois Biol. Monogr. *1,* No. 3, 1–96.

Drummond, F. H. 1937. Cestoda. In Lady Julia Percy Island Reports of the Expedition of the McCoy Society for Field Investigations and Research. Proc. Roy. Soc. Victoria (Australia) *49,* 401–404.

Dujardin, F. 1837. Sur l'embryon des Entozoaires et sur les mouvements de cet embryon dans l'oeuf. Ann. sci. nat. zool. *8,* 303–305.

Dujardin, F. 1838. Observations sur les ténias et sur le mouvement de leur embryon dans l'oeuf. Ann. sci. nat. zool. *10,* 29–34.

Dujardin, F. 1845. Histoire naturelle des helminthes ou vers intestinaux. Paris.

Du Noyer, M. Rondeau, and J. G. Baer. 1928. Etude comparée du *Taenia saginata* et du *Taenia solium.* Bull. sci. pharmacol. *35,* 209–234.

Duvernoy, G. L. 1842. Note sur un nouveau genre de ver intestinal de la famille des Ténioides, le Bothrimone de l'esturgeon (*Bothrimonus sturionis*). Ann. sci. nat. zool. *18,* 123–126.

Edgar, S. A. 1940. Artificial evagination of larval tapeworms. Trans. Kansas Acad. Sci. *43,* 397–399.

Edgar, S. A. 1941. Use of bile salts for the evagination of tapeworm cysts. Trans. Am. Microscop. Soc. *60,* 121–128.

Editorial. 1931. *Diphyllobothrium latum.* Am. J. Clin. Path. *1.*

Editorial. 1934. The broad tapeworm in dog and pig. Lancet *227* (5784), 35–36.

Eguchi, C. 1926. Studies on *Dibothriocephalus latus* with a special reference to its life-history in Japan. Bull. Path. *3.*

Ehrstrom, R. 1926. Zur Kenntnis der Darmparasiten in Finnland. Acta Med. Scand. *64,* 29–68.

Eichler, W. 1940. Korrelationen in der Stammesentwicklung von Wirten und Parasiten. Z. Parasitenk. *12,* 94.

Einarsson, M. 1926. L'échinococcose en Islande. Sur la mode de contamination humaine. Ann. parasitol. humaine et comparée *4.*

Eisenbrandt, L. L. 1936. Precipitin reactions of helminth extracts. Proc. Soc. Exp. Biol. Med. *35,* 322–325.

Eisenbrandt, L. L. 1938. On the serological relationships of some helminths. Am. J. Hyg. *27,* 117–141.

Ekbaum, E. K. 1933a. A study of the cestode genus *Eubothrium* of Nybelin in Canadian fishes. Contrib. Can. Biol. Fish. *8,* 89–98.

Ekbaum, E. K. 1933b. *Citharichthys stigmaeus* as a possible intermediate host of *Gilquinia squali* (Fabricius). Contrib. Can. Biol. Fish. *8,* 99–100.

Ekbaum, E. K. 1935. Notes on the species of *Triaenophorus* in Canada. J. Parasitol. *21,* 260–263.

Ekbaum, E. K. 1937. On the maturation and the hatching of the eggs of the cestode *Triaenophorus crassus* Forel from Canadian fish. J. Parasitol. *23,* 293–295.

Elek, S. R., and L. E. Finkelstein. 1939. *Multiceps serialis* infestation in a baboon. Zoologica *24,* 323–328.

Erickson, A. B. 1938. Parasites of some Minnesota Cricetidae and Zapodidae and a host catalogue of helminth parasites of native American mice. Am. Midland Naturalist *20,* 575–589.

Erlanger, R. S. von. 1890. Der Geschlechtsapparat der *Taenia echinococcus.* Z. wiss. Zool. *50,* 555–559.

Eschricht, D. F. 1841. Anatomisch-physiologische Untersuchungen ueber die Bothryocephalen. Nova Acta Acad. Leopold-Carol nat. curios. *19*, Suppl. 2. 161 pp.

Essex, H. E. 1927a. The structure and development of *Corallobothrium*. Illinois Biol. Monogr. *11*, 257–328.

Essex, H. E. 1927b. Early development of *Diphyllobothrium latum* in northern Minnesota. J. Parasitol. *14*, 106–109.

Essex, H. E. 1928a. On the life-history of *Bothriocephalus cuspidatus* Cooper, 1917, a tapeworm of the wall-eyed pike. Trans. Am. Microscop. Soc. *47*, 348–351.

Essex, H. E. 1928b. An interesting cestode larva from the liver of the common bullhead (*Ameiurus nebulosus*). J. Parasitol. *15*.

Essex, H. E. 1929a. *Crepidobothrium fragile* n. sp., a tapeworm of the channel catfish. Parasitology *21*, 164–167.

Essex, H. E. 1929b. A report on fishes from the Mississippi River and other waters with respect to infestation by *Diphyllobothrium latum*. Minnesota Medicine, March 1929.

Essex, H. E. 1929c. The life-cycle of *Haplobothrium globuliforme* Cooper, 1914. Science *69* (1800), 677–678.

Essex, H. E. 1932. A new larval cestode, probably *Hymenolepis cuneata*, a tapeworm of a wild duck. J. Parasitol. *18*, 291–293.

Essex, H. E., and G. W. Hunter. 1926. A biological study of fish parasites from the central states. Trans. Illinois Acad. Sci. *19*, 151–181.

Essex, H. E., and T. B. Magath. 1931. A comparison of the viability of ova of the broad tapeworm, *Diphyllobothrium latum*, from man and dogs . . . Am. J. Hyg. *14*, 698–704.

Essex, H. E., J. Markowitz, and F. C. Mann. 1931. Physiological response and immune reactions to extracts of certain intestinal parasites. Am. J. Physiol. *98*, 18–24.

Evanno (no initials). 1933. Sur la sparganose oculaire. Bull. acad. vet. France *6*, 355–356.

Evans, R. G. P. 1934. Hydatid disease of the lung, with a case report. Lancet *226* (5781), 1281–1283.

Evans, W. M. R. 1940. Observations upon some common cestode parasites of the wild rabbit, *Oryctolagus cuniculus*. Parasitology *32*, 78–90.

Eysenhardt, C. G. 1829. Einiges ueber Eingeweidewürmer. Verhandl. Berlin Ges. naturf. Fr. *1*, 144–152.

Fabricius, O. 1780. Fauna Groendlandica, systematice sistens animalia Groendlandiae occidentalis hactenus indagata . . . 452 pp. Hafniae et Lipsias.

Fabricius, O. 1794. Bidrag til Snylte-Ormenes Historie. Skrivter af Naturhistorie Sel skabet 3, Kjobenhavn (oploest den 28 December 1792).

Fain, A. 1947. Un cas de sparganose chez l'homme . . . Ann. soc. med. trop. Belg. *27*, 65–69.

Fain, A. 1950. *Inermicapsifer cubensis* (Kouri, 1938), presence du cestode *I. cubensis* synonyme de *Inermicapsifer arvicanthidis* (Kofend, 1917) chez un enfant indigene et chez un rat (*Rattus r. rattus* L.) au Ruanda-Urundi (Congo Belge). Bull. soc. path. exot. *43*, 438–443.

Fairley, K. D., and C. H. Kellaway. 1933. The value of laboratory investigations in the diagnosis of hydatid infestation. Australian and New Zealand J. Surgery *11*, 236–243.

Fairley, N. H. 1922. Researches on the complement fixation reaction in hydatid disease. Quart. J. Med. Oxford *15*, 244–267.

Fasten, N. 1922. The tapeworm infection in Washington trout and its related biological problems. Am. Naturalist *16*, 439–447.

Fastier, L. B. 1949. The effect of physical agents on hydatid scolex viability. Parasitology *39*, 157–163.

Faust, E. C. 1920. Two new Proteocephalidae. J. Parasitol. *6*.

Faust, E. C. 1921. Preliminary survey of the parasites of vertebrates of North China. China Med. J. *35*, 1–15.

Faust, E. C. 1925. On a case of triradiate *Taenia solium* from North China. China Med. J. *39*.

Faust, E. C. 1928. Infestation experiments in man and other mammalian hosts with the Sparganum stage of oriental Diphyllobothriidae. Proc. Soc. Exp. Biol. Med. *26*, 252–254.

Faust, E. C. 1929a. What is *Sparganum mansoni*? J. Trop. Med. Hyg. *32*, 76–77.

Faust, E. C. 1929b. Human helminthology. Philadelphia.

Faust, E. C., H. E. Campbell, and C. R. Kellogg. 1929. Morphological and biological studies on the species of *Diphyllobothrium* in China. Am. J. Hyg. *9*, 560–583.

Faust, E. C., and C. M. Wassel. 1931. Preliminary survey of the intestinal parasites of man in the central Yangtze valley. China Med. J. *35*, 532–561.

Faust, E. S. 1908. Ueber chronische Oelsaürevergiftung. Arch. Exp. Path. Pharmakol. Suppl. Band, 1908, pp. 171–175.

Faust, E. S., and T. W. Tallqvist. 1907. Ueber die Ursachen der Bothriocephalusanämie. Arch. Exp. Path. Pharmakol. *57*, 367–385.

Fenstermacher, R. 1934. Further studies on diseases affecting moose. Bull. 308 Minnesota Agr. Exp. Sta. St. Paul. 26 pp.

Fenstermacher, R., and W. L. Jellison. 1933. Diseases affecting moose. Bull. Minnesota Agr. Exp. Sta. St. Paul. 20 pp.

Filippi, C. 1892a. Nota preliminare sul systema riproduttore della *Taenia botrioplitis*. Bull. soc. Roma stud. zool. An. I, 75–79.

Filippi, C. 1892b. Ricerche istologiche ed anatomiche sulla *Taenia botrioplitis* Piana. Atti reale accad. Lincei Roma *7*, 249–294.

Fillippi, F. de. 1854. Mémoire pour servir à l'histoire génétique des trématodes. Ann. Sci. Nat. *11*, 255–284.

Flattley, F. W. 1922. Considerations on the life-history of tapeworms of the genus *Moniezia*. Parasitology *14*, 268–281.

Flössner, O. 1923a. Neues ueber die Echinokokkusflüssigkeit. Münchener med. Wochschr. *70*.

Flössner, O. 1923b. Neue Untersuchungen ueber die Echinokokkenflüssigkeit. Z. Biol. *80*.

Flössner, O. 1925. Neue Untersuchungen ueber Echinokokkenflüssigkeit. Z. Biol. *82*.

Flury, F. 1912. Zur Chemie und Toxicologie der Ascariden. Arch. exp. Path. Pharmakol. *67*.

Foggie, A. 1933. On a cestode parasite of the domestic pigeon (*Columba livia*). Ann. Mag. Nat. Hist. (Ser. 10) *12*, 168–172.

Forel, F. A. 1868. Preparations microscopiques d'une nouvelle espèce de *Triaenophorus*. Bull. soc. vaudoise sci. nat., Lausanne 9, 696.

Forti, A. 1932. L. F. Marsilii e Schistocefalo dello Spinarello. Arch. zool. Italiane *16*, 1437–1439.

Fortner, H. C. 1923. The distribution of frog parasites of the Douglas Lake region, Michigan. Trans. Am. Microscop. Soc. *42*, 79–90.

Fortuyn, A. B. D., and L. C. Feng. 1940. Inheritance in mice of resistance against infection with the eggs of *Taenia taeniaeformis*. Peking Nat. Hist. Bull. *15*, 139–145.

Foster (no initials). 1916. Two new cases of polyradiate cestodes with a summary of the cases already known. J. Parasitol. *2*.

Fraipont, J. 1880. Recherches sur l'appareil excreteur des trématodes et des cestodes, 2me communication; 3me communication. Bull. acad. roy. Belg. *50*, 265–270.

Fraipont, J. 1881. Recherches sur l'appareil excréteur des trématodes et des cestodes; deuxieme partie. Arch. biol. *2*, 1–40.

Friedheim, E. A. H., and J. G. Baer. 1933. Untersuchungen ueber die Atmung von *Diphyllobothrium latum* (L.). Ein Beitrag zur Kenntnis der Atmungsfermente. Biochem. Z. *265*, 329–337.

Friedheim, E. A. H., B. Susz, and J. G. Baer. 1933. Sur l'energie d'activation et le coefficient de temperature d'une réaction biologique. (La respiration des larves de *Diphyllobothrium latum.*) Compt. rend. soc. phys. hist. nat. Genève *50*, 177–182.

Friis, S. 1870. En hidtil ubeskreven Baendelorme hos Fugle. Vidensk. Meddel. naturh. Foren. Kjoebenhavn (aar 1869) *1*, 121–124.

Frisch, J. L. 1727. De taeniis in anserum intestinis. Miscell. Berolinensis incrementum scientiarium ex scriptis Soc. Reg. Sc. exh. Contin. *3*, Berolini, p. 42; Phys. u. med. Abh. k. Acad. Wiss. Berlin *1*, 155–156.

Frisch, J. L. 1734a. Die mustelae fluviatilis rapacitate et de taeniis in stomacho hujus piscis. Miscell. Berolinensis incrementum scientiarium . . . *4,* 392–393, 395–396.

Frisch, J. L. 1734b. De taeniis in pisciculo aculeato qui in Marchia Brandenburgia vocatur "Stecherling." Miscell. Berolinensis incrementum scientiarium . . . *4,* 395–396.

Frisch, J. L. 1740. De Taenia capitata. Miscell. Berolinensis incrementum scientiarium . . . *6,* 129.

Fritsch, G. 1886. Die Parasiten des Zitterwelses. Sitzber. kgl. preuss. Akad. Wiss. Jahrg. 1886, pp. 99–108.

Froehlich, J. A. 1789. Beschreibungen einiger neuen Eingeweidewürmer. Der Naturforscher Halle *24,* 101–162.

Froehlich, J. A. 1791. Beiträge zur Naturgeschichte der Eingeweidewürmer. Der Naturforscher Halle *25,* 52–113.

Froehlich, J. A. 1802. Beiträge zur Naturgeschichte der Eingeweidewürmer. Der Naturforscher Halle *29,* 5–96.

Fuhrmann, O. 1895a. Die Taenien der Amphibien. Vorläufige Mitteilung. Zool. Anz. *18,* 181–184.

Fuhrmann, O. 1895b. Die Taenien der Amphibien. Zool. Jahrb. Anat. & Ont. *9,* 207–236.

Fuhrmann, O. 1895c. Beitrag zur Kenntnis der Vögeltaenien I. Rev. suisse zool. *3,* 433–458.

Fuhrmann, O. 1896a. Beitrag zur Kenntnis der Vögeltaenien II. Rev. suisse zool. *4,* 111–133.

Fuhrmann, O. 1896b. Beitrag zur Kenntnis der Bothriocephalen I. Centralbl. Bakt. Parasitenk. *19,* 546–550.

Fuhrmann, O. 1896c. Beitrag zur Kenntnis der Bothriocephalen II. Centralbl. Bakt. Parasitenk. *19,* 605–608.

Fuhrmann, O. 1897. Sur un nouveau Taenia d'oiseau. Rev. suisse zool. *5,* 107–117.

Fuhrmann, O. 1898a. Ist *Bothriocephalus Zschokkei* mihi synonym mit *Schistocephalus nodosus* Rud.? Centralbl. Bakt. Parasitenk. *23,* 550–551.

Fuhrmann, O. 1898b. Ueber die Genera *Prosthecocotyle* Monticelli und *Bothriotaenia* Lönnberg. Vorläufige Mitteilung. Zool. Anz. *21,* 385–388.

Fuhrmann, O. 1899a. Das Genus *Prosthecocotyle.* Zool. Anz. *22,* 180–183.

Fuhrmann, O. 1899b. Das Genus *Prosthecocotyle.* Centralbl. Bakt. Parasitenk. *25,* 863–877.

Fuhrmann, O. 1899c. Mitteilungen ueber Vögeltaenien. I. Ueber *T. depressa* Siebold. Centralbl. Bakt. Parasitenk. *26,* 83–86. II. Zwei eigentümliche Vögeltaenien. Centralbl. Bakt. Parasitenk. *26,* 618–622. III. *T. musculosa* mihi et *T. crateriformis* Goeze (*Monopylidium* nov. gen.). Centralbl. Bakt. Parasitenk. *26,* 622–627.

Fuhrmann, O. 1899d. Deux singuliers Taenias d'oiseaux: *Gyrocoelia perversus* n. g. n. sp. et *Acoleus armatus* n. g. n. sp. Rev. suisse zool. *7,* 341–451.

Fuhrmann, O. 1899e. On the anatomy of *Prosthecocotyle torulosa* (Linstow) and *Prosthecocotyle heteroclita* (Dies.). Proc. Roy. Soc. Edinburgh *22,* 641–651.

Fuhrmann, O. 1900a. Neue eigentümliche Vögelcestoden. Ein getrenntgeschlechtlicher Cestode. Zool. Anz. *23,* 48–51.

Fuhrmann, O. 1900b. Zur Kenntnis der Acoleinae. Centralbl. Bakt. Parasitenk. *28,* 363–376.

Fuhrmann, O. 1901a. Neue Arten und Genera von Vögeltaenien. Vorläufige Mitteilung. Zool. Anz. *24,* 271–273.

Fuhrmann, O. 1901b. Bemerkungen ueber einige neuere Vögelcestoden. Centralbl. Bakt. Parasitenk. *24,* 757–763.

Fuhrmann, O. 1902a. Sur un nouveau Bothriocephalide d'oiseau. Note préliminaire. Archiv. parasitol. humaine et comparée *3,* 440–448.

Fuhrmann, O. 1902b. Sur deux nouveaux genres de cestodes d'oiseaux. Note préliminaire. Zool. Anz. *25,* 357–360.

Fuhrmann, O. 1902c. Die Anoplocephaliden der Vögel. Centralbl. Bakt. Parasitenk. *32,* 122–147.

Fuhrmann, O. 1903. L'évolution des Taenias et en particulier de la larve des Ichthyotaenias. Arch. sci. phys. nat. *16,* 1–3.

Fuhrmann, O. 1904a. Ein merkwürdiger getrenntgeschlechtlicher Cestode. Vorläufige Mitteilung. Zool. Anz. *27*, 327–331.

Fuhrmann, O. 1904b. Neue Anoplocephaliden der Vögel. Vorläufige Mitteilung. Zool. Anz. *27*, 348–388.

Fuhrmann, O. 1904c. Ein getrenntgeschlechtlicher Cestode. Zool. Jahrb. Syst. *20*, 131–150.

Fuhrmann, O. 1904d. Die Tetrabothrien der Säugetiere. Centralbl. Bakt. Parasitenk. *35*, 744–752.

Fuhrmann, O. 1905a. Ueber ost-asiatische Vögelcestoden. Reise von Dr. Walther Volz. Zool. Jahrb. Syst. *22*, 303–320.

Fuhrmann, O. 1905b. Das Genus *Diploposthe* Jacobi. Centralbl. Bakt. Parasitenk. *40*, 217–224.

Fuhrmann, O. 1906a. Die Taenien der Raubvögel. Centralbl. Bakt. Parasitenk. *41*, 79–89.

Fuhrmann, O. 1906b. Die *Hymenolepis* Arten der Vögel. Centralbl. Bakt. Parasitenk. *41*, 352–358, 440–452; *42*, 620–628, 730–755.

Fuhrmann, O. 1907a. Die Systematik der Ordnung der Cyclophyllidea. Zool. Anz. *32*, 289–297.

Fuhrmann, O. 1907b. Bekannte und neue Arten und Genera von Vögeltaenien. Centralbl. Bakt. Parasitenk. *45*, 512–536.

Fuhrmann, O. 1908a. Nouveaux Ténias d'oiseaux. Rev. suisse zool. *16*, 27–73.

Fuhrmann, O. 1908b. Das Genus *Anonchotaenia* und *Biuterina*. Centralbl. Bakt. Parasitenk. *46*, 622–631; *48*, 412–428.

Fuhrmann, O. 1908c. Cestoden der Vögel. Zool. Jahrb. Suppl. 10. 252 pp.

Fuhrmann, O. 1909a. Neue Davaineiden. Centralbl. Bakt. Parasitenk. *49*, 94–124.

Fuhrmann, O. 1909b. Cestoden. In Wissenschaftliche Ergebnisse der Schwedischen Expedition nach dem Kilimandjaro, dem Meru und den umgebenden Masai Steppen Deutsch Ost-Afrikas, 1905–1906. Pp. 11–22.

Fuhrmann, O. 1909c. *Triaenophorus robustus* Olsson dans les lacs de Neuchâtel et de Bienne. Bull. soc. sci. nat. Neuchâtel *36*, 86–89.

Fuhrmann, O. 1909d. La distribution faunistique et geographique des cestodes d'oiseaux. Bull. soc. sci. nat. Neuchâtel *36*, 90–101.

Fuhrmann, O. 1910a. Die Cestoden der Vögel des Weissen Nils. In L. A. Jägerskiöld, Results of the Swedish Zoological Expedition to Egypt and the White Nile. 1910. 55 pp.

Fuhrmann, O. 1910b. Vögelcestoden, Nova Guinea. In Résultats de l'expédition scientifique néerlandaise à la Nouvelle Guinée, 1910. Zoologie *9*, 467–470.

Fuhrmann, O. 1911. Vögelcestoden der Aru-Inseln. Abhandl. Senckenberg. nat. Ges. *34*, 251–266.

Fuhrmann, O. 1912. Vögelcestoden. In Ergebnisse der mit Subvention aus der Erbschaft Treitl unternommenen zoologischen Forschungsreise Dr. F. Werners nach dem aegyptischen Sudan und Nord-Uganda. Sitzber. Akad. Wiss. Wien Math. naturw. Klasse, Abt. I. *121*, 181–192.

Fuhrmann, O. 1913a. Nordische Vögelcestoden aus dem Museum Goteborg. Medd. Göteborgs Musei Zoologiska, Afdelning I. 41 pp.

Fuhrmann, O. 1913b. Sur l'origine de *Fimbriaria fasciolaris* Pallas. 9me congrès international de zoologie, Monaco, 1913. Pp. 435–457.

Fuhrmann, O. 1914. Ein neuer getrenntgeschlechtlicher Cestode. Zool. Anz. *44*, 611–620.

Fuhrmann, O. 1916. Eigentümliche Fischcestoden. Zool. Anz. *46*, 385–398.

Fuhrmann, O. 1918. Cestodes de la Nouvelle-Caledonie et des Iles Loyalty. In Nova Caledonia F. Sarasin et J. Roux. *2*, 399–449.

Fuhrmann, O. 1920a. Considérations générales sur les Davainea. Festschrift fur Zschokke, Bale, 1920. 19 pp.

Fuhrmann, O. 1920b. Die Cestoden der Deutschen Südpolar Expedition, 1901–1903. In Deutsche Sudpolar-Expedition, 1901–1903 (1920). Zoologie *16*, 469–524.

Fuhrmann, O. 1921. Einige Anoplocephaliden der Vögel. Centralbl. Bakt. Parasitenk. *87*, 438–451.

Fuhrmann, O. 1923. Encore le cycle du *Bothriocephalus latus*. Revue médicale de la Suisse romande, 43me annee. Pp. 573–575.

Fuhrmann, O. 1924a. *Hymenolepis macracanthos* v. Linstow, avec considérations sur le genre *Hymenolepis*. J. Parasitol. *11*, 33–43.

Fuhrmann, O. 1924b. Questions de nomenclature concernant le genre *Raillietina* Fuhrmann (syn: *Davainea* Bl.). Ann. parasitol. humaine et comparée *2*, 313.

Fuhrmann, O. 1924c. Two species of reptilian cestodes. Ann. Trop. Med. Parasitol. *18*, 505–513.

Fuhrmann, O. 1925a. (In collaboration with J. G. Baer.) Report on the Cestoda. In Zoological results of the third Tanganyika expedition conducted by Dr. W. A. Cunnington. Proc. Zool. Soc. London, 1925, pp. 79–100.

Fuhrmann, O. 1925b. Le phénomène des mutations chez les cestodes. Rev. suisse zool. *32*, 95–97.

Fuhrmann, O. 1925c. Sur le développement et la reproduction asexuée des *Idiogenes otidis* Kr. Ann. parasitol. humaine et comparèe *3*, 143–150.

Fuhrmann, O. 1926. Cestodes. In Catalogue des invertébrés de la Suisse, fasc. 17, Musée d'Hist. nat. de Genève, 1926. 150 pp.

Fuhrmann, O. 1927. Brasilianische Cestoden aus Reptilien und Vögeln. Abhandl. Senckenberg. nat. Ges. *40*, 389–401.

Fuhrmann, O. 1931. Dritte Klasse des Cladus Plathelminthes. Cestoidea: Cyclophyllidea. In Handbuch der Zoologie . . . gegründet von Dr. Willy Kukenthal . . . herausgegeben von Dr. Thilo. Krumbach, Vol. 2, Berlin und Leipzig. Pp. 141–416.

Fuhrmann, O. 1932. Les Ténias des oiseaux. Mémoires de l'Université de Neuchâtel *8*, 381 pp.

Fuhrmann, O. 1933a. Cestodes nouveaux. Rev. suisse zool. *40*, 169–178.

Fuhrmann, O. 1933b. Deux nouveaux cestodes de mammifères d'Angola. Bull. soc. sci. nat. Neuchâtel *58*, 97–106.

Fuhrmann, O. 1933c. Un cestode aberrant. Bull. soc. sci. nat. Neuchâtel *58*, 107–120.

Fuhrmann, O. 1934. Vier Diesing'sche Typen (Cestoda). Rev. suisse zool. *41*, 545–564.

Fuhrmann, O. 1935a. Rectification de nomenclature. Ann. parasitol. humaine et comparée *13*, 386.

Fuhrmann, O. 1935b. Les Ténias des oiseaux. Bull. ornithologique de la Suisse romande *1*, 114–157.

Fuhrmann, O. 1936a. *Gynandrotaenia stammeri* n. g. n. sp. Rev. suisse zool. *43*, 517–518.

Fuhrmann, O. 1936b. Un singulier Ténia d'oiseaux, *Gynandrotaenia stammeri* n. g. n. sp. Ann. parasitol. humaine et comparée *14*, 261–271.

Fuhrmann, O. 1937. Un cestode extraordinaire, *Nematoparataenia southwelli* Fuhrmann. Compt. rend. du XIIme congrès international de zoologie, Lisbonne, 1935 (1937). Pp. 1517–1532.

Fuhrmann, O. 1943a. (In collaboration with J. G. Baer.) Cestodes. Mission biologique Sagan-Omo (Ethiopie méridionale), 1939, dirigée par le professeur Eduardo Zavattari. Bull. soc. sci. nat. Neuchâtel *68*, 113–140.

Fuhrmann, O. 1943b. Cestodes d'Angola. Rev. suisse zool. *50*, 449–471.

Fujita, A. 1922. On the parasites of Japanese fishes. Dobutu Gaku Zassi *34*.

Gaehtgens, W. 1943. Serodiagnostische Untersuchungen ueber Taenieninfektionen . . . Arch. Hyg. Bakt. *129*, 133–157.

Gaiger, S. H. 1915. A revised check-list of the animal parasites of domesticated animals in India. J. Comp. Path. Therap. London *28*, 67–76.

Galli Valerio, B. 1900. Notes de parasitologie. Centralbl. Bakt. Parasitenk. *27*, 305–309.

Galli Valerio, B. 1902. *Bothriocephalus latus* Brems. chez le chat. Centralbl. Bakt. Parasitenk. *32*, 285–287.

Galli Valerio, B. 1904. Notes de parasitologie. Centralbl. Bakt. Parasitenk. *35*, 81–91.

Galli Valerio, B. 1905. Einige Parasiten von *Arvicola nivialis*. Zool. Anz. *28*, 519.

Galli Valerio, B. 1905–1913. Notes de parasitologie. Centralbl. Bakt. Parasitenk. *39*, 230–247; *47*, 608–612; *50*, 538; *56*, 43–47; *60*, 358; *65*, 304–311; *69*, 496–504.

Galli Valerio, B. 1935. Notes parasitologiques. Schweizer Arch. Tierheilk. 77, 643–647

Garcia, E. Y., and C. M. Africa. 1935. *Diphyllobothrium latum* (Linnaeus, 1758) Lühe, 1920 in a native Filipino. Philippine J. Sci. *57*, 451–456.

Garrison, P. E. 1907. Preliminary report on . . . new species of *Taenia*. Philippine J. Sci. *2*, 537–550.

Gasowska, M. 1932. Die Vögelcestoden aus der Umgebung von Kiew (Ukraine). Bull. internat. acad. Polonaise sci. lettr. Year 1931, Ser. B, *11*, 599–627.

Gassner, F. X., and F. Thorp, Jr. 1940. Studies on *Thysanosoma actinioides*. J. Am. Vet. Med. Assoc. *96*, 410–411.

Gastaldi, B. 1854. Cenni sopra alcuni nuovi elminti della *Rana esculenta*, con nuove osservazioni sul *Codonocephalus mutabilis* Diesing. 14 pp. Torino.

Gauthier, M. 1923. Développement de l'oeuf et l'embryon du Cyathocéphale parasite de la truite. Compt. rend. *177*.

Gauthier, M. 1925. Endoparasites de la truite indigène (T. *fario* L.) en Dauphiné. Compt. rend. assoc. France avanc. sci. *49*, 442–444.

Gedoelst, L. 1911. Synopsis de parasitologie de l'homme et des animaux domestiques. 332 pp. Liege.

Gedoelst, L. 1916. Notes sur la faune parasitaire du Congo belge. Rev. zool. Afric. *5*, 1–96.

Gedoelst, L. 1920. Un cas de parasitation de l'homme par l'*Hymenolepis diminuta* (Rudolphi). Compt. rend. soc. biol. *83*, 190–192.

Germanos, N. K. 1895. *Bothriocephalus schistochilos* n. sp. Ein neuer Cestode aus dem Darm von *Phoca barbata*. Jenaische Z. Med. u. Naturw. *30*, 1–38.

Gervais, H. 1870. Sur les entozoaires des Dauphins. Compt. rend. *71*, 779–781.

Gervais, P. 1847. Sur quelques entozoaires taenioides et hydatids. Mém. acad. sci. lettr. Montpellier *1*, 85–103.

Gläser, H. 1909. Die Entwicklungsgeschichte des *Cysticercus longicollis* Rud. Z. wiss. Zool. *92*.

Gmelin, J. F. 1790. Caroli à Linné. Systema Naturae, Tom. I. Pars 6 (Vermes). Leipzig.

Goette, A. 1921. Einziges aus der Entwicklungsgeschichte der Cestoden. Zool. Jahrb. Anat. *42*, 213–228.

Goeze, J. A. E. 1782. Versuch einer Naturgeschichte der Eingeweidewürmer thierischer Körper. xi + 471 pp. Blankenburg.

Goldberg, O. 1855. Helminthum dispositio systematica. 130 pp. Dissertation, Berlin.

Goldschmidt, R. 1900. Zur Entwicklungsgeschichte der Echinococcusköpfchen. Zool. Jahrb. *13*, 466–492.

Goldschmidt, R. 1902a. Untersuchungen ueber die Eireifung, Befruchtung und Zellteilung bei *Polystomum integerrimum*. Z. wiss. Zool. *72*, 397–444.

Goldschmidt, R. 1902b. Bau und Entwicklung von *Zoogonus mirus*. Centralbl. Bakt. Parasitenk. *32*, 870–876.

Goldschmidt, R. 1909. Eischale, Schalendruse und Dotterzellen der Trematoden. Zool. Anz. *34*, 481–497.

Goodall, R. H., and H. Krischner. 1930. Biological tests for hydatid disease. Am. J. Trop. Med. *10*, 71–76.

Goodsir, J. 1841. On *Gymnorhynchus horridus*, a new cestoid entozoon. Edinburgh Philosophical J. *31*, 9–12.

Gordadze, G. N., A. N. Kamalova, and S. M. Bugianishvili. 1944. *Taenia* infections in man in Georgia. Med. Paras. and Paras. Diseases (Russian) *13*, 64–66.

Gordon, H. McL. 1932. A note on the longevity of *Moniezia* spp. in sheep. Australian Vet. J. *8*, 153–154.

Gorodilova, L. I. 1944. Epidemiology and control of *Hymenolepis* infections. Med. Paras. and Paras. Diseases (Russian) *13*, 18–26.

Goto, S., and N. Ishii. 1936. On a new cestode species, *Amphilina japonica*. Japanese J. Exp. Med. *14*, 81–83.

Gough, L. H. 1911. A monograph of the tapeworms of the subfamily Avitellinae, being a review of the genus *Stilesia* and an account of the histology of *Avitellina centripunctata* (Riv.). Quart. J. Microscop. Sci. *56*, 317–383.

Gough, L. H. 1912. The anatomy of *Stilesia globipunctata*. Parasitology *5*, 114–117.

Gower, W. C. 1938. An unusual cestode record from the porcupine in Michigan. Papers Michigan Acad. Sci. Arts. Lett. *24*, 149–151.

Gower, W. C. 1939. A host-parasite catalogue of the helminths of ducks. Am. Midland Naturalist *22*, 580–628.

Graña, A. 1944–1948. Series of studies on the biological diagnosis of hydatid infestation in man. J. Immunology *48*, 203–211. Prensa Medica Argentina *31*, 680–688; *31*, 733–737. Arch. Uruguay. Med. Cir. y Espec. *24*, 231–236, 473–475, 559–565; *27*, 667–670. Medicina, Buenos Aires *4*, 290–296; *5*, 365–368. Am. J. Physiol. *143*, 314–323; *148*, 243–252. Boll. soc. cirug. Uruguay *16*, 213–216. Ann. Allergy *4*, 207–212. Arch. Surgery *52*, 523–537, 713–728.

Graña, A., and C. Oehninger. 1944. Constitución quimica y propiedades biológica de la membrana hidática. Arch. Uruguay Med. Cir. y Espec. *24*, 231–236.

Grassi, G. B. 1867. Bestimmung der vier von Dr. E. Parona in einem kleinen Mädchen sus Varese (Lombardei) gefundenen Taenien (*Taenia flavopunctata*? Dr. E. Parona). Centralbl. Bakt. Parasitenk. *1*, 257–259.

Grassi, G. B. 1885. Contribuzione allo studio della nostra fauna. Atti. accad. Gioenia *18*, 241–252.

Grassi, G. B. 1887. Entwicklungsgeschichte der *Taenia nana*. Centralbl. Bakt. Parasitenk. *2*, 94–95.

Grassi, G. B. 1888a. La pulce del cane (*Pulex serraticeps* Gervais) e l'ordinario ospite intermedio della *Taenia cucumerina*. Nota preventiva. Bull. soc. entom. Ital. *20*, 66.

Grassi, G. B. 1888b. Beiträge zur des Entwicklungscyclus von fünf Parasiten des Hundes (*Taenia cucumerina* Goeze; *Ascaris marginata* Rud.; *Spiroptera sanguinolenta* Rud.; *Filaria immitis* Leidy; und *Haematozoon* Lewis). Centralbl. Bakt. Parasitenk. *4*, 609–620.

Grassi, G. B. 1888c. *Taenia flavopunctata* Weinl., *Taenia leptocephala* Creplin, *Taenia diminuta* Rud. Atti reale accad. sci. Torino *23*, 492–501.

Grassi, G. B., and G. Rovelli. 1889a. Embryologische Forschungen an Cestoden. Centralbl. Bakt. Parasitenk. *5*, 370–377.

Grassi, G. B., and G. Rovelli. 1889b. Embryologische Forschungen an Cestoden (Schluss). Centralbl. Bakt. Parasitenk. *5*, 401–410.

Grassi, G. B., and G. Rovelli. 1892. Ricerche embriologische sui Cestodi. Atti accad. Gioenia *4*, 1–109.

Green, N. K., and R. A. Wardle. 1941. The cultivation of tapeworms in artificial media. Can. J. Research, Section D, *19*, 240–244.

Grembergen, G. van. 1945. Le metabolisme respiratoire du cestode, *Moniezia benedeni* (Moniez, 1879). Enzymologia *11*, 268–281.

Grimm, O. 1872. Zur Kenntnis einiger wenig bekannten Binnenwürmer. Nachr. k. Ges. Wiss. Gottingen *12*, 240–246.

Grube, E. 1855. Bemerkungen ueber einzige Helminthen und Meerwürmer. Arch. Naturgeschichte *21*, 137–158.

Grube, E., and G. R. Wagener. See Wagener, 1852b.

Grüber, A. 1878. Ein neuer Cestodenwirt. Zool. Anz. *1*, 74–75.

Grüber, A. 1881. Zur Kenntnis des *Archigetes Sieboldii*. Zool. Anz. *4*, 89–91.

Guberlet, J. E. 1916a. Morphology of adult and larval cestodes from poultry. Trans. Am. Microscop. Soc. *35*, 23–44.

Guberlet, J. E. 1916b. Studies on the transmission and prevention of cestode infection in chickens. J. Am. Vet. Med. Assoc.

Guberlet, J. E. 1919. On the life-history of the chicken cestode, *Hymenolepis carioca*. J. Parasitol. *6*, 35–37.

Guiart, J. 1927. Classification des Tétrarhynques. Assoc. franc. pour l'avanc. des sci. 50me session, Lyon (1926). Paris, 1927. Pp. 397–401.

Guiart, J. 1931. Considérations historiques sur la nomenclature et sur la classification des Tétrarhynques. Bull. institut océanographique, Monaco, No. 575, pp. 1–27.

Guiart, J. 1933. Contribution à l'étude des cestodes de Calmars, avec description d'une espèce nouvelle, *Diplobothrium pruvoti*. Arch. zool. exp. et gén. *75*, 465–473.

Guiart, J. 1935a. Le véritable *Floriceps saccatus* de Cuvier n'est pas la larve géant de

Tétrarhynque vivant dans le foie du mole (*Mola mola*). Bull. institut océanographique, Monaco, No. 666, pp. 1–15.

Guiart, J. 1935b. Cestodes parasites provenant des campagnes scientifiques du Prince Albert Ier de Monaco. Résultats des campagnes scientifiques accomplies sur son yacht par Albert Ier, Monaco, Fasc. 111, pp. 1–115.

Guiart, J. 1938. Etude parasitologique et épidémiologique de quelques poissons de mer. Bull. institut océanographique, Monaco, No. 755, pp. 1–15.

Gulati, A. N. 1929. Description of a new species of tapeworm, *Dipylidium catus* n. sp., with a note on the genus *Dipylidium* Leuckart, 1863. Bull. Agr. Research Pusa *190*, 1–14.

Guyer, M. F. 1898. On the structure of *Taenia confusa* Ward. Zool. Jahrb. Syst. *11*, 469–492.

Gwynn, A. M., and A. G. Hamilton. 1935. Occurrence of larval cestode in the red locust (*Nomadacris septemfasciata*). J. Parasitol. *27*, 551–555.

Hager, A. 1941. Effects of dietary modifications of host rats on the tapeworm *Hymenolepis diminuta*. Iowa State College J. Sci. *15*, 127–153.

Hall, M. C. 1898. The flukes and tapeworms of cattle, sheep and swine, with special reference to the infection of meats. Bur. Animal Industr. U. S. Dept. Agr. *19*, 11–136.

Hall, M. C. 1908. A new rabbit cestode, *Cittotaenia mosaica*. Proc. U. S. Nat. Museum *34*, 691–699.

Hall, M. C. 1910a. A new species of cestode parasite (*Taenia balaniceps*) of the dog and of the lynx, with a note on *Proteocephalus punicus*. Proc. U. S. Nat. Museum *39*, 139–151.

Hall, M. C. 1910b. The gid parasite and allied species of the cestode genus *Multiceps*. I. Historical review. U. S. Bur. Anim. Indust. Bull. 125. 68 pp.

Hall, M. C. 1911a. The gid parasite and allied species of the cestode genus *Multiplex* [*sic*]. (Editorial abstract.) Am. Vet. Rev. N. Y. *38*, 591–592.

Hall, M. C. 1911b. The coyote as a host of *Multiceps multiceps*. (Secretary's abstract of paper read before the 6th Meeting Helminthological Society, Washington, Apr. 11.) Science *33*, 975.

Hall, M. C. 1912. A second case of *Multiceps multiceps* in the coyote. Science *35*, 556.

Hall, M. C. 1915. The dog as a carrier of parasites and disease. U. S. Dep. Agr. Bull. 260, pp. 1–27.

Hall, M. C. 1916a. A new and economically important tapeworm, *Multiceps gaigeri*, from the dog. J. Am. Vet. Med. Ass. *50*, 214–223.

Hall, M. C. 1916b. A synoptical key to the adult taenioid cestodes of the dog, cat and some related carnivores. J. Am. Vet. Med. Ass. *50*, 356–360.

Hall, M. C. 1917. Parasites of the dog in Michigan. J. Am. Vet. Med. Ass. *51*, 383–396.

Hall, M. C. 1919. The adult taenioid cestodes of dogs and cats, and of related carnivores in North America. Proc. U. S. Nat. Museum *55*, 1–94.

Hall, M. C. 1920. Intestinal parasites found in eighteen Alaskan foxes. J. Am. Vet. Med. Ass.

Hall, M. C. 1926a. Developments in anthelminthic medication. Am. J. Trop. Med. *6*, 247–260.

Hall, M. C. 1926b. Some practical principles of anthelminthic medication. J. Parasitol. *13*, 16–24.

Hall, M. C. 1929a. Parasites and parasitic diseases of sheep. U. S. Dep. Agr. Farmers Bull. 1330.

Hall, M. C. 1929b. A new cestode reared in the dog, *Multiceps packi* sp. nov. J. Parasitol. *16*, 49.

Hall, M. C. 1929c. Arthropods as intermediate hosts of helminths. Smithsonian Miscell. Coll. *81*.

Hall, M. C. 1934a. Parasites and parasitic diseases of dogs. U. S. Dep. Agr. Circular 338.

Hall, M. C. 1934b. The discharge of eggs from segments of *Thysanosoma actinioides*. Proc. Helm. Soc. Washington *1*, 6–7.

Hall, M. C., and H. P. Hoskins. 1918. The occurrence of tapeworms, *Anoplocephala* spp., of the horse in the United States. Cornell Veterinarian *8*, 287–292.

Hall, M. C., and M. Wigdor. 1918. A bothriocephalid tapeworm from the dog in North America, with notes on cestode parasites of dogs. J. Am. Vet. Med. Ass. *53*, 355–362.

Hamann, O. 1885. *Taenia lineata* Goeze, eine Taenie mit flächenständigen Geschlechtsöffnungen. Z. wiss. Zool. *42*, 718–744.

Hamann, O. 1890. In *Gammarus pulex* lebende Cysticercoiden mit Schwanzanhangen. Jena Z. Naturwiss. *24*, 1–10.

Hamann, O. 1891. Neue Cysticercoiden mit Schwanzanhangen. Jena Z. Naturwiss. *25*, 553–564.

Hamann, O. 1893. *Taenia lineata* Goeze, eine Taenie mit flächenständigen Geschlechtsöffnungen. Z. wiss. Zool. *56*.

Hamid, A. 1932. A cestode, *Oochoristica khalili* n. sp., from a snake, *Psammophis schokari* Forskal. J. Parasitol. *24*, 238–240.

Hamill, J. M. 1906. On the mechanism of protection of intestinal worms, and its bearing on the relation of enterokinase to trypsin. J. Physiol. *33*, 479–492.

Hamilton, P. C. 1940. A new species of *Taenia* from a coyote. Trans. Am. Microscop. Soc. *59*, 64–69.

Hannum, C. A. 1925. A new species of cestode, *Ophiotaenia magna* n. sp., from the frog. Trans. Am. Microscop. Soc. *44*, 148–155.

Hansen, M. F. 1947. Three anoplocephalid cestodes from the prairie meadow vole, with description of *Andrya microti* n. sp. Trans. Am. Microscop. Soc. *66*, 279–282.

Hansen, M. F. 1948. *Schizorchis ochotonae* n. g. n. sp. of anoplocephalid cestode. Am. Midland Naturalist *39*, 754–757.

Harkema, R. 1936. The parasites of some North Carolina rodents. Ecological Monographs *2*, 151–232.

Harkema, R. 1942. The mourning dove, a new host of the anoplocephalid tapeworm, *Aporina delafondi* (Railliet). J. Parasitol. *28*, 495.

Harkema, R. 1943. The cestodes of North Carolina poultry, with remarks on the life-history of *Raillietina tetragona*. J. Elisha Mitchell Sci. Soc. *59*, 127.

Harman, M. T. 1913. Method of cell division in the sex cells of *Taenia taeniaeformis*. J. Morph. *24*, 205–243.

Harnisch, O. 1932–1937. Series of articles on the oxygen consumption of various parasitic helminths. Z. vergl. Physiol. *16*; *19*, 310–348; *22*, 50–66; *23*; *24*, 667–686. Verhandl. deutsch. Zool. Ges. *39*.

Harper, W. F. 1933. A cysticercoid from *Helodrilus* (*Allolobophora longus* Cede) and *Lumbricus terrestris* L. Parasitology *25*, 483–484.

Harris, J. R., and M. D. Hickey. 1945. Occurrence of Diphyllobothriidae in Ireland. Nature, London, *156* (correspondence), 447–448.

Hart, J. F. 1936a. Cestoda from fishes of Puget Sound. II. Tetrarhynchoidea. Trans. Am. Microscop. Soc. *55*, 369–387.

Hart, J. F. 1936b. Cestoda from fishes of Puget Sound. III. Phyllobothrioidea. Trans. Am. Microscop. Soc. *55*, 488–496.

Hart, J. F., and J. E. Guberlet. 1936. Cestoda from fishes of Puget Sound. I. Spathebothrioidea, a new superfamily. Trans. Am. Microscop. Soc. *55*, 199–207.

Hartmann, P. J. 1695. De Vesicularibus vermibus in mure. Miscell. acad. nat. curios. Lips. & Francof. (1694). Decur. 3, An. 2. Pp. 304–305.

Harwood, D. P. D. 1932. The helminths parasitic in the amphibia and reptilia of Houston, Texas and vicinity. Proc. U. S. Nat. Museum *81*, 1–71.

Harwood, D. P. D. 1933. The helminths parasitic in a water moccasin, with a discussion of the characters of Proteocephalidae. Parasitology *25*, 130–142.

Harwood, D. P. D. 1938. Reproductive cycles of *Raillietina cesticillus* of the fowl. Livro Jubilar do Professor Lauro Travassos. Rio de Janeiro, 1938. Pp. 213–220.

Hassall, A. A. 1893. A revision of the adult cestodes of cattle, sheep and allied animals. U. S. Bur. Anim. Indust. Bull. 4.

Hassall, A. A. 1896a. Check list of the animal parasites of chickens. U. S. Bur. Anim. Indust. Circular 9, pp. 1–7

Hassall, A. A. 1896b. Check list of the animal parasites of turkeys. U. S. Bur. Anim. Indust. Circular 12, pp. 1–3.

Hassall, A. A. 1896c. Bibliography of the tapeworms of poultry. U. S. Bur. Anim. Indust. Bull. 12, pp. 81–88.

Hassall, A. A. 1896d. Check list of animal parasites of ducks. U. S. Bur. Anim. Indust. Circular 13, pp. 1–7.

Hassall, A. A. 1896e. Check list of animal parasites of geese. U. S. Bur. Anim. Indust. Circular 14, pp. 1–5.

Hassall, A. A. 1896f. Check list of animal parasites of pigeons. U. S. Bur. Anim. Indust. Circular *15*.

Haswell, W. A. 1902a. On a *Gyrocotyle* from *Chimaera ogilbyi*, and on *Gyrocotyle* in general. Proc. Linnean Soc. New South Wales *27*, 48–54.

Haswell, W. A. 1902b. On a cestode of *Cestracion* . . . Quart. J. Microscop. Sci. *46*, 399–415.

Haswell, W. A., and J. P. Hill. 1893. On *Polycercus*: a proliferating cystic parasite of the earthworms. Proc. Linnean Soc. New South Wales *8*, 365–376.

Hawkins, P. A. 1942. *Sigmodon hispidus hispidus*, a new host for the strobilocercus of *Taenia taeniaeformis*. J. Parasitol. *28*, 94.

Hawkins, P. A. 1948. *Moniezia expansa* infections in sheep. J. Parasitol. *34* Suppl., 33.

Hearin, J. T. 1941. Studies on the acquired immunity to the dwarf tapeworm, *Hymenolepis nana* var. *fraterna*, in the mouse host. Am. J. Hyg. *33*, 71–87.

Heilmann, P. 1932. Beitrag zur Pathologie der Hirncercose. Virchow's Arch. path. Anat. *286*, 176–182.

Heilmeyer, L. 1932. Blutfarbstoffwechselstudien. Die Regenerations und Farbstoffwechselvorgänge beim Morbus Biermer sowie bei einer Botriocephalusanämie vor und nach Leberbehandlung. Deutsch. Arch. Klin. Med. *173*, 128–163.

Hein, G. E. 1927. Cedar oil as an aid in finding parasitic ova in faeces. J. Lab. Clin. Med. *12*, 1117–1118.

Hein, W. 1904a. Beiträge zur Kenntnis von *Amphilina foliacea*. Z. wiss. Zool. *76*, 25–26.

Hein, W. 1904b. Zur Epithelfrage der Trematoden. Z. wiss. Zool. *77*.

Hemming, F. 1947. Note 7. On an error . . . In Opinions and declarations rendered by the International Commission on Zoological Nomenclature. I (25), pp. 297–302.

Henneguy, L. F. 1902. Sur la formation de l'oeuf, la maturation et la fécondation de l'oocyte chez le *Distomum hepaticum*. Compt. rend. *134*, 1235–1238.

Henneguy, L. F. 1906. Recherches sur le mode de formation de l'oeuf ectolecithe du *Distomum hepaticum*. Arch. anat. microscop. *9*.

Henry, A. 1927. Tetrathyridium et *Mesocestoides*. Bull. soc. cent. méd. vét. *102*.

Henry, A. 1931. Les parasites et maladies parasitaires du Ragodin. Bull. soc. nat. acclimation France *78*.

Herde, K. E. 1938. Early development of *Ophiotaenia perspicua* La Rue. Trans. Am. Microscop. Soc. *57*, 282–291.

Hickey, J. P. 1920. The diagnosis of the more common helminthic infestations of man. U. S. Treasury Dep. Pub. Health Rep. 35. Reprint 596. Pp. 1383–1400.

Hickey, M. D., and J. R. Harris. 1947. Progress of the *Diphyllobothrium* epizootic at . . . Wicklow, Ireland. J. Helm. *22*, 13–28.

Hiles, J. 1926. Serological studies on hydatids. J. Helm. *4*, 143–178.

Hiles, J. 1927. Serological tests for hydatid disease. Proc. Roy. Soc. Med. London *20*, 708–713.

Hill, J. P. 1895. A contribution to a further knowledge of the cystic cestodes. Part II. On a monocercus from *Didymogaster*. Proc. Linnean Soc. New South Wales *9*, 49–84.

Hill, W. C. 1941. *Gryporhynchus tetrorchis*, a new dilepidid cestode from the great blue heron. J. Parasitol. *27*, 171–172.

Hilmy, J. S. 1929. *Bothriocephalus scorpii* (Muller, 1776) Cooper, 1917. Ann. Trop. Med. Liverpool *23*, 385–396.

Hilmy, J. S. 1936. Parasites from Liberia and French Guinea. Part III. Cestodes from Liberia. Publ. Egyptian Univ. Fac. Med. *9*, 1–72.

Hjortland, A. L. 1928. On the structure and life-history of an adult *Triaenophorus robustus*. J. Parasitol. *15*, 38–44.

Hoder, F. 1933. Der Nachweis der Echinokokkenkrankung durch immunbiologische Methoden. Fortschritte der Medizin. *51*, 959.

Hoeden, J. van der. 1925. Der Gehalt der Echinokokkenflüssigkeit an Echinokokkeantigen und Eiweiss. Münch. Med. Wochschr. *72*, 1022.

Hoek, P. P. C. 1879. Ueber den encystirten Scolex von *Tetrarhynchus*. Niederlandisches Arch. Zool. *5*, 1–18.

Hoeppli, R. 1925. *Mesocestoides corti*, a new species of cestode from the mouse. J. Parasitol. *12*, 91–96.

Hoeppli, R. 1927. Ueber Beziehungen zwischen dem biologischen Verhalten parasitischer Nematoden und histologischen Reaktionen des Wirbelkorpers. Arc. Schiffs. Trop. Hyg. *31*. 88 pp.

Hoeppli, R. 1933. Myeloid changes in the spleen of experimental animals due to infection with *Cysticercus fasciolaris* and to emulsions prepared from tapeworms. Chinese Med. J. *47*, 1146–1163.

Hoff, E. C., and H. E. Hoff. 1929. *Proteocephalus pugetensis*, a new tapeworm from the stickleback. Trans. Am. Microscop. Soc. *48*, 54–61.

Hoff, F., and H. Sauerstein. 1936. Ueber Bothriocephalus Anämie. Klin. Wochschr. *15*, 131–135.

Hofmann (no initials). 1901. Einiges ueber die Wanderung von Taenienembryonen. Thierarztl. Wochenschr. Berlin *36*, 537–541.

Hofsten, N. von. 1912. Eischale und Dotterzellen bei Turbellarien und Trematoden. Zool. Anz. *39*, 111–136.

Hölldobler, K. 1937. *Cysticercus multiformis* nov. spez., eine noch nicht beschriebene Finnenform einer Cyclophyllidea. Z. Parasitenk. *9*, 523–528.

Holten, H. S. 1802. Beskrivelse over en ny Fisk fra Portugal, og tvende i samme fundne ubekiendte Indvoldeorme. Skrivter af Naturhistorie Selskabet. Kjobenhavn *5*, 19–28.

Honess, R. F. 1937. Un nouveau cestode: *Fossor angertrudae* n. g., n. sp. du blaireau d'Amérique *Taxidea taxus taxus* (Schreber, 1778). Ann. parasitol. humaine et comparée *15*, 363–366.

Honigberg, B. 1944. A morphological abnormality in the cestode *Dipylidium caninum*. Trans. Am. Microscop. Soc. *63*, 340–341.

Hornell, J. 1904. Report on the *Placuna placenta* Pearl Fishery of Lake Tampalakamam. Rep. Ceylon Marine Biol. Lab. *1*, 41–54.

Hornell, J. 1912. New cestodes from Indian fishes. Rec. Ind. Museum 7, 197–204.

Horowitz-Wlassowa, L. 1926. Zur Frage des serologischen Nachweises der Echinokokkeninfektion. Deutsch. Med. Wochenschr. *52*, 147–148.

Horsfall, M. W., and M. F. Jones. 1937. The life-history of *Choanotaenia infundibulum*, a cestode parasitic in chickens. J. Parasitol. *23*, 435–450.

Houdemer, E., Dodero (no initials), and E. Cornet. 1933. Les sparganoses animales et la sparganose oculaire en Indochine. Bull. soc. medico-chirug. Indochine *11*, 425–451.

Houttuyn, M. 1775. Linnes Natursystem von Ph. L. St. Muller. Vol. 2, p. 904.

Hsü, H. F. 1935. Contribution à l'étude des cestodes de Chine. Rev. suisse zool. *42*, 477–570.

Hubbard, W. E. 1933. A remarkable infection of tapeworm larvae in a whipsnake. Am. Midland Naturalist *19*, 617–618.

Hubbs, C. L. 1927. The related effects of a parasite on a fish. J. Parasitol. *14*, 75–84.

Hubscher, H. 1937. Notes helminthologiques. Rev. suisse zool. *42*, 459–482.

Hudimi, T., and B. Nishazaki. 1934. Ueber den Fibrinogen und Thrombingehalt im Blut bei Kaninchenclonorchiasis. Okayama-Igakkai-Zasshi *46* (in Japanese, with German summary, p. 972).

Hudson, J. R. 1934a. Notes on some avian cestodes. Ann. Mag. Nat. Hist. (Ser. 10) *14*, 314–318.

Hudson, J. R. 1934b. A list of cestodes known to occur in East African mammals, birds and reptiles. J. East Africa and Uganda Nat. Hist. Soc., No. 49/50, p. 208.

Hughes, R. C. 1940a. The genus *Hymenolepis* Weinland, 1858. Oklahoma Agr. Exp. Sta. Tech. Bull. 8, pp. 1–42.

Hughes, R. C. 1940b. The genus *Oochoristica* Lühe, 1898. Am. Midland Naturalist *23*, 368–381.

Hughes, R. C. 1941a. The Taeniae of yesterday. Oklahoma Agr. Exp. Sta. Tech. Bull. 38, pp. 1–83.

Hughes, R. C. 1941b. A key to the species of tapeworms in *Hymenolepis*. Trans. Am. Microscop. Soc. *60*, 378–414.

Hughes, R. C., J. H. Baker, and G. B. Dawson. 1941a. The tapeworms of reptiles. Part I. Am. Midland Naturalist *25*, 454–468.

Hughes, R. C., J. H. Baker, and G. B. Dawson. 1941b. The tapeworms of reptiles. Part II. Host catalogue. Wasmann Collector *4*, 97–104.

Hughes, R. C., J. H. Baker, and G. B. Dawson. 1942. The tapeworms of reptiles. Part III. Proc. Oklahoma Acad. Sci. *22*, 81–89.

Hughes, R. C., and R. L. Schultz. 1942. The genus *Raillietina* Fuhrmann, 1920. Oklahoma Agr. Exp. Sta. Tech. Bull. 39, pp. 1–53.

Hungerbühler, M. 1910. Studien an Gyrocotylen und Cestoden. Ergebnisse einer von L. Schultze ausgeführten Zoologischen Forschungsreise in Sudafrika. Jenaische Denkschr. *16*, 494–522.

Hunnicutt, T. N. 1935. An anaemia associated with a fish tapeworm (*Diphyllobothrium latum*) infestation. J. Am. Med. Assoc. *104*, 1984–1986.

Hunninen, A. V. 1935a. A method of demonstrating cysticercoids of *Hymenolepis fraterna* (*H. nana* var. *fraterna* Stiles) in the intestinal villi of mice. J. Parasitol. *21*, 124–125.

Hunninen, A. V. 1935b. Infections of abnormal hosts with the mouse strain of *Hymenolepis fraterna*. J. Parasitol. *21*, 312.

Hunninen, A. V. 1935c. Studies on the life-history and host-parasite relations of *Hymenolepis fraterna* (*H. nana* var. *fraterna* Stiles) in white mice. Am. J. Hyg. *22*, 414–443.

Hunninen, A. V. 1936. An experimental study of internal auto-infection with *Hymenolepis fraterna* in white mice. J. Parasitol. *22*, 84–87.

Hunter, G. W., III. 1927a. Notes on the Caryophyllaeidae of North America. J. Parasitol. *14*, 16–26.

Hunter, G. W., III. 1927b. Studies on the Caryophyllaeidae of North America. Illinois Biol. Monogr. *11*, 1–186.

Hunter, G. W., III. 1928. Contributions to the life-history of *Proteocephalus ambloplitis* (Leidy). J. Parasitol. *14*, 229–242.

Hunter, G. W., III. 1929a. New Caryophyllaeidae from North America. J. Parasitol. *15*, 185–192.

Hunter, G. W., III. 1929b. A case of accidental parasitism. Science *69*, 645–646.

Hunter, G. W., III. 1929c. Life-history studies on *Proteocephalus pinguis* La Rue. Parasitology *21*, 487–496.

Hunter, G. W., III. 1932. An artificial lake with a low percentage of infected fish. Trans. Am. Microscop. Soc. *51*, 22–27.

Hunter, G. W., III. 1937. Parasites of fishes in the lower Hudson area. Annual Report (26th) of the New York State Conservancy Department Biological Survey Supplement.

Hunter, G. W., III. 1942. Studies on the parasites of fresh water fishes of Connecticut. Connecticut Geol. and Nat. Hist. Survey Bull. *63*, 228–288.

Hunter, G. W., III, and R. V. Bangham. 1933. Studies on the fish parasites of Lake Erie. II. New Cestoda and Nematoda. J. Parasitol. *19*, 304–311.

Hunter, G. W., III, and A. V. Hunninen. 1934. A biological survey of the Raquette watershed. X. Studies of the plerocercoid larva of the bass tapeworm, *Proteocephalus ambloplitis* (Leidy) in the small-mouthed bass. Annual Report (23rd) of the New York State Conservancy Department Biological Survey Supplement. Pp. 255–261.

Hunter, G. W., III, and W. S. Hunter. 1929. Further studies on the bass tapeworm, *Proteocephalus ambloplitis* (Leidy). Annual Report (18th) of the New York State Conservancy Department Biological Survey Supplement. Pp. 198–207.

Hunter, G. W., III, and W. S. Hunter. 1930. Studies on the parasites of fishes of the Lake Champlain watershed. Annual Report (19th) of the New York State Conservancy Department Biological Survey Supplement. Pp. 241–260.

Hunter, G. W., III, and W. S. Hunter. 1931. Studies on fish parasites in the St. Lawrence watershed. Annual Report of the New York State Conservancy Department Biological Survey Supplement. Pp. 197–216.

Hunter, G. W., III, and W. S. Hunter. 1934. A biological survey of the Raquette watershed. IX. Studies on fish and bird parasites. Annual Report (23rd) of the New York State Conservancy Department Biological Survey Supplement. Pp. 245–254.

Hunter, G. W., III, and J. S. Rankin. 1940. Parasites of northern pike and pickerel. Trans. Am. Fish. Soc. *69*, 268–272.

Hussey, K. L. 1941. *Aporina delafondi* (Railliet), an anoplocephalid cestode from the pigeon. Am. Midland Naturalist *25*, 413–417.

Ihle, J. E. W. 1927. Two Cestoden gevonden in een exemplar van *Mola mola*. Tijdschr. Nederlandsche Dierk. Ver. No. 20, *17*.

Ihle, J. E. W., and M. E. Ihle-Landenberg. 1932. Ueber einen neuen Cestodarier (*Klosterina kuiperi* n. gen. n. sp.) aus einer Schildkrote. Zool. Anz. *100*, 309–316.

Ihle, J. E. W., and G. van Oordt. 1925. Eenige Cestoden van Vogels. Tijdschr. Diergeneesk. Deel. 52, Aflevering 20, Jahrg. 1925.

Ijima, I. 1905. On a new cestode larva parasitic in man (*Plerocercoides prolifer*). J. Coll. Sci. Imp. Univ. Tokyo *20*, 1–21.

Inamdar, N. B. 1933. A new species of avian cestode from India. Ann. Mag. Nat. Hist. (Ser. 10) *11*, 610–613.

Inamdar, N. B. 1934. Four new species of avian cestodes from India. Z. Parasitenk. *7*, 198–206.

Inamdar, N. B. 1942. A new species of avian cestode from India. J. Univ. Bombay *11*, 77–81.

Inamdar, N. B. 1944. A new species of avian cestode, *Ophryocotyloides bhalerao* . . . Proceedings Indian Science Congress. Part III, p. 89.

Ingles, L. G. 1936. Worm parasites of California Amphibia. Trans. Am. Microscop. Soc. *55*, 73–92.

Isaacs, R., C. C. Sturgis, and M. Smith. 1928. Tapeworm anemia: therapeutic observations. Arch. Internal Med. *42*, 313–321.

Isobe, M. 1926. The significance, physiochemical conditions, and pharmacological studies in the movement of the hexacanth embryo. Acta Schol. Med. Univ. Kioto *8*, 519–536.

Ivervs, J. 1904. Sur un cestode du *Rhombus maximus*. Compt. rend. congrès internat. zool. Berne, 1904. Pp. 702–703.

Iwata, S. 1933. Some experimental and morphological studies on the post-embryonal development of Manson's tapeworm, *Diphyllobothrium erinacei* (Rudolphi) . . . Japanese J. Zool. *5*, 209–247.

Iwata, S. 1934. Some experimental studies on the regeneration of the plerocercoids of Manson's tapeworm, *Diphyllobothrium erinacei* (Rudolphi), with special reference to its relationship with *Sparganum proliferum* Ijima. Japanese J. Zool. *6*, 139–158.

Jacobi, A. 1896. *Diploposthe*, eine neue Gattung von Vogeltaenien. Zool. Anz. *19*, 268–269.

Jacobi, A. 1897a. *Diploposthe laevis*, eine merkwürdige Vogeltaenien. Zool. Jahrb. Anat. *10*, 287–306.

Jacobi, A. 1897b. *Amabilia* und *Diploposthe*. Centralbl. Bakt. Parasitenk. *21*, 873–874.

Jacobi, A. 1898. Ueber den Bau der *Taenia inflata* Rud. Zool. Jahrb. Syst. *12*, 95–104.

Jameson, H. L. 1912. Studies on pearl oysters and pearls. (1) The structure of the shell and pearls of the Ceylon pearl oyster (*Margaritifera vulgaris* Schumacher) with an examination of the cestode theory of pearl formation. Proc. Zool. Soc. London, 1912. Pp. 260–358.

Janicki, C. von. 1902. Ueber zwei Arten des Genus *Davainea* aus celebensischen Säugern. Arch. parasitol. humaine et comparée *6*, 257–292.

Janicki, C. von. 1904a. Weitere Angaben ueber *Triplotaenia mirabilis* J. E. V. Boas. Zool. Anz. *27*, 243–247.

Janicki, C. von. 1904b. Zur Kenntnis einiger Säugetiercestoden. Zool. Anz. *27*, 770–782.

Janicki, C. von. 1904c. Bemerkungen ueber Cestoden ohne Genitalporus. Centralbl. Bakt. Parasitenk. *36*, 222–223.

Janicki, C. von. 1905. Beutlercestoden der Niederländischen Neu-Guinea Expedition. Zugleich einiges Neue aus dem Geschlechtsleben der Cestoden. Zool. Anz. *29*, 127–131.

Janicki, C. von. 1906a. Studieren an Säugetiercestoden. Z. wiss. Zool. *81*, 505–597.

Janicki, C. von. 1906b. Die Cestoden Neu Guineas. Nova Guinea. Résultats de l'expedition scient. Néerl. à la Nouvelle-Guinée en 1903. V, Livr. 1, pp. 181–200.

Janicki, C. von. 1906c. Zur Embryonalentwicklung von *Taenia serrata* Goeze. Zool. Anz. *30*.

Janicki, C. von. 1907. Ueber die Embryonalentwicklung von *Taenia serrata* Goeze. Z. wiss. Zool. *87*.

Janicki, C. von. 1908. Ueber den Bau von *Amphilina liguloidea* Diesing. Z. wiss. Zool. *89*, 568–597.

Janicki, C. von. 1909. Ueber den Prozess der Hullmembranenbildung in der Entwicklung des Bothriocephalen. Zool. Anz. *34*, 153–156.

Janicki, C. von. 1910. Die Cestoden aus *Procavia*. Jenaische Denkschr. med. naturw. Ges. *16*, 373–396.

Janicki, C. von. 1918. Neue Studien ueber postembryonale Entwicklung und Wirtswechsel bei Bothriocephalen. I. *Triaenophorus nodulosus* (Pallas). Correspondenz-Blatt für Schweizerärzt, Basel.

Janicki, C. von. 1919. Neue Studien ueber die postembryonale Entwicklung und Wirtswechsel bei Bothriocephalen. II. *Ligula*. Correspondenz-Blatt für Schweizerärzt, Basel.

Janicki, C. von. 1920. Grundlinien einer "Cercomer Theorie" zur Morphologie der Trematoden und Cestoden. Festschrift für Zschokke, No. 30. 20 pp. Basel.

Janicki, C. von. 1926. Cestodes s. str. aus Fischen und Amphibien. In L. A. Jägerskiöld, Results of the Swedish zoological expedition to Egypt and the White Nile, 1901. Part 5, pp. 1–58. Uppsala.

Janicki, C. von. 1928. Die Lebensgeschichte von *Amphilina foliacea* G. Wagener, Parasiten des Wolga-Sterlets. Nach Beobachtungen und Experimenten. Arbeiten Biologischer Wolga-Station No. 10, Saratov.

Janicki, C. von. 1930. Ueber der jungsten Zustande von *Amphilina foliacea* in der Fischleibeshohle, sowie generelles Auffassungs des Genus *Amphilina* Wagener. Zool. Anz. *90*.

Janicki, C. von, and F. Rosen. 1917. Le cycle évolutif du *Dibothriocephalus latus* L. Recherches expérimentales et observation. Bull. soc. sci. nat. Neuchâtel *42*, 19–53; and Correspondenz-Blatt No. 45, für Schweizerärzt, Basel.

Jarvi, T. H. 1909. Die kleine Maräne, *Coregonus albula* L., als der Zwischenwirt des *Dibothriocephalus latus* L. in den Seen Nord-Tawastlands (Finnland). Medd. soc. Fauna et Flora Fens. Helsingfors *35*, 62–67.

Jellison, W. L. 1933. Parasites of porcupines of the genus *Erethizon* (Rodentia). Trans. Am. Microscop. Soc. *52*, 42–47.

Jellison, W. L. 1936. The occurrence of the cestode, *Moniezia benedeni* (Anoplocephalidae), in the American moose. Proc. Helm. Soc. Washington *3*, 16.

Jenkins, J. W. R. 1923. On a new species of *Moniezia* from the sheep, *Ovies aries*. Ann. Appl. Biol. *10*, 267–286.

Jepps, M. W. 1937. Note on Apstein's parasites and some very early larval Platyhelminthes. Parasitology *29*, 554–558.

Jewell, M. E. 1916. *Cylindrotaenia americana* nov. spec. from the cricket frog. J. Parasitol. *2*, 180–192.

John, D. D. 1926. On *Cittotaenia denticulata* (Rud. 1804) with notes as to the occurrence of other helminthic parasites of rabbits found in the Aberystwyth area. Parasitology *18*, 436–454.

Johnston, T. H. 1909a. On a cestode from *Dacelo gigas* Bodd. Records Australian Museum 7, 246–250.

Johnston, T. H. 1909b. Notes on Australian Entozoa. No. I. Records Australian Museum 7, 329–344.

Johnston, T. H. 1909c. Notes on some Australian parasites. Agr. Gazette New South Wales *20*, 581–584.

Johnston, T. H. 1909d. On a new reptilian cestode. Proc. Roy. Soc. New South Wales *43*, 103–116.

Johnston, T. H. 1909e. On a new genus of bird cestodes. Proc. Roy. Soc. New South Wales *43*, 139–147.

Johnston, T. H. 1909f. On the anatomy of *Monopylidium passerinum* Fuhrmann. Proc. Roy. Soc. New South Wales *43*, 405–411.

Johnston, T. H. 1909g. The Entozoa of Monotremata and Australian marsupials. No. I. Proc. Linnean Soc. New South Wales *34*, 514–523.

Johnston, T. H. 1910. On Australian avian Entozoa. Proc. Roy. Soc. New South Wales *44*, 84–122.

Johnston, T. H. 1911a. The Entozoa of Monotremata and Australian marsupials. No. II. Proc. Linnean Soc. New South Wales *36*, 45–57.

Johnston, T. H. 1911b. New species of avian cestodes. Proc. Linnean Soc. New South Wales *36*, 58–80.

Johnston, T. H. 1911c. *Proteocephalus gallardi*; a new cestode from the black snake. Ann. Queensland Museum, No. 10, pp. 175–182.

Johnston, T. H. 1912a. On a re-examination of the types of Krefft's species of Cestoda. Records Australian Museum *9*, 1–35.

Johnston, T. H. 1912b. New species of cestodes from Australian birds. Memoirs Queensland Museum *1*, 211–215.

Johnston, T. H. 1912c. Internal parasites recorded from Australian birds. The Emu *12*, 105–112.

Johnston, T. H. 1912d. A census of Australian reptilian Entozoa. Proc. Roy. Soc. Queensland *23*, 233–249.

Johnston, T. H. 1913a. Notes on some Entozoa. Proc. Roy. Soc. Queensland *24*, 63–91.

Johnston, T. H. 1913b. Cestoda and Acanthocephala. Rep. Australian Inst. Trop. Med., 1911. Pp. 75–96.

Johnston, T. H. 1914a. Second report on Cestoda and Acanthocephala in Queensland. Ann. Trop. Med. Parasitol. *8*, 105–112.

Johnston, T. H. 1914b. Some new Queensland endoparasites. Proc. Roy. Soc. Queensland *26*, 76–84.

Johnston, T. H. 1914c. Australian trematodes and cestodes; a study in zoogeography. Med. J. Australia *1*, 243–244.

Johnston, T. H. 1916a. Helminthological notes. Memoirs Queensland Museum *5*, 186–196.

Johnston, T. H. 1916b. A census of the endoparasites recorded as occurring in Queensland, arranged under their hosts. Proc. Roy. Soc. Queensland *28*, 31–79.

Johnston, T. H. 1916c. Endoparasites of the dingo, *Canis dingo* Blumb. Proc. Roy. Soc. Queensland *28*, 96–100.

Johnston, T. H. 1918a. Notes on certain Entozoa of rats and mice, with a catalogue of the internal parasites recorded as occurring in rodents in Australia. Proc. Roy. Soc. Queensland *30*, 53–78.

Johnston, T. H. 1918b. The endoparasites of the domestic pigeon in Queensland. Memoirs Queensland Museum *6*, 168–174.

Johnston, T. H. 1924. An Australian caryophyllaeid cestode. Proc. Linnean Soc. New South Wales *49*, 339–347.

Johnston, T. H. 1931. An amphilinid from an Australian tortoise. Australian J. Exp. Biol. and Med. Sci. *8*, 1–7.

Johnston, T. H. 1934. Remarks on some Australian Cestodaria. Proc. Linnean Soc. New South Wales *59*, 66–70.

Johnston, T. H. 1935. Remarks on the cestode genus *Porotaenia*. Trans. and Proc. Roy. Soc. South Australia *59*, 164–167.

Johnston, T. H. 1937. Entozoa from the Australian hair seal. Proc. Linnean Soc. New South Wales *62*, 9–16.

Johnstone, J. 1905–1912. Internal parasites and diseased conditions of fishes. From Herdman's Reports on the Lancashire sea fisheries – Scientific investigations . . . Trans. Biol. Soc. Liverpool, Vols. *19–26*.

Johnstone, J. 1912. *Tetrarhynchus erinaceus* Van Beneden. I. Structure of larva and adult worm. Parasitology *4*, 364–415.

Johnstone, J., A. Scott, and W. C. Smith. 1924. The parasites and diseases of the cod. Fishery Investigations of Great Britain *6* (No. 7), 15–27.

Johri, L. N. 1933. On the genus *Houttuynia* Fuhrmann, 1920 (Cestoda), with a description of some species of *Raillietina* from the pigeon. Zool. Anz. *103*, 89–92.

Johri, L. N. 1934. Report on a collection of cestodes from Lucknow. Records Indian Museum *36*, 153–177.

Johri, L. N. 1935. On cestodes from Burma. Parasitology *27*, 476–479.

Johri, L. N. 1939. On two new species of *Diorchis* (Cestoda) from the Indian Columbiformes. Records Indian Museum *41*, 121–129.

Johri, L. N. 1941. On two new species of the family Hymenolepididae Fuhrmann, 1907 (Cestoda) from a Burmese cormorant, *Phalacrocorax javanicus* (Horsfield, 1821). Philippine J. Sci. *74*, 83–89.

Jones, A. W. 1943. *Protogynella blarina* n. g. n. sp., a new cestode from the shrew, *Blarina brevicauda* Say. Trans. Am. Microscop. Soc. *62*, 174–178.

Jones, A. W. 1944a. *Diorchis reynoldsi* n. sp., a hymenolepidid cestode from the shrew. Trans. Am. Microscop. Soc. *63*, 46–49.

Jones, A. W. 1944b. *Diorchis ralli* n. sp., a hymenolepidid cestode from the king rail. Trans. Am. Microscop. Soc. *63*, 50–53.

Jones, A. W. 1945. Studies in cestode cytology. J. Parasitol. *31*, 213–235.

Jones, A. W. 1946. The scolex of *Rhabdometra similis*. Trans. Am. Microscop. Soc. *65*, 357–359.

Jones, A. W. 1948. Speciation in the Cestoda. J. Parasitol. *34* Suppl., 16–17.

Jones, A. W., and H. L. Ward. 1945. The application of cytological techniques to cestodes and other helminth material. J. Parasitol. *31* Suppl., 16.

Jones, M. F. 1929a. *Schistotaenia macrorhyncha* Rud. J. Parasitol. *15*, 1–18.

Jones, M. F. 1929b. Tapeworms of the genera *Rhabdometra* and *Paruterina* found in the quail and yellow-billed cuckoo. Proc. U. S. Nat. Museum *75*, 1–8.

Jones, M. F. 1929c. *Aphodius granarius* (Coleoptera), an intermediate host for *Hymenolepis carioca* (Cestoda). J. Agr. Research *38*, 629–632.

Jones, M. F. 1930a, 1930b, 1930c, 1930d. Notes without title on the life-cycle of *Raillietina cesticillus*. Proc. Helm. Soc. Washington, J. Parasitol. *16*, 158; *16*, 158–159; *16*, 164; *17*, 57.

Jones, M. F. 1931a. On the loss of an experimentally produced infestation of tapeworms in a chicken. Proc. Helm. Soc. Washington, J. Parasitol. *17*, 234.

Jones, M. F. 1931b. On the life histories of species of *Raillietina*. Proc. Helm. Soc. Washington, J. Parasitol. *17*, 234.

Jones, M. F. 1932. Additional notes on intermediate hosts of poultry tapeworms. Proc. Helm. Soc. Washington, J. Parasitol. *18*, 307.

Jones, M. F. 1933a. On the systematic position of *Davainea fuhrmanni* Williams, 1931. Proc. Helm. Soc. Washington, J. Parasitol. *19*, 255.

Jones, M. F. 1933b. Notes on cestodes of poultry. Proc. Helm. Soc. Washington, J. Parasitol. *20*, 66.

Jones, M. F. 1934. Cysticercoids of the crow cestode, *Hymenolepis variabilis* (Mayhew, 1925) Fuhrmann, 1932 (Hymenolepididae). Proc. Helm. Soc. Washington *1*, 62–63.

Jones, M. F. 1935. The cestode, *Hymenolepis microps* (Hymenolepididae) in ruffed grouse (*Bonasa umbellias*). Proc. Helm. Soc. Washington *2*, 93.

Jones, M. F. 1936a. *Metroliasthes lucida*, a cestode of galliform birds, in arthropod and avian hosts. Proc. Helm. Soc. Washington *3*, 26–30.

Jones, M. F. 1936b. A new species of cestode, *Davainea meleagridis* (Davaineidae) from the turkey, with a key to the species of *Davainea* from galliform birds. Proc. Helm. Soc. Washington *3*, 49–52.

Jones, M. F., and J. E. Alicata. 1935. Development and morphology of the cestode, *Hymenolepis cantaniana,* in coleopteran and avian hosts. J. Washington Acad. Sci. *25,* 237–247.

Jones, M. F., and M. W. Horsfall. 1935. Ants as intermediate hosts for the two species of *Raillietina* parasitic in chickens. Proc. Helm. Soc. Washington, J. Parasitol. *21,* 442–443.

Jones, M. F., and M. W. Horsfall. 1936. The life-history of a poultry cestode. Science *83,* 303–304.

Joyeux, C. 1916. Sur le cycle évolutif de quelques cestodes. Note préliminaire. Bull. soc. path. exot. *9,* 578–583.

Joyeux, C. 1919. *Hymenolepis nana* (v. Siebold, 1852) et *Hymenolepis nana* var. *fraterna* Stiles, 1902. Bull. soc. path. exot. *12,* 228–231.

Joyeux, C. 1920. Cycle évolutif de quelques cestodes. Recherches expérimentales. Bull. biol. France Belg. Suppl. 2, pp. 1–219.

Joyeux, C. 1921. Développement direct d'un *Hymenolepis* (Teniades) dans les villosités intestinales du hérisson. Bull. soc. path. exot. *14,* 386–390.

Joyeux, C. 1922. Recherches sur les ténias des Anseriformes. Développement larvaire d' *Hymenolepis parvula* chez *Herpobdella octoculata* (L.). Bull. soc. path. exot. *15,* 45–51.

Joyeux, C. 1923a. Recherches sur la faune helminthologique africaine. Arch. inst. Pasteur Tunis *12,* 119–167.

Joyeux, C. 1923b. Présence de *Dinobothrium plicitum* Linton, 1922 chez *Cetorhinus maximus* (L.). Ann. parasitol. humaine et comparée *1.*

Joyeux, C. 1924a. List de quelques helminthes recoltés dans les colonies portugaise d'Afrique. Ann. parasitol. humaine et comparée *2,* 232–235.

Joyeux, C. 1924b. Cestodes des poules d'Indochine. Ann. parasitol. humaine et comparée *2,* 314–318.

Joyeux, C. 1924c. Recherches sur le cycle évolutif des *Cylindrotaenia.* Ann. parasitol. humaine et comparée *2.*

Joyeux, C. 1925. Parasites des poules dans la province de Schinchiku (Formose). Ann. parasitol. humaine et comparée *3,* 103.

Joyeux, C. 1926. Sur quelques cysticercoïdes de *Gammarus pulex.* Arch. Schiffs. u. Tropenhyg. *30,* 433–451.

Joyeux, C. 1927a. Recherches sur le cycle évolutif d'*Hymenolepis erinacei* (Gmelin, 1789). Arch. Parasitol. *5,* 20–26.

Joyeux, C. 1927b. Recherches sur le fauna helminthologique algèrienne (cestodes et trématodes). Arch. inst. Pasteur Algèrie *5,* 509–528.

Joyeux, C. 1927c. *Diphyllobothrium mansoni* (Cobbold, 1883) (Note préliminaire). Bull. soc. path. exot. *20,* 226–228.

Joyeux, C. 1927d. Les ténias extra-intestinaux. Bull. inst. clinica quirurgica, Nos. 21–25.

Joyeux, C. 1928. La classification des cestodes d'après quelques travaux récents. Ann. parasitol. humaine et comparée *6,* 132–136.

Joyeux, C. 1929. Procédé pour rechercher les cysticercoïdes des petits crustacés. Ann. parasitol. humaine et comparée *7,* 112–115.

Joyeux, C. 1930. Sur quelques helminthes recoltés dans la region de Villers-sur-Mer. Bull. soc. Linn. Normandie (Trav. orig.) *3,* 8–12.

Joyeux, C. 1931. A propos d'une nouvelle classification du genre *Davainea* R. Bl. s. lat. Bull. soc. zool. France *55,* 44–57.

Joyeux, C. 1932a. Note rectificative au sujet des crochets du rostre chez *Raillietina* (*R.*) *insignis* (Steudner, 1877). Bull. soc. zool. France *57,* 397.

Joyeux, C. 1932b. Les donnés parasitologiques concernant le kyste hydatique du poumon. Arch. méd. gén. et coloniale *1,* 277–283.

Joyeux, C., and J. G. Baer. 1927a. Etude de quelques cestodes provenant des colonies françaises d'Afrique et de Madagascar. Ann. parasitol. humaine et comparée *5,* 27–36.

Joyeux, C., and J. G. Baer. 1927b. Recherches sur quelques espèces du genre *Bothridium* de Blainville, 1824 (Diphyllobothriidae). Ann. parasitol. humaine et comparée *5,* 127–139.

Joyeux, C., and J. G. Baer. 1927c. Sur quelques larves de Bothriocephales. Bull. soc. path. exot. *20*, 921–937.

Joyeux, C., and J. G. Baer. 1928a. Sur quelques cestodes de la région d'Entebbe (Ugande). Ann. parasitol. humaine et comparée *6*, 179–181.

Joyeux, C., and J. G. Baer. 1928b. Note sur quelques helminthes recoltés en Macedoine. Bull. soc. path. exot. *21*, 214–220.

Joyeux, C., and J. G. Baer. 1928c. Recherches sur le cycle évolutif d'*Hymenolepis fraterna*. Compt. rend. soc. biol. *99*, 1317–1318.

Joyeux, C., and J. G. Baer. 1928d. Rectification de nomenclature. Ann. parasitol. humaine et comparée *6*, 144.

Joyeux, C., and J. G. Baer. 1928e. Note d'helminthologie tunisienne. Arch. inst. Pasteur Tunis *17*, 347–349.

Joyeux, C., and J. G. Baer. 1929a. Les cestodes rares de l'homme. Bull. soc. path. exot. *22*, 114–156.

Joyeux, C., and J. G. Baer. 1929b. *Raillietina* (*R.*) *celebensis* Janicki, 1902 et *Raillietina* (*R.*) *baeri* Meggitt & Subramanian, 1927. Bull. soc. path. exot. *22*, 675–677.

Joyeux, C., and J. G. Baer. 1929c. Recherches expérimentales sur le larve plerocercoïde de *Diphyllobothrium ranarum* (Gastaldi, 1854). Compt. rend. soc. biol. *101*.

Joyeux, C., and J. G. Baer. 1929d. Etudes sur le ré-encapsulement de *Sparganum ranarum* (Gastaldi, 1854). Compt. rend. soc. biol. *101*.

Joyeux, C., and J. G. Baer. 1930a. Cestodes. In Mission Saharienne Augieras-Draper, 1927–1928. Bull. muséum nat. hist. nat. (Paris) 2me Ser., II, pp. 217–225.

Joyeux, C., and J. G. Baer. 1930b. On a collection of cestodes from Nigeria. J. Helm. *8*, 59–64.

Joyeux, C., and J. G. Baer. 1931. Evolution des plerocercoïds de *Diphyllobothrium* (Cestodes, Pseudophyllidiens). Compt. rend. soc. biol. *103*.

Joyeux, C., and J. G. Baer. 1932. Recherches sur les cestodes appartenant au genre *Mesocestoides* Vaillant. Bull. soc. path. exot. *25*, 993–1010.

Joyeux, C., and J. G. Baer. 1933a. Sur le cycle évolutif d'un Ténia de serpent. Compt. rend. *196*, 1838–1839.

Joyeux, C., and J. G. Baer. 1933b. Le ré-encapsulement de quelques larves de cestodes. Compt. rend. *197*, 493–495.

Joyeux, C., and J. G. Baer. 1934a. Sur quelques cestodes de France. Arch. muséum nat. hist. nat. Paris *11*, 157–171.

Joyeux, C., and J. G. Baer. 1934b. Les hôtes d'attente dans le cycle évolutif des helminthes. Biologie médicale, Paris, *24*, 482–506.

Joyeux, C., and J. G. Baer. 1935a. Cestodes d'Indochine. Rev. suisse zool. *42*, 249–273.

Joyeux, C., and J. G. Baer. 1935b. Un Ténia hyperapolytique chez un mammifère. Compt. rend. soc. biol. *120*, 334–336.

Joyeux, C., and J. G. Baer. 1935c. Recherches sur le cycle évolutif d'*Hymenolepis pistillum* Dujardin. Compt. rend. *201*, 742–743.

Joyeux, C., and J. G. Baer. 1935d. Notices helminthologiques. Bull. soc. zool. France *60*, 482–501.

Joyeux, C., and J. G. Baer. 1936a. Recherches biologiques sur la ligule intestinal: ré-infestation parasitaire. Compt. rend. soc. biol. *121*, 67–68.

Joyeux, C., and J. G. Baer. 1936b. Quelques helminthes nouvelles et peu connus de la musaraigne, *Crocidura rassula* Herm. Rev. suisse zool. *43*, 25–50.

Joyeux, C., and J. G. Baer. 1936c. Helminthes des rats de Madagascar. Contribution à l'étude de *Davainea madagascariensis* (Davaine, 1869). Bull. soc. path. exot. *29*, 611–619.

Joyeux, C., and J. G. Baer. 1936d. Cestodes. Faune de France *30*, 1–613. Paris.

Joyeux, C., and J. G. Baer. 1937a. Recherches sur l'évolution des cestodes de gallinacés. Compt. rend. *205*, 751–753.

Joyeux, C., and J. G. Baer. 1937b. Evolution du *Taenia taeniaeformis* Batsch. Compt. rend. soc. biol. *126*, 359–361.

Joyeux, C., and J. G. Baer. 1937c. Sur quelques cestodes de Cochinchine. Bull. soc. path. exot. *30*, 872–874.

Joyeux, C., and J. G. Baer. 1937d. Remarques morphologiques et biologiques sur quelques cestodes de la famille des Taeniidae Ludwig. Papers on helminthology published in commemoration of the 30-year jubileum of K. J. Skrjabin and of 15th anniversary of the All-Union Institute of Helminthology. Pp. 269–274. Moscow.

Joyeux, C., and J. G. Baer. 1938a. Sur le développement des Pseudophyllidea (Cestodes). Compt. rend. soc. biol. *127*, 1265–1266.

Joyeux, C., and J. G. Baer. 1938b. L'évolution des plerocercoïdes de la Ligule intestinale. Compt. rend. soc. biol. *129*, 314–316.

Joyeux, C., and J. G. Baer. 1938c. Recherches sur le début du développement des cestodes chez leur hôte définitif. Pp. 245–249 of Livro Jubilar do Professor Lauro Travassos. 1938. xx + 589 pp. Rio de Janeiro.

Joyeux, C., and J. G. Baer. 1938d. Sur quelques cestodes de Galliformes. Travaux de station zoologique, Wimereux, *13*, 369–389.

Joyeux, C., and J. G. Baer. 1939a. Sur quelques cestodes de Madagascar. Bull. soc. path. exot. *32*, 39–43.

Joyeux, C., and J. G. Baer. 1939b. Sur quelques cestodes de Charadriiformes. Bull. soc. zool. France *64*, 171–187.

Joyeux, C., and J. G. Baer. 1939c. Recherches biologiques sur quelques cestodes Pseudophyllidea. Volumen Jubilare pro Professore Sadao Yoshida. 1939. 2 vols. Vol. 2, pp. 203–210. Osaka.

Joyeux, C., and J. G. Baer. 1940a. Anatomica y posicion sistemica de *Raillietina* (*R.*) *quitensis* Leon, 1935, cestode parasito del hombre. Rev. med. trop. y parasitol. bact. clin. y lab. Havana *6*, 79–88.

Joyeux, C., and J. G. Baer. 1940b. Un cestode nouveau parasite du plongeon. Bull. soc. sci. nat. Neuchâtel *65*, 21–24.

Joyeux, C., and J. G. Baer. 1940c. Sur quelques cestodes. Rev. suisse zool. *47*, 381–388.

Joyeux, C., and J. G. Baer. 1945. Morphologie, évolution et position systèmatique de *Catenotaenia pusilla* (Goeze, 1782), parasite de rongeurs. Rev. suisse zool. *52*, 13–51.

Joyeux, C., and J. G. Baer. 1949a. L'hôte normal de *Raillietina* (*R.*) *demarensis* (Daniels 1895) en Guyane hollandaise. Acta Tropica *6*, 141–144.

Joyeux, C., and J. G. Baer. 1949b. A propos des Ténias du genre *Inermicapsifer* récemment découverts chez l'homme. Bull. soc. path. exot. *42*, 581–586.

Joyeux, C., and J. G. Baer. 1950a. The status of the cestode genus *Meggittiella* Lopez-Neyra, 1942. Proc. Helm. Soc. Washington *17*, 91–95.

Joyeux, C., and J. G. Baer. 1950b. Sur quelques espèces nouvelles ou peu connues du genre *Hymenolepis* Weinland, 1858. Bull. soc. Neuchâtel sci. nat. *73*, 51–70.

Joyeux, C., and J. G. Baer. 1950c. Le genre *Gyrocotyloides* Fuhrmann, 1931 (Cestodaria). Bull. soc. Neuchâtel sci. nat. *73*, 71–79.

Joyeux, C., J. G. Baer, and J. Gaud. 1950. Recherches sur des cestodes d'Indochine et sur quelques *Diphyllobothrium* (*Bothriocephales*). Bull. soc. path. exot. *43*, 482–489.

Joyeux, C., J. G. Baer, and R. Martin. 1933a. Recherches sur les sparganoses. Bull. soc. path. exot. *26*, 1199–1208.

Joyeux, C., J. G. Baer, and R. Martin. 1933b. Sur le cycle évolutif des *Mesocestoides*. Compt. rend. soc. biol. *114*, 1179–1180.

Joyeux, C., J. G. Baer, and R. Martin. 1936. Sur quelques cestodes de la Somalie-Nord. Bull. soc. path. exot. *29*, 82–96.

Joyeux, C., J. G. Baer, and R. Martin. 1937. Sur quelques cestodes de la Somalie-Nord (deuxième notice). Bull. soc. path. exot. *30*, 418–422.

Joyeux, C., and R. Ph. Dollfus. 1931. Sur quelques cestodes de la collection du Musée de Munich. Zool. Jahrb. Syst. *62*, 109–118.

Joyeux, C., R. Du Noyer, and J. G. Baer. 1931a. Etude sur le ré-encapsulement des *Sparganum*. Congrès International Microbiologie, Paris. 1930.

Joyeux, C., R. Du Noyer, and J. G. Baer. 1931b. Les Bothriocéphales. Bull. sci. pharmacol. *38*, 175–235.

Joyeux, C., and H. Foley. 1929. Recherches épidémiologiques sur l'*Hymenolepis nana* et sur *Hymenolepis fraterna*. Arch. inst. Pasteur Algérie *7*, 31–50.

Joyeux, C., and H. Foley. 1930. Les helminthes de *Meriones shawi* Rozet dans le nord de l'Algérie. Bull. soc. zool. France *55*, 353–374.

Joyeux, C., C. Gendre, and J. G. Baer. 1928. Recherches sur les helminthes de l'Afrique occidentale français. Coll. soc. path. exot. Monographie 2. 120 pp.

Joyeux, C., and E. Houdemer. 1927. Sur quelques larves de Bothriocéphales. Bull. soc. path. exot. *20*.

Joyeux, C., E. Houdemer, and J. G. Baer. 1932. Etiologie de la sparganose oculaire. Marseille méd. *69*, 405–409.

Joyeux, C., E. Houdemer, and J. G. Baer. 1934. Recherches sur la biologie des *Sparganum* et l'étiologie de la sparganose oculaire. Bull. soc. path. exot. *27*, 70–78.

Joyeux, C., and N. I. Kobozief. 1927. Recherches sur l'*Hymenolepis microstoma* (Dujardin, 1845). Compt. rend. soc. biol. *97*, 12–13.

Joyeux, C., and N. I. Kobozief. 1928. Recherches sur l'*Hymenolepis microstoma* (Dujardin, 1845). Ann. parasitol. humaine et comparée *6*, 59–79.

Joyeux, C., and P. Mathias. 1926. Cestodes et trématodes recoltés par le professeur Brumpt au cours de la mission du bourg de Bizas. Ann. parasitol. humaine et comparée *4*, 333–336.

Joyeux, C., and J. Millot. 1925. Sur un cysticercoide nouveau parasite de *Herpobdella atomaria* Carena, 1820. Travaux station zoologique Wimereux *9*, 98–101.

Joyeux, C., J. Richey, and Schulman. 1922. Description d'un cénure trouvé chez la souris blanche de laboratoire. Bull. soc. zool. France *47*.

Joyeux, C., and J. Timon-David. 1934a. Sur quelques cestodes d'oiseaux. Ann. muséum hist. nat. Marseille *26*, 1–26.

Joyeux, C., and J. Timon-David. 1934b. Note sur les cestodes d'oiseaux recoltés dans la région de Marseille. Ann. muséum hist. nat. Marseille *26*, 5–8.

Joyeux, C., and J. Timon-David. 1936. Cestodes d'oiseaux de la région marseillaise. Ann. faculté sci. Marseille *52*, 1–13.

Kahane, Z. 1880. Anatomie von *Taenia perfoliata* Goeze als Beitrag zur Kenntnis der Cestoden. Z. wiss. Zool. *34*, 175–254.

Kataoka, N., and K. Momma. 1933. A cestode parasitic in *Plecoglossus altivelis.* Annotationes Zoologicae Japonenses *14*, 13–22.

Kataoka, N., and K. Momma. 1934. A preliminary note on the life-history of *Proteocephalus neglectus*, with special reference to its intermediate host. Bull. Jap. soc. sci. fish. *3*, 125–126.

Kates, K. C., and C. E. Runkel. 1948. Observations on oribatid mite vectors of *Moniezia expansa* on pastures, with a report of several new vectors from the United States. Proc. Helm. Soc. Washington *15*, 19–33.

Kawanishi, K. 1932. Experimental studies on the morphological changes of the blood, and clinical symptoms, in infections with *Taenia solium* of man. Taiwan Igakki Zasshi *31*, 93–94.

Kay, M. W. 1942. A new species of *Phyllobothrium* van Beneden from *Raja binoculata* (Girard). Trans. Am. Microscop. Soc. *61*, 261–263.

Kellaway, C. H., and K. D. Fairley. 1932. The clinical significance of laboratory tests in the diagnosis of hydatid disease. Med. J. Australia, 19th Year, *1*, 340–342.

Kent, F. H. N. 1947a. Etudes biochimiques sur les protéines du *Moniezia* parasites intestinaux du mouton. Bull. soc. sci. nat. Neuchâtel *70*, 85–108.

Kent, F. H. N. 1947b. Sur l'existence de cénapses glygéno-protéiques dans un cestode (*Moniezia expansa*). Compt. rend. *225*, 602–604.

Kent, F. H. N. 1948. Etude biochimique sur le glycogène de *Taenia saginata.* Schweiz. Z. Path. Bakt. *11*, 329–335.

Kent, F. H. N., and M. Macheboeuf. 1947a. Recherches sur les protéines des cestodes. Schweiz. Z. Path. Bakt. *10*, 464–469.

Kent, F. H. N., and M. Macheboeuf. 1947b. Sur l'existence de cénapses protéin-acides biliaires dans les cestodes (*Moniezia expansa* et *Taenia saginata*). Compt. rend. *225*, 539–540.

Kent, F. H. N., and M. Macheboeuf. 1948. Existence de sels biliaires et de cérébrosides associés à des protéines chez *Moniezia expansa.* Experientia, Basel, *4*, 193–194.

Kerr, K. B. 1935. Immunity against a cestode parasite, *Cysticercus pisiformis*. Am. J. Hyg. *22*, 169–182.

Kerr, T. 1935. On *Linstowia echidnae* (Thompson, 1893) Zschokke, 1899: a cestode from the Australian ant eater. Ann. Mag. Nat. Hist. (Ser. 10) *15*, 156–160.

Kholodkovski. See Cholodkovsky.

Kessler, K. T. 1868. Beiträge zur zoologischen Kenntnis des Onegasees und dessen Umgebung. Beil. arb. Russ. naturf. Vers. St. Petersburg. 183 pp.

Kiessling, F. 1882. Ueber den Bau von *Schistocephalus dimorphus* Creplin und *Ligula simplicissima* Rudolphi. Arch. Naturg. *1*, 241–280.

Kingisepp, G. 1933. Zur Frage der experimentellen Anämien durch Parasitengifte. Arch. exp. Path. Pharmakol. *170*, 733–743.

Kingscote, A. A. 1931. The occurrence of tapeworms of the genus *Anoplocephala* in the horse. Report Ontario Vet. College, 1931, pp. 61–62.

Kintner, K. E. 1938. Notes on the cestodes of English sparrows in Indiana. Parasitology *30*, 347–357.

Kiribayashi, S. 1933. Studies on the growth of *Hymenolepis nana* with special reference to the possibility of differentiation of *H. nana* var. *fraterna* (Stiles). Taiwan Igakki Zashii *32*, 117–118.

Kirschenblatt, J. D. 1938. Die Gesetzmässigkeiten der Dynamik der Parasitenfauna bei den Mäuseähnlichen Nagetieren (Muriden) in Transkaukasien. Diss. Univ. Leningrad.

Klaptocz, B. 1906a. Ergebnisse der mit Subvention aus der Erbschaft Treitl unternommenen zoologischen Forschungsreise Dr. Franz Werner's in den aegyptischen Sudan und nach Nord-Uganda. Cestoden aus Fischen, aus *Varanus* und *Hyrax*. Stizber. Akad. Wiss. Wien Math. naturw. Klasse Abt. I. *115*, 1–24.

Klaptocz, B. 1906b. Ergebnisse . . . Cestoden aus *Numida philorhyncha* Licht. Sitzber. Akad. Wiss. . . . *115*, 963–974.

Klaptocz, B. 1906c. *Polyonchobothrium polypteri* (Leydig). Centralbl. Bakt. Parasitenk. *41*.

Klaptocz, B. 1906d. Neue Phyllobothriden aus *Notidanus (Hexanchus) griseus* n. g. Arb. zool. inst. Wien *16*, 325–360.

Klaptocz, B. 1908. Ergebnisse . . . Vogelcestoden. Arb. zool. inst. Wien *17*, 40 pp.

Klopina, A. 1919. Two new species of the genus *Caryophyllaeus* parasitic in Cyprinidae (in Russian). Bull. acad. sci. Petrograd, 1919, pp. 97–110.

Knoch, J. 1862. Die Naturgeschichte des Breiten Bandwurms, mit besonderer Berücksichtigung seiner Entwickelungsgeschichte. Mem. acad. imp. sci. St. Petersbourg *5*, 1–134.

Knoch, J. 1866. Die Entwicklungsgeschichte des *Bothriocephalus proboscideus* (*B. salmonis* Koellikers) als Beitrag zur Embryologie des *Bothriocephalus latus*. Bull. acad. imp. sci. St. Petersbourg *9*, 290–314.

Knoch, J. 1870. Neue Beiträge zur Embryologie des *Bothriocephalus latus*, als Beweis einer directen Metamorphose des geschlechtsrufen Individuum aus seinem bewimperten Embryo, Zugleich ein Beitrag zur Therapie der Helminthiases. Bull. acad. imp. sci. St. Petersbourg *14*, 176–188.

Kobayashi, H. 1931. Studies on the development of *Diphyllobothrium mansoni* Cobbold, 1882 (Joyeux, 1927). IV. Hatching of the egg onchosphaera and discarding of the ciliated coat. V. The first intermediate host (in Japanese). Taiwan Igakki Zasshi *30*, 15–16, 24–27.

Kobozieff, N. 1933. Les helminthes et le cancer chez les souris. Contribution expérimentale à l'étude du rôle des helminthes dans la pathogénie des cancers: cestodes et cancers chez la souris. Bull. assoc. française pour l'étude du cancer *22*, 152–171.

Koelliker, R. A. von. 1843. Beiträge zur Entwicklungsgeschichte wirbelloser Thiere. Arch. Anat. Physiol. Med., pp. 68–141.

Kofend, L. 1917. Cestoden aus Säugetiere und aus *Agama colonorum*. Vorläufige Mitteilung. Anz. Akad. Wiss. Wien Math. naturw. Klasse Abt. I. *54*, 229–231.

Kofend, L. 1921. Cestoden aus Säugetiere und aus *Agama colonorum*. Wissenschaftliche Ergebnisse der mit Unterstützung der Akademie der Wissenschaft in Wien aus der Erbschaft Treitl von F. Werner unternommenen zoologischen Expedition nach dem Anglo-Aegyptischen Sudan (Kordofan) 1914. Denkschr. Akad. Wiss. Wien Math. naturw. Klasse Abt. I. *98*, 1–10.

Kofoid, C. A., and E. E. Watson. 1910. On the orientation of *Gyrocotyle* and of the cestode strobila. Advance print from Proc. 7th Internat. Zool. Congress, Boston, 1907. 5 pp. Aug. 1910.

Köhler, E. 1894. Der Klappenapparat in den Excretionsgefässen der Tänien. Z. wiss. Zool. *57*, 385–401.

Kolenati, F. A. 1856. Die Parasiten der Chiropteren. 51 pp. Brunn.

Kolenati, F. A. 1857. Die Parasiten der Chiropteren. 51 pp. Dresden.

Koropov, V. 1935. Etude éxpérimentale de l'influence exercée par les produits des helminthes sur le système cardiovasculaire (in Russian, French summary). Med. Parasitol. and Paras. Diseases *4*, 288–298.

Kostylev, N. 1915. La *Taenia crenata* Goeze comme une espèce indépendante. Ann. musée zool. acad. sci. imp. St. Petersbourg *20*, 127–129.

Kotlan, A. 1921. Új-Guinea Madár-Cestodák. I. Papagály-Cestodák. (Bird cestodes from New Guinea. I. Parrot cestodes.) Ann. hist. nat. musée nat. Hungarici *18*, 1–20.

Kotlan, A. 1923a. Ueber *Sparganum raillieti* Ratz und den zugehörigen Geschlechtsreifen Bandwurm, *Dibothriocephalus raillieti* Ratz. Centralbl. Bakt. Parasitenk. *90*.

Kotlan, A. 1923b. Avian cestodes from New Guinea. II. Cestodes from Casuariformes. Ann. Trop. Med. Parasitol. *17*, 45–57.

Kotlan, A. 1923c. Avian cestodes from New Guinea. III. Cestodes from Galliformes. Ann. Trop. Med. Parasitol. *17*, 59–69.

Kotlan, A. 1925. On *Davainea proglottina* and its synonyms. J. Parasitol. *12*, 26–32.

Kouri, P. 1944. Tercer informe en relacion al *Inermicapsifer cubensis* (Kouri, 1938). Rev. med. trop. paras. bact. clin. y lab. *10*, 107–112.

Kouri, P., and J. M. Doval. 1938a. Le raillietinosis humaine en Cuba. Bol. mens. clin. asoc. Damas la Covadonga *5*, 121–134.

Kouri, P., and J. M. Doval. 1938b. Tres casos di parasitismo humano por especies de la familia Davaineidae. Rev. med. trop. y parasitol. Havana *4*, 207–217.

Kouri, P., and I. Rappaport. 1940. A new human helminthic infection in Cuba. J. Parasitol. *26*, 179–181.

Kowalewski, M. 1889. Ein Beitrag zur Kenntnis der Excretionsorgane. Biol. Centralbl. *9*, 33–47.

Kowalewski, M. 1894. Helminthological studies. I. (In Polish with French resumé.) Bull. intern. acad. sci. Cracovie, pp. 278–280.

Kowalewski, M. 1898. Sur la tête du *Tenia malleus* Goeze. Arch. parasitol. humaine et comparée *1*, 326–329.

Kowalewski, M. 1904. Helminthological studies. VIII. On a new tapeworm, *Tatria biremis* gen. nov. et sp. nov. (in Polish with English summary). Bull. intern. acad. sci. Cracovie, pp. 367–369.

Kowalewski, M. 1905. Helminthological studies. IX. On two new species of tapeworms of the genus *Hymenolepis* (in Polish with English summary). Bull. intern. acad. sci. Cracovie, pp. 532–534.

Kowalewski, M. 1906. Mitteilungen ueber eine *Idiogenes-species*. Zool. Anz. *29*, 683–686.

Kowalewski, M. 1907. Helminthological studies. X. Contribution à l'étude de deux cestodes d'oiseaux (in Polish with French resumé). Bull. intern. acad. sci. Cracovie, pp. 774–776.

Krabbe, H. 1865. Helminthologiske undersogelser i Danmark og paa Island, med saerligt Hensyn til Blaerormlidelserne paa Island. Kgl. Danske Videnska. Selskab, Skrifter, Naturvidenskab. math. Afdel. *7*, 347–408.

Krabbe, H. 1866. Om nogle Baendelormammers udviklung til Baendelorme. Vidensk. Medd. naturh. Foren Kjobenhavn, pp. 1–10.

Krabbe, H. 1867. Trappens Baendelorme. Vidensk. Medd. naturh. Foren Kjobenhavn, pp. 122–126; and (translation) Ann. Mag. Nat. Hist. (1869) *4*, 47–51.

Krabbe, H. 1869. Bidrag til Kundskab om Fugl enes Baendelorme. Kgl. Danske Videnska. Selskab, Skrifter, Naturvidenskab. math. Afdel. *8*, 249–363.

Krabbe, H. 1879. (Cestodes collected in Turkestan by A. A. Fedchenko.) (Fedchenko's travels in Turkestan. 3. Vermes. Pt. 1.) Izvest. imp. obsh. liub. esterstoozn . . . Moscow *34*, 1–23.

Krabbe, H. 1882. Nye Bidrag til Kundskab om Fuglenes Baendelorme. Kgl. Danske Videnska. Selskab, Skrifter, Naturvidenskab. math. Afdel. *1*, 349–366.

Kraemer, H. 1892. Beiträge zur Anatomie und Histologie der Cestoden der Süsswasserfische. Z. wiss. Zool. *53*, 647–722.

Krause, K. 1927. Contribution à l'étude du *Diphyllobothrium latum* (L.) en Palestine. Description d'anomalies chez ce cestode. Ann. parasitol. humaine et comparée 5.

Krefft, G. 1871. On Australian Entozoa. Trans. Entom. Soc. New South Wales 2, 206–232.

Kreis, H. A. 1937. Würmer als Parasiten. Ciba Z. jahrg. 5, Nummer 51, pp. 1746–1773. Basel.

Kreis, H. A. 1944a. Parasitismus und seine Beziehungen zum Menschen. "Ars Medici," Organ des praktischen Arztes. Nr. 10, Jahrg. 34, pp. 545–553.

Kreis, H. A. 1944b. Die Rolle der parasitischen Würmer in den Tropen. Acta Tropica *1*, 231–262.

Kreis, H. A. 1947. Helminthologische Probleme bei unseren Haustieren. Schweizer Arch. Tierheilk. *89*, 421–437.

Krull, W. H. 1939. On the life-history of *Moniezia expansa* and *Cittotaenia* sp. (Cestoda, Anoplocephalidae). Proc. Helm. Soc. Washington *6*, 10–11.

Krull, W. H. 1940. Investigations on possible intermediate hosts, other than oribatid mites, for *Moniezia expansa.* Proc. Helm. Soc. Washington 7, 68–70.

Küchenmeister, G. F. H. 1852. Ueber die Umwandlung der Finnen in Bandwürmer. Vierteljahr. Schriften. Prakt. Heilk. 9 Jahrg. Prag *33*, 106–158.

Küchenmeister, G. F. H. 1853. Experimente ueber die Entstehung der Cestoden zweiter Stufe zunachst des *Coenurus cerebralis* . . . Z. klin. Med. Breslau *4*, 448–451.

Küchenmeister, G. F. H. 1855a. Ueber eine Abart der *Taenia coenurus* d. h. des Bandwurms von der die Quese des Shafes und des Rindes herstemmen . . . Allgemeine deutsche Naturhistorie Zeitung, Vol. I. Hamburg.

Küchenmeister, G. F. H. 1855b. Die in und an dem Körper lebenden menschen vorkommenden Parasiten. Leipzig. English translation by E. Ray Lankester.

Küchenmeister, G. F. H. 1856. Ueber die Umwandlung der Blasenwürmer in Taenien insbesondere des *Coernurus cerebralis* Gervais. Wien med. Wochschr. *6*, 319–320.

Küchenmeister, G. F. H., and F. A. Zürn. 1881. Die Parasiten des Menschen. x + iv + 582 pp. Leipzig.

Kuczkowski, St. 1925. Die Entwicklung im Genus *Ichthyotaenia* Lönnberg. Ein Beitrag zur Cercomertheorie auf Grund experimenteller Untersuchungen. Bull. intern. acad. polon. sci. Classe sci. math. B., Année 1925, pp. 423–446.

Kuitunen, Kuitunen-Ekbaum. See Ekbaum.

Kulmatycki, W. J. 1924. *Caryophyllaeus niloticus* sp. n. Results Swedish Zool. Exped. Egypt. White Nile, 1901, ed. by Jägerskiöld, Uppsala, No. 27a. Pp. 1–19.

Kunsemüller, F. 1903. Zur Kenntnis der polycephalen Blasenwürmer, insbesondere des *Coenurus cerebralis* Rudolphi und des *C. serialis* Gervais. Zool. Jahrb. *18*, 507–538.

Kuntz, R. E. 1943. Cysticercus of *Taenia taeniaeformis* with two strobilae. J. Parasitol. *29*, 424–425.

Kurimoto, T. 1899. Ueber eine neue Art *Bothriocephalus.* Verhandl. 17 Congr. inn. Med., Wiesbaden. Pp. 452–456.

Kurimoto, T. 1900. *Diplogonoporus grandis* (R. Blanchard). Beschreibung einer zum ersten Male im menschlichen Darm gefundenen Art *Bothriocephalus.* Z. klin. Med. *40*, 1–16.

Laczko, K. 1880. Beiträge zur Kenntnis der Histologie der Tetrarhynchen hauptsächlich des Nervensystems. Zool. Anz. *3*, 433–439.

Lamarck, J. B. P. A. de Monet. 1816. Histoire naturelle des animaux sans vertébrés. Paris.

Lamont, M. E. 1921. Two new parasitic flatworms. Occ. Papers Museum Zool. Univ. Michigan, No. 93. 4 pp.

Landois, H. 1877. Ueber den Baren-Grubenkopf, *Bothriocephalus ursi* n. sp. Jahrbuch westfalischer Province. Verhandl. Wiss. Kunst. Munster *18*, 281–290.

Lang, A. 1881. Untersuchungen zur vergleichenden Anatomie und Histologie des Nervensystems der Plathelminthen. 3. Das Nervensystem der Cestoden im Allgemeinem und dasjenige der Tetrarhynchen im Besonderen. Mittlzool. sta. Neapel *2*, 372–400.

Lang, R. 1929. Vergleichende Untersuchungen an Hühnercestoden der Gattung *Raillietina*. Z. Parasitenk. *1*, 562–611.

Larrousse, F. 1929. Hôtes intermédiaires nouveaux d'un cestode de la souris, *Hymenolepis microstoma* (Dujardin, 1845). Compt. rend. soc. biol. *100*.

Larrousse, F. 1932a. Parasites vermineux, cristaux fuchsinophiles acido-resistants et réactions hyperplastiques. Compt. rend. soc. biol. *109*, 666–668.

Larrousse, F. 1932b. Remarques au sujet du sarcome à cysticerques dans le foie du rat. Ann. parasitol. humaine et comparée *10*, 330–333.

Larsh, J. E., Jr. 1941. *Corallobothrium parvum* n. sp., a cestode from the common bullhead, *Ameiurus nebulosus*. J. Parasitol. *27*, 221–227.

Larsh, J. E., Jr. 1942. Transmission from mother to offspring of immunity against the mouse cestode, *Hymenolepis nana* var. *fraterna*. Am. J. Hyg. *36*, 187–194.

Larsh, J. E., Jr. 1943a. The relationship between the intestinal size of young mice and their susceptibility to infection with the cestode *Hymenolepis nana* var. *fraterna*. J. Parasitol. *29*, 61–64.

Larsh, J. E., Jr. 1943b. Serological studies on the mouse strain of the dwarf tapeworm, *Hymenolepis nana* var. *fraterna*. Am. J. Hyg. *37*, 289–293.

Larsh, J. E., Jr. 1943c. Increased infectivity of dwarf tapeworm (*Hymenolepis nana* var. *fraterna*) eggs following storage in host feces. J. Parasitol. *29*, 417–418.

Larsh, J. E., Jr. 1943d. Comparing the percentage development of the dwarf tapeworm, *Hymenolepis nana* var. *fraterna*, obtained from mice of two different localities. J. Parasitol. *29*, 423–424.

Larsh, J. E., Jr. 1944a. Comparative studies on a mouse strain of *Hymenolepis nana* var. *fraterna*, in different species and varieties of mice. J. Parasitol. *30*, 21–25.

Larsh, J. E., Jr. 1944b. Studies on the artificial immunization of mice against infection with the dwarf tapeworm, *Hymenolepis nana* var. *fraterna*. Am. J. Hyg. *39*, 129–132.

Larsh, J. E., Jr. 1944c. The relation between splenectomy and the resistance of old mice to infection with *Hymenolepis nana* var. *fraterna*. Am. J. Hyg. *39*, 133–137.

Larsh, J. E., Jr. 1944d. Alcoholism in mice and its effect on natural and acquired resistance to *Hymenolepis nana* var. *fraterna*. J. Parasitol. *30* Suppl., 14.

Larsh, J. E., Jr. 1945a. Immunity relations in human cestode infections. J. Elisha Mitchell Scientific Society *61*, 201–210.

Larsh, J. E., Jr. 1945b. Effect of alcohol on natural resistance to dwarf tapeworm in mice. J. Parasitol. *31*, 291–300.

Larsh, J. E., Jr. 1945c. The relationship in mice of intestinal emptying time and natural resistance to *Hymenolepis*. J. Parasitol. *31* Suppl., 19.

Larsh, J. E., Jr. 1946a. A comparison of the percentage development of a mouse strain of *Hymenolepis* in alcoholic and non-alcoholic rats and mice. J. Parasitol. *32*, 61–63.

Larsh, J. E., Jr. 1946b. The effect of alcohol on the development of acquired immunity to *Hymenolepis* in mice. J. Parasitol. *32*, 72–78.

Larsh, J. E., Jr. 1946c. A comparative study of *Hymenolepis* in white mice and golden hamsters. J. Parasitol. *32*, 477–479.

Larsh, J. E., Jr. 1946d. The relationship in alcoholic mice of reduced food intake and decreased resistance to *Hymenolepis*. J. Parasitol. *32* Suppl., 10.

Larsh, J. E., Jr. 1946e. The use of vitamins in mice to prevent alcoholic debilitation to *Hymenolepis*. J. Parasitol. *32* Suppl., 10–11.

Larsh, J. E., Jr. 1947a. The relationship in mice of intestinal emptying time and natural resistance to *Hymenolepis*. J. Parasitol. *33*, 79–84.

Larsh, J. E., Jr. 1947b. The role of reduced food intake in alcoholic debilitation of mice infected with *Hymenolepis*. J. Parasitol. *33*, 339–344.

Larsh, J. E., Jr. 1947c. The effect of thyroid and thiouracil on the natural resistance of mice to infection with *Hymenolepis*. J. Parasitol. *33* Suppl., 24–25.

Larsh, J. E., Jr. 1948. The role of certain vitamins in alcoholic debilitation of mice infected with *Hymenolepis*. J. Parasitol. *34* Suppl., 31.

Larsh, J. E., Jr. 1949a. Tests in mice to determine the relationship of intestinal emptying time and natural resistance to infection with the pig ascarid. J. Parasitol. *35* Suppl., 35.

Larsh, J. E., Jr. 1949b. The effect of pregnancy on the natural resistance of mice to *Hymenolepis* infection. J. Parasitol. *35* Suppl., 37.

Larsh, J. E., Jr. 1950. Relationship in mice of intestinal emptying time and natural resistance to pig *Ascaris* infection. Science *111*, 62–63.

Larsh, J. E., Jr., and A. W. Donaldson. 1944. The effect of concurrent infection with *Nippostrongylus* on the development of *Hymenolepis* in mice. J. Parasitol. *30*, 18–20.

Larsh, J. E., Jr., and M. S. Gravatt. 1948. A comparative study of the susceptibility of guinea pigs and hamsters to an infection with pig *Ascaris*. J. Elisha Mitchell Society *64*, 196–203.

Larsh, J. E., Jr., and J. R. Hendricks. 1947. The localization of adult *Trichinella spiralis* in the intestinal tract of young and old mice. J. Parasitol. *33* Suppl., 24.

Larsh, J. E., Jr., and J. R. Hendricks. 1949. The probable explanation for the difference in the localization of adult *Trichinella spiralis* in young and old mice. J. Parasitol. *35*, 101–106.

Larsh, J. E., Jr., and D. E. Kent. 1949. The effect of alcohol on natural and acquired immunity of mice to infection with *Trichinella spiralis*. J. Parasitol. *35*, 45–53.

Larsh, J. E., Jr., and J. Nichols. 1949. Effect of adrenalectomy on eosinophil response of rats infected with *Trichinella spiralis*. Proc. Soc. Exp. Biol. and Med. *71*, 652–654.

La Rue, G. R. 1909. On the morphology and development of a new cestode of the genus *Proteocephalus* Weinland. Trans. Am. Microscop. Soc. *28*, 17–49.

La Rue, G. R. 1911. A revision of the cestode family Proteocephalidae. Zool. Anz. *38*, 473–482.

La Rue, G. R. 1914a. A revision of the cestode family Proteocephalidae. Illinois Biol. Monog. *1*, 1–349.

La Rue, G. R. 1914b. A new cestode, *Ophiotaenia cryptobranchi* nov. spec. from *Cryptobranchus allegheniensis* (Daudin). 16th Report Michigan Acad. Sci., p. 11.

La Rue, G. R. 1919. A new species of tapeworm of the genus *Proteocephalus* from the perch and rock bass. Museum Zool. Univ. Michigan Occ. Papers, No. 67.

Laser, H. 1944. The oxidative metabolism of *Ascaris suis*. Biochem. J. *38*, 333–339.

Lavruff, S. 1908. Resultate der Untersuching des Wurmerfaunas der Wolga-Flusses . . . Saratow Frd. obsi. jest. *5*.

Law, R. G., and A. H. Kennedy. 1933. *Echinococcus grandulosus* in a moose. North Am. Veterinarian *14*, 33–34.

Lawler, H. J. 1939. A new cestode, *Cylindrotaenia quadrijugosa* n. sp. from *Rana pipiens,* with a key to Nematotaeniidae. Trans. Am. Microscop. Soc. *58*, 73–77.

Leared, A. 1874. *Bothriocephalus latus*. Trans. Path. Soc. London *25*, 263–264.

Le Bas, G. Z. L. 1924. Experimental studies on *Dibothriocephalus latus* in man. J. Helm. *2*, 151–166.

Le Blond, C. 1836a. Quelques observations d'helminthologie. Ann. Sci. Naturelles, Paris. Zoologie *6*, 289–307.

Le Blond, C. 1836b. Entozoaire parasite d'un congre. L'institut, No. 153, p. 116.

Le Clerc. 1715. See Van Cleave, 1935.

Leidy, J. 1851. Contributions to helminthology. Proc. Acad. Nat. Sci. Phil. *5*, 204.

Leidy, J. 1855. Notices on some tapeworms. Proc. Acad. Nat. Sci. Phil. *7*, 443–444.

Leidy, J. 1856. A synopsis of Entozoa and some of their congeners observed by the author. Proc. Acad. Nat. Sci. Phil. *8*, 42–58.

Leidy, J. 1871. Notices of some worms. *Dibothrium cordiceps* . . . Proc. Acad. Nat. Sci. Phil. *23*, 305–307.

Leidy, J. 1872. On *Ligula* in a fish of Susquehanna. Proc. Acad. Nat. Sci. Phil. *24*, 415–416.

Leidy, J. 1875. Notes on some parasitic worms. Proc. Acad. Nat. Sci. Phil. *27*, 14–16.

Leidy, J. 1886a. On *Amia* and its probable *Taenia*. Proc. Acad. Sci. Phil. *38*, 62–63.

Leidy, J. 1886b. *Bothriocephalus* in trout. Proc. Acad. Nat. Sci. Phil. *38*, 122–123.

Leidy, J. 1887a. Notices on some parasitic worms. Proc. Acad. Nat. Sci. Phil. *39*, 2–24.

Leidy, J. 1887b. Tapeworms of birds. J. Comp. Med. Surg. *8*, 1–11.

Leidy, J. 1888. Parasites of the pickerel. Proc. Acad. Nat. Sci. Phil. *40*, 169.

Leidy, J. 1890. Parasites of *Mola rotunda*. Proc. Acad. Nat. Sci. Phil. *42*, 281–282.

Leidy, J. 1891. Notices of Entozoa. Proc. Acad. Nat. Sci. Phil. *42*, 410–418.

Leidy, J. 1904. Researches in helminthology and parasitology, arranged and edited by J. Leidy, Jr. Smithsonian Miscell. Coll. *46*, 199–207.

Leidy, J., II. 1924. The haematoxins of intestinal parasites. A critical summary with notes and some cases. J. Parasitol. *10*.

Leigh, W. H. 1939. Variations in a new cestode of the genus *Raillietina* (*Skrjabinia*) from the prairie chicken. J. Parasitol. *25* Suppl., 10.

Leigh, W. H. 1940. Preliminary studies on the parasites of upland game birds and fur-bearing mammals. Bull. Illinois Nat. Hist. Survey *21*, 188–194.

Leigh, W. H. 1941. Variations in a new species of cestode, *Raillietina* (*Skrjabinia*) *variabila* from the prairie chicken in Illinois. J. Parasitol. *27*, 97–106.

Leiper, R. T. 1918. Diagnosis of helminthic infections. Proc. Zool. Soc. London, 1918.

Leiper, R. T. 1935. Helminth parasites in the living okapi. Proc. Zool. Soc. London, 1935, 947–949.

Leiper, R. T. 1936a. Crustacea as helminth intermediaries. Proc. Roy. Soc. Med. *29*, 1073–1084.

Leiper, R. T. 1936b. Some experiments and observations on the longevity of *Diphyllobothrium* infections. J. Helm. *14*, 127–130.

Leiper, R. T., and E. L. Atkinson. 1914. Helminths of the British Antarctic Expedition, 1910–1913. Proc. Zool. Soc. London, 1914. Pp. 222–226.

Leiper, R. T., and E. L. Atkinson. 1915. Parasitic worms . . . Report of the British Antarctic "Terra Nova" Expedition, 1910–1913. Nat. Hist. Reports, Zoology, *2*, 19–60. London.

Lemaire, G. 1926. Recherches sur la permeabilité des kystes hydatiques et sur la nature du poison hydatique. Presse médicale, Paris, *34*, 1187–1188.

Lemaire, G. 1928. Les fonctions toxiques du liquide hydatique. L'Algérie médicale, May, 1928, pp. 1–16.

Lemaire, G. (in collaboration with M. E. Bressot and M. G. Esquier). 1928. Kyste hydatique central du foie. L'Algérie médicale, extrait, May, 1928, pp. 1–4.

Lemaire, G. (in collaboration with M. Dumolard). 1929. Kyste hydatique de l'oreillete droite. L'Algérie médicale, extrait, May, 1928, pp. 1–8.

Lemaire, G., and Ribere (no initials). 1935a. Methode simple et aseptique pour les essais de culture *in vitro* des scolex, applicable à l'étude des phénomènes biologiques susceptible d'être observé de part et d'autre d'un ultra-filtre. Compt. rend. soc. biol. *118*, 1080–1082.

Lemaire, G., and Ribere (no initials). 1935b. Sur la composition chimique du liquide hydatique. Compt. rend. soc. biol. *118*, 1578–1579.

Lemaire, G., and J. Thiodet. 1926. Sur la nature du poison hydatique. Compt. rend. soc. biol. *95*, 166–168.

Lemaire, G., J. Thiodet, and Derrieu (no initials). 1926. Sur la nature du poison hydatique. Compt. rend. soc. biol. *95*, 1485–1487.

Leon, L. A. 1938. Contribución al estudio de la parasitologia sudamericana. El género *Raillietina* y su frecuencia en el Ecuador. Rev. med. trop. y parasitol. bacteriol. clin. lab. *4*, 219–230.

Leon, L. A. 1949. Nuevas consideraciones sobre la raillietinosis humana y nuevos aportes al conocimiento de la *Raillietina* (*R.*) *quitensis*. Rev. Kuba med. trop. y parasitol. *5*, 1–4.

Leon, N. 1907a. Sur la fénestration du *Bothriocephalus latus*. Zool. Anz. *32*, 209–212.

Leon, N. 1907b. *Diplogonoporus brauni*. Zool. Anz. *32*, 376–379.

Leon, N. 1908. Ein neuer menschlicher Cestode. Zool. Anz. *33*, 359–362.

Leon, N. 1909a. Deux bothriocephales monstreux. Centralbl. Bakt. Parasitenk. *50*, 616–619.

Leon, N. 1909b. Ueber eine Missbildung von *Hymenolepis*. Zool. Anz. *34*, 609–616.

Leon, N. 1910. Un nouvel cas de *Diplogonoporus brauni*. Centralbl. Bakt. Parasitenk. *55*, 23–27.

Leon, N. 1916. *Dibothriocephalus taenioides*. Centralbl. Bakt. Parasitenk. *78*, 503–504.

Leon, N. 1920. Notes sur quelques vers parasites de Roumanie. Ann. Sci. Univ. Jassy *10*, 308–313.

Leon, N. 1925. Accouplement et fécundation du *Dibothriocephalus latus*. Ann. parasitol. humaine et comparée *3*.

Leon, N. 1926. Sur la bifurcation du *Dibothriocephalus latus*. Ann. parasitol. humaine et comparée *4*.

Le Roux, P. 1927. Helminths collected from the domestic fowl (*Gallus domesticus*) and the domestic pigeon (*Columba livia*) in Natal. 11th and 12th Reports of the Director of Veterinary Education and Research, Union of South Africa, Pretoria, pp. 210–217.

Leske, N. G. 1780. Von dem Drehen der Schafe und dem Blasenwurme im Gehirne derselben als die Ursache dieser Krankheit. 52 pp. Leipzig.

Lespes, P. G. C. 1857. Notes sur une nouvelle espèce du genre *Echinobothrium*. Ann. sci. nat. zool. (Ser. 4) 7, 118–119.

Lesuk, A., and R. J. Anderson. 1941. Concerning the chemical composition of *Cysticercus fasciolaris*. II. The occurrence of a cerebroside containing dihydrosphingosin and of hydrolecithin in *Cysticercus* larvae. J. Biol. Chem. *139*, 457–469.

Leuckart, F. S. 1820. Das Genus *Bothriocephalus* Rud. Zoologische Bruchstücke I. viii + 70 pp. Helmstadt.

Leuckart, K. G. F. R. 1848. Beschreibung zweier neuen Helminthen. Arch. Naturgeschichte, XIV Jahrg., *1*.

Leuckart, K. G. F. R. 1850. Helminthologische Notizen. Arch. Naturgeschichte, XVI Jahrg., *1*, 9–16.

Leuckart, K. G. F. R. 1852. Parasitismus und Parasiten. Arch. physiol. Heilk. Stuttgart *11*, 199–259.

Leuckart, K. G. F. R. 1855. Erziehung des *Cysticercus fasciolaris* aus dem Eiern von *Taenia crassicollis*. Z. wiss. Zool. *6*, 139.

Leuckart, K. G. F. R. 1856. Die Blasenwürmer und ihre Entwicklung. Zugleich ein Beitrag zur Kenntnis der *Cysticercus*-Leber. 162 pp. Giessen.

Leuckart, K. G. F. R. 1862–1863. Die menschlichen Parasiten und die von ihnen herrührenden Krankheiten. Ein Hand- und Lehrbuch für Naturforscher und Ärzte. First Edition. viii + 766 pp. Leipzig and Heidelberg.

Leukart, K. G. F. R. 1863. Die menschlichen Parasiten. Arch. Sci. phys. nat. n. ser. *16*, 243–245.

Leuckart, K. G. F. R. 1865. Bericht ueber die wissenschaftlichen Leistungen in der Naturgeschichte der niederen Thiere während der Jahre 1864 und 1865 (Erste Hälfte). Arch. Naturgeschichte, 31 Jahrg., Bd. 2, pp. 165–268.

Leuckart, K. G. F. R. 1869. Bericht ueber die wissenschaftlichen Leistungen in der Naturgeschichte der niederen Thiere für 1868 und 1869 (Erste Hälfte). Arch. Naturgeschichte, 35 Jahrg., Bd. 2, pp. 207–244.

Leuckart, K. G. F. R. 1878. *Archigetes Sieboldi,* eine geschlechtsreife Cestodenamme. Z. wiss. Zool. *30* Suppl., 593–606.

Leuckart, K. G. F. R. 1879. Die Parasiten des Menschen und die von ihnen herrührenden Krankheiten. Second Edition, Part I. xii + 856 pp. Leipzig and Heidelberg.

Leuckart, K. G. F. R. 1881. Die Parasiten des Menschen . . . Part II.

Leuckart, K. G. F. R. 1886a. Die Parasiten des Menschen . . . Part III. xxxi + 1000 pp.

Leuckart, K. G. F. R. 1886b. The parasites of man and the diseases which proceed from them. English translation by W. E. Hoyle. Edinburgh.

Leuckart, K. G. F. R. 1887. Zur Bothriocephalusfrage. Central. Bakt. Parasitenk. *1*.

Leuckart, K. G. F. R. 1891. Ueber *Taenia madagascariensis* Dav. Verhandl. deutsch. Zool. Ges., pp. 68–71.

Leuckart, K. G. F. R., and A. Pagenstecher. 1858. Untersuchungen ueber niedere See-Thiere: *Echinobothrium Typus*. Arch. Anat. Physiol. *25*, 600–609.

Levander, K. M. 1904. Nagra ord i anledning af forekomsten af stora larver af *Ligula intestinalis*. Medd. Soc. Fauna Flora Fenn. *30*, 109–112.

Levander, K. M. 1906. Om larver af *Dibothriocephalus latus* L. hos insjolae (Ueber Larven von *Dibothriocephalus latus* L. bei *Salmo lacustris*). Medd. Soc. Fauna Flora Fenn. *32*, 93.

Levine, P. P. 1938. Observations on the biology of the poultry cestode, *Davainea proglottina*, in the intestine of the host. J. Parasitol. *24*, 423–431.

Lewis, A. E. 1926a. Helminths of wild birds found in the Aberystwyth area. J. Helm. *4*, 7–12.

Lewis, A. E. 1926b. Helminths collected from horses in the Aberystwyth area. J. Helm. *4*.

Lewis, A. E. 1927a. A study of the helminths of dogs and cats of Aberystwyth, Wales. J. Helm. *5*, 175–182.

Lewis, A. E. 1927b. A survey of Welsh helminthology. J. Helm. *5*, 121–132.

Lewis, R. C. 1914. On two new species of tapeworms from the stomach and small intestine of a wallaby, *Lagorchestes conspicillatus*, from Hermite Island, Monte Bello Islands. Proc. Zool. Soc. London, pp. 419–433.

Leydig, F. 1853. Ein neuer Bandwurm aus *Polypterus bichir*. Arch. Naturgeschichte *19*, 219–222.

Li, H. C. 1929. The life-histories of *Diphyllobothrium decipiens* and *D. erinacei*. Am. J. Hyg. *10*, 527–550.

Limbourg, J. P. de. 1767. Observationes de ascaridibus et cucurbitinis, et potissimum de *Taenia*, tam humana quam leporina. Philos. Trans. *56*, 126–132.

Lincicome, D. R. 1939. A new tapeworm, *Choanotaenia iola*, from the robin. J. Parasitol. *25*, 203–206.

Lindner, E. 1921. Die Bedeutung des Cysticercus-Schwanzes. Biol. Zentr. *41*, 36–41.

Linnaeus, C. 1758. Systema naturae per regna tria naturae, secundum classes, ordines, genera, species, cum characteribus, differentiis, synonymis, locis. Editio decima, reformata. Vol. I, 823 pp. Holmiae.

Linnaeus, C. 1767. Systema naturae per regna tria naturae . . . Editio duodecima, reformata. Vol. I, pp. 533–1327. Holmiae.

Linstow, O. F. B. von. 1872a. Ueber den Cysticercus *Taenia gracilis*, eine freie Cestodenamme des Barsches. Arch. mikroskop. Anat. Entwicklungsmech. *8*, 535–537.

Linstow, O. F. B. von. 1872b. Sechs neue Taenien. Arch. Naturgeschichte *38*, 55–58.

Linstow, O. F. B. von. 1875. Beobachtungen an neuen und bekannten Helminthen. Arch. Naturgeschichte *41*, 183–207.

Linstow, O. F. B. von. 1876. Helminthologische Beobachtungen. Arch. Naturgeschichte *42*, 1–18.

Linstow, O. F. B. von. 1877a. Helminthologica. Arch. Naturgeschichte *43*, 1–18.

Linstow, O. F. B. von. 1877b. Enthelminthologica. Arch. Naturgeschichte *43*, 173–197.

Linstow, O. F. B. von. 1878a. Compendium der Helminthologie. Ein Verzeichniss der bekannten Helminthen die frei oder in thierischen Körper leben, geordnet nach ihren Wohnthieren, unter Angabe der Organe, in denen sie gefunden sind, und mit Beifügung der Litteraturquellen. xxii + 382 pp. Hannover.

Linstow, O. F. B. von. 1878b. Neue Beobachtungen an Helminthen. Arch. Naturgeschichte *44*, 218–245.

Linstow, O. F. B. von. 1879a. Helminthologische Untersuchungen. Jahresber. Ver. vaterl. Naturkunde Württemberg, Stuttgart, *35*, 313–342.

Linstow, O. F. B. von. 1879b. Helminthologische Studien. Arch. Naturgeschichte *45*, 165–188.

Linstow, O. F. B. von. 1880. Helminthologische Untersuchungen. Arch. Naturgeschichte *46*, 41–54.

Linstow, O. F. B. von. 1882. Helminthologische Studien. Arch. Naturgeschichte *48*, 1–25.

Linstow, O. F. B. von. 1884. Helminthologisches. Arch. Naturgeschichte *50*, 125–145.

Linstow, O. F. B. von. 1888. Report on the Entozoa. Reports of the Scientific Results of the Challenger Expedition: Zoology *23*, 1–18. Edinburgh.

Linstow, O. F. B. von. 1889a. Helminthologisches. Arch. Naturgeschichte *55*, 235–246.

Linstow, O. F. B. von. 1889b. Compendium der Helminthologie. Nachtrag. Die Litteratur der Jahre 1878–1889. xvi + 151 pp. Hannover.

Linstow, O. F. B. von. 1890. Beitrag zur Kenntnis der Vogeltaenien. Arch. Naturgeschichte *56*, 171–188.

Linstow, O. F. B. von. 1891. Ueber den Bau und die Entwicklung von *Taenia longicollis* Rud. Ein Beitrag zur Kenntnis der Fischtänien. Jena Z. Med. u. Naturw. *25*, 565–574.

Linstow, O. F. B. von. 1892a. Beobachtungen an Vogeltänien. Centralbl. Bakt. Parasitenk. *12*, 501–504.

Linstow, O. F. B. von. 1892b. Beobachtungen an Helminthen Larven. Arch. mikroskop. Anat. Entwicklungsmech. *39*, 336–343.

Linstow, O. F. B. von. 1892c. Helminthen von Süd-Georgien nach der Ausbeute der deutsche Station von 1882–1883. Jahrb. Hamburg Wissenschaft. Anstalten, *9*, 59–77.

Linstow, O. F. B. von. 1893a. Zur Anatomie und Entwicklungsgeschichte der Tänien. Arch. mikroskop. Anat. Entwicklungsmech. *42*, 442–459.

Linstow, O. F. B. von. 1893b. Helminthologische Studien. Jena Z. Med. u. Naturw. *28*, 328–342.

Linstow, O. F. B. von. 1895. Ueber *Taenia* (*Hymenolepis*) *nana* v. Siebold und *murina* Dujardin. Jena Z. Med. u. Naturw. *30*, 571–582.

Linstow, O. F. B. von. 1896. Helminthologische Mitteilungen. Arch. Naturgeschichte *48*, 328–342.

Linstow, O. F. B. von. 1900a. *Tetrabothrium cylindraceum* Rud. und das Genus *Tetrabothrium*. Centralbl. Bakt. Parasitenk. *27*, 362–366.

Linstow, O. F. B. von. 1900b. *Taenia africana* n. sp. eine neue Tänie des Menschen aus Afrika. Centralbl. Bakt. Parasitenk. *28*, 485–490.

Linstow, O. F. B. von. 1900c. On *Tetrabothrium torulosum* und *Tetrabothrium auriculatum*. Proc. Roy. Soc. Edinburgh *23*, 158–160.

Linstow, O. F. B. von. 1901a. *Taenia horrida, Tetrabothrium macrocephalum* . . . Arch. Naturgeschichte *67*, 1–9.

Linstow, O. F. B. von. 1901b. *Taenia asiatica,* eine neue Tänie aus Menschen. Centralbl. Bakt. Parasitenk. *29*, 982–985.

Linstow, O. F. B. von. 1901c. Die systematische Stellung von *Ligula intestinalis* Goeze. Zool. Anz. *24*, 627–634.

Linstow, O. F. B. von. 1901d. Beobachtungen an Helminthen des Senckenbergischen Naturhistorischen Museums des Breslauer Zoologischen Instituts und andern. Arch. mikroskop. Anat. Entwicklungsmech. *58*, 182–198.

Linstow, O. F. B. von. 1901e. Helminthen von den Ufern des Nyassa-Sees. Beitrag zur Helminthenfauna von Süd Afrika. Jena Z. Med. u. Naturw. *35*, 426–427.

Linstow, O. F. B. von. 1901f. Entozoa des zoologischen Museums der kaiserlichen Akademie der Wissenschaft zu St. Petersburg. Bull. acad. imp. sci. St. Petersburg *15*, 271–292.

Linstow, O. F. B. von. 1902a. *Taenia trichoglossi*. Centralbl. Bakt. Parasitenk. *31*, 32.

Linstow, O. F. B. von. 1902b. Zwei neue Parasiten des Menschen. Centralbl. Bakt. Parasitenk. *31*, 768–773.

Linstow, O. F. B. von. 1902c. Eine neue Cysticercus-Form, *Cysticercus Brauni* Setti. Centralbl. Bakt. Parasitenk. *32*, 882–886.

Linstow, O. F. B. von. 1902d. *Echinococcus alveolaris* und *Plerocercus lachensis*. Zool. Anz. *26*, 162–167.

Linstow, O. F. B. von. 1903a. Entozoa des zoologischen Museums der kaiserlichen Akademie der Wissenschaft zu St. Petersburg. II. Ann. muséum zool. acad. imp. sci. St. Petersburg *8*, 265–294.

Linstow, O. F. B. von. 1903b. Neue Helminthen. Arch. Naturgeschichte *71*, 267–276, 352–357.

Linstow, O. F. B. von. 1903c. Drei neue Tänien aus Ceylon. Centralbl. Bakt. Parasitenk. *33*, 532–535.

Linstow, O. F. B. von. 1903d. Helminthologische Beobachtungen. Centralbl. Bakt. Parasitenk. *34*, 526–531.

Linstow, O. F. B. von. 1903e. Parasiten, meistens Helminthen, aus Siam. Arch. mikroskop. Anat. Entwicklungsmech. *62*, 108–121.

Linstow, O. F. B. von. 1904a. Ueber zwei neue Entozoa aus Acipenseriden. Ann. muséum zool. acad. imp. sci. St. Petersburg *9*, 17–19.

Linstow, O. F. B. von. 1904b. Beobachtungen an Nematoden und Cestoden. Arch. Naturgeschichte *70*, 305–307.

Linstow, O. F. B. von. 1904c. Neue Helminthen aus West Afrika. Centralbl. Bakt. Parasitenk. *36*, 379–383.

Linstow, O. F. B. von. 1904d. Neue Beobachtungen an Helminthen. Arch. mikroskop. Anat. Entwicklungsmech. *69*, 494–496.

Linstow, O. F. B. von. 1904e. Neue Helminthen. Centralbl. Bakt. Parasitenk. *37*, 678–683.

Linstow, O. F. B. von. 1905a. Helminthologische Beobachtungen. Arch. mikroskop. Anat. Entwicklungsmech. *66*, 355–366.

Linstow, O. F. B. von. 1905b. Helminthen der russischen Polar-Expedition 1900–1903. Mem. acad. imp. sci. St. Petersburg *18*, 1–16.

Linstow, O. F. B. von. 1905c. Neue Helminthen. Arch. Naturgeschichte *71*, 267–276.

Linstow, O. F. B. von. 1905d. Helminthen aus Ceylon und aus Arktischen Breitens. Z. wiss. Zool. *82*, 182–193.

Linstow, O. F. B. von. 1906a. Helminths from the collection of the Colombo Museum. Ceylon J. Sci. *3*, 163–188.

Linstow, O. F. B. von. 1906b. Neue und bekannte Helminthen. Zool. Jahrb. *24*, 1–20.

Linstow, O. F. B. von. 1906c. Neue Helminthen. Centralbl. Bakt. Parasitenk. *41*, 15–17.

Linstow, O. F. B. von. 1907. Helminthen von Herrn Eduard Jacobson in Java gesammelt. Notes Museum Jentink. Leiden *29*, 81–87.

Linstow, O. F. B. von. 1908a. *Hymenolepis furcifera* und *Tatria biremis,* zwei Tänien aus *Podiceps nigricollis.* Centralbl. Bakt. Parasitenk. *46*, 38–40.

Linstow, O. F. B. von. 1908b. Recent additions to the collection of Entozoa in the Indian Museum. Records Indian Museum II, p. 108.

Linstow, O. F. B. von. 1909a. Neue Helminthen aus Deutsch Südwest Afrika. Centralbl. Bakt. Parasitenk. *50*, 448–451.

Linstow, O. F. B. von. 1909b. *Davainea provincialis.* Centralbl. Bakt. Parasitenk. *52*, 75–77.

Linton, E. 1887. Notes on two forms of cestoid embryos. Am. Naturalist *21*, 195–201.

Linton, E. 1889a. Notes on Entozoa of marine fishes. Ann. Rep. U. S. Comm. Fish and Fisheries for 1886, Washington, 1889, *14*, 453–511.

Linton, E. 1889b. A contribution to the life-history of *Dibothrium cordiceps,* a parasite infesting the trout of Yellowstone Lake. Bull. U. S. Comm. Fish and Fisheries *9*, 337–358.

Linton, E. 1890. Notes on Entozoa of marine fishes. II. Ann. Rep. U. S. Comm. Fish and Fisheries for 1887, Washington, 1890, *15*, 719–899.

Linton, E. 1891a. Notes on Entozoa of marine fishes. III. Ann. Rep. U. S. Comm. Fish and Fisheries for 1888, Washington, 1891, *16*, 523–542.

Linton, E. 1891b. On the anatomy of *Thysanocephalum crispum* Linton, a parasite of the tiger shark. Ann. Rep. U. S. Comm. Fish and Fisheries for 1888, Washington, 1891, *16*, 543–546.

Linton, E. 1891c. On two species of larval *Dibothria* from the Yellowstone National Park. Bull. U. S. Comm. Fish and Fisheries, Washington, 1891, *9*, 65–79.

Linton, E. 1892. Notes on avian Entozoa. Proc. U. S. Nat. Museum *15*, 87–113.

Linton, E. 1893. On fish Entozoa. Ann. Rep. U. S. Comm. Fish and Fisheries for 1889–1891, Washington, 1893, pp. 545–564.

Linton, E. 1897a. Notes on larval cestode parasites. Proc. U. S. Nat. Museum *19*, 787–824.

Linton, E. 1897b. Notes on cestode parasites of fishes. Proc. U. S. Nat. Museum *20*, 423–456.

Linton, E. 1897c. Notes on trematode parasites of fishes. Proc. U. S. Nat. Museum *20*, 507–548.

Linton, E. 1900. Fish parasites collected at Woods Hole in 1898. Bull. U. S. Comm. Fish and Fisheries for 1899, Washington, Sept. 1, 1900, *19*, 267–304.

Linton, E. 1901. Parasites of fishes of the Woods Hole region. Bull. U. S. Comm. Fish and Fisheries for 1899, Washington, 27 June, 1901, *19*, 405–492.

Linton, E. 1905a. Parasites of fishes of Beaufort, North Carolina. Bull. U. S. Bur. Fish. for 1904, Washington, 1905, *24*, 321–428.

Linton, E. 1905b. Notes on cestode cysts. *Taenia chamissonii,* new species, from a porpoise. Proc. U. S. Nat. Museum *28*, 819–822.

Linton, E. 1907a. Notes on *Calyptrobothrium,* a cestode genus found in the torpedo. Proc. U. S. Nat. Museum *32*, 275–284.

Linton, E. 1907b. Notes on parasites of Bermuda fishes. Proc. U. S. Nat. Museum *33*, 85–126.

Linton, E. 1907c. A cestode parasite in the flesh of the butterfish. Bull. U. S. Bur. Fish. for 1906, *26*, and Bur. Fish. Document No. 611, Washington, p. 111.

Linton, E. 1907d. Preliminary report on animal parasites of Tortugas. Fifth Yearbook of Carnegie Institution for 1906, Washington, pp. 112–117.

Linton, E. 1908. Preliminary report on animal parasites of Tortugas. Sixth Yearbook of Carnegie Institution for 1907, Washington.

Linton, E. 1909. Helminth fauna of the Dry Tortugas. I. Cestoda. Carnegie Institution, Washington, Pub. 102, pp. 157–190.

Linton, E. 1910. Notes on the flesh parasites of marine food fishes. Bull. U. S. Bur. Fish. for 1908, *28*, and Bur. Fish. Document No. 714, pp. 1197–1209.

Linton, E. 1911. Notes on the distribution of Entozoa of North American marine fishes. Proc. 7th Intern. Zool. Congress, Boston, 1907, pp. 686–696.

Linton, E. 1913a. Cestoda. In Summer, Osburn and Cole, Catalogue of marine fauna of Woods Hole and vicinity. Bull. U. S. Bur. Fish., Washington, for 1911, *31*.

Linton, E. 1913b. Cestode cysts in the flesh of marine fishes. Trans. Am. Fish. Soc. 42nd Ann. Meeting, pp. 119–127.

Linton, E. 1914. On the seasonal distribution of fish parasites. Trans. Am. Fish. Soc. *44*, 48–56.

Linton, E. 1915. Cestode cysts from the muskrat. J. Parasitol. *2*, 46–47.

Linton, E. 1916. Notes on two cestodes from the spotted sting ray. J. Parasitol. *3*, 34–38.

Linton, E. 1921. *Rhynchobothrium ingens* sp. nov., a parasite of the dusky shark, *Carcharinus obscurus.* J. Parasitol. *8*, 23–32.

Linton, E. 1922a. A contribution to the anatomy of *Dinobothrium,* a genus of selachian tapeworms. Proc. U. S. Nat. Museum *60*.

Linton, E. 1922b. A new cestode from *Liparis liparis.* Trans. Am. Microscop. Soc. *41*.

Linton, E. 1922c. A new cestode from the maneater and mackerel sharks. Proc. U. S. Nat. Museum *61*.

Linton, E. 1923. A new cetacean cestode (*Prosthecocotyle monticellii* sp. n.) with a note on the genus *Tetrabothrius* Rud. J. Parasitol. *10*, 51–55.

Linton, E. 1924a. Notes on cestode parasites of sharks and rays. Proc. U. S. Nat. Museum *64*, 1–114.

Linton, E. 1924b. *Gyrocotyle plana* sp. nov., with notes on South African cestodes of fishes. Fish. Marine Biol. Survey. S. Africa. Rep. 3, No. 8. 27 pp.

Linton, E. 1925. A new diecian cestode. J. Parasitol. *11*, 163–168.

Linton, E. 1927. Notes on cestode parasites of birds. Proc. U. S. Nat. Museum *70*, 1–73.

Linton, E. 1928. Larval cestodes (*Tetrarhynchus elongatus* Rudolphi) from the liver of the pelagic sunfish (*Mola mola*) collected at Woods Hole, Massachusetts. Trans. Am. Microscop. Soc. *47*, 464–467.

Linton, E. 1934. A pseudophyllidean cestode from a flying fish. Trans. Am. Microscop. Soc. *53*, 66.

Linton, E. 1941. Cestode parasites of teleost fishes of the Woods Hole region, Massachusetts. Proc. U. S. Nat. Museum *90*, 417–442.

Llambias, J. 1926. Alterations de la membrane hydatique. Compt. rend. soc. biol. *95*.

Loennberg, E. 1889a. Bidrag till kännedomen om i Sverige förekommande Cestoder. Bihang. till K. Svenska Vetenskaps. Akad. Handlingar. *14*, 1–69.

Loennberg, E. 1889b. Ueber eine eigentümliche Tetrarhynchidenlarve. Bihang. till K. Svenska Vetenskaps. Akad. Handlingar. *15*, 1–48.

Loennberg, E. 1890a. Ueber *Amphiptyches* Wagener und *Gyrocotyle urna* (Grübe und Wagener) Diesing (eine vorläufige Mitteilung). Biol. Föreningens Förhandlingar, Stockholm, *2*, 53–61.

Loennberg, E. 1890b. Helminthologische Beobachtungen von der Westküste Norvegens. Bihang. till K. Svenska Vetenskaps. Akad. Handlingar. *16*, 1–47.

Loennberg, E. 1890c. Bemerkungen zum "Elenco degli elminti . . . dal Dott. F. S. Monticelli." Biol. Föreningens Förhandlingar, Stockholm, *3*, 4–9.

Loennberg, E. 1891a. Mitteilungen ueber einige Helminthen aus dem zoologischen Museum der Universität zu Kristiania. Biol. Föreningens Förhandlingar, Stockholm, *3*, 64–78.

Loennberg, E. 1891b. Anatomische Studien ueber Skandinavische Cestoden. I. Svenska Vetenskaps. Akad. Handlingar. *24* (1), 1–109.

Loennberg, E. 1892a. Anatomische Studien ueber Skandinavische Cestoden. II. Zwei Parasiten aus Walfischen und zwei aus *Lamna cornubica*. Svenska Vetenskaps. Akad. Handlingar. *24* (2), 1–28.

Loennberg, E. 1892b. Einige Experimente Cestoden künstlich lebend zu erhalten. Centralbl. Bakt. Parasitenk. *11*, 89–92.

Loennberg, E. 1892c. Ueber das Vorkommen des breiten Bandwurms in Schweden. Centralbl. Bakt. Parasitenk. *11*, 189–192.

Loennberg, E. 1893. Bemerkungen ueber einige Cestoden. Svenska Vetenskaps. Akad. Handlingar. *18*, 17 pp.

Loennberg, E. 1894. Ueber eine neue Tetrabothriumspecies und die Verwandtschaftverhältnisse der Ichthyotaenien. Centralbl. Bakt. Parasitenk. *15*, 801–803.

Loennberg, E. 1896. Cestoden: Magalhaenische Sammelreise. I. 9 pp. Hamburg.

Loennberg, E. 1897. Beiträge zur Phylogenie der Plathelminthen. Centralbl. Bakt. Parasitenk. *21*, 674–684.

Loennberg, E. 1898. Ein neuer Bandwurm (*Monorygma chlamydoselachi*) aus *Chlamydoselachus anguineus* Garman. Arch. math. naturv. Kristiania *20*, 1–11.

Loennberg, E. 1899. Ueber einige Cestoden aus dem Museum zu Bergen. Bergens Museum Arbog, 1898, No. 4, pp. 1–23.

Loeper, M., and P. Soulie. 1932. Les aspects cliniques et les causes possibles des accidents digestifs provoqués par le ténia. Compt. rend. 2me congrès intern. pathologie comparée *2*, 187–196.

Loewen, S. L. 1929. A new cestode, *Taenia rileyi* n. sp., from a lynx. J. Parasitol. *21*, 469–471.

Loewen, S. L. 1934. A new cestode from a bat. Trans. Kansas Acad. Sci. *37*, 257–261.

Loewen, S. L. 1940. On some reptilian cestodes of the genus *Oochoristica* (Anoplocephalidae). Trans. Am. Microscop. Soc. *59*, 511–518.

Long, J. H., and F. Fenger. 1917. On the normal reaction of the intestinal tract. J. Am. Chem. Soc. *39*, 1278–1286.

Long, L. H., and N. E. Wiggins. 1939. A new species of *Diorchis* (Cestoda) from the canvasback. J. Parasitol. *25*, 483–486.

Longo, D. 1932. Intradermoreazioni specifiche e aspecifiche nell' echinococcosi. Policlinico (Sezione Medica) *39*, 202–208.

Loos, A. 1892. Ist der Laurersche Kanal der Trematoden eine Vagina? Centralbl. Bakt. Parasitenk. *13*, 808–819.

Lopez-Neyra, C. R. 1916. Notas helmintologicas. Bol. real. soc. espan. hist. nat. Madrid *16*, 457–462.

Lopez-Neyra, C. R. 1918. Notas helmintologicas (2. ser.). Bol. real. soc. espan. hist. nat. Madrid *18*, 143–155.

Lopez-Neyra, C. R. 1920a. Notas helmintologicas (3. ser.). Bol. real. soc. espan. hist. nat. Madrid *20*, 75–90.

Lopez-Neyra, C. R. 1920b. Estudio critico de las Davaineas parasitas de las gallinas en la region Granadina. Rev. real. acad. cien. exact. fis. y nat. Madrid *18*, 23 pp.

Lopez-Neyra, C. R. 1923. Apuntes para un compendio de helmintologica Iberica. Asociacion espanola para el progreso de las sciencas, pp. 93–111.

Lopez-Neyra, C. R. 1927a. Considérations sur le genre *Dipylidium* Leuckart. Bull. soc. path. exot. *20*, 434–440.

Lopez-Neyra, C. R. 1927b. Sur les cysticercoïdes de quelques *Dipylidium*. Ann. parasitol. humaine et comparée *5*, 245–248.

Lopez-Neyra, C. R. 1927c. Sobre le evolucion de la *Joyeuxia chyzeri* v. Ratz. Bol. real. soc. espan. hist. nat. Madrid *27*.

Lopez-Neyra, C. R. 1928. Recherches sur le genre *Dipylidium* avec descriptions de quatre espèces nouvelles. Bull. soc. path. exot. *21*, 239–253.

Lopez-Neyra, C. R. 1929a. Revision del genero *Dipylidium* Leuckart. Mem. real. acad. cien. exact. fis. y nat. Madrid *32*, 1–112.

Lopez-Neyra, C. R. 1929b. Consideraciones sobre el genero *Davainea* y description de dos especies nuevas. Bol. real. soc. espan. hist. nat. Madrid *29*, 345–359.

Lopez-Neyra, C. R. 1930. Davaineidos parasitos humanos y sus relaciones con los de los mamiferos. Bol. univ. Granada, 1930 (8), pp. 1–31.

Lopez-Neyra, C. R. 1931a. Relations du *Davainea madagascariensis* et des espèces parasites des mammifères. Considérations sur les *Davainea*. Ann. parasitol. humaine et comparée *9*, 162–184.

Lopez-Neyra, C. R. 1931b. Revision del genero *Davainea* Leuckart. Mem. real. acad. cien. exact. fis. y nat. Madrid *1*, 1–179.

Lopez-Neyra, C. R. 1931c. La *Davainea formosana* y sus relaciones con los davaineidos de los roedores. Arch. ital. zool. Napoli Torino *15*, 465–473.

Lopez-Neyra, C. R. 1931d. Estudios sobre el proceso de fimbriarizacion. Los generos *Fimbriaria* e *Hymenofimbria* como deformidades de *Hymenolepis* y *Diorchis*. Medicina de los paises calidos *4*, 1–18.

Lopez-Neyra, C. R. 1931e. Sobre la clasificacion que propusimos del genero *Davainea*. Medicina de los paises calidos *4*, 494–501.

Lopez-Neyra, C. R. 1931f. La *Fimbriaria fasciolaris* y sus relaciones con el *Diorchis acuminata*. Bol. univ. Granada No. 13, pp. 131–156.

Lopez-Neyra, C. R. 1932a. Sur la classification du genre *Davainea* (s. l.). Bull. soc. zool. France *56*, 534–541.

Lopez-Neyra, C. R. 1932b. *Hymenolepis pittalugai* n. s. et ses rapports avec les espèces similaires (*H. macracanthos*). Ann. parasitol. humaine et comparée *10*, 248–256.

Lopez-Neyra, C. R. 1934. Sobre la clasificacion que propusimos de *Davainea* S. L. Respuesta a Fuhrmann. Bol. univ. Granada *6*, 47–55.

Lopez-Neyra, C. R. 1935a. Sobre algunos generos de Dilepididae. Bol. acad. cien. exact. fis. y nat. Madrid *1*, 9.

Lopez-Neyra, C. R. 1935b. Sobre una tenia critica del alcaravan. Bol. soc. espan. hist. nat. Madrid *35*, 203–216.

Lopez-Neyra, C. R. 1936. *Fernandezia goizuetai* nov. gen. nov. sp., parasite intestinal del zorzal y revision de los "Ophryocotyliinae." Rev. acad. cien. exact. fis. y nat. Madrid *33*, 5–18.

Lopez-Neyra, C. R. 1941. Especies nuevas o insuficientemente conocidas correspondientes al genero *Hymenolepis* Weinland (s. l.). Revista Iberica de Parasitologia *1*, 133–170.

Lopez-Neyra, C. R. 1943. Raillietinosis humanas en la zona tropical. Medicina Colonial, Madrid, *1*, 215–242.

Lopez-Neyra, C. R. 1944. *Nematotaenia tarentolae* n. sp., parasite intestinal de geckonidos. Revista Iberica de Parasitologia *4*, 123–137.

Lopez-Neyra, C. R. 1949a. Raillietinosis humanas. Estudios de parasitologia comparada sobre Raillietinae parasita humanas y en especial de las formas neotropicales. Revista Iberica de Parasitologia 9, 229–362.

Lopez-Neyra, C. R. 1949b. La parasitologia humana en el Marruecos espanol. Revista Iberica de Parasitologia 9, 373–443.

Lopez-Neyra, C. R. 1950. Revision del genero *Cotugnia*, motivada por el estudio de una especie nueva hallada en la tortola de Granada. Revista Iberica de Parasitologia *10*, 57–96.

Lopez-Neyra, C. R., and J. M. Muñoz-Medina. 1921. *Dipylidium quinquecoronatum* nov. sp., parasito intestinal del gato domestico. Bol. real. soc. espan. hist. nat. Madrid *21*, 421–426.

Lorincz, F., G. Burghoffer, and G. Bodrogi. 1932. Beitrag zur Echinokokkenkrankheit in Ungarn. Centralbl. Bakt. Parasitenk. *124*, 16–22.

Loveland, A. E. 1894. On the anatomy of *Taenia crassicollis*. J. comp. med. vet. arch. Philadelphia, Feb. 1894, *15*, 67–89. Suppl. note by C. W. Stiles, p. 85.

Loveridge, A. 1923. Notes on East African birds (chiefly nesting habits and endoparasites) collected 1920–1923. Proc. Zool. Soc. London, 1923, p. 899.

Lovern, J. A. 1940. The lipins of the earthworm. Biochem. J. *34*, 709–711.

Lucet, A., and E. Marotel. 1904. Les cestodes du dindon, nature zoologique et role pathogène. Rev. méd. vét. Paris *81*, 162–168.

Ludwig, H. 1886. Dr. Johannes Leunis Synopsis der Thierkunde. Ein Handbuch für höhere Lehranstalten und für Alle welche sich wissenschäftlich mit der Naturgeschichte der Thiere beschäftigen wollen. 3 gänzlich umgearbeitete, vermehrte Auflage, Vol. II. xv + 1231 pp. Hannover.

Lühe, M. 1893. Beiträge zur Kenntnis des Rostellums und der Skolexmuskulatur der Taenien. Zool. Anz. *17*, 279–282.

Lühe, M. 1894. Zur Morphologie des Tänienskolex. 133 pp. Inaugural Dissertation Univ. Königsberg.

Lühe, M. 1895a. Zur Kenntnis der Muskulatur des Taenienskörper. Zool. Anz. *19*, 260–264.

Lühe, M. 1895b. Mitteilungen ueber einige wenig bekannte bzw. neue südamerikanische Tänien des K. K. naturhistorischen Hof-Museum im Wien. Arch. Naturgeschichte *61*, 199–212.

Lühe, M. 1895c. Das Nervensystem von *Ligula* in seinem Beziehung zur Anordnung der Muskulatur. Zool. Anz. *19*, 383–384.

Lühe, M. 1897a. *Bothriocephalus zschokkei* Fuhrmann. Centralbl. Bakt. Parasitenk. *22*, 430–434.

Lühe, M. 1897b. Die Anordnung der Muskulatur bei dem Dibothrien. Centralbl. Bakt. Parasitenk. *22*, 739–747.

Lühe, M. 1898a. Beiträge zur Helminthenfauna der Berberei. Sitzber. kgl. preuss. Akad. Wiss. *40*, 619–628.

Lühe, M. 1898b. Die Gliederung von *Ligula*. Centralbl. Bakt. Parasitenk. *23*, 280–286.

Lühe, M. 1898c. *Oochoristica* nov. gen. Taeniadarum (Vorläufige Mitteilung). Zool. Anz. *21*, 650–652.

Lühe, M. 1899a. Zur Anatomie und Systematik der Bothriocephaliden. Verhandl. deutsch. zool. Gesell. *9*, 30–55.

Lühe, M. 1899b. Beiträge zur Kenntnis der Bothriocephaliden. I, II. Bothriocephaliden mit marginalen Genitalöffnungen. Centralbl. Bakt. Parasitenk. *26*, 702–719.

Lühe, M. 1899c. Zur Kenntnis einiger Distomen. Zool. Anz. *22*, 524–539.

Lühe, M. 1900a. Ueber *Bothrimonus* Duvernoy und verwandte Bothriocephaliden. Zool. Anz. *23*, 8–14.

Lühe, M. 1900b. Untersuchungen ueber Bothriocephaliden mit marginalen Genitalöffnungen. Z. wiss. Zool. *68*, 97–99.

Lühe, M. 1900c. Beiträge zur Kenntnis der Bothriocephaliden. III. Bothriocephaliden der landbewohnenden Reptilien. Centralbl. Bakt. Parasitenk. *27*, 209–217, 252–258.

Lühe, M. 1901. Referat ueber v. Ariola's Revisione della famiglia Bothriocephalidae s. str. (*Bothriotaenia longispicula* Stoss = *Acoleus longispiculus* Stoss.). Centralbl. Bakt. Parasitenk. *29*, 415.

Lühe, M. 1902a. Ueber die Fixierung der Helminthen an der Darmwandung ihrer

Wirte und die dadurch verursachten pathologisch-anatomischen Veranderungen des Wirtsdarmes. Verhandl. Intern. Zool. Congr. Berlin, 1901, pp. 698–705.

Lühe, M. 1902b. *Urogonoporus armatus*: ein eigentümlicher Cestode aus *Acanthias*, mit anschlüssenden Bemerkungen ueber die sogenannten Cestodarter. Arch. Parasitol. Paris *5*, 209–250.

Lühe, M. 1902c. Revision meines Bothriocephaliden-systems. Centralbl. Bakt. Parasitenk. *31*, 318–331.

Lühe, M. 1902d. Bemerkungen ueber die Cestoden aus *Centrolophus pompilius*. 1. Zur Synonymie der *Centrolophus*-Cestoden. Centralbl. Bakt. Parasitenk. *31*, 629–637.

Lühe, M. 1910a. Cestoden. In A. Brauer, Die Süsswasserfauna Deutschlands. Heft *18*, pp. 1–153.

Lühe, M. 1910b. Cystotänien südamerikanischer Feliden. Zool. Jahrb. Suppl. *13*, 687–710.

Lungwitz, M. 1895. *Taenia ovilla* Rivolta, ihr anatomischer Bau und die Entwicklung ihrer Geschlechtsorgane. Arch. wiss. prakt. Thierheilk. *21*, 105–159.

Luther, A. 1909. Ueber *Triaenophorus robustus* Olsson und *Henneguya zschokkei* Gurley als Parasiten von *Coregonus albula* aus dem See Sapsojärvi. Medd. soc. Fauna Flora Fenn. Helsingfors *35*, 58–59.

Luttermoser, G. W. 1940. The effect on the growth rate of young chickens of infections of the tapeworm, *Hymenolepis carioca*. Proc. Helm. Soc. Washington 7, 74–76.

Luttermoser, G. W., and R. W. Allen. 1942. The influence of diets high and low in protein on the growth rates of chickens infected with the tapeworm, *Raillietina cesticillus*. Poultry Science *21*, 111–115.

Lyman, R. A. 1902. Studies on the genus *Cittotaenia*. Studies Zool. Lab. Univ. Nebraska, No. 48, and Trans. Am. Microscop. Soc. *23*, 173–190.

Lynch, J. E. 1945. Re-description of the species of *Gyrocotyle* from the ratfish, *Hydrolagus colliei* (Lay and Bennet), with notes on the morphology and taxonomy of the genus. J. Parasitol. *31*, 418–446.

Lyon, M. W., Jr. 1926. Native cases of infestation by fish tapeworm, *Diphyllobothrium latum*. J. Am. Med. Ass. *86*, 264–265.

Lyster, L. L. 1940. Parasites of some Canadian sea mammals. Can. J. Research, Sect. D. Zoological Sciences, *18*, 395–409.

MacArthur, W. P. 1933, 1934. Articles on the correlation between cysticercosis and epilepsy in man. Clinical J. *63*, 133–138; Trans. Roy. Soc. Trop. Med. Hyg. *26*, 525–528; *27*, 343–363; J. Roy. Army Med. Corps *62*, 241–259.

MacCallum, G. A. 1917. Some new forms of parasitic worms. Zoopathologica (New York Zoological Society) *1* (No. 2), 43–75.

MacCallum, G. A. 1921. Studies in helminthology. Zoopathologica (New York Zoological Society) *1* (No. 6), 229–294.

MacCallum, G. A., and W. G. MacCallum. 1912. On the structure of *Taenia giganteum*. Zool. Jahrb. Syst. *32*, 379–388.

MacDonough, E. J. M. 1927. Parasitos de peces comestibles. II. Larvas de un cestode trypanorhynchido de la pescadilla. Semana Medica, Buenos Aires, *34*, 373–376.

MacDonough, E. J. M. 1932. Parasitos de peces comestibles. VI. Sobre una "Ichthyotaenia" y oncosfera del pejerrey. Semana Medica, Buenos Aires, *39*, 1917–1921.

Maclaren, N. 1903. Ueber die Haut der Trematoden. Zool. Anz. *26*, 516–524.

MacLulich, D. A. 1943. *Proteocephalus parallacticus*, a new species of tapeworm from lake trout, *Cristivomer namaycush*. Can. J. Research, Sect. D., Zoological Sciences, *21*, 145–149.

Macy, R. W. 1931. A key to the species of *Hymenolepis* found in bats, and the description of a new species, *H. christensoni*, from *Myotis lucifugus*. Trans. Am. Microscop. Soc. *50*, 344–347.

Macy, R. W. 1947. Parasites found in certain Oregon bats with the description of a new cestode, *Hymenolepis gertschi*. Am. Midland Naturalist *37*, 375–378.

Macy, R. W., and R. L. Rausch. 1946. Morphology of a new species of bat cestode,

Hymenolepis roudabushi, and a note on *Hymenolepis christensoni* Macy. Trans. Am. Microscop. Soc. *65,* 173–175.

Magalhaes, P. S. de. 1892. Notes d'helminthologie brésilienne. Bull. soc. zool. France *17,* 145–146.

Magalhaes, P. S. de. 1898. Notes d'helminthologie brésilienne. Deux nouveaux ténias de la poule domestique. Arch. Parasitol. *1,* 442–451.

Magalhaes, P. S. de. 1899. *Davainea oligophora* de Magalhaes, 1898 et *T. cantaniana* Polonio, 1860. Arch. Parasitol. *3,* 480–482.

Magalhaes, P. S. de. 1905. Notes d'helminthologie brésilienne. Arch. Parasitol. *9,* 305–314.

Magalhaes, P. S. de. 1918. Notes d'helminthologie brésilienne. Ann. Policlinica Geral do Rio de Janeiro, Anno *3,* 28 pp.

Magalhaes, P. S. de. 1919. Notes d'helminthologie brésilienne. Le *Davainea bothrioplitis* (Piana, 1881–1882). Arch. Parasitol. *16,* 481–502.

Magath, T. B. 1924. *Ophiotaenia testudo,* a new species from *Amyda spinifera.* J. Parasitol. *11,* 44–49.

Magath, T. B. 1929a. Experimental studies on *Diphyllobothrium latum.* Am. J. Trop. Med. *9,* 17–48.

Magath, T. B. 1929b. The early life-history of *Crepidobothrium testudo* (Magath, 1924). Ann. Trop. Med. Parasitol. *23,* 121–127.

Magath, T. B. 1931. *Diphyllobothrium latum.* Am. J. Clin. Path. *1,* Editorial, 187–189.

Magath, T. B. 1936. Hydatid (*Echinococcus*) disease in Canada and the United States. Am. J. Hyg. *25,* 107–134.

Magath, T. B., and P. W. Brown. 1927. Standardized method of treating tapeworm infestations in man to recover the head. J. Am. Med. Ass. Chicago, *88,* 1548–1549.

Magath, T. B., and H. E. Essex. 1931a. Concerning the distribution of *Diphyllobothrium latum* in North America. J. Preventive Med. *5,* 227–242.

Magath, T. B., and H. E. Essex. 1931b. A comparison of the viability of ova of the broad fish tapeworm, *D. latum,* from man and dogs . . . Am. J. Hyg. *14,* 698–704.

Malkani, P. G. 1933. A rapid method of evaginating the scolices in parasitic cysts. Indian Vet. J. *9,* 193; *10,* 122–124.

Manson, P. 1882. Case of lymph scrotum associated with filarial and other parasites. Lancet, London, *2,* 616–617.

Manson, P. 1903. Tropical diseases. xiv + 756 pp. London.

Maplestone, P. A. 1921. Notes on Australian cestodes. Parts I and II. Ann. Trop. Med. Parasitol. Liverpool *15,* 403–412.

Maplestone, P. A. 1922a. Notes on Australian cestodes. III. *Cotugnia oligorchis* n. sp. Ann. Trop. Med. Parasitol. Liverpool *16,* 55–60.

Maplestone, P. A. 1922b. Notes on Australian cestodes. VI. *Schizotaenia cacatua* n. sp. Ann. Trop. Med. Parasitol. Liverpool *16,* 305–310.

Maplestone, P. A., and T. Southwell. 1922c. Notes on Australian cestodes. IV. *Gyrocoelia australiensis* Johnston. Ann. Trop. Med. Parasitol. Liverpool *16,* 61–68.

Maplestone, P. A., and T. Southwell. 1922d. Notes on Australian cestodes. V. Three cestodes from the black swan. Ann. Trop. Med. Parasitol. Liverpool *16,* 189–198.

Marchi, P. 1869. Sopra una *Taenia* della *Loxia curvirostra.* Atti. soc. Ital. sci. nat. *12,* 534–535.

Marchi, P. 1878. Sur le développement du cysticerque des geckos en cestode parfait chez les *Strix noctua.* Compt. rend. assoc. franc. avanc. sci. 7, 757.

Markov, G. 1938. The survival of a broad tapeworm's plerocercoids (*Diphyllobothrium latum* L.) in artificial media. Compt. rend. acad. sci. U.R.S.S. *19,* 511–512.

Markowski, S. 1928. Evolution de *Cladotaenia cylindracea* (Bloch). Ann. parasitol. humaine et comparée *6,* 431–439.

Markowski, S. 1933a. Untersuchungen ueber die Helminthfauna der Raben (Corvidae) von Polen (in Polish with German summary). Compt. rend. acad. polon. sci. Classe sci. math. nat. *5,* 65 pp.

Markowski, S. 1933b. Contribution à la connaissance de développement de la larve *Tetrathyridium variabile* (Diesing, 1850) (in Polish with French summary). Compt. rend. acad. polon. sci. Classe sci. math. nat. *5,* 5–6.

Markowski, S. 1934. Beitrag zur Kenntnis der Entwicklung der Larve *Tetrathyridium variabile* (Diesing, 1850) (German summary of 1933b). Mem. acad. polon. sci. Classe sci. math. nat.

Marotel, G. 1898. Sur une téniadé du *Bothrops lanceolatus* (note préliminaire). Compt. rend. soc. biol. *50*, 99–101.

Marotel, G. 1899a. Etude zoologique de l'*Ichthyotaenia calmettei* Barrois. Arch. Parasitol. *2*, 34–42.

Marotel, G. 1899b. Sur une téniadé du Blaireau. Compt. rend. soc. biol. *51*, 21–23.

Marotel, G. 1899c. Sur deux cestodes parasites des oiseaux (note préliminaire). Compt. rend. soc. biol. *51*, 935–937.

Marotel, G. 1912. Nouveau parasite de mouton. Soc. sci. vet. Lyon.

Marotel, G. 1913. Nouveau mode de presentation des cestodes . . . 9me congr. intern. zool. Monaco, pp. 662–663.

Marshall, W. S., and N. C. Gilbert. 1905. Notes on the food and parasites of some freshwater fishes from the lakes at Madison, Wisconsin. Ann. Rep. U. S. Bur. Fish. for 1904. Pp. 513–522.

Matevosyan, E. M. 1942. An analysis of the specific components of the genus *Diploposthe*: cestodes from Anatidae. Compt. rend. acad. sci. U.R.S.S. *34*, 265–268.

Matz, F. 1892. Beiträge zur Kenntnis der Bothriocephalen. Arch. Naturgeschichte *58*, 97–122.

Mayhew, R. L. 1925. Studies on the avian species of the cestode family Hymenolepididae. Illinois Biol. Monog. *10*, 1–125.

Mayhew, R. L. 1929. The genus *Diorchis*, with descriptions of four new species from North America. J. Parasitol. *15*, 251–258.

Mazzocco, P. 1923. Composition du liquide hydatique. Compt. rend. soc. biol. *88*, 342.

McClure, W. B., and L. Teskey. 1934. A case of infestation with *Diphyllobothrium latum*. Can. Med. Ass. J. *31*, 64–65.

McCoy, O. R. 1935. The physiology of the helminth parasites. Physiological Reviews *15*, 221–240.

McIntosh, A. 1937. New host records for *Diphyllobothrium mansonoides* Mueller, 1935. J. Parasitol. *23*, 313–315.

McIntosh, A. 1938. Description of the adult stage of *Taenia twitchelli* from an Alaskan wolverine. Proc. Helm. Soc. Washington *5*, 14–15.

McIntosh, A. 1940. A new taenioid cestode, *Cladotaenia foxi*, from a falcon. Proc. Helm. Soc. Washington *7*, 71–74.

McIntosh, A. 1941. A new dilepidid cestode, *Catenotaenia linsdalei*, from a pocket gopher in California. Proc. Helm. Soc. Washington *8*, 60–62.

McIntosh, W. C. 1864. Notes on the food and parasites of the *Salmo salar* of the Tay. Proc. Zool. Soc. London (Zool.) 7, 145–154.

McLeod, J. A. 1933. A parasitological survey of the genus *Citellus* in Manitoba. Can. J. Research, Sect. D, Zoological Sciences, *9*, 108–127.

McMullen, D. B. 1936. A note on the staining of the excretory system of trematodes. Trans. Am. Microscop. Soc. *55*, 513–515.

Meggitt, F. J. 1914a. The structure and life-history of a tapeworm (*Ichthyotaenia filicollis* Rud.) parasitic in the stickleback. Proc. Zool. Soc. London, pp. 113–138.

Meggitt, F. J. 1914b. On the anatomy of a fowl tapeworm, *Amoebotaenia sphenoides* v. Linstow. Parasitology 7, 262–277.

Meggitt, F. J. 1915. A new species of tapeworm from a parakeet, *Brotogerys typica*. Parasitology *8*, 42–55.

Meggitt, F. J. 1916. A contribution to our knowledge of the tapeworms of fowls and sparrows. Parasitology *8*, 390–410.

Meggitt, F. J. 1920a. A new species of cestode (*Oochoristica erinacei*) from the hedgehog. Parasitology *12*, 310–313.

Meggitt, F. J. 1920b. A contribution to our knowledge of the tapeworms of poultry. Parasitology *12*, 390–410.

Meggitt, F. J. 1921a. On two new tapeworms from the ostrich, with a key to the species of *Davainea*. Parasitology *13*, 1–24.

Meggitt, F. J. 1921b. On a new cestode from the pouched rat, *Cricetomys gambianum.* Parasitology *13,* 195–204.

Meggitt, F. J. 1924a. Cestodes of mammals. 282 pp. London.

Meggitt, F. J. 1924b. On two new species of Cestoda from a mongoose. Parasitology *16,* 48–54.

Meggitt, F. J. 1924c. On the collection and examination of tapeworms. Parasitology *16,* 266–268.

Meggitt, F. J. 1924d. Tapeworms of the Rangoon pigeon. Parasitology *16,* 303–312.

Meggitt, F. J. 1924e. On the life-history of a reptilian tapeworm (*Sparganum reptans*). Ann. Trop. Med. Parasitol. *18,* 195–204.

Meggitt, F. J. 1924f. On the occurrence of *Ligula ranarum* in a frog. Ann. Mag. Nat. Hist. (Ser. 9) *13,* 216–219.

Meggitt, F. J. 1925. On the life-history of an amphibian tapeworm, *Diphyllobothrium ranarum.* Ann. Mag. Nat. Hist. (Ser. 9) *16,* 654–655.

Meggitt, F. J. 1926a. The tapeworms of the domestic fowl. J. Burma Research Soc. Rangoon *15,* 222–243.

Meggitt, F. J. 1926b. On a collection of Burmese cestodes. Parasitology *18,* 232–237.

Meggitt, F. J. 1927a. A list of cestodes collected in Rangoon during the years 1923–26. J. Burma Research Soc. Rangoon *16,* 200–210.

Meggitt, F. J. 1927b. Remarks on the cestode families Monticelliidae and Ichthyotaeniidae. Ann. Trop. Med. Parasitol. *21,* 69–87.

Meggitt, F. J. 1927c. On cestodes collected in Burma. Parasitology *19,* 141–153.

Meggitt, F. J. 1927d. Report on a collection of cestodes mainly from Egypt. I. Families Anoplocephalidae, Davaineidae. Parasitology *19,* 314–327.

Meggitt, F. J. 1927e. Report on a collection of cestodes mainly from Egypt. II. Cyclophyllidea: family Hymenolepididae. Parasitology *19,* 420–448.

Meggitt, F. J. 1928. Report on a collection of cestodes mainly from Egypt. III. Cyclophyllidea (conclusion); Tetraphyllidea. Parasitology *20,* 315–328.

Meggitt, F. J. 1930. Report on a collection of cestodes mainly from Egypt. IV. Conclusion. Parasitology *22,* 338–345.

Meggitt, F. J. 1931. On cestodes collected in Burma. II. Parasitology *23,* 250–263.

Meggitt, F. J. 1933. Cestodes collected from animals dying in the Calcutta Zoological Gardens during 1931. Records Indian Museum *35,* 145–165.

Meggitt, F. J. 1934a. The theory of host specificity as applied to cestodes. Ann. Trop. Med. Parasitol. *28,* 99–105.

Meggitt, F. J. 1934b. On some tapeworms from the bull snake (*Pityopsis sayi*) with remarks on the species of the genus *Oochoristica* (Cestoda). J. Parasitol. *20,* 182–189.

Meggitt, F. J. 1940. On two tapeworms from a Burmese snake. Ann. Mag. Nat. Hist. (Ser. 11) *5,* 225.

Meggitt, F. J., and Maung Po Saw. 1924. On a new tapeworm from a duck. Ann. Mag. Nat. Hist. *14,* 324–326.

Meggitt, F. J., and K. Subramanian. 1927. The tapeworms of rodents of the subfamily Murinae, with special reference to those occurring in Rangoon. J. Burma Research Soc. Rangoon *17,* 190–237.

Mégnin, P. 1880. De la caducité des crochets et du scolex lui-même chez les ténias. Bull. soc. zool. France *5,* 117–129; Compt. rend. *90,* 715–717; and J. Anat. Physiol. *17* (1881), 27–44.

Mégnin, P. 1883. Notes sur les helminthes rapportés des côtes de la Laponie par M. le professeur Pouchet. Bull. soc. zool. France *8,* 153–156.

Mégnin, P. 1891. Un nouveau ténia du pigeon ou plutôt une espèce douteuse de Rudolphi rehabilitée. Compt. rend. soc. biol. *3,* 751–753.

Mégnin, P. 1899. Un ténia du pigeon ramier (*Palumbus torquatus*), *Davainea bonini* n. sp. Vol. jub. cinquantenaire, soc. biol., pp. 279–281.

Mehlis, E. 1831. Anzeige zu Creplin's Novae observationes de Entozois. Okens Isis, pp. 190–199.

Meier, N. T. 1913. Einige Versuche ueber die Regeneration parasitierender Platodes und deren Zuchtung in künstlichem Medium. Zool. Anz. *42,* 481–487.

Meijer, W. C. P. 1933. *Cysticercus cellulosae* bij den hond. Nederlandsch.-Indische Bladen voor Diergeneeskunde en Dierenteelt. *45*, 135–137.

Meijer, W. C. P., and Sahar (no initials). 1934. Over een lintworm van den hond, *Diphyllobothrium raillieti* Ratz, en het bijbehoorende plerocercoid, *Sparganum raillieti* Ratz, van het varken. Nederlandsch.-Indische Bladen voor Geneeskunde en Dierenteelt. *46*, 1–12.

Meinkoth, N. A. 1947. Notes on the life-cycle and taxonomic position of *Haplobothrium globuliforme* Cooper, a tapeworm of *Amia calva* L. Trans. Am. Microscop. Soc. *66*, 256–261.

Meissner, G. 1854. Zur Entwicklungsgeschichte und Anatomie der Bandwürmer. Z. wiss. Zool. *5*, 380–391.

Meixner, J. 1926. Beitrag zur Morphologie und zum System der Turbellaria-Rhabdocoela. II. Ueber *Typhlorhynchus nanus* Laidlaw und die parasitischen Rhabdocoelen nebst Nachträgen zu den Calyptorhynchia. Z. Morph. Okol. Tiere *5*, 577–624.

Melnikow, N. F. 1869. Ueber die Jugendzustände der *Taenia cucumerina*. Arch. Naturgeschichte *35*, 62–69.

Mendelsohn, W. 1933. Cultural characteristics of cysticercus cysts and two cysticercus tumours. Am. J. Cancer *17*, 442–461.

Mendelsohn, W. 1934. The malignant cells of two crocker cysticercus sarcomata. Am. J. Cancer *21*, 571–580.

Mendelsohn, W. 1935. A method for the cultivation under sterile conditions of the larvae of *Taenia crassicollis*. J. Parasitol. *21*, 417.

Menon, T. B., and G. D. Veliath. 1940. Tissue reactions to *Cysticercus cellulosae* in man. Trans. Roy. Soc. Trop. Med. Hyg. *33*, 537–544.

Messineo, E., and D. Calamida. 1901. Ueber das Gift der Taenien. Centralbl. Bakt. Parasitenk. *30*, 346–347.

Metchnikow, E. 1869. Entwicklungsgeschichtliche Beiträge. Bull. acad. imp. sci. St. Petersbourg *13*, 284–300.

Meyner, R. 1895. Anatomie und Histologie zweier neuer Tänien Arten des Subgenus *Bertia*. Inaugural dissertation, Univ. Leipzig, and Z. Naturwiss. *68*, 1–106.

Michajlow, W. 1932a. *Triaenophorus crassus* Forel (*T. robustus* Olsson) et son développement. Ann. parasitol. humaine et comparée *10*, 257–270.

Michajlow, W. 1932b. Les adaptations graduelles des copépodes comme premiers hôtes intermédiares de *Triaenophorus nodulosus* (Pall.). Ann. parasitol. humaine et comparée *10*, 334–344.

Michajlow, W. 1933a. Les stades larvaires de *Triaenophorus nodulosus* (Pall.). Ann. parasitol. humaine et comparée *11*, 339–358.

Michajlow, W. 1933b. Sur les stades larvaires de *Triaenophorus nodulosus* (Pall.). Le procercoïde. Compt. rend. acad. polon. sci. lettre. Classe sci. math. nat. No. 6, p. 8.

Miller, H. M., Jr. 1930. Experiments on immunity of the white rat to *Cysticercus fasciolaris*. Proc. Soc. Exp. Biol. Med. *27*, 926–927.

Miller, H. M., Jr. 1932a. Superinfection of cats with *Taenia taeniaeformis*. J. Prev. Med. *6*, 17–29.

Miller, H. M., Jr. 1932b. Further studies on immunity to a metazoan parasite, *Cysticercus fasciolaris*. J. Prev. Med. *6*, 37–46.

Miller, H. M., Jr. 1932c. Transmission to offspring of immunity against infection with metazoan (cestode) parasite. Proc. Soc. Exp. Biol. Med. *29*, 1124.

Miller, H. M., Jr. 1932d. Acquired immunity against a metazoan parasite by use of non-specific worm materials. Proc. Soc. Exp. Biol. Med. *29*, 1125–1126.

Miller, H. M., Jr. 1932e. Therapeutic effect of specific immune serum against a metazoan parasite (*Cysticercus fasciolaris*). Preliminary paper. Proc. Soc. Exp. Biol. Med. *30*, 82–83.

Miller, H. M., Jr. 1934. Specific immune serums as inhibitors of infections of a metazoan parasite (*Cysticercus fasciolaris*). Am. J. Hyg. *19*, 270–277.

Miller, H. M., Jr., and C. W. Dawley. 1927. Some effects of *Cysticercus fasciolaris* on the white rat. Read before Am. Soc. Parasitologists Dec. 1927, abstr. J. Parasitol. *14*, 122.

Miller, H. M., Jr., and M. L. Gardiner. 1932a. Protection of the rat against infection with a larval tapeworm by serum from immune rats. Proc. Soc. Exp. Biol. Med. *29*, 779–780.

Miller, H. M., Jr., and M. L. Gardiner. 1932b. Passive immunity to infection with a larval tapeworm of the albino rat. Science *75*, 270.

Miller, H. M., Jr., and M. L. Gardiner. 1932c. Passive immunity to infection with a metazoan parasite, *Cysticercus fasciolaris*, in the albino rat. J. Prev. Med. *6*, 479–496.

Miller, H. M., Jr., and M. L. Gardiner. 1934. Further studies on passive immunity to a metazoan parasite, *Cysticercus fasciolaris*. Am. J. Hyg. *20*, 424–431.

Miller, H. M., Jr., and K. B. Kerr. 1932. Attempts to immunise rabbits against a larval cestode, *Cysticercus pisiformis*. Proc. Soc. Exp. Biol. Med. *29*, 670–671.

Miller, H. M., Jr., and E. Massie. 1932. Persistence of acquired immunity to *Cysticercus fasciolaris* after removal of the worms. J. Prev. Med. *6*, 31–36.

Miller, J. N., and W. P. Bunner. 1942. The effect of mutilation on the tapeworm *Taenia taeniaeformis*. Ohio State J. Sci. *42*, 117–121.

Miller, R. B. 1943–1945. Studies on cestodes of the genus *Triaenophorus* from fish of Lesser Slave Lake, Alberta. Can. J. Research, Sect. D, Zoological Sciences.

1943a. I. Introduction and the life of *Triaenophorus crassus* Forel and *T. nodulosus* (Pallas) in the definitive host, *Esox lucius*. *21*, 160–170.

1943b. II. The eggs, coracidia and life in the first intermediate host of *Triaenophorus crassus* Forel and *T. nodulosus* (Pallas). *21*, 284–291.

1945a. III. Notes on *Triaenophorus nodulosus* (Pallas) in the second intermediate host. *23*, 1–5.

1945b. IV. The life of *Triaenophorus crassus* Forel in the second intermediate host. *23*, 105–115.

1945c. V. Description and life history of *Triaenophorus stizostedionis* n. sp. *23*, 117–127.

Miller, R. B. 1944. Suggestions for experiments in the control of the pike-whitefish tapeworm, *Triaenophorus crassus*. Rep. Fish. Branch Dept. Lands and Mines, Province of Alberta (Canada). June 1944.

Miller, R. B. 1945d. Effect of *Triaenophorus* on growth of two fishes. J. Fish. Research Bd. Canada *6*, 334–337.

Miller, R. B. 1946. The life-history of the pike-whitefish tapeworm, *Triaenophorus crassus*. Rep. Fish. Branch Dept. Lands and Mines, Province of Alberta (Canada). March 1945 (published 1946).

Millzner, T. M. 1926. On the cestode genus *Dipylidium* from cats and dogs. Univ. Calif. Publ. Zool. *28*, 317–356.

Minckert, W. 1905. Mittheilungen zur Histologie der Cestoden. I. Ueber Epithel verhältnisse und Struktur der Körpercuticula. Zool. Anz. *29*, 401–408.

Misra, V. R. 1945. On a new species of the genus *Oochoristica* from the intestine of *Calotes versicolor*. Proc. Indian Acad. Sci. Sect. B, *22*, 1–5.

Mlodzianowska, B. 1931. Ueber die jungsten Entwicklungsstadien von *Cysticercus fasciolaris* Rud., der Larve von *Taenia taeniaeformis* Bloch, auf Grund von experimentelle Untersuchungen. Bull. intern. acad. polon. sci. *11*.

Moghe, M. A. 1925a. *Caryophyllaeus indicus* n. sp. (Cestoda) from the catfish (*Clarias batrachus* Bl.). Parasitology *17*, 232–235.

Moghe, M. A. 1925b. A new species of *Monopylidium*, *M. chandleri*, from the red-nettled lapwing (*Sarcogrammus indicus* Stoliczkad), with a key to the species of *Monopylidium*. Parasitology *17*, 385–400.

Moghe, M. A. 1925c. Two new species of cestodes from Indian Columbidae. Records Indian Museum *27*, 431–437.

Moghe, M. A. 1926a. Two new species of cestodes from Indian lizards. Records Indian Museum *28*, 53–60.

Mohge, M. A. 1926b. A contribution to the cestode fauna of India. Privately printed. Pp. 1–13. Nagpur.

Moghe, M. A. 1926c. A supplementary note on *Monopylidium chandleri* and other related species. Parasitology *18*, 267–268.

Moghe, M. A. 1931. A supplementary description of *Lytocestus indicus* Moghe (syn. *Caryophyllaeus indicus* Moghe, 1925), Cestoda. Parasitology *23*, 84–87.

Moghe, M. A. 1933. Four new species of avian cestodes from India. Parasitology *25*, 333–341.

Moghe, M. A., and N. B. Inamdar. 1934. Some new species of avian cestodes from India, with a description of *Biuterina intricata* (Krabbe, 1882). Records Indian Museum *36*, 7–16.

Mola, P. 1903. Su di un cestode del *Carcharodon rondoletii* M. Hle. Arch. zool. Napoli *1*, 345–366.

Mola, P. 1906. Di alcuni specie poco studiate o mal noti di cestodi. Annuairio del musei zoologico della R. Univ. di Napoli (N. S.) *2*, 1–12.

Mola, P. 1907a. La ventosa apicale a che e omologa. Zool. Anz. *30*, 37–44.

Mola, P. 1907b. Sopra la *Davainea circumvallata* Krabbe. Zool. Anz. *30*, 126–130.

Mola, P. 1907c. Les organes genitaux de *Taenia nigropunctata* Crety et en particulier l'organe paruterin. Compt. rend. *145*, 87–90.

Mola, P. 1907d. Di un nuovo cestode del genero *Davainea* Blanch. Biol. Zentr. *17*, 575–578.

Mola, P. 1907e. Un nuovo elminto della *Gallinula chloropus*. Bull. acad. roy. Belg. *64*, 886–898.

Mola, P. 1907f. Ueber eine neue Cestodenform. Centralbl. Bakt. Parasitenk. *44*, 256–260.

Mola, P. 1907g. Nota intorno ad una fauna de cestodi di pesce fluviatili. Boll. soc. zool. Ital. *8*, 67–73.

Mola, P. 1908a. *Choanotaenia infundibulum* Bloch. Inst. zool. anat. reale univ. Sasseri, pp. 167–177.

Mola, P. 1908b. Due nuova forme di Tetraphyllidae. Boll. soc. adriat. sci. nat. *24*, 1–16.

Mola, P. 1912. *Davainea pluriuncinata* (Crety) e sinonima della *D. circumvallata* Krabbe. Arch. Parasitol. *15*, 432–441.

Mola, P. 1913. Nuovi ospitti di uccelli. Contributo al genero *Hymenolepis*. Biol. Zentr. *33*, 208–222.

Mola, P. 1919. Cestodes avium. Contributo alla fauna elmintologica Sarda. Arch. Parasitol. *22*, 577–578.

Mola, P. 1921. Une nuova classifica di cestodi. 10 pp. Sassari.

Mola, P. 1927. Vi e sinonima tra *Davainea bothrioplitis* (Piana) e *Davainea echinobothrida* (Megnin). Studi Sassaresi *5*, 487–491.

Mola, P. 1928a. Vermi parassiti dell' Ittiofauna italiana. Contributo all patologia ittica. Boll. di pesca, di piscicoltura e di idrobiologia. Anno 4, fasc. 4, 48 pp.

Mola, P. 1928b. Per una nuova classifica dei cestodi. 22 pp. Sasseri.

Mola, P. 1929a. Il nuovo genero *Viscoia* Mola, 1929 (Nota). Studi Sassaresi 7.

Mola, P. 1929b. Descriptio platodorum sine existis. Zool. Anz. *86*, 101–113.

Molin, R. 1857. Notizie elmintologiche. Atti reale ist. Veneto sci. Pt. 2. *16* (1856–1857), 146–152, 216–233.

Molin, R. 1858. Prospectus helminthum quae in prodromo faunae helminthologicae venetae continentur. Sitzber. Akad. Wiss. Wien Math. naturw. Classe Abt. I. *30*, 127–158.

Molin, R. 1859a. Cephalocotylia e nematoidea. Sitzber. Akad. Wiss. Wien Math. naturw. Classe Abt. I. *38*, 7–38.

Molin, R. 1859b. Prospectus helminthum quae in parti secunda prodromi faunae helminthologicae venetae continentur. Sitzber. Akad. Wiss. Wien Math. naturw. Classe Abt. I. *38*, 287–302.

Molin, R. 1860. Prodromus faunae helminthologicae venetae. Denkschr. Akad. Wiss. Wien Math. naturw. Classe Abt. II. *18*, 230–233.

Molin, R. 1861. Prodromus faunae helminthologicae venetae adjestic disquisitionibus anatomicis et criticis. Denkschr. Akad. Wiss. Wien Math. naturw. Classe Abt. II. *19*, 189–338.

Moll, A. M. 1917. Animal parasites of rats at Madison, Wisconsin. J. Parasitol. *4*, 89–90.

Moniez, R. 1877. Sur l'embryogénie des cestoïdes. Compt. rend. *85*, 974–976.

Moniez, R. 1879a. Note sur le *Taenia Krabbei* espèce nouvelle de Taenia armé. Bull. scientifique département du Nord, Lille (2me sér.) *2*, 61–163.

Moniez, R. 1879b. Note sur deux espèces nouvelles de Ténies inermés. Bull. scientifique département du Nord, Lille (2me sér.) *2*, 163–164.

Moniez, R. 1879c. Note sur le *Taenia Giardi* et sur quelques espèces du groupe inermés. Compt. rend. *88*, 1094–1096.

Moniez, R. 1879d. Note sur l'histologie des Tétrarhynques. Bull. scientifique département du Nord, Lille (2me sér.) *2*, 393–398.

Moniez, R. 1880a. Essai monographique sur les cysticerques. Travaux de l'institut zoologique de Lille de la station maritime de Wimereux, Paris *3* (1), 1–190.

Moniez, R. 1880b. Etudes sur les cestodes. Bull. scientifique department du Nord, Lille (2me sér.) *3* (6), 240–246; *3* (9), 356–358.

Moniez, R. 1880c. Note sur les vaisseaux de l'*Abothrium gadi*. Bull. scientifique department du Nord, Lille (2me sér.) *3* (9), 448.

Moniez, R. 1881. Mémoires sur les cestodes. Travaux de l'institut zoologique de Lille et de la station maritime de Wimereux, Paris *3*, 1–238.

Moniez, R. 1882. Sur quelques types de cestodes. Compt. rend. *154*, 661–663.

Moniez, R. 1889. Sur la larve du *Taenia Grimaldii* n. sp., parasite du dauphin. Rev. biol. Nord France *2*, 825–827.

Moniez, R. 1891a. Note sur les helminthes. Rev. biol. Nord France *4*, 22–34, 65–79, 108–118.

Moniez, R. 1891b. Le *Gymnorhynchus reptans* Rud. et sa migration. Compt. rend. *112*, 669–672; *113*, 870–871.

Moniez, R. 1892a. Note sur les helminthes. Rev. biol. Nord France *5*, 25–26.

Moniez, R. 1892b. Note sur les helminthes. Rev. biol. Nord France *5*, 150–151.

Mönnig, H. O. 1926a. Three new helminths. Trans. Roy. Soc. South Africa *13*, 291–298.

Mönnig, H. O. 1926b. Helminthological notes. The anatomy and life-history of the fowl tapeworm (*Amoebotaenia sphenoides*). 11th and 12th Reports, Dir. Vet. Educ. Research, Union South Africa. Pretoria. Pp. 199–206.

Mönnig, H. O. 1928. Check list of the worm parasites of domesticated animals in South Africa. 13th and 14th Reports, Dir. Vet. Educ. Research, Union South Africa. Pretoria. Pp. 801–837.

Mönnig, H. O. 1934. Veterinary helminthology and entomology. xvi + 404 pp. London.

Monticelli, F. S. 1888a. Contribuzioni allo studio della fauna elmintologica del Golfo di Napoli. I. Ricerche sulle *Scolex polymorphus* Rud. Mitt. zool. Stat. Neapel *8*, 85–152.

Monticelli, F. S. 1888b. Intorno allo *Scolex polymorphus* Rud. Boll. soc. nat. Napoli *2*, 13–16.

Monticelli, F. S. 1889a. Notes on some Entozoa in the collection of the British Museum. Proc. Zool. Soc. London, pp. 321–325.

Monticelli, F. S. 1889b. Elenco degli Elminti raccolti del Capitano G. Chierchia durante il viaggio di circumnavigazione della R. corvetta "Vettor Pisani." Boll. soc. nat. Napoli *3*, 67–71.

Monticelli, F. S. 1889c. *Gyrocotyle* Diesing, *Amphiptyches* Grube et Wagener. Nota preliminare. Atti reale accad. Lincei Classe sci. fis. mat. e nat. Rend. adunanza solenne *5*, 228–230.

Monticelli, F. S. 1889d. Sul sistema nervosi dell' *Amphiptyches*. Zool. Anz. *12*, 142–144.

Monticelli, F. S. 1890a. Note elmintologiche. Boll. soc. nat. Napoli *4*, 189–208.

Monticelli, F. S. 1890b. Alcuni considerazioni biologichi sul genere *Gyrocotyle*. Atti soc. ital. sci. nat. Milano *32*, 327–329.

Monticelli, F. S. 1890c. Elenco degli elminti studiati a Wimereux nella primavera del 1889. Bull. sci. France Belg. *22*, 417–444.

Monticelli, F. S. 1891. Un mot de reponse à Monsieur Loennberg. Bull. sci. France Belg. *23*, 353–357.

Monticelli, F. S. 1892a. Notizie su di alcuni specie di Taenia. Boll. soc. nat. Napoli *5*, 151–174.

Monticelli, F. S. 1892b. Appunti sui Cestodaria. Atti accad. sci. fis. mat. e nat. Napoli *5*, 1–11.

Monticelli, F. S. 1892c. Sulla cosidetta subcuticola dei Cestoda. Rend. accad. sci. fis. mat. e nat. Napoli *6*, 158–166.

Monticelli, F. S. 1892d. Nota intorno a due forme di Cestodi. Boll. mus. zool. anat. comp. univ. Torino *7*, 1–9.

Monticelli, F. S. 1892e. Sul genere *Bothrimonus* Duv. e proposte per una classificazione dei Cestodi. Monit. zool. ital. *3*, 100–158.

Monticelli, F. S. 1893. Intorno ad alcuni elminti della collezione del museo zoologico del la reale universite de Palermo. Il naturaliste siciliano, Palermo *12*, 167–180.

Monticelli, F. S. 1899. Sul *Tetrabothrium Gerrardii* Baird. Atti soc. mat. e nat. Modena (Ser. 4) Ann. 32, *1*, 9–26.

Monticelli, F. S., and C. Crety. 1891. Ricerche intorno alla sottofamiglia Solenophorinae Montic. Crety. Mem. reale accad. sci. Torino *31*, 381–402.

Moore, J. T. 1914. *Sparganum mansoni,* first reported American case. Am. J. Trop. Diseases *2*.

Moore, W. 1915. Rate of growth of the beef tapeworm in human beings. J. Parasitol. *2*, 96.

Morell, A. 1895. Anatomisch-histologische Studien an Vogeltänien. Arch. Naturgeschichte *61*, 81–102.

Morenas, L. 1932. Utilisation du liquide de cysticerque (*Cysticercus tenuicollis*) comme antigène dans la réaction de Casoni. Compt. rend. soc. biol. *110*, 321–322.

Morenas, L. 1933. Considérations sur le diagnostic biologique de la cysticercose cérébrale. Lyon Medical *151*, 636–637.

Morgan, B. B., and E. F. Waller. 1940. Severe parasitism in a raccoon (*Procyon lotor lotor* Linnaeus). Trans. Am. Microscop. Soc. *59*, 523–547.

Morse, M. 1911. Cestode cells in vitro. Science *24*, 770–772.

Motomura, I. 1929. On the early development of the monozoic cestode *Archigetes appendiculatus,* including the oögenesis and fertilisation. Annot. Zool. Japonenses *12*, 109–129.

Mrazek, A. 1890. O. cysticerkoidech nasich koryžu gladkovuduič̌h. Vestnik Ceskoslov. Akad. Zemedelske (Bulletin of the Czechoslovak Academy of Agriculture) *1*, 226–248.

Mrazek, A. 1891. Recherches sur le développement de quelques Ténias des oiseaux (in Czech with French summary). Vestnik Ceskoslov. Akad. Zemedelske *1*, 97–131.

Mrazek, A. 1896. Zur Entwicklungsgeschichte einiger Tänien (German summary). Vestnik Kralovske Ceske spolecnosti nauk *2*, 1–16.

Mrazek, A. 1897. *Archigetes appendiculatus* Ratz. Vestnik Kralovske Ceske spolecnosti nauk *3*, 1–47.

Mrazek, A. 1901a. Ueber die Larve von *Caryophyllaeus mutabilis* Rud. Centralbl. Bakt. Parasitenk. *29*, 485–491.

Mrazek, A. 1901b. Ueber das Verhalten der Langsnerven bei *Abothrium rectangulum* Rud. Centralbl. Bakt. Parasitenk. *29*, 569–571.

Mrazek, A. 1907. Cestodenstudien. I. Cysticercoiden aus *Lumbriculus variegatus.* Zool. Jahrb. Syst. *24*, 591–624.

Mrazek, A. 1908. Ueber ein neuer Art der Gattung *Archigetes.* Vorläufige Mitteilung. Centralbl. Bakt. Parasitenk. *46*, 719–223.

Mrazek, A. 1916. Cestodenstudien. II. Die morphologische Bedeutung der Cestodenlarven. Zool. Jahrb. Anat. *39*, 515–584.

Mrazek, A. 1927. Organisace a ontogenie larvy druhu *Tatria acanthorhyncha* (Wedl.) (Anatomy and ontogeny of the larva of *Tatra acanthorhyncha* Cestoda.) Vestnik Kralovske Ceske spolecnosti nauk, 1926, pp. 1–12.

Mueller, J. F. 1927. Two new species of the cestode genus *Mesocestoides.* Trans. Am. Microscop. Soc. *46*, 294.

Mueller, J. F. 1928. The genus *Mesocestoides* in mammals. Zool. Jahrb. Syst. Okol. *55*, 403–418.

Mueller, J. F. 1930. Cestodes of the genus *Mesocestoides* from the opossum and the cat. Am. Midland Naturalist *12*, 81–90.

Mueller, J. F. 1935. A *Diphyllobothrium* from cats and dogs in the Syracuse region. J. Parasitol. *21*, 114–120.

Mueller, J. F. 1936. Comparative studies on certain species of *Diphyllobothrium*. J. Parasitol. *22*, 471–478.

Mueller, J. F. 1937a. Spargana in *Natrix*. Science *85*, 519–520.

Mueller, J. F. 1937b. A repartition of the genus *Diphyllobothrium*. J. Parasitol. *23*, 308–310.

Mueller, J. F. 1937c. New host records for *Diphyllobothrium mansonoides* Mueller, 1935. J. Parasitol. *23*, 313–315.

Mueller, J. F. 1937d. The hosts of *Diphyllobothrium mansonoides* (Cestoda: Diphyllobothriidae). Proc. Helm. Soc. Washington *4*, 68.

Mueller, J. F. 1938a. The life history of *Diphyllobothrium mansonoides* Mueller, 1935, and some considerations with regard to sparganosis in the United States. Am. J. Trop. Med. *18*, 41–66.

Mueller, J. F. 1938b. Studies on *Sparganum mansonoides* and *Sparganum proliferum*. Am. J. Trop. Med. *18*, 303–328.

Mueller, J. F. 1938c. An additional species of *Diphyllobothrium* (subgenus *Spirometra*) from the United States. Livro Jubilar Prof. Travassos Rio de Janeiro, Brasil, III, pp. 337–341.

Mueller, J. F., and O. D. Chapman. 1937. Resistance and immunity reactions in infections with *Sparganum mansonoides*. J. Parasitol. *23*, 561–562.

Mueller, J. F., and F. Coulston. 1941. Experimental human infection with the *Sparganum* larva of *Spirometra mansonoides* (Mueller, 1935). Am. J. Trop. Med. *21*, 399–425.

Mueller, J. F., and F. Goldstein. 1939. Experimental human infection with *Sparganum mansonoides* (Mueller, 1935). J. Parasitol. *25* Suppl., 31–32.

Mueller, O. F. 1776. Zoologicae Danicae . . . xxxii + 282 pp. Havniae.

Mueller, O. F. 1780. Vom Bandwürmern. Naturforscher, Halle, *14*, 129–203.

Mueller, O. F. 1782. Vom Bandwurme des Stichlings und vom milchtigten Plattwurme. Naturforscher, Halle, *18*, 21–37.

Mueller, O. F. 1787. Verzeichniss der bisher entdeckten Eingeweidewürmer der Thiere . . . Naturforscher, Halle, *22*, 33–86.

Mueller, O. F. 1788. Zoologicae Danicae . . . I, 52 pp. II, 56 pp. Havniae.

Mühling, P. 1898. Die Helminthen-Fauna der Wirbeltiere Ostpreussens. Arch. Naturgeschichte, 1898, 118 pp.

Muñoz Fernández, E., and R. Saucedo Aranda. 1945. Accion intestinal de cestodes. Rev. Iberica Parasitol. Volume extraordinary, pp. 312–315.

Murie, J. 1870. On a probably new species of *Taenia* from the rhinoceros. Proc. Zool. Soc. London, pp. 608–610.

Nagaty, H. F. 1929. An account of the anatomy of certain cestodes of the genera *Stilesia* and *Avitellina*. Ann. Trop. Med. Parasitol. *23*, 349–380.

Narihara, N. 1937a. Studies on the post-embryonal development of *Hymenolepis diminuta*. I. On the hatching of the eggs (in Japanese, with English summary, pp. 730–731). Taiwan Igakkai Zasshi *36*, 713–729.

Narihara, N. 1937b. Studies on the post-embryonal development of *Hymenolepis diminuta*. II. On the development of the cysticercoid within the definitive host (in Japanese, with English summary, pp. 780–784). Taiwan Igakkai Zasshi *36*, 732–780.

Neslobinsky, N. 1911a. Zur Kenntnis der Vogeltaenien Mittelrusslands. Centralbl. Bakt. Parasitenk. *57*, 436–442.

Neslobinsky, N. 1911b. *Dilepis brachyarthra* Chol. und *Dilepis undulata* Schr. Centralbl. Bakt. Parasitenk. *59*, 416–417.

Neumann, L. G. 1888. Traité des maladies parasitaires non-bacteriennes des animaux domestiques. 2nd ed. 1892. 673 pp. Paris.

Neumann, L. G. 1891. Observations sur les Ténias du mouton. Compt. rend. soc. hist. nat. Toulouse *24*, 6–9.

Neumann, L. G. 1892. Sur la place de *Taenia ovilla* Riv. dans la classification. Compt. rend. soc. hist. nat. Toulouse *26*, 12–14.

Neumann, L. G. 1896. Note sur les téniadés du chien et du chat. Mém. soc. zool. France 9, 171–184.

Neumüller (no initials). 1932. *Echinococcus granulosus* (*Taenia echinococcus*) beim Fuchs, ein Beitrag zur Entstehung der Hülsenwurmkrankheit. Z. Fleisch. u. Milchhyg. *43*, 3–4.

Neveu Lemaire, M. 1912. Parasitologie des animaux domestiques. Paris.

Neveu Lemaire, M. 1936. Traité d'helminthologie médicale et vétérinaire. Paris.

Newton, M. V. B. 1932. The biology of *Triaenophorus tricuspidatus* (Bloch, 1779) in western Canada. Contrib. Can. Biol. Fish. 7, 341–360.

Nice, S. J. 1949. Improved methods of activating tapeworm embryos. Bios *20*, 128–133.

Nicholson, D. 1928. Fish tapeworm; intestinal infection in man; the infestation in Manitoba lakes. Can. Med. Ass. J. *19*, 25–33.

Nicholson, D. 1932a. The *Triaenophorus* parasite in the flesh of the tullibee (*Leucichthys*). Can. J. Research, Sect. D, *6*, 162–165.

Nicholson, D. 1932b. *Diphyllobothrium* infection in *Esox lucius*. Can. J. Research, Sect. D, *6*, 166–170.

Nickerson, W. S. 1906. The broad tapeworm in Minnesota, with the report of a case of infection acquired in the state. J. Am. Med. Ass. *46*, 711–713.

Nicoll, W. 1907. A contribution towards a knowledge of the Entozoa of British marine fishes. Part I. Ann. Mag. Nat. Hist. (Ser. 7) *19*.

Nicoll, W. 1909. A contribution towards a knowledge of the Entozoa of British marine fishes. Part II. Ann. Mag. Nat. Hist. (Ser. 8) *4*, 1–25.

Nicoll, W. 1910. On the Entozoa of fishes from the Firth of Clyde. Parasitology *3*, 322–356.

Nicoll, W. 1913. Recent progress in our knowledge of parasitic worms. Parasitology *6*, 141–152.

Niemec, J. 1885. Recherches sur le système nerveux des Taenias. Rec. zool. Suisse *2*, 589–648.

Niemec, J. 1888. Untersuchungen ueber das Nervensystem der Cestoden. Arb. zool. Inst. Wien 7, 1–60.

Nigrelli, R. F. 1938. Parasites of the swordfish, *Xiphias gladius* Linnaeus. Am. Museum Novitates, No. 996. 16 pp.

Nitsche, H. 1873. Untersuchungen ueber den Bau der Tänien. Z. wiss. Zool. *23*, 181–197.

Nitzsch, C. L. 1820. *Acanthocephalus.* In J. S. Ersch und J. G. Gruber, Allgemeine Encyclopaedie der Wissenschaften und Künste. Bd. 4, pp. 258–259. Leipzig.

Nitzsch, C. L. 1824. *Bothriocephalus.* In J. S. Ersch und J. G. Gruber, Allgemeine Encyclopaedie der Wissenschaften und Künste. Bd. 12, pp. 94–99. Leipzig.

Nordmann, A. von. 1832. Micrographische Beiträge zur Naturgeschichte der wirbellosen Thiere. Heft 1, x + 118 pp. Heft 2, xvi +150 pp. Berlin.

Nordmann, A. von. 1840. Histoire des vers (Vermes). In Histoire naturelle des animaux sans vertébrés de J. B. P. A. de Lamarck. 2nd ed. T. III, pp. 542–686. Paris.

Northrop, J. H. 1926. The resistance of living organisms to digestion by pepsin and trypsin. J. Gen. Physiol., Baltimore, *9*, 497–502.

Nosik, A. F. 1940. Epizootology, diagnosis and treatment of *Echinococcus* in dogs (in Russian). Sovetskaya Veterinariya No. 4, pp. 37–40.

Nunez, J. O., and M. C. Lopez. 1934. Investigaciones sobre la intradermoreaccion aplicada al diagnostico de la equinococcosis. Anales de medecine intern. *3*, 609–615.

Nybelin, O. 1914. Notizen ueber Cestoden. I. Ueber *Progynotaenia odhneri* einen neuen Vogelcestoden aus Schweden. Zool. Bidrag. Uppsala *3*, 225–228.

Nybelin, O. 1916. Neue Tetrabothriiden aus Vögeln. Zool. Anz. *47*, 297–301.

Nybelin, O. 1917. Australische Cestoden. Results of D. E. Mjoeberg's Swedish Scientific Expeditions to Australia, 1910–1913. Kgl. Svenska Vetenskapsakad. Handl. 52, No. 14. 48 pp.

Nybelin, O. 1918a. Zur Frage der Entwicklungsgeschichte einiger Bothriocephaliden. Göteborgs Kgl. Vetenskapsakad. Handl. *19.*

Nybelin, O. 1918b. Zur Anatomie und systematischen Stellung von "Tetrabothrium norvegicum" Olsson. Göteborgs Kgl. Vetenskapsakad. Handl. *20,* 25 pp.

Nybelin, O. 1919. Zur Entwicklungsgeschichte von *Schistocephalus solidus.* Centralbl. Bakt. Parasitenk. *83,* 295–297.

Nybelin, O. 1922. Anatomisch.-systematischen Studien ueber Pseudophyllidien. Göteborgs Kgl. Vetenskapsakad. Handl. *26,* 169–211.

Nybelin, O. 1927. *Anoplocephala gorillae.* Arkiv. Zoolog. *19.*

Nybelin, O. 1928. Zwei neue Cestoden aus Bartelwalen. Zool. Anz. *78,* 309–314.

Nybelin, O. 1931. Säugetier- und Vogelcestoden von Juan Fernandez. Nat. Hist. Juan Fernandez and Easter Island. Ed. Dr. Carl Skottsberg, Uppsala. Vol. 3, Zool., pp. 493–524.

Nybelin, O. 1942. Zur Helminthfauna der Süsswasserfische Schwedens. II. Die Cestoden des Welses. Göteborgs Kgl. Vetenskapsakad. Handl. Ser. B, *1,* 1–24.

Obersteiner, W. 1914. Ueber eine neue Cestodenform *Bilocularia hyperapolytica* nov. gen. nov. spec. aus *Centrophorus granulosus.* Arb. zool. Inst. Univ. Wien *20,* 109–124.

Obitz, K. 1934. Recherches sur les oeufs de quelques Anoplocephalides. Ann. parasitol. humaine et comparée *12,* 40–55.

Odhner, T. 1889. Zur morphologischen und phylogenetischen Beurtheilung des Bandwurmkörpers. Arb. zool. Inst. Univ. Wien *8.*

Odhner, T. 1894. Beiträge zur Phylogenie der Plathelminthen. Centralbl. Bakt. Parasitenk. *21.*

Odhner, T. 1904. *Urogonoporus armatus* Lühe, 1901, die reife Proglottiden von *Trilocularia gracilis* Olsson, 1869. Arch. Parasitol. *8,* 465–471.

Odhner, T. 1912, 1913. Die Homologien der weiblichen Genitalwege bei den Trematoden und Cestoden . . . Zool. Anz. *39,* 337–351.

Oelkers, L. 1889. Ueber das Vorkommen von Quexsilber in den Bandwürmern eines mit Quexsilber behandelten Syphilitikers. Ber. deutsche chem. Ges. *22,* 3316–3317.

Oerley, L. 1885a. A Czapaknak es Rajanak belfergi. (The entozoa of skates and rays.) Termeszetrajzi fuzetek Budapest *9,* 97–126.

Oerley, L. 1885b. Die Entozoen der Haie und Rochen. Termeszetrajzi fuzetek Budapest *9,* 216–220.

Oesterlin, M., and T. von Brand. 1933. Chemizische Eigenschaften des Polysaccharides einiger Würmer, und der Oxyfettsauren von *Moniezia expansa.* Z. vergl. Physiol. *20.*

Ohira, T. 1935. On the active immunisation of animals against tapeworms. Trans. 9th Congress Far Eastern Association of Tropical Medicine *1,* 601–604.

Okumura, T. 1919. An experimental study of the life history of *Sparganum mansoni* Cobbold (a preliminary report). Kitasato Arch. Exp. Med. *3,* 190–197.

Oldham, J. N. 1929. On *Hymenolepis sinensis* n. sp., a cestode from the grey sandhamster (*Cricetulus griseus*). J. Helm. 7, 235–246.

Oldham, J. N. 1930. The helminth parasites of marsupials. Imp. Bur. Agr. Parasitol. Notes and Memoranda No. 10. 62 pp. Repr. from J. Helm. *8.*

Oldham, J. N. 1931a. On the arthropod intermediate hosts of *Hymenolepis diminuta* (Rudolphi, 1819). J. Helm. *9,* 21–28.

Oldham, J. N. 1931b. The helminth parasites of common rats. J. Helm. *9,* 49–90.

Oldham, J. N. 1931c. Hand-list of helminth parasites of the rabbit. Imp. Bur. Agr. Parasitol. Notes and Memoranda No. 2. 12 pp. Repr. from J. Helm.

Oldham, J. N. 1931d. The helminth parasites of deer. Imp. Bur. Agr. Parasitol. Notes and Memoranda No. 4. 248 pp. Repr. from J. Helm.

Olsen, O. W. 1930. *Deltokeras multilobatus,* a new species of cestode (Paruterinae, Dilepididae) from the twelve-wired bird of paradise (*Selucides melanoleucus* Daudin, Passeriformes). Zoologica (New York Zoological Society) *24.*

Olsen, O. W. 1937a. A new species of cestode, *Dendrouterina nycticoracis* (Dilepididae) from the black-crowned night heron (*Nycticorax nycticorax hoacti* [Gmelin]). Proc. Helm. Soc. Washington *4,* 30–32.

Olsen, O. W. 1937b. A new species of cestode, *Dendrouterina lintoni* (Dilepididae) from the little green heron (*Butorides virescens* [Linn.]). Proc. Helm. Soc. Washington *4*, 72–75.

Olsen, O. W. 1938. Anoplocephaliasis in Minnesota horses. J. Am. Vet. Med. Ass. *92*, 557–559.

Olsen, O. W. 1939a. The cysticercoid of the tapeworm, *Dendrouterina nycticoracis* Olsen, 1937 (Dilepididae). Proc. Helm. Soc. Washington *6*, 20–21.

Olsen, O. W. 1939b. Schizotaeniasis in muskrats. J. Parasitol. *25*, 279.

Olsen, O. W. 1939c. *Tatria duodecacantha,* a new species of cestode (Amabiliidae Braun, 1910) from the pied-billed grebe (*Podilymbus podiceps podiceps* [Linn.]). J. Parasitol. *25*, 495–499.

Olsen, O. W. 1940. *Diplogynia americana,* a new species of cestode (Hymenolepididae) from the eastern little green heron (*Butorides virescens virescens* [Linn.]). Trans. Am. Microscop. Soc. *59*, 183–186.

Olsson, P. 1868a. Entozoa, iakttagna hos Skandinaviska Hafsfiskar. Platyhelminthes I. Lunds. Univ. Årsskr. *3*, 41–59.

Olsson, P. 1868a. Entozoa, iakttagna hos Skandinaviska Hafsfiskar. Platyhelminthes (Forts.). Lunds. Univ. Årsskr. *4*, 1–64.

Olsson, P. 1868b. Berättelse om en zoologisk resa till Bohüslän och Skagerack sommaren 1868. Öfversigt Kgl. Svenska Vetenskapakad. Handl. *25*, 471–485.

Olsson, P. 1869. Om entozoernas geografiska utbredning och foerekomst hos olika djur. Forhandl. skandinavisk. Naturforsk. *31*, 481–515.

Olsson, P. 1876. Bidrag till Skandinaviens helminth fauna. I. Kgl. Svenska Vetenskapsakad. Handl. *14*, 1–35.

Olsson, P. 1893. Bidrag till Skandinaviens helminth fauna. II. Kgl. Svenska Vetenskapsakad. Handl. *25*, 1–41.

Olsson, P. 1896. Sur *Chimaera monstrosa* et ses parasites. Mém. soc. zool. France 9, 499–512.

Ortiz, C. I. 1945. Communicacion preliminar sobre una posible neuva parasitosis intestinal en Venezuela. Bol. Laboratorio Clinica "Luis Razetta" *6*, 287–291.

Ortlepp, R. J. 1926. On a collection of helminths from a South African farm. J. Helm. *4*, 127–142.

Ortlepp, R. J. 1933. *Joyeuxia fuhrmanni* Baer, 1924, a hitherto unrecorded cestode parasite of the domesticated cat in South Africa. Onderstepoort J. Vet. Sci. Animal Ind. *1*, 97–98.

Ortlepp, R. J. 1934. Echinococcus in dogs from Pretoria and vicinity. Onderstepoort J. Vet. Sci. Animal Ind. *3*, 97–108.

Ortlepp, R. J. 1937. South African helminths. Part I. Onderstepoort J. Vet. Sci. Animal Ind. *9*, 311–336.

Ortlepp, R. J. 1938a. On two cestodes recovered from a South African kite. Livro Jubilar do Professor Lauro Travassos. 1938, xx + 589 pp. Pp. 353–358. Rio de Janeiro.

Ortlepp, R. J. 1938b. South African helminths. Part II. Some taenias from large wild carnivores. Onderstepoort J. Vet. Sci. Animal Ind. *10*, 253–274.

Ortlepp, R. J. 1938c. South African helminths. Part III. Some mammalian and avian cestodes. Onderstepoort J. Vet. Sci. Animal Ind. *11*, 23–50.

Ortlepp, R. J. 1938d. South African helminths. Part IV. Cestodes from Columbiformes. Onderstepoort J. Vet. Sci. Animal Ind. *11*, 51–61.

Ortlepp, R. J. 1938e. South African helminths. Part V. Some avian and mammalian helminths. Onderstepoort J. Vet. Sci. Animal Ind. *11*, 63–104.

Ortlepp, R. J. 1939. South African helminths. Part VI. Some helminths, chiefly from rodents. Onderstepoort J. Vet. Sci. Animal Ind. *12*, 75–101.

Ortlepp, R. J. 1940. South African helminths. Part VII. Miscellaneous helminths, chiefly cestodes. Onderstepoort J. Vet. Sci. Animal Ind. *14*, 97–110.

Ortner-Schonbach, P. 1913. Zur Morphologie des Glykogens bei Trematoden und Cestoden. Arch. Zellforsch. *11*, 413–449.

Osler, C. P. 1931. A new cestode from *Rana clamitans* Latr. J. Parasitol. *17*, 182–185.

Otto, G. F. 1936. Human infestation with the dwarf tapeworm (*Hymenolepis nana*) in the southern United States. Am. J. Hyg. *23*, 25–32.

Owen, R. 1832. Notes on the anatomy of the flamingo, *Phoenicopterus ruber* Linn. Proc. Zool. Soc. London, pp. 141–142.

Owen, R. 1834. On the anatomy of *Corythaix porphyreolopha*. Proc. Zool. Soc. London, pp. 3–5.

Owen, R. 1835. Description of a new species of tapeworm. Trans. Zool. Soc. London *1*, 385–386; Isia, 1835, p. 434.

Pagenstecher, H. 1858. Beitrag zur Kenntnis der Geschlechtsorgane der Taenien. Z. wiss. Zool. *9*, 523–528.

Pagenstecher, H. 1871. Ueber *Echinococcus* bei *Macropus major*. Verhandl. naturh.-med. Ver. Heidelberg *5*, 181–186.

Pagenstecher, H. 1872. Ueber *Echinococcus* bei *Tapirus bicolor*. Verhandl. naturh.-med. Ver. Heidelberg *6*, 93–95.

Pagenstecher, H. 1877. Zur Naturgeschichte der Cestoden. Z. wiss. Zool. *30*, 171–193.

Palais, M. 1933. Les anomalies des cestodes. Recherches expérimentales sur *Hymenolepis diminuta* (Rud.). Ann. fac. sci. Marseille *6*, 111–163.

Palais, M. 1934. Résistance des rats à l'infestation d'*Hymenolepis diminuta*. Compt. rend. soc. biol. *117*, 1016–1017.

Pallas, P. S. 1760. De infestis viventibus intra viventia. Diss. med. inaug. Ludg. Batav.

Pallas, P. S. 1766a. Miscellanica zoologica . . . xii + 224 pp. Hagae Comitum.

Pallas, P. S. 1766b. Elenchus zoophytorum sistens generum adumbrationes generaliores et specierum cognitarum succinctas descriptiones, cum selectis auctorum synonymis. xvi + 451 pp. Hagae Comitum.

Pallas, P. S. 1781. Bemerkungen ueber die Bandwürmer in Menschen und Thieren. Naturgesch. Oekon. St. Petersb. and Leipzig. I, pp. 39–112.

Pallas, P. S. 1811–1812. Fauna Asiatico-Rossica. 2 vols. Petropolis.

Parisot, J., and P. Simonin. 1920a. Toxicité et effets physico-pathologique du liquide vésiculaire de *Cysticercus pisiformis*. Compt. rend. soc. biol. *83*, 739–741.

Parisot, J., and P. Simonin. 1920b. Toxicité et action sur les appareils circulatoire et respiratoire de l'extrait total de *Taenia saginata*. Compt. rend. soc. biol. *83*, 937–941.

Parodi, S. E., and V. Widakowich. 1917. Cestodes del genero *Bothriocephalus* parasitos de algunas especies de nuestros felinos salvajes. Rev. jard. zool. Buenos Aires *13*, 222–227.

Parona, C. 1883. Osservazioni intorno ad un caso di cisticerco nel mufflone de Sardegna. Ann. reale accad. agr. Torino *26*, 3–9.

Parona, C. 1885. Di alcuni elminti raccolti nel Sudan orientale da O. Beccari e P. Malgretti. Ann. museo civico storia nat. Genova *22*, 424–445.

Parona, C. 1887a. Elmintologia Sarda. Contribuzione allo studio del vermi parassiti in animali di Sardegna. Ann. museo civico storia nat. Genova *24*, 275–384.

Parona, C. 1887b. Res ligusticae. II. Vermi parassiti in animalia della Liguria . . . Ann. museo civico storia nat. Genova *24*, 765–780.

Parona, C. 1893. *Hymenolepis monezi* n. sp. parasita del *Pteropus medius* ed *H. acuta* (*Taenia acuta* Rud.) dei pipistrelli nostrali. Atti soc. Ligust. sci. nat. Genova *4*, 202–206.

Parona, C. 1894. L'elmintologia italiana da suoi primi tempi all' anno 1890. Storia, sistematica, corologia e bibliografia. Atti Univ. Genova *13*, 733 pp.

Parona, C. 1896a. Nota intorno agli elminti del museo zoologico Torino. Boll. museo zool. anat. comp. Torino *11*, 6 pp.

Parona, C. 1896b. Intorno ad alcuni distomi nuovi o poco noti. Atti soc. Ligust. sci. nat. Genova *7*, 162–180.

Parona, C. 1898. Elminto raccolti dal Dottore Elio Modigliani alle isole Mentawei, Engano e Sumatra. Ann. museo civico storia nat. Genova *19*, 102–124.

Parona, C. 1899. Catalogo di elminti raccolti in vertebrati dell' isola d'Elba dal Dott. Giacomo Damiani. Atti soc. Ligust. sci. nat. Genova *10*, 85–100.

Parona, C. 1900a. Helminthum ex Conradi Paronae. Museo Catalogus Cestodes. 6 pp. Genova.

Parona, C. 1900b. Di alcuni elminti del museo nacional di Buenos Aires. Communicaciones museo nacional Buenos Aires *1*, 190–197.

Parona, C. 1900c. Catalogus helminthum ex Conradi Paronae Museo. Sect. II. 6 pp. Genova.

Parona, C. 1901a, 1901b. Di alcuni cestodi brasiliani raccolti dal Dott. Adolfo Lutz. Boll. museo zool. anat. comp. Genova, No. 102, 12 pp. (1901a); e Atti soc. Ligust. sci. nat. Genova *11* (1901b).

Parona, C. 1902a. Catalogo di elminti raccolti in vertebrati dell' isola d'Elba. Boll. museo zool. anat. comp. Genova, No. 113, 20 pp.

Parona, C. 1902b. Due casi rari di *Coenurus serialis* Gerv. Boll. museo zool. anat. comp. Genova, No. 118, pp. 1–6.

Parona, C. 1903. Elminti. Osservazioni scientifiche esegniti durante la spedizione potare de S. A. R. Luigi Amedeo si Savoia, Duca degli Abruzzi, 1899–1900. Milano. Pp. 633–635.

Parona, C. 1909. Vermi parassiti di vertebrati. In Spedizione al Ruwenzori . . . Parte scientifica 1, pp. 415–422. Milano.

Parrot, L., and C. Joyeux. 1920. Les cysticercoïdes de *Tarentola mauritanica* L. et les Ténias du chat. Bull. soc. path. exot. *13*, 687–695.

Pasquali, A. 1890. Le Ténis de polli di Massaua. Descrizione de una nuova specie. Giorn. intern. sci. med. Napoli *12*, 905–910.

Patwardhan, S. S. 1935. On two new species of cestodes from a snipe. Zool. Jahrb. Syst. *66*, 541–548.

Pavlova, P. 1935. De la toxicité du *Diphyllobothrium latum* (in Russian; French summary). Terapevticheskiy Arkhiv. *14*, 850–855.

Pearse, A. S. 1924a. Observations on parasitic worms from Wisconsin in fishes. Trans. Wisconsin Acad. Sci. *21*, 147–160.

Pearse, A. S. 1924b. The parasites of lake fishes. Trans. Wisconsin Acad. Sci. *21*, 161–194.

Peery, H. J. 1939. A new unarmed tapeworm from a spotted skunk. J. Parasitol. *25*, 487–490.

Penfold, H. B. 1936. The treatment of patients infested with *Taenia saginata*, with special reference to certain unusual results. Med. J. Australia, 23rd Year, pp. 385–398.

Penfold, H. B. 1937a. The signs and symptoms of *Taenia saginata* infestation. Med. J. Australia, 24th Year, I, pp. 531–535.

Penfold, H. B. 1937b. The life-history of *Cysticercus bovis* in the tissues of the ox. Med. J. Australia, 24th Year, I, pp. 579–583.

Penfold, W. J., and H. B. Penfold. 1936. The diagnosis of *Taenia saginata* infestation. Med. J. Australia, 23rd Year, I, pp. 317–321.

Penfold, W. J., H. B. Penfold, and M. Phillips. 1936a. A survey of the incidence of *Taenia saginata* infestation in the population of the State of Victoria from January, 1934, to July, 1935. Med. J. Australia, 23rd Year, I, pp. 283–285.

Penfold, W. J., H. B. Penfold, and M. Phillips. 1936b. Acquired active immunity in the ox to *Cysticercus bovis*. Med. J. Australia, 23rd Year, I, pp. 417–423.

Penfold, W. J., H. B. Penfold, and M. Phillips. 1936c. Ridding pasture of *Taenia saginata* ova by grazing with cattle or sheep. J. Helm. *14*, 135–140.

Penfold, W. J., H. B. Penfold, and M. Phillips. 1937a. *Taenia saginata*: its growth and propagation. J. Helm. *15*, 41–48.

Penfold, W. J., H. B. Penfold, and M. Phillips. 1937b. The criteria of life and viability of mature *Taenia saginata* ova. Med. J. Australia, 24th Year, I, pp. 1–5.

Penfold, W. J., H. B. Penfold, and M. Phillips. 1937c. Artificial hatching of *Taenia saginata* ova. Med. J. Australia, 24th Year, II, pp. 1039–1042.

Penner, L. R. 1938. A hawk tapeworm . . . J. Parasitol. *24* (suppl.), p. 25.

Perez-Vigueras, I. 1936. *Proteocephalus manjuariphilus* n. sp. (Cestoda), parasito de *Atractosteus tristoechus* (Bloch and Schn.) (Pisces). Rev. parasitol. clin. y lab. Havana 2, 17–19.

Perrenoud, W. 1931. Recherches anatomiques et histologiques sur quelques cestodes de Sélaciens. Rev. suisse zool. *38*, 469–555.

Perrier, E. 1873. Déscription d'un genre nouveau de cestoïdes (Genre *Duthiersia* E. P.). Arch. zool. exp. gén. 2, 349–362.

Perrier, E. 1897a. Traité de zoologie. Part II, pp. 1345–2136. Paris.

Perrier, E. 1897b. Classification des cestoïdes. Compt. rend. *86*, 552–554.

Perroncito, E. 1879a. Di una specie di Taenia (*T. alba*). Ann. reale accad. agr. Torino *21*, 127–130.

Perroncito, E. 1879b. Ueber eine neue Bandwurmart (*Taenia alba*). Arch. Naturgeschichte *45*, 235–237.

Perroncito, E. 1882. I parassiti dell' Uomo e degli animali utili. 506 pp. Milano.

Perroncito, E. 1886. Trattato teorico-prattico sul mallatie piu communi degli animali domestici. 434 pp. Torino.

Peters, B. G. 1936. Some recent developments in helminthology. Proc. Roy. Soc. Med. *29*, 1074–1084.

Peters, W. 1857. Ueber eine neue durch ihre riesige Grösse ausgezeichnete *Taenia*. Monatschrift kgl. preuss. Akad. Wiss., November 1856, p. 469.

Peters, W. 1871. Note on the *Taenia* from the rhinoceros lately described by Dr. J. Murie. Proc. Zool. Soc. London, 1871, pp. 146–147.

Petrov, M. I. 1938. New diphyllobothriids of man (in Russian with English summary). Med. Parasitol. and Parasitic Diseases (U.S.S.R.) *7*, 406–413.

Petruschevsky, G. K. 1931. Ueber die Verbreitung der Plerocerkoide von *Diphyllobothrium latum* in den Fischen der Newabucht. Zool. Anz. *94*, 139–147.

Petruschevsky, G. K. 1933. Ueber die Infektion der Fische des Onega Sees mit Plerocerkoide von *Diphyllobothrium latum*. Bouchte d. Biol. Borodin Station *6*.

Petruschevsky, G. K., and E. D. Boldyr. 1935. Propagation du bothriocephale (*Diphyllobothrium latum*) et de ses larves plerocercoïdes dans la région du nord-ouest de l' U.R.S.S. Ann. parasitol. humaine et comparée *13*, 327–337.

Petruschevsky, G. K., and I. Bychowskaja-Pavlovsky. 1933. Ueber die Verbreitung der Larven von *Diphyllobothrium latum* in Fischen aus Karelien. Bouchte d. Biol. Borodin Station *6*.

Petruschevsky, G. K., and W. Tarassow. 1933a. Die Bekämpfung des *Diphyllobothrium latum* in Karelian. Arch. Schiffs.-u. Tropenhyg. *37*, 1–8.

Petruschevsky, G. K., and W. Tarassow. 1933b. Versuche ueber die Ansteckung des Menschen mit verschiedenen Fischplerozerkoiden. Arch. Schiffs.-u. Tropenhyg. *37*, 370–372.

Piana, G. P. 1882. Di una nuova specie di Taenia del Gallo domestico (*Taenia botrioplitis*) e di un nuova cisticerco . . . Mem. accad. sci. ist. Bologna, 1880–1881, pp. 84–85.

Pickhardt, O. C. 1933. Removal of *Echinococcus* cyst: its influence on specific blood reaction. Ann. Surgery *97*, 119–121.

Pierantoni, U. 1928. *Bertia hamadryadis* n. sp. di cestode anoplocefalo parassita di *Hamadryas hamadryas*. Ann. museo zool. reale univ. Napoli *5*, 1–3.

Pintner, T. 1880. Untersuchungen ueber den Bau des Bandwurmkörpers mit besonderer Berücksichtigung der Tetrabothrien und Tetrarhynchen. Arb. zool. Inst. Univ. Wien *3*, 163–242.

Pintner, T. 1889. Neue Untersuchungen ueber den Bau des Bandwurmkörpers. I. Zur Kenntnis der Gattung *Echinobothrium*. Arb. zool. Inst. Univ. Wien 8, 371–420.

Pintner, T. 1890. Neue Beiträge zur Kenntnis des Bandwurmkörpers. Arb. zool. Inst. Univ. Wien *9*, 57–84.

Pintner, T. 1893. Studien an Tetrarhynchen nebst Beobachtungen an andern Bandwürmern. I. Mitteilung. Sitzb. akad. Wiss. Wien Math.-naturg. Klasse, Abt. I, *102*, 605–650.

Pintner, T. 1896a. Versuch einer morphologischen Erklärung des Tetrarhynchrüssels. Biol. Zentr. *16*, 258–267.

Pintner, T. 1896b. Studien an Tetrarhynchen . . . II. Mitteilung. Ueber eine Tetrarhynchenlarve aus den Magen von *Heptanchus.* nebst Bemerkungen ueber das Exkretionssystem verschiedener Cestoden. Sitzb. akad. Wiss. Wien Math.-naturg. Klasse, Abt. I, *105*, 652–682.

Pintner, T. 1899. Die Rhynchodäaldrusen der Tetrarhynchen. Arb. zool. Inst. Univ. Wien Math.-naturg. Klasse, Abt. I, *12*, 1–24.

Pintner, T. 1903. Studien an Tetrarhynchen . . . III. Mitteilung. Zwei eigentümliche Drüsensysteme bei *Rhynchobothrius adenoplusius* n. und histologische

Notizen ueber *Acanthocephalus, Amphilina* und *Taenia saginata.* Sitzb. akad. Wiss. Wien Math.-naturg. Klasse, Abt. I, *112*, 541–597.

Pintner, T. 1906. Das Verhalten des Exkretionssystem in Endgliede von *Rhynchobothrium ruficollis* (Eysenhardt). Zool. Anz. *30*, 576–578.

Pintner, T. 1909. Das ursprüngliche Hinterende einiger Rhynchobothriumketten. Arb. zool. Inst. Univ. Wien *18*, 113–132.

Pintner, T. 1912. Eigentümlichkeiten des Sexualapparates der Tetrarhynchen. Verhandl. III. Intern. Zool. Congress zu Graz, 1910. Pp. 776–780. Publ. Jena, 1912.

Pintner, T. 1913. Vorarbeiten zu einer Monographie der Tetrarhynchoideen. Sitzb. akad. Wiss. Wien Math.-naturg. Klasse, Abt. I, *122*, 171–254.

Pintner, T. 1914. Zur Anatomie und Systematik der Tetrarhynchen. Verhandl. 85. Versammlung deutsche Naturforsch. und Arzte, Wien 1913. 4 pp. Publ. Leipzig, 1914.

Pintner, T. 1924. Die Entstehung der Rüssel der Tetrarhynchiden. Zool. Anz. *59*, 100–104.

Pintner, T. 1925a. Bemerkenwerte Strukturen im Kopfe von Tetrarhynchoideen. Z. wiss. Zool. *125*, 1–34.

Pintner, T. 1925b. Topographie des Genitalapparats von *Tetrarhynchus ruficollis* (Eysenhardt). Zool. Jahrb. Anat. *47*, 212–245.

Pintner, T. 1926. Das System der Platodaria. Arch. Naturgeschichte *91*, 1–240.

Pintner, T. 1927. Kritische Beiträge zum System der Tetrarhynchen. Zool. Jahrb. Syst. *53*, 559–590.

Pintner, T. 1928a. Helminthologische Mitteilungen. I. Zool. Anz. *76*, 318–322.

Pintner, T. 1928b. Die sogenannte Gamobothriidae Linton, 1899. Zool. Jahrb. Anat. *50*, 55–116.

Pintner, T. 1929a. Studien ueber Tetrarhynchen . . . IV. Mitteilung. Ueber einige Diesing' sche Originale und verwandte Formen. Sitzb. akad. Wiss. Wien Math.-naturg. Klasse, Abt. I, *138*, 145–166.

Pintner, T. 1929b. Tetrarhynchen von den Forschungsreisen des Dr. Sixten Bock. Göteborgs Kgl. Vetenskapsakad. Handl. Ser. B, 1, pp. 1–46.

Pintner, T. 1929c. Helminthologische Mitteilungen. II. Zool. Anz. *84*, 1–8.

Pintner, T. 1929d. *Tetrarhynchus erinaceus.* Anzeiger akad. Wiss. Wien *61*, Nr. 17, 2 pp.

Pintner, T. 1930a. Tetrarhynchen aus Pacific Grove, California, U.S.A. Anzeiger akad. Wiss. Wien *67*, Nr. 3, 2 pp.

Pintner, T. 1930b. Weiteres ueber Anatomie und Systematik der Tetrarhynchen. Anzeiger akad. Wiss. Wien *67*, Nr. 8, p. 70.

Pintner, T. 1930c. Wenigbekanntes und Unbekanntes von Rüsselbandwürmern. I. Anzeiger akad. Wiss. Wien *67*, Nr. 15, p. 148.

Pintner, T. 1931a. Wenigbekanntes und Unbekanntes von Rüsselbandwürmern. II. Sitzb. akad. Wiss. Wien Math.-naturg. Klasse, Abt. I, *140*, 777–820.

Pintner, T. 1931b. Ueber fortgesetzte Tetrarhynchenuntersuchungen. Anzeiger akad. Wiss. Wien *68*, Nr. 10, 72–75.

Pintner, T. 1931c. Ueber fortgesetzte Tetrarhynchenuntersuchungen. II. Anzeiger akad. Wiss. Wien *68*, Nr. 16, 141–142.

Pintner, T. 1932a. Weiteres ueber Strukturen im Tetrarhynchenkopfe. Anzeiger akad. Wiss. Wien *69*, Nr. 18, 189–190.

Pintner, T. 1932b. Sinnespapillen am Genitalatrium der Tetrarhynchen. Zool. Anz. *98*, 295–298.

Pintner, T. 1933. Zur Kenntnis des Exkretionssystems der Cestoden. Sitzb. akad. Wiss. Wien Math.-naturg. Klasse, Abt. I, *142*, 205–211.

Pintner, T. 1934a. Bruchstücke zur Kenntnis der Rüsselbandwürmer. Zool. Jahrb. Anat. *58*, 1–20.

Pintner, T. 1934b. Ueber Entwicklungsvorgänge in der Cestodenkette. Anzeiger akad. Wiss. Wien *71*, Nr. 19, 256–258.

Pintner, T. 1935a. Ueber die Gewebe des Cestoden. Anzeiger akad. Wiss. Wien *72*, Nr. 1, 6–7.

Pintner, T. 1935b. Berechtigung. Zool. Anz. *109*, 271–272.

Plater, F. 1656. Praxeos Medicae Opus. Basel.

Plotnikov. See Petrov.

Plotz, M. 1932. *Diphyllobothrium latum* infestation in the eastern seaboard. Twenty-one cases from New York. J. Am. Med. Ass. *98*, 313–314.

Poche, F. 1922. Zur Kenntnis der Amphilinidea. Zool. Anz. *54*, 276–287.

Poche, F. 1923. Ueber die systematische Stellung des Cestodengenus *Wageneria* Mont. Zool. Anz. *56*, 20–27.

Poche, F. 1924. Die Entstehung der Rüssel der Tetrarhynchiden. Zool. Anz. *59*, 100–104.

Poche, F. 1925. Zur Kenntnis von *Amphilina foliacea.* Z. wiss. Zool. *125*, 585–619.

Poche, F. 1926a. Das System der Platodaria. Arch. Naturgeschichte *91*, 458 pp.

Poche, F. 1926b. On the morphology and systematic position of the cestode, *Gigantolina magna* (Southwell). Records Ind. Museum *28*, 1–27.

Poche, F. 1928. Zur Erklärung der Configuration des Exkretionssystems in den freien Proglottiden von *Wageneria* und ueber die Berechtigung der Gattung *Wageneria* (Tetrarhynchoidea). Livro Jubilar Pro Lauro Travassos.

Podiapolsky, B. 1924. Zur Kenntnis der parasitischen Würmer bei Ratten (in Russian). Rev. Microbiol. et Epid. Saratov *3*, 280–290.

Podjapolskaja, W. P., and M. P. Gnedina. 1932. *Diphyllobothrium tungussicum* n. sp. ein neuer Parasit des Menschen. Centralbl. Bakt. Parasitenk. *126*, 415–419.

Polk, S. J. 1941. *Dilepis hilli,* a new dilepidid cestode from a little blue heron. Wasmann Collector *4*, 131–133.

Polk, S. J. 1942a. The genus *Dilepis* Weinland, 1858. Wasmann Collector *5*, 25–32.

Polk, S. J. 1942b. *Hymenolepis mastigopraedita,* a new cestode from a pintail duck. J. Parasitol. *28*, 141–145.

Polk, S. J. 1942c. A new hymenolepidid cestode, *Hymenolepis dafilae,* from a pintail duck. Trans. Am. Microscop. Soc. *61*, 186–191.

Polonio, A. F. 1860a. Catalogo dei cefalocotilei italiani e alcuni osservazioni sul loro svilupp o. Atti soc. ital. sci. nat. Milano *2*, 217–229.

Polonio, A. F. 1860b. Novae helminthum species. Lotos (Prague) *10*, 21–23.

Polonio, A. F. 1860c. Eine neue Art von *Ligula.* Lotos (Prague) *10*, 179–180.

Pont, A. M. del. 1906. Sobre una nueva especie de Taenia (*Taenia furnarii*). Anales del Circulo Med. Argentinos (Buenos Aires), 15 pp.

Popoff, F. 1924. *Caryophyllaeus skrjabini* Pop. eine neue Cestode von *Abramis brama* (in Russian with German summary). Russische Hydrobiology. Zeitschrift herausgegeben von den Biologische Wolga Station.

Popov, P. 1935. Sur le développement de *Diplopylidium skrjabini* n. sp. Ann. parasitol. humaine et comparée *13*, 322–326.

Porter, A. 1918. A survey of the intestinal Entozoa . . . among natives in Johannesburg. Publn. South African Inst. Med. Res. *11*.

Posselt, A. 1934. Es giebt keine Uebergangs- oder Zwischenformen zwischen beiden Arten des Blasenwurmes (*Echinococcus cysticercus* und *Echinococcus alveolaris*). Frankfurter Z. Path. *47*, 194–230.

Potemkina, V. A. 1941. Contribution to the biology of *Moniezia expansa* (Rudolphi, 1810), a tapeworm parasitic in sheep and goats (in Russian). Compt. rend. acad. sci. U.R.S.S. *30*, 474–476.

Potemkina, V. A. 1944a. On the decipherment of the biological cycle in *Moniezia benedeni* (Moniez, 1879), a tapeworm parasitic in cattle and other domestic animals (in Russian). Compt. rend. acad. sci. U.R.S.S. *42*, 146–148.

Potemkina, V. A. 1944b. Contribution to the study of the development of *Thysaniezia ovilla* (Rivolta, 1878), a tapeworm parasitic in ruminants. Compt. rend. acad. sci. U.R.S.S. *43*, 43–44.

Potter, C. C. 1937. A new cestode from a shark (*Hypoprion brevirostris* Poey). Proc. Helm. Soc. Washington *4*, 70–72.

Pratt, H. S. 1909. The cuticula and subcuticula of trematodes and cestodes. Am. Naturalist *43*, 705–720.

Prenant, A. 1886. Recherches sur les vers parasitiques des poissons. Bull. soc. sci. Nancy *7*, 206–230.

Prenant, M. 1922. Recherches sur le parenchyme de Plathelminthes. Arch. morph. gén. éxp. *5*.

Price, E. W. 1932. A new host for *Duthiersia fimbriata*. Proc. Helm. Soc. Washington, in J. Parasitol. *19*, 84.

Pullar, E. M. 1946. A survey of Victorian canine and vulpine parasites. Australian Vet. J. *22*, 12–21.

Purvis, G. B. 1932. Cestodes from domestic animals in Malaya, with descriptions of new species. Veterinary Record *12*, 1407–1409.

Pushmenkov, E. P. 1945. A contribution to the knowledge of the development cycle of the larvae of cestodes parasitic of the liver of the reindeer. Compt. rend. acad. sci. U.R.S.S. *49*, 303–304.

Querner, F. 1925. Revision zweier von Diesing beschriebenen Rhynchobothriens (*R. tenuicolle* et *R. caryophyllum*). Ann. Nat. Museum Wien *38*, 107–117.

Rackemann, F. M., and A. H. Stevens. 1927. Skin tests to extracts of *Echinococcus* and *Ascaris*. J. Immunol. *13*, 389–394.

Railliet, A. 1886. Eléments de zoologie médicale et agricole. Fasc. 2. Pp. xv + 801–1053. Paris.

Railliet, A. 1889. Sur la classification des téniadés. Centralbl. Bakt. Parasitenk. *26*, 32–34.

Railliet, A. 1890. Les parasites des animaux domestiques au Japon. Naturaliste, Sér. 2, *4*, 142–143.

Railliet, A. 1892a. Sur un ténia du pigeon domestique répresentant une espèce nouvelle (*Taenia delafondi*). Compt. rend. soc. biol. *4*, 49–53.

Railliet, A. 1892b. Notices parasitologiques: *Taenia tenuirostris* Rud. chez l'oie domestique: rémarques sur la classification des cestodes parasites des oiseaux. Bull. soc. zool. France *17*, 115–117.

Railliet, A. 1893. Traité de zoologie médicale et agricole. 2nd ed. 736 pp. Paris.

Railliet, A. 1896a. Quelques rectifications de nomenclature des parasites. Rec. méd. vét. *3*, 157–161.

Railliet, A. 1896b. Sur quelques parasites du dromadaire. Compt. rend. soc. biol. *48*, 489–492.

Railliet, A. 1899a. Anomalies des scolex chez le coenurus sériale. Compt. rend. soc. biol. *51*, 18–21.

Railliet, A. 1899b. Sur les cestodes du Blaireau (*Meles taxus*). Compt. rend. soc. biol. *51*, 23–25.

Railliet, A. 1899c. Sur la classification des téniadés. Centralbl. Bakt. Parasitenk. *26*, 32–34.

Railliet, A. 1899d. Sur la synonymie du genre *Tetrarhynchus* Rud., 1809. Arch. Parasitol. *2*, 319–320.

Railliet, A. 1899e. Encore un mot sur le *Davainea oligophora* Polonio. Arch. Parasitol. *2*, 482.

Railliet, A. 1916. The food of slugs and the development of Anoplocephalidae. Ann. App. Biol. *3*.

Railliet, A. 1921. Les cestodes des oiseaux domestiques. Détermination pratique. Rec. méd. vét. *97*, 185–205.

Railliet, A., and A. Henry. 1905. Etude du Taenia recuelli au Tonkin par M. le Dr. Lacour. Ann. hyg. med. colon. *8*, 288–293.

Railliet, A., and A. Henry. 1909. Les cestodes des oiseaux par O. Fuhrmann. Rec. méd. vét. *86*, 337–338.

Railliet, A., and A. Henry. 1911. Helminthes du porc recueillis par M. Bauche en Annam. Bull. soc. path. exotique *4*, 693–699.

Railliet, A., and A. Henry. 1912a. Helminthes recueillis par l'expédition antarctique français du Pourquoi-Pas. I. Cestodes d'oiseaux. Bull. musée nat. hist. nat. *18*, 35–39.

Railliet, A., and A. Henry. 1912b. Helminthes recueillis par l'expédition antarctique français du Pourquoi-Pas. II. Cestodes de phoques. Bull. musée nat. hist. nat. *18*, 153–159.

Railliet, A., and A. Henry. 1915. Sur un cénure de la gerbille à pieds velus. Bull. soc. path. exotique 8, 173–177.

Railliet, A., A. Henry, and J. Bauche. 1914. Sur les helminthes de l'éléphant d'Asie. I. Trématodes et cestodes. Bull. soc. path. exotique 7, 78–83.

Railliet, A., and A. Lucet. 1891. Développement expérimental du *Cysticercus tenuicollis* chez le chevreau. Bull. soc. zool. France *16*, 157–158.

Railliet, A., and A. Lucet. 1892. Sur le *Davainea proglottina* Davaine. Bull. soc. zool. France *17*, 105–106.

Railliet, A., and A. Lucet. 1899. Sur l'identité du *Davainea oligophora* Magalhaes, 1898 et du *Taenia cantaniana* Polonio, 1860. Arch. Parasitol. *2*, 144–146.

Railliet, A., and M. M. Marullaz. 1919. Sur un cénure noveau du bonnet chinois (*Macacus sinicus*). Bull. soc. path. exotique *12*, 223–228.

Railliet, A., and A. Mouguet. 1919. Cénure du coypou. Bull. soc. cent. méd. vét. *72*, 204–211.

Ramsdell, S. G. 1928. A note on the skin reaction in *Taenia* infestation. J. Parasitol. *14*, 102.

Rankin, J. S. 1937. An ecological study of parasites of some North Carolina salamanders. Ecological Monographs 7 (2), 171–262.

Ransom, B. H. 1900. A new avian cestode, *Metroliasthes lucida* n. g. n. sp. Trans. Am. Microscop. Soc. *21*, 213–226.

Ransom, B. H. 1902. On *Hymenolepis carioca* (Magalhaes) and *H. megalops* (Nitzsch) with remarks on the classification of the group. Trans. Am. Microscop. Soc. *23*, 151–172.

Ransom, B. H. 1904a. Notes on the spiny-suckered tapeworms of chickens (*Davainea echinobothrida* = *Taenia botrioplites*) and *D. tetragona*. U. S. Bur. Anim. Indus. Bull. 60, pp. 55–72.

Ransom, B. H. 1904b. An account of the tapeworms of the genus *Hymenolepis* parasitic in man, with several new cases of the dwarf tapeworm (*H. nana*) in the United States. U. S. Pub. Health Service Hyg. Lab. Bull. 18, pp. 1–138.

Ransom, B. H. 1905. The tapeworms of American chickens and turkeys. 21st Ann. Rep. U. S. Bur. Anim. Indust., pp. 55–69.

Ransom, B. H. 1907. Tapeworm cysts, *Dithyridium cynocephali* n. sp., in the muscles of a marsupial wolf (*Thylacinus cynocephali*). Trans. Am. Microscop. Soc. *27*, 31–32.

Ransom, B. H. 1909. The taenioid cestodes of North American birds. U. S. Nat. Museum Bull. *69*, 1–141.

Ransom, B. H. 1911. A new cestode from an African bustard. Proc. U. S. Nat. Museum *40*, 637–647.

Ransom, B. H. 1913a. The name of the sheep measle worm (*Taenia ovis*). Science *38*, 320.

Ransom, B. H. 1913b. *Cysticercus ovis*, the cause of tapeworm cysts in mutton. J. Agr. Research *1*, 15–58.

Ransom, B. H. 1916. (Note without title.) Proc. Helm. Soc. Washington, in J. Parasitol. *2*, 93–94.

Ransom, B. H. 1926. Yellow-bellied sapsucker infested with tapeworms. Can. Field Naturalist *40*, 67.

Rao, M. A. N., and L. S. P. Ayyar. 1932. Triradiate tapeworms from hounds and jackals. Ind. J. Vet. Sci. *2*, 397–399.

Rasin, K. 1931. Beiträge zur postembryonal Entwicklung der *Amphilina foliacea* . . . Z. wiss. Zool. *138*.

Ratz, S. von. 1897a. Beiträge zur Parasitenfauna der Balatonfische. Centralbl. Bakt. Parasitenk. *22*, 443–453.

Ratz, S. von. 1897b. *Diplopylidium chyzeri* n. sp. (in Hungarian, with German summary, pp. 259–266). Termeszet. fuzetek. Budapest *20*, 197–203.

Ratz, S. von. 1900a. Drei neue Cestoden aus Neu-Guinea. Vorläufige Mitteilung. Centralbl. Bakt. Parasitenk. *28*, 657–660.

Ratz, S. von. 1900b. Trois nouveaux cestodes de reptiles. Compt. rend. soc. biol. *52*, 980–981.

Ratz, S. von. 1900c. Parasitoligiai jegyzetek. Veterinarius, Budapest, *23*, 525–534.

Ratz, S. von. 1912. Une larve plerocercoïde du porc. Presse Medicale *20*, 867–868.

Ratz, S. von. 1913. Ein Plerocercoid vom Schwein. Centralbl. Bakt. Parasitenk. *47*, 523–527.

Ratzel, F. 1868. Zur Entwicklungsgeschichte der Cestoden. Arch. Naturgeschichte *34*, 138–149.

Raum, J. 1883. Beiträge zur Entwicklungsgeschichte der Cysticerken. Inaugural Dissertation, University of Dorpat.

Rausch, R. 1946. *Paranoplocephala troeschi,* a new species of cestode from the meadow vole, *Microtus p. pennsylvanicus* Ord. Trans. Am. Microscop. Soc. *65*, 354–356.

Rausch, R. 1947a. *Andrya sciuri* n. sp., a cestode from the northern flying squirrel. J. Parasitol. *33*, 316–318.

Rausch, R. 1947b. *Bakererpes fragilis* n. g. n. sp., a cestode from the nighthawk (Cestoda: Dilepididae). J. Parasitol. *33*, 435–438.

Rausch, R. 1947c. A redescription of *Taenia taxidiensis* Skinker, 1935. Proc. Helm. Soc. Washington *14*, 73–75.

Rausch, R. 1947d. Observations on some helminths parasitic in Ohio turtles. Am. Midland Naturalist *38*, 434–442.

Rausch, R. 1948a. *Dendrouterina botauri* n. sp., a cestode parasitic in bitterns, with remarks on other members of the genus. Am. Midland Naturalist *39*, 431–436.

Rausch, R. 1948b. Notes on cestodes of the genus *Andrya* Railliet, 1883, with the description of *A. ondatrae* n. sp. (Cestoda: Anoplocephalidae). Trans. Am. Microscop. Soc. *67*, 187–191.

Rausch, R. 1948c. Observations on cestodes in North American owls with the description of *Choanotaenia speotytonis* (Cestoda: Dipylidiinae). Am. Midland Naturalist *40*, 462–471.

Rausch, R. 1949a. Some additional observations on the morphology of *Dendrouterina botauri* Rausch, 1948 (Cestoda: Dilepididae). J. Parasitol. *35*, 76–78.

Rausch, R. 1949b. *Paradilepis simoni* n. sp., a cestode parasitic in the osprey. Zoologica *34*, 1–3.

Rausch, R. 1949c. Observations on the life-cycle and larval development of *Paruterina candelabraria* (Goeze, 1782) (Cestoda: Dilepididae). Am. Midland Naturalist *42*, 713–721.

Rausch, R., and B. B. Morgan. 1947. The genus *Anonchotaenia* (Cestoda: Dilepididae) from North American birds, with the description of a new species. Trans. Am. Microscop. Soc. *66*, 203–211.

Rausch, R., B. B. Morgan, and E. L. Schiller. 1948. Studies on species of *Paranoplocephala* parasitic in North American rodents (Cestoda: Anoplocephalidae). J. Parasitol. *34* Suppl., 23.

Rausch, R., and E. L. Schiller. 1949a. A critical study of North American cestodes of the genus *Andrya,* with special reference to *A. macrocephala* Douthitt, 1915 (Cestoda: Anoplocephalidae). J. Parasitol. *35*, 306–314.

Rausch, R., and E. L. Schiller. 1949b. A contribution to the study of North American cestodes of the genus *Paruterina* Fuhrmann, 1906. Zoologica *34*, 5–8.

Rausch, R., and E. L. Schiller. 1949c. Some observations on cestodes of the genus *Paranoplocephala* Luehe, parasitic in North American voles. Proc. Helm. Soc. Wash. *16*, 23–31.

Rausch, R., E. L. Schiller, and B. B. Morgan. 1948a. Studies on the cestode genus *Paruterina* (Cestoda: Dilepididae). J. Parasitol. *34* Suppl., 23.

Rausch, R., E. L. Schiller, and B. B. Morgan. 1948b. Variations in *Andrya macrocephala* Douthitt, 1915 (Cestoda: Anoplocephalidae). J. Parasitol. *34* Suppl., 23.

Rausch, R., and J. D. Tiner. 1949. Studies on the parasitic helminths of the north central states. II. Helminths of voles (*Microtus* spp.). Am. Midland Naturalist *41*, 665–694.

Read, C. P. 1949a. Preliminary studies on the intermediate metabolism of the cestode *Hymenolepis diminuta.* J. Parasitol. *35* Suppl., 26–27.

Read, C. P. 1949b. Fluctuations in the glycogen content of the cestode *Hymenolepis diminuta.* J. Parasitol. *35* Suppl., 38.

Read, C. P. 1950. The vertebrate small intestine as an environment for parasitic helminths. Rice Institute Pamphlet. Vol. 37 (2), iv + 78 pp.

Rebello, S., S. F. Gomes da Costa, and J. T. Rico. 1928a. Réactions des cestodes etudiées par la méthode graphique (*Taenia serrata* et *Dipylidium caninum*). Compt. rend. soc. biol. *98*, 470–473.

Rebello, S., S. F. Gomes da Costa, and J. T. Rico. 1928b. Sensibilité des cestodes à l'action des anthelminthiques. Compt. rend. soc. biol. *98*, 473–475, 995–997.

Rebello, S., S. F. Gomes da Costa, and J. T. Rico. 1933. Sur l'emploi des cestodes humains (*Taenia saginata*) comme réactif pharmacologique pour l'étude des anthelminthiques. Compt. rend. soc. biol. *130*, 509–510.

Rebrassier, R. E. 1932. The anthelminthic value of Kamala for tapeworms in chickens. J. Am. Vet. Assoc. *80*, 895–903.

Redi, F. 1684. Osservazioni di Francesco Redi accademico della Crusca intorno agli animali viventi che si trovano negli animali viventi. ii + 253 pp. Florence. Second edition published at Naples, 1687, 116 pp.

Rees, F. G. 1933. Studies on *Cittotaenia pectinata* (Goeze, 1782) from the common rabbit, *Oryctolagus cuniculus*. Part I. Anatomy and histology. Part II. Developmental changes in the egg and attempts at direct infestation. Proc. Zool. Soc. London, 1933, pp. 239–257.

Rees, G. 1941a. The musculature and nervous system of the plerocercoid larva of *Dibothriorhynchus grossum* (Rud.). Parasitology *33*, 373–389.

Rees, G. 1941b. The scolex of *Aporhynchus norvegicus* (Olss.). Parasitology *33*, 433–438.

Rees, G. 1943. The anatomy of *Anthobothrium auriculatum* (Rud.) from *Raja batis* L. Parasitology *35*, 1–10.

Rees, G. 1944. A new cestode of the genus *Grillotia* from a shark. Parasitology *35*, 180–185.

Reeves, J. D. 1949. A new tapeworm of the genus *Bothriocephalus* from Oklahoma salamanders. J. Parasitol. *35*, 600–604.

Reid, W. M. 1940. Some effects of short starvation periods upon the fowl cestode *Raillietina cesticillus* (Molin). J. Parasitol. *25* Suppl., 16.

Reid, W. M. 1942a. The removal of the fowl tapeworm, *Raillietina cesticillus*, by short periods of starvation. Poultry Science *21*, 220–229.

Reid, W. M. 1942b. Certain nutritional requirements of the fowl cestode *Raillietina cesticillus* (Molin) as demonstrated by short periods of starvation of the host. J. Parasitol. *28*, 319–340.

Reid, W. M. 1948. Penetration glands in cyclophyllidean onchospheres. Trans. Am. Microscop. Soc. *67*, 177–182.

Reid, W. M., and J. E. Ackert. 1937. The cysticercoid of *Choanotaenia infundibulum* (Bloch) and the housefly as its host. Trans. Am. Microscop. Soc. *56*, 99–104.

Reid, W. M., J. E. Ackert, and A. A. Case. 1938. Studies on the life-history and biology of the fowl tapeworm *Raillietina cesticillus* (Molin). Trans. Am. Microscop. Soc. *57*, 65–76.

Reid, W. M., and J. I. Boles. 1949. Antibiotics as bacteriostatic agents for the cultivation of cestodes *in vitro*. J. Parasitol. *35* Suppl., 37.

Reinhardt, R. 1933. Arekolin als Antitaenikum. Berliner Tierärztl. Wochenschr. *49*, 129.

Reinitz, G. 1885. Mitteilungen ueber einer bisher noch wenig bekannten Blasenwurm. 43 pp. Dissertation, University of Dorpat.

Rendtorff, R. C. 1948. Investigations on the life-cycle of *Oochoristica ratti*, a cestode from rats and mice. J. Parasitol. *34*, 243–252.

Rennie, J., and A. Reid. 1912. The Cestoda of the Scottish Antarctic Expedition (Scotia). Trans. Roy. Soc. Edinburgh *48*, 441–454.

Richards, A. 1909. On the method of cell division in *Taenia*. Biol. Bull. *17*.

Richards, A. 1911. The method of cell division in the development of the female sex organs of *Moniezia*. Biol. Bull. *20*, 125–178.

Richardson, L. R. 1937. Observations on the parasites of the speckled trout in Lake Edward, Quebec. Trans. Am. Fish. Soc. *66*.

Rico, J. T. 1926. Sur les propriétés ant-helminthiques de l'*Allium sativum*. Compt. rend. soc. biol. *95*, 1597–1599.

Riehm, G. 1881a. Untersuchungen an den Bandwürmern der Hasen und Kaninchen. Z. Ges. Naturw. Berlin *6*.

Riehm, G. 1881b. Studien an Cestoden. Z. Ges. Naturw. Berlin *6*, 545–610.

Riehm, G. 1882. Fütterungsversuche mit *Ligula simplicissimus*. Z. Ges. Naturw. Berlin 7, 274–276, 328–330.

Rietschel, P. E. 1934. Ueber eine neue *Hymenolepis* aus einem Kolibri. Zugleich ein Beitrag zum Rechts-Links-Problem bei den Cestoden. Zool. Anz. *105*, 113–123.

Rietschel, P. E. 1935. Zur Bewegungsphysiologie der Cestoden. Zool. Anz. *111*, 109–111.

Rietz, J. H. 1930. Animal parasites of chickens in Ohio and West Virginia. J. Am. Vet. Med. Ass. 77, 154–156.

Riggenbach, E. 1895a. *Taenia dendritica* Goeze. Centralbl. Bakt. Parasitenk. *17*, 710–716.

Riggenbach, E. 1895b. Beiträge zur Kenntnis der Tänien der Süsswasserfische. Vorläufige Mitteilung. Centralbl. Bakt. Parasitenk. *18*, 609–613.

Riggenbach, E. 1896a. Das Genus *Ichthyotaenia*. Rev. suisse zool. *4*, 165–275.

Riggenbach, E. 1896b. Bemerkungen ueber das Genus *Bothriotaenia* Railliet. Centralbl. Bakt. Parasitenk. *20*, 222–231.

Riggenbach, E. 1898. *Cyathocephalus catenatus*. Zool. Anz. *21*.

Rigney, C. C. 1943. A new davaineid tapeworm, *Raillietina* (*Paroniella*) *centuri* from the red-bellied woodpecker. Trans. Am. Microscop. Soc. *62*, 398–403.

Riley, W. A. 1919a. *Dibothriocephalus latus*, the fish tapeworm of man. Fins, Feathers and Fur, March (No. 17).

Riley, W. A. 1919b. The longevity of the fish tapeworm in man, *Dibothriocephalus latus*. J. Parasitol. *5*, 193–194.

Riley, W. A. 1921. An annotated list of the animal parasites of foxes. Parasitology *13*, 86–96.

Riley, W. A. 1924. *Diphyllobothrium latum* in Minnesota. J. Parasitol. *10*.

Riley, W. A. 1933. Reservoirs of *Echinococcus* in Minnesota. Minnesota Medicine *16*, 744–745.

Riley, W. A. 1939a. The need for data relative to the occurrence of hydatids and of *Echinococcus granulosus* in wildlife. J. Wildlife Management 3, 255–257.

Riley, W. A. 1939b. Maintenance of *Echinococcus* in the United States. J. Am. Vet. Med. Ass. *95*, 170–172.

Riley, W. A., and W. R. Shannon. 1922. The rat tapeworm, *Hymenolepis diminuta*, in man. J. Parasitol. *18*, 109–117.

Rindfleisch, E. 1885. Zur Histologie der Cestoden. Arch. mikrosk. Anat. *1*, 138–142.

Riser, N. W. 1942. A new proteocephalid from *Amphiuma tridactylum* Cuvier. Trans. Am. Microscop. Soc. *61*, 391–397.

Riser, N. W. 1949. Observations on the nervous system of the cestodes. J. Parasitol. *35* Suppl., 27.

Rivas, D. de. 1926. The thermal deathpoint of protozoan and metazoan parasites and the application of intra-intestinal therapy to the treatment of parasitic and other affections of the intestine. Am. J. Med. Sci. *171*, 464–465.

Rivas, D. de. 1935. Clinical parasitology and tropical medicine. Philadelphia.

Rivolta, S. 1878. Di una nuova specie di taenie nella pecora, *T. ovilla*. Giorn. anat. fis. pat. anim. Pisa *10*, 302–308.

Rix, E., and M. E. Laas. 1936. Ueber die auf das Gewebenswachtum wirksamen Stoffe von *Ascaris lumbricoides* und *Taenia saginata*. Arch. exp. Zellforschung *18*, 467–474.

Rizzo, C. 1933. La diagnosi biologica di cisticercosi del nevrasse. A proposito di un quarto caso die cisticercosi cerebrale diagnosticate in vita. Riv. patol. nerv. ment. *41*, 193–216.

Roberts, F. H. S. 1932. A survey of the helminth parasites of the domestic fowl and domestic pigeon in Queensland. Queensland Agr. J. (n. ser.) *38*, 344–347.

Roberts, F. H. S. 1934. Worm parasites of domesticated animals in Queensland. Queensland Agr. J. *41*, 245–252.

Roboz, Z. von. 1882. Beiträge zur Kenntnis der Cestoden. Z. wiss. Zool. *37*, 263–285.

Rodgers, L. O. 1941. A new dilepid tapeworm from a cardinal. Trans. Am. Microscop. Soc. *60*, 371–374.

Roederer, J. G. 1762. Zwei Gattungen von *Fasciolis* (secretary's abstract). Göttingen Anz. v. gelehrt. Sachen (1761–1762), *61*, 537–539.

Rollings, C. T. 1945. Habits, foods and parasites of the bobcat in Minnesota. J. Wildlife Management *9*, 131–145.

Romanovitch, M. 1915. Quelques helminthes du Renne (*Tarandus rangifer*). Compt. rend. soc. biol. *78*, 451–453.

Ronka, E. K. F. 1934. Infestation with *Diphyllobothrium latum*, fish tapeworm. New England J. Med. *210*, 582–583.

Rosen, F. 1919. Recherches sur le développement embryonnaire des cestodes. I. Le cycle évolutif des Bothriocephales. Bull. soc. sci. nat. Neuchâtel *43*, 1917–1918 (1919), pp. 241–300.

Rosen, F. 1920. Recherches sur le développement embryonnaire des cestodes. II. Le cycle évolutif de la Ligule et quelques questions générales sur le développement des Bothriocephales. Bull. soc. sci. nat. Neuchâtel *44*, 1918–1919 (1920), pp. 259–280.

Rosenqvist, E. 1903. Ueber den Eiweissstoffwechsel bei der perniciösen Anämie, mit specieller Berücksichtigung der Bothriocephalus-Anämie. Z. klin. Med. *49*, 193–320.

Rosseter, T. B. 1890. Cysticercoids parasitic in *Cypris cinerea*. J. Microscop. Nat. Sci. London, pp. 241–247.

Rosseter, T. B. 1891. Sur un cysticercoïde des Ostracodes capable de se développer dans l'intestine du canard. Bull. soc. zool. France *16*, 224–229.

Rosseter, T. B. 1892. On a new cysticercus and a new tapeworm. J. Quekett Microscop. Club London *4*, 361–366.

Rosseter, T. B. 1893. On the cysticercus of *T. microsoma* and a new cysticercus from *Cyclops agilis*. J. Quekett Microscop. Club London *5*, 179–182.

Rosseter, T. B. 1894. On *Cysticercus quadricurvatus* Ross. J. Quekett Microscop. Club London *5*, 338–343.

Rosseter, T. B. 1897a. *Cysticercus venusta* (Rosseter). J. Quekett Microscop. Club London *6*, 305–313.

Rosseter, T. B. 1897b. Cysticercus of *Taenia liophallus*. J. Quekett Microscop. Club London *6*, 314–317.

Rosseter, T. B. 1897c. On experimental infection of ducks with *Cysticercus coronula, Cyst. gracilis, Cyst. tenuirostris*. J. Quekett Microscop. Club London *6*, 397–405.

Rosseter, T. B. 1898. On the generative organs of *Drepanidotaenia venusta*. J. Quekett Microscop. Club London *7*, 10–23.

Rosseter, T. B. 1900. The anatomy of *Dicranotaenia coronula*. J. Quekett Microscop. Club London *7*, 355–370.

Rosseter, T. B. 1903. On the anatomy of *Drepanidotaenia tenuirostris*. J. Quekett Microscop. Club London *8*, 399–406.

Rosseter, T. B. 1904. The genital organs of *Taenia sinuosa*. J. Quekett Microscop. Club London *9*, 81–90.

Rosseter, T. B. 1906a. On *Drepanidotaenia undulata* (Krabbe). J. Quekett Microscop. Club London *9*, 269–274.

Rosseter, T. B. 1906b. On a new tapeworm, *Drepanidotaenia sagitta*. J. Quekett Microscop. Club London *9*, 275–278.

Rosseter, T. B. 1907. On the tapeworm, *Hymenolepis nitida* Krabbe and *H. nitidulans* Krabbe. J. Quekett Microscop. Club London *10*, 31–40.

Rosseter, T. B. 1908. On *Hymenolepis fragilis*. J. Quekett Microscop. Club London *10*, 229–234.

Rosseter, T. B. 1909. *Hymenolepis acicula sinuata*, a new species of tapeworm. J. Quekett Microscop. Club London *10*, 393–402.

Rosseter, T. B. 1911. *Hymenolepis upsilon*, a new species of avian tapeworm. J. Quekett Microscop. Club London *11*, 147–160.

Roudabush, R. L. 1941. Abnormalities in *Taenia pisiformis*. Trans. Am. Microscop. Soc. *60*, 371–374.

Rudin, E. 1914. Studien an *Fistulicola plicatus* Rud. Rev. suisse zool. *22*, 321–363.

Rudin, E. 1916. *Oochoristica truncata* Krabbe. Zool. Anz. *47*, 75–78, 81–85.

Rudin, E. 1917. Die Ichthyotaenien der Reptilien. Rev. suisse zool. *25*, 179–381.

Rudolphi, C. A. 1793. Observationes circa vermes intestinales. Pars I. 46 pp. Diss. praes. Quistorp. Gryphiswaldiae.

Rudolphi, C. A. 1801. Beobachtungen ueber die Eingeweidewürmer. Archives für Zoologie und Zootomie (Braunschweig) *2* (1), 1–65.

Rudolphi, C. A. 1802. Fortsetzung der Beobachtungen ueber die Eingeweidewürmer. Archives für Zoologie und Zootomie (Braunschweig) *2* (2), 1–67; *3* (1), 61–125.

Rudolphi, C. A. 1803. Neue Beobachtungen ueber die Eingeweidewürmer. Archives für Zoologie und Zootomie *3* (2), 1–32.

Rudolphi, C. A. 1804. Bemerkungen aus dem Gebiet der Naturgeschichte, Medicin und Thierärzneykunde, auf einer Reise durch einen Theil von Deutschland, Holland und Frankreich. I. Theil, viii + 296 pp. Berlin.

Rudolphi, C. A. 1805. Bemerkungen aus dem Gebiet . . . II. Theil, xvi + 222 pp. Berlin.

Rudolphi, C. A. 1808. Entozoorum sive vermium intestinalium historia naturalis. I. xxvi + 527 pp. Amstelaedami.

Rudolphi, C. A. 1809. Entozoorum sive vermium intestinalium historia naturalis. II. Pars. 1, xxvi + 457 pp. Amstelaedami.

Rudolphi, C. A. 1810. Entozoorum sive vermium intestinalium historia naturalis. II. Pars. 2, xii + 386 pp. Amstelaedami.

Rudolphi, C. A. 1819. Entozoorum Synopsis cui Accedunt mantissa Duplex et Indices Locupletissimi. x + 811 pp. Berolini.

Ruether, R. 1901a. *Davainea mutabilis*. 20 pp. Dissertation, University of Giessen, Hannover.

Ruether, R. 1901b. *Davainea mutabilis*. Beitrag zur Kenntnis der Bandwürmer des Huhnes. Deutsch. Thierärztl. Wochenschr. *9*, 353–357, 362–364.

Ruszkowski, J. S. 1925. Essai du procédé de Leslie Sheather pour concentrer les oeufs d'helminthes destinées à l'expérimentation. Ann. parasitol. humaine et comparée *3*, 388–391.

Ruszkowski, J. S. 1927. Etudes sur le cycle évolutif et sur la structure des cestodes de mer. I. *Echinobothrium benedeni* n. sp. ses larves et son hôte intermédiaire, *Hippolyte varians* (Leach). Bull. intern. acad. polon. sci. Classe sci. math. nat. B., pp. 629–641.

Ruszkowski, J. S. 1932a. Le cycle évolutif du cestode *Drepanidotaenia lanceolata* (Bloch). Bull. intern. acad. polon. sci. Classe sci. math. nat. B., pp. 1–8.

Ruszkowski, J. S. 1932b. Etudes sur le cycle évolutif et sur la structure des cestodes de mer. II. Sur les larves de *Gyrocotyle urna* (Gr. et Wagen.). Bull. intern. acad. polon. sci. Classe sci. math. nat. B., pp. 629–641.

Ruszkowski, J. S. 1932c. Etudes sur le cycle évolutif et la structure des cestodes de mer. III. Le cycle évolutif du tétrarhynque *Grillotia erinaceus* (van Ben., 1858). Compt. rend. mensuels sci. math. nat. acad. polon. Classe sci. lettr. Nov. 1932, Nr. 9, p. 6.

Ruszkowski, J. S. 1934. Etudes sur le cycle évolutif et la structure des cestodes de mer. III. Le cycle évolutif du tétrarhynque *Grillotia erinaceus* (van Ben., 1858). Mem. intern. acad. polon. sci. Classe sci. math. nat. B., Nr. 6, pp. 1–9.

Sachs, H., and A. Klopstock. 1928. Beiträge zum serologischen Verhalten der Bandwurmlipoïde. Z. Immunitätsforsch. (Jena) *55*, 341–357.

St. Remy, G. 1900. Contributions à l'étude du développement des cestodes. I. Le développement embryonnaire dans le genre *Anoplocephala*. Arch. Parasitol. *3*, 292–315.

St. Remy, G. 1901a. Contributions à l'étude du développement des cestodes. II. Le développement de *Taenia serrata* Goeze. Arch. Parasitol. *4*, 143–156.

St. Remy, G. 1901b. Contributions à l'étude de développement des cestodes. III. Le développement embryonnaire des cestodes et la théorie des feuillets germinatifs. Arch. Parasitol. *4*, 333–352.

Salensky, W. 1874. Ueber den Bau und die Entwicklungsgeschichte der *Amphilina* (*Monostomum foliaceum* Rud.). Z. wiss. Zool. *24*, 291–342.

Salisbury, L. F., and R. J. Anderson. 1939. Concerning the chemical composition of *Cysticercus fasciolaris*. J. Biol. Chem. *129*, 505–517.

Sambon, L. W. 1924. *Cysticercus fasciolaris* and cancer in rats. J. Trop. Med. Hyg. *27*.

Sandground, J. H. (No date.) A new mammalian cestode from Brazil. Med. Rep. Hamilton Rice Exped. to the Amazon. Harvard University Press.

Sandground, J. H. 1928. Some new cestode and nematode parasites from Tanganyika Territory. Proc. Boston Soc. Nat. Hist. *39*, 131–150.

Sandground, J. H. 1929. A consideration of the relation of host-specificity of helminths and other metazoan parasites to the phenomena of age-resistance and acquired immunity. Parasitology *21*, 227–255.

Sandground, J. H. 1933. Two new helminths from *Rhinoceros sondaicus*. J. Parasitol. *19*, 192–204.

Sandground, J. H. (No date on reprint.) Notes and descriptions of some parasitic helminths collected by the expedition. Reprinted from Report of the Harvard African Expedition upon the African Republic of Liberia and the Belgian Congo.

Sandground, J. H. 1936. On species of *Moniezia* (Cestoda, Anoplocephalidae) harboured by the hippopotamus. Proc. Helm. Soc. Washington *3*, 52–53.

Sandground, J. H. 1937. On a coenurus from the brain of a monkey. J. Parasitol. *23*, 482–490.

Saunders, L. G. 1949. A survey of helminth and protozoan incidence in man and dogs at Fort Chipewyan, Alberta. J. Parasitol. *35*, 31–34.

Sauter, K. 1917. Beiträge zur Anatomie, Histologie, Entwicklungsgeschichte und Systematik der Rindertaenien. Dissertation, München.

Savazzini, L. A. 1929. *Cylindrotaenia americana* en nuestro *Leptodactylus ocellatus*. Semana Med. (Buenos Aires) *36*, 868–870.

Schapiro, H. 1887. Heilung der Biermischen perniciösen Anämie durch Abtreibung von *Bothriocephalus latus*. Z. klin. Med. *13*, 416–429.

Schapiro, M. M. 1937. A quantitative study of egg production in *Taenia saginata*. J. Parasitol. *23*, 104–105.

Schauinsland, H. 1883. Beitrag zur Kenntnis der Embryonalentwicklung der Trematoden. Jenaische Z. Naturwiss. *16*, 465–527.

Schauinsland, H. 1885. Die embryonale Entwicklung der Bothriocephalen. Jenaische Z. Naturwiss. *19*, 520–573.

Schauinsland, H. 1886. Ueber die Körperschichten und deren Entwicklung bei den Plattwürmern. Sitzb. Ges. Morph. Physiol. München *2*, 7–10.

Schauman, O. 1894. Zur Kenntnis der sogenannten Bothriocephalus-anämie. 214 pp. Helsingfors.

Schauman, O., and T. W. Tallqvist. 1898. Ueber die blutkörperchenauflosenden Eigenschaften des breiten Bandwurms. Deutsche Med. Wochenschr. *24*, 312–313.

Scheuring, L. 1929. Beobachtungen zur Biologie des Genus *Triaenophorus* und Betrachtungen ueber die jahrzeitliche Auftreten von Bandwürmern. Z. Parasitenk. *2*, 157–177.

Schiefferdecker, P. 1874. Beiträge zur Kenntnis des feineren Baues des Taenien. Jenaische Z. Naturwiss. *8*, 459–487.

Schiefferdecker, P. 1875. Ueber eine eigentümliche pathologische Veränderung der Darmschleimhaut des Hundes durch *Taenia cucumerina*. Arch. Path. Anat. *62*, 475–487.

Schilling, T. 1904. Ueber Echinokokkusflüssigkeit. Zentralbl. Inn. Med. *25*, 833–836.

Schmelz, O. 1941. Quelques cestodes nouveaux d'oiseaux d'Asie. Rev. suisse zool. *48*, 143–199.

Schmidt, F. 1888. Beiträge zur Kenntnis der Entwicklung des Geschlechtsorgane einiger Cestoden. Z. wiss. Zool. *46*, 155–187.

Schmidt, F. L. 1940. A new cestode, *Cladotaenia oklahomensis*, from a hawk. Trans. Am. Microscop. Soc. *59*, 519–522.

Schmidt, H. B. 1926. A simple method for finding *Dibothriocephalus latus* eggs in the stools. J. Lab. Clin. Med. *11*, 891.

Schmidt, J. E. 1894. Die Entwicklungsgeschichte und der anatomische Bau der *Taenia anatina* (Krabbe). Arch. Naturgeschichte *60*, 65–112.

Schneider, A. 1885. Neue Beiträge zur Kenntnis der Plathelminthen. Zoologische Beiträge herausgegeben von Dr. Anton Schneider, Breslau. Bd. I, Heft 2, pp. 116–126.

Schneider, G. 1902a. Ueber das Vorkommen des Bandwurms *Bothriotaenia proboscidea* Batsch im Magen und Darm von Ostseeheringen (*Clupea harengus membras* L.). Sitzber. Gesell. naturforsch. Freunde Berlin, 1902, pp. 28–30.

Schneider, G. 1902b. Ichthyologische Beiträge. III. Ueber die in Fischen des finnischen Meerbusens vorkommende Endoparasiten. Acta soc. fauna flora Fenn. *22*, 1–87.

Schneider, G. 1902c. *Bothrimonus nylandicus* n. sp. Arch. Naturgeschichte *68*, 72–78.

Schneider, G. 1903. Beiträge zur Kenntnis der Helminthfauna des finnischen Meerbusens. Acta soc. fauna flora Fenn. *26*, 1–34.

Schneider, G. 1904. Ueber zwei Endoparasiten aus Fischen des finnischen Meerbusens. Medd. soc. fauna flora Fenn. *29*, 75–76.

Schneider, G. 1905. Die Ichthyotaenien des finnischen Meerbusens. Festschrift für Palmen, Helsingfors, I, pp. 1–31.

Schofield, F. W. 1931. Heavy mortality among ducklings due to *Hymenolepis coronula*. Rep. Ontario Vet. College, 1931.

Scholz, G. 1936. Allergische Reaktionen bei mit Zestoden befallenen Hunden. 29 pp. Inaugural Dissertation, Berlin.

Schopfer, W. H. 1924. La permeabilité et l'osmose chez les parasites intestinaux (Nematodes: *Ascaris*). Verh. Schweiz Natf. Ges. Aarau *105*, 188–189.

Schopfer, W. H. 1925a. Recherches sur le liquide de *Cysticercus tenuicollis*. Actes Soc. Helv. sci. nat. Aarau *106*, 158–159.

Schopfer, W. H. 1925b. Urée chez les cysticerques. Arch. sci. phys. Genève (5) 7, 155–156.

Schopfer, W. H. 1925c. Sur la présence d'acide urique dans le liquide de *Cysticercus tenuicollis*. Arch. sci. phys. Genève (5) 7 Suppl., 128–131.

Schopfer, W. H. 1925d. Recherches sur la concentration moleculaire des sucs des parasites. Parasitology *17*, 221–231.

Schopfer, W. H. 1926a. Recherches sur la permeabilité des membranes de *Cysticercus tenuicollis* pour les sels de cuivre. Actes Soc. Helv. sci. nat. Aarau *107*, 219–221.

Schopfer, W. H. 1926b. Recherches physico-chimiques sur les parasites. Nouveaux résultats. Compt. rend soc. phys. hist. nat. Genève *43*, 64–67.

Schopfer, W. H. 1926c. Sur le comportement des *Ascaris* dans les liquides intestinaux hypotoniques. Compt. rend. soc. phys. hist. nat. Genève *43*, 101–103.

Schopfer, W. H. 1926d. Recherches sur la permeabilité des membranes de Cysticerque (*Cysticercus tenuicollis*) pour divers sels. Compt. rend. soc. phys. hist. nat. Genève *43*, 121–123.

Schopfer, W. H. 1926e. Recherches sur le comportement de *Cysticercus tenuicollis* dans les serums normaux et dilués. Arch. sci. phys. nat. Genève (5) *8*, 136–139.

Schopfer, W. H. 1926f. Recherches physico-chimiques sur les liquides de parasites (*Ascaris*). Parasitology *18*, 277–282.

Schopfer, W. H. 1927a. Résultats généraux sur la concentration moleculaire des liquides de parasites. Compt. rend. soc. phys. hist. nat. Genève *44*, 47.

Schopfer, W. H. 1927b. Recherches physico-chimiques sur quelques parasites de poissons marins et d'eau douce. Compt, rend. soc. phys. hist. nat. Genève *44*, 135.

Schopfer, W. H. 1927c. Sur l'indice de réfraction du liquide de cysticerque et ses variations. Arch. sci. phys. nat. Genève (5) *9*, 56–63.

Schopfer, W. H. 1929. Le liquid de cysticerque consideré comme dialysate. Rev. suisse zool. *36*, 221–228.

Schopfer, W. H. 1932. Recherches physico-chimiques sur le milieu intérieur de quelques parasites. Rev. suisse zool. *39*, 59–194.

Schopfer, W. H. 1933. Recherches physico-chimiques sur le milieu intérieur de quelques parasites. Protoplasma *18*, 628–631.

Schrank, P. F. von. 1788. Verzeichnis der bisher hinlanglich bekannten Eingeweidewürmer nebst einer Abhandlung ueber ihre Anverwandtschaften. 116 pp. München.

Schrank, P. F. von. 1790. Fortekning pa nagra hittils obeskrifne intestinalkrak. Kgl. Svenska Vetenskapsakad. Hand. 11, Stockholm. (Verzeichnis einiger noch unbeschriebenen Eingeweidewürmer. Kgl. schwed. Akad. d. Wiss. neue Abhandl. 1790.) (German translation by Kaestner and Link, Bd. 11, Leipzig, 1792, pp. 111–118.)

Schrank, P. F. von. 1796. Helminthologische Beobachtungen. v. Schrank, Sammlung naturhistorischer und physikalischer Aufsatze. 456 pp. Nurnberg.

Schrank, P. F. von. 1803. Fauna boica, durchgedachte Geschichte der in Bayern einheimischen und zahmen Thiere. viii + 272 pp. Landshut.

Schultz, G. 1927. The twentieth helminthological expedition in U.S.S.R. in Novotscherkassk. In The results of twenty-eight helminthological expeditions in U.S.S.R. (Russian text with English abstract.) Moscow.

Schultz, R. L. 1939a. *Hymenolepis scalopi* n. sp. Am. Midland Naturalist *21*, 641–644.

Schultz, R. L. 1939b. A new tapeworm from Swainson's hawk. Trans. Am. Microscop. Soc. *58*, 448–451.

Schultz, R. L. 1940a. Some observations on the amabiliid cestode, *Tatria duodecacantha* Olsen, 1939. J. Parasitol. *26*, 101–103.

Schultz, R. L. 1940b. The genus *Diorchis* Clerc, 1903. Am. Midland Naturalist *23*, 382–389.

Schultze, T. F. S. 1825. Ueber die Begattung der Bandwürmer. Ann. ges. Heilkunde *2*, 127–128.

Schumacher, G. 1914. Cestoden aus *Centrolophus pompilus* L. Zool. Jahrb. Syst. *36*.

Schwartz, B. 1919. A blood destroying substance in *Ascaris lumbricoides*. J. Agr. Research *16*, 253–258.

Schwartz, B. 1921a. Effects of secretions of certain parasitic nematodes on coagulation of blood. J. Parasitol. *7*, 144–150.

Schwartz, B. 1921b. Hemotoxins from parasitic worms. J. Agr. Research *22*, 379–432.

Schwartz, B. 1924. A new proliferating larval tapeworm from a porcupine. Proc. U. S. Nat. Museum *66*.

Schwartz, B. 1925. *Metroliasthes lucida*. J. Parasitol. *12*, 112.

Schwartz, B. 1927a. A subcutaneous tumour in a primate caused by tapeworm larvae experimentally reared to maturity in dogs. J. Agr. Research *35*, 471–480.

Schwartz, B. 1927b. The species of *Dipylidium* parasitic in dogs and cats in the United States. J. Parasitol. *14*, 68–69.

Schwartz, B. 1927c. The life-history of tapeworms of the genus *Mesocestoides*. Science *66*, 17–18.

Schwarz, R. 1908. Die Ichthyotaenien der Reptilien und Beiträge zur Kenntnis der Bothriocephalen. 52 pp. Inaugural Dissertation, University of Basel.

Scott, H. H. 1923. Contribution to the experimental study of the life-history of *Hymenolepis fraterna* and *Hymenolepis longior* in the mouse. J. Helm. *1*.

Scott, H. H. 1924. Stages in the direct development of *Hymenolepis longior* Baylis. J. Helm. *2*, 173–174.

Scott, J. W. 1913. Experiments with tapeworms. I. Some factors producing evagination of a cysticercus. Biol. Bull. *25*, 304–312.

Scott, J. W. 1930. The development of two new *Cladotaenia* in the ferrugineous roughleg hawk. J. Parasitol. *17*, 112.

Scott, J. W. 1941. A new genus and species of tapeworm from the bighorn sheep. Anat. Record *81*, 65–66.

Seddon, H. R. 1931. The life of *Moniezia expansa* within the sheep. Ann. Trop. Med. Parasitol. *25*, 431–435.

Seibert, H. C. 1944. Notes on the genus *Diplotriaena* with the description of a new species. Trans. Am. Microscop. Soc. *63*, 244–253.

Sekulowicz, S. 1932. Etudes sur le développement et sur la biologie de *Caryophyllaeus laticeps* (Pallas). Compt. rend. mensuels sci. Classe sci. math. nat. acad. polon., 1932 (8), p. 4.

Self, J. T., and T. J. McKnight. 1950. Platyhelminthes from fur bearers in the Wichita Mountains Wildlife Refuge, with especial reference to *Oochoristica* spp. Am. Midland Naturalist *43*, 58–61.

Seno, H., M. Kitagawa, and S. Iwamato. 1925. The effect of continued cold on the viability of the plerocercoid of *Dibothriocephalus latus*. J. Imp. Fish. Inst. Tokyo *20* (4).

Setti, E. 1891. Sulle tenie dell' *Hyrax* dello Sciosa. Atti. soc. Ligust. sci. nat. geogr. Genova *2*, 86–92.

Setti, E. 1892. Elminti dell' Eritrea e delle regioni limitrofe. Boll. museo zool. Genova *4*.

Setti, E. 1895. *Dipylidium gervaisi* n. sp. Atti soc. Ligust. sci. nat. geogr. Genova *6*, 99–106.

Setti, E. 1897. Nuovi elminti dell' Eritrea. Atti soc. Ligust. sci. nat. geogr. Genova *8*, 198–247.

Setti, E. 1898. Nuove osservazioni sui cestodi parassiti degli iraci. Atti soc. Ligust. sci. nat. geogr. Genova 9, 188–202.

Setti, E. 1899a. La pretesa *Taenia mediocanellata* dell' *Himantopus candidus* e invece la *T. vaginata*. Boll. museo zool. Genova, No. 69, pp. 1–4.

Setti, E. 1899b. Une nuova tenia nel cane (*Taenia brachysoma* n. sp.). Atti soc. Ligust. sci. nat. geogr. Genova *10*, 11–20.

Seurat, G. 1906. Sur un cestode parasite des huîtres perlières déterminant la production des perles fines aux Iles Gambier. Compt. rend. *113*, 801–803.

Shaw, J. N. 1924. *Hymenolepis tenuirostris,* the apparent cause of losses among geese. J. Parasitol. *17*, 115.

Shaw, J. N., B. T. Simms, and O. H. Muth. 1934. Some diseases of Oregon fish and game, and identification of parts of game animals. Bull. Oregon Agr. Exp. Sta. *322*, 1–23.

Shepard, W. 1943. A new hymenolepidid cestode, *Hymenolepis parvisaccata,* from a pintail duck. Trans. Am. Microscop. Soc. *62*, 174–178.

Shigenobu, T. 1932. Ueber die quantitativ Veränderung einiger Substanzen des Blutes bei der Kaninchenclonorchiasis (in Japanese with German summary). Okayama Iggakkai Zasshi (J. Okayama Med. Soc.) *44*, 1099–1112.

Shikhobalova, N. P., and N. V. Popova. 1937. The action of the albuminous and lipoidal substances of broad tapeworm on the blood of experimental animals. Papers on helminthology on commemoration of the 30 year jubileum of K. J. Skrjabin. Pp. 587–606. Moscow, 1937.

Shipley, A. E. 1898. On *Drepanidotaenia hemignathi,* a new species of tapeworm. Quart. J. Microscop. Sci. *40*, 613–621.

Shipley, A. E. 1900a. Entozoa. Fauna Hawaiiensis 2 (4), 427–441.

Shipley, A. E. 1900b. A description of Entozoa collected by Dr. Willey during his sojourn in the western Pacific. Willey Zoological Results, Cambridge. Part V, pp. 531–536.

Shipley, A. E. 1901. On a new species of *Bothriocephalus.* Proc. Cambridge Phil. Soc. *11*, 209–211.

Shipley, A. E. 1902. On a collection of parasites from the Soudan. Arch. Parasitol. *6*, 604–612.

Shipley, A. E. 1903a. Some parasites from Ceylon. Ceylon J. Sci. *1*, 1–11.

Shipley, A. E. 1903b. On the ento-parasites collected by the "Skeat Expedition" to Lower Siam and the Malay Peninsula in the years 1899–1910. Proc. Zool. Soc. London, 1903 (2), pp. 145–156.

Shipley, A. E. 1905. Notes on a collection of parasites belonging to the museum of University College, Dundee. Proc. Cambridge Phil. Soc. *13*, 95–101.

Shipley, A. E. 1907. Cestodes. In National Antarctic Expedition, 1901–1904, Natural History, Zoology.

Shipley, A. E. 1909. The tapeworms (Cestoda) of the red grouse (*Lagopus scoticus*). Proc. Zool. Soc. London, 1909, pp. 351–363.

Shipley, A. E., and J. Hornell. 1904. The parasites of the pearl oyster. In Herdman, Report to the government of Ceylon on the pearl oyster fisheries of the Gulf of Manaar. Royal Society London, Part II, pp. 77–106.

Shipley, A. E., and J. Hornell. 1905. Further report on parasites found in connection with the pearl oyster fisheries in Ceylon. Herdman, Report . . . Part III, pp. 49–56.

Shipley, A. E., and J. Hornell. 1906. Report on cestode and nematode parasites from the marine fishes of Ceylon. Herdman, Report . . . Part V, pp. 43–96.

Sholl, L. B. 1934. Marked taeniasis in a dog. J. Am. Vet. Med. Ass. *84*, 805–806.

Shorb, D. A. 1933. Host parasite relations of *Hymenolepis fraterna* in the rat and the mouse. Am. J. Hyg. *18*, 74–113.

Shuler, R. H. 1938. Some cestodes of fish from Tortugas, Florida. J. Parasitol. *24*, 57–61.

Siebold, C. T. von. 1837a. Zur Entwicklungsgeschichte der Helminthen. In K. F. Burdach, Die Physiologie als Erfahrungswissenschaft. Vol. II, pp. 201–206. Leipzig.

Siebold, C. T. von. 1837b. Bericht ueber die Leistungen im Gebiete der Helminthologie. Arch. Naturgeschichte *3*, 254–280.

Siebold, C. T. von. 1842. Bericht ueber die Leistungen . . . Arch. Naturgeschichte *8*, 263.

Siebold, C. T. von. 1843. Bericht ueber die Leistungen . . . Arch. für Anatomie, Physiol. und wissensch. Medicin. Jahrgang, 1843, pp. 1–87.

Siebold, C. T. von. 1848. Lehrbuch der vergleichenden Anatomie der wirbellosen Thiere. xiv + 679 pp. Berlin.

Siebold, C. T. von. 1850. Ueber den Generationswechsel der Cestoden nebst einer Revision der Gattung Tetrarhynchus. Z. wiss. Zool. *2*, 198–253. (Translated by Camille Dareste as Mémoire sur la génération alternante des cestodes suivi d'une revision du genre *Tetrarhynchus*. Ann. sci. nat., 3 ser., *15*, 177–248 [1851].)

Siebold, C. T. von. 1853. Ueber die Verwandlung der Echinococcus-Brut in Taenien. Z. wiss. Zool. *4*, 409–424.

Siebold, C. T. von. 1854. Ueber die Band- und Blasenwürmer nebst einer Einleitung ueber die Entstehung der Eingeweidewürmer. 115 pp. Leipzig. (French translation in Ann. sci. nat., 4 ser., *4*, 48–90 [1855].)

Sievers, O. 1935. Serologische Untersuchungen ueber Bandwurmantigene und ihre Antikörper. Z. Immunitätsforsch. u. Exp. Therapie *84*, 208–224.

Sievers, O. 1938. Serologische Prüfungen der Sera von *Bothriocephalus latus* Trägern. Acta Med. Skand. *96*, 289–303.

Sima, I. 1937. A Taenia és *C. pisiformis* elleni immunitás. Állatorvosi Lapok *60*, 1–4.

Simer, P. H. 1930. A preliminary study of the cestodes of the spoonbill, *Polyodon spathula* (Wal.). Trans. Illinois Acad. Sci. *22*, 139–145.

Simms, B. T., and J. N. Shaw. 1931. Studies on the fish-borne tapeworm, *Dibothrium cordiceps*. J. Am. Med. Ass.

Simon, F. 1937. A new cestode, *Raillietina centrocerci*, from the sage grouse, *Centrocercus urophasianus*. Trans. Am. Microscop. Soc. *56*, 340–342.

Simon, F. 1940. Parasites of the sage grouse, *Centrocercus urophasianus*. Univ. Wyoming Publn. *7*, 75–100.

Singer, K. 1935. Experimentelle Beiträge zum Problem der Pathogenese der perniziösen Anämie. II. Mitteilung. Zur Kenntnis der Anämie bei künstlich mit *Bothriochepalus latus* infizierten agastrischen Hunden sowie der Sekretionsverhältnisse des Castleschen Prinzips bei dieser Tierart. Z. gesamt. Exp. Med. *95*, 752–771.

Singh, K. S. 1948. On a new cestode, *Gangesia lucknowia* (Proteocephalidae) from a freshwater fish, *Eutropiichthys vacha* Day, with a revised key to the species of the genus. Indian J. Helm. *1*, 41–46.

Sinitsin, D. F. 1896. Entoparasitic worms of birds in the vicinity of Warsaw (Russian text with French summary). Travaux lab. zool. univ. Varsovie, 29 pp.

Sinitsin, D. F. 1931. A glimpse into the life-history of the tapeworm of the sheep, *Moniezia expansa*. J. Parasitol. *17*, 223–227.

Skinker, M. S. 1935a. A new species of *Oochoristica* from a skunk. J. Washington Acad. Sci. *25*, 59–65.

Skinker, M. S. 1935b. A re-description of *Taenia tenuicollis* Rudolphi, 1819, and its larva, *Cysticercus talpae* Rudolphi, 1819. Parasitology *27*, 175–185.

Skinker, M. S. 1935c. Miscellaneous notes on cestodes. Proc. Helm. Soc. Washington *2*, 68.

Skinker, M. S. 1935d. Two new species of tapeworms from carnivores and a re-description of *Taenia laticollis* Rudolphi, 1819. Proc. U. S. Nat. Museum *83*, 211–220.

Skrjabin, K. J. 1913. Fischparasiten aus Turkestan. I. Hirudinea et Cestodaria. Arch. Naturgeschichte 79, 2–10.

Skrjabin, K. J. 1914a. Vergleichende Charakteristik der Gattungen *Chapmania* Mont. und *Schistometra* Cholodk. Centralbl. Bakt. Parasitenk. *73*, 397–405.

Skrjabin, K. J. 1914b. Zwei neue Cestoden der Hausvögel. Z. Infektionskrankheiten, parasitische Krankheiten, und Hygien der Haustiere *15*, 249–260.

Skrjabin, K. J. 1914c. Zwei Vogelcestoden mit gleicher Scolexbewaffnung und verschiedener Organisation, *Hymenolepis collaris* Batsch und *Hymenolepis compressa* Linton. Centralbl. Bakt. Parasitenk. *74*, 275–279.

Skrjabin, K. J. 1914d. Beitrag zur Kenntnis einiger Vogelcestoden. Centralbl. Bakt. Parasitenk. 75, 59–83.

Skrjabin, K. J. 1914e. Vogelcestoden aus Russisch Turkestan. Zool. Jahrb. Syst. 37, 411–492.

Skrjabin, K. J. 1915. *Hymenolepis fasciata* Rud. (in Russian). Messe med. vet. soc. Petrograd 27, 225–229.

Skrjabin, K. J. 1922. Material zur Monographie der Vogelcestoden. II. Die Gattung *Thelazia.* Ann. mus. zool. acad. sci. Russia.

Skrjabin, K. J. 1923. Studien zur Erforschung der parasitischen Würmer der Raubtiere. I. Ein neuer Hundebandwurm: *Dipylidium rossicum* n. sp. Arch. wiss. u. prakt. Veterinarkunde *1*.

Skrjabin, K. J. 1924a. Faune des vers parasites dans les steppes du Turkestan. I. Parasites des rongeurs (in Russian). Moscow.

Skrjabin, K. J. 1924b. *Progynopilidium noelleri* n. g. n. sp., ein neuer Bandwurm der Katze. Berlin. tierarzt. Wochschr. *40*.

Skrjabin, K. J. 1933. Au sujet d'un nouveau remaniement de la systématique de la famille des Anoplocephalidae Cholodk., 1902. Bull. soc. zool. France *58*, 84–86.

Skrjabin, K. J., and E. M. Matevosyan. 1942a. Stages in the postembryonic development of cestodes of the family Hymenolepididae and an attempt to establish morphological types of their larvicysts. Compt. rend. acad. sci. U.R.S.S. *35*, 83–85.

Skrjabin, K. J., and E. M. Matevosyan. 1942b. Typical morphological modifications of the chitinous organs of the scolex in cestodes from the family Hymenolepididae (in Russian). Compt. rend. acad. sci. U.R.S.S. *35*, 86–88.

Skrjabin, K. J., and N. P. Popoff. 1924. Bericht ueber die Tätigkeit der helminthologischen Expedition in Armenien, 1923. Russk. Zhurnal Trop. Med. *1*, 58–63.

Skrjabin, K. J., and R. E. Schulz. 1926. Affinités entre *Dithyridium* des souris et le *Mesocestoides lineatus* (Goeze, 1782) des carnivores. Ann. parasitol. humaine et comparée *4*, 68–75.

Skrjabin, K. J., and R. E. Schulz. 1928. Ueber den Umfang der medizinischen Helminthologie. Russk. Zhurnal Trop. Med. *6*, 145–152.

Skvortsov, A. A. 1942. Egg structure of *Taeniarhynchus saginatus* and its control (in Russian with English summary, pp. 17–18). Zoologicheskii Zhurnal *21*, 10–18.

Slater, W. K. 1925. The nature of the metabolic processes in *Ascaris lumbricoides.* Biochem. J. *19*, 604–610.

Sleggs, G. F. 1927. Notes on cestodes and trematodes of marine fishes of southern California. Bull. Scripps Inst. Oceanography, Tech. Ser. 1 (6), pp. 63–72.

Sluiter, C. P. 1896. *Taenia plastica* n. sp., eine neue kurzgliedrige Taenie aus *Galeopithecus volans.* Centralbl. Bakt. Parasitenk. *19*, 941–946.

Smith, A. J. 1908. Synopsis of studies in metazoan parasitology in the McManus Laboratory of Pathology, University of Pennsylvania. Univ. Penn. Med. Bull. *20*, 262–282.

Smith, A. J., H. Fox, and C. Y. White. 1908. Contributions to systematic helminthology. Univ. Penn. Med. Bull. *20*, 283–294.

Smorodinzev, I. A., and K. W. Bebeschin. 1935a. Beiträge zur Chemie der Helminthen. Mitteilung II. Untersuchungen der chemischen Zusammensetzung einselner Teile des *Taenia saginata.* Biochem. Z. *276*, 271–273.

Smorodinzev, I. A., and K. W. Bebeschin. 1935b. The content of glycogen in tapeworms (Cestoides) (in Russian). Compt. rend. acad. sci. U.R.S.S. *3*, 413.

Smorodinzev, I. A., and K. W. Bebeschin. 1936a. La composition chimique des oeufs de *T. saginata* et de *D. latum* (in Russian). Compt. rend. acad. sci. U.R.S.S. *4*, 29.

Smorodinzev, I. A., and K. W. Bebeschin. 1936b. Beiträge zur Chemie der Helminthen. Mitteilung III. Die chemische Zusammensetzung des *Taenia solium*. J. Biochem. Tokyo *23*, 19–20.

Smorodinzev, I. A., and K. W. Bebeschin. 1936c. Beiträge zur Chemie der Helminthen. Mitteilung IV. Die chemische Zusammensetzung des *Diphyllobothrium latum*. J. Biochem. Tokyo *23*, 21–22.

Smorodinzev, I. A., and K. W. Bebeschin. 1936d. Beiträge zur Chemie der Helminthen. Mitteilung V. Die chemische Zusammensetzung der *Ascaris lumbricoides*. J. Biochem. Tokyo *23*, 23–25.

Smorodinzev, I. A., and K. W. Bebeschin. 1936e. Les protéinases des ténias. Bull. soc. chim. biol. *18*, 1097–1105.

Smorodinzev, I. A., and K. W. Bebeschin. 1936f. La teneur en glycogène des ascarides (in Russian). Compt. rend. acad. sci. U.R.S.S. *2*, 189–191.

Smorodinzev, I. A., and K. W. Bebeschin. 1939a. La teneur en lipoïdes dans le corps du *Taeniarhynchus saginatus*. Bull. soc. chim. biol. *21*, 478.

Smorodinzev, I. A., and K. W. Bebeschin. 1939b. Les lipoïdes de *Taeniarhynchus saginatus*. Bull. soc. chim. biol. *21*, 1194.

Smorodinzev, I. A., K. W. Bebeschin, and P. I. Pavlova. 1933. Beiträge zur Chemie der Helminthen. Mitteilung I. Die chemische Zusammensetzung von *Taenia saginata*. Biochem. Z. *261*, 176–178.

Smorodinzev, I. A., and P. I. Pavlova. 1936a. Répartition de l'azote des fractions albumineuses dans le corps des Ténias. Ann. parasitol. humaine et comparée *14*, 489–494.

Smorodinzev, I. A., and P. I. Pavlova. 1936b. La composition chimique des oeufs de *Taeniarhynchus saginatus* et de *Diphyllobothrium latum*. Compt. rend. acad. sci. U.R.S.S. *3*, 29–31.

Smyth, J. D. 1946. Studies on tapeworm physiology. I. The cultivation of *Schistocephalus solidus in vitro*. J. Exp. Biol. *23*, 47–70.

Smyth, J. D. 1947a. Studies on tapeworm physiology. II. Cultivation and development of *Ligula intestinalis in vitro*. Parasitology *38*, 173–181.

Smyth, J. D. 1947b. The physiology of tapeworms. Biological Reviews *22*, 214–238.

Smyth, J. D. 1947c. Studies on tapeworm physiology. III. Aseptic cultivation of larval Diphyllobothriidae *in vitro*. J. Exp. Biol. *24*, 374–386.

Smyth, J. D. 1948. Development of cestodes in vitro: production of fertile eggs: cultivation of plerocercoid fragments. Nature *161*, 138.

Smyth, J. D. 1949. Studies on tapeworm physiology. IV. Further observations on the development of *Ligula intestinalis* in vitro. J. Exp. Biol. *26*, 1–14.

Smyth, J. D. 1950a. Parthenogenetic development of eggs of a cestode cultured aseptically *in vitro*. Nature (correspondence) *165*, 492–493.

Smyth, J. D. 1950b. Studies on tapeworm physiology. V. Further observations on the maturation of *Schistocephalus solidus* (Diphyllobothriidae) under sterile conditions *in vitro*. J. Parasitol. *36*, 371–383.

Smyth, J. D., and C. A. Hopkins. 1948. Ester wax as a medium for embedding tissue for the histological demonstration of glycogen. Quart. J. Microscop. Sci. *89*, 431–436.

Soler, M. de los Angeles. 1945. El genero *Nematotaenia* y descripcion de una nueva especie. Rev. Iberica Parasitol. Tomo Extraordinario, pp. 67–72.

Solomon, S. G. 1932. On the experimental development of *Bothridium* (= *Solenophorus*) *pythonis* De Blainville, 1824 in *Cyclops viridis* Jurine, 1820. J. Helm. *10*, 67–74.

Solomon, S. G. 1934. Some points in the early development of *Cysticercus pisiformis* (Bloch, 1780). J. Helm. *12*, 197–204.

Solonitzin, J. A. 1933. Mehrfacher Tetrathyridies der serösen Höhlen des Hundes.

Z. Infektionskrankheiten, Parasitäre Krankheiten und Hygiene der Haustiere *45*, 144–156.

Sommer, F. 1874. Ueber den Bau und die Entwicklung der Geschlechtsorgane von *Taenia mediocanellata* und *Taenia solium*. Z. wiss. Zool. *24*, 490–563.

Sommer, F., and L. Landois. 1872. Ueber den Bau der geschlechtsreifen Glieder von *Bothriocephalus latus*. Z. wiss. Zool. *22*, 40–99.

Sondhi, G. 1923. Tapeworm parasites of dogs in the Punjaub. Parasitology *15*, 59–66.

Sonsino, P. 1889a. Ricerchi sugli ematozi del cane e sul ciclo vitali della *Taenia cucumerina*. Atti soc. Tosc. sci. nat. Pisa *10*, 20–64.

Sonsino, P. 1889b. Studie e notize elmintologiche. Atti soc. Tosc. sci. nat. Pisa *10*, 224–237.

Sonsino, P. 1895. Di alcuni entozoi raccolti in Egitto, finora non descritti. Monitore zool. ital. Firenze *6*, 121–125.

Southwell, T. 1910a. On the determination of the adult of the pearl-inducing worm. Report on certain scientific work done on the Ceylon pearl banks during the year 1909. Ceylon Marine Biological Reports, Part IV, No. 6, pp. 169–172.

Southwell, T. 1910b. A note on endogenous reproduction discovered in the larvae of *Tetrarhynchus unionifactor* inhabiting the tissues of the pearl oyster. Report on certain scientific work . . . Part IV, No. 7, pp. 173–174.

Southwell, T. 1911a. Description of nine new species of cestode parasites including two new genera from marine fishes of Ceylon. Report on certain scientific work . . . Part V, pp. 213–215.

Southwell, T. 1911b. Some remarks on the occurrence of cestodes in Ceylon. Ceylon J. Sci. 7.

Southwell, T. 1912. A description of ten new species of cestode parasites from marine fishes of Ceylon, with notes on other cestodes from the same region. Report on certain scientific work . . . Part VI, No. 22, pp. 259–278.

Southwell, T. 1913a. Parasites from fish. Notes from the Bengal Fisheries Laboratory. Rec. Indian Museum *9*, 79–103.

Southwell, T. 1913b. On some Indian Cestoda. Pt. I. Rec. Indian Museum *9*, 279–300.

Southwell, T. 1913c. A brief review of the scientific work done on the Ceylon pearl banks since the year 1902. J. Econ. Biol. *8*, 22–34.

Southwell, T. 1915. Notes from the Bengal Fisheries Laboratory, Indian Museum. No. 2. On some Indian parasites of fish, with a note on carcinoma in trout. Records Indian Museum *11*, 311–330.

Southwell, T. 1916. On some Indian Cestoda. Pt. II. Records Indian Museum *12*, 1–20.

Southwell, T. 1921a. A note on the occurrence of certain cestodes in new hosts. A new species of cestode (*Anoplocephala vulgaris*) from an African rhinoceros. Ann. Trop. Med. Parasitol. *14*, 295–297, 355–364.

Southwell, T. 1921b. Cestodes from Indian poultry. Ann. Trop. Med. Parasitol. *15*, 161–166.

Southwell, T. 1921c. Cestodes from African rats. Ann. Trop. Med. Parasitol. *15*, 167–168.

Southwell, T. 1921d. A new species of Cestoda from a cormorant. Ann. Trop. Med. Parasitol. *15*, 169–171.

Southwell, T. 1921e. Fauna of the Chilka Lake. On a larval cestode from the umbrella of a jelly fish. Mem. Indian Museum *5*, 561–562.

Southwell, T. 1922a. Cestodes in the collection of the Indian Museum. Ann. Trop. Med. Parasitol. *16*, 127–152.

Southwell, T. 1922b. Cestodes from Indian birds; with a note on *Ligula intestinalis*. Ann. Trop. Med. Parasitol. *16*, 355–382.

Southwell, T. 1924a. The pearl-inducing worm in the Ceylon pearl oyster. Ann. Trop. Med. Parasitol. *18*, 37–53.

Southwell, T. 1924b. Notes on some tetrarhynchid parasites from Ceylon marine fishes. Ann. Trop. Med. Parasitol. *18*, 459–491.

Southwell, T. 1925a. On the genus *Tetracampos* Wedl, 1861. Ann. Trop. Med. Parasitol. *19*, 71–79.

Southwell, T. 1925b. A monograph on the Tetraphyllidea. Liverpool School of Tropical Medicine, Memoir No. 2. Liverpool University Press.

Southwell, T. 1925c. On a new cestode from Nigeria. Ann. Trop. Med. Parasitol. *19*, 243–246.

Southwell, T. 1925d. The genus *Tetracampos* Wedl, 1861. Ann. Trop. Med. Parasitol. *19*, 315–317.

Southwell, T. 1926. Cestodes in the collection of the Liverpool School of Tropical Medicine. Ann. Trop. Med. Parasitol. *20*, 221–228.

Southwell, T. 1927. On a collection of cestodes from marine fishes of Ceylon. Ann. Trop. Med. Parasitol. *21*, 351–373.

Southwell, T. 1928a. Cestodaria from India and Ceylon. Ann. Trop. Med. Parasitol. *22*, 319–326.

Southwell, T. 1928b. Cestodes of the order Pseudophyllidea recorded from India and Ceylon. Ann. Trop. Med. Parasitol. *22*, 419–448.

Southwell, T. 1929a. On the classification of the Cestoda. Ceylon J. Sci. *15*, Pt. I, 49–72.

Southwell, T. 1929b. Notes on the anatomy of *Stilesia hepatica* and on the genera of the sub-family *Thysanosominae* (including *Avitellininae*). Ann. Trop. Med. Parasitol. *23*, 47–66.

Southwell, T. 1929c. A monograph on cestodes of the order Trypanorhyncha from Ceylon and India, Pt. I. Ceylon J. Sci. *15*, Pt. III, 169–312.

Southwell, T. 1930. Cestoda. Vol. I. In The fauna of British India. i–xxxi + 391 pp. London.

Southwell, T., and A. Adler. 1923. A note on *Ophiotaenia punica* (Cholodkovsky, 1908) La Rue, 1911. Ann. Trop. Med. Parasitol. *17*, 333–335.

Southwell, T., and I. S. Hilmy. 1929a. On a new species of *Phyllobothrium* (*P. microsomum*) from an Indian shark. Ann. Trop. Med. Parasitol. *23*, 381–383.

Southwell, T., and I. S. Hilmy. 1929b. *Jardugia paradoxa*, a new genus and species of cestode with some notes on the families Acoleidae and Diploposthidae. Ann. Trop. Med. Parasitol. *23*, 397–406.

Southwell, T., and A. Kirshner. 1937a. Description of a polycephalic cestode larva from *Mastomys erythroleucus* and its probable identity. Ann. Trop. Med. Parasitol. *31*, 37–42.

Southwell, T., and A. Kirshner. 1937b. On some parasitic worms found in *Xenopus laevis*, the South African clawed toad. Ann. Trop. Med. Parasitol. *31*, 245–265.

Southwell, T., and A. Kirshner. 1937c. Parasitic infections in a swan and in a brown trout. Ann. Trop. Med. Parasitol. *31*, 427–433.

Southwell, T., and F. Lake. 1939. On a collection of Cestoda from Belgian Congo. Ann. Trop. Med. Parasitol. *33*, 107–123.

Southwell, T., and P. A. Maplestone. 1921. A note on the synonymy of the genus *Zschokkeella* Ransom, 1909 and of the species *Z. guineensis* (Graham, 1908). Ann. Trop. Med. Parasitol. *15*, 455–456.

Southwell, T., and P. A. Maplestone. 1922. Notes on Australian cestodes. Ann. Trop. Med. Parasitol. *16*, 189–198.

Southwell, T., and B. Prashad. 1918a. Notes from the Bengal Fisheries Laboratory. No. 4. Cestode parasites of *Hilsa*. Records Indian Museum *15*, 77–88.

Southwell, T., and B. Prashad. 1918b. Notes from the Bengal Fisheries Laboratory. No. 5. Parasites of Indian fishes, with a note on carcinoma in the climbing perch. Records Indian Museum *15*, 341–355.

Southwell, T., and B. Prashad. 1918c. Methods of asexual and parthenogenetic reproduction in cestodes. J. Parasitol. *4*, 122–129.

Southwell, T., and B. Prashad. 1920. A revision of the Indian species of the genus *Phyllobothrium*. Records Indian Museum *19*, 1–8.

Southwell, T., and B. Prashad. 1923. A further note on *Ilisha parthenogenetica*, a cestode parasite of the Indian shad. Records Indian Museum *25*, 197–198.

Southwell, T., and A. J. Walker. 1936. Notes on a larval cestode from a fur seal. Ann. Trop. Med. Parasitol. *30*, 91–100.

Spasski, A. A. 1948a. A new cestode family, Skrjabinochoridae n. fam., characterised by complete absence of uteri. Dokladi Akademii Nauk SSSR *59*, 409–411.

Spasski, A. A. 1948b. *Mathevolepis petroschenkoi* n. g. n. sp., a new cestode genus with uterine canals for the development of the eggs. Dokladi Akademii Nauk SSSR *59*, 1513–1515.

Spasski, A. A. 1948c. Change of function of the attachment apparatus in the cestode, *Insinuarotaenia schikhobalovi* n. g. n. sp. Dokladi Akademii Nauk SSSR *59*, 825–827.

Spätlich, W. 1909. Untersuchungen ueber Tetrabothrien. Ein Beitrag zur Kenntnis des Cestodenkörpers. Zool. Jahrb. Anat. *28*, 539–594.

Spencer, W. B. 1889. The anatomy of *Amphiptyches urna* (Grube and Wagener). Trans. Roy. Soc. Victoria *1*, 138–151.

Spengel, J. W. 1905. Die Monozootie der Cestoden. Z. wiss. Zool. *82*, 252–287.

Sprehn, C. E. W. 1932. Lehrbuch der Helminthologie. xvi + 998 pp. Berlin.

Sproston, N. G. 1948. On the genus *Dinobothrium* van Beneden (Cestoda) with a description of two new species from sharks . . . Parasitology *39*, 73–90.

Srivastava, H. D. 1939. A study of the life-history of a common tapeworm, *Mesocestoides lineatus*, of Indian dogs and cats. Ind. J. Vet. Sci. *9*, 187–190.

Stafseth, H. J. 1935. On the control of tapeworm infestation in chickens, with notes on the pathology of the intestines of the hosts. Michigan Agr. Exp. Sta. Tech. Bull. No. 148, 46 pp.

Stafseth, H. J., and W. W. Thompson. 1932. The effects, treatment, and prevention of worm infestation in poultry. J. Am. Vet. Ass. *80*, 467–474.

Stammer, H. J. 1936. Die Entoparasiten der in Schlesien 1935 beobachteten Flamingos. Berichte des Vereins Schlesischer Ornithologen *21*, 15–17.

Steck, W. 1926. Ein einfaches direktes Verfahren zur Ermittlung der Wurmeiermenge im Kote. Schweiz. Arch. Tierheilkunde, Zurich *68*, 561–563.

Steelman, G. M. 1939a. *Oochoristica whitentoni,* a new anoplocephalid cestode from a land tortoise. J. Parasitol. *25*, 479–482.

Steelman, G. M. 1939b. A new cestode from the Texas horned lizard. Trans. Am. Microscop. Soc. *58*, 452–455.

Steelman, G. M. 1939c. A new cestode, *Diorchis longibursa*, from the coot. Am. Midland Naturalist *22*, 637–639.

Steenstrup, J. J. S. 1842. Ueber den Generationswechsel oder die Fortpflanzung und Entwicklung durch abwechselnde Generationen, eine eigentumliche Form der Brutpflege in den niederen Thierclassen. Auf Verlassung des Verfasser nach dem Manuscripte desselben uebersetz von C. H. Lorenzen. xvii + 140 pp. Copenhagen, 1842.

Steenstrup, J. J. S. 1857. Jagttagelser og Bemaerkninger om Hundesteilens Baendelorm, *Fasciola intestinalis* Linn., *Schistocephalus solidus* (C. F. M. Prod. Z. D.). Overs. o. d. k. Dansk. Vidensk. Selsk. Forh. Copenhagen, 1857, pp. 186–195.

Steenstrup, J. S. S., and C. F. Lütken. 1898. Spolia Atlantica. Bidrag til Kundskab om Klump-eller Maanefiskene (Molidae). D. Kgl. Danske Videnskab. Selsk. Skr. *6*, 1–102.

Stephens, J. W. W. 1908. Two new human cestodes and a new linguatulid. Ann. Trop. Med. Parasitol. *1*, 549–556.

Steudener, F. 1877. Untersuchungen ueber den feineren Bau der Cestoden. Abh. naturf. Ges. Halle *13*, 277–316.

Stewart, M. A. 1939. The validity of *Dipylidium sexcoronatum* von Ratz, 1900 (Cestoda). J. Parasitol. *25*, 185–186.

Stiles, C. W. 1892a. Notes sur les parasites. 13: Sur le *Taenia giardi*. Compt. rend. soc. biol. *4*, 664–665.

Stiles, C. W. 1892b. Notes sur les parasites. 14: Sur le *Taenia expansa* Rudolphi. Compt. rend. soc. biol. *4*, 665–666.

Stiles, C. W. 1893. Ueber die topographische Anatomie des Gefässsystems in der Familie Taeniadae. Centralbl. Bakt. Parasitenk. *13*, 437–465.

Stiles, C. W. 1895a. Notes on parasites. A double-pored cestode with occasional single pores. Centralbl. Bakt. Parasitenk. *17*, 457–459.

Stiles, C. W. 1895b. Notes on parasites. 38: Preliminary note to "A revision of the adult leporine cestodes." Veterinary Magazine *2*, 341–346.

Stiles, C. W. 1896. A revision of the adult tapeworms of hares and rabbits. Proc. U. S. Nat. Museum *19*, 145–235.

Stiles, C. W. 1903. The type species of the cestode genus *Hymenolepis*. U. S. Pub. Health Service, Hyg. Lab. Bull. *13*, 19–21.

Stiles, C. W. 1906. Illustrated key to the cestode parasites of man. U. S. Pub. Health Service, Hyg. Lab. Bull. *25*, 1–104.

Stiles, C. W. 1908. The occurrence of a proliferating cestode larva (*Sparganum proliferum*) in man in Florida. U. S. Pub. Health Service, Hyg. Lab. Bull. *40*, 5–18.

Stiles, C. W., and C. E. Baker. 1935. Key-catalogue of parasites reported for Carnivora (cats, dogs, bears, etc.) with their possible health importance. Nat. Inst. Health Bull. *163*, 913–1223.

Stiles, C. W., and A. Hassall. 1893. A revision of the adult cestodes of cattle, sheep and allied animals. U. S. Bur. Anim. Indust. Bull. No. 4, pp. 1–134.

Stiles, C. W., and A. Hassall. 1894. A preliminary catalogue of the parasites contained in the collections of the U. S. Bureau of Animal Industry, U. S. Army Medical Museum, Biological Department of the University of Pennsylvania (Leidy collection), and in the collections of Stiles and of Hassall. Veterinary Magazine *1*, 245–253.

Stiles, C. W., and A. Hassall. 1896a. Report upon present knowledge of the tapeworms of poultry. U. S. Bur. Anim. Indust. Bull. No. 12.

Stiles, C. W., and A. Hassall. 1896b. Notes on parasites. 47: Priority of *Cittotaenia* Riehm, 1881 over *Cittotaenia* Railliet, 1891. Veterinary Magazine *3*, 407.

Stiles, C. W., and A. Hassall. 1899. Internal parasites of the Pribilof fur seal. Report of Fur Seal Investigations, Washington: The fur seals and fur seal islands of the North Pacific Ocean *3*, 99–177.

Stiles, C. W., and A. Hassall. 1902. *Bertiella*, new name for the cestode genus *Bertia* Bl., 1891. Science *16*, 434.

Stiles, C. W., and A. Hassall. 1902–1912. Index catalogue of medical and veterinary zoology. Parts 1–36. U. S. Bur. Anim. Indust. Bull. *39*, 1–2703.

Stiles, C. W., and A. Hassall. 1912. Index catalogue of medical and veterinary zoology. Subjects: Cestoda and Cestodaria. U. S. Pub. Health Service, Hyg. Lab. Bull. *85*, 1–467.

Stiles, C. W., and A. Hassall. 1926. Key catalogue of the worms reported for man. U. S. Pub. Health Service, Hyg. Lab. Bull. *142*, 69–196.

Stiles, C. W., A. Hassall, and M. O. Nolan. 1929. Key catalogue of parasites reported for Primates (monkeys and lemurs) with their possible public health importance, and key catalogue of Primates for which parasites are reported. U. S. Pub. Health Service, Hyg. Lab. Bull. *152*, 409–601.

Stiles, C. W., and M. Orleman. 1925. The cestode genus *Hydatigera* Lamarck, 1816, species *reditaenia* Sambon, 1924. J. Trop. Med. Hyg. *28*, 249–250.

Stiles, C. W., and M. Orleman. 1926. La nomenclature des genres de cestodes *Raillietina*, *Ransomia* et *Johnstonia*. Ann. parasitol. humaine et comparée *4*, 65–67.

Stiles, C. W., and E. C. Stevenson. 1905. The synonymity of *Taenia* (*T. crassicollis*, *T. marginata*, *T. serialis*) and *Echinococcus*. U. S. Bur. Anim. Indust. Bull. *80*, 1–14.

Stiles, C. W., and L. Taylor. 1902a. An adult cestode (*Diplogonoporus grandis*) which may possibly occur in returning American troops. U. S. Bur. Anim. Indust. Bull. *35*, 41–47.

Stiles, C. W., and L. Taylor. 1902b. A larval cestode (*Sparganum mansoni*) of man which may possibly occur in returning American troops. U. S. Bur. Anim. Indust. Bull. *35*, 47–56.

Stoll, N. R. 1935–1937. Tapeworm studies on *Moniezia expansa*. I. Restricted pasture sources of *Moniezia* infection in sheep. Am. J. Hyg. *21*, 628–646, May

1935. II. Persistence of the pasture stage of *M. expansa*. Am. J. Hyg. *22*, 683–703, November 1935. III. Sheep parasitised with one *Moniezia expansa* each. J. Parasitol. *22*, 161–179, April 1936. IV. *Moniezia expansa* of sheep strain contracted by calf. J. Helm. Soc. Washington, January 1937. V. Absence of *Moniezia expansa* from the sheep intestine early after infection. Am. J. Hyg. *26*, 148–161, July 1937. VI. Beginning of reproductive maturity of *Moniezia expansa* in sheep. Sonderabdruck aus der Festschrift Nocht, 1937, herausgeg. vom Inst. Schiffs.- und Tropenkrankheiten in Hamburg. VII. Variation in pasture infestation with *M. expansa*. J. Parasitol. *24*, 527–545, December 1939.

Stoll, N. R., and W. G. Hausheer. 1926. Concerning two options in dilution egg-counting: small drop and displacement. Am. J. Hyg. *6*, 134–145.

Stossich, M. 1882. Prospetto della fauna del mare Adriatico. Parte IV. Vermes. Boll. soc. adriat. sci. nat. Trieste *7*, 168–242.

Stossich, M. 1890. Elminti veneti raccolti dal Dr. Alessandro Conte di Ninni. Boll. soc. adriat. sci. nat. Trieste *12*, 49–56.

Stossich, M. 1891. Elminto veneti raccolti dal Dr. Alessandro Conte di Ninni, e descritti da Michaele Stossich. Boll. soc. adriat. sci. nat. Trieste *13*, 1–8.

Stossich, M. 1895. Notize elmintologiche. Boll. soc. adriat. sci. nat. Trieste *16*, 33–46.

Stossich, M. 1896a. Ricerche elmintologiche. Boll. soc. adriat. sci. nat. Trieste *17*, 121–136.

Stossich, M. 1896b. Elminti trovati in un *Orthagoriscus mola*. Boll. soc. adriat. sci. nat. Trieste *17*, 189–191.

Stossich, M. 1898. Saggio di una fauna elmintologica di Trieste e provincie contemini. Prog. civ. scuola sup. Trieste, 162 pp.

Stossich, M. 1899. Appunti di elmintologiche. Boll. soc. adriat. sci. nat. Trieste *19*, 1–6.

Stossich, M. 1900. Osservazioni elmintologiche. Boll. soc. adriat. sci. nat. Trieste *20*, 89–103.

Stroh, G. 1932. *Coenurus cerebralis* bei der Gemse. Berliner Tierarztl. Wochenschr. *48*, 465–466.

Stunkard, H. W. 1926. The tapeworms of the rhinoceroses, a study based on material from the Belgian Congo. Am. Museum Novitates No. 210, 17 pp.

Stunkard, H. W. 1932a. The resistance of European rabbits and hares to superinfestation by different species of the genus *Cittotaenia*. J. Parasitol. *19*, 156.

Stunkard, H. W. 1932b. Attempts to grow cestodes *in vitro*. J. Parasitol. *19*, 163.

Stunkard, H. W. 1934. Studies on the life-history of anoplocephaline cestodes. Z. Parasitenk. *6*, 481–507.

Stunkard, H. W. 1937a. The life cycle of *Moniezia expansa*. Science *86*, 312.

Stunkard, H. W. 1937b. The physiology, life cycles and phylogeny of the parasitic flatworms. Am. Museum Novitates No. 908, 27 pp.

Stunkard, H. W. 1937c. The life cycle of *Moniezia expansa*. Biol. Bull. *73*, 370.

Stunkard, H. W. 1937d. The life cycle of anoplocephaline cestodes. J. Parasitol. *23*, 569.

Stunkard, H. W. 1938a. Parasitic flatworms in Yucatan. Publn. Carnegie Inst. Washington, No. 491, pp. 33–50.

Stunkard, H. W. 1938b. *Oochoristica parvula* n. nom. for *Oochoristica parva* Stunkard, 1938 pre-occupied. J. Parasitol. *24*, 554.

Stunkard, H. W. 1939a. The development of *Moniezia expansa* in the intermediate host. Parasitology *30*, 491–501.

Stunkard, H. W. 1939b. The role of oribatid mites as transmitting agents and intermediate hosts of ovine cestodes. Verhandl. VII. Intern. Kongr. Entom. Berlin, 1938, *3*, 1671–1674.

Stunkard, H. W. 1939c. Observations on the development of the cestode, *Bertiella studeri*. Abstracts, 3 Intern. Congr. Microbiol., New York, p. 179.

Stunkard, H. W. 1939d. The life cycle of the rabbit cestode, *Cittotaenia ctenoides*. Z. Parasitenk. *10*, 753–754.

Stunkard, H. W. 1940a. The morphology and life history of the cestode, *Bertiella studeri*. Am. J. Trop. Med. *20*, 305–333.

Stunkard, H. W. 1940b. Observations on the development of the cestode, *Bertiella studeri*. Proc. 3 Intern. Congr. Microbiol., New York, pp. 461–462.

Stunkard, H. W. 1940c. Tapeworm infections in the West Indies. Rev. med. trop. parasitol. bact. clin. y lab. *6*, 283–288.

Stunkard, H. W. 1941. Studies on the life history of the anoplocephaline cestodes of hares and rabbits. J. Parasitol. *27*, 299–325.

Stunkard, H. W. 1945. The Syrian hamster, *Cricetus auratus*, host of *Hymenolepis nana*. J. Parasitol. *31*, 157.

Stunkard, H. W. 1947. On certain pseudophyllidean cestodes from Alaskan pinnipeds. J. Parasitol. *33* Suppl., 19.

Stunkard, H. W. 1948. Notes on *Diphyllobothrium stemmacephalum* Cobbold, 1858. J. Parasitol. *34* Suppl., 16.

Stunkard, H. W., and W. F. Lynch. 1944. A new anoplocephaline cestode, *Oochoristica anniellae*, from the Californian limbless lizard. Trans. Am. Microscop. Soc. *63*, 165–169.

Stunkard, H. W., and J. J. Milford. 1937. Notes on the cestodes of North American sparrows. Zoologica *22*, 177–183.

Stunkard, H. W., and H. W. Schoenborn. 1936. Notes on the structure, distribution and synonymy of *Diphyllobothrium lanceolatum*. Am. Museum Novitates No. 880, 9 pp.

Subramanian, K. 1928. On a new tapeworm (*Raillietina Rangoonica*) from the fowl. J. Burma Research Soc. *18*, 78–79.

Subramanian, K. 1939. Studies on cestode parasites of fishes. I. *Biporophyllaeus madrassensis* gen. et sp. nov., with a note on its systematic position. Rec. Indian Museum *41*, 131–150.

Subramanian, K. 1941. Sympathetic innervation of proglottides in *Avitellina lahorea* Woodland. Current Science *10*, 441–443.

Sugimoto, M. 1934. Morphological studies on the avian cestodes from Formosa (in Japanese). Rep. Govt. Res. Inst. Dept. Agr. Formosa *64*, 1–52.

Sumner, F. B., R. C. Osburn, and L. J. Cole. 1913. A biological survey of the waters of Woods Hole and vicinity. Part II, Sect. III. A catalogue of the marine fauna. Bull. Bur. Fish. Washington *31* (1911), Part II (1913), 547–794.

Sunkes, E. J., and T. F. Sellers. 1937. Tapeworm infestation in the southern United States. Am. J. Pub. Health *27*, 893–898.

Swales, W. E. 1934. *Rhabdometra odiosa* (Leidy, 1887) Jones, 1929, a cestode parasite of *Pedioectes phasianellus* in Quebec. J. Parasitol. *20*, 313–314.

Swingle, L. D. 1914. The morphology of the sheep tapeworm, *Thysanosoma actinoides*. Bull. Agr. Exp. Sta. Wyoming, No. 102.

Szidat, L. 1938. *Brachyurus gobii* n. g. n. sp., eine neue Caryophyllaeiden-Art aus dem Gründling, *Gobio fluviatilis* Cuv. Zool. Anz. *124*, 249–258.

Szpotanska, I. 1917. Un nouveau genre, sous-genre et quelques nouvelles espèces de la famille Tetrabothriidae. Societas Scientiarum Varsoviensis *10*.

Szpotanska, I. 1925. Etude sur les Tetrabothriidae des Procellariiformes (in Polish with French summary). Bull. intern. acad. polon. sci. Classe sci. math. nat. B, 1925, pp. 673–727.

Szpotanska, I. 1929. Recherches sur quelques Tetrabothriidae d'oiseaux. Bull. intern. acad. polon. sci. Classe sci. math. nat. B, 1928, pp. 129–152.

Szpotanska, I. 1931a. Quelques espèces nouvelles ou peu connues des Hymenolepididae Fuhrmann (Cestodes). Ann. Mus. Zool. Polonici *9*.

Szpotanska, I. 1931b. Note sur un espèce du genre *Liga*. Ann. Mus. Zool. Polonici 9.

Szpotanska, I. 1932. Kilka nowych lub malo znanych gatunkow z podrodziny Hymeno lepididae Fuhrmann. Ann. Mus. Zool. Polonici *9*, 247–266.

Szpotanska, I. 1934. Z badan nad anatomja *Hymenolepis villosoides* Solowiow. Ann. Mus. Zool. Polonici *10*, 327–332.

Taliaferro, W. H. 1929. The immunology of parasitic infections. New York.

Tallqvist, T. W. 1907. Zur Pathogenese der perniziösen Anämie mit besonderer Berücksichtigung der *Bothriocephalus*-Anämie. Z. klin. Med. *61*, 427–532.

Talysin, T. 1930. *Dibothriocephalus minor* Chol., der kleine Bandwurm Transbaikaliens. Z. Parasitenk. *2*, 535–550.

Talysin, T. 1932. *Dibothriocephalus strictus* n. sp., Menschenparasit des Baikalgestades. Z. Parasitenk. *4*, 722–729.

Talysin, T. 1934. Zur Frage der morphologischen Charakteristik der Strobila bei *Diphyllobothrium minus* Chol. Zool. Anz. *106*, 209–215.

Tarassow, W. 1933a. Ueber die Verbreitung von *Diphyllobothrium latum* und andere Darmparasiten bei der Bevölkerung des Gebiets der Seegruppen Kontschosero. Berichte Borodin Biol. Sta. No. 6.

Tarassow, W. 1933b. Die Behäftigung der Bevölkerung Kareliens mit Eingeweidewürmer. Berichte Borodin Biol. Sta. No. 6.

Tarassow, W. 1934a. Das Schwein und der Hund als engültige Träger des *Diphyllobothrium latum*. Arch. Schiffs.-Tropenhyg. *38*, 156–159.

Tarassow, W. 1934b. Beiträge zum Problem des Kampfes gegen *Diphyllobothrium latum* im Nord-Westgebiet. Arch. Schiffs.-Tropenhyg. *38*, 477–486.

Tarassow, W. 1937. De l'immunité envers le bothriocephale *Diphyllobothrium latum* (L.). Ann. parasitol. humaine et comparée *15*, 524–528.

Taylor, E. L. 1928. *Moniezia*, a genus of cestode worms and the proposed reduction of its species to three. Proc. U. S. Nat. Museum *74*, 2612–2628.

Taylor, E. L. 1933. *Davainea proglottina* and disease in fowls. Vet. J. *89*, 500–504.

Taylor, E. L. 1934. *Fimbriaria fasciolaris* in the proventriculus of a swan . . . Parasitology *26*, 359–360.

Templeton, R. 1836. A catalogue of the species of annulose animals, and of rayed ones, found in Ireland. Magazine of Natural History, London, *9*.

Theiler, G. 1924. On the classification of the cestode genus *Moniezia* (Blanchard, 1891). Ann. Trop. Med. Parasitol. *18*, 109–123.

Thienemann, J. 1906. Untersuchungen ueber *Taenia tenuicollis* Rud. mit Berücksichtigung der übrigen Musteliden-Taenien. Berlin.

Thomas, L. J. 1927. A new bothriocephalid from *Diemictylus viridescens* with notes on the life history. J. Parasitol. *14*, 128.

Thomas, L. J. 1929. Notes on the life history of *Haplobothrium globuliforme* Cooper, a tapeworm of *Amia calva*. Anat. Rec. *44*.

Thomas, L. J. 1930. Notes on the hatching of *Diphyllobothrium latum* eggs. J. Parasitol. *16*, 244–245.

Thomas, L. J. 1931. Notes on the life history of *Ophiotaenia saphena* from *Rana clamitans* Latr. J. Parasitol. *17*, 187–195.

Thomas, L. J. 1934a. Further studies on the life cycle of a frog tapeworm, *Ophiotaenia saphena* Osler. J. Parasitol. *20*, 291–294.

Thomas, L. J. 1934b. Notes on the life cycle of *Ophiotaenia perspicua*, a cestode of snakes. Anat. Rec. *60*.

Thomas, L. J. 1936. A new source of *Diphyllobothrium* infection. Science *85*, 119.

Thomas, L. J. 1937a. *Bothriocephalus rarus* n. sp., a cestode from the newt *Triturus viridescens* Raf. J. Parasitol. *23*, 119–123.

Thomas, L. J. 1937b. Environmental relations and life history of the tapeworm, *Bothriocephalus rarus* Thomas. J. Parasitol. *23*, 133–152.

Thomas, L. J. 1941. The life cycle of *Ophiotaenia perspicua* La Rue, a cestode of snakes. Rev. med. trop. y parasitol. bact. clin. y lab. *7*, 74–78.

Thomas, L. J. 1946. New pseudophyllidean cestodes from the Great Lakes region. I. *Diphyllobothrium oblongatum* n. sp. from gulls. J. Parasitol. *32*, 1–6.

Thomas, L. J. 1947. Notes on the life cycle of *Schistocephalus* sp., a tapeworm from gulls. J. Parasitol. *33* Suppl., 10.

Thomas, L. J. 1949. Interrelations of *Diphyllobothrium* with fish-eating birds of North Lake Michigan. J. Parasitol. *35* Suppl., 27.

Thompson, D. W. 1893. Note on a tapeworm from echidna (*Taenia echidna* n. sp.). J. Roy. Microscop. Soc. *3*, 297.

Todtmann, W. 1913. Die Schalenbildung der Eicocons bei Turbellarien. Arch. Hydrobiol. Stuttgart *8*.

Todtmann, W. 1914. Die Bildung der Eischale bei *Gyratrix hermaphroditus* Ehrb. Arch. Hydrobiol. Stuttgart 9.

Tomita, S. 1937. Clinical observations on patients infested with *Hymenolepis nana*, with special reference to changes in their blood picture (in Japanese with English summary, p. 1056). Taiwan Igakkai Zasshi *36*, 1043–1055.

Tosh, J. R. 1905. Internal parasites of the Tweed salmon, chiefly marine in character. Ann. Nat. Hist., Ser. 7, *15*, 115.

Töttermann, G. 1937. Experimentalla undersökningar över *Bothriocephalus latus* roll i den perniciösa patogenes (English summary). Nordisk Med. Tidskr. *14*, 1320–1322.

Töttermann, G. 1938. Ueber die Pathogenese der Wurmanämie. Acta Med. Scand. *96*, 268–288.

Töttermann, G. 1939. Ueber Sternalmark und Blut bei Wurmträgern (*Bothriocephalus latus, Taenia mediocanellata*). Acta Med. Scand. Suppl. No. 104, 176 pp.

Töttermann, G. 1944a. On the Price-Jones curve in tapeworm-anemia. Acta Med. Scand. *117*, 135–144.

Töttermann, G. 1944b. Anemia hyperchromica diphyllobothrica. Acta Med. Scand. *118*, 402–409.

Töttermann, G. 1944c. On the occurrence of pernicious tapeworm-anemia in *Diphyllobothrium* carriers. Acta Med. Scand. *118*, 410–416.

Töttermann, G. 1944d. Furthermore on the question of pathogenesis of pernicious tapeworm-anemia. A preliminary report. Acta Med. Scand. *118*, 422–429.

Töttermann, G. 1947. Is the broad tapeworm the causal agent of hypochromic anemia? Ann. Medicinae Internae Fenniae *36*, 185–190.

Töttermann, G., and E. Kirk. 1939. Om innehället av lipoider i *Bothriocephalus latus* (German summary, p. 2716). Finska Läkaresällskapets Handlingar 82 (9), published in Nordisk Medicin *3*, 2715–2716.

Tower, W. L. 1900. The nervous system in the cestode, *Moniezia expansa*. Zool. Jahrb. *13*, 359–381.

Trawinski, A. 1936. Ueber Anwendung der Präzipitations reaktion zum Nachweis der Schweinzystizerkose. Centralbl. Bakt. Parasitenk. *136*, 116–120.

Trowbridge, A. H., and H. M. Hefley. 1934. Preliminary studies on the parasite fauna of Oklahoma anurans. Proc. Oklahoma Acad. Sci. *14*, 16–19.

Tseng, Shen. 1932a. Studies on avian cestodes from China. Part I. Cestodes from charadriiform birds. Parasitology *24*, 87–106.

Tseng, Shen. 1932b. Etude sur les cestodes d'oiseaux de Chine. Ann. parasitol. humaine et comparée *10*, 105–128.

Tseng, Shen. 1933a. Studies on avian cestodes from China. Part II. Cestodes from charadriiform birds. Parasitology *24*, 500–511.

Tseng, Shen. 1933b. Study on some cestodes from fishes. J. Sci. Nat. Univ. Shantung, Tsingtao, China, *2*, 1–21.

Tsuchiya, H., and E. H. Rohlfing. 1932. *Hymenolepis nana*, report of additional cases and an experimental transmission from man to rat. Am. J. Diseases Children *43*, 865–872.

Tsunoo, S., S. Yokota, S. Asai, and M. Morokuma. 1934. Ein kasuisticher Beitrag zu *Diplogonoporus grandis*. Nagasaki Igakkwai Zasshi *12*, 1200–1202.

Tubangui, M. A. 1925. Metazoan parasites of Philippine domesticated animals. Philippine J. Sci. *28*.

Tubangui, M. A. 1931. Worm parasites of the brown rat (*Mus norvegicus*) in the Philippine Islands, with special reference to those forms that may be transmitted to human beings. Philippine J. Sci. *46*, 548–553.

Tubangui, M. A. 1938. Pseudophyllidean cestodes occurring in the Philippines. Livro Jubilar Lauro Travassos, 1938, pp. 489–494.

Tubangui, M. A., and V. A. Masilungan. 1937. Tapeworm parasites of Philippine birds. Philippine J. Sci. *62*, 409–438.

Turner, A. W. 1926. Sensitising powers of proteins of parasites as tested by the isolated uterus reaction. Proc. Roy. Soc. Victoria n. s. *38*, 24–54.

Turner, E. L., D. A. Berberian, and E. W. Dennis. 1933. Successful artificial immunization of dogs against *Taenia echinococcus*. Proc. Soc. Exp. Biol. Med. *30*, 618–619.

Turner, E. L., E. W. Dennis, and D. A. Berberian. 1935. The value of the Casoni test in dogs. J. Parasitol. *21*, 180–182.

Turner, M. 1919. On a coenurus in the rat. Ann. App. Biol. *6*, 136–141.

Turner, M., and R. T. Leiper. 1919. On the occurrence of *Coenurus glomeratus* in man in West Africa. Trans. Roy. Soc. Trop. Med. and Hyg. *13*.

Tyson, E. 1683. *Lumbricus latus* or . . . the joynted worm . . . Philosophical Transactions, London *13*, 113–144.

Tyson, E. 1691. *Lumbricus hydrotropicus* or an essay to prove that the hydatids . . . are a species of worms or imperfect animals. Philosophical Transactions, London *17*, 506–510.

Udekem, J. de. 1855. Notices sur deux nouvelles espèces de scolex. Bull. acad. roy. Belg. *22*, 528–533.

Vaillant, L. 1863. Sur deux helminthes cestoïdes de la genette. Inst. Paris *31*, 87.

Vaillant, L. 1864. Note sur les hydatides développés chez un oiseau et des vers cestoides trouvés chez la genette ordinaire. Compt. rend. soc. biol. *5*, 48.

Van Cleave, H. J. 1927. Ctenophores as the host of a cestode. Trans. Am. Microscop. Soc. *46*.

Van Cleave, H. J. 1933. An index to the International Rules of Zoological Nomenclature. Trans. Am. Microscop. Soc. *52*, 322–325.

Van Cleave, H. J. 1935. Some interesting pre-Linnean names. Trans. Illinois Acad. Sci. *28*, 263–265.

Van Cleave, H. J. 1941. Relationships of the Acanthocephala. Am. Naturalist *75*, 31–47.

Van Cleave, H. J., and J. F. Mueller. 1932. Parasites of the Oneida Lake fishes. Part I. Descriptions of new genera and new species. Roosevelt Wild Life Annals *3*, 1–71.

Van Cleave, H. J., and J. F. Mueller. 1934. Parasites of Oneida Lake fishes. Part III. A biological and ecological survey of the worm parasites. Roosevelt Wild Life Annals *3*, 161–334.

Van Gundy, C. O. 1935. *Hymenolepis anthocephalus*, a new tapeworm from the mole shrew, *Blarina brevicauda* Say. Trans. Am. Microscop. Soc. *54*, 240–244.

Vaullegeard, A. 1895. Métamorphose et migration du *Tetrarhynchus ruficollis* (Eisenhardt). Bull. soc. linn. Normandie *8*, 112–143.

Vaullegeard, A. 1899. Recherches sur les Tétrarhynques. Mém. soc. linn. Normandie *19*, 187–376.

Venard, C. E. 1938. Morphology, bionomics and taxonomy of the cestode *Dipylidium caninum*. Ann. New York Acad. Sci. *37*, 273–328.

Venard, C. E. 1940. Studies on parasites of Reelfoot Lake fish. I. Parasites of the large-mouthed black bass, *Huro salmoides* (Lacépéde). Report of the Reelfoot Lake Station (Tennessee Academy of Science) *4*, 43–63.

Venard, C. E., and P. L. Ellis. 1933. On cestodes from dogs. Veterinary Alumni Quart. (Ohio State University) *21*, 20–23.

Vergeer, T. 1928a. *Diphyllobothrium latum* (Linn., 1758), the broad tapeworm of man; experimental studies. J. Am. Med. Ass. *90*, 673–678.

Vergeer, T. 1928b. Canadian fish, a source of the broad tapeworm of man in the United States. J. Am. Med. Ass. *90*, 1687–1688.

Vergeer, T. 1928c. An important source of broad tapeworm in America. Science *68*, 14–15.

Vergeer, T. 1928d. New sources of broad tapeworm infestation. J. Am. Med. Ass. *91*, 396–397.

Vergeer, T. 1928e. Dissemination of the broad tapeworm by wild carnivora. Can. Med. Ass. J. *19*, 692–694.

Vergeer, T. 1929a. The broad tapeworm in America. J. Infect. Diseases *44*, 1–11.

Vergeer, T. 1929b. The dog, a reservoir of the broad tapeworm. J. Am. Med. Ass. *92*, 607–608.

Vergeer, T. 1930. Causes underlying increased incidence of broad tapeworm in man in North America. J. Am. Med. Ass. *95*, 1579–1581.

Vergeer, T. 1934. *Diphyllobothrium laruei* sp. nov. and *Sparganum pseudosegmentatum* sp. nov., two cestodes from the Great Lakes region. Anat. Rec. *40*.

Vergeer, T. 1935. The origin of the genus *Diplogonoporus* Loennberg, 1892. J. Parasitol. *21*, 133–135.

Vergeer, T. 1936. The eggs and coracidia of *Diphyllobothrium latum*. Papers of the Michigan Acad. Sci., Arts and Letters *21*, 715–726.

Vergeer, T. 1942. Two new pseudophyllidean tapeworms of general distribution in the Great Lakes region. Trans. Am. Microscop. Soc. *61*, 373–382.

Verma, S. C. 1926. On a new proteocephalid cestode from an Indian freshwater fish. Allahabad University Studies *2*, 353–362.

Verma, S. C. 1928. Some cestodes from Indian fishes including four new species of Tetraphyllidea and revised keys to the genera *Acanthobothrium* and *Gangesia*. Allahabad University Studies *4*, 119–176.

Vialli, M. 1925. La pressione osmotica negli invertebrata. Arch. fisiol. Firenze *23*, 577–596.

Viborg, E. N. 1792. Efterretning om den Kongl. Danske Veterinair Skoles Indretning. Kjobnhavn. Paa Tydsk i Samml. für Tierarzte *1*.

Viborg, E. N. 1795. Nachricht von der Eintrichtung der Königl. Dänischen Thierarzten Schule nebst einigen Anmerkungen von ähnlichen Anstalten. Sammlung von Abhandlungen für Tierärzte und Oekonomen aus dem Dänischen. I. 324 + 2 pages. Copenhagen.

Vigener, J. 1903. Ueber dreikantige Bandwürmer aus der Familie der Taeniiden. Jahrb. Nassauischen Vereins für Naturkunde *56*, 115–177.

Vigueras, I. P. 1934. Sobre la presencia en Cuba de *Diphyllobothrium mansoni* (Cobbold). Mem. Soc. Cubana Hist. Nat. *8*, 351–352.

Vigueras, I. P. 1941a. Nota sobre varios vermes encontrados en el "flamenco" (*Phoenicopterus ruber*). Mem. Soc. Cubana Hist. Nat. *15*.

Vigueras, I. P. 1941b. Nota sobre *Hymenolepis chiropterophila* . . . Rev. Univ. Habana, 1941.

Viljoen, N. F. 1937. Cysticercosis in swine and bovines, with special reference to South African conditions. Onderstepoort J. Vet. Sci. Anim. Indust. 9, 337–570.

Villot, F. C. A. 1875. Recherches sur les helminthes libres ou parasites des côtes de la Bretagne. Arch. zool. éxp. gén. *4*, 451–482.

Villot, F. C. A. 1882a. L'appareil vasculaire des trématodes consideré sous le double point de vue de sa structure et ses fonctions. Zool. Anz. *5*, 505–508.

Villot, F. C. A. 1882b. Classification des cystiques des ténias fondée sur les divers modes de formation de la vésicule caudale. 9 pp. Montpellier.

Villot, F. C. A. 1883a. Classification des cystiques . . . Rev. sci. nat. Montpellier *2*, 109–117.

Villot, F. C. A. 1883b. Mémoire sur les cystiques des ténias. Ann. sci. nat. zool. *15*, 61 pp.

Vincentiis, C. de. 1887. Sui cisticerchi ocularia . . . e sulla struttura fine dell' uova mature di *Taenia saginata*. Estratto della Rivista Internaz. med. chir. Napoli *4*, 69–79.

Voge, M. 1946. A new anoplocephalid cestode, *Andrya neotomae*, from the wood rat, *Neotoma fuscipes*. J. Parasitol. *32*, 36–39.

Vogel, H. 1929a. Helminthologische Beobachtungen in Ostpreussen insbesondere ueber *Dibothriocephalus latus* und *Opisthorchis felineus*. Deutsch. Med. Wochenschr. *55*.

Vogel, H. 1929b. Beobachtungen ueber *Dibothriocephalus latus*. Arch. Schiffs.-Tropenhyg. *33*, 164–168.

Vogel, H. 1929c. Studien zur Entwicklung von *Diphyllobothrium*. Z. Parasitenk. 2 (2), 213–222.

Vogel, H. 1930. Studien zur Entwicklung von *Diphyllobothrium*. Z. Parasitenk. 2 (5), 629–644.

Vogel, R. 1921. Ein Cysticercus des Regenwurmes als Jugendform der Vogeltaenie, *Dilepis undula* (Schrank). Centralbl. Bakt. Parasitenk. *85*, 370–372.

Volz, W. 1899. Die Cestoden der einheimischen Corviden. Zool. Anz. *22*, 265–268.

Volz, W. 1900. Beitrag zur Kenntnis einiger Vogelcestoden. Inaug. Dissertation, Basel; Arch. Naturgeschichte, pp. 115–174.

Vosgien (no initials). 1911. Le cysticercus cellulosae chez l'homme et chez les animaux. Thése de la Faculté de Médicine, Paris. See Brumpt, 1936.

Waele, A. de. 1933. Recherches sur les migrations des cestodes. Bull. acad. roy. Belg. *19*, 649–660, 837–848, 1126–1135.

Waele, A. de. 1934. Nieuwe bevindingen over der levenscyclus der Cestoden. Natuurw. Tijdschr. (Belg.) *16*, 60–69.

Waele, A. de. 1936. Le mécanisme physiologique des migrations et de la specificité chez les cestodes. Compt. rend. XII Congr. Intern. Zool., Lisbon, 1935, pp. 313–328.

Waele, A. de, and L. Dedeken. 1936. Le phénoménon de l'évagination chez *Cysticercus bovis* et la migration du parasite chez l'homme. Mém. musée roy. hist. nat. Belg., Sér. 2, Fasc. 3, pp. 369–373.

Wagener, G. R. 1848. Enthelminthica. Dissertatio inauguralis . . . Universität. Friderica Guilelma ut summi in Medicina et Chirurgica Honores rite sibi concedantur . . . 31 pp. Berolini, 1848.

Wagener, G. R. 1851. Enthelminthica. I. Ueber *Tetrarhynchus.* Briefliche-Mitteilung an den Herausgeber. Pisa, 1 Jan. 1851. Arch. Anat. Physiol. u. wiss. Medicin, Berlin, Jahrg. 1851, pp. 211–220.

Wagener, G. R. 1852a. Enthelminthica. III. Ueber einen neuen in der *Chimaera monstrosa* gefundenen Eingeweidewurm. Arch. Anat. Physiol. u. wiss. Medicin, Berlin, Jahrg. 1852, pp. 543–554.

Wagener, G. R. 1852b. Die Entwicklung der Cestoden. Tagesberichte ueber die Fortschritte der Natur- und Heilkunde, R. Froriep, Weimar, *3*, 65–71.

Wagener, G. R. 1854. Die Entwicklung der Cestoden nach eigenen Untersuchungen. Verhandl. kaiserl. Leopold Carol Akad. Naturforscher; Nova Acta Akad. Caesar Leopold-Carol naturw. curiosorum *24* Suppl., 21–91.

Wagener, G. R. 1857. Beiträge zur Entwicklungsgeschichte der Eingeweidewürmer. Natuurk. Verhandel. van de hollandsche Maatschap der Wetenschap. te Haarlem II Verzam., XIII Deel, 1857, pp. 1–112.

Wagener, G. R. 1858. Enthelminthica. V. Ueber *Amphilina foliacea mihi* (*M. foliaceum* Rud.), *Gyrocotyle* Diesing und *Amphiptyches* Gr. W. Arch. Naturgeschichte *24*, 244–249.

Wagin, W. 1933. Zur Frage der Helminthfauna Pinnipedia (in Russian with German summary, pp. 61–62). Trans. Arctic Inst. Leningrad *3*, 51–60.

Wagner, O. 1917. Ueber Entwicklungsgang und Bau einer Fischtaenie (*Ichthyotaenia torulosa* Batsch). Jenaische Z. Naturw. *55*, 1–66.

Wallace, F. G. 1934. Parasites collected from the moose, *Alces americanus,* in northern Minnesota. J. Am. Vet. Med. Ass. *84*, 770–775.

Wallace, J. C., and M. Grant. 1922. Infestation by broad tapeworm. J. Am. Med. Ass. *78*, 1050.

Walter, H. 1866a. Helminthologische Studien. Berlin. Offenbacher Ver. Naturk. 1865–1866, *7*, 51–79.

Walter, H. 1866b. Nachtragliche Mittheilung zu Helminthologische Studien. Berlin. Offenbacher Ver. Naturk. 1865–1866, pp. 133–134.

Walton, A. C. 1939. The Cestoda as parasites of Amphibia. Contributions Biological Laboratories Knox College No. 64, 31 pp.

Walton, A. C. 1941. Notes on some helminths from California Amphibia. Trans. Am. Microscop. Soc. *60*, 53–57.

Ward, H. B. 1894a. A preliminary report on the worms (mostly parasitic) collected in Lake St. Clair, in the summer of 1893. Michigan Fish. Comm. Bull. *4*, 49–54.

Ward, H. B. 1894b. Some notes on the biological relations of the fish parasites of the Great Lakes. Proc. Nebraska Acad. *4*, 8–11.

Ward, H. B. 1895. The parasitic worms of man and the domestic animals. Report Nebraska Board Agr., pp. 225–338.

Ward, H. B. 1896. A new human tapeworm. Western Medical Review *1*, 35–36.

Ward, H. B. 1898. The parasitic worms of domesticated birds. Studies Zool. Lab. Univ. Nebraska, 118 pp.

Ward, H. B. 1901. Internal parasites of Nebraska birds. Proc. Nebraska Ornithol. Union *2*, 63–70.

Ward, H. B. 1906. A new bothriocephalid parasite of man. Science n. s. *23*, 258.

Ward, H. B. 1908. Some points in the migration of Pacific salmon as shown by its parasites. Studies Zool. Lab. Univ. Nebraska, 9 pp.

Ward, H. B. 1910. Internal parasites of the Sebago salmon. Proc. 4th Intern. Fish. Congress in Bull. U. S. Bur. Fisheries (1908) *28*, 1151–1194.

Ward, H. B. 1911. The discovery of *Archigetes* in America, with a discussion of its structure and affinities. Science n. s. *33*, 272–273.

Ward, H. B. 1912a. Means for the accurate determination of human internal parasites. Illinois Med. J.

Ward, H. B. 1912b. The distribution and frequency of animal parasites and parasitic diseases in North American freshwater fishes. Trans. Am. Fisheries Soc. 1911 (1912), pp. 207–241.

Ward, H. B. 1912c. Some points in the general anatomy of *Gyrocotyle*. Zool. Jahrb. Suppl. 15, Festschr. 60 Geburtstag J. W. Spengel.

Ward, H. B. 1913. Cestoda. Buck's Ref. Handbook of Med. Sci. *2*, 761–780.

Ward, H. B. 1916. Intestinal parasites in children. Arch. Ped. *33*, 116–123.

Ward, H. B. 1917. On the structure and classification of North American parasitic worms. J. Parasitol. *4*, 1–11.

Ward, H. B. 1918. Parasitic flatworms. In Ward and Whipple, Fresh-water biology, pp. 365–453. New York.

Ward, H. B. 1923. (Discussion of case of *D. latum*. Proc. Helm. Soc. Washington.) J. Parasitol. *9*, 244.

Ward, H. B. 1926. Animal parasites. Abt's Pediatrics *8*, 912–1065.

Ward, H. B. 1927. A study on the life history of the broad fish tapeworm in North America. Science *66*, 197–198.

Ward, H. B. 1929. Studies on the broad fish tapeworm in Minnesota. J. Am. Med. Ass. *92*, 389–390.

Ward, H. B. 1930. The introduction and spread of the fish tapeworm (*Diphyllobothrium latum*) in the United States. De Lamar Lectures 1929–1930. Baltimore.

Ward, H. B. 1935. The longevity of *Diphyllobothrium latum*. Recueil des travaux dedié au 25me anniversaire scientifique du Professeur Eugene Pavlosky, 1909–1934. Pp. 286–294. Moscow.

Wardle, R. A. 1932a. The Cestoda of Canadian fishes. I. The Pacific coast region. Contrib. Can. Biol. Fish. n. s. 7, 223–243.

Wardle, R. A. 1932b. The Cestoda of Canadian fishes. II. The Hudson Bay drainage system. Contrib. Can. Biol. Fish. n. s. 7, 379–403.

Wardle, R. A. 1932c. On the technique of tapeworm study. Parasitology *24*, 241–252.

Wardle, R. A. 1932d. The limitations of metramorphic characters in the differentiation of Cestoda. Trans. Roy. Soc. Canada *26*, 193–204.

Wardle, R. A. 1932e. Significant factors in the plerocercoid environment of *Diphyllobothrium latum*. J. Helm. *11*, 25–44.

Wardle, R. A. 1933. The parasitic helminths of Canadian animals: The Cestodaria and Cestoda. Can. J. Research *8*, 317–333.

Wardle, R. A. 1934. The viability of tapeworms in artificial media. Physiol. Zool. *7*, 36–61.

Wardle, R. A. 1935a. The Cestoda of Canadian fishes. III. Additions to the Pacific coastal fauna. Contrib. Can. Biol. Fish. *8*, 79–87.

Wardle, R. A. 1935b. Fish tapeworm. Biol. Board Canada Bull. *45*, 1–25.

Wardle, R. A. 1937a. The physiology of the sheep tapeworm, *Moniezia expansa*. Can. J. Research *15*, 117–126.

Wardle, R. A. 1937b. The physiology of tapeworms. In Manitoba essays, 60th anniversary commemoration volume, University of Manitoba, pp. 338–364.

Wardle, R. A., M. J. Gotschall, and L. J. Horder. 1937. The influence of *Diphyllobothrium latum* infestation upon dogs. Trans. Roy. Soc. Canada *31*, 59–69.

Wardle, R. A., and N. K. Green. 1941a. Tapeworm anaemia: the influence of tapeworm fatty acid ingestion upon the host blood picture. Trans. Roy. Soc. Canada *35*, 85–97.

Wardle, R. A., and N. K. Green. 1941b. The rate of growth of the tapeworm, *Diphyllobothrium latum* (L.). Can. J. Research *19*, 245–251.

Wardle, R. A., and E. L. McColl. 1937. The taxonomy of *Diphyllobothrium latum* (L.) in western Canada. Can. J. Research *15*, 163–175.

Wardle, R. A., J. A. McLeod, and I. E. Stewart. 1947. Lühe's "Diphyllobothrium" (Cestoda). J. Parasitol. *33*, 319–330.

Warthin, A. S. 1928. Increasing human incidence of broad tapeworm infestation in the Great Lakes region. J. Am. Med. Ass. *90*, 2080–2082.

Watson, E. E. 1911. The genus *Gyrocotyle* and its significance for problems of cestode structure and phylogeny. Univ. California Publn. Zool. *6*, 353–468.

Webster, J. D. 1942. The type of *Gyrocoelia milligani* Linton, 1927. J. Parasitol. *28*, 230.

Webster, J. D. 1943. A revision of the Fimbriariinae (Cestoda, Hymenolepididae). Trans. Am. Microscop. Soc. *62*, 390–397.

Webster, J. D. 1944. A new cestode from the bobwhite. Trans. Am. Microscop. Soc. *63*, 44–45.

Webster, J. D. 1947. Helminths from the bobwhite in Texas . . . Trans. Am. Microscop. Soc. *66*, 339–343.

Webster, J. D. 1948. Two cestodes from a nighthawk. J. Parasitol. *34*, 93–95.

Webster, J. D. 1949a. Fragmentary studies on the life history of the cestode *Mesocestoides latus*. J. Parasitol. *35*, 83–90.

Webster, J. D. 1949b. Records of *Ophryocotyle* . . . Trans. Am. Microscop. Soc. *68*, 104–106.

Webster, J. D., and C. J. Addis. 1945. Helminths from the bob-white quail in Texas. J. Parasitol. *31*, 286–287.

Wedl, K. 1855. Helminthologische Notizen. Sitzber. Akad. Wiss. Wien, Math. naturwiss. Klasse, Abt. I, *16*, 371–395.

Wedl, K. 1856. Charakteristik mehrerer grössenteils neuer Taenien. Sitzber. Akad. Wiss. Wien, Math. naturwiss. Klasse, Abt. I, *18*, 5–27.

Wedl, K. 1861. Zur Helminthenfauna Aegyptens (2 Abt.). Sitzber. Akad. Wiss. Wien, Math. naturwiss. Klasse, Abt. I, *44*, 463–482.

Weerekoon, A. C. J. 1944. A new avian cestode, *Cotugnia platycerci*, from Stanley's Rosella parakeet, *Platycercus icterotis*. Ceylon J. Sci. *22*, 155–159.

Weimer, B. R., R. S. Hedden, and K. Cowdery. 1934. Flatworm and roundworm parasites of wild rabbits of the northern Panhandle. Proc. West. Acad. Sci. *7*, 54–55.

Weinland, D. F. 1857. Observations on a new genus of taenioids. Proc. Boston Soc. Nat. Hist. *6*, 59–63.

Weinland, D. F. 1858. An essay on the tapeworms of man. x + 93 pp. Cambridge, Massachusetts.

Weinland, D. F. 1861. Beschreibung zweier neuer Taenioiden aus dem Menschen. Versuch einer Systematik der Taenien ueberhaupt. Nov. Act. Akad. nat. curios. Jenae *28*, 24 pp.

Weiss, M. A. 1910. Sur les cestodes de deux genettes capturées en Tunisie. Bull. soc. hist. nat. Afrique du Nord *1*, 113–115.

Weithofer, M. 1916. Wissenschaftliche Ergebnisse der mit Unterstützung der Kaiserliche Akademie der Wissenschaft in Wien aus der Erbschaft Treitl. von F. Werner unternommenen Zoologische Expedition nach dem anglo-aegyptischen Sudan (Kordofan) 1914. Vogelcestoden aus Sennar und Kordofan. Akad. Anz. Akad. Wiss. Wien *53*, 312–313.

Welch, F. H. 1876. The anatomy of two parasitic forms of the family Tetrarhynchidae. J. Linnean Soc. London *12*, 329–342.

Wenninger, F. J. 1929. The anatomy of *Stenobothrium macrobothrium* Diesing. Am. Midland Naturalist *11*, 503–533.

Werner, P. C. F. 1782. Vermium intestinalium praesertim Taeniae humanae brevis expositio. 144 pp. Leipzig.

Wernicke, R., and E. Savino. 1923. Quelques propriétés physiques du liquide hydatique. Compt. rend. soc. biol. *88*, 243.

Wetzel, R. 1932. Zur Kenntnis des weniggliedrigen Hühnerbandwurmes, *Davainea proglottina.* Arch. Wiss. Prakt. Tierheilk. *65*, 595–625.

Wetzel, R. 1933. Zur Kenntnis des Entwicklungskreis des Hühnerbandwurmes, *Raillietina cesticillus.* Deutsche Tierärztl. Wochenschr. *41*, 465–467.

Wetzel, 1934. Untersuchungen ueber den Entwicklungskreis des Hühnerbandwurmes *Raillietina cesticillus* (Molin, 1858). Arch. Wiss. Prakt. Tierheilk. *68*, 221–232.

Wharton, D. R. A. 1930. Immunological studies with tapeworm antigens. Am. J. Hyg. *12*, 511–536.

Wharton, D. R. A. 1931. Skin reactions in rabbits infected with the larval form of *Taenia serrata.* Am. J. Hyg. *14*, 477–483.

Wilhelmi, R. W. 1940. Serological reactions and species specificity of some helminths. Biol. Bull. *79*, 64–90.

Will, H. 1893. Anatomie von *Caryophyllaeus mutabilis* Rud. Ein Beitrag zur Kenntnis der Cestoden. Z. wiss. Zool. *56*, 1–41.

Willemoes-Suhm, R. 1869. Helminthologische Notizen. I. Zur Entwicklung von *Schistocephalus dimorphus* Creplin. Z. wiss. Zool. *19*, 470–472.

Williams, O. L. 1931. Cestodes from the eastern wild turkey. J. Parasitol. *18*, 14–20.

Williams, S. R. 1939. Variation in *Moniezia expansa* Rudolphi. Ohio J. Sci. *39*, 37–42.

Wilmoth, J. H. 1945. Studies on metabolism of *Taenia taeniaeformis.* Physiol. Zool. *18*, 60–80.

Winfield, G. F., and C. F. Chang. 1936. *Raillietina* (*Raillietina*) *sinensis,* a new tapeworm from the domestic fowl. Peking Nat. Hist. Bull. *11*, 35–37.

Wisniewski, L. W. 1928. *Archigetes cryptobothrius* n. sp., nebst Angaben ueber die Entwicklung im Genus *Archigetes* R. Leuck. Zool. Anz. 77, 113–124.

Wisniewski, L. W. 1930. Das Genus *Archigetes* R. Leuck. Eine Studie zur Anatomie, Histogenese, Systematik und Biologie. Mem. acad. polon. sci. Classe sci. math. nat. B, *2*, 1–160.

Wisniewski, L. W. 1932. Zur postembryonalen Entwicklung von *Cyathocephalus truncatus* Pallas. Zool. Anz. *98*, 213–218.

Wisniewski, L. W. 1933. *Cyathocephalus truncatus* Pallas. I. Die Postembryonalen Entwicklung und Biologie. II. Allgemeine Morphologie. Bull. acad. polon. sci. Classe sci. math. nat. B, *3*, 237–252, 311–327.

Wisseman, C. L., Jr. 1945. Morphology of the cysticercoid of the fowl tapeworm, *Raillietina cesticillus* (Molin). Trans. Am. Microscop. Soc. *64*, 145–150.

Witenberg, G. 1932. On the cestode subfamily *Dipylidiinae* Stiles. Z. Parasitenk. *4*, 542–584.

Witenberg, G. 1934. Studies on the cestode genus *Mesocestoides.* Arch. Zool. Ital. *20*, 467–509.

Wolf, E. 1906. Beiträge zur Entwicklungsgeschichte von *Cyathocephalus truncatus* Pallas. Zool. Anz. *30*, 30–37.

Wolffhügel, K. 1898a. Vorläufige Mitteilung ueber die Anatomie von *T. polymorpha* Rud. Zool. Anz. *21*, 211–213.

Wolffhügel, K. 1898b. *Taenia malleus* Goeze, Repraesentant einer eigenen Cestodenfamilie: Fimbriariidae. Vorl. Mitteilung. Zool. Anz. *21*, 388–389.

Wolffhügel, K. 1899a. Beiträge zur Kenntnis der Anatomie einiger Vogelcestoden. Zool. Anz. *22*, 117–123.

Wolffhügel, K. 1899b. Rechtfertigung gegenueber Cohns Publikation "zur Systematik der Vogeltaenien II." Centralbl. Bakt. Parasitenk. *26*, 632–635.

Wolffhügel, K. 1900a. Beitrag zur Kenntnis der Vogelhelminthen. 204 pp. Inaug. Dissert. Basel.

Wolffhügel, K. 1900b. *Drepanidotaenia lanceolata* Bloch. Centralbl. Bakt. Parasitenk. *28*, 49–56.

Wolffhügel, K. 1903. *Stilesia hepatica* nov. spec. ein Bandwurm aus den Gallengängen von Schäfen und Ziegen Ostafrikas. Berlin Tierärzt. Wochenschr. *43*, 1–16.

Wolffhügel, K. 1904. Ein interessantes Exemplar des Taubenbandwurmes *Bertia Delafondi* (Railliet). Berlin Tierärzt. Wochenschr. *44*, 1–10.

Wolffhügel, K. 1911. Los Zooparasitos de los animales domesticos en la Republica Argentina. Rev. centro estudiantes agron. y vet., Buenos Aires. 104 pp.

Wolffhügel, K. 1916. Cestode nuevo, parasito del estomago succenturiado de un cisne (*Cygnus melanocoryphus* Molin). Rev. med. vet. *1*, 22.

Wolffhügel, K. 1920. Die Parasiten der Haustiere in Südamerika, besonders in den La Plata Staaten. Festschr. f. Zschokke No. 29, 4 pp.

Wolffhügel, K. 1936. *Fimbriariinae* (Cestoda). Z. Infektionskr. u. Hyg. Haustiere *49*, 257–292.

Wolffhügel, K. 1938. Nematoparataeniidae. Z. Infektionskr. u. Hyg. Haustiere *53*, 9–42.

Wolffhügel, K., and Vogelsang. 1926. *Dibothriocephalus decipiens* (Diesing), su larva *Sparganum reptans* en al Uruguay. Rev. med. vet. *8*.

Woodberry, L. A. 1932. The development of *Diphyllobothrium cordiceps* (= *Dibothrium cordiceps*) in *Pelicanus erythrorhynchus*. J. Parasitol. *18*, 304–305.

Woodger, J. H. 1921. Notes on a cestode occurring in the haemocoele of house-flies in Mesopotamia. Ann. Applied Biol. *7*, 345–351.

Woodland, W. N. F. 1923a. On *Amphilina paragonopora* sp. n. and a hitherto undescribed phase in the life history of the genus. Quart. J. Microscop. Sci. *67*, 47–84.

Woodland, W. N. F. 1923b. On some remarkable new forms of Caryophyllaeidae from the Anglo-Egyptian Sudan, and a revision of the families of the Cestodaria. Quart. J. Microscop. Sci. *67*, 435–472.

Woodland, W. N. F. 1923c. On *Ilisha parthenogenetica* Southwell and Baini Prashad, 1918, from the pyloric caeca of a fish, *Clupea ilisha* (Ham. Buch.) and a comparison with other plerocercoid larvae of cestodes. Parasitology *15*, 128–136.

Woodland, W. N. F. 1924a. On the life-cycle of *Hymenolepis fraterna* (*H. nana* var. *fraterna* Stiles) of the white mouse. Parasitology *16*.

Woodland, W. N. F. 1924b. On the development of the human *Hymenolepis nana* (Siebold, 1852) in the white mouse, with remarks on "H. fraterna," "H. longior" and "H. diminuta." Parasitology *16*.

Woodland, W. N. F. 1924c. On a new species of the cestodarian genus *Caryophyllaeus* from an Egyptian siluroid. Proc. Zool. Soc. London, 1924, pp. 529–532.

Woodland, W. N. F. 1924d. On a new *Bothriocephalus* and a new genus of Proteocephalidae from Indian freshwater fishes. Parasitology *16*, 441–451.

Woodland, W. N. F. 1925a. On some remarkable *Monticellia*-like and other cestodes from Sudanese siluroids. Quart. J. Microscop. Sci. *69*.

Woodland, W. N. F. 1925b. *Tetracampos* Wedl, 1861, as a genus of the Bothriocephalidae. Ann. Trop. Med. Parasitol. *19*, 185–189.

Woodland, W. N. F. 1925c. On *Proteocephalus marenzelleri*, *P. naiae* and *P. viperis*. Ann. Trop. Med. Parasitol. *19*, 265–279.

Woodland, W. N. F. 1925d. On three new Proteocephalids (Cestoda) and a revision of the genera of the family. Parasitology *17*, 370–394.

Woodland, W. N. F. 1926. On the genera and possible affinities of the Caryophyllaeidae; a reply to Drs. O. Fuhrmann and J. G. Baer. Proc. Zool. Soc. London, 1926, pp. 49–69.

Woodland, W. N. F. 1927a. On three new species of *Avitellina* (Cestoda) from India and the Anglo-Egyptian Sudan, with a redescription of the type species *A. centripunctata* (Rivolta, 1874). Ann. Trop. Med. Parasitol. *21*, 385–414.

Woodland, W. N. F. 1927b. A revised classification of the tetraphyllidean Cestoda, with descriptions of some Phyllobothriidae from Plymouth. Proc. Zool. Soc. London, 1927, p. 519.

Woodland, W. N. F. 1927c. On *Dinobothrium septaria* van Beneden, 1889 and *Parabothrium bulbiferum* Nybelin, 1922. J. Parasitol. *13*, 231–248.

Woodland, W. N. F. 1928a. On a new genus of avitelline tapeworm from ruminants in East Africa. Parasitology *20*, 56–65.

Woodland, W. N. F. 1928b. On some new avian cestodes from the Sudan. Parasitology *20*, 305–314.

Woodland, W. N. F. 1929a. On a new species of *Rhabdometra* with a note on the nematodiform embryos of *Anonchotaenia globata*. Proc. Zool. Soc. London, 1929, pp. 25–29.

Woodland, W. N. F. 1929b. On some new avian cestodes from India. Parasitology *21*, 168–179.

Woodland, W. N. F. 1930a. On three new cestodes from birds. Parasitology 22, 214–229.

Woodland, W. N. F. 1930b. On the genus *Polypocephalus* Braun, 1878 (Cestoda). Proc. Zool. Soc. London, 1930, pp. 347–354.

Woodland, W. N. F. 1933a. On the anatomy of some fish cestodes described by Diesing from the Amazon. Quart. J. Microscop. Sci. *76*, 175–208.

Woodland, W. N. F. 1933b. On two new cestodes from the Amazon siluroid fish *Brachyplatystoma vaillanti* Cuv. Parasitology *25*, 485–490.

Woodland, W. N. F. 1933c. On a new subfamily of Proteocephalid cestodes – the Othinoscolecinae – from the Amazon siluroid fish *Platystomatichthys sturio* (Kner). Parasitology *25*, 491–500.

Woodland, W. N. F. 1934a. On the Amphilaphorchidinae, a new subfamily of proteocephalid cestodes, and *Myzophorus admonticellia* gen. et sp. n., parasitic in *Pirinampus* spp. from the Amazon. Parasitology *26*, 141–149.

Woodland, W. N. F. 1934b. On six new cestodes from Amazon fishes. Proc. Zool. Soc. London, 1934, pp. 33–44.

Woodland, W. N. F. 1934c. On some remarkable new cestodes from the Amazon siluroid fish, *Brachyplatystoma filamentosum* (Lichtenstein). Parasitology *26*, 267–277.

Woodland, W. N. F. 1935a. Some more remarkable cestodes from Amazon siluroid fish. Parasitology *27*, 207–225.

Woodland, W. N. F. 1935b. Additional cestodes from the Amazon siluroids, Pirarara, Dorad and Sudobim. Proc. Zool. Soc. London, 1934, pp. 851–862.

Woodland, W. N. F. 1935c. Some new proteocephalids and a ptychobothriid (Cestoda) from the Amazon. Proc. Zool. Soc. London, 1935, pp. 619–623.

Woodland, W. N. F. 1935d. A new species of avitelline tapeworm, *Avitellina sandgroundi*, from *Hippotragus equinus*. Ann. Trop. Med. Parasitol. *29*, 185–189.

Woodland, W. N. F. 1937a. Some cestodes from Sierra Leone. I. On *Wenyonia longicauda* sp. n. and *Proteocephalus bivitellatus* sp. n. Proc. Zool. Soc. London, 1936, pp. 931–937.

Woodland, W. N. F. 1937b. Some cestodes from Sierra Leone. II. A new caryophyllaeid, *Marsypocephalus*, and *Polyonchobothrium*. Proc. Zool. Soc. London, 1937, pp. 189–197.

Woodland, W. N. F. 1938. On the species of the genus *Duthiersia* Perrier, 1873 (Cestoda). Proc. Zool. Soc. London, 1938, pp. 17–36.

Woodland, W. N. F. 1941. A revision of the African and Asiatic forms of *Duthiersia* (Cestoda). Proc. Zool. Soc. London, 1940, pp. 207–219.

Wright, R. R. 1879. Contributions to American helminthology. Proc. Can. Inst. *1*, 54–75.

Wunder, W. 1939. Das jahreszeitliche Auftreten des Bandwurmes (*Caryophyllaeus laticeps* Pall.) im Darm des Karpfens (*Cyprinus carpio* L.). Z. Parasitenk. *10*, 704–713.

Yamaguti, S. 1934. Studies on the helminth fauna of Japan. Part 4. Cestodes of fishes. Japan. J. Zool. *6*, 1–112.

Yamaguti, S. 1935a. Studies on the helminth fauna of Japan. Part 6. Cestodes of birds, I. Japan. J. Zool. *6*, 183–232.

Yamaguti, S. 1935b. Studies on the helminth fauna of Japan. Part 7. Cestodes of mammals and snakes. Japan. J. Zool. *6*, 233–246.

Yamaguti, S. 1938. Studies on the helminth fauna of Japan. Part 22. Two new species of frog cestodes. Japan. J. Zool. *7*, 553–558.

Yamaguti, S. 1939. Studies on the helminth fauna of Japan. Part 28. *Nippotaenia chaenogobii*, a new cestode representing a new order from freshwater fishes. Japan. J. Zool. *8*, 278–289.

Yamaguti, S. 1940. Studies on the helminth fauna of Japan. Part 30. Cestodes of birds, II. Japan. J. Med. Sci. *1*, 175–211.

Yamaguti, S. 1942. Studies on the helminth fauna of Japan. Part 42. Cestodes of mammals, II.

Yamaguti, S. 1945. On the meaning to be attached to the expression "Le plus anciennement designe" used in Article 25 of the International Code, with special reference to the case of *Ophiotaenia ranarum* Iwata and Matuda, 1938, and *Ophiotaenia ranae* Yamaguti, 1938 (Class Cestoidea, Order Tetraphyllidea). Bull. Zool. Nomenclature *1*, 102.

Yamaguti, S., and I. Miyata. 1937. A new tapeworm (*Oochoristica ratti*) of the family Anoplocephalidae, from *Rattus rattus rattus* and *Rattus r. alexandrinus.* Japan. J. Zool. *7*, 501–503.

Yamaguti, S., and I. Miyata. 1940. *Nippotaenia mogurndae* n. sp. (Cestoda) from a Japanese freshwater fish, *Mogurnda obscura* (Temm. et Schleg.). Japan. J. Med. Sci. *1*, 213–214.

Yaroslavsky, W. A., and A. I. Solowieff. 1930. *Dibothriocephalus dividocapitis* nov. spec. Berliner Tierärzt. Wochenschr. *46*, 296–298.

Yokogawa, S. 1933. Report on experiments with *Sparganum mansoni* undertaken in an endeavour to clarify the nature of *Sparganum proliferum.* Taiwan Igakkai Zasshi *32*, 114–116.

Yokogawa, S., and H. Kobayashi. 1930. On the species of *Diphyllobothrium mansoni sensu lato.* Trans. 8th Congr. Far Eastern Assn. Trop. Med. Siam *2*.

Yorke, W., and T. Southwell. 1921. Lappeted *Anoplocephala* in horses. Ann. Trop. Med. Parasitol. *15*, 249–264.

Yoshida, S. 1914. On a second and third case of infection with *Plerocercoides prolifer* Ijima found in Japan. Parasitology *7*.

Yoshida, S. 1917a. The occurrence of *Bothriocephalus liguloides* Leuckart, with special reference to its development. J. Parasitol. *3*.

Yoshida, S. 1917b. Some cestodes from Japanese selachians. Parasitology *9*, 560–592.

Yoshino, K. 1933. Studies on the post-embryonal development of *Taenia solium.* Taiwan Igakkai Zasshi *32*, 139–141.

Yoshino, K. 1934. On the evacuation of eggs from the detached gravid proglottids of *Taenia solium* and on the structure of its eggs. Taiwan Igakkai Zasshi *33*.

Young, M. R. 1938. Helminth parasites of New Zealand. Publn. Imperial Bur. Agr. Parasitol. (Helminthology), pp. 1–19.

Young, R. T. 1908. The histogenesis of *Cysticercus pisiformis.* Zool. Jahrb. Anat. *26*, 183–254.

Young, R. T. 1912a. The epithelium of Turbellaria. J. Morph. *26*, 255–268.

Young, R. T. 1912b. The somatic nuclei of certain cestodes. Arch. Zellforsch. *6*, 140–168.

Young, R. T. 1913. The histogenesis of the reproductive organs of *Taenia pisiformis.* Zool. Jahrb. Anat. *35*, 355–418.

Young, R. T. 1919a. The degeneration of yolk glands and cells in cestodes. Biol. Bull. *36*, 309–311.

Young, R. T. 1919b. Association of somatic and germ cells in cestodes. Biol. Bull. *36*, 312–314.

Young, R. T. 1923. Gametogenesis in cestodes. Arch. Zellforsch. *16*, 419–437.

Young, R. T. 1935. Some unsolved problems of cestode structure and development. Trans. Am. Microscop. Soc. *54*, 229–239.

Young, S. 1934. Ueber das Wachstum der *Diphyllobothrium mansoni* (Cobbold, 1883) Joyeux, 1928 im Darme des Endwirtes (Hundes) und die von diesen Bandwurm hervorgerufene Anämie. J. Shanghai Sci. Inst. *1*.

Zeder, J. G. H. 1800. Erster Nachtrag zur Naturgeschichte der Eingeweidewürmer, mit Zufassen und Anmerkungen herausgegeben. xx + 320 pp. Leipzig.

Zeder, J. G. H. 1803. Anleitung zur Naturgeschichte der Eingeweidewürmer. xvi + 432 pp. Bamberg.

Zeliff, C. K. 1932. A new species of cestode, *Crepidobothrium amphiumae,* from *Amphiuma tridactylum.* Proc. U. S. Nat. Museum *81*, 1–3.

Zernecke, E. 1895. Untersuchungen ueber den feinern Bau der Cestoden. Zool. Jahrb. Anat. *9*, 92–161.

Ziegler, H. E. 1905. Das Ektoderm der Plathelminthen. Verhandl. deutsch. zool. Gesell. 15 Sammlung, Breslau.

Ziluff, H. 1912. Vergleichende Studien ueber die Muskulatur des Skolex der Cestoden. Arch. Naturgeschichte, 1912, pp. 1–33.

Zimmermann, H. R. 1937. Life-history studies on cestodes of the genus *Dipylidium* from the dog. Z. Parasitenk. 9, 717–729.

Zograf, N. J. 1886. Structure de la forme cystique de *Gymnorhynchus reptans* Rud. Isvestia soc. imp. sci. nat. Moscow *50*, 259–284.

Zograf, N. J. 1890. Zur Frage ueber die Existenz ectodermatischer Hüllen bei erwachsenen Cestoden. Biol. Zentralbl. *10*, 422.

Zschokke, F. 1884. Recherches sur l'organisation et la distribution zoologique des vers parasites des poissons d'eau douce. Arch. Biol. *5*, 153–241.

Zschokke, F. 1885. Ueber den Bau der Geschlechtswerkzeuge von *Taenia literata*. Zool. Anz. *8*, 380–384.

Zschokke, F. 1887a. Studien ueber den anatomischen und histologischen Bau der Cestoden. Centralbl. Bakt. Parasitenk. *1*, 161–165, 193–199.

Zschokke, F. 1887b. Helminthologische Bemerkungen. Nitt. Zool. Sta. Neapel 7, 264–271.

Zschokke, F. 1888a. Ein Beitrag zur Kenntnis der Vogeltänien. Centralbl. Bakt. Parasitenk. *3*, 2–6, 41–46.

Zschokke, F. 1888b. Ein weiterer Zwischenwirt des *Bothriocephalus latus*. Centralbl. Bakt. Parasitenk. *3*, 417–419.

Zschokke, F. 1888c. Recherches sur la structure anatomique et histologique des cestodes des poissons marins. Mém. inst. national génevois *17*, 396 pp.

Zschokke, F. 1890a. Ueber Bothriocephalen-larven in *Trutta salar*. Centralbl. Bakt. Parasitenk. 7, 393–396, 435–439.

Zschokke, F. 1890b. Erster Beitrag zur Parasiten-Fauna von *Trutta salar*. Verhandl. naturf. Gesellsch. Basel *8*, 761–793.

Zschokke, F. 1891. Die Parasiten-fauna von *Trutta salar*. Centralbl. Bakt. Parasitenk. *10*, 694–699, 738–745, 792–801, 829–838.

Zschokke, F. 1892. Seltene Parasiten des Menschen. Centralbl. Bakt. Parasitenk. *12*, 497–500.

Zschokke, F. 1895. *Davainea contorta* sp. aus *Manis pentadactyla* L. Centralbl. Bakt. Parasitenk. *17*, 634–645.

Zschokke, F. 1896a. Zur Faunistik der parasitischen Würmer von Süsswasserfischen. Centralbl. Bakt. Parasitenk. *19*, 772–784, 815–825.

Zschokke, F. 1896b. Die Taenien der aplacentalen Säugetiere. Zool. Anz. *19*, 481–482.

Zschokke, F. 1898a. Weitere Untersuchungen an Taenien der aplacentalen Säugetiere. Zool. Anz. *21*, 477–479.

Zschokke, F. 1898b. Die Cestoden der Marsupialia und Monotremata. Denkschr. med. naturw. Gesellsch. Jena *8*, 358–380.

Zschokke, F. 1899. Neue Studien an Cestoden aplacentaler Säugetiere. Z. wiss. Zool. *65*, 404–446.

Zschokke, F. 1902a. *Hymenolepis* (*Drepanidotaenia*) *lanceolata* als Schmarotzer im Menschen. Centralbl. Bakt. Parasitenk. *31*, 331–335.

Zschokke, F. 1902b. *Hymenolepis* (*Drepanidotaenia*) *lanceolata* aus Ente und Gans als Parasit des Menschen. Zool. Anz. *25*, 337–338.

Zschokke, F. 1903a. Ein neuer Fall von *Dipylidium caninum* (L.) beim Menschen. Centralbl. Bakt. Parasitenk. *34*, 42–43.

Zschokke, F. 1903b. Die Arktischen Cestoden. In Römer und Schaudin. Fauna Arctica *3*, 1–30.

Zschokke, F. 1903c. Marine Schmarotzer in Süsswasserfischen. Verhandl. naturf. Gesellsch. Basel *16*, 118–157.

Zschokke, F. 1904a. Die Darmcestoden der amerikanischen Beuteltiere. Centralbl. Bakt. Parasitenk. *36*, 51–62.

Zschokke, F. 1904b. Die Cestoden der südamerikanischen Beuteltiere. Zool. Anz. *27*, 290–293.

Zschokke, F. 1905a. Das Genus *Oochoristica*. Z. wiss. Zool. *83*, 51–67.

Zschokke, F. 1905b. *Dipylidium caninum* (L.) als Schmarotzer des Menschen. Centralbl. Bakt. Parasitenk. *38*, 534.

Zschokke, F. 1907. *Moniezia diaphana* n. sp. Ein weiterer Beitrag zur Kenntnis der Cestoden aplacentaler Säugetiere. Centralbl. Bakt. Parasitenk. *44*, 261–264.

Zschokke, F. 1917. *Dibothriocephalus parvus* J. J. W. Stephens. Rev. suisse zool. *25*, 425–440.

Zschokke, F., and A. Heitz. 1914. Entoparasiten aus Salmoniden von Kamschatka. Rev. suisse zool. *22*, 195–256.

Zurn, F. A. 1882. Die tierischen Parasiten und Krankheiten des Hausgeflügels. 237 pp. Weimar.

Zwicke, C. 1841. De entozois corporis humani. 32 pp. Dissertation, Berlin.

Index

Page numbers in italics refer to tables and figures. These numbers are not repeated if the page contains also relevant text material. For Part II, where arrangement is by classification, only major subdivisions have been indexed.

Abothriinae, 649
Abothrium, 649–50, *651*
Abothros, 299
Acanthobothrium, *259*, 260–63
Acanthotaenia, *209*, 211–14
Acanthotrias, 424
Ackert, J. E., and Reid, W. M., quoted on cysticercoid larvae, 78–91
Acoleidae, 521–23
Acoleorhynchus, 301
Acoleus, 522, *523*
Acrobothrium, 264
Adelobothrium, 279, *281*
Adenocephalus, 581, *582*
Aleurotaenia, 496–97
Alimentary tract, evidence of, 150
Alimentation, 105–8, 144, 150–51
Alyselminthus, 424, 576
Amabilia, *523*, 524
Amabiliidae, 523–24
Amerina, 516
Amoebotaenia, *480*, 484
Amphicotyle, 642–43
Amphicotylidae, 641–42
Amphicotylinae, 642
Amphilina, 656, *657*
Amphilinidea, 653–56
Amphilininae, 656–58
Amphoterocotyle, 342–43
Amphoteromorphus, 194–95
Anchistrocephalus, 640–41
Ancistrocephalus, 640
Andrya, 353–55, *356*
Angularella, *480*, 481
Angularia, 481
Anomotaenia, 491–92, *493*
Anonchocephalus, *640*, 641
Anonchotaenia, 514–17, *515*
Anootypus, 381
Anophryocephalus, *336*, 341
Anoplocephala, *356*, 358
Anoplocephalidae, 347–51, *352*, *353*
Anoplocephalinae, 351–53
Anoplotaenia, 401–2
Anthemobothrium, 279, *281*, 282–83
Anthobothrium, *21*, *25*, 31, *239*, 241–42
Anthocephalus, *34*, 306
Antonow, A., investigation of host-metacestode relationship, 127
Anurina, 516
Apical organ, 151, 182
Aploparaksis, *452*, 471
Apolysis, 9–10, 294, 562: correlation with longevity, 117; part in determining origin, 152
Aporhynchus, 317
Aporidea, 534–37
Aporina, *349*, 359
Aprostatandrya, 354–55
Archigetes, 13, 18, 26, *542*, 543–44
Armandia, 315
Ascometra, 520
Ascotaenia, 378
Aspidorhynchus, 301
Atelemerus, 635
Austramphilina, 658
Austramphilininae, 658
Autecology, 92–122
Avitellina, *21*, *25*, 30, 38, 380–81

Baer, J. G., hypothesis on origin, 145
Baeria, 366
Baeriella, 364
Baerietta, *345*, 346–47
Bakererpes, 484–85
Balanobothrium, 265–68
Balanotaenia, *547*, 549
Bancroftiella, 489, 491
Basement membrane, 13–14
Bathybothrium, 649, *651*
Batrachotaenia, 224
Bertia, 362
Bertiella, 362–64
Biacetabulum, *542*, 544
Bilateral symmetry, 150
Biology, 92–141
Biporophyllaeus, *664*, 665
Biporophyllidea, 664–65
Biuterina, 446–47
Biuterina, 446–47
Biuterinoides, 448–49
Bladder worms, *84*
Body, 9–13
Bombicirhynchus, 318

Bonsdorff, B., experiments on effect of tapeworm infection, 138–40
Bothria, 7–8
Bothridia, 8–9, 229, 291
Bothridiotaenia, 342
Bothridium, 579, *580*
Bothrimonus, 557–58
Bothriocephalidae, 623–34
Bothriocephalus, 625–32
Bouchardia, 303
Bouchardidae, 303
Brand, T., findings on respiration, 110
Braun, M., classification, 160
Braunia, 579
Braun-Lühe classification, 160
"Bronn's Thierrich," 160
Brumptiella, 436
Bullock, F. D., and Curtis, M. R., experiments to determine malignancy, 129

Calliobothrium, *27*, 258, *259*
Callitetrarhynchinae, 305–8
Callitetrarhynchus, 306, 307
Calycobothrium, 282
Campbell, D. H., investigations of host-oncosphere relationships, 123–24
Capingens, *550*, 551
Capingentidae, 550–51
Carpobothrium, 239, 241
Carus, J. V., classification, 159–60
Caryophyllaeidae, 541–48
Caryophyllaeides, *542*, 544
Caryophyllaeus, *35*, 36, 45, *46*, 546–48
Caryophyllidea, 540–51
Catenotaenia, *81*, *82*, *83*, 381, *385*, *387*
Catenotaeniidae, 381–88
Caulobothrium, 238
Cephalobothriidae, 276–85
Cephalobothrium, 277
Cephalochlamys, 617, *618*
Ceratobothrium, *266*, 269
Cerebral cysticercosis, 421
Cestoda, 175–652: theory of common origin with Trematoda, 142–47; common origin with Turbellaria, 148–54
Cestodaria, 653–65: relation to Cestoda, 142–50
Chaetophallus, *336*, 341
Chandler, A. C.: observations on alimentation, 106–7; experiments on premunition, 133
Chapmania, 444, *445*
Chemistry of tapeworms, 70, 92–105
Child, C. M., research on proglottisation and segmentation, 10–11
Chitinolepis, 457
Chitinorecta, 492
Chlamydocephalus, 617
Choanotaenia, 7, *80*, *493*, 497–501
Christianella, 315–16
Cittotaenia, *43*, *363*, 365–66
Cladogynia, 482
Cladotaenia, 405–6, *407*
Classification: determining validity of a character, 162; limitations of character for specific discrimination, 163–67; value of metromorphic characters of internal morphology, 167–69; importance of host location, 169; scheme used in this book, 173–74. *See also* History and classification
Claus, C., hypothesis on origin, 142–43
Clelandia, 482
Clestobothrium, *621*, 623
Coenomorphinae, 301–3
Coenomorphus, 302–3
Coenurus, *84*, 90, 412
Congeria, 301
Copeosoma, 533
Corallobothrium, 64, 195–96, *197*
Cordicephalus, 588–91, *589*
Cotugnia, *434*, 436
Cotylorhipis, 479, *480*
Crepidobothrium, 65, 222–25, *225*
Crusz, H., research on cysticercus development, 91
Culcitella, 520–21
Cultivation of tapeworms, 92–98
Curtis, M. R., and Bullock, F. D., experiments to determine malignancy, 129
Cuticle, 13, 16–17
Cyathocephalidae, 544–55
Cyathocephalus, 51, 63, 554, *555*
Cyclobothrium, 282
Cyclophyllidea, 321–533
Cyclorchida, *447*, 448
Cyclustera, 491
Cylindrophorus, *266*, 268–69
Cylindrotaenia, 344–46, *345*
Cysticercoid, 73–85, *74*, *76*, *80*
Cysticercus, 85–91, *86*, 90, 99
Cysticercus, 424–26
Cystotaenia, 424

Dasyrhynchidae, 305–8
Dasyrhynchinae, 305–8
Dasyrhynchus, *304*, 305–6
Dasyurotaenia, 405
Davainea, *434*, 436
Davaineidae, 428–33
Davaineinae, 435–36
Davaineoides, 437
Deltokeras, 447–48, *448*
Dendrouterina, 448–89, *489*, *490*
Deschiens, R., opinion on pathogenic substances of verminous origin, 133
Diagonobothrium, 285
Diancyrobothriidae, 567
Diancyrobothrium, 567
Diandrya, *356*, 357
Dibothriocephalidae, 572–618
Dibothriocephalus, 5, 12, 16, *34*, *37*, *41*,

50–51, *52*, 55, 58, 59, 60, *66*, 67, 118, 135, 605–6
Dibothriorhynchidae, 301–3
Dibothriorhynchus, 302
Didymobothrium, 557
Diesing, K. M., classification, 159
Digramma, 576, *577*
Dilepididae, 475–94
Dilepidinae, 477–94
Dilepis, 486–87
Dinobothrium, 245–46
Diochetos, 374
Dioicocestidae, 526–28
Dioicocestus, 526, *527*
Diorchis, *464*, 469–71, *479*
Diphyllobothrium, 585–87, *586*
Diplobothrium, 282, *283*
Diplocotyle, 556–57
Diplocotylidae, 555–58
Diplogonadism, 12, 31
Diplogonimidae, 301–3
Diplogonimus, 302–3
Diplogonoporus, 587–88
Diplogynia, *529*, 530–33
Diplootobothrium, 318, *319*
Diplophallus, 529
Diploposthe, 528, *529*
Diploposthidae, 528–33
Diplopylidium, 502–3, *506*
Dipylidiinae, 495
Dipylidium, 57, 75, *76*, 505, *506*
Discobothrium, *283*, 284
Discocephalum, 270
Disculicepitidae, 272
Disculicepitidea, 270–72
Disculiceps, *271*, 272
Diseases caused by infestation, 128
Distoichometra, *345*, 346–47
Distribution in primitive hosts, 146
Dittocephalus, 618
Djombangia, 549
Drepanidotaenia, *452*, 458
Dubium, 592
Duthiersia, 580–81

Echeneibothrium, 236–37, *238*, *239*
Echinobothrium, 284–85
Echinococcus, 391–99, *392*, *393*, *394*, *395*
Echinocotyle, 458–59
Echinophallidae, 634–36
Echinophallus, 635
Echinorhynchotaenia, *480*, 481
Echinorhynchus trichiuri, 302
Eggs, 46–54
Electrotaenia, 210, *211*
Endorchis, 193, *194*
Eniochobothrium, 282–83, *283*
Environmental exchanges, 104
Ephedrocephalus, *190*, 192
Euapolysis, 10
Eubothrium, 164, 643, *644*, *646*
Eugonodaeum, 495
Eutetrarhynchidae, 315–16
Eutetrarhynchus, *313*, 315
Excretory system, *see* Osmoregulatory system

Female reproductive system, 36–44
Feng, L. C., and Fortuyn, A. B., experiments on immunity, 125
Fimbriaria, 472–74, *473*
Fimbriariella, *473*, 474
Fimbriariinae, 472–74
Fimbriaroides, *473*, 474
Finna, 424
Fischiosoma, 424
Fistulicola, 640
Floricepitidae, 311–12
Floriceps, *304*, 306
Fortuyn, A. B., and Feng, L. C., experiments on immunity, 125
Fuhrmannella, 355–57
Fuhrmannetta, 437
Fuhrmanniella, 450

Gangesia, 208–10, *209*
Gastrotaenia, 537
Gephyrolina, 656–57
Gid, 413
Gidhaia, 358, 479
Gigantolina, *657*, 658
Gigantolininae, 658
Gilquinia, *313*, 317
Gilquiniidae, 316–17
Glandicephalus, 582–83, *584*
Glaridacris, *547*, 548
Glycogen content, experiments on, 109–10
Gmelin, J. F., classification, 158
Goeze, J. A. E., natural history of parasitic worms, 158
Goeziana, 424
Gough, L. H.: discussion of sucker muscles, 20–22; description of nervous system, 30; description of female genitalia, 38–39
Grillotia, *307*, 310–11
Grillotiinae, 310–11
Growth, 118–22
Gryporhynchus, 490
Gymnorhynchidae, 311–12
Gynandrotaenia, 532
Gyrocoelia, *527*, 528
Gyrocotyle, 659–63, *660*
Gyrocotylidea, 658–63
Gyrocotyloides, 663

Haeruca, 424
Halsiorhynchus, 314
Halysis, 424, 576
Haplobothriidae, 567–72
Haplobothrium, 568, 577
Haploparaksis, 471

Haploparaxis, 449, 471
Hearin, J. T., experiments on immunization, 132
Helictometra, 378
Hemiparonia, 359
Hepatotaenia, 364
Hepatoxylidae, 301–3
Hepatoxylon, *300*, 302–3
Hermaphroditism, 12, 31
Heterotetrarhynchus, 310–11
Hexacanalis, 277, *278*
Hexacanth embryo, *see* Oncosphere
Hexastichus, 380
History and classification, 155–69. *See also* Classification
Holdfast organ, 4–9, 20, 149: shape and size, 6; sucker, 6–7; bothriate, 7–8; bothridiate, 8; teratological distortions, 11–12; musculature of trypanorhynchan type, 22–23; part in determining origin, 143–44, 149–50
Hooks, 291, 389, 430, 453
Hornellobothrium, 284
Host relationships: with oncosphere, 122–25; with metacestode, 125–29; with strobilar stage, 129–41
Houttuynia, 442–43, *443*
Human infestation, 45, 126, 127: symptoms, 134–41
Hydatidosis, 395–400
Hydatigena, 424
Hydatigera, 48, *49*, *50*, 87, 88, 103, 406–8, *409*
Hydatis, 424
Hydatula, 424
Hygroma, 424
Hymenolepididae, 449–56
Hymenolepidinae, 456–57
Hymenolepis, 81, 459–69, 462, *464*, 468
Hyperapolysis, 10
Hypocaryophyllaeus, 544–45
Hyracotaenia, 374–77

Ichthyotaenia, 176
Ichthyotaeniidae, 176
Icterotaenia, 499, 500
Idiogenes, 444, *445*
Idiogeninae, *444*
Idiogenoides, 436
Ilisha, *71*, 72
Immunity, 123, 130, 131–34
Inermicapsifer, 374–77, *376*
Infula, 526–27
Insinuarotaenia, 391

Jardugia, 529–30
Johnstone, J.: description of nervous system, 28–30; description of female genitalia, 39
Joyeuxia, 509–12
Joyeuxiella, 509–12, *512*

Khawia, 549
Killigrewia, 359–60
Kotlania, 436
Kowalewskiella, 501
Krabbea, 588
Krimi, 486
Küchenmeister, F. G., experiments with *Cysticercus cellulosae*, 45

Lacistorhynchidae, 308–11
Lacistorhynchinae, 309–10
Lacistorhynchus, *307*, 309
Larsh, J. E.: experiments on immunity, 125; infestation experiments, 132
La Rue, G. R., description of holdfast musculature, 19–20
Laser, H., findings on respiration, 109
Lateriporus, 482–84, *483*
Laterorchites, *483*, 485
Laterotaenia, 494
Le Bas, G. Z., experiments on human infestation, 136–37
Lecanicephala, 273–85
Lecanicephalidae, 275
Lecanicephalum, *271*, 275–76
Length, criterion of growth, 118–19
Leptotaenia, *531*, 532–33
Life cycle, 45–91: studies on, 46
Liga, *486*, 490–91
Ligula, *14*, 576–79, *578*, *580*
Linnaeus, C., nomenclature, 157
Linstowia, 367–68
Linstowiinae, 367–77
Lintoniella, 196, *197*
Loennberg, E., on origin, 148–49
Longevity, 116–18
Lühe, M., description of uterine tract, 42–43
Lytocephalus, 617–18
Lytocestidae, 548–50
Lytocestoides, 549
Lytocestus, *547*, 549

Male reproductive system, 31–36
Malika, 497, *513*
Manaosia, 224, *225*
Marsipometra, 651–52, *652*
Marsipometrinae, 650–52
Marsypocephalus, 189, *190*
Megacephalos, 424
Megathylacus, 207–8, *209*
Meggittia, 436
Mesocestoides, 325–29, *326*
Mesocestoididae, 325–29
Metacestode, 57–58: relationship with host, 125–29
Methyl green–pyronin technique, 55–57
Metroliasthes, 517, *518*
Miller, H. M.: investigations of host-oncosphere relationships, 123; experiments on premunition, 130–31

Mola, P., classification, 161–62
Molicola, 306
Moniezia, 100, 110, *116*, *356*, 357–58
Moniezioides, 364
Monobothrioides, 549–50
Monobothrium, 545–46
Monoecocestus, 355, *356*, 522
Monopylidiinae, 495
Monopylidium, 498
Monorchis, 449
Monorygma, 231
Monozootic concept, 152
Monticellia, 177, 189, *191*
Morphic variation, 165
Movement, 110–16: in artificial media, 114–15
Multicapsiferina, 368
Multiceps, 412–13, *415*
Multitesticulata, 500
Muscles, 19–24
Myzophorus, 234
Myzophyllobothrium, 235–36

Neck, 9
Nematoparataenia, 534, 535–37
Nematotaenia, 344, *345*
Nematotaeniidae, 343–47
Neotenia, 424
Neoteny, 153
Neotetrabothrius, 342–43
Nervous system, 28–31
Neuromuscular cells, 14
Neyraia, *447*, 448
Niemac, J., description of nervous system, 30–31
Nippotaenia, *536*, 538–39
Nippotaeniidae, 538–39
Nomenclature, *see* Classification
Nomimoscolex, 193–94, *195*
Notopentorchis, 521
Nybelin, O.: quoted on origin, 142; belief that tapeworm is monozootic, 152
Nybelinia, *69*, 111, *112*, *113*, *300*, 301
Nybelinidae, 299–301

Octopetalum, 518, *519*
Odhner, T., quoted on origin, 142
Oligorchis, 458, *464*
Onchobothriidae, 254–69
Onchobothrium, 259, 260
Onchodiscus, 624–25, *633*
Oncomegas, 320
Oncosphere, 54–57, 149: relationship with host, 122–25
Onderstepoortia, 502
Oochoristica, 368, *370*, *371*, *373*
Oogenesis, 46
Ophiotaenia, *21*, *34*, *62*, 184, 214–26, *215*, *220*
Ophiovalipora, 488
Ophryocotyle, 433, *434*
Ophryocotylinae, 433–35
Ophryocotyloides, 435
Oriana, 282
Origin and evolution, 142–54: difficulties in making hypotheses, 149–53; controversy on monozootic *vs.* polyzootic, 152–53; postulates for further study, 153–54
Ortner-Schönbach, P., findings on respiration, 109–10
Orygmatobothrium, 253–54, *254*
Osmoregulatory systems, 4, 24–28
Otobothriidae, 317–18
Otobothrium, 317–18, *319*

Palaia, 224
Pancerina, 367
Panuwa, 513–14
Parabertiella, 360
Parabothriocephaloides, 633
Parabothriocephalus, *633*, 634
Parabothrium, 650, *651*
Parachoanotaenia, 500
Parachristianella, 316
Paracladotaenia, 402–3
Paradilepis, *486*, 487–88, *488*
Paralinstowia, 368
Paranoplocephala, *356*, 360–61
Parataenia, 275–76, *276*
Paratetrabothrius, 342
Parenchyma, 16–19
Paricterotaenia, *483*, 485, 500
Paronia, *363*, 365
Paroniella, 437
Parorchites, 494
Paruterina, *519*, 521
Paruterininae, 514–21
Parvirostrum, 494
Parvitaenia, 492–94
Pedibothrium, 255, *256*
Pelichnibothrium, 236, *237*
Peltidocotyle, *190*, 191
Pentorchis, 480–81
Phanobothrium, 283
Phoreiobothrium, 269
Phylogeny, 148
Phyllobothriidae, 232–53
Phyllobothrium, 246–53, *247*, *248*, *250*
Phyllobothrium delphini, 231
Phyllobothrium loliginis, 232
Pierretia, 299–301
Pillersium, 285
Pintner, T., classification, 161
Pintnerella, 320
Pithophorus, 234–35, *235*
Platybothrium, 264–65, *265*
Platyelminthes, 4
Plerocercoid larval forms, 66–73, *67*, *68*, *69*, *70*, *71*, *72*

Plerocercoides, 592
Plerocercoides portieri, 232
Poche, F., classification, 160–61
Poecilancistrium, 318, *319*
Polycephalus, 424
Polycercus larval form, 81, *84*, 85
Polyonchobothrium, 620–23, *621*
Polypocephalus, 278, *280*
Polyzootic concept, 152
Porogynia, 443
"Pratt's theory," 60
Priapocephalus, *336*, 340
Procercoids, 58–66
Prochoanotaenia, 500
Prochristianella, 316
Prodicoelia, 579
Progamotaenia, 364–65
Proglottisation, 9, 152: difference from segmentation, 9–10; physiological reasons for, 10–11; part in determining origin, 152
Progrillotia, 311
Progynopylidium, 503–4
Progynotaenia, 530–31, *531*
Progynotaeniidae, 522
Proorchida, 488
Proparuterina, 494
Prosobothrium, 284, *285*
Prosthecocotyle, 342–43
Proteocephala, 175–225
Proteocephalidae, 187–225
Proteocephalus, 196, *197*, *198*, *199*, *200*, *201*, *204*
Proterogynotaenia, *531*, 532
Proto-cestode, 148–54
Protogynella, *531*, 532
Prototaenia, 361
Pseudandrya, 484
Pseudangularia, 481–82
Pseudanoplocephala, 360
Pseudapolysis, 10, 113
Pseudhymenolepinae, 474–75
Pseudhymenolepis, 475
Pseudobothrium, 648–49
Pseudochoanotaenia, 496
Pseudoligorchis, 457–58
Pseudolytocestus, *550*, 551
Pseudophyllidea, 559–652
Pseudotobothrium, 318
Psychiosoma, 424
Pterobothriidae, 312–15
Pterobothrium, *313*, 314
Ptychobothriidae, 618–23
Ptychobothrium, 619–20, *622*
Pyramicocephalus, 576, *577*

Raillietina, 437–42, *438*, *440*
Rees, G.: description of osmoregulatory system, 27; description of nervous system, 31
Reid, W. M., and Ackert, J. E., quoted on cysticercoid larvae, 79–81
Reproductive system: male, 31–36; female, 36–44
Respiration, 108–10
Rhabdometra, 518–20, *519*, *520*
Rhopalothylacidae, 320
Rhynchobothrium, 318
Rhytelminthus, 636
Rhytis, 636
Rietschel, P. E., on movement, 111
Rudolphi, K. A.: as founder of zoological classification, 155; classification, 158–59
Rudolphiella, *190*, 192
Rufferia, 301
Rufferidae, 299–301

Sbesterium, 305
Schistocephalus, 615–17, *616*
Schistometra, *445*, 446
Schistotaenia, 524
Schizorchis, 353
Schizotaenia, 355
Sciadocephalus, *225*, 226
Scolex, *see* Holdfast
Scolex pleuronectis, 229–31, *230*
Scyphocephalus, 375
Scyphophyllidium, 234, *235*
Segmentation, 9: difference from proglottisation, 9–10; physiological reasons for, 10–11; part in determining origin, 152
Senga, 620, *621*
Sex organs: male, 31–36; female, 36–44
Shipleya, 527–28
Shipleyia, 527–28
Silurotaenia, 210, *211*
Similuncinus, *493*, 496
Skin, 13–17
Skorikowia, 471
Skrjabinia, 437
Skrjabinochora, 325
Skrjabinochoridae, 325
Solenophorus, 579
Solenotaenia, 176, 178, *222*, 226
Southwell, T., classification, 162
Southwellia, 487, 513
Sparganum, 592
Sparganum proliferum, 70, *71*
Spartoides, *550*, 551
Spathebothridea, 552–58
Spathebothriidae, 552–54
Spathebothrium, 553
Spengel, J. W., hypothesis on origin, 142–43
Sphaeruterina, *519*, 521
Sphyriocephala, 303
Sphyriocephalidae, 303–5
Sphyriocephalinae, 303–5

Sphyriocephalus, 303, *304*
Sphyronchotaenia, 444, *445*
Spiniloculus, *256*, 257
Spirometra, 591–95, *594*, *601*
Staphylocystis, 81
Starvation: effect on glycogen content, 110; as cause of expulsion, 113
Staurobothrium, *281*, 282
Stenobothrium of Diesing, 299–301
Stenobothrium of Pintner, 301
Stilesia, 379
Stocksia, 549
Strobila, *see* Body
Strobila chemistry, 100
Strobilocephala, 340–41
Strobilocephalus, *336*, 340–41
Strobilocercus, 407
Subcuticle, 14–15
Suckers, 6–7
Surface, 98–99
Symptoms, of infestation, 134–41
Synbothrium, 314
Syndesmobothrium, 314
Synecology, 122–41
Syngenes, 301
Systema Naturae, 157

Taenia, 417–19, *418*, *419*, *420*
Taeniarhynchus, 403–4, *404*
Taeniidae, 388–428
Taeniola, 424
Taprobothrium, 632, *633*
Tarassow, W., effects of self-infection, 137
Tatria, *523*, 525–26
Taufikia, 358–59
Taxonomy, *see* Classification
Teleostotaenia, 179
Tentacles, 288–93
Tentacularia, 299, *300*
Tentacularia pillersi, 318
Tentaculariidae, 299–301
Tetrabothriidae, 333–43
Tetrabothrium, 342–43
Tetrabothrius, *336*, 342–43
Tetracampos, *266*, 269, 622
Tetradiscocotyla, 533
Tetrafossate tapeworms, 153
Tetragonocephalum, *271*, 275
Tetrantaris, 302
Tetraphyllidea, 227–28
Tetrarhynchus brevibothria, 320
Tetrarhynchus megacephalus, 302
Tetrarhynchus viridis, 303
Tetrathyridium, 327
Thysanocephalum, *256*, 257
Thysanosoma, 378
Thysanosominae, 377–81
Thysanotaenia, 377
Tötterman, G., experiments on human infestation, 137–38
Trachelocampylus, 424
Trematoda, 19: theory of common origin with Cestoda, 142–47
Triaenophoridae, 636–41
Triaenophorus, 636, *637*
Trichocephaloidis, 482, *483*
Tricuspidaria, 636
Trigonocotyle, *336*, 341
Trigonolobum, 320
Triplotaenia, 366
Triuterina, 353
Trypanorhyncha, 286–320
Turbellaria, 19: common origin with Cestoda, 148–54
Tylocephalum, 277–78, *279*, *280*

Uncibilocularis, 256–57
Unciunia, 479–80, *480*
Urocystidium, 522

Valipora, 482, *483*
Van Cleave, H. J., quoted on Linnaeus nomenclature, 157
Vaullegeardidae, 311–12
Venard, C. E., study of life cycle, 75–77
Vergeer, T., quoted on embryonic envelope, 50–51
Vermaia, 224
Viscoia, 500
Vitta, 494

Wagner, O., description of osmoregulatory system, 26
Wardium, 450
Wardle, R. A., findings on respiration, 110
Wardle, R. A., and Green, N. K.: experiments on human infestation, 137; assertions on effects of infection, 141
Weight, *see* Growth
Weinlandia, 449
Welsh, G. H., 156
Wenyonia, 541, *542*
Wenyonidae, 541
Wisniewski, L. W.: description of parenchyma formation, 18–19; description of osmoregulatory system, 26
Woodland, W. N., description of fauna, 146–47
Wyominia, 379

Yorkeria, 258, *259*
Young, R. T.: list of main problems of structure and development, 12–13; opinion on origin of sex organs, 32; comments on oogenesis, 46–47

Zeder, J. G., classification, 155
Zosteropicola, 516, 520
Zschokkea, 368
Zschokkeella, 368
Zygobothrium, 193, *194*